The Palgrave Macmillan
Dictionary of Political Thought

REFERENCE

The Palgrave Macmillan Dictionary of Political Thought

3rd edition

Roger Scruton

First published 1982 by The Macmillan Press
Paperback edition first published 1983 by Pan Books Ltd
Second edition published 1996 by Macmillan General Books
Third edition 2007

Published by
PALGRAVE MACMILLAN
Houndmills, Basingstoke, Hampshire RG21 6XS and
175 Fifth Avenue, New York, N. Y. 10010
Companies and representatives throughout the world

PALGRAVE MACMILLAN is the global academic imprint of the Palgrave Macmillan division of St. Martin's Press, LLC and of Palgrave Macmillan Ltd. Macmillan® is a registered trademark in the United States, United Kingdom and other countries. Palgrave is a registered trademark in the European Union and other countries.

ISBN-13: 978–1–4039–8951–2   hardback
ISBN-10: 1–4039–8951–6   hardback
ISBN-13: 978–1–4039–8952–9   paperback
ISBN-10: 1–4039–8952–4   paperback

This book is printed on paper suitable for recycling and made from fully managed and sustained forest sources.

A catalogue record for this book is available from the British Library.

Library of Congress Cataloging-in-Publication Data

Scruton, Roger.
  The Palgrave Macmillan dictionary of political thought / Roger Scruton.—3rd ed.
      p. cm.
  Includes bibliographical references and index.
  ISBN 1–4039–8951–6 (cloth)—ISBN 1–4039–8952–4 (paper)
      1. Political Science—Dictionaries. I. Title.

JA61.S37 2007
320.03—dc22   2006044838

10   9   8   7   6   5   4   3   2   1
16   15   14   13   12   11   10   09   08   07

Printed and bound in Great Britain by Antony Rowe Ltd, Chippenham and Eastbourne

A Note on Composition

The first draft of this dictionary was written continuously, so as to achieve maximum consistency of style and minimum overlap. The articles were sent out separately to the advisers, two of whom were asked to comment on each article. The final draft was then composed, taking into account, as far as possible, all the comments received. The list of entries was gradually amended and developed in the course of writing, partly in response to suggestions received, partly in response to a developing perspective. Because of the novelty of the project, and the attempt to bring together disparate but related disciplines, it cannot be hoped that a uniform standard has been reached throughout, or that some fundamental items of political thought have not been overlooked. However, a certain synthesis has emerged, which may permit development and clarification in any future edition.

I have benefited greatly from the comments offered, and from friendly advice given by Michael Oakeshott, Amartya Sen, John Vickers and William Waldegrave. In particular, I have received inestimable benefit from the painstaking work of Sally Shreir, who read through the whole dictionary suggesting countless additions, improvements and amendments. Without her help and guidance this project would have been far more arduous and far less rewarding than it has been. It is not to be expected, however, that all errors have been eliminated, and I alone am responsible for those that remain, as well as for the tone and manner of the work, and for any expressions of opinion or manifestations of outlook.

ROGER SCRUTON
London, 1982

Note

Cross-references are indicated by an asterisk; they occur only when a major intellectual connection is in issue. Reference to authors and texts have been kept to a minimum, but are included wherever an idea seems to be specific to the thoughts of a particular school or person.

Because this is a dictionary of concepts, it has been necessary to provide not only definitions but also the sketches of arguments. These are necessarily incomplete, and may also be one-sided. The intention is to illustrate the concept, rather than to persuade the reader, and it should be borne in mind that no article can do more than suggest the arguments given for or against any particular position.

Preface to the First Edition

'Political thought' denotes something that all human beings engage in, whether or not knowingly. It also denotes various specialized academic disciplines which seek to explore, to support or to undermine our everyday political persuasions. Several such disciplines have contributed their terminology to this dictionary, among them political science, philosophy, sociology and economics. In addition the reader will find terms from the practical arts of law, politics and religion, together with words designed at least to draw attention to, if not to resolve, important modern controversies.

An apology may not be necessary for what follows, but some explanation of the aims and principles of such a dictionary may help the reader to gauge its utility. It is impossible to include in one small volume reference to all the concepts involved in the practice of politics, or in its related academic disciplines. The intention has been to extract, both from active debate, and from the theories and intuitions which surround it, the principal ideas through which modern political beliefs find expression. The emphasis of the dictionary is conceptual rather than factual, exploring the formulation of doctrines rather than their specific application. Political events are mentioned only when they cast light on intellectual conceptions. For this reason the few proper names contained in the dictionary are those of thinkers rather than those of political figures. Likewise nations, treaties, battles and laws are seldom mentioned, and, while it has been necessary to include discussions of the major movements and parties in contemporary politics, the detailed history of the modern world has been passed over, as outside the scope of a dictionary of concepts.

Political terms are often as obscurely understood by the person who uses them as by the person who is puzzled in hearing them used. The main purpose of this dictionary is to provide not just definitions but, where possible, clarifications of political terminology. Sometimes, as in the case of Marxism, the task is made easier by the existence of a definite and articulated theory, which the dictionary articles need only condense into appropriate form. In other cases (and this is particularly true of the main items of conservative thought) the absence of theory presents a peculiar difficulty. Here the dictionary must itself attempt a small part of a task that has not been accomplished, and perhaps not even been attempted, with the rigour that the subject demands. For this reason, while many entries will be recognized as summaries of existing theories, others will appear to present conceptual novelties. It is hoped that the two kinds of entry will so interlock as to give structure and coherence to the whole. It goes without saying that every attempt has been made to be impartial, and to provide equal, and equally clear, expression to the major beliefs and concepts which enjoy favour in the modern climate of political opinion. But impartiality is itself a kind of partiality, and readers should approach the dictionary with as many quotation marks at their disposal as they might require for their peace of mind.

Some doubt may be felt as to the number of disciplines which have been called upon in the construction of this work. Why, for example, should the social sciences figure so prominently in a book designed to clarify the language of actual political discourse? It would certainly be odd to include, in a dictionary of mathematical concepts, entries dealing with the sociology of mathematical thought and practice. For what bearing could such entries have on concepts like those of number, proof, validity and integration? A sociological explanation of our mathematical habits casts no light upon their true internal logic. However, the same is not true of politics. Political thought, unlike mathematics, is permeable to its own explanation. A sociology of political belief will not leave its subject unaffected. Consider the concept of 'commodity fetishism'. While this purports to provide an explanation of certain persistent economic beliefs and practices, it contains within itself a novel way of criticizing what it explains. No sooner did the concept exist than it was used to give expression and support to political beliefs which seemed to gain in cogency through the adoption of this technical term. Similarly no exposition of modern political thought can avoid encroaching on those disciplines – economics, sociology and political science – which have political thought as part of their subject-matter. Both the language and the art of politics are formed and reformed under pressure from these disciplines, borrowing their concepts, their theories, their truths and above all their confusions in the compulsive search for self-justification.

It should not be thought, however, that the subject-matter of this dictionary is either recondite or truly theoretical. On the contrary, it belongs to the mental repertoire of all active, thinking beings, and it is to be hoped that, by treating impartially conceptions which enter, however hazily, into so many current debates and disagreements, this dictionary will make some small contribution to their clarity.

Preface to the Second Edition

In the 13 years since the first edition of this work was published, momentous events have occurred, and the language of politics has evolved in response to them. The collapse of the Soviet Union has entirely changed the confrontation between left and right, while the growth of European federalism has precipitated institutions, strategies and concepts whose bewildering character is only partly explained by the desire to bewilder. As in every period, reason and folly march in tandem, and neither has a monopoly over the language. In order to take proper note of their common progress I have deleted some entries, expanded others, and added definitions of terms which have come into prominence. I have also added summaries of political thinkers whose work has been especially influential in recent debates.

I have drawn on the advice of three people: Sean Sayers and Ian Steedman, both of whom were advisers to the original edition, and Robert Grant. As before, I have tried to be impartial without being bland, and to put concepts and arguments in the place of obfuscation and dogma. My advisers are not responsible for any local failure to achieve those goals, having done their very best to advance them.

ROGER SCRUTON
Malmesbury, September 1995

Preface to the Third Edition

A further ten years have elapsed since this book was last revised, and they have had as great an impact on political thought as the momentous years between the First and Second Editions. The eruption into Western politics of Islamic thought and Islamist movements has awoken us to the realities of religion and to the human need for it; the ever-expanding claims of the European Union have brought with them a new bureaucratic language; communism has died as an ideology, while Marxism and neo-Marxism survive only in isolated pockets of the Western academy and in the testimony to their former power provided by works such as this one.

Meanwhile the emergence of neo-conservatism in America, and capitalism without democracy in China, have created new kinds of international politics, and new ways of brokering the relations between states. Moreover, no observer can have failed to notice that political thought is being rapidly driven from public life, to be replaced by something that we might call 'business thought'. The deep and difficult arguments about constitutions and their legitimacy, about law and its sources, about property and its rights, about power and authority – arguments that have occupied the major thinkers in our political and philosophical tradition and which formed the original subject-matter of this book – seem to have no place in the thinking of today's politicians. Their concern is not with government, but with management; they are not interested in truth or doctrine but only in 'spin'; and the concepts with which they try to understand society come to them from business schools and management gurus rather than from the great works of political and sociological thought which inspired the original edition of this dictionary.

In this edition I have tried to take account of these developments, and also to amplify the aspects of the book that are the least vulnerable to the flow of events and the whims of fashion. I have therefore deleted ephemeral material and added more entries on thinkers and theories that have a permanent place in intellectual history.

I have retained much that is of no practical relevance, now that Marxism is unbelievable and socialism more or less dead. My excuse for doing so is that this is a dictionary of thought, not of action, and thoughts may be interesting and influential, even in times when they have lost their immediate use.

I have drawn on the advice of Robert Grant, Jonathan Rée and Frank Buckley, three people with contrasting views and outlooks, who have helped me to suppress my prejudices and to maintain, as best I could, the attitude of impartial curiosity that has been the principal motive of this work.

Malmesbury, Wiltshire and *Sperryville, Virginia, Spring 2006*

Abdication

The voluntary relinquishing of the throne by a reigning monarch. Not the simple thing that it appears to be, since the monarch is *head of state and, in a *constitutional monarchy, possesses discretionary powers that are vital to the functioining of government (*see* *prerogative). The monarch will normally have been trained to exercised these powers in council, and his accession to the throne would have been associated in the popular mind with their *legitimacy. Abdication casts a shadow, therefore, over the legitimacy of government, and may lead to a national crisis, as did the abdication of Edward VIII in the UK in 1936.

abnormality

A deviation from a *norm. Abnormality is to be distinguished from eccentricity, which is the presence of noteworthy and uncommon characteristics in a *normal individual. Eccentricity is usually permitted if harmless, abnormality often regarded with suspicion whether harmless or not. Different political arrangements draw the line between the two in different ways, and the problem of defining what is normal in human nature makes dispute inevitable. Moreover the human desire to hold others responsible for the characteristics which distinguish them gives a motive to confusion. An abnormality is not part of the moral character, but part of the amoral circumstances, of the person who possesses it. To represent it as a harmful eccentricity is to justify treatment intended either to conceal the victim, or to force him to change. This thought has been extremely important in *politicized theories of *psychotherapy. The idea of the individual as essentially *responsible for his eccentricities underlies some doctrines of *authenticity.

abortion

The issue of abortion is intractable, partly because of the absence of any other case to which it can be assimilated. The relationship between a woman and her unborn child is both non-transferable and original: the child comes into existence in and through the woman, and the question of its rights and welfare cannot be considered in complete isolation from the question of the rights and welfare of its mother. Some deny that an unborn child is a *person, and on that ground deny it the *right to life. On this view the only question of *rights* is that which concerns the woman: does she have a 'right to choose' whether to give birth? If the pregnancy is unwanted, what right has another to compel her to proceed with it? It seems arbitrary, however, to say that the divide between person and non-person occurs at birth. The alternative positions are many. some see the foetus as a person, but believe that the case is one of *conflicting* rights. Others argue that the language of rights is wholly inadequate to capture the nature of the *obligation towards the unborn child.

In the US abortion has become a defining issue in politics. The decision of the Supreme Court in the case of *Roe* v. *Wade* (1973) conferred what is tantamount to a constitutional right to abortion. According to the leading judgement in that case, delivered by Mr Justice Blackmun, the foetus has no rights at all under US law, since it is not a citizen, while the mother has a *right to *privacy (not explicitly mentioned in the Constitution) which would be violated by the attempt to forbid abortion. Many liberals defend the decision, and are prepared to campaign vigorously to prevent the Supreme Court from qualifying it, while conservatives tend to believe that the case was wrongly decided, or at any rate decided on grounds that are without authority in the Constitution. As a result the issue of abortion has become a political battleground in the United States, with implications for social policy, sexual relations and constitutional law of a kind that go to the heart of the conflict between the liberal and conservative visions of modern society. The decision in *Roe* v. *Wade* is now under challenge, with some liberals prepared to concede that the case was wrongly decided, and that 'abortion rights' should be granted by the legislature rather than read into the Constitution by the Supreme Court. This has been the procedure in other jurisdictions that permit abortion, and many Americans, both liberal and conservative, are wary of attempts by the Supreme Court to pre-empt the legislature over matters that are so profoundly controversial.

Whatever the rights and wrongs of abortion, there is no doubt that its acceptance in modern societies indicates a radical change of attitude towards the unborn, who are no longer protected as other human beings are protected. Some conservatives argue that a society which adopts this attitude to future generations has

discarded the feeling of *piety, and compromised its chances for survival. Liberals often retort that there is no place for piety in a secular society, and that the issue must be settled by considering the rights of existing citizens. Feminists in particular have campaigned for the right to abortion, by way of affirming the feminist principle that it is the woman, and no one else, who has rights over her body.

See, in general, *consequentialism, *rights, *judicial activism.

absolutism

The theory and practice of absolute *government, i.e. government which is not *limited by any *agency internal to itself. Absolute government should be distinguished from absolute *power. Power is always contained, limited or diverted by other powers within the state; but government can be absolute even without possessing absolute power. It is so whenever there are no constitutional *checks and balances, so that no exercise of government can be criticized or opposed in the *name* of government. The principal limitation of government is the law. Defenders of absolutism, such as *Bodin and *Hobbes, have often been motivated by the thought that all government requires *sovereignty – meaning a body of decisions which cannot be questioned. Since sovereignty must be exercised through law, the sovereign himself cannot be criticized *by* the law, which is no more than his own command. On this view law is authoritative simply by virtue of the status of the agent who commands it, and not by virtue of its content or of its moral or intellectual credentials.

Absolutism must be distinguished from *totalitarianism. It involves, not the total supervision by a central power of all the functions of society, but simply the possession of an unfettered power of government, which may or may not be used, and which need not be applied universally, or in every area of social existence. Sometimes, as in the European absolutism of the seventeenth and eighteenth centuries, this power may be used in order to limit the concentration of power in bodies that are not themselves sovereign, such as the nobility, the church, or the empire. Sometimes it may be used to eliminate *opposition and to establish a complete *dictatorship, as with Hitler and Stalin. Absolute rule may vest in an individual, in an *office (absolute monarchy), in a party (*democratic centralism), or in a system of administration (classical Chinese *bureaucracy).

abundance

Goods are abundant in a society whenever any member of it can obtain such of those goods as he desires by working no more than he wishes. It is sometimes thought to be a criterion of *welfare that all goods which people need should also be abundant, and that the economy should have this abundance of necessaries as its aim. (*See* *need.) The view that human needs expand indefinitely leads to scepticism about this criterion. It is also sometimes argued that the abundance of luxuries (i.e. goods which are not needed but only desired) may be an evil: *see* *consumerism.

academic freedom

1. Freedom to pursue teaching, learning and research without regard for the public utility of what is taught or studied, and unconstrained by external directives (whether from the state or from elsewhere) as to the form, content or conclusions of the subject. This freedom includes the freedom to publish the results of research.

2. Specifically, the freedom of an educational body to provide its own constitution, appoint its own staff and students, and determine its own curriculum, whatever the *ideological content of what is taught. It is a disputed question whether this specific freedom does exist, or can or ought to exist. It implies that those who buy or provide the services of academics should have no power to prescribe the nature of the service rendered. Hence the provision of academic freedom requires the abolition of any contractual relation between the academy and the public.

The issue of academic freedom is to be distinguished from that of whether academic institutions ought to raise their funds, and recruit their students, without aid or direction from the state. On the other hand, it is naive to suppose that the state will provide the funding for an institution over which it exerts no right of control.

Academic freedom has been defended by *classical liberal thinkers such as *J.S. Mill, on the ground that knowledge advances best when freely pursued, and when released from the need for political or ideological conformity. Moreover, the best guard against error is the freedom to question, and this freedom is at the root of the academic life. That vision of 'the advance of knowledge', as *Bacon called it, seems to be only imperfectly endorsed in Western universities today, where pressures to ideological conformity in the name of *political correctness are constantly in the news. On the other hand, those pressures are felt most strongly in departments of the *humanities, and it is sometimes argued that these departments are, by their very nature, devoted less to the 'advance of knowledge' than to the propagation of moral and intellectual *values. Hence it is difficult to know exactly what would be meant, by teaching in the humanities in which ideological conclusions are avoided.

acceleration principle (or: accelerator principle)

The hypothesis in economics, that investment in an industry varies according to the rate of change (rather than according to the level) of its output. Under standard conditions a certain amount of capital will be required to produce a particular rate of output. If this rate of output changes then, *ceteris paribus*, the amount of capital invested must also change. It is, however, not possible to assume that the relation between them is one of direct proportionality.

This hypothesis plays an important part in theories of the *trade cycle. It implies that an increase in demand for any product brings about an increase in demand for the machines etc. used to make it. Thus a small change in the output of consumer goods tends to result in a much bigger (i.e. accelerated) change in the output of the goods used to make them. Conversely a small fall in the output of consumer goods may result in a much larger fall in the output of capital goods. It is also argued that the 'accelerator' can be brought into play by a very slight *variation* in the rate of change of output of a consumer good. Thus if output of a particular product increases by five per cent in one year and continues to increase, but only by four per cent, in the next year, this may precipitate an actual *fall* in the output of capital goods, and in the amount of capital invested.

access

The concept of access has become increasingly important in sociological studies of political power, since, it is argued, 'power of any kind cannot be reached by a political interest group or its leaders without access to one or more key points of decision in government' (David B. Truman: *The Governmental Process: Political Interests and Public Opinion*, 1951). Access is the probability of obtaining the attention and influencing the decisions of the relevant officers of government. 'Effective access' is usually given as a function of three variables: the strategic position of the group within society, the internal characteristics of the group, and the nature of the institutions of government. A group may be without access (such as the lowest *caste in a caste system), with effective access, or with 'privileged access' (which arises when decision makers automatically take a group's interests into account). The UK aristocracy has had privileged access, and also 'direct' access, to power through the House of Lords, whereas most other classes have had varying degrees of effective but indirect access.

Sociologists further distinguish 'loose' from 'taut' patterns of access, the first existing when there is a multiplicity of points of access to political decisions, the second when there are defined channels of *representation through which groups exert their influence. Access seems to have shifted, in the US and postwar Europe, from *party to *pressure group, perhaps as a result of modern *bureaucracy, and of the decline of trust in representation.

accession

The act of joining the *European Union through a 'Treaty of Accession' with the existing member states. The Treaty requires the 'accession state' to adopt a *rule of law, to respect the *European Convention on Human Rights, to be democratic and with a competitive *market economy, and to accept the *acquis communautaire* of the EU. Often interim arrangements and periods of adjustment form part of the Treaty, which must be ratified by all member states.

accommodation

1. In sociology, the state or process of social adjustment to conflict. To be distinguished from adaptation (structural changes brought about by biological variation and selection), *assimilation (the process whereby two groups or cultures fuse), and *acculturation. Accommodation allows two groups to harmonize overtly, while leaving the real source of conflict unresolved. Thus first generation immigrants may be accommodated by adopting the food, clothes etc. of the country in which they find themselves, but they may not be acculturated, where this implies full participation in the culture of the native population.

2. In politics, accommodation is usually distinguished from *confrontation and from *conciliation. It is the process whereby hostile powers establish a *modus vivendi* which enables each to fulfil as many of its purposes as it can without overt *aggression towards the other.

accountability

Sometimes distinguished from responsibility. A is accountable to B if B may sanction and forbid his actions. It does not follow that B is responsible for A: chains of responsibility run downwards by *delegation, chains of accountability upwards; if the two chains coincide, then this is a political achievement.

acculturation

The process whereby an individual or group acquires the cultural characteristics of another through direct contact. Acculturation is a one-way process, whereby one culture absorbs another, and is to be distinguished from the two-way process of *assimilation, in which homogeneity results from changes in both. The phenomenon is of increasing political significance, as war, communication and migration force the states of the world to decide whether to open or to close their frontiers to one another. Their decisions may often be affected by the extent to which acculturation of new arrivals is considered possible.

accumulation

The amassing of *capital, for purposes of either investment or consumption expenditure. If there is to be a 'means of production' over and above what is provided by nature, then there must be accumulation, in the form of 'produced means of production'. In a *capitalist economy accumulation is in private hands; in a *socialist economy, in theory, every accumulation of any significance is *socially owned. In between those two, infinite varieties of *mixed economy can be envisaged.

Moral and political discussions of *private property often involve objections to certain levels of accumulation. Some think that all accumulation gives the person who has *control over it a further control over the lives of others. (*See* *exploitation.) Some also believe that the laws of inheritance ought not to permit constant accumulation of property across generations. Nevertheless it is difficult to envisage systems of private property rights without rights of transfer of property, and if transfer is permitted, then accumulation is always possible. Modern uses of *taxation can often be seen as attempts to permit maximum mobility of private property through exchange, while preventing accumulations beyond a certain level. (*See also* *primitive accumulation.)

acquis communautaire

The legal, political and procedural inheritance of the European Union, acquired through the process of union, and by the centralisation of powers and procedures hitherto exercised by the member states. The term was formally adopted by the EU only in the *Maastricht Treaty of 1992, which made clear for the first time that the *acquis communautaire* denotes an irreversible process, so that powers once lost to the European process cannot thereafter be retrieved from it. The *acquis* now amounts to 100 000 pages of legal and regulatory edicts.

act of state

1. Philosophical. Any act which can be attributed to no single citizen or group of citizens, and which is done for reasons connected with the interests, rights, privileges etc. of a *state, can be considered to be an act of state. Thus a declaration of war, while conveyed between statesmen and usually through diplomatic channels, is the act of one state towards another, it being impossible for any *agency less than the state to declare war. Some acts of state are directed towards other states, as in the example. Others are directed towards citizens and subject associations. It is the state that punishes the criminal, that expropriates the property owner, that nationalizes industries and enacts laws. The state can act through its officers, or through a monarch; it may also endorse or *ratify the actions of private citizens undertaken independently (as when the state annexes as a colony land captured by an adventurous citizen). In general a state has all the capacities for agency that an individual person has. Its actions may be intentional or unintentional, reasonable or unreasonable, moral or immoral. It may also *have* reasons for what it does, and respond to reasons for or against courses of action (the idea of a 'process' of government). Thus, it is often said, the state has will and responsibility, and this is one argument for thinking that, like a company in law, it is to be regarded

more as an autonomous person than as an organic aggregate of subjects. This thought is given elaboration in the philosophies of *Rousseau and *Hegel.

2. Legal. Acts of state are usually defined legally so as to include only actions *between* states. Thus in English law an act of state is an act of the sovereign power performed by virtue of the *prerogative, and in the course of its relations with other powers or with the *subjects of other powers. It cannot be challenged in the courts since it lies outside their jurisdiction. Hence in English law (as also in US law), there can be no act of state against an individual citizen or subject (i.e. one who owes allegiance), and the plea of act of state can never be used by government officers in defence of an encroachment on a subject's rights. Certain provisions in other constitutions might be interpreted as allowing the same effective immunity for government actions against citizens as is granted to government actions against other states: e.g. rights to enter and search without warrant, to imprison without trial, and so on, in cases of sedition.

activism

The German *Activismus* was used at the end of the First World War to denote the active engagement of *intellectuals in political transformation. 'Activists' are distinguished by the extent of their involvement in politics, and by the methods that they are inclined to sanction in pursuit of transformation, rather than by the nature of their views. They are not necessarily *extremists, nor are they necessarily opposed to constitutional forms of political change. *Sorel, however, defended activism in terms that also sanction extremism, arguing that activism is a necessary part of any serious political standpoint, since doing is everything, and thought only a *rationalization of what is done. On such a view it is incoherent to present a recipe for, or exhortation to, political transformation in advance of the attempt to precipitate it. Activism becomes essential to politics, and, Sorel thought, essentially violent.

actually existing socialism

Term used in the former communist countries to describe them as they really were, rather than as the official theory required them to be. Its use was largely ironical, and more or less confined to the writings of *dissidents.

addiction

A condition in which desire for some specific object of consumption becomes deep-rooted, recurrent and immovable, despite all rational considerations that weigh against it. The term is used somewhat loosely, to cover the habits of smokers, alcoholics and drug-abusers, as well as cravings for sex, music, television or even affection. It is important to distinguish those habits that significantly alter the physiological processes of the addict – such as heroine-addiction – from those which merely stimulate the craving for pleasure. The first replace vital functions of the body, and so cannot be set aside without painful and often fatal withdrawal symptoms. Some addictions seriously affect character – alcoholism, for example, and heroin addiction. Hence almost all governments have adopted policies to combat this kind of addiction. Others merely damage the body, like smoking or the addiction to fast food, though so far only the first of those has incurred legal restrictions. The most contentious instance, politically speaking, is television. Recent research seems to establish that television is genuinely addictive, setting up reward patterns in the brain that need to be constantly stimulated, and also that it has an adverse effect on character (enhancing belligerence and impatience) and also on learning (shortening the attention span, and rendering abstract argument more difficult to absorb). The potentially disastrous long-term effects are probably not susceptible to political remedy, however.

additional member system

A system of *proportional representation in which members of the chamber of deputies are allotted to parties from two lists of candidates: those who stand in the *constituencies, and who must be voted in by the local electorate; and additional candidates whose numbers are chosen in order that the party representation in the chamber will be proportional to the total number of votes cast in its favour, regardless of its performance in the constituencies. Each party submits a list of candidates from which these additional seats will be filled, and can thereby guarantee the presence of its key members in the chamber, even if they could not be elected in any constituency. The system is used in Germany and also in the Czech Republic and Hungary.

adjudication

The settlement of a dispute by judicial decree, hence, in English and US law, the judgement or decision of a court.

More broadly the term is used to refer to the process of settling disputes peacefully by referring them to some body with authority to make a decision or award binding upon the parties. Thus it covers awards made by mixed commissions and arbitral tribunals as well as those made by the courts. It is a method of resolving conflicts, to be contrasted with such processes as *arbitration and *mediation, in that it issues in a statement of *rights under the law. Its nature is of great concern to students both of *jurisprudence, and of politics. It represents a particular style of government that may not exist in all places and in all times, and which may be criticized and defended for the characteristics that distinguish it. Some argue that the settling of all disputes by adjudication may confer legislative power upon judges, and thus violate the supposed requirement of a *separation of powers. Others argue that disputes should be capable of settlement by less tortuous or costly means, and that too great an emphasis on adjudication serves to limit the possibilities of settlement. Advocates of the politics of *confrontation may argue that adjudication is a way of ensuring the peaceful victory of the powers that be, through their servants, the *judiciary. Advocates of the politics of *conciliation, by contrast, value adjudication as one among many possible means of translating powers into rights while avoiding *violence. (*See* *judiciary, *law.)

administered prices

*Prices which are determined by the policy of some agency which can control them, rather than by *market forces, or by whatever other less deliberative mechanism might be held to determine them. Prices can be administered by a *monopoly, by an *oligopoly, by a *cartel, or by a government.

administrative law

The branch of law which governs the activities of state administrative bodies, such as ministries, state departments, local government, commissions, and agencies. To be distinguished from *constitutional law, which is concerned not with the subordinate organs of government but with the supreme executive and legislative bodies. (There is also a large grey area between the

two.) In modern government there is increasing *delegation both of government power, and, through delegated legislation, of government authority. Hence the question arises of what remedy the citizen has against a body which acts, or purports to act, with the authority of the state. In France, as a result of traditional centralization, reinforced by Napoleonic edicts, administrative bodies are now subject to strict control by special administrative courts, and by the *conseil d'état*. Hence no special remedy is provided whereby the aggrieved citizen can obtain relief from an ordinary court of law. In the UK and the US there are, by contrast, established procedures of appeal to the courts, regarded as important parts of the constitutional freedom of the subject.

In the US, the supervision of the Supreme Court can prevent administrative bodies from acting *ultra vires*, it being always possible for the aggrieved citizen to seek *judicial review on the grounds that he has been denied *due process of law. In the UK the courts can overturn administrative decisions by special prerogative writs. These are summonses issued to the administrative body on behalf of the aggrieved party, calling on it in the name of the Crown to account for its actions. Among such writs is the celebrated *habeas corpus, and also mandamus (ordering a public officer to perform some neglected function), and certiorari (asking for the records of a decision to be submitted). (As the Latin names testify, these writs are of ancient provenance, and were partly responsible for the emergence of the English style of government, in which the Crown is represented as the servant of the subject against his oppressors.)

Of particular relevance in any subsequent proceedings are the principles of natural justice: has the administrative body effectively 'stood in judgement' on the plaintiff? If so, did it allow him the right of hearing? Did it review the relevant evidence? And so on. This survival of the doctrine of *natural justice in administrative law is vital if the state is to be seen as dealing at all levels on open terms with its citizens.

Adorno, Theodor, W. (1903–69)
German philosopher, social theorist and musician, who developed a Marxist critique of popular culture. A founding member of the *Frankfurt school, Adorno emigrated to the US upon Hitler's rise to power. The 'commodity culture' by which he found himself, in his new home, surrounded, elicited from him many acerbic and often penetrating pages of condemnation, and even if the Marxist trappings of his thought now seem dated, his defence of musical *modernism against musical *fetishism has had a lasting impact on Western culture. Adorno argued that 'late capitalism', as he called it, has generated, as part of its *ideology, a 'mass culture', the function of which is to distract people from the truth of their condition, and to provide them with a blanket of sentimental clichés. By contrast modernist art is concerned to see through the 'fetishized' products of popular culture, and to reveal the exploitation and oppression on which they depend. *See also* *authoritarian personality, *critical theory, *progress.

adversarial system
The mode of legal procedure in criminal cases whereby the prosecution (the state) acts through a counsel who is opposed in court by another counsel acting on the instructions of the accused. Each party is 'represented' before a third (the judge and jury) whose impartiality is necessary to justice, and whose existence and

independence are often taken to be fundamental constituents in the *rule of law. The adversarial system is to be contrasted with the *inquisitorial system common in countries with Roman-law or Napoleonic jurisdictions, and with systems that involve 'confessional' trials, trials by ordeal, and *show trials, where the individual is pitted directly against the state as his accuser and required to exonerate himself or be condemned. In show trials prosecutor and judge are identical, although this identity might be masked – for example by the presence of a judge who is acting under instructions from the prosecution. Some argue that there can be no true adversarial system unless the defendant who cannot afford a lawyer to represent him has an automatic right to public defence (US) or legal aid (UK).

The expression is sometimes used to describe a political system in which *opposition has a recognized function, with a place within the institutions of government, perhaps supported from public funds.

advertising
The declaration that goods or services are available for purchase, usually accompanied by attempts to persuade the public to buy them. The nature of advertising changed radically during the course of the twentieth century, with the development of new techniques of persuasion. Advertising has helped to form the character of *capitalist societies, and achieved a place in the life of the individual not unlike the place accorded to *propaganda in communist systems. It is the object of controversy on many grounds. Some argue, for example, that advertising is an economic evil, since it creates a barrier to entry into a market, preventing firms which cannot afford expensive advertising campaigns from selling their products. Others retort

that advertising promotes competition, and permits the emergence of self-supporting media of communication, thereby eliminating the need for state funding and promoting freedom of information.

Some of the hostility to advertising reflects the view that it radically alters the perceived quality of purchase and exchange, by imbuing them with acquisitive and *fetishistic impulses. Thus products become desired not because of their ability to satisfy human needs, but for reasons wholly unconnected with that, such as the desire for enhanced *status, the sense of a 'magic' power, the desire merely to have and to hold that which one is taunted for not possessing. Many go further and argue, with Vance Packard (*The Hidden Persuaders*, 1957) and *Galbraith, that advertising *creates* the wants that it offers to satisfy, and whose satisfaction it keeps just beyond our reach, by making sure that new wants are always created in the place of old. Thus it has an 'enslaving' effect, not unlike that described by nineteenth-century theories of *alienation. To this argument it may be replied that advertising provides useful information to consumers which they could easily obtain in no other way. It therefore enhances economic freedom. Moreover, the evils complained of by Packard and Galbraith are due less to advertising than to the particular styles and the particular media employed by it.

In the case of risky products, such as tobacco, alcohol and junk food, governments have begun to institute advertising bans, on the assumption that the appetite for these things is partly the result of advertising, which glamorizes the product and endows it with a false aura of sophistication. Against such bans it is argued that advertising does not sell the product but only the brand, and the effect of a ban is simply to freeze the market, so abolishing competition, while actual consumption remains unaffected. All such claims are hotly disputed; as a result advertising remains a serious subject of political controversy.

From the economic point of view advertising is sometimes seen as a form of indirect *taxation, whereby the mass media are subsidized by the consumer: hence the association of the two in the term 'admass', coined by J.B. Priestley in 1955, in order to describe the emerging tyranny of the mass media and advertising. However, advertising has a far older history than the mass media, and has produced its own art forms, such as the shop signs and street cries of medieval Europe.

aesthetics and politics

The term 'aesthetic', introduced into modern philosophy by A.G. Baumgarten (1714–62), is now normally used to denote a kind of imaginative experience, whose object is conceived as an end in itself. It arises from the contemplation of appearances, in which questions of ultimate purpose and scientific truth are held in suspension. It was plausibly suggested by *Kant that such experience is not only essential to the life of a *rational being, but also itself inherently rational, issuing in judgements held forth as objectively binding. Moreover, despite its abstraction from particular purposes, aesthetic experience provides an intimation of the inherent 'purposiveness' of reality. Two questions arise: what are the political consequences, and what the social and political causes, of aesthetic *values so conceived?

(i) The political consequences. Some argue that, despite its non-functional character, aesthetic experience is essential both to understanding and to acting on the world. In every action appearance has a dominant part to play, since it is largely through appearances that we respond to our environment. Hence the saving of appearances may be a persistent political purpose: it is this, for example, which explains much of the concern of 'conservationists' for landscape and townscape. When people agitate on behalf of some valley that is threatened by development, they are certainly not agitating on behalf of its rights. Nor are they truly concerned with the rights of themselves or future generations. The beauty of the landscape itself seems to give sufficient reason to act. Some argue, however, that such aesthetic activism has its ultimate *raison d'être* in social life. The regard for beauty reflects a deep need for social harmony, and in agitating on behalf of aesthetic values people are really agitating on behalf of the forms of life which are consonant with them. It is certainly indisputable that appearances are of overwhelming importance in social existence, and that the sense of manners, etiquette, and 'good form' are both intimately related to the aesthetic, and also integral to our understanding of one another as persons. Hence demands for aesthetic continuity can plausibly be seen as extensions of a sense of social 'belonging'; aesthetic values seem to nourish our understanding of the ends of social existence, and therefore inevitably qualify our pursuit of the political means. Such arguments were very popular in the nineteenth century, for example among *cultural conservatives, among certain kinds of pastoral socialists, and among thinkers like *Ruskin, *Morris and the critics of *industrialism. Such thinkers also extolled the aesthetic interest of the cognoscenti, as an index of the social needs of the common people. Their vision of the political significance of aesthetic value formed part of a general theory of the interdependence between high and common *culture.

The early twentieth century also saw the rise of an 'aestheticised' politics, in which the role of artist was consciously adopted by politicians as a model. This aestheticizing of politics was particularly influential in the birth of Italian fascism, with Mussolini expressly promoting himself as a 'sculptor whose material is humanity'. The futurist Marinetti, who saw all life as an opportunity for aesthetically interesting gestures, lent his support to this kind of politics, and it found exemplary expression in the poet Gabriele d'Annunzio's expedition to capture and hold the city of Fiume (now in Croatia), after the First World War, in defiance of Italy's obligations under the Treaty of Versailles. D'Annunzio reigned in Fiume for 15 months, decorating himself with titles, and dramatizing the process of government to give it the air of a work of art.

(ii) Social and political causes. It is evident that aesthetic values may reflect *ideological commitments. Some argue that the 'aesthetic' way of seeing things arose, like its name, in the *bourgeois period of Western civilization, as part of the *ideology (in the Marxist sense) of capitalist society. Aesthetic values arise in the mind of the person who wishes to consolidate his economic position by a species of passive and 'functionless' contemplation that shows to be harmonious what is in reality far from being so. This is then seen as part of an ideological attempt to *naturalize reality with consoling representations; other social orders will not require, and therefore will not produce, this kind of mystery. (Thus Bertolt Brecht: *The Messingkauf Dialogues*, 1939, published 1967. The theme has been taken up in our time by the literary critic Terry Eagleton (*The Ideology of the Aesthetic*, 1990) and the sociologist Pierre Bourdieu (*Distinction*, 1988).) That is one example of a theory which tries to find the causes of our love of beauty in social and political circumstances. Others, unpersuaded by that, may nevertheless see individual aesthetic outlooks as reflecting both particular political arrangements, and also the position of the individual within them. The eighteenth-century aesthetic of nature, for example, may be represented as an offshoot of aristocratic control exerted over the landscape. In contemplating the beauty of nature, the aristocrat was consoled by a vision of the 'natural' quality of his power. (*See also* *architecture, *art.)

affirmative action

Action taken in order to advance, rather than merely to conform to, the political vision underlying a doctrine of legal rights. Thus, if it is determined that, in matters of employment, blacks and women are to be given the same rights as white men, then affirmative action on the part of an employer involves not merely conforming to the code by giving equal consideration to all candidates independently of race and sex, but also actively seeking applications from women and blacks, so 'affirming' the underlying political vision which, if merely 'conformed to', might result in the perpetuation of existing inequalities. Affirmative action is sometimes defended as a necessary part of enforcing just distribution, sometimes criticized as a form of unjust discrimination in favour of those whose position is advanced by it. It is to be distinguished from a system of 'quotas', which requires a particular outcome, rather than a particular effort, and also from the practice of *reverse discrimination. Affirmative action is also sometimes justified as a way of correcting historical injustices, by giving favourable consideration towards people who belong to groups that have been discriminated against in the past.

affluence

The condition in which all human needs are easily satisfiable and generally catered for, and in which productive activity is directed increasingly to the production of luxuries (i.e. goods for which there is no natural *need).

In *The Affluent Society*, 1958, J.K. Galbraith argued that, when widespread poverty and want are abolished, people come to have a standard expectation of comfort. In such a society received ideas of economic theory (which tend to involve the assumption that at least *something* necessary is also scarce) cannot be applied. It is no longer rational for the *private sector to pursue increasing production or for the *public sector to refrain from interference in the economy. In fact, however, firms continue to seek the expansion of demand, and continue to see the public sector as an obstacle to the needed diversion of resources. This unbridled private expansion can persist only by the creation of artificial or 'synthesized' demands, through *advertising and the expansion of the credit system. Because of the neglect of public works the result is a condition of private affluence accompanied by public squalor: private cars but not enough roads for them, private wealth but insufficient police to protect it, and so on. Galbraith's argument seemed more plausible when it was first published, since it appeared at a time of rapid economic growth, before the necessary public adjustments had occurred. Since then Western societies have had to come to terms with affluence, and the pressures that it places on natural resources, on the environment and on cultural traditions.

In all discussions a distinction must be drawn between affluence that is concerned only with *consumption, and that which directs itself towards a style of life, involving, say, sumptuous ceremony and display. It is contended, e.g. by *Veblen, that the latter is simply a conspicuous version of the former. However, Veblen also argues that such conspicuous consumption provides part of the motive of accumulation and so cannot be eliminated from the productive process, which requires accumulation if it is to proceed at all. Others argue that, until naturalized by the trappings of civilization and leisure, conspicuous consumption is merely the object of envy, and so of social discontent.

'Aflaq, Michel (1910–89)

Syrian writer and political activist, educated in French schools in Syria and at the Sorbonne, of Greek Orthodox extraction, who founded the *Ba'ath movement for the 'resurrection' of the Arab peoples, with a view to uniting the Arabic-speaking world behind a reforming nationalist ideology, and in opposition to the colonial ventures of the European nation-states. 'Aflaq was a defender of free speech, civil rights and secular law, and was briefly, in the 1950s, minister of education in Syria. He argued in favour of an Arab, as opposed to a merely Muslim, identity, and hoped to reconcile Muslims, Christians and Jews in the foundation of viable jurisdictions in the post-colonial era. However, the movement that he founded, which took power in Syria and Iraq, soon found his views unacceptable and he retired from political life. When he died in Iraq he was granted a monumental funeral by the Ba'athist regime of Saddam Hussein, and the message was put out that he died a convert to Islam, having recognized that his defence of an Arabic politics dictated such a course. This message is now doubted, however, since 'Aflaq's voluminous writings have a strong undercurrent of attachment to the Christian legacy, and he continued to defend

*laïcité, as a precondition of reconciliation between the faiths.

agency

The faculty of action. Changes are divided into things that happen and things that are done, and philosophers and jurists dispute over the grounds and significance of the distinction. Only some forces in the world are also agents: the wind, for example, does nothing, although it causes much to happen. Some argue that the distinctive feature of agency is that it involves intention or decision: this is disputed by others, who argue that the crucial idea is *responsibility, so that things done include many of the consequences of negligent but unintentional behaviour.

Agency belongs to many bodies and organizations besides human beings: e.g. to companies, states, committees and meetings. Perhaps this is because all such bodies are also *corporate persons; or perhaps agency and personality are independent ideas. The distinction between actions and happenings is of immense importance: the first are justified, and criticized, by reasons; they define the responsibility and answerability of an agent; they give grounds for reciprocal actions which punish, repair, restore or reward. The political problems are typified by *revanchism, which holds a present generation responsible for things done by its ancestors, and takes revenge accordingly.

agenda

Latin: things to be done, but used in English as a singular noun. A well-conducted meeting needs an agenda, meaning a list of matters to be considered or decided. But the term is now more widely used, to denote the goals which animate people in their thought and action, and which may not be immediately apparent. In politics it is very important to know, not only the thoughts and declared policies of a party, but also its underlying agenda.

A 'hidden agenda' is one that is deliberately concealed, usually by adopting another, harmless-seeming agenda which is designed to deceive outsiders. Communist Parties have acted on the principle that the real agenda should be revealed only to those who can be trusted to act on it, and that it must be kept hidden from all opponents until resistance is futile.

aggregate demand

The total demand for goods and services produced within a single economy, including demands of households for consumer goods, of firms for investment, of government for goods, investment etc. and export demands. Many economists hold that aggregate demand determines the level of production and hence employment. Followers of *Keynes, in particular, believe that the analysis of aggregate demand is essential to the understanding of *national income and *unemployment. Whether aggregate demand has an automatic tendency to achieve the level giving full employment of labour and of productive capacity is, however, a central point of controversy within economic theory.

aggregate supply

The total supply of goods and services to meet the *aggregate demand within an economy; i.e. domestic products + imports.

aggression

A term fundamental to international disputes, which, since the First World War, has come to replace the idea of an 'offensive' act. It is argued that 'an acceptable definition of aggression and a reliable procedure for determining when an act of aggression has

occurred are essential to a practicable system of collective security' (W.M. Honan: *International Conflict and Collective Security*, 1955). However, the United Nations Charter failed to define aggression, stipulating only that the Security Council and the General Assembly are authorized to call *specific* actions aggression. Two definitions were put forward in 1933, one by the Committee on Security Questions of the Disarmament Conference, the other by a 'Convention for the definition of Aggression', subscribed to by Afghanistan, Estonia, Latvia, Persia (Iran), Poland, Romania, Turkey, Yugoslavia and the USSR. While the subsequent history of those states may be held to illustrate the futility of definitions in international politics, certain distinctions were made that have been incorporated into more recent definitions. It is now normal to distinguish direct aggression between states (e.g. armed invasion, whether or not preceded or accompanied by a declaration of war) from indirect aggression (e.g. the provision of arms and relief to an existing aggressor); aggression may be military or, as in a blockade of ports or an embargo, economic – although to what extent a blockade may go without being an act of aggression is a matter of dispute (*see* *pacific blockade). Aggression may involve regular armies answerable to the sovereign power, or more or less autonomous groups of guerrillas. All attempts to arrive at a definition are motivated by the desire to outlaw aggressive war (*see* *just war), under the supposition that if there were no aggressors, but only states prepared for 'self-defence', then there would be no wars. Aggression is, therefore, the initiating act expressive of an intention to fight. The problem is to identify its instances, in particular to show how indirect aggression is manifested by such complex agencies as states.

Moreover, the adoption of pre-emptive measures by a peace-loving state, in order to avert a threat from a potential belligerent, may involve violent military intervention, but with the intention of preventing, rather than initiating, a fight. The problems of definition in this area have therefore come very much to the fore in the aftermath of the American-led invasion of Iraq.

agitprop
The acronym for the Department of Agitation and Propaganda, set up in 1920 as a section of the Central Committee Secretariat of the Soviet Communist Party, and which gradually spread its influence into all areas of Soviet life and into many of the spheres of international politics, where it advanced behind *front organizations. Now often used as a general term for left-wing agitation and propaganda, when these involve any substantial degree of organization, and also for certain kinds of cultural activity designed to establish a widespread acceptance of leftwing *ideology.

agrarian movements
Movements, popular in the early to mid-twentieth century, which extol the rural way of life as a model to be followed, and which represent the countryside and its economy as a source of wholesome values that have been eroded by technology and urban lifestyles. To a great extent literary in inspiration, the agrarian movements have been influential in France (led by the writers Jean Giono and Gustave Thibon), in England (under the influence of the *Soil Association and the writer H.J. Massingham), and in the American South (led by the Southern Agrarians and the poet Allen Tate). The *Wandervogel* movement in Germany, which began life as a youth movement at the end of the nineteenth century,

becoming an indigenous answer to the Boy Scouts after the disaster of the First World War, injected a strong agrarian streak into German politics, and was in due course hijacked by the Nazi Party, to become part of the 'blood and soil' ideology that was soon to lead to another and yet more disastrous war. As a result agrarian movements are viewed with suspicion in modern Germany, and have given way to *green politics, which attempts to distance itself from all forms of rural nostalgia and to see the land and its culture as simply one aspect of the global environment.

agrarian parties
Parties founded expressly in order to represent rural interests. Unfamiliar in the British context (although the Conservative Party has always had rural leanings and disproportionate rural support) and unknown in the US, agrarian parties have nevertheless been a familiar feature in agricultural countries with large rural populations. Their influence is now declining, as parties seek to free themselves from association with particular classes, groups or interests so as to appeal to the nation as a whole. In Poland, Hungary and Romania, however, 'peasant' or 'smallholders' parties are for the time being major forces in the political process, while traditional agrarian parties still have considerable following in Scandinavian countries.

agribusiness
A term introduced to denote the new kind of food production, in which large estates – often owned by non-resident or corporate landlords – are devoted exclusively to the production of crops or livestock, and in which the land is treated as a capital asset like any other, to secure the maximum return on investment. Agribusiness favours large holdings, mechanized

production, a minimal labour force, and the use of fertilizers and pesticides to secure a reliable production of foodstuffs. It has become an object of controversy among those who believe it to be destructive of the natural and social ecology of the countryside. Others argue that the economies of scale introduced by agribusiness will facilitate the diversion of resources to environmental protection, as well as stimulating a viable rural economy.

agriculture

A term which should perhaps be contrasted with *agribusiness, so as to denote the small-scale production of food by resident farmers, whose interest in the land is also an interest in their home and in the place where they have settled with their families. Agriculture is not so much an economic function as a way of life, and the movement to maintain that way of life in the face of adverse economic trends has been an important force in recent politics – notably in Europe, under the *Common Agricultural Policy. The deliberate destruction of agriculture, and its replacement by state-controlled agribusiness, has been widely regarded as the primary social and economic disaster of the communist system. (*See* *collectivization.) In so far as the *agrarian movements survive today, it is in the guise of attempts to 'put the culture back in agriculture'.

ahistorical (sometimes anhistorical)

A theory is described as such when it treats its subject-matter either as though it had no history, or as though its history played no important part in the explanation of its nature. It is often said that the *liberal theory of human nature and political institutions is ahistorical. The intention is to accuse liberalism of describing our social and political nature without reference to the fact that these develop

historically, or to the fact that historical development determines both what is politically possible and what is politically justified. Marxists often go on to add that this ahistorical vision is itself the reflection of a particular set of historical circumstances – say, those which obtained in eighteenth- or nineteenth-century Europe, and perhaps even now in America. Such circumstances (it is argued) enable people to envisage a universal human type, whose essence, while in fact the product of a particular phase of historical development, is perceived as changeless, sempiternal, the common property of every economic and political order.

Some confusion results from the fact that any description of the essence of something (be it human nature or the nature of a plant or animal) must have universal validity: i.e. it cannot be specific with relation to time. If it is of the essence of human nature to develop through time, then this is a timeless truth about human nature. A liberal theory may well rely on just such a timeless truth in constructing its fundamental theory of rights and duties, without incurring the charge of being 'ahistorical': yet this charge is sure to be levelled at it, simply on account of its search for universality.

aid

On the assumption that the world divides into 'developed' and 'developing' nations, and that it is better for a nation to be developed than not, the idea of international aid has come to have considerable importance in political thinking. (*See* *development.) It has been argued before the UN Conference on Trade and Development that growth in real terms in nations recognized as 'developing' can be secured only by a level of imports which exceeds their capacity to export. Hence, without foreign aid, they must inevitably decline further in real income level, as a result of the very process of trade that promises to improve their status. This idea has been used to suggest a variety of conclusions, for example: (i) that it is an inevitable effect of free trade to impoverish further the poorer nations (an argument analogous to Marx's attempt to show that private ownership of the means of production inevitably leads to the creation of a propertyless class); (ii) that there is a moral duty on richer nations to provide aid; (iii) that development is impossible without actual colonization. Others (e.g. P.T. Bauer: *Dissent on Development*, 1971) argue that the economic theories underlying the accepted wisdom concerning aid and development are in fact contentious, that it is aid which, in removing the incentive to exploit resources, leads to impoverishment, and that aid merely lines the pockets of a ruling élite, without producing a real investment. *See also* *North/South divide, *thirdworldism, *three worlds theory.

akrasia

A term of ancient Greek philosophy, normally translated as 'weakness of will', and indicating an area of philosophical difficulty in the understanding of human motivation. As rational beings we choose what we think to be good. So how can we think something to be good and not choose it? One answer is that our will is 'overcome' by other and non-rational forces, so that, when we choose something that we also condemn, we are not acting rationally. But in that case, are we really *choosing*? This problem, which sometimes seems sophistical, was identified by Aristotle as a major obstacle to a comprehensive theory of rational agency.

al-Banna, Hassan (1906–49)

Egyptian schoolteacher, *Islamist and political activist, founder of the *Muslim Brotherhood. Stimulated by the British occupation of Egypt into resisting both foreign government and foreign ways, al-Banna was deeply preoccupied with the condition of the new urban poor who had migrated from the countryside to the shanty towns of twentieth-century Egypt. He believed that they were being uprooted from a way of life which was essential to them, that they must be provided with education, resources and the religious instruction that would enable them to form coherent communities, and that they should be guided along the path of righteousness and organized in the pursuit of an Islamic state. The Muslim Brotherhood was to be both teacher and vanguard of this disenfranchised proletariat, and by acts of violence directed against foreigners, infidels and the traitors within, it was to secure an Islamic Republic that would serve as a model to the Arab world. Under al-Banna's leadership the brotherhood grew to a mass movement, with half a million members in Egypt and branches in other Arab countries. It also began to embark on selective assassinations – including, in 1948, the Prime Minister of Egypt. In 1949 al-Banna was himself assassinated, many assume by the Egyptian secret services, which were attempting to bring the Brotherhood under control.

alien

A person who, by the law of one state, is not a national or citizen of that state, though he may be resident there. The decision whether to admit aliens falls within the privilege of each sovereign state, and no state can be forced by international law to do so. The matter is, however, a subject of fierce domestic disagreement. The *jus gentium* in *Roman law evolved partly in order to determine the political rights of aliens, and most states now recognize some standard of humane behaviour towards aliens on their soil.

The legal idea of an alien is bound up with those of *jurisdiction (i.e. the idea that a state has sovereign authority over a particular *territory*) and *allegiance (i.e. the idea that persons owe duties to *specific* sovereign states). In some versions of liberal internationalism, for which jurisdiction and allegiance ought to aspire to be international, the idea of an 'alien' is inherently retrograde. (*See* *Kant.)

The legal idea should be distinguished sharply from the social and political conception that certain people, classes, or races are 'alien' from the point of view of a society by which they are surrounded. In the legal sense a person is 'alien' to the state; in the socio-political sense he is 'alien' to society. That is to say, his customs, allegiances, behaviour (perhaps even the colour of his skin), mark him out as something strange, and perhaps unacceptable, in the consciousness of those with whom he must mix.

alienation

A term used to describe a state of mind or of being, and owing its modern significance to three related ideas, all of them with discernible medieval antecedents:

1. In *Hegel two terms tend to be translated as 'alienation': *Entäußerung* (objectification), and *Entfremdung* (self-estrangement). The theory – which is not particularly associated with either term – occurs as part of a general account of the progress of spirit (*Geist*) towards knowledge of, and unity with, the 'Absolute Idea'. Spirit begins in subjectivity, and proceeds towards objective existence; spirit creates its world in the act of knowing it, and both history and individual development are to be seen as the construction and overcoming of successive 'objectifications'. At a

certain 'moment' of consciousness, the spirit divides the world into good and bad, ideal and reality, saved and fallen. This divorce is experienced as a divorce between the self and the objectifications which it has 'posited' as not-self. The fracture between the ideal objectification and the fallen self is experienced as a thoroughgoing imperfection in all conscious life: Hegel calls this state the 'unhappy consciousness'. Estrangement from the self is conjoined with estrangement from others. Since it is the essence of spirit to identify itself with the ideal, the world is seen as devoid of spirit, which lies beyond humanity, and not in it. Men are seen as objects, while spirit is seen as realized only in the being of a transcendent God. The practice of religion is the attempt to overcome this rift, to see man as no longer trapped in nature, and no longer aspiring hopelessly to overcome it. Alienation is overcome by the recognition of the immanence of God, and the self-transcendence of man, through the sacramental customs of religion. Hegel had Christianity in mind, and in particular the doctrine of the incarnation of God in Christ, who reconciles in his person the human and the divine.

2. In the early writings of *Marx, alienation (*Entfremdung*) is alienation from *species-being (*Gattungswesen*) – a term borrowed from Feuerbach (*see* *Young Hegelians) to describe the distinctive character of human social existence. Feuerbach had secularized some of the theological ideas of Hegel, and thus paved the way for Marx's view, according to which alienation is no longer inherent in man's 'being in the world', but only in his being in a *particular historical* world. Man's essence lies in his species-being, so that alienation from species-being is alienation from the human essence, and hence from self. This process

occurs when people are compelled to see themselves as objects, as means to ends, with no satisfactions that they can identify as their own. They then cease to have reality for themselves; instead they project their essence and value into the objects which they pursue. Human life is seen only as a means, whereas objects are seen as ends, with an intrinsic value which in reality cannot belong to them. Since the prime activity of species-being is *labour, the primary mode of alienation is alienated labour, through which people are compelled to instil the world with the forms of alienated consciousness. Marx saw this state as associated with *private property, which compels the *division of labour, and the institution of the *wage contract. By forcing people to sell themselves (i.e. in another, legal, sense, to 'alienate' their *labour power), it also compels them to engage in the production of goods which have no *use-value for them, but only *exchange-value. Such goods do not reflect back to the producer an image of himself, since they bear the imprint of no natural satisfaction. In pursuing and producing them, a person sees himself as a means to an end that is not his own. Hence he becomes an object to himself, and looks on others likewise. Only with the abolition of private property will man be restored to himself, and to the 'species-being' which constitutes his satisfaction. *See also* *master and slave.

3. In *Freud and post-Freudian psychology, alienation is seen as the condition in which people are placed by civilization, through the necessity to conform to roles and expectations, and to *repress and transform vital instincts and impulses, so that in becoming acceptable to others they become strangers to themselves.

Many modern thinkers (e.g. *Marcuse and Erich Fromm (1900–80))

attempt to synthesize the Marxian and Freudian ideas. For them 'capitalist man' is a being crippled through the fatty degeneration of the will, driven to see himself always as an object and never as the originator of his acts, a person who is no longer a true person because he cannot be what he really is: he loses interest in life because it is not *he* who lives it. In this speculative social criticism alienation is often contrasted with an ideal of *authenticity or *self-realization. In none of the established usages is the notion very clear, but in all of them it expresses the search for a theory that will describe the condition of the modern self, and also explain its sense of being 'separated' from some truly human way of being.

allegiance

The bond which attaches the subject to the sovereign, and also to fellow subjects. This bond can be conceived in two ways. First, as a power, consisting in emotional attachment to certain familiar conditions and expectations, of which the state is the symbol and expression. Secondly, as a duty towards the sovereign power. In the latter construction, it gives rise to the well-known problem of *political obligation: how can allegiance be *owed*, and what justifies us in asserting this? Liberals and others have attempted to find the answer in theories of the *social contract; Marxists and anarchists have looked forward to the creation of a state of affairs in which the problem of political obligation would not arise, believing that the highest form of society is one without sovereignty, and therefore with nothing towards which allegiance might be owed.

Conservatives, by contrast, have made the concept of allegiance, conceived as a power, fundamental to their description of the experience of society. Allegiance becomes the inescapable precondition, both of the contract which liberal thinkers suppose might justify it, and of the renunciation of sovereignty to which the anarchist aspires. Allegiance is an emotional condition, which creates the possibility of political obligation, but has no independent ground. Some – for example *Hegel in *The Philosophy of Right* – have tried to argue that the power and the obligation are one, and both examples of *piety. On this view the attempt to found political obligation in contract or consent is based on the spurious view that voluntary activity is the only thing that can put a citizen under an obligation. But it is essential to many institutions – for example the *family – that people should recognize and defer to obligations which do not arise through voluntary action. This sense of obligation towards what is safe and familiar is an ineliminable part of social consciousness and cannot be further justified. According to such views, allegiance is the true fact of the matter in political life, and any attempt to replace it with contract, consent, or some unforeseeable alternative (such as would be involved in the total abolition of sovereignty) misrepresents the fundamental bond of society, and misdescribes the subject-matter of politics. The problem for such views lies partly in determining the object of allegiance: is allegiance towards individuals, towards *society, towards the *state, or what? Moreover, how can it be brought into being if it does not already exist? Also, while 'allegiance' may describe the citizen's *sense* of obligation towards the state, it does not seem to describe, on this theory, any proven obligation.

All those problems have come to the fore in current disputes over *immigration. How do we secure the allegiance of immigrants who retain their old customs, old affections, and old sense of belonging in another and differently governed place? At least, if allegiance is based in a contract, we can persuade them to sign; but if it lies deeper than rational choice, and is rooted in custom, proximity and lifestyle, we cannot assume that an immigrant will possess it.

alliance

Specifically, a nation is an ally of another if bound to it by some treaty for mutual defence. More loosely, 'allies' are those who recognize the threat of a common aggressor, and agree under certain terms to take concerted action, diplomatic, economic, or military, to counter it. 'The Allies', used to name the association of nations fighting the Axis powers during the 1939 war, is a term the emotional resonance of which survives in 'The Western Alliance'. This now names the loose association of nations united to some extent by treaty (e.g. NATO), to some extent by a common apprehension of danger, most of all by similar conceptions of political *legitimacy, and by mutually dependent economies. It is disputed whether the creation of alliances is beneficial either to world peace or to the common interests of the international community, but even without the existence of alliances, the division of the world into *blocs, *spheres of influence, and spheres of *coercion and domination would presumably produce similar effects.

al-Qa'eda

Arabic: the base. Name bestowed by its founder, Osama bin Laden, on a worldwide *Islamist movement whose ostensible purpose is to free the holy places of Arabia (specifically Mecca and Medina) from all taint of heathen occupation, but which has expanded to become the major network of international *terrorism in the contemporary world, recruiting disaffected Muslims from all over the globe, in a terminal struggle against Western civilization and *jahiliyya*. The name indicates that the pious Muslim, who has resolved to give his life to the cause, has found a sufficient foundation for his life wherever he should choose to be, and has no need of a domicile, a nation, a jurisdiction or any law other than that laid down by the Holy Koran. His duty is to love his fellow believers, to hate the infidel and if possible to die in the cause. The principal intellectual influence on al-Qa'eda has been *Wahhabism, and its doctrine of the unity of God and the inviolability of his commands.

alternative society
A term used in the popular exposition of a certain kind of extreme liberalism (fashionable in the US and other highly developed urban-industrial societies during the 1960s), according to which the aim of individual life is to lead an 'authentic life style', achieved through independent personal choice. There is no reason to conform to the 'structures' of the 'system' into which one is born that is more compelling than the impetus to enact the authentic life style of one's own devising, and so to create, in community with one's fellows, the 'alternative society' and its associated *counter-culture. This counter-culture will be offensive to the guardians of the 'establishment', since it will threaten the easy solution by which they have chosen to live. (The terms in inverted commas are part of the rhetoric that confers on the original thought the appearance of system.)

The advocacy of the alternative society derives in part from *Sartre's existentialism, in part from the psychotherapeutic doctrines of *Reich and R.D. Laing, and in part from the radical social criticism of *Marcuse.

Criticized from the right by the defenders of traditional order, it was also fiercely denounced from the left, for example by *Lasch.

alternative vote
The system of *proportional representation in which voters rank candidates in order of preference. If no candidate has a majority of first preferences, then the least successful candidate is eliminated, and the second preferences of his supporters added to the initial totals. The re-allocation of votes is repeated until a winner emerges.

Althusser, Louis (1918–90)
*Neo-Marxist French philosopher, who attempts to combine 'scientific Marxism', with the *structuralism of *Lévi-Strauss. Althusser argues, in *For Marx* (1965), that there is a fundamental discontinuity ('epistemological break') between *Hegel and Feuerbach, on the one hand, and Marx on the other. He dismisses the early (pre-1845) writings of Marx as 'humanist', and finds the true, 'scientific' Marxism in the writings that follow. Althusser's major deviations from Marx's historical materialism may be attributed to his conception of 'structural causation', which he argues to be implicit in the mature 'scientific' theories of Marx. Revolution and all social transformation are brought about through *contradiction, and the 'principal contradiction' is that identified by Marx, between *productive forces and *production relations. However, this principal contradiction is 'inseparable from the total structure of the social body in which it is found'. The social body contains other contradictions, existing at several distinct levels within the *superstructure, and interacting systematically, as they struggle to align themselves: so contradictions pass from one level to another. Because the various contradictions

develop unevenly it is possible that an economically backward country might present the sudden confluence of contradictions necessary for successful revolution (the case of Russia). Althusser calls this 'fusion of accumulated contradictions' 'over-determination', borrowing a term from *Freud. Thus while the economy may exert a powerful sway over social conditions, it alone can never be taken as the cause of social transformation (although Althusser affirms somewhat half-heartedly the thesis of *Engels, that 'economic necessity . . . in the last analysis always prevails'). Althusser was briefly influential, but suffered an eclipse during the 1980s, and is now increasingly regarded as an historical curiosity. His dense, paranoid prose style, and blindness to any debates other than those current in the French Communist Party suggest, at the very least, an obsessive personality. In later life Althusser developed a psychotic illness which caused him, in 1981, to strangle his wife.

altruism

The disposition to care for others, or to act knowingly in their interests. The term has been appropriated by ethologists, to describe organisms which exist partly through giving help to members of their species. In *game theory, altruistic strategies are contrasted with selfish strategies, such as that known as 'tit-for-tat', in which every hurt inflicted by one party is answered with a hurt inflicted by the victim. Axelrod and others have tried to show that, in the long run, organisms that adopt an altruistic response to their kind are better able to adapt to competition than those who play tit-for-tat, and that the emergence of altruism is therefore a long-term effect of natural selection. *Sociobiologists have attempted to extend ethological theories of the 'altruistic organism' to

the human species, in order to explain our liking for each other as a convenient evolutionary device. Whatever the value of such explanations, it is clear that altruism is a serious motive in human affairs, and one that must affect the calculations of politicians and economists. Some economists argue that *classical theorists such as *Smith did not take sufficient account of it; others try to integrate altruism into economics by ascribing to it a distinctive function, whereby it generates the *optimum economic behaviour in a group. (See, e.g. E.S. Phelps (ed.): *Altruism, Morality and Economic Theory*, 1975.)

Philosophers distinguish two distinct motives that go by the name of altruism: the emotional motives, of love, liking and *friendship, whereby another's interest is automatically mine; and the moral motive, of respect or considerateness, whereby another's interest becomes a reason for me, while not necessarily becoming mine. See *charity, *Kant.

amendment

The process of legislative amendment has become increasingly important in modern democracies. Bills introduced into the legislature by governing parties are gradually subjected to dilution or qualification, through the influence of individual members and *committees, and often in response to organized *pressure groups. It is therefore impossible to predict the precise form of the legislation that will emerge, even from a determined government with a strong majority.

Amendment has played a decisive role in US history and government, since it was by the process of constitutional amendment that the Declaration of Rights was incorporated into the Constitution, with incalculable results. (See *Bill of Rights.)

amnesty

From the Greek meaning oblivion or forgetfulness. An amnesty is a general determination that whole classes of offenders shall not be prosecuted. It is juridically distinct from a pardon, which is the annulment of a penalty already prescribed. Only the criminal consequences of the absolved act are destroyed, and third parties may still have recourse to a civil action for damages.

Amnesties are offered to prisoners of war and of conscience, or to *political offenders. They may be general or particular, absolute or conditional. There is considerable dispute over who, and in what circumstances, is entitled to offer them. In the US, it seems undecided whether an amnesty is an executive rather than a legislative act. The first theory attributes the power of amnesty to the President, the second attributes it to Congress.

The term is also used, as in 'Amnesty International', to denote the general overlooking of accusations founded merely in differences of opinion between the accused and the state. Liberty of *conscience, it is thought, requires that a sincerely held belief cannot be sufficient grounds for punishment.

anarchism

The belief either that government is intrinsically evil, or that historical circumstances have conspired to make it so, together with the further belief that it is preferable and possible to abolish government, either completely, or at least in part. The anarchist believes in a *society without the institutions of a *state, and tends, also, to reject all forms of *authority that interfere with the spontaneous actions and associations of individuals. Typical anarchist beliefs are these:

(i) People are benign by nature and corrupted by government.

(ii) The state is exploitative, and oppressive, whereas society is natural and free.

(iii) Man is a social animal, fulfilled through voluntary cooperation, but frustrated by all *coercion.

(iv) Reforms 'from above' bear the imprint of the authority that initiates them, and are therefore worthless.

(v) Social change must be brought about through revolutionary action, perhaps even *violent action.

Not all those beliefs are held by every anarchist. *Godwin, for example, believed in a society of small producers, united by cooperation, but without a state, and sought to achieve this by enlightened social reform. The Russian anarchist *Bakunin advocated 'anarchism, collectivism, atheism', in a synthesis that required immediate violent revolution. Others could be called anarchists despite rejecting all of (i) to (v): *Nietzsche, for example, who lauded the strength and egoism of the individual will, and sought to free it from all attachment to the 'herd-like' necessities whereby the multitude are governed. Much nineteenth-century anarchism was hostile towards private property, or towards some kinds of private property, as a kind of concealed slavery. *Proudhon, who attempted to make anarchism into a conscious mass movement, proposed the maxim that 'property is theft'. However, he also thought that property is a necessary part of freedom, and therefore attacked *monopoly and usurpation as the principal evil forms of it. Bakunin advocated *common ownership of the means of production, but was prepared to concede private ownership in the 'means of consumption'. Godwin accepted most kinds of private ownership, on a small scale. Modern thinkers influenced by anarchism (e.g. the non-anarchist *Nozick) are usually of a *liberal persuasion, and are therefore more tolerant towards private property, on account of the interference in freedom that its abolition seems to entail.

Another important aspect of nineteenth-century anarchism was the hostility towards organized religion: Tolstoy, for example, who believed in a society of love, argued that 'true' religion involves a complete negation of the state and all its institutions. Most anarchists have either accepted that position, or gone further, and argued that no religion is true. Violent anarchists, such as *Sorel, have been influential during the twentieth century, and the nineteenth-century anarchists were extremely important in providing concepts to *Marx, whose '*withering away of the state' is directly inspired by their ideals.

In all its forms anarchism must assume that there is a condition of human society (or even human solitude) in which material needs and collective responsibilities will be met spontaneously, without coercion. Most anarchists are therefore disposed to reject the view of Hobbes, that the life of man outside the protection of the sovereign is 'solitary, poor, nasty, brutish and short'. The objections contained in Hobbes's remark are endorsed by many, who also see history as confirming them. Without violence, it is argued, the destruction of the state is inconceivable, and with violence, a new state must immediately replace that which is destroyed. Furthermore, the advocacy of violence seems to go against those very assumptions about human nature on which anarchism bases its vision of a new society. In the face of such difficulties certain anarchists assert that the social condition of man has first to be improved by the massive discipline of industrial production before the state can wither away and 'true human nature' reassert itself. Perhaps the view

most radically opposed to anarchism is *Hegel's, that 'true human nature' requires the state, not only as the means to its security, but as the highest expression of its freedom.

anarcho-capitalism

A theory advanced by the American economist and political scientist Murray N. Rothbard (1926–95), who believed that capitalist production, left to itself and without the interference of the state, would generate all the laws and procedures necessary to peaceful and prosperous coexistence. The market would generate a consensual morality, a law of contract and tort, and an allocation of responsibilities and liabilities that would be sufficient to rectify injustices and to maintain a mutually profitable equilibrium among its participants. Interference from the state is the great enemy, not only of a free economy, but of the more fundamental freedoms from which social responsibility spontaneously emerges. At a certain stage in his career Rothbard suggested an alliance between libertarians of the right, such as himself, and those of the left with genuine anarchist tendencies.

anarcho-syndicalism

A movement arising in the later nineteenth century from a fusion of anarchist and *trade union (syndicalist) principles, and led at first by James Guillaume, a Swiss disciple of *Bakunin, and later guided and endorsed by *Sorel. Anarcho-syndicalism advocated the use of trade union power, in order to oppose and destroy state power in all its forms. In Sorel's hands it was exhorted to *violence, and action (culminating in the final and decisive 'general strike') which would be tantamount to violence. Sorel's philosophy is often thought not to be a genuine *anarchism, since he advocated the use of organized groups in order to overthrow the established order. (*See further* *syndicalism.*) The anarcho-syndicalist movement thought of trade unions as the nuclear bodies of a future society, which must prepare themselves as cohesive fighting units, in order to work for the overthrow of the capitalist state. It formed the basis of pre-Francoist trade unionism in Spain, and of the US 'Industrial Workers of the World' (the 'wobblies'), but it was opposed in the UK by the existing trade union formations. Its ideals have persisted, even though the movement has perished, and in France *industrial action may still sometimes be viewed as a direct or indirect *confrontation with the state, whether or not the state is also the employer against which the action is directed.

Anglicanism

The system of religious doctrine and practice upheld by Christians in communion with the see of Canterbury, and hence by the Church of England, and its offshoots in former colonies and dependencies. The doctrine is derived from a fusion of evangelical authority and respect for local custom. The proof of doctrinal validity is to be sought in the first four centuries of Christian teaching, before the institutional structure of the Roman Catholic Church had diverted that teaching to its own peculiar usage; while in all matters of liturgy, ceremony, and the legal and social status of religious belief, local custom and tradition are respected as containing the only objective authority. Anglicanism thus comes to stand for a particular vision of the social role of the church. The 'Church of England', is not only common to Englishmen (and, by extension through the (Episcopal) Church of Scotland, Church of Ireland etc., to Scots, Irish etc.), but also legally established

within, and influenced through, a national government. It thereby attempts to incorporate into its constitution a vision of the harmony between secular and religious obligations, encapsulated in the doctrine that the head of state (the sovereign) is also the leader of the church. In the UK constitution some bishops hold seats in Parliament as of right, and all bishops are appointed by the sovereign with the advice of the Prime Minister. Equally, liturgical and doctrinal reforms require the consent of the sovereign in Parliament, a fact that has recently been resented by the Anglican Church on the grounds that it provides an impediment to reforms dictated by its evangelical mission. Clearly, the coexistence of that mission with a respect for established usage, and the incorporation of both into a legal and political superstructure of the kind currently existing in the UK, are delicate social and political artifacts. The social order that they reflect remains an object of *nostalgia on the part of some English conservatives, although others argue that it is either extinct or on the verge of extinction. (*See* *common prayer, *liturgy.*)

The spread of Anglicanism through the British Empire has led to the existence today of a world-wide Anglican communion, officially under the tutelage of the see of Canterbury, but severed from the political allegiance implied in the role of the Queen, as simultaneously Head of the Church and Head of State. This strange state of affairs has generated considerable strain, as the American branch (called Episcopalian) tends towards the new secular causes, such as *gay marriage, while the African branch retains much of the fervent Evangelical faith with which Anglicanism was first preached on that continent.

animal liberation

The movement for 'animal liberation' exists in many forms. At its most radical it involves a complete identification with the animal kingdom, a refusal to eat animals or to use them in any way that involves constraint, together with agitation – even violent agitation – on behalf of a new social and political order in which animals will finally enjoy their 'rights'. This radical form is a reincarnation of the revolutionary spirit, with animals taking the place of the proletariat; as such it belongs to the *victim culture of the modern city. Less radical forms of the movement may be content merely with *pressure groups, working towards legislative control of the way in which animals are reared, slaughtered or hunted. *See* *animals.

animal rights

See *animals.

animals

Movements to protect animals from mistreatment began in the early nineteenth century and have gathered momentum in recent years, giving currency to many controversial ideas. Some argue that animals, like people, have *rights and that it is therefore morally unacceptable to use them for our purposes. Against this it may be held that creatures have rights only if they also have duties, and that it makes no sense to attribute duties to non-rational animals. Moreover, the assumption that animals have rights would make them full members of the moral community, bound by the very same morality that constrains our own behaviour. On this view, predators would live under a permanent cloud of guilt, and the whole animal kingdom would be crying out for justice against its criminal members.

These philosophical difficulties do nothing to avert the charge that animals are often used cruelly and in morally unjustifiable ways. The question has therefore arisen as to *how* exactly they are to be treated, what laws should govern our behaviour towards them, and to what extent animals are to be protected by the state. Clearly, animals are not citizens, and play no part in the political process. Nevertheless, they are indefinitely vulnerable to human mistreatment, and most people favour some kind of legal framework to guarantee their protection. However, the case of wild animals must be distinguished from that of domestic animals.

There are two common motives for protecting wild animals: concern for the individual animal, and concern for the species. Someone might be opposed to angling or *hunting on the grounds that the animals suffer unduly and merely for the sake of human pleasure. An ecologist might favour angling and hunting on the grounds that these practices serve the long-term interests of the hunted species by endowing human beings with a motive to preserve their habitats. Legislation to protect endangered species is now common throughout the civilized world; and proposals to abolish hunting and shooting have met with favour in several European countries, notably Germany (under the Nazis) and more recently Belgium, Holland and (in the case of hunting) the United Kingdom.

Domestic animals are already under our protection. For many people, therefore, the question of how we should treat them is more urgent than the question of hunting and fishing. How should farm animals be reared, for example, and how should they be slaughtered? Should we use animals as the subjects of painful or crippling experiments – for example when testing drugs? How, and to what extent, should animals (horses and dogs, for example) be trained in order to satisfy our interests?

Arguments in this area are clouded by emotion. Unless we are able to determine how we differ from the animals, and how we resemble them, we shall be unable to know the extent of our moral duties towards them. The religious view that human beings have an immortal soul, capable of good and evil, which will be judged for all eternity, whereas animals are merely alive, gives grounds for a coherent moral distinction. But it is a controversial view, and those who do not accept it may find themselves at a loss to know *why* they should view animals so differently from people. Indeed, the loss of the religious worldview is one explanation for the upsurge in the movement to protect and favour animals. (*See also* *ecology, *speciesism.)

annexation

Primarily a term in *international law, denoting the *act of state whereby territory not previously held under the sovereignty of that state is acquired. Annexation confers all powers of use, exclusion, alienation, titles to public property rights, etc., on the annexing state. Allegiance of the inhabitants of the annexed territory is automatically assumed by the new sovereign, and although existing law and *local government organization in principle remain intact, they do so only in so far as this does not conflict with the interests of the annexing state. Thus annexation is to be distinguished from the establishment of a *protectorate, or military occupation, these latter procuring for the dominant state an extension of authority, but not full *sovereignty. It is also distinct from colonization, in that actual occupation either by the authorities of the annexing state or by its citizens is not required.

Within international law annexation can only be validated when consented to by the state whose territory is annexed (in whole or in part), or (in the case of a territory not formerly held by another state) when consented to by the international community. The consent of a predecessor state may be given tacitly, under *coercion, or in the form of a *treaty. In either case, the inhabitants of the annexed territory are without rights of *self-determination. Originally annexation was intended as a mechanism whereby the discovery of new land could be both facilitated and credited to the adventuring state; it is now simply one among many means whereby major powers incorporate the territories of smaller powers.

anomie (also: anomy)

Greek: without law. 'Anomy' appeared in English in the sixteenth century and was frequently used in seventeenth-century theology to mean disregard of law, particularly divine law. The French *anomie* was appropriated by *Durkheim to denote the social condition in which no established code prevails or is accepted as objectively binding, either because traditions of social conformity have broken down, or because the sense of an authority independent of the individual impulse has been dissolved. *Anomie* may be a form of personal disorganization, when the individual can recognize no social *norm as constraining him, or a form of social disorganization, when norms are in conflict or have lost authority. Durkheim argued (*Suicide*, 1897) that *anomie* is a characteristic of an immature industrial society, that has yet to develop a suitable moral climate. However, in a late essay (*The Dualism of Human Nature*, 1914) he seemed to admit the possibility that the *anomie* which he discerned in modern society, where the *division of labour isolates every individual from his fellows, and where authoritative institutions exert no necessary influence, may not be overcome, and may become perpetual.

Anomie may be described as the public aspect of *alienation and also as a reaction to *disenchantment.

anthropology

The science of man, which has divided into several distinct but related studies, and developed an emphasis upon societies considered to be either *prehistorical or in some way removed from too much interaction with the modern world. Anthropology has tended to concentrate on such *primitive societies, not because they are thought to require analysis in ways inapplicable elsewhere but, on the contrary, because of the assumed ease with which they might generate universal conclusions. In studying what is unfamiliar and difficult to conceptualize, the anthropologist hopes to discover hypotheses concerning *human nature and society everywhere. The following distinct branches are now recognized:

(i) physical anthropology, which merges with human biology, and deals with the physical characteristics of the species;

(ii) cultural anthropology, which studies the artifacts of separate *cultures, and looks for their general function or significance in the lives of those who make use of them;

(iii) social anthropology, which probably includes cultural anthropology, but ranges more widely, in order to explore all aspects of man's social existence, and to explain the forms which it takes;

(iv) philosophical anthropology, which is not so much a branch of anthropology as an extension of philosophy to the universal but disputed truths of human nature, in order to provide the basis for moral and political theory.

Social and cultural anthropology tend to be comparative, and this has led to the ascendancy of cultural *relativism in anthropological studies. The two principal modern schools are *structuralism, associated with the work of Lévi-Strauss, and 'functionalism', associated with Bronislav Malinowski (1884–1942). The first looks for 'meanings', the second for *functional explanations. The method of functional explanation – whereby social characteristics are explained in terms of their functional relation to the well-being of society – has impinged on *sociology and had considerable influence in all areas of political thought. Other notions important to anthropology also have wide political significance, among them *custom, *culture, *myth, *ritual and *tradition. Anthropology has *organicist adherents, who emphasize the fragility of primitive communities and conclude that social order is organic, change in one part having unforeseeable and perhaps dangerous consequences in another. It is common for anthropologists to caution themselves against conservative conclusions, however, since what is unforeseeable to them may not be unforeseeable to the people they study, and the sense of organic complexity may be no more than an ignorance of function or a blindness to significance.

anthropomorphism

The tendency to see non-human forms and animals as endowed with human characteristics, both physical and mental, but especially with will, emotion and intelligence. It is variously held to be good, bad and indifferent that men should project their own natures into their surroundings, but it is almost universally agreed that such is inevitable (at least under 'existing social conditions').

anti-

A prefix often used to denote a form of hostility supposed to express something other than a reasoned aversion to its object. Usually – as in some of the examples that follow – the explanation of the hostility is held to lie in social and economic circumstances, perhaps because these might show not only that the aversion is unreasoned, but also that it is unreasonable. *See also* *-phobia.

anti-Americanism

Hostility towards the material success and military power of the US, often accompanied by contempt towards the culture and institutions that they have protected. Anti-Americanism is a growing phenomenon, despite the fact – or maybe because of the fact – that the vast majority of people who wish to emigrate from their country of origin, wish to emigrate to the US. French anti-Americanism has a pronounced cultural slant, involving hostility to the *kitsch of American popular culture, and to the supposed naivety of US dealings with people from other cultures. Islamic anti-Americanism seems to have other and more frantic causes, related to the ability of the American media to project the sensuous attractions of the Western way of life around the globe. (*See* *jahiliyya*.)

anti-clericalism

A liberal movement, which aims to reduce the political influence of the clergy and of religious institutions. Anti-clericalism is evident in much medieval literature, but its origins as a political movement lie in the eighteenth-century *Enlightenment. It became an active force during the French Revolution, and in the Third Republic, was deeply intertwined with Italian, Spanish and other forms of *nationalism, inspired Bismarck's *Kulturkampf* against the Catholic church, and currently appears both outside the church and within it (in the *secularization of religious practice and doctrine).

anti-communism

The aversion towards *communism, specifically in the US, has been thought by many, whether or not themselves communists, to have a character so intense and hysterical as to be insufficiently explained by the sincere belief that communism is a bad form of government. *McCarthyism, for example, has sometimes been thought to be not merely opportunistic but also founded in self-deception. It has been accused of concentrating on obnoxious deviations from communist principles (such as *Stalinism) and ignoring the genuine and perhaps redeeming ideals which those deviations mark, in order to generate an atmosphere of hysterical fear and hatred. Explanations of this alleged hysterical character vary; some invoke the threat that communism poses to private property, others invoke its anti-individualistic message (thus explaining the prevalence of anti-communism in the US and its relative absence from Europe). The thought that communism, properly understood, could not be loathed *as such* is perhaps a curiosity of mid-twentieth-century American liberalism, although it has had widespread influence.

antinomianism

General name for the view – specifically advocated by *Gnostics and again at the Reformation – that Christians are set free by grace from the need to observe any moral law. Hence any view that claims absolute right of action on the grounds of absolute truth of doctrine.

anti-semitism

The most notorious form of *racism in politics, which has had a long history, culminating in the Nazi *holocaust, and continuing as a vital force in the modern world, e.g. in Eastern Europe (notably Poland), in the former Soviet Union, and in the Middle East, where it is partly the effect, and partly the cause, of opposition to *Zionism.

Anti-semitism has many forms. It may attribute to the Jews a debased and subject moral character, or a character of innate degeneracy (as in the Nazi ideology); it may equally accuse the Jews of cunning, success, power and conspiracy; or of a disposition to accumulate benefits through usury and injustice. Anti-semitism must be distinguished from the religious hostility to the Jews as those who had denied, and continue to deny, Christ. The two hostilities may fuel one another but, strictly speaking, the religious hostility is removed by conversion to the Christian faith, while racism remains indifferent to any change that is within its victim's power (which is one reason why it is comforting: the enemy will never deceive you by turning out to be your friend). Explanations of anti-semitism are as varied as the phenomenon. It is sometimes thought to be based on the hostility of the *petit bourgeois* towards those of his own social class who are able to obtain a livelihood through capital investment; on this view it is the hostility of the borrower towards the lender (made acute by hyperflation) which tries to rationalize its own intensity by finding an irredeemable moral, rather than a redeemable institutional, fault. Others (e.g. *Sartre) have tried to explain the phenomenon in terms of fantasies of the Jew's sexual prowess, thus aligning anti-semitism with some kinds of hostility towards those judged to be 'primitive'. No explanation seems wholly satisfactory. Some account must be taken of habit: once a particular group which cannot defend itself is picked out as the enemy, the habit of so identifying it begins to grow. Moreover there seems to be an inveterate need for societies in a state of acute crisis to look for the 'enemy within' who causes it.

None of those theories accounts for the growth of anti-semitism in the Muslim world today or for the renewed spread of anti-semitism across the European continent. Both those phenomena correspond, however, to the state of mind that Nietzsche called *ressentiment* – the desire of the weak and inadequate to pick on a victim yet weaker than themselves.

anti-social behaviour

A euphemism that refers to the breakdown of social feelings in modern societies and the indifference with which people – and young people especially – view their own immorality, and the disorder and suffering that it causes. The search for the cause of anti-social behaviour has led in many directions, though the hypothesis that it is one result of the decline of religion gains some credibility from the fact that it is frequently cured by conversion to a disciplined faith. This has been made apparent in the US by the success of religious movements in overcoming socially destructive behaviour in the inner cities. Others attribute anti-social behaviour to the breakdown of the family, and in particular to the rise of the fatherless family, in which no model of discipline and stability is provided to the children. See *underclass.

antitrust

Originally US legislation designed to control large business groupings and to prevent the formation of uncompetitive markets through *monopolies (which were often known in the nineteenth century as *trusts on account of their legal status). Antitrust legislation is now adopted as a substantial part of much European company law, as a result of EU legislation and policy. The Sherman Anti-Trust Act 1890 marked the first significant break with the practice of *laissez faire* in the US, and indicated the widespread admission that law can create and control the conditions of a market, and that it may be in the public interest for the state thereby to exert substantial indirect control over the economy. *See also* *oligopoly.

apartheid

Afrikaans term meaning 'aparthood', and denoting the policy of racial segregation as practised by the National Party in South Africa between 1948 and the late 1980s. Officially it was a policy of 'separate but equal development'; it involved legislation controlling places of residence, schools, universities, and recreational facilities; as well as laws prohibiting mixed marriages, and controlling voluntary associations. The major intention was to allow political power only to the white population, and to deny to the remainder all rights that would be tantamount to political *access, including the right to vote at an election. Blacks were confined to certain autonomous 'homelands', alleged to be their 'true' historical places of residence, leaving the remaining areas to be enjoyed by whites in untroubled sovereignty. The substantial difference between the natural assets and *infrastructure of the two kinds of area was often noted; the historical justification were for the most part considered to be either lies or *myths. The myths used to support the withholding of political rights from blacks had no application to the situation of the 'coloureds' who, having nothing where they were, suffered the additional grievance of having nowhere to go. (The coloureds are Afrikaans-speaking, and for the most part Calvinist people, descended

from Malaysians brought to the Cape Colony as slaves; the category also included others of mixed descent, including many who are indistinguishable in every observable respect from blacks or whites.)

apolitical

A stance is called apolitical if it does not have, as part of its main purpose, intentions regarding the political order: i.e. regarding the institutions through which power is exercised. Since all social change is likely to have some *effect* on those institutions, and may even cause a necessary revision in their structure, it is always possible to give a political interpretation of a stance that is apolitical. On some views every social act or gesture also has a political meaning, in the sense of intimating some measure of criticism or acceptance of established institutions, and some idea, however sketchy, of institutions that would bring it to fulfilment. On this view there may be no important differences between those acts that have a political *intention*, and those which merely have political consequences. Typically, practices that regard *opposition as an unacceptable feature of government do not recognize the possibility of apolitical associations.

apologetics

Originally the branch of theology concerned with making religious doctrine acceptable to non-believers. All *doctrine stands in need of apology, and it is one of the characteristics of modern political thought that substantial analogues of Christian apologetics have been associated with it. It is normal for apologetics to require 'sacred texts' that are both definitive (when rightly interpreted) and also open to interpretation (and so applicable even when apparently false). It then attempts to establish the public *possibility* of beliefs associated with those texts. Thus French **gauchisme* of the 1960s and 1970s managed to make Marxism acceptable to the *consumer society by rewriting it as a status-conferring intellectual *commodity. Apologetics should be distinguished from *propaganda, which seeks to make doctrine not acceptable but accepted. Propaganda always simplifies, where apologetics complicates and sophisticates, its subject.

apparat

The class of full-time servants of the Communist Party (the *apparatchiki*, those belonging to the apparatus), which evolved in the USSR as a distinctive feature of *Lenin's 'party of the new type'. Professional communists with unquestioning loyalty to the party were sought throughout the USSR and its satellites as the core of the *civil service, and the necessary means of achieving and maintaining government by the Communist Party. However, you could be an apparatchik without being a member of the party and increasingly, as time went on, the loyalty of the apparat was purchased by privileges, rather than recruited through belief.

apparatchik

See *apparat.

appeasement

Used in the 1920s to denote policies aiming to remove by common agreement the grievances generated by the peace settlement of 1919 – especially the grievances felt in Germany. The policy of appeasement, systematically pursued in the UK, facilitated Hitler's accumulation of power in the 1930s and the USSR's accumulation of power after the Second World War. Appeasement involves concessions in response to explicit or implied threats; it acts to the detriment of a power

that does not threaten, and to the benefit of a state which makes *non-negotiable demands.

appropriation

Taking something as property. The term has various technical usages, e.g., in law, the setting aside of property or money for a particular purpose (as in bankruptcy proceedings). It also denotes a state action authorizing expenditure of public funds to be made for stated purposes. In the US appropriations are authorizations to make expenditures from the general funds of the Treasury, or from the various special funds. In the UK, by the Appropriation Act, Parliament appropriates the supply which it grants to particular purposes. Both are in theory *legislative acts, but whereas the US Congress has a relatively free hand in determining what appropriations shall be, the UK Parliament may only decrease or delete items. Thus, so long as the *cabinet commands a majority in the House of Commons, and may make any appropriation vote a matter of confidence, it can determine the outcome. Hence appropriation in the UK has some of the character of an *executive act. The legislative nature of appropriation in the US is illustrated by the distinction between the enabling act, which establishes policy and authorizes an executive agency to do things, and the appropriation which is necessary to provide money in support of it.

approximation of laws

The policy of states, subject to treaties of commercial intent, whereby laws governing or influencing commercial transactions are aligned, thus founding common expectations and facilitating trade across frontiers. The Treaty of Rome provides extensively for approximation, involving what some regard as an effective abrogation of *sovereignty on the part of its signatories, since laws dealing with highly sensitive domestic issues – such as taxation and mobility of labour – are subject to amendment and *ratification under the terms of the treaty. *See also* *European Community, *European Union.

Aquinas, St Thomas (1226–74)
The greatest of medieval theologians, who attempted to synthesize the newly rediscovered philosophy of *Aristotle with the articles of Christian faith, and so generated an authoritative system of theological, moral, and political doctrine, known after its inventor as Thomism, which has served as the foundation for *Roman Catholic teaching. His political philosophy consists largely of an exposition and development of the theory of *natural law.

There are four kinds of law: eternal law, natural law, divine law, and human law (or *positive law). Eternal law is another name for God's conception of the ends of creation; natural law consists of the principles that rational beings will recognize and obey by nature – i.e. it is that part of the eternal law that is revealed to reason in its earthly condition. Divine law consists of God's commandments, as revealed in the scriptures, and human law (positive law) consists in the particular legal enactments that rational beings make for the good government of their institutions. Unlike the later thinkers who regarded positive law as filling in the gaps left by natural law, Aquinas often seems to argue as though natural law is sufficient in itself to generate all positive laws. If we conjoin it with the particular 'determinations' that characterize this or that social or political arrangement, then the natural law will generate the human laws which, in those circumstances, uniquely specify what

is just. Thus by the natural law, all property belongs to men in common, provided that no one has been induced to labour in anticipation of a right of ownership. Once such anticipations arise, however, and once the institutions are created through which they are expressed and transmitted, the natural law generates a human law of private property, which can be violated only at the cost of injustice. A positive law that is unjust is, by this standard, felt not to be binding, indeed, not to be a genuine law, so that tyrannical law is not so much law as the perversion of law.

Aquinas favoured limited *monarchy as the ideal form of government. He also repeated arguments, to be found in Aristotle and elsewhere, for the primacy of marriage and the *family in social order, and for the primacy of *offices in forming a political *constitution. Since there is a limit set by reason to the forms of legitimate political constitution, a constitution is legitimate only when each law is a 'dictate of reason in the ruler', in which case the proper effect of law is to lead the subject to his true *virtue. In the state 'each person is related to the entire community as the part to the whole', and the state is 'the perfect community'. This Aristotelian conception of the organic perfection of political order was taken to considerable lengths. Thus Aquinas was prepared to argue that 'the individual is to the perfect community as the imperfect to the perfect', thus foreshadowing *Hegel's view of the state, as in some sense the completion and fulfilment of man's earthly existence. However 'man is not ordained to the body politic in respect of all he is and has': i.e. there are limits to what a sovereign may legitimately require of his subjects. For example, all subjects have a right to resist government that has become severely oppressive. More importantly, the state cannot claim authority in matters of religion, so that, within the limits of legitimacy, it is necessary that the division between church and state be upheld, the former possessing the authority of the eternal law, the latter the authority of man's local and particularized attempts to conform to it. The church can therefore stand in judgement over princes, but cannot legislate for them except in so far as they are disposed to transgress nature's commands.

Aquinas is noteworthy for his attempt to extend the concept of natural law into the sphere of international relations, first by discussing the answerability of all princes to divine authority, secondly by laying down rules of just dealing between states. For example, he attempted to define the nature of a *just war, insisting on the distinction between war entered into in a just cause, and war prosecuted according to innate principles of just dealing between enemies (*jus ad bellum*, and *jus in bello*). This distinction and its application underlie much of the intellectual structure of the modern law of war.

Aquinas also redefined and extended the theory of the *just price, and had much to say concerning property rights, favouring local production for use over international trade, and justifying slavery, provided it were merely a form of economic domination, and did not violate principles of natural justice. (His view here was in part an apology for Aristotle, in part the expression of the theory that some people could not flourish without being guided and even controlled by others.)

arbitrage

One of the forces bringing about equality of price between markets. If goods sell in one *market at a price lower than their price in another, then 'arbitraging' may occur: that is, goods may be bought in the first market and sold in the second. The effect of this is to raise the price in the first market and lower it in the second, so that the two tend towards equality. The key element in arbitrage is that the amount of profit be determined with certainty. Because arbitrage profits involve no risk, they are hard to obtain, and such profits as do exist are normally no more than a recompense for the detailed attention and time involved in seeking out the opportunity. If that were not so goods would automatically have found their way to the market where they could most profitably be sold.

arbitrary

The exercise of *power is called 'arbitrary' when no independent reason can be given for its exercise which has weight for anyone other than the person who wields it. A power applied according to a law is not arbitrary, although someone may wish to question whether the law which validates it has any independent *authority. (*See* *autocracy.)

arbitration

The submission of a dispute, whether commercial, industrial or international, to the decision of a person or body other than a court of competent jurisdiction. Arbitration is to be distinguished from *conciliation and from *mediation on account of its quasi-judicial nature, and on account of the fact that the award rendered in arbitration is, in substance, final. Arbitration may be voluntary or (as sometimes when a government intervenes in an industrial dispute) compulsory. In either case the terms of the final settlement will normally be enforced by any subsequent judicial proceeding, unless it can be shown that they were formally defective, e.g. on account of a breach of *natural justice. Despite this, it is an unsettled question whether arbitration is itself a kind of *adjudication: there are similarities of form, and of result; but it seems that the courts can enquire into proceedings of arbitration and adjust the result in ways that are not normally available to a court of appeal.

In international relations arbitration is a much more obviously judicial procedure. It has been significant since classical times (as exemplified in the habit of small independent cities of submitting disputes to the senate in Rome). The precedent in modern international relations was set by the Jay Treaty between Britain and the US in 1794, allowing for arbitration by mixed commission. In 1899 The Hague conference erected at The Hague the Permanent Court of Arbitration, which has settled some 20 important issues. It is disputed whether arbitration by this court is the same as 'judicial settlement' by the International Court of Justice. Some argue that it is in effect the same, and that it is necessary to assert this if arbitration is to have the intended effect. The proposal to make arbitration obligatory was voted down at The Hague conference, but states may elect to make arbitration obligatory in dealings between them.

architecture

Described by *Ruskin (*The Seven Lamps of Architecture*, 1849) as the most political of the arts, and embroiled in political controversy throughout modern times. Being public, overt and semipermanent, architecture exerts a certain dominion over the visual life of people; this enables it to translate political dogma into symbolic form, and to validate stylistic expression through the perceived association with political ideals. Neo-classicism – the stylistic affectation of a discipline and order intrinsic to the buildings of Greece and Rome – has been the standard architecture of the political demagogue, being associated with the French Revolution, national socialism, fascism and Stalinism, and valued for its solemn logic, and for its representation of existing public institutions as timeless and changeless. (Though in America neo-classicism has retained another meaning, as the style of cities, so that every American shopping mall will have details lifted from the classical repertoire, as a way of suggesting an urban settlement rather than a temporary set of warehouses around a parking lot.)

By contrast, the gothic style was propagandized in the nineteenth century as the symbol of a civil society which neither required nor tolerated the decrees of an absolute ruling power, but which arose organically out of common expectations, common beliefs and a shared experience of labour. Socialist thinkers such as Viollet-le-Duc in France and *Morris in England thus advocated the gothic as the symbolic form of natural, classless labour, working outside the tyranny of private property and enforced public order. Ruskin, too, advocated the gothic style, though he valued it as the expression of a hierarchical and religious community, in which labour was sacred, and building an act of *piety.

The Modern movement of Le Corbusier, the Russian constructivists and the Bauhaus was influenced by neo-classical ideas, and also by vaguer political aspirations based on the desire totally to remake the human environment, in order to erase the images of luxury and decadence that characterized humanity's former incompetence.

In all such ideas the assumption is not just that architecture symbolizes a political expectation, but also that, by imposing itself on public perceptions, it helps to realize that expectation.

In modern times theories of a 'functionalist' kind have been influential. These may take two forms: first, that function is the primary requirement that a building must fulfil, and aesthetic standards are subordinate to it; secondly, that aesthetic standards are fulfilled simply *by* fulfilling function, perhaps in the most visually explicit way. The second view is certainly false; the first highly disputable. Some argue that such ideas have led to a decline in respect for aesthetic values among architects, and that, in the absence of that respect, the true function of a building can never be known. Aesthetic implications are present in every human endeavour, and attention to them is necessary if the final purpose is to be understood. On this view, architecture illustrates in most vivid form the intrinsic relation between aesthetic value and social and political action. (*See* *aesthetics and politics.)

Widespread dissatisfaction with the buildings of architectural *modernism has recently led to the emergence of *postmodernist styles, which are more playful, more tolerant of ornamentation, and more in keeping with the classical layout of our cities. Some value these styles for their eclecticism, and for their supposed endorsement of the *postmodern culture which gave rise to them. There has also been a powerful movement of reaction against modernist ideas of *planning: *see* *New Urbanism.

Arendt, Hannah (1906–75)
German-born philosopher, social critic and historian, whose *Origins of Totalitarianism* (1951) was the first major attempt to come to terms with a distinctive feature of modern politics, and to trace the causes of the greatest political catastrophe that humanity has ever suffered. The work emphasizes the role of nineteenth-century *nationalism in feeding the *collectivist aspirations of modern politicians, and has

been criticized for its insufficient emphasis on *Lenin and the 'party of the new type' which he introduced, and which was to be the model followed by all subsequent totalitarian governments. But it remains influential, partly because of the breadth of learning, culture and observational powers that it displays.

Arendt's most important philosophical work is *The Human Condition* (1958), which offers a hierarchical vision of the active life, with the statesman at the top, the craftsman and artist as intermediaries, and the labourer at the bottom. The ascending hierarchy of labour, work and action implies that freedom and autonomy can be realized only in a fully political existence, in which a shared public life gives meaning to our private endeavours. This vision of politics is reminiscent of *Plato, and was further expanded in *On Revolution* (1963) and *Between Past and Future* (1961, 1968).

In 1963 Arendt published *Eichmann in Jerusalem*, an account of the new form of evil introduced by bureaucratic forms of government, in which crime becomes a de-personalized routine, and people are reduced to things, and disposed of as things. The 'banality of evil' which we have seen in modern times is, for Arendt, a kind of consummation of evil, and the most terrifying lesson of modern politics. The book, which was also a commentary on the Eichmann trial in Jerusalem, caused great controversy, and led Arendt to consider the whole question of human freedom and responsibility, in her final work, *The Life of the Mind*, published posthumously in 1978. *See also* *essence/appearance, *people, *revolution, *work.

aristocracy
Greek: rule by the best. *Aristotle contrasted aristocracy, in which virtue is the title to power, with *oligarchy,

in which the title resides in wealth. Both are forms of 'rule by the few', but only in the former case is rule by the few in the interests of the many. Aristotle's concern was with an *ideal type; nevertheless it is normal to make a corresponding distinction among actual governments, between those where power belongs to a minority *class with hereditary privileges (aristocracy), and those where power belongs to a minority group or party, without hereditary restrictions on membership (oligarchy). In this sense, there are two kinds of aristocracy: that of some Greek city-states, and related arrangements, in which the *ruling class held power without the sanction of a *monarch; and that familiar in Europe, in which aristocratic entitlements have generally been conferred or confirmed by the sovereign. The second is the more familiar, and has three aspects:

1. The legal-political aspect. The dominant features have been (a) a ruling class identified first through the possession of land and secondly through rules of succession (usually by *kinship); (b) the consequent conferring of dignities and entitlements by the sovereign which confirms a given aristocrat and his successors in the political position acquired; (c) a title bestowed on the aristocrat, signifying that, just by virtue of being successor to the powers identified in (a) and (b) (however time may have depleted and exhausted them) he may hold office in government (e.g. he may take his place in a house of *peers, or become a member of the sovereign's privy council). The net result is the existence of a hereditary *establishment and hereditary entitlements to land, goods and offices. It has usually been possible for outsiders to gain access to the aristocracy, although *social mobility in this respect has varied from place to place and time to time.

2. The economic aspect. It is almost universally accepted that the above pattern of legal relations is associated with, and perhaps also explained by, economic relations. In Marxian theory, for example, 1. is the description of a legal and political *superstructure which expresses and is explained by relations of power, in particular, by the power of the person who controls land over the person who is forced to work on it. Hence this particular kind of aristocracy is seen as an expression of *feudal relations of production, surviving as a genuine concentration of influence only to the extent that landed property confers powers distinct from those conferred by movable goods (in particular, petty sovereignty over a segment of *territory). The Marxian explanation is often criticized, mostly because it fails to explain the persistence of European (and especially British) aristocracy after the abolition of feudal tenures. (*But see* *nobility.)

3. The social aspect. This is perhaps most vivid in the popular imagination, which identifies aristocracy with all hereditary privilege and the leisure, luxury and manners generic to it. Hence aristocracy comes to stand for an idea of 'breeding', which has sometimes served as a rationalization of hereditary entitlement. There are aristocratic virtues and vices, and these have a distinct character in imaginative and moral thinking, exemplified in the mysteries of title that made it necessary for Dracula to be a count.

The old sense of aristocracy as 'rule by the best' is sometimes attached to the arrangement described, perhaps on the ground that, given the necessary imperfection of all human beings and human arrangements, the best we can hope for is that a class should be bred with the habit of power, and rewarded with the dignities and privileges necessary to make it accept the limitation of that power, and the responsibility of office. The main question is whether or not hereditary entitlement furthers rule in the interests of the many. (*See* *hereditary principle.)

Aristotle (384–322 BC)

Greek philosopher and pupil of *Plato, who gave, in his *Politics* and elsewhere, a renowned and subtle account of political institutions. Aristotle held that man is a rational animal and, as such, also a political animal: it is inevitable and right that he should seek to fulfil himself through living as part of a state (Greek: *polis). Only in the perfect state can perfect human *virtue be exercised, and each kind of state will have its own peculiar virtues and vices. Aristotle classified states according to two variables: who holds power? And: in whose interest is it exercised? There are three politically possible answers to the first question (one, some and all), two politically possible answers to the second (the holder of power, and everyone). The ideal is *aristocracy: the state in which the best, who are inevitably few in number, exercise power in the interests of all. However, since that ideal is hard to achieve, and even harder to sustain, Aristotle advocated a form of mixed government, or 'polity', in which all citizens 'rule and are ruled by turn', and power is monopolized by no particular class. Aristotle was a vigorous critic both of *democracy, and of the kind of collective *education advocated by *Plato. He defended the family as the nucleus of political organization, and argued for a connection between family and *household, and therefore for the necessity of *private property. He also argued that some men are naturally slaves in that they depend upon the will of others for their guiding force, so that the *division of labour required in every state may be both natural and just.

Aristotle defined a citizen as anyone who can 'hold office', and his description of the ideal system of offices provides the foundation for many modern forms of *constitutionalism. The power of individuals in government is both curtailed and guided through offices, which are in turn governed by law, so that, in the Aristotelian polity, laws are supreme, and the outcome of the concentration of power in offices is a *rule of law. Moreover, government is given a character that endures from generation to generation, despite the successive changes in office holders, so that settled expectations begin to arise, and the bond between the rulers and the ruled becomes intelligible to both. In the context of his account of citizenship Aristotle raised in its modern form the question of *political obligation. He argued that political obligation is founded in distributive *justice, which is the principle that unites citizen to citizen and all to the state. Distributive justice involves 'treating equals equally'. This is possible only in the context of judicial procedure, together with the means to determine the individual rights and duties with respect to which citizens are to be compared. Aristotle favoured, as a source of such rights and duties, custom and customary law over the written statutes that can be made and remade by fiat of those in power. His defence of custom and his emphasis on the value of political stability are underpinned by a conception of the state as 'organic'. The whole, he argued, is 'prior to' its parts, which therefore depend upon it. In politics this means that the individual is incomplete until he takes part in political organization. When that organization is not merely political but also just, then the citizen may be not only complete, but also fulfilled.

armies

These take many forms. It is normal to distinguish the standing army (where an organization of armed men is kept permanently ready for war), the professional army (in which soldiers are regarded as committed to the army as to a *profession, usually with a long contract of service), the conscript army (in which citizens are 'called up', i.e. obliged to leave their occupations for some limited, or in war unlimited, period of 'military service'), and the *guerrilla army. The last fights without an overt structure of military institutions, and without subscribing to the conventions and laws of international war. It may not have a defined hierarchy of officers, it may not have uniforms, and it usually fights not openly but covertly, selecting targets so as to cause maximum damage with minimum *confrontation.

Countries with large standing armies and compulsory military service in effect subject all their citizens (or at least all their male citizens) to some years of military discipline, thus giving them a taste of the attitude to *authority and to social life that is characteristic of highly disciplined institutions with violent purposes. This was the *Spartan ideal of education, which is still adopted both as a means to an end, and also as an end in itself. The soldier acquires a distinct attitude towards offices and those holding them, towards discipline and social order, and towards actual, potential or imaginary 'enemies of the state' (or, in modern parlance, 'enemies of the people'). It is characteristic of tyranny to exploit that attitude. Conversely, the drafting into the army of men imbued with civilian values can radically change the ideology through which military institutions are guided.

Armed forces, being a symbol of national or imperial power, are among the most important components of the state. The existence of strong external purposes, together with a discipline which attaches the soldier to them, makes it both necessary for an army to be subject to the sovereign power, and possible for it not to be. In times of civil strife and disorder an army will always take power, not because it wants to, but because power will attach to it for a longer time than power can attach to anything else. This thought was important in motivating *Trotsky's formation of the Red Army.

armistice

The suspension of fighting pending a definite peace settlement: the term refers either to an agreement between belligerents, or to the condition existing during the term of that agreement. Armistice must be distinguished from *capitulation and *surrender, in that it is essentially bilateral, with mutual concessions and mutual restrictions, and from a treaty of peace, in that it does not end the legal state of war. It is valid only when made by the highest authorities in belligerent states, and may be repudiated if made, e.g., by military commanders.

A war that ends without armistice (e.g. those against Germany and Japan in the Second World War) ends to the disadvantage of the vanquished, though not necessarily to the advantage of the victor.

arms control

Expression introduced in the 1950s by US strategists, to denote all the ways whereby one or more states may intentionally restrain the development, testing, deployment, and danger of armaments, with the aim of reducing the likelihood and the hazards of warfare. It covers disarmament, agreements for restraint (such as the SALT agreement between the US and the

USSR and the 1968 non-proliferation treaty), and unilateral acts, such as the decision by the US and others in 1969 to suspend research into biological weapons and to destroy stocks of them. Some include under 'arms control' all attempts to 'neutralize' other states, i.e. to prohibit them from joining particular military alliances.

Arnold, Matthew (1822–88)
English poet, critic and social theorist, and foremost nineteenth-century advocate of *cultural conservatism. In *Culture and Anarchy*, 1869, Arnold defined *culture as 'a pursuit of our total perfection by means of getting to know, on all matters which most concern us, the best which has been thought and said in the world, and, through this knowledge, turning a stream of fresh and free thought upon our stock notions and habits'. Arnold argued that culture, and access to culture, were essential for the right direction of political power, and that, without them, there could be no true conception of the ends of human conduct, but only a mechanistic obsession with the means. He criticized many of the 'stock notions' of nineteenth-century *liberalism and *utilitarianism, both on account of their materialistic and rationalistic visions of human progress, and also on account of their *individualism. The concept of *freedom upon which so much liberal thought depends seemed to Arnold to be too abstract – 'a very good horse to ride, but to ride somewhere' – and to contain no serious reasons for opposing the state in its name. The state, he argued, is 'the representative acting-power of the nation', and therefore must have power to act both in the name of freedom, and in the name of order. Without it public life must always be diverted towards the interests of one

or other class (of which Arnold distinguished three, the 'barbarians' (aristocracy), the 'philistines' (middle class) and the 'populace' (working class)). When this happens, the result is anarchy; however, within each class there is a spirit opposed to anarchy, and dedicated to the common good and public order: this is the spirit that culture awakens, nourishes and refines. To achieve political order, therefore, the state must guarantee that the conditions for *humane education are as widely available as possible.

Arrow's theorem
A theorem in the theory of *social choice which demonstrates that it is impossible to design a 'constitution' that will generate complete and consistent rankings of alternative states of a society according to the preferences of its members, while satisfying certain further conditions. Due to the mathematical economist K.J. Arrow (b. 1925), this theorem is one of the most important theoretical results in welfare economics. The proof begins from the idea of a *social welfare function (interpreted as a set of rules for transforming the desires of individuals into concrete social choices). It then proceeds to lay down certain plausible-seeming conditions that such a function should satisfy – for example, that no member of the group should be allowed to dictate the outcome. It is shown that no such social welfare function can meet those conditions. Some economists have rejected one or more of Arrow's conditions, others have disputed their interpretation, or their applicability to politics, while others have accepted his result as showing the inherent impossibility of legislating on the basis of social choice. Others have read the result as indicating the need for a wider informational base for social

choices, going beyond Arrow's use of individual preferences without any interpersonal comparison of utilities.

art

1. There are three major views concerning the political significance of art: (i) that it is, can be, or ought to be an *expression* of political consciousness; (ii) that it is, can be, or ought to be an *agent* of political transformation; (iii) that it is, can be, or ought to be *autonomous in a way that denies the possibility of a political meaning.

Advocates of the third view defend their position from the philosophical premise that art must be appreciated not as means but as end, so that the attempt to subordinate it to political aims and ideologies is an attempt to deny its nature. Theories and practices such as *socialist realism and *fascist neo-classicism exhibit the inevitable degeneration, vulgarity and bad taste that ensue upon the attempt to *politicize art. According to R.G. Collingwood (*The Principles of Art*, 1938) this attempt turns art into magic, and so destroys it.

Defenders of the first view may well accept that art must be treated as end and not means, while suggesting that to appreciate an object as the expression of a state of consciousness is not necessarily to treat it as a means. It is hard to imagine art that does not gain at least some of its significance from its expressive power. And how can there be an expressive activity that is divorced entirely from social and political consciousness? (i) and (iii) may therefore be compatible.

It is characteristic of modern *totalitarianism to believe some variant of (ii). Art has an overwhelming influence on the minds and opinions of the educated. Hence it has been regarded as an important political force, perhaps even as one of the ferments that create the 'subjective conditions'

of revolution (*see* *cultural revolution, *Lenin). The difficulty for that view lies in drawing the line between art and *propaganda, and in doing justice to the extreme complexity of our responses to the first in comparison with the simplicity of our responses to the second. Conservatives and revolutionaries have alike found confirmation for their views in Shakespeare, and the great artistic rumination on the tyranny of *exchange-value – Wagner's *Ring* – has always had as many admirers on the Right as on the Left, eliciting in both the sense that this work has, as Wagner put it, the 'ring of truth'.

2. Political constraint on art. Art brings about peculiar transformations of human consciousness. Attempts to diagnose the effect also lead to proposals to restrain it. *Plato would have banned all art from his Republic – save only those forms of music that seemed suitable to moral development. Plato's recommendations have sometimes been followed – notably during the 'Cultural Revolution' in China. But it is more common to pay lip-service to artistic freedom, and to argue that political interference in artistic activity is unwise or impossible, except in so far as it falls under the idea of legitimate *censorship.

3. Marxist theory of art. For classical Marxism art is part of *ideology and therefore has the unspoken but discoverable function of consolidating the political *superstructure out of which it is created. This explains why, e.g., modernist literature has so often concealed a highly conservative message (as in T.S. *Eliot's *Four Quartets*, or in Joyce's covert vindication of bourgeois values in *Ulysses*). It is part of the *romantic character of contemporary *neo-Marxism that it accepts this view with reluctance, believing that art, because it must always revolutionize itself, cannot fail to be an agent of revolution. Hence the idea (*see*, e.g., Ernst Fischer: *Art Against Ideology*, 1955; Raymond Williams: *Marxism and Literature*, 1977) that art, or true art, is essentially 'anti-ideological', concerned not to consolidate the existing political structure but rather to give expression to a 'truth' beyond ideology, a truth that in someway subverts the complacencies of bourgeois society.

4. Decadence. Theories of artistic decadence have emphasized *sentimentality, *kitsch, and the coarsening of moral and spiritual values under the influence of mass communication. Conservatives like *Arnold and Eliot have joined Marxists like *Adorno and *Benjamin and liberals like Croce and Lionel Trilling in seeking for an explanation of decadence, and a discipline that will stand firm against it, so as to rescue art from the diseases of popular culture. These thinkers have in consequence had a powerful influence on political thinking in the twentieth century, as intellectuals have sought to come to terms with a democratic culture that most of them find hard to share and harder still to enjoy. Briefly influential too was the Nazi attack on *entartete Kunst,* the supposedly decadent art of the modernists – an art attacked equally by Stalin and his successors in the name of popular culture. In this way artistic decadence has been an important theme in modern political thought, with widely divergent views as to what is and what is not an instance of it.

Asiatic despotism

Probably synonymous with *oriental despotism. A name sometimes given to the various forms of *despotism exemplified in Asia, from the time of the Mongol invasions onwards, in which rigid institutions combined with close surveillance of all citizens, were used to uphold unstable and

therefore ruthlessly *autocratic power. The ruling class of bureaucrats was dominated by a sovereign whose powers depended mainly on the army, but also on the sanction of religious institutions, of which he was the nominal head. All insubordination was suppressed by terror, law was not respected, and decrees and institutions would be put aside as the sovereign required. This form of government was related by *Marx to *Asiatic modes of production, since the constant dissolution and refounding of the state and the unceasing changes of dynasty left the economic order untouched by the 'storm clouds in the political sky'. East European *anti-communists (e.g. *Miłosz) sometimes describe the government that was imposed on the states of Eastern Europe by the communists as a form of Asiatic despotism.

Asiatic modes of production

Description often given of the self-sufficient communities of Central, Southern and Eastern Asia, in which village economy persists with minimum *division of labour, and in which production of food and other necessaries ossifies around traditional forms, remaining resistant to innovation.

assimilation

The process whereby an immigrant community adopts the outward forms and political allegiance of a host community, without necessary absorbing the majority culture or adopting the majority religion. (*Cf.* *acculturation.) Unassimilated minorities, which define their allegiance either in contrast to, or in opposition to, the allegiance of the majority, constitute a potential threat to social and political stability, as recent events have amply demonstrated. The received view in Europe is that assimilation is therefore necessary if immigration is to be acceptable. Note, however, that anybody who said as much 20 or even ten years ago risked the charge of *racism. That peculiar fact needs an explanation; so far none has been provided.

association

The forming of a *society. A *state determines a *civil society, and within that civil society there are usually many subject associations. Lawyers, sociologists and philosophers have debated over the nature and variety of these associations, and the distinctions which they make are of the first importance in politics, in providing the models for various views of the state, and in upholding and criticizing conceptions of the role and importance of subordinate institutions. The following distinctions are particularly important:

(i) Voluntary and non-voluntary. A voluntary association (e.g. a club) is one that is constituted by the willing acceptance of its members. A non-voluntary association (e.g. a *family) exists and persists whether or not accepted. (Children may be unable to give consent, adults unable to withhold it.) In law, therefore, obligations attaching to voluntary association are contractual, whereas those of the family are not.

(ii) Purposeful and purposeless. Some associations (e.g. businesses, sports clubs) have specific purposes and expire when those purposes are fulfilled or removed. Others do not, and persist even in the absence of an identifiable aim. Among the second kind of association one must again include the family, together with certain clubs and societies of a purely conversational and friendly character. The point here is not that the family generates no purposes, or that family activities are without purpose, but rather that there is no *external* purpose, nothing that some *other* association might have fulfilled just as well. What purposes there are have to be defined by reference to the family, and not vice versa. Some sociologists theorize the distinction here in terms of *Gemeinschaft* and *Gesellschaft*. *See also* *friendship.

(iii) Incorporated and unincorporated. A legal distinction between an association that has formed itself (usually by 'articles of association') into a *corporate person, with liabilities, assets, rights, obligations and *agency of its own, and associations which have not made that transition, and in which responsibility and accountability still remain with the individual members. The law chooses to regard all unincorporated associations as based in a contractual relation between members, property being vested in trustees, and legal action effected through representatives. (*See further* *incorporation.)

(iv) Constituted and unconstituted. An association may have a *constitution directing its procedures, or it may vary in accordance with the wishes and conflicts of the day. A club exemplifies the first condition, a family the second. In the former case there is an analogy of *positive law, in the latter case there is only *natural law.

All those distinctions are different and none of them is simple. The complexity partly explains the difficulty of the question, What kind of association is a state? The state might, for example, be voluntary, purposeful, and unconstituted, as some *social contract theories suggest that it is or ought to be. Or it might be non-voluntary, purposeless and constituted, as some followers of *Hegel prefer to argue. In either case it may have some of the characteristics of an autonomous legal person. If we think of the state as irreducible to its members this might be because we think that there are associations which create new entities out of old ones, as a new legal person is created by a partnership. In which case some kinds of association may be 'ontologically creative'. But which kinds, and why? These questions are considered under various headings in this dictionary. (*See* *institution, *state.)

Many theorists of *absolutism (e.g. *Hobbes) are suspicious of large associations, on account of their ability to challenge the sovereign power. For related but different reasons *totalitarianism aims to bring all associations within the orbit of the state, so that they take their nature, constitution and purposes from the central power. The 'freedom of association' is therefore an important issue in modern politics, sometimes taken to concern a basic *freedom without which elementary *human rights cannot be respected. The issue is inextricably bound up with that of the *autonomous institution. Institutions are associations which have achieved an identity independent of their members, and which can therefore become active forces which change the purposes of their members. In order to deny institutional *autonomy, it is usually necessary to restrict the freedom of association. Many who disapprove of totalitarian government may nevertheless seek this restriction, in order to abolish, e.g., private education, or monopoly.

Association of Trial Lawyers of America (ATLA)

A US-based coalition of lawyers, law professors and others, which describes itself as 'working to promote justice and fairness for injured persons', and which has actively resisted *tort reform in the US. ATLA's members include many who earn large fees from 'class actions', such as those involving asbestos, in which people join together to file suits for compensation against firms chosen as much for their ability to pay as for any faulty behaviour. In view of the negative attitude towards this kind of legal action on the part of the US Republican Party it is not surprising that ATLA is a major funder of the Democratic Party in Congressional elections.

asylum

A place of refuge. States can grant asylum to citizens of foreign jurisdictions, which means to offer them protection from threats made by that jurisdiction by conferring a right of residence. The UN Convention on Refugees and Asylum of 1951 obliges its signatories to offer asylum to migrants who are fleeing from oppression in their homeland, under certain conditions. This Convention was signed at a time when there were few migrants in the world. It is currently invoked by tens of thousands of 'economic migrants' coming to Europe in search of a better life, since it offers a quick and legal route to a right of residence. The Convention enables dictators to export their opponents without earning the bad name that comes from killing them. And it has filled the cities of Europe with people who, while claiming asylum from their hosts, are also actively preparing *jihâd against them. Hence the UN Convention has come in for serious criticism as an example of the way in which transnational legislation can undermine the preconditions of stable national government.

asylum-seeker

An immigrant, legal or illegal, who is seeking to take advantage of the UN Convention (*see* *asylum) in order to claim residence in the country to which he has come.

Atatürk, Kemal (1880–1938)
Turkish military leader and statesman.
See *Eastern question, Kemalism,
Laicism.

atavism
1. The theory that ancestral types may
appear as 'throwbacks' (based on a
hypothesis of the geneticist Grygor
Mendel, sometimes given as grounds
for *racist ideology, and influential in
nineteenth-century *criminology).

2. The tendency of primitive forms
of consciousness to emerge (in various
disguises) in the thoughts and actions
of otherwise civilized beings, as when
black skin is regarded as testimony to a
'black' character, or ownership of
property is regarded as sufficient
grounds for assault. The first case
shows a survival of what Sir James
Frazer calls 'contagious magic' (*The
Golden Bough*, 1900), while the second
shows a return to the ancient idea of
'hubris', according to which pride and
power offend the gods and bring down
judgement.

Athenian democracy
The form of government that existed
periodically in Athens during the fifth
and fourth centuries BC. All adult male
citizens were able to vote in the assembly, where, in most cases, officials were
chosen by lot, in boards of ten, one
from each tribe. The chief administrative officials were the *archons* (ceremonial), the *strategoi* (military), and the
taniai (treasurers); but there were
others, and Athenian democracy is
remarkable for its proliferation of
offices and for the seriousness with
which official duties were regarded.
Three other features should be noted:
the power of orators (such as
Alcibiades and Demosthenes) who
were able to sway opinion in the
assembly, and had the kind of influence on political life that is today
attributed only to the *media; the

absence of any independent political
and economic status for women; the
economic and political dependence of
the state upon *slavery; and the
*ostracism of prominent citizens,
which served as a safety-valve for
*envy. Slaves, not being citizens, had
no vote. Nevertheless the Athenians
were proud of their constitutional freedoms, and of the respect for the individual which allowed them to be, in
the words attributed to Pericles by
Thucydides, 'free and tolerant in our
private lives, in public affairs obedient
to the law'.

Aufhebung
See *dialectic.

Augustine, St (354–430)
Augustine of Hippo was a doctor of the
church, and the first thinker to
attempt a systematic Christian philosophy of society. He exerted a profound
and lasting influence on all Christian
thought and practice, invented confessional literature, and was a political
thinker of considerable consequence.
In the *City of God* he attempted to
reply to the pagans who had attributed
the fall of Rome in 410 to the abolition
of heathen worship. Augustine set out
the fundamental contrast between the
law of this world and that of the heavenly city towards which all citizens
should aspire. From this description of
the 'Kingdom of God' he derived an
ideal system of laws and offices,
adapted to the temporal world. The
state mediates, or ought to mediate,
between the earthly realm of sin and
disharmony and the heavenly realm of
absolute righteousness. All institutions
of the state are forms of dominion
(sovereigns over subjects, owners over
property, masters over slaves) and
dominion, in so far as it is a form of
order, is good, although it is an order
conditioned by the relative unright-
eousness of its participants.

The ideal order of property, for example, is that everyone should possess everything in common. Its actual order is determined by the need to subject property to the discipline of justice, in a world infected by the imperfections of avarice and greed. The state is necessary to this discipline, but not all states are equally acceptable. The ideal is rule of free men by free men through deliberation (which is the rule prescribed both by nature and by God); when that rule is displaced by masters whose authority is purely coercive, then natural order and divine law are simultaneously violated. The absolute righteousness of the City of God is an idea that corresponds to the ideal of justice given in Plato's *Republic* (by which Augustine was considerably influenced); it is also the ancestor of Christian theories of *natural law. The relation of the temporal city to the City of God is not a sequential relation. Augustine argues instead that the righteous already inhabit the City of God, and that it is present among us, as a noumenal reality to which we can reach out through our own moral and spiritual efforts.

Augustine attempted to discover principles of international dispute, and presented an interesting analysis of *peace, as containing three degrees: the peace of God (*see* *pax), the peace of the just, and the peace of the unjust (i.e. of those who would make war if they were not afraid of the consequences). He also gave a theory of history which attempted to reconcile God's *providence and foreknowledge with the metaphysical *freedom of human agency.

Augustinianism is the general name for the tradition of Christian politics inspired by the *City of God*, and in particular for the attempts to extract from Augustine a coherent doctrine and policy governing relations between *church and state.

Austin, John (1790–1859)
English legal philosopher. *See* *command, *jural relations, *law, *philosophic radicals, *positivism.

Austrian school

A school of economic thought originating in the work of Carl Menger (1840–1921), who developed the still widely influential *marginal utility theory of *value. His work was further developed by Friedrich von Wieser (1851–1926), Eugen von Böhm-Bawerk (1852–1914) and *Mises (1881–1973), and the tradition has continued into our own time, gaining renewed political influence in the thought of the philosopher-economist *Hayek, who has tried to combine the original empirical theory of value with philosophical considerations concerning freedom, the nature of the state, and the structure of markets, so as to provide an elaborate philosophical underpinning for modern liberal *capitalism. (*See also* *calculation debate, *capital.)

autarchy

Greek: self-government. Ambiguous term which may mean either absolute government (*see* *absolutism), or self-government (*see* *autonomy, political), or self-sufficiency (*see* *autarky).

autarky

Self-sufficiency; etymologically distinct from *autarchy. Now used primarily in an economic sense to denote the fact or the aim of national self-sufficiency in food, raw materials and production. The aim of autarky is part of the politics of *isolationism, and goes with resistance to *free trade, and to any form of economic or political dependence on other sovereign powers. It was defended as an essential part of national sovereignty by *Fichte.

authenticity

The ideal, associated with the *existentialist philosophies of *Sartre and

*Heidegger, according to which an individual must create himself in and through his own decisions. His freedom lies precisely in the fact that his identity is not (or need not be) determined by any arrangement external to himself. The 'inauthentic' individual is the one who abandons the responsibility to make himself what he really is and takes refuge in an external command, precept, role or moral code, wrongly imagined to be objectively binding, but in fact simply masking, without overcoming, the 'anxiety' of being (usually written 'Being'). Anxiety is confronted and overcome only in the choice that wills, not only the act, but the whole person implied in it. This ideal of authenticity, freed from its metaphysical overtones, often occurs as one of the postulates of modern *liberalism. It has been given a new lease of life by the Canadian political philosopher Charles Taylor who argues, in *Sources of the Self*, 1992, that the search for political order and the search for a freely constituted and responsible sense of self are, in the last analysis, one and the same.

authoritarian personality

Sometimes identified as a distinct human type (e.g. by *Adorno, in *The Authoritarian Personality*, 1948), and one which has made a substantial negative contribution to politics in modern times. The authoritarian personality is the one who introduces questions of authority into all areas of social life, and in particular into areas where they are inappropriate or unnecessary, with the result that nothing happens by willing cooperation or natural sympathy, but only by command and obedience. The martinet, the unbending father, the dictatorial schoolmaster, the bullying sergeant-major – life and literature abound in relevant examples, and there is no shortage of theories to

explain and criticize what may in fact be a natural and necessary human feature. Probably there is no more vivid example of the authoritarian personality in the field of artistic and musical criticism than that of Adorno himself.

authoritarianism

1. The advocacy of government based on an established system of *authority, rather than on explicit or *tacit consent. Authoritarians believe either that it is good that government should be ordered in this way, or at least that it is necessary. The sources of both beliefs are to be found in two common thoughts: first, that people need authority, and secondly that authority is not the outcome but rather the precondition of consent. More radical authoritarians may sometimes argue that there is no rational source of *political obligation, and hence there is a need to ensure stability against the advance of sceptical reflections; respect towards established institutions is thought to be at least necessary, if not sufficient, for this end.

2. The state of mind, and habits of action, associated with the *authoritarian personality.

authority

That feature of a person, role, office or government which authorizes (i.e. makes legitimate, either in reality or in appearance) the acts and commands exercised in his or its name. Authority attaching to a person, not as the holder of an office, but as the particular person that he or she is, is sometimes said to arise from *charisma. This suggestion derives from *Weber (*Theory of Social and Economic Organization*, 1922), who distinguished three kinds of authority: legal-rational (in which acts are authorized by normative rules), traditional (in which immemorial tradition confers legitimacy), and charismatic. This classification is made from a sociologist's point of view, and distinguishes not so much kinds of authority, as explanations of the *belief* in it.

In all cases authority must be distinguished from *power, being a relation *de jure* and not necessarily *de facto*: authority is a right to act, rather than a power to act. It may be accompanied by power, and so upheld, or without power, and so ignored. One of the most important powers that uphold authority is the power of people's belief in it thus, in a sense, authority can create its own power, and this gives rise to a disposition to use the two terms as though they were synonymous.

From the philosophical point of view three questions must be distinguished: (i) what causes the belief that certain individuals, institutions etc. have authority? (ii) What, if anything, shows that belief to be true? (iii) What, if anything, shows that people ought to subscribe to it?

Questions (ii) and (iii) are not identical. Many who do not think that there is such a thing as authority, nevertheless think that we ought to preserve our belief in it, perhaps on grounds of utility, or public order. The following three observations relate severally to the three questions distinguished:

(i) The causes of the belief in authority are more varied than Weber's division suggests. *Habit is one cause, *custom another (both subsumed under *tradition by Weber). It may even be that the rational perception of a genuine and objectively existing *right of government is also the explanation of the belief in it. Or it may be, by contrast, that the best explanation is *functional: i.e. the belief is held because it performs a function, say, in upholding an economic order, or in upholding the individual's security within it. (*See* *ideology.)

(ii) The grounds of the belief in authority are explored by theories of *political obligation. Theories of *social contract and *consent argue that rights of action must be conferred on institutions, offices or persons by willing agreement of those subject to them, while theories of *prescriptive right argue that, in appropriate circumstances, history alone is sufficient to confer legitimacy. About this question many remain wholly sceptical.

(iii) Some find the value of the belief to stem from its being a necessary condition of government, and hence of the security brought by government. Others argue that people need to believe in an external authority if their lives are to possess inner order, the moral life being impossible without the external symbols of its objectivity. (This second view was perhaps *Hegel's.) Others, perhaps confusing authority with the power which it requires for its enactment, regard all authority as either valueless (because arbitrary) or deleterious (as an interference, or attempted interference, with *freedom). It is often said – in particular by conservatives – that modern societies suffer from a deficit of authority, and that this is the true explanation of both *alienation and *anomie.*

autocracy

Literally self-rule, used to mean rule by an agent who holds all power himself, and who exercises that power in an *arbitrary manner. There may be a constitution and laws which *seem* to limit or guide his power, but in fact these can be revoked at will by the autocrat, and also disobeyed by him, there being no independent mechanism for enforcing them. Most theorists hold that true autocracy requires the concentration of power in a *single* person, and not, for example, in a *party or *caucus. Although parties may rule in a manner that admits no limitation by law, their multiple agency serves partly to restrict their power.

The principal feature is that the ruler may affect each of his subjects at any time in any way that he pleases, and in a manner that admits of no redress. Autocracy should therefore be seen as the perversion of *absolutism, in which power is not only absolute but also arbitrary.

autonomy

Greek: living under one's own laws; hence self-government. The following are important political applications of the idea:

(i) Autonomy of the individual. This is captured by the doctrine that the *rational individual may, in the words of *Kant, 'will the maxim of his action as a law for himself'. It is held that rational beings (or *persons) do not merely respond to the promptings of appetite and desire, but also to self-imposed commands, and this is what distinguishes free action from subjection to the 'laws of nature'. Kant argued that a rational being not only may, but also must, be autonomous in this sense, and that he can be so only if his action is governed by a universal law. *Freedom thus becomes a kind of *obedience. Kant's discussion of autonomy underlies much political theory, both *liberal and anti-liberal, since it seems to generate an idea of freedom that is distinct from *licence. Moreover, it connects the freedom of the individual with a philosophy of the nature of the individual, and this philosophy, or some variant of it, has emerged in the present century as fundamental to some liberal conceptions of man. (*See also* *authenticity.)

(ii) Autonomy of the state. The autonomy of a state is partly a matter of power (of whether it has the external and internal strength to make and enforce its own laws), and partly a matter of recognized *authority (whether it is regarded by other states as the *legitimate government in a particular *territory). The first is a matter of degree: clearly, the power of a *satellite country or a *protectorate to make its own laws is limited by the surveillance of a more powerful external influence, as the power of every state to enact laws is limited by the variable tolerance of its citizens. The second is absolute in international law, since it is tantamount to the legal idea of *sovereignty. Sovereignty is both the necessary and the sufficient condition for the legal existence of a state.

(iii) Regional autonomy. The idea of autonomy has recently been extended to discuss the politics of *devolution. By granting or recognizing a power to make laws to local bodies (e.g. councils, regional assemblies), a state confers or recognizes regional autonomy. All such grant or recognition is on sufferance, since a lawmaking power that cannot be overridden by the central government tends to produce a separate state (perhaps united by *federation) rather than a regional government. Hence complicated examples of regional autonomy often present an appearance of federation. Consider the states of the US, or the striking legal status of Scotland: such quasi-states are immensely difficult to describe. (*See* *devolution.)

(iv) Autonomy of *groups, and *minorities. Unlike regions, groups and minorities have no necessary claims to territory, hence they cannot be granted *jurisdiction over territory, even of a modified kind. However, it has been argued that religious organizations manifest a genuine lawmaking power that is independent both of territory and of the state (*see* *church and state); from the legal point of view, therefore, they are said to provide the only true examples of autonomy within a jurisdiction. (*See also* *millet system.)

(v) Autonomy of institutions. An institution may be called autonomous for any one of three reasons: (a) when it has the capacity to make its own statutes and byelaws; in this sense universities are usually autonomous; (b) when it is outside the direct control of some higher political body (such as a *party or government agency): in this sense universities are autonomous only to some extent and only in certain places and disciplines; (c) when it has its own peculiar or internal aims and purposes: i.e. when there is something that it does which could be done by no other institution. (All universities are autonomous in this sense, as are football teams and families.)

The maintenance of autonomous institutions of all three kinds, with their own traditions of thought, feeling and action, is often put forward as a central aim of some kinds of social *conservatism. The persistence of such institutions is regarded as guaranteeing a social and political continuity which is not enforced (but only subsumed) by the state. Thereby, it is hoped, two conservative ideals – *limited government and social continuity – which seem to be in conflict, might be reconciled. (For an important application of this view, *see* *Tocqueville.)

Specific demands for autonomy, in particular regional autonomy, will reflect the prevailing political tensions of an epoch. It is often argued that a measure of regional autonomy is always necessary when there are *separatist tendencies, since, without it, local feelings will take an overtly nationalist form.

B

a'ath
Arabic: resurrection. Name of a movement founded by *Aflaq, who wished to rouse the Arabs of the former Ottoman Empire to a consciousness of their Arab identity, and to build a new kind of nationalist politics, in which the Arabs would assert their territorial, cultural and political rights against the Western colonial powers. Out of the *ba'ath* movement there grew a *ba'ath* *party, strongly influenced in the 1950s and 1960s by the Soviet communist party, and attempting to unite Marxist social analysis with a *pan-Arab idea of cultural, social and political unity, based on the common history and traditions of the Arab peoples. It thus sought to combine socialism with the pursuit of national unity, and while resisting the appeal to *Islam as the fount of political and social ideals, celebrated it as a product of the Arab national genius.

In practice, *ba'ath* parties have been instruments of terror and oppression, whenever they have succeeded in gaining power. The two most important instances in the modern world – the *ba'ath* parties of Syria and Iraq – have sustained one-party states, with extensive secret police forces using torture and assassination in order to eliminate all actual or potential opposition. The two most prominent leaders of these parties – Hafiz el-Assad of Syria and Saddam Hussein of Iraq – were tribal politicians in the classical Arab mould, distinguished from their historical predecessors only by their apparent lack of moral or religious scruple. The overthrow of Saddam Hussein by the American-led invasion has led to the dissolution of the Iraqi *ba'ath* party, though the death of Hafiz al-Assad has not yet altered the position of the party in Syria, where it effectively holds Bashar, Hafiz's son, hostage as President.

Babeuf, François Gracchus (1760–97)
See *babouvism.

babouvism
Extreme *egalitarianism, along the lines proposed by François Babeuf (1760–97) in his *Conspiracy of Equals*. This was a leading document for the secret societies of the nineteenth century, which advocated absolute equality of incomes, and prepared the ground, for conspiratorial and insurrectionary movements of *socialist persuasion.

Bacon, Sir Francis, Viscount Verulam (1561–1626)
English philosopher, essayist, jurist, and Lord Chancellor. Bacon's *The Advancement of Learning*, 1623, is one of the foundational texts of modern science, arguing for a new approach to explanation, in which quantitative laws would replace arduous classifications, and in which relations of cause and effect would marginalize the *teleological explanations favoured by medieval science. Bacon was an *empiricist, who repudiated all claims to knowledge that did not have experience and experiment as their ultimate authority. As well as being a founding father of modern science,

and a distinguished judge (though one who lost office on charges of corruption), he is universally esteemed as one of the greatest essayists and prose stylists in English. *See also* *balance of power, *equity, *humanities.

bad faith
(French: *mauvaise foi.*) *See* *Sartre.

Bagehot, Walter (1826–77)
English essayist and critic, who was perhaps the first writer to give an impartial overview of the English Constitution, and to show that – even though unwritten – it has a logic and authority of its own. *See* *bicameral government, *cabinet, *checks and balances, *peer.

Bakunin, Mikhail (1814–76)
Russian revolutionary, often known as 'the father of modern *anarchism', whose conflict with Marx in 1869–71 broke up the First *International. Bakunin advocated violent struggle and individual acts of *terrorism in order to bring about revolutionary change, the principal goal of which would be the immediate elimination of all political, social and religious institutions, and their replacement with a free federation of independent associations in which all would have equal rights and equal privileges, including that of secession. Bakunin was opposed to the systematic and statist implications of Marx's thinking, and gave a prophetic critique of the likely outcome of Marx's *dictatorship of the proletariat. His own thinking, however, was too scattered and euphoric to provide the clear revolutionary alternative that he wished for. He played a leading role in the revolutionary uprising in Dresden in 1849, in which he was associated with Richard Wagner, and was sentence to death when the uprising was suppressed. His sentence was later commuted to exile.

balance of payments
The balance of payments accounts of a state record the economic transactions that its residents undertake with foreigners within a given period. Economists distinguish 'autonomous' and 'accommodating' items. The former include the imports and exports of goods and services, property income, and investments in long-term assets. The surplus or deficit on those items which are considered not to be within the direct control of the government of a state must be financed. *See also* *balance of trade, *exchange control.

balance of power
An important concept in the description of international relations, but also of uncertain meaning. It may refer:

(i) to a policy on the part of states that deliberately aims to prevent the preponderance of any one state or *bloc, and to maintain approximate equilibrium in military potential;

(ii) to an observed principle of international politics,, whereby any state which threatens to increase its power becomes at once subject to increases in countervailing power from potential belligerents;

(iii) to a political system characterized by a particular configuration of power relationships.

A distinction is usually made between *multipolar equilibrium, and simple or bipolar equilibrium. In the first a balance may be maintained either peacefully (e.g. through economic rewards and punishments), or through the use of force (as when a troublemaker is made to confront the coalition of the remaining states: e.g. the War of the Grand Alliance, 1688–97). Since the First World War critics of the European multipolar balance have often claimed that a multipolar balance eventually becomes a bipolar balance of competing alliances, thus precipitating an arms race, and war. Defenders of the multi-polar balance have attributed the long periods of peace in Europe to its existence. Both sides admit that international configurations that can be called balanced are both likely to be unstable, and not certain to be peaceful. Defenders of the balance of power in Europe have included Bolingbroke, *Bacon and *Hume (who wrote a famous essay on the subject). Critics have included *Rousseau and *Kant, who denounced it as an immoral sport of sovereigns (cf. *Augustine's idea of the 'peace of the unjust').

balance of trade

The balance between the cost of a state's imports and the receipts for its exports, over a given period. The balance of trade is just one element of the *balance of payments. *Friedman has argued that, if currencies are free-floating, and not supported by state intervention, then trade is self-equilib-riating, since the currency value will rise or fall in response to the surplus or deficit in trade, so cancelling out any imbalance. Even if that is not true, it remains an important question whether imbalances matter. Thus the US economy runs on a large and seemingly permanent deficit, exporting currency in order to cover the cost of imports. Since those who receive the currency will have an interest in maintaining its value, it is assumed that they will not dump the currency on the international money market. There are many economists who disagree with that assumption.

balanced budget

The central budget of a government is in balance when current receipts are equal to current expenditure: i.e. when the sum of taxes equals the government's expenditure on goods and services. Followers of *Keynes argue that budget surpluses and deficits can

be used to manage the economy, so that a balanced budget is not necessarily desirable.

Balfour Declaration

See *Zionism.

balkanization

Term coined by German socialists to describe the effect of late-nineteenth-century Tsarist policy on the Balkan states bordering the Russian Empire, and later used to denote the divisive effects upon those states of the treaty of Brest-Litovsk (1918). Hence: division of a region into a number of small, autonomous states, often mutually hostile, in order to remove the possibility of a serious military threat from any of them. Since the collapse of Yugoslavia, the Balkan states have shown a remarkable ability to balkanize themselves.

banking

The business of safeguarding deposits and lending money at interest. The 'banking system' consists of the totality of institutions officially recognized as determining standard transactions of this kind (but does not include, for example, building societies).

The central government agencies may try to use the 'banking system' as a mechanism of monetary control (*see* *monetarism, *money supply). In offering overdrafts and loan facilities banks can augment the money supply, while by raising interest rates they may decrease it. The normal object of such a banking system is to put most of the money at its disposal to use, by lending at interest, while retaining a minimum cash balance with which to meet its obligations to depositors.

Most modern governments attempt to exert control over the creation of credit by the banking system. Thus a central bank (such as the Bank of England, or the more complex system of banks in the US known as the Federal Reserve System, whose board is appointed by the President, with the approval of the Senate) may attempt to determine rates of interest, for example, by its activities in financial markets. These 'minimum lending rates' may be enforced either directly, by legal stipulation, or indirectly, by economic pressure (exerted in the UK by dealings between the Bank of England and discount houses). An increase in the minimum lending rate causes other interest rates to rise, so making borrowing less attractive and curtailing the money supply. Economists dispute over whether this method of control is effective in the absence of additional government measures. In particular the rise of transnational banks and finance houses has led to transactions that bypass the control of any particular government.

International politics is affected, not only by the existence of such transnational corporations, but also by the perhaps more political International Bank for Reconstruction and Development (the *World Bank), designed to encourage investment in *developing countries. The World Bank diverts funds from contributing countries (who contribute according to their share in world trade) to those who, for lack of *capital, are unable to embark on socially necessary projects. (See further *world organizations.) The effect of such institutions is much debated. Some argue, for example, that they permit capital accumulation without *revolution, and so enable the developing countries to make a peaceful transition to *capitalist (or at any rate modern) modes of production. Others argue that, since they deal in Western currencies, and notably in dollars, transnational financial institutions constitute a covert mortgaging of the countries that they subsidize to the Western economic system. Moreover,

since their transactions pass through the hands of (usually unelected) elites, they entrench the power of those elites, by giving them extensive foreign bank accounts.

bankruptcy

The procedure whereby the courts take possession of the property of a debtor, in order to hold it in *trust for his creditors, by way of partial settlement of their claims. The procedure, which has been the subject of legislation in England since 1542, and of federal legislation in the US since 1800, can be initiated by a petition from a creditor or by the debtor himself. In the US 'filing for bakruptcy' has become a fairly normal way of bringing a business to an end. *Limited liability means that the owner of a bankrupt business may be able to protect his other assets from sequestration by the court, although certain forms of fraudulent dealing can lead to charges of 'criminal bankruptcy'. Bankruptcy was described by *Fourier as 'a more despicable form of theft than highway robbery, yet one which people have become used to and tolerant of: so much so that they even regard some as *honest bankruptcies*, when the speculator only takes half the sum.' (*Theory of the Four Movements*.)

Although clearly subject to abuses, the law of bankruptcy is an important part of a free economy, provides signals to the potential investor and ensures that failing businesses are quickly removed from the market. The absence of bankruptcy laws in communist systems meant the absence of any reliable signal of failure, and the consequent misallocation of funds to enterprises that swallowed them without result. At a certain point the entire economy was *de facto* bankrupt, though without the ability to declare itself such.

Barrès, Maurice (1862–1923)
French novelist, polemicist and politician whose ardent defence of French nationalism had a great impact on French politics in the early twentieth century. He was an early critic of the 'cult of self', to which he devoted a trilogy of novels (*Le Culte du moi*, 1888–91), in which an egoistic hero gradually discovers the truth that there is no self without other, and no happiness without love. Barrès believed the cult of self had undermined the social order of France, producing a widespread *déracinement* (uprootedness) in ordinary people, and that the pursuit of individual pleasure had poisoned the sources of social responsibility. The soul of France, he believed, could be rediscovered only through social conflict and struggle. His defence of this idea rested on social *Darwinism, and assumed France to be an organic community united by a cult of the Land and the Dead. True regeneration of the nation required, for Barrès, political reform, and constant vigilance against liberalism, democracy and Marxism. This nationalist vision was enshrined in another trilogy, *Les Bastions de l'est*, 1905–21.

Barrès's *anti-semitism, his populism and his invocation of instinct against the uprooted 'rationalism' of liberal thought have led many to see him as a precursor of *National Socialism. However, in his analysis of the Great War and the defeat of France (*Chronique de la grande guerre, 1920–24*), Barrès repudiated his anti-semitism, and identified weaknesses in the French body politic that have endured to this day. There is nothing in his writings to suggest that he would have endorsed the kind of barbarism that was later to arise in Germany.

barter
The voluntary exchange of goods without the intermediary of *money.

Systems of barter become cumbersome as soon as there are large surpluses to be disposed of or a systematic *division of labour in production; the natural tendency in those circumstances is for some standard object of human covetousness (e.g. gold) to become a standard object of exchange. Some argue that, in barter economies, production is undertaken predominantly to meet the subsistence needs of the producer himself, and that in such an economy *Say's law will be observed.

base and superstructure
A distinction introduced into political thought by *Marxism, and made by *Marx in the *Preface to a Critique of Political Economy*, 1859. According to Marx it is necessary to distinguish the economic base of the social order from the legal, political and cultural superstructure which rests upon it. The base consists of the relations between people (or between classes of people) which determine their various powers of control over the means of *production, distribution and exchange: these are the *production relations, through which *productive forces operate. The superstructure consists in legal, political and social institutions that express, enforce and consolidate the relations of economic power that pertain to the base. Marxists believe that changes in the base explain corresponding changes in the superstructure, but not (or at any rate, not primarily) vice versa. Hence the most fundamental historical processes are economic ones, legal and political changes being merely changes in the social embodiment of those more basic things. If it were shown that the historical development of legal and political institutions were *autonomous, or that economic relations were normally, or at any rate not abnormally, the effects and not the causes of legal and political thought

and action, then the Marxist thesis would be refuted.

The theory is criticized as inverting the true order of causality. Critics believe that it is changes in the legal and cultural 'superstructure' that release the energies of people; economic growth is caused by those changes and does not produce them.

Baudrillard, Jean (1929–)
French sociologist and cultural critic, who has given ironically endorsing accounts of the consumer society, and of the meaning of objects in an economy of waste. He celebrates the mass media for their freedom from moral, aesthetic and cultural constraints, and generally promotes a *postmodern toleration of every habit that challenges the norms of bourgeois society. The consumer society, he argues, is one in which illusion and reality encounter each other on equal terms, and the role of the cultural critic is to decipher the new world that is precipitated from their clash. Much criticized for his pseudo-scientific and nonsense-riddled prose, Baudrillard has also been admired for his sociological serendipity. See also *consumer society, *postmodernism.

Beauvoir, Simone de (1908–86)
French novelist, essayist and philosopher who, in *The Second Sex* (1949), gave the classical philosophical statement of modern *feminism, in terms that reflect the existentialist philosophy of her lifelong companion *Sartre. In a world shaped and fashioned by men, de Beauvoir argued, woman is compelled to assume the status of the Other. She becomes an Object, while man (the first sex) enjoys the privileges of the *Subject, who retains his freedom and autonomy, and is able to build an individual life without permission from his fellows. Female emancipation means the assumption by women of the autonomy and freedom that have been hitherto monopolized by men. Since freedom cannot be achieved without an equal assumption of responsibility, women must be prepared to accept the burdens of freedom if they also want the benefits. But since the benefits include personality itself, no reasonable woman would refuse to pay the price.

behaviouralism
The view, briefly fashionable in America, that social and political theories should be based in a study of the observable behaviour of people, and not on their expressed convictions. Associated with the work of David Easton (*The Political System*, 1981), it favours quantitative and statistical analysis over the grand ideological theories.

behaviourism
The psychological theory that the scientific study of the mind must be confined to the study of behaviour (including language), without reference to the deliverances of introspection; alternatively, the philosophical theory that there is nothing to the mind besides behaviour, so that introspection is the observation of nothing. The psychological theory – or at least the method associated with it – has been extended into the socio-political sphere by B.F. Skinner, in order to give expression to a theory that is at once *utopian in its aspirations and *materialist in its assumptions. The leading idea is that behaviour is formed in response to previous behaviour, and to the 'rewards' or 'reinforcements' of the environment that *condition it, so that the self-consciousness of the subject plays no important part in the process of social development. Hence political activity should be directed towards creating the conditions that reinforce the behaviour desired. This

raises the question, Desired by whom? Some find the pseudoscientific optimism of *Beyond Freedom and Dignity*, 1971, to be, in the light of that question, an apology for *tyranny. Others are concerned rather to reject the theory of *human nature on which it is based.

Bell, Daniel (b.1919)
American sociologist. *See* *cultural contradictions of capitalism, *end of ideology, *third way.

bell curve
When a variable attribute such as IQ is distributed in a population, then more members of the population will be at or near to the statistical norm than those to either side of it. If you map numbers of people against level of IQ, therefore, the resulting curve will have a bell shape, and the apex of this bell will indicate the norm. The expression became familiar and controversial with the book published by Richard Herrnstein and Charles Murray, *The Bell Curve*, 1994, in which the performance of American blacks and whites in IQ tests and related measures were compared, through plotting the bell curves for each group. The results were controversial, not merely because they suggested that whites performed systematically better in the relevant tests, but because they caused people to ask whether the tests measured anything of real significance, other than the ability to conform to expectations formed by a white middle-class culture.

belligerency
The legal condition or status of the parties to public war. There seem to be two requirements: an actual contest of arms, and an intention, recognition or declaration of this sufficient to attribute the contest to the parties. In international contests belligerency usually begins with a formal declaration of war, or is preceded by an ultimatum with conditional declaration.

To recognize the belligerency of two parties to a civil war is to concede that the international law of belligerency applies to them, whereas to recognize *insurgency is not to suppose that this law yet applies. The law of belligerency lays down rights and duties to be recognized by all states deeming themselves *neutral to the combat, and also rights and duties to be honoured (ideally) by the parties themselves. In international law only some states are qualified to make war – i.e. to be 'belligerents'. 'Insurgent' governments can become belligerents through the act of 'recognition' bestowed on them by other qualified states.

Benda, Julien (1867–1956)
French philosopher and essayist. *See* *humanitarianism, *intégrisme*, *intellectuals, *jingoism, *trahison des clercs*.

beneficial interest
See *trust.

Benjamin, Walter (1892–1940)
German literary and cultural critic, who blended the Marxist humanism of the *Frankfurt school with Jewish mysticism, in an attempt to understand the nature of art in capitalist society. In 'The Work of Art in the Age of Mechanical Reproduction' (in *Illuminations*, 1968), Benjamin argues that new techniques of visual reproduction (photography and film in particular) have both democratized the aesthetic experience, and also demystified the process of artistic creation. In this way they have introduced new potentials for communication, as well as new threats of *fetishism. Benjamin's unsuccessful attempt to flee Nazi Europe to the United States led in 1940 to his suicide. See also *politicization.

Bentham, Jeremy (1748–1832)
English philosopher, economist and legal theorist, proponent of the principle of *utilitarianism, according to which the happiness of the community should be the sole aim of morality and of law. Bentham proposed a quantitative idea of happiness, as pleasure (*see* *hedonism), and a procedure for calculating the benefit of a course of action in terms of such factors as the quantity of pleasure, its probability, its proximity and duration in time. This (the 'felicific calculus') was one of the first experiments in *cost/benefit analysis. Bentham's merits as a legal and constitutional theorist stem partly from the minuteness of detail and classificatory completeness with which he approached legal and social analysis. He upheld a theory of legal *positivism, and opposed all ideas of *natural right, as well as the theory of the *social contract. He argued that *rights and obligations are created by *convention, and that the sole criterion to be applied in determining the merit of laws and maxims is the criterion of utility. He went on to deduce (*Introduction to the Principles of Morals and Legislation*, 1789) that laws should be certain, and therefore written; that they should be enforceable, and therefore adapted to the actual state of society and to the movement of social reform; and that they should be calculated to maximize the overall prospect of pleasure. On such a basis Bentham constructed a liberal-reformist doctrine of the law and judicial procedure that has remained influential into the present century. He attempted to synthesize utilitarianism with the economic theories of *Smith, and put forward a plan for a *welfare state with free education, sickness benefits, minimum wages and guaranteed employment. See also *animals.

Berlin, Sir Isaiah (1909–2002)
Latvian-born British philosopher and historian of ideas, and articulate exponent of *liberal *pluralism. In 'The Hedgehog and the Fox' (1953) Berlin contrasts the monism of those who, like the hedgehog in Archilochus's line, 'know one big thing', and the pluralism of the fox, who knows many things, suggesting that these correspond to two permanent temperaments, which may also conflict in a single person, as they did in Tolstoy. Liberal pluralism, for Berlin, meant accepting not merely competing values, but also irresoluble conflicts between them: we could live with others' values, however, provided we recognize the social and epistemological benefits of competition, and the need for all institutions to be constantly revised to accommodate the changing aspirations of people.

In 'Two Concepts of Liberty' (1968) Berlin famously distinguished negative freedom – the freedom from external constraint – from 'positive' freedom, meaning the freedom to realize one's full potential, or in some other way to achieve fulfilment. Political systems that promise positive freedom, such as the corporatism of *Hegel or the *communism of *Marx, have a pronounced and predictable tendency to promote the restriction or extinction of negative freedom. But the true aim of liberal politics is negative freedom – the removal of contraints – rather than the ill-conceived and paternalistic attempt to get us to 'be what we truly are'. Moreover, the promise of positive freedom is not one that we can rationally act upon: always it involves a dangerous element of utopianism and a denial of the known facts of human nature.

Berlin was a towering presence in British culture, who did much to create the liberal consensus of the academy in the aftermath of 1968.

Bernstein, Eduard (1850–1932)
German political theorist who tried to update Marxist theory, in the light of his observations concerning the development and stabilization of modern capitalist society. He advocated the gradual reform of capitalism in a socialist direction, and thereby entered history as the originator of Marxist *revisionism. *See also* *Kautsky.

bicameral government
The system of government in which the *legislature, the *executive, or both, are distributed over two houses, an upper house and a lower house. The best-known examples of such arrangements – the UK *Parliament (involving House of Commons and House of Lords), and the US *Congress (involving House of Representatives and Senate) – have been taken as models for bicameral government in other countries, the second being adapted to the government of *federal states, the first having a kind of organic unity which fits it to the government of autonomous and traditionally unified societies. In theory each house acts as a check on the other, preventing hasty legislation, and enforcing deliberation. In practice, and for a variety of reasons, there is often a creeping tendency for the power of the upper house to decline, unless some countervailing force upholds its status. This force may be found in a procedure for election (as in the US *Senate), in executive control over membership, or in enhanced dignity and status, such as has been traditionally associated with the British House of Lords. Not all dignity is a form of political power, and already in 1867 Bagehot (*The English Constitution*) divided the instruments of government into the 'dignified' and the 'effective', implying that the House of Lords belongs to the first and not to the second kind. Bagehot also went on to argue for the indispensable place of that 'dignified' part in securing acceptance of the powers exercised by the effective, and this thought has often been reiterated by defenders of the *Westminster model of bicameral government.

Defenders of bicameral government on the US model often refer to the *checks and balances supposedly introduced by it. Those who defend the Westminster model are often more concerned with its ability to generate a settled political establishment, which unifies the diverse allegiances within the state, offers a sop to ambition, and defuses the enthusiasm of revolutionary powers. Both forms seem to have the indirect effects of giving power to the *judiciary, and of making it comparatively easy to recognize and seek redress for official acts which are performed *ultra vires*. In the UK it has always been very important that subjects should be able to affirm their rights against an action by one house by petitioning the other.

Opponents of bicameral government are apt to be impatient with the delays that it may impose on legislation, with the difficulty with which an upper house can be persuaded to condone substantial changes in constitution or social structure, and with the complexity of *representation when the decisions of representatives stand to be ratified or amended by another body. Thus *Sieyès remarked that 'if the upper house agrees with the lower it is superfluous; if it disagrees, it ought to be abolished'. Opponents may also argue that bicameral government prevents the exercise of absolute power even in times when such power is necessary, and that no satisfactory qualification for membership of an upper house has been, or could be, devised.

Perhaps the most debated question concerning this issue is the last one:

what should qualify a person for membership of an upper house? Is hereditary right acceptable (*see* *hereditary principle*)? Should there be *elections? Executive privilege of appointment? The problem here is how to make the upper house into a genuine revising chamber, with some kind of sanction that enables it to represent constitutional continuity, while preventing it from becoming the principal forum of political decision-making. *See* *peer.

bien-pensant

French: someone with the 'right ideas'. Used ironically to denote anyone whose opinions are adopted in order to conform to what is socially acceptable – specifically among those who are well-off, *liberal and *half-educated. *See also* *political correctness.

bilateralism

1. The advocacy of joint policies between states, e.g. in matters of aggression, defence or trade, perhaps requiring complex constitutional devices in order to secure *approximation of laws.

2. Specifically, the agreement between two states to extend to each other privileges in trade which are not extended to others (e.g. favourable tariffs). Such agreements (unlike the opposed multilateralism) act as a *de facto* restriction on international trade, and are generally opposed by those not party to them. A General Agreement on Tariffs and Trade (GATT) was therefore agreed at the *Bretton Woods conference in 1944 and signed in 1947 committing the signatories to the expansion of multilateral trade and the reduction of exclusive agreements. This was replaced in 1995 by the *World Trade Organization. The Soviet Union and its satellites engaged in extensive bilateral agreements, in order to incorporate their national plans into definite and predictable patterns of international trading.

bill

A draft or proposed piece of legislation, put before *Parliament, *Congress or some other legislative body for consideration, either by a Minister concerned with public policy, or by a 'private member' of the parliament or assembly, or by petition from a member of the public. When passed by the legislative body, a bill becomes an act.

bill of rights (also: declaration of rights)

Any attempt to formulate systems of *natural rights that can be recognized by, and enforced against, particular governments. The *Constitution of Virginia*, 1776, and the French *Declaration of the Rights of Man and of the Citizen*, 1789, incorporated such declarations, and succeeded, in the first case, in enforcing them. The US Bill of Rights (or first ten amendments) is founded on eighteenth-century ideas of natural right which have their origin in *Locke. It is a constitutional device rather than a specific legal enactment, and thus has provided a genuine limit to state power, providing rights which can be fought for in open court, whatever the authority of the power that seeks to deny them. The English 'Bill of Rights' of 1689 is, by contrast, only a legal enactment, and can itself be overruled or qualified by subsequent parliamentary decisions. It is therefore not part of the constitution and provides no permanent guarantee of the rights which it designates (which include *habeas corpus). The USSR and its Eastern European dependencies had constitutions incorporating declarations of rights (partly in order to achieve nominal conformity with the United Nations Charter of Human Rights).

However, they were ineffective, and attempts by the citizen to assert them against official power led to charges of *sedition and even *show trials. Moreover, a bill of rights is effective only if there is also *judicial independence, so that judges have power to uphold the rights specified when they are sued for. If a judge is under instruction from the state in all actions to which the state is party, then a bill of rights does not exist as a genuine constitutional device, but only as a legal fiction.

Several suggestions have been made as to the desirability of a constitutional bill of rights in the UK. It should, however, be recognized that rights have traditionally been guaranteed in the UK not by constitutional declarations, but by customary *procedures*. Thus the existence of an independent judiciary, the priority of *equity over *common law and *statute, and the entrenched disapproval of retroactive legislation, act together to provide strong barriers against parliamentary despotism, and this fact is illustrated throughout the history of English *constitutional law. The 'Bill of Rights' exists partly as a reminder of these procedures, and partly as a reassertion of the *sovereignty of Parliament against the claims of the *monarchy. It should also be recognized that a written declaration of the American variety is a guarantee of rights only when it can be upheld, and this requires just the kind of procedural detachment from executive power that is displayed by the UK judiciary.

Bismarck, Prince Otto von (1815–98)
German statesman and Chancellor. See *anti-clericalism, *culture, *health, *Kulturkampf, *Realpolitik, *welfare state.

black consciousness
A movement originating among urban blacks in the US, and spreading to Africa, which urges the formation among black peoples of a consciousness of their identity and political aspirations which will be independent of the *values, aims and manoeuvres of the white nations, and independent of ways of thinking redolent of a colonial past. The idea of black consciousness is often embellished with theories of *oppression, which imply that blacks have accepted pictures of their own role and position which consolidate the existing domination by whites and reflect the ruling white *ideology. The elimination of this subservient consciousness is seen as a necessary preliminary to the pursuit of real political power. See also *négritude.

black economy
See *shadow economy.

Blackstone, Sir William (1723–80)
English jurist, politician and judge, author of the celebrated *Commentaries on the Laws of England* (4 vols, 1765–69), which set out the traditional *Tory defence of the English *common law and British constitution, as practical applications of the principles of *natural law. Blackstone sees the British constitution as a solution, tested by time and custom, to the problems of social conflict and the needs of orderly government, and praises the *common law as an all-pervasive check on tyrannical ambition. The *Commentaries* were the first attempt to give a comprehensive statement of English law, along with a vindication of its genius.

Blanquism
The theory and practice of revolution by *coup d'état*, carried out by a secret *élite of armed conspirators, rather than by any mass organization. Named after the French revolutionary Louis Auguste Blanqui (1805–81), who influenced several generations of

French radicals, Blanquism views a temporary élite dictatorship as a necessary means of extinguishing any remaining strains of capitalism and of imposing a revolutionary programme on the people, regardless of their support for it. The entire concentration of the doctrine is on the means of revolution; the end is taken more or less for granted.

Blanqui bequeathed to Marxism such fundamental concepts as *class struggle, and *dictatorship of the proletariat. Blanquism played a part in the formation of *syndicalism in France, and anticipated the actual strategy of *bolshevism.

bloc

French for block. From the habit in continental government of divergent political groups or parties gathering together to support the government in power. The term was later extended to cover groupings in an *opposition, and then transferred to international relations in order to denote political and economic concertedness of states, whether or not bound to each other by *treaty or *alliance. For example, all nations incorporated into, or overrun by, the USSR since the 'October Revolution' were, by consent or compulsion, likely to act in concert on most military, economic and political issues, and so constituted a 'bloc'.

Blocs must be distinguished from coalitions: the former are united by interest, but do not require either a truce between the parties, or a common policy.

block voting

The practice of *voting in collusion with others, and according to an agreed common policy. A block vote may involve the members of a given *faction voting against their judgement; the practice is therefore often condemned as being against the spirit of voting. It was heavily criticized in the Federalist Papers, and suggestions were made as to how a constitution might be designed to prevent it. However, the universal emergence of *parties has made block voting of *some* kind a normal accompaniment of democratic procedure. Some argue that it is necessary if any kind of representation is to be effective. Nevertheless, the block vote accorded to trade unions in the Labour Party constitution led to much bitter controversy, and widespread disaffection among would-be Labour supporters. The revised constitution under *New Labour has no provision for block voting.

blockade

The right of a belligerent to forbid access to and egress from enemy territory, usually by sea, whether on the part of the enemy or on the part of a *neutral. Under *international law such a right must be enforced impartially against all enemy and neutral nations. The Declaration of London, 1908, attempted to restrict rights of blockade, but was never *ratified. *See also* *pacific blockade.

Bodin, Jean (1530–96)

French political philosopher and one of the first theorists of modern *absolutism. In his *Six livres de la république*, 1576, Bodin provided an original and highly influential examination of the concept of *sovereignty, defined as the 'most high and perpetual' power in a commonwealth and the entity which has the absolute right and duty of law-giving. Law is the expression of the sovereign's will, and binds the subject regardless of his consent. The sovereign power is, however, subject to the constraints of *natural law, and while violation of that law may absolve the subject of his duty to obey, it does not confer on him a right to rebel (political order being a benefit so great that no man has a right to overthrow it); it may, however, give to neighbouring sovereigns a right to interfere in the cause of *justice. The sovereign cannot be subject to his own laws, since they express his will, but the holding of power demands respect for the institutions of civil life, among which the family and private property are given particular emphasis.

Bodin's defence of absolute monarchy was far from a justification of *autocracy. He regarded faction and civil strife as the major causes of cruelty and injustice. To prevent them, he argued, a political arrangement must balance interests against each other, and so still their conflict. It is only when there is absolute sovereignty that there is the authoritative source of conciliation. Hence Bodin combined his absolutist doctrine with the advocacy of *minority rights in matters of religion, judicial independence, and constraints against taxation. He also gave one of the first accounts of *international law, regarded as specifying the rights of a sovereign not over his subjects but against other sovereigns. The fundamental aim in all aspects of his theory was to develop a concept of sovereignty that would uphold the privileges of the French monarch, at a time of factional insurrection and religious dissent, precipitated in part by the Huguenot rebellions.

body politic

An *organicist term for *civil society. The term was popular among seventeenth-century writers, and is interesting for its implications as to how social order was conceived. Historians of ideas sometimes comment on the subsequent replacement of this and related metaphors by those of a more mechanical kind; e.g. 'the ship of state', *'checks and balances'. The

influence of Newtonian mechanics is sometimes stressed, along with the emergence of the *universalist, and atomistic, vision of social order that appealed to the *Enlightenment.

Bolingbroke, Henry St John, Viscount (1678–1751)

English statesman and political philosopher. See *balance of power, *establishment, *patriotism.

bolshevism

The revolutionary wing of the Russian Social Democratic Party became known as *bolsheviki* ('members of the majority') in 1903, at the second Party Congress in London. The *bolsheviki* were led by *Lenin in opposition to the *mensheviks – i.e. members of the minority. (In actual fact, at the moment of split, the mensheviks were in the majority, the adoption of the name 'bolshevik' by the Leninist faction being a ploy of *newspeak.) The name was retained in the official designation of the Soviet Communist Party from 1912 until 1952, and 'bolshevism' is now accepted as a standard term for *Leninism as practised by that party, and as theorized in the works of Lenin himself. It involves the advocacy of violent revolution as opposed to the gradual change sought by the mensheviks, together with a stringent form of *democratic centralism: all powers are to be assumed by the state in the name of the proletariat which is to dictate during the aftermath of revolution. The bolsheviks eventually seized power by *coup d'état*, and proceeded to eliminate all remaining *opposition to their rule.

Bonapartism

Attachment to and advocacy of the policies of Napoleon Bonaparte, involving belief in (a) a strong post-revolutionary concentration of power, (b) a centralized administration and '*carrières ouvertes aux talents*', (c) a system of honours and dignities issuing from the sovereign power, (d) a correspondingly ceremonial and majestic *state, (e) a foreign policy of aggression and conquest rather than defence, with a global *sphere of influence, (f) the embodiment of the power of state in the personality of a leader, who will represent *majesty in concrete form. While Bonapartism can still be seen as a characteristic of the French presidential system (albeit in diminished form), it owed its original success to the military genius of Napoleon, and to the ease with which he was able to revive and modernize the principles of *aristocratic government.

Bork, Robert H. (1927–)

American judge, solicitor general and jurist who has defended a conservative reading of the American Constitution, arguing that the duty of the judge is to construe the original intention of the Founders strictly, and not to import interpretations that reflect his own desires and prejudices while being at variance with the letter and the spirit of the original document. Although there is latitude for disagreement, and the Constitution can be extrapolated to deal with circumstances that the Founders did not or could not foresee, all such extrapolation must be guided by respect for the overall intentions of the Constitution. The habit of importing interpretations of constitutional clauses in order to satisfy this or that (usually liberal) prejudice is in fact tantamount to repudiating the constitution entirely, and refusing to recognize it as setting limits to legislative and judicial powers. Moreover, it is to authorize judicial legislation in defiance of the will of Congress and the elected representatives of the people. Therefore it is a violation of the democratic traditions of the American people. Bork has been a particularly

trenchant critic of the decision in *Roe* v. *Wade* (see *abortion). His more philosophical writings, in which he defends the spiritual and moral inheritance of America against modern corruption, have placed him firmly in the conservative camp. As a result Bork's nomination to the Supreme Court by President Reagan was so vehemently opposed by the liberal *establishment that the appointment could not be ratified.

bourgeois/bourgeoisie

French: town-dweller, and the class thereof. The term bourgeois has two uses which have been conflated for reasons that are self-evident.

1. As appropriated by *Marx, the term denotes a particular economic position, and the *class created by that position, viz. the class of property-owners under capitalist and proto-capitalist systems of production. Private property in the means of production seems to be the essential feature of this class, and the one that gives its structural description. However, Marx and *Engels also have in mind another way of identifying this class: as the 'class' of *small* property-owners, which arose during the Middle Ages and came to displace the existing *aristocracy from positions of eminence which they had formerly occupied, so that 'the bourgeoisie has at last, since the establishment of modern industry and of the world market, conquered for itself, in the modern representative state, exclusive political sway. The executive of the modern state is but a committee for managing the common affairs of the whole bourgeoisie' (*The Communist Manifesto*). The vision recurs repeatedly in Marx and subsequent writers, of a class that has *come* to hold a certain dominant position in production relations, and therefore in the state. This suggests that there is a way of identifying a class which does not

make reference to its economic position, and which also enables us to think of it as possessing power, or even *agency, of its own.

2. The term has also been used to describe the traditional division between the class of gentlemen and aristocrats, and that of their rivals, the bourgeoisie, who had newly arrived in a position of eminence through the profits of trade. This usage is exemplified in Molière's ironical title *Le bourgeois gentilhomme*, 1670. It is essentially the expression of a *contrast* between new, urban-based wealth, and old, land-based power. The *bourgeoisie is conceived, in this usage, as a *middle class, and its association with the life and *ethos of the town is far more important than its economic position. Ridicule and hostility towards the bourgeoisie have been important parts of French intellectual life since the seventeenth century, and the game of *épater le bourgeois* (Flaubert's expression) was extended in the nineteenth century to Germany, where bourgeois culture had taken over much of the impetus provided by the *romantic movement, and in place of the bungling absence of style that had been satirized by Molière had effectively created a style of its own (the so-called 'Biedermeier' style – from the fictional Gottlieb Biedermaier, imaginary representative of middle class respectability, lampooned by Ludwig Eichrot (1827–92) and others in the periodical *Fliegende Blätter*).

Emerging from 2. during the nineteenth century was the sense of the 'bourgeois' as a special kind of creature, whose thoughts, feelings and relations demanded new and so far unstudied explanations. The bourgeois is characterized by a particular kind of family relations, particular thoughts, feelings and attachments, and a characteristic *ideology. *Weber emphasized the extent to which the rising middle classes were the standard bearers of the new, 'intra-mundane' ideals of the personal and the *business ethic. Others have continued the game of ridicule, best exemplified, perhaps, by *Sartre, in *Saint Genet*, 1952, where the bourgeois is characterized by his rejection of, and hostility to, crime, by his predilection for lasting heterosexual, as opposed to transient homosexual, relations, by his fear and suspicion of all that 'inverts' a fragile vision of 'normality'. This is a long way from the Marxian idea: to suppose that these attitudes (which are not unknown even among members of the working class) are specific to private property in the means of production is, to put it mildly, far-fetched.

Nevertheless, there are intuitive connections between the two ideas, which explain many of the current usages of the term. The major difficulty is that there are two rival ways of identifying and theorizing classes. According to one way (class = position in economic relations), classes cannot 'rise'; according to the other (class = life-style, kinship relations, and ethic), they can.

bourgeois democracy

Term of *newspeak used by communists and their fellow travellers to denote (and to decry) the European, and by implication American, systems of *representation, as these have emerged and evolved during the last two centuries. Bourgeois democracy has been typically contrasted with *people's democracy, in which there may be no elections to office, but in which power is supposedly exercised in the interests of the people as a whole, and not in the interests of any particular class. Likewise, 'bourgeois civil liberties'.

bourgeois economics

Term used by Marxists to denote the kind of economic theory developed by the nineteenth-century successors of Adam Smith (including *J.S. Mill, although more usually rather less self-critical figures), which treats exchange and *exchange-value as fundamental economic facts, and the laws of the *market as laws of nature. It is criticized for representing the historical conditions of capitalist modes of production as permanent features of human life: 'The aim is . . . to present production – see, e.g. Mill – as distinct from distribution etc., as encased in eternal natural laws independent of history, at which opportunity *bourgeois* relations are then quietly smuggled in as the inviolable natural laws on which society in the abstract is founded' (Marx, *Grundrisse*).

boycott

Named after its original victim (Captain Boycott, an Irish landlord's agent isolated by the Irish League in 1880), a boycott implies the severance of all relations, whether economic, social or political, in order to force a recalcitrant party to change its actions or policies. Boycotting of an individual citizen or legal *person may sometimes be lawful, but it is also frequently a *conspiracy to injure. In international law it seems not to be recognized as a form of action distinct from *embargo, *sanctions etc. It is, however, fairly normal practice in international diplomacy to boycott the delegate of a state whose policies are the object of disapproval.

In *industrial action, boycotting has assumed some importance, especially in the US, although some US states have made the 'secondary boycott' (boycott of firms who patronize or supply an offending employer) illegal.

Bracton, Henry de (d. 1268)

English jurist, credited with the authorship of *De legibus et consuetudinibus angliae* (On the Laws and Customs of England), in which the law of England is represented as independent of the royal power, and standing in judgement over it. The king is the servant of the law, whose duty is to enforce the law impartially and justly: in doing so, he makes himself God's minister or 'vicar' on earth. Bracton's defence of the common law of England, as arising through a cooperative process in which all subjects take part, and standing higher in power and authority than the sovereign's pleasure, was the archetype for many subsequent explanations of the traditional freedoms of the English.

brands and branding

Branding is the process whereby a business emancipates itself from a particular product and becomes identified instead with a label or brand. Naomi Klein, in *No Logo*, 2000, argues that the big corporations have realized that the production and sale of goods bring with it enormous liabilities with no corresponding profits. Far better to invest resources in a brand, and to use that brand like a magic wand to transform cheap goods produced anywhere into expensive goods marketed somewhere. Many corporations have thereby 'transcended' their products and own little of value apart from the intellectual property invested in their brand. Klein goes on to argue that this produces a kind of illusionist economy, with deleterious effects on the minds of consumers, the appearance of cities, the quality of products and the conditions of work forces in poorer countries. The thesis is controversial and over-stated; but there is truth in it too.

breach of the peace

In UK law any disturbance of the public order, including particular offences such as affray and riot. If a breach is feared persons or associations may be bound over to keep the peace. This is an effective judicial power which may be used to political ends, for example in preventing potentially riotous demonstrations.

Bretton Woods

The Bretton Woods Conference of July 1944 established a global monetary order, in anticipation of the German defeat. Its principal creations were the *World Bank and *International Monetary Fund. It also established a system of fixed exchange rates that lasted for some 30 years, with all currencies pegged to the dollar. The weakening of the dollar during the 1970s caused the system to collapse.

brigandage

Terrorism and violence conducted with the aim of material gain, and outside the law. Originally brigands were small groups of bandits operating in areas of China, India, Mexico, and elsewhere, where the topography and climate facilitated their exploits. There seem to be two kinds of brigandage: that arising from the dispossession, impoverishment, or persecution of some individual, group or class, which, in desperation, turns to violence; and that arising during the transition from military to civil government, when soldiers fear to lay down their arms, and also resent the loss of power that is consequent on doing so. The second kind has been important in the aftermath of wars employing mercenary soldiers, and is of some importance today in Africa and South America. The activities of brigands have frequently come to be identified with the social aspirations of one part of a divided community, brigandage has therefore often found partisan protection, either on the part of a dominant group who use it to harass their opponents, or on the part of a foreign power with an interest in *subversion.

brinkmanship

Term coined by the game-theorist T.C. Schelling, based on a remark of John Foster Dulles, to denote the art of advancing to the brink of war but not engaging in it. An important feature of a certain style of foreign policy, associated with the *cold war. The motivating thought seems to be that a policy of brinkmanship, coupled with the tenacious advocacy of *non-negotiable demands, must always succeed against a policy of compromise.

brotherhood of man

Slogan of the French Revolution, meant to denote a community of interests among all human beings, arising from the fact, and the perception, of equality. It has seemed impossible that this ideal should be realized if there are conflicting interests stemming from class-membership, or from the holding or not holding of *property, and it is a persistent idea that only the abolition of private property and the class divisions associated with it can bring about this community of human interests. The fact that at least some people are more attached to their own interests than to those of others has not (historically) been regarded as important by defenders of the ideal, although it has led some to regard the ideal as *utopian. To many feminists, the allegedly *sexist language of the slogan vitiates its claim to represent an ideal of equality.

Buchanan, James M. (1919–)
American economist and political theorist. See *public choice.

Buddhism

A religious system founded in India during the fifth century BC by Siddharta Gautama (563–483 BC), who called himself the Buddha ('enlightened one'), and who preached to all willing devotees a middle path between the extremes of bodily indulgence, self-mortification and speculative philosophy. Buddhism sees the individual life as inextricably linked, both to the future incarnations of the individual (*karma*), and to the lives of all other persons and animals (*dhata*). Purity and renunciation are essential to securing a worthwhile future existence. The sense of the connectedness with other lives fosters compassion and charity, and has led to strong feelings of solidarity in Buddhistic communities. The most important type of community is the *sangha*: a social group bound together for mutual moral and spiritual enhancement. The monastic members contribute the 'gift of truth', while the lay members are responsible for the 'gift of provision'. The community is envisaged as bound together by a mutual indebtedness, religious, moral and economic, while the aim of all association is friendship and love, which transcend barriers of race, class, country and time. Hence Buddhism denies the religious authority of the brahmans (the hereditary spiritual class), and does not view the *caste system as necessary to personal salvation. It views the power of the state as based on a historically evolved contractual relationship between the sovereign and the people, which requires that the sovereign should, by executive skill and moral example, strive to earn his position.

The essence of the doctrine lies in respect for life, and absolute equality. All forms of slavery are forbidden, and the ideal community is one of complete *social justice. After the Buddha's death, however, sectarian proliferation ensued, and Buddhist communities gradually returned to hierarchical principles of organization. The religion remains as a permanent invocation to renounce the world, and to refine away the dross of *karma* so as to reach the ideal blessedness of *nirvāna*, in which the individual soul loses all that distinguishes it, and is liberated from the cycle of birth and death. Nirvana is attained by the eightfold path of morality described in the *Samyutta-nikāya*: right views, right intention, right speech, right conduct, right occupation, right effort, right mindedness, and right concentration.

budget (Literally: purse.)
A plan of income and expenditure for a future period; essential in all arrangements where income and expenditure are not simultaneous. The extent of government expenditure over the last few decades has meant that the government's budget has become an important instrument of policy. *Fiscal changes are often governed by the desire to modify budget surplus or deficit in the hope of achieving social and political objectives (such as a reduction in unemployment) or, alternatively, in the interests of a balanced budget.

Bukharin, N.I. (1888–1938)
Russian *bolshevik, close friend and collaborator of *Lenin, social scientist and economist. Bukharin was the first editor of *Pravda* and later became the official theorist of Soviet communism. Between 1925 and 1928 he was co-leader, with Stalin, of the Communist Party, and main architect of the more moderate economic policy which was then adopted. By 1928 he had become the main leader of the anti-Stalin faction, and continued to be seen as the symbol of the *bolshevik struggle against Stalinism until long after Stalin had had him shot.

Bultmann, Rudolf (1884–1976)
German theologian. *See* *demythologization.

bureaucracy
Rule by administrative offices; also, loosely, the assemblage of such offices. In a bureaucracy actual power is vested in those who are, from the legal point of view, administrative intermediaries between *sovereign and *subject. They (normally the civil servants, although there can also be military and religious bureaucracies) can delay or advance the causes of both sovereign and subject to an extent that gives them *de facto* control over major political transformations. *Weber (*Wirtschaft und Gesellschaft*, 1921) argued that the conflict between capitalism and socialism will be extinguished by the triumph of bureaucracy, which would prove indispensable for the rational attainment of the goals of any organization in industrial society. The result would be the creation of an increasingly centralized, increasingly impersonal, and increasingly 'routinized', kind of *authority.

Since administrators can master their tasks only slowly, they must perforce remain in office longer than most politicians remain in power: their activities therefore impose a continuity on successive governments which has an effect not unlike that of an unwritten *constitution. The UK *civil service – with its complex *career structure – is well known for its ability to assert continuity against every kind of radical reform, a point argued in its favour by C.H. Sisson (*The Spirit of British Administration, and some European Comparisons*, 1959). The power of the US President to appoint advisers and officers within the civil service enables him, to some extent, to break down the administrative prerogative. By appointing 'special advisers' from outside the civil service, the government of Tony Blair has tried to follow the American model, in order to give legitimacy to far-reaching constitutional changes.

In totalitarian states, by contrast, it is impossible to distinguish government from administration, appointment to political office and to administrative office being alike determined by the ruling party. In one sense this provides the nearest approach to complete bureaucracy that has yet been achieved. In another sense, however, it is further removed from bureaucracy than any form of government known in the West, since it prevents the existence of genuinely administrative, as opposed to political, decisions. The policies of the party are enacted at every level, from *Politburo to factory floor. This amalgamation of politics and administration has sometimes been thought to be a feature of *oriental despotism.

bureaucratization
According to *Weber, technological advances, and other material changes, make modern societies unmanageable without a complex administrative machine. Gradually the functions of society are removed from private hands and small-scale initiatives and 'bureaucratized'. This process will gradually eliminate the most important distinctions between capitalist and socialist societies, and replace traditional ideas of *legitimacy with a 'legal-rational' substitute.

Burke, Edmund (1729–97)
Irish statesman, philosopher and political theorist who, despite affiliations to the *Whig faction of Lord Rockingham, became, through his writings, a founding father of modern intellectual *conservatism, his *Reflections on the Recent Revolution in France*, 1790, being often cited by adherents to that cause. Burke's thought is unsystematic but highly imaginative, attempting a synthesis of the Whig principle of freedom with the *Tory principle of order.
(i) Advocacy of social continuity.

*Revolution is an evil, not only because of its violence, but also because it inevitably leads to the seizure of power by those who can neither employ it harmoniously nor renounce it peacefully. *Reform too is dangerous if taken to radical extremes, for it may then bring about a social order that can be neither understood nor accepted by its participants. Continuity is necessary if the values which motivate present action are to be understood and realized in the future, and in this sense one must 'reform in order to conserve'.

(ii) Critique of *individualism. Individuals find fulfilment only in society and only in the participation in norms, customs and institutions which reflect back to them a sense of their unity with their fellows. (Hence the family, not the individual, is the basic unit of social order.) Outside society individuals may have desires, but they cannot have long-term aims, values, achievements or rewards. The social nature of man is given as a further argument for continuity. In common with some of the *empiricist philosophers, for whom he was the greatest political spokesman, Burke regarded human nature as a permanent but uncomprehended datum, and social and political order as a delicate achievement that is more easily destroyed than created, and which we should value too much to meddle with unthinkingly.

(iii) Critique of the *social contract theory. Society is a partnership across generations, in which the dead and the unborn are equal partners with the living. To treat it as a contract among present members is to jeopardize the social, material and spiritual inheritance of which we are temporary trustees.

(iv) The defence of *monarchy and *aristocracy. Inequality is inescapable in society, and guidance and leadership essential. There is also a natural sense of dependence, subordination and affection which are aroused by ability, virtue, age and social *grace. The relationship between the leader and the led may therefore be institutionalized and rendered acceptable through a hereditary aristocracy, which should leave some room for the upward mobility of new talent. Monarchy is the true central institution of political order, because it provides a 'natural' object for obedience and reverence.

(v) Defence of *private property. Burke was influenced by liberal economic theory in the style of *Smith, and thought that it is the nature of property to be both private and unequally distributed. He argued in favour of the inheritance and *accumulation of wealth, and regarded the impediments to universal *franchise in the English constitution as justified by the need to see that property (upon which all stability depends) is adequately represented, and so achieves political responsibility proportionate to its actual power. Parliament thus represents, not individuals, but social rank and economic influence.

(vi) Defence of *tradition and *custom, against the rational schemes of revolutionaries. Burke valued tradition as the repository of social knowledge. Traditions embody, he believed, the collective solutions, evolved over many generations, to problems that could be neither solved nor grasped by a single human mind. In contrasting traditional with rational solutions he echoed Smith's theory of the *invisible hand, and anticipated *Hayek's account of evolutionary rationality.

Burke's political vision was diverse and diffuse; the potential conflict between liberal economics and social conservatism was never resolved, partly because his thoughts arose from intuitions about the nature of *society which were never encapsulated in a developed theory of the nature, function and legitimacy of the *state. Politics, for Burke, was a matter of 'prudence and practicability'. Conservatives value his writings for their eloquent elevation of the given, the concrete, the known and familiar, over the abstract, the unknown and the merely projected.

Burnham, James (1905–87)
American sociologist, active before the Second World War in the communist movement, who turned his back on all forms of Marxism and socialism and wrote in defence of the American liberal tradition. In *The Managerial Revolution* (1942) Burnham argued that the tendency of socialism in all its forms is not to produce a classless society, as it promised, but on the contrary to generate a new and intransigent ruling class of bureaucrats – the managerial elite. This class would automatically demand a planned economy, restrictions on creativity and enterprise and encroachments on democratic rights. He criticized the *New Deal as a large and dangerous step in the managerial direction and in *The Struggle for the World* (1947) laid out a battle plan for what was to be known as the *cold war.

business cycle
Americanism for *trade cycle, gaining popularity because of the narrow implications of the word 'trade'.

business ethic
The code of conduct and *ideology which govern the transactions involved in business under conditions of open competition, private ownership, and sale and purchase in a market. It involves a respect for contract, for open dealing, for the payment of debts and the pursuit of debtors. It has also been thought to involve an assignment of monetary values to all forms of human relationship (cf. the 'goodwill' of a business, which may be bought and sold), and a respect for human fellowship as much for its expression of such monetary values, as for its independent moral lustre.

Sociologists often distinguish the business from the *professional ethic. Whereas the *professions are essentially engaged in furnishing services, business deals largely in goods; thus in business sound credit arrangements and fair profits can be emphasized to a greater degree than is compatible with professional practice.

butskellism
A British variety of *centrist politics, named after the *moderate conservative R.A. Butler, and the moderate socialist Hugh Gaitskell. It involves the search for common ground between advocates of private *property and advocates of the *welfare state, in order to find the *consensus that will facilitate constitutional government and reconcile the major interests that have emerged in the UK since 1945. *See* *mixed economy.

Cabal

Originally from Hebrew *qabbālāh*, which denotes the oral tradition handed down from Moses to the Rabbis of the Mishnah and the Talmud. The tradition has secret and mystical components, so that the kabbala or cabbala came to mean, in medieval parlance, the mystical study of hidden things. Hence a cabal is a secret or private intrigue, usually of a sinister character. The term was already in use by the beginning of the seventeenth century and was applied in the reign of Charles II to the small committee of the Privy Council called the 'Committee for Foreign Affairs', which was the precursor of the modern *cabinet. (It so happened that, at a certain point, the initials of the five ministers concerned also formed the word 'cabal'.) Thereafter the term passed into common political usage.

cabinet

The immediate entourage of ministers who confer directly with the *Prime Minister (as in the UK) or *President (as in the US). In the UK, cabinet ministers are almost always members of *Parliament, and make collective decisions in secret which are then imposed on the ruling *party in Parliament (including remaining non-cabinet ministers) through the action of the 'whips'. Hence the cabinet acts as the prime concentration of *executive power. The US constitution makes no mention of a 'cabinet', and the ministers concerned stand only in an advisory relation to the President.

They have to work to establish their own links with *Congress and the President is therefore less constrained to listen to them, since they may not represent an independent political following. The cabinet is therefore much less powerful, and the President correspondingly more so. The role of the cabinet in UK politics has been frequently remarked on, as revealing both the flexibility, and the inscrutability, of the UK constitution. See, for example, W. Bagehot: *The English Constitution*, 1867.

cadre

French military term (= 'framework') for the collected officers of a regiment. Appropriated *circa* 1930 by the Soviet and Chinese Communist Parties, to denote the individual workers, functionaries and intellectuals affiliated to the party and active in promoting its policies. Now generally used to denote organized *activists (whether individuals or groups) who take concerted measures to promote common political ends. In the US the term was misconstrued as analogous to Spanish *padre* and mispronounced accordingly.

caesaropapalism

The system whereby a *sovereign power has supreme control over the church within its dominions, and exercises this control in matters (e.g. doctrine, discipline and liturgy) normally reserved to ecclesiastical authority. Generally used to refer to the powers exercised by the Byzantine Emperors over the Eastern patriarchates, it can also be used to describe the power of the Communist Party over the same patriarchates in Russia and the Ukraine, and (to a far less extent) the power of the UK *Parliament over the Church of England, which has to seek the consent of the Queen in Parliament for major doctrinal, liturgical and constitutional change. In the Byzantine case, justification was attempted through the claim that the Emperor had derived his imperial power from God, who had enjoined him to safeguard the souls as well as the bodies of his subjects.

calculation debate

The 'calculation debate' was initiated by *Mises, *Hayek and other economists of the *Austrian school in response to early twentieth-century socialist proposals for a centrally planned economy. The Austrian response to these proposals is that they pose an insoluble problem when it comes to calculating how to allocate resources. This response turns on three crucial ideas. First, economic activity depends upon knowledge of other people's wants, needs and resources. Secondly, this knowledge is dispersed throughout society and not the property of any individual. Thirdly, in the free exchange of goods and services, the price mechanism provides access to this knowledge – not as a theoretical statement, but as a signal to action. Prices in a free economy offer the solution to countless simultaneous equations mapping individual demand against available supply. When prices are fixed by a central authority, however, they no longer provide an index either of the scarcity of a resource or of the extent of others' demand for it. The crucial piece of economic information, which exists in the free economy as a social fact, has been destroyed. Hence when prices are fixed the economy either breaks down, with queues, gluts and shortages

replacing the spontaneous order of distribution, or is replaced by a black economy in which things exchange at their real price – the price that people are prepared to pay for them. This result has been abundantly confirmed by the experience of socialist economies; however, the argument given in support of it is not empirical but a priori. It is based on broad philosophical conceptions concerning socially generated and socially dispersed information.

Calhoun, John Caldwell (1782–1850)
American statesman, vice-president of the US (1825–32), who produced, in his *Disquisition on Government* and *Discourse on the Constitution and Government of the United States* (both posthumous), a defence of the Southern States and the conservative outlook which they typified. He wrote acerbically against the idea of human equality, and in favour of competition, hierarchy and a society of ranks. He even offered justifications for slavery, although he is now principally studied for his defence, on philosophical and constitutional grounds, of *states' rights, including the right of several states to secede from the Union. His defence is phrased partly in terms of the idea of 'concurrent majority', still defended by certain conservative thinkers in the US. In defining a majority we should not consider numbers only; we must take into account the various interests at stake. Legislation by majority vote is legitimate only if supported by a majority within each relevant interest i.e. by a 'concurrent' majority. Hence each major interest in the nation retains a *veto on legislation. Only in this way, Calhoun thought, will the loyalty of the interests be retained. (But how do you define an 'interest'? And how stable are interests, in the flux of modern politics?)

caliphate

Arabic: *khalifah*, successor. The system of potentially international government by which, under the original custom of *Islam, the faithful were ruled by the 'successor' of the prophet, chosen from the tribe of the prophet, and usually establishing his claim by descent from or kinship with Muhammad. Originally the Abassid caliphs in Baghdad exerted considerable political power, and could be thought of as the genuine rulers over the territories that had fallen to their government. Gradually, however, the rise of contestants for power led to a reduction in the political power of the Caliph, until, in medieval times, his role was merely to authorize the actual rule of princes (sultans) by confirming their titles – sometimes under coercion. His role was compared at the time to that of the Pope in Christendom; the comparison is misleading, however, since the office of Caliph was without specific priestly duties, nor did the Caliph have the kind of universal responsibility for the souls of the faithful that was vested in the Pope. He was a figurehead, symbol of the unity of Islam, and principal channel through which divine authority extended to the rule of princes. In due course rival caliphs emerged, and eventually princes began to dispense with the nominal separation of *power and *authority contained in the duality of sultan and caliph, and themselves assumed both titles, usually with very slender claims to legitimacy under *Islamic law. The caliphate endured under the Ottoman sultans, who ruled always as 'successors to the prophet', but it was abolished by the Turkish National Assembly in 1924. Attempts to revive it (for example, to the benefit of the last kings of Egypt) have proved abortive, though the establishment of a world-wide caliphate is currently one of the professed goals of the *Islamist movement. Historically, the caliphate remains one of the most important examples of the manner in which, under ostensibly religious government, power and authority inevitably begin to diverge (*see* *church and state).

*Shi'ism does not recognize the caliphate as such, but speaks instead of the imamate – or the sequence of imams who were the true successors of the prophet, of whom, in the most common version, there were only 12, the last entering an extended period of occultation that will last until the end of the world.

Calvinism

The theological system of Jean Calvin (1509–64) which is accepted by most non-Lutheran reformed churches. Calvin accepted the *Lutheran doctrines of justification by faith alone, of the absence of free will since the Fall, of the absolute authority of the Bible in all matters of belief and conduct, and added the peculiar belief in the gratuitous predestination of the 'elect' to salvation, and of others to damnation. He denied the reality of divine grace, and advocated in his *Institutes*, 1536, a species of partial theocracy which he himself exercised for a while in Geneva. Calvinism, unlike Lutheranism, attempted to give a complete account of human institutions and social life, in order to replace the one that had been previously provided by the Catholic church.

Man is a creature of fellowship, who has equal need of both church and state. The concern of the church is with spiritual salvation, of the state with the regulation of external conduct and the just ordering of society (where justice includes distributive justice, so that it is the business of the state to ensure equitable distribution of benefits). Church and state must promote each other's welfare, and hence it is right that blasphemy (e.g.)

should be a civil crime; however, the two systems should be structurally independent, so that officials of the church do not acquire through their office a place in the state, nor officials of the state a place in the church. The ideal government is one chosen by the people from those members of the *aristocracy best suited to wielding political power. Calvin also believed in a version of the doctrine of *natural law, and thought that the magistrate held his authority ultimately from God, who is the source of the natural law.

Complex political practices have emerged from Calvinism, and from its attempts to sustain itself against the *universalist and secular thinking of the *Enlightenment. These remain influential in those parts of the world where Calvinism spread in the wake of the second 'Helvetic confession' of 1566, among them Scotland and Northern Ireland. In 1622 Calvinism became the state religion of Holland and thence passed to the Dutch colonies, notably to South Africa, where the Calvinist Dutch Reformed Church still holds considerable influence among the Afrikaans-speaking population, both white and coloured, although the once popular opinion (put about by Dr Livingstone) that the Calvinist doctrine of the elect was responsible for the harsh treatment of blacks by the Voortrekkers is now doubted.

A revival of Calvinist theology in the present century (notably in the writings of Karl Barth (1886–1968)) has led to attempts to renew the Calvinist vision of political life. Thus the Amsterdam philosopher H. Dooyeweerd, in his *New Critique of Theoretical Thought*, 1933, produced a Calvinist account of sovereignty, attempting to give a revised doctrine of the spheres of church and state, perhaps in order to reconcile the fundamentalist Christianity advocated by the one with the unchristian practice of the other. Faith, according to Dooyeweerd, is an 'ontological decision' presupposed in all Christian action; but it displays itself differently in the several autonomous spheres. Reality has 'modalities', each of which is explored by a separate science, and each of which has its own point of view and sovereignty. (A basis for this proposition is derived from *phenomenology.) Violation of the sovereignty of one sphere by the principles of another induces a confused vision of the Christian mission, which is to understand and love the world as God's creation. Each special sphere is subject to the authority of religion as recorded in the Bible. However, it proceeds according to principles of its own, and hence must be accepted in the form which those principles give to it.

This modern Calvinist *ideology opposes state intervention in the economy, since this violates the sovereignty of contrasting spheres. It has been used to suggest an argument against mixed marriages, and in favour of separate development (*see* *apartheid). However, it is only under a very crude interpretation that such a conclusion can be drawn from it. For the separation of spheres is not a separation of realms (whether worldly or spiritual, economic or legal, black or white), but a separation of ways of perceiving and acting on a single reality.

Cambridge school

A school of economic thought influenced by economists at the University of Cambridge, England, following the ideas of *Keynes, and developing the Keynesian emphasis on *macroeconomics over *microeconomics. It has opposed various *neo-classical theories, and attempted to provide an acceptable theory of the economic role of the state, and so align economics with a political vision adapted to the circumstances of modern government. It has generated various theories of economic growth and development, and has given a reasoned basis for the *mixed economy. Some of its adherents have supported certain socialist policies, in respect of ownership of the means of production and the distribution of wealth. Hence it was a powerful influence on the thinking of Labour governments in the UK during the 1960s and 1970s. It has been criticized for its comparative neglect of microeconomics. Principal members of the school include Joan Robinson (1903–83) and Nicholas Kaldor (1908–86).

Camus, Albert (1913–1960)

Algerian-born French writer and philosopher, who dramatized in his novels and plays the fundamental experience, as he saw it, of modernity, which is the sense of the absurd. Faced with a universe that responds to all his questions with a profound and unmeaning silence, man finds himself alone with his freedom, forced to choose between alternatives for which no reason can be given. Despite this bleak vision of the human condition, Camus devoted himself, first to the French war-time Resistance against Nazi occupation and subsequently to a kind of *humanist politics, based on the absolute values of freedom and love. He entirely rejected the post-war leaning of the French *intelligentsia towards communism, and as a result was ostracized by *Sartre and his followers. While advocating an attitude of rebellion towards all arbitrary authority, Camus recognized the difficulties that beset an ordinary human life, and looked on bourgeois society with a compassion that was deeply offensive to Sartre's *existentialism.

Canetti, Elias (1905–94)

Expatriate Bulgarian sociologist and writer of Spanish-Jewish descent. *See* *crowds, *leadership.

canon law

Originally, the system of law constituted by ecclesiastical legislation for the government and administration of the Christian church.

Formed from an amalgamation of *Roman law, New Testament doctrine, and ideas of the apostolic fathers, the canon law was systematized in the twelfth century by Gratian, became increasingly refined and codified, and presented the most developed system of international *jurisdiction that the world has known, losing its direct, but none of its indirect, influence in the affairs of sovereign states at the Reformation, after which only the *Roman Catholic and *Anglican churches continued to acknowledge the authority of the canon. By the Act of Submission 1532 the English clergy agreed not to make any new canons without royal permission, so that the canon thereafter gradually lost its authority in the Anglican communion.

The canon law incorporates elaborate doctrines of evidence, inquisition and *natural justice, and laid the foundations for modern procedure in criminal trials. It also created the laws of marriage, property and succession that were to pass into European and later American legislations, and, because of its international character, contained the first attempts to specify rights of action between states, and the first legal definitions of *sovereignty.

capacity in law

The ability to bear rights and disabilities in law. Capacity is usually restricted in the case of infants, minors and people of unsound mind. It has an active and passive side, and the two may not exactly correspond: thus, in UK law, a minor has the right to enter into a contract, but not the liability to bear its enforcement. Capacity is part of the complex idea of the legal *person, and its definition reflects an intuitive understanding of *responsibility.

capital

In economics, sometimes defined as 'produced means of production', that is, commodities that have been produced and which are themselves employed in the production of other commodities. A distinction is sometimes drawn between fixed capital (buildings, machinery etc.) and circulating capital (e.g. semi-finished products). Alternatively it has been suggested that the essence of capital is time, in particular the way in which the passage of time can be put to productive use in capitalist production. Labour is applied, and consumption is forgone, in order to yield greater benefits in the future. On this view, capital need not involve 'produced means of production'. For example, allowing wine to mature would also be an accumulation of capital. Thus the *Austrian school sees the capitalist method of production as a 'roundabout method' that involves 'waiting': the more waiting the more production. Yet another view is that capital is wealth: i.e. command over current output. This last view defines capital in a financial sense rather than as a feature of production.

According to Marx there is an ideological distortion in regarding capital – in the form of inanimate objects like machines and *money – as an independent *productive force. This view (sometimes stigmatized as 'capital *fetishism'), is held to neglect the fact that, without *labour, none of this accumulated stock could produce anything. If capital is to play a genuine part in production, labour must be regarded as intrinsic to it. Hence Marx distinguished 'constant' from 'variable' capital, their ratio being the 'organic composition' of capital. The first includes raw materials, machinery, and all parts of the means of production which produce no alteration in exchange-value, the second consists of labour power, which both reproduces itself, and also generates the *surplus value necessary for capitalist accumulation. Constant capital is not a productive force, but a means of production, which, being controlled by the capitalist, enables him to extract labour hours from the worker.

Opponents of the Marxist position sometimes argue that the distinction between constant and variable capital is based on a false dichotomy, between the part played by machinery and land and the part played by labour, in the process of production. (Consider the crop which grows unattended, or the factory which is set in motion at the touch of a switch.)

Various questions have exercised political thinkers since the first attempts were made to distinguish capital from property as such. For example: how is capital possible? This is the question which concerned many nineteenth-century political economists. What does capital do? This is a question of interest to modern economists (*see* *capital theory). Is capital necessarily private? (*See* *state capitalism.) Ought it to exist? If there can be production without capital, then this last is one of the most important questions of political philosophy. If there cannot be production without capital, then it is irrelevant.

The necessity for accumulation, saving and investment in economic life has its parallel in other sphers of human activity. Sociologists now speak of *social capital and even *human capital, on the assumption that both societies and individuals invest in attributes that render them more successful in the long run. In similar vein *sociobiologists refer to the genetic 'investment' of a species, and the genetic capital represented by its current stage of evolution.

capital punishment

Any punishment which inflicts death on the recipient. The death penalty has been removed from many legal systems, on the ground that it is never justified to deprive another human being of life, regardless of the nature of his offence. The matter continues to be controversial, however, since natural feelings for justice demand that we make a distinction between offences which can, and those which cannot, be committed without forfeiting the *right to life. *See* *punishment.

capital theory

A branch of economics which explores the implications of the existence of *capital for the theory of prices, the theory of production, and the theory of income distribution. Difficult technical questions arise concerning the role of time and uncertainty. In addition there are problems concerning the factors that determine the relative distribution of income among holders of capital and suppliers of labour, and these questions touch directly upon the central questions of political theory. The theories of capital advanced by the *Austrian school of economists hold that capitalist production involves the sacrifice of leisure and consumption for greater gain in the future. Both the person who invests, and the workforce that he hires, are making sacrifices for the sake of future benefits; and the profit of the investment is not different in principle from the wage earned by the worker, in representing a future compensation for a present cost.

capitalism

Term given currency by *Saint-Simon, and now used in two ways:

1. An economic arrangement, defined by the predominant existence of capital and *wage labour, the former consisting of accumulations in the hands of private (i.e. non-government) owners, including *corporations and *joint stock companies, the latter consisting in the activities of labourers, who exchange their *labour hours (or, according to *Marxian theory, their *labour power) for wages, paid from the stock of capital. The capitalist receives not a wage but a *profit, by realizing in a *market the value of the goods produced. Capitalism presupposes private property in the means of production, a market economy, and the *division of labour. It does not necessitate, but it may be thought to encourage, *factory production.

2. According to Marxist theory capitalism marks a transient stage of historical development, and is further characterized by the formation of capitalist and labouring *classes. The former – the *bourgeoisie – accumulates all *surplus-value, while the latter – the *proletariat – accumulates nothing, and so remains propertyless. Marx himself did not often use the term 'capitalism', but the theory is in essence his.

In both explanations 'capitalism' denotes a theoretical concept, used in the description and explanation of social arrangements that may have many aspects besides those mentioned. It is unclear whether there is or has been any society that corresponds exactly either to the Marxist or to any other conception of capitalism. It is more accurate to say that both definitions are attempts to specify an *ideal type. Moreover, some (e.g. *Weber, *Sombart), have argued that crucial elements of this type are to be found in almost all historical societies.

At least the following varieties of capitalism are recognized: commercial capitalism (in which large-scale operators control exchange), industrial capitalism (dominated by large-scale private production), finance capitalism (controlled by bankers and creditors), *state capitalism, and welfare capitalism (in which the state intervenes in the economy in the interests of social *welfare). The emphasis on large-scale production and ownership reflects the observations (and obsessions) of nineteenth-century economists. Modern capitalism seems increasingly to involve a growing *service economy, a heterogeneous mass of small-scale private owners and shareholders, and small-scale ('self-employed') producers. It is doubtful whether nineteenth-century theories, such as those of Marx, have any application to this new phenomenon.

Capitalism is defended either because it is seen as a necessary consequence of private property (which is in turn defended either as socially necessary (*Hegel) or as the subject of a *natural right (*Locke)), or else because it is seen as integral to the market economy. In the latter case the defence may rest on the view that a market economy has an intrinsic capacity to maximize production, and results in a rational (perhaps even *optimal) distribution of scarce resources, and so increases the material well-being of capitalist and labourer alike; or else on the more philosophical idea that the market is the economic realization of some ideal of political *freedom. Some (e.g. *Hayek) add that any attempt to destroy capitalism will lead only to a transference of power from the individual to the state, and so increase the power of the latter to the point where it is bound to be a form of *despotism. It will also destroy the information-base on which rational economic decision-making depends. (*See* *calculation debate.) Others (for example, advocates of *anarcho-capitalism) see capitalism as the foundation of responsible accounting, and of the economic and social virtues (thrift, honesty, accountability) that stem from it. *Weber suggested that democracy in its clearest form can only occur under capitalism, while others have tried to argue that capitalism is the true cause of *limited government.

Against those arguments *socialists have tended to urge that capitalism, which involves the accumulation of profits in hands other than those of the producer, is inherently unjust (*see* *exploitation); that its lack of *planned economy causes imbalances and inequitable distributions; and that it creates only an illusion of democracy, since it transfers power to the class of capitalists, who remain essentially without answerability to their employees.

capitulations

1. Grants of extra-territorial privileges by one state to the subjects of another; specifically, exemption from jurisdiction by *municipal courts. Much used throughout the history of empire building, capitulations existed into the twentieth century, and represented the view that law is a personal relation between subject and sovereign, attaching to the former wherever he might be. They disappeared only with the increasing *irredentism in the nations and peoples that they were used to exploit.

2. In international law, conventions between armed forces of belligerents stipulating terms of surrender of specific towns, ships and troops.

career politics

Political process that admits of description in terms appropriate to a *profession, with recognized procedures for admission into government or party, and recognized methods of self-advancement. Career politics may permit complete change of party and political doctrine in mid career (cf. the changing allegiances of President Mitterand of France). It is becoming the standard mode of political activity in Western Europe, and is perhaps to be contrasted with prevailing eighteenth- and nineteenth-century practice, in which many assemblies were constituted by unpaid representatives, and many seats were made available by tradition or patronage and occupied by citizens who had a settled expectation of a certain level of power, but often no particular desire to increase it. It is sometimes thought that such 'amateur' politics is the real index of the *hegemony of a *ruling class which, since it already possesses power, does not need to exert itself unduly in the pursuit or exercise of office. It can then regard public office as existing 'for its own sake' (which phrase the *reductionist will interpret as 'for the sake of the ruling class'). Against that, it is argued that career politics has the tendency to fill the legislature with a new *political class, consisting of people who know nothing of life save the business of politics itself, and are therefore increasingly cut off from the real aims and tribulations of the people for whom they legislate. Moreover, since they advance their careers by legislating, careeer politicians become in due course a threat to the rest of us, constantly increasing the burden of legislation and never taking any real account of the cost of it. This threat is particularly felt in the US, where a congressman can attach his name to a piece of legislation, and so become a known feature of the political landscape.

caring society

Phrase introduced into modern UK politics by liberal-socialist journalism, in order to denote, not a specific form of *society, but rather a particular kind of *state, actively engaged in providing for the needy, the ill, the aged and the underprivileged, by taxing the wealthy, able, middle-aged and established. Its opponents describe the caring society as one that cares for bureaucrats, by making as many people as possible dependent upon their decisions.

Carlyle, Thomas (1795–1881)

Scottish historian and social critic, *Calvinist by upbringing, who sought in German romantic literature (especially in Goethe) a justification for the passionate rejection of all procedures (whether religious or rationalist) for the solution of political problems. Carlyle followed *Coleridge in attempting to adapt the German vision of the organic complexity of society to the critical Anglo-Saxon spirit. He wished for a society which contains the guarantees of community and stability that others had sought in the state, and this led him to reject all materialist doctrines of the nature of man. He was also suspicious of *democracy, of *laissez-faire economics, of liberal legal philosophy, and of all attempts to override the fact of man's social existence in favour of some *individualistic picture of human nature. He admired Frederick the Great, longed for a German conquest of Europe, and sought in German philosophy and literature that sense of the wholeness and mystery of human fulfilment which he found lacking in prevailing *Benthamite and *utilitarian conceptions of human nature.

Carlyle's *History of the French Revolution*, 1837, attempted to portray political events dramatically, as the expression of a social condition. In this and subsequent works he elaborated his vision of society as an organism, with birth, maturity, convulsion, and death. He expressed an antagonism to the *Enlightenment, and a belief that liberal opinion is a luxury, made possible by diseased social conditions, and presaging social ruin.

Carlyle's criticisms of liberalism were more influential than his favoured ideal: a society founded on the worship of heroes, involving a new aristocracy construed on the model of the Calvinist elect, and with a social and economic order of a quasi-feudal kind.

cartel

An arrangement, usually between suppliers possessing some degree of mutual independence, who agree together to set prices for their products and perhaps quotas for output and investment. Legally enforceable cartels are impossible in the UK and US, being in breach of the laws controlling *monopoly, and of *antitrust legislation; they may also, in certain circumstances, constitute a *conspiracy at common law. Nevertheless cartels exist informally without the support of any enforceable contract. There are also international cartels which escape the controls of any particular *jurisdiction. *See* *oligopoly.

caste

The hereditary *class system of India consists of castes, in which each person is socially equal to every other member of his caste, having the same religious rights, and often following the same occupation or profession. There are thought to be some 3000 castes in India, reflecting stratifications of tribe, race, occupation, territory and religion (J.H. Hutton: *Caste in India*, 1951). Until recently, social mixing between castes has been difficult or impossible, and attempts to enforce it by law have met with powerful resistance. From the outside the caste system exhibits one of the most rigid of class structures, with minimum *social mobility, and maximum hereditary determination. Because it includes a definite economic stratification, it lends itself to *functional

explanation in terms of economic role, though in a modern economy, in which *information technology is revising and marginalizing traditional skills, it is rapidly becoming dysfunctional. Moreover, the complexity of the system is such as to defy easy analysis in economic terms.

Castroism (also *Fidelismo*)

The ideology and practice introduced into the government of Cuba by Fidel Castro, since his seizure of power by *coup d'état* in 1959. Castro seems not to have been a communist when he first took power, but, in a speech in 1961, he declared himself to be a *Marxist-Leninist, and thereafter began to rationalize his own *coup d'état* as a Marxist-Leninist *revolution. This revolution had been achieved in Cuba not by economic development, but by popular support for a guerrilla army, acting to restore rights and privileges to a people whose economic condition was in fact primitive. (*See* *focoism.) The political system in Cuba was sustained through incessant military activity abroad, vigorous personal leadership (*jefatura*), and abundant aid from the USSR; it evolved in the direction of centralized government, without formal *opposition, and with effective state control over most economic activity. The collapse of the Soviet Union has left Cuba increasingly isolated. Its military ventures have ceased, its economy is fragile, and much of its population has fled from the island. Castroism lives on, however, and has found a new advocate in President Chavez of Venezuela.

casuistry

Originally a casuist was a theologian, or similar learned person, who resolves conflicts of duty and questions of *conscience. Casuistry denotes the art of so describing reality, and so prescribing action, that a given set of principles can be adhered to in actual circumstances. A casuist attempts to show how a particular principle applies in a particular case, and also to extract principles that will rationalize the moral intuitions that particular cases prompt. (*See* *double effect.*)

In a wider sense 'casuistry' has come to be a derogatory term, for the practice of reconciling reality with *doctrine. Thus it is part of the casuistry of capitalism to argue that the seemingly unjust distributions that result from it are not unjust at all, but the necessary consequence of just (because freely contracted) relations. It is part of the casuistry of Leninism to argue that cruelties perpetrated against opponents are justified by the 'revolutionary morality' that looks to the communist future.

casus belli

Latin: cause, or ground, of war. In international law, a situation put forward by a state as justification for war. According to the UN Charter the only recognized *casus belli*, apart from those authorized by the Security Council or General Assembly, is self-defence.

catastrophe theory

A controversial branch of applied mathematics, developed by the French mathematician René Thom, which studies the transition of systems from one dynamical configuration to another. A 'catastrophe' arises when such a transition generates points of instability within the system. On passing through such a transition (as when a wave transgresses the topological laws of surface formation at its climax) a 'catastrophe' ensues, the movement of the system being determined by a distinct law from that which had previously governed it. The theory has been applied to economics, social development and the study of political

institutions. Such sciences often deal with laws of development which apply up to a certain point, but which predict only a collapse of existing structures beyond that point. The Marxist theory of revolution as precipitated by a dynamical *contradiction has been seen as a kind of catastrophe theory. The more adventurous applications of the theory remain, however, highly controversial.

Catholic Action

Organized action of a social and political kind on the part of *Roman Catholic laity. The term derives from a movement founded in 1922 by Pope Pius XI, to encourage flexible lay *propaganda under the direction of the clergy. *See* *Opus Dei.

Catholicism

See *Roman Catholicism.

caucus

Originally US term, denoting a private meeting of members of a party prior to an election, in order to harmonize interests and policy. Since 1878 it has been used in the UK and US to denote the influencing of government by secret, semi-secret or exclusive organizations within the officially recognized party-political system, as when a group of 'hard-liners' meet in advance of official gatherings in order to decide on concerted action, while keeping other party members in ignorance of their aims and methods.

caudillo

Spanish: a chief. Title assumed by General Franco, as *de facto* ruler of Spain, in 1938. Now used to denote the leader of any Spanish-speaking (typically Latin-American) country, who, upon rising to power, rewards the friends and cronies who had helped him. Hence *caudillismo*, the art of obtaining and retaining power through a network of confederates, in the manner of many South American politicians.

cause of action

The facts which give a citizen the right to bring an action in law. (Hence 'just cause'.)

censorship

The office of censor was a Roman magistrate, first held in 443 BC, with the function of reviewing the rolls of citizens, knights and senators (the *census), regulating morals and ritually purifying the people. From this office derives the modern use of the term 'censorship' to denote the practice of examining, restricting and prohibiting public acts, expressions of opinion, and artistic performances. It takes the following forms:

(i) Direct interference by the state prior to publication of offending material ('preventive' censorship). This was common in the USSR and its satellites, but not in the UK, US or Western Europe, and is thought to be unconstitutional in the US (*see* *prior restraint). It has been all but abolished in the UK with the disappearance of the office of Lord Chamberlain in 1968 – always excepting 'classified' material (*see* *official secrets), publication of which cannot be justified before a court of law. However, the British Board of Film Censors retains the power to prevent the distribution of films judged to be offensive.

(ii) Subsequent prosecution before a court of law ('punitive' censorship). This is the standard action of the state in the UK and US against *obscenity, blasphemy, and *sedition. Usually various defences are recognized, and the outcome depends upon judicial process.

(iii) Indirect control through responsible but autonomous bodies, such as the churches, and the Press Council, which have no legal, but some coercive, power.

(iv) Indirect control through private actions for libel (which is to be contrasted with 'seditious libel', a UK action brought by the state, corresponding to the 'slander of the state' familiar in communist countries). Private action for libel may be expensive and troublesome, and it is sometimes thought not to provide sufficient protection for the 'right of *privacy', and so to require supplementation by the creation of a criminal offence.

(v) Self-imposed censorship, as in the 'decision not to publish' based upon settled expectations as to what is socially and politically acceptable.

The justifications for state censorship will, as with all questions of state action against the citizen, lean on either utility or justice (or both), and will differ depending upon which concept is principally emphasized. Censorship may be held to contribute to political stability (and therefore to the sum of present *utility), but does it follow that the state has a right to censor? (May it not be an injustice against those who desire to publish or become acquainted with the material in question?) When liberal thinkers emphasize the limitation that censorship places on human freedom they usually (*see* *Mill) interpret the concept of freedom so that questions of freedom and questions of justice are intimately conjoined (people being *free* to the extent that there is no interference with their rights of action).

Mill argued in another way against censorship, suggesting that human knowledge advances through exposing opinions to refutation, so that the distinction between truth and error can be clearly seen. Censorship interferes with that process, by arbitrarily declaring in advance that this or that opinion is erroneous or forbidden. It therefore has an inherent tendency to marginalize truth and the pursuit of truth, and to put conformity in their place. For a long time Mill's argument was orthodox among liberals. However, the growth of *political correctness, and the domination of universities by politicized factions, has led to a growing tendency to censor opinions, reading matter and appointments, particularly in American academic institutions. Moreover, legislation in European countries designed to appease Muslim opinion, has made certain forms of anti-religious utterance into crimes, and the idea of *hate speech is now being incorporated into legal provisions, with the express aim of silencing certain forms of discourse. The issue of censorship is therefore again a live issue in political debate. *See* *law and morality, *pornography.

census

Under Roman law, the registration of citizens and their property, for purposes of taxation and suffrage. Now used more widely, to denote any act (usually an *act of state) whereby information is collected relating to the number, situation and outlook of citizens. The importance of censuses and *opinion polls in modern politics furthers the view that the legitimacy of government depends on the opinions and situation of the governed.

Centesimus annus

The Latin title of an *encyclical, issued by Pope John Paul II in 1991 to mark the hundredth anniversary of *Rerum novarum*, the celebrated encyclical of Pope Leo XIII in which the pontiff gave an explicit statement of the Church's social policy, in response both to the massive changes resulting from the industrialization and urbanization of modern societies and to the socialist policies that were being proposed to deal with them. *Centesimus annus* gives a qualified endorsement of capitalism, while broadly supporting the welfare state. It draws important lessons from the collapse of communism, concerning the political chaos that ensues, when man's spiritual life is officially denied or opposed. And it presents a call for dialogue and compromise as the instruments of social peace. The encyclical represents an attempt to distance the church, both from the radicalism of *liberation theology, in which Marxist categories are brandished in seeming ignorance of the spiritual disaster that their adoption has entailed, and from the complacency of traditional Catholic social teaching, which regards business and the economy as no concerns of the Church. It also conveys Pope John Paul II's distinctive vision of the human being, as living in a world that is phenomenologically distinct from the world occupied by things and animals – a vision that shows the influence of *Scheler.

centralization

The process whereby executive, administrative, economic and juridical power is concentrated in a centre, defined either geographically (e.g. as the capital city), or in terms of some single organization (such as a civil service, or a *party). Centralism, sometimes seen as an administrative necessity, is in conflict with the demand for *devolution, and for laws, institutions and economic relations which reflect more nearly the disparate local identities that may compose a state. In places where local affiliations are strong (e.g. parts of Africa) – centralization can often be achieved only by force, law alone carrying no weight of authority. *Tocqueville distinguished two distinct kinds of centralization, that of administration, and that of political power, and praised the US for the extent to which it had achieved decentralization of the second kind.

centre

The supposed political position somewhere between the *left and the *right, where political views are either sufficiently indeterminate, or sufficiently imbued with the spirit of compromise, to be thought acceptable to as large a body of citizens as would be capable of accepting anything. The 'centre' is an important concept in UK politics, and the persistent aim for it – while it may involve divesting oneself of all coherent political beliefs – is nevertheless considered justifiable to the extent that politics is constituted, not by consistent doctrine, but by successful practice. The centre is seen as representing political stability, social continuity, and a recognized *consensus. It is also thought (but this is a confusion) that the centre position will be *moderate. 'Retreat from the centre' is an expression used by P. Mayer to denote the disposition among many modern politicians and intellectuals to regard the 'centre' position as unsafe, because of the abandonment of principle, and the complexity of untrustworthy *alliances that it requires, and because the confession of ignorance and uncertainty, while honest, is neither politically nor intellectually respectable.

centrism

1. The doctrine that one should pursue the political *centre.

2. A movement within the Polish Communist Party, associated with Gomułka, which sought to liberalize Poland after Stalin's death.

ceremony

The public practice whereby something is displayed, enacted or recalled, in such a way as to endow it with a symbolic value and a lasting social significance. Some follow Yeats ('A Prayer for my Daughter') in associating the decline of ceremony with a loss of innocence and grace in social relations, seeing ceremony as the force which, enacting a shared condition, makes social nature intelligible. Others regard ceremony as a form of constraint, and therefore inherently in need of justification, perhaps all the more so because of the extent to which the interests of an *establishment may be advanced by exploiting the common need for and pleasure in ceremonial events.

Some liberals consider that ceremony is a feature of *civil society, and not one for which the state should take responsibility: ceremony must therefore be either spontaneous or false. But this seems to overlook the existence of ceremonies of state. These are nowhere more emphasized than by *totalitarian regimes, which attempt to create highly symbolic demonstrations of unity designed to impress on the subject the ineluctable nature of the political order which surrounds him, and also to celebrate and exhibit for the benefit of external powers both the reality of that order and the subject's all-consuming commitment to it. In this case ceremony is monopolized by the state, to form part of the enterprise of *government through symbols. But liberal democracies may also depend in mysterious ways upon ceremonies of state. The ceremonial institution of monarchy in the UK seems to inspire more affection than any other aspect of the constitution, and more respect than any political party, perhaps because it manifests itself so briefly, and to so little effect.

Ceremonies are important examples of activities which are entirely focused on themselves, having the kind of 'purposefulness without purpose' which Kant ascribed to the object of *aesthetic interest. Hence they fulfil the conservative ideal of action which inspires maximum loyalty while doing minimum damage.

chain of command

Suppose A has power and authority to command B; B to command C; C to command D, and so on. Suppose too that B is answerable to A for C's actions, C answerable to B for D's and so on. Then there exists a 'chain of command' from A downwards. Some forms of *constitutionalism insist that the true aim of government is to maintain this chain of command, by guaranteeing that when any place in it falls empty, it is at once filled by someone similarly *empowered*, and similarly *answerable*. An *office in politics may then be defined as a place in the chain of command, with recognized procedures for entry into and departure from it.

charisma

New Testament Greek: a gift of divine grace. Term used by *Weber to denote a kind of *power over others which is also perceived as *authority by those subject to it. The holder of charisma may be a human being, in which case his authority might be interpreted in terms of a myth of his divine mission, insight, or moral attributes. Alternatively, it is sometimes said, charisma can attach to an office, in which case it may be associated with an idea of that office as enshrining the history, legitimacy and mystery of a social order. Weber distinguishes charismatic from traditional and legal-rational kinds of authority. However, it is not clear how far the 'charisma of office' can be detached from the disposition to feel the power of, and attribute authority to, traditions and systems of law. See *routinization.

charity

1. In moral contexts, 'charity' denotes the Christian virtue of love of one's neighbour (from Latin *caritas*, a translation of the New Testament Greek *agape*). This is a distinct mode of love, being neither erotic, nor familial, nor friendly, nor reducible to any universal sense of duty (though *see* *Kant, who thought otherwise). St Paul wrote that 'though I bestow all my goods to feed the poor, and though I give my body to be burned, and have not charity, it profiteth me nothing' (I Cor. 13, 3). The famous declamation from which this comes conveys the widely accepted view that, while the end result of charity may be the betterment of the human condition, this is not its motive. What leads a person to charity is concern for *this* (irreplaceable) person, or *this* (irreplaceable) group of people, in *this* predicament. To put it another way, the end of charity is universal, but its motive is concrete. The maxim that 'charity begins at home' is a simple way of giving voice to this idea. *See* *humanitarianism.

2. In political discussion, charity has sometimes been held to depend upon social arrangements involving private *property. It requires that people be able to *provide* for others, which in turn requires the exercise of *gift. Universal redistribution, making the needs and powers of all people equal, might also be seen as tending, to the abolition of the charitable motive, which is (to put it tendentiously) that of rejoicing in the power conferred by property through the act of giving it away. Perhaps, therefore, charity is what *Hume called an 'artificial virtue', one reflecting an actual social condition which it may not be desirable to uphold.

3. In legal contexts, the specificity of the charitable motive, together with the universality of its end, are obliquely acknowledged in its definition. A charity must benefit (according to UK and US law) some body of the public, but not necessarily a considerable body. To prove charitable status it must be shown that the motive is either sufficiently general, or specific

only in the way that charity is specific. Thus the benefit conferred should not be by way of ancillary reward to a group of employees, nor a gift by way of friendship, nor any other gesture of self-interest or personal affection. The founding of a school, a hospital, a church are all allowed by this criterion, as are far more specific intentions, such as the relief of poverty in a particular parish.

Both English and US law have followed judicial interpretation of a definition of charity given in the preamble to the Charitable Uses Act 1601, which defines charity by a list of examples, many of them now redundant. By a quirk of legal history, it is uncertain whether this act has now been abolished. In the US case the legal category of charity has recently been absorbed into that of *non-profit organizations, and the law set upon an independent footing. In the British case, judicial interpretation has allowed four kinds of charitable use: relief of poverty, advancement of learning and education, advancement of religion, and other purposes in similar spirit. Any charity, being already of public benefit, is exempt from tax. It therefore becomes a substantial political issue whether certain institutions (e.g. private schools) should be given charitable status, or even whether the law of charity, and the fiscal privilege associated with it, should survive. Moreover, as a *common law matter, the actual recognition of something as a charity is a matter for *judicial decision, and judicial decisions, say some, must inevitably reflect the interests of the property-owning class to which judges belong. Moves to undo the law of charity have been contemplated by socialist parties in the West, and no such law existed in any system constructed on the Soviet model. In Britain charities are now subject to supervision by the Charities Commission, which lays down guidelines as to the goals, conduct and accountability of trustees. The Commission is not a judicial body, however, and its rulings are anticipations of what a court would decide, rather than legal rulings.

In *post-communist societies, the restoration of charitable and other 'non-profit' institutions has become a major social and political objective, the experience of communism having demonstrated how destructive it is to deprive people of the possibility to offer and receive help in an organized way. This restoration is also resisted by the new kind of political leader, who fears the effect of *NGO politics in spreading unsatisfiable demands among the people. This reaction has been particularly strong under Vladimir Putin in Russia.

Many thinkers of a liberal persuasion object to the existing law of charity, in that it extends fiscal benefits to institutions which may be of no true public value, and withholds them from associations based on *self-help, since the motive of these is too interested to be charitable. Thus the British Limbless Ex-Servicemen's Association is a charity, while the National League of the Blind, being organized around the principle of self-help, is not.

charter

1. In law, a deed, granted as a rule by the sovereign power, conferring powers, rights, privileges and immunities on a subject institution or township. An important instrument in the *delegation of authority.

2. Charters of Liberties, of which two were issued by English Kings (Henry I and Stephen) at their coronations while one was imposed on King John by his rebellious barons (the 'Unknown Charter' of 1215, which was reworked later that year as Magna Carta). A Charter of Liberties and Privileges was the first enactment of

the first assembly of New York Colony, passed 1683, and later disallowed by the English Parliament.

3. Magna Carta: the 'great charter' issued by King John in 1215 under pressure is the most famous instance of a Charter of Liberties, and effectively granted to the free subjects of the King the sovereignty over their own lives that the King had threatened to confiscate, and lay down rules of legal procedure and administration that put an effective shield between the subject and the Crown. Although rooted in feudal conceptions, and the work of a privileged class, Magna Carta is rightly esteemed as laying the foundations for a new kind of sovereignty, in which both sovereign and subject are governed by law, and in which access to the law is the subject's inalienable right.

4. UN Charter. The Charter of the United Nations Organization, drafted in 1945, consisting of a preamble and seventy articles, setting out principles of action in respect of threats to peace, instruments and procedures of international justice, and general rules for economic, social and political cooperation. Powers conferred on the Security Council (China, France, the USSR, UK and US, together with six others elected for terms of two years) exceed any that have previously been exercised by an international body, and use of these powers has changed the pattern of international politics, by giving to certain states with conflicting interests the role of supervising peace and war. The Security Council can operate only because each power has a *veto, which can effectively prevent any power from being overruled in any matter that is important to its foreign policy. The Charter thus confers as much responsibility on the major powers as is prudent, given their determination to have their own way in all things that matter.

5. Charter movements. Movements organized around a charter, in which rights, freedoms or privileges are claimed from a ruling power. Examples have included *Chartism, the Charter 77 movement in communist Czechoslovakia (which demanded that the authorities uphold and respect rights which had already been declared in law) and Charter 88 in the UK (which is asking for a written *constitution and a new *bill of rights for the British people).

Chartism
Working-class organization founded in England in 1838, in order to express dissatisfaction with the 1832 Reform Bill, the 1834 Poor Law and the general condition of the trades and crafts under a regime of high food prices and industrial competition. It also pressed for further electoral reform. Chartism is named from the 'People's Charter' of 1838 which demanded, among other things, universal male suffrage without qualification of property. It impressed on British labour the necessity for political status as a means towards economic advancement, and thus set the pattern for UK labour movements, involving gestures towards trade union organization, provisions for strike action, and the recruiting of a broad base of support among the urban working class. With the return of prosperity after 1842 interest in the Charter dwindled, and Chartism had ceased to be a significant political movement by 1850.

chattering classes
Expression, probably invented by the British journalist Frank Johnson, to denote the class of opinionated and *bien pensant people who take every opportunity to display a tender social conscience and to harangue those who offend against it, while leading

comfortable middle class lives insulated from the negative effects of their favourite policies. The assumption is that the chattering classes will support liberal, statist and egalitarian politics, as the best way of maintaining their privileges, including the freedom to chatter.

chauvinism

Term derived from the name of Nicolas Chauvin, a French soldier fanatically devoted to Napoleon, and originally used to signify *idolatrie napoléonienne*. It was later applied to bellicose and uncritical devotion to one's country or leader, when sufficiently *xenophobic. It was further extended – as in the usage 'male chauvinism' – to denote any equally bellicose and uncritical attitude that exalts the virtues of one group (in this case men) and disparages those of another (in this case women). The general principle behind the extension is this: chauvinism is held to be a kind of self-protective hostility, which conceals the inability of the subject to enter into relations with others on equal terms. By representing the world as fraught with immovable inequalities, it appeases anxiety by making equal relations impossible.

checks and balances

A phrase which probably derives from *Jefferson, *Notes on the State of Virginia*, query XII: 'the powers of government should be so divided and balanced among several bodies of magistracy, as that none could transcend their legal limits, without being effectively checked and restrained by the others' (the direct influence on Jefferson being *Montesquieu). The phrase was similarly used by Walter Bagehot (*The English Constitution*, 1867), to denote constitutional devices whereby any power within a state can be prevented from becoming absolute by being

balanced against, or checked by, another power. Such constitutional devices include the *separation of powers, *judicial review, and *bicameral government. Collectively they determine the process whereby a constitution imposes its own mould on all decisions and actions propagated through it, and reduces the prominence of particular parties, offices and individuals. Bagehot himself thought that there was a fundamental difference between the UK and the US constitution in respect of checks and balances, the first being such that the 'supreme determining power is upon all points the same', while in the second 'the supreme power is divided between many bodies and functionaries', a feature which he thought responsible for much US indecisiveness in the mid-nineteenth century, since all power, even the sovereign power, as it is exercised in international relations, could be checked absolutely. Ultimately, Bagehot thought, the maintenance of checks and balances involves adherence to 'the principle of having many sovereigns, and hoping that their multitude may atone for their inferiority'. Others have objected to the mechanical model of society assumed in the phrase. 'The trouble with the theory is that government is not a machine but a living thing . . . No living thing can have its organs offset against each other as checks, and live' (Woodrow Wilson). *See also* *body politic.

Chesterton, G.K. (1874–1936)

English wit and man of letters, who defended the Christian legacy against modernist ideas, attacked socialism, *egalitarianism, and the democratic culture, and in a series of charming and often powerful writings, in every genre from the epic poem to the detective novel, presented his sometimes quaint but always penetrating defence of the medieval legacy in laws, customs and institutions. Chesterton defended orthodoxy against heresy, and tradition against innovation in almost every sphere (*Heretics*, 1905, *Orthodoxy*, 1908) and became a Roman Catholic in 1922. He clashed publicly with *Shaw over the latter's defence of socialism, and presented the classic case against socialism, as the confiscation of human freedom and dignity by the state.

Chicago school

In economics, the school of *free-market thinking associated with the University of Chicago, and in particular with *monetarism, as defended by *Friedman and George Stigler (1911–91).

Chiliasm

The doctrine of the millennium: the belief that Christ will return and reign in bodily presence for a thousand years. Identical with *millenarianism. Chiliastic movements arose in the Middle Ages, and often took on anarchistic and revolutionary forms, in the attempt to provide a political preparation for the coming of Christ.

children

The place of children in society, the extent of their legal protection and the duty to educate and socialize them are longstanding topics of political thought. *Plato, in the *Republic*, advocates the collective nurture of children by the state, since the future of society is too dependent on the education of the next generation to entrust this matter to the whims of parents. Although modern people are on the whole repelled by Plato's suggestion, they nevertheless accept that their children should be in the hands of the state for much of the day, engaged in education controlled by the state and

financed by the state. This development is recent: compulsory education was introduced into European jurisdictions only during the course of the nineteenth century, and the provision of schools by the state, and the legal control of the curriculum came even later. In the US there is a growing reaction against this process (*see* *home schooling), on the grounds that children belong to their parents, and the state is as likely to corrupt as to improve them.

The protection of children from abuse, whether physical, mental or sexual, forms an important goal of all systems of domestic law, and is also the subject of the United Nations Declaration of the Rights of the Child of 1959, a document that has defined the rights of the child so widely (to include health, education, family, and even love) that until recently it has had little influence on the domestic policies of its signatories.

Attitudes to children have begun to shift, however, as the state becomes more and more involved in their upbringing – itself a consequence of the weakening of family ties. Indeed, in many areas it often seems as though the state is opposed to the family, standing as a shield between the child and parental authority. In the UK, for example, the state protects the child who, despite being below the age of consent for sex, has secretly sought an abortion. The doctor consulted, the law says, is not obliged to reveal the girl's condition. This is so, even though the girl, being below the age of consent, is the victim of a crime.

Likewise many states, the UK included, have adopted laws forbidding or strictly limiting the use of corporal punishment, even in the home. Conservatives tend to argue that corporal punishment is natural, vivid, and part of the normal process whereby a child comes to defer to parental authority, and that the alternatives are either ineffective or in some way destructive of the child, by inducing a habit of sentimentality and premature excuses. The discussion of this and related issues is complicated by the comparative lack, in modern societies, of a coherent account of the distinction between the child and the adult. What is it that the adult possesses and the child does not? The obvious answers: *rationality, *responsibility, *accountability, *freedom, all raise philosophical questions that ordinary people, unaided by religion, find difficult to answer. Hence the increasing recourse to the law, to settle matters that were once settled uncontentiously by custom. At the same time, the expansion of the concept of 'child abuse', to cover not only sexual molestation and other criminal acts, but also strict discipline and the occasional smack, has led not only to notorious injustices in the American courts, but also to a crucial obscurity concerning the rights and wrongs of child-rearing.

Chomsky, (Avram) Noam (b. 1928)
American linguistician and political activist, who has been a tireless critic of his country's foreign policy, and (according to his foes) a tireless supporter of its enemies. Chomsky's intellectual reputation is based on his contributions to linguistics. The surface grammar of language, he argues, cannot be understood in terms of rules for joining individual words together in well-formed strings. Grammatical sentences must be seen as the result of transformations effected upon a deep structure, by the iteration of 'transformational rules'. (*Aspects of the Theory of Syntax*, 1955.) Deep structures are syntactical categories implanted in the brain by evolution, and are, or contain, linguistic 'universals' – ways of conceptualizing

the world in common to all language users. Hence the uniform linguistic development of children, whatever their language and whatever their culture.

Chomsky's linguistic theory is developed with considerable subtlety and has had a lasting impact on the subject. Its connection to his political beliefs is unclear; nor are the beliefs based in any articulated theory. His view of America as driven by the commercial interests of its ruling circles into imperialist adventures, and his disposition to hold his country and its elected representatives to account for crimes committed around the world, have brought him large and passionate groups of both supporters and opponents. To his supporters he is a brave and outspoken champion of the oppressed against a corrupt and conspiratorial political class. To his opponents he is a self-important ranter, whose one-sided vision of politics is chosen not for its truth but for its ability to shine a spotlight on himself. Whichever view you take, Chomsky is a leading figure in American public life, and an unparalleled stimulus to argument.

Christendom
'The realm of Christ': the collective name for nations and states the subjects of which profess Christianity. It was an important conception in international politics, when such subjects, by virtue of their faith, were bound by allegiance to the Pope. It was also of some importance subsequently, for as long as it could be assumed that the nations of Christendom would act in concert on international issues which relate to faith and doctrine, but was revealed as a moribund idea by the Holy Alliance in the nineteenth century. The concept remains interesting partly because it contains the idea of international *jurisdiction, and

partly because it indicates a common source of law throughout Western countries, and a common ground for the belief in *natural law.

Christian democrats

The *moderate Roman Catholic parties in Belgium, France, the German Federal Republic (most German Protestants are in the former East Germany), Italy and the Netherlands. Originally *left, or left of *centre parties (e.g. as founded in Uruguay in 1910, and in Italy in 1919), they tended at first to enter into alliances with *socialist and *communist parties. Even in 1965 the Chilean Christian Democrat Party was prepared openly to condemn capitalism as 'merciless' and 'degrading of human dignity', although it also condemned communism as a form of slavery. Since 1945, especially in Europe, Christian democrats have tended to be moderate *reformist parties, professing *Christian affiliation, and representing, especially in Italy, a middle class anxious for stability, and hostile both to socialism and to communism. Christian democrat parties have emerged in post-communist Europe, but only in Slovakia and the Ukraine have they been an important political force. In the contemporary situation, Christian democrat parties are all centre-right in their orientation.

Christian socialism

A nineteenth-century movement of social reform within the *Anglican Church, which owed its inspiration to *Carlyle, and its opportunity to *Chartism. It saw the Anglican Church as having a vital role to play, both spiritual and social, in rectifying the social injustice and suffering caused by industrial capitalism. Its own vision of the alternative tended towards nostalgic medievalism, involving an admiration

for crafts as opposed to manufactures, and a belief in cooperative production and ownership. Christian socialists sought to spread their movement to working people, in order to give enactment to their (perhaps somewhat *bourgeois) views of the dignity of labour. Neither the establishment of cooperatives nor the institution of evening classes were able to persuade the workers to adopt the prescriptions offered to them. The first English appearance of the concept of *social justice is in the writings of Christian socialists.

Christianity

The most important force in shaping the constitutions of the states of Europe, and the intermediary through which Roman law and classical morality and institutions were imposed upon our ancestors. The belief in the *church as the body of Christ in the world led to the doctrine of *ecclesiastical jurisdiction, and hence to the modern forms of *international law. It also gave rise to the problem of the relation between church and state, left largely unresolved into the present century, and thence to the medieval formulations of the problem of *political obligation. The politically significant aspects of Christian doctrine are impossible to summarize, but the following deserve mention:

(i) As in all monotheistic religions, ultimate allegiance is owed not to the *sovereign but to God, whose kingdom is not of this world. The supreme guiding principle in individual life is personal salvation, which is God's sole purpose in the creation of any individual soul, and this must therefore be put before all worldly causes. However:

(ii) Christianity has from the beginning recognized a distinction between secular and religious authority, and upheld a regime of secular law as the preferred form of earthly government. (*See* *Two Swords doctrine.)

(iii) *Charity is the fount of virtue, and pride is the fount of sin: this doctrine requires the relief of the miseries of others, and a reluctance to pursue worldly glory or power (except as a means to the exercise of charity and to the worship of God). A policy of concern for, and identification with, the underprivileged (sometimes advanced as The Imitation of Christ) has often seemed to follow from this.

(iv) The doctrine of the incarnation, i.e. that God is identical with Christ and dwells among us, as a suffering and redeeming presence, reinforces the belief that man in his compassionate aspect is nearer to God, whereas man in his pride is cast out.

The fourth doctrine, glossed in various ways, may provide the (mystical) thought which both reconciles the other three, and also licenses political action. For example, the traditional *Roman Catholic doctrine of the church as the bride of Christ has enabled people to pursue worldly power and authority in the name of religion, and to avoid the conflict of allegiance between this world and the next. Recent Christian thinkers, more vividly impressed by the duty of charity than by the transcendence of God, have interpreted the incarnation as an invitation to political activity in the name of *social justice. (*See* *liberation theology.) The moral teachings of the Sermon on the Mount – in which humility, meekness, poverty, and the position of the underdog are all condoned or praised – could be interpreted in an opposite sense, as inviting us to ensure that as many people as possible possess those attributes, and so come closer to salvation. Like all great religions, Christianity contains enough contradictions on these fundamental issues to enable its individual consolations to extend to people of all persuasions and in every age, so dignifying every manner of worldly activity

– from the provision of guns to terrorists to the assertion of absolute monarchical power – with the character of spiritual vocation. However, in its contemporary form, Christianity tends to emphasize the features that distinguish it from its nearest rival, *Islam, namely: the centrality of forgiveness, toleration towards other faiths, the belief in secular law and secular government, and the reality of the Incarnation. For many Christians all four ideas are contained in the last one: the idea that God has taken on human form, and dwells among us.

See also *crusade.

church

1. Any linked configuration of religious institutions, usually with a professional priesthood.

2. In traditional and Christian teaching, the church is not just a voluntary *association of individual believers, but a *corporation, endowed with the Holy Spirit, and constituting the bodily presence of God in the world. It is characterized by unity, holiness, catholicity, and apostolicity, the last including the 'apostolic succession' under which the Pope claims authority in an unbroken chain, through St Peter, from Christ. The *Reformation introduced the modern conception of the church as an invisible body, constituted of the saved, whose membership is known only to God; together with the rival conception of the church as a visible body whose institutional form must vary from country to country, in order to preserve its spiritual essence in the contrasting conditions that surround it, and in order to avoid being subject to a potentially corrupting worldly power. (For a yet more localized conception, *see* *Anglicanism.) In both cases the church is given a partially transcendent identity, which separates it from its members and so ensures its notional survival through every diminution in its worldly influence.

3. In many nonconformist Christian practices, the term 'church' is used simply to denote a voluntary association of believers, for the purposes of religious instruction and celebration. It may not involve a professional priesthood, may have no hierarchy of authority, and no rules other than adherence to certain items of doctrine. The association is more like a club than it is like the church, as traditionally described.

church and state

The relation between church and state has been one of the most lasting issues in European politics, and continues to be a dominant political problem in the *post-communist states of Europe. Either a church is so constituted as to be subject to the sovereign power, in which case it is 'established', or it is not, in which case it exists within the state not merely as an *autonomous institution but as a rival source of authority. Certain theories of *sovereignty (for example, that of *Hobbes) hold the second alternative to be inherently destructive, since if the authority of some power is not absolute then that power cannot be sovereign. Other theories attempt to explain how people can owe *political* *allegiance to one power and religious allegiance to another, even though, over many issues, the two could conflict. (*See* *Two Swords doctrine.) The church can give spiritual and moral guidance only at the risk of affecting actions in which the state has an interest. The clash between the two institutions becomes apparent when the state forbids the church some function considered necessary to its mission – e.g. education. If the state is able in fact and not just in law to do this, then the state has *de facto* sovereignty, such as was exercised through

the French Law of Associations 1901, which effectively brought all the activities of religious congregations within the governance of the state. Equally, the two institutions may gain power from their harmony, and a church, in teaching obedience and humility, may act as a politically conservative force.

Full legal establishment of a church may result from its attempt to enshrine its own authority in law – as advocated by *Hooker in his defence of Anglicanism – or from the state's attempt to subjugate, and even to eliminate, the power of the church – as in the USSR, where ecclesiastical constitution and even liturgy were governed by the state, while all religious education was forbidden, and atheism propagated as part of the ideological commitment expected of the citizen. The peculiar balance found for several centuries in the Anglican Church is a reflection of a widespread political and religious consensus, the dissolution of which has led to a new crisis (however diminished) in the relations of church and state. Equally, the persistent failure of the Polish state (as governed by the Communist Party) either to *ratify or to oppose the authority of the church led to a similar crisis of a far more cataclysmic kind.

The nature of such crises was frequently discussed by medieval thinkers, and notably by *Dante, in his *De Monarchia, circa* 1309: the church, as God's will in the world, calls on us freely to accept its yoke, and so to recognize that its authority binds not through tyranny but through love. The church cannot impose itself by force without negating the principle of its own authority. But the authority of the church is to be distinguished from the power of worldly princes. The latter is good only to the extent that it freely aligns itself with the former: otherwise it is a perverted power, which negates the freedom of its subjects. Hence power and authority must be separated by the two institutions, so as the better to combine; the first lies with princes, the second with the church. Hence in making *itself* into a princedom the church, Dante argued, had offended against its mission.

Cicero, Marcus Tullius (106–43 BC)
Roman orator and statesman, who devoted his enforced retirement to composing works of philosophy, law and politics in which he attempted to adapt and systematize ideas already expounded by the Greeks, in particular by *Plato and the *Stoics. His writings were extremely influential in transmitting Hellenic conceptions of the state to later thinkers, and his advocacy of the synthesis of *philosophy and *rhetoric provided the foundation for many subsequent theories of political education.

The highest human *virtue resides in the possession and employment of knowledge in practical affairs: philosophy provides the knowledge, while rhetoric makes it effective. The individual virtue generated by their union defines also an ideal of political order: a constitutional republic, in which not force but persuasion is the instrument of power and where monarchy, aristocracy and democracy are combined in a stable equilibrium. The best means to the acquisition of virtue is *liberal education, in which theoretical knowledge and practical skill are organically mingled. Cicero gave an extended account of the virtuous man (*De Officiis*), emphasizing the public responsibility which conditions his private satisfactions. In his two political works, the *Republic* (largely paraphrased from Plato and surviving only in fragmentary form) and the *De Legibus* (also surviving only in part), Cicero gave a developed account of what public responsibility amounts to.

The second work introduced with admirable clarity the distinction between *power and *authority, as it has entered into much subsequent political thinking. It also provided an extended celebration of Roman law as an exemplification of constitutional authority, expounded the principles of Stoic philosophy as a basis for political life, and thereby transmitted Stoic theories of *natural law to Christian thinkers.

Cicero's works have been thought (partly on his own admission) to be more eloquent than original. Nevertheless, their influence – on medieval thought through the famous 'dream of Scipio' contained in *The Republic* (in which Plato's views of the soul, of love and of eternity are given dramatic cogency), and on Renaissance thought through the *De Officiis* – has been as great as that of any of the Roman texts, passing ancient ideas of virtue and order into the repertoire of Christian philosophy.

citizen
1. The legal conception of an individual who owes *allegiance to, and receives protection from, a *state. Conditions of citizenship are determined for each state in accordance with its own legal provisions, and it is not necessary that everyone who resides within the *jurisdiction of a particular state should be a citizen of that state, even when he is a 'national' of that state and citizen of no other. Such 'statelessness' is now rare, although it was common in the ancient world. International law, however, does not recognize the distinction between citizenship and nationality and regards the first as completely determined by the second.
2. An ideological preference for the term 'citizen' over the rival 'subject' has been frequent since the American and French revolutions, it being

assumed that the latter suggests a condition of subservience which the former does not. More philosophically, one can be a 'citizen' only within a certain *constitution, which defines the rights and duties of citizenship, but one can be *subject* to an unconstituted power. In political philosophy it has therefore been of great importance since ancient times to attempt to give the basis of citizenship and so justify any given legal determination. *Aristotle defines a citizen as anyone who can 'hold office', and subsequent extensions of this idea have involved the thought that citizenship (as opposed to subjecthood) is possible only where there are sufficient *offices open to all. This thought is fundamental to modern *constitutionalism, and, provided the term 'office' in not interpreted too narrowly, can be seen to capture much of the idea of mutual *responsibility invoked in the legal definition.

citizenship

The condition of the true citizen (sense 2.) – i.e. the person who is a responsible member of society, obedient to the law, with a developed sense of responsibility towards others, and who can be trusted to hold public office. Proposals to combat *anti-social behaviour, and to promote the *assimilation of immigrant groups, through 'citizenship education' are now being adopted in the UK. Proponents argue that citizenship can be taught independently of religion, private morality and family values, to provide a uniform secular background of legal norms, sufficient to generate social cohesion. Opponents argue that the concept of citizenship is too abstract and philosophical, too much a product of Enlightenment ideas which are themselves the offshoot of Judaeo-Christian morality, to form the basis of *socialization in modern conditions.

city

The city was the original political entity – the place where people settled together and shared their economic, religious and social life, and where they bound themselves by common rules and laws. (*See *polis.*) In more recent times the city has become an object of intense political concern for two reasons: the migration of populations to cities (where they may or may not be citizens); the effect on cities of the immense concentration of power within their perimeters. Modern cities tend to be places with large immigrant communities, some of them not assimilated to the majority way of life, in which relations between people become increasingly fluid and negotiable. People who live in cities do not see the world as rural people see it. Theirs is a society of strangers, and the distance between them and their neighbours is amplified by the *modernist styles of architecture that have been introduced under the pressure of population growth. (*See *planning.*) Legislation that seems natural and right to urban people may not seem natural or right to those who live and work in the country, and tensions between the two communities have been amplified in recent years by the decline of farming, and the outward spread of the suburbs. (*See *suburbanization.*) In the UK the championing of the city against the countryside has been an important socialist cause (as in Raymond Williams, *The Country and the City*, 1975), leading most recently to a ban on *hunting. Conversely, the championing of the country against the city has been one of the enduring marks of English conservatism. (*See *town and country.*)

city state
*See *polis.*

civic
Latin: *civicus*, belonging to citizens. Now usually used in the sense 'of, or

pertaining to, a town or city', as in 'civic feeling', 'civic pride', 'civic amenities', which denote specific relations between people and their place of residence. Some argue that it is only when towns inspire civic feeling that the state can command loyalty. Hence the nature and origin of civic feeling have been of concern to political thinkers. The following have been suggested as contributing to it: established and diversified employment, recognized local customs, civic ceremonies, congenial and stable architecture, and, of course, prosperity and trade. By contrast, migrancy, unemployment, large-scale demolition and neglect, the absorption of *local government into national party politics – all these things might seem to take civic feeling away. The conditions mentioned have been held to stem from the rapid flow of *capital from place to place, together with local specialization in production, which causes towns to flourish and collapse in ways unintelligible to their occupants; though doubtless this is only one among several possible explanations. The Marxist idea of *proletarian consciousness is meant to suggest that the worker under developed capitalist conditions can acquire no civic but only a *class sentiment, since he is forced to find his identity not in local attachments, but in the governing principle of his life – his place in the process of production.

civil association
See *Oakeshott.

civil disobedience
Expression given currency by *Thoreau, in an essay entitled 'Resistance to Civil Government', 1849, defending a decision not to pay taxes to a government which sanctioned slavery. The strategy of civil disobedience was made famous by the Indian statesman *Gandhi, who first employed it in 1913, and in 1920 the Indian National Congress voted overwhelmingly to adopt the strategy in order to undermine British imperial government. The phrase is now used to denote any non-violent acts of overt and deliberate lawbreaking, or acts of contested legality, which have the aim of bringing to public notice either the actual illegitimacy of certain laws, or their lack of moral or rational justification. Its success is dependent on the extent to which it can prevent or delay the judicial process. It is clear that in the most tyrannical states civil disobedience is unthinkable as a strategy of political action, since it will be scotched as soon as it is attempted.

The question whether and when civil disobedience is permissible is one part of the general question of *political obligation. One necessary condition of legitimacy is voluntary surrender to punishment. The one who breaks a law and then tries to evade punishment is an ordinary criminal, who does nothing to bring the law into disrepute. The one who surrenders to punishment is both breaking the law and at the same time enforcing it – against himself. His law-abiding character, displayed in the act of disobedience, shows the law to be oppressive, and his own conduct to be motivated by conscience and high principle.

Recent advocates of civil disobedience – such as *King – have therefore scrupulously insisted on voluntary surrender and a plea of guilty.

civil law
1. In all legal systems, the branch of law dealing with actions between subjects – whether individuals or corporations – and including tort, contract, property law and the laws of trusts. It is to be distinguished from criminal law, in which the state

engages in an action against one or more subjects, and administrative and constitutional law, which govern the actions of the state itself.

2. The term 'civil law' is also used to denote the *Roman law, and those legal systems which derive from it. Civil-law (or *civilian) jurisdictions still abound in the modern world, and are to be contrasted with systems founded in *common law, in *Napoleonic law, or in the *shari'ah* of *Islam.

civil liberties
See *civil rights, *liberties.

civil rights
Those *rights that belong to the citizen by virtue of his citizenship alone, and which are protected by law. To be distinguished from *human rights, which may or may not be so protected, and which (if they exist) belong to all people everywhere, whether or not enshrined in law. In US political practice the two kinds of right are not always distinguished, partly because it is thought that the Constitution, through its *bill of rights and certain acts of Congress, makes all human rights into civil rights. Moreover, to deny a civil right is to deny a human right – i.e. the right to be given what has been promised. In the UK the reference to civil rights is less frequent than that to civil *liberties. Whether or not the two ideas are the same is a disputed question. On some views rights are always permissions: i.e. they consist in injunctions to others (including the state) to allow the individual to proceed about some action. On this view, 'civil rights' and 'civil liberties' are different terms for the same thing. However, it is clear that not all rights which are claimed are like that. Some speak, for example, of a *right to work, which imposes on others not just the obligation to leave me free to work, but also the obligation to provide work so

that I may exercise this freedom. Others go further, and speak of rights to health, happiness, children and a host of other things that it may be beyond human possibility to provide. (Is this view coherent? For this and related questions, *see* *rights.)

The civil rights movement came into existence in the US in order to enforce rights guaranteed by the Constitution but, by historical and political circumstances, denied to blacks. It culminated in the Civil Rights Act 1964, containing additional provisions against discrimination. However, it is clear that the passing of a new law cannot in itself give effect to laws which already exist but have proved ineffective. Hence the concentration of the activities of the movement on seeing that the law is not only clear, but also enforced.

Movements in the USSR and its satellites to uphold rights guaranteed under the written constitution, or by virtue of the Helsinki Accord, 1975, were generally treated as subversive and 'anti-socialist', and suppressed accordingly. The systematic nature of the state opposition to such movements eloquently illustrates the proposition that a piece of paper *describing* a constitution does not *create* a constitution, and without the fulfilment of further conditions (such as *judicial independence) remains a piece of paper. The relative effectiveness of the US movement is perhaps partly a consequence of the fact that the rights pursued really are *guaranteed* by the Constitution, and can be fought for in open court.

civil service
The body of full-time officers (other than political or judicial officers) employed by the state in the administration of civil (as opposed to military) affairs. While containing many (and increasingly many) branches, it is

fundamentally divided between the administration of home and of foreign affairs.

The genesis of the modern forms of civil service marks a radical change in the manner and content of government. In the UK the hierarchical nature of the institutions of administration – with complex rules of answerability, careers open to talent, successive dignities and honours expected if not by right at least by convention, the whole culminating in the permanent 'under-secretaries' answerable to ministers of the crown – all this evolved from the structure of the nineteenth-century Indian civil service and its predecessor, the administrative section of the British East India Company. It is significant that an under-secretary is called 'permanent', in order to distinguish him from the merely transitory minister from whom in theory he receives instructions, but to whom in practice he may often dictate. The French civil service reflects an older structure, having emerged under the absolute monarchs of the seventeenth and eighteenth centuries, while in the US the composition and structure of the civil service still express presidential patronage and nomination, careers being pursued at the lower rather than at the higher level of office.

The growth of the modern civil service raises large questions of *legitimacy and *right. For example, does a civil servant have a right to strike against his employer (the state)? US law says no, while UK law says yes (with certain important exceptions), perhaps because the question has never been fully considered by Parliament. Even in the UK the civil service is divided among itself as to the extent to which it should exercise this right. Does a civil servant have a right to engage in party political activity? Both US and UK law say no, on the grounds that this undermines the principle of *representation, transferring political activity from the chamber of elected representatives to the hidden corridors of administrative power. Clearly, whatever view is taken, concern over this question indicates that the civil service is not *merely* an administrative organ, and thus the prospect of a systematically disloyal civil service is one that no government, and no state, can contemplate with indifference. Some have held out this fact in support of the US system, in which the senior offices of the service are filled by political appointment, or even in support of *democratic centralism, according to which the party in power also fills every important office in the administrative machine.

civil society

1. Term increasingly popular in the eighteenth century, and introduced into political theory largely as a result of *social contract theory. It denotes the state of society in which patterns of association are accepted and endorsed by the members. Most users of the term were influenced by *state of nature theory, seeing the individual as an atomic constituent of the civil society, which is composed by contract, consent or submission from these self-dependent atoms.

2. In *Hegel: civil society is not *formed* by contract but is the *sphere* of contract, i.e. of free association between individuals. As such it is not a complete entity but one aspect (or 'moment') of the political order, another aspect of which is the *state. (Hegel's term is *bürgerliche Gesellschaft*, which could also be translated 'bourgeois society', or 'the society of the town'.) As a result of Hegel's view many political theorists now distinguish 'civil society' from 'state', using the first to denote forms of association

which are spontaneous, customary, and in general not dependent upon law, and the second to denote the legal and political institutions that protect, endorse, and bring to completion the powerful but inarticulate forces of social union. Accepting such a distinction it would perhaps be right also to accept another: that between 'civil society' and 'society' *simpliciter*, the first denoting only those associations which *also* have a political aspect, the second denoting all associations generally.

3. During the years prior to the collapse of communism, opposition to communist government in Eastern Europe often proposed 'civil society' as an ideal, meaning a society organized by free association and spontaneous institution building, outside the control of the state, and independent of the ruling party. In this use the term 'civil society' refers to a de-politicized society – a society into which political power does not excessively intrude.

civilian

1. Traditionally, one who studied the *civil law. Hence:

2. 'Civilian system': any system of law founded in *civil, i.e. Roman, law.

3. In theological usage, one who bases his values in secular considerations, especially in the virtues of *civility, as opposed to divine command.

4. (Now most frequent): a person or body not engaged in military activities. (Hence, by extension, 'non-military', as in 'civilian clothes'.)

Modern political questions about the status of civilians (sense 4.) in time of war are fraught with difficulty, just as are the associated questions concerning the existence and nature of universal *human rights, to be respected in every circumstance. This is evidently a consequence of the modern practice of 'total war' which involves acts of aggression against

every citizen of a hostile state, whether or not he or she is engaged in military acts. Moreover democracy, which has the express aim of identifying all citizens with the state, makes it much harder to separate those who are actually conducting a war from those who are being dragged along by it. (*See* *armies.)

civility

1. Term often used by sixteenth-century political writers to denote civil order and government.

2. The virtue of the citizen, hence the kind of behaviour appropriate to 'good citizenship'. In particular, those parts of 'good manners' which enable people to accept one another as members of a common social order, and so treat one another with due regard for social well-being and quotidian moral rights.

civilization

1. The condition of society which is generally contrasted with its undeveloped, or 'barbarous', condition and in which, it is supposed, refined and rare advantages exist, usually in conjunction with refined and rare disasters.

The concept has played an important part in defining the aims of nineteenth- and twentieth-century politics, and various attempts have been made to define it more precisely. Thus *Coleridge (*On the Constitution of Church and State*, 1830) distinguishes civilization, which is the 'mixed good' consequent on general material and scientific progress, from 'cultivation', which is the unmixed good of a mind in which feeling, thought and potential have developed in harmony (*see* *culture). From the point of view of usage this distinction is an artificial one, but from the point of view of theory it is of some importance. Thus it is integral to many forms of *cultural conservatism to oppose the unqualified pursuit of material advance, and to seek to overcome political instabilities and political dissatisfactions not through economic growth, but through education. The education in question will be *humane, united to a tradition of thought and action, and expressive of a partly sceptical, partly dignifying vision of the complexity of human arrangements. Such an education, it is sometimes thought, is as likely to be impeded as propagated by material and scientific development: this is the thought behind Coleridge's distinction. *See also *Kultur/Zivilisation, *Spengler.

2. A social entity that manifests legal, cultural, religious and customary continuity over an extended period and extended geographical area: as in Roman civilization, Egyptian civilization, and so on.

civitas

Latin term used concretely to denote the union of citizens within a state or commonwealth, and abstractly to denote the condition and rights of the citizen. In *Cicero, the term is of great importance in translating all those notions that had been associated by the Greeks with the *polis, and which were later associated with the *state.

clash of civilizations
*See *Huntington.

class

1. A general term subsuming all those distinctions between people that involve unequal but systematic distributions of *privileges, thus covering distinctions of rank, *caste, *estate, *status, degree, and class in sense 2., but not distinctions of *group, *role or *office.

2. Usually a theoretical term, occurring as part of an *explanation* of systematic inequalities. When so used it becomes necessary to distinguish the

easily observable features which make us believe a person to be of a certain class from those features, perhaps not easily observable, which determine to what class he actually belongs. Thus in England someone may be assigned to a certain class on the basis of accent, manners, title, and membership of a social circle. In America material wealth, the nature of work, and access to leisure and luxury are likely to be given greater prominence. Theorists dispute, however, over the underlying distinctions (if there be any) of which these features are signs. Consider English upper-class characteristics: are these signs of *power or of *authority? Are they signs of economic or political position? Do they convey a particular *class consciousness that causes those who possess it to enter into privileged relation with others of their kind? Sociological theories attempt to answer such questions, some (e.g. *Weber) finding the essence of class to reside in 'life chances', some finding it in separate social or economic functions, and so on. One difficulty for such theories is that part of what makes a person upper class may be that he is taken as such by others who are upper class. So that access to a class is often achieved by representing oneself as already belonging to it. *See* *social mobility.

3. In *Marxian and similar theories, the term 'class' is used as a technical term associated with a theory of ownership and control. It denotes positions in the system of *production relations, which are held to explain all such characteristics of class-recognition as those referred to above. If an 'upper-class mentality' appears to survive in the absence of any shared economic position then this is only a lingering after-effect that will vanish as economic reality makes itself perceivable. (Thus the Faubourg society described by Proust is merely the ghost

of an upper class, sitting crowned upon the economic grave thereof.) For the Marxist the principal theoretical classifications are those of *master and *slave, *patrician and *plebeian, *lord and *serf (in *feudalism), and *bourgeois and *proletarian (in *capitalism).

Whether or not the Marxist theory is accepted, economic position is given increasing prominence in theories of class membership. Thus it is usual in England to speak of the lower (or working) class, the lower middle class, the middle middle class, the upper middle class, and the upper class. And since these are loosely identified in practice with labour in the first case, trade in the second, profession in the third, rent and credit in the fourth, and landed nobility in the fifth, it is tempting to think that what is being described are fundamental distinctions of economic function. Those impressed by this idea have sometimes thought that two variables are needed in order to explain actual social inequalities: class and status (thus Weber).

In all usages it is important to distinguish theories which make it possible for classes as a whole to move from some lower to a higher position, and those which define classes in *terms* of their position, so that classes cannot move. Although Marx adopts a definition of the second kind, there is a tendency in Marxist writing to dramatize history by speaking of whole classes as though they move upwards and downwards through the social and economic hierarchy. This may be true of individual members of a class, but it can never be true of the class.

class consciousness

A term that seems to be used in two senses, to denote either:

1. the individual's sense of himself as belonging to a social *class, or

2. those features of the individual's outlook and understanding which are

to be explained by his membership of a social class.

The first is sometimes distinguished from the second by referring to it as consciousness of class *identity*. This may, for example, be manifest in loyalty to one's own class, and hostility to, or suspicion towards, members of another. Depending on the theory of class adopted, either 1. or 2. or both may be taken as in part *constitutive* of class (as in E.P. Thompson: *The Making of the English Working Class*, 1968), or as ancillary to (and perhaps explained by) class (as in classical *Marxism, which distinguishes, in this respect, the class-in-itself from the class-for-itself). The second idea is more congenial to those who wish to separate matters of consciousness from the 'material conditions' which underlie them (*see* *materialism). But it imposes the very real task of describing the precise nature of class consciousness, and explaining such things as social aspiration (the desire to change one's class, when this does not seem to be primarily a desire to change one's material condition), *snobbery (whether normal or inverse), and the relative absence of class consciousness in the US (as contrasted with the UK) despite very great differences of material wealth, and despite the economic relations definitive of *capitalism.

class struggle

According to *Blanquism and to much *socialist theory, the class *conflict that is the driving force of history, being at the root of all major changes in law, institutions, morality and religion.

*Marxists see the class struggle as intensifying under capitalism to the point of *revolution, when the whole social order is overturned in the interests of a rising class. According to this theory the class struggle is always a reality in capitalist society, but is not always apparent to its participants, since antagonistic *class consciousness may not arise, the *bourgeois devices of *legitimation sufficing to establish an uneasy acceptance of the *status quo*. By contrast with the Marxist position, *Weber saw the principal class struggle as that between creditors and debtors, with the conflict under capitalist conditions between employers and workers as merely a special case. On this view the rising class seeks always to expropriate those to whom it is indebted, while the established class seeks to sustain the law that would guarantee repayment.

No theory of the class struggle has been wholly satisfactory, partly because it is hard to accept that there always is such a thing or to accept that those conflicts which influence history can all be seen in terms of class. It is not obvious, for example, that class struggle underlies all *sectarian and religious strife, or the alleged war between the sexes; nor is it obvious that a description in such terms would be explanatory. It seems that electorates dislike 'class politics', as divisive and irrelevant. It was therefore only when the Labour party discarded its advocacy of the class struggle that it was perceived as a 'natural party of government'. *See* *New Labour.

classical economics

The school of eighteenth- and nineteenth-century economists who, in opposition to the *physiocrats, emphasized the importance of manufacture and production but who, like the physiocrats, emphasized liberty and property over agriculture in the determination of prices, prosperity and distribution. Its principal exponents – among them, *Smith, *Ricardo, *Malthus, and the *Mills – shared the assumption that competition is the foundation of economic activity, and in their several ways gave

grounds for the belief that market conditions, operating without interference from the state, would generate economic stability. If, at times, the market does not work for the common benefit, state interference must nevertheless be contemplated only with hesitation, since it tends to lead to inefficiency or stagnation. For Adam Smith, for example, it is not only natural but also right that economic activity should be guided by self-interest alone. (*See* *invisible hand.)

The classical theories were refined and perpetuated by J.S. Mill, and dominated political and economic thinking in the US and the UK in the nineteenth century. They lost credibility with the experience of *recession and the Great Depression in the 1930s, which prompted interest in the theories of *Keynes and the *Cambridge school. These attempted both to explain such facts as recession, and to justify state intervention in the economy, as a means of maintaining *aggregate demand. In more recent times, however, classical economics has enjoyed a resurgence, and reappears in the work of the *Austrian and *Chicago schools. *See also* *neoclassical economics.

classical liberalism

Liberalism as expounded by the thinkers of the *Enlightenment tradition, from *Locke and *Montesquieu to *Hayek, as opposed to liberalism in the sense current in the US, where it refers to attitudes of a left-leaning and statist kind. *See* *liberalism, sense 2.

Clause 4

See *New Labour.

clerisy

See *Coleridge.

climate change

In so far as climate change presents an issue for political thought it is the issue of whether political decisions can affect it, and if so, whether the will exists to take those decisions. Leaving aside all dispute about the facts – i.e. the extent of climate change, its causes and its likely effects – the question remains whether anything short of a global treaty could control or reverse the process, and whether a global treaty is possible. Energy consumption in the US is driven by consumer demand, which in turn determines voting patterns, so that a party that placed severe restrictions on energy would very soon be out of office. Energy consumption in China is driven by communist central planning, which is entirely insensitive to the protests of anyone, let alone ecological activists who run the constant risk of arrest. In these circumstances it is unclear what a treaty can achieve, given that the US and China are the world's largest consumers of energy.

cliometrics

From Clio, the muse of history. Study of historical processes through the use of statistics and statistical methods: a growing discipline which downplays the effects of great men and women, great battles and great kings and queens and instead studies parish registers, hospital records, church archives and other sources of information about the lives of ordinary people.

closed shop

The restriction of employment in a particular place to members of a particular *trade union or unions. The practice is legally disapproved in both the UK and US, on a variety of grounds, both under statute, and under the common law of *contract, its opponents describing the closed shop as an interference in individual liberty and a restriction of the free economy. In both jurisdictions,

however, professional associations are permitted, even when membership is a necessary title to practice. (For example, English solicitors must belong to the Law Society, which can strike them off for malpractice.) Is this a similar interference in individual freedom, and a similar restriction of the free economy? (Compare also the role of qualifications in creating a barrier to entry in the medical, teaching and psychoanalytical professions.)

coalition

A temporary political alliance of distinct parties or persons, who preserve their separate political identities. Coalitions may be formed for electoral purposes, for the purpose of creating a government that has sufficient power and unity to rule, or for the purpose of defeating a government (as in the 'negative coalitions' of post-war France). In the US a coalition is usually a cross-party grouping in Congress, formed in response to a particular issue, but with no long-term political objective.

A coalition government is tied by a power of *veto, since any party within it may threaten to withdraw if its policies are opposed. Hence a coalition must act in a way that is more acceptable to its members than their own withdrawal.

The theory of coalitions is a branch of *game theory, and considers the rationality of strategies that involve forming or leaving coalitions with a view to maximizing the economic or political pay-off.

Coase theorem

In an article published in 1960 the British economist Ronald Coase argued that, when governments distribute property then, in the absence of transaction costs, all allocations of rights are equally efficient, since interested parties will bargain privately to correct any *externality. In the presence of transaction costs, the most efficient allocation is to the party who assigns the most utility to the property in question. Coase developed his theorem, as it was later called, in the context of discussing government allocation of radio frequencies; it is now considered as a fundamental (though not universally accepted) conjecture in understanding government regulation of a market economy.

codification

The verbal formulation of the whole or part of the law of a state, with a view to replacing all existing *statutes, *common law, customary law, and so on: a practice introduced in Babylon in 2100 BC, and since often repeated. The tradition of codification in France began with the *ordonnances* of the seventeenth century, and culminated after the Revolution in the *Napoleonic law, which served as a model for many of the codified legal systems adopted by the nation states of Europe during the nineteenth century. Codification in Germany and Austro-Hungary proceeded on the model of codified *Roman law. It was advocated for English law by *Bentham. However, attempts to achieve codification of the UK legal system have made no progress, due to the extent and complexity of the *common law, the ascendancy of *equity, and the appreciation of the value of the present fairly flexible relations between judiciary and Parliament. US law is partly codified, but relies heavily on English common law, from which it ultimately derives.

Codification has seemed to many besides Bentham to be legally and politically desirable, since it leads to settled expectations and easy predictions; some have thought that it might even serve to make recourse to the courts unnecessary. Others have objected that it must always be too rigid to allow for proper treatment of *hard cases, and that it misrepresents the true nature of law, which is partly implicit in the procedures of adjudication, discovered by the judge in practice as much as invented by the *legislator in statutory decrees.

coercion

Any force or threat of force that reduces the freedom of an action, so that, in performing it, an agent acts less freely than he might have done, although not unintentionally. (You can be *forced* to do something which you do not do intentionally, but coercion is essentially a constraining of intentional action.) In law physical coercion makes an act legally ineffective, moral coercion does not. This reflects a distinction that we need to make, between forces that *interfere with freedom by removing it, and those which merely narrow the range of autonomous choice.

Followers of *Kant would not regard moral coercion as a form of coercion, but as a form of *influence. A person, can either be influenced by reasons, in which case he retains his identity as a moral agent and the freedom that is inherent in it, or else he cannot, in which case he has lost freedom and moral integrity together. As Kant's position shows, the philosophical definition of coercion is hard to provide. The criminal law, for example, ought not to be a system of coercion, for if it were, it could never be freely obeyed; the truly autonomous agent ought then to choose to defy it. One way of looking at it is to say that the law is *two* systems, one of *authority, which influences the rational agent to obey the law, another of *power, which coerces the agent not so influenced to act in accordance with it.

cold war

Term invented by the US financier and presidential adviser Bernard Baruch in 1947, and given currency by the journalist Walter Lippmann. It denotes a state of hostility between rival *blocs (specifically the Western and the Soviet), involving economic, political and subversive action, but without overt war.

Responsibility for the condition of cold war is variously attributed to Stalin's ambitiousness, to the activities of international capitalism, to the activities of international communism (and in particular to the series of *coups d'état organized by communists in collaboration with the USSR in Eastern Europe), to American foreign policy in the Far East, to USSR foreign policy in Europe, and so on. It is clear, however, that it could not exist without there being two immensely powerful antagonists each of whom wants to exercise a power that the other seeks to deny him. The view that the cold war was caused by 'capitalist encirclement' of the USSR was once popular among members of the Western left. The view of most writers from the ex-Soviet territories is that the cold war was caused by the communist party, its expansionist programme, its non-negotiable goal of total domination and its strategy of systematic deceit.

Coleridge, Samuel Taylor (1772–1834) English poet, philosopher and social theorist. Coleridge made one of the first attempts to adapt the philosophical vision of *Kant, Schelling, and the early German *idealists to the description and evaluation of the social condition of England, thereby taking a stand against what he saw as the fragmented vision of society and the individual characteristic of *empiricism. He was particularly hostile to the *utilitarian theories of *Bentham, and argued that human *values cannot be understood in terms of pleasure and pain. Coleridge argued vehemently against Jacobinism and its attempt to replace the language of social *privilege with the language of *natural right, rejected the idea of human *progress as a linear movement dependent only on the growth of scientific knowledge, and felt that the enlightened *rationalism of his contemporaries ignored the instinctive, pious relations between people that form the true bond of society. He was also opposed to the influence of *laissez-faire and *classical economics, and advocated government intervention in the economy in order to relieve poverty and hardship and to provide education.

Coleridge defended the institutions of *Anglicanism and, in *On the Constitution of Church and State*, 1830, pointed to the need to reconcile the demands of political order and constitution with the more instinctive needs that are embodied in religious institutions. Here, as elsewhere, he defended the view that *culture is an indispensable mediator between explicit law and implicit social feeling, and argued for the political importance of the 'clerisy', or learned class, in whom the culture of a nation is enshrined, and who, in taking decisions informed by that culture, act in tune with the deeper, unspoken instincts of the governed:

'The clerisy of a nation, or national church, in its primary acceptation and original intention, comprehended the learned of all denominations; – the sages and professors of the law and jurisprudence; of medicine and physiology; of music; of military and civil architecture; of the physical sciences; with the mathematical as the common *organ* of the preceding; in short, all the so-called liberal arts and sciences, the possession of which constitutes the civilization of a country, as well as the theological.'

That passage illustrates both the impulsive nature of Coleridge's thought, and also his distinctively modern faith in the role of the *intellectual, for whom he was the first true propagandist, despite his somewhat medievalist conception of the established church. His arguments for the indispensability of culture shaped many of the nineteenth-century expressions of *cultural conservatism, and also awoke *Mill to the shortcomings of the utilitarian creed. Coleridge's importance lies largely in his perception of the opposition between the empiricist and idealist visions of *human nature, and his recognition that the first typically involves a massive simplification of the facts which it claims to know by observation.

collective bargaining

The practice of settling wage claims, conditions of work, productivity and related matters through bargaining between *trade unions, representing employees, and organizations representing employers. The effect is that terms of employment are settled by *influence, *confrontation and *conciliation, after the contract of employment. The resulting terms are not (in law) terms of a contract of employment unless afterwards incorporated therein.

It could be held that the practice of collective bargaining effectively abolishes the contract of employment, and establishes (*de facto if not *de jure) a new kind of relation between employer and employee, which has no clear precedent in law. See *industrial law.

collective choice

An ambiguous term, used in a variety of contexts, and in connection with a variety of theories. These theories fall broadly into two kinds:

1. Theories of *social choice, which attempt to derive 'social choices' from individual choices, in accordance with principles which justify the first in terms of the second.

2. Theories of 'collective action', which attempt to describe and explain the ways in which *groups conduct their affairs, and the ways in which the actions of groups emerge from the actions of their members.

The first is a normative study, belonging to logic, political philosophy, and welfare economics. The second is a partly descriptive, partly normative, study, belonging to sociology and political science. However, it overlaps with the theory of social choice, to the extent that, in this area, description depends on the answer to normative questions: i.e. whether a choice is described as made *by* a group will depend in part on whether it can be justified in terms of the choices of the members. The second kind of theory (here considered) deals, then, with such questions as the following: how do people with an interest in a decision also influence that decision? And, when is a decision really the decision of a *group* rather than of some agent, individual or *pressure group within it? In many ways the second question is the most interesting, since, if there is no clear answer to it, then there is no clear answer to some of the most important questions of political theory. Thus advocates of *collectivization wish to see collective *control over the means of production, and this involves determining when actions proceed from a genuine collective choice, and when they are imposed. In practice all of the following have been called collective choice: state decisions made by a politburo in secret; votes of activist élites at open meetings; block votes; decisions taken without consultation with, but 'on behalf of' some group and so on.

Consider the procedure of voting exemplified by the UK Trades Union Congress. Each delegate casts a vote that is weighted according to the size of his union; it is therefore possible for a decision repugnant to a majority of trade unionists to be taken with the authority of their 'majority vote'. In what way can that decision be said to be a 'collective choice' made by the trade union movement as a whole?

The question illustrates the extent to which normative and descriptive questions here arise together. *Rousseau made an important distinction between the *general will, and the will of all, arguing that the first need not coincide with the second. The general will is that which is expressed in group choices; the will of all is that which is arrived at by aggregating the several individual choices. Some argue that there can only be genuine collective choices if there is also a general will, in the sense of a new kind of *agency distinct from the agencies of the members of a group. A *constitution is required to establish that agency, and the real test of the existence of collective choice lies in the nature of that constitution. (For example, is it such that the majority consented to be governed by it, or would consent if asked?)

By contrast, there seem to be things that happen as a result of individual choices which, while in some sense expressing the 'will of all', are not really the expression of a general will. This can occur when the result issues, not from a constitution, but from a mechanism. Thus, consider the *market system, as conceived by *classical economists. Here the actual behaviour of commodities is influenced by *every* choice made by sellers and purchasers, and determined by all of them. Some might argue that this could only be a real collective choice if it were mediated by a constitution: that is, by a system of rules, to which

the members of society might consent. But if people had the choice as to whether to submit to the market mechanism or not they might refuse. Although their decisions determine the behaviour of the market, the existence of the market is not their decision. *See also* *invisible hand.

collective consciousness
See *Durkheim.

collective goods
See *public goods.

collective responsibility
The principle that each member of a decision-making body should hold his membership on condition of accepting full *responsibility for all of the body's decisions. This principle, imposed on families by the primitive legislation of tribes, is also imposed on the UK cabinet by itself.

collective security
Term denoting strategies which states have adopted in order to cooperate in the prevention of *war, usually by adopting a centralized system of *security arrangements. The UN Security Council was established with collective security as its principal aim. However, since each member may *veto any decision, efforts at collective security can succeed only in so far as they are in the interests of all the parties. Hence the difficulty, some say, of dispensing with a policy of *deterrence.

collectivism
The theory and practice that advocate the 'collective' as the economic, social and political unit, as opposed to *individualism, which advocates the individual, and *state socialism, which advocates the state. A collective is an autonomous *association of individuals which is not *private in the manner of the *family, but which has a variable

membership determined partly by local attachments. 'Collectivism' was originally employed to denote the kind of anarchist socialism advocated by *Bakunin, which opposed itself to both *Proudhon and *Marx. The theory and practice have shown little consistency, however, and the term now seems to have three distinct meanings:

1. (Narrow.) The theory that the economy should be owned and controlled collectively, so that all major decisions are the result of *collective choice rather than individual preference.

2. (Broad.) Any socio-political system in which, whether or not there is collective control in sense 1., individuals act collectively in social, cultural or productive activity, perhaps under the directives of a *party, but in the name of a 'collective'. Fine semantic distinctions matter very much in describing those arrangements which might be called 'collectivist' in this sense.

3. Sometimes the term 'collectivist' is used to denote any view which allows that a collective may have rights that can override the rights of individuals. For example, some think that the state has rights; others think that lesser forms of association, such as institutions of education, religion, or recreation, also have them. A theory which holds that these rights are not always defeasible in favour of the rights of individuals may, on this usage, be called 'collectivist'. Recent human rights legislation in Europe has shown a tendency to uphold '*group rights' – for example the rights of religious and ethnic minorities, which are not accorded to everyone. This form of collectivism is both widespread and widely criticized.

Confusion between the senses is very common; thus many seem to think that criticisms of 3. apply also to 1. and 2. In fact the three ideas are quite independent, and the use of the term 'collectivism' would perhaps better be confined to 1. alone.

collectivization

The act of bringing property under collective control (see *collectivism 1.). Often used to denote the agricultural practice of those states governed on the Soviet model, in which private landowners were expropriated in order to establish collective farms. In the USSR the *kolhoz* (collective farm) was, in law, if not in fact, the joint property of its members, each of whom was entitled to a share of its profits; it is to be distinguished from the *sovkhoz*, or state farm, which is the property of the state and worked by employees of the state. The legal owners of a *kolhoz* did not have the right to sell it to anyone else, other than the state, which could determine the conditions of sale unilaterally. Whether one can speak of joint ownership in such conditions is disputable. (*See* *property.)

When voluntary, collectivization is usually described as the formation of a *cooperative. This is in part to indicate the revocable nature of the act, in part to record the fact that this transaction can occur independently of any substantial political change in surrounding institutions, and in part to indicate that the members of a cooperative retain the right of transfer which the members of a *kolhoz* must forgo.

The collectivization of agriculture in the Soviet Union is now widely acknowledged to have cost many millions of lives, to have ruined the rural economy and to have led to the long-term dependence of the country on agricultural imports. (*See* *kulaks.) There is little evidence that the policy has been less cruel or more effective elsewhere.

college

1. Educational. A particular form of educational *institution, in which members are voluntarily associated for the purposes of teaching, learning, and research, and which also has a domestic aspect – as exemplified in the colleges of older universities. Colleges developed originally out of monastic communities, and the resulting institutions are peculiar in aiming to provide extensively for the social and personal needs of their members. In the UK they tend to be *corporations (traditionally incorporated by charter, though now becoming private limited companies), with a highly developed social *ethos, and a capacity to influence their members in ways that are not narrowly educational. They have therefore formed the model for certain ideals of association. (*See* *collegialism.)

2. Electoral. *See* *electoral college.

collegialism

The theory that the church or state or both are, or ought to be, voluntary *associations, whose social and political structure is to be construed on the model of a *college, united for the pursuit of recognized ends, but generating also an ethos which is something more than devotion to those ends.

colonialism

The theory and practice of *colonization.

colonization

The establishment of a 'colony', i.e. a collection of people whose origin is in some 'mother country', and who retain the language and customs of that country, but whose social and economic life is sustained in the place to which they have moved. Modern colonialism has usually also been imperialistic, hence the term has come to denote the particular kind of *imperialism associated with the European colonies in Africa and South-East Asia. Typically this provided for partially autonomous legal and social institutions in the colonized country, in so far as this was compatible with overriding military, political and economic objectives, combined with the retention by the mother country of supreme legislative and political powers and by the colonial community of social and political rights not normally extended to natives. It has been, in effect, a form of subjugation, in which, throughout the period of colonization, the colonized country has been without independent *sovereignty (an attribute which it often did not have in any case, and gained only in the wake of decolonization). Colonization also brought about highly contested boundaries between colonized countries, which reflected the limits of colonial expansion, of economic interest, or of military capacity, rather than any indigenous sense of racial, cultural or historical identity.

It is sometimes argued that the function of colonies in recent history has been to provide raw materials for manufacturers in the mother country. If this were so, then decolonization would leave a country with developed facilities for exporting raw materials, but no facilities for employing them in production. Hence the economic (and ultimately political) dependence on the mother country (or some substitute) would survive. The argument is, however, disputed, since it is clear that the availability of cheap labour in the colonies has led to the export of capital from the mother country, and the import of *manufactured* goods. It may nevertheless be the case that *markets* formed under colonial administration are so structured as to make *autarky difficult. Moreover, cultural hegemony, through language and through a residual community of former colonists, together with the siting of educational and legal institutions in the mother country, create their own form of dependence. Thus the process of 'appeal to the Privy Council' survived until recently in many former colonies of the UK, so that the law of those countries was subject to judicial review in the former mother country.

Leninist theories of imperialism argue that it is capitalism, with its insatiable appetite for markets, that makes colonization necessary. This seems difficult to reconcile with the fact that colonization may be inspired by political motives (as in the Soviet colonization of the Baltic states and Eastern Europe), social motives (as in the original colonization of North America), religious motives (as in the Arab conquest of North Africa), or no motives at all (i.e. 'in a fit of absence of mind', as Joseph Chamberlain described the process whereby Britain acquired its empire).

The effect of nineteenth-century colonization on modern politics has been incalculable, and awareness of this has been responsible for several recent coinages. Thus some speak of neo-colonialism, meaning that kind of economic and cultural infiltration of *developing countries which depends neither on force nor on political alliance, but simply on the operation of skilfully managed market forces. Others refer to 'colonial ingratitude', in order to describe the resentment of colonies to the development of their resources by a colonizing power, even though this development has been to the economic advantage of the colonized country, and is recognized as such. Colonization has been a fertile source of excuses for subsequent oppression and mismanagement, and the once fashionable view that colonization was the cause of under-development has given way to the more sombre thought that

colonization has often been the brief moment of light in an otherwise self-perpetuating darkness.

Comecon
Council for Mutual Economic Aid, set up by the USSR in 1949 in response to the Marshall Plan, with the intention of reducing the dependence of communist countries on trade with the West. It involved the major members of the Soviet bloc, Cuba having joined later, and Yugoslavia being represented as an 'observer'. Comecon presented a striking example of an attempt to bring economic relations into line with political ones. It contrasts with the *European Union, in which a legal superstructure has developed in order to bring political relations into line with economic ones.

Comintern
See *internationals.

comity
Friendship and good behaviour between states: international good manners. The necessary precondition for the operation of *international private law (as when the citizen of one state seeks to enforce a contract made with the citizen of another).

command
To command is to issue directives to another, and to demand that he obey them. The usual implication is that a command, to be legitimate, must be issued by someone with *authority so to do, and, to be effective, must be issued by someone with *power to enforce obedience. Hence most exercises of command are also exercises of authority and power. Actions done in response to a command are done knowingly and intentionally, although in certain circumstances a person commanded to do something

(e.g. a soldier) may be less free than someone merely *influenced to do it, and less *responsible for the outcome.

Tacit command arises when a power of command has to be assumed in the explanation or justification of some human relation, even though it is never explicitly formulated in directives. Some argue that the correct way of describing, and perhaps also of justifying, the relation of *political obligation is in terms of a power of command vested in the sovereign, associated with a posture of *obedience in the subject. Such a theory may wish to add that the command is not usually explicit, but only tacit (cf. *tacit consent).

Command theories of political obligation have their analogue in 'command theories of law', such as that presented by the jurist John Austin: laws are to be understood as generalized commands, issuing from the sovereign power, and enforced by sanctions upon all who are subject to that power. On this theory all actual law is *positive law.

command economy

An economy, such as that imposed and maintained by the *communist party in the former Soviet Union, in which all major enterprises are centrally controlled, and in which economic activity is initiated and governed by *commands issuing from the central organization, rather than by *market forces.

commensalism

A term of sociology, denoting a relation that involves both competition and cooperation among those who occupy similar specialized positions within a *division of labour. Some writers do not distinguish commensalism from symbiosis; however, the latter is normally taken to be a relation between those occupying dissimilar kinds of functional position within a system. Thus commensal relations underlie the *class structure, while allowing for *social mobility, whereas symbiotic relations underlie the structure of corporate groups.

commercialism

The disposition to see all social and political activity in commercial terms, and all political values as their 'cash equivalents', all political aims being identified with the commercial activities which most nearly correspond to them. For example, conservation is identified with the aims of the tourist trade. The argument as to whether or not the countryside should be protected by law is resolved by balancing the profits which would ensue upon its exploitation, from the profits that would accrue to the tourist trade should it be conserved.

commissar

An officer, especially during and after the 1917 revolution in Russia, commissioned by a soviet, a government or a party, in order to organize social, political and military activities, and to supervise indoctrination. A 'people's commissar' in the USSR was the head of a government department.

commitment

Usually used in a sense corresponding to the French *engagement*, as this term occurs in the *existentialist philosophy of *Sartre, to denote complete identification with a cause or way of life. Commitment is the expression of existential freedom, and the answer to the anxiety into which that freedom plunges me. Although I cannot be sure, for example, that the cause of revolution is just and humane, I must not hesitate for ever to espouse it, lest I should lose my nature as a political agent. There comes a point where commitment is necessary. The nature of political reality is clear only to the person who is engaged in it, since only he *exercises* his freedom, and only in the exercise of freedom can that reality be understood. Hence the value of commitment can be understood only after it has come into being.

Commitment is analogous to *faith: it involves will, but its end-point cannot be known or aimed at before it is reached. To be committed is not simply to do this or that thing in a cause, but to consign one's whole self to a cause, and so to will both the act and the state of being which it expresses. Usually commitment is to one of the causes associated with the political *left, for reasons partly made clear in the definition of *praxis.

committees

A committee is a body formed, elected or appointed to make decisions on a certain matter. It investigates the facts, and also makes decisions, in so far as it is within its power to do so. The decisions of a committee are examples of conscious *social choice, but are usually made on behalf of people who are not themselves members of the committee but only *represented on it.

In the workings of the UK Parliament and the US Congress, committees have a specialized function. They do not in theory make legislative decisions, but offer recommendations and advice. A 'committee stage' is necessary before any bill can pass into law, and during this stage amendments are likely to be proposed, and will usually be accepted by the legislative body, on the understanding that the committee has had the time and expertise to look more deeply into the consequences of the proposed legislation. The power of the committees in the US Congress is so great that it is often suggested that they are the *de facto* legislature on any issue which passes through their hands.

A 'steering committee' is one charged with preparing the *agenda for the decisions by the main body which appoints it. Such a committee inevitably has considerable *influence, if not *control, over the final outcome. The theory of committees is an important part of the theory of *social choice.

commodities

1. Particular kinds of raw material and 'primary product', such as grain, rubber, iron – anything, in other words, produced immediately from land.

2. More normally in economics (especially in *price theory), a commodity is an object of exchange. A commodity is associated with two *values, called by classical economists *exchange-value, and *use-value, and by many modern economists *price and *utility. Thus a £10 note has exchange-value but next to no use-value, while a glass of water can have great use-value but can be exchanged (in normal conditions) for nothing.

commodity fetishism

Defined by *Marx in *Capital*, vol. 1, as the disposition of commodities to conceal the social nature of their production. Through the seemingly autonomous laws of the *market, *exchange-value appears as an objective and intrinsic property of commodities, inducing the labour of the person who seeks to acquire them. In fact, however, this value is itself (according to the *labour theory) *produced* by human labour. The labour of men therefore appears not as a human attribute but as an illusory power in the things which men produce. Moreover this power in things appears to generate fluctuations of the market, price rises, unemployment, etc. whereas in fact the true causality of all these effects lies in the social processes of production and exchange.

Common Agricultural Policy (CAP)

A *protectionist policy to support *agriculture (or at any rate *agribusiness) in the *European Union. Established in 1958 by the Treaty of Rome it was for many years the only significant policy of the European Community, accounting for over two-thirds of the budget. The CAP has been welcomed as a way of supporting European agriculture in conditions of unprecedented competition from farmers with more favourable climate, soil, labour costs, etc. It has been criticized as exerting a vast distorting pressure on trade, with periodic dumping of surpluses, exorbitant subsidies and a rise in the cost of food. The CAP has encountered strong pressure from the *GATT and *WTO, and reform is constantly promised, and constantly deferred.

Common Fisheries Policy (CFP)

In contrast to the *Common Agricultural Policy, the European CFP is not designed to protect European fisheries from competition but rather to make the fisheries of maritime member states available to the wider membership. The CFP was hastily improvised in the early 1970s, when the UK, Ireland and most of Scandinavia were actively seeking membership. To join the European Community the applicant states had to accept that their fisheries (greatly coveted by existing members) would henceforth be a 'common resource'. Iceland and Norway refused the deal, Britain, Denmark and Ireland accepted it. The resulting bitterness, as British and Irish fisheries collapsed, has inflicted lasting damage on the European project.

common good

Political theorists sometimes distinguish conceptions of legitimacy and political obligation based in an idea of *consent, from those based in the idea of a common good. Thus T.H. Green argued that 'the state is an institution for the promotion of a common good' (*Lectures on the Principles of Political Obligation*, 1879–80), and tried to give to the idea of a 'common good' sufficient elaboration to justify the obedience of the citizen and the extent of the law. A common good may mean at least two things: a benefit to the civil society as a whole, and a benefit to each of its members. That these need not be the same is indicated by the case of a partnership. At a certain point a partnership may thwart the purposes of its members: the good of the partnership (its active engagement in profitable business on its own account) may then run counter to the good of each partner. This possibility arises in every association of individuals that creates a new locus of *agency, so enabling us to distinguish the 'common good' from the 'good of all', rather as *Rousseau distinguished the *general will from the will of all. (An analogous dichotomy arises in considering the idea of the *public interest.) Green seemed to interpret the common good in the second way, as involving the good of each citizen individually, and argued that the state can promote the common good only by creating the universal conditions for the growth and exercise of *virtue. Some of the paradoxes of *utilitarianism are avoided by the Kantian view that the conditions for the growth of virtue in any one individual are the conditions for the growth of virtue in all. (The common good is that which ministers to common – i.e. universal – human nature.) Any other human good might be such, however, that to extend its provision as widely as possible requires depriving at least one individual of the opportunity to acquire it. In that case, the 'common good' might begin to appear as the good of civil society as a whole, and not as the good of each and every member of it.

common law

Term used in several senses, but now principally defined by two contrasts:

1. Common law v. *equity. The common law is the part of the law, whether written or abstracted from cases, in which determinate legal remedies are sought and applied on the basis of definite breaches of law, the law describing the nature, scope and application of the remedy. Remedies in equity are more flexible, and are available even in the absence of breaches of law. (See *injunction.) They also, in UK law, take precedence over remedies in law.

2. Common law v. *statute. Common law is used to denote case law, i.e. the part of law that is defined through, and discoverable through, judicial decision, as opposed to the law that is laid down by the *legislature.

It is part of the peculiar form of *judicial independence existing in the UK that common law in sense 2. is so important, and that common law in both senses may be overridden by equity. In French and German law the term 'common law' (*droit commun* and *Gemeinsrecht*) is used in a different sense, to denote law common to the whole state as opposed to regional law. Legal *positivists think of common law as 'judge-made' law, and regard it as having validity only because the legislature extends a blanket endorsement to it. Others (e.g. *Blackstone, *Hayek) regard common law as a paradigm of judicial reasoning, a field of discovery, independent of the legislature and directly answerable to the sense of *justice. For such thinkers common law is more truly law than the pronouncements of a legislature, and common-law jurisdictions such as the English and the American are nearer to the demands of justice than any system founded in legislation alone.

common market

A common market is a kind of *customs union, since its precondition is the diminution or abrogation of the powers of member states to levy duties on imports other than the common duties. However, its provisions may extend beyond those normally envisaged in such a union, and involve everything that might promote exchange within a group of states, with the hope that the increase of exchange will generate an increase in economic activity and living standards.

The history of common markets is complex. Modern examples include Benelux (agreed pre-war), the Central American Common Market (1960) and the Andean Pact (1969). The most significant development in their form and nature has been the creation of the European Economic Community (now the *European Union) by the Treaty of Rome (1957) as amended by subsequent agreements and in particular by the *Maastricht Treaty. This provides not only for the free movement of goods, services, capital and labour throughout the member countries, but also for an elaborate administrative, legislative and judicial procedure, raising questions of *sovereignty and *international law that are perhaps without historical precedent. Thus the European Union has a parliament, with elected representatives, a court of law, and an enormous machinery of law-making and law-enforcement which, while ostensibly concerned to facilitate trade, in fact penetrates into the reaches of civil life, dictating the standard quantities and sizes of commodities, the forms and procedures of sale, and the size and nature of transportation. It indirectly affects the development of regions, investment policy, supply, demand and mobility of labour, throughout the member countries. And through the *Common Agricultural Policy it controls the production of food in ways which have had major social consequences.

To some extent nations have always had to bend *municipal law in the interests of commerce, security and (more recently) international agreements. However, by the Treaty of Rome, law is not merely recommended to the member states by the European parliament, but is also *made for* those states by the Council of Ministers, through the *legal instruments laid down in the Treaty. These now generate over half of all new laws passed in the Member States.

common ownership

Property rights in x are said to be held in common if:

1. more than one individual has a right of property in x, and no individual with such a right may be prevented from exercising it by any other; or alternatively if:

2. more than one individual has a right of property in x, and no individual may detach his right of property by consent or transfer, so as to convert it into a *private right.

UK and US law do not permit common ownership in sense 2. but insist that common ownership is a form of *trust. Each owner is then private owner of a portion of the property, and can either force sale in order to realize that portion, or detach it directly for his own exclusive use. The principle of common land in feudal land law seems to be that it was held in common in sense 2. so that the rights of all owners were violated by enclosure. *See* *property.

common pool resources

Resources from the use of which it is difficult to exclude people, since they cannot easily be allocated under a system of private rights, but which are nevertheless (unlike *public goods) depleted by use. Examples include the oceans and their contents. *See* *tragedy of the commons.

Common Prayer

The Book of Common Prayer is the official service book of the Church of England, compiled because of Archbishop Cranmer's wish to replace the Latin service books with a vernacular text. Issued in 1549, and revised by an Act of Uniformity in 1662, it has recently been provided with an Alternative Service Book, in an attempt to make the liturgy applicable to the experience of a modern worshipper. The battle over this revision illustrates the peculiar constitutional problem of *Anglicanism, which can revise its liturgy and practice only with the consent of the Queen in Parliament. It also illustrates a problem that has dominated conservative thinking throughout the nineteenth and twentieth centuries, that of cultural continuity.

Some argue that fundamental beliefs, such as those enshrined in a religion, are not easily detachable from the words, forms and *ceremonies in which they are embodied. Hence changes in those forms and ceremonies, and in particular the provision of a whole new *language and vocabulary of worship, cannot be assumed to leave the content of religious and moral belief significantly unaltered. Whether or not this is so is a deep philosophical problem, concerning the nature of religious and moral sentiment. The issue is of serious concern in the US, where traditional forms of religion, whether episcopalian or nonconformist, continue to provide the imagery and the vocabulary with which common predicaments are described.

commonwealth

1. In *Hobbes and other seventeenth-century writers, the term is used to imply that the members of some social order have a common weal, or social well-being, which it is in their collective interest to preserve. The existence of such a social well-being determines the need for politics: it is a further question what laws and institutions (if any) would minister to it. Hence the term 'commonwealth' came to be used also to mean 'state' and preserves this meaning in such titles as 'The Commonwealth of Puerto Rico'.

2. Now generally used to refer to two historical phenomena: (a) The government of the Cromwells (the Commonwealth and Protectorate) which existed between the execution of Charles I and the restoration of Charles II. This government involved the survival of the legal powers of *monarchy in the absence of legitimate succession, and also, according to some, an enhanced need for their violent exercise in those circumstances. (b) The free association of sovereign states that had been members of the British Empire. A loose, but at one time powerful, association, united by similar legal and political institutions, but bound by no constitution or rules of membership. The UK monarch was widely recognized by the member states as head, although it is not clear what this meant. The monarch cannot be head of the Commonwealth, since that is a position that bears no legal *sovereignty. Nor can she be head of each state, since that is legally impossible, and formally rejected e.g. by India, which has declared itself a republic.

The principal consequences have been legal (the persistence of appeals to the UK Privy Council, the establishment of privileges in respect of UK nationality, etc.); and economic (the establishment in 1969 of the Commonwealth Development Corporation, to channel funds to the *developing countries in the Commonwealth, and the various *bilateral agreements under the Finance Act 1957 ('Commonwealth Preference')). There is no implication of a common *foreign policy. The rise of the EU and other transnational institutions, blocs and alliances, and the widespread adoption by Commonwealth countries of one-party rule, have led to the virtual demise of the Commonwealth in its original form.

communalism

The theory and practice of the *commune, whether or not conjoined with *communism as the prevalent political condition.

commune

An *association whose members own everything in common (*see* *common ownership), including the product of their labour. Such associations have been advocated as a political *ideal since ancient times, but received renewed support in the works of *Owen and *Fourier. The Paris Commune of 1871 was a popular uprising which led to the brief autonomous government of the city by the *communards*. It declared that the city should be owned uniquely, entirely and in common by its people, with no citizen having a greater right to any part of it than any other. Whether through impracticality or misfortune, the objective was not realized. Communes of such a type were favoured by *Marx, and some were formed in Russia immediately after the October Revolution. However, they were soon turned into 'collective farms' and similar institutions installed or maintained by coercion.

It is doubtful that the modern 'commune', composed of refugees from the *bourgeois way of life, has much in common with the ideals proposed under this label. All attempts to relinquish private property and to hold everything in common encounter problems of organization: who is to direct the process, and how?

communication

The transmission of information, ideas, emotions, values and attitudes. Since communication is essential to all social order, the theory of communication presents large political issues, including the following.

(i) The nature of *language, and its relation to *ideology. Some argue that the very act of speech, because of its social nature, is a political act, and so laden with ideological implications. This thought tends to take two forms: (a) language as such is ideological, so that political meanings are attributed to every utterance, however innocent it may seem; (b) ideological significances are to be found in the language, accent, and subjects of conversation of a particular class or classes. Class-membership is 'signalled' in speech, and this is held automatically to give an ideological meaning to its signals.

(ii) Control over the means of communication. This was advocated by *democratic centralism as a necessary part of its political aim, and in any case is almost invariably exercised by parties who rule in the name of that idea. Here 'communication' does not mean language, but rather the *media of mass communication. In democracies, the concern is often expressed that the 'media barons' exert an *oligopoly over the means of communication, and that *dissident opinions are increasingly difficult to express. This book, however, contains thousands of them.

(iii) Specific questions as to *how* means of communication are controlled (i.e. owned, licensed, censored etc.) in democratic regimes.

(iv) Questions concerning the use of particular media. For example, the internet opens whole new possibilities of propaganda, education, display, trade and military manoeuvre, and it is not unreasonable to suppose that these possibilities change the character of political organization, just as they change the character of social life.

(v) More general issues concerning the media, in particular those illustrated in Marshall McLuhan's slogan that the medium is the message, and those concerning the effect of 'saturation' by communications – as when a person spends half of his life in front of a television.

(vi) The problem posed by political communication. This is held to be a two-way process, between sovereign and subject and subject and sovereign. In democracies the way is (or should be) open in both directions, whereas in some kinds of *despotism it is open only in one. How is it to be kept open? And should the way up be the same as the way down? (*See* *representation.)

communism

1. A social and economic arrangement defined by the fact that no participant owns significantly more than any other, either because all property is held in common, or because the institution of property does not exist, or (Marx) because ownership is confined to the means of consumption and is excluded from the means of production and exchange. To be distinguished from arrangements in which property is not owned in common but by some impersonal, but nevertheless autonomous body, such as the state. (*See* *socialism, *state capitalism, *state socialism.) Also to be distinguished from arrangements in which equality of ownership is established by isolated, or periodic, acts of redistribution, whether by common consent, by taxation, or by act of state. In all such arrangements, it has been thought, the

principle of communism is not achieved, since the individual is permitted to indulge a right of ownership, and may well feel an injustice in its abolition. Moreover, periodic equalization is compatible with the institutions of barter and exchange, each of which is held to be alien to the communist ideal.

According to Marxist theory, socialism is a stage of development, and leads to communism, hence the frequent Marxist distinction between the two. True communism (or 'full communism') is incompatible with any form of exchange. It is the real economic expression of *democracy and is characterized by the slogan 'from each according to his ability, to each according to his need' (Marx: *Critique of the Gotha Programme*). The emphasis on need signifies the disappearance of *exchange-value, and its supersession by *use-value alone. It is this in particular which distinguishes communist society from the forms of 'redistributionism' which might otherwise be confused with it.

2. Any movement which aims to bring about the state of affairs described above, or which represents that state of affairs as a political ideal. There have been many such movements in history, but the principal one in modern times began with the European revolutions of 1848 and the publication in that year of the *Communist Manifesto* by Marx and Engels. The word 'communism' occurs frequently in their writings, but for a long time the word 'socialism' was preferred as the name of the ideal, the principal Marxist parties calling themselves *social democrats. Their political organization began with the first of the *internationals, founded in London in 1864 with the support of Marx. The Third international, or Comintern, founded in Moscow in 1919, in the wake of the 1917 revolution, displayed

the final preference for the word 'communism'. This word was adopted by *Lenin and *Trotsky in order to distinguish their ideals from the less pure intentions, as they saw them, of the European socialists and social democrats, and also in order to emphasize an affinity with the Paris Commune of 1870, which, according to Marx, involved a genuine gesture in the direction that he favoured. The Comintern gave the impetus and name to communist parties throughout the world, and since then the term 'communism' has been synonymous for many with the form of government of which Lenin was the principal inventor, namely:

3. The system of government in which a *communist party rules, without permitting legal *opposition.

Communist Manifesto
Composed by *Marx and *Engels and published in German in 1848, at the behest of the Communist League, and in English in 1850, the *Communist Manifesto* was the principal document involved in the launching of the *Communist Party as an international organization in the following century.

In the first part an impressive summary is given of Marx's theory of history, in which the development of *productive forces under capitalism is described, together with the resulting destruction of all feudal relations and hierarchy, all true national boundaries, and all traditional modes of trade, life and consciousness. The necessary consequence is said to be the emergence of the urban *proletariat, which comes to be organized 'into a class, and consequently a party'. The manifesto, having described the alleged condition of the proletariat, goes on to affirm the identity of interest between the Communist Party and the proletariat everywhere. The 'theoretical conclusions' of the communists are said to be founded on 'actual relations springing from an existing *class struggle'.

The remainder of the manifesto is given over to examining the proposals made by the Communist Party in support of the proletariat. These include the abolition of all 'bourgeois property, and 'in this sense, the theory of the communists may be summed up in a single sentence: Abolition of private property'. The contention is that *private property relations condemn the proletarian to be propertyless, by forcing him to accept the minimum wage. Hence he has nothing to lose by their abolition, and everything to gain from the *common ownership that will eventually displace them. Moreover, this common ownership is historically necessary, since it, and it alone, is compelled by the continuing and necessary development of the productive forces which, unleashed by capitalism, are like some uncontrollable demon now working for capitalism's crisis and destruction.

The manifesto also proposes the abolition of 'bourgeois' law and education, the abolition of the *family, a heavy progressive income *tax, and centralization of capital and *communication in the hands of the state. It concludes by analysing the various kinds of theoretical and sentimental *socialism current in its day, finds fault with all of them, and advocates the overthrow by force of all existing social conditions, since 'the proletarians have nothing to lose but their chains'. The fact that the manifesto proposes no institutions or laws, no procedures other than violent destruction, and no rules for compromise or adjudication, is neither commented upon in the text nor noticed by those who have sworn by it.

communist parties

The word 'communism' was used in its current sense as early as 1840, and the *Communist Manifesto* spoke of 'the Communists', referring to them as a *party. Communist parties in the modern form are, however, a twentieth-century invention, emerging as a result of the split between *bolshevism and the *social democrats at the Second *International, after which *Lenin set about organizing his 'party of the new type'. The Soviet attempt to make communism into a complete system of government was inspired by Lenin's theory of the party, and has dominated the history of communist parties throughout the world. The subsequent conflict between *Stalin and *Trotsky found echoes in intellectual and political movements within Western parties right up to their final collapse in the early 1990s, as did the disputes over *revisionism, the personality cult, and the role of national as opposed to international aims and aspirations.

The British Communist Party was founded in 1920, and, under Lenin's advice, unsuccessfully sought affiliation with the Labour Party, first in 1921, and then in 1922 and 1936. It has never been represented in the House of Commons by more than a few members, and its influence as a party steadily declined until its dissolution in 1991. Trotskyists with communist commitments turned their attention to the *labour movement and for a while succeeded in turning trade union and Labour Party policies in directions once advocated by the Communist Party. The American party suffered much from *McCarthyism and other forms of *anti-communism, and is now moribund. The French Communist Party has existed since 1920, became highly influential after the Second World War under the *Stalinist M. Thorez (*regnabat* 1930–64), and maintained close working-class connections. The non-Stalinist party of Georges Marchais (born 1920) repudiated the *Marxist-Leninist doctrine of the *dictatorship of the proletariat, and its relations with the USSR were increasingly strained. Perhaps the strongest of the Western European communist parties is the Italian, founded in 1921 by *Gramsci, and at one time able to receive one-third of the votes cast at a general election, and to secure control of many important municipal councils. It seems unlikely that the French and Italian communist parties will now be able to play an independent role in the brokering of power, although the Italian party retains control of many municipalities.

The communist parties in Eastern Europe have suffered many calamities; first, the murder in 1919 of the founders of the German party, Rosa *Luxemburg and Karl Liebknecht; secondly, the triumph of *Nazism; thirdly, the forced imposition of Soviet dominion after the war, which turned the Communist Party into an instrument of imperial government. Its position should, however, be seen in the context of fairly effective indigenous support, and the brief ascendency of communist parties in the 1920s, when Hungary experienced communist government, and neighbouring states felt the considerable influence which that government exercised.

For the Chinese Communist Party, *see* *Maoism. *See also* *Eurocommunism.

communitarianism

A social philosophy which has emerged in reaction to the failure of *socialism, on the one hand, and the supposed dangers of *libertarianism on the other. Communitarians are prominent among American political scientists, and include such established academic figures as Michael Walzer, Michael Sandel, Charles Taylor, and Amitai Etzioni, whose journal *The Responsive Community* has served as a platform for the development and propagation of communitarian ideas. Libertarians – especially those on the *right, who seek to liberate people from state control and who value individual freedom above all other social goals – have been careless of our need for *community and for an *identity that is greater than the individual will. Libertarian ideas promote the fragmentation of society, and the pursuit of profit at the expense of social life. Classical *liberalism was equally careless of community, on account of its *individualist philosophy of the human person, and its failure to see that the person is a social artefact, whose freedom is acquired only in the condition of society. On the other hand, socialists, who emphasize the need for community, wrongly assume that the state can act to restore or preserve our communal identity in the face of social fragmentation. In doing so, they transfer too much power to the state, and bring about the political alienation of the ordinary citizen. The ideal should be that of a *civil society, neither led nor controlled by the state, but existing as something over and above the sum of the individuals who compose it, a source of meaning and value that will endow the individual life with purpose and enable people to flourish according to their nature.

Some people see communitarianism as a belated recognition by left-liberal thinkers of truths which have traditionally been expressed by *conservatives. However, conservatives are likely to criticize communitarians as sentimentalists who wish to have just as much community as will make the life of the left-wing intellectual comfortable, while being unwilling to pay the price – which is hierarchy, authority, exclusion, a common morality and perhaps even common religious beliefs and customs.

Communitarians reply that we live in a secular world, and the old idea of community is no longer available in any case, so that the conservative response offers no alternative.

community

A term denoting a social *group, usually identified in terms of a common habitat (such as town, village, or district), and implying both a body of common interest, a degree of social cooperation and interaction in the pursuit of them and a sense of belonging among the members. By extension, any self-identifying group of people with similar interests who attempt to advance those interests by establishing themselves in a common place, e.g. a community of artists, or of scholars.

The term has many rather vague uses and is sometimes used as a translation of *Gemeinschaft. It is also used in the political context to imply a community of interests among people who may form no genuine community in the above sense at all, and who may even be deeply divided among themselves – as in 'gay community', 'Muslim community', etc., where the use of the word is part of an attempt to normalize and make socially acceptable groups that have been the target of hostility.

community law

The directly applicable law of the European treaties and their instruments (on which, *see* *European Union). In the event of conflict it takes precedence over *municipal law. (This is clearly necessary for the effectiveness of the treaty, but may also be an abrogation of *sovereignty on the part of its signatories.) In general, community law becomes part of the law of the UK if it is, in its nature, or under the treaty, self-executing, or is the subject of a separate parliamentary enactment, or

is implemented by statutory instrument (see European Communities Act 1972, S. 2(2)). It was established in *H.P. Bulmer Ltd* v. *T. Bollinger SA*, 1974, that European law is to be construed by UK courts, not according to strict and literal interpretation, but in accordance with the practice of European courts, and the spirit of the Treaty of Rome, so that even judicial procedure is now constrained by that treaty. See further *acquis communautaire, *legal instruments.

community politics

Used to describe UK Liberal Party politics in by-elections during the early 1970s, the term now has a wider application, to denote the political emphasis on matters of local concern, and the attempt to acquire support for national policies by representing them as bearing directly upon comprehensible (whether or not connected) interests of the small and localized *community.

commutative justice

Justice arising in connection with exchange and mutual dealings, as opposed to *distributive justice. The expression used to translate *Aristotle's idea of 'the justice that is corrective in transactions between people' – as in punishment, or compensation – as opposed to the justice that governs the distribution of goods among those who have a claim to them.

company

Nowadays, usually a form of *corporation, whose legal identity is secured by the provisions of company law, and whose essence consists in the uniting of members for a common purpose. Under the UK Limited Liability Act 1855, shareholders can limit their liability in law for actions of the company, thus constituting the company as an independent agent, which can contract debts and obligations which no shareholder is required to honour, and even commit crimes of which no shareholder is guilty (and be fined or dissolved in consequence). Similar legislation has now been adopted by almost all jurisdictions.

Thanks to company law and limited liability, the principal agent in modern capitalist production is no longer the individual, and capital itself is largely detached from individual ownership, leading an autonomous (or seemingly autonomous) life of its own, so that even those who control its employment (the managers) are themselves employees, bound by a labour contract to the impersonal company which they serve. (*See* *separation of ownership from control.*) All organization and accounting of incorporated companies is closely controlled by statute, in order to avoid the evident opportunities for fraud presented by limited liability.

compensation criterion (sometimes: compensation principle)
A criterion for the social desirability of an economic *policy, first proposed by *Kaldor. If those who gain from a policy could compensate in full those who lose, and yet still remain better off, then the policy is preferable to one which leaves things as they are. The principle might be compared with that offered by *Pareto optimality, which says that a policy is beneficial if no one is made worse off and someone made better off, but which, unlike the compensation principle, refers to the actual rather than to the hypothetical distribution of benefits resulting from a policy. Such principles are much used in welfare economics, which normally requires some standard of optimal satisfaction of competing claims.

The compensation principle has been much criticized, first because

hypothetical benefits seem to be an incoherent object of social policy, secondly because of the paradox, noted by T. Scitovsky, that it might recommend *both* a change from A to B, *and* a change from B to A. Further inconsistencies have been noted by P.A. Samuelson, W.M. Gorman, and others.

competition
A process in which many agents rival one another, e.g. to sell their products or their labour. The general precondition of a *market economy, competition clearly admits of degrees, and hence for the sake of economic analysis is studied in relation to an ideal of 'perfect competition', in comparison with which all actual competition is 'imperfect'. Perfect competition in a market requires (among other things) the following conditions: a large number of buyers and sellers (so that the amount bought by any buyer is negligible relative to the total transaction), homogeneous goods, perfect information possessed by all regarding selling and buying opportunities, absence of transaction costs, and freedom of entry into the market. From these and other assumptions about preferences and production conditions it can be shown that, if perfect competition pervades the economy as a whole, there will exist a set of prices at which *supply and *demand are in *equilibrium for every commodity in the economy. Yet further assumptions (e.g. concerning adjustment processes) would be needed for it to follow that the economic system will tend to equilibrium rapidly or at all.

The existence of *monopoly and *oligopoly, and the many legal, economic, and political barriers to entry into a market that have arisen in the modern world, make the theory of perfect competition more or less inapplicable, except as the study of an *ideal type, although some markets approximate to it. However, such factors have not eliminated competition altogether, but require recognition of its imperfect character; the many political and moral questions posed by the widespread dependence on competition as a controlling and motivating economic force remain. The assumption of much political theory during the eighteenth and early nineteenth centuries was that competition would also generate the *just price, since all factors contributing to the destruction of free contractual arrangements between buyers and sellers would have been removed. However, that is at best only true if the basic distribution of property rights is not unjust. It remains an open question whether normal competition generates injustice, and whether, and to what extent, it provides the conditions in which some members of society are inevitably *exploited to the benefit of the remainder.

Defenders of competition are apt to praise the 'competitive spirit', either as the source of all progress and invention, or as the necessary affirmation of the individual will (*see* *Nietzsche). It is argued that, without it, people are either less prosperous, or less dominant over nature, and in any case in a state of imperfection or decline. This reference to the competitive spirit is an important part of the *ideology of capitalism, and also an important concept for certain religious and moral criticisms that are made of it.

Comte, Auguste (1798–1857)
French philosopher and exponent of *positivism (a philosophy first enunciated in modern form by *Saint-Simon, whose secretary Comte was), and inventor of the term *sociology, together with many parts of the study that now goes by that name.

Comte's early writings were influenced by *counter-revolutionary thought of the early nineteenth century. While he admired many of the ideals of the French Revolution, he sought to reconcile them with a respect for social order and *progress. His search for a 'middle way' between *Jacobinism and conservatism led to his development of positivism, which aimed to derive political doctrine from a science of society. He argued that social evolution proceeds through three stages, the theological or fictitious, the metaphysical or abstract, and the scientific or positive. Comte saw himself as advocating the transition from the second stage to the third, in which all phenomena subject to invariable natural laws would become the subject of scientific investigation. Man finally comes of age in this 'positive' era, and loses his dependence on religion as on all other forms of systematic illusion. However, man also requires a philosophy of life that will facilitate the transition and maintain social order. Comte therefore proposed the development of a secular system of 'common moral ideas', based on an appreciation of the normative character of all social relations, and the impossibility of social order without a publicly accepted system of values. This and similar items of sociological analysis greatly influenced *Durkheim.

In Comte's later writings, the attempt to find a system of values that would reconcile order and progress led in a new direction – that of the 'church' of positivism. 'Positive' is a term used to denote knowledge and understanding which confines itself to the actual empirical world, and refuses to transcend it in search of hidden causes and final ends. All genuine human knowledge is scientific and methodical, and no question that cannot be answered by science has an answer. The nineteenth-century man possesses an ever-growing understanding of his position, and on the basis of this can plan a total reordering of society to meet actual and scientifically determinable needs. Thus Comte summarized this aspect of his political vision (the theology of science) in the slogan: 'science whence comes prediction; prediction whence comes action'. His vision also had dogmatic and liturgical aspects, involving the worship of humanity. Comte tried to develop institutions of a quasi-ecclesiastical kind with which to transmit this faith, the result being described by T.H. Huxley as 'Catholicism minus Christianity'.

Comte was an eccentric but influential thinker, and fragments of his thought found their way into many nineteenth-century political theories, from *utilitarianism to the sociology of *Marx, with whom Comte shared the ambition to strip away the veil of illusion from human things, and to reveal them, and to act on them, as they really are.

conciliarism

The theory, developed by medieval theologians and jurists, that a council (specifically a council of the *church) may in certain circumstances be a manifestation of the Holy Spirit. The properly constituted council exists as a *corporate person, whose authority is independent of that bestowed on or exercised by any individual, being diffused throughout its members. Conciliarism posed a challenge to the idea of papal authority, and laid the foundations for modern *constitutionalism. It was defended in a radical form by several early Renaissance political theorists, notably *Marsilius of Padua, whose defence was important in shaping the modern concept of *corporate personality.

conciliation

Conciliation is the attempt by a third party to resolve a dispute. It is to be distinguished from *arbitration, on the one hand, and *mediation on the other. It is unlike arbitration in that it involves no award by the third party, and is in no sense a judicial or quasi-judicial process; it is unlike mediation in that it is not a passive intercession, but rather an active attempt to resolve a conflict. On some views conciliation provides the model for all *politics, which involves reconciling conflicting forces and opposing interests.

Methods of conciliation have been laid down in UK law since the Conciliation Act 1896; they are now largely governed by the Advisory, Conciliation and Arbitration Service, set up in 1976. In international law, conciliation is the process of settling a dispute by submitting it to a commission of enquiry, whose findings take the form of recommendations rather than legally binding judgements or awards.

concordat

A treaty between the papacy and a 'temporal' *sovereign concerning ecclesiastical affairs. Examples include that with Napoleon of 1801, accepted by most subsequent French regimes, except in periods of fervent *anti-clericalism; that of 1929 with Mussolini; that of 1933 with Hitler; and that with the Hungarian communist government in 1964, ostensibly securing freedom of worship. A concordat will tend to involve some compensatory concession by the church,' e.g. articles establishing the degree of allegiance owed by the church to the particular state.

concurrent majority

See *Calhoun, *ultra vires*.

conditioning

1. Term from empirical psychology used to denote the establishment of a

connection between stimulus and response, with the implication that this connection comes about through repetition and in a mechanical way that involves no reflection or intention on the part of the subject. (The term derives from the theory of learning advanced by the Russian psychologist I.P. Pavlov (1849–1936), for whom the 'conditioned reflex' was the paradigm of the learned response.) Hence, any attempt to control human behaviour by repetition of mechanical and mesmerizing routines.

2. The term is also extended to refer to behaviour induced by punishment and reward (called 'operant conditioning' by B.F. Skinner) although this may be theoretically quite different from Pavlov's 'classical' or 'respondent' conditioning. It is further extended to denote all learning processes which result in the acceptance rather than in the active questioning of existing conditions – with the implication that acceptance is a kind of mechanical, 'Pavlovian' or 'Skinnerian' submission to the force of habit. 'Social conditioning' can thus come to denote any form of *education which leads to a conservative attitude to the *status quo, whether or not that education involves serious learning as opposed to unthinking routine. See *behaviourism.

Condorcet, Marie Jean, Marquis de (1743–94)
Social and political theorist, supporter of the French Revolution, who was executed in the Terror. See *counter-revolutionary, *progress, *voting paradox.

confederacy
In *international law, an *association of *states for mutual benefit and protection.

confederation
An association of sovereign states with common means of effecting common purposes. The difference between a confederation and a *federation lies in the greater emphasis on the independence of the members in the first case, and on their unity of purpose and organization in the second. Thus the US was a confederation of states up to 1789, and thereafter a federation, until the Southern states seceded and formed a new confederation in 1861.

The distinction is brought out by the German distinction between a *Staatenbund* (confederation of states), and a *Bundestaat* (a federated state). In the second case there is a tendency towards the existence of only *one* *sovereign state (as in the US); in the first case there is the determined persistence of many.

conflict model of society
The sociological term for theories of history and society which see social behaviour and transformation as the outcome of conflicts between rival interests and forces, and which place less emphasis on planning, friendship, peace and creativity. The extreme example of a conflict model is *dialectical materialism.

conflict of laws
An alternative name for international private law. Suppose a citizen of the UK negligently damages property belonging to a citizen of France in the US. Which legal system provides the French citizen with a remedy and why? The rules of conflict are not themselves international but internal to each body of national law, regulating disputes between contending factions which arise within the *jurisdiction. Hence, to answer the question, one must first determine which jurisdiction is to be recognized (in this case, the US). The principal questions determined by the rules of conflict are (a) jurisdiction, (b) which system of law applies and (c) whether any

foreign judgement has to be accorded decisive authority.

confrontation

The point of conflict between two interests, when all *conciliation, *mediation, *arbitration, *adjudication and *bargaining have been put aside, and where *force is mutually recognized as the only remaining course of action. Some see *politics as the science of avoiding confrontation; others see it as the art of provoking it.

Confucianism

The philosophy and outlook of Confucius (K'ung Fu-Tzu, (551–479 BC)), who emphasized in his *Analects* the importance of moral *values in all social and political order. He defended the 'Way' ('Tao') of the ancients to an age that had lost religious motivation, arguing that *custom and *ceremony are the most important forces of social order and good government. Confucius represented the *hierarchical structure of traditional Chinese society as natural, while arguing that the criterion of membership of the *ruling class should be moral rather than hereditary, so that kings should 'reign not rule'. Each citizen must assume the moral obligations of his *role and station, in order to create the harmonious order in which true *virtue (*jen*, or humanity), can be practised.

Confucius's disciple Mencius (Mengtzu, (371–289 BC)) tried further to politicize the Confucian doctrine, and to persuade the rulers of the warring Chinese states to adopt the way of virtue, arguing that obedience to virtue is spontaneous and requires no force.

'Neo-Confucianism' is the name sometimes given to the successive attempts, from the Sung revival (eleventh century) onwards, to reintroduce the Tao into political thought and action, and *Maoism has even been seen as a late manifestation of this movement, although in the 1970s Mao was concerned to discredit Confucianism as anti-Marxist, and his 'cultural revolution' was directed as much against Confucianism as against anything else that might bring some last shred of consolation to the ordinary Chinese subject.

congress

A coming together of people, and now used to refer to certain established institutions, among which two deserve special mention:

1. The institution of the US government as formed and defined by Article 1 of the US constitution. This article vests all *legislative power in a 'Congress of the United States', consisting of the *Senate and a House of Representatives, the division into two bodies being designed to reflect certain principles of *bicameral government. Congress can legislate on all matters listed in Article 1, s. 8, such as taxation, commerce, war and peace, but not on certain matters contained in s. 9. Nor has it any power to legislate in a manner that would conflict with the *bill of rights.

Management of Congress lies to a great extent within the governance of the chairmen of 'standing *committees', chosen by seniority in office. Each committee has (with certain exceptions) a majority from the party which has a majority in the House of Representatives. The importance of committees in Congress contrasts with their relative unimportance in UK parliamentary government. The congressional committees are so ordered and constituted as to be able to carry through the necessary legislation without interference from outside, each item of legislation having a standing committee appointed to discuss it. This leads to the efficient and rapid consideration of many bills at once, but it also circumvents the general discussion of each. This circumvention is accepted partly because of widespread trust in the constitutional process, combined with a high degree of *consensus as to the form, manner and content of policy in all sections of the House. Neither this trust in constitution, nor the consensus that goes with it, exists in the UK Parliament.

2. Name of the Indian party considered to be the paramount power in obtaining independence in 1947, when led by Nehru. It arose out of the Indian National Congress, an institution founded by an Englishman (A.O. Hume) in 1885 in order to educate Indians first for the civil service and later for government, and which thus became the focus both for Indian claims to autonomy and for supporters of constitutional government after autonomy.

congressional committees
See *congress 1.

congressional government
Term used to denote the type of government that separates the *executive from the *legislature and makes each independent of the other. To be contrasted with *cabinet government, which has an executive chosen by, and/or responsible to, the legislature.

conscience
If someone believes an action to be morally right or wrong, and is therefore motivated to promote or resist it, then he is moved by conscience. Some philosophers (e.g., Bishop Butler, 1692–1752) consider conscience to be a motive quite different from any other, sharply to be distinguished from passion, self-interest, or the 'cool self-love' that proceeds from a reasoned estimate of one's highest well-being. Others describe it as a

desire (albeit of a peculiarly irresistible kind). Still others think of conscience not as a motive, so much as a species of appraisal or judgement, which tells us what is right without providing the spur to pursue or to avoid it.

*Kant, following Butler and other eighteenth-century moralists, argued that conscience must, of its nature, override all other considerations, not in the sense of prevailing against them, but in the sense of silencing them. Thus, while it may not have absolute *power to determine what I do, it has, of its nature, absolute *authority. The person of conscience is the person in whom the power to act on this authority is always present.

Some residue of such an idea is present in the thinking of those who hold that it is always an injustice to force someone to act against his conscience, since, if he has any rights, he must have the right to do as he thinks right. However, this sorts ill with the intuition that there can be error, and even corruption, of conscience, and that someone may conscientiously set about the performance of acts which it is morally and not just politically desirable to restrain. Nevertheless the phrase 'prisoner of conscience' points to a widespread view that in certain cases, where there is agreement of a special kind (perhaps of the kind referred to in doctrines of *natural justice) that an act is wrong, then it is a fundamental violation of right to imprison someone who not only thinks that it is wrong, but also refuses to do it. Hence the importance of a category of *conscientious objection, as specifying a limit to *political obligation.

conscientious objection
Objection to a *command on grounds of *conscience: specifically objection to *conscription on the ground that it is morally forbidden to be an agent of

*war. Sovereign powers occasionally allow conscientious objection as a sufficient reason for avoiding military service, but usually require, perhaps as proof of sincerity, but more probably in order to discourage the habit, evidence of serious *commitment to a specific, and preferably arduous, religion. Conscience that rests in moral values alone, unsupported by religious *faith, tends to be regarded with suspicion, although it is now formally accepted as a valid ground of objection by the US Supreme Court.

conscription

Compulsory enlistment for military duties was a familiar feature of war in ancient times and responsible for many of the features of the *Spartan constitution and the Jewish *theocracy. The practice was revived in modern times by the French Revolution, with its *levée en masse* of August 1793.

Most major wars are now fought by conscript armies, and conscription is often maintained in peacetime in countries which value its discipline, as one of the effective substitutes for a sentiment of *political obligation. Some argue that conscription is a good thing, war being too serious a matter to be left to professionals; others oppose it, on the grounds that it makes *total war difficult to avoid. Once used by one side, however, it is inevitable that conscription will be used by the other.

Moreover, the ethic of modern *patriotism, which legitimates such practices as conscription, has made it difficult for many to think of conscription as anything other than a natural right of the *sovereign, or to regard the *mercenary soldier (i.e. the one who kills not because commanded, but merely for financial gain) with very much sympathy.

consensus

The converging of opinion upon a common judgement. The term entered political thought through *Cicero, who wrote of the *consensus juris*, or agreement in judgement, which he thought to be a necessary condition for the existence and endurance of a republic.

A consensus will come into being automatically where there are common interests, a common understanding of those interests, and of the fact that they are shared, and a common agreement on the means to advance them. But that is not the most important example. A consensus can exist despite conflicting interests; (a) because this fact is not understood (some *Marxists argue that it is part of the function of *ideology to *conceal* conflicts of interest); (b) because differences of interest are balanced by compensating differences of opinion concerning the means necessary to secure them; (c) because of the abrogation of individual interest, in favour of some common conception of the public good – as in time of war.

An important example of the third kind of consensus is provided by *tradition, which may, at least on occasion, represent certain forms of action as legitimate, others as not, and operate as a perceived (if not always understood) background to public political speculation. Conflicts will then be resolved within a given framework perceived as defining possibilities, and there will be an immediate consensus against any act that violates it. This is the kind of consensus which has been called 'public spirit' – the *virtue of *republics, according to *Montesquieu. It is perhaps to this public spirit that appeal is made by that form of *centrism known as 'consensus politics'. This has the appearance of a search for policies designed to please as many and to offend as few as possible. It is in fact a form of political action which moves, whether towards conservation or towards change, always by emphasizing the correct *form* of what is done, and its consistency with well-tried and commonly approved procedures.

consent

1. A mental act on the part of an *autonomous *rational agent, on the basis of understanding, whereby he agrees to participate in some action or common enterprise. Consent is to be distinguished from the decision not to resist another's act, which, if extracted by *coercion (e.g.), cannot be called consent. Consent involves taking *responsibility for an outcome, which therefore becomes 'the doing' of the consenter, even though he may not be the originator of the act which produces it. Hence, it is commonly thought, there can be no injustice to someone in compelling him to receive that to which he has already consented.

2. In law, consent is a material element in certain relations of *contract, *marriage, and sexual intercourse, which determines the nature of what is done. The legal concept of an 'age of consent' is designed to capture in a formula the two ideas of autonomy and rationality, it being assumed that both these qualities are acquired or developed through the normal process of maturation. The concept of an age of consent also serves as a *legal fiction, whereby minors may be protected from the consequences of a reckless act.

3. In political theory consent is often proposed as a criterion of *legitimacy, or as the basis of *political obligation, as in theories of the *social contract. *Locke distinguishes actual from *tacit consent, the latter being genuine consent which is, however, not overtly expressed in any gesture

(unless, perhaps of a purely ceremonial kind), but which can be inferred from the conduct of the citizen. Thus a person who, knowing himself to be free to withdraw from a social arrangement, nevertheless chooses to remain within it, can be taken to have consented to it. The precise meaning of 'tacit consent' remains disputed, as does the claim that the idea provides a criterion of legitimate government.

Consent to political action is a complex matter, and it is not at all clear that there is any process – democratic or otherwise – that incontestably confers it. *See* *collective choice, *democracy, *mandate.

consequentialism

The view that the merit of an action is determined by its consequences, and not, for example, by the motive that compels it, or the character from which it springs. According to this view the fundamental concept of *morality is not obligation but *value (Greek *axios*), hence the occasional use of the terms 'axiology' or 'axiological ethics' to denote consequentialism, in contrast to 'deontology' (Greek *deontos*, a duty), or 'deontological ethics', in which the fundamental concept is obligation. *Utilitarianism is an example of a consequentialist system of ethics, and like other systems it generates paradoxes that are hard to overcome. For example, the good consequences of an action may be enormous, but unintended, distant, and unknown to the agent; whereas the bad may be intended, known, but temporary and slight. Does it follow that the agent acted rightly?

Consequentialism exists in various forms. One form argues that the value of an action is determined not by consequences but by intention; however, the intention is meritorious only to the extent that it is directed towards the good: in which case not actual but *intended* consequences become the criterion of merit. A still milder form of consequentialism argues only that the rational being ought to consider all the consequences of his acts, and should not regard a question of morality as closed. Hence there can be no absolute or inviolable obligations. In all versions consequentialism endorses some version of the maxim 'if the means accuse, the end excuses', and has therefore proved useful to *terrorists, *tyrants, and politicians generally (*cf.* *Lenin's 'revolutionary morality'). Moralists often argue that the pattern of thought involved in consequentialism is the sign of a corrupt mind, since it permits the evasion of every obligation in the interest of some further, however remote or hypothetical, good. But even if this is so, it may be difficult for a politician to take the 'deontological' view. Politics is a complicated *kind* of *agency; it seems *always* to involve balancing one outcome against another, so that, without a consequentialist ethic, it is almost impossible for the politician to avoid *dirty hands. *See* *Machiavelli, *realism.

conservatism

The social and political outlook that embodies a desire to conserve existing things, held to be either good in themselves, or better than the likely alternatives, or at least safe, familiar, and the objects of trust and affection. Conservatism has three distinct parts: an attitude to society, an idea of government, and a political practice. All three are informed by, but not reducible to, scepticism, in particular towards proposals for radical change, towards *utopian theories and ideals, and towards liberal and socialist ideas of human nature.

(i) The attitude to society. Typically conservatives regard society as an achievement, which, for all its imperfections, is likely to be preferable to the pre-social or post-social *state of nature. (*See* *Hobbes.) They might also hold (as against certain forms of *liberalism) that society is in some sense antecedent to the individuals who compose it, the individual being a social artifact, the product of historical conditions that ally him to customs, values and expectations without which he is seriously damaged or incomplete. (*See* *Burke, *Hegel.) These customs, values and expectations are therefore intrinsically objects of respect, and can be rejected only by casting oneself loose from the social order that makes consistent rejection possible. What then remains to a conservative when the customs and values which command his support begin to lose their authority? Modern conservatism has arisen in response to that problem, emphasizing the need for the *legitimation of values, either through the renewal of *traditions, through religious doctrine or, more commonly, through some idea of *natural justice that will provide local allegiances with their universal ground.

(ii) The idea of government. The question for a conservative is what to conserve, and how? The question is answered through an idea of 'government by institutions', and an associated theory of the nature and function of *institutions. Power should be vested in *offices, and in individuals only as the holders of offices. These offices should be attached to institutions that fit closely to the customs and values of *civil society, arising out of them, and conserving them. Hence conservative opposition to the attempt 'to form political institutions on abstract principles or theoretical science, instead of permitting them to spring from the course of events, and to be naturally created by the necessities of nations' (Disraeli). The state is the highest institution, but can pursue the ends of conservative government only if it presides over many and diverse institutions that are the property of *civil society rather than the state. Such institutions will conserve their own principles of development, and the role of government will be in part to protect them from arbitrary encroachment and erosion, and to provide the legal framework within which they might develop in answer to the needs and expectations of their members. The theory of the 'subject institution' occupies much of conservative thought, and signals the deep opposition between conservative and *totalitarian doctrine (a totalitarian state being one in which no institution is both subject and autonomous). (See *Machiavelli.)

The state, like other institutions, is defined by offices, and therefore by a constitution permitting redress for *ultra vires acts. This constitution does not have to be written, but it must act so as to reconcile and harmonize existing interests and activities, while providing ceremonial and expressive form to sovereignty and authority. It is usual for a modern conservative to advocate the division of power within a state, as being the best method of reconciling unity of government with individual liberty, and with the diversity of subject institutions. The state, like society, will be seen as a complex entity more easily damaged than improved, with laws of development and self-preservation that need to be respected. It will also be seen as more closely connected with civil society than many liberal theories represent it to be.

(iii) Political practice. Conservatism is inevitably pragmatic and local in its practice, reluctant to espouse overarching solutions and often willing to concede that there are problems and difficulties which no merely political action can solve. It is anxious to resolve conflicts within the framework of inherited institutions and the *rule of law. It believes in the exercise of power, and also in the need to conceal power through the diversity of government and the creation of a far-reaching *establishment. Its emphasis on natural social relations is often held to require the defence of *private property; even if this is so, it seems clear that conservative practice does not necessitate the defence of modern *capitalism.

Conservatism is usually criticized as the *ideology of class domination, and as the political practice which ensures that those presently holding power will continue to do so, while extracting a spurious and deceived consent from the classes that are subject to, and victims of, their rule. It is usually defended as a genuine and undeceived kind of democracy, the form of government that respects human nature, and answers to the real human need for order, hierarchy, freedom and the *Permanent Things. See also *cultural conservatism. *neoconservatism.

conservative parties

The UK, Canada, certain other *Commonwealth countries, and certain *constitutional monarchies contain influential political parties that call themselves Conservative. (In Canada the name was for a while changed to the oxymoronic 'Progressive Conservative' for fear that the conservative emphasis of party policies might be construed as *reactionary. This has not prevented the Party from suffering catastrophic defeats in recent elections, and it has now (2006) been returned to office under its old title.) Conservative parties outside the sphere of European constitutional monarchy are rare, and, since *conservatism must necessarily take a different form from place to place, usually without much resemblance to the UK example. The US *Republican Party is usually described as conservative, and consciously adopts and propagates conservative policies and doctrines, although this was not always so.

The UK Conservative Party (more accurately, Conservative and Unionist Party, signifying its constitutional unity with the Liberal Unionists who had defended the Union with Scotland and Ireland) represents an alliance in defence of established institutions which, since its announcement in Peel's Tamworth Manifesto of 1834, has gradually transformed itself into an active democratic force. It has been committed to slow reform, *conciliation, a *mixed economy, and the maintenance of *hierarchical and *parliamentary institutions of government. More recently, however, it has favoured *privatization of the economy, and *democratization of social and political institutions. Its modern form is partly due to Disraeli, who turned the party in the direction of universal adult suffrage, and emphasized, in his 'One Nation' doctrine, the supposed unity of interest that binds the working class and the old aristocracy together and leads them to seek a common remedy against the evils of modern *capitalism, and against the socially divisive beliefs and practices of the rising middle class. The party's links with conservatism are, however, uncertain. Its recent sympathy for liberal, and in particular *laissez-faire, doctrines, in both politics and economics, distances it from its nineteenth-century origins. Its triumphant profile in the years of *Thatcherism were followed by severe defeats from *New Labour, and the party is now searching for a new identity, much as the Labour Party did following the defeats inflicted on it by Margaret Thatcher.

consociationalism

Term introduced by A. Lijphart (*Democracy in Plural Societies: A Comparative Exploration*, 1977) to describe a form of government particularly suited to divided or multicultural societies, in which power-sharing at the executive level is combined with devolution of powers to the communities in all matters over which they can govern themselves. Practised in Lebanon after the Second World War, it has also been observed in Austria during the same period, in Belgium, Luxemburg and Canada.

consolidated fund

Prior to 1787 different government funds in Great Britain were maintained for different purposes: the funds were then consolidated in a particular account of the exchequer, into which taxes are paid and from which government expenditure is drawn. Parliament passes at least two Consolidated Fund Acts in each session, in order to release money for public uses and to borrow money by the issue of treasury bills. Recent proposals by the Liberal Democrat Party in the UK to 'earmark' taxes according to the purposes to which they will be applied involve a partial return to eighteenth-century practice.

conspicuous consumption

See *Veblen.

conspiracy

In law, an agreement between two or more persons to effect some unlawful purpose. The crime is complete when the parties have agreed, and does not require further action.

The law of conspiracy raises an interesting political question, since it implies that it may be a crime to conspire to commit an act that is not in itself a crime but only a tort (civil wrong) against its victim, or even a mere 'corruption of public morals' (according to the House of Lords in *Shaw* v. *DPP*, 1962, followed in *Knuller* v. *DPP*, 1973, though the case is sometimes disapproved, e.g. in Parliament, 3 June 1964). Some object to this on the (mistaken) ground that conspiracy, like attempt, is a *lesser* crime than the overt act. The UK and US laws of conspiracy thus permit criminal action against those who plan a civil mischief, such as a vociferous protest or the occupation of an embassy (*R.* v. *Kamara*, 1974). Should this be permitted? Or does it license too many judicial invasions of the civil right to do wrong?

conspiracy theory of history

The theory that effects which fall to the benefit of some *class (usually the *ruling class) are produced by *conspiracy of that class. Often attributed to *Marxists, the conspiracy theory is in fact precisely what Marx's theory of history was designed to replace, by showing that the benefit of a ruling class will be secured, in the short term, independently of the intention to secure it, and despite any (benevolent) intention to relinquish it.

Constant de Rebecque, Henri Benjamin (1767–1830)

Swiss-born French writer, usually referred to as Benjamin Constant, whose defence of *liberalism was one of the most important attempts to confront the errors of the French Revolution and its Napoleonic aftermath, and to diagnose the dangers in the social philosophy of *Rousseau. Constant drew a celebrated distinction between ancient and modern liberty. The ancients had understood liberty in terms of citizenship – the right to participate in public decision-making. But this guarantees none of the private rights and protections that constitute liberty in its modern sense. The ancient idea is essentially aristocratic, and presupposes a slaveholding society given to frequent wars. The modern idea is pacific, presupposing equality, law-abidingness and the desire on the part of each citizen to pursue his own interests without interference from his neighbours. The modern state is shaped by the needs of commerce, and when ancient ideas of liberty are imposed upon it – as by Rousseau and the Revolutionaries – the countervailing pressures do not exist that would protect private rights against a factitious public duty. The result is a dangerous concentration of power in the hands of fanatics, whose appeal to the *general will does nothing to justify their conduct.

constituency

1. In the theory of *elections, a constituency is composed of all those entitled to vote for a particular candidate, and whom the candidate, once elected, represents in the legislative body. (*See* *representation.) In the UK and US constituencies are defined geographically, and the representative or Member of Parliament is assumed to have a duty towards all his constituents, regardless of their vote.

2. More loosely, *parties or politicians have constituencies, meaning the class of people who tend regularly to support them. One of the major tasks facing a political party in modern conditions is to identify its constituencies, answer to their needs and retain their loyalty. *Labour parties and *agrarian parties began by specifying their constituencies in terms of class. But the evidence suggests that constituencies in modern conditions are composed of multifarious interests that cannot be identified so simply, and that a party identified with a social class is destined for defeat.

constituent assembly

An assembly drawn together for the purpose of adopting a *constitution. The first to go by this name was the French National Constituent Assembly of 1789, which drew up the first constitution after the Revolution. The first to establish a durable constitution, however, was the Norwegian Constituent Assembly of 1814, which adopted the constitution that is still in place today. Other important examples are the German National Assembly which met in Weimar in 1919, and which adopted the fatal Weimar Constitution, the Irish Constituent Assembly (the Third Dáil) of 1922, setting up the Irish Free State which broke away from the UK, and the Constituent Assemblies of India (1946) and Pakistan (1947), which began the process of constitutional and autonomous government on the Indian sub-continent.

constitution

1. The body of rules governing the structure, organization and procedure of any corporate body. A constitution sometimes has a special form, as in the charter of a university, or the articles of association of a company. Or it may have to be inferred from practice, being encapsulated in no particular document or authority.

2. (A special case of 1.) The fundamental political principles of a state, which determine such matters as the composition, powers and procedure of the *legislature, *executive and *judiciary, the appointment of officers, and the structure of *offices which authorize, express and mediate the exercise of power. Constitutions may be written or unwritten, they may depend upon explicit rules or unspoken conventions, they may be *republican or *monarchical, or *democratic (although probably not *autocratic), and so on.

Various questions arise concerning the nature of political constitutions that require careful discussion. For example: what is an unwritten constitution, and is it preferable to a written constitution? What is necessary for a constitution? What is necessary for a constitution to be enforced, and what is the status of a constitution that cannot be enforced? Can a constitution without a *bill of rights be effective in safeguarding the fundamental rights and freedoms of the citizen?

It is probably a fallacy to suppose that a constitution becomes more definite and more invulnerable through being written, since no written document makes sense without interpretation, and interpretation here means judicial interpretation, in which the written rule is interpreted in the light of actual, and dynamic, social expectations, and in which a tradition of judicial reasoning is incorporated into the current construction of every clause. The *US constitution, which is written, is now virtually unintelligible except in the light of highly complex judicial applications, and congressional amendments. The *UK constitution, which is unwritten, is neither more nor less unintelligible for that fact, and differs largely in the great role played by conventions in determining procedure. Thus it is a convention and not a law that the sovereign should invite the leader of the majority party in the House of Commons to be Prime Minister. It would probably be wrong to say that this is therefore *not* part of the constitution, since it plays precisely the same fundamental role in determining the nature and function of government as do the rules in the US constitution for the election of a President. It is sometimes put forward as an argument in favour of the unwritten constitution that it can provide a better safeguard of citizens' rights and liberties, precisely because it hesitates to formulate them, and so never exposes them to hasty or tyrannical elimination. The constitution remains procedural, and rights are guaranteed by the priority given in judicial reasoning to factors of *equity and *natural justice. However, a written constitution may protect all rights by *entrenched clauses, and even protect those clauses from amendment. Nevertheless, it should be remembered that a clause can never be so deeply entrenched that it could not die the death of judicial qualification.

A written constitution is genuine only if it can be enforced. The question then arises, enforced by whom? The obvious answer is, by the citizen, by action in open court. (Which is why judicial construction becomes all-important, whether the constitution be written or not.) If the only persons empowered to enforce the constitution are the state and its officers, then the constitution provides no genuine limitation of their actions. It may *describe* their procedure, but it cannot prescribe for it. In which case it would seem wrong to say that there *is* a genuine constitution. Such reflections naturally prompt the thought that, without *judicial independence, a constitution, even if written, remains a kind of fiction. Thus the *USSR constitution, which was a document specifying many of the rights of citizens, could be upheld in a court of law. But if the state had an interest in the outcome, then the judge acted under instructions from the state, and there was no genuine *adjudication. In such a case the constitution can provide no guarantee of the ordinary citizen's rights, even if it purports to prescribe them.

constitutional government

The mode of *limited government in which the *constitution, together with the law and offices that are prescribed by it, provide the limit and ratification of every exercise of power, and in which it is impossible for any officer to transgress the constitution without thereby ceasing to hold power legitimately, and so being removable from office. *Hobbes, *Locke, *Montesquieu and their many followers developed theories of constitutional government, versions of which are now widely accepted as giving both a true representation of political liberty, and the preferred way of exercising political power so that it expresses not the will of those who wield it, but the rights of the citizens whom it governs. Constitutional government nowadays tends to require the *separation of powers, the *rule of law, and the exercise of power through office. Fundamental to all these things is the citizen's ability to proceed against *ultra vires* acts, together with the procedural rules that make legitimate powers discernible. Constitutional government disappears once the edict of an individual or a party becomes overriding in all matters of state, or whenever particular interests that conflict with an alleged 'constitution' cannot in fact be contained by it. Almost all modern states have written constitutions relating to every exercise of power. It seems, however, that only a minority of them are constitutional.

constitutional law

The branch of law that governs the formation, reformation and application of a *constitution. Although a written constitution may to some extent clarify the subject matter of constitutional law, the legal determination of which matters are, and which are not, constitutional (as opposed, say, to *administrative) is always to some extent open to contention. The unwritten constitution of the UK is expressed through a complex and often highly ambiguous constitutional law, which allows much latitude to the courts in determining the constitutional validity of particular acts. For example, parliamentary *privilege is frequently abused for personal, demagogic, or political ends. It is not certain that this is a breach of the constitution. Nor is it clear who, if anyone, has a cause of action, how the action would be adjudicated, or what would be the remedy.

constitutional monarchy

A *monarchy which is not absolute, but *limited by a *constitution, so that, while the *sovereignty of the state is personified in a monarch, the powers of that monarch are determined not by the monarch but by the law. Usually the monarch may be removed from office if he refuses to obey that law even if there is no law which expressly permits this. A constitutional monarchy is a peculiar artifact, in which most executive powers are exercised in the name of the monarch, despite the fact that the monarch himself is unable either to exercise or to forbid them. The residual power that he does possess (e.g. to form a government in times of national emergency) may nevertheless be vital to the government of the state, just as his ceremonial function may be vital to the social order that is thereby governed. *See* *prerogative.

constitutionalism

The advocacy of *constitutional government, i.e. of government channelled through and limited by a constitution. The major current of Western political thought in the seventeenth and eighteenth centuries was constitutionalist, and included *Hobbes, *Locke, *Montesquieu and the *Founding Fathers of the US. There seem to be two distinct thoughts underlying constitutionalism: that a constitution is necessary in order to limit government, and that it is necessary if there is to be government by *consent. While some theorists concentrate on limiting devices (such as the *separation of powers), others concentrate on the devices necessary to obtain and elicit consent (such as *representation). Hence modern constitutionalism has tended to absorb both the traditional attacks on *absolutism, and the subsequent defences of *democracy.

consumer

1. In economics: whoever realizes the *use-value of a good, say, by eating food, by hanging and admiring a picture on his wall, by wearing clothes. The consumer represents the last point of the process of *production, distribution and exchange, and consumption is the aim of economic activity. The theory of consumer behaviour is a major aspect of *neo-classical economic theory. The 'means of consumption' are all those appurtenances which surround and facilitate consumption – such as a house, its furniture, and the means whereby food is prepared and clothing stored. Many socialists, who oppose private ownership in the means of production, distribution and exchange, yet favour private ownership in the means of consumption, as indispensable to human freedom and peaceful existence. (Though how far the means of consumption can be separated from the means of production is a matter of debate: for example, the car owned by a salesman may be used for his business as well as for the pleasure of his family.)

2. The term 'consumer' is *value-free in economic theory, but has a highly value-laden use in certain kinds of political discourse, notably those which recognize a distinction between the 'consumer' attitudes towards objects, and those other, less covetous,

or more contemplative attitudes, in which moral and other values play a significant role. Economists make a distinction between consumer durables (objects which can be used, and still retain a use-value so as to be the subject of possible barter and exchange), and non-durables, which, like food, vanish in the act of consumption. But this does not capture the significant distinction between the value of a house and the value, say, of a friend.

'Consumerism' is a label that is beginning to be applied to those political outlooks that see acquisition and consumption as the principal ends of existence. It is therefore more or less standardly a term of abuse. *See* *consumer society.

consumer organizations

Organizations, which may be either voluntary or (as in the case of the UK Consumer Protection and Advisory Committee) established under government supervision, designed to inform *consumers and to protect them against *restrictive practices, and other factors that lead them to pay more than they need, or obtain less value than they might.

consumer society

A society in which activity is directed to an inordinate extent to the accumulation and consumption of material goods, and in which the ability to consume is held forth as a standard of social achievement to be emulated, being the reward of labour and also its aim. A loose expression used in the criticism, e.g., of *market economies, under the regime of which the motive of labour has often seemed to be little more than the fulfilment of transitory and inessential appetites. The perennial moral conviction that, as Wordsworth expressed it, 'getting and spending we lay waste our powers' is

thus used to criticize the structure of a certain economic arrangement, usually on the supposition that there is some alternative which escapes the criticism (*cf.* *commodity fetishism).

consumer surplus

The excess of the maximum amount a *consumer is prepared to pay for a certain quantity of a good (rather than to forgo that whole quantity) over the amount that he actually pays for it. Such a surplus exists because what a consumer is willing to pay for one extra unit of some good, of which he is already consuming n units, is less than he would have been prepared to pay for the nth unit when consuming $n-1$. (Example: suppose that sausages cost 10p each and that I buy three of them at a total cost of 30p. I might have been induced to part with 20p by the prospect of the first sausage (when I had none), another 15p by the prospect of the second (when I had one), and 10p by the prospect of the third (when I had two), so that the total value to me of the three is 45p and the consumer surplus is 15p. In general consumer surplus arises because of diminishing *marginal utility.)

Consumer surplus provides a monetary measure of the benefit that a consumer derives from the supply of a product, given the terms on which it is made available. It seems therefore to offer the possibility of assessing the net effect on welfare of policies that alter the terms on which different products are supplied. Economists have argued that some systems of *taxation are worse than others because they lead to a greater loss of consumer surplus.

containment, policy of

The policy pursued by the US since 1947 of containing the spread of communism within existing territorial limits, either by armed intervention

(Korea, Vietnam), or by economic and technical assistance (as in Marshall Aid and the Colombo Plan), or by military strength and a network of alliances. The first having failed in Vietnam, and the second having led to a disastrous reaction by non-communist Muslim fundamentalists in Iran, it is no longer clear that such a policy is feasible. Nor, since the collapse of communism and the rise of international terrorism, are its benefits obvious.

contract

In law a contract is an agreement between two or more persons intended to create a legal (and legally enforceable) obligation between them. Contracts can be express, as when promises are uttered and exchanged. Or they may be implied, as when two parties act in full knowledge of each other's aims and behaviour, at least one party knowing that the other is doing what he does only on the assumption of a return which he has been led to expect. (Many quotidian sales and purchases involve such an element of implied contract.) Contracts may also be conditional, as when I agree with you the terms of a contract which is to become binding upon the fulfilment of a condition. A contract may be void (without legal effect) – as in the case of a contract to commit a crime – or voidable – as in the case of a contract made under *duress, or a contract with an infant, which is voidable at the infant's request. Contract must always be distinguished from precontractual negotiations, such as offers, invitations to treat, and tenders, which are not enforceable in law.

Behind the legal idea of contract lies an important moral idea – that of the *autonomous agent who puts himself under obligations through his own voluntary acts, and whose knowing, intentional behaviour can, when based in requisite understanding, be *sufficient* to bind him morally to the performance of some act. He is not bound when his autonomy is violated – e.g. by *coercion, *force, intimidation or fraud. Nor is he bound if he is not, or not yet, fully autonomous (the case of an infant), or when his rationality or understanding are impaired. The idea of the autonomous being who *creates* his obligations is a vital one in modern political theory, since it provides the basis for many ideas of *political obligation and *legitimacy – such as those derived from the postulation of a *social contract.

*Associations can be distinguished into the contractual and the non-contractual. In the first, as in a partnership, members are bound to each other by a contract, the terms of which have been agreed, and can be released from the association by a countervailing agreement among the parties concerned. In the second, as in a *marriage, while there may be a contract to enter into the association and a contract *ancillary* to the association (providing e.g. for the nurture of children), the association itself is neither created, nor modified, by that contract, nor does it have terms that can be negotiated, renegotiated or negated. Its obligations arise in another way – one might say, from its autonomous nature, and not from the agreement of the parties. This difference between contractual and non-contractual associations is also vital to political theory, since a quite different structure of human relations pertains to the two kinds of union. Much will depend, therefore, upon whether one takes the first or the second as the model for the organization either of *civil society or of the *state.

Contract with America

A political manifesto, drawn up by the Republican congressman Dick Armey, and released by the Republican Party during the course of the 1994 US Congressional Election. The Contract promised smaller government and lower taxes, support for entrepreneurs and the entrepreneurial culture, limits to *United Nations influence on US foreign policy, *tort reform and reform of the welfare system. It expressed support for family values and religious initiatives, and promised to return to *civil society the powers that had been stolen from it by the *state.

contradiction

In logic a contradiction consists of the conjunction of a proposition with its negation – i.e. any proposition of the form '*p* and not-*p*'. Since the two conjuncts cannot both be true, the state of affairs described by a contradiction is impossible, a fact that has led some philosophers to conclude that there can be contradictions in thought but not in reality. By contrast, *Hegel's conception of the *dialectic, and various theories that have sprung from it, have fostered the belief that there *can* be contradictions in reality.

One suggestion is this: a person contradicts himself when he believes two incompatible things, and also when he *intends* each of two logically incompatible things, as when he intends to give all his money to the poor and also to buy a new car. When exposed, a contradiction becomes untenable (if the agent seems still to hold on to it, then this is proof that he does not understand it, and therefore does not really hold on to it). But a contradiction can persist just so long as it is, through ignorance, idleness, or self-deception, concealed. I may intend both to pay my debts and to enjoy myself, and persistently neglect the facts which show that I cannot do both.

By extension we can think of human *institutions as exemplifying contradictions. This is a more interesting case, since here the persistence of the contradiction need not depend upon there being some *individual* who is in contradiction with himself. Thus if I aim at *x*, and you aim at not-*x*, we are not in contradiction, but only in *conflict*. However, if an institution is such as to require that part of its membership act so as to produce *x* (whether or not knowingly) while part act so as to produce not-*x*, then it would seem reasonable to say that the institution contains a contradiction, just as an individual who aims simultaneously at *x* and not-*x* is in contradiction (and not just in conflict) with himself. An example might be an educational institution, which is so structured that all pupils learn to question the authority of their teachers, and yet which aims also to inculcate an attitude of unquestioning obedience. It is logically impossible to realize the two purposes, but it is possible for an institution to exist guided and convulsed by the separate pressures that tend towards the incompatible outcomes.

In some such sense it could be that complex social relations involve real (but concealed) contradictions, and not merely conflicts, among rival members or rival groups. For example, the view, held by some *Marxists, that *capitalism contains a contradiction (manifest, e.g., in the *class struggle) might be true. It would be true if it were of the *essence* of capitalism to generate incompatible aims among those bound by this form of *production relation.

Whether there can be contradictions in the material world independent of human thoughts, aims, institutions and relations, is more doubtful. Hegel's belief in such contradictions is usually considered as inseparable from his view that reality is not material. *Engels's enthusiastic affirmation of a true *dialectical *materialism* has usually been found more puzzling. However it was accepted by *Mao, who argued that contradiction is the law of all material development, under socialism and communism as much as under capitalism. He saw this law confirmed by the destruction of all that surrounded him, and failed only to acknowledge that the cause of this destruction was himself.

control

1. Of agents. One agent controls another when the first can provide the necessary and sufficient conditions for the second's actions. Actions that are controlled are intentional, but not free, although the relation of control may be the result of a free choice in both parties (as in a military commission). Control is distinct from *influence, and also from *coercion: it may lack the element of *force that is present in coercion, and is, moreover, a dispositional extended relation, governing a plurality of actions. You could be coerced only once and commanded only once, but it is doubtful that you can be controlled on only one occasion.

2. Of things. An agent controls a thing when (and to the extent that) he can do with that thing as he wishes. Thus control is a matter of degree, restraints on its exercise arising perhaps from law, perhaps from facts of nature. Only an *agent* can have control, since control is exercised in intentional acts. Sometimes 'control' is used in an absolute sense – as in 'controlling interest' – where it signifies that there is no greater control vested in any other agent.

The concept of control is important in discussing the *separation of ownership from control, collective control (which is applicable only if we can speak of *collective choice), and the distinction between the *rights and *powers of ownership.

convention

1. In the general acceptance of the term, convention is distinguished from both *custom and *law, although all three terms are used to describe regularities in the intentional behaviour of rational beings. Convention has the fragility and changeability of law, together with the inexplicit, natural-seeming character of custom. It may be a motive in the mind of someone who could not state or describe it, but like law, it contains an *obligation which is independent of *habit. Its arbitrariness, like the arbitrariness of *positive law, is readily understood, so that conventions change not only in the course of nature but also at will (for example, changes in dress precipitated by tailors: but *see* *fashion). At the same time there may be transactions of such complexity that they can be governed, if at all, only by convention, and not by law alone. This is fairly evidently true of the workings of an unwritten *constitution. It is a convention in the UK that the monarch must accept the advice of the ministry for the time being, but any attempt to embody this convention in a law would undermine the constitutional supremacy of the monarch and so make the convention inapplicable. The example shows the large part that conventions may play in politics: it may often be a political act of the greatest importance to uphold or defy them. The constitutional stability of the UK is perhaps partly to be explained by the manner in which rapid changes of law take place against a slowly shifting background of conventions, themselves upheld by customs sufficiently inarticulate to remain outside the forum of speculative reform.

2. The term may also denote an international meeting to discuss some matter of common interest, and is further used to describe agreements

(specifically, in *international law) which may or may not also be given legal force: such as The Hague Convention and the Geneva Conventions. (*See* *asylum.)

convergence thesis

Following *Weber, political scientists have sometimes argued that *capitalist and *socialist societies will gradually converge, as *bureaucratization, large-scale planning and impersonal forms of social order exert themselves. The convergence thesis was applied to Western and Soviet-style economies by certain academic *sovietologists. To those who have lived under a communist regime the thesis is ridiculous, and its falsehood is now obvious to everyone, even to sovietologists.

convertibility

A currency is freely convertible if it can be openly sold against other currencies, at prices determined by the market. Many states either forbid or severely control the buying and selling of their currency, thus imposing artificial rates of exchange, which form a tax on all purchases made by a foreign buyer. The ability of a currency to maintain its exchange rate in a free market is one index of the health of the national economy that it represents. This ability is, however, influenced by other factors, including history, symbolism and assessments of social and political stability.

cooperative movement

A political movement founded on the belief that the means of production, distribution, exchange or consumption should be owned and controlled by cooperatives, i.e. by voluntary associations owned not by investors but either by the members themselves or by patrons, and run by directors, who are also members. The aim is to secure equality by a periodic *redistribution of *profits and to eliminate *competition between the members. The cooperative is a mode of ownership which is both compatible with (indeed, a form of) private property, and at the same time not dependent on any division between owner and employee.

The movement began with the Rochdale Equitable Pioneers in 1844, who hoped to realize, within the framework of nineteenth-century industrialism, the ideals formulated by *Owen and *Fourier. The movement flourished in the UK and US (especially in the Midwest), and more recently in France, Italy and (to some extent) Germany. In the UK the emphasis has been on cooperative associations of consumers, whereas on the Continent it has been on cooperative production. From 1918 onwards cooperative movement candidates for the UK Parliament have contested elections in alliance with the *Labour Party, and the movement now has little independent political identity. However it remains an important ideal, and the modern form of cooperative known as a 'housing association' has to some extent influenced the character of land tenure in UK cities.

coordination

The process whereby distinct actions or operations are brought into line, so as not to impede, or actively to assist one another. For example, the French rule of traffic control: *priorité à droite*. Coordination problems are an important topic of study in *game theory, and recur throughout the political realm.

Copenhagen consensus

A project launched by the Danish Environmental Assessment Institute which aims to define global problems, to evaluate alternative proposals and to present reasonable solutions. It addresses issues of world health, the environment, water shortages, education, world trade, and so on, and in general promotes free market rather than statist solutions, to the indignation of many environmentalists.

corporal punishment
See *children.

corporate personality
1. In law, a corporate person is an *association, such as a firm, a school or a church, which has been incorporated, so as to become a *person in law, with rights, duties, privileges and obligations that can be the subject matter of legal dispute. The rights and liabilities of a corporate person are not identical with the rights and liabilities of its members, and may survive even when there *are* no members, as when the directors of a firm all resign without appointing successors, even though the firm is still trading, with debts and claims that have not been honoured.

2. Morally speaking, corporate persons exist even if there is no law that recognizes them. All reasonable people assume that schools, churches, clubs and societies have moral relations with their members and with other institutions. Not only do they have rights and liabilities in law; they also have duties and rights of a moral kind. You can *owe* to them debts of gratitude, for example; you can feel bound in duty and allegiance towards them; you can resent and disapprove of them; you can praise them and blame them – and all this in the sense that implies a full personal relationship. It seems, therefore, that our world contains persons who are not human, and not incarnate in any animal organism. These persons make free choices, and are held responsible for them; they are objects of affection, anger and esteem. And it is partly through our relationships with them

that our own personalities are formed. Is this mysterious? *Hegel and his followers say not, since for them the life of the spirit (or *Geist*) is constantly realizing itself in ever more 'objective' forms, and must do so if the 'subjective spirit' is to enjoy its freedom. *Empiricists tend to be more sceptical. Attitudes to the idea of corporate personality greatly affect the conceptions of the *state that are prevalent in political philosophy.

Roman law recognized two kinds of association – the *societas* and the *universitas*, the first being constituted by a contractual relation between its members, who are the sole owners of its property, the second being able to hold property of its own. The *universitas* is the original of modern ideas of corporate personality, and gave its name to the most important modern instance – the *alma mater* which has formed the leading personalities of European culture. In English law many associations that are persons in the moral sense (for example, clubs and small-scale charities) are 'unincorporated' from the legal point of view. This anomaly matters less on account of the law of *trusts. English law also recognizes the 'corporation sole', i.e. the corporation with at most one member, the most important instance of which is the *Crown. This corporate person goes on existing between the death or abdication of one monarch and the coronation of the next, and all subjects owe their allegiance to it during this vacant time, just as it retains the duty to protect them and to enforce the law.

corporate social responsibility
Known in business as CSR, the expression denotes the practice, of increasing importance in the modern economy, of setting aside a portion of the profits from a business in order to support 'good causes' that would be recognized

as such by those in whose eyes the business wishes to appear as a responsible citizen. Ostensibly a worthy use of funds, CSR also has the aspect of a protection racket, through which a business buys off potentially hostile *pressure groups and *single-issue fanatics, by contributing to their favourite causes, regardless of whether this is in the long-term interests of the general public or the shareholders of the firm. Thus the major petroleum companies devote their CSR funds to environmental projects, retain environmentalists as consultants, and advertise themselves as ecological heroes – which does nothing to reduce the emissions from the consumption of fossil fuels, but everything to massage the lobbyists whose livelihood has come to depend on opposing fossil fuels. Critics of CSR therefore see it as a process whereby business is led to endorse vociferous *political correctness at the expence of genuine public spirit and old-fashioned charity. Defenders reply that without the vociferous lobbyists there would be no pressure on businesses to behave as citizens at all. *See* *stakeholder.

corporate state

A state in which government represents and is answerable, not to the individual citizen, but to the various *corporations of which the individual is a functional part. The corporations are *autonomous in the manner of the medieval *estates and *guilds, and have an analogous political role, mediating between the individual and the central power, and generating independent allegiances which will be pooled and reconciled in the common submission to a single government. The idea of the corporate state has its origins in medieval Roman Catholic ideas of government, and was later applauded (although not usually put into practice) by *fascism, and by the governments that grew out of the fascist movement. It has been partly put into practice (although neither applauded nor acknowledged) by successive governments in the UK, which have formed policy in consultation with, e.g., the Trades Unions Congress, the Confederation of British Industry, and other bodies that represent corporate powers rather than individual citizens. The rise of organized *lobbying has also involved a move towards a new kind of corporate state.

corporation

1. In law: a group of individuals, or a series of holders of an *office, that is deemed to possess *corporate personality. Corporations must be distinguished from unincorporated associations, in which no independent legal entity is created or deemed to exist In UK law corporations are of two kinds: aggregate, to which more than one individual may belong (e.g. a *company), and sole, in which one individual at a time holds an office that is passed to a successor (for example, the *Crown which is a distinct legal entity from the human being who wears it; or a minister).

2. More widely, any organization that acquires a corporate identity, whether or not it counts as a corporation in law. For example, a trade union, which acts and suffers very much as a single entity. In this sense 'corporation' is used in the above definition of *corporate state, to denote any entity that has some control over its members and acts on their behalf (whether or not they also have control over it), and which is also an *autonomous or at any rate partly autonomous institution. Some think that all corporations in sense 2. ought to be corporations in sense 1., so that their actions should be wholly circumscribed by law. But it is impossible in

practice and difficult in theory to see how this might be done.

corporatism (or: corporativism)
The theory and practice of the *corporate state as developed in *fascist Italy (and also, in more tempered form, in the Spain of General Franco). Inspired by aspects of Roman Catholic social doctrine, this attempted to justify the organization of the economic system into 'corporations' subordinate to the state, and also argued that such an economic system would render political *representation superfluous. The economy was divided into associations (called 'syndicates') of workers, employers and the professions; only one syndicate was allowed in each branch of industry, and all officials were either fascist politicians or else loyal to the fascist cause. According to law the syndicates were autonomous, but in fact they were run by the state. The 'corporations' united the syndicates in a given industry, but made no pretence at autonomy from the state. The theory held that, because the people are not politically articulate, their interests could be consulted only through institutions related directly to their occupations. A small ruling *élite of politically competent leaders would, if placed in charge of those institutions, both guide and be guided by the people.

The term 'corporativism' was also used by *Gramsci, partly in order to criticize the fascist theory of the corporate state, and partly in order to describe what he took to be a general feature of the development of capitalist society, in which workers see their interest in terms of their place within a corporation, rather than in the universal terms required for political understanding. He defined the awakening of a class to *politics in terms of its ability to 'go beyond corporativism'.

The tendency of modern democractic governments to consult corporate bodies representing defined interests within the state, such as the Trade Unions Congress in the UK, confederations of industry and other organised lobby groups has meant the emergence of a new kind of 'bottom up' corporatism, in distinction to the 'top down' approach of the fascists. Some writers distinguish the two as 'liberal' and 'authoritarian' corporatism respectively.

corruption
In the political context corruption means using public office for private gain, whether financial or social, and without due regard for the public duties attached to the office in question. A politician who accepts bribes in order to legislate in the interests of the donor is corrupt in that sense, as is a politician who trades publicly administered privileges for sexual favours. In certain parts of the world corruption is endemic, not because of any moral depravity in the politicians, but because of social expectations that undermine the very idea of public office and its duties. For example, it is expected of a politician in many parts of Africa that he use his office to help members of his family and tribe: not to do so would be a gesture of intolerable ingratitude, and a politician who maintained the standards of honesty expected at Westminster would be regarded as cold-hearted and even suspected of alien allegiances.

Corruption is a matter of degree, and there are an increasing number of marginal cases that make it very difficult to distinguish the innocent from the guilty. The distinction between legitimate *lobbying and downright bribery is not always easy to draw, as recent cases in the US Congress show. Furthermore, in the UK, people can obtain personal privileges and legislative goals by giving funds to political parties: a great many peerages are purchased in this way, and the Political Animal Lobby, which gave a million pounds to the Labour Party, was rewarded with the ban on *hunting for which it had lobbied. The Party responded to criticism, however, by saying that it would have banned hunting in any case, so that it was not influenced by the gift. This excuse, universally available, is what makes the matter difficult to decide in any particular case.

cosmopolitanism

1. Belief in the ancient *Stoic ideal of the 'cosmopolis', or 'world-state', to which all human beings or *rational creatures necessarily belong, and which they must attempt to realize in their actions, regardless of the local conditions which may frustrate them. The ideal underlies *Augustine's theocratic universalism, and *Dante's conception of 'world empire'. Its greatest advocate in modern times has been *Kant, whose prescription for a 'perpetual peace' involves the generation of an international federation of peace-loving states obedient to the conception, incipient in the thinking of every moral agent, of a 'kingdom of ends' in which everything is as it ought to be, and ought to be as it is.

The Stoic ideal underlies a more derogatory usage:

2. The belief in, and pursuit of, a style of life which is cosmopolitan in the sense of showing an acquaintance with, and an ability to incorporate, the manners, habits, languages and social customs of cities throughout the world. To be distinguished from *internationalism and from sense 1. (both involving the belief in and pursuit of a single way of life valid for all people everywhere) in its emphasis on the city (Greek: *polis*) and its culture, and in its desire for a kind of virtuosity,

which does not so much align people as distinguish them. In this sense, the cosmopolitan is often seen as a kind of parasite, who depends upon the quotidian lives of others to create the various local flavours and identities in which he dabbles. Hence:

3. A term of abuse, used by totalitarians of all shades, to identify the slippery, treacherous enemy within, the 'rootless cosmopolitan' (Hitler) or 'cosmopolitan bourgeois' (Stalin), who usually turns out to be cultured, liberal and Jewish.

cost

The cost of an action or policy consists in any harm received, any outlay incurred or any benefit forgone in its exercise. There are as many kinds of cost as there are varieties of human benefit and *harm.

Economists distinguish historical costs – actual costs incurred at the time of a transaction – from the current costs of that transaction. See *cost–benefit analysis, *opportunity cost.

cost–benefit analysis

Analysis of a social or economic policy in terms of *costs and benefits, where these are construed as widely as is thought necessary to capture the issues which the policy involves. Cost–benefit analysis does not (and should not) confine itself to immediate economic losses and gains, but endeavours to include as many as possible of the harms and benefits that will ensue upon a given policy, including long-run costs and benefits. The policy is then deemed to be reasonable only if there is a balance of benefit over cost, *optimal only if there is a greater balance of benefit over cost than might be achieved by any alternative policy.

Cost–benefit analysis is a useful tool in economics, but its wider application depends upon two assumptions: (i) that costs and benefits are all quantifiable – an assumption easy to make in the case of marketable and reproducible products, but difficult where objects held to have absolute *value (for example, human lives) are involved; (ii) that the various costs and benefits are also commensurable with one another, so that, for example, the cost of forgoing a dinner might be set against the ultimate benefit of losing weight. *Bentham invented a 'felicific calculus' which was the first systematic attempt at cost–benefit analysis, and which he sought to extend to cover the entire fields of moral, legal and political reasoning. He was able to satisfy the two assumptions above, first by estimating all costs and benefits in terms of a *single* polarity of variables – pleasure and pain – and secondly by assuming that all pleasures, whether actual or hypothetical, can be measured against each other. (Thus the pursuit of a pleasure is reasonable to the extent that it is probable, large, near at hand, and so on.) This, combined with the *utilitarian criterion of optimality, enabled Bentham to quantify every political and moral problem, and sketch solutions to such problems that have never ceased to arouse incredulity, not the least on account of the number of acts deemed rational for which it would be absurd to postulate pleasure as a motive. This has led many to say that we cannot expect the realm of human values to be so readily subjected to mathematical discipline, and that the utility of cost–benefit analysis is confined almost wholly to the economic sphere. Which is not to say that the costs and benefits of a policy should not be pondered in advance of embarking on it, but only that we should not assume that it will always be *irrational* to refuse to weigh some value in terms of benefits. But *see* *rationality.

Council of Europe

Founded in 1949, as a forum through which the European states could solve their problems by *consensus rather than force, the Council of Europe was and remains independent of the *European Union, representing an alternative model of European cooperation, and one that respects the sovereignty of nation states. Its principal products have been the *European Convention on Human Rights, the European Social Charter and the Convention on Data Protection. Its Court of Human Rights in Strasbourg has no powers of enforcement, but issues judgements that are nevertheless taken as authoritative by the nations that subscribe to the Convention – which includes some outside the EU itself, such as Norway and Turkey.

Council of Ministers

See *European Union.

Council for Mutual Economic Aid

See *Comecon.

counter-culture

Term popularized by T. Roszak (*The Making of a Counter-Culture*, 1969), and used to denote the deliberate fostering and creation of a *culture suited to an *alternative society, in overt defiance of traditional forms, customs, manners and values. It is usually assumed that a counter-culture must be expressive of the ethos of liberty, toleration, and community based on mutual respect. It principally expresses itself in aggressive gestures designed to offend those who are merely tolerant towards (as opposed to committed to) its values.

counterfinality

The tendency of an act or policy to thwart its own aim. Counterfinality arises frequently in cases of *social choice, and is exemplified in various problems of *game theory, such as the *prisoner's dilemma, and in social *contradictions.

counter-revolutionary

Term first used in 1793, by *Condorcet, who defined it as a 'revolution in the contrary direction'. However *Maistre, who advocated counter-revolution, described it as 'not a contrary revolution, but the contrary of a revolution' (1796). The term has since been made current by *Marxist thought and practice. It has two distinct meanings:

1. (Maistre.) A person, act or attitude opposed to some given *revolution, or to revolution as such.

2. (Condorcet,) A person, act or attitude that seeks to produce some *new* revolution designed to overthrow the order established by the last, perhaps in the hope of restoring (in whole or in part) the original government that preceded it.

The term was also used as a term of abuse in Soviet *propaganda, to denote any rebellion against Soviet dominion, even on the part of those who never had a revolution, never wanted one, and asserted only what they considered to be *human rights.

countervailing power

The forces that arise, particularly in *mixed economies, to counterbalance the bargaining power of large buyers, sellers and producers: e.g. the *trade unions, organizations of distributors and consumers, government operations against *monopolies and *administered prices, and so on. The term was introduced by J.K. Galbraith (*American Capitalism: The Concept of Countervailing Power*, 1952) in order to describe the new kind of economic organization that seemed to have emerged in the place of *laissez-faire* capitalism, and to have superseded classical market competition. He argued that the state should always intercede on the part of the weaker power.

country

1. Country, as opposed to town: those parts of a territory in which there are few and small residential areas, and in which the major part of the *land is given over to agricultural uses. The country is normally characterized by a lower *social mobility than the town, a greater attachment to traditional modes of production, to custom, and to social *hierarchy, and (normally) a greater conservatism of political outlook. The town, by contrast, exhibits social mobility, highly divided and diversified labour, *bourgeois attitudes towards trade and production, and a constant friction between social classes. Theories of the emergence of town from country emphasize these factors, and (as a rule) the distinct economic relations that they exemplify. See *town and country.

The country and the landscape (countryside) remain immensely important as symbols in British social and political life. The obsession with country life in British literature has been interpreted (e.g. by Raymond Williams) as a sign of its ideological nature – a constant turning away from the realities of the modern city towards a vanished social order, whose unreality protects it from criticism. Others see country life in Britain as the vital and self-renewing thing that it always was, and the tendency of British writers – and especially children's writers – to turn their attention to it as nothing but a recognition of realities. The dispute here is mirrored in the US, in the intellectual and political conflict over the *agrarian movements.

2. A 'country' may also be an independent *sovereign state, identified, however, not in terms of its political

features, but in terms of its *territory and *jurisdiction. The frequency of this usage emphasizes the important role that territorial conceptions play in identifying and explaining political entities. It also illustrates an area of potential confusion in political thought, since the relation between state and country seems not to be determinate. Thus Russia is the same country now as in the novels of Tolstoy; but is it the same state? Could A be the same state as B but a completely different country? (Suppose a given set of political institutions is simply transported, together with language and customs, from one part of the world to another: *cf.* the founding of Israel, which some believe did not occur in the twentieth century.) The problems here are not unlike those that arise in trying to describe the relation between a human *person and his body.

3. Sometimes the word 'country' is used to denote *only* the territorial aspect of a state, so that a country remains the same whatever the political institutions that govern it, and whatever people should reside within its borders. This raises the question of how countries may be counted (for normally they are counted *in terms of* the political divisions that create boundaries). Take the former Czechoslovakia: was it one country? Or two (since it incorporated two *nations)? Or three (Bohemia, Moravia, Slovakia)? Or arbitrarily many? Each way of counting seems to point back to some present or previous political division.

4. In UK electioneering parlance, the 'country' signifies the *electorate, and 'going to the country' is a somewhat antiquated way of describing an appeal to the electorate (usually through the declaration of a general *election) to support the existing government.

coup d'état

A change of government by *force, resulting in a change of constitution, and brought about by those who already hold some form of power, whether military or political. The instigation of a coup thereby transforms the terms on which their office is held from a public trust into a private possession. A *coup d'état* supposedly differs from *revolution in that the latter is effected by the people, or at least by those who hold no power under existing arrangements, and perhaps represent themselves as 'leaders of the people' in order to gain it.

Examples of *coups d'état* include Napoleon I's seizure of power in 1799, Napoleon III's in 1851, Mussolini's in 1925, and in all probability (although the case is disputed) the seizure of power by the *bolsheviks in October 1917.

coup de Prague

In 1948, the Czech and Slovak *communist parties, having become the largest single body within a constitutional assembly of elected *representatives, created a single party state by a combination of demonstrations, threats, and violence, while maintaining for a time the outward appearance of constitutional legitimacy. A *coup de Prague* therefore means any quasi-constitutional seizure of power, backed by subversion and force, which effectively abolishes the constitution.

courts

Originally a court was a monarch's or great lord's palace; the name was then transferred to the society surrounding him, to some of the institutions of *parliament (*cf.* the Spanish *cortes*), and now generally to all institutions in which people sit in judgement over each other. Certain distinctions among types of court are important in understanding the practice of *adjudication:

(i) Criminal *v.* civil. The first deals with accusations of crime brought either by the state (perhaps through a representative, such as the UK Director of Public Prosecutions) or by a private citizen; the second deals with a *dispute* between parties over some matter governed by *law.

(ii) Courts of general *v.* courts of special jurisdiction. The first can deal with more or less any kind of case, the second only with specific matters (e.g. matrimonial disputes) mentioned in their constitution.

(iii) Superior *v.* inferior courts. A superior court is one that deals with more important cases, involves more qualified and specially selected officers and judges, and so on. An inferior court may involve an unqualified (and unpaid) magistrate, sitting as judge, and often its decisions may be made subject to review by a superior court. The distinction here must not, however, be confused with that between:

(iv) Appellate *v.* trial court. Judgements of the first bind the reasoning of the second (*see* *precedent), and, in appropriate circumstances, appeal can be made from a decision of the second to the first. Appellate systems may be many-tiered, as in the UK, where appeal can be made (provided permission is granted) from the Court of Appeal to the House of Lords. The last-named court is also the upper chamber of Parliament, and embodies in institutional form the traditional right of the *subject to appeal to his *sovereign.

(v) In the US, distinction must also be made between federal and state courts. Since there are separate systems of law for each state, in addition to the federal system which governs the US as a whole, separate courts are required, with officers of distinct competence and authority.

Among courts of special jurisdiction, certain examples stand out as being of independent political interest. Courts martial, for example, have a structure that fits them for the direct imposition of a discipline that is more surveillant than the ordinary *law. Here the courts are instituted *within* the armed forces, under the special discipline there applicable, and appeal is not normally granted to any court of more general jurisdiction. Compare the recently instituted industrial tribunals (*see* *industrial law), from which appeal is normally possible. These were established in the UK in 1964, and consist of three members, of whom the chairman alone need be legally qualified; they exercise jurisdiction under statutes dealing with a wide variety of disputes between employer and employee – such as complaints of unfair dismissal – which are not covered by the contractual relation between them. In both these cases we find forms of adjudication that have developed, not so much because of the content of special laws, as because of the need to adapt the administration of justice to special institutions. There are now also international courts of special jurisdiction, including the European Court of Human Rights (est. 1954), which has no power to enforce its judgements (*see* *Council of Europe).

The French Revolution introduced a new judicial institution, the 'revolutionary court or tribunal', in which states, or even private citizens, declare themselves to be enacting in judicial form the precepts or ideals of an existing or projected *revolution. Here people are tried for offences which may be wholly unspecific, and which often do not correspond to any law knowable to the offender or interesting to his accuser. A right of defence may not exist and prosecutor and judge are almost invariably identical, if not in person at least in aim. In such arrangements, it is often argued, elementary principles of *natural justice are ignored, so that it is a misnomer to speak of the result as a form of adjudication. To call such tribunals 'courts' is therefore sometimes criticized as a misleading if not dangerous usage, whereby violence is turned into justice by purely semantic means. The reply, that the real difference between violence and justice *is* merely semantic, consisting in the choice of terminology best suited to the interests of a ruling or oppressing class, is seldom withheld.

covenant

In law, an 'agreement under seal' (i.e. ceremonially sealed by the signatories), or, in a deed relating to land, or implied in such a deed, a condition binding on one or the other of the parties and attached to the land. The term 'covenant' was also used more generally, to denote any particularly binding promise, such as God's covenant to Noah. It is used in this sense by *Hobbes, for example, in describing the *social contract, and has also passed into modern political usage, to denote an obligation which establishes (and therefore is not created by) *international law. Thus the 'Covenant of the League of Nations' refers to the original charter which formed the first part of the Treaty of Versailles, 1919, and which created the League of Nations as an international body.

craft

The skilful adapting of means to ends. The craftsman is normally thought of as the *complete* producer of a *commodity, who does everything necessary to its manufacture. He is therefore distinguished from the *detail labourer, who plays only a *part* in the production of any commodity, and who, while employed as a means, need have no perception of the end which he thereby furthers. Thus a craftsman (such as a shoemaker) must be the master not of one skill but of many related skills. It may also be, as some have argued, that his work absorbs him and satisfies him more completely than the work of the detail labourer, so that he may escape from the *alienation to which the latter is habitually subject.

The last suggestion underlies much of the admiration for, and desire to restore, craft in the place of detail production among romantic socialists and cultural conservatives in the nineteenth century. Chief among these were *Ruskin, *Morris and the Pre-Raphaelites, who offered penetrating psychological analyses of the phenomenon that they advocated, but few feasible projects that would tend to restore it. More recent thinkers, rejecting their ideas, have nevertheless often tried to imagine ways in which the wholeness and satisfyingness of craft can be instilled into the industrial process. In all such discussions, the important fact has been, not the mechanical nature of detail labour, so much as its unnatural isolation from the process as a whole, and the supposedly incoherent view of his own *agency that the labourer thereby obtains. The rise of the *service economy has to some extent rendered these discussions irrelevant.

creationism

The belief that the world and all things in it have been created, typically by a single God with the attributes specified by the leading monotheistic religions. Creationism, once accepted as common sense, has been thrown in doubt by *Darwinism, which seems to explain the appearance of design in our world without reference to a creator. But *see* *intelligent design.

credibility

Used of a policy (especially a policy of defence) to denote its ability to persuade those who need to be persuaded that it will, in the declared circumstances, be put into effect. The term is also used of a politician, to denote his ability to persuade others that he will govern according to a professed programme or *ideology; while a 'credibility gap' (US term) exists whenever there is a perceived disparity between official utterances and the facts surrounding them.

crime

In law, any offence declared by the *legislature as contrary to law, whether or not it constitutes a moral wrong, and whether or not some other party has a cause of civil action in respect of it. Any conduct may be declared criminal by law, and while many moral evils are also crimes, the categories of the morally wrong and the legally criminal are almost nowhere coextensive. (*See* *law and morality.) Indeed, if *civil disobedience is ever justified, this must be because there are actions which are morally obligatory, and yet also crimes.

The most important distinguishing characteristic of crime is that it confers on the state the legal right to punish the offender (rather than the legal duty to compel him to compensate the person he has wronged, though in primitive systems of law the precise character of this distinction is often obscured). One must distinguish, in UK and US law, *common law crimes from *statutory crimes, the former including murder, theft and rape, and corresponding for the most part to antecedent moral intuitions about what must not be done. (It should be noted that theft has been lifted out of the common law of England by statutes designed to systematize judicial findings.) It is also necessary to distinguish crimes according to their seriousness. English law used to recognize treason, felonies

and misdemeanours, allowing to the third a very low degree of culpability: in other legal systems (that of the US, for example) this idea of the 'petty crime' is still enshrined in law.

The most important intellectual construct involved in the understanding of crime is that of the uniting of the guilty act (*actus reus*) and the guilty mind (*mens rea*). In English and US law most important crimes require both components. For example, the *actus reus* of murder is the causing of the death of an innocent. The *mens rea* is intending death, or intending to cause 'grievous bodily harm'. Both parts of the definition of a crime may present great problems of application: what is meant by 'causing' in the definition of the *actus reus*? And what is meant by 'intending' in the definition of the *mens rea*? Such questions, ultimately philosophical, occupy much of the subject-matter of *jurisprudence, and indicate the extreme complexity of our ordinary understanding of human acts. The element of *mens rea* may cover very complex states of mind, such as negligence (a disposition that involves no specific intention), a general desire to harm, and so on. Defences of insanity, diminished responsibility and the like involve trying to disprove *mens rea*.

There exist crimes for which no element of *mens rea* is required, crimes of *strict liability. In UK and US law only statutory crimes can be such, and then only when the absence of the requirement of *mens rea* is made explicit in the statute; else, by judicial construction, the element of *mens rea* will, in the interests of *natural justice, be inferred (see the House of Lords judgement in *Sweet* v. *Parsley*, 1970). Such statutory crimes are normally (but not always) of the kind that might otherwise have been described as misdemeanours – parking offences, and the like. Some legal systems, however, seem to permit strict liability even for serious offences, and so to issue severe punishments for wholly unintended acts. (Examples: Chinese and Soviet law, the *sharî'ah*.)

criminal law

The branch of law dealing with *crime and *punishment. In England the criminal law is founded in *common law, substantially modified by statute in 1861, and further in the twentieth century. In Scotland criminal law is still, for the most part, common law, while the English common law of crime persists in the US, adapted in certain respects to the different circumstances there prevailing. In most cases the application of criminal law is governed by the following basic principles of *justice:

(i) *Nulla poena sine lege.* No act can be punished unless a law exists that forbids it, however immoral, anti-social or destructive it may be.

(ii) Criminal law must be clear and unambiguous, so as to give 'fair warning'.

(iii) Criminal statutes are to be construed strictly and not extended by analogy.

(iv) *Retroactive legislation is impermissible, unless expressly authorized by statute.

Such provisions are widely held to capture an important element in the idea of *natural justice, and impose real constraints on judicial construction. They are tantamount to the theory that when deciding a case, the judge does not make law, but discovers it. This theory is, however, a theory about what must be thought by the participants in the judicial process, not a theory about what must be true for that process to be possible. See further *hard cases.

criminology

The scientific study of criminal behaviour, often thought to have been founded by Cesare Lombroso (1835–1909), who attempted to trace criminal conduct to certain physical and biological characteristics of the criminal (*see* *atavism). In fact the study had already been begun in the eighteenth century with Cesare Beccaria's *On Crimes and Punishments*, 1764, an application of *hedonist principles to the study of the causes of crime, and had been continued subsequently by *Bentham.

Modern criminology is of wide scope, and concerns itself with almost every question concerning crime and punishment, including why criminal law becomes law, why societies punish criminals in the way they do, and the nature and effects of the various kinds of punishment. Emphasis has shifted from the exclusive concentration on the criminal, towards a more general sociological analysis. An extreme version of this shift is to be found in the work of the French philosopher and social historian *Foucault, who shifts the emphasis from: what causes the criminal to behave as he does to: what causes society to punish him – for, on Foucault's view, neither crime nor punishment can be judged against some absolute standard of normality.

crisis management

After the Cuban missile crisis of November 1962 the US Secretary of Defense (McNamara) said that 'there is no longer any such thing as strategy, only crisis management', meaning that diplomatic relations reveal their meaning and potential only in crisis, and all foreign policy is focused on surviving crises.

crisis of capitalism (or: crisis of capitalist production)

An expression used by Marx, and by many Marxists, to denote the situation in which capitalism, having harnessed *productive forces and turned them to its own ends, must go on to develop those forces beyond its power to contain them, so that the *production relations of capitalism begin to fetter the productive forces. Finally, the fetters burst asunder, along with all the social and political *superstructure that rests on them. Socialists differ as to the extent of their belief in such crises, and as to the precise explanation offered for their occurrence. In all versions of the theory the crisis is supposed to be inevitable, either because it is of the essence of capitalism to foster growth beyond the limits that can be contained by it, or because capitalism generates social oppositions that can only exacerbate over time.

Defenders of capitalism argue in reply either (a) that capitalism is a self-equilibrating system, that avoids major crises, or (b) that crises are part of the *health* of capitalism, and that systems which strive to avoid them will eventually collapse. It seems that the Marxist theory of crisis has now entered a crisis, in that nobody seriously believes it, other than those who have devoted their lives to teaching it.

crisis of socialism

Term used by opponents of Marxism to point to the supposed facts:

(i) that the predicted internal collapse of capitalism (*see* *crisis of capitalism) has not occurred;

(ii) that in those societies called socialist there is never a satisfactory rate of growth, but rather a constant tendency to overproduction of some essential goods, and underproduction of others.

Some add that it is only under *market conditions that *equilibrium is possible, that market conditions are not possible without private property, and that out of private property capitalism must inevitably develop. The crisis of socialism became a reality in

the 1980s, with the social, economic and political collapse of communism, and the near-universal recognition that market relations and private property are indispensable parts of any viable economic order.

critical theory

The theoretical outlook associated with Max Horkheimer, *Habermas, *Adorno and other members of the *Frankfurt school who, while professing allegiance to Marxist methods of historical analysis, have seen the principal significance of Marxism as residing not in the theory of history, nor in the explanation of economic value and the process of production, but in the conceptual tools which it provides for the critical analysis of consciousness – e.g. *false consciousness, *alienation and *ideology. The early Marx is valued partly because he bears the imprint of *Hegel's speculative cultural analysis, and partly because he views the conflicts involved in capitalism through their effects in the consciousness of its denizens. Many other sources also enter into critical theory, including 'systems theory' or *cybernetics, and *hermeneutics. The master-thought seems to be this: that consciousness stands to be interpreted, and in its interpretation the moral nature of social arrangements is revealed, in addition to their relationship to the economic system in which they occur. Associated with this 'diagnostic' analysis of consciousness is the attempt to explain *crisis and *catastrophe in all their forms, and on all the levels of self-awareness at which they are revealed. Among the products of critical theory only Adorno's and Eissler's music criticism has had a lasting influence. However, the emigration of the Frankfurt school's leading members to the US gave them a kind of after-life, through the New School of Social Thought, which they founded there in New York.

Croce, Benedetto (1866–1952)
Italian *idealist philosopher and politician, who wrote works of aesthetics, criticism and cultural history. These were influential partly on account of their attempt to translate idealist thought into a style accessible to all educated people. Croce developed a theory of expression, as the necessary embodiment without which the mental life of the subject is formless and uncomprehended, and in terms of this theory attempted to show the importance of individuality in our knowledge of each other and the world. He affirmed the importance of the 'spirit' in human affairs and in history, and developed a theory of history according to which all true history is contemporary history – i.e. history as now perceived. He believed that history is the 'story of liberty', in which the moral life of humanity achieves its elaboration. The true bearer of moral value and moral freedom is the individual, although he achieves his fulfilment in the 'ethical universal', which is the state as conceived by the historian, as an expression of spirit, rather than the state as conceived, e.g., by the fascist demagogues, as an instrument of control. (Croce's initial support for fascism became overt hostility in 1925, when the first fascist dictatorship was established. Thereafter he was chief intellectual spokesman for liberalism in Italy, denounced by both Mussolini and *Gramsci.)

Croce's version of *liberal individualism was expanded in such a way as to preserve the traditional Hegelian defence of social existence and shared institutions. He gave an important assessment of the value of art and culture, and was influential on both liberal and conservative thought during the first half of the twentieth century. He is now chiefly consulted for his pioneering work on aesthetics

(*Estetica*, 1902), which introduced concepts that influenced the entire twentieth-century development of the subject.

crowd
A mass of people gathered together, but without formal bonds of *association, which neverthelss responds collectively, so as to present itself as a single force. The emergence of the crowd as an *agent of revolution during the French Revolution transformed the contemporary perception of political events, and the important role of crowds in modern politics has stimulated the study of their social and political significance. Crowds are more powerful than individuals, in that they are larger, and also capable of generating a sense of release from all moral and social restraint; hence crowds show virtues of sacrifice and vices of cruelty which no individual can show and which most people regard with amazement or abhorrence when not themselves absorbed into a mass of people. Crowds are also less powerful than individuals, in that they are without definite will or purpose until one is provided, and are open to irrational persuasion, influence and leadership: hence crowds can be controlled in ways that an individual may resist, partly because they generate public acceptance of all common conduct. Thus crowds can be used by a leader as a means to enhance and exercise his own power, and may yet have comparatively little power of their own should the leader be removed.

Sociological studies have varied from the specific – concentrating, for example, on such phenomena as crowd hysteria – to the highly general, as exemplified by Elias Canetti in *Crowds and Power*, 1960. Canetti argues (contentiously) that the instinct to form into a crowd is founded on a spontaneous reversal of the normal fear of being touched. In this reversal individuals 'discharge' their differences and become miraculously equal, borrowing power from their sudden union. This experience is supposed to explain many political phenomena: not only war, racial persecution, ceremony, and the peculiar kinds of 'closed' crowd known as religious congregations, but also such institutional crowds as the UK *Parliament, whose behaviour is explained by the fact that parliamentary *privilege encloses its members in a crowd by extending an indefinite permission to each of them. Even the sense of justice is traced by Canetti to the feelings of equality experienced at their most vivid among crowds, while submission to the crowd identity is offered as an explanation of *leadership, of the social reality of *command, of the strange rapt attention of the theatre audience, and of the power of the conductor of an orchestra. It is arguable, however, that such a theory is too general to be explanatory.

Crown

In UK legal and constitutional usage, 'the Crown' denotes the *office of the *sovereign and all acts of the sovereign in so far as they issue from that office. Legally speaking, the Crown is a 'corporation sole' (see *corporate personality). Property held by the Crown may in fact not be enjoyed by the sovereign personally, and acts in the name of the Crown may be unknown to the sovereign. The concept is that of an office, and does not denote the office-holder in any other way. The rules for succession to this office are of great constitutional significance, and have, since the Act of Settlement 1700, the Union with Scotland Act 1706, and the Union with Ireland Act 1800, been settled by *statute. The sovereign of the UK has many constitutional functions that are

embodied, by statute, custom and convention, in the powers, rights and obligations of the Crown. The obligations include the upholding of the Church of England, of which the monarch is head, of the Presbyterian Church of Scotland, and of the Christian religion generally; the administration of justice, the upholding of parliamentary statutes, and the acts required as commander-in-chief of the armed forces. The whole government of the UK is carried on in the name of the Crown, and this confluence of functions in a single office is designed partly to convey a sense of political unity and *sovereignty. Despite the *delegation of almost all statutory powers through ministers, it is possible that enough customary and *prerogative powers remain to render the sovereign more than a symbol of sovereignty. He may for example be able to act so as to restore political unity in a time of crisis (as did King George V in 1931, under the *prerogative). However, in most respects, 'the Crown' names a collection of *legal fictions.

crusade

1. Historically, the 'crusade' was a military expedition carried out in the name of the cross – in other words by way of a defence of Christianity. Historians generally acknowledge eight, possibly nine, crusades, of which the first four were decisive in affecting relations between Christians and Muslims then and now. The first was a delayed reaction to the destruction of the Church of the Holy Sepulchre in Jerusalem in 1009, ordered by the Fatimid Caliph of Cairo, al-Hakim bi-Amr Allah, an event which profoundly shocked the Christian world, and caused a long debate as to whether it was permissible to take up arms in the cause of Christ. The church was rebuilt and pilgrimages resumed, but sporadic

Muslim harassment of Christians caused growing antagonism in Europe, so that when the Byzantine Emperor Alexius I appealed in 1095 to Pope Urban II for military aid to prevent his empire finally falling to the Seljuk Turks (much of it having already been lost to them in 1071 at the Battle of Manzikert), the Pope preached the cause of a crusade, in which many of the highest nobility and military chiefs of Europe took part. The result was the reconquest of the Holy Land, and the establishment of the Kingdom of Jerusalem. Subsequent crusades were not so successful, and the third, launched in 1187 after Saladin had recaptured Jerusalem and led by several sovereigns, including King Richard I of England, was forced to turn back on account of disease, heat and lack of proper provisions. The fourth crusade of 1204 is notorious for the licentious and undisciplined behaviour of the troops who signed up to it, and who – having got as far as Constantinople – satisfied themselves with the sack and pillage of the city, notwithstanding their mission to defend it. Subsequent crusades include that launched against the heretical Cathars (a *manichean sect) of Provence (the Albigensian crusade of 1209), which was carried out with singular ruthlesness. The crusades are often cited as a cause of antagonism between Muslim and Christian, and as an example of belligerent interference by Christians in the 'House of Islam'. On the other hand, Islam was established in the Middle East by conquest, and the original Christian populations were reduced to *dhimmi* status and often persecuted. Assigning blame is therefore a contentious and ultimately futile exercise.

2. A general term for any passionate pursuit of a cause which has a moral or spiritual dimension.

cult of personality

Phrase coined at the USSR Communist Party conference of 1956, primarily to denote and explain away the style of government exercised by Stalin, but of wider application. It seems to refer to the concentration of political power and authority in a person, rather than in the office which he occupies, accompanied by an enforced adulation of that person on the part of ordinary citizens, and massive propaganda designed to display his superhuman virtues.

Having found this explanation for *Stalinism, the Communist Party remained haunted by the question of whether the 'Stalinist superstructure' was the necessary outcome of the socialist economic base. If historical materialism were true, then Stalinism was inevitable; if it was not inevitable, then historical materialism could not be true. The problem was made acute for the party by *Engels' officially accepted theory of 'so-called great men': 'If a Napoleon had been lacking another would have filled the place . . . the man was always found as soon as he became necessary.'

cultural conservatism

A species of *conservatism characterized by the emphasis on the continuity of a *culture (usually a high culture), both as good in itself, and as a major cause of social and political stability. England in particular has a long tradition of cultural conservatism, stretching from the beginning of the *romantic movement to the present day, and involving such thinkers as *Coleridge, *Arnold, Cardinal Newman, *Carlyle and *Ruskin in the nineteenth century, followed by less broad but often equally influential twentieth-century figures, among whom F.R. and Q.D. Leavis must be given prominence. F.R. Leavis was equally the heir to a parallel American tradition, typified by

Emerson and Henry James, and bequeathed to English thought by T.S. Eliot, whose *Notes Towards the Definition of Culture*, 1945, remains one of the outstanding documents of this way of thought. Not all cultural conservatives have been political conservatives. Notable among the exceptions are *Morris and *Leavis.

American cultural conservatism is directed towards conserving the fragments of old European culture, usually with an exile's consciousness of the difficulty of the task; but, like the English version, it tries to justify itself by making large and often striking claims for the role of culture in determining the quality of life, not just of those who possess it, but also of those who do not. The monument to that doctrine is the academic subject of English as taught, at least until recently, in many English and American universities, through which the political battle between *élitist and *egalitarian values has been fought out almost entirely in terms of standards of literary taste, and, conversely, literary taste has been represented as a major vehicle of social and moral consciousness.

Perhaps the most important text of cultural conservatism is Matthew Arnold's *Culture and Anarchy*, 1869, in which high culture is represented as the repository of 'sweetness and light', the guarantee that we may still pass on to future generations the inheritance of enlightened social order, calm government, and true human values, which is celebrated in the greatest works of art. High culture is therefore the antidote to anarchy, as well as containing within itself the refutation of utilitarianism, and of every other doctrine expressive of the *philistine consciousness.

Cultural conservatism involves a belief in the power of consciousness to determine political order, and thus stands opposed to most of the materialist visions of history. It has often been criticized for its alleged intellectual snobbery and élitism, and alternatively as a forlorn attempt to endow art and high culture with functions that can only be filled by religion, thus conserving religious feeling in secularized form. It has also been thought to provide an intellectual backing to conservatism, while remaining aloof from all explicit *doctrine. The ruling thought has been: if we do not conserve culture, what else can we conserve?

cultural contradictions of capitalism

Expression introduced by the American sociologist Daniel Bell, echoing the Marxist theory of the *contradictions of capitalism, but referring to the conservative complaint against capitalism, that while it sustains the economic order, it corrodes the cultural legacy that makes economic order durable. The solution is not to repudiate capitalism, but to emphasize and amplify the means of cultural communication, so that the virtues and emotions of a serious moral order can be passed from one generation to the next.

cultural revolution

Term introduced by *Lenin, in order to argue that revolution requires the fulfilment of both 'objective conditions' (material transformation), and 'subjective conditions' (the way in which social reality is perceived). Cultural revolution is a necessary part of achieving appropriate subjective conditions, and involves the breaking down of the habits and artifacts of bourgeois *culture, so as to deprive the old economic order of its cultural support.

The 'cultural revolution' initiated in China in 1968 by Chairman *Mao, ostensibly designed to purge the communist state of Western and bourgeois influences, but directed at all forms of traditional learning and expertise, involved the use of 'Red Guards', licensed to destroy and humiliate whoever stood out as a representative of old and respected forms of learning, or who dabbled in the small-scale economic life outside the state on which the populace depended for its sparse supply of goods. The destruction, which lasted for six years, ruined what there was of the Chinese economy, caused untold suffering and uncounted deaths, and was praised throughout the ranks of Western left-wing intellectuals, notably by *Sartre.

culture

1. In *anthropology and *sociology, 'culture' denotes indifferently all manifestations of social life which are not merely concerned with the reproduction and sustenance of human beings. Thus customs, habits of association, religious observances, even specific beliefs, may be spoken of as part of a culture. The ruling idea here is that there are activities which embellish and colour the process of collective survival, and give to it its distinctive local forms. Culture is often argued to have a role in the creation and conservation of a social order, and might even be susceptible to *functional explanation. Alternatively, for the anthropological *structuralist, it is to be understood first as a complex of symbols, and only secondly in terms of any function that it may (perhaps as a consequence) perform.

2. Outside that wide, and perhaps over-wide, technical usage, the term 'culture' is usually reserved for habits, customs and attitudes that are specific to *leisure. In this usage it is common to distinguish 'high' from 'common' culture, the first requiring educational attainments for its exercise and understanding, the second requiring no more than membership of society. To the first belong all activities in which true *aesthetic interest is exercised, and aesthetic values pursued; to the second belong dancing, entertainment, and sport, in which relaxation and social contact are the principal aims. The distinction between the two is neither sharp nor obviously significant. Some regard the attempt to make it more precise as a form of *élitism, on the supposition that the culture called 'high' will inevitably be put forward as preferable, despite the knowledge that its products may often be inaccessible to the majority.

The distinction between high and common culture is nevertheless important to political thinking. Many modern governments regard themselves as under an obligation to support high culture (which, because of its limited appeal, may wither away in the absence of other forms of patronage), but usually have very little coordinated policy towards common culture, which is generally assumed to be capable of supporting itself. (But *see* *leisure, *sport.) According to *cultural conservatism high culture, in forming the outlook of the educated class, will, through the inevitable dominance of that class, shape the expectations and customs of society.

A culture can be said to be 'common' to a nation, class or social group when there is a shared familiarity with its products and practices, so that widespread reference and allusion are made to it, causing it to be a major determinant of the form and content of communication.

Among modern political movements concerned with culture, *nationalism has been the most prominent, and cultural conservatism has often formed an integral part of it. One may also mention Bismarck's 'war of culture' (*_Kulturkampf_), in which he sought to wrest the formation of the educated classes from the control of the Roman Catholic Church, and the similar wars against cultural independence on the part of *Lenin, Hitler, Stalin and *Mao. _See also_ *cultural revolution, *multiculturalism.

culture/civilization

See *Kultur/Zivilisation.

culture wars

Conflicts currently waged in US universities and media, and to a smaller extent elsewhere, between conservatives and *liberals over cultural matters thought to impinge on the conduct and aims of politics. These involve the controversies over *multiculturalism, over *neo-conservatism, over *feminism and *gay rights, over the university curriculum and all other cultural matters in which liberals strongly think one thing, and conservatives strongly think another. The culture wars have had an enormous impact on American intellectual life, raising both the temperature and (possibly) the intellectual level of public debate.

custom

A form of repeated rational action, in which past performance provides the reason for present repetition, by showing 'what is done'. Custom is distinguished from *law, in that it need not be enforced by the *state or by legal penalties; from *convention, in that it need not be exact or rule-guided; from *habit, in that it is, nevertheless, something that only rational beings engage in, and can be attributed to non-rational animals only in a metaphorical sense. To do what is customary is to act intentionally, and for a specific reason, namely, that this is what is done. The reason may be a bad one, but it has the merit of referring beyond the agent to an implied social world and its justifying context. Custom forms a background from which law may emerge, as the crystallization of settled expectations. Without custom, it is argued, law and government would be difficult if not impossible; at the same time, to attempt to impose custom by law is inherently self-defeating, since it involves removing the freedom of action which makes custom possible. Attachment to custom is an important conservative ideal; it is often held to show that an action can be wholly justifiable, even though of only local validity, and not perceivable as valid by the person who does not engage in it. Customs are therefore sometimes extolled as providing the conservative substitute for *doctrine.

customs union

An association of states for the purpose of *free trade among themselves, and in which the member states apply common laws and regulations to trade with non-members. The second condition distinguishes a customs union from a free-trade area, in which members may still make what provisions they choose for trade with non-member states. A free-trade area may be less stable, in that these differing relations with the outside world may cause internal frictions. For example, goods may enter through member states which impose low duties, and so cause an imbalance of trade with states which charge higher duties. A *common market goes beyond a customs union in permitting free movement of all economic inputs, including labour, capital, and the means of distribution.

cybernetics

Greek: _kubernēs_, a steersman. The study of the control and internal governance of systems (e.g. organisms, and machines exhibiting 'artificial intelligence'), where the various operations interact reciprocally and systematically. The term was invented in 1947 by Norbert Wiener and Arturo Rosenthal, and denotes not an existing but a projected science. Sometimes the expression 'systems theory' is preferred, and sometimes the two expressions are distinguished, the one being used to denote some branch, or supposed branch, of the science denoted by the other. It is held that systems can be more or less 'closed' to influence from outside, so that many of the laws of their operation and development can be understood in terms of the reciprocal interaction among component parts. It is further held that the laws governing such systems are universal, and do not apply merely to the organic realm, as traditionally defined. The term 'feedback' has been coined to denote the return of a part of the output of a system as a new input: positive feedback increases the input, negative feedback decreases it. Negative feedback is therefore inherently stabilizing, and acts so as to reduce activity, while positive feedback may be inherently destructive. The governor of a machine will be designed to produce negative feedback, braking the machine as it races; some think that the capitalist economy exhibits positive feedback (growth stimulating further growth) in a manner that would perhaps warrant the prediction of a *crisis of capitalism. As the last example indicates, social arrangements are 'systems' in the relevant sense and this has led many sociologists and political thinkers to regard cybernetics as a useful tool in explaining social and political processes, although some doubt that there is anything to be said for this approach that will serve to distinguish it from the ancient theory of *organicism.

D **ante Alighieri** (1265–1321) Florentine poet who, in his *De Monarchia, c.* 1309 presented a philosophical description of *monarchy, and of the state, influenced by *Aristotle and *Cicero, but containing many distinctively modern features. He argued that peace is a necessity if human powers are to be realized, and that there can be no guarantee of peace while there are national rivalries: hence the world should be governed by one prince, who is supreme over nations, and also untempted by cupidity, having no further territory to gain. Salvation for human society requires the restoration of the Empire, which will generate the true order of government and also save the papacy from corruption. Dante argues that both institutions – empire and papacy – are sanctioned by divine ordinance, and both are necessary, the one holding all legitimate temporal power, and the other all legitimate spiritual power. The papacy cannot wield temporal power without also losing spiritual authority, in particular its authority to adjudicate disputes by referring them to the law of God. Its attempt to transform itself into a princedom was therefore a lapse from its divine mission and apostolic constitution. The dualistic vision of the origins of *power and *authority was developed against the background of a philosophy of *natural law, inspired by *Aquinas. Dante's discussion was highly influential in establishing the modern conceptions of the relation between religious and political allegiance, and of *political obligation. *See also* *church and state, *Two Swords doctrine.

Darwinism

The name for any *evolutionary theory conceived in the spirit of Charles Robert Darwin (1809–82), who argued in *The Origin of Species*, 1859, that evolution proceeds by natural selection, generated by random mutation and the 'survival of the fittest'. Darwin's theory is an application of *functional explanation to biology; it is therefore sometimes imitated by those who wish to extend such explanation to the social sciences. It had direct impact on politics in giving credence to certain *racist ideologies, or to philosophies that emphasized the importance of racial character in determining political conditions and social responses. It also led to 'social Darwinism', a theory influential in the late nineteenth century, which argued that societies, like species, are subject to the law of natural selection, and are therefore inherently progressive, later examples always showing greater adaptation to circumstances than earlier ones. This transfer of evolutionary theory to the social sphere, while founding a certain callow optimism, seems to be based on confusion, concerning first the kind of organization, and secondly the time-scale of development, of that to which it is applied. Nevertheless, versions of the Marxist theory of history that incorporate an idea of functional explanation seem to bear a marked similarity to Darwin's theory.

The attempt to understand the

social nature of the human being in terms of the evolutionary adaptation of the human species has led to several new applications of the Darwinian theory, for example in *sociobiology and also in the theory of the *meme. As a result of these theories Darwinism is once again an important force in political thinking.

de jure/de facto

A *power exists *de jure* if its exercise is authorized by *law. To say that it exists *de facto* is to say only that it exists, with the usual implication that the question of its *legitimacy has either not arisen or been settled in the negative. *See* *rights and powers.

death

Since it is the fact about the human condition that least bears contemplation, death tends to play a subdued part in political thinking, although images of death pervade political writings, lying behind Marx's description of revolution as 'the midwife of history' (so that the old society is also killed by its monster child), and also behind the many adulations of *terror, as a purging and salutary tonic.

It is possible to distinguish outlooks that encourage the acceptance of death (either as the prelude to immortality, or as the sobering premise of moral reflection) from those that abhor it, and which attempt to provide a consoling picture of social existence without reference to this fundamental fear. The first often feature as underlying philosophies of conservatism, and are typically dismissed as *reactionary by those who seek for more mortal perfections. They have a tendency to reconcile people to their condition, and to induce a stoic (some would say complacent) acceptance of the inadequacy of present arrangements. They also tend to encourage belief in *providence and *destiny, as taking history

out of human hands and ensuring the constant re-enactment of an imperfect social order.

Typically such views are religious, *Buddhism providing perhaps the most important example, though *Heidegger's advocacy of 'being-towards-death' is a purely secular attempt to place the acceptance of death at the heart of our projects. Heidegger is unusual; secular doctrines usually attempt to replace the religious conviction of man's 'fallen' condition by a belief in human powers and in *progress, so blotting out the thought of death with the idea of a future society characterized by material and spiritual satisfaction. The image of perpetual youth in some *utopian writings, and in the idea of the *alternative society, is a striking example of this attempt to remove hesitation, by forbearing to mention the fundamental source of human anxiety. It is often argued by conservatives that it is at least as important to accept death as to provide for life, and that a doctrine (such as *Marxism-Leninism) which seeks to remove the consolations that have aided in the acceptance of death, on the grounds that they have impeded the adequate or equal provisioning for life, is founded in a mistaken vision of human self-consciousness. Thus, from *Burke to *Eliot, conservative thinkers have emphasized the fundamental need for religion in social order, and have criticized their opponents for overlooking this need. Others, while not prepared to endorse religion on these grounds, have nevertheless been prepared to concede the necessity for social arrangements that permit and facilitate *mourning*, and the ritual and ceremony that provide its social and cathartic significance. This concession is not necessarily a small one, since it requires endorsing both a measure of freedom of association, and respect for tradition; thus funeral ceremonies became, at one point, a focus of the clash between *Maoism and *Confucianism in modern China.

To take seriously the analogy between the *body politic and the human organism inevitably leads to the view that the first, like the second, is mortal. It must therefore strive (but not officiously) to stay alive, and perhaps also to accept its death as inevitable. In opposition to that idea there is a long tradition of *constitutionalism which regards a constitution as a means of securing permanence. Thus *Cicero wrote: 'death of the state is its punishment, even though it seems to relieve all individuals of punishment; for a political body must be so constituted that it might be eternal'. This thought partly explains the reluctance among many progressive thinkers to accept the organicist position, and the tendency to substitute for it a more mechanical, or at any rate unilinear, view of the movement of history.

Death and dying have come to the centre of political debate with the movements to legalize *euthanasia, and with the problems arising from longevity and the ageing of human communities. Do states, in modern conditions, need in some way to manage death, or are all attempts to do so intolerably offensive to our moral instincts?

death taxes

Taxes payable by the estate of someone on his death. *J.S. Mill advocated the confiscation of property at death, on the grounds that no one other than the deceased was entitled to it, and justice required that everybody be given an equal start in life. Death taxes (or death duties as they are known in UK law) have been criticized as an excessive intervention of the state in the economy, which removes an important source of private capital that might otherwise be responsibly invested by the heirs. Some have argued that the total abolition of such taxes, by stimulating the economy with a constant reinjection of private capital, would in fact lead to more taxes (in the form of income tax) paid to the State. Moves to abolish death taxes are significant in the US; elsewhere death taxes remain punitive, ensuring, in the UK, the collapse of the landed aristocracy, as well as massive outflows of capital to tax havens abroad. The first of those results has led to a continuing problem as to who will maintain the landscape and how.

decadence

The condition of society in which *values, customs and certainties are in decline, not because of economic collapse, but because of moral and spiritual exhaustion. Characteristic of decadence is the affectation of traditional values on the part of those who no longer sincerely believe in them, and also their deliberate (perhaps even orgiastic) violation by those who thereby hope to awaken in themselves some titillation of guilt, and so experience the faint after-image of conviction. Another, less sophisticated, manifestation is the wholesale pursuit of physical and sensual gratification, combined, perhaps, with an inability to understand the higher forms of human interest, or why, indeed, the word 'higher' should be chosen to denote them.

Gibbon (*The Decine and Fall of the Roman Empire*) famously attributed the fall of Rome to decadence; and the decadence of human society has been a favourite theme of moralists ever since human society began. Whether things are actually worse now than they were in the time of Jeremiah is perhaps not in point; it may be fair to say, however, that the accusation is more widespread, very often with 'Western society' as its principal object (*see* *Islamism). Some theorists have taken an 'ontogenetic' view of civilization, according to which each phase of development has a life process, with a primeval, middle, and decadent stage. Thus *Hume, Burckhardt, *Vico, and *Spengler each thought of decadence as part of an ubiquitous process of cyclical fulfilment and decay; for *Bodin, *Montesquieu, Turgot, and *Comte, however, periods of decadence are only incidental aberrations from an indomitable advance. Modern social scientists often explain decadence in terms of 'dysfunctionality': i.e. decadence arises when a social and political superstructure has ceased to fulfil the social and perhaps economic functions required of it, and can therefore no longer command the wholehearted support of the members of society.

decentralization

The process whereby *centralization is reversed, so that power is shifted from central political and administrative bodies, answerable to a single executive, to a multitude of quasi-autonomous bodies, concerned with the formulation and application of policy in particular regions and in answer to local and variable requirements.

Decentralization has often been put forward as a remedy against the concentration of power, and as a means of ensuring that the needs and expectations of the common citizen are respected. It is not clear that it need have either effect, since *sovereignty requires that the original concentration of power be conserved, even if mediated by new local institutions. Decentralization seems to occupy a point midway between mere 'deconcentration' (the *delegation of power to local officers) and *federation

(the division of internal sovereignty). *See* *devolution, *federation, *local government.

decision theory

A branch of applied mathematics, designed to formalize the notion of *rational choice under conditions of risk and uncertainty. It incorporates the theory of probability, and attempts to compute the relative *costs of different courses of action on the basis of their probable outcome. (Bayesian decision theory is characterized by adherence to the theorem in probability theory put forward by Thomas Bayes (1702–61).) Decision theory is a part of *cost–benefit analysis, being largely confined to the study of the relative importance of probabilities, given an assignment of costs. It aims to provide axioms and rules of inference which convey the structure of rational choice, but is applicable only on the assumption that rational choice concerns itself with quantifiable costs and benefits that may be balanced against each other. *See also* *game theory, *preference, *utilitarianism.

declaration of rights

See *bill of rights.

Declaration of the Rights of Man and of the Citizen

Document put out by the French Revolutionary Assembly in 1789, in lieu of a constitution, which declared all the rights – both *natural and *civil – that were being conferred on the citizen by the new Revolutionary order, including the right to life, limb and property, the right to a fair trial, and many or most of the rights advocated by Enlightenment thinkers who had addressed the question of citizenship and *republican government – notably *Locke, *Montesquieu and *Rousseau. Like many such documents the Declaration was accompanied by no attempt to set up the institutions that would make it possible for citizens to claim their rights in a court of law, and within two years French citizens were being regularly killed, maimed, robbed and imprisoned without trial in the name of the state.

deconstruction

A philosophy, associated principally with *Derrida and his academic followers, which attempts to mount a comprehensive critique of Western culture, and to propose a method for studying the products of that culture which will neutralize their claim to authority. According to Derrida, Western culture is 'logocentric' – that is, it is founded on the authority of the spoken word (*logos*), and therefore devalues the written word, which abolishes the 'self presence' that we encounter in the spoken word and substitutes an absence in its stead. The written text stands as a screen between the reader and the author, who disappears behind it, and leaves the text as the sole guide to its meaning. (The thesis of the 'death of the author'.) How then should texts be read? According to Derrida (borrowing from the Swiss linguist Ferdinand de Saussure (1857–1913)), meaning attaches to a sign only in the context of other signs that might replace it in a sentence. The meaning of 'hot' is given by the contrast (*différence*) between 'hot' and 'cold', 'hot' and 'warm', etc. Language is a system of differences, and the meaning of every word is given by the other words that it excludes. Hence all meaning waits on the 'other' sign, the sign that completes a word by opposing it but which cannot be written down without itself becoming incomplete. Meaning is therefore always deferred, vanishing as we seem to reach it; and if we stop at a particular place, saying *now* we have it, *now* the meaning lies

before us, then this is our decision, which may have a political purpose but which is in no way dictated by the text. Hence the ambiguous noun '*différence*' must here be taken in both its senses, as difference and deferral, a fact which Derrida signals by spelling the word '*différance*'.

How, then, should we approach the text? We must try to subvert its claim to meaning by 'deconstructing' it, showing that the very attempt to mean something will also express the opposite meaning. Derrida goes further, arguing that all discourse is founded in metaphor – a view that he takes from *Nietzsche. Hence to study a text is to jeopardize its claim to objectivity by de-coding the metaphors upon which it is built and showing that everything questionable has already been assumed in the very discourse that forbids the question.

Originally applied to literary theory, deconstruction spread like wildfire through the humanities and social sciences, and led even to a 'deconstructionist' approach to politics, in which the 'politics of difference' is advocated as the answer to the oppressive structures of Western civilization. Its critics say that deconstruction is a meaningless hotchpotch, to which the deconstructionist replies that 'they would, wouldn't they?' However, it is doubtful that its appeal stems from any compelling rational grounds for believing it.

Briefly fashionable in humanities departments, deconstruction now seems to be losing its following, having promised much and delivered little.

decree

A legal rule which has all the authority of legislation, but which is issued directly by a minister or state department, without the deliberation of a legislative body. Government by decree is normal in Middle Eastern politics. It is also familiar in some parliamentary democracies, although here the power to issue decrees is itself derived, either from the *constitution or from some enabling legislation of the national parliament. The constitution of the French Fifth Republic grants to ministers a power to make decrees which cannot be questioned in the National Assembly. In the UK ministers can add details to legislation but must present these details to Parliament for approval. EU *directives also have the force of decrees, since national legislatures are compelled by treaty to incorporate them as law, with or without discussion.

deep ecology

The branch of the *ecological movement that seeks a complete reorientation of human social and political life, so as to achieve a new balance with nature before it is too late. Deep ecologists believe that most environmental protection is skin deep, and that the damage now being done to other species, to the atmosphere and to the ecological balance is so great that nothing short of a wholly new life-style could possibly rectify it. Critics accuse deep ecology of *millenarian hysteria. The reply is that, for the first time in history, we *know* that the end is nigh.

deferred gratification

A benefit that is forgone for the sake of a greater future reward. All coherent economic activity depends upon deferred gratification, since without it *consumption would annihilate *investment. For economists of the *Austrian school it is deferred gratification rather than private ownership that is the primary feature of capitalist investment.

deficit financing

The deliberate policy whereby a government spends more than its income. It takes the form of a budget financed by borrowing or by expanding the *money supply, usually with the object of raising the general level of purchasing power so as to stimulate economic activity and increase employment. The use of deficit financing as part of monetary policy was advocated by *Keynes.

deflation

1. The opposite of *inflation, signifying falling as opposed to rising prices.

2. The condition of reduced economic activity, where there is *unemployment and unused productive capacity.

*Neo-classical economists argue that if prices (including wages) are perfectly flexible, real economic activity is independent of the price level, and depends solely on relative prices. They would tend to employ the first definition. The second definition, however, is more common.

de Gaulle, General Charles (1890–1970)

French statesman, leader of the Free French forces during the Second World War, and President of France. De Gaulle was a visionary politician and a highly cultivated man, who became a symbol for many French people of their country's standing in the world. His *Mémoires de guerre*, 1954–59, paint an idealized portrait of France, the country of Jeanne d'Arc and Victor Hugo, of the Revolution and its Napoleonic aftermath, and of the attempt to embody the spiritual condition of Europe. When de Gaulle (who had been President in the immediate aftermath of the Second World War) stepped again into the political arena to become President in 1958, after the humiliating retreat from Indo-China, he restored belief in the institutions and identity of France, and oversaw the emergence of France as a major actor in what was to become the European Union. He saw the purpose of the European project as that of safeguarding the continent from American and Russian domination, not as the formation of a federal union or superstate, and was a fervent advocate of nationality and national parliaments. His vision of France was both romantic in its rhetoric and realistic in its politics, and his time in office led to the formation of a Gaullist Party, and a Gaullist philosophy, which have remained dominant to this day. (*See* *Gaullism.)

deism

A system of natural religion, classically expounded in J. Toland's *Christianity not Mysterious*, 1696, and highly influential in eighteenth-century France and Germany. According to deism, reason is the necessary and sufficient guarantee of faith, and tells us that God exists, that the world is governed by a natural moral law, and that future punishments and rewards will be based on observance of that law. God is the all-wise, all-benevolent and omnipotent creator, but it is inconsistent with His nature that he should further intervene in creation. This *demythologized belief, which sweeps the world clean of miracles and mysteries, and makes direct appeal to the deity absurd, had a profound influence on *Enlightenment thought, and notably on the moral and religious ideas of *Voltaire and *Kant. It accompanied the similar demythologizing of the idea of *political obligation, and furthered the *secularization of political doctrine, and the growth of religious *toleration.

delegation

The transfer of authorized power to a subordinate person or body, who acts not merely as the channel for that power, but as its agent, making deci-

sions in its name. A delegate is authorized to act only in accordance with specific instructions, or a specific ideology. Delegation therefore differs from *representation, without being as rigidly controlled as *mandation. The most important forms of delegation are military – from commanding to subordinate officer – and constitutional, from *Parliament or *Congress, for example, to bodies which are given powers to legislate in their name. (Although since Congress does not have the full *sovereignty of Parliament, it seems that its powers of delegation are limited: *Schechter Poultry Corp.* v. *US*, 1935.) Delegated legislation has become increasingly important in the UK since the Reformation, and in particular since 1832, with the growth of government influence in all spheres of administration. It is frequently criticized on account of the uncertain validity of any controversial enactment, and the uncertain competence of the legislator. In all criticism the main demand is for adequate parliamentary or congressional control. In the UK, however, challenge in the courts is often hindered by provisions which say that legislation made by the delegate is as valid as the empowering statute, or that confirmation by a minister is to be conclusive evidence that the requirements of the statute have been complied with.

A delegate is bound by the long-standing rule of law that he cannot himself unless specifically authorized delegate the power conferred on him (*delegatus non potest delegare*), which provision is necessary if there is to be genuine delegation, as opposed to the universal diffusion of the power of the state, and genuine *answerability for the exercise of that power.

The concept is to some extent clarified by the distinction between delegation and representation, a distinction emphasized in a celebrated speech by *Burke. Delegation confers power through the directives of an original; representation confers powers, in addition to those conferred by the original, which belong to the institutional structure through which representation is effected. In the latter case the two powers may act so as to limit each other, so that a representative cannot be bound to carry out all the directives of those whom he represents, whereas a delegate must do all that he is required to do, and sometimes nothing that he is not specifically required to do.

demagogue
Greek: a leader of the people. Now used to signify a person able to obtain political *power through *rhetoric, by stirring up the feelings of his audience and leading them to action despite the considerations which weigh against it. The demagogue is often held to require *charisma and qualities of *leadership. He at least needs to appear cogent in answer to every question, and to appear absolutely convinced of the truth of what he utters, master of himself, his audience, and his mission. In addition a demagogue is usually thought to be motivated more by the desire for power than by concern for the common good, to be prepared to appeal to irrational motives, and to be bent on policies that are disastrous for the people as a whole. He benefits by representing himself as possessing knowledge of the future, and a theory which validates that knowledge, and by urging the people to take action against powers that have conspired to delude and oppress them.

demand
The willingness and ability to pay for goods and services. A 'demand curve' is a geometric representation of the relation (the demand function) between *price per unit of product and the quantity demanded by the consumer.

The demand curves of all consumers are aggregated to obtain the market demand curve which will, in general, reflect the 'law of demand': the lower the price, the greater the quantity of the product demanded (although naturally the price cannot normally become negative). Exceptions to this law include goods purchased for ostentation, where price is thought to be a sign of quality, or the ability to pay to be a sign of social distinction. An apparent exception is provided by some kinds of speculative buying, in which a rise in price causes speculators to think that prices might rise yet further.

demand-pull inflation
See *inflation.

democracy
Literally, government by the *people as a whole (Greek: *demos*) rather than by any section, class or interest within it. The theory of democracy is immensely complicated, partly because of difficulties in understanding who the people are, and which acts of government are truly 'theirs' rather than those of some dominant group or interest. (*See* *collective choice.) The first distinction to be made is that between *direct and representative democracy: in the first all citizens participate in decision-making, say by voting and accepting a majority verdict. In the second case, the people choose (say by voting) representatives who are then answerable to them, but at the same time directly involved, and usually without further consultation, in the practice of government (*see* *representation, *and cf.* *delegation).

Apart from that distinction, however, there is little agreement as to what is important in constituting a regime as democratic. This is partly because of two conflicting criteria that might be employed in the assessment of any political decision: by whom was it taken? (which raises the problem of *collective choice) and: whose interest does it serve? (which raises the problems of social welfare, and *social choice). It is normal in the West to use the first criterion, and to call a state democratic if there is *some* way of attributing every major political decision to the people, either because they take part in making it, or because it ultimately depends upon their *consent. It was normal in the Soviet bloc to use the second criterion, and to regard decisions as democratic if they furthered (or perhaps only if they were intended to further) the interests of the people, even though taken by a ruling party which forbad popular membership of its ranks. (*See* *democratic centralism.)

As soon as societies become large, with large-scale *division of labour and complex patterns of *distribution, direct democracy seems hardly feasible. The question of principal importance then seems to be, what makes a *constitution* democratic? It is to this question that the theory of Western constitutional democracy addresses itself, burdened also by ancillary questions inherited from the long history of European constitutional government, in which what first existed as a right of appeal of every subject to the sovereign, was gradually transformed into *limited government with representational assemblies whose consent had to be sought for every legislative and executive decision. It is clear that to limit, in this way, the power of government is not of itself to transfer that power to the people, and while regular *elections and universal *suffrage are now seen as essential features of a democratic constitution, they are only one part of a mode of government that may yet be undemocratic in every other particular. In

particular every constitution requires a framework of *offices and *conventions which will not be subject to easy emendation by popular choice. Hence power and privilege intrinsic to that framework (e.g. that vested in a *civil service) will rarely be seen as a reflection of popular choice, however necessary it may be to making that choice effective. Moreover, a democratically elected government may proceed to enact, during its term of office, policies which are manifestly in conflict with the wishes and the interests of the people.

In representative democracies various criteria have been laid down for determining when an election really does reflect the choice of an electorate. Furthermore, attempts have been made to impose democratic organization on all subject institutions within a democracy, in order to avoid the obvious objection that the state represents only one among many concentrations of political power. The desire to extend democratic decision-making through every *autonomous body has led to much heart-searching in recent politics, partly because it has seemed that, without that extension, democracy is seriously incomplete. This thought lies behind many justifications once given for socialism, state control of the economy being justified as a kind of 'economic democracy'. This kind of argument is often dismissed as an apology for dictatorship. Many (e.g. *Hayek, Michael Novak, and *Friedman) add that true economic democracy arises only when each person's economic choices are both freely made and effective in influencing prices, and that these conditions require a free market.

Although democracy is almost universally assumed to be the only acceptable form of government today (even if only in the spirit of Winston Churchill's remark that every other form of government is worse), it should be pointed out that, until the French Revolution democracy was regarded with almost universal suspicion, and that it only slowly gained in credibility during the course of the nineteenth century.

democratic centralism
Term adopted by the *Communist Party in the USSR and elsewhere to designate the variety of decision-making recommended by *Lenin, and supposedly practised in Soviet government. It is held to involve free political discussion within the party, and free elections to party offices, combined with a one-party state and a strict hierarchical discipline. 'Centralism' means the concentration of all power in the central party organization, which is made responsible for the organization and development of every institution in which political influence may arise, from the school to the factory floor, and from the family to the police force, and which is therefore intolerant of every autonomous body within its sphere of influence. What the word 'democratic' could mean in such a context is debatable.

democratic deficit
The absence of popular accountability in any institution that claims to possess it. A repeated complaint made against the *European Union is that it appropriates powers and privileges without being accountable for their exercise, and that it avoids or ignores the votes of those in whose interests it purports to be acting. Hence the democratic deficit has become a standing issue in discussions of the EU.

democratic despotism
Term introduced by *Tocqueville (*L'ancien régime et la Révolution*, 1856) in order to signify the kind of *despotism that supposedly proceeds from too fervent and too uncritical an adherence to the doctrine of the *sovereignty of the *people: 'No gradations in society, no distinctions of classes, no fixed ranks – a people composed of individuals nearly alike and entirely equal – this confused mass being recognized as the only legitimate sovereign, but carefully deprived of all the faculties which could enable it either to direct or even to superintend its own government. Above this mass, a single officer, charged to do everything in its name without consulting it. To control this officer, public opinion, deprived of its organs; to arrest him, revolutions, but no laws. In principle a subordinate agent; in fact a master.'

democratic parties
Parties are normally formed in order to propose policies to an electorate and to pursue power as a means to put those policies into practice. This process may or may not occur within a framework which merits the label 'democratic'. A democratic party must nevertheless claim to uphold that framework, and this is often taken to mean upholding free and periodic elections, so that the party is committed also to guaranteeing that it may be expelled from office should it lose public support. This commitment is perhaps the only thing which all 'democratic' parties tend to share, and its existence goes no further than democratic parties in Western constitutional states.

The US Democratic Party deserves individual mention on account of its special relation to constitutional government as this has evolved in the twentieth century. It was founded in 1828 and dominant until 1860, when it became identified with the South, and was unable to return a President to office until Cleveland in 1885. Since then the Democratic Party has steadily lost its conservative and agrarian image (which has instead been adopted by the rival Republican Party) and identified itself with a kind of enlightened *dirigisme*, in which American ideals of liberty and self-determination are combined with active government concern for the poor and the dependent. It thus emerged after the Depression as the champion of government intervention, and embodied in the *New Deal of President Roosevelt (1933–45) the first systematic programme of social welfare for the US as a whole. The arguments before the Supreme Court that much of the programme of the New Deal was in fact unconstitutional show the extent to which a like background of policy is imposed on the two major parties in the US by the supervision of the constitution. Nevertheless the image of the Democratic Party as to the *left of the Republican has survived since that time, and determines to some extent the nature of the support that is offered to it, as well as the policies that it advances when in office. At the same time, however, it must be remembered that, in the US, 'changing one's political complexion is made easier by the fact that the conservative-liberal distinction does not coincide with party lines. The Democratic ranks are heavy with liberals, the Republican with conservatives. Each party, nevertheless, harbours an important minority of the opposite persuasion' (R.V. Denenberg: *Understanding American Politics*, 1976, 2nd edn 1980).

democratic socialism

*Socialism pursued by *democratic means – e.g. through persuasion of the electorate in a state ruled by representative institutions. ('The parliamentary road to socialism'.) Normally contrasted with socialism and communism imposed by force, following a revolution or *coup d'état*. ('The revolutionary road to socialism'.) Not to be confused with *social democracy. Democratic socialism has been professed by many Western parties, e.g. the UK Labour Party prior to the emergence of *New Labour, but very few such parties profess it today. Some dismiss the idea as an oxymoron, for example *Solzhenitsyn, who compared 'democratic socialism' to 'boiling ice'.

democratization

The introduction of features of *collective choice into institutions and associations that are not themselves parts of government: e.g. places of work, schools and universities, churches and local communities. Democratization is a major political movement in Western countries, and is often seen as an essential feature of *gradualist social reform in accordance with a respect for existing institutions.

demystification

The process of removing the mystery from things, specifically from social things, usually by attempting to reveal the true causes of social beliefs and behaviour. This may sometimes be equivalent to *demythologization, but is of wider application, arising from every item of social consciousness, however innocent of *myth. Demystification involves the critical analysis of thoughts and ideas held to conceal social realities, and its most influential examples are the Marxist theories of *ideology and *false consciousness. The varieties of demystification are, however, considerably wider, ranging from *critical theory, *deconstruction and other products of academic reflection, to the *nihilism of the 'romantic twilight', and the invigorating *egoism recommended in the twentieth century by the ideologists of fascism and national socialism. In the face of this attempt to remove all mysteries from human things – which some see as founded in a deeper hostility to human *values – many conservative thinkers have emphasized the difficulty of living without mystery, some even going so far as *Plato, and advocating the *noble lie.

demythologization

Term introduced by the German theologian Rudolf Bultmann (1884–1976) to denote the systematic removal from the New Testament teaching of elements of *myth. Bultmann regarded belief in the bare fact of Christ crucified as sufficient for *Christian *faith, and considered that it was necessary to reinterpret as allegorical all those elements of the gospel which could not command rational assent in a modern believer. The idea of a demythologized religion has existed for at least two centuries, was given evangelical form by *deism, and found early systematic expression in *Kant's *Religion within the Limits of Reason Alone*, 1793. However, once Bultmann had made the term fashionable, its use was rapidly extended beyond theology to describe a persistent, and characteristically *modern, outlook on the world. The demythologized worldview is one in which all appearances are reviewed and amended in the light of science, and in which no supernatural beliefs are allowed to gain a foothold. Symbolic modes of thought and behaviour are perceived as such and not regarded as intimations of a world order other than that discoverable to science. The extreme form of this attitude has often been criticized under the name of *scientism, and sociologists influenced by *Weber have sometimes argued that the element of 'enchantment' in human thinking is socially indispensable. Nevertheless, even if no adequate substitutes for myth are available, it does not follow that a rational being can suspend his disbelief in it. *See also* *desacralization, *disenchantment.

deontology

The study of, or emphasis upon, *duty as the foundational concept in ethics. To be distinguished from *consequentialism, which emphasizes the good results of what we do, rather than the dutiful motive, as the foundation of a positive moral judgement.

dependence

A state is politically dependent when its power structure and institutions are controlled from outside, economically dependent when exports and imports are necessary for survival. Both forms of dependence may be enforced by another state, either by conquest or by *Finlandization. All states are now dependent to some degree, although the ideal of political and economic *autarky is not without adherents (*see* *isolationism). The major distinction lies between those which are dependent on *one*, more powerful, state (such as the former communist states of Eastern Europe were) and those which are multilaterally dependent, in the manner of most states in the democratic West. Originally, however, a dependency was not a sovereign state, but one which owed allegiance directly to a dominant sovereign power. (See, e.g., G.C. Lewis: *An Essay on the Government of Dependencies*, 1841.) In UK law this sense remains, and a 'dependency' is a state or region not annexed by the *Crown but subject to UK *jurisdiction (it is thus a wider term than *colony).

Recent international power struggles are sometimes thought to have shown a change from old methods of securing political dependence through threat or conquest, to the newer techniques of subversion, and economic dependence, brought about, say, by the saturation of a market.

dependency culture

Term introduced by American sociologists (e.g. Charles Murray, *Losing*

Ground: American Social Policy 1950–1980, 1984) to denote the *culture arising from *welfare provisions, which effectively relieve a whole class of the population of the need to work and induce an attitude of dependency on state institutions. The term is usually intended in a pejorative sense, on the assumption that those who become dependent on the state are apt to remain so. The sense of responsibility for their own lives becomes atrophied, initiative and risk-taking dwindle, and the normal process of building a home and family is neglected in favour of cheap and renewable pleasures. Whether the accusation is fair may be doubted. However, Murray presents empirical evidence for the conclusion that the poorer classes in America (urban blacks in particular) have become trapped by the dependency culture, and as a result burdened with enormous social costs – such as illegitimacy, juvenile crime, boredom and drug abuse – which far outweigh the material benefits of welfare. *See also* *underclass.

dependency theory
A theory developed during the 1970s (e.g. by Immanuel Wallerstein) in order to explain the failure of the former colonial countries to develop despite the provision of aid. The basic claim is that the former colonies remain dependent on international finance and Western money markets, and that all aid goes to fuelling this dependency and furthering the economic ascendency of Western multinationals. Third-world countries are thereby maintained in a state of immiseration, to the benefit of the capitalist world. The theory has much in common with the Marxist theory of *exploitation, and is now widely rejected. *See* *developing country *thirdworldism.

depression
The state of an economy in which labour and the means of production remain unemployed for an extended period (as opposed to *recession, where the unemployment is of shorter duration). The most significant example in recent times, which has had incalculable political consequences, was the Depression of 1929–34 – the 'world slump' – which, beginning in America, transmitted itself through international banking and uncontrolled credit transfers to central Europe and then to the UK, so that its political effects were immediate and striking throughout the capitalist world – notably in the *New Deal in the US, in the rise of *national socialism in Germany, and in the political instability of central Europe.

déracinement
French: uprootedness. Term introduced by *Barrès, and used by French political thinkers (especially *Weil) to describe the state of people torn loose from their cultural, religious and moral origins, led to question the validity of all instinctive relations, and deprived of the forms of life through which to rehearse and renew their social nature and attachments.

derogation
The temporary exemption from some regulation or provision, as in the derogations to its Treaties offered by the *European Union by way of easing the passage of new member states.

Derrida, Jacques (1930–2004)
Algerian-born French philosopher and critic. *See* *deconstruction.

desacralization
The process whereby the sense of the sacred and the holy is gradually driven from the experience of social relations: as when marriage, once thought of as

a *sacrament and a vow before God, becomes instead a secular *contract, with terms that might be altered or rescinded by agreement. It is an important question how much desacralization a society can bear without moral disintegration.

Descartes, René (1596–1650)

French philosopher and mathematician. *See* *false consciousness, *human nature, *natural light, *rationalism.

desegregation

The process, begun in the US in the 1950s, of attempting to procure for blacks, not just the nominal freedom and equality guaranteed under the constitution, but actual political equality with whites, by abolishing the established separation of educational, recreational and other facilities.

deskilling

The process whereby, in advanced societies, skills are gradually lost from the wider community, as labour-saving devices and advanced technology take over the day-to-day tasks that were previously performed by people. This process, aided, some say, by the 'dumbing down' of the school curriculum and the destruction of hobbies by television, has created a society most of whose members lack the elementary skills needed for survival outside the pampered circumstances of their upbringing – for example, the ability to cook, to grow food, to use tools, to mend machinery, to sew, knit or build in wood.

despotism

From Greek, *despotēs*, meaning originally a master (for example, of a household, and so of slaves), and applied to the *absolute ruler of a people whose condition could be compared to that of *slavery. Now often applied to any form of *arbitrary or *tyrannical government, but perhaps better used to mean a form of government that is not inherently *limited by law, custom or effective *opposition, so that the power of state can encroach wherever and whenever this should please those who wield it. To be distinguished from *absolutism, which may involve real limitations on the power of government, but where those limitations are not specifically enshrined in law.

Since *Montesquieu's celebrated analysis of despotism (*De l'ésprit des lois*, 1748) it has seemed evident that a necessary condition for its existence is the concentration of powers in a single person, office or political *agent, so that there is no internal constraint on or correction of the exercise of power. (*See* *separation of powers.) The concentration of power does not have to be in an individual. The original Greek meaning suggests that the important feature of despotism is the condition of those subject to it, and it makes little material difference to that condition that all power should be concentrated in a committee, or a party, rather than an individual, except in so far as this multiplicity of *command may permit the subject to secure relief, either by exploiting disagreements, or by obtaining some covert form of *representation.

Despotism requires that power be not only concentrated but also without effective opposition within the state. It is also arbitrary, in the sense of standing above law, at least to some degree: however, it is not easy for any power to be wholly arbitrary without arousing opposition stronger than itself, hence actual despotism always exists in conjunction with a system of law, however primitive, whereby to *legitimate its own exercise, and transgresses the law only when this is thought to be essential to maintaining its supremacy. Hence a fiction of *legality is usually maintained.

Some writers have referred to 'enlightened despotism', to indicate, for example, the peculiar kind of absolute monarchy exercised in Prussia under Frederick the Great. In such cases it is supposed that the individual character of the despot is such as to ensure that concentrated power is used in the pursuit of ends that are worthy in themselves, and perhaps likely to recommend themselves to a liberal conscience, while needing despotic power for their realization.

destabilization

The process whereby the subject institutions of a state, and its lawful *associations (e.g. schools, businesses, armed forces) are deliberately set against the state, by agitation and *propaganda, so that the political order should become unstable, permitting conquest or *annexation by another external or internal power. Destabilization played a significant part in communist foreign policy, and is currently an important tactic of *Islamists in the Middle East.

destiny

An impersonal force that orders the affairs of men, so as to propel them through life independently of their will, but in a manner illustrative of their character, and perhaps symbolic of their condition. The idea has existed in mystical form (which makes destiny unknowable), in religious form (which transforms destiny into *providence), and in the form of scientific or quasi-scientific theories about the nature of history (*see* for example, *historical materialism, *Spengler). Most people believe that some things that happen to them are independent of their will; the singular character of a belief in destiny is the conviction that all the *important* things that happen in human affairs are independent of the will. The intermediate position is that

of common sense, which holds that there is a basic 'human condition'. This is, and perhaps ought to be, independent of the will; in the context of the human condition, projects may be undertaken which can fail for the smallest reason or succeed despite the odds. Extreme forms of liberal anarchism dislike such ideas, and are reluctant to countenance the existence of unchangeable features of humanity. Matters previously assigned to destiny are, it is supposed, or ought to be, brought within the arena of *consent. Noteworthy among these matters is sexuality, previously thought to define the condition from which the individual begins, now sometimes thought to be a matter of personal choice, which may be 'tacitly consented' to, but which might easily be changed.

The idea of destiny (*moira*) played an important role in the ancient Greek understanding, both of the individual life and of the life of the *polis. The tragedians see *moira* as a fundamental part of each person's self-identity – not a force working from outside, but a force that has possession of an individual's soul and choices, so that he is both free and unfree in acting it out. The *polis* is intimately bound up with the fate of its leading families, as in Aeschylus's *Oresteia*, and plays its own role in releasing them, at last, from the bond of *moira*, by offering justice and deliberation in its place.

detail labour

*Labour that is directed entirely to some detail in the process of production, and which therefore produces a *commodity only in combination with other labour of a similar kind. A production line creates successive tasks for detail labour, and exemplifies the 'detail division of labour'. This is to be distinguished from the social *division of labour, since it is characteristic, not of *market conditions as such, but of the industrialization of production, and can, presumably, exist without a market economy.

Detail labour has been the object of much distaste, on the part of socialists and conservatives alike, both of whom have tended to see in it a dehumanization of the labourer and a source of *alienation. It is sometimes opposed to *craft, which is held to be complete and completely intelligible to the labourer, in the way that a production line cannot be. While the consequent attempt to restore craft-like modes of production (*see* *Morris) has often been criticized as short-sighted and quixotic, there seems to be general agreement that *something* is wrong with production that requires a person, for much of the day, to devote himself completely to an action that is incomplete.

According to *Marx detail division constitutes a 'separation of the labourer from the means of production', which brings about a condition of enslavement to the means of production, since it alone can give completion to his task. Marx's critique was anticipated by Adam *Smith, who lamented the idiocy and enslavement consequent upon detail labour, while asserting that 'in every improved and civilized society this is the state into which the labouring poor, that is, the great body of the people, must necessarily fall' (*Wealth of Nations*, v, i, ii). Whatever the truth in this lament, it seems that only a small proportion of the work force in most modern economies is employed at any moment in detail labour. Indeed, the shift from the production of goods to the *service economy makes this whole debate largely irrelevant.

détente

French: the reduction of tension between states. The term has been used largely in connection with US–USSR relations since the late 1960s, in which a policy of *peaceful coexistence was professed by both parties, and seemingly pursued, through arms limitation talks and the Helsinki Accord, 1975, on security and cooperation in Europe.

determinism

1. The philosophical doctrine that everything that happens is determined by that which preceded it. More precisely: nature is governed by 'deterministic' laws, such that, given a complete description of the world at one time and a statement of those laws, a complete description of the world at any later time may be deduced. Determinism is sometimes thought to imply that all events happen by necessity, and that nothing could be other than it is. However, this obscures an important distinction, between *fatalism, and what *J.S. Mill called 'philosophical necessity', which denotes only the operation of universal natural laws.

Philosophers debate over (a) whether or not determinism is, or could be, true (for example, does the dominance of irreducibly statistical laws in microphysics refute it?); (b) if it is true, is it compatible, or incompatible, with human freedom? The thesis of 'compatibilism', variously advanced by *Spinoza, *Hobbes, *Hume, *Kant, and Mill, argues that human freedom does not require any violation of the causal order, and so is compatible with the truth of determinism.

2. In political thought 'determinism' is normally used more narrowly, to denote the view that human choice is not itself a main causal factor in the generation of social and political arrangements. Whether or not we have free will, history is determined independently of its exercise, for example, by economic processes which continue and develop however

we choose to act on them. (*See* *histor-ical materialism.*)

*Vulgar Marxism, which is in part distinguished by that view, also argues that since human consciousness is a product of material conditions, those conditions cannot themselves be brought about by consciousness (i.e. by intentional action). Implausible though such a view may be, it has a certain appeal, since it seems to entail that the political action of one's opponent is based on an illusion. It also entails that political action of one's own is based on the same illusion, but this consequence is not always so clearly perceived.

deterrence

To deter is to dissuade an agent from a course of action by alerting him to consequences that he does not desire. In the theory of *punishment, deter-rence is often presented as a, or the, major justification of the practice, and in that context must be carefully distinguished from retribution, vengeance, and correction. The term has achieved wider political currency from modern *strategies of defence, notably in the context of the threat of nuclear war. Strategists distinguish active or extended deterrence (which threatens retaliation to any act of aggression, whether against the state in question or against its allies), from minimum or finite deterrence, intended to protect only the state which adopts it. Graduated deterrence is the systematic strategy of demon-strating an intention to punish hostile acts in accordance with their serious-ness, while mutual deterrence is the relation that exists between two hostile powers that effectively deter each other from war.

devaluation

An increase in the amount of domestic currency required to purchase a unit of foreign currency. Since devaluation raises the price of foreign goods and services at home, while lowering the prices of domestic goods and services to purchasers abroad, it tends to increase the volume, though not necessarily the value in money terms, of exports, and correspondingly discourages imports. Social, economic and political reasons may make governments reluctant actively to devalue. Instead a government may 'float' the currency, leaving the level of the exchange rate to be determined in the international market. *See* *exchange control.

developing country

A phrase imprecisely used, and vari-ously defined. Generally, a developing country is one that is poor in terms of *per capita* income, and whose economic structure is backward. One theory is that developing countries have not yet reached the stage of *development sufficient to yield domestic savings which will finance further *economic growth. That defin-ition assumes that growth has no natural limits, and that the presence of self-stimulated growth is the main thing that separates the rich from the poor among nations. Some regard the word 'developing' as evasive, since it begs the question as to the real posi-tion of the nations relative to one another. A like evasion may seem to be involved in 'underdeveloped', 'back-ward', and so on. The implicit assump-tion is that a universal process, which has occurred elsewhere, is here only in its initial stages, and that all that is necessary in order that the poorer nations should come into line with the richer is that this process should be actively stimulated. Although many of the 'developing' nations have indeed experienced economic growth, it has been at a much slower rate than that of the developed nations, thus causing the gap between the two to widen (i.e. their relative growth rate has declined). Some believe the process of trade that has this result to be for that reason unjust. Various attempts have been made – e.g. through *aid – to alleviate the condition of the poorer nations (e.g. by the United Nations, through its Conference on Trade and Development, UNCTAD). Any solution that does not envisage substantial improvements in the *infrastructure of poorer countries is at best a temporary measure, and some argue that this improvement cannot be achieved by aid alone. *See* *three worlds theory.

development

Usually used to denote the process of *economic growth in *per capita* *income, and the fundamental changes in economic structure that generate that growth. Generally these include: *industrialization, the migration of *labour to industrial areas, *division of labour, etc.; the consequent revisions in economic relations, especially in the modes of tenure of *land; the steady increase in *investment.

Economic development has a precise significance. Some also speak of cultural and political development. In the first case it is not clear what is meant, since *culture, in its normal acceptation, is not something that exhibits continuous progress. On whatever scale we might measure cultural sophistication, however, cultural and economic sophistication need not go together. (Compare the fragmentary culture of modern capitalism with the sophisticated culture of the undeveloped countries of the European Middle Ages.) In the case of political development the idea of a continuous progression seems, at least in some contexts, to be more persuasive. For example, the steady limitation of the powers of European monarchs, the rise of representative institutions, and the development of constitutional constraints and democratic procedures, have all seemed at one time or another to have a kind of inevitability, and a character of steady achievement through *rationalization. For this reason some political analysts speak of constitutional, representative, and democratic institutions as more 'developed' than say *absolutism or *oriental despotism. So long as the term is not held to have any implications beyond its reference to the history of European monarchy this is not misleading. However, it is only on the assumption of what has been called the *Whig interpretation of history that such 'development' can be seen as a universal human value. *See* *end of history.

deviationism

Term introduced in 1921 in a resolution passed by the tenth congress of the Russian Communist Party, and used to denote the tendency within any *communist party to stray from officially sanctioned belief or policy. There are two major types of deviationism: 'dogmatism', or blind adherence to Marxist theory regardless of facts, and 'empiricism', or respect for the facts so great as to lead to a rejection of Marxist theory. In addition, deviationism can be either 'right' or 'left', depending upon whether what is advocated is tougher or milder action (the terms 'adventurism' and 'capitulationism' are also used to denote these two contrasting tendencies). Deviationism, unlike *revisionism, was not so serious a crime that it could not be atoned for and corrected.

devolution

The transfer of legal and political powers to some subordinate institution, while retaining, in theory, complete political control over their exercise. The subordinate institution usually has a *territorial significance, and is designed to correspond to an existing or emergent sense of social and historical *identity. It usually has both *executive and *legislative powers, and thus the result of devolution is to create a subordinate political identity – usually in order to cater for feelings of local allegiance which are too strong to suffer direct government, and too feeble to express themselves in concerted *irredentism.

The process of devolution in the UK has been designed as a compromise, with powers delegated to the Scottish Parliament and the Welsh Assembly, without relinquishing the sovereignty vested in the UK Parliament in Westminster. The constitutional status of the subordinate assemblies seems therefore to be uncertain: their powers are neither *merely* delegated, nor truly autonomous, since the UK Parliament can presumably always reclaim the powers that it has delegated. The problem posed by the lack of an English Parliament is one that the UK government has not yet attempted to address.

Dewey, John (1859–1952)
American philosopher, psychologist, and theorist of education, an exponent of a modified *pragmatism, who opposed what he saw as the artificial divide between theoretical and practical knowledge fostered by *empiricist theories of the mind. Dewey argued that knowing is doing, and the objects of knowledge are the consequences of operations performed by the knower: education involves learning how to turn the world into an object of knowledge. Dewey's educational theories were extremely influential in the earlier part of the twentieth century. His social and political thought is important partly because of its attempt to reconcile *liberal individualism with a philosophy of the individual that recognizes the individual to be, as

such, an abstraction. While the locus of all action is the individual agent, the thoughts and values of that agent are to be understood only by situating him in the dynamic social context of which he is a part. Dewey saw the major problem of contemporary American society as lying in the need to rework tradition (specifically, traditional customs, institutions and ways of perceiving the world) into a scientific and technological vision of reality. He believed that philosophy is the true critical instrument whereby human life, culture and institutions can be understood, and tried to advocate educational ideas that would reconcile the pragmatist approach to science and knowledge with a respect for culture and *humane education generally. His emphasis on the active nature of experience owed much to *Kant and *idealism, although his sense of the individual as in part the active creator of the social world was more redolent of native American optimism than of the idealist philosophies of society which it distantly echoes. Dewey's emphasis on 'child-centered' education and his belief that children learn by self-expression and experiment changed the attitude to education in both the US and the UK – some say with disastrous consequences. (*See* *education.)

dhimmî
Arabic, from *dhimmah*, a covenant: one who has been granted protection under covenant; specifically an adherent of one of the faiths tolerated within the *dar al-Islam* (the 'House of Submission'). On Koranic authority both Christianity and Judaism are beneficiaries of the covenant; in Persia the benefit was extended to Zoroastrians and in the Indian principalities during periods of Muslim rule to Hindus and Buddhists (though grudgingly). The *dhimmî* must pay a

poll tax in order to secure his exemption from forced conversion to the faith, and traditionally the procedures for collecting this tax were designed to humiliate and to remind the *dhimmî* of his servitude. Attempts by a *dhimmî* to convert Muslims were punishable (traditionally by death), and the right to build places of worship is not acknowledged, though traditionally allowed on sufferance. Contracts between a Muslim and a *dhimmî* were unenforceable by the *dhimmî*, who was present always as a passive partner to the deal. The exacting provisions of the *dhimmah* were softened under the Ottomann *millet system, though their force is still felt in the Middle East today, notably in Egypt, where the indigenous Copts, survivors of a pre-Islamic Christian community, are subject to systematic discrimination. Likewise in modern Iran Christians and members of the Baha'i faith have been subjected to persecution, and neither seems to enjoy any real protection under the law.

D'Hondt system

A system, invented by a nineteenth-century Belgian, for distributing posts between different groups in an elected assembly or government. Suppose three parties hold respectively 100, 60 and 30 seats in an assembly, with the right to appoint six cabinet members between them. Divide the number of seats held by each party first by two, then by three etc., in order to allocate posts after the first three according to numerical results. Thus the first position goes to Party A (100 members), the second to Part B (60) members and the third to Party C (30 members), the fourth to Party A (100/2 being greater than 60/2,) as does the fifth (100/3 being greater than 60/2), with the sixth going to Party B (60/2 being greater than 100/4); Party C remains with the one post. The system is used by the European Parliament and was used by the Northern Ireland Assembly before its dissolution in 2000.

dialectic

A term derived from Greek philosophy (literally: argument), and used in a variety of interconnected ways throughout the history of Western thought:

1. *Plato. The dialectic is the process of question and answer, whereby the philosopher draws his interlocutor to see for himself the truth of which the philosopher wishes to persuade him. The 'Socratic method' consists in first prompting a response, and then, by showing it to be erroneous, turning the disputant's mind in the direction of a truth that he will recognize as true without recourse to received ideas, prejudice or external authority. The 'dialectic' is supposed to show that the rational ability to perceive truth is innate, and needs only to be awakened by philosophical reflection.

2. *Kant. The dialectic is the 'logic of illusion', the process of contradictory and fallacious reasoning which follows upon the attempt to know the world absolutely, through pure reason alone, and without reference to the experience and point of view of the knowing subject. A dialectical contradiction is one in which each premise is founded on a false supposition, itself derived from the vain attempt to see the world from a 'transcendental' perspective, as a 'thing in itself'.

3. *Hegel, influenced by Kant, was concerned, however, not to bury but to praise the 'dialectical' modes of reasoning. In Hegel 'dialectic' describes both the relation between premises and conclusions in a logical argument, and also the process of historical development in reality. The essence of the dialectical movement is 'the negation of the negation', or the

'labour of the negative', whereby truth is approached by the successive generation of the negation of each concept postulated in the attempt to capture it. A concept is posited: it describes reality only partially and generates out of itself its own negation. The conflict between the two concepts is resolved (transcended) by the process of dialectical union, whereby a new, more adequate representation of the world is derived. And so on. (Later idealists sometimes used the terms 'thesis', 'antithesis', 'synthesis' to denote the three parts of the argument. The precedent for this usage lies in the work of Hegel's predecessor *Fichte.) History moves in like manner, from crude formless gestures, by way of dialectical contradictions in action, to the fully realized consciousness of science, embodied in the institutions of a state. The oppositions that determine all development, whether in logical or mathematical argument, or in the human soul and society, are to be construed not as conflicts, but as *contradictions. Through resolving such contradictions spirit achieves a 'lifting up' (*Aufhebung*) to a higher level.

4. In *Marxist thought. Partly on account of Hegelian influence on both *Engels and *Marx, partly because of Russian Marxist intellectuals who refused to see any absolute divide between Hegel and Marx, the 'dialectic' has been thought to be fundamental, first to the Marxist theory of history, secondly to the hoped-for Marxist 'method' in all the human sciences. The contradictions, for Marx, however, are to be found in *material* reality, and in thought only as a consequence of that reality. (*See* *dialectical materialism.) Dialectic describes the movement of history, as generated by forces which contradict each other, but which also grow from each other. Thus capitalism generates *bourgeoisie and *proletariat, which grow in response to each other, cannot exist without each other, but remain in irreconcilable conflict until the new order emerges from their revolutionary ruin. It is supposed that this innate contradiction has an essentially *dynamic* character, as in Hegel: it is *because* of contradiction that things must change.

The dialectical 'method' is sometimes put forward as including various other theses from Hegel's logic, such as the 'transition from quantity to quality'. (Example: the addition of successive parts to a frame at a certain point produces a bicycle.) There are no abrupt transitions, only new perspectives brought about by successive change. This, and various other Hegelian ideas, are sometimes advanced as 'laws of dialectics', held to apply to subjects as disparate as formal logic and sociology.

dialectical materialism

Term coined by Josef Dietzgen (1828–88) and used by the Russian Marxist Plekhanov as a name for Marx's theory of history and consciousness, as expounded by Marx's friend and collaborator, *Engels. The term is now best used as a name for Engels' own version of the theory (as expounded, e.g., in the posthumous *Dialectics of Nature*, 1925). Like Marx, Engels believed that 'consciousness does not determine life, but life determines consciousness' (Marx: *The German Ideology*). *Hegel had described the movement of history as the movement of consciousness (or 'spirit') alone, arguing that this movement must proceed according to the logical order of the *dialectic. Engels agreed that the movement of history is dialectical, but denied that it is spiritual. Hence the name 'dialectical materialism'.

Dicey, Albert Venn (1835–1922)

English jurist whose celebrated examination and defence of the British constitution (*Introduction to the Study of* *the Law of the Constitution,* 1885) has influenced all subsequent thinking about the nature of constitutions, and about the relevance or otherwise of a written document. Dicey argues that written clauses cannot protect a citizen from oppression if no procedure exists whereby the citizen himself can enforce them against the state and its agents. The unwritten constitution of the United Kingdom, precisely because it is reluctant to state the rights of the citizen and operates by *convention rather than rule, presents a far greater obstacle to tyranny than the written constitution of Revolutionary France. This is in part because the rights that it guarantees are embedded in the very *procedure* of government and made available to the citizen by the *common law and *equity, over which governments have little or no control.

dictatorship

In the Roman Republic a dictator was a magistrate with extraordinary powers, appointed in times of civil or military crisis. He was nominated by a consul on the recommendation of the senate and confirmed by the Comitia Curiata. The office lasted for six months, but was usually laid down when the crisis was passed: other magistrates were subject to the dictators. No dictator was chosen after 202 BC, but Julius Caesar assumed dictatorial powers for ten years in 46 BC, and shortly before his assassination was given them for life.

Hence, a system of government in which one person, office, faction or party is empowered to dictate all political action and compel obedience from all other citizens. The term is not truly distinct in modern usage from 'despotism', although possibly it has the added implication that the ruling agent is active in commanding things, and not merely obstructive in resisting them. Just as there can be 'enlightened

despotism', so can there be 'benign dictatorship', and indeed such was the Roman conception of the office that bore this name. Dictatorship may exist *de jure, as in the Roman office, or merely *de facto,* as in most modern versions.

dictatorship of the proletariat

An expression used by *Marx, and adapted from *Blanqui, who had written of the need for a 'revolutionary dictatorship'. Marx never explained what he meant by 'dictatorship' (and sometimes spoke only of the 'rule' of the proletariat); nevertheless the expression came to have a definite rhetorical significance in subsequent Marxist thinking, in order to denote the nature and the legitimacy of state power during the period of transition from revolution to true communist society.

difference

See *deconstruction, *diversity, *Girard.

difference principle

A criterion of *social justice according to which situation *a* is to be preferred to situation *b* only if the least advantaged member of society is better off in *a* than the least advantaged individual would be in *b*. To be contrasted with *Pareto optimality, and classical *utilitarian conceptions of social welfare. The difference principle has been incorporated by *Rawls into his theory of *justice, where it is used to specify the supposed requirement of social justice, against a prior principle determining individual *rights. 'The intuitive idea is that the social order is not to establish and secure the more attractive prospects of those better off unless doing so is to the advantage of those less fortunate' (J. Rawls: *A Theory of Justice,* 1971) – an intuitive idea that is also endorsed by many of the utilitarian justifications of capitalism and private property.

differentials

A feature of the 'reward system' in employment that has become increasingly important in political thought and practice. It seems that many people respond more vigorously to an erosion in the 'differentials' that distinguish them from the groups with which they normally compare themselves, than to many absolute changes in their living standards. The existence of a graduated system of reward, with various levels fixed relatively to one another, has therefore been held to be a functional requirement in economic life.

Dilthey, Wilhelm (1833–1911)

German philosopher and social theorist, influenced by *Kant, and one of the founders of the modern conception of *Verstehen*. The world is to be understood in two ways – according to scientific explanation and prediction, and according to the peculiarly human form of understanding (*Verstehen*) which is exemplified in our perception of each other, and which can be extended to all social and therefore all historical phenomena. *Verstehen* is the comprehension of a mental content – e.g. an idea, experience or intention – as this is manifest in empirically given expressions. It is not that there are two worlds, but rather two ways of understanding the world. The 'human' way of understanding is cultivated through those studies – the *Geisteswissenschaften* – which explore the concepts and relations that are integral to *Verstehen*: this is the true reason for thinking that *humane education is essential for the correct perception of the 'human world', and so of all social and political reality. The human world is a world of significances, and no human significance can be fully grasped by scientific abstractions. Every expression must be returned to its social, historical and cultural context, if its full meaning is to be revealed, and hence *Verstehen* must be educated through comparison and analysis. Without that education history and society will remain only partly intelligible. Dilthey argued against *empiricism and *individualism, and extended his theory of understanding to institutions and legal systems. He was a founder of modern *hermeneutics, and profoundly influenced the course of sociology, through his admirer *Weber.

dilution of labour

The assignment of work customarily assigned to one category of labourer to workers of another kind – specifically, the extraction from the process of production of those parts that can be performed by unskilled labourers, in order to economize on the use of skilled labour. Such economizing has been one of the major results of productivity bargaining in recent years.

diminishing returns, law of

The hypothesis that if one *factor of production is continually increased by constant amounts, while other factors remain unaltered, then – at least after some point – the resulting increases in output become steadily smaller. (For example, the constant increase in the amount of corn fed into a mill, with no increase in the number of people employed there, will produce a steadily diminishing increase in the amount of flour produced.)

This 'law' is not really a universal rule, but typically it is true. It is in fact a common-sense assumption, perhaps better captured in ordinary maxims of practical wisdom than in the technicalities of economic theory. Nevertheless, it has been given technical exposition and support by many economists.

diplomacy

The art of conducting negotiations between *states. Modern diplomacy began with the creation of permanent missions between states in the fifteenth century, but diplomatic representation is very ancient, in the form of envoys from sovereign to sovereign. The Congress of Vienna established grades of diplomatic office, and laid down rules of correct behaviour and immunity. Diplomatic privileges traditionally included *droit de chapelle* (entitlement to practise own religion), *droit de quartier* (immunity from local police), and *droit de l'hôtel*, or extraterritoriality, under which the embassy is regarded as a place exempt from local *jurisdiction and *taxation. All these are summed up under the label 'diplomatic immunity', although the extent of that immunity is now disputed. For example, does extra-territoriality give an embassy the right to construct buildings in defiance of local planning law? Diplomacy is a mode of settling disputes without recourse to *force, or to *international law. If international *adjudication were systematic and generally enforceable, then presumably diplomacy would be less necessary. One of the most important functions of any diplomatic approach is to persuade the other party to accept a settlement under international law. Thus even the application of law may require diplomacy.

direct action

Action to secure a political objective taken outside the constitutional framework, and indifferent to existing legal constraints. Direct action may be non-violent, as advocated by Gandhi and various *civil rights movements (*see* *civil disobedience, *passive resistance), or violent – in which case its extreme forms include *rebellion and *revolution.

Among familiar forms of direct action are *terrorism and strikes carried out by workers who have no legal right to strike. (*See* *industrial action.)

direct democracy

Any system of government in which all decisions are made by *collective choice of the citizens, and not through representatives. Direct democracy is contrasted with representative democracy (*see* *representation), and it is widely assumed that it is feasible only if the body to be governed is small, and so able to register its preferences by repeated voting. One of the most historically important systems of direct democratic government was that instituted in Athens (*see* *Athenian democracy). Some argue that only in a direct democracy is there any guarantee that the *people are *sovereign; others (including, e.g., *Paine, and *J.S. Mill) have argued for the superiority of indirect systems, which permit the emergence, at key positions in government, of experts who may be answerable to the people but who are not merely puppets of the people.

directive

Order given from an authority to some person, office or organization that is bound to obey it. Directives form the principal instrument of legislation in the *European Union, and are issued by the Council of Ministers to member states, instructing them to pass legislation to a certain effect. Even if a national government hesitates to enact the relevant legislation, the *European Court of Justice will usually assume that the rights and duties that would have been created by it already exist and so grant a cause of action to those who are adversely affected by the absence of the law. This 'direct effect' of the directives compromises national sovereignty; but then so does the existence of the directives themselves, since national legislatures are bound to enact them, regardless of their opinion as to the wisdom of doing so. Moreover, directives issue from the Council of

Ministers, which is an appointed and not an elected body. Not surprisingly, therefore, they have become an object of controversy. They should be distinguished from EC *regulations, which operate throughout the EC without the need for any local legislative enactment. *See* *legal instruments.

dirigisme

From French *diriger*, to direct. A term originally used to describe the policy of French monarchs and controllers of finance during the seventeenth century, and now used to denote the state of affairs in which the *state controls the economy by detailed intervention in economic affairs, e.g. through *nationalization, and through laws restricting private ownership, or by compelling companies to trade on certain terms, in certain areas, and with a certain work force. Its extreme form has sometimes been called *state capitalism by those socialists who have wanted to distinguish between the ideal of common ownership and the practice of state control.

Sometimes the term is used, in the context of French politics, to denote the active intervention of the state in areas of social life other than the economic – e.g. education, local planning and administration, recreation.

dirty hands

It has been argued (e.g. by *Sartre) that politics requires the politician to dirty his hands and that this is either a justification of the dirt or a reason to stay away from politics. A *consequentialist will ultimately take the first line, but his opponent, who believes in the absolute authority of a moral rule, will find it hard to avoid the second. It may be, however, that *casuistry concerning the ideas of *responsibility and *double effect may help the moral absolutist to follow the consequentialist into the breach. *See* *morality and politics.

disability

The impairment in physical or mental powers, through illness, accident or inherited condition. The status of people with disabilities has changed radically in recent times, as a result of concerted political campaigns. Some argue that disabled people have a right to the public provision of amenities that will assist them and minimize the effect of their disabilities. This argument has been widely accepted, though not without opposition from those who believe that it is a recipe for *rights inflation, as well as imposing unacceptable burdens on both public and private providers.

disarmament

The renunciation of military means, either by agreement with a potential aggressor, or independently (*unilateral disarmament). Proposals for general (= applying to all states) and comprehensive (= applying to all weapons and forces) disarmament have been repeatedly made and discussed, for example by the League of Nations in 1927 and 1934. The United Nations set up in 1946 the Atomic Energy Commission for the elimination of the use of atomic energy for destructive purposes, and in 1947 the Commission for Conventional Armaments, 'for the general regulation and reduction of armaments and armed forces'. The commissions were separately established in order to secure maximum chance of agreement over the two issues, but were merged in the UN Disarmament Commission in 1951 when no agreement had been reached. The USSR argued that disarmament must come first and verification afterwards, and pressed for an agreement on that basis; the West argued that without provisions for verification all agreements were useless. The problem of verification continued to dominate discussion, and remained largely unresolved, despite later concessions by the USSR in the final act of the Helsinki Accord, 1975, and in 'strategic arms limitation' talks between the USSR and the US, resulting in agreements in 1972 and 1974. *See* *arms control.

discourse theory

Social and literary criticism inspired by the work of *Foucault, which takes the 'discourse' of a writer or of an epoque as its object of study, and which attempts to show the ways in which argument, conceptualization and language itself are organized around prevailing structures of social power. Much US academic feminism can be seen as a form of discourse theory, whose aim is to show the way in which a patriarchal vision of the human condition has been inserted into, and concealed within, the accepted descriptions of social facts.

discrimination

The according of differential treatment to persons, bodies, or groups, usually with the implication that there is not sufficient ground for doing this in the actual differences between them. Thus 'discrimination' tends to mean irrelevant, and also invidious, distinction. Some argue that irrelevance implies invidiousness, since if the differences between *a* and *b* are irrelevant to deciding the question of what treatment should be ministered to either, then it is unjust to discriminate between them. (*See* *justice.) Intuitions about 'invidious' distinctions are frequently built into law – as in the UK Race Relations Act 1976, and Sex Discrimination Act 1975. *See* *racism, and *sexism.

A distinction may be thought to correspond to some deep division of nature between people, and so to give grounds for differential treatment. While the search for that deep division may involve the rationalization of an irrational prejudice (e.g. in the Nazi ideology of race), it may also involve

serious hypotheses concerning large and undecided questions (e.g. in the normal grounds for treating children differently from adults, or mentally retarded people differently from mentally normal people).

Those seeking to rectify the long-term effects of discrimination have frequently argued for a policy of *reverse or 'positive' discrimination. This policy is a major object of controversy in the US.

disenchantment

German: *Entzauberung.* Term given a specialized sense by *Weber, to denote the perception of the world conferred on the modern consciousness by the loss of wonder, and by the conviction that a scientific explanation can be offered for every observable fact. Disenchantment is not, normally, the outcome of any deliberate process of *demystification, or *demythologization, but consists in an irreversible shift in consciousness, with consequences that are felt throughout the realm of moral and political values, and without discernible remedy. Weber thought that it was an inevitable consequence of the acceptance, under modern conditions, of a 'legal-rational' vision of social arrangements.

The 'literature of disenchantment', thought to include such writers as Kafka, Beckett, and Rilke (whose self-conscious efforts to re-enchant his world have often been held up as an object lesson in heroic failure), is one of the most striking features of modern high culture, giving expression to, and perhaps relief from, a condition that is sometimes thought to lie at the heart of twentieth-century social consciousness.

Disraeli, Benjamin, Earl of Beaconsfield (1804–81)
British statesman and novelist, who established the British Conservative

Party as a champion of *democratization and social and electoral reform. *See* *conservatism, *conservative parties, *industrial law, *industrial revolution, *land, *Toryism, *trade union.

dissident

Normal translation of German *Andersdenkende*, Russian *inakomyslyashtie*, one who thinks differently, one who dissents from official ideas. It was defined variously in communist countries, e.g. by Jan Tesář (1979) as 'openly expressed political disagreement with the government in a totalitarian system', and although clearly there can be received ideas (and therefore dissent from them) in the absence of *totalitarianism, it is largely in order to indicate the peculiar muffled fervour of dissent in totalitarian countries that the term has been used. In this context some have distinguished 'intrastructural' from 'extrastructural' dissent, the former being dissent 'within the system' as when the ideology, codes of conduct, and political expectations of the Communist Party are quietly but deliberately flouted by someone holding office in a communist state.

Often the dissident is attempting to enforce, or encouraging the state to enforce, existing laws (usually laws concerning *civil rights). (*See* *charter.) Either the state, in adopting such laws, intended them to be obeyed, in which case there is no dissent from them, but only official lawlessness, or it did not, in which case it is in contradiction with itself, and so must be dissented from by every rational being. In this way the term 'dissident' has a misleading implication of eccentricity, for although it may be foolhardy to *express* dissent, e.g. from the edicts of a ruling Communist Party, it may also be impossible not to feel it. Indeed, it has often been thought necessary to personal existence that the citizen in a totalitarian country should withhold his assent from much that occurs in public life, and much that he is forced overtly to condone. Thus 'the essence of dissent is the consciousness that there is no salvation except in the citizen himself, in the restoration of his feelings of self-hood (*svébytnost*) and civic responsibility' (Jan Tesář). That quotation from a Czech dissident expresses two aims of dissent: the struggle for the *autonomy of the self, as this is described by *Kantian thinkers, and the expression of that struggle through an attitude of *responsibility towards *civil society. In external things, however, the only hope is for what *Masaryk called 'small-scale work' (*drobná práce*) – the gradual bending of all public acts and institutions towards the truths that are officially denied. Some of the most important concepts in contemporary political thought have emerged from the writings of dissidents in communist countries – notably *Havel and *Solzhenitsyn.

distribution

1. Economics. The theory of distribution concerns itself with explaining how the returns to the several *factors of production (*land, *labour and *capital) are determined. Some theories focus on aggregate rent, wages and interest, while others seek to provide a far more detailed explanation; e.g. why is a professor of Greek paid more than an agricultural labourer? (Clearly the first, unlike the second, is neither essential to survival, nor in great demand.) Distribution theory has been, and remains, a controversial and unsettled area of economics.

2. More generally, political theory distinguishes distribution of goods from their production, exchange and consumption, as separate but perhaps mutually dependent parts of the process whereby nature is put to use. (*See*

*production, distribution, exchange, consumption.)

3. The question of the extent to which patterns of distribution of wealth, goods and power should be altered in the interests of justice is one that underlies much recent socialist thinking. *Aristotle's conception of distributive justice has often been taken to suggest that the concept of justice can be applied to a distribution, quite independently of its application to the acts, or supposed acts, which brought that distribution about. The question of the coherence of that conception therefore lies at the heart of much political disagreement. (*See* *justice, *social justice.)

distributive justice
See *justice.

diversity
In the context of modern politics the pursuit of diversity means the attempt to make institutions and associations more fully representative of the social, ethnic and sexual distinctions prevalent in society as a whole – thus to secure the appointment of women, ethnic minorities and people of working class origins to positions previously monopolized by white upper class males. The policy, actively embraced by *New Labour, by the *multicultural movement in the US and by the *European Union, can lead to absurd or socially divisive results, as when women or people from ethnic minorities are advanced within some profession despite their lack of qualifications. (*See* *reverse discrimination.) Diversity is sometimes defended on the ground that in modern societies a new form of *identity is emerging in which difference plays a constitutive role: so that people identify with institutions and associations precisely because they come to perceive through them their own difference and distinctness, recognizing difference as a permanent feature of the human condition.

divine right
The idea that a *sovereign rules by divine ordinance, or perhaps that he is himself a divinity. The theory of a divine right seems at one stage to have been widely accepted, and was consciously reintroduced by Augustus to the government of Rome as a necessary part of the *legitimation of his new-found *absolutism. In a speech before parliament in 1610, James I argued that 'Kings are not only God's lieutenants upon earth and sit upon God's throne, but even by God himself they are called gods', adding that kings 'exercise a manner or resemblance of divine power on earth'. He and his family went on to illustrate and apply what Alexander Pope was later to describe as 'the right divine of kings to govern wrong', and a defence of the doctrine – *Eikon Basilike* (Greek: *The King's Picture*) – wrongly attributed to Charles I, achieved great popularity upon the latter's execution, partly because it explained to the English public the quasi-religious horror that was then experienced. The doctrine was defended in modified form by Sir Robert Filmer (*Patriarcha*, 1680), to be attacked by *Locke, and in this version can be seen as an extended metaphysical attempt to make sense of political obligation without referring to contract or consent. Since allegiance to the sovereign defines the political condition of man, and since there is no contract or consent outside that condition, allegiance must be founded in some obligation deeper than those which have arisen through the voluntary undertakings of the subject. Whence came this obligation if it were not divinely imposed? Filmer's view was that no account of political authority could escape reference to

divine *command, and that too great a separation between divine and civil obedience was dangerous both to civil and to religious institutions.

division of labour

If each person produces all that he needs and nothing that another needs, then no one works for another. If, however, someone acquires a skill at some particular employment such as chair-making, he may devote his time to that and exchange chairs for other goods, made by people of similarly specialized employment. Thus there arises the 'social division of labour', a phenomenon noted by *Plato in the *Republic* as fundamental to the institutions of a stable state, and one of the bonds of mutual dependence which necessitate a common system of law. The phenomenon was explored by Adam *Smith as a necessary accompaniment of market conditions, and the essence of manufacturing, and by Marx, as a distinctive feature of private property relations; it has also been a subject of considerable speculation on the part of modern sociologists, in particular *Durkheim (*De la division du travail sociale*, 1893).

It is necessary to distinguish the social division of labour just described, from the detail division of labour which occurs within a factory. Here the process of production is broken down into fine constituents, and each assigned to a different labourer. *See* *detail labour.

division of powers

See *separation of powers.

doctrinaire

Introduced into French usage *circa* 1815 to describe a party which attempted to mediate between extreme and warring *factions, the term is now generally used to denote any outlook or activity that is characterized by rigid adherence to *doctrine, regardless of whether circumstances show that doctrine to be impracticable, irrational or misguided.

doctrine

Literally 'teaching', the term 'doctrine' has been transferred from religious to political usage to denote any attempt to give system or coherence to political *ideals and practice. It is to be distinguished from the theory which explains doctrine (if there be such), and also from the policy which puts it into practice, since it aims to provide a set of reasoned beliefs and attitudes, that will recommend itself through its own intrinsic qualities, and not because it is in anybody's interest either to believe or to act as though he believed it.

Political visions differ in the extent to which they think that doctrine is desirable or possible, and the extent to which they think that doctrine can or ought to be detached from the specific historical conditions in which it is expressed. It is characteristic of certain forms of conservatism to oppose this detachment, and to argue that principles and policies must be allowed to form themselves in response to the actual conditions in which they are applied, and ought not to be formulated as abstract truths applicable to all people everywhere. (*See* *Burke, *Oakeshott.) Sometimes this opposition to doctrine is itself given a doctrinal character – an absolute truth about the human condition of universal application. Sometimes (as with *Hume) it is put forward as part of a sceptical attitude towards the human pretension to knowledge.

Liberalism and socialism are more eager in their search for doctrine, and give descriptions of human ideals and fulfilment that purport to be of universal validity. (*See* *universalism.)

dogma

In Christian theology, the term denotes a truth of religion guaranteed as such by divine revelation, and defined in detail by the *church. Dogma commands assent from the believer, since it is what has to be believed if the religion is to be adopted at all. Similarly, in politics, one may distinguish defining beliefs from peripheral beliefs in any particular standpoint, and it is part of political theory to discern which beliefs are held dogmatically, and which can be changed without fundamental damage to the outlook. The equal right to *welfare is, for example, an item of socialist dogma, while the advocacy of religious *toleration is probably not. Likewise the right of *private property is an item of conservative dogma, while the advocacy of a *laissez-faire economy is not. Sometimes these fundamental beliefs are called axioms, on the ground that *dogmatism is a vice, while not all such ultimate principles are invidious.

The defining characteristic of dogma is that it is ultimate, whereas the defining characteristic of *doctrine is that it is systematic.

dogmatism

The tendency to treat one's own beliefs, whatever their origin and nature, as matters of *dogma, and so to hold on to them irrationally, in the conviction that one's standpoint depends in its entirety on their preservation.

More widely, the inability to relinquish some conviction, in the face of however much evidence to the contrary. Dogmatism implies a belief in *doctrine, which gives system to all beliefs, and so shows each belief to be immovable. It is to be distinguished from bigotry, the acceptance of a dogma in the absence of any interest in doctrine.

domestic

In politics the domestic is to be contrasted with the 'external' or *international, while in economics such expressions as 'domestic product' can be defined without reference to international trade. It should not, however, be assumed that there is any real independence of domestic from international issues or that the character of a domestic government can be determined quite independently of the *foreign policy with which it is conjoined; nor should it be assumed that the structure and volume of domestic product are independent of foreign trade.

domino theory

Expression publicized by the US National Security Council in 1950, and later much used by President Eisenhower, to denote an interdependence of neighbouring states, especially in *developing countries, of such a kind that, faced with internal crises of a similar nature (specifically, the upsurge of guerrilla warfare, armed infiltration, and communist activism), the collapse of one will lead to the progressive and consecutive collapse of its neighbours. The expression summarizes certain intuitive observations, and is not in fact the name of any formulated theory designed to explain them.

double effect

A principle of *casuistry, popularized by Roman Catholic teaching, which argues that an agent is not necessarily responsible for the unwanted side-effect of an intentional action, even though he foresees that effect and does nothing to avoid it. The important factor is not the side-effect, but the effect at which the agent aims. Suppose you are driving a trolley and the brakes fail. You see three men working on the track before you, but can switch to a side track to avoid them; unfortunately there is also a man working on the side track. You switch to the side track, thus doing something with the foreseeable result that someone will be killed. It seems hard to say that you are responsible for his death, or in any other way blameworthy, since you at no point aimed to produce it. This principle is important in discussing such problems as that of *dirty hands.

draconian laws (alternatively: draconic laws)

Literally laws of the kind given to Athens by the archon Draco in 621 BC. Now used as a general designation for any legislation that is severe, inflexible, and of wide application, on the (probably false) assumption that such were the laws of Draco. (*See also* *legislator.*)

Dreyfus, Alfred (1859–1938)

French artillery officer of Jewish extraction, falsely accused and convicted of betraying military secrets, whose case became a cause célèbre in France, on account of the anti-semitism exploited by his accusers, and of the passionate defence of him by Zola (*J'accuse*, 1898), *Péguy and others. Dreyfus was pardoned in 1906; but his case had precipitated one of the first modern discussions of national identity and the place of Jews within it.

drugs

See *addiction.

due process (i.e. of law)

The conduct of legal proceedings according to established principles designed to safeguard the legal *rights of the individual. The concept is rooted in English common law, and finds expression in Magna Carta, 1215, article 39 (on which *see* *charter), which establishes that there shall be no imprisonment without trial and that the accused shall have a right to trial by jury. It was adopted by the US constitution, Fifth Amendment (1791), and extended to state action by the Fourteenth Amendment (1867). It is now established that no federal or state government can act so as to deprive a person of 'life, liberty or property, without due process of law'.

The alleged refusal of due process has become one of the major causes of action in US *administrative law. Partly as a result of that, the complaint is now interpreted very widely, so that any legal proceeding which does not conform to intuitive requirements of *natural justice is held to violate the right to due process.

dumping

Selling in a foreign market at a price below that charged at home, or even below cost of production. An exporting state or company may tolerate the short-run losses due to dumping in order to eliminate foreign competition and so secure a monopoly, or in order to dispose of temporary surpluses. The General Agreement on Tariffs and Trade (GATT), 1948, permits defence against dumping by the levy of a duty, and dumping is expressly forbidden within the EU by the Treaty of Rome. (*See also* *international trade.*)

duress

In law: *force applied or threatened in order to *coerce, and actually coercing, someone to act in a certain way. Duress includes threats to deprive of economic benefits, and threats to spouse, parent or child. Any act performed under duress is legally altered, and a contract obtained by duress is voidable. This legal idea has its moral counterpart, and it is sometimes offered as an objection to certain *social contract theories of *political obligation that the contract which they envisage as lying at the heart of social arrangements is one that exists by duress. (This particularly weighs against *Hobbes's view, that people are bound by contract to the warring sovereign whose peace they have accepted.)

Durkheim, Émile (1858–1917)

French sociologist, a founder of modern sociology, and influential both in his attempt to synthesize theory with statistical research and in his use of the *katascopic approach. Durkheim held that the *milieu social* is as much a reality as the physical environment, but it is a 'reality *sui generis*', which cannot be reduced to physical terms. *Social facts exist independently of the individual, and exert a unique kind of constraint upon his action. Durkheim investigated such constraints, as disclosed within a system of *division of labour, where order is embodied in contractual relations. Durkheim argued that, although a contract is backed by the sanction of the law, it is the non-contractual element of a contract that both impinges most directly on the personality of the individual and also renders the contract binding. Laws can have authority only when underpinned by the 'moral authority' of internalized *norms. In industrial society, shifts in economic relations had broken down the older 'mechanical solidarity' of the 'horde', and largely replaced it with the 'organic solidarity' of the division of labour. What was previously a true 'collective consciousness', which united all members of society in a single system of values, had become a divided complex of competing norms, attached to functional groups and classes. The sole remaining common sentiment was that of humanity. But this idea was itself threatened, Durkheim thought, by pathological conditions of society, exemplified in *suicide, and characterized by *anomie*.

Durkheim introduced the idea of *functional explanation into social sciences, and argued that there are genuinely social causal relations: i.e., one social fact may cause another such fact, according to laws of social development, and these laws, together with the facts that they explain, may not be reducible to any laws or facts concerning the behaviour of individuals. Thus Durkheim rejected *individualism. He also criticized *utilitarian doctrines, and in particular the claim that increased division of labour and economic progress must necessarily bring increased happiness: on the contrary, the enforced fragmentation of industrial production gives people an individuality they can neither want nor bear, since it detaches them from the social order in which their norms are validated.

Durkheim offered a theory of the religious sentiment, as expressing a need for community, and for a criterion of social membership. He explored the 'elementary forms of the religious life' as ways in which the destiny of the community is made real in our emotions and also safeguarded against internal and external threats.

duty

Duties may be moral, religious, legal, personal, social or political; they may be founded in nature or in convention; they may be overriding or overridable, conditional or unconditional, absolute or relative. The philosophical theory of *deontology regards duty and the associated idea of obligation as the fundamental concepts of morality, specifying both a reason and a motive for action. Typically such a philosophy also elevates duty over all other motives, and endows it with an absolute, unconditioned and overriding claim to obedience (*see* *Kant). To argue in such a way is, by implication, to deny the validity of *utilitarianism, as of every form of *consequentialism or *teleology, as answers to the questions of morality. Deontology will also regard legal and political perspectives as subordinate to the moral perspective, and will, typically, attempt to generate a *natural law theory of political obligation. Philosophers dispute over whether *rights and duties are correlative – i.e. whether every right defines a duty and every duty a right – or whether there can be duties where no one has a right to their obedience, or rights where no one has a duty to respect them. (*See* *jural correlates.) Theories of natural and of human rights often neglect to settle this dispute, and therefore occasionally seem to be claiming rights while saying nothing about who has the duty to respect them or to see that they are satisfied. Hence recent scepticism towards the advocacy of rights, which often seems to be a way of claiming benefits while offering nothing in return for them. By placing the concept of duty first, and deriving that of a right from it, we emphasize the fact that the benefits of political existence also have a cost, and the cost is a heavy one.

Since only rational beings seem to have duties, many philosophers have tried to refer the motive of duty to reason alone, and to argue that the true objectivity of moral judgement is to be found in its appeal to duty, which is no other than an appeal to reason. (The most important example of such a philosopher is Kant, although Kant had often been anticipated, notably by *Aquinas.) Others, in the spirit of *Hume's scepticism concerning moral judgement, have argued that reason alone cannot be a motive to action, and therefore that the appeal to duty adds no independent authority to any moral law but at best merely reiterates it. In this way the concept of duty has often served as

a focus for disputes both about the objectivity of morals, and about the nature of practical reason.

Dworkin, Ronald (b. 1931)

American jurist whose theories of rights and of judicial reasoning have had considerable impact upon recent jurisprudence, not least because of Dworkin's own attempt to use them in the defence of left-liberal causes. (*Taking Rights Seriously*, 1977.) Rights in law are not privileges or benefits granted by the law which can be downgraded in case of conflict or exchanged for benefits of another kind. When one party to a dispute shows that he has a right to x then the dispute is at an end, and the law must grant him x. ('Rights are trumps.') Conflicts of rights cannot be settled by a profit and loss account, but only by setting the law aside.

Although the adage says that 'hard cases make bad law', it is from the study of *hard cases, Dworkin believes, that the structure of legal reasoning is most clearly understood. In a hard case, a judge must make a decision concerning the rights and liabilities of the parties, without the aid of any explicit legal enactment. His judgement is not an exercise in 'discretion', since that would be tantamount to saying that he is inventing the rights and duties which he then imposes. Rather, the judge makes use of certain principles which are superior to the rules contained in the law and derive from the nature of judicial reasoning. Even in a hard case, the rights and duties of the parties are discovered, not invented.

Dworkin expands the argument with a view to showing that standard forms of legal *positivism are untenable, and that law should be understood more as a continuous dialogue or tradition than as a set of edicts issuing from a sovereign power. Some critics argue that his conservative vision of the law, which is derived almost exclusively from English and American (i.e. *common law) sources, sits ill with the liberal causes that he seeks to defend in terms of it. Nevertheless, Dworkin's polemical writings on civil disobedience, positive discrimination and *abortion have been immensely influential, aiming to present the liberal case at a level of sophistication that it does not always attain.

dyarchy

Term coined by the German historian Th. Mommsen 'to refer to the Roman principate, in which *sovereignty seemed to be shared between two separate *agencies, the *princeps* and the senate. Applied also to the particular form of constitutional government introduced by the UK Government of India Act 1919, which divided the provincial executive powers into two.

dynasty

Greek: *dunastēia*, lordship. A class of sovereigns or rulers, whose succession is determined by blood relationship. Dynasties often seem to have a durable political character, so that the politics of a Stuart monarch might be explained by his being a Stuart, and of a Tokugawa Sho'gun by his being a Tokugawa. How far such explanations are genuine and how far they are the residue of discredited beliefs about *heredity is a moot point: to the extent that they are genuine, it seems that there are not only rulers but also ruling families. *See* *Ibn Khaldûn.

dystopia

A negative *utopia. Modern literature abounds in dystopian fantasies – for example Orwell's *1984* and Aldous Huxley's *Brave New World*.

Eastern question

The many and related political problems in South-Eastern Europe and Asia Minor caused in the nineteenth century by the weakness of the Ottoman Empire and the rivalry of its powerful neighbours and successors, by the desire of European powers to curb Russian influence, and by the desire of Russia to *destabilize the Balkan states (see *balkanization). To some extent these problems still exist, but have taken on a completely different complexion since the success of Kemal Atatürk in saving the nucleus of a Turkish nation state after 1918, the expansion and then collapse of the Soviet Empire, and the self-balkanization of the Balkan states following the collapse of Yugoslavia.

ecclesiastical jurisdiction

*Courts have been founded by various religions – notably the Jewish, Muslim and Christian – with the intention of resolving spiritual disputes, whether affecting clergy or laity, by *adjudication. Since 'spiritual' disputes can be interpreted so as to cover everything from crime to the terms of a contract, the establishment of such courts has frequently amounted to a claim to jurisdiction over *territory where the church itself is not in fact *sovereign. This claim was always resisted by the state in England, but the resistance was successful partly because the *canon law and the ecclesiastical procedures and judgements that had grown from it were incorporated in part into the *common law of the land. The ecclesiastical courts were still able to reserve for themselves jurisdiction over certain matters, so that, for example, a clergyman could be punished for criminal behaviour only in an ecclesiastical court (giving rise to the much abused plea of 'benefit of clergy').

Two political consequences of ecclesiastical jurisdiction deserve mention here in that they provide precedents and examples for subsequent legislation. The first is the international character of the law applied, and the impossibility of construing its legitimacy as arising from the exercise of territorial sovereignty. (Although the doctrine of 'papal sovereignty' contains a faint echo of territorial privilege.) Hence ecclesiastical jurisdiction automatically gives rise to the idea of a *natural law, i.e. a law which is not merely *positive, since it transcends the edicts of all temporal powers. The second is the attempt of the ecclesiastical courts to impose doctrines of fair dealing between master and servant, and between parties to a contract, e.g. by the various attempts to forbid usury (still incorporated into *Islamic law), and by the theory of the *just price, according to which, in conditions of scarcity and unequal bargaining power, the court can be appealed to in order to settle a just price for a commodity, based on need, and on the assumption of normal conditions and open-handed dealing.

ecology

Term originally used by Ernst K. Haeckel in 1873, to denote the branch of biology which deals with the inter-relationship between organism and environment (Greek, *oikos*, a home or living place). The term has been adopted by political movements which regard the conservation of the environment as an all-important, perhaps the single most important, political goal: hence the various 'ecology parties' which fight (usually with little success) for representation in European national assemblies. These are sometimes romantic in temperament, anti-industrial, with liberal or socialist leanings in matters of property and law, and favour strict legal control over every activity that can in any way alter the balance of nature, or either reduce or pollute natural resources. Often the underlying idea here is one of justice: the earth is held in trust by those who presently occupy it, and cannot be appropriated for their sole use without violating the rights of succeeding generations. In the US, however, where a majority of people seem to favour strict environmental laws, major support for ecology movements comes also from well-to-do conservative elements.

In recent times the environment has become a major left-wing cause, along with *animals and *minorities. In Germany, in particular, the 'red and green' alliance is now a rooted tenant in the political landscape. The reason for this is not hard to find: damage to the environment comes from those with the capacity to cause it; to oppose such people is to take a stand against property and power. It is therefore to fall within the broad camp of the left, as this has defined itself over two or more centuries.

This does not alter the fact that the greatest environmental catastrophes in our time have been perpetrated by socialist and communist governments, on account of the accumulation of centralized power and the lack of answerability that have been intrinsic to socialism and communism in our times. This prompts a difficult question: since they will require massive state intervention, 'green' policies may very well create the very machine that they oppose. In the face of this problem, many people advocate conscious steps towards a society of small-scale private enterprises, governed by strict laws which nevertheless safeguard the right of private property and create obstacles to the growth of state power, or state enterprises.

As that paragraph suggests, green policies may be high on the agenda of the left at the present time, but they are by no means exclusively left-wing. *Nazism, with its cult of nature and the soil, was perhaps the first political movement to place environmental considerations at the top of its agenda – along with animals. (One of the Nazi Party's first moves, once in power, was to ban *hunting.) There have been right-wing romantic Greens, as well as left-wing revolutionary Greens; capitalist Greens and socialist Greens; mystical Greens and secular Greens; sober Greens and *millenarian Greens. (*See* *deep ecology; *New Age; *Soil Association.) All that can be said with confidence is that no politics henceforth can ignore the environment, since almost everyone is aware of its fragility and alarmed at the continued abuse of it. On the other hand, short-term benefits take precedence over long-term costs, and the abuse will continue just so long as people adopt the lifestyle of *economic man. Hence the environment displays in a vivid form some of the problems and paradoxes of *social choice – notably the *prisoner's dilemma, the *free rider problem and the *tragedy of the commons.

economic growth

The process whereby productive activity, and with it *national income, increase. The analysis of economic growth is one of the major preoccupations of political theorists and economists, partly from the questionable assumption that well-being requires growth, partly from the simpler view, upheld by some macroeconomic theories, denied by others, that full employment depends upon a steadily increasing output (*see* *unemployment). The first of these views, often criticized by moralists and philosophers, has also been abandoned by some economists. E.J. Mishan, for example, argues on various grounds that it is perfectly rational to prefer current to future consumption, and so to refrain from the investment required for growth. The reason for this may be present pleasure, or it may be more far-reaching and speculative, such as a concern for the effects of excessive growth on the environment, and on the social structure through which production is channelled (*The Cost of Economic Growth*, 1969).

Some theorists distinguish various stages of growth – for example Marx, whose theory of history implies that there are dearly marked divisions in economies, such as that between the feudal and the capitalist, which come about quite rapidly, but also as a result of a gradual growth of the underlying economic forces. The antecedents of the Marxian theory are to be found in various eighteenth-century ideas concerning the 'four stages' of development. More recently, and less systematically, W.W. Rostow has distinguished six stages of growth (*Stages of Economic Growth*, 1960):

(i) Traditional arrangements in which custom prevents growth.

(ii) The preconditions for 'take-off', notably the preparations for modern technological development.

(iii) Take-off, in which the economy generates a surplus sufficient to provide its own investment.

(iv) The 'drive to maturity', in which there is a shift from import to export.

(v) Economic maturity.

(vi) High mass consumption.

The division here is not supposed to be arbitrary, the assumption being that there are different underlying economic structures proper to each stage. Economists have criticized Rostow's analysis, however, partly for the unclarity of the idea of 'take-off' and also for its inability to explain quite what happens between (i) and (ii). In Marx six stages are also distinguished – primitive communism, slavery, feudalism, capitalism, socialism, and mature communism – but Marx's theory seems to correspond only to a segment of the history of Europe, and then only approximately. It is normal to distinguish the stages of growth in *developing countries from those in 'mature' capitalist countries, on the assumption that the conditions of the first are to some extent dependent on conditions already reached in the second. In the light of that distinction, theories such as Marx's would seem to be of only limited application, while the classification provided by Rostow seems to have more heuristic than explanatory value. (*See also* *three worlds theory.)

economic man (*homo economicus*)
The abstraction employed by much economic theory, which offers to explain the economic behaviour of actual human beings in terms of an *ideal type of rational choice. The economic man plays an important part in *classical and *neoclassical economics. He is motivated by interests or preferences, which he attempts to optimize; he therefore obeys the axioms of *decision theory, and is deflected from his purposes by no interests other than his own. Some economists argue that this creature

differs from the rest of us only in his enhanced rationality, for, even when motivated by *values, we are obedient only to interests of our own. Others argue that values cannot be fitted into the usual theories of economic motivation, and that economic man is no more than a 'rational fool' (Amartya Sen).

economic warfare

Not usually a form of *war, and not in itself an act of belligerency in *international law, the mounting of trade embargoes against, the forbidding of exports to and imports from, a potentially hostile state, may nevertheless be described as economic warfare when practised sufficiently consistently and backed up by measures designed to undermine the economy of that state and compel it to sue for terms. Hence representatives have argued before the United Nations special committees for the definition of *aggression (e.g. in 1956), that certain kinds of economic pressure constitute aggression.

economics

There is no agreed definition of the subject of economics. Most suggested definitions fail to cover everything that is studied as economics. Thus L. Robbins's famous definition ('economics is the science which studies human behaviour as a relationship between ends and scarce means which have alternative uses') comprehends *microeconomics, but not *macroeconomics. Some idea of the latter is conveyed by the title of Adam *Smith's famous book, *An Inquiry into the Nature and Causes of the Wealth of Nations*, which appeared in 1776.

All political thinkers are faced by the question of the extent to which their science is distinct from, incorporates, or is incorporated by, economics. Social policy always requires expenditure, and often has economic effects; all policy therefore has an economic aspect, even if it is not concerned with economic ends. Hence the permanent tendency of governments to occupy themselves with questions of economics, resulting perhaps in direct government intervention in the economy, or in a kind of dogmatic non-intervention which has just as large immediate and intended effects.

Historical materialists go further in asserting the interdependence of politics and economics, arguing that political institutions and political decisions are always the effects of economic causes, so that there are no political facts which are not, at some level of explanation, economic facts. On such a view the study of politics might seem to be entirely subsumed under economics, at least so far as concerns explanation and understanding. However, even if historical materialism were true, such a conclusion would not follow. Consider human relations. Conversation and friendship are rationally conducted only by someone who attends to the surface expression of human life, and who ignores the physiological processes which determine that expression. Likewise, there may be a rational art of politics that proceeds without reference to the underlying mechanisms that determine it. (*See also* *essence/appearance, *Verstehen*.)

Since economic ills are politically undesirable, the curing of the economy must be an essential part of politics, even if only the precondition of its successful exercise. If our view of human nature allows more to well-being than the provision of goods and services, and if we believe that politics must concern itself with well-being as a whole, then we must nevertheless admit that economics cannot constitute the whole of politics. At best there may be that kind of dynamic synthesis of the two which has sometimes been called *political economy, and which sees the government of a state in terms which apply equally to the management of a *household. *But see* *positive economics.

ecumenical movement

Greek: *oikoumene*, the inhabited earth. The movement within the Christian churches towards a visible union of all believers in Christ. While a permanent feature of *Christianity (enshrined in the idea of a 'catholic' church), the movement has been a major force only since the division within the church at the Reformation, and took its principal modern impetus from the World Missionary Conference held in Edinburgh in 1910. The modern attempt to represent liturgical and doctrinal differences as peripheral, in comparison with the defining belief in Christ crucified, has seemed to some to herald the resumption of true Christian belief, to others to indicate only that Christian belief has ceased very much to matter, even to those who profess it. It has often been argued that the strongest religious sentiments emerge in hostilities between those who are united in all beliefs except one or two irrational embellishments, and that the cessation of hostilities is brought about only by the loss of the metaphysical assumptions that made them possible. On this view it is to be expected that the ecumenical movement within Christianity, unlike the continuing conflict between Sunni and Shi'ite Muslims, presages the political decline of religious doctrine.

education

The process whereby *rational beings are instructed, and through which they acquire the beliefs, emotions and *values pertaining to a *culture. How can the state stand apart from that process or regard its result with indifference? The question, explored with great vigour and skill by *Plato, has continued to occupy the thought and practice of philosophers and politicians, and is now everywhere bound up with political choices.

The definition of 'education' is no easy matter. It is now normally seen as the more formal and structured part of *socialization, and is thus defined by *Durkheim: 'Education consists of a methodological socialization of the young generation' (*Education and Sociology*, 1922). However, what distinguishes education from training, for example, or from *conditioning? One suggestion is that education essentially has a *person as its object, whereas training and conditioning may be directed towards (non-personal) animals. On one view this means that education must show an awareness of, and a respect for, the personhood of its recipient. Those philosophies which connect the ideas of person and rationality would perhaps gloss this suggestion as follows:

(i) In education, the rationality of the recipients is engaged. For example, they are given *reasons* for believing, doing and feeling things, and are not simply manipulated or bludgeoned into some finished state of unthinking acceptance of doctrine.

(ii) In education, the *autonomy of the recipients is respected. They are treated as beings with *responsibility for their own acts and judgements, and encouraged to view themselves as such.

Clearly both (i) and (ii) are matters of degree, and in the early stages of education it is to be assumed that the rationality and autonomy of the pupil are only incipient. The major political question that arises out of any such definition is this: to produce autonomous individuals, do we need autonomous schools? Conservatives and classical liberals say yes; socialists and US-style liberals say no.

Massive *indoctrination is usually thought to violate both the conditions offered, and this has been offered in the US as an argument for *withdrawing* state support from schools which practise indoctrination (specifically religious indoctrination) on the ground that the state has an obligation to provide education, and also to foster *toleration by means of it.

Socialists tend to argue that the autonomy of the schools means the *hegemony of a class. Better teachers gravitate towards the more expensive schools, and parents and teachers conspire together to give the school and its curriculum an *elitist character. This idea has been used (notably by the UK Labour Party) as an argument against both private schools and 'streaming' in state schools. (NB in UK usage, a 'public school' is a private school, whereas in US usage it is a school supported by and answerable to the state legislature.) Conservatives stress that the argument, even if valid, is irrelevant, since the question concerns educational values, and what is necessary to secure them. Socialists, they respond, put *social engineering above education; in doing so they inevitably condone the dumming down of the curriculum and the widespread loss of knowledge.

What are educational values, and what *should* be taught in schools? Both Plato and *Aristotle argued that *virtue is the main aim of education; later thinkers extended the idea of virtue to include *rhetoric, and this outlook was transmuted into the advocacy of *humane education and high culture by such nineteenth-century thinkers as *Arnold and *J.S. Mill. All such ideas have seemed to their critics to involve an element of élitism. Arguments as to how schools should be funded, and whether parents should have a 'right to choose' how to educate their children, often turn on this point. A 'right to choose' that extends only to one class is often seen as a mere extension of the power whereby that class controls the remainder. Hence the ferocious and ongoing battle over schooling and the role of the state in controlling and imposing it. (*See* *home schooling.)

The political questions of when children should attend school and for how long, and whether this attendance should be compulsory, are also bound up with the nature and value of education. In practice the 'school leaving age' has been determined in accordance with two intuitions: (a) children should stay at school until they have learned what is necessary for responsible autonomous existence; (b) they should be kept in school just so long as they would be a social nuisance elsewhere. It is often argued that both these aims would be better fulfilled in many cases by apprenticeship than by school. A radical decline in literacy and numeracy among children leaving state schools has recently been observed throughout the Western world. Conservatives often attribute this decline to the inherent inefficiencies and corruptions of state institutions. Others refer to changes in the way that children are socialized, and notably to the negative impact of television on their mental development.

egalitarianism

A somewhat vague term, best taken to denote the belief that people are or ought to be equal in at least some, possibly every, respect relevant to political decision-making. Specifically, the belief that there are no relevant differences whereby one person can be supposed to have a greater inherent *right to some benefit than another. From that it is sometimes held to follow that an unequal distribution of benefits is either unjust, since it distinguishes people on grounds which do not determine their rights, or else inherently in need of justification. *See* *justice.

At least the following assumptions seem to be involved in the usual forms of egalitarianism:

(i) The ultimate justification for any *distribution of benefits is to be given in terms of the rights of those receiving them.

(ii) Distribution is always within political *control, and so is always, by design or by neglect, the result of political activity.

(iii) There is some common property in all people which is the single ground of whatever rights they possess.

(iv) This common property is possessed to an equal extent by all people.

All of these assumptions may be doubted, but it is clear that (iii) and (iv) are of perennial appeal, and have been subjects of many attempted *a priori* justifications, notably by *Kant, who identifies the common property as practical reason, made manifest in the *autonomy of rational choice. (i) must be justified in terms of a theory of distributive justice, sufficient to eliminate all conflicting reasons (such as those stemming from *need, from *utility, or from *natural right) for distribution. In order to make (ii) seem plausible it has been common to argue that egalitarian doctrine applies, not to those benefits which are bestowed by nature, but only to those which arise from artifice. Often the principle offered here is that of *equal opportunity, meaning to refer to the opportunities available for social, political and material advancement. It is, however, true that almost any human benefit, including physical beauty and intelligence, might be conferred or withdrawn by political agency, assuming sufficient human competence. It might then seem as though the logical

consequence of egalitarianism is some kind of genetic engineering, in which it is ensured that everyone has his own regulation measure of beauty, intelligence, and innate capacity for well-being. However, this idea normally evokes revulsion, even among the most hardened egalitarians – for it suggests a controlling power, as in Huxley's *Brave New World*, who therefore stands above the equal beings over whose destiny he rules. It therefore seems that egalitarianism stands in need of a procedure for determining which benefits are to be attributed to humans as their responsibility, and which to be withheld as part of the sacred reserve of 'nature'.

Much modern egalitarianism seems to stem not from *universalist doctrines about rights so much as a *nihilistic disbelief in them. If there are no rights, no obligations, no values, but only subjective preferences, then no one has the right to anything. From which it follows that no one has the right to any more of anything than anybody else. This conclusion might then be confused with the positive doctrine (in fact incompatible with the nihilist premise) that it is *wrong* for anyone to possess more of some good than any other. Strictly speaking, given the premise, it is neither right nor wrong.

Opponents of egalitarianism might reject any of (i) to (iv). Commonly they argue that distribution can be made equal only by violating natural rights of ownership; alternatively, that utility, or human fulfilment, requires an element of struggle, competition, success and failure in the pursuit of all goods, and a background of accepted disabilities from which to embark on this struggle. (For the first, *see* *Nozick; for the second, *Nietzsche.) Moreover, in all its forms egalitarianism, to become a political reality, would require powers of enforcement that, by their very nature, create huge inequalities between the enforcers and the enforced. Nothing is more obvious in socialism than the existence, and frequent oppressiveness, of these inequalities.

egoism

The view which either describes self-interest as the true principle of *morality, or else recommends the abolition of morality in favour of a life lived for self alone. It has been advocated in modern times, to considerable political effect, partly by way of exaggerating the merits of *individualism against *collectivism, partly by way of advancing a peculiarly modern and irreligious worldview that is nevertheless held to be compatible with the reassertion of human dignity. Principal exponents of that second thought have been the *Young Hegelian Max *Stirner, *Nietzsche and *Rand. All three believed that modern socialism is nothing more than the survival of religious feeling in a bowdlerized and *sentimental form, and that its doctrines should be interpreted not in terms of what they express, but in terms of what they conceal: an envy of strength, pride and resolution; a desire to level by destroying what is superior; a small-minded resentment of the individual who is prepared to assert himself against the crowd; a wish to cripple human nature by forcing it into a single universal mould of fettered altruism. Neither Stirner nor Nietzsche could be thought of as offering a defence either of conservatism or of capitalism, their views being too resolutely self-centred to make the transition to systematic political theory. Their closest affinity is with modern *existentialism. Rand, however, saw capitalism as the logical consequence of egoism, and also the vindication of it, the proof that the egoism of the strong works to the benefit of the rest of us.

Various philosophies attempt to reconcile egoism and *altruism, either by arguing that it is in the long-term interest of the individual to adopt the principles and habits of an altruistic moral code (a view supported, e.g., by *Hobbes, and sometimes known as 'rational egoism'), or because the individual pursuit of self-interest acts (perhaps by an *invisible hand) in the long-term interest of society (a view associated with certain defences of the *market, notably that given by *Smith, and also with *Mandeville's ironical defence of 'private vices').

election

The process whereby an electorate chooses, by *voting, officers either to act on its behalf, or to *represent it in an *assembly, with a view to *government or *administration. The elements of an election are: rules of eligibility for candidates, rules for membership of the electorate, voting procedures, and officers empowered to enforce them (such as the 'returning officer' in UK law), laws relating to practice and designed, e.g., to prevent corruption, intimidation and excessive expenditure or unfair advertising. How these elements should be further specified, if the election is to result in an outcome that is in a real sense the choice of the electorate, is one of the problems of *collective choice. Many theorists try to find the distinction between *democracy and its alternatives in the nature of the procedure of an election: others seek it in the structure of the kind of *representation that results. Others look elsewhere altogether.

As an example of the issues raised by electoral procedure it is instructive to compare two electoral systems, those of the UK and the former USSR. In the UK the title of candidate is open, both in theory and in practice, to anyone who is able to place a deposit with the returning officer (with a few exceptions, such as members of the House of Lords and lunatics), and any candidate may announce his candidature publicly, it being an offence in law to prevent him from doing so. In the USSR there was a *de jure* right for anyone to stand as a candidate, but anyone whose name was not on the list chosen by the local committee of the Communist Party announced his candidature only at personal risk, and anyone who voted for him exposed himself to the same risk, should his vote be known. Membership of the electorate in the USSR was extended to all citizens, male or female, who had reached the age of 18, and all those that were entitled to vote did vote, since not to cast one's vote was to authorize the electoral officer to cast it for you, in favour of the candidate chosen by the Communist Party. In the UK voting is not permitted to members of the House of Lords, but is now open to the remainder of the population of 18 or over, by virtue of the successive Reform Acts which have extended the *franchise. Voting procedure was open in the USSR, but the ballot was designated secret by the law (article 95 of the constitution); however, anyone who made use of the procedure for casting his vote secretly was noted by the electoral officer, and reported to the Party officials, who would afterwards ensure that he regretted his decision. Finally, UK law circumscribes the amount and character of campaigning that any party may make in an election, so permitting minority parties to assert themselves as vigorously as any other, should they have the means. In the USSR all parties other than the Communist Party were illegal, and there was no legal limit to the amount of propaganda that it could issue.

It can be seen that the two practices are completely different, the one being an instrument (however crude) whereby a government subjects itself to public opinion and suffers the verdict, the other being an instrument for the ritualistic rehearsal of the rule of a single party. The important features which distinguish them seem to be the permission or lack of permission for candidates other than those officially endorsed to stand and to campaign for election, and the adherence or non-adherence to the rule of the secret ballot. It is these two conditions which are usually referred to by the designation of 'free election'. On the other hand, the impossibility of winning an election in Western countries without an enormous expenditure of money on advertising and publicity, entails that only established parties with extensive private support have a chance, and (in the US that) only wealthy people are able to put their names forward as candidates.

electoral college
An institution of officers (who may themselves be elected to office) responsible for electing a president, governor, prime minister, party leader, or other figure of high political power, who will obtain authority not only over them, but also over the interests they represent. The Pope is elected by a college of cardinals, and the US President, by article II of the US constitution, by an electoral college composed of electors from each state equal in number to the total representatives of that state in the two main houses of *Congress. This procedure, which divides the election of the President from the votes cast by the *electorate, means that votes cast for a President in the college will tend to exaggerate the degree (and even to belie the absence) of popular support for the President.

An electoral college may fulfil either or both of two functions: that of making important groups with an interest in the outcome of a choice party to that choice, and that of removing key choices from direct popular control.

electorate

The class of citizens entitled to vote in an *election, by whatever procedure.

Eliot, Thomas Stearns (1888–1965)

American-born poet, dramatist and critic, an articulate conservative, and a powerful influence over conservative thinking in both Britain and America. Eliot was a *modernist in literature, who did more than any other contemporary writer to rescue English poetry from its late Victorian archaisms and return it to the mainstream of European literature. He developed a laconic and allusive style, much influenced by Baudelaire, Laforgue and French symbolism, but addressed directly to the spiritual crisis, as he saw it, of modern civilization. In *The Waste Land* (1922) Eliot evokes the barren soulscape of the city, summoning the feelings of loss and emptiness that followed the hollow victory of the First World War, and providing an unforgettable image of a place, a civilization and a society suspended in the void and longing for renewal. The poem appeared in the first issue of *The Criterion*, a journal founded in London by Eliot to propagate his distinctive vision of literature, through which he was to remake the canon of English classics and entirely change educated perception of what mattered in the literature of the past. In due course Eliot was drawn towards the Anglo-Catholic religious tradition, became an articulate apologist for the doctrine and ritual of the Anglican church, and defended a kind of melancholy retreat into high culture as the spiritual resource with which to combat the godlessness of modern society. In *Four Quartets* (1944 onwards) Eliot presents this quasi-monastic vision in verse of enormous power, that helped to shape much conservative thinking in the decades following the Second World War. In an earlier essay (*After Strange Gods*, 1935) Eliot had let slip various remarks that could be interpreted as *anti-semitic, and this has had a negative impact on his reputation in recent years. *See* *art, *cultural conservatism, *death, *élite, *emigration, *myth, *Permanent Things.

élite

Literally, that which has been chosen, and generally signifying the class of persons within a society who are in a position to view themselves in just that way, as chosen, either by others or by nature, to lead or govern. Some adhere to a more specialized meaning, and distinguish government by an élite – that is, by a class that is *chosen* for the purpose, say, by some ruling party – from government by a *ruling class, which obtains its powers by *prescription. (Thus T.S. Eliot, in *Notes Towards the Definition of Culture*, 1945, who distinguishes the élites of *Stalinist governments from the ruling classes that have held power elsewhere.) More generally, the term is used of any body of people who act in concert, whether or not knowingly, to maintain a shared position of social and/or political *privilege. *See also* *new class, *oligarchy.

élitism

1. The view that *élites are desirable. The term is also used of any defence of the institutions and social relations which facilitate *oligarchy, or which pertain to a *ruling class. Élitism in this sense is usually contrasted with *egalitarianism, and is defended on a variety of grounds. Thus it may be argued that government by an élite is in the interests of the people, that the institutions which generate élites can

be destroyed only by acts of injustice, or that important moral and social motives, such as pride, emulation and dignity, require the formation of élites if they are to be widely experienced. (*See* *hierarchy.)

2. The view that élites are inevitable, sometimes known as 'scientific élitism', and associated with the names of *Pareto, Mosca, and R. Michels (whose theory of the *iron law of oligarchy is discussed under that heading). Pareto distinguished the 'governing élite' from the 'non-governing élite', and both from the remainder (the non-élite). He argued that all organization, including the organization of a democracy, will generate both kinds of élite, the one dominating politics, and the other society (*Mind and Society*, 1935, vol. III). Some recent sociologists have extended Pareto's dual theory, arguing that in all developed societies there is a plurality of competing élites, which rise to eminence through the several systems of control. Politics is only one such system; others include management, trade union organizations, military organizations, and cultural and educational institutions. (*See also* *power élite.)

3. The attitude of favouring, whether expressly or by implication, the formation and well-being of social élites. In this sense 'élitism' is often used (especially on the left) as a term of abuse, on the grounds that this attitude helps to promote distinctions of class, race or gender, fosters inequality and retards the cause of *social justice. Élitists may reply that it does no such thing, provided entry into the élite is open to all. Or they may reply, being élitists, 'So what?'

emancipation

The act of freeing a human being or class of human beings from the *control of another, usually when this control is enshrined in some legal privilege or right. In the case of emancipation in *Roman law various standard procedures of *manumission were developed, whereby the slave ceased to be the legal property of another. This transition from control to autonomy has been achieved in modern times largely by abolishing the existence of laws which permit human beings to be property (although note that these laws still permit some kinds of *person* to be property, such as companies). Thus emancipation of slaves in America and serfs in Russia proceeded by government decree; however, the resurgence of laws restricting the occupation, place of residence, opinions and lifestyle of the Soviet worker involved the restoration of (partial) property rights in his body and labour, the new owner being the state rather than a nobleman. The 'emancipation' of women means, not the abolition of legal property rights in women, but the abolition of those legal, social and moral bonds which can often have the appearance of property rights: the release of women from the control of fathers, lovers, husbands and brothers is therefore a *de facto* rather than a *de jure* emancipation, and on some views not even that. *See* *slave.

emergency

A situation in which something must be done immediately if a catastrophe is to be avoided. Emergencies test the strength, flexibility and utility of political systems, and on some views provide the test of who really governs (*see* *Schmitt), or else the test of political legitimacy. Thus a political system that creates regular emergencies – whether by accident or by design – is often thought to be less legitimate than one in which emergencies seldom arise. In either case we must distinguish emergencies generated within the political system from those which come from outside – whether natural like a typhoon, or artificial like aggression from a neighbouring state. All states must be prepared for external emergencies. It is a peculiar feature of many modern systems – notably *fascism and *communism – that they foster constant internal emergencies, and seem to depend upon them for their continued existence. In general revolutionary parties seize power in an emergency (often created by themselves) and have a tendency to perpetuate that emergency, as one ground of support for their usually drastic policies. *See* *terrorism.

emergency powers

Powers granted to a government or executive power which allow normal procedures (e.g. of legislation and adjudication) to be bypassed or suspended. In constitutional states, the granting of emergency powers is circumscribed by the constitution, and usually depends upon, or is controlled by, the legislative assembly. Emergency powers may be exercised in the UK either under the royal *prerogative, or else by the declaration by the government of a state of emergency, followed by legislation granting the requisite powers. The US constitution makes no mention of emergency powers, although they have been exercised, as when President Lincoln suspended the right of *habeas corpus during the civil war.

emerging state

A *state that is in the process of securing for itself legal, constitutional, and usually economic *autonomy, by asserting itself against the vestiges of a previous colonial regime, or against the dependence on the power, protection and economic support of its neighbours.

emic/etic

A distinction in social *anthropology. An emic analysis of a culture uses symbols and concepts which belong to the culture itself, whereas an etic analysis views it from outside. *See* *Verstehen.

emigration

Departure of a person from the country where he has citizenship to another, with the intention of permanent residence abroad, and usually with the intention of relinquishing his original rights and duties of citizenship. The permitting of emigration is regarded by many (e.g. *Locke) as a necessary condition of legitimate power, since to forbid it is to forbid all choice to the citizen regarding the political structure to which he will be subject. It is therefore sometimes advocated as a basic *human right, and was acknowledged as such even in the constitution of the USSR, which restricted it in reality.

The 'émigré' consciousness has played an important part in forming the political outlook of modern Europe. Some even argue that Western culture has become dominated by émigrés (Stravinsky, T.S. *Eliot, *Hayek, Joyce, Nabokov, Picasso, Wittgenstein, *Popper, and many others) who have sought to find outside the country of their origin the ideal memory of a civilization that has been lost, neglected or betrayed. This is sometimes offered (e.g. by Perry Anderson: 'Components of the National Culture', *New Left Review*, 1968) as part of an explanation of the alleged *reactionary nature of the postwar intellectual establishment in Europe (the 'white émigré' syndrome). European émigrés in the nineteenth century included, however, most of the founders of modern socialism, including *Marx, *Engels and *Lenin.

eminent domain

The power of a *sovereign state to take *private property for public use, subject to making reasonable compensation, as distinct from *seizure or *expropriation. This power is recognized as a (conditional) right by certain theories of *natural law (e.g. those of *Grotius and *Pufendorf); it is familiar in English law from the seventeenth century and from earlier practice, and is even permitted (subject to *due process) by the US constitution, Fifth and Fourteenth amendments. It is an important qualification to every private property right, and records the fact that no property right can easily be made absolute against the state, since the existence of a state (i.e. of a set of enforceable legal rights) is a precondition of property in any form. The power of eminent domain may be delegated, and commonly is delegated to local government bodies. Hence there is an emerging controversy in the US over whether eminent domain should be used only in order to acquire land required for some socially necessary project (such as road-building), or whether it can be used to acquire land for development. If the latter is permitted, then city authorities can effectively confiscate any property they wish, provided they show an intention to use it more profitably than the current owners.

emotive meaning

Term introduced by the British philosopher C.L. Stevenson (*Ethics and Language*, 1944) to distinguish the meaning of moral and other evaluative terms, from the meaning of ordinary narrative and scientific discourse ('descriptive meaning'). When I describe something I express my beliefs about its nature and properties. When I use evaluative language I express my attitudes – for example, of approval or disapproval. Terms with emotive meaning therefore standardly express either pro- or con- attitudes towards the things to which they

apply. A term may have both a descriptive and an emotive meaning: for example, the term 'Chink' applied to a person of Chinese origins, which both describes him as such and expresses the speaker's contempt for the Chinese. Although there seems to be an important truth behind Stevenson's theory, it has been subjected to such criticism by philosophers that it is now impossible to accept it in its original form.

empire

Literally, rule or territory of an emperor (Latin: *imperator*), a title now of vague meaning, attached to certain kinds of *monarchy, but almost entirely in disuse. The term has been applied to states characterized:

(i) by their magnitude in area, population and power, including several *nations, peoples or subordinate states of different race or culture; and/or:

(ii) by their origin in conquest by a dominant tribe or nation which continues to form the ruling group and to monopolize *coercion; and/or:

(iii) by their political structure vesting supreme authority in a single supreme government (the imperial or *metropolitan power) from whose grant all local authority is derived; and/or:

(iv) by a theory of potentially universal jurisdiction, sanctioned by a religion, law or ideology that transcends national boundaries.

Hence *imperialism, the general name for a pursuit of power (whether economic, social or political) which acknowledges no national boundary as its natural limit. The main feature of empire is the disregard or disrespect for the *sovereignty of weaker powers, sometimes accompanied by a belief in the innate superiority of either the race, the history, the institutions or the ideology of a governing people. Empires may be imposed by conquest, or acquired by default, as when the British Empire expanded during the nineteenth century through the adventures of traders and colonists, who called upon the Crown to impose the laws necessary for their security and business.

empiricism

The thesis that all knowledge of matters of fact is based on, or derived from, experience, so that all claims to knowledge of the world can be justified only by experience. Empiricism argues that *a priori* knowledge either does not exist, or is confined to 'analytical' truths, which have no content, deriving their validity merely from the meanings of the words used to express them; hence metaphysics, which seeks to combine the *a priori* validity of logic with the contentful character of science, is impossible. Principal empiricists have included many British philosophers (notably William of Ockham, Berkeley, *Hume, and *J.S. Mill), and also the logical *positivists. The influence of empiricism on Anglo-Saxon political thought has been very great, through what it affirms, through what it denies, and most of all through what it refuses to attend to. The following ideas might (with varying degrees of plausibility) be attributed to empiricist influence:

(i) Experience is intelligible in isolation, or 'atomistically', without reference to the nature of its object or to the circumstances of its subject. Thus it makes sense to suggest that the object and the subject can be eliminated from all description of experience: in particular there is no need to refer to the social conditions of an experience in order to describe its content. (This seems to be implied by Hume's theory of the relation between 'idea' and 'impression', as well as by Russell's 'Logical Atomism', and other related theories.)

(ii) The subject of experience is the passive 'recipient' of data that are imprinted upon his intelligence irrespective of his activity, so that the subject brings nothing *to* experience and gains everything *from* it. (But *see* *pragmatism, which in some versions tries to combine empiricist ideas with the denial of (ii).)

(iii) The individual is fulfilled when the totality of his desires are fulfilled, so that there is no satisfaction of the *whole* of the human personality over and above the satisfaction of its parts. (This thesis is sometimes thought to be an essential part of *utilitarianism, at least of the kind defended by *Bentham.)

(iv) The individual is the fundamental component of, and in every important way more basic than, society: he is intelligible in isolation, and social phenomena are to be understood only by reference to him and to others of his kind. (*See* *individualism.)

(v) 'Reductionism': specifically, the view that facts about society are 'reducible' to facts about the individuals that compose it. This is contrasted with the position (variously espoused by *idealists and by some *phenomenologists) that the individual is intelligible only when referred to the social arrangement in which he is embedded (*see* (iv) above), so that any attempt to 'reduce' a society to its individual members will involve a vicious circle.

These and other theories all presuppose an 'atomistic' view of the world, of the relation between individual and society, and of the relation between the individual and the state. In practice not all those ideas have been espoused together, so that (iv) and (v), e.g., were rejected by Hume, who accepted (i) and (ii), while (iii) was accepted by Mill, who expressed considerable doubt about (i) and (ii). Nevertheless, there does seem to be a general tendency among philosophers who are empiricist in the strict sense given by (i) and (ii) to construe social and political institutions in an individualistic way, as agglomerates of separately intelligible parts. This has led political discussion to associate with the empiricist outlook a particular vision of the social world: composite, sceptical, individualistic, and with no patience for *social facts. In the political sphere the methodological opposite of this is *Hegel.

In the scientific sphere, empiricism generates a characteristic view of causation, which seems to be an almost inevitable consequence of its theory of knowledge. The world consists of a set of contingently connected objects and states of affairs, united by regularities rather than by necessities, and unrelated to any transcendental cause or destiny. Science investigates matters of fact, through observation and the postulation of regular connections; the aim of science is prediction, and judgements of *value have no place in it, being merely subjective preferences in the investigator, which describe no objective states of affairs.

employers' associations

Associations such as the UK Confederation of British Industry which attempt to reach agreement over strategy and tactics, in *collective bargaining, among those who are offering employment. A stone tablet recently unearthed among the ruins of Sardis testifies to the existence of such associations in the ancient world; their modern form is due partly to the ability of *trade unions to carry a dispute from one place of employment to another, partly to the recognition by employers of the need to *lobby government as a united front.

employment

The general theory of employment concerns itself with the economic conditions for full employment, and the explanation of, and remedies for, *unemployment, together with whatever consequences may flow from either of these conditions. The theory requires, therefore, a definition of full employment: does this mean employment of all those who *might* work, or only of some section (the 'work force')? If the latter, how is the work force to be defined? How many hours does a person have to work per week in order to be considered employed? (Official figures for the unemployed refer as a rule only to those with *no* employment, whether full-time or part-time.) Is there any requirement that his work fulfil a function, or do those also serve who only stand and wait? (The case of the match-sellers in the Strand who appeared in abundance during the Depression, or of many workers in the supposedly fully employed work forces of communist countries, who were night-watchmen where there was nothing to watch.) *Keynes defined involuntary unemployment as unemployment of those willing to work at the existing wage. Recognizing that it takes time to switch from one job to another, one might then define full employment in terms of an equality between jobs available and those who are involuntarily unemployed. However, in recent years, with growing sensitivity to the potential conflict between the goals of full employment and price stability there has been a tendency to define the employment objective as 'the lowest level to which involuntary unemployment can be reduced without bringing about an unacceptable rise in the price level'. (*See also* *overfull employment.)

Even without a definition of full employment, it is possible to study the factors that affect the *level* of employment within an economy. Keynes famously argued that one of the most important of these is the level of *aggregate demand. This hypothesis, combined with the plausible assumption that a government may act so as to increase aggregate demand, say by commissioning public works, or selectively reducing *taxation, lends economic support to the political doctrine that unemployment is the affair of government, and to be remedied by government action. It is also plausible that, the higher the level of employment, the greater the bargaining power of the work force, and the higher the consequent rate of increase in wages and so in prices; if that is so, then *inflation and employment rise together, although, beyond a certain point, inflation may produce such uncertainty as to discourage investment and therefore production, and so bring about a fall in demand, which in turn generates unemployment. Such assumptions are not everywhere accepted. Nevertheless almost all theories of employment recognize the existence of *some* connection between a high level of employment and high inflation, and propose remedies in consequence. (*See* *Phillips curve.)

A 'war economy' generates employment while imposing wage and price controls, thereby disciplining the work force not to increase its demand for wages. Even without a war economy, the production of armaments may serve to maintain the level of employment, since like the Egyptian production of pyramids discussed by Keynes, it is an activity 'the fruits of which, since they could not serve the needs of man by being consumed, did not stale with abundance' (*General Theory of Employment Interest and Money*, 1936). (On the political question posed by unemployment, and the distinctions between the various types of unemployment, *see further* *unemployment.)

Énarque

Colloquial name for a graduate of the French École Nationale d'Administration, an élite institution devoted to preparing young people for careers in public administration. *Énarques* call each other *tu*, and effectively divide the great departments of state among themselves.

encyclical

Letter issued by the Pope and sent round to all bishops and senior clergy, defining or emphasizing aspects of Roman Catholic teaching, often on issues of contemporary social and political significance. Known always by the first words of their Latin versions, encyclicals have several times had an important role in defining political issues and focusing political action – notably *Rerum novarum* and *Centesimus annos.

Encyclopaedists

Thinkers associated with the great French *Encyclopédie*, begun as a commercial undertaking, with the intention merely to translate Ephraim Chambers's *Cyclopaedia* (1728), but gradually taking on the character of a revolutionary intellectual and political project, in which the Newtonian science and Lockean philosophy would be systematized for the benefit of the public, and in which the *Enlightenment would find an influential and popular voice. Denis Diderot became principal editor in 1747, and he and Jean d'Alembert worked to endow the Encyclopaedia with the controversial and sceptical character for which it was known. Important thinkers who contributed include the Baron d'Holbach (who, despite his name, was German), *Voltaire, *Montesquieu, Quesnay, Turgot, *Rousseau, along with Diderot and d'Alembert themselves. The work's agnostic, and sometimes downright hostile, approach to the Christian religion was edited out by the original printer, to Diderot's indignation. Even so, it was *mal vu* by the Jesuits, and caused a storm in political circles.

end of history

Thesis associated with the Hegelian philosopher *Kojève, and adopted by *Fukuyama, according to which history is a process of attrition, whereby conflicts, local concentrations of power and hierarchical structures give way under the pressure of the demand for equal respect. The arrival of global democracy and universal equality of status signals the end of history.

end of ideology

Thesis associated with the US sociologists Seymour Martin Lipset and Daniel Bell, observing social and political changes in the 1950s, who argued that the old ideological conflicts between socialism and capitalism were at an end, and that a rational and pragmatic approach to both economic and political questions had replaced them. See Daniel Bell, *The End of Ideology: On the Exhaustion of Political Ideas in the Fifties*, 1960.

end state

Political philosophers sometimes distinguish those theories of justice and legitimacy that find these qualities in the nature of the act, from those which find them in the state which results from it. Only if this 'end state' (term made current by *Nozick) shows an *equitable distribution, some argue, can the transaction that leads to it be considered legitimate or just. Others regard this restriction as both too severe and also inherently disrespectful of individual rights, and attempt to develop concepts of justice and legitimacy that will eliminate reference to the final distribution in

favour of reference to the procedure that leads to it. (*See* *procedural justice, *Rawls.) The dispute here is fundamental to the modern debate concerning *social justice, and also to *consequentialism.

enforcement of morals

A controversy in the early 1960s between the leading UK philosopher of law, H.L.A. Hart, and a leading judge, Patrick, Lord Devlin, concerning the extent to which the law can rightfully enforce conformity to a moral code; *see* *law and morality.

Engels, Friedrich (1820–95)

Lifelong friend and collaborator of *Marx, Engels was a well-to-do factory owner of Prussian origin, who spent much of his life in England, beginning his literary career with a highly influential account of the fate of the industrial working class as he observed it in Manchester (*The Condition of the Working Class in England*, 1845). He was co-author of many of the famous documents in which Marx's philosophy was expounded, notably *The German Ideology*, 1846, and the *Communist Manifesto*, 1848. Engels himself contributed both style and clarity to these original formulations, and influenced Marx profoundly by drawing attention to the problems of *political economy. Despite an early essay on this subject, however, he left the main enterprise of attacking the assumptions of *classical economics to Marx. Nevertheless, his thought has been extremely influential, and he can be considered the originator of *dialectical materialism as a distinct form of Marxism. This philosophy achieves independent (if somewhat wild) expression in Engels's late work *Anti-Dühring*, 1877–78, in which the dialectical method is extended beyond the description of human actions and institutions to the explanation of physical reality. Engels's dialectical philosophy was further expounded in the posthumous *Dialectics of Nature*, and may be summarized in the three 'dialectical' laws: the transition of quantity into quality, the interpenetration of opposites, and the law of development through contradiction (or the negation of the negation); together with the idea that categories do not have fixed and immutable referents so that 'the world is not to be comprehended as a complex of ready-made *things* but as a complex of *processes*'.

In *The Origins of the Family, Private Property and the State*, 1884, Engels endorses the suggestion originally made by *Hume, that monogamous marriage is the result of the subjection of one sex by another, in order to provide heirs of undisputed paternity. He adds that 'the first class-antagonism in history ... is the antagonism between man and woman in monogamous marriage, and the first class-oppression is that of the female sex by the male'. His analysis of the interpenetration of property and family relations, and their connected developments, later proved highly influential.

As editor of Marx's posthumous work (including *Capital*), Engels probably had a great influence on the final form of the Marxian critique of political economy, but it is at present impossible to assess the extent of this influence. He was also an *activist, and an expositor of revolutionary tactics, although he lived the life of a fox-hunting, claret-drinkng country squire. His writings, because of their popular appeal, have been highly influential in the conduct and philosophy of modern *revolutions.

English law

Since the *UK system of law is a composite body, formed by an historical process of amalgamation, it is still necessary to distinguish English law (applicable in England and Wales) from Northern Irish law, and *Scots law. While the differences over a wide range of criminal and civil matters are now slight, there remain areas – such as the law of land – in which English and Scots law differ significantly, reflecting the greater adherence of the former to *common law, and the *Roman law influence on the latter. Moreover English law, as a distinct common-law tradition, is the foundation of US law, and of legal systems adopted in many parts of the former British Empire. It remains, therefore, as a major influence on modern politics, providing concepts and forms of action that have no equivalent in other systems – notably the concept of the *trust.

Enlightenment

German: *Aufklärung*; French: *Lumières*. A name often given to the period in European history which succeeded the rise of modern science in the seventeenth century and culminated in the French Revolution, and which was characterized, so far as the educated part of society was concerned, by a scepticism towards traditional authority in matters of religion and politics, an openness of outlook, and a respect for reason as the guiding principle and defining property of the human condition. While the Enlightenment expressed itself in a variety of ways, according to national character and local conditions, its most thoroughgoing manifestations are probably French, in the works of *Voltaire and Bayle, and German, in the philosophy of *Kant who, in 1784, wrote: 'Enlightenment is the liberation of man from his self-caused state of minority ... the source [of this minority] lies not in a lack of understanding, but in a lack of determination and courage to use it without the assistance of another.' The Enlightenment was prodigious of political theory, much of it liberal, universalist, secular, and anti-authoritarian. *See*, e.g., *Kant, *Paine, *Rousseau.

In a more general sense the term 'enlightenment' is used (along with 'toleration', 'freedom of thought', 'open-mindedness') to denote the ideals of what is sometimes called the 'liberal enlightenment' view of politics. This sees a major cause of social evil in prejudice, intolerance, superstition, and attachment to custom, habit and traditional forms of association (interpreted as expressions of an outlook that forswears reason for an unthinking immersion in actual social conditions). The assumption is presumably that if all people were to think about and to question the prejudices whereby they live, then the result would be greater political understanding, and greater social harmony. Many conservatives (e.g. *Burke) argue that this assumption is itself an unargued prejudice, that it is more reasonable to suppose that matters as complicated as those involved in politics are harder to understand by reflective thought than by active engagement, that social disharmony is more often the result of critical thought than is social harmony, and that prejudice is the natural condition of every social being. But if true, then that conservative view must itself be impossible to understand through argument, so that both it and the position that it attacks must be represented as vague and vaguely articulated attitudes, rather than as *doctrines over which there might be reasoned disagreement.

entente

From French: *entendre*, to understand; and compare the etymology of *détente*. Literally, an understanding that falls short of a binding *treaty or alliance between states, especially as used in *entente cordiale.* This phrase was coined in the 1840s to denote the friendly understanding between Britain and France in matters of *foreign policy, and revived as a description of their relationship in the Anglo-French *entente* of 1904. An 'Anglo-Russian *entente*' of 1907 was, like its namesake, founded in a convention agreed between the parties, but it was far less effective in bringing the two parties together.

enterprise

1. Any business undertaking in which someone risks *capital in the hope of a *profit.

2. More generally, the state of mind which makes such risk-taking likely or possible.

Enterprise is 'free' when the laws of property permit the private deployment of capital in business and the private appropriation of some part of the product. The virtues of 'free enterprise' – either as an expression of a more general spirit of freedom, or as a causally efficacious factor in production and distribution, or (*Hayek, e.g.) as the indispensable vehicle of socially necessary information – are habitually referred to in defence of the capitalist economy.

enterprise culture

An expression that became current during the 1980s to denote the set of attitudes, activities and institutions suitable in the post-socialist society. In an enterprise culture the habit of risk-taking is revived, along with the willingness to take responsibility for one's life and actions. The state is increasingly pushed out of the economic realm, and social initiatives become a matter of individual choice and free association between responsible people. Whether such a culture can re-emerge, after the *dependency culture with which it is contrasted, is a debatable question. It is often said that modern education and democratic politics produce an aversion to *risk which weakens the spirit of enterprise and undermines the ability of people to take responsibility for their own lives.

entrenched clauses
Those clauses in a written *constitution that require special legislative procedures if they are to be repealed or amended, and which are thereby protected from hasty or frequent alteration. For a fuller measure of protection the special procedure is sometimes made applicable not only to the clauses themselves but also to the clauses that provide the special procedure of protection – this is known as double entrenchment, which pushes the weak point further back. (Only an infinite regress of entrenchments could provide any protection beyond that of procedural delay, as the example shows.) The UK *Parliament is odd in that it has deeply embedded constitutional devices, which it is almost impossible to change without violence to sovereignty, and yet no possibility of entrenching legislation.

entrepreneur
French: literally, the person who undertakes to do something, specifically to take risks for the sake of gain. A name given in economic theory to the one who takes the initiative in bringing *factors of production, or buyers and sellers, together. He need own nothing to start with, but exerts some control which falls to him by virtue of his initiating role. His return is in the form of *profit or loss, rather than wages, rent or interest: i.e. it is fundamentally non-contractual, which is why he is usually seen as 'taking a risk'.

The entrepreneur corresponds to the traditional 'capitalist' of nineteenth-century theory, and like the capitalist is largely an intellectual abstraction, in that risk-taking and control of the means of production are now often separated, usually because risk remains with shareholders who have limited and typically only 'negative' control over production. *See also* *separation of ownership and control.

entropy
Term of thermodynamics. A measure of the disorder among the component parts of a system – for example among the molecules in a cloud of gas. The second law of thermodynamics states that entropy is always increasing – i.e. that all systems randomize in time. Some have seen this law as applicable also to human societies, and even see the modern world as a proof of it. (*See* *globalization.) The term is also used to similar effect in *cybernetics, where it denotes a measure of the tendency of any closed system to move from a less to a more probable state. (Again, failing the injection of information, the most probable state is complete randomness.)

entryism (alternatively: entrism)
The tactic of gaining clandestine admission to political organizations not directly concerned to advance one's aim in order to bend their purposes in one's favoured direction. (Usually, in the direction of *subversion or communist *revolution.) The term is now used widely, to mean any form of covert subversion (usually, but not necessarily, from the *left), effected by duplicity and through membership of some institution dedicated to purposes to which one does not adhere.

environmentalism
1. The theory that character is determined more by the environment

(specifically the social environment) of the individual than by genetic inheritance.

2. Concern for the environment, for the balance of nature and for the renewal of natural resources. *See* *ecology, *green.

envy

The desire to possess the goods and advantages of another, which may or may not involve the desire to dispossess him. Envy has been described by Helmut Schoeck (*Envy (Der Neid)*, 1966) as a fundamental social emotion, and one that all societies need to manage in order to survive and flourish. Hence we adopt 'envy-avoiding stratagems', concealing our goods, advantages and talents, and approaching others with humility, praising them for the virtues that they may not possess. Envy has often been identified as one of the motives of *egalitarianism, and also of *socialism in the political sphere. In all its forms, however, it is wise to distinguish the desire to gain what another possesses from the desire merely to take it away from him. See *ressentiment*.

equal opportunity

It is often supposed that both the state and social conditions exert control, either positively or negatively, over *access to institutions which confer social or political power, and over the distribution of legal rights. The advocates of 'equal opportunity' hold that all citizens should be equally well placed to obtain such social or political benefits. In its usual form, this thesis holds that only 'relevant' considerations should be held to impede or influence the advance of any particular person. Otherwise scarce advantage may accrue to someone who does not deserve it so much as another, from whom it is withheld. What is the criterion of relevance? It is

normal to argue that no one should be in a better position simply because he *already* possesses greater privilege or power. That criterion might recommend itself on grounds of 'natural justice; nevertheless it is not always easy to apply. For example, is intelligence a relevant feature whereby to distinguish applicants to a university? If so, is it not a power already possessed, independently of the benefit applied for? Perhaps the criterion refers, however, only to man-made powers; but again, education already acquired is, common sense suggests, both a man-made power and a relevant feature in conferring advantages. Here the advocate of equal opportunity will have to ask whether that prior education was itself acquired by equal opportunity, and so on. Often this cumulative questioning of all advantage ends by advocating *reverse discrimination, as the only feasible way of overcoming, in the long run, the unequal opportunities that are socially prevalent.

It is somewhat easier to agree that certain features are *not* relevant to bestowing an advantage; e.g. in the case considered, it is not relevant that the applicant's father is a party member or a governor of the university. But what about the case, much disputed, in which the applicant's father is an old member of the college to which he applies? Is it always and inevitably correct to rule that consideration out as irrelevant? To say yes is to take a *universalist view of institutions which some would rebut, on the grounds that it makes institutions unintelligible. For why, in that case, confine the applicants to citizens of one country? And consider institutions like the club and the family, both of which may have political power and privilege as a side-effect, but in which social and primary relations *must* be relevant. Much argument over equal opportunity in education seems to concern the extent to which it is legitimate to consider a school or university as bound by *private rather than *public obligations.

It is sometimes argued that supporters of equal opportunity must also support *meritocracy, as the inevitable result of opportunities being not only made available, but also seized.

equal pay

The principle, urged especially by *feminists, that people who do the same job should gain the same reward (specifically, regardless of sex, and by implication, regardless of any other feature judged irrelevant to the quality of the performance). The principle was incorporated into the first constitution of the International Labour Organization, and also in the Declaration of Philadelphia 1944 and the UK Equal Pay Act 1970, which also demanded equal terms and conditions of employment. Similarly for 'equal time', and so on. One of the problems with the application of such a principle lies in determining when two pieces of work are equal – i.e. in determining what is meant by 'same job'. Moreover, it seems that employers may often escape the force of the principle by redefining the jobs performed by women, so that while they are the same in fact, they are not the same in law, as those performed by men.

Some argue that there are tasks which are better done by one sex than by the other, but that nevertheless the two sexes should get the same pay for the same amount of time expended at them, since it is invidious to pay workers differently for the same job unless there is a specific agreement concerning quotas. Such questions raise intricate issues not only of *justice, but also of *utility, since it is clear that there are long-term effects on social life (particularly on the relations between

the sexes, and on the nature of the family) that are brought about by all such economic equalities.

equal protection

The idea that the rights and liberties of all citizens should receive equal protection from the law, enshrined in the Fourteenth amendment to the US Constitution, which was passed in 1868 in order to protect former slaves from state legislatures that sought to abridge their *civil rights. *Judicial activism has led to an increasing use of this clause, in order to break down real and apparent *discrimination, whether racial or sexual. Thus in *Brown* v. *Board of Education of Topeka* (1954) racial segregation in schools was ruled unconstitutional, under the Fourteenth amendment. In general, equal protection is now interpreted in the US to extend far more widely than the merely formal equality before the law that it once denoted. Any custom, institution, or legal enactment which has the persistent effect (whether or not intended) of allowing to one race or sex greater scope to enjoy its rights or liberties than is allowed to another may fall before the Fourteenth amendment. This result is not without its critics, who regard it as an unwarranted extension of a purely formal provision in the Constitution, so as to generate new and intrusive laws without the consent of the legislature.

equality

Advocacy of equality as a political ideal is often thought to be a peculiarly modern attitude, although the connection between equality of treatment and *justice is enshrined in the idea of *equity, and has a philosophical ancestry that reaches back at least as far as *Aristotle. In his account of justice in Book III of the *Nicomachean Ethics*, Aristotle argues that no distinction ought to be made between people who are equal in all respects relevant to the kind of treatment in question – a conclusion that can be given an *egalitarian and an anti-egalitarian emphasis, depending upon the scope of 'relevant'.

1. Equality before the law. This obtains whenever an individual's *rights in law are determined simply by his being subject to the sovereign power which legislates, and to no other factor. There is never full equality in this respect, children and lunatics being treated differently from adults of sound mind, women (as a rule) differently from men, peers (in the UK) differently from commoners, citizens differently from slaves. Hence those who fight for equality before the law usually try to determine which of these distinctions are *relevant* to legal right and privilege, which are not. *De jure* equality must then be distinguished from *de facto* equality: both rich and poor have equal *rights* in law, but it would be wrong to claim that they have equal *power* to enforce them (*see* *isonomy).

2. Political equality. Equality in respect of the ability to vote someone to office, and to stand for office oneself. This exists when the only impediment to any subject acquiring political power is his own incompetence, and the only impediment to his acquiring competence his own lack of talent. Political equality was one of the main aims of the French Revolution and was later encapsulated in the Napoleonic idea of the 'career open to talent'. It exists in varying degrees in different places but never, it would seem, absolutely. In the UK, for example, certain offices of state – notably that of *sovereign, and others whose entry requirements are hereditary – are not open to everyone.

3. Material equality. While 1. is an ancient ideal, and 2. frequently advocated, there is considerable dispute over whether a political arrangement can provide, or even ought to try to provide, material equality to those who belong to it. Does it do this by constant acts of *redistribution? Then how is this compatible with *natural justice, or with respecting the rights of people to do what they please with what is theirs? Does it do this by the abolition of *private property? Then how is this compatible with the minimal *freedom over our immediate environment that we all require? And how can this abolition be brought about without massive coercive powers and therefore inequality of another kind? (*See* *justice, *private property.) However, it is also often argued that material equality is a prerequisite of other equalities; in which case this seeming conflict among political values cannot be easily dismissed or contained.

4. *Equal opportunity: this is usually suggested as a milder, or more politically feasible, alternative to 3., which takes the guarantee of equality as far as any merely political action can or ought to take it. The advocacy of equality may be based on doctrines of equal rights (*see* *egalitarianism), upon a philosophy of a common *human nature (as by *Cicero, and *stoicism), or on *Realpolitik, out of a fear that too much inequality leads to resentment and to social upheaval. The rejection of equality may be made in the spirit of 'free *enterprise', or in the name of a philosophical *egoism which rejects the idea of a 'common human nature' (*cf.* *Nietzsche), or in the name of a natural justice that seems threatened by too much interference in the supposedly natural inequalities that arise between people.

equilibrium

1. The state of balance between opposing forces. Political equilibrium must be distinguished from political stability, in which there may be no forces tending to pull asunder, although it is one plausible theory of *politics that it is the art of bringing about an equilibrium between forces within a social order, and so generating stability from potential chaos. Equilibrium is the professed aim of much international politics, and is implied by the *balance of power.

'Social equilibrium' has equally been of concern to sociologists and political theorists, some, e.g. Talcott Parsons (*Towards a General Theory of Action*, 1951), arguing that all social systems have a tendency towards equilibrium, others, e.g. Marx, arguing that capitalism, for example, exhibits at best a dynamic equilibrium, as opposed to the static equilibrium of the *Asiatic mode of production. One of the most influential definitions of social equilibrium is that given by *Pareto: a social system is in equilibrium if, when 'it is artificially subjected to some modification different from the modification it undergoes normally, a reaction at once takes place tending to restore it to its real, normal state' (*The Mind and Society*, 1916).

2. In economics, the concept of equilibrium is of great importance, since it plays a crucial role in the explanation of actual movements and fluctuations, being the ideal point of rest from which the system would have no intrinsic tendency to depart. (Note that the system may or may not tend *towards* such a state, even if one exists.) The analysis of equilibrium (equilibrium analysis) and of differences between equilibria (comparative statics) is fundamental to much economic theory. Equilibrium in economies characterized by perfect *competition may be defined as that state in which, for every commodity and resource, total *supply and *demand are exactly equivalent, and

the plans of all agents are fulfilled. If this equivalence exists, then, given that the only force which prompts a market to move is excess of supply over demand, or demand over supply, there will be a stasis, that lasts as long as the equivalence remains. Thus change in the system may be analysed as a movement towards or away from the equilibrium, while lack of change is explained by the fact of equilibrium. One kind of stasis that has lent itself to economic analysis is 'competitive equilibrium', in which no agent believes that prices vary with the amount that he individually buys or sells, all firms strive to maximize profit, and all individuals optimize their preferences. While actual situations may differ from that mathematical ideal, it can prove useful as a model for the behaviour of some markets.

'Equilibrium price' – the price of a commodity in equilibrium conditions – is an important concept in *price theory.

equilibrium model of society

The theory, to be contrasted with the *conflict model of society, that societies have a natural tendency towards *equilibrium, and that political institutions and processes develop partly in order to facilitate the return to equilibrium in times of strain or conflict. Some version of the equilibrium model underlies most modern conservative outlooks; it is also implicit in the *progressivist theories of *Comte and Spencer, and in some of the anti-revolutionary theories of socialist transformation, such as that of *Kautsky.

equity

1. General. Equity is another name for just dealing, and must not be confused with *equality. While it is tautologous to say that treating people equitably is just, it is certainly not tautologous,

although some think it true, to say that it is just to treat them equally.

2. In legal usage, 'equity' has a distinct, highly technical sense which, while derived from 1., cannot be summarized in terms of *justice alone. Equity is a sub-system of English and related legal systems, derived partly from principles of *natural justice, and partly from the peculiar historical circumstances which led to the adoption of those and related principles by the Court of Chancery in England. This court arose in the sixteenth century in order to deal with matters that had previously been the subject of appeals to the sovereign through the Chancellor. Dispute between its *jurisdiction and that of the *common law was frequent, but resolved by James I on the advice of Chancellors Ellesmere and *Bacon, who decreed that equity should always prevail, thus ensuring that principles of natural justice may always enter into and determine the result of judicial decisions, even when common law and *statute seem to rule against them. This seems to be part of the far-reaching powers conferred by judicial independence as it exists in the UK and US (which also incorporates equitable doctrines into its law). The UK Judicature Acts 1873–5 abolished separate jurisdictions, so that the ascendancy of equitable principles is now exemplified in all the courts. Certain maxims have emerged which indicate the manner in which natural justice is envisaged by the judicial mind. These 'maxims of equity' include the following: equity looks to the intent rather than to the form; he who seeks equity must do equity, and must come with clean hands; equity looks on that as done which ought to be done. In general these maxims act so as to embed and enforce judicial reasoning. Equity also provides specific remedies, such as *injunction, which are not available in the common law.

3. The law of trusts. Repeated application of equitable reasoning leads to the creation of whole new categories of legal rights, independent of those created by statute. This 'creative' aspect of equitable reasoning has been of great influence in diversifying, complicating, and adjusting claims to property. Thus equitable ownership can exist in property whose legal title vests in another: in such a case the courts grant to the equitable owner the right of use and transfer, subject to certain conditions. This is the kind of ownership known as a *trust. Doctrines of trust dominate UK and US property law, and even now enable the creative interpretation of property relations – as when a 'constructive trust' is invoked in order to give to an exploited mistress a right of property in her lover's home (*Davis* v. *Johnson*, 1978).

Erasmus, Desiderius (1466–1536)
(Erasmus of Rotterdam)
Early humanist and scholar, a monk by education but a critic of the monastic life who lived the life of a man of the world. Erasmus was opposed to the dogmatism of *Luther, upheld the doctrine of human free will (*see* *freedom, metaphysical), and, in a series of biting satires, endeavoured to point out both the necessary imperfection of human institutions, and also the folly of attempting to overthrow them in the name of some intellectually satisfying but untried absolute. While he criticized the formalism of the Roman Catholic Church, and upheld the aims of the *Reformation, he viewed the veneration of the individual *conscience with distaste, as the mark of a fool attempting to make his folly sovereign, and argued for continuing papal authority in matters of faith. He became one of the earliest defenders of ecclesiastical and political reform in a conservative spirit, sceptical of all

recipes for perfection, and anxious to see piecemeal change within the framework of existing institutions. He was often condemned for his scepticism by those impatient of hesitation, but did much to create, by means of it, the climate of opinion that we most easily recognize as modern, in particular by presenting an image of an outlook that is serious, and committed, but without *doctrine.

Erastianism

The ascendancy of the state over the church in ecclesiastical matters, so that doctrine and ritual may be (to some extent) influenced and modified at the dictate of the state. Named after the Swiss theologian Th. Erastus (1524–83). Erastianism has been an important element in *Anglicanism, and a similar, but older, idea has influenced the present constitution and practice of the Russian Orthodox Church.

eschatology

The part of theology which deals with the final destiny both of the individual and of mankind. Sometimes applied by analogy to those parts of socialist theory (whether *utopian or scientific) which deal with the ultimate state at which we should aim, or towards which we are inexorably proceeding. Thus Norman Cohn (*The Pursuit of the Millennium*, 1957) has described medieval revolutionaries as inspired by 'eschatological fantasy', and compared Nazism to communism on the ground of their supposed like recourse to 'eschatological drama'. (*See also* *millenarianism.)

essence/appearance

A distinction of Hegelian provenance, and sometimes referred to in *Marxian economics and neo-Marxist political theory. The terms come from metaphysics, where they denote the distinction between the constitution or essence of an individual and the properties whereby we recognize it. In Hegel they are used to conflate two separate distinctions, that between essence and accident, and that between reality and appearance, the temptation to make this conflation seeming to be deep-rooted in idealist metaphysics. In Marxian economics the distinction is between the *values of commodities (as given by the labour necessary to produce them) and their *prices (which are the appearances of values). People think of price as the essence of value partly because they fall victim to *commodity fetishism.

In the social sphere, the distinction is usually between the reality of social and historical arrangements and the beliefs, concepts and experiences through which they are perceived by their participants. Thus behind the 'appearance' of free contractual relations between employer and employee lies, some argue, the conflicting essence of their relation, which is one of unilateral coercion through need. To which it may sometimes be replied that 'in the realm of human affairs being and appearance are one' (Hannah Arendt *On Revolution*, 1963), and that one no more proves the unreality of a contract by showing it to be an appearance than one proves that because redness is a secondary quality (a quality that exists by virtue of our disposition to perceive it) nothing is red. Nevertheless, the distinction is of considerable interest, and features, for example, in the *bolshevik view that society contains 'objective' enemies of the *proletariat – that is, those who, whatever their thoughts and intentions, must, by virtue of their real position in *class terms, act so as to oppress those who occupy the real position of the oppressee. This concept was extremely useful in the *show trials of the 1930s and exerts a lasting influence.

essentially contested concept

Expression introduced by the philosopher W.B. Gallie to describe concepts that are used without precise criteria, but with a precise social purpose. For example, the concept of justice is used with a view to allocating praise and blame; but the criteria for its application will always be contested, precisely because this purpose cannot be freed from human conflict. Such a concept is 'essentially contested' in that no procedure exists that will finally settle disputes over its application. Other examples that have been proposed are the concepts of *freedom, *authority and *power. But whether the idea is coherent may be doubted: for a concept whose instances cannot be agreed surely has no place in the public language. If the meaning of *words* is sometimes in dispute this is only because the concepts expressed by them are immutable.

established church

A church that enjoys legal or constitutional privileges. In the UK the *Anglican Church is established, although this seems to imply no disabilities in the subject who is not himself a member of it. In Norway the Lutheran Church is established, but has a far more limited constitutional role than that bestowed by tradition and convention on the Anglican Church, some of whose bishops sit in the House of Lords as legislators.

establishment

A term that is ambiguous between (i) established *power, (ii) established *right, and (iii) a third thing, lauded by certain conservatives (such as *Burke and Bolingbroke), which consists in a certain kind of synthesis of (i) and (ii) under a *rule of law. The 'right' referred to in (ii) may go beyond the narrow idea of legal right, perhaps so as to embrace conceptions of

natural justice (as in Burke). Thus, one conservative writes: 'Establishment comprises both power and authority. It is a plausible assumption that power and authority mutually require each other. Power without authority is "unhappy" power. It is "at large" in the world, distributing violence without earning respect. The transformation of power into authority confers recognition, and so removes the element of arbitrary force. Power and authority seek each other. Their search is the process of politics, while establishment is the condition which their meeting creates' (Roger Scruton: *The Meaning of Conservatism*, 1980, 161–2). That conservative view is prescriptive, in that it recommends establishment, as the process of entrenching power within a system of rights, so as to provide both an internal and external corrective to, and justification for, its exercise. Others use the term descriptively, simply to describe the 'powers that be' (sense (i) above), independently of their legal or moral status, while yet others use the term largely as a term of abuse, in order to pinpoint and criticize influences that have no *other* claim to legitimacy than the fact of leaning on established power, while remaining inaccessible to the mass of people whose lives are governed by them.

However the term is used, it is clearly necessary to distinguish full legal establishment, where an institution is recognized and protected by the law, and its powers and privileges defined in law, from *de facto* establishment of the kind evinced by the Roman Catholic Church in Poland, which has the power, but not the right to influence government policy.

The term was originally popularized through an article in the *Spectator* by Henry Fairlie, 1955, who gave to it its slightly pejorative sense, and identified in the UK such institutions as the Monarchy, Parliament, the Church of England, the BBC and the public schools as among its components. In the US the components must be differently defined (whether for praise or abuse), while in the USSR and its satellites the establishment (in this sense) normally consisted of only one institution, the Communist Party.

estates of the realm

The classes of citizens recognized by the medieval English Parliament as having distinct rights and duties and requiring (or deserving) *representation in Parliament in distinct ways. Three such classes were identified originally: the clergy, the barons and the commons, and this division persists in the modern UK Parliament, the House of Lords being composed of *peers (Lords Temporal, and Lords Spiritual, the latter being bishops), the House of Commons being forbidden to peers. The term 'estates of the realm' was used from the early fifteenth century onwards, some say by analogy with the French *états generaux*, in which the sovereign would summon to a parliament, representatives of the various estates (usually the three mentioned). Russian law traditionally recognized four 'estates': nobility, clergy, working townsmen, and peasantry, and some vestiges of legal and political distinctions between them survived until the Revolution. In the UK the press has been called (by *Carlyle) the fourth estate, the trade unions the fifth.

étatisme

Term used by French writers from the 1920s onwards to refer to the direct intervention by the state in the economic life of a capitalist society, by *nationalization, by the administering of prices and control of wages, and by social welfare legislation. In a wider sense it signifies the vesting of power

in the state, as a necessary condition of political transformations. *Étatisme* is declared to be one of the 'six arrows' of the Turkish Republican People's Party, and was given its most consistent exposition, in both theory and practice, during the 1930s in Turkey.

ethics

1. Often used in a specific sense – as in *business ethic, *professional ethic – to mean the standards characteristic of an activity or profession, whether or not those standards reflect any accepted or acceptable morality in those who obey them.

2. More generally, any system of moral *values held forth as meriting intrinsic obedience, and not on account of some purpose that obedience might serve.

3. Now most usually used as a technical term of *philosophy, to denote the philosophical study of morality. As such, it has developed two branches: normative ethics, and meta-ethics. Normative ethics attempts, by philosophical reflection, to expound or criticize systems of moral values, e.g. by exploring consistency, conformity to human nature, ability to bring order to the experience of the moral agent. Meta-ethics engages in critical reflection on the meaning of moral judgements, on the kinds of justification that might be given for them, and on the crucial question of whether that justification might ever be objectively binding. The two branches are related. For example, a philosophy that upholds the meta-ethical doctrine of subjectivism (according to which there is no validity to any moral judgement beyond the subjective disposition to accept and act on it) is likely to find normative ethics peculiarly difficult, having deprived itself by its own arguments of the right to legislate for others. Conversely any system of normative ethics would seem to

require and to stem from a view as to the justification of moral judgement.

The subject-matter of moral judgement is extremely hard to identify. It includes judgement of the ultimate value of certain courses of action, specific judgements as to what ought to be done here and now, principles of conduct, and specifications of those qualities of human mind and character that are intrinsically admirable (the *virtues). It is common to contrast ethical systems founded in the study of *human nature and virtue (such as that of *Aristotle), with those founded in the reasoned analysis of moral principles (such as that of *Kant). It is also common to distinguish those systems which argue that the value of every act is ultimately to be found in its consequences for human welfare (*see* *consequentialism), from those which argue that actions, or the motives which generate them, may sometimes possess value intrinsically, and which therefore attempt to derive a system of morality from the study of *duty (*see* *deontology). It is sometimes argued that, in the political sphere, only the consequentialist attitude is appropriate, since in this sphere the end must be allowed to justify the means. Deontologists oppose such a view as intrinsically immoral, (*see* *morality and politics), and argue that if there are any moral values at all, then there will be circumstances when they simply cannot be overriden by any reasoning from consequences.

A major source of philosophical controversy concerns the relation between fact and value, and that between 'is' and 'ought'. Are the distinctions here real, and do they imply that there is no inference from judgements of fact to judgements of value? *See* *value, *value-free.

ethiopianism

Term principally applied to quasi-nationalist movements among blacks in America and West India, which look to Africa (i.e. 'Ethiopia') as a symbol of a social and political condition to be recaptured through political action. A specific form ('Rastafarianism') represents the former emperor of Ethiopia as a semi-divine being, the rightful protector of African *civilization, and the symbolic representative of the type of *Christianity indigenous to Africa and closest to the message of the gospels.

ethnic

Greek: *ethnos*, a tribe. Belonging to a *race or kind. Ethnic groups and ethnic minorities exist by virtue of long-standing association across generations, complex relations of *kinship, common *culture, and usually religious uniformity and common territorial attachments.

ethnic cleansing

Term introduced during the war between ethnic communities in the Balkans which began in 1992 following the collapse of communism. It denotes a policy whereby, by the use of force, threat or terror, ethnic groups are expelled from the territory where they reside, in order to leave it exclusively occupied by the ethnic group of the aggressor.

Under other names the policy has been a long-standing feature of national and international politics. Although the methods employed are usually cruel and immoral, the long-term effect may be positive – for example, in Cyprus in 1974, when action by the Turkish army to expel the Greek population from the North of the island and transport the Turkish population from the South brought to an end a conflict that had cost thousands of lives.

ethnicism

1. Originally heathen *superstition, or (used without pejorative implication)

the religion of any society that does not subscribe to some variety of Judaeo-Christian belief.

2. Now more frequently, the desire (to be distinguished from that involved in *ethnocentrism) to conserve or recapture a political identity based upon race, region, or any *tradition which has its rationale in membership of an ethnic group (= a group whose members are identified not in terms of political institutions, but in terms of blood relation, *language and regional attachment).

ethnicity

Those social and cultural characteristics that people possess by virtue of their membership of an *ethnic group. The desire to enhance ethnicity, and give it a prominent place in politics, is a major factor in modern political movements among *minorities. *See* *négritude.*

ethnocentrism

Term used by W.G. Sumner (*Folkways*, 1906), to denote attitudes which uncritically or unjustifiably suppose the superiority of the subject's own *ethnic group. Now generally employed in a somewhat pejorative sense. (*See* *multiculturalism.)

ethnographical principle

The principle that persons of the same race, language or ethnic group should be united in a common state, with its own *territory and *jurisdiction, so that political boundaries should coincide with the intuitively accepted sense of 'who belongs where'. The violation of this principle in the colonization of Africa has been widely deplored for its after-effects, as has its violent assertion by Israel in defiance of opposition from her neighbours. The principle can be seen as one of the motivating ideas behind *nationalism, and is rejected by all those who think

that social and political sentiments are, and ought to be, distinct.

ethos

Greek: character. Following *Aristotle (*Rhetoric*, II, xii–xiv), used to denote the characteristic 'spirit' or 'tone' of an *association, *institution, *society, *culture or *people. An ethos is a prominent *social fact, which is often held to explain things which can be explained by no individual action or state of mind. Explanations in terms of ethos are sometimes dismissed as mere re-descriptions (as in 'the pursuit of profit is part of the ethos of capitalism'), but they may be more than that, especially for those who believe in the 'collective consciousness' discussed by such sociologists as *Durkheim.

eudaimonia

Greek: enjoying a good *daimon* or protecting spirit. The term used by Aristotle as we might use 'happiness', and defined as the final end of rational conduct, and also as 'an activity of the soul in accordance with virtue' (*Nicomachean Ethics*). 'Eudaimonism' is the philosophy that places the pursuit of happiness at the top of the social and political agenda, and is recognizable in the American Declaration of Independence, with its assertion that 'all men are endowed by their creator with certain inalienable rights, and . . . among those are life, liberty and the pursuit of happiness'.

eugenics

Greek: good breeding. The social and political philosophy that gathered momentum in the wake of *Darwinism, and which argued for a social policy dedicated to breeding human beings who would make a positive contribution, in whatever way, to the society of which they form a part. Not the same as *racism, but nevertheless symbiotic with it, eugenics was briefly fashionable among socialists and utopians such as *Shaw and *Sanger, and was subsequently adopted in a virulently racist form by Hitler.

Eurocommunism

Term probably coined by F. Barbieri in 1967 but later used to denote the attempted synthesis of *liberalism and *communism promulgated by Western European communist parties since 15 November 1975, when the French and Italian parties issued a joint declaration of policy. Their 'Eurocommunist Manifesto' recognized the right of other parties to exist, abandoned the postulate of the *dictatorship of the proletariat, advocated democratic elections, the 'parliamentary road to socialism and communism', the guarantee of civil liberties, and the right of *opposition. Denounced by the USSR as *revisionism, Eurocommunism nevertheless gained a considerable following, especially among those who wished to take advantage of the common political institutions and lawmaking capacity of the European Community, in order to advance the condition of the working class throughout its member states. Eurocommunists were notable for their frequent denunciations of USSR foreign and domestic policy and their respect for political institutions denounced in the USSR as *bourgeois democracy. Nevertheless, the collapse of the USSR seems to have coincided with the final collapse of Eurocommunism.

European Commission

The leading institution of the *European Union, operating together with the Council of Ministers as the *de facto government of the EU. The 20 commissioners are nominated by member states, for five year terms, and the portfolios are divided into 'Directorates-General', each of which has a private office. The Commission is the 'guardian of the treaties', with sole right to initiate legislation. Its accountability is minimal, though the *European Parliament has been able to force its resignation *en bloc*, following an independent report condemning its collective incompetence and irresponsibility. (However, the Commissioners, having resigned, remained in office as 'acting Commissioners', there being no provision for their replacement.) In general the EC has been blamed both for the dictatorial ways of the EU, for its *democratic deficit, and for the repeated inability of the auditors to pass its accounts. Nevertheless its Presidents and members have remained at the helm through all scandals, and only the European Parliament has been able to limit its powers – by a small amount.

European Community (EC)

Strictly speaking, the European Communities: the institutions that were subsequently to be incorporated into the *European Union, and which were created at least partly with that intention. The EC comprised three institutions – the European Coal and Steel Community (established 1951), the European Economic Community (*Common Market) and the European Atomic Energy Commission. The last two were established in 1957, by the Treaty of Rome (in fact two treaties); all three were merged in 1967, and because few people knew the extent or nature of the European institutions that grew in subsequent years, the whole system was commonly referred to as the European Community. Under the *Maastricht Treaty, the communities were reformed as a single entity, called the European Union (EU), and the people of the member states were described in the treaty as 'citizens' of the European Union. Whether the result is a genuine political union, and whether it has bestowed a new citizenship on the peoples of Europe, is hotly disputed (*See* *European Union.*)

The major item of policy established by the EC was the *Common Agricultural Policy – a scheme for the subsidizing of food production, which still consumes two-thirds of the European budget. This is paradoxical, in that the original intention of the Treaty of Rome was to create a common market, encouraging free trade, private enterprise and a market economy throughout the continent. The result has been described by critics as an elaborate *protectionism which gives vast economic and social power to the European bureaucracies, penalizes innovation and promotes the stagnation of the rural economy. Originally favoured by defenders of capitalism and the market, therefore, the EC subsequently enjoyed the favour of socialists and large-scale corporations, who saw in it, respectively, an opportunity for *social engineering, and a safe and subsidized market with few internal barriers.

European Court of Human Rights

Judicial body establish by the *Council of Europe, and neither related to the *European Court of Justice nor part of the EU machine. The Court's jurisdiction is limited to states which have signed the European Convention on Human Rights.

European Court of Justice

See *European Union.

European Economic Area (EEA)

The treaty establishing the EEA, signed in 1992, was designed to create a Europe-wide *free trade area, on terms dictated by the *European Community. The signatories are bound by Community legislation and accept most of the *acquis communautaire*, in return for enjoying free trade provisions with the member states.

European Law

There is no legislature as such in the *European Union. Law issues in the form of *legal instruments from the *European Commission or the Council of Ministers, in the form of Treaties which add to or amend the Treaty of Rome, and in the form of judgements of the European Court of Justice, which ruled in 1963 that '. . . the Community constitutes a new legal order . . . for the benefit of which the States have limited their sovereign rights'. In other words, European law takes precedence over national law, whenever there is a conflict between them – a position made explicit in the proposed European Constitution, but not yet officially accepted by all the member states. The process of law-making in the EU is more or less secret; new legislative initiatives must originate in the Commission, which operates as a closed bureaucracy; the Council of Ministers sits in private and rarely issues minutes of its meetings; the ECJ does not publish dissenting judgements.

European Union

The EU comprises, in its political aspect:

(i) The Council of Ministers, consisting of representatives of the several national governments. Major executive decisions are made by this council, and can become *directives, which must then be enacted as law by the national legislatures.

(ii) The *European Commission. This is the administrative heart of the EU, and is the source of European legislation. (*See* *legal instruments.) The Commission can prepare draft legislation for the Council of Ministers, and prepares the annual EU budget, from which its own staff are paid.

(iii) The European Parliament, with members (MEPs) elected from each country. It began life as an advisory rather than a legislative assembly; however, the Single European Act, adopted by the UK in July 1987, grants legislative power to the Parliament, since it provides that legislative proposals from the Parliament can be overturned only by a unanimous vote of the Council of Ministers. The Parliament now also has the final say as to which countries may join the EU.

(iv) The European Court of justice, which forms the judicial branch of the EU. This has 27 members, drawn from the national judiciaries of the member states, and adjudicates disputes under European treaties, regulations and *directives. Its constitution enables it to serve as a court of final appeal in any matter between a citizen and his government concerning which the EU has issued some regulation or directive. Because the Treaty of Rome contains clauses dealing with *civil liberties, the court can in many cases grant or uphold rights that a national government wishes to deny. It has no powers of enforcement, but members of the EU are reluctant to be seen to disobey its decisions.

To some a dream, to others a nightmare, complete political union remains a vague – or at least under-described – *end state, to which the EU may, whether by accident or design, be tending. At least the following steps have been proposed, and in some cases implemented in whole or in part:

(i) *Monetary union. This has been achieved in part through the adoption of the single currency (the Euro) by many member states. However, the fiscal consequences of this move, which effectively forbid a member state from devaluing its currency, even though this is the best and possibly only way to return to competitiveness, are beginning to be acutely felt, especially in Italy.

(ii) A single internal market – the goal of the UK Single European Act

1987, designed to introduce complete mobility of the *factors of production within the EU, and now enacted by all national legislatures.

(iii) A European *federation, with national states reduced to a condition of *local government, like the several states of the Union in the US. There seems to be little agreement among those who propose such a federation as to its precise relation to the member states. Vague talk of *subsidiarity fails to reassure those who believe that national *sovereignty is the *sine qua non* of a free people, while the result of Union is perceived differently by those (such as the Italians) whose experience of stable government is minimal, and those (such as the British) who have experienced little else.

(iv) A single Constitution, defining executive, legislative and judicial powers, and appropriating these where necessary from the member states. The document described as a 'Constitutional Treaty', some 15 times the length of the US Constitution, was recently rejected by referendums in France and the Netherlands. However, referendums that go against the unifying process are usually ignored or reversed by the EU machine, and this will probably be no exception.

(v) The *acquis communautaire*, whereby powers appropriated from, and laws passed for, the member states cannot be regained or overthrown by those states. This – the 'ratchet' process – suggests that political unity of some kind is the inevitable long-term result of the European process.

(vi) Integration at every level – local government, foreign policy, social provisions, defence, agriculture, energy and so on – often through independent commissions.

Debates over the EU are now at the top of the political agenda. The issues seem to be the following:

(i) The implied loss of national

*sovereignty. The effect of the powers listed above is that national legislatures are compelled to legislate whether they like it or not on issues which may be of acute national concern.

(ii) The lack of accountability of the *European Commission.

(iii) The alleged wastefulness and corruption of the European subsidy machine.

(iv) The allegedly insensitive nature of the regulations and directives issued by Brussels.

(v) The allegation of a hidden *agenda, according to which complete political union is the secret goal. (*See* *Monnet.)

(vi) The seeming loss of democratic control over the legislative process. (*See* *democratic deficit.)

(vii) The scale and ambition of many legislative proposals – such as the Social Chapter of the *Maastricht Treaty, which contains clauses deeply distasteful to free-market *conservatives.

(viii) The attempt by the EU to create centres of power and decision-making both above and below the national level, so as to defuse the belligerent feelings that derive from too vehement a sense of national identity. (*See* *subsidiarity.)

All those issues go to the heart of politics, and, however the European experiment is finally judged, there is no doubt that it has been the greatest stimulus to political thinking since the *cold war.

Europeanism

The attitude which sees the well-being, destiny and *institutions of the major European states as so closely linked by geographical and historical circumstances that no cogent political action can be successfully pursued in one state without some reference to, and attempt to achieve integration with, the others. For the advocates of a fully

federal *European Union, Europe, which created the *nation state, should also transcend it, and bear political witness to the fact of its common outlook, culture and heritage, through the creation of common legal, economic and political institutions. While based in a *common market, the EU has evolved a set of political institutions, which have the *approximation of laws as their aim, and which impinge on local customs, habits and political procedures in a manner which tends towards their abolition. This is welcomed by many Europeanists, as a furtherance of true political unity (*see* *Monnet).

Europeanism was also a strong undercurrent in *dissident movements in Eastern Europe, since it affirmed the existence of an identity other than that insisted on by the Communist Party, and provided a real cultural and territorial claim with which to support the somewhat abstract assertion of *human rights. Hence, for many people in *post-communist countries, membership of the European Union has a significance which goes far beyond questions of economic prosperity.

euthanasia

Greek: good death. Term used since 1869 to denote the termination of human life in order to relieve the suffering of the victim, usually with his consent. Euthanasia raises in a vivid form certain questions concerning *persons, and the extent to which our duties towards them may be dissolved or overridden by their actual or supposed consent. It is normal to phrase questions concerning euthanasia in terms of the language of rights – have I the right to do this to someone, if he consents? What if he does *not* consent (supposing him to be unconscious and destined to a life as a vegetable)? Perhaps human vegetables are not persons, and have no rights? The language of rights is perhaps misleading, since the question can be phrased without it: ought I, and ought he, ever to do this, even if life holds nothing for him?

Distinction is made between the issue of euthanasia and that of *abortion, on the grounds that (i) in euthanasia consent of the victim is possible or may be inferred; (ii) abortion always requires a positive interference in the course of nature, whereas euthanasia may involve the opposite – a decision to cease medication and to let nature take its course.

evangelism

1. The dedicated preaching of the gospel; transferred to political contexts to denote political action which favours persuasion through *doctrine, rather than through *force, material inducement, or *conciliation. Some think that only the last is a truly *political approach to human conflict.

2. (= evangelicalism.) Term denoting various *activist tendencies within the Christian (specifically *Protestant) churches, which emphasize the contents of the gospel, rather than custom or institution, as the true source of spiritual authority.

evil

Not all bad things are evil; though in the case of people 'evil' seems to be a kind of metaphysical superlative of 'bad'. The evil person is not just careless of others' well-being, heartless, cowardly, self-indulgent or mean. He is actively involved in the destruction of others, dedicated, like Mephistopheles in Goethe's *Faust*, to the negation of human life, love and hope. Hence the category of evil is important in all human perception, as a kind of anti-reality, a horizon above the pit of nothingness, a temptation which beckons us to our destruction. Condemning a

political ideology as evil means identifying it with this nothingness. Sometimes the identification will be *part* of the ideology, as in the Russian *nihilism of the nineteenth century. Sometimes it is an identification made from the observer's perspective, as with *Nazism and *communism – or at least communism as perceived by its victims. Much of *Islamism can be understood as a reaction to habits and social conditions (particular those associated with the Western way of life) which are perceived, not as bad or imperfect, but as evil – and therefore as an existential threat to the ordinary Muslim. And *Islamism is in turn perceived as evil by those whom it targets.

'The problem of evil' in theology uses the term in a different sense. This does not refer to 'the Devil's work', but to the problem of reconciling the goodness and omnipotence of the Creator with the manifold suffering and destruction that occurs in the world.

evolutionary psychology
See *sociobiology.

evolutionary sociology
See *sociobiology.

evolutionism

1. Belief that major social and political changes are to be understood as forms of 'evolution', whereby social structures gradually adapt themselves to material conditions, and steady improvements in institutions emerge from failed attempts. The evolutionary view of society has a long history, and versions were common in the eighteenth century, put forward, for example, by *Montesquieu and *Kant. *Saint-Simon argued that there is an evolutionary sequence through which all mankind must pass, and *Comte suggested that there are three universally observable

stages of human development in the social sphere. Herbert Spencer (1820–1903) extended some of Comte's ideas in *Principles of Sociology*, 1867, arguing that social life has a natural tendency to develop from simple to complex forms, and steadily to enrich its variety. He had begun to develop his influential account of this before Darwin's *Origin of Species*, 1859, and later argued that Darwin's theory confirmed his own, thus founding the ideology of social *Darwinism, according to which adaptation of society to material conditions is to be understood in terms of the 'survival of the fittest'. *Marxism has an evolutionist side, but argues that, while society develops, it does not develop in a uniform way, and in particular undergoes periods of *revolutionary* transformation, when laws of steady development no longer apply, since the whole social organism has become dysfunctional. Modern evolutionists include the Catholic theologian Teilhard de Chardin (1881–1955), who attempted to reconcile evolutionary and *creationist philosophies.

2. Any *reformist doctrine that believes in a slow and continuous process as the only way to initiate beneficial change, and which therefore opposes *revolution, or the violent overthrow of existing institutions. Roughly speaking, the *social democrat parties have become evolutionists, and have been condemned as such by the *communist parties, which represent their own aims as revolutionary. Eduard Bernstein's *Evolutionary Socialism*, 1899, which advocated evolutionism from within the Marxist camp, has always been particularly distasteful to communists, and, since Lenin's attacks on it, was taken as the major text of *revisionism.

*Hayek defends what he calls 'evolutionary rationality' against the rational plans of socialists and others for the *end state of human society. Evolutionary rationality pertains to customs, institutions and traditions which have the innate ability to adjust to the flow of events, and to arrive at a reasonable solution to shared problems by an *invisible hand.

excess profits
1. The medieval doctrine of the *just price was an application of the view that there is a price for each commodity at which it could exchange without *exploitation of the buyer or deprivation of the seller. To sell above that price is to make a profit unjustly. This idea of a just price – to be determined by principles of justice which are independent of actual supply and demand – survives in the wartime concept of 'excess profits', according to which a government may determine, by criteria which do not refer to actual market forces, the level above which profit may not go without incurring a penalty. During 1939–46 excess profits were subject in the UK to an 'excess profits tax', designed to prevent the exploitation of the ordinary consumer. (*See* *usury.)

2. In economics, 'excess profit', also called 'supernormal profit', has a technical sense, for which *see* *profit.

excess supply or demand
Two kinds of economic disequilibrium (*see* *equilibrium). In the presence of excess demand the amount of a good or service which buyers seek to purchase at a given price exceeds the amount which sellers are able or prepared to sell at that price, so that (other things being equal, and failing, e.g., government constraint) prices will generally tend to rise until equilibrium is attained. In the presence of excess supply, conversely, prices tend to fall.

exchange control

The control by the *state of dealings in gold and foreign currencies, exercised through the banking system. Exchange control may affect, or even be used to fix, the rate of exchange, for example, when the price of domestic currency is artificially raised for foreign traders in order to increase holdings of *hard currency. And it may affect capital transfers, as when the transfer of domestic currency abroad is forbidden or limited. The second form of exchange control is the subject of much political controversy. It had been practised by UK governments continuously since the end of the war, until its abolition in 1979. It was then argued that the economic benefit of the measure had never been proven, and that, while it limited the citizen's ability to convert domestic assets into foreign assets, it also deterred foreign investors from converting foreign assets into domestic ones, so achieving no real improvement in the *balance of payments. The persistence of exchange control was said by some to be a form of *protectionism, which could not achieve its intended effect. It was also argued to be an unwarranted interference in individual *liberty, and became the occasion of many traditional arguments on behalf of *free trade. The abolition of exchange control brings about a 'floating' exchange rate. According to economists of the *Chicago School floating exchange rates will tend of themselves to bring the balance of payments into equilibrium.

From 1979 the states of the *EU have operated an 'exchange rate mechanism', designed to create a zone of currency stability following the collapse in the early 1970s of the dollar-based system agreed at *Bretton Woods. The participating currencies were to be given a central exchange rate against the ECU (European Currency Unit), and central banks would intervene to maintain stability. The UK entered the ERM in 1990, at a time of recession, and following massive speculation on the pound was forced out of the system in 1992, at vast cost meanwhile to the exchequer in the vain attempt to maintain the official exchange rate. The system remained in being, however, until replaced by the single currency and partial *monetary union.

exchange economy

An economy in which there is specialization of activity and therefore social *division of labour, which creates the need for exchange, usually through the creation of a *market. The interdependence of division of labour and a system of exchange was pointed out by *Smith, and it persists whether or not there is state intervention in the economy.

There is also a technical meaning of the term within economics, according to which an 'exchange economy' is a hypothetical economy in which there is exchange without production. (A possible example of this is the prisoner-of-war camp after the receipt of food parcels.)

exchange-value

A term of *classical economics. The exchange-value of a commodity consists of the quantity of some other commodity against which it will exchange in *equilibrium conditions. When the other commodity is money, exchange-value becomes *price. Exchange-value is a principal subject-matter of quantitative economics, and must be distinguished from (another term of classical economics) *use-value, which requires independent theoretical treatment.

executive

The branch of government concerned with implementing domestic and foreign policy, and applying law. According to one version of the doctrine of the *separation of powers, the executive is contrasted with the *legislature, whose function is not to implement but to decide on policy, not to apply but to determine the law, and with the judiciary, whose function is to decide disputes as to the meaning or the applicability of the law.

In the UK the executive branch of government includes the *Crown, and the ministers of the Crown, and the *civil service (including the Foreign Office). It has two peaks of power: the *cabinet, which pursues party politics, influences as best it can the decisions taken in *Parliament, and then advises the Crown; and the civil service, which is in theory a servant of the Crown, but in practice exercises, through inertia, or habit, an executive power of its own.

Because of the influence of the doctrine of the separation of powers upon the US *constitution, the term 'executive' is used widely, to refer to all the powers of the President and his cabinet, whether or not those powers correspond precisely to any theoretical division between those which are and those which are not of an executive kind. These executive powers of the President are subject to constant scrutiny (with various sanctions, culminating in *impeachment) by both houses of Congress. The President appoints his own staff to the executive office, which may contain as many as 2000 members, each engaged in mediating between the central apex of executive power and the various departments and agencies through which it is exercised. The constitution permits the establishment of 'executive agencies' designed to apply the legislation passed by Congress: these include the National Security Council and the CIA.

'Executive agreements' are agreements made between the US President and another head of state: they have the validity and effect of a *treaty, but do not require *ratification by the Senate. By analogy, some writers refer to 'executive war', meaning war precipitated and conducted by the President, whether in his role as commander-in-chief, or by his constitutional executive powers, which is pursued despite dissent from the people and from the two assemblies. The war in Vietnam had, at certain stages, such a character, but also resulted in legislation restricting the power to make executive war.

exile

Conceived by the Greeks and Romans as a form of punishment appropriate to grave offences, and used as such in the USSR, where 'exile' meant forced confinement in an inhospitable place, exile is now often the preferred response to *oppression. Voluntary exile – prolonged and perhaps permanent absence from one's country of origin – is therefore a common condition, with its own *ethos, and *culture, and a powerful influence in public affairs. Exile is a special case of *emigration, where what is sought is not primarily the advantages of the place to which one goes, but essentially freedom from whatever disadvantages prevailed at home. Some argue that the exile character is shaped by the thought of betrayal of those who have not been able to escape, and that this thought explains the exile's sense of impotent homelessness. Governments in exile are, perhaps for this reason, seldom respected either by those in exile themselves, or by those at home.

Exile with loss of citizenship is normally called expatriation, whether or not the loss was voluntary.

existentialism

Term adapted from the Danish philosopher Søren Kierkegaard (1813–55), and now denoting the philosophy of personal existence which he introduced, according to which the subjective consciousness of the individual, and his solitary 'leap into the unknown', constitute the sole legitimate premise of all metaphysical and ethical speculation. The term is also used of the philosophies of *Heidegger and *Sartre, together with many of those who have been influenced by them and, through them, by the *phenomenology of Edmund Husserl (1859–1938). Heidegger poses the 'problem of being', and distinguishes between various kinds of being (e.g. *Sein, Dasein* and *Existenz*), with which we, as self-conscious agents, are familiar, but which need to be uncovered by philosophical reflection. It is only in the *authentic choice, whereby we take *responsibility for our own being, that our freedom is expressed and our anxiety in the face of nothingness overcome. This choice seems to precipitate a reflective posture – which Heidegger calls 'being towards death' – in which the fact of mortality becomes the premise of all practical reasoning, and the clue to acceptance of 'being in the world'. (*See* *death.) Similar ideas, less obscurely formulated, occur in the work of Sartre, but associated there with an energetic form of political *activism, based nevertheless on the premise that an individual is answerable to himself alone, and has no responsibility greater than the responsibility to be who he (really) is. (*See* *commitment.)

If there is a political posture characteristic of existentialism it is to be found in that last phrase, and in the various embellishments that are offered to the idea of the human being as self-created. Sartre argues, for example, that the central fact about human beings is that they have no nature (or 'essence') but only existence. Hence there is no *natural law,

and no objective morality. The individual is alone in the world, burdened by a freedom which he cannot shift since it is the precondition of all his acts, and for which he must take full and elaborate responsibility.

At the same time there is no responsibility outside the act of commitment; a political stance may provide the channel through which commitment can flow, in which case it may fulfil the obligatory existential choice of the godless agent. There is, however, a contradiction involved in this attempt to recognize absolute sovereignty only in the unmediated, untheorized, undoctrinal choice, while urging that such a choice must be, or at any rate ought to be, directed towards a political (specifically communist) end. Sartre's theory that contradiction is the inevitable result of the attempt to relate to anything other than oneself at least makes this course no more irrational than any other; in his followers, however, it is sometimes difficult to see the grounds for nevertheless fervent recommendations. Marxists often argue that the existentialist emphasis on subjectivity and the suffering consciousness is in fact incompatible with their vision of political agency, and incompatible with *historical materialism. For Sartre, however, existentialism is, in the last analysis, only an 'enclave within Marxism'. Other writers (notably *Arendt and *Camus) have argued for an 'existentialist politics', in which the individual confronts his historical condition by taking full responsibility for it in his public life.

'Christian existentialism' is the name of the style of subjectivist *demythologizing theology that takes its inspiration from Kierkegaard, and which extols the agonized individual who loses all for the sake of a faith that is inexpressible.

expansionism

Term coined about 1900 to refer to the advocacy of, or furtherance of, a policy of expansion, especially territorial expansion, either by inducing economic dependence in neighbouring states, or by the *subversion of their political systems in order to make them politically dependent, or by direct conquest. Economic expansionism, such as witnessed in postwar Japan, involves the constant expansion of markets, in order to capture an ever larger share of world trade.

exploitation

1. In common parlance, John exploits Alfred when John uses Alfred to John's advantage, and Alfred's detriment, without making just recompense (perhaps making no recompense whatsoever). Hence applications of the idea of exploitation presuppose a standard of 'just recompense'. Exploitation may involve deception (as in fraud), or *force (as in *slavery), or 'undue influence' (as when a husband exploits his wife): but its essence does not consist in any of these, which are invoked only to explain the position of the victim. Some find its essence in the idea of 'just recompense' just referred to; others in the *Kantian notion that some forms of treatment involve using others as means and not as ends – a notion itself designed to explicate the idea of injustice.

One explanation of how exploitation may arise is in terms of unequal bargaining power. This has been invoked as common ground by many of those who would criticize the institution of *wage labour. The crucial problem is clearly that of determining when, and how, unequal bargaining power leads to injustice. Some say that a labourer is compelled by necessity to sell his *labour power, whereas his employer is not compelled by any similar necessity to contract for it, and

that this alone is sufficient to generate injustice. However, without further theory, that is extremely contentious: for it would have the consequence that there could never be a *just price for any commodity that is needed by the purchaser, so that the buying and selling, for example, of food, will always involve an injustice, whatever the price. Some might still be prepared to accept this consequence, but most attempt to give further theories of the wage relation. It is sometimes argued that the employer need only give (and therefore will only give) to the labourer sufficient to enable the reproduction of his labour power – i.e. what he needs for survival. But those who argue this way (including *Marx) make the important proviso that custom, local conditions and expectancy determine what is needed by the labourer: in which case this says very little about the actual amount (relative or absolute) that the capitalist must offer. Besides, it is to be supposed that unionization removes this element of absolute dependence on the employer's whim, as do laws governing the minimum wage and labour hours. In short, the unequal bargaining power that remains is rather like that which exists in (almost) every *contract. Is it necessary that it leads to exploitation?

2. Classical *Marxism says yes, but only by introducing a new concept of exploitation so as to imply that, whenever there is private property in the means of production, there is also exploitation. This theory is sometimes thought to be part of the *labour theory of value, but is in fact independent. It argues first that *capital is not a *productive force, but only a pattern of *production relations, with the important feature that it facilitates a particularly high level of production. Nevertheless, the only producer in the capitalist enterprise is the labourer –

capital (in the form of machinery, etc.) being no more than the means to increase the efficiency of his labour. But the labourer does not keep the full product of his labour – part of it is kept by the capitalist, in the form of *surplus-value. This will be true whether or not the labourer receives more than the amount necessary to reproduce himself and his labour power. (In terms of the labour theory of value the point is sometimes put thus: surplus-value is the extraction of hours of unpaid labour.) Thus the labourer is deprived of some portion of the product which he, and he alone, produces. The 'rate of exploitation' is defined in terms of the ratio of the time worked to the time required for the labourer to produce the equivalent of what he receives.

While this theory speaks of exploitation, it is clear that it is stated and defended without reference to the concept of justice. If it is true, it does not follow that the labourer is exploited in sense 1. unless it is also argued, e.g., that he has a *natural right to the product of his labour. That position has been argued, e.g. by *Locke, but as part of a philosophical *defence* of private property in the means of production, and also by some of the early socialist followers of *Ricardo.

export and import
Exports are goods and services produced in one country, and sold in exchange for the goods, services, credit or currency of another: imports are what the other country thereby receives. Invisible exports are such items as financial services, shipping services, royalties, legal fees; they may constitute a considerable amount of a state's *national income, as, in the UK, upon whose banking and legal systems much of international trade ultimately depends. Re-export is the export of imported commodities without significant alteration, as in much of the UK trade in tea.

expropriation
Depriving some person or corporation of private property, usually by government agency, with no recompense. To be distinguished from *nationalization and *eminent domain, where recompense (which may or may not relate to the actual value of the property) is offered. Is there a distinction between *taxation and expropriation? If not, does that show that the former is unjust, or that the latter may sometimes be just? Some (e.g. *Nozick) regard taxation as a forced parting with property legitimately acquired; others regard all rights of private property as inherently defeasible in the interests of the state (through whose protection they are held), so that neither taxation nor expropriation is in itself unjust, but unjust only when independent circumstances (involving, e.g., the disregard for genuine *natural rights) might make them so.

externalities
(Also known as 'neighbourhood effects'.) Consequences of some activity which are not part of the direct economic benefit or cost to the agent, but which either benefit or harm others. In particular, costs which are transferred to others, such as the cost of pollution in industrial production. It is sometimes thought that there can be no coherent ecological politics unless and until all actors in the economy are forced, by law, to 'internalize' their costs – in other words to meet the full cost to others, whether now or in the future, of what they do. Whether or not such a politics is any more than a *utopian fantasy, it is clear that the ability of producers and consumers to externalize their costs (e.g. by using non bio-degradable wrappings) is the

principal source of environmental damage.

A distinction is sometimes made between moral and physical externalities. Moral externalities comprise the mental effects of a transaction on people who are not party to it, such as the effect of aesthetic degradation on those who live in badly planned towns. Moral externalities can in turn have their physical effects – for example, the vandalism of town centres that occurs when they lose all semblance of a civilized settlement.

extradition

The delivery by one state to another of a person against whom the second state desires to proceed under its own criminal law. In the UK extradition is permitted only under statute, where there is an extradition treaty with the other state. In the US there can be inter-state extradition, governed by the 'Inter-state Comity' Clause (art. IV, s. 2). This clause has been held by the Supreme Court, however, to be discretionary, so that the governor of one state may refuse to return a prisoner to another whence he fled, without giving reason.

Extradition is not normally allowed, under any legal system, for *political offences, although what constitutes a political offence remains uncertain. This exception is thought necessary for a variety of reasons, but most of all in order to remove from *adjudication by the courts matters which concern diplomatic relations and foreign policy.

extremism

Vague term, which can mean:

1. Taking a political idea to its limits, regardless of 'unfortunate' repercussions, impracticalities, arguments, and feelings to the contrary, and with the intention not only to confront, but also to eliminate, *opposition.

2. Intolerance towards all views other than one's own (for which, *see* *toleration).

3. Adoption of means to political ends which disregard accepted standards of conduct, in particular which show disregard for the life, liberty and *human rights of others.

Fabianism

The Roman general Q. Fabius Maximus, surnamed 'Cunctator' ('the delayer'), won his campaigns by slow attrition of the enemy. Accordingly, those British socialists who wished to see their aims achieved by a policy of gradual reform within existing institutions and constitutional government, rather than by revolutionary upheaval, called their society, founded in 1884, the Fabian Society, wishing to imitate the Roman general in success as well as in name. The society has never had many members, but it has included influential intellectual figures (among them, Sidney and Beatrice Webb, H.G. Wells and G.B. *Shaw), along with many Labour Party politicians. It has tirelessly pursued the task of making socialism intellectually and politically (some would also add, perhaps unfairly, socially) respectable, and, through its influence in universities (notably in Oxford) was able to win over to the Labour Party many of those best situated to obtain parliamentary seats. It has therefore been important in forming the UK Labour Party during the mid-twentieth century. It is characterized by wide-ranging, relatively undoctrinaire, and imaginative social analysis, but not by any doctrine besides the central one implied in its name.

faction

Any group organized for political ends, which defines itself at least partly by its opposition to some rival group. A faction is usually *within* a *party, *institution, or *government, and is identified by perceived common purpose rather than by rules of membership. Were a faction to achieve the level of political ascendancy necessary to announce its aims, and to invite membership, then it would tend to become a *party. Systems which do not permit *opposition parties nevertheless have still to contend with opposing factions.

Fear of, and hostility towards, faction motivated much of sixteenth- and seventeenth-century *absolutism, and subsequent *constitutionalism often had, as one of its aims, the stilling of faction through permanent procedures of balance and *conciliation. The transformation of faction into legitimate opposition is often seen as one factor in political *equilibrium.

factors of production

Defined by the economist Alfred Marshall (1842–1924) as 'the things required for making a commodity', they are often grouped by economists into *land, *labour and *capital, on the assumption that these three are roughly independent factors involved in production, and that no one of them is effective alone: land provides *raw material, capital the instruments of production, and labour the necessary activity which brings these together to produce a saleable *commodity. 'Factors' are usually distinguished from 'inputs'. An input is a commodity or service, a factor of production is the recipient of some category of income (rent, wages or profit).

It is sometimes thought that this division reflects either economic error, or political prejudice, or both, in that it seems to imply (or in *certain applications* seems to imply) that the contributions of the factors are comparable, so that capital, for example, merits a return just as much as does labour. *Marxists argue that the owner of *capital, unlike the owner of *labour power, does not actually *do* anything – ownership exhausts his contribution, which is thereby not a contribution at all, but an indefinite tax on another's labour. By contrast thinkers of the *Austrian school argue that capital embodies the sacrifice of present consumption for the sake of future gain, and this sacrifice is comparable to that of the labourer, who exchanges present leisure for a future wage.

It may also be noted that much modern economics makes no use of the notion of aggregate 'factors' of production, and that the whole attempt to divide the inputs of capital and labour has an antiquated and Victorian air, with labour now often considered as a form of *human capital, and the whole economic process depending in its turn on *social capital.

factory legislation

Since the beginning of the *industrial revolution in the UK there have been repeated attempts on the part of government (often acting under pressure from concerned philanthropists such as *Owen, or from increasingly organized working-class pressure) to ensure that *factory production should conform to some standard of humane conduct towards the labourer. Such legislation has been a major channel through which objections to unfettered capitalism – whether motivated by socialist distaste for *exploitation, or by conservative distaste for social disruption and uprootedness – have found expression. In the first acts (from that of 1802 introduced by Peel to that of 1867) the principal concern was to shorten the working day and to prevent the exploitation of children; later the emphasis shifted to provisions for health, safety and the conditions of work. In the US legislation was more tardy, and while the State of Massachusetts paved the way in a series of statutes beginning in 1836, there was no coherent body of federal legislation until the twentieth century. Even in 1916 and 1919 federal laws limiting child labour were held to be unconstitutional, and a proposed child labour amendment to the constitution was rejected in 1924. Not until the Depression did US legislation catch up with that of the UK.

factory production

That mode of production characterized by the gathering of labourers into a single place, in order to engage in *detail labour, for fixed hours, in a process which may or may not include all the operations required for the production of a *commodity. Factory production, which brings people into close relation with machines, is characteristic of a certain kind of *technological advance, itself characteristic, according to some theories, of capitalism. Its aspect of enslavement and *alienation which struck such horror into nineteenth-century observers (and presumably into nineteenth-century victims, although they had less time to be articulate about it), is one that serious modern political doctrines have attempted to confront, either by advocating the abolition of factory production (a thesis often denounced as utopian or at any rate romantic), or by suggesting modes of ownership or control that will mitigate it (although how it is mitigated by, e.g., *common ownership of the factory is a problem to which socialism returns an answer that many find unpersuasive), or (what is perhaps most reasonable) by advocating further advances that will enable people to master the machines that presently seem to master them. The emergence of the *service economy has to some extent made these issues irrelevant.

failed state

A state, typically founded in the aftermath of colonial rule, in which the infrastructure of law, government and policy-making fails to take root, so that criminal gangs, religious sects, tribal chieftains and assorted external powers compete for control, usually at great cost to the indigenous population. Examples include Sudan, where *Islamists seized power in the North, tyrannizing over Christians and animists in the South, and encouraging Arab tribes in the Darfur region to enslave and massacre the indigenous non-Muslim population. The situation may now be improving, following a peace agreement between North and South. But the infrastructure of a modern state no longer exists to guarantee the result. Some argue that failed states show the need for *pre-political order, and come about through the attempt to impose the order of a state in the absence of a continuous (for example national) society.

fairness

Popular term meaning *justice, perhaps with a slight leaning towards the *distributive conception expressed by that term. Thus the theory of 'justice as fairness' advocated by *Rawls can be seen partly as advancing a claim for the primacy of distributive conceptions in settling claims over what is just, while also emphasizing that just agreements involve the discounting of all 'unfair' advantage. On the other hand, the ideas of 'fair comment' (a defence to a claim of damages in libel), 'fair trading' (concept introduced into UK law in 1973 in order to protect consumers from certain kinds of *exploitation), and 'fair wages' (introduced into UK law in 1891 in order to protect labourers from exploitation in times of over-full employment) use the term 'fair' to denote justice in transaction rather than in distribution. (On the distinction here see *justice.) The distributive conception is more obviously evinced by the 'fairness' doctrine in US communications law, which requires the *media of mass communication to apportion their time 'fairly' to the various candidates and parties seeking election during a political campaign. Significantly, fairness is not taken to mean that all parties should be given a share of time, or that times allotted to the various parties should be equal.

The child's cry 'It is not fair', like the more sophisticated 'It is not just that . . .', suggest a demand that the world be so arranged that justice be done. Some think that such a complaint is not only childish, but also incoherent; others see in it the basic motive of all serious political action.

fair trade

Trade in which parties do not seek to exploit each other beyond what is necessary to make an honest profit. Difficult to define precisely (though see the previous entry), fair trade is nevertheless an important concept in debates concerning the *developing nations, which are by their nature in a weak position when it comes to establishing terms of trade with nations in the developed world. In particular, they frequently lack the legal and institutional infrastructure that will enable them to fight off predatory assertions of property rights in their inventions and produce. (See *World Trade Organization, *trade-related intellectual property.)

faith

Regarded by the Christian churches as a supernatural rather than a natural act, faith arises from God's action on the soul, and involves an act of the will, and something surpassing an act of understanding, on the part of the subject, who voluntarily reaches out for and encounters the deity, without knowing, until he has become acquainted with God, exactly what it is that he is believing, and afterwards, in all probability, being unable or reluctant to put what he believes into words.

The underlying doctrine of faith is this: there are systems of belief so integral to the identity of the person who subscribes to them, and so far beyond intellectual definition, that they must be understood at least partly in terms of the will: an act of will is their precondition and also their result. The knowledge that results from the undertaking of faith is more like knowledge of a person ('acquaintance') than it is like knowledge of a fact, and for this reason it seems absurd to transcribe the deliverances of faith into propositions that may be doubted or believed, according to the evidence. Such an assimilation of doctrinal commitment to acts of will has its equivalent in the realm of politics, for example, in neo-conservative ideas of *tradition, in *neo-Marxist notions of *praxis and in *existentialist theories of *authenticity and *commitment.

falangism

The *falange española* (Spanish phalanx), or falangists, were founded in 1933 by José Antonio Primo de Rivera (son of Primo de Rivera, Spanish dictator 1923–30), in order to secure working-class support for the local brand of *fascism. It continued its activities throughout the republican period, emphasizing traditional, as much as the new fascist and *collectivist, modes of social unity, and was finally successful in the civil war, under the determined leadership of General Franco. Hence 'falangism' now denotes the particular synthesis of fascism and traditionalism exemplified by Franco's subsequent dictatorship, with its emphasis on Spanish national character, on close moral and political ties between people and leadership, and on a fundamental unity between the state and all autonomous institutions, including the church. In the wake of Primo de Rivera's original movement, falangist movements arose elsewhere, notably in Lebanon, where the name was retained (*Phalange* in French, *kataëb* in Arabic), long after the movement had adapted to postwar conditions and the defeat of fascism, retaining solely the idea of a nation unified by faith and tradition, and guided by strong leadership and military strength.

falling rate of profit

It was several times predicted by nineteenth-century economists that, in the long run, the rate of profit of all enterprises will tend to fall, and the *accumulation of capital come to an end. *Ricardo derived this prediction from the fact that natural resources are limited: gradually more inferior land must be brought under the plough, and since the net product per labourer falls as cultivation is extended, while the exchange-value of capital against agricultural products rises, the margin of profit must inevitably dwindle. The prediction is no longer widely accepted, and those who accept it do not necessarily forecast the doom of capitalism. Some – for example, *Keynes, and many of his followers – look forward to a natural end to accumulation, and to the pursuit of profit that accompanies it.

false consciousness

Term of *Marxist theory, already current in 1893, when *Engels wrote, in a letter to Mehring: 'Ideology is a process accomplished by the so-called thinker consciously indeed but with a false consciousness.' It has many earlier equivalents in *Hegel, and in *Feuerbach's analysis of *fetishism, and was popularized by writers such as *Lukács and *neo-Marxists, particularly those of the *Frankfurt school. If, as the *German Ideology* says, life determines consciousness and not consciousness life, then each mode of life will generate its own characteristic form of consciousness. Whether or not some form of *determinism is true, it is clear that this view of consciousness raises a problem concerning truth: in particular, how can one pursue truth – how can one know, that is, that the world is as one's consciousness represents it to be? The problem is made acute by the suggestion that falsehood may be generic to a particular kind of consciousness, so that even its weighing of the evidence will not guarantee the truth of its conclusions, since that very reasoning will be infected by the intrinsic falsehood that governs it.

Various responses have been made to that suggestion. One – which is at least as old as Descartes – is to argue that truths of method are ultimately self-guaranteeing, so that, with proper discipline, it is always possible for a rational being to have access to the truth, provided only that he follow the method prescribed by reason itself. (Some philosophers have also wished to derive, from this *autonomy of reason, a guarantee of human *freedom.) Others have accepted in part the argument given by the critics of 'false consciousness', and accepted too a rather striking conclusion of the *historical materialism with which it is associated: if one's vision of the world is determined by one's mode of life, specifically by one's position in the economy and hence one's class, then, since thought alone cannot change that position, thought alone cannot change one's vision of reality. Hence there is no purely intellectual pursuit of truth, at least concerning matters of social and political perception. In which case not only are there modes of consciousness which are inherently false; there is also no way to change them except by action. This active move towards a mode of consciousness that is, or can be, true is sometimes called *praxis. A false consciousness is one that does not make particular errors of fact so much as general errors of reasoning and perception. Since those errors will be integral to an economic position (e.g. that of the *bourgeoisie) they can be eliminated only by changing that position. That is only one example of the survival in Marxism of essentially religious ideas – in this case the idea that you come to truth through changing your life, and not through rational argument. (*See* *faith.)

family

From Latin *famulus*, meaning a servant, the term *familia* came to denote the *household, and then, by extension, the particular system of human relations that prevails among its occupants. The word now has two senses: (i) to refer to a system of *primary relations among people related by blood and marriage and living together (for some part of their lives) in social and economic interdependence; (ii) to refer to blood relations as such, as they extend through generations, traced according to either paternity or maternity (depending upon the prevailing social emphasis), and according to socially recognized principles of exclusion and inclusion. In the first sense (here discussed) sociologists distinguish the nuclear from the extended family. The first is composed from immediate kin, usually monogamous parents and their children; the second involves, in principle at least, all those alive who have any degree of close kinship, through parenthood, brotherhood or sisterhood, and focuses upon the principal breadwinners, who are under an obligation to provide far-reaching support for those suitably related to themselves. In the extended family – characteristic of an agricultural economy, but also determined by cultural expectations – it is normal for three or four generations to live under the same roof, in the nuclear family there are at most two. Economic explanations and radical critiques often argue for the *bourgeois nature of the nuclear family, although there is no widespread agreement about this.

In political theory the family, and the household, have played an important part, thus:

(i) *Aristotle gave a celebrated defence of marriage, the family and the household in his *Politics*, as part of his answer to *Plato's advocacy of collective nurture, education and ownership in *The Republic*. He suggested connections between the relations of domestic love and those of private property which have proved both shocking and consoling to subsequent thinkers. In the course of his discussion he adumbrated many of the arguments of later conservatives both for the family as an institution, and for private property as an immovable part of it.

(ii) *Hegel provided perhaps the most important political analysis of the family in the literature. He repeated Aristotle's arguments concerning the relation between family, household and property, and added some striking theses of his own: (a) the family is a *necessary* part of individual development, from the sphere

of undifferentiated union with others to that of competitive conflict and voluntary association with them (the sphere of *civil society), and thence to the fully conscious union contained in the *state; (b) the bond of the family is not contractual but based in *piety, and this form of involuntary allegiance provides the model for political allegiance generally.

(iii) *Engels, influenced by Hegel's defence of the family, argued that the three institutions of private property, the family, and the state are connected, and that family relations develop in response to property relations. He also argued for the simultaneous abolition of the three institutions, relying on anthropological data, and upon Marxist economic analysis.

In more recent times conservatives, echoing Aristotle, have upheld the family as a social institution apparently common to all classes, and integral to social and political order, while various radical thinkers of the left follow Engels in attacking it, and in prophesying its collapse, as an institution dependent on bourgeois attitudes and bourgeois economic relations. Sometimes (as in R.D. Laing and A. Esterson: *Sanity, Madness and the Family*) the attack has been associated with neo-Freudian doctrines of repression, and with the idea that the individual is inevitably crippled by this arrangement which surveys his personal development, and requires from him conformity to a source of authority outside himself. Such radical critiques, which have their origins in the educational theories of *Rousseau, are sometimes dismissed by conservatives as romantic and sentimental. However, they connect with both *feminist arguments concerning the 'patriarchal' nature of our institutions, and the arguments of *Foucault concerning the omnipresence of power and dominion. They have therefore retained some of their appeal, and feed into current anxieties as to whether the family can really survive in *postmodern conditions.

Breakdown of the nuclear family has become a live political issue, with the rise of the single-parent household, usually with a mother who has had children by one or more men who left her and never married her. Social studies by Charles Murray and others have shown a striking tendency among the children of such households to crime, depression, drug abuse, educational failure and casual relationships. Hence the family, and how to retain or restore it, has become an active issue in policy-making. *See* *dependency culture.

family values

The *values supposedly inculcated by the traditional two-parent family, in which long-term commitment forms the background to a regime of sobriety, piety and healthy bonding between children and their peers. The 'family values movement' in the US has been influential in defending the family against state interference, in supporting initiatives for *home schooling, in pressing for a traditional Judaeo-Christian approach to education and in resisting pressures for the normalization of homosexuality.

famine

Theories of famine include those of a *Malthusian kind, which see the cause as over-population, and those of a *libertarian kind, which see famine as stemming from the kind of misallocation of resources that always ensues, when people rely on some other form of distribution than the market. No doubt there are cases that can be assimilated to both those explanations. However, the most politically significant famines of recent times

have been deliberately induced: for example, that engineered by Stalin in the Ukraine in order to break all resistance to his rule, and the local famines in Maoist China, through which the countryside was kept in a state of total dependence on the central system of command. Famine has always been used as a weapon in war-time; the use of it as a peace-time instrument of control is perhaps one of the original inventions of communism.

fascism

From Latin: *fasces*, the bundle of rods with a projecting axe-head, carried before the consuls as a sign of the state authority of Rome, and adopted as a symbol of social unity (the bundle) under political leadership (the axe). The name was given by Mussolini to the movement which he led to power in Italy in 1922, but is now used more widely, to include German *Nazism, and Spanish *falangism, on the basis more of a common *ethos than a common *doctrine. Fascism is characterized by the following features (not all of which need be present in any of its recognized instances): *corporatism; *nationalism; hostility to *democracy, to *egalitarianism, and to the values of liberal *enlightenment; the cult of the *leader, and admiration for his special qualities; a respect for collective organization, and a love of the symbols associated with it, such as uniforms, parades and army discipline. In Germany the cult of *violence, together with a violent *anti-semitism, were added to these features, with notorious results. The *anti-communist and anti-liberal stance of fascist movements, together with the loathsomeness of many actual examples, have made the fight against fascism a rallying point for left and liberal causes, so that the label 'fascist' may often be applied very loosely, to denote almost any doctrine that conflicts with left-liberal ideology. In this expletive use the term conveys no very clear idea, a fact which perhaps explains its popularity.

From the intellectual point of view fascism remains an amalgam of disparate conceptions, often ill-understood, often bizarre. It is more notable as a political phenomenon on which diverse intellectual influences converge than as a distinct idea; as a political phenomenon, one of its most remarkable features has been the ability to win massive popular support for ideas that are expressly anti-egalitarian (*see* *Reich). Mussolini's own ideas were derived from a heady mixture of popular science, *Marx, *Sorel and *Nietzsche. He advocated regeneration through conquest and perpetual struggle, and spoke, in speeches seething with sexual imagery, of the need to overcome degeneracy and impotence, to make sacrifices for the nation, and to connect to the great 'dynamo' of fascism. Fascists are 'not republicans, socialists, democrats, conservatives or nationalists. They represent a synthesis of all the negations and the affirmations.' In other words, the ultimate doctrine contains little that is specific, beyond an appeal to energy and action: it is, one might say, the form of an *ideology, but without specific content (other than can be provided by admiration towards the leader). This perhaps explains some of its appeal; it seemed to make no demand other than those which the individual himself would make had he the energy. It then provided the energy.

fashion

A fashion is a class of intentionally adopted appearances, in dress, thought or behaviour, which aims to signify membership of a dominant or influential group and to exemplify one's merit as a member of that group. A fashion therefore creates a pattern of social relations focused on display. An intellectual fashion is a theory or doctrine that is adopted not for its truth, but for its appearance, and because it signifies membership of a dominant intellectual coterie. Fashion is traditionally the property of a *ruling class, and part of its procedure of *legitimation. It is now a more widespread phenomenon, partly because of *social mobility, partly because of the influence of the *media in simultaneously standardizing and accelerating changes in socially available appearances.

fatalism

The thesis that every event is determined irrespective of human choice. The thesis is stronger than *determinism, which does not (usually) claim that human choice is without effect, but only that it, too, is determined by preceding circumstances. If fatalism is true then what will be must be. We may try to alter the future, but our trying too is predestined, and outside of our control. Action may then seem to be irrational; the least that can be said is that, believing some such thing, you have a strong motive to resign yourself, an exercise for which fatalistic philosophies usually provide recipes, often on the *Stoic model.

According to *Durkheim, fatalism is the refuge adopted by a consciousness that feels itself powerless; *suicide may be explained by a fatalistic vision, in which case it is to be contrasted with the supposedly more frequent kind of suicide that results from *anomie.

Federal Reserve System

See *banking.

federalism

1. A system of *government, such as exists in the US, in which a central (or 'federal') government, both *legislature

and *executive, exists side by side with state or provincial government, again with both executive and legislative powers. Both federal and state governments will derive what powers they have from the single federal *constitution, but both are supreme in their particular fields, so that (in theory at least) the state government cannot be construed as a *delegation of federal power. The *US model depends upon a written constitution, and upon highly complex political and judicial procedures for the resolution of conflicts, and for the reassertion, when necessary, of the ultimate *sovereignty of the federal government. A more loosely defined federal system exists in Germany, with powers devolved to the separate *Länder* (states) from the Federal legislature, which, however, remains supreme in all matters regarding national unity, identity, sovereignty and defence. It is therefore a poor example for those who advocate federal government as an *alternative* to concentrated and centralized power.

2. The advocacy of 1. as a model of government, in particular as a way of abolishing nation states in favour of a mutually beneficial central government. In the context of *European Union, the advocacy of federalism involves active opposition to national *sovereignty, in favour of a unified system of European government. If national governments retain any powers, this will be by virtue of a principle of *subsidiarity. In the context of US internal politics, federalism is a force tending in the opposite direction – towards fragmentation rather than unification. A federalist is typically an advocate of *states' rights, perhaps going so far as to argue that the federal government has its powers by delegation from the states, and not vice versa. In other words, a federalist wishes to defend the United States as a *confederation, rather than as a sovereign federal state.

Federalist Papers

A series of 85 articles by Alexander Hamilton, *Madison and John Jay, published under the pseudonym of Publius, in support of the campaign for the ratification of the US Constitution in 1787–88. They are widely admired and studied for their distillation of the principles of classical *liberalism as these applied to the American experience.

federation

The act of forming a political unity under a federal government (*see* *federalism), and hence the unity thereby formed. Thus Syria and Egypt for a while (1958–61) formed a federation, the United Arab Republic, in order to encircle Israel and to promote pan-Arabism, with powers united under a single political authority. A federation, in which there is a single *sovereign power, must be distinguished from a *confederation. The essential difference is that the central authorities in a federation have a direct power over the citizens of its component provinces or states, and can legislate for all of them at once. Switzerland, which is called a confederation, is thus really a federation, while the unity actually achieved by Syria and Egypt after a while began to seem more like that of a confederation.

feedback

The return of part of a system's output to change its input. A technical term of systems theory, or *cybernetics, widely misused to mean a response, public or private, to a question, action or policy.

fellow-traveller

From the Russian *poputchik*, used by *Trotsky (*Literature and Revolution*,

1923) to denote the intellectual supporters of the Russian Revolution whose support, however absolute-seeming, was always in fact conditional upon unstated demands of a more or less sentimental, 'bourgeois', or conciliatory kind. The term was later extended to describe sympathizers with communism (specifically with the social system of the USSR as they took it to be), whether they confessed their sympathy or did not confess it or even openly denied it. It is now used yet more widely, to cover those who sympathize with, and advance, a political cause, while not overtly belonging to it.

feminism
The advocacy of the *rights of women and of their social, political and economic equality with men. Originally a movement among the half-emancipated women of the educated classes, it has become part of a wider *women's movement, which is often activist, and which sometimes bases its stance on the belief that society, as presently known in the West, enshrines a persistent *sexism, and moreover constantly frustrates the right of a woman to be a person, and to control her own destiny. In its widest reach it argues not only that women have been accorded rights inferior to those of men, but also that in all social relations their status is implicitly taken to be, or treated as, inferior, and that this has led to their being dominated, both overtly and covertly, by men, in all their activities, thoughts and emotions.

Among the claims frequently made by modern feminists the following are of note: first, that the biological differences between men and women do not explain all the observed differences in their social status, role and behaviour; these latter differences must therefore be seen as a social creation, which it lies within our power to remove. Secondly, that the natural differences between the activities, physical attributes, and responses of men and women should not be taken as grounds for assigning a lower value to the 'feminine' attributes than we assign to the 'masculine'. Thirdly, that women should not be urged to think that fulfilment for them is only possible in relation with men. In particular, women should cease to think of their *identity as given by their appearance in the eyes and minds of men; hence it should be as respectable and fulfilling for a woman to associate only with her own sex as it could be for a man.

In addition, different tendencies within feminism place emphasis on various theoretical claims. 'Socialist feminism' argues that the present position of women is partly to be explained in terms of the capitalist economy, which require that women be bred for a certain role in the order of private property, work, and child-rearing, and that a necessary step on the road to the elimination of invidious sexual discrimination is the elimination of the social and economic system that makes such discrimination functionally necessary.

'Radical feminism', associated with American writers such as Andrea Dworkin and Catherine MacKinnon, is distinguished by the belief that the status of women is not dependent upon but rather far more fundamental than any economic system. For the radical feminist women are inevitably dominated by men when they attempt to enter into society with them, since men have an almost instinctive tendency to set up social relations and to construct institutions that are balanced in their own favour. Radical feminists often argue for complete *separatism, in which women will seek the society of their own sex to the exclusion of the other, and in which lesbian relationships will be the norm, men being perhaps used for their spermatozoa, but not for their companionship. Radical feminism, particularly in its French variant associated with the names of Julia Kristeva, Hélène Cixous and Luce Irïgaray, has made much of the idea of *gender as a social construct, arguing as though the entire human world could be made in either masculine or feminine versions, and that the true aim of feminism is to seize the culture, and make it speak with a feminine voice.

Anti-feminist arguments usually rely on the thought that it is no accident that the relations between men and women are as they are, and that there is a 'natural' order in which both sexes are fulfilled by mutual dependence. They may add that the appearance of male dominance is only an appearance, and perhaps that it is part of the *bourgeois nature of feminism so easily to mistake appearance for essence.

fetishism

Term current in the eighteenth century, and popularized by the anthropologist E.B. Tylor (1832–1917), who used it to denote the worship of inanimate objects, by ascribing to them a spirit, or by regarding them as endowed with magical powers. This attitude was already described by several thinkers of the *Enlightenment, and had been castigated, e.g. by *Kant, in his attack on all forms of religion that express themselves through sensory forms inadequate to the metaphysical idea of a transcendent being. (Kant's criticism had in turn been presaged by *Spinoza.) The term passed into philosophical usage through Kant's denunciation, and was extended by *Feuerbach to the whole of *Christianity (and, by implication, to the religious attitude as such). It was then borrowed by *Marx, in order to criticize, not religion, but the capitalist economy and the attitudes and beliefs associated with it, which in Marx's view, had about them much of the force and the illusion of religious superstition. *See* *commodity fetishism. Finally, the term reappears as an important feature of *Freud's psychology of sexual behaviour, denoting the transference of sexual response to inanimate objects, or to parts of the body (such as the feet) not directly connected with the normal sexual act.

feudalism

1. A social and economic arrangement, characterized by a strict hierarchical organization, from *lord down to *serf, with as many intermediate steps as the penury of the dominant class, or the power of the subordinate class, could interpose. The serf (or villein) is attached to the land (or the manor), and has no right to move outside the jurisdiction of the manorial court. This court regulates his conduct and settles his disputes with his fellow serfs; since it is presided over by his lord, it will not settle disputes with *him*. The serf works the land, keeping some of the product for himself, and yielding a portion (or *corvée*) to his lord, who remains, in law, the sole owner of the land. Feudalism is characterized by production for use rather than exchange, and by the relative absence of *wage labour or freedom of movement.

2. In Marxist theory, feudalism is the system of *production relations just described, divested of any reference to law, religion, or bonds of obligation. The transition from feudalism to *capitalism is supposedly necessitated by the development of *productive forces to the point where *division of labour, and hence a *market economy, become necessary. At this point market towns are formed, and the serfs are cast out from their tenancies, to form the *industrial army necessary for *factory production. The economic relations of capitalism then come into being.

3. From the points of view both of law and of history 1. must be seen as the sketch of an *ideal type, and 2. as a fantasy. The obligation of the serf to his lord was in fact matched by an obligation of the lord to deal justly with his serf. This second obligation could be enforced by ecclesiastical courts or by direct appeal to the sovereign. Hence relations between serf and lord were mediated by complex bodies of ecclesiastical and secular law, the serf often being able to obtain security of tenure equivalent to a property right. Moreover, in so-called feudal societies exchange was common, a merchant class existed, and the power of the clergy was usually sufficient to limit and diversify the powers of the feudal lords. Classes in feudal society came to depend upon a system of *estates in which hereditary rights and uncodified obligations played as great a part as economic potential in determining the social position of the individual. Feudal modes of land tenure were finally abolished in England by the Tenures Abolition Act 1660, but the economy had ceased to be feudal several centuries before.

Feuerbach, L.A. (1804–72)
German philosopher, whose book *The Essence of Christianity* (1841) set about to demythologize the Christian religion, arguing that its saints and divinities are simply the projection of human virtues which, by setting them up as objects to be worshipped, we remove from ourselves, so suffering a moral decline. *See* *alienation, *Althusser, *false consciousness, *fetishism, *myth, *species being, *Young Hegelians.

Fichte, Johann Gottlieb (1762–1814)
German idealist philosopher, whose metaphysics of the Self was profoundly influential on the development of German romantic thought. Fichte's political philosophy was a ragbag of vehement ideas, the influence of which is quite out of proportion to their intellectual merit. In *The Closed Commercial State* (1800) he defends *autarky, centralization of commercial life, and a kind of *corporate state with a pronounced military aspect. And in *Addresses to the German Nation* (1807–08) he diagnoses the defeat of the German princedoms by Napoleon, and exhorts the German people to identify itself as a single nation with a unique spiritual mission. Fichte argues that the nation is the individual's 'own extended self', and the realization of his freedom in a higher sphere. For the sake of this higher freedom, the individual should be prepared to relinquish his 'empirical' self, and it is this readiness to sacrifice which guarantees a nation's survival. In later writings, Fichte extended his *nationalism into the sphere of international relations, arguing that there is no law or right between nations, but only the 'right of the stronger'.

Fichte's writings are obscure and full of foreboding. But he has been rightly identified as a leading voice in political romanticism, the Founding Father of German nationalism, and a prophet of much that was to come. *See also* *dialectic.

fifth column
The Spanish nationalist general, Emilio Molo (1887–1937), when asked at a press conference which of four army columns he expected to capture Madrid, answered 'the fifth column', meaning organized sympathizers within the city. Hence: sympathizers within an opposition camp who organize its subversion.

Filmer, Sir Robert (d. 1653)
English writer and royalist. *See* *divine right.

Finlandization

Following many years of dispute and war with the USSR, in which Finland had been compelled to concede large areas of territory, the postwar Prime Minister (and subsequent President) Suho Passikivi pursued a policy of *neutralism in order to escape total incorporation into the Soviet Union. Astute policies of friendly agreement, trade concessions, and yielding to pressures to buy and sell to the USSR led to an increasing dependence of Finland on the USSR and to a conformity of Finnish foreign (and to a slight extent domestic) policy to Soviet requirements. This process of becoming covertly dependent upon, and responsive to the demands of, a powerful neighbour, for fear of being forced to concede much more, has become known as 'Finlandization'.

fiqh

Arabic, comprehension, from *faqiha*, to understand: the name used for the general science of jurisprudence relating to *Islamic law. Because the law has been laid down for all time by God, the fact that there are areas in which no law has yet been discovered, or where existing laws seem to be in conflict either with themselves or with what is necessary for human well-being or survival, jurisprudence was for the first centuries of Islam a powerful and creative political force, generating the four recognized schools or sects (*madhdhâhib*, singular *madhhab*). These four schools – Hanbali, Hanafi, Shafi and Maliki, named after their founders – may produce conflicting judgements, but all are recognized by most Muslims as authoritative. The schools of jurisprudence, like Islamic philosophy, assume that all law that is genuine law originates as a divine command, as revealed through the Koran or the *sunnah* (the deeds and sayings of the Prophet), and as deduced by analogy (*qiyas*) or consensus (*ijma'*). Apart from these four sources (*usul*, singular *asl*), no other source of law is recognized.

Around the beginning of the tenth century the view arose among Sunni jurists that every issue concerning the law and its application had been resolved by the *ijtihâd* (independent effort of reasoning) of learned and righteous scholars from one or other of the four schools, and that Muslims could henceforth be governed by a settled community consensus or *taqlid*. Hence there could be no further scope for *ijtihâd* and henceforth 'the gates of *ijtihâd* are closed'. This proverbial saying has remained authoritative among many Muslims, but was defiantly rejected by *Ibn Taymiyya and has never been accepted by the *Shi'ites.

firm, theory of

A branch of *microeconomics concerned to explain and predict the economic behaviour of firms. The traditional theory considered firms as vehicles for the maximization of profit, and made the further assumptions that firms possess full information and complete certainty, although the theory can be extended to take account of probabilities and 'information gaps'. The firm used to be taken as a self-contained system, and the theory would not attempt to explore problems of internal organization, such as the *separation of ownership from control, or the differences of structure which arise from public as opposed to private ownership. Moreover, standard theories assumed market conditions, and did not attempt to explain the behaviour of firms in systems of ownership which reduce or eliminate *competition, such as complete *socialization or *oligopoly.

More recently, however, the theory of the firm has often dropped the all-important assumption that firms are primarily concerned to maximize profits in competitive markets. The behaviour of firms in other types of market (e.g. oligopoly) has been extensively studied. Moreover, many modern theories have suggested that firms – or their managers – maximize not profits, but growth, or sales, or *managerial utility. Some theories have dropped the assumption that firms maximize at all, and have proposed that the managers of firms are primarily concerned to achieve or maintain certain levels or targets (e.g. a satisfactory market share or stock market valuation). Sometimes hybrid models, which combine 'satisficing' and maximizing behaviour, are proposed – e.g. the model which assumes that the firm maximizes its rate of growth subject to the maintenance of satisfactory profits.

First World
See *three worlds theory.

fiscal drag
If tax rates are progressive, then, in times of *inflation, wage increases might take people into higher tax brackets, even though their real incomes are not rising, a situation that will not be remedied before the next budget. This tends to create a fall in demand, which acts as a drag on further growth. In order to counteract the *deflation that results from this, governments may be asked to reduce taxation, or else to increase government expenditure so as to increase the level of *aggregate demand.

fiscal policy
That part of government policy which is concerned with raising revenue for government purposes, largely through *taxation, and with deciding on its expenditure. Many modern governments used to adopt a fiscal policy which aimed to exert some control over the level of *aggregate demand, and hence employment, the theory justifying such action being derived directly or indirectly from the work of *Keynes. Many economists opposed this, and for a while fiscal policy served as a focus for the debate between Keynesians and *monetarists, a debate that absorbed much intellectual energy in the UK and elsewhere. Keynesian ideas are less popular today, with many factors, such as rapid movements of capital and *globalization, making it all but impossible for governments to exercise the kind of control over demand that Keynes advocated.

flexible response
See *massive retaliation.

focoism
From Spanish: *foco*, a focal point. Used to denote the kind of *guerrilla warfare strategy advocated by Che Guevara, and by Fidel Castro, as appropriate to revolutionary activity in Latin American countries (see *Castroism). The aim is to establish small centres of insurrection in the countryside, to extend revolutionary activity from these bases, and only later to capture the government and administrative machinery.

focus group
A group of individuals selected and brought together by researchers in some topic of social or political interest, in order to discuss and comment, from personal experience, on the topic. A focus group is a form of group interview, with the important addition that the data consist not only in the opinions of the members but also in

the way those opinions change in the course of their interaction. Focus groups have become a key instrument in certain kinds of sociological research, as well as providing important information to politicians, concerning the way they are perceived and the likely impact of their policies.

force

A term that is as difficult to define as *aggression, and as important in the description of international behaviour, as well as in the description and justification of every political arrangement. Force that subdues the agent against which it is used is also called *coercion; force which is opposed freely will amount to coercion only when the will of the resistant is overcome. There seem to be two ideas involved in that of force: an active and a passive. To force someone to do something involves making alternatives sufficiently undesirable to him that he will do what one desires. In other words the active idea of force is that of deliberately restricting available courses of action. The passive idea is that of being forced to do something, even though there is no *agency which is doing the forcing. Here the idea is more closely connected with that of need.

By either definition it is as much an act of force to deprive a neighbouring state of all supplies of food or water, as it is to invade that state with show of arms. But delicate issues of *responsibility arise in the application of all such definitions. I may have something which you require for your needs, but do not, simply by the fact of possessing it, *deprive* you of what you need: some relationship of mutual acquaintance and responsibility is required before I can in any way be held to be *doing* something to you by peacefully enjoying something which is necessary for your survival (else we should all in effect be murderers).

In international law the ascendancy of ideas of agency has led to the restriction of the notion of force to 'the use of force', a notion that is held to correspond to ideas of aggression, invasion and attack. Some have asserted that 'use of force' in article 2 of the United Nations Charter includes *both* the use of arms, and any violation of international law which involves an exercise of *power within the territory of another state, even without the use of arms. Others argue that this is too broad an interpretation, and that a 'use of arms' is necessary. But this raises similar problems. Is there a use of arms when an invading army, encountering no resistance, does not fire a single shot? The International Law Commission so held when considering the German occupation of Bohemia and Moravia in 1939.

forced saving

Saving which is the result of a deficient supply of goods for consumption, rather than an actual desire to save. In a *free market forced saving exists only in a state of disequilibrium since at *equilibrium the plans of all agents are fulfilled, while in a fully *planned economy it can arise repeatedly and endure for long periods. However, in many planned economies (e.g. that of the former USSR) citizens are forbidden to hold more than a certain sum in savings, and must surrender the remainder to the state.

Fordism

Term coined by *Gramsci in order to describe the designs and achievements of the American car manufacturer Henry Ford, as manifested in his Detroit factory at the beginning of the twentieth century. Ford practised what he called 'scientific management', paying his workers always more than the average in return for industrial peace, standardizing hours, work load and tasks and in general prompting the caricature of factory production that Charlie Chaplin put across in *Modern Times* (1936).

foreign policy

Even if one thought *government to be unnecessary or undesirable in *domestic affairs, or that some form of *minimal state is the most extensive government that could be justified, the existence of other, independent states not so persuaded, and possessed of burgeoning political and economic ambitions, implies the need for sufficient government at home to permit serious policy abroad. In practice this means a lot of government, since it is impossible to commit people to *war, to an agreement concerning *trade, or to economic sanctions, without exercising extensive domestic control. (The neglect of such issues may be responsible for the air of unreality surrounding some theories of *anarchism, and of the minimal state.)

It is sometimes argued (for example by *Machiavelli) that foreign policy is also a major instrument of domestic government, for example by creating fervent union between citizens united behind a common cause. The mutual dependence of domestic and foreign policy can be seen in the constitutional and political changes that have been precipitated in the UK by the loss of empire, and in the US by the entry into and exit from the Second World War, by the subsequent cold war in which traditional *isolationism was cast aside, and by the current *war on terror.

Foreign policy must therefore inevitably be affected by the structure of domestic government. Monarchy, which permits and indeed encourages alliance through marriage, has a peacemaking device which is not available to other forms of government; despotism, in which a single person holds power for life, or in which a single party holds power indefinitely, permits long-term foreign policy of a kind that is pursued only with great difficulty by governments whose leadership is regularly subjected to re-election. European aristocracy, under which a small number of influential families held domestic power while maintaining lasting international contact, permitted treaties and alliances that are now achieved only with the greatest difficulty. The greatest domestic effects of foreign policy stem from the need for continuity: it is this that has given to the UK Foreign Office a power which persists through changes of government, and which it is difficult, if not impossible, for any actual government to oppose.

Foreign policy provides the most vivid examples of *acts of state, and of the character of the state as an international *person, with *rights, *agency, *responsibility and *answerability as well as *power.

formalism

1. A tradition in *aesthetics and art criticism which finds the merit, or the meaning, of a work of art in features of its form or structure, rather than in its representational content. Members of the school of Russian formalists which existed in Petrograd and Moscow before the Revolution in many cases welcomed the Revolution, and imagined that it would free the study of art from bourgeois preoccupations with subject-matter and morality, by exposing the literary and artistic structure as conveying the essential, and *ideological, significance of the creative act. Most members of the school were subsequently exiled or executed and all were forbidden to teach. One, however, Mikhail Bakhtin, was permitted to survive in the heartlands of Russia, and was later even permitted to publish, becoming in due course a

major influence on literary theory in Western universities; others escaped to Paris and were there influential in founding the school of *structuralist criticism.

2. As a term of abuse, used by both the *Communist and the *Nazi parties, to designate art whose perfection lies in its form, and which detaches itself from the representation of social matters and from the propagation of social values – specifically values of international, or of national socialism. Communist propaganda contrasted 'formalism' with *socialist realism, and castigated the former for its bourgeois detachment, and for the sterile aestheticism which refuses social responsibility. The label 'formalist' has been applied to most significant twentieth-century art, in particular to abstract painting, cubism (especially Braque), constructivist sculpture and architecture, and the music of the second Vienna school, which has been thought to be particularly pernicious, partly because it pursues new and not easily understood musical structures, and partly because it is accompanied by theories which say that this is precisely what it *should* do.

3. A school of *sociology, associated with the name of Georg Simmel, which emphasizes the importance of the form of social relations, rather than the particular people united by them, and which attempts to explain social development in terms of *competition, cooperation, *commensalism, etc., so developing a 'geometry of social life'.

Foucault, Michel (1926–84)
French social philosopher and historian whose writings have been seminal in recent radical movements on the left, and who was a major force in French intellectual life after the eclipse of *existentialism.

Foucault's writings cover many subjects, and are usually centred on the historical transition from the 'classical' to the 'bourgeois' era of our civilization. (These terms are deliberately vague; in so far as they correspond to anything definite it is to the transition from aristocratic to meritocratic government that occurred – so Foucault seems to assume – at the French Revolution.) In remarkable and imaginative forays into the by-ways of historical scholarship, Foucault examines the history of madness, of medicine, of punishment, of sexuality and of knowledge itself, arguing that the institutions, concepts and beliefs of each period are dictated by the needs of the prevailing social *power. Foucault originally described his method as an 'archeology of knowledge' and his subject-matter as truth – truth considered as the product of 'discourse', taking both form and content from the power that speaks through the prevailing language. (*See* *discourse theory.*) In *Les Mots et les choses* (1966), he argues that man is a recent invention – meaning that it is only since the Renaissance that the fact of being human (rather than, say, a farmer, a soldier or a nobleman) has acquired any special significance. The sciences which have taken man as their subject-matter are already outmoded as forms of 'knowledge': they must give way under the impulse of a new *episteme* (i.e. structure of 'knowledge') to something which we cannot yet name. Each new *episteme* is the servant of some rising power and has, as its principal function, the creation of a 'truth' which serves the interests of a ruling class or power-structure.

This updating of the Marxian theory of *ideology has been very influential, partly because of the easy (its critics would say mechanical) way in which it can unmask the institutions and ideals of 'bourgeois' society.

Foucault did not hesitate to see through as many of these institutions and ideals as he could, in order to lay bare the workings of power in its 'capillary' form – the form which pervades all action and discourse, and turns the human world to the service of its masters. Those who speak against the prevailing power are denounced as 'criminal' or 'mad', and confined to prisons and hospitals. Foucault's histories of those institutions and the practices employed in them are designed to show that the criminal and the madman are so described and so treated because they are a threat to the voice of 'reason', where 'reason' is simply another name for the 'discourse' which renders power and property legitimate. He identifies as prominent madmen the writers and philosophers who share his own view of bourgeois society – for instance the Marquis de Sade and *Nietzsche, with whom he consciously compared himself.

In his later work on the history of sexuality (*Histoire de la sexualité*, 1984), Foucault asks the question why the sexual act has been 'problematized' in our society, and tries to show that this 'problematization' is by no means universal, being unknown, for example, among the ancient Greeks. His intention is to show that the 'moral' sanctions which surround the sexual act are merely ideological devices whereby bourgeois society perpetuates itself. The implication is that we can defy sexual morality and the concept of 'normality' on which it depends, and that this defiance will signal a liberation of the self from a defunct *episteme*. Unsurprisingly, therefore, Foucault, who was himself homosexual, has become an iconic figure in the movement for *gay rights. *See also* *criminology, *psychotherapy.

Founding Fathers

Name generally given to the 55 delegates who were present at the drawing up of the US constitution by the Philadelphia Convention in May 1787. *Jefferson was not in fact there, but was represented by James *Madison and George Whyte, and was acquainted with more of the delegates, all of whom were committed to the notion of a stronger union.

four freedoms

Proclaimed by President Roosevelt in a speech to the US Congress on 6 January 1941, by way of summarizing certain values for which (in his own opinion, and in the opinion of many others) the US government stands. The *freedoms advocated were these: (i) freedom of speech and expression; (ii) freedom to worship God in one's own way; (iii) freedom from want (to be ensured by economic understanding between nations); (iv) freedom from fear (to be ensured by disarmament). The list is interesting in that it introduces two ideas of freedom: freedom *from* ((iii) and (iv)), and freedom *to* ((i) and (ii)). Freedom from want and from fear are, on one plausible account, the end of political activity, and require far-reaching and officious management of social and political arrangements, whereas freedom of speech and worship are to be secured by the limitation of political activity. Two of these freedoms therefore require a positive duty on the part of others (perhaps of all others), while the other two require only a refusal to meddle.

The doctrine of the 'four freedoms' seems to involve a rhetoric that ranges freely over *right and *obligation: this may be one explanation of the fact that, in subsequent international agreements, the *right to work has gained acceptance as a right on the same footing as, e.g., the rights to speak one's mind, and to practise one's religious conviction, even though the latter rights involve only a concession, and not an active undertaking, from those not concerned to exercise them.

'Four freedoms' were also advocated by Liu Shao-Ch'i (1898–1973) in China, in 1953: to rent and to sell land; to hire labour; to engage in sideline economic pursuits; and to lend money at interest. Since these freedoms amount to rights of private property in land, they were attacked by *Mao, and never implemented. Liu was denounced during the *Cultural Revolution as a 'capitalist roader' and expelled from the party.

Fourier, Francois Marie Charles (1772–1837) (not to be confused with Baron Jean-Baptiste-Joseph Fourier (1768–1830), inventor of Fourier analysis in geometry)
French social critic, and utopian socialist, active during the post-revolutionary period, who devoted his energies to the description of schemes for the salvation of mankind. Since the world had been created by a benevolent God, the actual misery of human beings could be explained only on the assumption that men had not carried out God's plans for them. These plans had been rediscovered by Fourier, but could be put into practice only by releasing man's 13 passions, repressed by civilization, but essential to the harmony which would come in place of it. The passions are: the five senses; the four 'group' feelings of ambition, friendship, love and family feeling; the three 'series' passions of intrigue, diversification (*la passion papillone*) and combination; and the passion for harmony which synthesizes all the others.

To release the passions, humanity would have to be organized into *phalanstères* (phalanxes, or 'phalansteries') each of about 1800 members, the

different characters and inclinations being scientifically combined in a complex system of groups and series, so that each person could express his inclination in everything that he did, and avoid every activity that did not suit him. Such phalanxes would be systems of common ownership, in which a certain level of private property would also be permitted, along with inequalities necessary to the exercise of human potential.

Fourier was an influential critic of existing social and economic conditions. His attempts to found a phalanx absorbed many of his energies. Others took up the cause, so that 'Fourierism' was for a while a popular kind of socialism, although the experimental phalanxes failed. The movement remains interesting largely because of its attempt to combine socialism with a detailed psychology of *self-realization.

fourth estate
See *estates of the realm.

France, constitution and laws
Since the Revolution France has been ruled in the name of many documents claiming to be 'constitutions' (and vividly illustrating the thesis that a mere document can be no such thing), and even the present 'fifth' Republic continues to revise itself in a manner that makes it difficult to distinguish between 'constitution' and *positive law. The French form of government is a paradigm of European *republicanism, and displays constant and far-reaching *reform within a seemingly immovable structure of republican dignities and concentrated power. The system is *bicameral, the National Assembly, or lower house, being the principal *legislative body, and the 'Council of the Republic' acting as a revising chamber with various dignifying functions. The *President is elected

directly (reform introduced in 1962; previously he was appointed for a seven-year period by both chambers of parliament). The President also appoints the prime minister and *cabinet, and now holds the principal *executive power, although dependent upon the support of the National Assembly for most legislative measures. The frequent 'constitutional' changes (which may concern matters such as the reorganization of *local government, or the *decentralization of administration) are often introduced as the result of *referendums. The present appearance of the French constitution is that of a *constitutional democracy with strong presidential control over the government, outweighing the influence of any single party. The parties themselves are numerous, but only the *Gaullist and *socialist parties can command an enduring substantial vote.

For French law, *see* *Napoleonic law.

franchise

The legal right to vote at an election. Since the late eighteenth century almost all states have moved gradually in the direction of an extended, rather than a contracted, franchise, and universal adult *suffrage is now the rule rather than the exception.

Frankfurt school

The school of social thought represented by the Institute for Social Research, founded in the University of Frankfurt in 1923 and exiled to New York during the Nazi period. Principal members have been *Horkheimer, *Adorno, *Benjamin, *Marcuse and *Habermas, all of whom have been separately influential, and each of whom has subscribed in part to the *critical theory advocated by Horkheimer, in which social and cultural phenomena are subjected to

detailed criticism, using concepts proper, so it is claimed, to a *Marxist analysis of consciousness. The Frankfurt school was instrumental in awakening interest in the early writings of *Marx, in which the influence of *Hegel's study of consciousness is still apparent, notably in the theory of *alienation. Its members opposed the *scientist interpretation and application of *historical materialism, which, they felt, both undervalues the role of consciousness in human affairs, and also encourages a naive and dogmatic *positivism, which is both doctrinaire in theory and highly destructive in practice. Since most members of the school have not believed in the possibility of a *value-free study of society, they have rejected the scientific claims of Marxism and attempted to adapt its concepts to the uses of cultural criticism, in order to examine institutions, practices and ways of thought that classical Marxism had referred to as *superstructure. In this way the Frankfurt school was one of the first to produce a theory of art which could claim to be Marxist in inspiration without being obviously naive about its subject-matter. However, this very result indicates the extent to which consciousness is taken seriously as a subject for sociological analysis, and in a way that is not obviously compatible with the main tenets of Marxism. It is also possible to discern elements of *cultural conservatism in the writings of Adorno, beside which his professions of left-wing allegiance seem more like fashion than conviction. Habermas's theory of *crisis attempted to preserve some of the structure of the Marxist theory of history, and to justify belief in the fact, if not in the value, of *revolution. In more recent writings, however, Habermas has been increasingly inclined to espouse a kind of liberal *constitutionalism. *See further* *crisis theory, *critical theory.

fraternity

The least discussed of the three aims of the French revolutionaries, although the most important, in that it attempts to specify the nature of the bond of society, without which, it is reasonable to assume, neither liberty nor equality would have value or be concrete objects of *policy. Fraternity is, literally speaking, the uniting of men in bonds of brotherly affection, though for most revolutionary purposes 'men' includes women, and 'brotherhood' sisterhood. In so far as this kind of affection extends further than immediate kin and personal friends, it is characteristic of members of a (small) tribe, and may also sometimes arise between people who act and suffer together in some dangerous enterprise, such as a battle. But whether such a feeling could actually form the bond of society within a modern democratic state is to be doubted. In contrast to the relations of *allegiance, *obedience and *political obligation, it seems to have a personal and limited character which would forbid its easy extension (except in forms that are sentimental and therefore uncommitted) to large groups of people. However, the original ideal of the advocates of fraternity was the replacement of particularized affections, such as those of the family, with sentiments thought to be more universal and less socially divisive. Some, remembering the crimes committed in the name of fraternity, prefer to drop this name from their political vocabulary, others retain it, at least for slogans and propaganda, but whether it now has a serious political application outside that use remains doubtful.

free enterprise

The situation in which people are permitted by law to begin *enterprises of production, distribution or exchange, and perhaps also to assert private rights of ownership over the result. It is often argued that it is impossible to deny this freedom without denying some (and perhaps all) of the traditionally valued *freedoms mentioned below. Socialists argue that free enterprise acts against the third of the *four freedoms, since it prevents the organization of an economy directed to freeing people from want. Economists of the *Austrian school (notably *Hayek) argue that free (i.e. private) enterprise is necessary if capital is to find its way to the uses where it may be most profitably applied, and that, in its absence, no coherent strategy of *investment can be devised. The experience of the *planned economy lends some support to this view.

free market

A *market in which distribution and exchange lie outside the *control of the *state, and are allowed to proceed according to private agreements. The free market is an essential part of *free enterprise and, according to a thesis accepted for different reasons by both the defenders and the opponents of capitalism, is impossible without private property in the means of production. A market is rendered unfree either through government interference in its operation (e.g. through *price control), or by the transfer of property to public or common ownership. (*See* *production, distribution, exchange, consumption.)

Like all *freedoms this one is a matter of degree; nevertheless it is defended and attacked with a fervour perhaps more appropriate to an absolute condition. Some (e.g. *Friedman and some earlier economists of the *Austrian school) argue that the free market permits economic growth, leads to stability, and respects fundamental rights that must otherwise be denied. Such arguments, expressed dogmatically, are apt to evoke a negative response. Some reply that a completely free market is unrealistic, in an age of industrialization, overpopulation and exhaustible resources; others argue more radically, against all forms of private ownership in the means of distribution. The opposition, when absolute, is no more likely to be persuasive than the defence. Are we to abolish the free market to the extent of removing every right of exchange? In which case, are we to envisage a society without sale or purchase, without *gift, and without barter? The prospect, when described in detail, is seldom found appealing.

Apart from social and political considerations, some economists argue independently for the free market, on principles inherited from *classical economics, defending it as a self-regulating mechanism with a natural tendency towards *equilibrium, perhaps generating, along with that equilibrium, the conditions of social and political order. To this should be added the powerful arguments of *Mises and *Hayek, that the essential economic information contained in *prices in a free market can be made available in no other way. See *calculation debate.

free rider
Suppose people living in a community pool their resources in order to pay a water company to extend a pipeline to their neighbourhood, thus sharing the costs of a common benefit. Joe, who also lives in the neighbourhood, refuses to contribute, but he is nevertheless in an equal position to benefit from the water supply once it has been provided. Joe is taking a 'free ride' on the collective action, and is an instance of the 'free rider' problem in the theory of *collective choice. In one sense Joe is more rational than his neighbours – since he obtains the same benefit without the cost. But are there ways of making him bear some part of this cost without violating his freedom? The 'free rider' problem is exhibited whenever a *public good is provided from private resources.

free trade
The condition in which there is a free flow of goods and services in international trade. No trade between two nations is today absolutely free, in the sense of being shielded from all interference arising from the national interest of the states taking part in it; nevertheless, within limits, free trade still exists between trading partners with demand for each others' goods. Disputes focus upon (a) the extent to which a state ought to permit, in the interests of its citizens, free trade with others; (b) the methods which should be used, if necessary, to limit it. Classical and neo-classical economics extended the doctrine of the free market into international affairs, but some modern theories of *development question the possibility of *equilibrium conditions arising naturally between the developed and the *developing countries. Others have argued for active government intervention in order to produce surpluses on the *balance of trade (see *mercantilism, *neo-mercantilism), or in order to protect domestic producers (see *protectionism). Both those policies involve rejection of the idea that free trade is the advisable condition of international exchange, and acceptance of *tariffs, import quotas, selective *customs unions, and similar measures.

A 'free trade area' is an association of states (usually neighbouring states) under a common agreement to remove all tariffs, quotas, and similar government barriers to free trade between themselves. Each state may continue to trade with non-members on its own terms.

The cause of free trade was advanced after the war by the *GATT, which has now been replaced by the *World Trade Organization, which works for a global free trade area, and which has, in consequence, become the subject of important political controversies.

freedom, metaphysical

It is necessary to distinguish the metaphysical problem of 'free will' from the problem of political freedom (discussed in the next entry). Metaphysical freedom is the freedom to do one thing rather than another; it supposedly enters into every intentional act, and provides the basis on which we hold people *responsible for the consequences of what they do. Perhaps the most important question concerning metaphysical freedom is whether it is compatible with the truth of *determinism. Thus if my action and all its consequences were determined by the state of the universe before my birth, does it still make sense to say that I acted freely or am responsible for what I did? The thesis of 'soft determinism' or 'compatibilism' says yes, while 'hard determinism' says no. Clearly the problem of free will is not the same as that of political freedom: it does not concern the nature and justification of political constraints on my action, but the action's status in the light of its cause. Acts which are indisputably free from political constraint raise the problem of metaphysical freedom just as much as those which are not: when I lift this glass to my lips, do I act freely, or do the causes which determine my action also compel it, so that my sense of choice is no more than an illusion?

It is probably true to say that modern philosophical discussions of this problem have shifted the emphasis from the concept of freedom to that of responsibility, partly under the influence of 'ordinary language' methods, and partly under the influence of studies in *jurisprudence which to a great extent have provided the model for those methods. What is at stake, it is thought, is not so much whether there are acts which are 'free' in some metaphysical sense, but whether there is a true human responsibility. For it is from our descriptions of people as responsible or otherwise that the human consequences – in the form of blame, praise, *punishment and reward – follow.

freedom, political

Freedom is often advanced as one of the *values integral to Western civilization, and its absence is often deplored in regimes said to be *totalitarian and communist.

There is a distinction to be drawn between a negative and a positive idea of freedom, the former conveyed in the expression 'freedom from', the latter in the expression 'freedom to'. (A version of this distinction was emphasized in an influential paper by *Berlin.) A person may be free *from* constraints and threats, in a world that leaves him free *to do* very little, say, because it contains no resources upon which he can exercise his powers. The distinction here is not hard and fast, and the two ideas are to some extent interconvertible. Nevertheless there is a difference at least of emphasis between those who discern political freedom in the absence of certain constraints, and those who discern it in the presence of certain powers and possibilities. In another sense, 'positive' freedom is often described as that state of a person in which his powers are fully exercised – i.e. in which external possibilities are matched by an internal capacity to realize the self and its aims within them. (*See* *self-realization.) The interplay of the various positive and negative ideas of freedom seems to be responsible for many of the tensions and conflicts which the concept of freedom contains.

(i) The liberal position. (Expounded, for example, by *J.S. Mill in *On Liberty*, 1859.) Simply expressed, this finds freedom in the power of the individual to assert himself against the state (or even against society, Mill for various reasons omitting this distinction). The power of the state is enshrined in law, so that the measure of the freedom of the individual is not the lenience, but the scope, of the law that governs him. Are there clearly defined areas of individual life which are not governed by law, so that real choices are left open by it? A further embellishment of the liberal view construes such freedom as itself the *aim* of law; law should not merely permit these areas of untrammelled choice, but also maximize them. The thought here is an ancient one, but was given rhetorical impetus by *Locke, in his distinction between *liberty and 'licence'. Freedom is not maximized simply by removing all law, since that is to leave the individual unprotected from the invasion of his freedom by his neighbours. The law aims to provide a system of constraints which, while limiting freedom in some respects, maximizes freedom over all. Licence is a freedom that is exercised only at risk to another's freedom: to forbid it is not to lower but to increase the sum total of individual liberty. Disputes then focus on the precise form of such a law, and whether or not it should be responsive to any requirements *other* than those of freedom. (*See* *harm, *law and morality.)

(ii) The conservative position. (Expounded, for example, by Sir James Fitzjames Stephen in *Liberty, Equality, Fraternity*, 1873, a reply to Mill.) This usually argues either that the liberal conception of freedom is mistaken, or that freedom has to be balanced against other values in a way that makes it legitimate to encroach on it. The first argument tends to emphasize that freedom is a value only for someone who can also value the activities which are permitted by it. (There is no value in a freedom which allows you to do only what you see no significance in doing.) True freedom is a more complex phenomenon than mere permission, and exists only where values exist. People have values as a result of their perception of themselves as belonging to a social order; if freedom is to be preserved social order must be preserved as its necessary precondition. But this order requires law, and lays down a separate criterion for the validity of law. The arguments here are not exclusive to conservatives, and are often construed as attacking not liberalism as such, but only the *individualism involved in the common versions of it.

(iii) The welfare socialist view. Neither of the above positions gives sufficient attention to the conditions for positive freedom. Absence of legal constraint gives you no power to do anything, unless the world also contains food, drink, and the conditions of healthy physical (perhaps even moral) action. Such things are provided by human labour. Hence, if people are to be free, in the positive sense of possessing power to fulfil their natures, they must suffer whatever constraints are necessary to organize their labour and ensure a satisfactory distribution of its product. In response to the massive interference with human choice that tends to result from this way of thinking, liberals, and even some conservatives, have had recourse to the idea of freedom as a *natural right, i.e. as something which cannot in any circumstances, without injustice and wrongdoing, be taken away. (*See* *freedoms.)

Other specific views are mentioned

elsewhere in this dictionary – e.g. under *Hegel (who argued that freedom consists, in the last analysis, not in the power to oppose the state, but in the disposition to obey it), *Mill, *Locke, *liberty, *liberalism, *individualism. In all discussions it is important to bear in mind that the freedom discussed is that of a *rational agent, who has autonomy, values, and long-term aims and projects. Hence the problem of freedom raises far-reaching problems of human nature, focusing on the tenability or otherwise of individualism.

freedom of information

See *secrecy.

freedoms

In political contexts, usually used to denote those choices which are, or ought to be, offered to the citizen as of *right. Doctrines of 'freedoms' are often extensions of ideas concerning *human or *natural rights; alternatively they may summarize traditions of *positive law, which have attempted to define the areas of human life from which the law withdraws or attempts to withdraw. Modern *constitutionalism, which seeks to define limits to government, often attempts to specify freedoms as one determinant of these limits. Often the choice of freedoms is dictated by a sense of the distinction between the public and the private that may be extremely hard to articulate in any other way. Common among these freedoms are freedom of speech, freedom of worship, freedom of association, freedom of assembly, freedom of contract and exchange, freedom of movement. Roosevelt's *four freedoms stepped outside the normal frame of reference of US constitutional thinking in referring not only to freedoms to *do* certain things should one choose, but also to freedoms *from*

certain handicaps and disasters, specifically hunger and fear.

freemasons

A religious brotherhood of stonemasons existed in medieval Europe, and was established in England in the twelfth century in order to safeguard the secrets of the stonemason's craft; it was abolished in 1547 but later reorganized, with educational and social aims, and without any specific connection with stonemasons. Later still it adopted the trappings of a highly symbolic, ceremonial but essentially monotheistic and even Christian religion, Mozart, Goethe and Tolstoy being among its more distinguished sympathizers. It preserved the air of secrecy, and soon became a closed society, opposed by the Catholic church, and also by Maria Theresa, Empress of Austria. While the nature of freemasonry as a social and political influence is difficult to determine, there is no doubt that, because of its secrecy, and its internal ethos of fraternity, it has often been suspected of fostering secret associations for political purposes, or in restraint of trade.

Freud, Sigmund (1856–1939)

Viennese scientist and founder of psychoanalysis. Although Freud never applied his mind systematically to politics, his theories have influenced political thought in countless ways. The following (contested) ideas have all been extremely important:

(i) The theory of unconscious determination. This has given additional impetus to the thought – common to many political theories, both conservative (e.g. *Burke) and revolutionary (e.g. *Marx) – that the real motives of political action are to be found elsewhere than in the conscious reasons that might be given for it.

(ii) The theory of *repression, according to which important instincts are denied direct expression by social pressures, and consequently submerge, to re-emerge in new and surprising forms. Some political theories have been built upon this and related ideas – see, for example, *Reich. It should not be assumed that repression is regarded everywhere as harmful; some (including Freud) regard it as a necessary process, whereby primordial instincts are transformed into the motivating force of *civilization.

(iii) The emphasis on fundamental instincts, such as the sexual 'libido', and the 'death instinct' or 'death wish', as providing the ultimate explanation of human conduct. This emphasis has often been opposed, as being fundamentally destructive of moral values, and of the picture of man as a rational animal which sustains them. Some have welcomed it for its pessimistic implications, and as a necessary corrective to the naiveties of *progressivism. Yet others (Freud again included) have found in the Freudian account of motivation a reason to doubt the economically based theories – such as *historical materialism – which see the activity of production as the generating force of history. For Freud, both *death and the sexual drive are more fundamental, and the conflicting instincts towards them, if conceived as fundamental forces in human history, must generate a historical movement that is far more complex than the linear progress imagined by the theories of nineteenth-century progressives and revolutionaries.

(iv) The theory of Freud's Civilization and its Discontents, 1933, which implies that the repression required to introduce the social forms of civilization also leads to a vast and potentially dangerous accumulation of unconscious forces, ready to erupt, and so to destroy what they have been channelled into creating. Freud did not regard this as an argument against repression, but merely as a tragic aspect of all civilized society. See also *psychotherapy.

frictional unemployment

*Unemployment resulting from the delays that people face, after leaving one employment, before entering another. Frictional unemployment can exist even where there are more jobs available than there are people seeking them. (Contrast *structural unemployment.)

Friedman, Milton (b. 1912)

American economist, leading member of the *Chicago school, who has been an ardent propagandist for *free market economics, as the uniquely efficient and (in Friedman's view) uniquely honest form of economic order. Friedman has criticized all forms of state interference in the economy, and extended the theory of the market into other areas of social life, arguing that a free market is the true source of responsible accounting in education, in local government, and in every area where people receive and offer benefits. See also *monetarism, *New Right.

friendship

Friendship is of various kinds: intimate, casual, supportive, comradely, erotic, platonic, and so on. In all cases it exhibits the following features: (i) friendship is an end in itself and does not exist for some further purpose. To the extent that I have a ruling purpose in my relations with another (other than his well-being, and his friendship), to that extent I am not motivated by friendship towards him. The attempt to formulate this feature more precisely underlies much of the thinking behind *Kant's second categorical imperative (Act so as to treat rational beings always as ends, and never as means only); (ii) friendship is possible only between persons, who are aware of each other as persons (contrast filial dependence, and unembellished sexual desire); (iii) friendship is incapable of unjust dealings – a friendly feeling evaporates when one party discovers that the other has exploited, lied to or manipulated him; moreover the other could not have been motivated by friendship in doing so (except in very special cases).

The idea of friendship has inspired certain conservative theories of the relation between *citizens (*Aristotle) and between each citizen and the *civil society (*Oakeshott). Friendship is non-contractual (there being no common and defining purpose), and yet both voluntary and impregnated by obligations (which arise in the course of it); it is a source of dependence, and also conditional upon just dealings; it is autonomous, containing no specific purpose upon the achievement of which it will be dissolved, and yet entirely rational and pursued through intentional action. Hence friendship demonstrates that there can be relations of dependence, expressing values of justice, which are not founded in contract and not transferable from object to object. Such relations (which fall within the ancient sphere of *piety) give a model for *political obligation, which is (on some accounts) similarly structured. Political obligation (on this theory more accurately described as *allegiance) is thereby shown to be as rational as friendship.

front organizations

Organizations which profess acceptable aims, in order to conceal the unacceptable aims which really motivate them. Usually the term describes organizations which are ostensibly liberal, democratic and constitutional, with respected and respectable members, controlled by *activists owing allegiance to the Communist Party. They were much used by the *Comintern, and were among the most successful of all instruments of USSR *foreign policy. They have also been used by *Trotskyists, and by the US Central Intelligence Agency.

Führerprinzip

Term adopted in Nazi Germany to denote the idea that a national *leader (*Führer*) is required, who would prove his merit through his personal *charisma, and so achieve and deserve absolute *authority over all citizens. In Hitler's words, this required: 'unrestricted authority downwards, unrestricted responsibility upwards'.

Fukuyama, Francis (b. 1952)

American sociologist and political scientist, influenced by *Kojève, whose book *The End of History and the Last Man*, 1992, argued that history has been shaped by the constant conflict between the desire to dominate and the need for recognition. The demand to dominate has been defeated by the economic triumphs of capitalist democracy, which gives each person a sovereign sphere of his own. Moroever, with the fall of communism, and the near universal adoption of democratic and egalitarian ideas of political order, the available forms of domination have been destroyed, along with the ideology that supported them. Hence history has come to an end. (*See* *end of history.) The ensuing non-conflictual order will be increasingly international, and also exhibit a steady loss of high culture, distinction and virtue, as we approach the condition of *Nietzsche's 'last man'. In subsequent writings, notably *On Trust*, 1996, Fukuyama has given trenchant defences of the capitalist economy, arguing that it both generates and also depends upon an extensive *social capital in the form of trust.

functional explanation

A type of explanation common in the social sciences, anthropology and biology, which attempts to incorporate into accepted models of scientific method the puzzling feature of *teleology. It can be illustrated by the theory of evolution. Birds try to escape their predators by flying, and it seems natural to say that they have wings *in order to* do this. That is the germ of a *teleological explanation, or explanation in terms of an end. We can rewrite this explanation and at the same time eliminate the reference to purpose, by using the idea of a function: wings have a function, in relation to the bird's need to survive. *That* wings have this function may then be invoked in order to explain the fact that birds possess them. Such an explanation no longer refers to an end (a succeeding state of affairs) but to a cause (a preceding state of affairs). It is because wings have this function in relation to the condition of birds at time t that birds have wings at time $t + \delta$. *How* the explanation works (i.e. what theory might be invoked to entail it) may vary from case to case. The further details of the theory of evolution, as given by *Darwin, are supposed to make the functional explanation more plausible. Thus, in the light of the theoretical hypothesis of natural selection, one can show *how* the function of wings determines their existence. But the functional explanation might have been correct, even though the theory of natural selection (which entails it) was not.

In a similar way, an anthropologist may explain ceremonies, and other social practices, in terms of a function that relates them to the well-being of a tribe. Such an explanation may eliminate all reference to purpose, in particular to the avowed purpose with which their practices are engaged in by the members of the tribe. The social cohesion, for example, that results from and explains a ceremony of propitiation will not typically be the purpose of those who engage in it, who seek not to unite with their fellows, but to propitiate a deity.

Some advocates of the materialist theory of history phrase the theory in terms of functional explanation. Social and political *superstructures have the function of consolidating some pattern of economic relations: this is what causes them to exist. Of course one may look for further explanations which show *how* that is possible. One may not find those further explanations, and yet still be persuaded that the functional explanation is true.

Many think that without some account of the mechanisms involved (such as is provided by the theory of evolution) functional explanations are not really explanations. On this view the use of functional explanation in the social sciences is illegitimate, involving an inference from the (uncontentious) idea that dysfunctionality causes the disappearance of something, to the (unwarranted) idea that functionality *causes* its appearance.

functionalism

See *anthropology, *architecture, *functional explanation.

fundamentalism

A term originally used of the various Protestant sects that arose in the sixteenth and seventeenth centuries, and which vied with each other over which sect was more true to the fundamental tenets of the faith, as laid down in the Gospels. The term has recently been extended to faiths other than Christianity, and notably to various forms of Islam, such as *Wahhabism and the Islamic activism of *Qutb and the *Muslim Brotherhood. It is doubtful that these exhibit a faith that is in any real way more attached to the 'fundamentals' of Islam than any rival. All Muslims are fundamentalists, in recognizing the Koran as the final authority in every matter with which it deals. French writers prefer the term *intégrisme* in order to emphasize the integrated world-view, allowing no intrusion from secular values, that is presented by the modern style of Islamic militancy.

G[8] The 'Group of Eight'. An informal but powerful forum of nations, whose original members (the G7) were Canada, France, Germany, Italy, Japan, the UK, and the US, who became the G8 when the Russian Federation joined them in 1998. The G7 arose from the 1973 oil crisis and the global recession that followed, and since 1975 the group has organized an annual economic and political summit, attended by heads of government and international officials, in which matters of common concern are discussed, with a view to coordinating policy. The G8 is not an international organization, and has no standing in international law. It is an association of sovereign states, which meet and act by mutual agreement. Nevertheless it has been viewed with suspicion by those who protest against *globalization, and is often thought to belong to the same transnational network as the *World Trade Organization.

Gadamer, Hans-Georg (1900–2001)
German philosopher, and one of the leading figures of postwar German culture, whose influence on philosophical discourse both within his homeland and in the wider world, was almost as great as that of his teacher, *Heidegger, whose *hermeneutical approach to human thought and institutions he adopted and expanded. In *Truth and Method* (1960), Gadamer attempts to show that the truths of history, social life and culture are not accessible to scientific observation, since they are revealed only through a kind of dialogue. This dialogue involves listening to the voice of history as enshrined in traditions and institutions, and to the voice of a culture as typified by its poetry. Historians, critics and artists all deploy the hermeneutical method, since it is from the repeated application of this method that their subject-matter comes into being. Much of the alienation and disorientation of modern society stems from the attempt to replace the natural tendency to enter into dialogue with the world with an unnatural obsession with scientific inference. The scientist who analyses the structure of your facial muscles does not understand you as I understand you, when I see you smile – though what he is studying is, from his viewpoint, exactly what I am studying too. Similarly, the historian is less concerned with the biological laws that govern human society than with the collective face that speaks to us across the centuries, and to which we also speak. Historical study is valuable not because it tells us what happened, but because, by bringing us into relation with others, it also tells us who we are.

Gadamer's qualified defence of prejudice, tradition, and cultural rootedness recalls the political philosophy of *Burke; but to defend those things in the context of postwar Germany was to present an unusual challenge to the prevailing culture. Gadamer had the knack of squeezing past all ideological censors, however. He was an eminent professor in Nazi Germany;

an eminent professor in Soviet-controlled East Germany; an eminent professor in Conservative Heidelberg; and still an eminent professor in the 1960s, when Heidelberg went red and then green. This last feat was greatly helped by his ongoing public debate with *Habermas, which ensured that Gadamer was not dismissed on the Left, despite the fact that some of his ideas might prove useful to conservatives, and despite the fact that he had remained on close terms with the ex-Nazi Heidegger to the very end of the latter's life.

Gaia hypothesis

An hypothesis put forward by James E. Lovelock (*Gaia: a New Look at Life on Earth*, 1979) according to which all living things on earth are really part of a single living thing, Gaia (Greek for Earth), which adjusts the planetary environment with a view to ensuring its own survival. Human interference with the environment, however, threatens to disrupt the *feedback mechanisms whereby Gaia returns to equilibrium. More metaphor than theory, the Gaia hypothesis has nevertheless been extremely influential among environmentalists and those who argue for a politics of *sustainability.

Galbraith, John Kenneth (1908–2006)

American economist. *See* *affluence, countervailing power, *use-value.

game theory

A branch of mathematics (developed by O. Morgenstern and J. von Neumann), originally developed as a theory of the market economy, but offering a way of formalizing many social and political problems and activities. A game includes a number of *players*, each having a choice between certain *strategies*, and receiving a *pay-off*, defined for each combination of strategies by the rules of the game. In the general case the pay-off to each is determined by the choices of all, and it is this feature that has led people to think that the theory of games might provide a suitable model for social interaction, in which the information-base of each person's choice alters according to the choices made by others, as in a market. It is an assumption of the theory, however, that each player chooses *rationally*, in the sense that he has a consistent *preference ordering among possible outcomes and attempts to secure the best pay-off to himself. Choices made without prior communication are *independent*. The game has a *solution*, if each player has a uniquely best (or 'dominant') strategy or if, after repeated play, an outcome emerges which no player has reason to avoid. Games are of varying degrees of complexity, and the theory can be extended to take account of those situations in which there are many players, and in which information is uncertain.

Distinctions are made between types of game. In *zero-sum games, the pay-offs to the players add up to zero or, more generally, to some constant amount. Such games are games of *conflict*: one player's gain is another's loss. In non-zero-sum games that is not the case, and there is a potential for mutual gain. At the extreme are games in which the players have identical preferences. Nevertheless there may be difficulties of *coordination* in such games if there is no possibility of communication. Such difficulties may be resolved by the emergence or establishment of some convention or habit, such as the English habit of keeping to the left in a subway. Alternatively there may be some obvious or *salient* feature which is conducive to coordinated choice, even in the absence of any formal communication. Games are described as *cooperative* or *non-cooperative* according to whether players have the ability to engage in preplay communication and to make joint binding agreements.

It is no part of game theory, as a branch of applied mathematics, to suggest that human nature conforms or ought to conform to the paradigm of *rationality from which it begins. But it is a significant addition to political thought only if there are political problems or strategies which possess the form of a game, and for which the theory can determine at least an ideal, if not an actual, outcome. Some writers urge that human nature and political institutions are too complex to permit such an easy mathematical reduction. Neumann (*The Theory of Games and Economic Behaviour*, 1944) believed that the market economy approximates to the model proposed by game theory. Others have gone so far as to suggest that almost all political choice could be seen on the model of the particular problem in game theory known as the *prisoner's dilemma.

Gandhi, Mohandas Karamchand (Mahatma) (1869–1948)
Indian statesman and philosopher, and leader of the nationalist movement which led India to independence from the UK in 1947. Gandhi's political philosophy has a religious root, and reflects Hindu and Buddhist conceptions of the destiny of man. The universe is governed by a Supreme Intelligence or Truth (*satya*), which is embodied in all living things. The spirit is corrupted by sensual indulgence, and it is this that will destroy the *West, which is destined to sink under the impulse of its own degrading materialism. The spirit is manifest in love, which is the 'law of our being'. But we can live by his law only if we follow the path of *ahimsa* or non-violence. The state is a concentration

of violence, which imposes its will by force: it should therefore be demolished and rebuilt as an aggregate of small-scale and consensual communities. In the face of the violent state the individual always retains his inalienable right to *civil disobedience on behalf of those things which are morally demanded of him. And when the state impedes the ways of love, then civil disobedience becomes the duty of the citizen. But this disobedience can be pursued only by *non-violent resistance.

The non-violent state exists in order to further the growth or transcendence (*sarvodaya*) of all its citizens. But what form should such a state take? Gandhi, who had begun from a quasi-anarchist view that the state should be no bigger than is required for the regulation of a society of small communities, was tempted in a socialist direction. He disliked wealth on moral and religious grounds, and hoped for a society based on a principle of charitable *trusteeship. But he also accorded to the state powers of nationalization, confiscation and industrial organization which would require massive coercive powers. This conflict in his political outlook was never resolved, and his contribution to modern political thought is largely to be found in the theories of civil disobedience and non-violence. Gandhi was heartbroken when the independence of India was at once followed by the bloody conflicts between Muslim and Hindu which continue to the present day, and he himself was assassinated by a Hindu fanatic for having dared to suggest that assassination was not the right way to go about the business of improving things.

GATT
The General Agreement on Tariffs and Trade, worked out at *Bretton Woods

and signed in 1947, now replaced by the *World Trade Organization. *See* *bilateralism.

gauchisme

French: leftism. A term in use since the nineteenth century, but now mostly used to denote the *anarchist movement within the intellectual and student *left in France, particularly as this was manifested in and around 1968. The essential elements seem to be exuberant contempt for *bourgeois values, *Marxizing theory, and strongly *romantic prescriptions in answer to the question, What is to be done?

Gaullism

French political movement centred on the policies, principles and character of General (later President) *de Gaulle (1890–1970), beginning with the Rassemblement du Peuple Français (1947), and supplying a majority in the National Assembly as the Union de la Nouvelle République (1958). It has survived the death of de Gaulle to become a major political coalition capable of commanding considerable support among the French electorate. It tends to change its name with almost every election, and became the Rassemblement pour la République when Jacques Chirac reformed the Gaullists in 1976. According to one observer such 'terminological problems' express 'both the party's essential continuity . . . and the uncertainty of its role and impermanence of its organizational structure' (Michael Steed: *Political Parties in the European Community*, 1979).

The distinctive philosophy of Gaullism emphasizes nationalism, leadership, and an independent foreign policy, conducted for the most part outside the structure of the Western alliance. The advocacy of a capitalist economy, traditional French *centralism, and Roman Catholic morality is combined with a strongly republican outlook which often appears conservative in its evident emphasis on military security, political stability and economic growth, but which also has some of the volatility of its Napoleonic archetype.

gay marriage

The movement for *gay rights in the US and elsewhere has recently begun to campaign for the legalisation of marriage between people of the same sex, on the grounds that civil marriage brings with it financial and social advantages which ought to be available to all, regardless of their *sexual orientation. If homosexual partners promise fidelity, and live together in mutual harmony, they have effectively done everything required of a heterosexual couple by the law of marriage. So why should they be denied the change in status? Against that some argue that civil marriage owes its privileges to another and deeper union, which is the religious *sacrament from which it borrows its clothes, and that this sacrament binds man and woman for life. However, the ease with which man and woman can obtain a civil divorce suggests that the sacramental character of marriage is in any case no longer honoured in the civil law.

The arguments here are deep and complex, depending on (among other things) the nature and comparison of homosexual and heterosexual desire, the place of children in marriage, and the role of marriage and the family in the transmission of *social capital.

gay rights

The rights due to individuals, either as *human rights or as the *civil rights of a jurisdiction, but which are not available to homosexuals, or else available only in some reduced and mutilated form, on account of the prejudice against their *sexual orientation.

Campaigns for gay rights often involve the attempt to win acceptance for homosexuality as *normal, believing that, until this acceptance is granted, people will always be acting so as to marginalize homosexuals. However, there is no right, either natural or positive, to be considered normal.

Geist

German: spirit or soul. Term used by *Hegel and his followers to refer to the basic substance, the inner nature of which is the object of all self-consciousness and which strives to realize itself both subjectively through our own *self-realizations, and also objectively through the dialectical transformations that constitute history. (Hence the Hegelian division of phenomena into those of subjective and those of objective spirit.) *See* *Volksgeist, *Zeitgeist.

Geisteswissenschaften

German: the sciences of spirit. Term coined during the nineteenth century, to denote those branches of study which have the human soul and human institutions as their subject-matter, it being assumed by followers of *Dilthey (himself a disciple of *Kant and Hegel) that these studies exemplify methods different from those employed in the physical sciences. *See* *Gadamer, *hermeneutics, *humane education, *Verstehen.

Gemeinschaft and Gesellschaft

German: community and society. Terms employed by the sociologist Ferdinand Tönnies (*Gemeinschaft und Gesellschaft*, 1887, tr. *Community and Association*, 1955) in order to distinguish two kinds of association, one based in bonds of affection, kinship, etc., the other in *division of labour, self-interest and *contract. The theory of the distinction concerns two *ideal types, and it is important in providing two contrasting models of political association and political obligation, the one (that of non-contractual allegiance) popular among traditional conservatives, the other (that of quasi-contractual obligation) popular among liberal individualists.

gender

1. Feminists and others make a distinction between sex (which is a biological fact about the individual), and gender, which is a human artefact. The masculine and feminine genders are shaped by society and culture, while male and female sexuality are, although to some extent malleable, based in sexual difference, which is a trans-historical fact. Not only can individuals choose their gender, they can also work to ensure that gender is changed – so that women, for example, are perceived differently. Many feminists believe that their principal task is not to work for women's *rights in a man-made world, but to create another world, made in part by women. In this world the feminine gender will be constructed in a new way, so that women will no longer be perceived as child-bearing, home-building, man-dependent creatures, but as autonomous agents who set their own agendas and depend only on themselves.

2. Use of the term has become confused by the widespread adoption – under the influence of feminist politics – of 'gender' as the word for sex, perhaps in order to indicate that sexual differences are not as absolute as they have traditionally been supposed, and that the distinction between man and woman is at every point negotiable.

3. Gender also refers to a distinction in grammar, more or less defunct in the English language, between the masculine, feminine and neuter noun, and the corresponding forms of the adjective. Only pronouns retain gender

distinctions in English (he/she/it etc.). Some languages have no gender distinctions – e.g. Turkish and Hungarian. Others (e.g. Arabic) allow masculine nouns with feminine adjectives and vice versa. These facts have not prevented feminists from seeing the generic use of the masculine pronoun in English, to refer indifferently to all human beings, as *sexist. The influence of feminism in this matter has been so great that it is now difficult to publish an article in an American academic journal without using the feminine pronoun when referring indifferently to all human beings. This dictionary uses the masculine pronoun, on the grounds that the feminine pronoun makes a loud political statement in a context where political statements (as opposed to reports of them) should be kept to the minimum.

gender politics

Politics which looks first to distinctions of sex as they are assumed or promoted by social policies and asks the question whether they are drawn as they should be, and if not, whether an effort is being made to change them. American feminists have been influential in pursuing gender politics, not only in the national political process, but also in all subordinate institutions where they have gained a foothold, notably in universities.

general strike

See *anarcho-syndicalism, *industrial action, *myth, *Sorel, *syndicalism.

general will (*volonté générale*)

Term introduced by Diderot and adopted by *Rousseau, who distinguished the 'general will', which is the will of a society in its political aspect, from the 'will of all', which is the majority preference on this or that occasion. The two may conflict (for example, a majority may seek to disobey a law enacted by a constitution to which all agreed under the terms of a *social contract). The general will is expressed in law and is thought to be a 'real force, superior to the action of any particular will'. In being forced to conform to the general will, Rousseau argued, a citizen is being 'forced to be free'.

The idea has been important in shaping modern political thought, particularly since it seems to capture a *paradox of democracy, namely, that citizens may consent to arrangements that thereafter constrain and restrict their choices. Subsequent applications range from *Hegel's theory of the personal *state, to modern theories of *social choice, which sometimes argue that results such as *Arrow's theorem show that there can be no consistent democratic constitution based on the 'will of all', but only on some impersonal (but dictatorial) general will.

genocide

Term coined by the US jurist Raphael Lemkin in 1944, to denote the deliberate destruction of a *race, usually motivated by a theory as to the nature of races whereby to distinguish the 'higher' from the 'lower' (eliminable) varieties. Classified as a crime under *international law by the UN General Assembly in 1948, it was defined so as to include forms of persecution designed to eliminate a race or ethnic group while falling short of mass murder (for example, compulsory sterilization, forcible transfer of children). *See* *holocaust, *racism.

gentleman

1. A man of 'gentle' birth. This originally signified a definite position in the social *hierarchy. A gentleman required inherited material wealth, usually in the form of land, and an education (when he had one) derived

from recognized institutions of learning closed to those who did not belong or aspire to the upper *class. It is questionable whether the *gentry now form a class in any precise or theoretical sense since (a) their economic position is fairly indeterminate; (b) it is easy to become or cease to be a gentleman; (c) the classification seems from its beginning to have been subordinate to an ideal of civilized conduct. Hence:

2. A man who displays certain distinctive social characteristics, being courteous, liberal, honest, and well-spoken. These virtues have been thought to be more easily achieved by someone who is both attached to the land and relieved of the necessity of working it. Such a man, who has neither the vulgarity of the merchant, nor the avarice of the farmer, may exhibit, even in those conditions of poverty and ill-fortune that are the test of virtue, the social graces of a gentleman.

The vagueness of 1. combined with the broad application of 2. have led to the sense that a man can become a gentleman simply by representing himself to be one. No man can become an aristocrat in that way. Hence the term has come to express an idea of *social mobility. By representing oneself as a gentleman in sense 2. one is better placed to become a gentleman in sense 1. But even if that is true, the social mobility of women is unlikely to be improved by it. (On the other hand, there is a parallel social ideal of the 'lady' which has been equally influential.)

Those who subscribe to a *power theory of politics will not regard sense 2. as denoting a politically significant category. Thus Bertrand Russell (an aristocrat, but no gentleman) wrote: 'whatever the prevalent conception of manners may be, it is only where power is (or lately was) hereditary that men will be judged by their manners

. . . What survives in the way of admiration of the "gentleman" depends upon inherited wealth, and must rapidly disappear if economic as well as political power ceases to pass from father to son' (*Power*, 1938).

gentry
The class of *gentlemen. Used specifically to denote the class of small entrepreneurial landlords which existed in England from the early Renaissance onwards, and which provided much of the base for the political power struggles that shaped and reshaped modern English parliamentary institutions. Hence the 'gentry controversy', a parochial dispute, initiated by R.H. Tawney and H.R. Trevor-Roper, concerning the role of this class in the mid-seventeenth-century civil war in England.

geopolitics
A science, or pseudo-science, associated principally with the names of R.J. Kjellen (1864–1922), Halford Mackinder and Karl Haushofer, which conceives geographical location as an important and perhaps major determinant of political identity, political thought and political action, and which sees *nations as organisms struggling with each other for the occupancy of space. Haushofer coined the term *Lebensraum* (space for living), which played an important role in the *Nazi rhetoric of conquest. Mackinder put forward the influential 'heartland' thesis in 1904, according to which European history has been shaped by the struggle to control the Eurasian land mass – a thesis that has considerable influence on US foreign policy in Europe.

gerontocracy
Greek: *geron*, an old man. Rule by the elderly, a frequent practice among primitive tribes and in those societies where it is considered that only age

can provide the knowledge, wisdom or influence necessary for government. For different reasons gerontocracy has become the characteristic form of government in China, as it was in the USSR, and many of the satellites of the USSR. Increasing longevity, which has made age an unreliable sign of wisdom or even of rational intelligence, has undermined the credibility of gerontocracy in modern societies.

gerrymandering

In 1811 Elbridge Gerry, Governor of Massachusetts, created abnormally shaped constituencies, which looked on the map like salamanders. The purpose was to bias the outcome of elections in his favour. Hence 'gerrymandering', the practice of manipulating constituencies so as to secure some desired result. In the UK the Boundary Commissioners are constantly taking account of changes in the distribution and concentration of population in order to secure a fair result. But it seems that they never exactly succeed, and all political parties have at one time or another blamed them for electoral defeat. By creating devolved assemblies in Scotland and Wales, but not in England, while allowing the Scots and Welsh to return members to the Parliament in Westminster, *New Labour has effectively prevented the English (a majority of whom vote conservative) from electing a conservative Parliament. This too has been described as gerrymandering, though it proceeds not by carving up constituencies but by creating and preventing national assemblies.

ghetto

Probably from Italian: *borghetto*, small (part of a) city. Originally used to denote the quarter of a town (principally in Italy) to which the Jews were by law confined, and now denoting any urban area in which people of one race or ethnic group congregate, either by consent, or by coercion, or by economic constraint. The usual implication is that the living conditions in a ghetto are less desirable than those in surrounding areas, and that the occupants of the ghetto form part of an underprivileged *minority.

Gierke, Otto von (1841–1921)

German jurist whose account of the law of associations (*Das deutsche Genossenschaftsrecht*, 1886–1913) contains a classic defence of a law shaped by and for the sake of society, as opposed to one imposed by and for the sake of the state. Gierke argues, from extensive historical examples, that the traditional German law of associations, like the English law of trusts, arose from the voluntary creation of institutions, each endowed with rights and duties, and with the moral identity of a *corporate person. These self-regulating institutions formed the stuff of social life, providing identity to their members, and serving as the repository of traditions and inherited knowledge. Their enemy was the *Enlightenment sovereign who wished to assert his right of control over all subject institutions, and who was able to do so in part because of the ascendancy of the idea of *natural right. While seeming to defend the individual against tyranny, the philosophy of natural right, by making all rights into the property of individuals, deprives associations of rights of their own and so leaves them unprotected against the sovereign power. The French Revolution had expressly tried to destroy all institutions and associations apart from those controlled by the state; and the Napoleonic law, subsequently spread to much of Europe, had implanted in the European legal systems a prejudice in favour of the state, together with a pernicious *individualism. It was therefore necessary to recapture the true German idea of society as something richer, healthier and more organic than the political machine established by Enlightenment conceptions of sovereignty.

Gierke's vision of the traditional 'German' law of associations contains elements of wishful thinking; however, his Hegelian vision of corporate personality was very influential, and entered British conservative thinking through *Maitland.

Giffen goods

Goods which do not obey the law that less is bought as price rises (the 'law of demand'). Named after Sir Robert Giffen (1837–1910), who observed that when the price of bread rose the labouring classes bought more of it, and when the price fell, less. Such goods are not now regarded as exceptions to the 'law of demand', which has been supplemented by the theories of *income effect and *substitution effect, whereby the behaviour of Giffen goods may be explained.

gift

The voluntary transfer of property to another, or into *common ownership, without receipt of any property in exchange. Gift between private persons requires private property, and its importance in expressing and cementing indispensable human relationships has provided one of the frequently used arguments for private property: the right of property being extolled as a necessary condition for its own renunciation, much as chastity has been extolled as the necessary condition for those relations which are founded on its demise. This sentiment received expression, for example, in *Hegel and *Burke. Conversely many who have been opposed to private property have for that reason been opposed to gifts, and in many socialist

communities gifts are severely curtailed by law; even capitalist economies may subject gifts to punitive *taxation in the interest of *social justice and *redistribution.

A specific form of gift – that from the dead to the living – has frequently evoked this hostility in an acute form, since it seems to be the principal means whereby the power of individual families and even classes is preserved. (*See* *death taxes, *hereditary principle.) Some think that it is unjust that one person should begin life with inherited wealth, others argue that it is in any case politically unacceptable that such constant accumulation across generations should be possible, and therefore advocate total or partial confiscation of wealth on death. Inheritance may, however, be both upheld and abolished in the name of a more feudal conception of private property. According to this conception property is held not absolutely, but subject to the will of the sovereign to whom allegiance is owed. Thus property is at best a right for life, with ownership reverting to the sovereign (i.e. the state) on death, to be redistributed in accordance with the will of the sovereign (i.e. in accordance with the law). The law may designate, for example, the eldest male son as heir, thus upholding inheritance. This does not alter the fact that transfer across generations has now ceased to be a gift, and has become, instead, the resumption of ownership by the sovereign, followed by its reallocation according to the law. This is probably the correct way to understand the medieval concept of 'entail', which makes the holder of an estate into a kind of trustee for those entitled in succession. This way of seeing inheritance also shows how it is possible for private property to be subject to state supervision, so that no interference in the right of property as commonly understood need be involved in any measures designed to prevent accumulation beyond a certain level (specifically beyond the level at which the subject begins to appear comparable in power to the sovereign).

No such intellectual construction can be used to rationalize the forbidding (or permitting) by law of gifts *inter vivos*, and the question of their admissibility continues, therefore, to raise important questions concerning the nature and justification of private property.

Girard, René (b. 1928)

French critic and anthropologist, whose novel theory of the sacred, put forward in *Violence and the Sacred*, 1972, has had a far-reaching influence on theories of religion and political violence. The core of religion is not belief in the transcendental but the experience of sacred awe – an experience that is fundamental, Girard believes, to human community. The sacred can be presented to us in many forms – in religious ritual, in prayer, in tragedy – but its true origin is in an act of communal violence. Primitive societies are invaded by 'mimetic desire', as rivals struggle to match each other's social and material acquisitions, so heightening antagonism and precipitating the cycle of revenge. The solution is to identify a victim, one marked by fate as 'outside' the community and therefore not entitled to vengeance against it, who can be the target of the accumulated blood-lust, and who can bring the chain of retribution to an end. Scapegoating is society's way of recreating 'difference' and so restoring itself. By uniting against the scapegoat people are released from their rivalries and reconciled. Through his death the scapegoat purges society of its accumulated violence. His resulting sanctity is the long-term echo of the awe, relief and visceral re-attachment to the community that was experienced at his death.

The need for sacrificial scapegoating is therefore deeply implanted in the human psyche, arising from the very attempt to form a durable community in which the moral life can be successfully pursued. One purpose of the theatre is to provide fictional substitutes for the original crime, and so to obtain the benefit of moral renewal without the horrific cost. Hence, according to Girard, we should see a tragedy like Sophocles' *Oedipus Tyrannus* as a re-telling of what was originally a ritual sacrifice, in which the victim is chosen so as to focus and confine the need for violence. Through incest, kingship, or worldly hubris the victim marks himself out as the outsider, the one who is not with us, and whom we can therefore sacrifice without renewing the cycle of revenge. The victim is thus both sacrificed and sacred, the source of the city's plagues and their cure.

Girard's theory has been taken to throw light on such phenomena as the scapegoating of the Jews, the Christian story of the Passion, the violence of Islamists against America, and the extraordinary power of terrorist regimes. It has been criticized as both too general to distinguish the many forms of violence and the many shades of religious feeling, and as too heavily influenced by the Christian doctrines for which Girard attempts to offer a kind of proof.

glasnost

Russian: 'publicity', from *glas*, voice. Term associated with the policies of Mikhail Gorbachev (b.1931), who assumed leadership of the USSR in 1985 and initiated a policy of 'speaking out' in a society where the communists had maintained their monopoly of power only by preventing this.

Commentators differ as to whether Gorbachev sought by this policy to destroy the power of the communists, to preserve it or to transfer it to another *oligarchy. In the event it was only after the fall of communism that independent newspapers could exist in the USSR, and the permission of glasnost extended no further than the party and its privileged associates.

Gleichschaltung

German: levelling or regularizing of government. The general idea of political coordination or bringing into line, so that policy decisions harmonize. The term was given a more sinister use by Hitler, to signify the systematic elimination of *opposition and of those who instigate it.

globalization

The process whereby barriers to trade, to the movement of populations, to the spread of information, disinformation, lies, truths and enquiries, to scientific knowledge and mass-produced ignorance – in short anything produced by or embodied in people – are rapidly being broken down. The causes of globalization are many, but obviously technological advances in *communication, transportation, and marketing have been crucial, as well as the implosion of regimes such as that of the *USSR which depended upon freezing populations, industries and ideas in a posture of xenophobic resistance to externally motivated change. The rise of *multinational business and *transnational institutions, the erosion of *local cultures and markets by migrations, the universal desire of people for freedom, opportunity and prosperity, not to speak of the growing *entropy of modern societies, have all made a contribution.

Some welcome globalization, as one aspect of the 'creative destruction' celebrated by *Schumpeter – the process that destroys old and dysfunctional systems and customs, and creates the conditions in which innovation can begin. Others welcome it as the *end of history, or as the beginning of a new and universal civilization, based on Western ideas of freedom, individuality and mobility. Others abhor it as the enemy of *tradition, *local custom and the gentle institutions of people who live close to the soil. Others still abhor it as a confidence trick practised by the multinational corporations in their desire to appropriate the resources of the *developing world. One aspect that tends not to be commented upon, is the contribution made by globalization to the *shadow economy, and also to the rise of international *terrorism, itself in a certain measure part of that shadow economy.

glory

Glory can name either the splendour, generosity and ostentation of a style of life, or the esteem due to *virtue, especially to courage and effort expended in a public cause. To some extent both those ideas have been subsumed under the traditional French political value of *gloire*, which at first referred to the reputation and dignity of the true public figure and later (after the trappings of monarchy had been borrowed by Napoleon) to that kind of public recognition and display which is the reward of heroic action. (The direct influence here was the Roman idea of *gloria* as the reward of virtue.)

In a lesser sphere the pursuit of glory has often been thought (e.g. by *Aristotle) to be an ineliminable part of the political motive, since it is nothing more than an attempt to represent objectively the subjective pride that is essential to virtue. In so far as all political order requires courage it also requires the motive of honour, and that in turn requires the satisfaction of honour, which is the public recognition that is symbolized in acts of display. Some have argued that the modern world has not escaped the need for that display. For example, some defend a system of *honours, on the ground that public service should find a reward in the form of recognition and social status, rather than in financial advantage or naked power. Glory, as an end in itself, thereby removes the motive from a certain kind of corruption.

gnosticism

A religious movement of pagan origins that influenced Christianity in the second century, and which held that no redemption is possible without 'gnosis' – the revealed knowledge of God and man's destiny – and (sometimes) that possession of gnosis is a sufficient guarantee of redemption. The term has been borrowed by Eric Voegelin to describe political doctrines which claim to reveal a truth about man and history sufficient to show the way to a secular redemption. Voegelin argues that the gnostic idea of salvation through knowledge, while quickly condemned as a heresy by the church, represents a permanent temptation of the human intellect, and is a source of dangerous fantasy in religion, morality, and politics.

Gobineau, Arthur (self-styled Comte de) (1816–82)

French political theorist, diplomat and polemicist, widely known as the father of modern *racism, who wrote powerfully and trenchantly of the condition of European civilization in the nineteenth century, and who also sought to develop a theory of *race that would explain the simultaneous technological advance and spiritual insecurity of the European powers, and the relative backwardness and innocence of the

Africans. Gobineau was fascinated by Arab and Middle-Eastern civilization, which presented a striking challenge to many of his theories, and was a tireless collector of anthropological evidence in his attempt to show that physical environment has no effect on culture, and that all flourishing and all degeneracy can be traced to the influence of race. He recognized three races – the white, the yellow and the black, in descending order of superiority – and argued that the luxury and *decadence of his countrymen were but one small consequence of the fact that the white race had all but disappeared in a mess of hybridization. All races achieve their characteristic greatness when unmixed, and hybridization is the downfall of all.

Godwin, William (1756–1836)

British political theorist and novelist, husband of *Wollstonecraft. In his *Enquiry Concerning Political Justice*, 1793, Godwin gave what was perhaps the first extended modern defence of *anarchism, based on principles of *natural justice, utility, and the *rights of man. He argued for 'primeval equality' – i.e. for the view that man outside society can recognize no distinctions among his kind that might justify unequal treatment. All inequality is created by the condition of society, which generates class distinctions, sentiments of nationality and territory, and all the aggressive activities that we have learned to associate with them. Only the total removal of political *institutions can restore people to their natural rights, and permit them to engage in genuine as opposed to constrained *social contract with their fellows. Godwin's anarchism was liberal in inspiration; however, since there is a right, in Godwin's view, only to what maximizes utility, his preferred list of natural rights does not resemble that normally offered by liberal theory. Despite his influence on the intellectuals of the romantic period (notably on the poets Shelley and Wordsworth), Godwin was never associated with any definite political movement.

good offices

In *international law 'good offices and mediation' signifies the intervention in a dispute by a *state not party to it, in order to procure a settlement. 'Good offices' are in theory distinct from 'mediation', the first denoting the preparatory moves towards securing negotiation between the parties, the second involving the actual initiation of the negotiations.

GOP

'Grand Old Party' – standard US *journalese for the US *Republican Party.

government

The exercise of *influence and *control, through *law and *coercion, over a particular group of people, usually formed into a *state. Government has many kinds, and the following distinctions should be noted:

(i) Constitutional and non-constitutional: in the first, power is limited by a *constitution, in the second it is not. Many governments pretend to be constitutional: a common sign of this is a written constitution, which carefully specifies the rights of the citizens while neglecting to mention how they might enforce them. (*See* e.g. many of the post-colonial African constitutions.)

(ii) Absolute and limited (*see* *absolutism and *limited government). This distinction concerns the extent to which a government's power is limited by other agencies within the state (law being principal among them), as opposed to other states.

(iii) Political and non-political, for which *see* *politics. Certain institutions, concerned with the *representation, *arbitration, *adjudication and *conciliation of interests within the state, are deemed to have a 'political' character, the most important of them being courts of law. Government can, however, exist without such institutions, and even without law – in which case it may be *despotic, or merely *primitive (as in the government of a tribe by a single chieftain in accordance with *custom).

(iv) In addition to those basic distinctions, various classifications of government have evolved, for example according to who holds power and in whose interest (the influence here being *Aristotle). The principal ones now recognized are *monarchy, *democracy, *aristocracy, *oligarchy, and *tyranny.

Theories of government are legion, but it is always important to distinguish between those which see government as a means to an end, and those which see it as an end in itself. *Hegel's theory is an example of the latter; standard *liberal and *socialist theories are examples of the former. If there are human ends for which government is necessary, then probably government must always be considered (at least to some extent) as a means to them. Thus if government is necessary for *peace, *friendship, *production and social life, then government must be conceived as a means to these basic and indispensable goods. But if *anarchism is right and those goods are obtainable without government, then government may yet be defensible as an end in itself – i.e. as defining a form of life (that of political *allegiance or *obligation) which is desirable in itself (say, because it is the full expression of man's *freedom – roughly Hegel's view). In reality most political practice recognizes that government is both a means to order, and an end of social existence, and has a dual value founded in compromise between these two.

Since the subject-matter of this dictionary is government, it would be impertinent to extend this entry.

government through symbols

The kind of government in which the state, its power, and its authority, are given periodic demonstration of a symbolic kind. The purpose may be to increase the *authority of the state, as in the ceremonies and pageants that occur in monarchies, and which involve not the display of power but only the rehearsal of traditional allegiances, or in the flags, national anthems, parades and tournaments upon which virtually every government relies for the image of legitimacy. In this sense all government needs symbols, since it is through symbols that values, including those of political obligation, are understood. Alternatively, the purpose may be to increase the *power of the state, as in the show trials organized periodically by communist states, or in the *autos da fé* of the church, which existed to inspire awe and terror in the citizens, and to remind them in a vivid form of their subjection to an overriding power.

grace

1. The supernatural assistance of God, bestowed with a view to the salvation of a human soul.

2. The ability to appear in society so as to attract the interest, sympathy and obedience of others, without offending their pride.

The second indicates a style of politics that has often appealed to Europeans; the first indicates a belief that has sometimes enabled them to achieve it.

gradualism

The view, sometimes associated with *social democracy, that the transformation of social and political life cannot be achieved by sudden *revolution, but can be achieved by steady and systematic 'permeation' of existing political institutions. *See also* *evolutionism, *Fabianism.

Also, more loosely, any political doctrine that advocates slow and steady rather than sudden and disruptive advances towards its aims. Gradualism has been a major cause of Fabians, and was passionately advocated by Sidney and Beatrice Webb, and by *Shaw.

Gramsci, Antonio (1891–1937)

Founder of the Italian *Communist Party, and imprisoned by Mussolini, Gramsci wrote works in prison which were subsequently to be highly influential (*Prison Notebooks*, 1948–51). He attempted to reformulate certain theses of *Marxism – in particular *historical materialism – in a way that would reflect native Italian conceptions of the role of institutions, consciousness and culture. A *humanist and hater of tyranny, Gramsci has achieved renown as a symbol of an intellectual communism of Italian manufacture. His term *hegemony has entered political rhetoric, although not always with a meaning of which he would approve. For Gramsci a hegemony consists of complex and concealed modes of *class domination, whereby positions of influence throughout society are always, by a hidden mechanism, filled by the members of an already ruling class. Hence an important task of the revolutionary is to infiltrate the *autonomous institutions (schools, councils, universities, the church) through which hegemony is covertly exercised, so as to remove their internal staying power and let loose the flood of revolution that is surging from below.

Revolution should involve the construction of a new hegemony, which will gradually expand, spreading the influence of the Communist Party into all areas of civil society. Gramsci wished for a revolution but not for a coercive state, and thought that through this new hegemony, which would involve the gradual *democratization of all institutions and the involvement of the whole people in all aspects of their life, the area of state coercion could be gradually eliminated. The ideal was not a state but a 'regulated society', in which *consensus would replace the rule of force. *See also* *corporatism.

grass roots
US political slang, originating *circa* 1912, and used to designate support for a policy or party within the ranks of citizens who do not possess any more power than is contained in the ability to vote. 'Grass roots politics' denotes a political practice that seeks to instigate and fulfil policy by influencing the opinion and involving the sentiments of those outside political office, and which usually represents itself as being at one with some popular *consensus. *See also* *populism.

Great Officers
In English parlance, Great Officers of the Realm (elsewhere Officers of State (Scotland) or Great Officers of State) are the holders of those political offices through which executive powers are exercised in the name of the sovereign. The usage is antiquated, and does not now correspond to the true centre of executive power (the *Prime Minister and *cabinet), but only to a traditional sense of the manner in which monarchical privilege is represented. In the UK the Great Officers include the Lord Chancellor (who is responsible for the execution of law and judicial process, but whose title and position are currently under review), the Lord President of the

Council, the Lord Privy Seal and 12 others. Only the first of these is of necessity a peer, and all are bound by an order of precedence. Absolutism in France was accompanied by the virtual disappearance of Great Officers of State (with the exception of the Chancellor), while in most other states the importance of these officers steadily diminished through the nineteenth century.

Greek constitutions
Since much of our political philosophy has it origin in discussions prevalent in ancient Greece, the constitutions of the Greek city states (*see* **polis*) are often taken as models with which to guide discussion of the *nation states which have long since succeeded them. The two principal Greek constitutions now discussed are those of Athens (*see* *Athenian democracy) and *Sparta: in the former a kind of partial *democracy prevailed, while in the latter intense political organization of all aspects of social life coexisted with extraordinary social divisions. Sparta was esteemed for its inner discipline by *Plato, who expressed, in the *Republic*, and the *Laws*, his admiration for a constitution that could so easily provide political answers to every social question. In the *Laws* Plato compares many Greek constitutions, and enables us to see how the familiar problems of political theory – the role of law, the problem of securing limited government, the nature and status of labour, and the problem of social class – are generic to government, and not peculiar to our time.

Extant are a constitution of Athens, attributed to Xenophon but in fact written by an Athenian oligarch about 425 BC, which disguises bitter criticism of democracy behind a 'descriptive' facade; an incomplete history and analysis of the Athenian constitution by *Aristotle, and a 'constitution of the

Lacedaimonians' (i.e. of Sparta) by Xenophon, which says, however, very little about its subject-matter. Plato's *Laws* remains therefore an indispensable source.

green

Description adopted by advocates of *environmentalism (sense 2.), in order to identify the key issues and policies that a modern society must consider. The German ecology party calls itself the 'Green Party', and other parties in Europe follow suit, although usually the label is unofficial. Some people who defend political action to protect the environment nevertheless object to the label 'green' for its romantic and sentimental overtones. To many hard-headed German conservatives the Green Party seems to express a longing to return to some pre-industrial idyll which, because it is no longer available, destroys all realism and wisdom in those who relentlessly pursue it. Others perceive in the 'greens' a kind of *single-issue fanaticism which is equally inimical to constructive politics. These suspicions are not allayed by the fact that green parties always seem to place themselves on the left of the political spectrum, even though the issues that preoccupy them are of concern to everyone. Whether the suspicions are fair is a moot point. The German greens are adamant that their party has nothing to do with the *agrarian nostalgia that played an important part in pre-war German politics: rather it belongs to a global movement, calling for rational solutions to problems that we avoid at our peril.

Green, Thomas Hill (1836–82)

English philosopher who sought to reconcile classical *liberalism with an *idealist metaphysics, and to replace the *individualism of Locke and Mill with a more *organicist theory of the relationship between individual and society. Although freedom under law is the true end of political order, it is only through the bond of *political obligation that it can be achieved. Individuals are not free in a state of nature, nor are they truly individuals outside the experience of society. People become free rational agents by a process of *self-realization, and this process can occur only through social relations in which rights are matched by obligations. Associations define new possibilities of action, new goods and new evils, and the state must take charge of the *common good if it is to sustain the social order through which self-realization is possible.

Green's vision of the relation between individual and society is largely Hegelian; but he wished to reject the conservative implications of Hegel's philosophy, without embracing the atomistic view of society that he perceived in *empiricist writing on politics. Hence he has been esteemed as much by constitutionally minded socialists as by conservatives, not least because his theory of the common good seems to authorize socialist policies of welfare legislation and economic planning.

Gresham's law

'Bad money drives out good', named after Sir Thomas Gresham (1519–79), a businessman and economic adviser to King Edward VI and Queen Elizabeth I of England. The idea is this: if the face value of two coins differs from the bullion value, then the one with the higher bullion value can be melted down and so will exchange against the other at an advantageous rate; eventually it will disappear from circulation. Sometimes, when the *exchange-value of a coin as bullion is more than its exchange-value as money, a law may be passed to *take* it out of circulation.

gross domestic product (GDP)

A measure of the total flow of goods and services produced by the economy – i.e. the aggregate value added – over a specified period (normally a year). Intermediate products (i.e. those which re-enter the production process) are not included. 'Gross' product does not allow for depreciation. The GDP is 'domestic' in that it is a measure of the actual level of production *within* the economy: contrast *gross national product.

gross national product (GNP)

*Gross domestic product plus *income accruing from overseas investments and minus income earned in the domestic market by those residing abroad.

Grotius, Hugo (Huig de Groot) (1583–1645)

Dutch jurist, philosopher and man of letters, a *humanist and disciple of *Erasmus, Grotius wrote a famous pamphlet in defence of the freedom of the seas (*Mare Liberum*, 1609) and, after escape from life imprisonment on political charges, wrote the first, and the greatest, exposition of modern *international law (*De Jure Belli ac Pacis: On the Law of War and Peace*, 1620–25). The purpose was to devise a system of international law suitable to the new *nation states of Europe, which would not rely upon *ecclesiastical jurisdiction, but harmonize with, and gain support from, normal principles of adjudication. Grotius argued that such a system of law must be founded in *natural law, which is instinct in human nature, and independent of the command of God: 'Natural law is so immutable that it cannot be changed by God himself.' This law has authority in all rational beings, and therefore can command assent at all times and places, irrespective of whether there is some power,

secular or ecclesiastical, able to give support to its manifest moral authority. Natural law is distinct from *positive law, and provides the criterion whereby positive law might be tested, and to which appeal may be made when the positive laws of separate nations conflict. One principle of natural law is of particular importance in international jurisdiction, as the foundation of all legal dealings between states: *pacta sunt servanda*, i.e. promises and treaties are to be adhered to. Other postulates offered by Grotius in the name of natural law are perhaps more parochial than this one, which he clearly regarded as the most important, in founding what he called the *jus voluntarium* (the 'voluntary legislation') characteristic of dealings between states. On the basis of his exploration of this concept, Grotius offered a famous analysis of the *just war, arguing that no war could be just if purely aggressive (*see* *aggression) and hence that only acts of defence and retaliation could be countenanced. Grotius's ideas on this subject have since been taken seriously, and to a great measure applied, through the legal determinations of the United Nations.

Grotius defended a *social contract doctrine although, unlike later theorists (such as *Hobbes, *Locke and *Rousseau), he believed that this contract actually occurred, preceding the state of society in every community governed by law (hence the natural law principle of *pacta sunt servanda* also provides the ultimate basis of *political obligation).

Grotius's writings were voluminous; he is notable for his attempt to give a full account of man as rational agent, and for the extent to which he presaged, in that account, many ideas that were to acquire their full modern dress in the moral philosophy of *Kant.

group

Usually defined by political scientists as a number of individuals with a common interest, whether or not associated for the pursuit of that interest. Groups vary according to size, organization and interest, and many contain subgroups and *factions. Studies of *collective choice make increasing reference to groups, and 'group theory' (exemplified, e.g., in Arthur Bentley: *The Process of Government*, 1949; and Sidney Verba: *Small Groups and Political Behaviour*, 1961) is now an important part of the sociology of politics. *See also* *interest group, *pressure group, *single-issue fanatic, *lobby.

group rights

Many thinkers agree that people have rights, either as human beings (*human rights or *natural rights) or as citizens (*civil rights). But do they, in addition, have rights as members of this or that group – say, as Jews, Gypsies, males, educated people? Liberal *individualists tend to view the idea of 'group rights' as invidious – a way of introducing *discrimination in the name of rights, and therefore committing injustice as though it were a form of justice. For example, it has been argued before the UK courts that Gypsies have a human right to their traditional life-style, and therefore to settle where they will, so that planning regulations that forbid non-Gypsies to settle and build in a particular place do not apply to Gypsies. Once allowed, such arguments allow privileges to be bestowed promiscuously on any group that can claim some special exemption on account of life-style, tradition or historical injustice. In which case, rights become instruments with which to discriminate in favour of some people and against others, purely on the grounds of their 'group', and lose their character as a universal shield against oppression. Some of these issues recur in discussions of *reverse discrimination.

growth

Growth usually means *economic growth, although naturally many other factors of social life exhibit principles of growth – e.g. population, knowledge, understanding, sympathy. *Progressivism, the view which sees all forms of growth as related and as occurring together, is to be contrasted with the view that economic growth is an independent social feature, that might occur whether or not there is any corresponding movement in political and social institutions, and without determining growth in anything else. The assumption that economic growth is essential to political stability has been called into question: *see* *limits to growth, *sustainability.

guerrilla warfare

Guerrilla is the Spanish term for a kind of irregular and usually undeclared warfare carried out by autonomous units without a coordinated high command but, it is assumed, with a concerted (and usually *revolutionary or *nationalist) purpose.

The 'urban guerrilla' was a familiar exponent of modern *terrorism, although he has been eclipsed by the new forms of terrorism, which do not glory in a military image, and pursue death as a form of religious redemption.

guestworker

German: *Gastarbeiter*. Citizen of a foreign state permitted to reside within the sovereign territory in order to work there, and who has a right to send money home but no right of residence beyond the cessation of his employment. In Germany, because of labour shortages, the policy of permitting foreigners (especially Turks, as a result of a long-standing informal, and sometimes formal, alliance) to enter the country as guestworkers has been endorsed by successive governments, despite popular opposition. The problems posed by the arrangement are many. For example, what happens to the children of a guestworker? What rights do they have to welfare, education and other civil privileges? Many German-born children of guestworkers speak only German, are of German culture and have no chance of a life outside Germany. Working-class resentment of these 'foreigners who are taking our jobs' can therefore lead, and in Germany has tended to lead, to acute ethnic tensions.

Guevara, Ernesto, 'Che' (1928–67)
Argentinian-born revolutionary. *See* *focoism.

guild socialism

A movement within the British *labour movement, guild socialism existed as an active force from 1906 to 1923 (becoming the National Guilds League), and as a dwindling idea thereafter. The central aim was to incorporate into the modern labour organizations the social concern and sense of wholeness characteristic of the *guilds, and to develop, out of small autonomous associations, modes of common ownership and control that would be organically linked to the leisure and social life of their members. These guilds were to be the true locus of economic activity, and also were to provide the basis for all social and political existence, with the state reduced to the status of arbitrator

and adjudicator of disputes and conflicts. Ideally, even parliamentary government could be abolished if power was properly vested in these self-sufficient social units. The principal exposition of the idea is A.J. Penty: *Restoration of the Guild System*, 1906.

guilds

Permanent voluntary associations serving a common interest of their members: this interest was usually occupational, but not always so (thus universities began in England as guilds). Deriving from the Roman *collegium* (*see* *college), guilds emerged in Europe at about the beginning of the eleventh century as organizations of skilled labourers and craftsmen concerned to promote the social, professional and religious interests of their members, to help those in need, and to promote their education and welfare. They could effectively forbid someone from practising a vocation by closing their doors to him, and anticipated in their dealings with their members some of the social and political organization of modern *trade unions, differing largely in the nature of the employments supervised by them, and in the greater emphasis on social, recreational and ceremonial embellishments to the life of labour and craft. They had their own bodies of customary law, and were later always governed, in England, by statute (e.g. the Statute of Artificers 1562). Guild organization broke down under the impact of *industrialization, *detail labour, and *laissez-faire.*

Habeas corpus

In English law, a *prerogative writ (i.e. a summons by a legal officer issued on behalf of the sovereign), calling for the liberty of a subject. Originally habeas corpus was a command to bring the person before a court; now it is simply a general order to release from imprisonment. The existence of this writ (named after its opening words in Latin: 'In that you have the body of . . .') is seen as one of the fundamental guarantees of traditional English liberty. It is older than Magna Carta, 1215, and was established in the seventeenth century as the appropriate process for securing release from illegal detention. The writ may now be validly used against the *Crown, its officers and ministers, and therefore vests absolute power in a judge to enquire into the validity of any restraint, except where ordered by a court of competent jurisdiction (when the enquiry would be tantamount to retrial), and in certain rather peculiar cases (as when a member of the House of Commons is committed to the Tower for breach of *privilege).

The writ also exists in the US, transplanted from English law, and now issued as an original proceeding by the Supreme Court. Abraham Lincoln worried about the suspension of the writ during the civil war emergency, and it then became a public issue of the first importance: to what extent does the US constitution guarantee the rights and liberties of the citizen in the absence of this writ? Habeas corpus has also become an issue recently because of its increasing use to take issues out of state courts and into federal courts, a practice that is frequently deplored by *federalists. No equivalent of habeas corpus exists in Napoleonic systems of law, and the proposed adoption by the EU of a continent-wide arrest warrant will effectively end habeas corpus in the UK. The current Prevention of Terrorism Act 2004, which allows detention without charge for 30 days, has in any case limited its effect – though this Act is widely regarded as an emergency provision, rather than a permanent feature of the legal landscape.

Habermas, Jürgen (b. 1929)

German philosopher and social theorist, the most important heir in postwar Germany to the social and political thinking of the *Frankfurt school. Habermas's early works, from the late 1950s and 1960s, are marked by the Marxist *humanism of his mentors, and in particular by the 'critique of instrumental reasoning' initiated by Max Horkheimer. In the bourgeois world everything, including man himself, is treated as a means to production, and production as a means to consumption. The world is 'instrumentalized', and all reasoning is in terms of means to an end. In such a world nothing is treated as an end in itself, not even the human being. Thought too is instrumentalized as *ideology, and the individual exists in a condition of *alienation. The primary problem for this bourgeois order is that of its *legitimation, and the crisis of legitimation dominates modern politics.

In later writings Habermas tries to give an account of social life that will show how alienation and instrumentalization might be overcome. His 'theory of communicative action' takes speech – and specifically conversation – as its model of a social activity pursued for its own sake and which is intrinsically meaningful to those who take part in it. (*The Theory of Communicative Action*, 1981.) The task of politics is to create the conditions in which no party to the social dialogue can exploit or silence any other, since each person has equal *access to the means of communication. Democracy is the system in which the voice of each citizen is heard as clearly as the voice of every other, and in which no voice is without an effect on the decisions made in its name.

Habermas tries to develop a theory of law and constitution which will answer to this liberal ideal, and in consequence has moved away from the vague and somewhat bureaucratic Marxism of his youth, towards a more *social-democratic view of the relation between the individual and the state. At the same time he has turned his attention to issues of cultural history and social theory, and attempted to give an account of the new conditions of *postmodern society, from which religion and morality have retreated and in which social equilibrium requires the balancing of fleeting and often contradictory appetites.

Habermas has been popular in left-wing circles, although his theory of communicative action comes close to the conservative ideas advocated by *Oakeshott. His voluminous writings, and equally voluminous references to academic sources in every relevant discipline, have conferred on him an unassailable academic status, even though, for many of his critics, the content of his thinking is far slighter than its form. *See also* *critical theory.

half-education
The complaint is often made by conservatives that democracy has a tendency to promote the half-educated to positions of power, the half-educated person being the one who knows just enough to question the traditional order and not enough to re-affirm it. For *Masaryk, half-education (*Halbbildung*) is the great disease of modern civilization, since it casts people loose from their roots while providing no alternative home or consolation. Hence it is the major cause of modern *suicide.

Hamilton, Alexander (1755–1805)
US statesman, a co-author of the *Federalist Papers, and founder and leader of the Federalist Party in Congress. Hamilton distrusted democracy, and believed in a strong central government, which would develop federal fiscal and economic policies to the benefit of manufacture and trade. Hamilton was killed in a duel with his rival Aaron Burr.

harassment
A form of *coercion, much practised, easily recognized, but difficult to define. A legal definition is offered by, and for the purposes of, the UK Protection from Eviction Act 1977, s. 1(3) which extends an intuitive idea from the Administration of Justice Act (s.40, forbidding harassment of debtors) to the harassment of occupiers, and makes it an offence to do acts calculated to interfere with the peace or comfort of an occupier and his family, with the intention of getting him to renounce his rights of occupancy. Recent uses of the expression '*sexual harassment' require a separate entry in this dictionary.

hard cases
From the maxim 'hard cases make bad law'; a phenomenon singled out by

the American jurist and philosopher *Dworkin (*Taking Rights Seriously*, 1977), as posing fundamental questions concerning the nature of *law and legal reasoning. A hard case is a case in law whose outcome seems not to be determined by an antecedent rule, and where, while the judge may follow a *precedent, the disparity between the present case and the one with which it is compared is too great to permit any simple assimilation of the one to the other. Attention to such cases brings into focus the all-important question: does the judge make, or discover, the law? On the one hand, there is no antecedent rule determining his decision (which makes it seem as though he makes the law to fit this case); on the other hand, he cannot *think* of himself as making the law, for that would suggest that the law came into existence after the action that is being tried, in which case injustice (in the form of *retroactive legislation) will be the inevitable consequence of his decision. The problem is rendered more, not less, acute, as *statute comes to replace *common law, since this seems to emphasize the conventional, man-made character of the law, and to cast doubt on the interpretation of judicial reasoning as a process of discovery.

hard currency

A currency, traded in a foreign exchange market, for which the demand is persistently high, on account of its purchasing power or stability. Governments with 'soft' currencies often control exchange in order to acquire hard currency at favourable rates (*see* *exchange control). The softness of a currency is often taken as a sign of the economic fragility of the state which issues it, so that the constant search on the part of *communist states for hard currency was often taken as an index of the economic instability or inefficiency of communist economies. The retort was sometimes made that this is a distortion, due to the fact that the institutions of international exchange are all in the hands of capitalists.

harm

A concept important in articulating *liberal conceptions of the nature and function of *law, and in formulating plausible limits to the scope of law. One popular idea (which finds expression in some of the writings of *J.S. Mill) is that the primary function of law is to prevent the individual from doing harm to others and to himself. Intuitively appealing though that conception is, it has presented immense problems in its application, for what constitutes harm? What harms a plant may not harm a dog, what harms a dog may not harm a person; and conversely. Roughly, x harms y whenever x prevents y from existing or flourishing according to y's nature; disputes about harm are therefore usually disputes about *human nature. Since the flourishing of a *person may not be identical with, and may be quite independent of, the flourishing of the human animal in which he is, as it were, incarnate, enormous philosophical controversies arise. For example, am I harmed by something just *because* I do not consent to it? What then is the criterion of my consent to a law? That I voted for the party whose majority secured its enactment? Clearly this criterion, when combined with the original liberal idea of the function of law, leads to enormous scepticism about laws which are both deeply entrenched in all legal systems, and perhaps even essential to good government. (And, in another, more plausible sense, people often consent to things which harm them.)

Some accounts of harm attempt to

do justice to the complexity of the idea of the person, by defining his harm as an invasion of his interests, where his interests, include, or are exhausted by, his *rights (sometimes his *natural rights). Then the true function of law may be construed as the protection of natural rights. This provides a more objective criterion than 'consent', and one that has often seemed plausible; but how are natural rights to be determined? This problem is perhaps as difficult as the one which 'harm' was invoked to solve.

Harrington, James (1611–77)
English political philosopher and scholar, who set forth, in his *The Commonwealth of Oceana*, 1656, a *utopian picture of the ideal *republican state. The work has a philosophical basis in *empiricism, and defines the types of rule (monarchy, oligarchy, etc.) in terms of the distribution of property among members of the state (thus presaging later theories of *class), while attempting to discover the general conditions for stability. Harrington was an admirer of *Machiavelli and also a philosophical *hedonist, who attempted to vindicate private property and to show that republican government in an essentially capitalist society – a 'commonwealth for increase' – would be the most stable political system. In the course of this he argued for a written constitution, *bicameral government, a *separation of powers, rotation of *offices, secret ballot, indirect election of a *president and many other extremely interesting features of the ideal constitution, which was to be, in his famous words, 'an empire of laws, not of men'. His work was to exert a powerful influence upon many of the Founding Fathers of the US constitution, and to influence the content of that constitution itself. Harrington was imprisoned on a trumped-up charge of treason in 1661, became insane while in prison, and never recovered his wits after his eventual release.

hate speech
A phrase without precise legal meaning which has nevertheless entered political discourse and begun to influence the law. Hate speech includes traditionally recognized forms of insult and abuse, but extends much further to include all kinds of idioms judged innocent by those who make use of them, but perceived as *racist, *sexist, *homophobic etc. by many who do not. The idea of hate speech has influenced recent legislation in the UK in ways that seem to threaten freedom of speech. Public criticism of homosexuality and of Islam are both now potentially criminal in UK law; interestingly the most fervent critics of homosexuality tend to speak in the name of Islam, and vice versa.

Havel, Václav (b. 1936)
Czech writer, former *dissident, and first post-communist President of Czechoslovakia, subsequently President of the Czech Republic. Havel's plays and essays, which were published abroad and in *samizdat during the communist period and subsequently openly in his homeland, contain one of the most important analyses of the nature of late-communist society. In *The Power of the Powerless*, 1978, and *The Politics of Conscience*, 1983, Havel describes this society as 'post-totalitarian', meaning that it no longer makes use of the full apparatus of totalitarian power – such as *terrorism, *show trials, and *genocide – but instead induces a state of mind in which citizens 'live within the lie' and so conform spontaneously to the needs of the bureaucratic state. The communist state does not require that people believe in it, but only that they pretend to believe; it does not openly

deny that it is corrupt and oppressive but merely prevents people from saying so; it does not police every activity, but induces people to police themselves, by ensuring that anybody at any place or time might be reporting back to 'them'. The peculiar *phenomenology of such a society has been matchlessly described in Havel's essays, and he shows the weight of self-induced suffering which must inevitably ensue when people lose all trust in others and live in a state of ironic detachment from themselves.

The communist order is threatened by two things: truth and responsibility. When people take responsibility for their lives, they wish to 'live in truth', to deal honestly with their neighbours, and to banish the lie from their daily actions. They find themselves committed to a politics of *conscience, which brings them inevitably into conflict with the totalitarian order (as Havel was brought into conflict with the Czech state, as a founder member of VONS (the Committee for the Defence of the Unjustly Prosecuted), a conflict that led to a long spell of imprisonment).

Although the post-totalitarian order is particularly destructive of the human conscience, Havel believes that the whole tendency of modern society is towards an anaesthetizing of conscience and an extinction of the sense of responsibility. This can be witnessed in capitalist societies too, and especially in the carelessness towards the earth and its future that is characteristic of industrial production. Human beings can be restored to their natural condition only if they cease to deny the validity of the transcendental and recognize that they are trustees of the earth and not sole proprietors.

As philosopher-statesman Havel recalls the first President of Czechoslovakia, *Masaryk. The principal influence on his political thinking, however, has been *Patočka.

Hayek, F.A. von (1899–1993)
Political philosopher and economist of the *Austrian school, whose denunciation (especially in *The Road to Serfdom*, 1945) of the *totalitarian systems of government imposed upon Europe by Lenin, Hitler and Stalin did much to create the postwar consciousness of liberty at bay. Hayek developed a theory of spontaneous order so as to justify not only the *free market but also the *common law and free association as the fundamental features of any rational and self-regulating society.

All social action requires information about the wants and needs of indefinitely many people; it also requires spontaneous solutions to conflicts. In a free market the price of every good is determined by the totality of human demands for it, and there can be no better indication of the sacrifice which others are prepared to make in order to obtain the good. The information contained in prices is therefore social, dynamic and practical: it is information concerning what to do in order to satisfy the distant wants of strangers. This information could not exist in a single head, since it is available only in the *process* of free interaction, in a society where people are free to buy and sell. Any interference with the market mechanism therefore destroys the information-base upon which rational economic decisions depend. *Planning, which attempts to reconstruct this information as a static set of data, is invariably irrational since, by fixing the direction and parameters of economic life, it destroys the information on which it depends.

The free market is an example of a spontaneous order, which arises by an *invisible hand from free association and which generates of its own accord the solutions to economic problems. In like manner, the common law generates a spontaneous legal order, which, because it grows from particular solutions to particular conflicts, inherently tends to restore society to a state of equilibrium – unlike *statute law, which tries to anticipate conflicts and thereby creates them.

A *classical liberal by inclination, Hayek sees the economic structure of capitalism, however modified by historical contingencies, as an essential part not only of economic prosperity, but also of the freedom of action to which all social beings aspire. Nevertheless, freedom is only possible when guaranteed by a constitution, and it is no easy matter to develop a constitution that permits liberty, while forbidding licence and anarchy. His later work, therefore – notably *The Constitution of Liberty*, 1961 – attempts to give an account of the ideal constitution of a modern capitalist state. The result is a mitigated traditionalism, in which many of the constitutional devices of the Anglo-American political tradition are upheld, as guarantees of stability which also permit the possibility of reform. Hayek supports democracy in principle, but argues that the mechanisms whereby power is exercised in democracies prevent the emergence of genuine *collective choice, and that no political system provides as real an instance of collective choice as is provided by the operation of a market. Moreover, whereas in an economic market each individual acts under a budget constraint, under most majority-rule democracies politicians are under no similar constraint, or at least, not immediately: hence the self-regulating conditions of the market cannot easily be achieved in the political sphere.

head of state

The individual who *represents the state according to law and in international relations. He or she need not in fact wield political power, and the function may be more or less ceremonial. Thus a head of state may be a hereditary *monarch, whose only political act is to *ratify the decisions of others. Alternatively he may be a *president, elected for a certain period, and with enormous *prerogative powers (as in the US), yet subject to review and limitation by a Supreme Court and Congress, in the light of a constitution that is designed precisely for that purpose. He may also be a *dictator or *tyrant, who cannot be removed from office by constitutional means, and who exercises power without fear of legal sanction.

Often supreme executive power may be vested in an individual who is not the head of state, but who submits his decisions to some president or monarch for ratification, even though the head of state has no choice but to ratify (on pain of removal from office, exile or death). In such a case the head of state may serve as a symbol of *authority, acting so as to give sanction to naked *power: but without *some* residual legal powers, it is difficult to see how he might do even this. Such is the attraction of power that popular sentiment is always apt to identify the head of state with the actual holder of power. Thus there arises in the UK what is – from the constitutional point of view – an illusion, namely, that the *Prime Minister is *leader of the nation.

The distinction between head of state and prime minister (or some equivalent distinction, involving the separation of the dignities and ceremonies of state from the actual exercise of power) is sometimes urged as a necessary constitutional device, providing a focus for national loyalties which stands apart from direct involvement in domestic politics, and therefore retains some power to unite warring factions. It also gives symbolic expression to the distinction between power and authority, and emphasizes that political offices are more durable and more important than their passing occupants. On this view it is *important*, and not just eccentric, that the UK head of state has a ceremonial role, is the titular head of the *Anglican Church, has a vestigial royal prerogative, accedes to office by hereditary entitlement rather than by the struggle for power – and so on. All those are, in *Bagehot's thinking, 'dignifying' attributes, which confer authority, and power only in so far as the constitution makes use of that authority.

health

One of the most important issues in modern politics has been that of *welfare provision, in particular provision for the health of citizens who cannot otherwise afford to obtain treatment for their illnesses. While measures to control the outbreak of disease have always been recognized as a public responsibility, the detailed provision of proper medical services to the poor emerged as a political objective only in the nineteenth century. It was introduced for the first time by Bismarck in Prussia, and then gradually imitated by Austro-Hungary, by Tsarist Russia, by England and – most recently – by France. The US continues to debate the merits of public healthcare ('Medicare' and 'Medicaid') as against private insurance. Although President Clinton's scheme for a national health system was defeated in 1995, state-funded hospitals have existed since the nineteenth century and play a major role in offering free treatment to those who cannot afford to pay for it.

Modern arguments tend to focus on the question whether a private medical service – one that is sustained through *contractual relations between doctor and patient, perhaps supported by schemes of private insurance – should survive at all. Arguments of justice, utility and freedom are offered on both sides. They may be summarized thus:

(i) For private medical care. (a) Justice. If someone is prepared to pay for a good, and another prepared to offer it, and if they freely contract between them, is there not an injustice to both parties in making that contract impossible? In particular, is it not unjust to the doctor, whose training (for which he sacrificed time and effort) gives him something that others both need and demand? Moreover, if doctors are supposed to provide their services to all comers for fixed reward, do they not have a right to refuse them? Or is the state entitled to compel them, just because of their qualifications, to work, and perhaps for a reward that lies outside the scope of their asking? (Various embellishments to this theme can be imagined, by taking particular cases, in the manner of *Nozick, and attempting to force the opponent to admit that the doctor's rights are being infringed.)

(b) Utility. If properly rewarded, and according to agreement, resources will be allocated more efficiently than they could be allocated by the state, and facilities would have a constant tendency to improve, through *competition. The poor too must benefit from this and those hours which a doctor may be required to work for the state will be more useful than in arrangements of fully socialized medicine.

(c) Freedom. Patients are less free when, whatever sacrifices they are prepared to make, nothing can be achieved in the way of superior treatment; doctors are less free when their labour hours are commandeered by the state.

(ii) Against private medical care. (a) Justice. Any kind of differential treatment makes it inevitable that better treatment will be available to the rich than to the poor. This means, in effect, that people will be offered differential medical treatment on grounds *other* than their state of health. But the only *relevant* ground for medical treatment is the state of health. All discrimination between people based in grounds irrelevant to the allocation of a good is an injustice. (*See* *social justice.) Hence the rights of the poor are infringed by private medicine.

(b) Utility. The complete socialization of medicine brings into the 'public sector' all the talent that might otherwise gravitate to the exclusive hospital. In comparison to the good done to private patients, the good done to everyone under socialized medicine must surely be greater. (The precise form of the argument here will depend upon which criterion of *optimality is to be chosen.) Moreover, it is in everyone's interest that the population as a whole should be healthy, and therefore both productive and able to defend the country in time of war.

(c) Freedom. The freedom of the rich is indeed enhanced by private medicine: but only at the expense of the freedom of the poor, whose possibilities are seriously diminished by all differentials of this kind.

The dispute captures, in miniature, two classical and recurring positions in the philosophy of social *welfare.

hedonism

1. Psychological: the view that people never pursue anything except pleasure, or the avoidance of pain. They may pretend to be pursuing nobler things, but this is an illusion; moreover, all the particular objects of desire are desired only because of the pleasure that they bring.

2. Philosophical: the view that pleasure and pain are the only criteria in terms of which the *value of any

action may be estimated, and hence must figure as the grounds of all practical reasoning.

Bishop Butler (1692–1752) rebutted psychological hedonism by pointing to the absurdity of the view that if I want a plate of fish, then what I want is really the pleasure produced by it. For then it would be irrational of me to respond with amazement to the offer of a book, a lover or a cocked hat in place of it. Philosophical hedonism has perhaps had more of a following, partly on account of the efforts of *Bentham, partly because it seems to promise a mathematical structure to practical reasoning. But it is probably no more plausible (*see* *value).

Hegel, G.W.F. (1770–1831)

German philosopher, founder, along with *Fichte, of modern *idealism, and perhaps the greatest influence on modern political thought in the German romantic tradition after *Marx, whose outlook he did much to make possible. Hegel's philosophy contains many parts, but of particular concern to politics are the following:

(i) The theory of the *dialectic. In Hegel this has two sides: (a) all reasoning is dialectical, proceeding from the positing of a concept, via the extraction of its negation and the consequent 'labour of the negative', to a new concept which transcends and makes 'determinate' the content of the first. Through the dialectical process a definite reality is gradually 'determined', the universality of the concept finds the 'particularity' of its object, and so generates knowledge. (b) Reality itself has the structure of thought (the fundamental thesis of idealism, which also identifies thought with reasoning). Hence all processes in the world, whether the world of nature or the world of history, exhibit the order and development of the dialectic, passing from 'undifferentiated' beginnings to ever more determinate ends. An example of this is the progress of man himself, from the primitive undifferentiated consciousness of the member of the tribe, to the final self-realized and self-conscious individual, who postulates his ideal aim and satisfaction as his own, and so challenges the world to match his individuality. (In the folds of this progression all human history lies concealed, although only its end result, the German *romantic *individualism exemplified at its highest in Hegel, is immediately knowable.)

(ii) The theory of *self-realization. The dialectical process in the individual is one of steady advance towards the determinate 'self', which is 'for itself'. The individual knows himself through his efforts to create a determinate reality: thus man realizes himself in labour, in art, in political life, and in each case the increasing self-knowledge and increasing power represent a gain in *freedom. (See *self-determination.) In this way Hegel came to view true (realized) human nature as an acquisition, rather than a gift, a fact which coloured his whole political philosophy. In particular he argued that social interaction *precedes* the creation of the individual, and so cannot be explained as a matter of individual choice. His complex account of self-realization includes the celebrated theories of *alienation, and of the relation between *master and slave.

(iii) The theory of history. History is the human spirit writ large – the 'march of reason in the world' – and its movement must inevitably exemplify the dialectical movement that is contained in every manifestation of the spirit. (See *Geist.) Hence it proceeds from undifferentiated union (the equivalent of the pure concept of 'Being' from which the dialectic begins), through struggle and opposition (see *master and slave), to

the highest forms of self-consciousness. Self-consciousness thereby emerges from the conflicts of religion (alienation), into the pure air of science, which sees everything as it is, since for science appearance has become transparent to essence. (See *essence/appearance.) At every period the spirit manifests itself as a specific *Zeitgeist, determining the forms of social life, political order, knowledge, religion and art. The *progressivist tendency in Hegel is mitigated by his sense that reflective knowledge arrives always too late ('the owl of Minerva spreads its wings only at the gathering of the dusk'), so that the understanding of the human condition vouchsafed to him was also the guarantee that he could not remedy it.

(iv) The theory of the state. In *The Philosophy of Right*, 1821, Hegel produced an extremely succinct exposition of law, politics, and morality, in which he proposed the state as the highest expression of man's freedom, resulting from the transcendence of the (philosophically antecedent) conditions of *family and (in dialectical opposition to it) *civil society. The elements of the theory are these: (a) The bond of the family is not contractual but one of *piety. The family is an indispensable 'moment' (a term not to be understood in a temporal sense) of political existence, without which the free being cannot emerge; (b) civil society is the sphere of justice, in which men freely secure and contract away their rights. Here the theory of the *social contract may seem to give a picture of social union, but only because those 'contracting' already possess the *autonomy which the family provides and which the state protects; (c) the unstable opposition between particularized loyalty to the family and universal loyalty to all free (contracting) beings is transcended and resolved in a new, self-conscious, but non-contractual, obligation that orders all conflicting claims – that to the state, as the body of institutions which express, uphold and endorse the laws through which conflict is resolved. The state becomes the highest expression of man's freedom, and allegiance to it a necessary condition of full self-realized individuality; (d) *private property is justified as a necessary part of the dialectical process displayed in (a) to (c), as are *marriage, retributive punishment and adherence to a written code of law.

hegemony

Greek: *hegemon*, a chief or ruler. Term used since the nineteenth century to denote the influence of one state over others; hence 'hegemonism', which describes the politics of those powers that cow their neighbours and dependants into submission.

In political thought the term is now as often used in the sense given to it by *Gramsci, in which it denotes the ascendancy of a *class, not only in the economic sphere, but through all social, political and ideological spheres, and its ability thereby to persuade other classes to see the world in terms favourable to its own ascendancy. Gramsci advocated the construction of a rival hegemony, through the infiltration and transformation of those small-scale institutions by which class ascendancy, once achieved, is sustained. This struggle for hegemony is seen as a transforming factor as important as any development of *productive forces, and corresponds to *Lenin's 'subjective conditions' for revolution.

Heidegger, Martin (1889–1976)

German philosopher and the founder of modern *existentialism. Heidegger's early works are inspired by the *phenomenology of Husserl, though written in a peculiar idiom which is entirely his own. In *Being and Time* (1927) Heidegger writes of the situation of *Dasein*, by which he means self-conscious existence, arguing that *Dasein* has both being (*Sein*) and the 'question of being'. The philosophical quest is an attempt to confront that question, to come to terms with the condition in which we are placed by our ability to ask 'why?'. Initially *Dasein* exists in a condition of 'thrown-ness' (*Geworfenheit*), in a world of objects whose essence consists in their 'being-to-hand'. The 'question of being' induces a condition of anxiety (*Angst*), which tempts *Dasein* into roles dictated by Others – by 'them'. The solution to this problem is not to adopt those roles, but to embark on the path of *authenticity. This leads at last, by devious routes, to an attitude of 'care' (*Sorge*), and thence to the condition which Heidegger calls resoluteness in the face of our 'being-towards-death', in which *Dasein* lives in conscious acceptance of its own finitude.

Heidegger's metaphysics is obscure and derived from idiosyncratic arguments concerning the etymology of words (usually words of ancient Greek). Its notorious conclusions (such as the dictum that 'Nothing noths' (*Das Nichts nichtet*)) and its fearsome abstraction have led to its being dismissed as nonsense by *positivists, and confined to the museum of culture by many continental writers. However, in later essays Heidegger escaped from the prison of his early style and developed his vision of philosophy as a form of *hermeneutics. He wrote pertinently of social matters, producing a profound critique of technological society, and an invocation of the true condition of the human being, as a creature who *dwells* in the earth and who must consecrate his being here. His essays on poetry, architecture and culture have been widely admired – by romantic *conservatives who find in them an invocation of natural society, by *green activists who find in them the philosophical justification for a politics which puts nature before people, and by *deconstructionists, who derive many of their concepts from Heidegger's approach to the written word. However, Heidegger's links with the *Nazis, thanks to whom he became Rector of Freiburg University during the 1930s, have cast a cloud over his reputation. Some commentators point to the fact that connection with, and even participation in, *totalitarian movements of the *left have never cast any comparable cloud over the career of those many intellectuals (*Lukács, for example) who stand accused of it. Nevertheless, it would be far more reasonable to condemn both Lukács and Heidegger than to absolve either.

hellenism

Admiration for, and imitation of, ancient Greek *virtues: in the political sphere this involves admiring and attempting to sustain the vision of public life celebrated by Thucydides in words attributed to Pericles: 'Our constitution is called a democracy because power is in the hands not of a minority but of the whole people. When it is a question of settling private disputes, everyone is equal before the law; when it is a question of putting one person before another in positions of public responsibility, what counts is not membership of a particular class, but the actual ability which the man possesses . . . and just as our political life is free, so is our day-to-day dealing between ourselves . . . free and tolerant in our private lives, in public matters obedient to the law' (*Peloponnesian War* 2, 37). Associated with that idealized vision of *Athenian democracy is the respect for the ancient virtues of courage, honour and endurance. In the writings of *Arnold,

Hellenism, as a social and political ideal, is contrasted with 'Hebraism', the detailed dependence on the dictatorial will of God.

helot

See *Sparta.

Helvétius, Claude-Adrien (1715–71)

French writer and philosopher, heavily influenced by the empiricist epistemology and psychology of *Locke, who was a major influence on French Enlightenment thought, and the founding father of *utilitarianism.

All human activity is directed towards physical pleasure (*sensibilité physique*), and all institutions should be judged in terms of their utility in providing it. Human beings can be changed for the better only by manipulating their passions, and not by exhortation or advice; nevertheless education is a universal benefit. The improvement of society requires the reform of political institutions, so as to ensure that the best people enjoy the most pleasure. In his posthumous work *De l'homme* (1772) Helvétius saw Christianity, with its other-worldly morality, and the French monarchy, with its outmoded feudal structures, as the two greatest obstacles to social and political reform.

Herder, Johann Gottfried von (1744–1803)

German philosopher and critic, a powerful intellectual opponent of the *Enlightenment, and a force behind the *romantic movement in Germany and central Europe. Herder emphasized the active nature of the human mind, and argued against *empiricist views of knowledge and experience, on account of their attempt to construe all knowledge as a passive reception, and also on account of their inability to explain the true complexity of *language, *culture and social life. He expounded an influential philosophy of history, and a view of language as expression, according to which the language of a people encapsulates not only its common experiences, but also its historical identity and an underlying consciousness of unity. This unity is expressed through cultural artifacts, but it is also in part constituted by them. Language is therefore seen as the repository of all that is distinctive of and precious to the group who speak it. In due course, as a result of Herder's influence, language was to become the object of solicitious political feelings. Thus he inspired many of the romantic *nationalist movements of central Europe, which sought to use language and culture to provide the 'natural' political boundaries which the various imperial alignments had obliterated. *See also *Volksgeist, *Volksstaat.

hereditary principle

The principle either that there are hereditary *natural rights (e.g. the right of a child to enjoy some part of its deceased parents' *property), or that there ought to be (for whatever reason) hereditary legal rights. (For the distinction here, *see further* *positive law.) The two important hereditary rights generally considered are: title to property, and title to *nobility (construed as conveying social and political *privilege). The second is sometimes thought to be a late arrival in European legal systems; according to *Maitland, for example, titles such as 'earl' originally denoted offices, and only later, under Norman influence, were these offices thought of as hereditary – a feature which Maitland significantly describes as the 'tendency of every office to become hereditary, to become property' (*Constitutional History of England*, 1908), as though the inheritance of property is so natural a thing as to *explain* the inheritance of political

rights and privileges. However, this extension of the hereditary principle to offices is probably only a rationalization of widespread feelings about family and kinship which manifest themselves even in expressly anti-aristocratic governments, such as those of the US and France.

Many who do not object to the inheritance of property rights as such, nevertheless object to the inheritance of political status (as under the *apartheid system) and especially the inheritance of office, as under the peerage system, even though the acquisition of property may confer political advantages that far outweigh the very slight political privilege conferred by membership of a house of *peers. In the last case, this is partly because *titles* of nobility have an independent significance, as part of a system of *honours – and it seems absurd that anyone should bear an honour that he has not earned. However, conservatives such as *Burke have thought that inherited status is useful for the generation of a permanent and competent political class, united by bonds of family across generations, and so committed to the maintenance of social continuity; this argument, if it justifies titles, also justifies inherited property.

The arguments over the hereditary principle in the UK are of less significance since the abolition of the hereditary House of Lords. It is clear that inheritance, whether of title or property, may lead to extraordinary powers being conferred on idiots, degenerates and fools. However, it is also clear that democratic election is equally likely to lead to great power being placed in the hands of idiots, degenerates and fools, so that arguments conducted at this level remain inconclusive, not to say ridiculous. It seems that the main conservative arguments *for* the principle concentrate rather on the ideas of continuity and *tradition, and the effect of hereditary office in defusing the urgency of the scramble for power, and tempering ambition and preferment with safe expectation and leisure – attributes which may be necessary in government, but not easily acquired through professional politics. The main liberal and socialist arguments against the principle seem to dwell first on ideas of *social justice, secondly upon the supposed obnoxiousness of class distinctions and class rule.

Hereditary *monarchy is probably the only remaining instance of the legal inheritance of a politically significant public office, though many ceremonial offices and functions are still inherited in the UK.

heredity and environment

Of vital consequence and almost impenetrable intricacy, the dispute as to the roles of heredity and environment in forming the moral and social attributes of people underlies many of the current conflicts of political opinion. *Racism emphasizes what it takes to be the overwhelming importance of heredity in determining not only intelligence and temperament, but also customs, character, morals – indeed, in its extreme form, everything from table manners to political doctrine. Likewise those accused of *sexism often complain that they seek only to affirm that the inherited characteristic of sex is sufficient to determine, independently of social environment, different patterns of thought, feeling and social response among men and women. (In other words, sex determines *gender.)

The revulsion against *eugenics is in part responsible for the current reluctance to consider heredity as a relevant factor in the treatment accorded to individuals. The obvious moral and scientific difficulties posed by the testing of any particular theory, combined with the somewhat obscure and perhaps irrelevant evidence provided by the breeding of 'character' in animals, must in any case lead to caution. (But see *bell curve.) It must also encourage the development of a theory of rights that does not depend upon the truth of any particular hypothesis. If, for example, you have to believe that there is no inherited difference in intelligence, aggressivity, etc. between blacks and whites in order to accord equal rights to both, that surely shows that your doctrine of rights – in pre-empting the answer to an unsettled scientific question – is confused, or at least ill-considered. (A sophisticated, perhaps sophistical, rejoinder has it that to treat such questions as though they are 'scientific' is *already* racist: see *scientism.)

hermeneutics

The science of interpretation, traditionally applied to the discovery of the real but hidden meanings of sacred texts (specifically the Gospels), but given a more universal interpretation by *Schleiermacher and then, much later, by *Heidegger. As currently understood, the term denotes the activity of understanding the world not as a physical system, but as an object of human thought and action (as *Lebenswelt* or 'human world'). The premises of modern hermeneutics (derived in part from the work of *Dilthey) are: (i) that scientific explanation is not the only form of understanding (see *Verstehen); (ii) that we understand the human world only through asking questions of it, and every question is determined in form and content by an interest that underlies it; (iii) that a question already embodies a partial interpretation of the thing questioned. From these premises arises the 'hermeneutical circle': no interpretation is possible until interpretation has begun. This is supposed not to be a vicious circle, but simply to reflect the fact that our world exists as an object of consciousness only in and through language, which is the continuous expression of our being.

The more specialized applications of hermeneutics in literary criticism have remained recondite and obscure. However, the underlying vision has had considerable influence on continental (especially German) social and political thought. Thus *Gadamer has propagated hermeneutics as a supposed 'method', appropriate to the social sciences, that will avoid the fallacies of *scientism. He has also attempted to give a philosophical account of the nature of *tradition. Since there is no *first* question asked of the human world but only a continuous flow of never-ending questions and answers, it is only through immersion in that continuity that social reality can be understood. The continuity involves language, culture and social interaction (both the last two themselves offshoots of language), and immersion in that continuity is what is meant by 'tradition'.

hierarchy

Greek: sacred rule. Term adopted to denote the power given by Christ to his apostles and their successors to form and govern the *church. It is now used more widely to denote any system in which the distributions of *power, *privilege and *authority are both systematic and unequal. The result is a society arranged according to 'degree', with power, privilege and authority varying together. Such an arrangement was defended by Shakespeare's Ulysses in *Troilus and Cressida*. Act I, scene iii: 'Take but degree away, untune that string, and/ Hark what discord follows!' – a speech that asserts an indissoluble connection between the existence of degree and the perception of the world in terms of *right and authority, rather than in terms of power. Thus for many of Shakespeare's day the structure of hierarchy seemed necessary in order for power to be perceived as legitimate rather than arbitrary, and hence for justice to be a live social value. *See* *legitimacy.

Hindu law

A system of law whose *jurisdiction is not determined by the boundaries of a state but by adherence to a religion. Its sources are in ancient Sanskrit texts (e.g. the Upanishads), and its aim, as in *Jewish or *Islamic law, is to provide practical guidance for those who seek to be righteous in the eyes of God. It upholds the *caste system, and determines family law and rights of inheritance. Following British rule in India, and the subsequent efforts to evolve a genuine national law, Hindu law fell into disrepute. It is to some extent protected from extinction by its obscurity, and by its organic closeness to the *customs around which it is built. The Janata Party (BJP) from time to time campaigns to revive Hindu law – a fact that Indian Muslims tend to view with alarm.

historical jurisprudence

The study that tries to find the nature and meaning of *law through its historical development, rather than through the reasoning given for the enactments of *legislators. It is associated with *Vico and *Montesquieu, and has been exemplified by thinkers as diverse as *Burke, who saw law as the final conscious reflection of a spirit that has its true significance in unconscious custom, and F.C. von Savigny (1779–1861), perhaps its most important exponent. Savigny argued against the Napoleonic codification of German law on the ground that law is discovered not made: in the course of this argument he produced a classic statement of the benefits of *common law and the harm of *statute. Recent exponents of the argument include *Hayek.

historical materialism

The fundamental tenet of *Marxism in all its 'classical' varieties. History is the product not of conscious decisions and ideas (*see* *voluntarism*), but of 'material' processes and conditions which can be identified and described without reference to the mental states of those who participate in them. (*See* *materialism*.) It is the changes in these material conditions which make necessary and bring about those changes in social, political and institutional *superstructures which in aggregate form the substance of history. The process of change has been variously described as *dialectical (*see* *dialectical materialism*), as one of unceasing development of *productive forces, and as a *class struggle in which the participants are driven by their economic condition to act as they do. Although it is likely that these ideas are not mutually compatible, Marxists have often assumed that they are.

historicism

A term with many meanings, of which the three principal ones are:

1. The view that no society or period of history can be understood exclusively in terms of ideas current at the time of understanding, but that each period must be seen in terms of ideas contemporary to it. (This may be advanced as part of the general doctrine of *Verstehen*, and clearly leads to paradoxical consequences if taken to extremes: for how can I understand the conceptions of a former time except by translating them into conceptions of my own?)

2. (In the writings of *Popper.) Any belief in over-arching laws of historical development, such as those expounded by *Hegel, *Marx and *Spengler, which claim to reveal the necessity in historical processes and which have the effect of subduing or undermining the belief in human *agency and ingenuity. Popper criticizes historicism as such, arguing that it is a mask for uncritical attachment to *totalitarian *ideology, using the 'inevitability' of history as the justification for acts of tyranny and arbitrary violence. He also criticizes individual historicist theories by attempting to show that they are so phrased as to be compatible with any seemingly recalcitrant experience, and so, being irrefutable, are empty of empirical content.

3. (Especially in architectural theory, e.g. that of the early Pevsner.) The love of and *nostalgia for the culture of a previous age, and the attempt to recapture it by stylistic imitation in the absence of the social conditions that made it possible, or which gave to it the character of a sincere expression. (Thus the Gothic revival has been criticized as historicist, although it is often replied that every architectural style has begun as 'historicist' in this sense: *see* *architecture*.)

historicity

1. Term used by *Heidegger to refer to the fact that human consciousness gains part of its significance from its nature as a historical phenomenon, immersed in temporal processes which are larger than itself. Human understanding involves grasping the historicity of experience and situating oneself in the flow of time.

2. In Marxist usage, the historicity of institutions means their nature as historical phenomena, to be understood in terms of the 'material conditions' that produced them.

historiography

See *history.

history

Now used in two senses: **1**. The process of change in human societies over time.

2. The art of describing that process. The term 'historiography' has recently been invented in place of sense 2.

Theories of history in sense 1. are attempts to give general 'laws of motion' for human societies. Examples include:

(i) Hegel's theory, that human history is the expression of *Geist, as it 'unfolds' through successive stages of its 'realization'. This theory is both *progressivist, and also *idealist.

(ii) *Historical materialism, as espoused by *Marx, which is *progressivist and *materialist.

(iii) Cyclical theories, such as those offered by *Vico and *Spengler.

(iv) *Conspiracy theories, which identify human intention as the motor of historical change.

Theories of history in sense 2. are attempts to distinguish the methods of the historian from those of the natural scientist. Some writers treat history as the writing of a chronicle of events: such was the ancient practice. Others believe that all history is also interpretation, and that history is distinguished from the writing of chronicles by the act of *Verstehen which is its pre-condition. (*See also* *hermeneutics.) It is probably true that the controversy over historical method now consumes much of the energy of historians, partly because there is so little further room for argument about the facts.

Hitler, Adolf (1889–1945)

German statesman and Nazi leader. *See* *absolutism, *appeasement, *concordat, *culture, *Führerprinzip, *Gleichschaltung, *Hayek, *ideology, *myth, *national socialism, *persuasive definition, *Spengler, *sport.

Hobbes, Thomas (1588–1679)

English political theorist and philosopher. A royalist, whose perception of the chaos and brutality of the Civil War, and consequent attempt to understand the conditions of peace and good government, was combined with a sceptical, largely *empiricist outlook on human knowledge and society. Hobbes wrote several political works, and his *Leviathan*, 1651, is one of the few universally recognized masterpieces of political theory (and also one of the great stylistic achievements in English). He attempted in that work to give a systematic account of *human nature, *sovereignty, *political obligation and *law, free from limitation to any particular social or political predicament. To understand sovereignty, he thought, we should first try to understand the condition of man without it. He believed in natural law, as a system of principles the validity of which all rational beings will recognize, but thought that natural law could not be enforced or obeyed in a *state of nature, which is a state of the 'war of every man against every man', since natural law has *authority, but no intrinsic *power. Security lies in a kind of *social contract, first, between people, to set up the sovereign who will command and protect them, and, perhaps derivatively, between each person severally and the sovereign power under which he places himself, and on whom he confers the power to enforce the contract with his fellows. (Although it should be noted that the sovereign is in some sense 'outside' the original contract and can therefore forfeit his right to obedience only if he fails entirely to deliver protection.) Sovereignty may be embodied in one person or in an assembly of people, but once established, it has absolute authority in making law, and can be rejected by the *subject only by an act of *rebellion which, in breaking the contract which confers supreme entitlement on the sovereign, must always amount to injustice.

The state of nature must be thought of, not as a state which precedes the institution of sovereignty, but as a state which will certainly follow upon its dissolution. It is also a state in which sovereigns exist in relation to each other, since here too there is no overriding sovereign whose command has the force of law. The complete absence of any power that will enforce rights in a state of nature confers an absolute obligation on the subject to obey the sovereign in return for whatever rights the sovereign may guarantee. It seems then, that there can be no justification for *civil disobedience, although Hobbes somewhat inconsistently goes on to argue that there are real limits imposed on the legitimacy of state action by that natural law which, without the state, could never be upheld.

Hobbes's thought shows considerable similarity to that of *Bodin, and together they have been thought of as the supreme theorists of *absolutism, although what emerges from Hobbes – on one reading at least – is an argument that justifies government absolutely, and *limited government as the preferred variety. He attempted to lay bare the components of the institution of sovereignty in a manner that is certainly original, and which has often been thought to be exemplary. His principle that there can be 'no obligation on any man which ariseth not from some act of his own' introduces a great strain into his theory, however, in that it seems to suggest that all legitimacy and political obligation must

eventually be traced to contract or consent. His attempt to find the basis of natural law in the inherent injustice of requiring a person to destroy his own life was influential on later thinkers – notably *Locke – but leads to obscure reasoning about all subsidiary 'natural rights'.

holism

1. The theory that the whole is more than the sum of its parts, exhibiting what *Hegel called the 'transition from quantity to quality'. Thus it might be argued that a society is something greater than the aggregate of individuals which composes it, since it has features, and performs actions, which cannot be attributed to any aggregate. (For example, a society has laws and institutions which outlast the individuals subject to them.)

One part of that metaphysical doctrine is the view (variously espoused by *Burke, *Hegel and certain *Marxists) that the individual acquires part of his nature from the historical totality of which he is part. Thus Robinson Crusoe according to *Marx (*Grundrisse*) is not really an 'atomic' individual, but rather a personification of all the social attributes of *bourgeois economy, arbitrarily transported to an empty place. To think that his nature, aims, intentions and values, and the conception of freedom so integral to his dramatic function, could belong to him independently of the historical condition that defines him, is like thinking that the hand of a human being might have performed all its functions even though severed from the body.

2. The view that, in some cases – e.g. that of organic life, perhaps that of social life – only 'holistic explanation' is possible. That is, the behaviour of each part must be explained in terms of a theory which makes essential reference to laws governing the whole.

3. A term of abuse sometimes used (e.g. by *Popper) for anti-individualistic philosophies of *history, with no more precise meaning than that which can be assigned to *collectivism in its more popular sense. *See* *individualism.

4. The philosophical system of Jan Smuts (1870–1950), South African statesman, who believed that the holistic laws of biological development had their counterpart in human society. He therefore emphasized the 'holistic factor' in history, in opposition to the supposed effect of individual decisions.

Clearly all of the above theories exhibit different departures from the same basic idea.

holocaust
Greek: the burning of everything. Term adopted by Jewish historians for the *genocide of the Jews practised by the *Nazis and named by the latter more euphemistically 'the final solution' (*Endlösung*). The term is traditional, but was first used in its modern sense by the Romanian Jewish writer Elie Wiesel.

home
See *household.

home rule
The aspiration of Irish *nationalists in the nineteenth century and adopted as a slogan by their successors in the twentieth. Home rule is contrasted with rule by the English from Westminster: it means rule of Ireland by the Irish, according to laws and institutions of their own. By extension, any rule which results in *autonomy after breaking from a colonial power.

home schooling
A movement begun in the US in the 1970s, and now gathering momentum, in which families, acting singly or in neighbourhood groups, educate their children at home, using textbooks and study guides provided by firms specializing in this form of teaching. Opposed by the US Department of Education as counter to laws imposing compulsory education, home schooling was held to be a right under the Constitution by the Supreme Court, following a long campaign by the Amish (a Christian community that has resolutely refused to belong to the modern world). To some extent the right exists elsewhere, notably in the UK, where it is subject, however, to severe scrutiny by the educational inspectorate, in order to ascertain that the parents are qualified to teach and able and willing to do so.

homophobia
Aversion to *homosexuality of a passionate kind, that might express itself in acts of violence, and in prejudicial treatment generally. The term has also been used to suggest that criticism of *homosexuality is either irrational, or based in a pathological condition which may be legitimately deprived of a voice. *See* *phobia.

homosexuality
The issue of homosexual conduct has come to the fore in recent political debates for four reasons:

(i) Liberalization of the law (in the UK by the Sexual Offences Act 1967) has brought with it a change in social attitudes, so that the stigma attached to homosexuality has to a great extent disappeared.

(ii) Campaigns for *gay rights – especially in the US – have taken on an increasingly radical character, arguing for an end to all forms of discrimination against homosexuality, and even for the legalization of *gay marriages.

(iii) The outbreak of AIDS, initially spread in Western countries by homosexual activity between males, has led to accusations and counter-accusations, often of a bitter kind.

(iv) The condemnation of homosexuality by orthodox *Islam has led to a growing conflict in Europe.

The issue of 'gay rights' should be distinguished from that of the 'gay culture'. Many people believe that homosexuals should suffer no legal disability and should be allowed to engage in homosexual conduct in private (provided that the act occurs between 'consenting adults'), without believing that homosexuality is either normal or morally acceptable. Such people might actively seek to confine homosexuality to the private sphere, to forbid or curtail its public display, and to prevent schools from teaching children that it is a normal or acceptable option on a par with heterosexual union. Proponents of 'gay pride' respond that, so long as homosexuality is regarded as abnormal or reprehensible, its practitioners will suffer from direct and indirect infringements of civil liberties, and that only a culture of display can secure for them the rights which are or ought to be guaranteed by the state.

The issues here are vast and complex. Traditional sexual morality was as severe towards adultery and fornication as towards homosexual intercourse. Indeed, it permitted intercourse only within marriage, and as a result would represent marriage as a higher state – even a *sacrament. Some argue that homosexual union between men shows a tendency towards promiscuity which is not only dangerous from the medical point of view, but also the true source of the disapproval with which homosexuality has traditionally been regarded. It is difficult to see what, in modern (perhaps we should say *postmodern) conditions follows from this, though the strong condemnation of homosexuality by *Islam is now a serious cause of social conflict in Europe. *See* *homophobia, *sexual conduct.

honour

The recognition bestowed on *virtue. Honour is part of reputation, and the pursuit of it is an art upon which the Greek *polis* depended. To acquire honour a person must persuade others both to recognize his superiority and to feel themselves not diminished but enhanced by it. This cannot be done without *grace, liberality and style. Honouring someone is in a certain sense the opposite of envying him. Hence the pursuit of honour is an important force in creating harmonious societies – a fact recognized by *Aristotle.

honours

The 'honours system', whereby public service is recognized through conferring an intangible benefit such as a title, membership of an order of knighthood, a medal, or some similar right to sport ribbons on one's chest and letters about one's name, is widely accepted as a necessary feature of government. In the US, however, it exists only in an attenuated form – this being regarded by some as the effect of democratic informality, by others as one of those far-reaching consequences of a *constitution which set out to remake the social world. In the UK, by contrast, it provides one of the essential motives both for civil servants, and for all others who may attract the attention of the public.

Against the honours system it is sometimes argued that it helps to form and perpetuate distinctions of *class (which is an argument only if such distinctions are bad); that it distributes privilege inequitably; that it forms and consolidates a ruling or dominant *establishment within the state (again only an argument if that can be shown to be bad). In its favour the argument is brought that it rewards loyalty to the state with a purely symbolic entitlement, and that the desire for this symbolic recognition is both purer than the pursuit of naked power or wealth, and more immediately consonant with the continuing loyalty of the subject who has acquired it: a title, for example, being a dignity to live up to, rather than an asset to dispense.

In the UK it should be noted that honours include peerages, and hence may involve the direct gift of political *office, even as a reward for writing operas (as in the case of Benjamin Britten). This anomaly has to some extent been rectified, now that peerages are liberally scattered among cronies, regardless of their personal merit or public service. Few, however, regard this as an improvement.

Hooker, Richard (1553–1600)
English divine and political theorist whose *Laws of Ecclesiastical Polity*, 1593 onwards, contains an examination of the theoretical principles behind the idea of an established church. Hooker reinterpreted the theories of *natural law, and other features of the political philosophy of *Aquinas, in order to fit them for the new constitutional position of the Anglican Church. He also anticipated many arguments that were to reappear in *Locke (whom he greatly influenced), and tried to demonstrate how the secular and religious authority could be combined into a single sovereign power, while still permitting a real distinction in practice between the legitimate and illegitimate exercise of power. While the body of his work is ostensibly concerned with the organization of a church under the principles of revealed religion, it contains many important disquisitions upon political problems generally, and on the concepts of *law, *justice, and *jurisdiction. Hooker, like Hobbes and Bacon, is esteemed as one of the great prose stylists in English.

Horkheimer, Max (1895–1973)
German philosopher and social scientist. *See* *critical theory, *Frankfurt school, *Habermas, *mass production.

hospitality
Hospitality is in many societies a sacred duty, and almost always so among *nomads. It requires that food, shelter and gifts be offered to someone who is not part of the *family or *community, simply because he finds himself temporarily in the same *household. Hospitality requires the relinquishing, passing or extending of a right of property, and anyone who argues that there should be no private property argues by implication that there should be no private hospitality. Hospitality is a form of *gift, but most gifts are not obligations. The difference presumably lies in the fact that, within the household, property is already embodied in a common right of use – 'mine', as *Hegel puts it, over-reaches itself into 'ours'. Hence, to invite someone into the household is to invite him to share in a common right, and the obligation arises ceremonially to confer that right upon him.

hostages
The practice of hostage-taking is ancient, and traditionally governed by the morality of the *jus in bello* (*see* *just war). Hostages could be voluntarily surrendered as a pledge of good behaviour or taken by force in order to secure it. For *Christian morality, however, the taking of hostages outside the rules of just war, and in order to secure some objective without the risk of fighting, has always been abhorrent. *Islamists in the modern world have damaged their cause by this practice, although it is uncertain

what tactic should be used in response to them. The rules of just war suggest that, while taking innocent people hostage against their will is wrong, the appropriate response to this wrong is to take hostages in turn and to bargain for the release of the original victims. But to carry this tactic through requires a ruthlessness that few democratically elected governments possess.

hours of work

Ever since the radical reformers and socialists of the nineteenth century advocated the 'shortening of the working day' as the first objective of *welfare legislation, a move towards limited hours of work has become the norm in developed economies. It seems that the normal working week has settled at about 40 hours since the last war. Among the professional classes the average is higher, indicating either increased incentive, or increased sense of obligation, to work, or perhaps a function that requires hours of work beyond those contracted for. European legislation restricting the hours of work has become extremely controversial, since it is a way in which a country with severe unemployment like France or Germany can undermine the competitiveness of one with full or near full employment like the UK.

household

With a few exceptions, recent political theory has neglected to discuss the institutions for which 'household' is the collective name, and which exemplify a peculiar synthesis of *private and *common ownership: private in that there is a *right to exclude; common, in that this right is shared indivisibly among members whose number may be indeterminate. Along with their defences of the *family as the first locus of social existence, *Aristotle and *Hegel each argued for this specific mode of ownership, Hegel finding in it new reason for the defence of private property. The household is the forum of consumption, and its stability is integral to social and political stability. However it is formed (whether out of one family or many, as a *commune or as a nuclear family, contractually or non-contractually), its behaviour and nature will be of equal interest to both economists and political theorists. One general political characteristic of the household has been the frequent absence of any legal determination of property rights within it, the presumption of common ownership being paramount (unless expressly disavowed, e.g. by a contract ancillary to marriage). Another traditional characteristic of some significance is the *division of labour within the household (often according to sex and age), which seems to be independent of the existence of a *market. A market can exist between members of a household only by dividing the household into several.

Houses of Parliament

See *Parliament.

human capital

Term that first appeared in 1961 in an *American Economic Review* article, 'Investment in Human Capital' by Theodore W. Shultz. Economists have since loaded much baggage on to the concept but most agree that skills, experience and knowledge, embodied in human beings, are a species of capital, which plays an indispensable part in the generation of profit. The point is that old divisions of the *factors of production, which separate *capital from *labour, fail to take note of the fact that both involve long-term and short-term investments, and contribute to the profit-making process in comparable ways. *See also* *social capital.

human nature

All political *doctrine must be founded in a theory of human nature, and disputes commonly reflect differences (whether or not argued) over what this nature is. Thus it seems that communism must assume that the aggressive, acquisitive, competitive and dominion-seeking feelings of human beings (which lead them to pursue and secure private property, status, and hegemony) are not natural, but the product of changeable social conditions. Likewise liberalism must assume that the desire for freedom is natural and fulfillable, and that its fulfilment will contribute to human happiness. Many conservatives argue as though human nature were entirely inscrutable, revealed by the actual facts of human history, but not easily describable except in terms which are either too platitudinous to found a distinctive doctrine, or too much the product of doctrine to have any universal value. It may certainly be true that the *monism of much socialist and liberal thought – the first emphasizing almost exclusively questions of ownership and control, the second those of liberty – must indicate a simplified view of the nature of the political being. But the scepticism of much conservative doctrine exemplifies a similar simplification, often emphasizing the ineffability of human things only in order to dignify its own reluctance to remedy them.

Philosophers have found a recurrent problem in the seeming duality of human nature. Human beings are organisms, obeying laws of growth and decline. They are also *rational beings, as are gods and angels. It seems difficult to resist the view that each of those attributes determines a nature or essence of the thing that possesses it. Thus there are well-known philosophical problems concerning the possibility that the organism might continue without the attributes of the rational being, or that the rational being might continue without the attributes of the organism. Is this vegetable really identical with John, the victim of the accident? And is this new body, which has all John's character, memories, intentions and thoughts, not perhaps really John, translated into a new existence? Those intuitive problems – which seem to suggest a separation between person and body – also give support to philosophical theories that define the rational agent wholly without reference to his body, either in the manner of Descartes (the 'Cartesian ego') or in the manner of *Kant (the transcendental self, which has a perspective *on* the empirical world, but no identity within it). Kant's idea of the rational being as entirely *autonomous, standing apart from the laws of empirical nature, provides the philosophical basis for the concept of autonomous choice, or choice in which the whole self is implicated. This concept is necessary in formulating the underlying values of liberalism. Hence the Kantian theory of human nature often recurs, in however transmuted a form, in modern political thinking. Followers of *Hegel object that the autonomous being of Kant is a social artifact; he should therefore be seen as the product of a political order and not as the atom from which that order is constructed. This reversal of metaphysical priorities brings about a profound shift in political focus. From this rival view of human nature the liberal standpoint is often found far less plausible. *Idealists have further criticized the political outlook of *empiricists and *utilitarians largely on account of a supposed naivety in the vision of human nature underlying it. The deep questions aroused by that conflict remain the overt or covert subject-matter of much modern debate.

human rights

A label designed (a) to denote the idea of *natural rights, (b) to propagate and win sympathy for that idea in the peculiar political atmosphere of the modern world. Since the doctrine of natural rights is rehearsed and endorsed in the US constitution (following the *Virginia Declaration of Rights* of 1776), and since fairly specific rights are therein associated with it and declared to be binding, the idea of human rights has also come to be seen as an *ideological conception, behind the veil of which the interests of *international capitalism take their devious way. Human rights of a fairly standard kind (including freedom of speech, worship, and peaceful assembly) are endorsed in the UN Charter (exercised through a UN commission that can at least report on their absence, if not assure their presence), and more recently in the Helsinki Accord of 1975, which tried to use international sanctions in order to compel the respect for human rights in states not given to upholding them.

The Helsinki agreement is interesting in that it posed a fundamental problem for the philosophy of *rights: are all rights really *freedoms, in the sense of being limitations on the acts of others? Or are some rights also duties, requiring the active provision of something not available without human effort? The first list of rights, proposed by nations of the Western alliance, followed the pattern of freedom – i.e. it consisted in a set of limitations on what the state might *do* to the citizens (e.g. arrest them arbitrarily, imprison them without trial, punish them for receiving 'forbidden' literature, and so on). The states of the Soviet bloc insisted that certain other rights should be added – notably the *right to work, which requires the state (or, if not the state, some other *agency) actively to provide opportunities, and not merely to

permit things to happen. It may be doubted that such a 'positive' conception of rights is coherent; nevertheless it proved useful in the subsequent international rhetoric.

The problems facing the defender of human rights are threefold: (a) Is the doctrine that there are natural rights defensible? (b) Which rights are natural, and which merely local? (c) Can a natural right always override a conventional (or legal) right that conflicts with or denies it? Most theories neglect to answer those questions and end up with lists of rights that are either too wide (e.g. the *four freedoms), or too narrow, to be universally applicable. (Consider the attempt to impose the idea of 'human rights' upon an Islamic state like Iran.) The UK Human Rights Act 1997, incorporating the rights specified under the *European Convention on Human Rights, has proved particularly controversial, since it has been used to override long-standing provisions of planning and administrative law on which important expectations have been built. This is partly because it seems to permit the assertion of *group rights, which privilege one group of citizens over others.

There is one human right which seems, however, to command universal assent when understood, and to precipitate the transition from *tyranny to constitutional government when upheld – the right to *due process and to the *judicial independence which that requires.

humane education

Term used since the early Renaissance to denote those subjects which were traditionally (in Roman schools of *rhetoric and their tributaries) thought to be integral to *liberal education: in its original form *studia humaniora*, 'the more human studies'. This last expression is Petrarch's, used by him to denote classical literature and scholarship, as opposed to the 'more divine' studies of theology and cosmology. Nowadays the term tends to denote those subjects that involve academic discipline, and perhaps an associated tradition of scholarship, but which do not exemplify scientific method. The scientific revolution (presaged in *Bacon's *Advancement of Learning*, 1605) brought with it the view that certain subjects have a peculiar claim to objectivity, and are characterized, first, by the attempt to understand the world as an entity independent of our ways of perceiving it, secondly, by a potential for progress (since discovery is cumulative – hence the title of Bacon's work). In the absence of these two features it is very unclear how we may speak of 'method' and 'objectivity', so that the 'humanities' stand in need of defence as educational subjects. The debate surrounding them has often assumed a political significance, partly on account of a surviving sense that political and administrative advancement has often been made easier for those versed in the humanities than for those with a knowledge of science. It is often argued that this reverses the natural priorities: scientific education fits people for public life, not by giving them meretricious gifts of rhetoric, but by conferring a real understanding of the material world, and of *technology. The reply often involves a general defence of the *Geisteswissenschaften*, perhaps by attempting to represent them as more appropriate to the understanding of the human world than any natural science (*see* *Verstehen*), or by arguing, in more traditional manner, for their role in inculcating *virtue, and transmitting *culture. The defence of humane education has been additionally complicated by the subversion of the traditional curriculum by *deconstruction, *feminism, and other *politicized theories.

humanism

1. The outlook, prevalent particularly in Renaissance Europe, and often summed up in the ancient apophthegm 'man is the measure of all things', which emphasizes the human, as opposed to or at least in addition to the divine, as a centre of significance, a repository of virtue, a source of strength, purpose and discovery, and a principle of artistic, moral and political expression.

2. The modern outlook, perhaps first given rhetorical expression by Baron d'Holbach and other eighteenth-century *Encyclopaedists, but more characteristic of the twentieth century than of any earlier period, which emphasizes the human as the *sole* and *sufficient* source of all our *values. For humanism, the moral atheist is the type of the enlightened man, and it is by looking to the human capacities for knowledge and virtue that hope will be regenerated and the misery of the human condition overcome. Such an attitude does not usually involve militant atheism, since that would indicate too stark an intolerance towards a common human weakness, and a departure from the principle urged by Terence in the words 'Homo sum; humani nil a me alienum puto' – 'I am a man and hold nothing human alien to myself.' Nevertheless the principal opponent, for the humanist, is the man of *faith, who regards our 'fallen' condition as a self-evident fact, and human effort as worthless without the assistance of *grace.

In an influential publication (*Letter on Humanism*, 1949) *Heidegger argued that humanism is a metaphysical illusion, since it depends upon an a priori definition of *human nature, something that it is impossible to possess and inauthentic to strive for.

humanitarianism

A term of vague meaning, defined by Julien Benda (*see* *trahison des clercs*) thus: 'I should like to draw a distinction between humanitarianism as I mean it here – a sensitiveness to the abstract quality of what is human, to Montaigne's "whole form of the human condition" – and the feeling which is usually called humanitarianism, by which is meant the love for human beings existing in the concrete.' Both senses, Benda affirms, are to be distinguished from *cosmopolitanism. The 'love for human beings existing in the concrete' is a vague idea, but presumably corresponds to the warmhearted and essentially particularized love that is also known as *charity. The contrast between this concrete love and the abstract virtue of duty to one's neighbour is a familiar theme of moral thought, some (e.g. *Kant) thinking that only the abstract duty can be meritorious, others (e.g. Dostoevsky) arguing that the abstract duty is worthless and that the only thing that matters is love for the individual, here and now, no other love being true to our mortal nature. Both the abstract and the concrete love are to be distinguished from another thing known as 'humanitarian sentiment', namely, compassion towards humanity as a whole, which *Rousseau called 'le zèle compatissant' ('compassionating zeal'), and which *Nietzsche dismissed as 'slave morality'. Benda's idea perhaps corresponds to none of the familiar usages, but rather to a modern sceptical, and perhaps somewhat anguished, version of *humanism, sense 1.

Hume, David (1711–76)
Scottish philosopher, historian, diplomat and essayist, whose radical *empiricism has had a far-reaching influence on modern thought. His political and economic writings do not represent a substantial part of his output: nevertheless their distinctive tone and vision have often been identified, both by conservatives and by liberals, as expressing thoughts fundamental to their outlook. Hume was a Tory, and thought that this particular, historically determined political vision was both consonant with his scepticism and also commendable to common sense. His influence was not, however, confined to British conservatism: several of the *Founding Fathers of the US found inspiration in Hume's defence of *mixed government, and many nineteenth-century *utilitarians saw Hume as their intellectual ancestor. Had Rousseau taken time off from sentimental compassion in order to experiment with friendship, he too might have been influenced; but despite Hume's exemplary kindness, Rousseau did not find cause to extend his compassionating zeal towards this particular benefactor.

Hume attacked the theory of the *social contract, arguing that the criterion of *tacit consent is inapplicable, most people being inevitably constrained by cultural, linguistic and habitual ties to stay where they are, whatever the government that should exert jurisdiction over them. He also argued that the only true basis for any conception of *legitimacy or *political obligation must be *utility, thus laying foundations for the utilitarian views of political order espoused by *Bentham and *Mill. (Although it is doubtful that Hume would have been in sympathy with nineteenth-century *utilitarianism, or that he would have condoned the particular idea of utility that it employed.) Hume believed that politics, as a 'moral' science, could be deduced from the study of human nature, and that controversies would dissolve if the true structure of the human sentiments could be discerned. The principal sentiments involved in political order he identified as sympathy and benevolence, and he regarded the sentiment and idea of justice as ultimately derived from them. Justice, he thought, required the establishment and defence of private rights, principal among which was the right of private property, for which he gave a classic utilitarian defence. He defended staunchly the liberties that he associated with the British constitution as this had emerged from the 'Glorious Revolution' and its aftermath, although he was extremely doubtful that those liberties could be easily guaranteed or that a formula could be found wherein to summarize them. His own preference was for a form of mixed *republican and *monarchical government, such as he argued was exhibited in Great Britain, where the two kinds of power oppose and limit each other.

The unsystematic nature of Hume's political reflections stems from his scepticism. Used against orthodoxies, that scepticism was devastating. His writings on economics include the first serious analysis of the *balance of payments mechanism, and were highly influential on *classical theorists.

hunter-gatherer

The condition of human communities prior to the adoption of systematic *agriculture. It is sometimes argued that, since for most of its evolution the human species was dependent upon hunting and gathering, our genetic make-up predisposes us towards the habits required for survival as a hunter-gatherer community, and that much utopian thinking shows an insufficient awareness of this fact. In particular, the tendency towards hierarchical order, gender roles, male bonding, animistic religion, and many other widely deplored aspects of human nature might have their origins in conditions that have now been almost universally superseded, but which have left inexpungeable residues in the human psyche.

hunting

In UK usage the pursuit of a wild animal using a pack of hounds, extended by US usage to include shooting and trapping. Hunting has been a subject of controversy since ancient times, though not always for the same reasons. Plato defended hunting with hounds in *The Laws*, on the ground that it was a training for young people in courage and in the knowledge of the landscape and habits of wild animals. However, it should be carried out with skill and determination, and not be allowed to degenerate into savage butchery. Nor should it involve the invasion of sacred places or the destruction of agricultural land. The idea that hunting involves a special kind of respect towards the quarry, and a self-limiting on the part of the hunter, has been more recently emphasized by Ortega y Gasset (*La caza*, 1943), and the peculiar relation between the hunter and the quarry that he has 'singled out' has been a recurring theme in Western art and literature.

In modern times hunting with hounds has been opposed both as a symbol of an old and class-ridden social order, and as a 'cruel sport'. Its defenders argue that it is open to all classes, is a source of social cohesion in rural areas, and is far less cruel than the alternatives, when judged as a form of population management. The UK Hunting Act 2004 outlaws 'hunting with dogs', but defines neither 'hunting' nor 'with', so leaving it uncertain whether the activities that it was intended to ban are now legal. The Act was passed in defiance of evidence placed before an official enquiry, without the consent of the House of Lords, and with no attempt to justify state interference in a long-established custom that most of the legislators had themselves never witnessed. Nevertheless it was welcomed by the defenders of *animal rights as a significant step towards extending towards wild animals the protection that had previously been enjoyed only by domestic animals and pets. The symbolic importance of the legislation is illustrated by the fact that it was debated in Parliament for over 220 hours, at a time when the decision to commit the country to war in Iraq occupied Parliament for a total of 18 hours.

Huntington, Samuel (b. 1927)
US political scientist, known for his work on *democratization, who has recently addressed the new international situation following the collapse of communism. In *The Clash of Civilisations and the Making of World Order*, 1996, he argues that the conflict of the cold war will be replaced by a violent and disorderly clash of civilizations, as the Islamic world reacts to the global transfer of Western attitudes, Western technology and Western secularization. In *Who Are We?*, 2002, Huntington addresses the question of American identity, in the wake of the terrorist atrocities of 11th September 2001. Huntington's argument centres on what he calls the American Creed, which he believes to derive from the 'Anglo-Protestant' culture of the original settlers. And he marshals the evidence of recent historical scholarship, which sees the development of American political institutions, and the forging of the American national idea, as continuous with the Protestant 'Awakenings' that repeatedly swept across the continent. To

separate this religious inheritance from the idea of America, to reconstitute as a purely secular body politic what began life as a sacred pledge, would be to deny the most vigorous input into the American experience.

Husserl, Edmund Gustav Albert (1859–1938)
German-speaking Moravian philosopher. *See* *existentialism, *Heidegger, *phenomenology.

Huxley, Aldous (1894–1963)
English novelist and critic. *See* *dystopia, *egalitarianism.

hyperflation
*Inflation that is so rapid as to move uncontrollably towards a radical breakdown in the monetary system, and the complete collapse of all long-term expectations concerning price, so that in a very short time money is no longer effective as a medium of exchange.

hypocracy
Recent American coinage, to mean 'rule by *hypocrisy'.

hypocrisy
According to La Rochefoucauld, hypocrisy is the tribute that vice plays to virtue. Without it, virtue would receive no political tributes at all, and a universal cynicism would cloud the collective consciousness. Hence not everyone is prepared to condemn hypocrisy in a politician, and a supreme form of it was defended by Plato (*see* *noble lie).

bn Khaldūn (1332–1406)
Tunisian courtier, judge and
historian, whose *Muqaddimah*,
or *Prolegomena*, contains one of
the first attempts at a scientific sociology, together with an influential
account of political order and its
decline. Khaldūn argues that societies
are governed by universal laws and are
not easily affected by individuals. Nor
should their distinctive features be
attributed to racial characteristics since
these too are only the temporary
effects of given geographical, social
and cultural circumstances. Khaldūn's
theory of the dynasty, as having a
natural term of life (three generations
of 40 years each), contains a premoni-
tion of many later theories of history,
and an interesting diagnosis of the
causes of the ascendancy and decline
of institutions. He distinguishes three
kinds of state: that based on the divine
law (*siyasa diniya*, the ideal *theocracy
of Islam), that based on a law established by human reason (*siyasa 'aqliya*,
which only approximates to the first),
and that based on the ideal state of the
philosophers. Each possibility represents an *ideal type; nevertheless
actual institutions will differ according
to which type is seen as their ultimate
aim and fulfilment. Khaldūn is interesting for his attempts to give a theory
of *positive law, and to integrate his
account of the state with an analysis of
production and taxation. He also
produced a striking account of *pre-
political order, arguing that human
collectivities (*'umrān*) emerge from
favourable climatic and environmental factors and are held together by a
bond of membership (*'asabiyya*, from
'asab, sinew) which inevitably weakens in political conditions, even
though it requires political organization if it is to achieve its full reality.

Ibn Taymiyya (1263–1328)
Muslim writer born in what is now
Syria, who laid down principles for an
Islamic *theocracy. Taymiyya held
that the *caliphate is not obligatory,
and indeed that there had been no
legitimate successor to the Prophet
following the first four 'righteously
guided' caliphs. The true heirs of the
Prophet are therefore the *'ulema*, the
class of religious and legal scholars
who are able to transmit the laws and
doctrines of the faith, and in particular
those of the Hanbali school of *fiqh* to
which he belonged. The state is not an
institution distinct from the faith, but
the means for upholding and enforcing religious obedience, in accordance
with the *sharî'ah*. Without religion the
state will degenerate into tyranny,
hence religion and political order are
mutually necessary to each other.
Taymiyya upholds the Islamic
doctrine concerning the treatment of
the *dhimmî*, according to which
Christians and Jews can reside within
the sovereign territory on terms of
subordination, and reaffirms what he
takes to be the Koranic view that all
others are in a condition of war against
the faith, until they have been forced
to adopt it. The theories of Taymiyya
are now enjoying a revival, largely
because Taymiyya, in reaction against
what he saw as the laxness of the *Sufi*
culture centred in the Persia of his day,

reaffirmed the true Koranic doctrine (as he saw it) of *jihâd*, according to which the 'struggle' on behalf of the faith is not the inner search for enlightenment of the Sufis, but an outward hostility to all that defies God's holy purpose, and which prevents the spread of Islam. Taymiyya was particularly incensed against apostates and Muslims who had adopted compromising ways, all of whom, he believed, should be mercilessly killed.

iconoclasm

Greek: the breaking of images, applied originally to the destruction of religious symbols and images, usually in obedience to the sentiment that to use an image in worship is to worship the image, and so be guilty of idolatry. (A sentiment which, while founded in a *non sequitur*, remains an immovable part of the nonconformist *Protestant outlook.)

The term is now used in two related senses: (i) to denote any destructive activity directed against the substance of a belief through ridiculing the symbols upon which it is nourished, and in which it finds expression; political iconoclasm is a significant modern pastime, usually severely punished in any state which relies on *government through symbols; (ii) since icons are, by extension, ideas, to denote the assailing and ridiculing of cherished beliefs.

ideal

Any state of affairs which exists as idea and aspiration, rather than as reality, usually put forward as an example of moral or political perfection. To possess ideals is to possess *values that are incommensurate with the actual, hence the opposite of the 'idealist' is the 'realist'. The realist tends to believe that small improvements and practical manoeuvres within the existing state

of affairs may constitute true moral virtue, whereas the idealist thinks of virtue in terms of a sacrifice demanded from the agent, who must act so as to defy reality.

To have values is not necessarily to have ideals: values may be informed by a sense of the actual, and of the difficulty of moving from it. Nevertheless at least one philosopher – *Kant – has argued that all values are in effect ideals, since all values postulate not what is, but what ought to be. Through them the agent is inevitably constrained to aim at the 'kingdom of ends' in which only reason is sovereign.

ideal types

A term introduced by *Weber, who defined an ideal type as 'an analytical accentuation of certain aspects of reality' – i.e. an abstraction adopted for explanatory purposes. The term is now used to describe theoretical *models of institutions, social relations, and political systems which are 'ideal' in the sense of being construed entirely according to the theoretical laws that explain them, and not according to observation of the actual world. At the same time the models are chosen so as to correspond as nearly as possible to the actual world. If there were an instance of such an ideal type in reality then we should be able to explain *all* its features; even if there is not such an instance, however, it is hoped that the proximity of real arrangements to an ideal type will explain their *principal* features. (Examples of ideal types include, e.g., *feudalism, *capitalism, and *communism as described by *Marx; the *family as described by Hegel, the US *state as described by its *constitution.)

There is a problem in the philosophy of science as to whether, and if so how, the postulation of an ideal type can really explain something that only imperfectly copies it. Is the case like that of axiomatic geometry, which, while it corresponds only roughly to the disordered lines of the perceivable world, nevertheless describes the laws which govern them? Unfortunately geometry is a descriptive science, and does not really explain why something that exemplifies its laws is as it is; the 'ideal type', however, is supposed to show *why* the actual events that mimic it develop as they do.

idealism

1. Metaphysical. The only things that exist (or which 'ultimately' exist) are ideas or mental entities, so that the whole structure of reality is to be understood in terms of consciousness. Thus, in Berkeley's philosophy, the world is held to consist of the infinite mind of God, the finite minds of his creatures, and the mental states ('ideas') of all of them. Berkeley is often cited as a paradigm metaphysical idealist although, from the political point of view, it is fair to say that he is without significance. The major forms of metaphysical idealism that have had political influence are those given by *Plato, *Kant, and *Hegel. Kant's 'transcendental idealism' argues that the world as known bears the imprint of the knower, so that all attempts to know the world 'as it is in itself' are empty. The one guarantee that we have of the existence of the 'thing-in-itself' comes through practical reason; hence the 'moral law' which guides practical reason is also the foundation of metaphysics. The resulting vision of the sovereignty of the moral law had profound political influence, in giving a reasoned foundation for *universalism and *natural law.

Hegel's 'objective' idealism begins from the premise that reason and the concepts of reason contain within themselves the seeds of knowledge: reason does not so much discover as 'posit' reality, which is a perpetually developing object of consciousness, deriving its nature from the concepts through which it is known. The development of reality is, like the development of an argument, *dialectical, and proceeds towards that absolute idea which is both the object and the subject of ultimate knowledge. The world, although it is none other than the absolute idea which knows it, is always known as *object*: so that objective reality is understood as distinct from, even though ultimately identical with, the knowing subject. The result of this thoroughgoing idealism is that, in Hegel's words, 'the real is rational and the rational real'. Hence, despite all appearances to the contrary, the world as object exhibits the 'cunning of reason'. This theory has far-reaching implications, among them:

(a) the structure of reason and its concepts is prior to that of history, so that the former explains the latter;

(b) the essence of historical processes may be concealed by their appearance, even (and especially) to the participants, who exist at a stage of rational development that does not enable them to perceive the underlying reality (it being part of reason's 'cunning' to hide itself from its progeny). (*See* *essence/appearance.)

*Historical materialism is a theory which, in its usual forms, accepts (b) (or something like it) while denying (a), the force of the word 'materialism' lying in the belief that ideas are powerless to produce events, and are at best the product of them. (a) and (b) are characteristic only of Hegel's idealism, and not, for example, of Plato's or Kant's. The underlying metaphysic is remarkable for its attempt to reconcile the two ideas contained in (a) and (b) – i.e. that the fundamental stuff of the world is consciousness, and that consciousness itself remains only imperfectly conscious of the world.

Sometimes, when *Marxists use the

term 'idealist', they mean to refer to any theory which rejects the thesis that 'life determines consciousness, not consciousness life', whether or not that theory involves the metaphysical commitment here identified as the defining feature of idealism. (Thus *Gramsci is sometimes called an idealist, since the Gramscian theory of hegemony attributes to the consciousness of a ruling class a large role in securing its ascendancy.) This usage is not really respectable, since what is meant can be said in another way, and the controversy referred to is saturated with dead philosophical arguments. (*See also* *materialism.)

2. Moral and political idealism. The pursuit of, and unwillingness to renounce, *ideals of conduct, even when present reality conflicts with them, and even when their future realization seems unlikely or impossible, perhaps with a reluctance to believe in that impossibility. In international affairs idealists are often contrasted with *realists, the former seeing international relations at least partly in terms of moral precepts, justice, trust and obligation, the latter seeing them only in terms of power.

3. Various attempts to combine 1. and 2. – for example the political idealism of *Green, who believed that metaphysical idealism underpinned idealist strategies in politics: social problems would be overcome and social progress achieved through the inevitable working out of political ideals.

identity

Normally used, in political contexts, to denote not the relation which everything bears to itself, but rather self-identification. Only conscious beings or things that contain conscious beings as members, such as societies, states, clubs and institutions, have identity. An institution has an identity, when

the members are able not only to distinguish it from other institutions, but also to convey its distinctive character in words, gestures and practice, so as to reassure themselves that it *should* exist and that they have reason to belong to it. Thus the emergence of a 'national identity' involves a growing sense among people that they belong naturally together, that they share common interests, a common history, and a common destiny.

The search for an 'identity' is of increasing importance in modern politics. Very often the identity is that of a *minority within the social order. For example *Rastafarianism has involved an attempt by urban blacks in the UK and elsewhere to acquire an identity that will render their social experience legitimate in their own eyes, as an experience of people who belong elsewhere and who are essentially displaced. The *Nation of Islam has been adopted for similar reasons by African-Americans. The experience of being 'strangers and sojourners' is so much a part of Jewish history that it is not surprising to find the question of identity also becoming increasingly prominent among writers of Jewish extraction – many of whom seek to reconcile a Jewish identity with political loyalty to a secular or Christian state.

*Communitarians and *conservatives both argue that modern *individualism, with its abstract and internationalist view of citizenship, fails to capture the loyalty of ordinary people. Political association depends upon a sense of identity – and this is inherently local, exclusive, founded in a tie of membership. The concept of identity therefore defines one of the major points of confrontation between the liberal-individualist worldview and its conservative or communitarian opponent. The debates surrounding the concept of identity are of importance for another reason, for they involve an attempt to understand and come to terms with the new forms of social order, in which religion is dwindling, social and physical mobility increasing, and the local character of *town and country eroding. On some views *nationalism involves a longing, in these new and trying circumstances, for an identity which will be a sufficient foundation for political loyalty, and will be defined not in terms of religion or status but in terms of place.

identity politics

Political action which places the pursuit of *identity at the top of its agenda, believing that no political programme can be successfully carried out if people do not first know who and what they are, and why they should take one another's interests so much into account as to ponder a common cause and a common *allegiance. While identity politics has occupied the leaders of *minorities, whose posture towards the existing order may often be oppositional, it is not exclusively a politics of protest. Majority movements of a *nationalist kind also make identity into the primary matter of politics.

ideology

Term coined by the French philosopher Destutt de Tracy in 1795, to denote the general science of ideas, which was to clarify and improve the public mind. Given currency by the rhetoricians of the French Revolution (*les idéologues*), by Napoleon, and by *Marx, the term developed in many directions and now has two principal and partly conflicting significances:

1. Any systematic and all-embracing political *doctrine, which claims to give a complete and universally applicable theory of man and society, and to derive therefrom a programme of political action. An ideology in this sense seeks to embrace everything that is relevant to man's political condition, and to issue doctrine whenever doctrine would be influential in forming or changing that condition. Most things taught in the name of *Marxism are ideology, and it is sometimes said that *totalitarian government – as opposed to 'liberal democracy' – stands in need of ideology to justify its endless intrusion into personal life. Ideology is the principal object of much conservative criticism (e.g. that given by *Oakeshott), largely on the grounds that political doctrine, if possible at all, is not detachable from the particular circumstances in which it is conceived, and can never be given the universal, all-embracing character to which ideology aspires.

2. In Marxist and *Marxian theories 'ideology' denotes any set of ideas and values which has the social function of consolidating a particular economic order, and which is explained by that fact alone, and not by its inherent truth or reasonableness. (*See* *functional explanation.) The function of ideology is to *naturalize the *status quo*, and to represent as immutable features of human nature the particular social conditions which currently persist. Ideology wins support for class rule, by persuading oppressed classes to accept the descriptions of reality which render their subordination 'natural'. It therefore has three principal functions: to legitimate, to mystify, and to console.

It is a part of classical Marxism to argue that ideology is necessary only under certain social conditions (specifically those of feudalism and capitalism) and that, with the coming of communism, the veil of ideology will be torn aside: society and human nature will at last be perceived as they really are. One of the problems faced by such a theory is this: how do we, who do not exist in that ideal or future state, distinguish the ideological from the nonideological among our beliefs? If we cannot make the distinction, how do we know that we are not, in all our social beliefs (including, say, the belief in communism), victims of a *false consciousness? One answer to those questions is contained in the doctrine of *praxis.

You do not have to be a Marxist to accept that there are ideologies in sense 2. All that is necessary is to make a distinction between two ways of arriving at a belief: the way of science, which is the pursuit of truth, and the way of ideology, which is the pursuit of some emotional benefit or consolation. We explain the belief that the earth is round by referring to the process whereby the truth that the earth is round generates the belief that it is so. We explain the feminist belief that women have the same mental capacities as men by referring to the 'will to believe' that finds consolation in just this doctrine, our explanation proceeding quite independently of any proof that the belief is true. On that view it is quite possible for a belief to be ideological *and* true; but in calling it ideological one is implying that its truth played no part in producing it.

imam

Arabic: leader (of a congregation), an examplary person or model, the person 'in front'. (From the same root as *ummah*, the Islamic community.) The term is now used in two senses: first to denote the person who leads the faithful in prayer; secondly to denote the supreme religious leader, the one appointed by God to lead the *ummah* in this world. In the first sense the office of imam is a feature of most Islamic sects, though with no universally agreed procedure for choosing or electing its occupant. The second idea

is a feature of *Shi'ite doctrine, which rejects the idea of the *caliphate (according to which the successor of the Prophet is also imam to all the faithful), and replaces it with that of the true Imams, appointed by God, of whom 12 are normally recognized.

immigration

The entrance into an alien country of people who intend permanently to reside there. The introduction of immigration controls into the law of most modern states has accompanied an increased possibility of movement between states. The traditional idea (given philosophical importance by *Locke in his theory of political obligation) that the freedom to emigrate is a necessary condition of legitimate government is still upheld in the law of most Western countries; but the freedom to immigrate, having no such doctrinal basis, is equally often denied there. Henry Sidgwick upheld it in the name of a liberal sentiment that was avowedly *universalist and *cosmopolitan: 'the business [of government] is to maintain order over the particular territory which historical causes have appropriated to it, but not in any way to determine who is to inhabit the territory, in order to restrict the enjoyment of its natural advantages to any particular portion of the human race' (*Elements of Politics*, 1891). To which the reply may be made that it is unlikely that 'historical causes' should mark out a territory for government without also marking out a people to be governed. *Nationalist philosophies of the state go further, arguing that some measure of ethnic or at least prepolitical unity is the precondition of government. On this view a state is possible only where there is customary conformity over a large area of social life.

To some extent this nationalist sentiment is falsified by the experience of America, which, being a society entirely constructed by immigrants, developed laws and institutions which made immigration acceptable. (A comparable example is provided by Brazil.) These led to the creation of a highly supple *federal structure. Ever new waves of immigrants were able to settle and to recognize the binding character of the *jurisdiction. However, immigration has now become an issue in the US, for two reasons: first, the new wave of immigrants consists largely of unskilled and poorly educated people, who are seen as a threat by their indigenous counterparts. Second, the quantity of newcomers is vastly greater today than in the days of Italian and East-European immigration of recent history.

In the nation states of Europe immigration, in particular from other continents, has long been an acknowledged political problem. Some argue that the aversion to it is largely a species of *xenophobia or even *racism, and that the European states (especially the UK) are obligated by their colonial past to overcome those feelings. Others argue, either in the spirit of nationalism, or more pragmatically, in terms of the limitation of resources, that unrestricted immigration is a social ill. The German and French laws, which in effect permit the temporary importation followed by the forced expulsion of cheap labour, are often held up as typifying the kind of exploitation that underlies immigration controls, although how one could persuade the present population of a state to accept immigration on terms that are not to its own advantage is a problem which such objections do little to overcome. *See* *guestworker.

The large-scale immigration into Europe of Islamic populations from North Africa, Pakistan and the Middle East has now led to a change in the language of public debate about this issue, with a general consensus in favour of the view that immigration must be followed by *assimilation, if the host society is not to be blown apart. But it is far easier to prevent immigration than to compel assimilation; hence the consensus, while nearer the truth than the old diatribes against the 'racism' of the host community, is nowhere nearer to a realistic solution.

impeachment

Broadly, a criminal accusation brought in a *legislative body. It is not the same as removal from office, but is more like a criminal indictment. In the UK, US, France and almost all South American states the function of accusation is vested in the lower house of the legislature and the function of trial and sentence in the upper house.

The ancient Greek *eisangelia*, whereby a citizen could be brought before the public assembly and accused of misconduct in public office, closely resembled impeachment. Its use in the UK was discredited by the impeachment of Warren Hastings, 1788, and has been rendered largely obsolete by the doctrine of ministerial responsibility and by *administrative law. It remains an important power of the US Congress, although the constitution provides that 'judgement shall not extend further than removal from office, and disqualification to hold and enjoy office of honour, trust or profit under the US'. Impeachment can be directed against the President, the Vice-President, the federal judiciary and federal officials, and provides a major constitutional limitation to *executive power, as was abundantly illustrated in the case of President Nixon and more recently in the case of President Clinton. It has been used in all only 13 times since Congress was established, but persists as the symbolic and effective expression of the sovereignty of Congress in a state which vests supreme executive power not in Congress but in a President.

The power to impeach has been frequently defended by advocates of *limited government. Perhaps the first important exposition of the reasoning behind this view occurs in *Machiavelli (*Discourses*, I, VIII).

imperfect competition (or:
monopolistic competition)

A technical term of economic theory, denoting a *market in which there are many firms whose outputs are close but not perfect substitutes, either because there is 'product differentiation' (differences of brand name, social appearance, etc.) or geographical fragmentation of the market. Since the products are not homogeneous one firm may raise its prices relative to its competitors without losing all its sales, so that its 'demand curve' (which relates price per unit to quantity sold) is downward sloping, rather than horizontal as in *perfect competition. The theory of imperfect competition, developed in the 1930s by E.H. Chamberlin and Joan Robinson, is an important part of the modern analysis of markets.

imperial preference

An economic doctrine, canvassed by Joseph Chamberlain in 1897, according to which British dominions and colonies were to be given economic preference through *protection, largely by imposing high tariffs on imports from outside the colonial network. Running counter to the *free trade advocates of the time, this doctrine received little support until the Depression. Analogous policies have been instigated by a variety of imperial powers, most recently by the USSR through the institutions of *Comecon.

imperialism

The extension of power through conquest, or the pursuit of 'empire', i.e. of a global influence so dominant as to amount to virtual *sovereignty wherever it is successful. Empire was advocated in the UK in the 1880s by Joseph Chamberlain, in opposition to the 'Little Englanders' who favoured a policy of *isolationism. Chamberlain argued that the expanding influence of France and Germany must be counterbalanced by the expanding influence of the UK. This defence facilitated the once fashionable economic analysis of imperialism as a search for captive markets, offered in 1902 by J.A. Hobson, who criticized imperialism as a form of *exploitation. The criticism was taken up by *Lenin, who in *Imperialism as the Highest State of Capitalism*, 1917, argued that imperialism is an economic necessity for the capitalist economy, in order to overcome the otherwise inevitable *falling rate of profit that spells its doom. (Lenin was thus able to explain why Marx's prediction of a falling rate of profit had not been fulfilled.) Imperialism is the last state since it leads to international competition in order to secure markets and exploit resources, and hence to 'imperialist war'. This, as Lenin later thought was demonstrated by the emergence of the Russian Revolution from the chaos of the First World War, creates the conditions for the seizure of power by the international proletariat.

Lenin's theory has provided support for the claim that innocent-seeming gestures on the part of capitalist powers are nevertheless expressions of imperialism (or at any rate 'neo-imperialism'). This complaint was given theoretical elaboration by K. Nkrumah (1909–72) in *Neo-Colonialism, The Last Stage of Imperialism*, 1965. However, armed invasion by communist powers is also part of the international role of the Communist Party, in offering assistance to the proletariat everywhere. Hence the term 'imperialist' acquired, in communist rhetoric, a distinctive and misleading flavour. Social and economic *influence from capitalist countries was called imperialism, while military *coercion from communist countries was described as liberation.

Although communism has collapsed, and with it the credibility of Lenin's argument, imperialism remains an object of censure among the *bien-pensants, on the assumption that an empire always involves some kind of dictatorship, a dangerous centralization of power, and an infringement of the *rights and *liberties of the subject peoples. This assumption is no longer credible. Central Europe under the Habsburg Empire is now widely acknowledged to have enjoyed rights, liberties and political freedoms that it had never enjoyed before, and which it lost very soon after the Empire collapsed in 1918. Habsburg imperialism helped to stem the tide of *nationalism, to avert civil wars and to extend a rule of law over people many of whom had shown no disposition to invent such a benefit for themselves.

Imperialism is once again an issue in international affairs, with critics of US foreign policy in the Middle East denouncing it as 'neo-imperialism', and Islamist groups like *al-Qa'eda consciously aiming to establish a new *caliphate that will exert imperial sway over the Muslim world.

implied powers

Powers of the US President and Congress implied but not specified by the constitution, specifically by virtue of the clause (Art. 1, s. 8) giving power to make 'all laws which shall be necessary and proper for carrying into execution the foregoing powers, and all other powers vested by this constitution in the Government of the United States, or in any Department or Office thereof'. Initially controversial, this clause has since been widely used to extend the powers of government.

impossibility theorems

See *Arrow's theorem, *Paretian liberal.

incentive

The expected benefit that induces someone to incur a *cost, especially a labour cost. The theory of incentives is an important part of the controversy between defenders of capitalist and socialist economies, it being argued in favour of capitalism that it alone is compatible with a realistic view of human inducements. Socialists used to argue that, under socialist conditions, a new human nature will emerge (see *new man), and that 'moral' and 'collective' incentives will then be stronger than their 'material' and 'individual' counterparts. People brought up in communist systems laugh at this argument, usually with some bitterness.

income

The flow of money, goods and services accruing to a particular economic unit (individual, household, group or shareholder) over a period of time, or the flow of money with which the economic unit acquires the flow of goods and services. (Hence the distinction between *real and money income.) Income is an important concept in modern economics, and it is often argued that much economic behaviour is to be explained in part by the attempt to maximize income, and that limits on income constrain consumption. The theory of what determines the aggregate flow of income within the economy forms an important part of *macroeconomics, largely pioneered by *Keynes, and now one of the major areas in which economic thinking influences political policy. According to the Keynesian theory the rate of production of goods and services, and hence the level of *national income, is determined – to put it simply – by the level of *aggregate demand, which is in turn dependent partly on the level of income (a mutual dependence known as the 'circular flow of income') and partly on the prevailing rate of *interest. Hence the factors determining the rate of interest become important in the theory of income determination. Among these factors the *money supply is often considered to be particularly important. Keynesians, however, tend to emphasize the role of government expenditure in raising aggregate demand by more direct and efficacious means.

income and capital

Much discussion of the politics of *distribution focuses upon the relative merits of redistributing *capital and *income, usually in the name of some egalitarian ideal. Many countries permit vast accumulations of capital, but tend to limit inequalities of income, usually by progressive *taxation. Taxes on capital result in a transfer of the economy from private ownership to state control. Hence they inevitably lead towards *monopoly. Experience of the effects of this is one of the major motives behind recent *privatization of capital assets. *See also* *death taxes.

income effect

The effect which a change in the price of a good has on a consumer's demand for it, by way of the change induced in his *real income. Thus, if the price of x drops by 10p a unit, someone who is used to buying ten units of x a week finds his real income increased by £1 per week because he could continue to

spend his income as before and still have £1 left over. The quantity of x purchased may rise, e.g. because x is something which the consumer wants more of than he could previously afford. Alternatively, it may fall, e.g. because x was an 'inferior good', destined to be replaced as soon as more real income becomes available to spend on better things. Thus the income effect might be positive, zero, or (less commonly) negative. The *substitution effect, via the change induced in relative prices, is, however, always negative. The combined effect is usually that price and quantity demanded are inversely related. (But *see* *Giffen goods.)

income tax

See *taxation.

incomes policy (or: prices and incomes policy)

A policy for controlling (and in practice usually restraining) *prices and *incomes in money terms, usually in order to achieve stability in the former and so to control *inflation. Such a policy seeks to control prices directly, and not by regulating the *money supply, or *aggregate demand. The hope is to preserve the balance of the economy intact as far as possible, and so to control inflation without precipitating *unemployment.

The wisdom of such a policy is disputed. However, the relative concreteness of the practice, together with its intelligibility, have led to the temporary imposition of an incomes policy by several postwar governments in the UK and the US. Many economists continue to argue that the objectives of stable prices, full employment and economic growth are, in the end, incompatible. It is debated whether temporary incomes policies can have more than temporary effects, and whether an incomes policy can be made permanent. (*See* *Keynes, *monetarism.)

incorporation
1. The creation of a *corporation – i.e. an *association which is a distinct legal entity, with *rights, *duties, and *agency of its own.

2. The doctrine of 'incorporation' in law holds that *international law is part of the law of a state only if made so by domestic enactment.

incrementalism
Term used to denote policy-making that settles always on small circumscribed objectives, while remaining as sensitive as possible to influences from existing policies and decisions. Thus C.E. Lindblom writes (*The Policy-Making Process*, 1968): 'usually – though not always – what is feasible politically is policy only incrementally, or marginally, different from existing policies'. Nevertheless this approach may be not only necessary, but also beneficial, since it concentrates the mind on what is knowable, not only theoretically, but also practically, and thus enables the policy-maker to estimate the effects of any particular decision. Lindblom cites, as an example, the practice of the Anti-trust Division of the Department of Justice, in extending laws controlling mergers and prices. *See also* *piecemeal engineering.

independence
1. The ability of a *state to exercise *rights of *government in its own *territory without encroaching on the rights of other states: an essential condition for the recognition of a state as a distinct legal *person in *international law. Independence implies that no other state has the legal right to interfere in the internal affairs of the state which possesses it, whether directly or indirectly.

2. Freedom from dependence – economic, military or political – on any other power. In this sense (*de facto* independence rather than *de jure*), no state has total independence, and independence is always a matter of degree.

index
1. A number (index number) which gives a synthetic 'average' level or value of a set of related items, used particularly to show changes over time, e.g. of the prices of different commodities, or the outputs of different industries. If the various items whose behaviour is thus aggregated show distinct tendencies over time, then the economist is faced with a statistical problem in determining how to encapsulate their economic behaviour in a single figure. This is the 'index number problem', which arises whenever different factors have to be weighed against each other, and a choice of mean has to be made.

2. In the Roman Catholic Church, a list of writings 'indicated' by ecclesiastical authority as forbidden to the faithful. The 'papal index' has been one of the most important forms of *censorship in European history, though it is no longer enforced by any state.

indexation
The linking of a monetary obligation to the price level, so that the former changes in proportion to the latter. Thus the indexation of pensions to the level of prices means that their real value will not be affected by the level of inflation at the time of their receipt. Some economists consider that the indexation of all monetary obligations helps to reduce expectations of inflation, and so contributes to the control of inflation. By the operation of English *common law the indexation of damages in civil action seems to be

automatic; in Brazil (e.g.) indexation of *all* monetary obligations is obligatory. Indexation can be partial, as in the Italian *scala mobile* for the indexation of wages.

indifference curve

A theoretical construct much used in economics. An individual is indifferent between two bundles of goods if he regards each as being at least as good as the other. On a graph of commodities demanded, a curve can then be drawn connecting the graphical representation of these points of 'indifference'. For example, if five apples and eight oranges were regarded as neither better nor worse than six apples and six oranges, then these figures determine two points on an indifference curve. The properties ascribed to these curves will reflect assumptions about the psychology of consumers. For example, an assumption that the curves are continuous implies that the consumer is always willing to receive a quantity of one of the goods as an exact compensation for some reduction in the quantity of the other. (*See also* *preference.)

The device of the indifference curve can be extended beyond economics in order to give theoretical representations of problems in morality and politics, where commitments to distinct values are in issue. (*See*, for example, Albert Weale, in R. Harrison, ed., *Rational Action*, Cambridge, 1979.) In morality it is often objected that values cannot be seriously weighed against each other by the moral agent, who, when asked to choose between respect for life and respect for liberty, say, may find himself in a dilemma, but not in a resoluble dilemma, since the two goods may not be commensurate. In politics, however, where it might be argued that responsibilities fall less directly, the economist's indifference curve may be a useful device.

Thus a government may be indifferent between 90% employment and 10% inflation on the one hand, and 95% employment and 20% inflation on the other. The construction of an indifference curve will then be significant, on the assumption that employment and inflation vary together.

indirect rule

A system of *colonial government by *delegation of power to indigenous institutions, modified so as to conform to the legal and constitutional requirements of the metropolitan government. Introduced into Nigeria by Lord Lugard in 1898, and thereafter widely imitated.

individualism

1. The attitude which sees the individual human person, his rights, and his needs, as taking precedence over all collectives (whether family, corporation, civil society or state), in moral and political decision-making. Usually justified by the basic theory that only individuals have rights (or, at any rate, only individuals have natural rights): the attribution of rights to a collective being simply a way of summarizing the rights held by individuals by virtue of their membership of it. (But *see* *group rights.) Important modern defenders of this kind of individualism include *Nozick and (probably) *Rawls.

2. The more metaphysical position that the individual human person may exist apart from any social arrangement, and is therefore intelligible, in principle, independently of society. On this view all *social facts are complex facts about individuals, societies themselves being nothing more than constructs out of the individual people who compose them. (*See* *reductionism.) Even *institutions – such as the law, and the state – are thought to have no reality independent of the individuals who compose

them, and so play no constitutive part in the nature of those individuals.

A characteristic individualistic doctrine is that of liberal individualism, which argues that the state must be seen as a system of constraints on the activities of the individual, justifiable only in so far as it protects his freedoms and rights, society being a voluntary association of individuals, which may be renounced by any of them by a simple change of mind. Only in this way, the liberal individualist argues, will we see the true basis of political obligation.

Anti-individualists tend to argue that the individual human being may indeed exist outside society, but the same is not true of the individual human *person*, since the essence of the person is social. This doctrine of 'social essence' has not always been put quite as clearly as that (*see*, for a particularly confused, but influential version, *species-being*). It claims that the person – the bearer of rights – is (i) a product of social and institutional arrangements, and (ii) able to flourish only in the appropriate social conditions. It is therefore wrong to think that individuals can be understood without reference to the social relations in which they participate. Moreover, in an important sense, institutions might have to be considered as prior to individuals, and so no more to be thought of as aggregates of individuals than organisms are to be thought of as aggregates of cells.

Individualism is central to many liberal and *Enlightenment theories, while anti-individualism is an important component, both of idealist theories of the state (notably *Hegel's), and of certain forms of *Marxism.

3. 'Methodological individualism'. The attempt to study society and social facts while making as little reference as possible to institutions and 'social wholes', and exploring instead the actions, intentions etc., of individual people. Methodological individualism was put forward by *Schumpeter as the basis of an objective social science, and adopted and systematized by *Mises in his economic theory, and by *Popper in his attacks on *historicism.

indoctrination

'Indoctrination' does not mean the transmission of *doctrine, nor even *education that has the transmission of doctrine as its ultimate purpose, but rather the inducement of specific beliefs and attitudes (which may lack system, cogency, or any other ingredient thought to be necessary to doctrine) by methods that are not genuinely educational, and which involve the abrogation of reason and intellectual autonomy on the part of the recipient. All education leads to the acquisition of at least some irrational beliefs; hence we cannot distinguish genuine education from its false substitute in terms of the end result but only in terms of the method used. Not respecting the autonomy of the recipient, indoctrination prevents the exercise of those rational faculties that it purports to develop; either the recipient remains sceptical of what he is told, or he believes it simply as *dogma. Indoctrination is designed to induce beliefs, whether or not they are true; to the extent that someone knows he is being indoctrinated, to that extent will he cease to believe what he is told without independent evidence.

The distinction between education and indoctrination has been central to recent discussions over the nature and goals of education. It has been argued that many of the subjects and methods proposed by radical reformers of the curriculum are masks for leftist indoctrination – the instant response being that the traditional curriculum is also a mask for indoctrination, only in the opposite direction. While there is no simple way out of this confrontation, it is worth pointing out the difference between a subject that is based on foregone conclusions and one that leaves students free to make up their minds. For example, a programme in 'feminist studies' indicates in its name, its literature and its curriculum that the student will either begin or end as a feminist. What should be the conclusion of an argument is here assumed as the premise – and at the same time protected from questioning. It is perhaps reasonable to suppose that this is the primary characteristic of indoctrination in all its forms. All education is based on unexamined premises – but only indoctrination involves foregone *conclusions*.

industrial action

Term originally used by the French *syndicalists in order to denote action located in the centre of production (the factory) designed to force the transfer of ownership from management to the *trade union. The term is now used more widely, to signify any form of strike, go-slow, or unilateral constraint on the part of the work force, designed to compel the other side (management, shareholders or the state) to comply with certain demands. These demands will include anything from a change in terms and conditions of work, to a change in government policy (increasingly, whether or not the state is in fact party to the wage contract, it being assumed that the state can be compelled to join any dispute in which the national interest is at stake). The object may also be more personal, such as the exclusion of a particular worker from the work force, for whatever reason (but *see* *industrial law). Action is 'official' if instigated or recognized by the appropriate trade union, otherwise 'unofficial'.

The following have formed parts of the repertoire of industrial action: strike, in which the work force joins together to withdraw labour; secondary strike, in which other work forces do likewise in order to prevent alternative modes of production or distribution; general strike, in which some large section of the entire work force of a state withdraws its labour, either to enforce a demand on the part of some section of it, or else to enforce a demand on the part of the whole; picketing, whereby workers attempt both to announce their action, and to persuade others neither to enter the place of work, nor in any other way to behave so as to make the action nugatory; secondary picketing, in which workers from one place of work picket another place whose productive activities thwart or hamper the aims of their action.

All the above were permitted, with qualifications, by UK statute, even though they all amount to *conspiracy in *common law. However, recent reforms have limited or, in some cases, forbidden actions of this kind. US labour law, which has provided the model for much legislation (including that in the UK), has evolved during the twentieth century, from a situation in which industrial action was almost invariably frustrated by the courts, through the granting of *injunctions, to one in which most common varieties of industrial action are permitted, circumscribed and controlled by statute. The famous Taft-Hartley Act 1947, enacted after Congress had overridden a presidential *veto, was much criticized by the trade unions, in that it attempted to define and make illegal certain types of 'unfair labour practice' and so to assert the rights of an individual against his union. It has been subject to amendments, but its provisions remain, so that the US law was until recently thought to be more biased in favour of management than is the UK law. Needless to say this is an area of great legal and constitutional intricacy, for which it is impossible to envisage a universal solution that might be applied regardless of the nature and constitution of the state as a whole.

In the postmodern economy, in which increasingly many people are either in temporary employment or self-employed, industrial action is rapidly disappearing, since its most important victim is now often the one who has recourse to it.

industrial democracy

Industrial production in which workers, whether or not they have ownership of the means of production, at any rate exert *control over it, by participating in the decisions governing its management. (*See further* *collective choice, *democracy, *democratization, *workers' control.) Workers may participate directly, through voting at the crucial decisions, or indirectly, through representatives (who may in turn be officers of a *trade union). The usual form of participation contemplated is one in which workers sit in a representative capacity on the board of directors of the firm, so taking part in all executive decisions. But a variety of other practices could be devised, each of which might equally be called industrial democracy. For example, workers might become shareholders in the firm, and thereby acquire both a vote and an interest in its collective decisions. Laws in Germany that compel employers to put workers or their representatives in board positions are largely socialist in inspiration; the capitalist alternative is to pay part of the workers' wages in shares; *see* *Mitbestimmung.

In favour of industrial democracy the following arguments are often

urged: it serves to identify the interests of the work force more closely with those of the company, and so increases the motive of labour; it removes the antagonism between labour and management, who can perceive more clearly their common interest; it awakens an interest in the end of production in the worker who had otherwise seen himself only as a means; it promises some relief from *alienation, perhaps by virtue of that last feature. Arguments offered against the arrangement are similarly various: it is said to violate the right of property, by vesting too much control in people who have neither ownership nor an interest in ownership (*see* *separation of ownership and control); it paralyses the firm by electing on to its board of directors workers who have no expertise in management; it *politicizes the wage contract, and puts the directors of the firm at the mercy of a trade union which may have no interest in the firm's survival; it exaggerates the antagonism between labour and management by acquainting the first with the superior position of the second; it perpetuates the subjection of the worker through creating a new illusion of interest in the machine that exploits him. And so on.

industrial law

Not a distinct branch of law, but a name for all those aspects of law that deal with industrial relations and disputes, with the formation and conduct of *trade unions, and with the dealings between employer and employee concerning hours of work, wages, and conditions of employment. Some 'industrial legislation' is in fact *factory legislation, which concerns not the specific contracts of employment, or the apparatus involved in forming, disputing or amending them, but those general conditions of work regarded as legally and politically acceptable.

Attempts to introduce law governing disputes between labour and management have been characteristic of modern *constitutionalist tendencies in government. These have abhorred disputes which, while ostensibly arising under contracts, are in fact irresoluble by the law of contract, and so resolve themselves through *confrontation rather than *adjudication. Some have seen practices such as the *closed shop, and certain forms of *industrial action such as secondary picketing and sympathetic strikes, as already containing elements of lawlessness, independent of any violent or anarchic use to which they might be put. At the same time it seems that trade unions cannot carry out their appointed task – which, on one interpretation at least, is that of giving to their members sufficient collective power to redress the imbalance of the wage contract – without acting in ways that the law of contract could not countenance. Thus already in the UK Trade Disputes Act 1906 unions were granted large privileges and immunities from legal liability in respect of actions done 'in the course of or in contemplation of' an industrial dispute. The principle of such immunity remains fundamental to UK industrial law. The justification refers to the particular nature of the wage contract, pointing out the extent to which it determines the life and livelihood of the labourer, and the inevitable element of *coercion introduced by this. On the other hand, immunities involve a systematic injustice towards those who do not enjoy them, and prevent the law from exerting its true social function, which is that of settling, rather than exacerbating, disputes. Hence in recent years steps have been taken to mitigate the effect of the 1906 legislation, in order to eliminate the confrontational character of industrial relations.

Industrial tribunals were established in the UK in 1964, to deal with complaints in the first instance arising under matters covered by industrial legislation – e.g. unfair dismissal. These have given additional credence to the view that industrial law is only nominally a branch of the law of contract, and is really a new and developing branch of the law, analogous to family law, which has grown up in response to a new and only partly contractual relation between people. The call to make the relation between employer and employee no more easily severable than that between husband and wife may be seen as a desire to inject into the relations of production what Disraeli called the 'feudal principle'. To which an advocate of the *free economy would object: do we really want to return to feudalism?

It is not surprising therefore that UK legislation of the 1980s aimed to restore some of the contractual character of the relation between employer and employee: first by outlawing practices designed to involve third parties in an industrial dispute (e.g. secondary picketing); second, by outlawing the *closed shop and similar practices which compel workers against their will to join a union; and third, by obliging trade unions to ballot their members before taking industrial action. Although these reforms were fiercely resisted by the trade union leadership, they commanded widespread support among union members, and were an important component of *Thatcherism, since endorsed by *New Labour.

industrial revolution
The introduction into many branches of manufacturing industry of innovations in technique (originally machinery, steam power, railways, etc.),

which occurred in Britain in 1760–1860, and which is called a *revolution because of the radical social transformation that it precipitated. (The phrase originated in France, and was used in order to compare the industrial revolution with the French Revolution.) The phenomenon fascinated subsequent political theorists, largely because it seems to demonstrate the demonic force of economic transformation, which precipitates changes in every aspect of social and political life. The industrial revolution involved demographic restructuring, changes in communications, in style of life, in obligations and relationships, in religion and morality, and in the nature of political institutions. It also created, or seemed to create, a new alignment of classes, and a new class antagonism. It was probably this, as much as the history of the French Revolution, that led to the Marxist analysis of society in terms of *base and superstructure, and to the theory of revolution that found the true determinants of revolutionary transformation in the economic base, rather than in the institutions that rest upon it. Modern historians dispute the Marxist claim that the industrial revolution led to a fall in the standard of living for industrial workers, although all agree that the experience of the industrial revolution is one of the most important factors in the emergence of the working class as a political force.

English conservatives of the nineteenth century tended to argue that political adjustments could ensure legal and social continuity even through this transformation, and Disraeli, in his famous 'One Nation' doctrine, perhaps gave the most politically effective expression to that idea. The adjustments in franchise, property law, and parliamentary institutions that were thereby made have often been thought to be instrumental in preventing true social revolution in the UK.

Later industrial revolutions include that in Germany beginning in the 1860s and 1870s, and that which, on some accounts, is being experienced throughout the modern world as a result of the *internet. *See* *technology.

industrialism

The advocacy and pursuit of *industrialization. Some romantic conservatives – notably *Carlyle and *Coleridge – condemned industrialism, not only because of its blindness to the dehumanizing effects of *factory production, but more particularly because of its erosion of natural bonds of attachment between people and between people and places. It was always a challenge for such thinkers to build their criticism into creative politics, and to offer a vision of the future that would not be merely pastoral.

The recent move from manufacturing to service industries in developed countries gives an antiquated character to industrialism, as well as to the theories that oppose it. *See* *service economy.

industrialization

The process whereby production becomes, not necessarily industrious, but industrialized – e.g. centres of *factory production arise, in which every kind of machine is involved in the production process, and new conditions of work created, together with the population demanded by those conditions. The social effects of rapid industrialization have often been studied – in particular the growth of large centres of production such as the English Victorian cities, the depopulation of the countryside, and the rapid erosion of all traditional bonds based on a sense of place and natural *piety, under the impulse of the new *mobility of labour.

Industrialization does not necessarily mean factory production: there can be industrialization in agriculture also, where the principal features are the growth of the farm, the use of ever larger and more efficient machinery, the breaking down of small fields and hedgerows, and the rationalization of crops. The short-term benefits of this are now widely believed to be outweighed by the long-term environmental and social costs. (*See* *agribusiness.)

infiltration

Used either of the clandestine movement of an army into territory occupied by an opponent, or else of the clandestine entry into a party, institution or faction, by agents of some opposing force. A specifically modern form of infiltration, interesting both for its theory and for its results, is *entryism.

inflation

The state of an economy in which prices are steadily rising, resulting in a steady fall in the value of money. Theories of its cause are often (at least since *Keynes) divided into 'cost-push' and 'demand-pull' theories. The first attributes inflation to increased costs of production independent of the state of demand. Thus if there were a general difficulty in obtaining some essential commodity, or if trade unions acted to push up the level of wages without guaranteeing any corresponding increase in productivity, this would automatically increase costs of production. Critics of the theory argue that the wage demands of trade unions are not so much a cause as an effect of inflation; such critics may espouse the 'demand-pull' theory, which holds that inflation is created by an excess of demand over the total of goods and services, at constant prices, independent of supply conditions. *Monetarism is such a theory, arguing

that inflation results to a great extent from governments increasing the supply of money, perhaps with the aim of increasing the level of demand.

Emphasis on demand-pull inflation partly explains the fashionable call to governments to cut public spending, while emphasis on cost-push partly explains the call for incomes policies. (Although, in both cases, views about the relation between government spending and *unemployment are highly influential.) On all these subjects *see* *Keynes, *monetarism, *price control.

The bad effects of inflation are variously identified: the possibility of *hyperflation, and the consequent collapse of the monetary system; the arbitrary and unplanned redistribution of income, e.g. away from those, such as pensioners, with incomes that are not indexed; the discouraging of saving and *investment, and the consequent exacerbation of the disparity between demand and supply; the deleterious effects on the *balance of payments, the exchange rate, and international trade; and so on. Virtually no political thinker welcomes inflation (unless he also welcomes political instability, say, because it prepares the way for *revolution), and modern governments seem to be united in the determination to reduce it. However, because of its redistributive effect it may be favoured by those (notably borrowers and mortgagees) who seek to gain from it, and these may constitute a group sufficiently large and powerful effectively to resist policies designed to counter inflation. Some economists (notably *Kaldor) have also favoured *mild* inflation, as a stimulus to growth, but the consensus seems to be that the stimulus is at best only temporary. In the long term inflation favours spending over saving, and therefore reduces the capital investment upon which economic *growth depends.

It should be noted that, perhaps because the two rival explanations given are (rightly or wrongly) often associated respectively with advocates of free-market capitalism and of social democracy, the discussion of the issue reaches further than questions of economics. Even there, it will tend to take into account the phenomenon of unemployment, since many theories seem to accept that employment and inflation rise together, so that the ideal of full employment and stable prices may be impossible to achieve. (*See* *Phillips curve.)

inflationary gap
The gap between *aggregate demand and aggregate supply which precipitates demand-pull *inflation.

influence
One of the basic concepts of political science but, like many such concepts, extremely difficult to define. It is left undefined in international law, and although municipal law makes use of such concepts as 'undue influence' it is usually assumed that an intuitive understanding of the idea will suffice. The major problems concern the relations and distinctions between influence and *control, *force, *coercion, *interference, and *power. As defined in this dictionary, influence is a *form* of power, distinct, however, from control, coercion, force and (probably) interference. It involves affecting the conduct of another through giving reasons for action short of threats; such reasons may refer to his advantage, or to moral or benevolent considerations, but they must have weight for him, so as to affect his decision. The influenced agent, unlike the agent who is coerced, acts freely. He may choose to ignore those considerations which influence him, and he may himself exert control over the influencing power, as in an unequal marriage.

As illustrations of the vital distinction between influence and control, consider the following two cases: the USSR claimed that Eastern Europe was a *sphere of influence. However, it *seemed* to be a 'sphere of control', in that the USSR could dictate a vast number of key political decisions within that sphere. Again *democratic centralism is said to be democratic because the people can influence all decisions; the Western theory of constitutional democracy assumes that influence is not enough: the people must exert some control over political decisions, for example, by being able to eject a representative from office. The theory of *representation and *election is therefore a theory not of popular influence but of popular control.

infrastructure
Literally an underpinning, or substructure; now used in three separate contexts in diverging ways:

1. Economics. The infrastructure of a state denotes underlying capital *accumulations, embodied in such things as roads, communications systems, and other capital items, including, on some accounts, such intangibles as *education and *law.

2. Military theory. The infrastructure of an army or military zone consists in bases, installations and so on, which support and supply the military activities of the soldiers that make use of them.

3. In politics. Sometimes the word 'infrastructure' is used to denote the *base of social institutions, in the context of a *determinist theory of their cause. Some also refer to 'ideological infrastructure', meaning to imply that, even in the realm of *ideology, there are more fundamental beliefs, values and perceptions, which connect together to support transient and fragile superstructures of thought and feeling. (For example, the infrastructure of

Christian belief underpins the many fleeting and sectarian enthusiasms that have transcribed it into action.)

injunction

A remedy, granted by courts on application from a plaintiff who stands to be injured by some action or inaction, whereby the courts order someone to refrain from doing (restrictive injunction) or to do (mandatory injunction) the thing in question. The remedy was not available in *common law, which is applied only *after* misdemeanour and never before it; however, it is a long-standing principle of *equity that, in cases where injury would be irreparable, continuous and inadequately remedied by damages, the courts have power to grant an injunction. They may also grant such ancillary relief (including damages) as is appropriate and just, but, because the remedy is equitable, they will also look to the conduct of the parties in deciding whether an injunction should be granted (i.e. the 'maxims of equity' apply).

Breach of injunction amounts to contempt of court and is therefore a criminal act, for which the usual penalty is imprisonment. Hence many have objected to the wide powers of injunction in the UK and US courts, on the ground that they can be used to import criminal sanctions into civil disputes. Injunction has been extensively used in the US, not only to ensure protection of rights guaranteed by the constitution, but also in highly controversial areas, such as labour disputes. *See also* *prior restraint/subsequent punishment.

injustice

See *justice.

inquisitorial system

The procedure in criminal cases adopted in most *civilian systems of law, to be contrasted with the *adversarial (or accusatorial) system of the *common law. Under the inquisitorial system the court itself, rather than counsels for the prosecution and the defence, interrogates witnesses, calls for evidence and examines the accused. The court is composed of a judge or a bench of judges and assessors, and must ascertain the facts, establish the verdict and pass judgement. In the adversarial system the case is argued by prosecution and defence before a judge and jury. The facts of the case, as well as the verdict, are decided by the jury on hearing the evidence presented by defence and prosecution. The judge, who normally sits alone, directs counsel and jury on points of law and procedure and passes sentence. The inquisitorial system bestows upon the prosecution the full power of the court; it also makes no use of juries and places the whole matter of the trial in the hands of lawyers and experts. The rule of common law, that the accused is 'innocent until proved guilty' does not apply, and convictions are generally far easier to secure.

institution

Widely defined by the *Oxford English Dictionary* as an established law, custom, usage, practice, organization, or other element in the political or social life of a people; a regulative principle or convention subservient to the needs of an organized community or the general ends of civilization. Some sociologists attempt to bring order into the discussion of institutions by distinguishing four types: the political (concerned with regulating the pursuit and exercise of *power), the economic (concerned with establishing and maintaining production and economic relations), the cultural (involving *education, *culture, and *leisure), and institutions of *kinship (including the *family). This division is helpful only to the extent that these four spheres of social life do not completely interpenetrate; moreover it is associated with no accepted theory of the general nature and function of institutions. Nevertheless the concept of an institution is indispensable to political thought, and it is important to clarify it. It is for example a frequent complaint made by conservatives that neither liberals nor socialists give a satisfactory account of institutions, or attempt to show how their respective ideals might be *embodied* in institutions. Whether or not the accusation is fair, the failure of *democratic centralism to generate any institution that commands the respect of those governed by it has frequently been noted, and has often been thought to be connected with the *Marxist attempt to eliminate reference to institutions from the description of the underlying forces of history. Among important features of institutions the following deserve mention:

(i) Institutions contain 'members', but are not identical with any member, even when there is only a single member, as in the institution of *monarchy.

(ii) Institutions have independent *agency, and sometimes even personality. There are things done and suffered by institutions which are not done or suffered by any of their members; and institutions may have rights and obligations that do not belong to any member. (Some *individualists doubt both these propositions.) The conferring of a degree is an act of a university, but not necessarily of any individual member of it, just as the condemning of a criminal is the act of a court, but not of any individual officer of the court. These two features seem to belong to institutions whether or not they are voluntary associations, whether or not they are

recognized as persons in law, and whether or not they are *incorporated. (Thus a football club may be *blamed* for damage caused by its members, even though it is a voluntary association without legal personality.)

(iii) Institutions may endure beyond the life of any particular member, and have a history which is not simply the history of their members.

(iv) Institutions manifest their existence through the intentional acts of their members; they also form and govern the intentions of their members, partly by influencing the conceptions from which the members act. A complex example of this is a parade: soldiers on parade are doing something which is unintelligible without the existence of military institutions; they are also doing it with an intention that can be expressed only in military terms.

Institutions may or may not have a *constitution; they may or may not have rules, laws and *conventions; they may or may not be *autonomous. The defence of autonomous institutions (and the required *freedom of association) is an important conservative and liberal cause. Autonomy can mean either or both of two things: (a) the autonomous institution is self-governing, answerable to no external constraints other than those contained in the criminal and civil law; (b) the autonomous institution has its own internal purposes which could not be fulfilled in some other way, but which require just *this* institutional arrangement (*see*, e.g., *education, *sport). The proliferation of both kinds of autonomy might be thought to be necessary for the accommodation of the diversity of social life, as well as for the protection of the realms of *leisure and the *private from the encroachments of the state. A state may also be defined as totalitarian on the grounds that it does not permit autonomous institutions in any sphere in which the state has an interest – e.g. in education, trade union organization, and so on.

The continuity of society is something that many conservatives extol, and which they seek to embody in the continuity of autonomous institutions (rather than in the state). Such thinkers are also apt to refer to the necessary fragility of institutions, which, like life, are always easier to destroy than to create, while being so deeply implicated in the moral development of the individual that he may well be unable to know what he loses in destroying them, or to envisage, except in negative terms, the value of a world that is not conditioned by their presence. (These conservative theories are to be found, for example, in *Burke and through him have been extremely influential.) However, it should not be thought that conservative thought has a monopoly over this concept, which is fundamental also to the 'constitution of liberty' which liberalism has, in its reflective moments, attempted to prescribe. *See* *Hayek.

institutional economics
School of economic thought (also known as institutionalism), which flourished in the US in the 1920s and which held, partly under the influence of *Veblen, that economists err in attempting to understand economic behaviour without taking account of the non-economic, specifically institutional, contexts in which it occurs. Institutional economics passed through a period of eclipse, but is once again attracting followers in both the US and the UK.

insurgency
A term used in *international law and generally in order to denote an uprising ('insurrection') against constituted

government which falls short of *revolution, *rebellion or *civil war. Hence 'insurgent', a belligerent in such an insurrection. To call the Afghan tribesmen who fought the Soviet-backed government 'insurgents' is to avoid the question of the legal status of their war. At the same time it is to suppose that the government against which they fought is not that of a foreign power, nor one established by *usurpation. Nevertheless in certain circumstances (e.g. for the purposes of negotiation, settlement, trade and cooperation) it may be necessary to deal directly and legally with 'insurgent governments', which may therefore be accorded *international personality.

integration
Different groups within a jurisdiction may have the same *rights in law, but nevertheless enjoy unequal *privileges, and disparate social, educational and recreational institutions. (Contrast *segregation.) Integration is the process whereby all such institutions are made available to all members of the state, regardless of creed, race, and origin, with the intention of forming a unified *civil society within the jurisdiction of a unified *state. The aim of integration may, however, partially conflict with that of *toleration, which requires some measure of respect towards those groups (whether ethnic, religious, or however formed) which determine among themselves to remain socially distinct from other groups within the state, and who, while perhaps anxious for equal legal rights, are equally anxious for separate social institutions. This problem is of considerable importance in the US, on account of the federal structure designed to allow for just such a separation between state and civil society, and on account of the constitution, which, through the bill of rights, acts so as to impose uniform legal expectations.

intégrisme

Term coined by the French *right-wing intellectual Charles Maurras, to denote the aim of bringing all distinct characteristics of a *nation within the purview of its political organization, so that, e.g., the *Roman Catholic Church in France would be regarded as an integral part of the political structure of the country, along with the language, customs and traditions of the people. A form of late *nationalism, it has also been denounced as *fascist by some of its opponents, on account of the attempt to incorporate the functions of *civil society into those of the *state. It may be that this accusation overlooks the distinction between asserting the political relevance of an institution or *social fact, and advocating state participation in it. Maurras and his followers evoked the famous charge of the *trahison des clercs*, from the pen of Julien Benda, a liberal intellectual who believed that no intellectual should lend his support to the politics of prejudice (unless the prejudice was liberal). *See also* *royalism.

The term has been re-deployed in recent years to denote the aims and beliefs of *Islamists motivated by a desire to subordinate all forms of social life to the imperatives of their religion: *see* *fundamentalism.

intellectual property

Assets of an intangible kind, in the form of inventions, symbols, literary artefacts, in which intellectual effort has been invested, perhaps with a view to exploiting the result for profit. The protection of intellectual property has become an ever more significant feature in modern economies, as corporations retreat from producing things and take to branding them instead (*see* *brands). The first attempts to claim property in intellectual assets took the form of patents,

the earliest recorded example being granted in England in 1449. Patents of 14 years were exempted from the English Statute of Monopolies 1623 (which ended the practice of monopolies granted by the Crown); the idea was to encourage private citizens to make their secrets known, in return for a short-term monopoly of their use. In this way patents were supposed to facilitate the spread of useful knowledge and to encourage trade. Hence patents were protected in the US constitution from the outset (Section VIII, paragraph 8).

As originally conceived neither patents nor copyright governed ideas: the one protected useful inventions while the other protected the written word. But already in the sixteenth century two Italian mathematicians, Tartaglia and Cardano, attempted to claim monopoly rights to a purely intellectual acquisition, the 'cossist algebra' – a form of calculation that speeded up book-keeping. The case never came to court, but it anticipates the current conflicts over access to code and software, concerning which *see* *Open Source. It could be said that it is fair to patent inventions, but not to patent discoveries, for which the reward is honour, not a right to exclusive use. But the distinction is not easy to make, and in one area – that of *trade related intellectual property (TRIPS) – the confusions are both rife and politically charged.

Intellectual property also includes trademarks and trade secrets. While a patent protects a product, a trademark merely protects a brand. At the same time it may represent an enormous investment of time and energy, and the theft of a brand through counterfeiting can lead to unsustainable losses, especially in industries that deal in products like fashionable clothing, in which the only real investment is the brand. Hence the perceived need to protect intellectual property world-wide. This has led to the TRIPS provisions in the *World Trade Organization treaties, and to the Patent Cooperation Treaty, enforced as part of the laws of each signatory, and administered by the World Intellectual Property Organization in Geneva.

intellectuals

Byron (who rhymed 'intellectual' with 'have they not hen-pecked you all?') was one of the first writers to use this term in its modern sense, so as to denote someone for whom ideas, science, art and culture are so important as to determine not only the aims of everyday life, but also the roots of political thought and action. The *clerisy of *Coleridge was described in terms that celebrate the role of the intellectual as guardian of cultural and social values (although from an established position *within* society, rather than from an oppositional vantage-point outside it), and throughout the nineteenth century intellectuals produced similar apologies for their own condition. In *Leninism the *intelligentsia are given a crucial role in the preparation and instigation of revolution, and are even regarded as suitable members of a subsequent (and, according to the theory, provisional) government. By contrast, conservative thinkers have often tended to dismiss intellectuals as either politically ineffective, or not to be trusted, since it is easier to go wrong when attempting to articulate a *doctrine than when following a *prejudice. The effect of the intellectual, on this view, is to draw a veil of abstraction around the immediacies of practical life, and to sever politics from the instincts of the people. That *populist idea can be found in *Burke, as part of his denunciation of the French Revolution and of the role of intellectuals in bringing about its worst

excesses. (Burke wrote of a 'literary cabal', motivated by an 'armed doctrine'.)

The view of Coleridge and *Arnold, which attributes to intellectuals the irreplaceable task of preserving the gift of culture, so as to secure it from the assaults of barbarism and from the blight of indifference, is equally, however, a conservative view, just as Julien Benda's attack on the intellectual presumption of a right to rule (*see* *trahison des clercs*) is an anticonservative defence of liberal values. (Though it is worth noting that the assumption of a right to rule is more characteristic of left-wing intellectuals (Benda included) than their right-wing opponents.) Since it is only intellectuals who are anxious to articulate, rather than to enact, political ideas, it is only they that will be bothered by this dispute over their own status. However, there is evidence that they are worried by it. Many left intellectuals, disturbed by the classical *Marxist position which seems to side-line their contribution to the march of history, have tried to develop theories of 'intellectual production', with which to justify their role. (*See* *technological determinism*.) Thus *Gramsci, for example, argued that intellectuals occupy key positions in the organization of society, and have a functional significance which confers on them vast *de facto* power, both economic and political.

intelligence

The gathering of 'intelligence' about a potential enemy, whether political, economic or military, is now one of the most sophisticated branches of *government. Governments anxious about the security of their rule also gather intelligence about those subject to it, to the point where every citizen may regard every other as a potential policeman. *See* *police state.

The organization of the various internationally operative intelligence agencies – such as the CIA – lies outside the scope of this dictionary; but it must be remembered, in any attempt to describe the nature of the modern state, that these agencies form an ever more powerful, and ever more autonomous, influence in the exercise of power. Fear of this autonomy in the CIA led to the formation in the US of a Senate committee (under Senator Church), which in 1976 called for stricter control of the intelligence service, and provisions for compelling it to be answerable to Congress. The accountability of the KGB was as inscrutable as the KGB itself, but it, and its predecessor the NKVD, together with the many subsidiary organizations through which they exerted themselves, have probably had a far greater influence in shaping modern history than the communist ideology which they purported to serve.

intelligent design

The claim that the Darwinian theory of evolution, while it explains the capacity of species to develop through random genetic change, does not give a complete account of the *origin* of species, and that the most likely explanation of that origin is in terms of design. Even if it is true that humanity reached its present state through a process of microevolution, of the kind hypothesized by Darwin, the starting point was itself an organism with features so remarkable that it is highly improbable that they were not designed. Various arguments are advanced in support of that claim. For example there is the incompleteness of the fossil record, from the Darwinian standpoint: an objection to his theory that Darwin himself recognized. There is also the difficulty of accounting for functional parts of an organism, such

as the eye, in terms of a gradual process of evolution: an organ cannot be half-way to being an eye. The eye is, so to speak, a target rather than a result, and difficult to conceive as a by-product of a process that is not intrinsically guided towards creating just such a thing.

Critics believe that the concept of probability invoked in that argument is without foundation, and that the difficulties for Darwin's theory are merely general problems arising when we seek to translate *teleological into *functional explanations, problems which can always be surmounted. The controversy has become significant, since it impinges on the teaching of science in American schools, with advocates of intelligent design vying with Darwinists for control over the curriculum. The controversy also hides a more urgent disagreement: between those who believe that schools should have nothing whatsoever to do with religion, under the 'no foundation' clause in the US constitution, and those who wish school education to prepare their children for a religious way of life. (*See* *secular government.*) However, it should be pointed out that the hypothesis of intelligent design is not in itself a religious claim, and requires no particular form, nor any form at all, of worship, piety or prayer.

intelligentsia

Russian term, current since the mid-nineteenth century, used to describe collectively all those *intellectuals who not only identify themselves as such, but do so in the course of attributing to themselves a particular social position independent of *class, and perhaps accessible from any class, together with a political outlook that reflects that position. Feebly defined as 'critically thinking personalities' by the Russian materialist and proto-Marxian philosopher D.I. Pisarev (1840–68), they were promptly portrayed (and condemned) as *nihilists by Ivan Turgenev, in his famous novel *Fathers and Sons* and by devils in Dostoevsky's novel of that title. Some find Turgenev's and Dostoevsky's vision confirmed in the role of the intelligentsia before, during and after the Russian Revolution.

interest

Return from the deployment of *capital over time; consequently the sum of money due after financial capital has been loaned for a given length of time. The 'classical theory' of interest given by *Smith and *Ricardo represents interest as an income which attaches to capital, rather as *rent attaches to *land, a view which explains interest only given a satisfactory theory of rent. The classical theory was developed further: the rate of interest was seen as being determined by the supply and demand for loanable funds. The former depended upon the expected profitability of investment which, according to the theory, depended upon the marginal productivity of capital. The latter depended upon consumers' rate of *time preference: goods available today have more value than goods available tomorrow.

The classical theories, and related ones, were criticized by Keynes, who tried to explain the rate of interest in monetary terms, developing a more complex analysis in terms of expectations, in which interest is regarded as the reward for sacrificing the liquidity of other assets. However, the marginal productivity theory of interest still retains some support.

The receipt of interest has always been the subject of moral condemnation – for example, by *Aristotle in the *Oeconomica*, and by traditional *Christian and *Islamic doctrines of *usury. However, in times of *inflation, there can be little inducement to

save without positive *nominal* interest, and, without private saving, new capital cannot be accumulated by the *private sector. So a condemnation of interest is sometimes thought to be tantamount to a conditional affirmation of socialism. For a brief survey of the arguments, *see* *just price, *ribâ*, *usury.

interest group

A *group, united by common interest, which has sufficient *identity to act on its own behalf (e.g. by electing officers, and representatives, establishing common funds, associations, and reports, engaging in active *propaganda) and which therefore has some *influence either on public opinion or on government. An interest group may have sufficient political *access to become a *pressure group; alternatively its political influence may be only indirect, e.g. through the mobilization of popular support. The theory of the interest group is an important part of modern political science, and vital to the explanation of *collective choice.

interests

When it is said that some action or state is 'in Mary's interest', or 'one of Mary's interests', any one of four things may be meant: Mary desires it; she intends it; she values it; or she needs it either intrinsically, or in order to satisfy one of her desires, intentions or values. Not everything desired is intended, not everything intended is valued, not everything valued is needed, and vice versa for the whole sequence. The distinctions here – familiar to a philosopher – may be overlooked in political discussion, even though the concept of a 'real interest' (sometimes used with sinister implications) has evolved in order to distinguish those things which are really in a person's interest from those things which he or she merely thinks to be so.

Real interests are best seen as *needs, and these are indisputably objective – i.e. whether or not Mary needs something is determined independently of Mary's thinking that she does; Mary may or may not be right about this. The same is not obviously true of Mary's desires, intentions, and values, which, like her beliefs, are or seem to be subjective: there is no distinction between what they are and what Mary thinks they are – although Freudian psychology might lead one to doubt this, at least over a certain range of cases.

In sociology interests tend to be identified with *revealed preferences: that is with all aims that are actually pursued, whatever their source and justification. A distinction is then made between individual and 'common' interests, the latter being definitive of *groups, and invoked in the explanation of *collective choice.

In all political thinking, however, the distinction between needs, values, intentions and desires should be observed, so that it may be necessary to penetrate below the sociologist's analysis. For one thing, since a person may neither desire nor value what he needs, his real interests may diverge from his pursuits: is it then justified to restrain him? Some forms of liberalism regard any obstruction to desires as an interference with freedom. Others – perhaps influenced by *Kantian theories of *autonomy – argue that an interference in desires which permits the realization of intentions does not reduce, but on the contrary enhances, freedom. Still others – again perhaps under Kantian influence – may argue that an interference in intentions that permits the greater realization of *values is not only not a violation, but a liberation, of human autonomy. The last view seems to permit considerable

invasion of ordinary human projects, but, says the Kantian, no *rational choice would ever be impeded by it, and this is the true justification of all those strictures that are contained in law.

In all discussions of this issue much will depend upon the philosophical question of the objectivity of values, and also on a conception of *human nature in terms of which the needs of the human being are to be specified. It is a frequent criticism of the application of preference theories to political decisions that the concept of a preference is indifferent between desires, intentions and values, while the aim of politics may be unintelligible if these are given equal weight, or even assumed to be commensurate.

interference

Left undefined in international law, but a term vital to the understanding of international relations. Interference is a form of *agency, which may involve *force or the threat of force, or the establishment of a system of *control or *coercion. It involves action designed to ensure compliance with certain requirements, in a sphere where another agent is morally, politically or legally *sovereign. It involves disrespect for sovereignty, and a refusal to recognize that things which affect your interest may not be your concern.

The precise nature of the agency involved is difficult to define. It seems to be a definite interference in the affairs of another state to make a show of arms and to threaten, or represent oneself as threatening, force, should that state change its form of government. On the other hand, to refuse to ratify a treaty or a trade agreement after a change of government, in order to register disapproval, seems not to be an interference, but merely an attempt to influence.

international capitalism

Term used to denote not a theory but a force (*cf.* *international socialism). The suggestion is that there is a natural tendency in capitalism to expand, whether behind the cover of *imperialism, or through the capture of markets, so inducing economic dependence upon absentee shareholders. The rise of the *multinational company has renewed the fear of international capitalism, and the desire to stem its advance – though not by socialism; rather by the restoration of the *local economies that are threatened by *globalization.

International Court of Justice

The judicial organ of the United Nations, established in 1946 at The Hague. All 15 judges must be from different countries, and have *judicial independence, not being representatives in any legal or political sense of the countries from which they are appointed. Jurisdiction is limited to civil cases brought by and against *sovereign states, although the statute which establishes the court contains an 'optional clause', whereby member states can choose to be bound by the court's decisions in any matter of international law, the interpretation of treaties, and so on.

The judgement is that of a majority, and the court is not bound by its own previous decisions: nevertheless it has written reports, and these have played a major part in the development of *international law.

International Labour Organization

Set up in 1919 by the Treaty of Versailles with the object of advancing the cause of *social justice by working towards an international code of labour law and practice, in the form of conventions (legal instruments to serve as models for national legislations) and recommendations. It attempts to provide an international forum for labour demands, and to recommend to governments what are in effect constitutional means of answering them, through law and *conciliation. Since 1946, the ILO has been a specialized agency of the United Nations.

international law

International law has two branches: public (applying between states), which is referred to in this entry, and private (applying to individuals), which is also known as *conflict of laws and described under that heading. In theory the first is a single body of law applying universally, while the second (which settles such questions as *jurisdiction) inevitably varies from place to place, being simply a branch of the law of the particular *sovereign state that applies it.

The possibility of an international law has been one of the great issues of Western political thought, not only since the collapse of *ecclesiastical jurisdiction, but also prior to that jurisdiction, when jurists and philosophers faced the question of adapting and justifying *Roman law in local conditions that differed markedly from those known to the Roman jurists.

The term 'international law' was coined in 1780 by *Bentham, but modern discussions have their roots much earlier, in the thought of *Aquinas, *Grotius, *Pufendorf, Vattel and *Kant, all of whom attempted to give theoretical foundations for international *jurisdiction. Grotius advocated a mixture of natural law and *positive law, as providing the basis for the law obtaining between states, so that it is now normal to divide theorists of the subject into positivists, naturalists and Grotians, the leading naturalist being Pufendorf (*De Jure Naturae et Gentium*, 1672), and the leading positivist Vattel (*Le droit des* *gens*, 1758). According to the positivists international law is a summary of treaties, customs and agreements between states, with no authority beyond that provided by the voluntary submission of the parties; while according to the naturalists there is a universal source of this authority in *human nature, which can be neither disobeyed in good conscience nor overriden by contract. On either view the question of the intellectual basis of the law must be distinguished from that of its effectiveness, and it is clear that, in the lack of any single sovereign power to enforce international law, the agreement of nations to abide by it (for whatever reason) is the only material force that can ensure its application. Complex problems of jurisprudence arise over the relation between international law and state (in this context usually called *municipal) law. Which takes precedence, and why? According to the 'monist' doctrine both systems of law are binding on those subject to them, so that international law automatically enters into the legal system of any state subscribing to it; according to the 'dualist' doctrine, the origins of the two kinds of law are so different as to define completely different spheres of action. Neither theoretical position alters the need to bring the two into harmony, since clearly any conflict will lead to municipal courts overriding decisions in international law, and hence to a *de facto* withdrawal of the state from the agreement to be bound by that law.

International Monetary Fund (IMF)
Set up as a result of a bilateral agreement between the US and the UK in 1944, at the *Bretton Woods Conference, the IMF came into operation in 1947, as a specialist agency of the *United Nations. Its aim has been to encourage international cooperation in the monetary field, removing *exchange controls, and stabilizing exchange rates, so as to permit multilateralism among those states which elected to belong to it. The fund is a substitute for the gold standard, which was effectively abandoned by the beginning of the 1930s. It is used to tide member states over temporary balance of payment difficulties, by allowing them to borrow money in exchange for their own currency, which they are then obliged to buy back in five years' time. The effect of the IMF has been considerable, and its use of revenue from gold sales to provide aid for developing countries has caused it to have a wide influence besides the real stabilization achieved in the currencies of its member states.

In order to fulfil its function, the IMF has been granted the power to impose restrictions on the economic policies of member states wishing to borrow large amounts of money from it. These restrictions involve measures to reduce inflation, to cut back government spending and to increase taxation, so as to bring about a more balanced national budget. They have been a major factor in preventing socialist governments from embarking upon state-funded programmes and have therefore been resented by the left. On the other hand, their beneficial effect on the balance of international trade is widely recognized and, since the collapse of *international socialism and the *Comecon system, most members of the former Soviet empire have elected to join the IMF.

The IMF is distinct from the *World Bank (the International Bank for Reconstruction and Development) also set up under the auspices of the United Nations in 1944. This has the function of raising loans for developing countries and has no monetary policy.

international organizations

Bodies set up by multilateral agreement between states, to be distinguished from transnational organizations, which simply operate in a plurality of states (in the manner of *international socialism), and *multinational corporations. Since the Congress of Vienna, international organizations have been of enormous importance in determining relations between states. The question of the *international personality of such organizations is often crucial – without it, they cannot be party to disputes under *international law. (Thus it seems that the British *Commonwealth lacks international personality, while the *United Nations possesses it.)

In addition to the United Nations and its subsidiary institutions (which include the *International Court of justice), the following international organizations have become politically important: the Food and Agriculture Organization, the *International Labour Organization and UNESCO (UN Educational, Scientific and Cultural Organization). These are not strictly part of the UN, but have been brought into relationship with it by agreements between them and the Economic and Social Council of the UN.

Among the specialized agencies of the United Nations, two of the most important are the World Health Organization and the *International Monetary Fund. Equally significant, though outside the UN structure, is the Organization for Economic Cooperation and Development (OECD), established in 1961 with the aim of encouraging economic growth and stability among member states while contributing to the economic growth of the developing countries, whether or not members.

international personality

Status of a legal *person in *international law – accorded to every *sovereign state, and denoting the external aspect of *sovereignty in so far as this is a legally recognizable attribute. A state can remain the same international person despite changes of name, *territory, *dynasty, form of government, *constitution, etc. The problem of the true identity of states is reflected in the difficulties posed by the international recognition of a new *regime. Recognition as an international person is, however, not the same as recognition as *legitimate: an *insurgent government and a legitimate government may equally acquire the status of legal persons. If that were not so, then there could be no *adjudication of their dispute.

Individuals may also have international personality, for the purpose of laws dealing expressly with their interests, such as the laws concerning human rights, but how that helps them to enforce international law against a resistant *municipal power is hard to say. It seems that the problem of enforcing human rights in those states where citizens are apt to express their grievances in terms of the definition of that concept embodied in the UN Charter, and thereby in international law, has remained unchanged by the existence of that law. This may be partly because individuals' rights are also determined by *municipal law, whereas the rights of a sovereign state are determined *only* by international law.

international socialism

The form of socialism advocated in the *Communist Manifesto*, which regards its aims as universal, and recognizes no national boundaries, seeking the emancipation of the *proletariat everywhere, from bondage imposed upon it by private property in the form of capitalism. The proletariat is sometimes held to be the only class that is truly international, having been stripped, according to the theory, of every asset that would attach its interests to a particular nation, territory, sovereign, or other object of localized political allegiance. *Cf.* *national socialism.

international trade
The exchange of goods and services between one state and another, which takes place because of differing costs of production, and because of the pursuit of a wider range of goods and services, and a greater quantity of both. The 'law of comparative advantage', due to Torrens and *Ricardo, holds that even when the costs of production are uniformly higher in one country than in another, mutual trade may be to the advantage of both. According to neoclassical theory, states will tend to export the commodities in the production of which their most abundant resources are most intensively employed. Hence trade will involve the exchange of 'labour intensive' goods, from states with a relatively large labour force, against raw materials and technology, from states in which those may be found and produced in relative abundance. *Mercantilism and *protectionism hold that too much unrestricted trade between states can sometimes be bad for at least one of the parties, and therefore advocate restrictions of *free trade, say, through tariffs. The controversy here, which is ancient, seems to continue unresolved. Extensive international trade has, however, often been seen as a vital adjunct to *international law, creating the mutual dependence between states that provides the ultimate sanction in any dispute. It is sometimes argued, however, that trade has a tendency to create its own kind of political

subservience: *see* *imperialism, *international capitalism.

internationalism
The belief that political activity should define its objectives not in terms of the constitution, history or geographical boundaries of any particular *nation, but in terms of a universal human condition.

Examples of internationalist theories include *Marxism (in its classical form), which thought of all political activity in terms of an international *class struggle (*see* *international socialism); the political theory of *Kant, who saw the aim of politics as the federation of *republics in a 'League of Nations', governed by objectively determined and universally applicable laws; and the medieval conception of *natural law, which associated an internationalist theory of the human condition with a defence of the twin international jurisdictions of the Holy Roman Empire and the *church. The last example is, however, deviant, in that it preceded the widespread *nationalism against which internationalism is in part a reaction.

Internationals
Term usually applied to a succession of international federations formed from parties dedicated to *international socialism, the first (the international 'Working Men's Association') being founded in London in 1864, with the support of Marx, the second in Paris in 1889, both being split by faction, decay and hostility between the participants, divided over matters equally of doctrine and of policy. The third, the Comintern, founded in Moscow in 1919, survived, due to ruthless leadership exercised first by Lenin and subsequently by Stalin, who dissolved it in 1943. Meanwhile the so-called Fourth International had been formed in

1938 by followers of *Trotsky, while an independent 'Labour and Socialist International' had been created in 1923 by a few powerless *social democrats. (There was also a 'fascist international' founded at the same time, although it had no influence.) Finally a Socialist International was founded in 1951 in Frankfurt, with members from 40 countries. The history of the internationals evolved around various disputes, principal being that concerning anarchism, which split the first, that between *bolsheviks and *mensheviks, which split the second, that between *Stalinists and *Trotskyists, which split the third. The fissiparous nature of the Internationals offered a lesson which only those who attended them seemed incapable of learning.

internet
The world-wide network of telecommunications, which enables people to communicate instantly around the globe. The internet has transformed every aspect of life, by accelerating all transactions that can be conducted at a distance. Some welcome this, arguing that it breaks down barriers between people, some deplore it, arguing that it erects new barriers between people, since it enables them to obtain all that they want from a position of cushioned solitude, and makes it possible to escape from commitments with the same rapidity as they are acquired. See *multinationals, *Open Source.

intervention
In *international law intervention means dictatorial *interference in the domestic or foreign affairs of a state by another, in such a way as to impair the first state's *independence. The law of intervention has in the past suffered from the defect that the legality of any act of intervention can always be put

beyond question by declaring it to be war. However, under contemporary law, war is illegal unless undertaken in self-defence.

interventionism
The belief in the right and necessity of government to interfere in the operation of the market in order to achieve economic or social ends. The means advocated might involve any or all of the following: *price control, *exchange control, *incomes policy, support for ailing industries, *nationalization. The outcome of such policies may be a *market economy with close state supervision, or it may be a *mixed economy.

investment
In economics, the expenditure on *capital goods rather than *commodities that are immediately consumed. In more common parlance, the purchase of any asset or the undertaking of any commitment which involves forgoing present for the sake of future benefits.

In forgoing present for future benefits (and therefore in preferring capital to consumption expenditure), a person makes a sacrifice of a kind necessary to continuing *production (cf. *Austrian school theories of capital). Hence the *interest on investment, if it represents the price at which an individual is prepared to forgo present enjoyment for future enjoyment (together with the risk of no enjoyment at all should the project fail), is simply the real price of investment (see *time preference, *usury).

invisible hand
*Adam Smith argued in The Wealth of Nations, 1776, that, under the mechanism of a *free market, the pursuit of profit leads each participant to act to the material advantage of society as a whole, as though 'led by an invisible hand to promote an end which was no

part of his intention'. This is a more optimistic formulation of the slogan 'private vices, public benefits', given prominence by *Mandeville, and some form of it may still be offered as part of the justification of the market economy – namely that it also embodies a mechanism which achieves common economic objectives to the greater satisfaction of its participants than any viable alternative.

Smith's idea was the precursor of *Hegel's 'cunning of reason'. Recently *Nozick has generalized Adam Smith's dictum, so as to describe as 'invisible hand explanations' all those theories that 'explain what looks to be the product of someone's intentional design as not being brought about by anyone's intentions'. Not surprisingly, he finds that such explanations are common throughout the *social sciences (*Anarchy, State and Utopia*, 1974). He was to some extent anticipated in this by *Hayek, who offers invisible hand theories not as explanations but as justifications of the 'spontaneous orders' which arise in response to shared problems – notably that of the *common law. However 'invisible hand' mechanisms do not necessarily work to the benefit of the participants. Not only are there cases of 'private virtues, public evils', as Mandeville recognized; there are also many examples of *counterfinality, e.g. the *prisoner's dilemma.

iron law of oligarchy

The law postulated by the German sociologist Roberto Michels that in all organizations power tends to fall into the hands of a small number of leaders, regardless of the formal constitution of the organization. Applying this 'law' to the German Socialist Party he argued that, in spite of its democratic constitution and revolutionary goals, it was doomed to acquire bureaucratic and also conservative leaders. As Michels put it, 'who says organization, says oligarchy' (*Political Parties*, 1920).

iron law of wages

Expression coined by *Lassalle, to denote the process whereby wages are supposedly kept down to the minimum required for the subsistence of the wage-labourer. The arguments for such a 'law' had been given by *Malthus and *Ricardo, who argued that if wages rise above subsistence level, the population will increase, and with it the supply of labour, so that, by the 'law of supply and demand', wages will fall back to the subsistence level. *Marx accepted the 'iron law', but not for those reasons: rather, he argued, there will always be a 'reserve army of labour' under capitalism, and hence a substitute for any labourer not prepared to work for the subsistence wage. The subsequent history of capitalism has refuted all versions of the law as thoroughly as the history of socialism has confirmed the *iron law of oligarchy.

irredentism

Originally, the policy and programme of the 'irredentists', i.e. those activists who, in 1878 and thereafter, strove to unify all Italian-speaking regions into a single Italian state. (Their slogan – *Italia irredenta* – means 'Italy unredeemed'.) Now used more generally to name any attempt to unify into one state regions, some of which are regarded as subject to a power with no title to rule them, and all of which are thought to belong, by tradition, law, custom, and language, or by nature, together; *cf.* *nationalism. Significant irredentist movements have arisen since the Second World War in Cyprus (the call for *enosis*, or union with Greece), in Northern Ireland (the Republican movement, which calls for union with the Republic of Ireland), and in Hungarian-speaking Transylvania (the call for union with Hungary).

isegoria

Greek; the equal right to be heard in the sovereign assembly of the state before any public decision is taken. An ideal and partial achievement of *Athenian democracy which is completely absent from all systems of *representation.

Islam

Arabic: submission. Like any religion Islam has had a profound influence on the political institutions of those peoples who have adopted it, and has produced its own legacy of political thought. This has taken three distinct forms: Islamic jurisprudence or *fiqh*; the study of philosophy; and the traditional handbooks or mirrors-for-princes. The early Islamic jurisdictions were founded on the theory of the *caliphate: the divinely sanctioned rule through the successor (*khalîf*) of the prophet. Actual powers in the Muslim world rapidly diversified, however, and the caliphate became an office with little or no temporal power; the question of the legitimacy of actual powers then became acute. The supreme source of authority was the *Islamic law, or *sharî'ah* (= divine legislation), and the *sunna* (= custom, generally used to refer to the precepts and examples that can be extracted from the exemplary life of the Prophet). The source of the law is revelation, through the Koran, through such subsequent texts and commentaries as can be supposed to have been guided by right apprehension of God's purpose and through the authenticated stories of the Prophet's life and sayings, known as *hadîth* (plural *huduth*). The authority of the law is therefore absolute, and all legitimacy must be derived from it. Originally it was thought that any officer, including the Caliph, could be legitimately deposed for an action contrary to the law; later it was realized that this

would be impracticable, and that it was necessary to derive a system of *legal fictions (*hiyal*), in order to reconcile the law with actual human necessities. The jurists became increasingly concerned with the problem of obedience to a power which is, from the point of view of the law, in the wrong hands. Their reflections were various, but in practice of little influence: the prince (*sultân*) continued to administer affairs according to his own law, which existed alongside the divine law, and which was regarded as justified in so far as the divine law left much human conduct undetermined. The radical divide between *Sunni and *Shi'ite has meant that the ways of reconciling divine law with human government have been explored from two closely related and therefore violently antagonistic perspectives, the one accepting the imperfection of human arrangements, the other rejecting it, while waiting the return of the occulted last Imam in the form of the Mahdi. (*See* *Shi'ism.)

The Sunni theory of the caliphate was expounded by Mâwardî (d. 1058), who argued that the caliphate is incumbent upon the Muslim community, but that it is governed by that section of the law which is devoted to man (the *mu'âmalât*) rather than that devoted to God (*ibâdât*). A caliph can be designated by the community or appointed by a ruling caliph: in this way Mâwardî took a step towards the view that the caliph is only spiritually speaking the successor of the Prophet, and can be appointed or elected to this role – a position later defended by al-Ghazâlî (d. 1111), who nevertheless believed that the Caliph ought to be descended from the Quraish, the tribe of the Prophet. As the power of the caliphs dwindled to zero, rival theories arose, such as that of Ibn Jamâ'a (d. 1333), who justified the *sultanate in terms derived from the Sunni legal tradition, and that of *Ibn Taymiyya who denied that the caliphate was mandatory altogether.

Medieval Islam produced important political thinkers, many of them (the *falâsifa*) directly inspired by the Greek philosophers. The *falâasifa* influenced all medieval thought, by transmitting the works of Plato, Aristotle and the neo-Platonists, along with their own detailed interpretations, to the Muslim and Christian worlds. The various attempts to reconcile the Greek vision of the state with the divine law caused renewed attention to the nature of law, as the fundamental principle of government. In his description of the virtuous city, al-Fârâbî (c. 873–950) presents the prophetic revealed law as the constitution of an ideal Platonic state, with Plato's philosopher-king as *imam. He even asserts that 'the meaning of imam, philosopher and lawgiver is one and the same'. The role of the prophet as lawgiver is justified since the soul of the prophet is united with the 'active intellect'. Although reason can supplement revelation, the true system is founded on revelation, since this alone can ensure the happiness of the citizens in the world to come. Avicenna (Ibn Sînâ) (980–1037), notable for his comprehensive synthesis of the neo-Platonic and Aristotelian traditions, argued more directly for the *sharî'ah* as the fount of political order. Philosophy acquaints us with the world of intelligibles and is the occupation of an illumined minority; the things of this world are organized by the prophet, who stands higher in the scheme of things than the philosopher, being in direct communication with God. Man is a political being, who is part of a state and who can exist in this world only through a state. But his salvation depends upon obedience to a higher law.

According to the Andalusian Averroës (Ibn Rushd) (c. 1126–98) philosophy shows the world as it is, but is inaccessible to the mass of mankind, who must therefore learn the truth not through Reason but through revelation, example, dogma and rhetoric. Philosophy does not refute dogma, since truths cannot contradict each other; but in an important sense it goes further in showing what the imagistic and narrative content of ordinary religion really means. The corollary, however, is exactly that drawn by Avicenna: that philosophy has no bearing on the public law, which must be derived by the familiar techniques of *fiqh*. (Averroës was a distinguished *qadi*, or Islamic judge.) Unlike the Greeks, the Muslim philosophers were committed to the view that this law applies not only in this world but also in the next, so that whatever political order is ideal in this world must also describe a possible order in the kingdom of God; hence the ideal states described by the *falâsifa* did not correspond very closely to any recognizable kind of human government. Subsequent thinkers, such as Ibn Taymiyya and the Machiavellian sceptic *Ibn Khaldūn made a point of offering more realistic descriptions of human motivation.

The mirrors-for-princes, typified by that wrriten by the Vizier Nizâm al-Mulk (d. 1092), see kingship as divided into three kinds: the religious, which is the best and leads to salvation for king and subject alike; the philosophical, based on reason and ensuring the good order of earthly government (with or without other-worldly salvation); and the passionate or capricious, which is the way to destruction. The books are garrulous, full of instruction and example, but with little systematic thought.

Modern Islamic thinkers have been of two kinds: those preoccupied with the problem of reconciling Muslim teaching with the modern world and the structure of the *nation state, and those who seek a return to the pure Islamic tradition, such as *Qutb and the followers of *Wahhabism. The Moslem League, led by Mohammed Ali Jinnah (1876–1948), was able to establish an independent Pakistan in the wake of the British withdrawal from India, and in 1956 a coalition of extremists and republicans turned this into an Islamic State, with a constitution based on a reading of the divine law. This was to provide an example for Muslims everywhere, notably in neighbouring Afghanistan (see *Taliban). But Pakistan has gone through a succession of internal conflicts and disorders, and the attempts to found Islamic states have elsewhere frequently led to tyranny and oppression. Many argue that Islamic law leaves much of human life undetermined and is therefore an insufficient basis for government in modern conditions. Others argue that Islam seems to have permitted the foundation and evolution of no institutions of government that might survive the collapse of the faith, so that Islamic states can maintain order only by a constant rehearsal of religious fervour, in a world that finds religious fervour difficult to muster. In this, it is sometimes said, Islam is sharply to be distinguished from *Christianity, which has formed bodies of law, institutions of government and education, and political procedures, all of which have survived the declining influence of the religion that founded them. (*See* *Two Swords doctrine.)

The recent upsurge of *Islamism – among Shi'ite Muslims in Iran and Lebanon, among remnants of the *Muslim Brotherhood, and among Wahhabite factions and groupings such as *al-Qa'eda – has entirely changed the political landscape, both in Islamic countries and in places which the Islamists have targeted. It has also led to a renewed attempt to construct jurisdictions based on *Islamic law, with political institutions framed according to Koranic precepts. The *theocratic guardianship of Ayatollah Khomeini shows the difficulty of reconciling Islamic conceptions of government with Western ideas of citizenship, and in particular with the citizenship of non-Muslims. Traditionally non-Muslims were accepted within the Islamic community (the *ummah*) only as *dhimmî* (i.e. those joined by a pact), whose legal status was a matter of dispute. It seems that only Christians and Jews ('people of the book') could enjoy real guarantees under traditional Islamic jurisdiction, but even so the extent of the pact of *dhimmah* was unclear.

The situation today should, however, be contrasted with the situation in the Ottoman empire, under which a real effort was made to emancipate law from Islamic narrow-mindedness and to produce a system in which people of different faiths and ethnic identities could enjoy both a workable civil and criminal jurisdiction applying to all subjects and specialized codes applicable to the particular religious communities. (*See* *millet system.) Although there is no doubt that Sunni Muslims were favoured over people of other faiths (including Shi'ites), the situation of the Middle East today represents a drastic political change, and one which threatens to promote a new level of intolerance in the Islamic world. The *rule of law has existed in recent years only in those states – notably Morocco, Egypt and Lebanon – which have either a large Christian minority or a well-entrenched legacy of colonial institutions, or which have consciously Westernized their institutions, like Turkey and the Iran that Khomeini destroyed.

Islamic law

Sharî'ah, divine law. An important example of a system of law which is religious in meaning, and which applies not by virtue of *citizenship or *allegiance to a state, but by virtue of religious affiliation, and which therefore generally depends upon an Islamic ruler to enforce it. It is applicable primarily between Muslims (although it contains provision for non-Muslims within the jurisdiction – *see *dhimmî*), and takes the concept of *obligation, rather than that of *right, as central. The law originates in the Koran and the *sunna* (the traditions arising from the life and example of Muhammad) and is regarded as immutable, since it consists in what Muhammad knew, by revelation, of the divine will. It makes room for property and contractual rights, and economic developments, partly by the extensive use of stratagems and legal fictions (*hiyal*) – particularly important being those invoked in reconciling the need for interest in capitalist economies with the law forbidding usury. The science of law (*fiqh*) became highly developed in the Middle Ages, with four recognized schools of jurisprudence aimed at reconciling scant but absolute revelations with the needs of a living human society. All four schools of *fiqh* admitted the possibility of independent judgement or *ijtihad* (literally 'effort', from the same root as *jihâd*), but the effort must be based on the four recognized sources of law – the Koran, the Sunna, analogy and consensus – and could not be used to introduce secular ideas of authority. Moreover, it has been held since the thirteenth century that 'the gate of *ijtihad* is closed', meaing that the *sharî'ah* can no longer be added to, but merely studied for whatever it may disclose.

Although states sometimes declare adherence to Islamic law, no state is governed exclusively by it, not even modern Iran. Moreover, certain provisions of Islamic law, under all interpretations, are in direct conflict with modern expectations – notably the harsh regime of punishments (including stoning for adultery and amputation for theft) – and these have been quietly dropped from the code by most of its modern advocates. The last systematic attempt to govern according to Islamic law was that of the *Taliban in Afghanistan.

Islamism

Term recently introduced in order to distinguish *Islam, as a religious creed and devout practice, from Islamism, which is the belligerent attempt to impose Islamic government and *Islamic law on people regardless of whether they consent to it. Its principal exponents in the modern world have been the *Muslim Brotherhood, founded in Egypt by *al-Banna, Hezbollah (the Party of Allah) in Lebanon, and *al-Qa'eda. Islamists believe that they are commanded to wage *jihâd against the infidel, and that the situation of the modern world, which has drifted away from God's commandments, authorizes radical destruction and martyrdom in the war against *jahilîyya (ignorance).

Some argue that the tendency towards Islamism is contained within Islam itself, with the doctrine of *jihâd* and the belief in the legitimacy of forced conversions and the punishment of apostasy. Most Muslims do not agree, and are anxious to distance themselves from Islamism, which they regard as both incompatible with modernity and a threat to their own position within it. (*See also* *fundamentalism, *Wahhabism.)

Islamo-fascism

Expression introduced by the French Middle-East scholar Maxine Rodinson

(1915–2004) to describe the Iranian Revolution of 1978, and now gaining currency, to describe the particular combination of top-down rule and intransigent *Islamism that seems to be the goal of Islamist movements.

isolationism

The doctrine that a state may best promote its own interests by refraining from interfering in those of others, and by keeping clear of the large issues of international politics. It was practised by Imperial China and the Japanese Shogunate, and often advocated in the UK in the nineteenth century (sometimes under the banner of 'splendid isolation'); but it is most widely known as a permanently recurring feature of US foreign policy, already advocated in Washington's farewell address of 1796, and confirmed in the *Monroe doctrine of 1823, which is sometimes said to have introduced a policy of 'hemispheric isolationism'.

isonomy

Greek: equality before the law. The ideal of isonomy is an ancient one, and its achievement is often regarded (especially by theorists of liberalism) as one measure of the legitimacy of the resulting government. For, in a condition of isonomy, the individual's dealings with the state (i.e. all dealings that are mediated by law) are not affected by who he is, by what power he has, or by what title, property or office distinguishes him.

The conditions of isonomy are difficult to determine. In one sense it could be said to be achieved so long as anybody who appears before a judge is given treatment according to the merits of his case. But in another sense that is not enough, since it could be that only the rich, powerful or politically influential are able to appear before a judge in the first place or able, at any rate, to ensure that they have the best advice when they do so. Thus some have argued that, without some effective system of legal aid, ensuring that any person, however lacking in privilege, may have access to the best legal advice, there can be no genuine isonomy. Even so, there will be many ways in which the influence of the influential may be felt, but perhaps it is vain to define isonomy so strictly that only the refutation of a tautology could bring it into being.

isoquant

In economics, a curve showing the various possible combinations of inputs required to produce a given output of a given product, e.g. the various combinations of quantities of capital and of labour that could produce a sack of coal. Perhaps 100 units of capital and 50 of labour produce the same as 75 units of each – in which case these two quantities define points on a single isoquant.

Isoquants are often supposed to exhibit a similar structure to *indifference curves, except that outputs are measurable and *utilities are not, so that quantities may be attached to isoquants but not to indifference curves. Isoquants feature in the theory of the *firm, and in summarizing the contributions made by the various *factors of production.

Jacobinism

Named after the Jacobin club in the French Revolution, a society of deputies, led by Robespierre, which acted so as to concentrate power in its own hands, believing that the truth of its vision was sufficient guarantee of its authority to act. Subsequently there were many such clubs, and the term Jacobinism has been used to denote any revolutionary movement which is determined to impose its aims at whatever cost, in the conviction that the end justifies the means, and that the people, being ignorant, must be compelled towards the aims of revolution and cannot be expected willingly to adopt them. The philosophy of the Jacobin club has often been thought to derive from *Rousseau, although the relation between Rousseau and Robespierre is certainly not closer than that between *Lenin, who described himself and his followers as 'Jacobins tied to the proletariat', and *Marx.

Jacquerie (sometimes: Jacquery)

From the French 'Jacques', nickname for a peasant, and originally describing the revolt of the peasantry against the nobles in northern France in 1357–58; subsequently used to denote the mass of people taking part in an uprising based in peasant support.

jâhiliyya

Arabic: the condition of ignorance. Term standardly used to describe the Arab world before the revelation granted to Muhammad, later adopted by *Qutb to describe the materialistic society of the West.

Jefferson, Thomas (1743–1826)

American essayist and statesman, drafter of the *Declaration of Independence*, 1776, President of the US (1801–9), and founder of the University of Virginia. Jefferson was a theorist of *constitution and *democracy, who, in his *Manual*, 1796, left a summary of the law and practice of *Congress which remains a standard work, and which is bound up and published with all the successive editions of the Rules of the House of Representatives and of the Senate. In his *Notes on the State of Virginia*, 1784, he had expounded his own version of the theoretical basis of the ideal American constitution, which, while democratic in form, contains a strong residue of respect for the agrarian mode of life, and for the stable structures of government that would support it. He defended *bicameral government, the office of a *supreme court, and a *bill of rights. He also conveyed respect for the English *common law, and for the rights that had been enshrined in it, so that the *Virginia Declaration of Rights*, 1776, which he prompted, contained a résumé of rights extracted from or continuous with those implied in the common law. His observation of the French Revolution convinced him that, although there are universally valid principles of human rights, the form of government must be tailored to the conditions of a given society, and not dictated by the logic of abstract ideas. He also believed that generations as well as individuals have rights, and that a constitution and laws should not be immovably imposed on succeeding generations. The eventual adoption of the Bill of Rights owes much to Jefferson, as does the US constitution as a whole. *See also* *Jeffersonian democracy.

Jeffersonian democracy

The kind of *democracy advocated by *Jefferson, involving universal *suffrage, *bicameral government, stable *institutions, declared *freedoms and *rights (it was Jefferson who criticized the constitution of 1789 for its failure to include a *bill of rights), *division of powers, and effective *checks and balances to the exercise of power. In particular, Jeffersonian democracy is distinguished by its emphasis on *federalism, and on the need for individual states to retain powers against the federal government, so as to be able to nullify the latter's unconstitutional acts. It thus sees the principal constitutional guarantee as lying in the decentralization of power.

Jesuit movement

The Society of Jesus was founded by St Ignatius Loyola in 1534 and approved by Pope Paul III in 1540. It aimed to revitalize the *Roman Catholic Church in face of the threat posed by the *Reformation, and to undertake missionary work designed to convert people to the faith. Members of the order wear no distinctive habit, and their obligations are entirely contained within this aim of conversion, so that they have become types of single-minded devotion to *doctrine. Their influence was widespread, in educational institutions, in the administering of 'spiritual exercises', in the conduct of missions, and in the subtle use of *casuistry with which to adapt their doctrine to every prior disposition to believe it. Their rapid advance accordingly invoked

considerable hostility, and the order was expelled from France in 1764, and then suppressed by Pope Clement XIV in 1773. Nevertheless they continued to function in a reduced way, were restored by Pope Pius VII in 1814, and still maintain missions and centres of learning throughout the world. Their methods, involving infiltration, and personal persuasion of those most able to exert public influence, have served as a model for many subsequent subversive movements.

Jevons, William Stanley (1835–82)

English political economist, logician and philosopher of science, and one of the inventors of the *marginal utility theory of *price. Jevons extended this theory to generate the marginal productivity theory of *interest, and thus prepared the ground for modern economic analyses of *capital, as a separate *factor of production. He was extremely influential on many members of the *Austrian school and on neo-classical theorists, and thereby many of his theories have entered into the modern theories of the market economy.

Jewish law

The law contained in the Torah of Moses, as glossed and supplemented by subsequent scribes, commentators and priests, which was partly committed to writing in the Mishnah (AD 200), and ultimately collected in the Babylonian Talmud of AD 600. Among systematic treatises, those of Moses Maimonides (1135–1205) – the *Mishnah Torah* – and Joseph Qaro (1488–1575) – *Shulchan 'Arukh* – are the most respected. Jewish law is construed as having its basis in divine revelation, but accommodates elaborate customary rules and procedures. Its effect on Christianity has caused it to exert an influence upon Western law generally, particularly in matters relating to marriage, to relations between *church and state, and to commercial contracts (where its international character has been influential in forming laws of contract that permit and support international trade).

jihâd

Arabic: struggle, by implication struggle on behalf of the faith. One of the sacred duties of the Muslim, as commanded by the Koran, but interpreted differently in different epochs and by different Islamic sects. According to some, the struggle could be conducted by peaceful dialogue with the unbeliever, a wrestling with error in which truth will be finally victorious. According to others – the *Sufi mystics, for example – the struggle is an inner struggle, in which the enemy is one's own sensuous nature, and the aim is illumination. Authority for this is found, not in the Koran, but in a *hadîth* of the Prophet who, on returning from the battle of Bard (the last of his battles against the polytheists) is reported to have said 'we are finished with the great *jihâd*; now we begin the greater'. However, in periods of fervour, *jihâd* is seldom interpreted so mildly and is now routinely understood as the imposition of *Islamic law by force of arms, or simply as the life-and-death confrontation with the heathen. The one who dies in the course of *jihâd* dies as a martyr (*shahid*, witness), and is promised a place in Paradise. This teaching has been emphasized by the radical *Wahhabi cult which, through its growing influence in the Islamic world, has served to overthrow long-standing rules of peaceful co-existence.

jingoism

From the refrain 'By Jingo!', attached to a music-hall song of 1878, which became the marching song of those citizens of the UK who in that year were spoiling for war with Russia. Hence: blustering, bragging *chauvinism, with aggressive inclinations of an *imperialist kind. Described by *Benda as 'the form of patriotism specially invented by democracies'.

joint stock company

A business association in which common stock, or *capital, is contributed by a group of persons. As a result, there may be effective *separation of ownership from control. The rise of the joint stock company in the seventeenth century proceeded without effective legal discipline until the South Sea Bubble of 1720. After that, company law, controlling the behaviour, and eventually limiting the liability, of members of a joint stock company, was introduced, thus ratifying the institutions of the modern economy. The phrase 'joint stock company' is now virtually obsolete.

journalese

Lazy use of language designed more to cut corners or to evoke stock responses than to observe and make sense of the facts. The terms 'left' and 'right', as now used and as partially defined in this dictionary, are terms of journalese, which help to engineer readers' reactions, but are systematically misleading as descriptions.

journalism

The production of news and comment for widespread publication. The issue of the freedom of the press (and by implication of the *media generally) is one that journalism, the express purpose of which is one of *communication, irrespective of literary, scientific or any other merit, raises in its acutest form. The liberty to publish news and information is in most places subsequent to control, either through the operation of independent statutes, or through the exercise of *de facto* powers of *censorship. Like all such liberties it must be thought of as a matter of degree, curtailed by laws of libel, decency, *privacy and *sedition. Nevertheless the 'freedom of information', guaranteed under the Helsinki final agreement, is one that is often defended as a basic *human right, and which has been opposed by many modern states (including half those that signed the Helsinki agreement) with a fervour that is sometimes thought to be a sign of political, if not mental, instability. (The accusation of mental instability is derived from the claim that only someone suffering from paranoid delusions, or whose life was in some similarly deranged way founded on a lie, would oppose the truth as though it were in itself a crime; this accusation against press censorship and the suppression of free information within the USSR was made with great force by *Solzhenitsyn.) A reply that is often made is that journalism in the West only *appears* to be objective, and that it is in fact so structured as constantly to reinforce a bias in favour of established interests. Hence 'freedom of information' never means more than freedom to disseminate established lies.

In the West discussion of this issue has involved the resurgence of a kind of *cultural conservatism, which represents journalism as too deeply degenerate for its freedom to be valuable, together with liberal attempts to define the ideal extent of the freedom of the press, and the true grounds for its restriction. To summarize these arguments is almost impossible, but some main points may be given here:

The cultural conservative argues that, whatever freedom exists, it can never have greater value than that of the activity it permits. The forces which direct a 'free press' are inevitably given to the promotion of lies, distortions and vulgarities. For there is a commercial necessity to appeal as widely and forcefully as possible. The existence of a large reading public makes high-toned journalism anachronistic and financially unrewarding. Moreover, the transference of journalism to media of mass communication such as television and the internet removes all qualifications (such as literacy, or education) which had previously been necessary for the reception of information about the public world. Content is determined by style, and the content of most journalistic utterance will accordingly be confined to those matters that have the widest appeal, irrespective of any intrinsic worth as subjects of communication. (Hence '*journalese' and 'journalistic' as terms of abuse.)

The liberal argument tends to begin from the idea that the widespread dissemination of information about the public world is not only a duty of those who possess it, but also a right of the recipient. This is particularly so in a democracy, where every citizen has to cast a vote at an election, and where every citizen therefore has a right to be informed of the likely consequences. Moreover, the dissemination of information has been seen as a fundamental factor in the breaking down of barriers, between individuals, classes, races, and societies, and it is – on one liberal view – only barriers that threaten civil and international peace. Vulgarity or paucity of literary merit are small prices to pay for such freedom of information, and even if it be true that journalism is too preoccupied with the immediate and the sensational to deliberate on its true significance, deliberation is in any case not its responsibility, but rather the responsibility of the citizen.

The liberal argument is, on the whole, accepted in the US and the UK, and what control there is is exercised through councils and professional bodies (such as the UK Press Council). These do not have any legal jurisdiction over journalism, but simply exert pressure to maintain certain standards of conduct among their members. However, many think that the individual has rights which are inherently threatened by journalism. The aim of journalism is to secure an audience, and the more sensational, violent and tragic an episode, the more likely that an audience will be secured. Hence the press constantly intrudes into the privacy of individuals, precisely at those points where privacy is most evidently necessary. Privacy and the press are therefore now important issues in public debate in the UK. Emphasis is beginning to shift from the rights to the duties of the journalist, in particular his responsibilities to the public, which involve the duty to tell the truth, but not the right to tell the truth about anything or anyone.

journeyman

A term that has an air of obsolescence, because the condition that it describes – that of the day labourer – is largely obsolescent. From *journée* (French: day), a journeyman is one qualified at a craft, trade or skill, who is able to work at it as a wage-labourer with frequent changes of employer, and who demands payment by the day. In the sixteenth and seventeenth centuries, journeymen formed a large and active rising class, and in their struggle for independence from their masters combined with security of employment, precipitated many important changes in the economy.

Judaism

Judaism, unlike *Zionism, does not stress the doctrine that the Jewish people constitute or should constitute a separate state or nation, but only

that they are bound individually and collectively by a single law (*see* *Jewish law) which is of international application. Being founded in *natural justice, divine revelation, tradition, and domestic custom, this law enters into conflict with surrounding *positive law, if at all, only through no fault of its own. Because of this, modern Judaism (in contrast to the Judaism of the Old Testament) has generated no political vision that is common to those who subscribe to it. However, profession of the Jewish faith, which has often been persecuted (*see* *antisemitism), may still awaken political suspicions, and while persecution of the Jews in Muslim countries has tended to represent itself as 'anti-Zionist', it has exhibited a disconcerting continuity with the anti-semitism of the past, so that now very few Jews remain in the Islamic world.

Judaism is not a single creed or a single practice. There is an overarching distinction between orthodox and liberal Jewry, the first adhering to Old Testament customs and rituals, maintaining a 'kosher' diet according to the dietary laws laid down in Leviticus, avoiding marriage with gentiles, and retaining the observances commanded to Moses, Abraham and the Prophets. Liberal Jews adopt a freer interpretation of the law, and are content to follow the customs of the surrounding society in most matters of diet and dress. Within this overarching distinction there are many sub-divisions of the Jewish faith, including that between the Sephardic Jews – the diaspora that spread through North Africa and Spain and adopted the outward trappings of Muslim society – and the Ashkenazy Jews – the diaspora that spread through Austria and Eastern Europe into Russia. There are distinct traditions of religious and secular wisdom, including the Hasidic tradition of

Eastern Europe, and distinct traditions of worship, some extremely exacting. In all its forms Judaism is remarkable for having survived in exile for two millennia, maintaining the ancient Hebrew language, and constantly building on the wisdom and mission of the Old Testament, according to which the Jews, as God's chosen people, are destined to bear endless suffering, and destined nevertheless to endure.

judicial activism

Expression employed, especially in the American context, to denote the use of the court by judges, particularly judges of the *Supreme Court, to advance public policies, whether or not these have been proposed or endorsed by the *legislature. In many recent decisions the Supreme Court of the US has used its position as final court of appeal in constitutional matters to overrule both state and federal legislation, often in highly controversial ways and with highly controversial reasoning. (One famous, and for many people notorious, instance is the judgement in *Roe* v. *Wade* – for which, *see* *abortion.) Some (notably *Dworkin) argue that an element of judicial activism is implied in the very role of the judge, and that the controversies aroused by recent decisions are intrinsic to the nature of constitutional government. Since a great many of the decisions have had the effect of interpreting the Constitution in a *liberal direction, they have been opposed by conservatives, who have argued that judicial activism, at least in its recent form, does not so much apply the Constitution as read into it meanings and intentions that it does not contain. The dispute here raises an interesting question of *hermeneutics. How exactly do you discover the meaning of a legal document formulated in conditions that no longer exist and yet designed to be applied *now*, in

conditions which the original authors could not have envisioned? Clearly, a constitution provides no limitation to state power if its terms can be interpreted in whatever way the Supreme Court decides: in such circumstances the only effect of a constitution would be to achieve a massive centralization of dictatorial powers in the Supreme Court and to make the legislature redundant. On the other hand, the constitution cannot be applied without interpretation, since its terms have changed meaning over time, and the intentions of the *Founding Fathers as to how the constitution should be applied in present-day circumstances are essentially unknowable.

Judicial activism, in the form of judicial legislation, is possible in any *common law system. In the British context, an activist judge is one who uses his powers in order to neutralize the effect of parliamentary *statutes. The rule in English law is that courts must, in interpreting statutes, look to the *intention of Parliament.* But sufficient hermeneutical licence exists for a judge to ignore that intention, using legal devices that lie outside parliamentary control – for example, the concepts and doctrines of *equity.

judicial legislation

See *judicial activism, *judiciary, *legislation.

judicial review

1. The challenging of acts performed by the *legislative branch of government before a judicial body. To the extent that this exists it grants a dominant role to the *judiciary in the exercise of political power. It is not officially recognized in UK law (although there is some dispute about this) nor is it explicitly sanctioned in the US constitution. Nevertheless, judicial review is practised by the *Supreme Court, and state constitutions are

generally interpreted as granting the power of judicial review to their own courts. It is arguable that, unless the judiciary has this power, the effect of a written constitution limiting the acts of a legislature is nugatory, since no body would exist to ensure that the constitution is applied. On the other hand, who is to supervise the Supreme Court? The old problem of 'quis custodiet illos custodes?' arises here in a particularly vivid form.

The situation in the UK has been significantly altered by the *European Union, which permits the validity of Parliamentary legislation to be examined before the *European Court of Justice (ECJ), which can overrule a statute if it violates the treaties of Union. UK judges may hear cases under this provision, in order to decide whether or not the ECJ would rule on them and if so how: hence UK judges now have a far-reaching *de facto* power of judicial review.

2. Sometimes the expression 'judicial review' is used more widely, to mean the judicial review of the exercise of any power of government, including the executive power, as expressed, for example, through administrative decisions. This is clearly both possible, and also necessary, if there are to be constitutional guarantees of individual *rights: *see* *administrative law, *judiciary.

judiciary

The judiciary comprises the whole body of judges within a legal system, and its nature, function, composition and procedure provide one of the focal points of modern political debate. Three main areas need to be reviewed; judicial independence, judicial legislation, and the class interests of the judiciary.

(i) Independence. According to the doctrine of the *separation of powers, the judiciary exercises a power within the state that is separable (whether or not separated) from the other powers of government – in particular from those of the *legislature and the *executive. To what extent is this idea a fiction? If it is not, to what extent ought it to be put into practice? If it is put into practice then how should it be done?

The idea of judicial independence seems not to be a fiction. However, it refers to a condition that may be extremely difficult to achieve, since it requires that the power that appoints a judge must also be prepared to yield to him. The problem of how to achieve this through a *constitution has exercised some of the most influential political thinkers in modern times, notably *Montesquieu, and the *Founding Fathers of the US. It is not necessary that there should be a written constitution; in both the US and the UK it seems that there are definite procedures whereby a citizen may obtain redress before a court for abuses of executive power (*see* *administrative law). It is perhaps easier to imagine judicial independence from the executive than from the legislative power; for obviously a judiciary ceases to be a power of the state altogether once it ceases to apply the law, as enacted by the legislative assembly. Nevertheless it may be independent to the extent that judicial decisions cannot be overturned by the legislature, i.e. if there is no *retroactive legislation, and also no appeal from the courts to the legislature. (By an accident of the UK constitution the House of Lords is both a legislating body and also the highest court of appeal but, by convention, its two functions are kept separate.) Judicial independence might exist *de jure* – it may for example be specified in a written document which purports to describe the constitution – but not exist *de facto*, say, because a judge is removed from office whenever his decision displeases the executive. However, it may be that judicial independence is a necessary condition for the *rule of law, and for a genuine constitution, in which case it could be said that, without it, the distinction between the *de jure* and the *de facto* is dissolved.

Ought judicial independence to exist? Some argue (as just noted) that without it there is no rule of law: law does not determine the outcome of any issue but only the will of those in power. Moreover, no constitution can guarantee rights if the citizen cannot contend for these rights in open court, and no citizen can contend for his rights against the executive power if the judge of his case is always identical with the executive power. (*See* *natural justice, *show trials.)

How is independence to be secured? This is in many ways the hardest question, since it really means, how is it to be secured without also dissolving the organic relations between the various powers of government? Components of judicial independence that are standardly accepted (although not necessarily by any one theorist) are: (a) promotion of judges on advice from the existing judiciary; (b) no retroactive legislation; (c) acceptance of the doctrine of *precedent, and *stare decisis*; (d) established judicial procedure that is not subject to constant executive and administrative review; (e) the possibility of *judicial review.

(ii) Judicial legislation. It seems that the separation of powers ought to vest the making of law outside the judiciary. However, the existence of *common law, of *equity, and the doctrine of precedent, together with the inescapable fact of *hard cases, all entail that, at least sometimes, a judge must come to a decision that is not uniquely determined by the existing pronouncements of the legislature. It

might seem, therefore, that in such a case, the judge *makes* the law (since nobody else does). Others reply that this does not follow: he discovers the law, or else draws out its implications. That philosophical dispute is extremely hard to resolve. (*See* *Dworkin, *hard cases.) In any case, there is much independent discussion of the extent to which this 'judicial legislation' is or should be, permitted. Some esteem it, on the conservative ground that judges tend to be freer from impetuous reformism than politicians, and usually have a better grasp of the effects of legislation in the lives of ordinary citizens. Some believe, with *Hayek, that judges in a common-law system do not legislate, but discover the system of 'abstract rules' that lies dormant within our free transactions. Legislation, for Hayek, is intrinsically suspect, since it involves the attempt to graft instrumental rules on to a spontaneous system of reasoned argument, in which justice is the ruling principle. (But *see* *judicial activism.) Others see judicial legislation as an obstacle to reform, and perhaps also as an instrument of class *hegemony, hence:

(iii) The class interests of the judiciary, which are now a frequent object of political comment. The judges in Western democracies belong inevitably to the professional classes. Opposition to their independence often comes from those who see this independence as an indefinite permission given to a particular class to advance itself behind the shield of law. *See* *rights and powers.

junk science
Term of *journalese to denote the eager adoption of results that claim to be scientific, but which have not been validated by serious scientific method. Junk science is accepted because it advances some favoured cause or

ideology – for instance, the junk science of *eugenics, acccepted by so many people during the first half of the twentieth century, or the junk science of the health fads accepted so widely today.

junta

From the Spanish, and originally referring to the local councils established in 1808 to conduct the war against Napoleon, a junta is a deliberative council or committee. Now generally refers to any form of government involving a committee which holds power as a body, and especially to forms of military government in which a ruling council of officers takes responsibility for all executive and legislative acts.

jural relations

Relations such as *right, *obligation, *privilege and inability which define the application of the law. The study of jural relations has a large philosophical component, and such analytical jurists as Austin and Hohfeld have attempted to describe the logical relationship among them. The following table is now widely accepted:

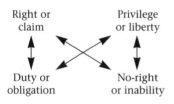

Right or claim — Privilege or liberty

Duty or obligation — No-right or inability

Vertical arrows indicate 'jural correlatives', in which application of either term to one party indicates the application of the other term to the other; diagonal arrows indicate 'jural opposites', in which application of one term to one party indicates the non-application of the other term to the other. Not all legal rights define a duty and some are correlated with a

privilege; hence the above table enables one to work out the implications of any given theory of legal rights.

jurisdiction

The sphere of authority exercised by a state. Hence, in *international law, the right of a *sovereign state to determine rights and duties of persons by legislation and to enforce those rights and duties. Jurisdiction extends over a certain *territory, and it seems that this territorial element in the concept has become essential to settling questions as to its application. The idea therefore forms an essential part of the notion of a state as embodied in a territory – although whether there can be territoriless sovereign states is not settled only by the question of whether there can be a state without jurisdiction. (*See* *millet system.) Jurisdiction may be qualified by rights of *asylum etc., and there may be disputes over jurisdiction, especially in the case of federations, in which the component states may possess local legislative systems in addition to the supreme legislature of the federation.

It is also common to speak of the 'jurisdiction' of a court, meaning the class of persons and issues which may be heard before it. Important problems of jurisdiction are raised by the powers of the *International Court of Justice, by *ecclesiastical jurisdiction and by the claims often made on behalf of *Islamic law.

jurisdictional dispute

1. In US labour law, a dispute between unions concerning which workers should belong to which union. The thought here is that a union exerts a kind of *jurisdiction over its members by virtue of its representative and disciplinary functions, and that two such jurisdictions cannot be exercised over the same member.

2. Sometimes also applied to a

dispute over whether an administrative body has acted *ultra vires*, i.e. beyond the powers conferred on it by law. Such a dispute may be called 'jurisdictional' because administrative bodies often exercise powers which are quasi-judicial, and it is in respect of these (i.e. of the quality of their 'jurisdiction') that the action of *ultra vires* is usually brought.

jurisprudence

The study of *law, not the actual law of any particular *jurisdiction, but law as such – its origin, form and nature. It is to be distinguished (but can be distinguished only with difficulty) from the philosophy of law, which deals with the meaning and justification of the underlying concepts of law, such as *right, *obligation, *responsibility and *justice. Jurisprudence is both comparative and historical; it takes certain basic concepts for granted and deliberates on the problems generated by their application in this or that field of legislation. A question of jurisprudence such as, What is responsibility in law? is partly philosophical – dependent upon an analysis of the extra-legal concept of responsibility – and partly legal – dependent upon a collection of (and extrapolation from) the actual criteria used by the courts in assigning responsibility. But it is not exclusively either, and this explains the peculiar nature of jurisprudence: it tries to bring the order and system of philosophy into the reasoning of the law, by subsuming that reasoning under principles for which a philosophical explanation can be at least envisaged, if not produced.

jury

A body of laymen summoned to a court of law in order to decide questions of fact in a judicial (usually, criminal) proceeding. Juries must not decide questions of law, and are always given legal guidance, either by the judge or by some officer of the court, in so far as this has a material bearing upon the matter that they must decide. The 'grand jury' in US criminal proceedings also has an accusatory function, but this does not give it authority in matters of law.

The institution of trial by jury was well established in medieval English law, but was increasingly confined to criminal cases; it is now exclusively an institution of Anglo-American law. It is often defended on the grounds that the participation of ordinary citizens in the administration of justice helps to enhance the reputation of the law, and also gives a criterion of the extent to which laws are in harmony with popular sentiment; moreover it provides some protection of the liberties of the accused. It is attacked on the ground of the frequent ignorance and prejudice of juries, who, while called upon to decide only questions of fact, nevertheless tend to see facts in terms of the legal consequences as they understand or misunderstand them.

In US *tort law juries have an important role to play, not merely in assigning responsibility for fault, but also in assessing damages. Moreover, lawyers can challenge proposed members of the jury, in order to exclude them, for example on the ground that they might be prejudiced. The astute use of challenges, together with rhetorical manipulation of jury sentiment in the courts, has given rise to astronomical awards of damages, in which juries side with the 'little man' against big business, regardless of fault. As a result there have been frequent calls (now being acted upon) for *tort reform in the US.

just price/just wage

In medieval political thinking frequent reference was made to the just price, as opposed to the actual price, of commodities (including labour – hence 'just wage'). Shortages, whether or not artificially created, the comparative immobility of the *factors of production and the frequent demographic catastrophes caused by plague and war meant that prices would fluctuate suddenly and uncontrollably. Sovereigns would sometimes attempt to impose a just price for essential foodstuffs and labour and would often appoint officers with the responsibility of determining what this price might be. (Justices of the Peace had this responsibility in England.) This early attempt at *price control was hampered by the lack of any criterion for settling the justice of a price in a situation of radical shortage. The most coherent suggestion is that the just price of a commodity is that which it *would* command in a situation where unusual or unforeseeable factors had not arisen to distort the market.

It is doubtful that such a criterion could be systematically applied, however, since all circumstances are to some extent unusual and unforeseeable. Nevertheless, there is an instinctive feeling that someone who exploits' another's misfortune in order to make a larger profit than customary is not acting justly. In so far as there is a concept of the just price, it is perhaps subservient to that of the just *person*, an unjust price being a price which only an unjust person would feel able to demand. *See* *Aristotle, *Aquinas, *exploitation.

just war

A conception frequently discussed by medieval philosophers and recently revived. *Canon law distinguished *jus in bello* (justice in the course of war) from the *jus ad bellum* (the just cause of war). A just cause may be pursued by unjust means – e.g. by the wholesale slaughter of non-combatants. *Aquinas summarized medieval thinking in his view that a war is just only if (a) there is sufficient *authority in the party who wages it; (b) there is just cause of offence (a *casus belli*), and (c) there is an intention to wage war solely for the sake of *peace, or for the suppression of the wicked and the sustenance of the good.

The major problems concern the idea of 'just cause' in (b), although many modern thinkers are unhappy, both about the concept of authority invoked in (a) (does the leader of an *insurgent army ever have authority? If so, in what sense?) and about the incorporation into (c) of some condition other than that of peace (who are the good? And who are the wicked?). The best example of just cause, and the one almost universally accepted, is that of unprovoked *aggression from some other state. Indeed, *Grotius, and many thinkers who followed in his steps, found this to be almost the sole just cause of war.

The question of *jus in bello* is at least as complicated as that of the just war. It seems intuitively evident that a just cause can be pursued unjustly, and attempts have therefore been made (e.g. through the 'Geneva Conventions') to limit the procedures that may legitimately be employed by belligerents, whatever the justice of their cause. Medieval thinkers proposed two criteria: proportionality of means, and the immunity of non-combatants. The Geneva Conventions have made efforts to define non-combatants and their rights more precisely. However, modern forms of warfare are such as to involve non-combatants almost automatically and this has radically altered the character of the soldier's moral perceptions.

justice

*Plato's *Republic* begins with the question, 'What is justice?', and with the famous refutation of the view that justice is the *interest of those with *power: in other words, it argues for the non-identity of rights and powers. (For the persistence of the doctrine refuted by Plato, *see* *rights and powers.) Since then, Plato's question has lain at the heart of all moral, political and legal philosophy, and is often considered to be the single most important question in political thought. *Aristotle, who thought of justice as the true subject-matter of political philosophy, and of its execution as a major purpose, perhaps *the* major purpose, of the *polis* (a view also expressed by Aeschylus in the *Oresteia*), made a famous distinction between *distributive and commutative justice, the first being concerned with the distribution of goods among a class, the second with the treatment of the individual in particular transactions (e.g. when punishing him). In the second case justice involves giving to someone what he deserves, or else what he has a *right to receive. In the first case it is, according to Aristotle, a matter of 'treating equals equally'. These are not necessarily the same idea (although it could be said that, in the abstract, equals do have a right to be, and deserve to be, treated equally). If I have to distribute a cake among five starving people, then they may each deserve the whole cake, but it may be unjust not to divide it.

The Aristotelian distinction survives in various forms, although it would now be very unusual for a philosopher to think that there are really two concepts of justice rather than two applications of a single idea. Contemporary use of the term *social justice makes extensive use of the distributive conception, while, in regulating actions between people, the commutative conception – justice as right or desert – seems to be prevalent. Many of the problems arise because the two may enter into conflict, as when

Robin Hood acts unjustly (by taking what he has no right to take) in order to bring about social justice (through *redistribution). Is this conflict real, or would deeper reflection resolve it? Theories divide over their answer to that question. Those who take patterns of distribution as their model (among whom the most influential recent theorist is *Rawls) might find themselves resolving this issue only to admit that Robin Hood acts justly (provided perhaps that he dignifies himself with the title of *sovereign and redistributes in the name of the *state); those who regard the respect for individual rights as the central idea in justice (such as *Nozick) might resolve the issue only to find themselves condoning distributions of goods so unequal as to be very oddly described as just. The important questions seem to be these:

(i) Is justice primarily the attribute of an act, of a person, or of a state of affairs? If of an act, then states of affairs (e.g. 'distributions' of goods) are just or unjust only to the extent that they are the outcome of just or unjust acts. If of a person, then rules of just action must be subordinate to a conception of human *virtue (e.g. an action is just if it would be recommended by the 'impartial judge' or the 'just person') – a conception which vastly complicates the discussion, and probably undercuts the desire of many modern philosophers to establish simple laws of justice. If of a state of affairs, then we might consider it unjust that one person is born more advantaged than another, even though human agency has nothing to do with it. Aristotle seems to have favoured the second idea; much dispute between socialists and liberals in modern politics comes from socialists being attached to the third of those ideas, and liberals (*Hayek, for example) to the first.

(ii) Is justice a forward-looking or a backward-looking conception? In other words, does it look to the results of an action, or to its antecedents? The connection with desert and right suggests the latter, and this is at the root of the conflict – which many philosophers have thought to exist – between justice and *utility, itself cited as one of the principal failings of *utilitarianism. But some theories of social justice seem to construe justice as a forward-looking conception, nevertheless.

(iii) Is justice a constitutive or a procedural concept? That is, is the difference between the just and the unjust to be found in the nature of the action, or in the manner of its execution? Study of the law has sometimes led to the opinion that laws themselves are never either just or unjust, but that the process of their application may be one or the other, since it is only when legal rights have been determined that we can speak of 'treating equals equally'.

(iv) What *is* it, to treat equals equally? What is the relevant respect in which people are to be compared? If there is *no* respect, then the result of this maxim is *egalitarianism; if the respect is that of legal rights, and there is no natural limit on those (but only the limits embodied in *positive law), then rights may be unequally determined, and a slave may be justly treated as a slave.

(v) Is there, in other words, *natural justice? And are there *natural rights?

(vi) If so, does that solve the question, Why be just? *See* *value, *virtue.

In all those questions the problem of the objectivity of the concept of justice is paramount. There is a further problem suggested by them: the nature of the 'sentiment of justice' (*cf.* *Hume). Is there a real fact of human nature here, or could that sentiment be educated away? It always seems as though political systems that override the sense of justice thereby render themselves precarious. Is this because that sense is at the root of sentiments of *allegiance? Or is there a genuine conception of *political obligation that requires justice to be preserved? *Cf.* *piety.

Kaldor, Nicholas, Lord (1908–86)
See *Cambridge school, *compensation, *inflation.

kangaroo court
A mock hearing in which all norms of justice and judicial procedure are ignored, and in which, as a rule, prosecutor, judge and executioner are one, and the verdict predetermined. The 'trial' by terrorists of their hostages is an example; most *show trials differ only in a fictional division between prosecutor and judge. (Originally US slang, already current in 1853.)

Kant, Immanuel (1724–1804)
German philosopher, and the deepest and most systematic thinker of the *Enlightenment. Kant lived in relative removal from the political upheavals of the eighteenth century, and wrote little of direct political import; nevertheless his direct and indirect influence on legal and political thinking has been enormous, and his philosophical exposition of the principles of *universalism is without compare. Kant believed that reason, which could lead to theoretical knowledge only when carefully circumscribed, has a natural tendency to transcend its limits, leading to empty and paradoxical beliefs that could never be rationally supported. (*Critique of Pure Reason*, 1781, 1787.) However, this very same reason has a legitimate practical employment, in which it is *autonomous, a law-maker to itself, both postulating and obeying the 'categorical imperative' of pure practical reason. This stipulates that one must act only on that maxim which one can at the same time will as a law for all rational beings. (*Critique of Practical Reason*, 1788.) Reason is the distinguishing feature of man and of human *agency, and the defining property of the *person, who is constrained by it to treat himself and all other persons as ends, and not as means only. However, the conditions for the harmonious exercise of practical reason are not present in nature, so that men must ascend towards reason with the aid of local and circumscribed political communities. These fail to instantiate the universalist *ideal of a 'kingdom of ends' in which reason alone is sovereign.

In the political sphere we should aim for a 'league of nations', in which autonomous republics combine together through a permanent treaty to avoid war. (*Perpetual Peace*, 1795.) The pre-condition of such a league is that its members be republican states – i.e. states in which the people are represented in government, and which provide guarantees of the political freedom of their citizens. Kant at first hailed the French Revolution as a sign of mankind's progress towards this condition of republican government, in which subjects would at last be citizens. However, news of the terror and the judicial murder of the king caused him to withdraw his approval, and he returned to a belief in mitigated monarchy as the best form of government for imperfect beings.

Underlying Kant's famous and influential defence of the *cosmopolitan idea are the ruling ideas of his moral philosophy.

(i) The premise of all morality is autonomy. Autonomy is the kind of freedom that is unique to the will of a rational being, and which generates the ability to 'will the maxim of an action as law' for oneself. I can will a maxim as law for myself only if I also will it as a universal law, since it is of the essence of reason to abstract from all 'empirical' conditions towards universal maxims. Hence from autonomy there stems:

(ii) The categorical imperative: I must act so as to will the maxim of my action as a universal law, and I can do this only if I respect the rationality of others (else my law is not addressed to universal reason); hence I must treat all rational beings as ends, and not as means.

(iii) The conflict between reason and the passions is one part of that between the rational will, which struggles always to realize the kingdom of ends, and the 'empirical conditions' which prevail in the realm of nature. Law will become truly universal only when it abstracts from those conditions and addresses itself to reason alone. Such a law can make no distinction among rational beings except in terms of the 'good' and the 'bad' will that motivates them. Moreover, as an expression of autonomy, it conflicts with the individual will only where that will is acting unfreely, in obedience to a force of nature, rather than to its own sovereign authority. Hence when this universal law is enforced it will not infringe the freedom of those who are governed by it, but only curb their unfree desires.

Those ideas provide a philosophical foundation for *liberalism in one of its most persuasive forms: they recommend a kind of law which aims at freedom, and which makes no arbitrary distinctions among those to whom it is applied. Freedom is the ability to realize oneself in autonomous choices.

(*See* *self-realization.*) But such choices will always contain an act of rational obedience towards the moral law. (The idea of freedom as obedience was later, in *Hegel and others, to be given interpretations that are far from liberal.)

On Kant's view the moral law, since it stems from reason alone, must be objectively binding on all rational beings, and there is no need to have recourse to theology in order to recommend it. Indeed, to invoke religion at this point is, Kant thought, to fall into the trap of 'heteronomy of the will'. (Making the rational will obedient to something other than itself.) Hence Kant is often held to have completed a task begun by *Grotius, giving a basis for natural law which does not invoke the will of God, but rather commands God himself to obedience. Moreover, the second formulation of the categorical imperative (the injunction to treat persons as ends and not as means only) has often been thought to capture the essence of the idea of justice, and has therefore been used as a basis for many philosophical theories of rights. (*See*, e.g., *Nozick.)

Kant offered a definition of the *Enlightenment, as the overcoming by mankind of its self-imposed minority, and noted that Enlightenment involves an attempt to transcribe moral ideas into legal norms; he also believed that legality would increasingly prevail over morality, as a result of Enlightenment ideas, but that it could never displace morality or make human beings any better than they were. He advanced a version of the *social contract, although in terms that are purely hypothetical. A law is legitimate, he argued, if the citizens *could* agree upon it in circumstances where reason prevails – even if those are not the actual circumstances in which the law is passed.

katascopic (Also: catascopic.)
Of a social theory: proceeding from a conception of society towards a description of the individual, as opposed to 'anascopic': extrapolating from the individual towards a conception of society. Since *Durkheim it has been common for *sociology to be katascopic.

Kautsky, Karl (1854–1939)
The leading 'classical' exponent, after Marx and Engels, of *Marxism. Kautsky was influenced by *Darwinism, and found the *materialist theory of history irresistible, believing it to be an extension into the socio-political realm of the same persuasive thought that had motivated the theory of evolution. He accepted the Marxian distinction between base and super-structure, the thesis that capitalism would be destroyed by internal *crisis, and the theory that *socialization of the means of production was alone sufficient to end the contradictions of capitalism. The principal contradiction, for Kautsky, was that between the ability of capitalism to produce ever increasing wealth, and its inability to distribute it. The grievance of the work force arose, he argued, not from absolute *poverty but from 'relative deprivation', a concept which has since proved useful in making socialist policies believable even in the absence of poverty.

Kelsen, Hans (1881–1973)
Austrian jurist and political theorist, who advanced a legalistic conception of the state as a system of *positive law, not founded in natural law or in any other conception of justice other than as a constraint upon procedure (*General Theory of Law and State*, 1945). Each system of positive law consists of norms imposed and enforced by the state, the validity of these norms consisting in their derivability from a basic norm (*Grundnorm*), such as the proposition that the constitution is supreme. The *Grundnorm*, which is the point beyond which justification cannot go, defines the essence of the state and the form of its (internal) *sovereignty. Hence states can be classified in terms of this *Grundnorm*, which might, e.g., enjoin subjects to obey a constitution, or a custom, or the will of a monarch.

While Kelsen's view of the state is legalistic, he refused to see law as anything but rationalized and systematized *convention, through which political power exerts itself. The value of this system is to be found, not in its conformity to any abstract ideal of justice, but in its ability to promote peace, order and well-being. Hence the ultimate justification offered for any system of law is *utilitarian. Kelsen's influence on German jurisprudence was enormous, and his conception of law as a political instrument, with no internal constraints such as those embodied in *natural law or *judicial legislation has been attacked as justifying the extreme presumption of modern governments, which issue commands and then call them law, as the Nazis did. *See* *Hayek.

Kemalism
Advocacy of the doctrines and policies of Kemal Atatürk (1880–1938), Turkish military leader and statesman, who abolished the *sultanate, and founded the modern Turkish republic in a spirit of Turkish *nationalism. Kemalism advocates the orientation of the state towards international relations, and the complete reorganization of all traditions and customs which hinder those relations, or retard the formation of modern political institutions. Hence, in order to create a modern state, a modern civil society must be simultaneously generated to be governed by it. All educational,

administrative and legal bodies must be *secularized, and domestic life must be *modernized, even down to the details of dress and sexual conduct (Atatürk is famous for forbidding the wearing of the fez, and for his rejection of the Islamic laws of marriage and sexual relations). The authority previously appropriated by the Muslim clergy and 'ulema must be confiscated from them and returned to the secular state.

One of the most striking features of Kemalism was the attempt to give a serious practical politics of *language: it set out to reform the Turkish language both in alphabet and vocabulary, rejecting Arabic words in favour of native (i.e. Anatolian) words, and Arabic script in favour of the Roman alphabet. Hence it was able to break at the roots the bond with Islamic culture, and turn Turkey's face towards the West, fortified by a growing spirit of national *identity. In doing so it severed modern Turkey from its traditional culture, a fact often regretted by those sufficiently well educated to know how great that culture was, but probably viewed with indifference by the Turk in the souk.

ketman

Persian term meaning concealment, used to denote a phenomenon recorded admiringly by *Gobineau: the elaborate concealment of one's deepest convictions, and the ironic and absolute pretence to adopt a rival system of beliefs. *Ketman* (in Arabic *taqîyya*) was practised by certain Middle-Eastern sects (especially Shi'ites and Druze) in the face of political, religious and philosophical persecution. The term has also been used by *Miłosz (*The Captive Mind*, 1955), in order to denote the stance of the intellectual in the modern communist state, forced to simulate adherence to political doctrines which conflict with everything that he believes to be true, and learning to take elaborate, self-mocking pleasure in the techniques of concealment.

Keynes, John Maynard, Lord (1883–1946)

English economist, who addressed himself to the problem of *unemployment, seeking both to explain and to remedy it, and who thereby invented the most influential (though not necessarily the most true) twentieth-century theory of *macroeconomics. Traditional economics had attempted to explain unemployment by the inflexibility of wages in the downswing of the *trade cycle, arguing that the principal solution to unemployment was to cut wages, so that the prospect of greater profits would induce businessmen to invest. Keynes argued against this, suggesting that a cut in wages would probably lower *aggregate demand, which is in turn a factor involved in the stimulation of the economy, so that a lowering of wages might well, by reducing aggregate demand, cause a further decline in employment. Hence Keynes advocated the active stimulation of demand by the government, for example by spending on public works. He advanced a theory designed to justify this, and also to solve many of the outstanding problems left by older theories of *money, *interest, and *investment (*The General Theory of Employment, Interest and Money*, 1936). This suggested, as against the older theories, that the quantity of money in the economy determines, not just the level of prices, but also the real rate of interest. In order to increase output and to diminish unemployment it was not that wages should be cut but rather that aggregate demand for goods and services should be increased.

The details of the theory are complex, and it has been both much criticized and much defended by subsequent economists. However, it has had considerable political influence. It suggested, first, that a free economy may, at a certain point, require considerable government intervention if it is to survive; secondly that, given that intervention, it may very well survive indefinitely. Hence predictions of a *crisis of capitalism are unfounded, and the much discussed *falling rate of profit does not spell the doom of capitalist enterprise. Keynes thus gave theoretical foundations for a *mixed economy and for *interventionism; these have since become features of most Western European forms of government, though by no means endorsed by all economists, and indeed now regarded with increasing scepticism.

Keynes's theory implies that heavy unemployment is not necessarily a temporary aberration from the normal situation, but may represent an equilibrium, if there is no government intervention to remedy the problem. If aggregate demand is too high, on the other hand, it is argued that demand-pull *inflation will occur. Moreover sustained full employment may lead to problems of inflation, due to the strengthened position of workers and trade unions. (*See also* *over-full employment.)

Keynesianism

Advocacy of the kind of doctrine and policy recommended by *Keynes in the *General Theory*, and in particular of government intervention in the economy in order to stimulate demand. More recently, however, a distinction has often been drawn between (vulgarized) 'Keynesianism', and the (more subtle) ideas of Keynes himself.

kibbutz

Hebrew: *kibbus*, a gathering. A kind of *cooperative agricultural settlement,

owned collectively by its members, in which the family is not abolished but replaced, as primary unit, by a form of *commune, forbidding all private property in the means of production. Children are educated collectively, and work is distributed without regard to class or influence. (Such is the theory, which advocates a kind of communal social life as an effective way of securing true community of interest in those concerned to operate an enterprise.)

The kibbutz system was introduced into Palestine in 1909, in order to provide Jewish settlements which would operate within a *market economy, while being politically and socially independent. Kibbutzim were to be socialist and egalitarian in their internal organization (thus instantiating an ideal of *market socialism). Later they were favoured as a way to maintain an active military presence in the countryside.

King, Martin Luther Jr (1929–1968)

US minister, civil rights campaigner and writer, influenced by the life and teachings of *Ghandi, who led the campaign against segregation in the American South during the 1950s and 1960s, and preached the doctrine of non-violent resistance. King was many times jailed and frequently assaulted. His *Letter from Birmingham Jail*, 1963, setting out the principles behind his campaign on behalf of American blacks, and the philosophy of *civil disobedience, was immensely influential and, in conjunction with his memorable 'I have a dream' speech delivered to the Civil Rights March in Washington in 1963, led to substantial legal reforms outlawing segregation and discrimination. King was awarded the Nobel Peace Prize in 1964 and assassinated four years later by an enraged white man.

kinship

The system of human relations derived from sexual reproduction, and including such relations as the *family. Anthropologists distinguish kinship (relation by blood) from affinity (relation by marriage). In practice, however, both relations are involved in a 'kinship system', which consists of a set of obligations, customs and social ties which unite people into a society of supposed blood relationship. Such systems are of great interest to anthropologists, and form what is perhaps the least institutionalized of political orders. Each member either is, or behaves as if he is, a relation, by blood or affinity, of every other, and owes his obligation to the leaders and to the tribe on that basis alone. Usually an aura of sanctity and religious prohibition surrounds and consolidates this vital bond of kinship, so making the obligations founded in it absolute and indefeasible. Such sentiments enable many tribes to dispense with developed systems of law, thus surviving as societies without the protective mantle of a state. This means that, legally speaking, they may be incorporated into a state without violation of sovereignty, since, from the legal point of view, they do not possess it. However, from the philosophical point of view, it is clear that statehood is a matter of degree, that many tribes do possess it to some degree, and that the prevalence of *custom and *tradition should not be thought of as a simple absence of institutions, but rather as the presence of institutions of a special kind.

The strain of adapting *allegiance so that it is directed towards a state and its attendant system of law has led to periodic attempts in civilized communities to reorganize the sentiments of *political obligation on the model of those deep bonds of kinship which seem to dispense with legalized conceptions of politics entirely. This attempt is characteristic of certain forms of conservative *organicism, of old-fashioned *nationalism and, in the limiting case, of *racism, where an attempt is made to underpin the entire structure of a modern state with a fiction of kinship.

kitsch

Austro-German term of obscure etymology, denoting styles in art, music, literature and popular culture which tell lies about the human condition – hiding the awkward facts of death, disloyalty, and devotion behind fantasies of harmlessness, or else presenting them under the aspect of false heroics that deny their threatening side. Difficult to define more precisely, kitsch is nevertheless instantly recognizable, and has had an enormous role to play in modern social and political life. It has often been noticed, for example, that the art of *socialist realism and the official art of the Nazis were through and through kitsch. It has been argued that the *animal rights movement has its origins in the kitsch of Walt Disney, and that kitsch art and kitsch language has played an important part in projecting the Iranian revolution of Khomeini. Whatever we think of those claims, kitsch is clearly of great political importance, though whether as cause or effect it is difficult to say. Communism has been defined (by the Czech writer Petr Fidelius) as 'kitsch with teeth'.

Kojève, Alexandre Vladimirovitch Kojevnikov (1902–1968)

Russian-born writer, philosopher and civil servant, whose seminal lectures on *Hegel helped to shape the intellectual climate of Paris after the Second World War. Kojève presented his own version of the Hegelian philosophy of history, derived from a rhapsodic elaboration of Hegel's dialectic of *master and slave, mixed with elements of

*Heidegger and *Nietzsche. History proceeds inevitably to its end, and involves three broad periods: that of mastery, that of slavery, and the *end of history, in which the conflict beween those two is overcome. The struggle between mastery and enslavement is intrinsic to our condition as self-conscious creatures. The human being is 'negativity incarnate', engaged in a constant struggle to win for himself the recognition of his existence as a subject – i.e. as a creature outside the natural order of things. The age of mastery in the ancient world is succeeded by an age of slavery, in which the slave morality of Christianity (itself a survival of the slave morality of the *stoics) gradually conquers the old ethics of virtue. But Christianity postulates a global society of equals, and therefore inaugurates the era of *Enlightenment, in which religion enters a decline. The death of God is the responsibility of intellectuals who, by showing human beings to be the incarnation of consciousness and creators of their own ideals, show God to be superfluous. When this happens we have reached the end of history, in which the slaves will be masters of their fate, recognizing in each other their equal value. The result will be a universal homogeneity under the supervision of a benign and democratic state.

Although a refugee from the Russian Revolution, Kojève was sympathetic to Marxism, even described himself as a Stalinist, while believing that capitalism would inevitably triumph over communism, since it was part of the promise offered to the slaves. He was an influential civil servant, who played a leading role in establishing both the *GATT accords and the *European Union. Although conservatives could hardly imagine a more dangerous figure, he enjoyed the friendship of one (*Strauss), and has been a profound influence over another (*Fukuyama).

Kropotkin, Peter Alekseievitch, Prince (1842–1921)
Founder of anarcho-communism, who attempted to base an anarchist theory of society on a methodical science of social relations. Kropotkin opposed *Darwinism and argued, on the basis of observation both of men and of animals, that 'mutual aid' was the true principle of individual and social development, and not the 'survival of the fittest'. In *Law and Authority, an Anarchist Essay*, 1886, he argues that custom and voluntary agreement, rather than law and normative authority, represent the creative forces of history. In *Mutual Aid, a Factor of Evolution*, 1890–6, he argues that sociability is, under all circumstances, the greatest advantage in the struggle for life, and therefore the natural condition of all evolutionary beings, who, were it not for the corruptions imposed by the state and law, would develop bonds of instinctive solidarity which would make government unnecessary. He advocated a form of 'anarchist communism', and opposed his view to that of Marx, which he regarded as 'statist'.

Kuhn, Thomas Samuel (1922–96)
American philosopher of science, whose *The Structure of Scientific Revolutions*, 1962, presents a theory of the advance of science that has had a far-reaching influence over the study of intellectual change. The view of *Popper, that the method of science is one of conjecture and refutation, assumes that the scientist knows exactly what would constitute a refutation of his theory. However, all theories can be adjusted so as to avoid refutation by alleged counter-instances. For example, the Ptolemaic

cosmology, which held that the planets move in circular paths, introduced 'epicycles' in order to account for the way in which planetary movements deviate from the circle, so saving the core of the theory. The adjustments serve to protect a 'paradigm', which is a dominant model of what the explanation *ought* to look like. The paradigm influences the way in which any evidence is interpreted, and therefore constantly saves itself from refutation. At a certain point, however, a 'paradigm shift' occurs, as when cosmology shifted from a geocentric to a heliocentric idea of planetary motion, or the theory of motion shifted from the absolute space of Newton to the relativity of Einstein. The shift of paradigm is a revolutionary occurrence that involves a total break with all that had preceded it, and a systematic redescription of the evidence. Kuhn has been taken as authority for the view that the choice of paradigm, being in some sense outside the theory, is either irrational, or motivated by grounds other than its explanatory power. Hence the theory of the paradigm shift has fed the *relativism of contemporary intellectual life. Whether Kuhn intended this is unclear, since his text is multiply ambiguous.

kulaks

Former peasants elevated into proprietors of medium-sized farms after the agrarian reforms of Stolypin in Russia in 1906. The kulaks became a kind of agrarian middle class, and they present perhaps the most striking example in modern politics of the deliberate creation of a class, the aim being political stability, the disintegration of the village commune, and the protection of the countryside against revolution. In 1929 Stalin ordered the 'liquidation of the kulaks'; ten million people are estimated to have died.

Kultur/Zivilisation

The distinction between *Kultur* and *Zivilisation* entered German romantic thinking through *Herder and *Kant and subsequently became a fundamental theme of nineteenth- and early twentieth-century German social thought. The obvious translation – 'culture' and 'civilization' – does not do justice to the motivation of the romantics, which was to distinguish the *universalist ideas of the *Enlightenment ('mere' civilization) from the rooted sense of *identity which they threatened. The liberal philosopher and educational reformer Wilhelm von Humboldt (1767–1835) identified civilization as the outward conformity to the arts of society, culture as the inner and subjective development of the individual, through art, religion and self-reflection. The *nationalists (following Herder) identified culture as the spirit of a people, embodied in their language, art and customs, and would often dismiss civilization as the enemy of culture – an attempt to replace instinctive togetherness with an abstract and individualistic system of rules. This way of making the distinction survived into the twentieth century, in the work of *Spengler. And even Thomas Mann, in so many ways a representative of Enlightenment values, wrote, at the outset of the First World War, that civilization and culture are opposites, implying that the war was a fight to the death between the two – the Germans representing culture, their enemies civilization.

Kulturkampf

German: war of culture. Repressive political movement against the Roman Catholic Church, instigated in 1871 by Bismarck, with the intention of wresting all educational and cultural institutions from the church, and conferring them instead upon the state. Bismarck became convinced of the error of his policy, and concluded a concordat with Pope Leo XIII. The term has, however, remained, designating one aspect of a complex phenomenon, equally exemplified in *cultural revolution, where an attempt is made to transfer political power through gaining control over *education and *culture.

Labour

The purposeful exercise of human capacity (whether physical or intellectual) in the transformation of nature into objects of *consumption or *exchange. Labour was made central to political thinking by *Locke's theory of property, has been regarded by many economists as one among several *factors of production, and is given the status of the primary *productive force by *Marx.

Labour time is the time spent in productive activity, whereas labour *power* is the capacity to produce through labour. The distinction between the two is a cornerstone of the theory of *surplus-value, in the version defended by Marx.

Nineteenth-century theories of labour as constitutive of the human personality, and the associated attempts to analyse the self-image of labour in its varied employments, have had considerable influence upon modern political thinking, notably through the theory of *alienated labour, which attempts to account for the distressed quality of the labour process under *factory production, sometimes in terms of the distinct mode of ownership that is associated with it. (*See* *Arendt, *work.) Indeed, nineteenth-century political thought has bequeathed a kind of 'labour mystique' to subsequent theory and practice. With the rise of the *service economy, this mystique has faded, a fact symbolized by the transformation of the UK *Labour Party into *New Labour.

labour law

The body of legal principles and rules governing the employment of *labour: more or less synonymous with *industrial law.

Legislation governing the terms of the *wage contract is of great antiquity, and a notorious medieval example (the Statute of Labourers 1349, which condemned labourers after the Black Death to work for wages current before it, in defiance of supply and demand) has been the subject of much political comment, partly because it is an early example of an *incomes policy. Most modern legislation has been aimed at improving the conditions of labour, and has arisen as a response to the *industrial revolution, and to the social changes consequent on large-scale *factory production and the employment of *detail labour. The first important statute in the UK was Pitt's Health and Morals of Apprentices Act 1802; but *see further* *factory legislation.

labour mobility

Labour mobility is of two kinds: (a) geographical, consisting in the power of the labour force to move from place to place, and (b) occupational, consisting in the power of workers to change occupations in response to changing needs and the availability of jobs. Art. 48 of the Treaty of Rome, 1957, attempts to guarantee mobility in sense (a) throughout the EEC (as it then was), but it has been considerably qualified by local immigration laws. After the *Maastricht Treaty the mobility of labour has radically increased within the European Union, producing the 'Polish plumber' problem, as workers from the former communist countries offer their services at a rate far below the customary level. Within any economy both forms of mobility affect the rate at which economic *equilibrium can be achieved after radical changes in the place and character of production.

labour movement

The movement which seeks to further the interests of the working class, usually by gaining political power (either through *representation or through direct *control) for workers. The antecedents of the labour movement are found in the rebellions of slaves in antiquity, and in the 'peasants' revolt' of medieval Europe. The modern labour movement is, however, to a great extent an offshoot of *industrialization and of the consequent severance of the labourer from all traditional relations of obligation towards his employer. It began in France and England, among reforming radicals, during the eighteenth century, and took early shape in English *Chartism and French *Babouvism. Its history through the nineteenth century is intermingled with that of *Owenism, *Marxism, *ouvrièrisme* (the French movement pressing for working-class representation within a republican constitution), the *trade union movement, and the various responses from governments. In the UK these responses included *factory legislation, and the eventual extension of the franchise in 1867, as a result of which a considerable portion of the working class was able to vote in parliamentary elections. This permitted the emergence of new political movements, such as the Labour Representation League, formed in 1869, working for the representation of the labour movement in Parliament but 'without reference to opinion or party bias'. The movement culminated in 1900 in the formation of the UK *Labour Party, which has provided the model for similar parties elsewhere. These began by seeking to give power to the working class, through representation within a *constitutional democracy, and to use existing institutions in order to work for the betterment of the pay and conditions of labour, while maintaining a broadly *socialist political perspective. The labour movement has also had a developed international character, and has sought at every stage to create links between workers which transcend national boundaries.

labour parties

The political arm of the *labour movement. The UK Independent Labour Party emerged from an informal coalition with the Liberals in 1893, while the Labour Party as we know it was founded in 1900, as a combination of all *democratic socialist groups in the UK, including trade unions, the *Fabian Society, the Independent Labour Party and the left-oriented Social Democratic Federation. Other labour parties were formed in imitation of it, in various parts of the British Empire and (subsequently) Commonwealth, and Norway and Israel have both developed labour parties on the UK model. In so far as they have achieved an identifiable political character it was, at least until recently, captured by the following features:

(a) explicit appeal to the working-class vote;

(b) affiliation with, and even partial direction by, the trade unions, with important constitutional provisions to preserve the relative autonomy of the parliamentary party;

(c) belief in representational government through democratic election, and in the constitution and institutions (such as parliament) that will be necessary for that end;

(d) belief in a planned economy, with the increasing use of government power to direct industry, to ensure *economic growth and full employment, and to bring about a more equitable distribution of property and opportunity. For the most part this has involved the advocacy of the nationalization of key private assets, and the furtherance of a mixed economy;

(e) belief in the redistribution of wealth, usually through taxation, and the abolition of privilege (especially privilege which stems from class) in all fields, especially education and the professions;

(f) belief in the development of a *welfare state;

(g) the commitment to democracy, not only as a principle of government, but also as a necessary part of the just administration of all institutions, however subordinate. This last feature is part of the undercurrent of liberalism which motivates much labour-party thinking.

On the whole, labour parties have shown themselves to be constitutionalist in their activities, fairly conservative in their economic policy, and highly respectful towards popular symbols of government, such as the UK monarchy. Conflicts within the UK party arose during the 1970s and 1980s, partly because those on the left either rejected that constitutionalist and parliamentarian stance, or else were believed to reject it by those on the right. The conflict led to the formation of the first *social democrat party within the UK Parliament.

The success of *Thatcherism and the world-wide flight from socialist ways of thinking have subsequently led to a radical redrawing of the Labour Party's programme. What used to be its two most fundamental commitments –

to *social ownership of the means of production ('Clause 4' of the original constitution) and to close ties with the trade union movement, amounting in certain matters to virtual control by the union élites – have now been effectively rejected, and the Party has reconstituted itself as a reforming liberal party. See *New Labour. Labour Parties elsewhere, for the most part taking the British party as their model, as in Australia and Israel, have likewise evolved away from socialism towards more pragmatic forms of policy-making.

labour theory of value

A theory developed by *Ricardo, according to which the *exchange-value of a commodity is determined by labour alone. The theory exists in at least three forms.

(i) Since exchange-value is an artefact, and cannot exist in nature, it must exist in virtue of some human activity. The only activity that could explain the rise of the institution of exchange is the activity that transforms nature into commodities. This activity is human labour. The theory exists in this form in Hegel, though it has antecedents in *Locke and even in *Plato. It may explain the institution of exchange-value, but not the actual price of any commodity.

(ii) The exchange-value of a commodity is uniquely determined (provided certain conditions are satisfied) by the quantity of labour that went into its production. Hence *price, or exchange-value in *equilibrium conditions, is directly proportional to labour hours.

(iii) (Marx.) The exchange-value of a commodity depends upon the labour time 'socially necessary' to produce the commodity. Marx sometimes speaks of value as 'congealed labour', a phrase that is ambiguous between (ii) and (iii). Marx differed from the previous classical economists in that he argued that the capitalist buys labour *power*, rather than labour.

In all versions the labour theory attempts to dispense with demand as an independent determinant of price. It also represents capital as economically subordinate, to be explained as a by-product of labour. It is objected to the labour theory that it neglects scarcity rents, that it must reduce qualitative differences of labour to quantitative differences, that the special assumptions required for its conclusions are not fulfilled in modern economies, and that its most plausible version, (iii), requires a theoretical apparatus that has not been provided for it. Another objection is that the labour theory of value provides no theory of price levels unless one already knows the *surplus value accruing to the supplier of each commodity. In short, the labour theory of value has had its day.

laicism

The belief that civil functions performed erstwhile by a priesthood ought to be transferred to the laity, especially functions of a judicial and educational kind. Its extreme form might involve *anti-clericalism and the advocacy of a *Kulturkampf against the church. It remains an important movement in Turkey and (to some extent) Tunisia. Laicism was regarded by *Kemalism as an essential part of the process whereby modern political institutions could be constructed, hence it remains one of the 'six arrows' of the Turkish Republican People's Party.

Lacan, Jacques (1901–1981)

French psychotherapist. *See* *psychotherapy.

laïcité

French: laicism, used to mean a principle of social and political organization, according to which religion and religious allegiance must be kept out of public life, and play no part – or at any rate no obvious part – in the institutions controlled by the state, including the state schools. This principle has been affirmed by successive French constitutions, and been accepted by the majority of citizens. However, the arrival of large numbers of Muslim immigrants from North Africa, many of whom wish to display their faith in their mode of dress, has led to conflict in the schools and elsewhere. *Laïcité* is also upheld by the Lebanese constitution, in conscious adoption of the French tradition.

laicization

The transference of religious duties from a clergy to the laity. Not to be confused with *laicism, which advocates the authority of the laity in social and political matters, but usually concedes the exclusive competence of the priesthood in all matters of religion. However, a clergy which sees as 'matters of religion' what others see as 'simple politics' will often react to laicism as though it involved laicization, and so attempt to forbid it.

Laing, Ronald David (1927–86)

British psychiatrist. *See* *alternative society, *family, *psychotherapy.

laissez-faire

An expression which perhaps originated in a remark made by a merchant on being asked by Colbert, finance minister to Louis XIV, what economic policy should be adopted: 'Laissez faire, laissez passer.' The slogan was taken up by the *physiocrats, who believed that the state's role was simply that of protecting property rights and the natural order. *Classical economics shared this hostility to *interventionism, and the slogan *laissez-faire* is still used to characterize some of the ideas of the *New Right, who believe with *Smith that a statesman who seeks to control the flow of capital within an economy 'would not only load himself with a most unnecessary attention, but assume an authority which could safely be trusted, not only to no single person, but to no council or senate whatever, and which would nowhere be so dangerous as in the hands of a man who had folly and presumption enough to fancy himself fit to exercise it' (*The Wealth of Nations*, IV, 2).

The theory of *laissez-faire* is part of a justification that is still offered for the free market, although few now think that it indicates a feasible policy. Two prominent conservative thinkers, *Hayek and *Oakeshott, have argued, for example, that *laissez-faire* requires regulation, if it is not to degenerate into a *monopoly, and is therefore an artificial and not a natural condition.

Lamarckism

The theory of evolution associated with the work of the French zoologist J.B.P.A. de Lamarck (1744–1829), according to which needs provide a motivating force behind evolutionary change, which does not therefore proceed in the random manner envisaged by some Darwinists. Lamarck believed in 'the inheritance of acquired characteristics': i.e. in the ability of an organism to pass on its achievements. Darwin himself was mildly attracted by Lamarckism, although it is not generally accepted by biologists. However, it has had its political followers, notable among them being Stalin, who adopted and, so to speak, enforced the version of Lamarckism known, after its propagator, as Lysenkoism. This view seemed to offer a biological basis for the reconciliation of *egalitarianism with human progress, since it suggested that an organism reared differently from its ancestors would tend to develop in a new way, and that distinctions between people might be eliminated by new conditions of development. (*See* *new man.) A Lamarckian version of Marx's theory of history might also seem attractive, since it would account for the very small number of variations among economic systems that actually exist.

land

Land includes, for economic, political and legal purposes, all that is contained within the soil, all that grows on it, and also, in law, all that has been built on it (*see* *land law.) Early debates over the economics of agriculture often posed the question of whether land could be considered to be a *factor of production distinct from *capital. The free exchange of privately owned land is, legally speaking, a relatively new development, dating in the UK from the Settled Land Act 1856. But since land itself is productive often only when serviced by labour, it stands in a relation to labour that is comparable to that of any other means of production.

Some have argued that, while private property in such things as houses, commodities, and even factories may be permissible in the interests of security and production, private property in land violates a fundamental need or right of *common ownership. (Arguments along these lines were offered by Henry George, in *Progress and Poverty*, 1879.) Proposals for the social ownership of land have therefore been frequent in modern politics, even in the UK where, technically, no land is held except on tenure from the Crown. The problems for this new attempt to divide land from 'movable' goods are twofold: (i) all goods are produced from raw materials that were, originally, land; hence there has to be a transition from common ownership to private ownership if the latter is to be possible, and hence there must be a right of transfer. With whom does this right lie? If it lies with society as a whole (or with the state as society's trustee or guardian), then in effect there is common ownership of everything; (ii) in order to live on and produce from the land some security of tenure is necessary, and what is security of tenure if not a (defeasible) right of private property? (*See* *private property.) In which case social ownership becomes a legal fiction, like the ownership of land by the Crown.

Nevertheless the distinction between land and other forms of capital remains deeply entrenched in much political thinking, and not merely because the first is an ambiguous term which sometimes refers to agricultural as opposed to factory production. Many conservatives, for example, distinguish between the psychological stances involved in the ownership of land and the ownership of movable capital. The first stands as a symbol for permanent attachment to a place, and submission to the *jurisdiction there obtaining, while the second represents the desire to accumulate power in a manner that may avoid the responsibilities that attach to it, and to move from jurisdiction to jurisdiction in order to escape them.

land law

The branch of law which deals with the tenure of land provides one of the most interesting fields of political archaeology, since it contains strata from every era of social development, in which are fossilized the legal foliage of former social and economic orders.

As an example of a politically significant transition it is instructive to consider the case of settled land in English law. Originally settled land passed intact to the legal heirs, so that the tenant for life was considered trustee for those who were to succeed him, with no right of use that would enable him to alter their right to the land and its fruits. The Settled Land Acts 1856, 1882 and 1890 established that the interests of the heirs could be 'over-reached', i.e. translated into a money interest, and would automatically be so translated whenever the tenant for life sold the land. Hence – whatever the form of the settlement – there would be no impediment to sale of the land by the present occupant, who would then hold money, rather than land, in trust for his successors. This legislation put land for the first time on an equal footing with all other property as an item of free exchange, so that land becomes simply a special case of capital.

Of equal interest is the feudal doctrine, still surviving in UK law, of 'estates in land'. Land, being definitive of *jurisdiction, is always held subject to *allegiance. However, according to the feudal doctrine, tenure and allegiance follow each other: the obligation owed by the 'tenant in chief' is direct to the sovereign, that by the one who holds from the tenant in chief is to him, and so on. One half of this idea survives in the fact that tenure is always a matter of degree, descending from freehold (which is subject only to forfeiture in favour of the sovereign), through leasehold, to sub-tenancies, down to the weakest form of security, known as 'squatter's rights'. This last arises sometimes from *prescription, and sometimes from the effect of the Statute of Forcible Entry 1381, which makes it a crime forcibly to evict someone without legal process, and which has thus protected most kinds of tenancy since the late Middle Ages. Defenders and attackers of private property should attend to the idea, still enshrined in this kind of law, that property rights often exist in varying degrees, and always involve a third term. Besides the person possessing them and the thing in which they are possessed, there is also the sovereign power from which they are held. (*See* *eminent domain*.)

The modern attempt to control relations between landlord and tenant by statute is an attempt to extend security of tenure and so rights in land to all citizens. It is sometimes held to violate the existing property rights of the landlord, although it is clear that every extension of ownership in land will violate the rights of *someone*, unless some land is unowned.

In the US the original settlements involved *common ownership of land; private property in land emerged only later, as a result of purchases from the common fund, and it is the economic success of private ownership in land in seventeenth-century Virginia that is partly responsible for the later universal approval and adoption of this transaction. Attempts in communist countries to forbid private ownership of land and to enforce *collectivization of agriculture have invariably led to social and economic disaster – in some cases to starvation.

land reform

The breaking up of large estates, *redistribution of *land, and the facilitating of legal transfer of land, with the object of bringing about fundamental changes in the structure of power. Land, being identified with the state through the existence of *jurisdiction, and with life through its essential role in the production of necessary goods, seems to be fundamental to all relations of property. It is perhaps less true than it used to be that power in the state belongs to the class of landowners, but it is still the case that all radical changes in social structure proceed at least in part by land reform, and opposition to land reform may be a sign of the desire to conserve an existing social hierarchy. *See* *hereditary principle.

landlocked state

A state with no coastal borders (e.g. Switzerland, Slovakia), and which is therefore dependent upon the co-operation of its neighbours for all communications by sea. The importance of maritime communications for commerce and imperial expansion is sometimes offered as one explanation of the relative unimportance of landlocked states in international politics.

Lange, Oskar Ryszard (1904–65)

Polish economist and politician. *See* *market socialism.

language

Language, as a symbol of social identity, came to have increasing political importance with the rise of *nationalism, so that the existence of a common language is now often thought to be an important precondition of political *identity. *Irredentism in the UK has been associated with moves to revive the Celtic languages, and the formation of the central European states after the dissolution of the Austro-Hungarian Empire took language as its starting-point. *Kemalism exerted towards the Turkish language much of its political energy, hoping to reform it in the direction of a desired political identity and away from cultural dependence upon the supposedly backward states of Islam. *Feminism also asserts a politics of language, sometimes arguing for the removal of distinctions of gender from English, or for the replacement of the masculine pronoun as the usual form of indefinite reference, on the ground that such grammatical habits merely perpetuate socially induced and 'irrelevant' distinctions between men and women, and also prevent the speaker from recognizing the arbitrariness of those distinctions. (*See* *gender.*) In opposition to such radical reformers the *cultural conservative is apt to defend the existing language as the embodiment of moral, spiritual and aesthetic values: the thought here has usually been vaguely expressed, and its implications are as obscure as those of the positions which it attacks. (*See* *newspeak.*)

Along with the many nationalist movements that take language as a political focus, there is also an international movement, which advocates an international language (Esperanto) that will be free from all the local and parochial affections that are contained in the older tongues. This movement seems to have flagged, perhaps because there were no native speakers to give it initial impetus. By contrast the use of Latin as a universal language by the Roman Catholic Church (now rejected by that institution, to the sorrow of many of its members) was enormously successful in helping it to found an international *jurisdiction, and to influence political and educational institutions everywhere.

Almost all discussions of the political significance of language engage in large and unfounded speculations, and, while there is no doubt that many of the above views are based in serious perceptions, it is extremely difficult to see how thought about this most difficult question should proceed. *See* *communication.

Lasch, Christopher (1933–94)
US social critic who, starting from a leftist and anticapitalist perspective, gradually distanced himself from the radical liberationist movements of the 1960s and 1970s, to become a trenchant critic of the 'culture of narcissism', as he called it, in a book of that title (1979). Lasch had been appalled by the leftist attacks on the family in the name of self-liberation, and in *Haven in a Heartless World* (1978) he points to the irreplaceable value of domestic love and security in the raising of children

and in the creation of the web of social support on which we all depend. His subsequent attacks on the *New Left and its rejection of disciplined schooling in favour of 'child-centred learning' earned him many supporters on the Right. However, he remained an anticapitalist, convinced that the laxity and self-indulgence of American culture stem not from egalitarianism but from the devotion to material comforts and material gain. His writings, riven by his own internal conflicts, became steadily gloomier, and his inability to distance himself from the modern world suggests that he never fully understood the healing power of laughter.

Lassalle, Ferdinand (1825–64)
German *socialist, revolutionary of 1848, and for some time a friend both of *Proudhon and of *Marx. He advocated a form of socialism in which private property would be permitted if legitimately acquired, but in which the *iron law of wages would be broken by the abolition of *wage labour and the wage contract. He defended *cooperatives, which were to be established with assistance from the state, and which, when combined with universal suffrage, would lead not only to the economic but also to the political dominance of the working class, and the effective end of capitalist exploitation. Lassalle's socialism attempted to give concrete descriptions of future society, and to adapt itself to existing political institutions, so that changes in law within the existing constitution might be sufficient to bring it about. Hence it gave rise to many concrete programmes of reform, including the famous 'Gotha Programme', criticized as theoretically incoherent by Marx.

late capitalism
Term introduced by Ernest Mandel, and used by *Marxist writers to denote the species of capitalism which has

developed since the *industrial revolution and which survives in modified form in the US and Western Europe. It is called 'late' in obedience to the Marxist conviction that it is doomed soon to disappear. Needless to say, the term is less and less used.

latitudinarianism

Term applied disapprovingly to those seventeenth-century Anglican divines who were without serious conviction in matters of liturgy and even of doctrine. Now often extended to denote any kind of doctrinal unconcern, especially in matters of religion and politics.

law

H. Kantorowicz (1877–1940) defined law as 'a body of social rules prescribing external conduct and considered justiciable'. This definition, satisfactory so far as it goes, does not go far: what is meant by 'social'? 'rules'? 'prescribing'? 'external'? 'conduct'? 'justiciable'? And 'considered' by whom? The following observations seem pertinent.

(a) 'social' denotes the fact that law applies to more than one person, and that the subjects of law are themselves social beings (perhaps because they are *rational beings);

(b) 'rules' must embrace custom (since there is customary law), unformulated maxims (since there is *common law), as well as *statute. The common element here is that of repeatability: the same action can be performed on a variety of occasions, and in principle by any number of people. Thus laws, however qualified, must always have a universal form;

(c) 'prescribing' means that laws are not indicative but imperative in mood: they do not describe but command (although this is in one sense denied by legal realists: *see* below). Hence, if there is a motive to disobey the law,

there must also be sanctions and *punishments to enforce it;

(d) 'external' is meant to exclude thought and belief and those emotions that are 'kept to oneself', and to apply only to behaviour that is recognized socially. The possibility of laws forbidding private thoughts and emotions is, however, a real one. It is sometimes thought that such laws would be deviant; however, many systems of law prescribe 'correct beliefs'. It is sometimes argued that such laws prescribe not beliefs but parades, rituals and customs which require at least an outward pretence of those beliefs;

(e) 'conduct' means conduct which issues from the *agency of a *person, and for which it is intelligible to hold the agent *responsible;

(f) 'justiciable' means susceptible to evaluation before a *court of law, empowered to enforce a judgement;

(g) 'considered' is the most difficult term in this list. The simplest answer is 'considered by the state in its legislative capacity', which clarifies the matter only to someone who has a grasp of the idea of the *state and its *legislature. Many nineteenth-century theorists, notably *J.S. Mill, wrote as though law is the expression of a social requirement, so that 'considered' is to be interpreted as 'considered by society' – which seems to conflict with the observation that society, unlike the state, is not a decision-making body, and becomes one only by also becoming a state.

Law as roughly defined above has been theorized in three distinct ways:

(i) Natural law theory. This sees all laws as attempts by human reason to approximate to those rules of *natural law which enshrine an ideal of good conduct, and which are universally acknowledged by rational beings. The theory has two forms, according to whether natural law is thought of as gaining its authority from God's command or from human reason. However, as *Kant pointed out, the first interpretation makes natural law into a species of *positive law, and so in effect abolishes it.

(ii) Legal positivism. First fully expounded in modern times by *Bentham and John Austin. This theory regards law not as an attempt to approximate to an objective law of nature, but simply as a human *convention or stipulation, whose authority derives from no other source than that of the legislating body which dictates it. On this view all law is by definition *positive law. But that does not mean that all law is *arbitrary. A law must still be validated by its pedigree, by the fact, for example, that it can be derived from a *Grundnorm* (*see* *Kelsen) or that it conforms to a 'rule of recognition' (a phrase used by H.L.A. Hart) which determines its constitutional validity. Nevertheless there is no extra-legal standard that a law must conform to in order to *be* a law. Such a view may yet be compatible with the theory of *natural law, as providing an independent criterion of the *merit* of any positive law. (Alternatively, a *utilitarian criterion may be invoked in the justification of any particular body of laws.) For the positivist, law is law by virtue of its form; for the naturalist, by virtue of its content.

(iii) Legal realism. A name sometimes given to the view which tries to discuss the basic *fact* of law, without reference to its prescriptive nature. Law is a form of social activity, with its attendant punishments and persuasions; since this is the only fact of the matter, then it is in these terms that law must be discussed. Law becomes 'the prophecies of what courts will do in fact and nothing more pretentious' (J. Holmes).

law and morality

What is forbidden by the law may be morally permissible and even morally obligatory; likewise what is morally forbidden may be permitted or even compelled by the law. To what extent should the two systems of *sanction correspond, and to what extent can they correspond? Those questions have been a major problem for modern political thinkers. Liberals in the Anglo-Saxon tradition have tended to follow *J.S. Mill (*On Liberty*, 1859) in thinking that law is essentially *public, whereas morality has large *private areas into which the law can intrude only by violating individual rights or freedoms, and so undermining its own legitimacy. For example, sexual morality has recently been regarded as a private affair, or as public only in so far as it involves *harm to one of the participants. If that is so, it is often argued, the harmless varieties of sexual conduct, however morally obnoxious they may be or be thought to be, ought not to be forbidden by law. The only criteria should be those of harm and *consent. By contrast, thinkers who do not feel the liberal confidence in the absolute independence of *society and *state, may think of the state and its law as the guardian of an entire social order, and of all the values, whether moral, religious, or political, which that social order requires. For example, it may be argued that social order can endure despite the violation of many moral sanctions, but that moral sanctions must be recognized by the law if they are to be commonly accepted, and must be commonly accepted if social cohesion is to be maintained. This was argued against Mill, on utilitarian grounds, by Sir James Fitzjames Stephen in *Liberty, Equality, Fraternity*, 1873. The controversy between Mill and Stephen was restated in contemporary terms by H.L.A. Hart, *Law, Liberty and Morals*, 1963 (taking the liberal position) and Patrick Devlin, *The Enforcement of Morals*, 1965, giving the conservative reply.

The conservative position may correspond in its conclusions to more authoritarian pronouncements, such as those made on behalf of a divine law. Thus in the modern *Islamic state, the distinction between morality and law is apt to seem artificial, as is the corresponding distinction between the public and the private, precisely because all human affairs are regulated by a law which has been supposedly laid down by God. (*See further* *freedom, *Islamic law, *liberalism, *liberty.)

law and economics
A school of thought, with many followers in the US but also gaining ground elsewhere, which applies the methods of economic analysis to the explanation and justification of legislation and legal judgements. The leading idea is that legal decisions – whether in the legislature or in the courts – change the costs and benefits attached to particular courses of action. The law should therefore work as markets work, to allocate resources efficiently. For example, the legal decisions in civil law, by compelling those who cause damage to bear the cost of it, promote the allocation of resources to those who use them profitably. The behaviour of judges and juries can also be explained by applying the principles of rational choice that apply in economics. (*See also* *public choice.) An Encyclopedia of Law and Economics now exists, edited from the University of Ghent, and since 1991 an American Association of Law and Economics has had annual meetings, with a journal now devoted to its theme. Influential adherents of the school include Judge Richard Posner (b. 1939), who helped to found the school while professor of law in the University of Chicago.

law and order
The rallying cry of a certain kind of *populist conservatism, although plausibly held to be a main concern of *politics everywhere. To the extent that order exists without law there is no state (and perhaps no need for one); to the extent that law exists without order then the state exists only as an ideal and not in reality.

Order without law may be spontaneous (the ideal of *anarchism), or forced (the actuality of *despotism). *Constitutionalists tend to argue that it is no accident that the preaching of anarchism leads to despotism.

law of uneven development
A supposed law, often alluded to by *Marx, and invoked, e.g. by *Trotsky, in order to explain and predict the course of *revolution in underdeveloped countries (especially Russia) and to reconcile the observed facts with the major claims of *Marxist theory. The idea is that, instead of developing uniformly from feudal to post-capitalist conditions, such societies develop in a way that, while beginning in feudalism, and ending in socialism, is in its intermediary stages 'planless, complex and combined' – 'combined' meaning that various stages in the process, such as *primitive accumulation and *industrialization, which should in theory be separated, occur in combination. The law is therefore sometimes called the 'law of uneven and combined development', and 'without this law . . . it is impossible to understand the history of Russia, and indeed of any country of the second, third or tenth cultural class' (Leon Trotsky: *History of the Russian Revolution*, 1930).

Leavis, F.R. (1895–1978)
English literary critic, who had an enormous impact on the study and teaching of English language and literature, and on intellectual life in the UK, and whose views have to a certain extent altered the political landscape.

Leavis believed that all culture depends upon the active renewal of a 'great tradition', that this process of renewal both purifies the language and makes it possible for people to think creatively and to feel unsentimentally. Art and literature are not recreations but crucibles in which life is tested, and their decline will register itself in the loss of seriousness and in a retreat from the commitments and connections that life demands. Leavis vehemently opposed the idea that there might be two cultures, one scientific and one *humane – an idea that had been put forward by the novelist C.P. Snow. Science, he argued, is not a part of culture, since it does not have the education of the emotions as its goal. In trying to say what and how culture affects the human person, Leavis made a substantial contribution to understanding the role of *humane education in a modern society. He also influenced a generation of teachers towards the view that the appreciation of literature is the best preparation for a responsible moral life. He was heir to the *cultural conservatism of *Arnold and *Eliot, but his own political pronouncements, such as they were, had more in common with *guild socialism than with anything recognizable as conservatism.

leadership

The capacity to inspire confidence in the rightness of one's purposes, courage in their collective execution, and *obedience in the face of any threat of resistance. (*Contrast* *demagogue.*) Leadership has sometimes been propounded as a supreme political virtue (*see* *Führerprinzip*, *vanguard*), although it is also one of the characteristics that make *politics impossible. Leadership is a matter of degree, and consists in the extent to which a single person can build *control on a foundation of *influence. Changes effected

through leadership may be vaster and, despite the hardship of those affected by them, more easily accepted than those which derive from the deliberation of a party or a bureaucracy. At the same time, they are often considered, in retrospect, to be the inevitable outcome of irresistible and impersonal forces. Many recent sociological studies of leadership have attempted to explain these and related facts. Some argue that leadership results from *charisma – although this seems not so much to explain the phenomenon as to redescribe it. Others now reject attempts to explain leadership in terms of the personal characteristics of the leader, and prefer to see leadership as a relation dependent upon social context, so that those who are leaders in one situation may not be leaders in another. (*See* R.M. Stogdill: *Personal Factors Associated with Leadership*, 1948.) Elias Canetti (*Crowds and Power*, 1960) has described the function of the leader as an integral part of a *crowd, and has argued that the principal quality that he requires, apart from those which make him prominent in the first place, is survival. By showing himself able to survive while others succumb to the greatest dangers he perpetuates the myth of a more than human virtue; to do this he may even deliberately set out to kill his closest supporters and recklessly to create the dangers which will test his power to survive. Such, for example, was the leadership of Hitler, Lenin and Mussolini.

left

The polar opposite of *right. The term originated in the habit of the democratic and liberal side of the French assembly, and of other European legislatures in the nineteenth century, of sitting to the left of the president's chair (a habit presaged in the French Estates General of 1789, in which the nobility sat on the King's right, and the 'third estate' on his left).

Terms like 'left', 'left of centre', and 'left wing' now denote a variety of things, and most of all a certain flavour of politics. They are terms of *journalese, without precise meaning, but used to suggest some combination of the following views (no one of which is necessary and each of which admits of degree):

(i) a hostility to *private property, and belief in *social ownership as the ideal alternative, with control by the state as a necessary means to that;

(ii) a hostility towards classes judged to be favoured by the political system;

(iii) a hostility towards *establishment in all its forms, and towards *offices, *honours, and other symbolic expressions of the dignity of government;

(iv) desire for a classless society, without *privilege, *patronage or a *hereditary principle;

(v) belief in *democracy, or at least in popular participation in government; or government by consent;

(vi) belief in certain *natural rights (or *human rights), particularly those associated with the victims of existing social arrangements, be they workers, women, immigrants or whatever;

(vii) a belief in *progress, to be furthered by *revolution or *reform;

(viii) *egalitarian leanings, together with a desire for *social justice;

(ix) anti-*nationalist (although not necessarily *internationalist) tendencies (although it should be noted that nationalists now constitute one of the largest classes on the left);

(x) belief in a *welfare state, and in state control over education, medicine, and important resources.

Not all of (i) to (x) are compatible in practice, although it is possible to believe that they are. Many people on the left would describe themselves as socialists; the 'revolutionary left' is composed of those who wish to bring socialism into being by revolution, the rest being content with reform conducted through existing institutions. Left-wing theory is the attempt to synthesize all or some of (i) to (x), eliminate inconsistencies, and provide an underlying justification in terms either of a theory of history or a theory of *justice, or both.

Because there is a clear spectrum of opinion identified by the two poles of 'left' and 'right' it is now normal to refer, e.g., to the left wing of right-wing parties, and the right wing of left-wing parties. Very roughly those who shift to the left see themselves as moving in the direction of *Rousseau's 'compassionating zeal' for the under-privileged, and away from respect for existing institutions, in particular those that confer power, property, privilege and social distinction. Those who shift to the right tend to regard compassionating zeal as a mask for *ressentiment.

left-liberal

Vague term denoting the spectrum of attitudes common among Western *intellectuals, and exemplified in the later expressions of English *Fabianism, and in the 'Lib-Lab' mentality. The main characteristic is an adherence to those items of *left-wing belief which are, or seem to be, compatible with certain basic *liberal convictions, notably the belief in *natural rights, in *freedoms (especially of thought, expression and association), and in legal *reform in the direction of increased *toleration. The attempt to reconcile those values with *social justice, and even with *egalitarian principles of distribution, has been responsible for many of the most important shifts in political opinion among Western intellectuals since the Second World War. Although left-liberal attitudes are often unsystematic there have been attempts to give them full theoretical foundation – e.g. in the theory of *justice espoused by *Rawls. These attempts are usually inspired by the sense that the two sets of values – those associated with the liberal account of rights and freedoms, and those associated with socialist ideals of equitable distribution and social justice – are ultimately derived from a single *universalist intuition, concerning the equal value of every individual. It ought therefore to be possible to reconcile them within a single political doctrine. It is often objected that such a reconciliation is impossible, since the powers required to ensure socialist distribution can be exercised only by violating liberal rights and freedoms.

leftism

1. The adherence to the opinions of the *left.

2. In Communist Party official language, 'leftism' named a heresy, associated with *Bukharin, the main characteristics of which were originally a disposition to take socialist policies too far, and to insist for example on the *democratization of all social activities, rather than on the important tactical and supervisory role of the *Communist Party and its institutions.

legal fiction

A pretence that an instance of A is really an instance of B so that the law relating to Bs, but not to As, can be applied to it. The invention of a 'legal fiction' is a much favoured mode of legal development, enabling new cases to be accommodated and distinguished, without changing the structure of the law. Examples include many of the procedures for *manumission in *Roman law and for loans at interest in *Islamic law. Among examples in modern UK and US law is the doctrine that adolescents under a certain age cannot consent to sexual intercourse.

legal instruments

Term used of the law issuing from the *European Union, which has three instruments to choose from – regulations, decisions and directives – the choice being largely at the discretion of the *European Commission. Regulations are automatically incorporated into domestic law throughout the EU; decisions are binding only on those to whom they are addressed, while directives are binding in terms of the result, but leave the mode of arriving at it to each member state.

legal privilege

A privilege in law is an authority to do something without fear of legal sanction. In UK law, members of *Parliament, barristers, *trade unions, and many others have privileges, protecting them against certain kinds of action which, could they be brought against them, would effectively prevent them from performing their functions. A privilege is sometimes described as a kind of *right; however, the withdrawal of a privilege is not the violation of a right, so this usage is misleading. (It is sometimes said that it is a right, but not a 'claim right'. *See* *jural relations.) There is, for example, no 'right to strike' in UK law (although it is often spoken of); there is, rather, a privilege granting immunity to strikers from certain kinds of legal proceeding that might otherwise have been brought against them. For the distinction here *see* *privilege.

legalism

Excessive veneration for the law, and its procedures, and a reluctance to depart from the letter of the law, or to bend it in some new direction. Often used in a derogatory sense to mean excessive preoccupation with the *legality of an action and an associated reluctance to assess it on its independent merits.

legality

Conformity to *law. The principal
ground on which a *subject may
legally challenge the validity of an act
of his *sovereign. The law, being an
expression of the will of the sovereign,
can be invoked against the sovereign
without derogating from the sovereign's authority: a challenge based on
illegality is simply a reminder to the
sovereign of the internal necessity to
be consistent. To the extent that such
a challenge is not possible (e.g. by
*judicial review, or by action on a
charge of *ultra vires) there is no true
legal determination of the relations
between subject and sovereign, and
the relation between them is one of
*despotism.

legislation

The 'making' of law (inverted commas
necessary since some believe that
some law, and maybe all true law, is
not made but discovered: see *judiciary, *law). This can involve any one
of the following procedures:

(i) Express decree by the *legislature, which decree may be oral or written, and will always stand in need of
subsequent interpretation by the judiciary. See *statute.

(ii) The establishment of a legal
custom, with no express enactment of
the legislature, but with an entrenched
obedience to *precedent: see *common
law.

(iii) A decision of the highest *court
of the *jurisdiction concerning a case
not covered by the existing legislation.
The most famous case of this in
English law is the decision of the
House of Lords in *Rylands* v. *Fletcher*,
1868, from which most of the modern
law of occupier's liability ultimately
stems.

The third case is sometimes called
'judicial legislation', and is a special
case of (ii); it is an instance of
common law without precedent. What

is the basis of such legislation? Is this
merely an undetermined decision by
the judges? Or are they working out
implications in the existing law? Is
their attitude one of invention or
discovery? (*See* *hard cases.) Some
thinkers dispute over the value of this
third kind of legislation, and whether
or not a *constitution should permit it
(assuming that it could absolutely
forbid it and still be a constitution).
The US constitution, for example (Art.
I, ss 1 and 7, and Art. VI), expressly
confines the word 'legislation' to Acts
of *Congress. But perhaps the only
thing that is thereby confined is a
word. The thing denoted by that word,
say some, takes place in the law courts
just as soon as there is a doctrine of
*precedent.

legislator

The giver of law. That law should be
given to a people, by a single legislator, sometimes seems strange to
modern ways of thinking, but the idea
of the wise legislator is an important
conception in ancient and medieval
theories of the state and also in the
thought of *Rousseau, who wrote of
the legislator as 'shaping the people
like a god'. The most famous legislators were Lycurgus of Sparta, and
Solon, who, at about 594 BC, was called
upon to terminate the civil strife in
Athens and give laws to the city,
replacing those of Draco: some of
these laws survive in fragments of
verse (it being part of the authority of
the legislator that he should express
himself in memorable idiom, so that
even the illiterate can make use of his
laws).

*Machiavelli believed in the legisla-
tor idea, and was able to say: 'that
republic, indeed, may be called happy
whose lot has been to have a founder
so prudent as to provide for it laws
under which it can continue to live
securely, without need to amend

them; as we find Sparta preserving hers for 800 years, without deterioration, and without any dangerous disturbances' (*Discourses*, I, II), and again: 'with very few exceptions, no commonwealth or kingdom ever has salutary institutions given to it from the first, or has its institutions recast in an entirely new mould, unless by a single person' (*ibid*. I, IX). The advocacy of legislation by a single person was not confined to Machiavelli: even *Harrington advanced this doctrine, on the grounds that a government should be made 'altogether and at once'. It is often remarked, however, that modern *revolutions, while they may end by giving power to a single person, seldom produce the 'immortal legislator' whom Robespierre sought.

legislature

The part of government which exerts a *legislative power, i.e. which is concerned with making and changing the law. Usually contrasted with the *executive, which applies the law, and engages in foreign and domestic *policy, and the *judiciary, which interprets the law and settles disputes. (For the theory of the relation between these, *see* *separation of powers.) There cannot be a *constitution without rules for determining who shall belong to the legislature. In the UK it is composed of the monarch, the House of Commons, and the House of Lords – i.e. 'The Queen in Parliament'. In the US it is composed of the President, the Senate and the House of Representatives. In both cases, however, *delegated legislation is (in certain conditions) permitted, so that other institutions are from time to time granted legislative powers, and ministers have powers to act by decree and directive which are also legislative. Moreover, the possibility of judicial legislation makes it difficult to draw the boundary between the legislature and the judiciary with any confidence.

Furthermore, the UK is bound by Treaty to incorporate into its law all those rules and regulations prescribed by the *legislative instruments of the *European Union. In a certain sense, therefore, the UK has acquired a second and higher legislature based in the *European Commission.

legitimacy

A power is exercised illegitimately if there is no right to its exercise; otherwise it is exercised legitimately. Thus the crucial concepts in understanding legitimacy are those of *power and *right.

The main question that has occupied political thinkers is that of the legitimacy or otherwise of powers exercised in the name of the state, or of government. What gives a state the right to exercise such powers over the citizen, and which of the powers so exercised are rightly exercised? These questions are related to that of *political obligation: what obliges the citizen to obey the state? (Right and *obligation being 'jural correlatives': *see* *jural relations.) Expressing the question in terms of legitimacy emphasizes the *agency of the state, and questions that agency directly.

It is necessary to distinguish four questions:

(i) What makes a government, or the powers exercised by a government, legitimate? This is a question of political philosophy – identical in content, if not in emphasis, to that of political obligation.

(ii) What makes people believe a government to be, or accept it as being, legitimate? This is a question to which politician, however sceptical or indifferent they may be towards the first question, will always give their attention. If a people have the rooted belief that only democratic election, say, or only hereditary succession, confers legitimacy, they can be governed in some other way only by force.

(iii) What is the legal determination of legitimate power? This is a question of law, perhaps of *positive law, the answer to which may vary from state to state. Thus a directive from the Crown *empowers* (i.e. confers legitimate power upon) its recipient in UK law. An exercise of power, if *ultra vires*, is by this criterion illegitimate. By extension, in *international law, the legitimate government may be distinguished from the illegitimate, by legal rules. These rules may in fact fly in the face both of the true grounds (if there be any) for legitimacy (question (i)), and of the true sentiments of those destined to accept the result (question (ii)).

(iv) What is the legal determination of legitimate succession to power? This 'hereditary' idea of legitimacy is the one most frequently discussed in practical politics. Thus democratic election is recognized by the US constitution as the legitimate means of transferring the executive power to a new President (in normal circumstances). But clearly the powers conferred by the constitution are not themselves made legitimate just because they are, in this sense, legitimately transferred. It might still be argued that the exercise of power over such and such a territory in accordance with this constitution is a violation of right (for example, the right of the original inhabitants of the American continent). Likewise, worries about 'legitimate succession' to the ruling house of the UK are not likely to impress someone who believes that monarchical government constitutes an illegitimate exercise of power.

It seems that illegitimacy, like injustice, is more easily recognized than its opposite, and that the resentment towards a government thought to be illegitimate is far stronger than the contentment with a government that does not wear such a stigma. This fact of human nature has been all-important in European politics, especially in determining allegiances during wars of succession.

legitimation

The process whereby power gains acceptance in the eyes of those who are governed by it, by generating a belief in its *legitimacy. The social phenomenon here is highly complex, but the political views divide between the following:

(i) legitimation is necessary only in some political conditions, dispensable in others;

(ii) legitimation is always necessary, and should proceed through *indoctrination or 'political education';

(iii) (the conservative view) legitimation is necessary, but should proceed independently of political doctrine, and by drawing upon civil institutions of a different order from the political.

There is a natural disagreement over whether or not it would be *better* to dispense with legitimation or to create the conditions in which legitimation can be dispensed with – for example by establishing government by *consent (supposing this to be possible, and also distinct from government by legitimation). Some also have argued that there is a *crisis of legitimation (e.g. *Habermas and other members of the *Frankfurt school) which now imperils our civilization.

legitimist

Someone who believes in, and guides his political action by, an idea of the legitimate transfer of power. (*See* *legitimacy, question (iv).) Usually used to denote someone attached to a *monarchical government, governed by rules of succession, and to a particular person or family supposed entitled under those rules, the violation of which he deplores and resists. Such a person opposes not only *republican revolution, but also the ascent of a new ruling house, of a usurper or 'protector', or of any person other than the one prescribed by the (usually hereditary) rules for the transfer of government. The depth of legitimist feeling is great, and has often been compared to family feeling, perhaps because both are species of *piety.

Leibniz, Gottfried Wilhelm (1646–1716)
German philosopher, mathematician, jurist, politician and scientist. *See* *rationalism, *theodicy.

leisure

Leisure is the freedom from the immediate need to *work; idleness is the lack of an occupation. The first is a value only to someone who thinks that he can be better occupied by not working. It is characteristic of a *profession that it may so invade the desires and ambitions of someone who pursues it as to eliminate the thought that he could be better employed in some other way, so that the professional may often not regard leisure as a value. The same does not seem to be true of the labourer, who is occupied by work, but whose work does not always generate a sense that he is well occupied. Does it follow that the labourer will desire leisure, or that he will know what to do with it when he has it? This question has become of increasing concern to political thinkers, since it seems that enforced idleness (or *unemployment) is now a normal condition; it generates social problems to the extent that there is no satisfactory form of leisure available to the unemployed.

Traditionally leisure was an attribute of *aristocracy, the privilege of a *ruling class. As such it was the subject of meticulous planning, an end in itself, developed into social life, manners, *ceremony, display, and high *culture, so that the whole of life was given over to an elaborate play of aesthetic values. Some often attempt to envisage more democratic versions of that same laboured inactivity, perhaps out of a respect for the culture that is enshrined in it, perhaps out of a sense that it constitutes a valuable achievement in itself. Others regard that course as politically impossible, perhaps even as morally undesirable, and consider that, in so far as there can be a politics of leisure, it should be confined to those activities – such as *sport – which engage the attention of all classes. The older style of leisure, many say, is inextricably bound up with class domination, and gains its character from the elaborate ceremonies whereby ruling classes assert their determination to exclude those regarded as unsuitable for membership, while flattering their own ascendancy with activities that celebrate their entitlement to it. Others, like *Veblen, regard the principal feature of a *leisure class as residing, not in culture, but in *conspicuous consumption, whereby those in whose hands wealth accumulates play a functional role in social organization, by spending as much and as fast as they can.

Some, such as *Morris, argue that work is necessary in order to keep people fixed in social relations, and as a result may think of leisure as an evil, finding the cure for *alienation, not in the provision of leisure, but in the transformation of work from something fragmented into something all-engrossing or at least fulfilling, in the manner of *craft.

leisure class

Expression coined by *Veblen (*Theory of the Leisure Class*, 1899), to denote the peculiarly inelegant class which, he thought, had appropriated the means of leisure in industrial countries and which had prevented full development of the potential that industrial production makes available. Despite its wasteful and stunted nature, having no style other than that of conspicuous consumption, this class performs the important economic function of returning the surplus product of production to the producers, by squandering it in a massive way, so stimulating again the process of production, and providing the employment through which producers subsist. It therefore maintains production at a level sufficient to reproduce itself, while preventing production from developing as it might.

Lenin (V.I. Ulyanov) (1870–1924)
Russian revolutionary, leader of the *bolsheviks during and after the Russian Revolution, and architect of modern communism. Lenin made some emendations to Marxist theory; these emendations did not, he thought, depart from the spirit of Marxism, but only made it possible to envisage its practice in twentieth-century conditions. In so far as Lenin's theory differs from the *dialectical materialism of *Engels, it is in such particulars as the following.

(i) The emphasis on revolutionary morality. 'Our morality is completely subservient to the interests of the one class of the proletariat'. What matters is always the end; and the means, however objectionable to the *bourgeois conscience, may still be justified by it. Action requires total commitment to the revolutionary purpose: 'everything that is done in the proletarian cause is honest'.

(ii) The theory of the *vanguard. The proletariat, left to itself, develops only 'proletarian consciousness'; hence a revolution of the proletariat is ineffective unless conducted by a vanguard of 'professional revolutionists', drawn primarily from the bourgeois *intelligentsia. They act and speak in the name of the working class, and subsequently hold power in trust for it. Together with the proletariat they must form themselves into a *party, and that party must be entirely united over all questions that really matter to the advance of revolution.

(iii) The doctrine of *democratic centralism: that the concentration of power in a centrally organized party is necessary both before and after a revolution, if the interests of the proletariat are to be served.

(iv) The attack on *revisionism, and on the view that there is a peaceful path to socialism, together with a reaffirmation of the doctrine of the *class struggle delivered by the *Communist Manifesto. (These issues were at the root of the break from the *mensheviks.)

(v) The theory of *imperialism, as the last stage of capitalism, and of Russia as the 'weakest link in the chain of imperialism'. This was expounded in such a way as to explain (in the face of Marxist theory to the contrary) why revolution might take place in Russia, even though capitalism had not reached its *crisis there; why the revolution, when it did come, would be anti-bourgeois and anti-capitalist, despite the fact that Russian society was to some extent pre-capitalist in form; and why it would lead to the victory of the proletariat, and to an affirmation of its international character.

(vi) The theory of the *withering away of the state. While this is mentioned by Marx and Engels, the theory has a vital role in Lenin's prognostications. After socialism has been achieved, 'full communism' gradually comes into being as the state and all its machinery, including law, wither away, having been necessary only so long as antagonistic *production relations endured, in order to compel people to act against nature. But before this withering is possible, the central machinery must be strengthened and subjected to the rule of the party. Since the withering away of the state involves the withering away of law, revolution involves a complete break with all forms of legal order.

(vii) The theories of *cultural revolution, and of the double causality of revolution. Classical Marxism describes the 'objective conditions' of revolution. Before revolution is possible certain 'subjective conditions' must be fulfilled: including the changed consciousness of the intelligentsia, and the emergence therefrom of the revolutionary vanguard.

The force of Lenin's personality, his conviction of his own rightness, and his remarkable qualities of *leadership, were responsible for the success of the Russian Revolution and the eventual victory of the bolsheviks. This practical success has led to the acceptance of theories which, had they been uttered by someone else, might have been found less persuasive. See *Leninism.

Leninism

Adherence to the doctrines and in particular to the revolutionary methods of *Lenin. The main features are: furtherance of communist revolution as part of a world-wide struggle against capitalist imperialism; attachment to the organizational principles of 'the party of the new type' (i.e. the party which incorporates all functions of the state, and which systematically eliminates opposition); *democratic centralism; emphasis on the role of the revolutionary *vanguard, whose constitution naturally tends to be differently described depending upon who is in charge of it.

Leninism became a world-wide movement in 1920, when Lenin himself imposed on the *Comintern his 'twenty-one conditions', which in effect stipulated that communist parties everywhere should organize themselves according to the principles that he had laid down for the Russian party. However, it is not solely because of this, but rather because of the extraordinary practical success of Lenin's party organization, that Leninism became a feature of so many communist movements. It was also admired and consciously imitated by Mussolini and Hitler, in their bids to create a unified structure of political command, and still has its followers in Latin America today.

levellers

A radical political *faction among artisans and apprentices in mid-seventeenth-century England, who played some part in the formation of Cromwell's army, and who attempted, during the Putney debates of October 1647, to elicit democratic, *egalitarian policies in the Parliamentarians. They advocated universal suffrage for 'freeborn Englishmen', as a guarantee of government by consent; though it seems that the class of freeborn Englishmen did not include women or servants or the unemployed. Levellers were as much concerned by the vast disproportion of wealth between the lower class and the upper middle class, as by the rights of Englishmen and the undemocratic nature of existing political representation. Nevertheless they began a continuing movement in British politics, which was to flow into the labour movement in the nineteenth century, and to survive in many of the levelling policies still proposed by *New Labour.

Lévi-Strauss, Claude (b. 1908)

French social anthropologist. See *structuralism.

liberal education

A label for the kind of *education that arose out of the Roman 'liberal arts' (aimed to train the 'orator' or man with the *virtues necessary for public life), and which was regarded as the appropriate education for a *gentleman. The form of liberal education has always been more precisely defined than its content: it consists in attendance at a reputable school and a reputable university and the dilution of study with recreation of an improving kind, such as music, debating, wide reading, and competitive sport. The content of liberal education has usually been thought to derive from the humanities, on the understanding that the gentleman is a more useful member of his class the more useless his education. (*See* *humane education.) However, in the US the phrase 'liberal education' is still widely used to describe any form of academic education as distinct from professional training: education designed for the citizen rather than the expert.

The idea has traditionally been that uselessness is an essential precondition of *culture, which is essential both to *rhetoric and to social grace, which are in turn essential to good government. Hence uselessness in education is the greatest utility in public life. None of those conceptions is now very fashionable, although educators are perhaps beginning to question the *relevance revolution, which sought to make all education directly useful to the pupil.

liberal individualism

A term used in the history of ideas in order to denote the combination of *liberal principles with a metaphysical grounding in *individualism, on the assumption that the two qualify each other in ways that are both intellectually and historically significant. The outlook of liberal individualism is often ascribed to *Locke and his successors, although some (e.g. C.B. Macpherson: *Possessive Individualism*, 1962) also ascribe it to *Hobbes. It tends to be associated with the rise of capitalism, and the market economy, though whether markets cause liberal individualism or liberal individualism markets is a disputed question.

liberal parties

The political heirs of the *Whigs in England came to refer to themselves in the 1830s as 'liberals', following an established continental usage, and in recognition of a similarity of outlook with those called liberal in France. Throughout the nineteenth century liberal parties were formed in Europe, and the UK 'National Liberal Federation' was formed in 1877, providing the main centre of opposition to the *Conservative Party. The party went into a decline, partly as a result of the ascendancy of the *Labour Party, and despite periodic revivals has not in recent years been a dominant political force, except on those occasions when an electorate wishes to express an attachment to *centre policies, having identified the two major parties as too far to the *left or to the *right of some convenient point of safety. The formation of a 'Liberal Democrat' Party, out of the debris of the short-lived Social Democrat Party and the traditional Liberal Party, has in recent years given renewed life to the centrist philosophy of the latter, although most commentators doubt that this new-style liberal party could obtain power, unless there is *proportional representation, or an alliance with another party. Needless to say, therefore, proportional representation is a major objective of the Liberal Democrats.

The US has no major party that calls itself liberal, but its constitution provides a kind of background of *classical liberal principles (in particular the declared protection of *human and *civil rights), which has imposed a uniformity of outlook on the two major parties, compelling them to accept or to seem to accept many of the fundamental tenets of *classical liberalism.

The politics of modern liberal parties tend to be open and corrigible. In so far as anything general can be said about them, it is that they have stood mostly for *free trade, pacific attitudes in international relations, political *reform within the framework of enduring *institutions, extension of the *franchise, the support for *civil rights, *human rights, and *minority rights, and, in recent years, a qualified support for the *mixed economy. They have also shown support for *decentralization, and *community politics, and, at times, *democratization of industry and commerce.

liberalism

1. In US popular usage, 'liberal' means *left-liberal, and is expressly contrasted with 'conservative'. In this usage a liberal is one who leans consciously towards the under-privileged, supports the causes of minorities and socially excluded groups, believes in the use of state power to achieve *social justice, usually in the form of *welfare programmes, and in all probability shares the *egalitarian and *secular values of the *modern, and maybe those of the *postmodern world-view. Although not a *socialist, the American liberal is certainly not averse to the power of the state, provided it is exerted by liberals, and provided the principal victims are conservatives.

2. In the context of political science, the term is used either to summarize a particular tradition of social and political thought (*classical liberalism) exemplified by many of the great writers in the field from *Machiavelli to *J.S. Mill, or else to denote the emphasis on the individual and his rights, as against the sovereign power and the duty towards it, in the shaping of political aspirations.

The history of liberalism, in sense 2., is contemporaneous with the history of *limited government, i.e. with the successful attempts of those subject to government to curtail its powers, and to secure for themselves *charters, *statutes, *institutions, and forms of *representation, that will guarantee the individual's *rights against the invasions of the *sovereign power. There are recognizably liberal thoughts expressed in Magna Carta, 1215, although the modern idea is usually thought of as a seventeenth- and eighteenth-century creation, partly because of the political theory then produced in support of it, partly because of the rapid changes in political institutions which hastened its advance, and partly because the underlying *individualism received confirmation in so many aspects of economic, social and political life. Principal exponents of aspects of liberalism are *Spinoza, *Locke, *Montesquieu, *Kant, *Bentham, *J.S. Mill, *Jefferson and *Madison, together with many other significant figures of the *Enlightenment and subsequently.

It is almost impossible to reduce liberalism, in sense 2., to a single theoretical position, although the following ideas are fundamental to most forms of it:

(i) Belief in the supreme value of the individual, his freedom and his rights.

(ii) Individualism, in its metaphysical variant (*see also* *liberal individualism).

(iii) Belief that the individual has *natural rights, which exist independently of government, and which ought to be protected by and against government.

(iv) Recognition of the supreme value of freedom, usually glossed as the ability to secure that to which one has a right, together with the view that government must be so limited as to grant freedom to every citizen; perhaps even that government is justifiable only to the extent that it maximizes freedom, or to the extent that it protects the free individual from invasions of his rights.

All the above ideas go together, and form a moral and metaphysical unity. In addition, the following propositions may sometimes be advanced in the name of liberalism (because of the supposed theoretical connection with the above four):

(v) An anthropocentric, rather than theological, view of human affairs, regarding human potential and achievement as the principal locus of *value (see *humanism).

(vi) *Universalism: i.e. a belief that rights and duties are universal, and stem from a human condition that transcends place and time. People should learn to renounce their particular local attachments so as to view things from the standpoint of an impartial *legislator.

(vii) Advocacy of *toleration in matters of *morality and *religion.

Liberalism expresses the political theory of limited government, and conveys the political sentiments of the *modern person, who sees himself as detached from *tradition, *custom, *religion and *prejudice, and deposited in the world with no guidance beyond that which his own reason can provide. Hence, if there is a reasoned account to be offered of fundamental human liberties and rights, the individual can judge the *legitimacy of political institutions by the extent of their respect for these liberties and rights, and extend his allegiance accordingly. The fundamental feature of all liberal theories of political obligation is that of overt or tacit consent, and the theory of the social contract is the prime example of a liberal justification of government. To make the underlying philosophy coherent it is necessary to say much about both the nature of the human individual, and the nature of freedom. One philosophy which brings these two subjects together is that of Kant, whose theory of the autonomy of the rational agent provides a grounding for all of the propositions given above, with the possible exception of the last. But this last – the advocacy of tolerance – is perhaps the least tenable, liberalism being itself a moral view, and often expressed with a bigoted aversion towards its opponents that is nothing if not intolerant.

One of the important modern problems for liberalism is that of the *free market. It was standardly assumed (or argued) by early liberals that the right of private property, and the freedom of exchange, are ineliminable postulates of individual freedom. If so, a free market seems to be the inevitable result of liberal ideals. (Thus liberalism has often been denounced as *bourgeois ideology, precisely because it justifies the existence of a capitalist economy.) However, growing acceptance among some liberals of the socialist arguments against the market economy has led them to attempt to reconcile their beliefs with redistribution and egalitarian *social justice. This has produced the now fairly orthodox *left-liberal position (i.e. liberalism in sense 1. above), which survives despite the unresolved conflict between individual freedom and social justice. Against that there has arisen in recent years, especially in the US, a *neo-liberalism, which places the free market and free trade once again at the centre of the liberal worldview.

The major effort of liberal political

theory is devoted to the problem of what the English jurist Henry de Bracton (d. 1268) called the 'constitution of liberty': i.e. the framework of political institutions which makes limited government possible, and which effectively preserves the individual and his rights from any invasion from above. (The antiquity of liberal ideas in English law is well illustrated by the quotation, which was adopted by *Hayek, as the title of a book devoted to a modern statement of the liberal idea.)

liberation

The act of freeing, e.g. a *slave from his bondage, an individual from his *conscience, a nation from its conquerors, an oppressed class from its rulers. Modern usages concentrate on two contrasting kinds of movement those designed to liberate the human individual from supposedly irrational and oppressive taboos and conventions; and those designed to overthrow supposedly oppressive regimes. (Roughly these may be contrasted as movements against *repression and movements against *oppression.) To the first kind belong women's liberation (although radical *feminists diagnose the condition of women in such a way that their movement is more naturally seen as of the second kind), 'gay liberation' and so on; to the second kind belong the 'wars of national liberation' undertaken in the name of a nation, or a people (although sometimes in the name of an oppressed working class or peasantry). The aim in a 'war of liberation' is to intervene in the affairs of a state so as to liberate the *civil society that lies in its bondage. Since a society, unlike a state, is not a legal *person, and has no rights in international law, the doctrine by implication throws aside the question of legality, and applies the idea of justice independently. The US-led intervention in Iraq was justified in this way, as the liberation of an oppressed society, rather than a pre-emptive strike against a potential aggressor.

liberation theology

A movement within the Roman Catholic Church, arising in part from the experience of the priesthood in rural South America, in which Marxist ideas are synthesized with Christian teachings to produce a mixture which is both politically potent and intellectually bizarre. The central claim of liberation theology is that Christ came not merely to redeem us, but also to liberate us; Christians are therefore called to promote the *liberation of their fellows from all the chains that oppress them. Christ's mission was among the poor, and many of his teachings suggest a hostility not only to the oppression of the poor by the rich, but to the very fact of riches. By liberating the poor from their oppressors, we can provide them with material and spiritual freedom, and so set them on the path to salvation. Christ's sufferings are mirrored in the sufferings of the poor, and it is because the poor are in this way closest to Christ that the priest must work among them.

The attempt to graft Marxist ideas on to Christianity is inherently paradoxical, since Marxism is a *materialism, which treats religion in all its forms as mere *ideology. Still more bizarre is the advocacy, by many proponents of liberation theology, of violent *revolution as a means of achieving the emancipation of the poor. On the other hand, the intellectual conflict between these positions does not destroy their emotional unity, and priests who work among the truly poor have tended to pass from Christian compassion towards their flock, to socialist indignation against their supposed oppressors, and thence to very unchristian desires for violent action.

Critics of liberation theology focus not only on the apparent contradiction between Marxist politics and Christian belief, but also on the confusion of *goals* which occurs when the Christian idea of redemption is mixed with the practice of revolutionary politics. Redemption is not of this world or in this world; yet politics belongs only here. So how can redemption be achieved by political action? And how do the poor become closer to God by achieving the material well-being which allegedly separates Him from the rich? In the light of these questions, the Catholic Church has tended to view liberation theology with suspicion, although the Church has not pronounced it to be heretical. The important encyclical of Pope John Paul II, *Centesimos annos*, makes gestures of reconciliation towards liberation theology, and acknowledges the difficulties experienced by South American priests working among the poor.

libertarianism
1. The form of liberalism which believes in freeing people not merely from the constraints of traditional political institutions, but also from the inner constraints imposed by their mistaken attribution of power to ineffectual things. The active libertarian is engaged in a process of *liberation, and wages war on all institutions through which man's vision of the world is narrowed (some would say focused) – among them the institutions of *religion, and the *family, and the customs of social, especially sexual conformity. Libertarianism is not so much a doctrine as an attitude, condemned by some as mistaking licence for *liberty, praised by others as the new temper of *humanism.

2. In economics, a radical form of the theory of *laissez faire*, which believes that economic activity must be actively liberated from the bondage of needless political constraints in order to achieve true prosperity.
3. Often used as a name for the metaphysical theory that *determinism must be false, on account of the fact of human *freedom.
4. Now often used to mean the view that human activity in general, and economic activity in particular, should be released from all control by the state other than the bare minimum required for social order. In this sense, libertarians are economic liberals who wish to extend the principle of the *free market into all areas of social life, advocating 'market solutions' to social problems, and arguing that the major problems of modern society come from the attempt to control social life from outside and to organize by planning what can only be organized by spontaneous agreement among participants.

Libertarianism in sense 4. has exerted considerable influence over recent politics, and formed one input into *Thatcherism. It should be distinguished from classical *liberalism, which merely emphasizes rights and liberties against the sovereign power and defends the free market only as part of the *right of *private property and not as the ruling principle of all social order. Libertarians are radicals whose posture towards the state is one of vigilant suspicion and whose philosophy is often secular, anti-authoritarian and even *Nietzschean, as in *Rand. Two core arguments are given in favour of libertarianism. First, the Nietzschean argument that societies need *leadership, but that the second-rate will conspire to prevent leaders from emerging and will use the state in order to penalize all forms of power, achievement and success other than those conferred by committees of the second-rate. Second, the more soothing argument (which generalizes from the theories of the *Austrian school of economics) that social order arises spontaneously and that the information necessary for harmonious social life exists *only* in spontaneous institutions and is always destroyed by planning. *See* *Hayek, *Mises, *Oakeshott.

5. There are those (e.g. *Chomsky) who define themselves as 'libertarian socialists', a usage which, given sense 4. of the term, would come close to self-contradiction. For the libertarian socialist the state is justified in pursuing goals of *social justice, but must not infringe individual liberty in any other way.

liberty

While 'liberty' (Latin root) is synonymous with 'freedom' (Saxon root), it has legal and historical associations that have caused it to be discussed in different contexts, and to accrue to itself different connotations. A theory of liberty is a theory of *political* *freedom; but it helps to clarify matters if the following historical applications of the idea are first attended to:

(i) Liberty and liberties. The 'liberties of the subject' under UK law are not guaranteed by any particular statute, but are implied in a general principle (itself an immemorial *custom) that people may do what they like, so long as no law prevents them, and that the attempt to prevent them, in the absence of a law, is either a civil or a criminal wrong, itself a valid cause of legal action. Periodic attempts to embody the 'liberties of the subject' in a statute (from Magna Carta, 1215, to the Act of Settlement 1701) have provided a repertoire of *rights, some of which entered the *Bill of Rights attached to the US constitution; they have also helped to give legal cogency to the view that *natural rights are respected in UK law. *See also* *freedoms.

(ii) Liberty and licence. An *ad hoc* distinction is often made (borrowing terms put to contentious use by *Locke) between liberty and licence, the first being a necessary condition of human fulfilment, the second a sufficient condition of human degeneracy. Intuitively the distinction is easy to grasp: it is an infringement of my liberty to prevent me from walking out of my house, but only the removal of licence to prevent me from then abusing, assaulting or murdering my neighbour. But the theory of this distinction remains one of the deepest intellectual preoccupations of liberalism. Both liberty and licence consist in extension of permission (or removal of constraint), but the intuition is that sometimes this extension is right, sometimes wrong: if, however, that is *all* that can be said, the invocation of liberty becomes vacuous, either as the justification of a particular legal code, or as the assertion of an enduring human *value. The most plausible step in a theory of the distinction is to say that liberty is the permission to do what you have a *right to do, while licence is the permission to do what someone (usually someone else) has a right that you do not do. This shifts the discussion to the theory of rights, and is one ground for thinking that the idea of freedom cannot be discussed without also discussing that of *justice.

(iii) Liberty and value. If liberty is to deserve the place habitually given to it in political thought it must be shown to be a value, either as a necessary means to moral action, or as an end of moral action. Some philosophers (notably *Kant) have argued that liberty becomes a value through a connection with *autonomy, which is a necessary (and according to Kant sufficient) condition for moral agency. It is one of the deep questions of political philosophy to connect liberty, as identified through the liberties mentioned in (i), with autonomy, as specified through a theory of the nature of *rational agency.

(iv) Liberty and constraint. Some have argued that liberties make no sense without constraints, since constraints are necessary in order to nurture the being who can value liberties. This issue, which identifies another deep problem in political philosophy, is discussed under *freedom and also under *Hegel.

Liebknecht, Karl (1871–1919)
German lawyer and left-wing activist. *See* *communist parties, *Kautsky, *Luxemburg, *Spartacists.

limitation
The doctrine in law that after a certain period an action cannot be brought. In English law the period is generally 12 years, but may for some types of action be less. The doctrine of limitation has been of great importance in establishing the right to the use of land. It implies that if someone has occupied land for 12 years, with the knowledge of the legal owner, but without paying rent and with no attempt on the part of the owner to remove him, then the owner's title to the land is effectively extinguished, since no action can be brought to enforce it. (In this connection *see also* *prescriptive right.) A law without limitation must inevitably lead to social upheavals, as the burden of extinct agreements becomes intolerable. In most jurisdictions, therefore, there is a 'statute of limitations', that can be invoked to pre-empt vexatious litigation over the irredeemable past. In some jurisdictions the statute is extended to criminal offences, though this is not widely approved.

limited government
Usually contrasted with absolute government (*see* *absolutism), and meaning any form of government in which the sovereign power (in particular the *executive power) is limited by *law, *constitution, or *institutions, presenting *checks and balances to its exercise. The forms of limited government are as varied as the ways of limiting power: sometimes power is limited through a constitution, sometimes through a balance against other powers. The two cases are importantly different, so much so that often only the first is called limited government. In the case of constitutional limitation the sovereign power possesses an *internal* constraint on its exercise: it is, in other words, limited by itself. It is the very same sovereign who exerts supreme political power who also upholds the constitution through which that power is restrained and channelled. Some think, however, that that is possible only if the constitution embodies a *separation of powers, so as in effect to decompose the sovereign power into separate elements, and balance the one against the other. In particular they tend to argue for *judicial independence, as giving a guarantee to the subject that he may enforce against the sovereign those rights and privileges which are granted in the constitution.

In the second case, of *de facto* limitation, there need be no constitutional balance, but simply a balance of powers. But some balance of power seems to exist universally; no government has been so despotic that the sovereign power has not had to limit its activities in the light of opposition from within society or the state (although some argue that both Hitler and Stalin came near to complete *autocracy, by generating effective machinery for eliminating opposition before it could gather momentum).

Those monarchies which are called 'absolute', on the ground that there are no legal constraints upon the sovereign, have usually been severely limited in fact, by the need to reconcile the aristocracy, the common people and (sometimes) the church, to all policies of the sovereign. In a similar way modern governments may be limited by the aims and activities of the trade unions (France), a military establishment (Turkey) or an organized lobby of corporations (the US), even though no legal powers of limitation have been granted to those bodies.

There is an interesting conceptual difference between limited government that arises as a result of the limitation of a power once deemed absolute (such as, on one interpretation, the *constitutional monarchy of the UK), and a limited government which arises from a constitution that grants no absolute power (such as the constitutional democracy of the US). Some argue that the second is a recent invention, made possible by building upon the experience and institutions of the first. Whether or not that is so, it is often said that the search for the conditions of limited government is the major task of political theory, for only in conditions of limited government is *politics (as opposed to *force) the condition of public life.

limited sovereignty doctrine

The view that certain states within the immediate *sphere of influence and protection of a larger power can retain their independence only by limiting their *sovereignty, so as to conform to the foreign policy of the larger power. Originally put forward in 1947 as a corollary of the *Truman doctrine, subsequently rejected as legally incoherent by most Western powers, the view was influential in the Soviet bloc, where it was known as the Brezhnev doctrine, following President Brezhnev's invocation of it to justify the invasion of Czechoslovakia in 1968.

limited war

War that is limited, usually by agreement between the parties, to certain objectives, or in which the *territory attacked and (most importantly) the weapons used are limited either unilaterally or by agreement. The practice of limiting armaments is not exclusively modern. There are anthropological examples of tribes who limit war by agreement with their customary opponents, say to certain seasons of the year, or to certain weapons. Nevertheless limitation is made particularly important by the invention of modern weapons. Suggestions concerning *arms control have therefore been in existence at least since the invention of gunpowder. See *war.

limits to growth

An argument put forward by the UK economist E.J. Mishan (*Limits to Growth*, 1969), to the effect that the emphasis of economic policy on securing economic growth as the first goal of government and the precondition of all other desirable objectives is both unsustainable and destructive. Nothing can grow indefinitely, and all growth involves a depletion of resources and unwanted side-effects, both environmental and social. By pursuing growth relentlessly, we sacrifice the peace and equilibrium of human communities, and fail to safeguard the true fund of economic knowledge – which is the knowledge that enables us to renew our resources and live without depleting them.

linkage politics

In the theory of systems analysis, or *cybernetics, a recurrent sequence of behaviour which originates in one system, and causes effects in another, is known as a linkage. The term has been extended to political thought, not with any precise theoretical intention other than to indicate that political bodies are also systems, and that actions between them may accordingly be recurrent and systematic in ways determined by their internal organization. Linkages are described as reactive (e.g. when increased armament in one *state causes increased armament in another); emulative (e.g. when industrial expansion in one state causes a desire for similar expansion among its neighbours); and 'penetrative', as in the penetration of the economies of southern African states by South Africa, or the penetration of the politics of the Caribbean states by Cuba and the US. Penetrative linkages are the most difficult to understand; and the adoption of this jargon seems to do little to explain them.

Lippmann, Walter (1880–1974)
American journalist. *See* *cold war, *public opinion.

liquidity
The ease with which an asset can be exchanged for money: determined by the structure of the market, and by the ease with which goods of the requisite kind exchange. 'Liquidity preference' is another name for the desire to hold money as opposed to, say, land (which has low liquidity), while 'liquidity ratio' is the proportion of a bank's assets that are held in liquid form (i.e. as cash, or money on short-term loan). The liquidity ratio is a measure of a bank's ability to meet immediate public demand for money.

litigation
To litigate is to refer a dispute to a court of law. In the UK and the US litigation is increasingly used, instead of *arbitration, *mediation or *negotiation, in disputes over contracts and other civil causes. Because damages in the US are decided by a jury, and because lawyers are free to advertise their services on the basis that there will be no payment incurred if the litigant loses, there has resulted a 'litigation explosion' of gigantic proportions, as members of the public sue large corporations in the hope of obtaining millions of dollars for footling injuries. Some commentators see this as the new *crisis of capitalism, as large firms are successively bankrupted by the costs of litigation. Others argue that this explosion has occurred because lawyers are no longer constrained by a *professional ethic. *See* *tort reform.

liturgy
In its primary meaning, the 'liturgy' denotes the prescribed form of worship within a *Christian *church (although it can also be used, especially in the Eastern churches, as a name for the eucharist). It has been a frequent object of political controversy, and, somewhat surprisingly, continues to be so, within both the *Roman Catholic and the *Protestant communities. It has always been accepted that liturgy must evolve in response to changing modes of expression, but the language of every religion tends to lag behind the spoken language; the sacredness of the message attaches to the words used to convey it, and this in turn makes people hesitate to change them. Words used in a religious ceremony are also spells, and must be precisely repeated if their effect is to be felt. (The phenomenon can be witnessed equally in ancient Egypt and modern England, in Islam and Christianity, in established and nonconformist churches.) Hence rapid changes have a disorientating effect which may lead to considerable resistance.

In UK the peculiar constitutional position of the *Anglican Church grants parliamentary control over liturgy. This was exercised in enforcing the language and doctrine of the Book of Common Prayer in the Acts of Uniformity 1549, 1552, and 1662, and more recently in the Worship and Doctrine Measure 1974. The subsequent controversy over the Book of Common Prayer became a cause for *cultural conservatism, and led to a private member's bill in the Commons and Lords. At the same time the 'liturgical movement' in the Roman Catholic Church, originating in nineteenth-century France, has sought to make the Roman liturgies both more true to their meaning and more useful to public worship than they had been thought to be, by transcribing them into the vernacular, using words of common speech, and music of common enjoyment, and encouraging participation as opposed to mute observation of the *ceremony. Large questions concerning the nature of religious *language have been raised both by those opposed to, and those in favour of, these changes, and the only uncontroversial position is that ascribed to itself by the Church of England in the preface to the Old Prayer Book: 'It hath been the wisdom of the Church of England, ever since the first compiling of her Publick Liturgy, to keep the mean between the two extremes, of too much stiffness in refusing, and of too much ease in admitting, any variation from it.'

lobby

Originally a monastic term, a *lobium* is a covered walk or cloister. The House of Commons has always had a large entrance hall open to the public, traditionally called the Lobby, where members could meet people not belonging to the house. Lobbies became a standard feature of legislatures, and those of the House of Commons and the US House of Representatives have given rise to the term 'lobby', to denote both the group of people pressing for a particular legislative result and also the practice of doing so. Lobbyists are more active and focused than *interest groups, since they concentrate their efforts purely on the legislative process and those engaged in it. In the US there is an official register of lobbyists, engaged full time in advocacy on behalf of their clients. The same profession is now growing in the UK, and interest groups now regularly employ full-time parliamentary lobbyists in order to press for legislation favourable to their cause. The practice is objected to, on the grounds that it gives an advantage to organizations that can afford to pay lobbyists and therefore runs counter to the spirit of democracy. It also leads to much legislative time and attention being spent on matters that are not of pressing public concern, and to a consequent dilution of the political process. Unfortunately, however, no lobby exists to lobby for the abolition of lobbyists.

local government

A public organization authorized to decide and administer a limited range of public policies pertaining to a circumscribed *territory within a larger and sovereign *jurisdiction. In the UK boroughs were originally granted independent status by royal charter, which recognized the limited autonomy that they had formerly practised; in time such charters became regularized and often allowed considerable discretion to those who received them. The modern history of local government dates, however, from the 1830s, and in particular from the Poor Law Act 1834, which assigned welfare administration to local 'Boards of Guardians', and the Municipal Corporations Act 1835, which defined a municipal corporation as a 'legal personification of the local community, represented by an elected council, and acting for, and responsible to, the inhabitants of the district'. The US system is largely modelled on the UK counterpart, but the relationship is with the government of a particular state, rather than with the federal government. Local governments enjoy legislative power in the UK and the US, although it is controlled by statute (e.g. the UK Local Government Act 1972). The local organizations are also dependent upon central funds for many of their activities, and therefore constrained to obey orders from above. However, such financial dependence exists to a lesser extent in the US; in addition, certain states grant 'home rule' to counties and municipalities by statute or by constitutional provisions, thus permitting autonomy in all matters that are not constrained by the general law of the state. In France the Napoleonic system of delegating responsibilities to the mayor of local communities has led to extensive powers of local legislation.

In the UK local councils are now elected along party lines, and even respond to party whips, where the parties are defined in terms of national politics rather than local issues. Many councils have also adopted *cabinet style government, in imitation of the procedure followed in the national Parliament. Thus local government may become a testing ground for politicians attempting to enter the national parliament, a fact that has greatly promoted the emergence of the new *political class. Local governments may attempt to defy the central government and its law, and now exert considerable powers over the ordinary citizen. Prior to the nineteenth century these powers were confined to those specified in the poor laws and the statutes relating to the

upkeep of highways, but as the first were extended through welfare legislation and the second through the distinctly modern law of *planning, and as the organization of the police and the provision for general education and also housing were entrusted to local administration, it became inevitable that a concentration of political power would result. But while the power of local government has increased, its local character has, in a sense, dwindled. Two changes have helped to bring this about: the creation of artificial boundaries, designed for administrative convenience rather than in obedience to any historically recognized local affiliation; and the generation of a large and unionized bureaucracy. It is, furthermore, a crime to withhold local taxes, so that the citizen's main powers of redress lie in *administrative law, or in the ability to vote at a council election. Local councillors in the UK are remunerated only with a small allowance to cover expences, which means that they are drawn either from the class of people with time on their hands, or from the class of people who know how to turn influence to profit.

In Europe, and the UK in particular, all this has generated a *de facto* delegation of power, together with an extensive limitation of *sovereignty, since the delegated powers are more or less impossible to recall once they are entrenched in the local machinery. Some defend this transfer of power as necessary to the creation of more local and particularized allegiances; others condemn it for the very same reason – namely that it destroys local allegiances by bringing local government into the hands of powers that are not truly local, and at the same time not truly bound to the sovereign power.

The argument is a vexed and bitter one. It is not possible to govern a modern state without extensive local government, but it is also impossible to govern it if local government is not responsive to the demands of a central power, nor answerable directly to the citizen. The situation in the UK has been complicated in recent years by the following factors:

(i) The relatively low turnout at local elections, which means that unrepresentative factions and parties have a comparatively greater chance of success at the local than at the national level.

(ii) The recognition by private *interest groups and militant political factions of the opportunity presented by local government, either to advance their interests or to make publicity for an unpopular cause.

(iii) The large powers of taxation vested in local authorities and the lack of any enforceable guidelines as to the purposes for which it might be used.

(iv) The delegation to local authorities of administrative decisions of great importance to future generations – concerning planning, the provision of education and the maintenance of libraries and museums.

The ensuing scandals are well known, and include the destruction of provincial towns and cities by property developers (elected as Councillors on a Party ticket) in the 1960s; the penetration of the Greater London Council by a radical left faction of the Labour Party, which used its powers to sabotage government policy during the early 1980s and so provoked the government to abolish the GLC; the election of a 'Militant Tendency' (i.e. *Trotskyite) council in Liverpool followed by a politics of direct confrontation with central government; the attempts by local governments to resist conservative educational reforms, so provoking legislation which enables schools to opt out of local government control. Indeed many of the most important issues in recent UK politics have involved confrontation between local and central government. Conservative administrations under *Thatcher tried, but failed, to make the system of local taxation more accountable to the taxpayer. Some have argued that the citizen should have more power to withhold local taxes – although clearly such a power would render all local administration highly precarious. Others argue that the politics of national parties ought to be forbidden at local elections, or that the scope of the activities designated as 'local' ought to be substantially reduced (for example, by making education and the police a national affair). There has been a move by *New Labour to centralize many of the powers currently exercised by local government: in particular powers concerning planning, house-building and material infrastructure. However, this has been regarded less as a benign attempt to remedy the defects of local government, than as a suspicious bid for centralized control.

localization

The opposite of *globalization, sometimes proposed as a remedy for the social chaos that globalization is alleged to cause. The advocacy of local communities, local markets, local production, local food and local institutions has become a cause among environmentalists and cultural conservatives. Inevitably tinged with romantic *nostalgia, the localization movement has nevertheless made trenchant criticisms of the damage done to local communities in *developing countries, by the premature globalization from outside of their fragile economies, and of the damage done to the environment generally, when local communities are not given the kind of control over it that they both need and deserve.

Locke, John (1632–1704)
English philosopher whose political writings contain one of the finest modern justifications of *limited government, and one of the first statements of the principles of modern *liberalism. Locke argued against the theory of *divine right, and defended a form of constitutional government within the framework of *natural rights; his theory was taken as an intellectual foundation by many of the *Founding Fathers of the US, and also by several of the French revolutionaries. His two *Treatises of Civil Government*, 1690, remain standard works of political theory, while his *Letter on Toleration*, 1689, contains a vigorous defence of the liberal principle of *toleration.

(i) There are natural rights which derive from a 'law of nature' implanted by God in all reasoning beings. It is given to reason to perceive these rights and they exist independently of any social order. Principal among them are the rights to life, limb and freedom of action: no one can deprive me of these without doing me wrong, unless I myself have done something to give him just cause (perhaps not even then, since Locke sometimes describes these rights as 'inalienable'). There is also a natural right to *private property: any object which is appropriated or produced by 'mixing my labour' with it is, given certain conditions, e.g. that it was not the subject of some prior right, mine, as much as the limbs that worked on it are mine. (This is a kind of 'labour theory of right' which indirectly inspired the *labour theory of value.)

(ii) Natural rights exist in a *state of nature, and do not require the absolute protection and control of *Hobbes's *sovereign for their recognition. They are specific individual rights and cannot be removed or limited except by the consent of those possessing them, a process which probably extends only to freedom of action and property, and not to life and limb (see above). All government, since it involves the limitation of the freedom of the subject and his subjection to a higher power, must, therefore, be the result of consent if it is to be legitimate, and no government is made legitimate in any other way. Locke brings powerful arguments against the idea of an independent *hereditary principle of government, and against other theories of legitimacy that try to bypass the need for consent on the part of the governed.

(iii) The model for legitimate government is therefore to be found in contract. The transition from the state of nature to the state of civil society would involve a legitimate transfer, renunciation and creation of rights were it to result from a *social contract (or 'compact'), by which free beings contract among each other to accept the curtailment of their rights in exchange for the benefits and security of society. This compact is not a historical event, but, as it were, a structure concealed within society, which is revealed, whenever there is genuine *political obligation, by a species of *tacit consent.

(iv) Tacit consent is demonstrated in a variety of ways, but one extremely important criterion is that a citizen, given the opportunity to remove himself to some 'vacant place' outside the sphere of political obligation, chooses not to do so. This shows that he remains bound by the duties of the subject by his own choice, so that those duties are genuine obligations that he has incurred. Even travelling on the highway through some foreign place obligates the individual to accept the law there obtaining. (This aspect of the theory was much criticized, notably by *Hume.)

(v) Civil society forms itself into

particular institutions of government which enshrine and protect the contractual relation among its members. Locke did not develop a complete theory of political institutions, but he advocated *limited government, *constitution, and some kind of *representation (confined, however, to property owners). He also suggested that liberties could be better protected and the social compact better upheld by an effective *separation of powers – he thereby introduced a notion that was to have radical influence, partly through the more careful and systematic theory of it given by *Montesquieu.

Locke's political philosophy has been seen as a defence of the 'Glorious Revolution' of 1688 (though it was probably conceived earlier), as an imaginative exposition of perennial ideas of liberty and justice, and as an apologetic for the legal system associated with a market economy.

logistics

US term, introduced during the Second World War, to denote the activity and principles of supply for the armed forces, including transport and distribution; now extended also to non-military contexts.

long run

In *price theory, the time period sufficient for a *firm to be able to vary all its *factors of production: labour, raw materials, capital. Some industries can change their complete structure and composition only over a period of many years; for others it may be possible to do this in a period of weeks. It is only when the long run is considered that fully comprehensive economic planning can be undertaken, and this fact has influenced economic thinking throughout the world, in the smallest manufacture as much as in the 'five year plans' of the major communist states. It may be that five years is still too short, although, as *Keynes famously put it, 'in the long run we are all dead'.

lord

1. A title, bestowed in UK law on *peers and also by courtesy on some of the children of some of the peers, and on judges of the Scottish Court of Session. A courtesy title brings no legal or political *privileges, whereas a peerage (which may also be held by a woman) originally denoted the right to sit in the House of Lords, and the loss of the right to vote for or sit in the House of Commons. The right to sit in the House of Lords is now confined to 'life peers' (i.e. those appointed to the office for life), and a limited group of hereditary peers elected by their fellows.

2. A social and economic position, formerly associated with 1. but no longer so associated, titles being created as *honours, and economic position determined by *market forces which ignore or override the feudal position associated with lordship. The lord was distinguished, under *feudalism, in three ways:

(i) economically, as the holder of manorial land, who takes a return or *corvée* on the product of all the land from his serfs;

(ii) legally, as the president of the manorial court, with jurisdiction over the serfs on his land, subject usually to rights of appeal to the sovereign;

(iii) politically, in so far as he could claim the privilege of a peer, which was granted by the crown in exchange for certain military duties.

(i), (ii) and (iii) did not always go together, and they converge probably only in the *ideal type of feudalism defined in this work They define collectively a highly organized idea of established property, in which some conservatives have occasionally seen relations of mutual *responsibility miraculously conjoined with distinctions of class, and in which others have seen carefully concealed habits of *exploitation.

The legality of the title of lord (sense 1.) is defined by the constitution, and upheld in the idea of constitutional monarchy; outside monarchy the use of such titles is either illegal (as in the US), or anachronistic; they have therefore largely fallen into disuse.

loyalists

Those who remain loyal, during some crisis, revolution or civil war, to an established, and usually monarchical, *regime. In Northern Ireland the term denotes those who profess loyalty to the Union, i.e. who believe that the sovereign of the UK is the legitimate sovereign over Northern Ireland. The term is sometimes put in inverted commas, to denote the paradox that someone, professing loyalty, might yet commit crimes (acts forbidden by the sovereign) in its name.

loyalty

The disposition to act and speak in the interests and defence of another, regardless of benefit or cost. Loyalty can be the expression of *friendship (i.e. a result of spontaneous liking or love), of *justice (i.e. a result of the judgement that loyalty is *deserved*), or of *piety (i.e. a result of some unchosen bond that transcends considerations of justice alone). Political creeds differ according to which (if any) of those models is taken as a basis for loyalty towards the state. Liberalism emphasizes *political obligation, and justice; some conservatives emphasize friendship (*see*, e.g., *Oakeshott), while others (not necessarily conservative) emphasize piety (*see*, e.g., *Hegel).

The difficulties posed by the idea were illustrated in the elaborate procedures adopted by Presidents Truman and Eisenhower for determining the 'loyalty' of the servants of the US government.

Luddite

Said to be named after Ned Ludd, a Leicestershire half-wit who destroyed some stocking frames in a rage in 1779, the Luddites were undisciplined bands of unemployed manual workers who, in the early nineteenth century, wreaked havoc on the machines to which they attributed their misfortunes. Now used as a general term to describe visceral hostility to technological change, on behalf of some threatened way of life.

Lukács, Georg, or György (1885–1971) Hungarian philosopher and literary critic, an important influence on *neo-Marxism, and one of the first *Marxist thinkers to displace the theory of *historical materialism from the central place that it had occupied in revolutionary thinking, and to elevate in its place a Marxist theory of consciousness. (*History and Class Consciousness*, 1923.) The idea of *reification is important to his theory, as describing the consciousness of man under capitalism. Lukács's great respect for *Hegel's analysis of the human spirit led him to anticipate the theories which later became familiar with the publication of *Marx's manuscripts of 1844. Lukács to some extent shared those parts of Marx's philosophy which stem from Marx's *Young Hegelian origins, especially the theory of *alienation. He argued that the Marxist theory of history is correct but incomplete, needing to be supplemented by a theory of how the world is seen by the various classes at the various points of historical development. The structure of consciousness must be different for each class, and alters as production relations change; but all classes in capitalist society possess their own kind of *false consciousness. What philosophers had seen as the problem of knowledge (is the world as it appears to me?) is better understood as the problem of *praxis: do I act on the world so as to see it without false consciousness? The problem for all criticism of consciousness is to show how a vision that is fundamentally class-determined may yet be demystified, so as to give knowledge of the real world of social relations.

Lukács went on to give an ambitious account of the nature of philosophy and of art, and he can be regarded as the most widely influential of Marxist literary critics. His particular insights (e.g. into the realism of Balzac) are often esteemed more than the ambitious theories from which he supposed them to derive. As an articulate apologist for *Stalinism, and a thinker with a large fund of dark hatred for what others regard as normal features of the human condition, Lukács has inspired as much distaste as intellectual admiration, and is said to have provided the model for Naphta in Thomas Mann's *The Magic Mountain.* He was also a ruthless *commissar in the short-lived communist government of Béla Kuhn after the end of the First World War, was an active conspirator in re-imposing communism on Hungary in 1945 (when he returned from exile in Moscow), and occupied ministerial positions thereafter, being the only member of Imre Nagy's government to be spared when the Soviet Army crushed the Hungarian uprising in 1956. Unsurprisingly, therefore, Lukács is a controversial figure in Hungary.

Lutheranism

Martin Luther (1483–1546), founder of the German Reformation, famous advocate of the doctrine of 'justification by faith alone' and the 'priesthood

of all believers', and passionate preacher of the sovereignty of *conscience, could hardly have had more political influence than he had, despite the fact that he and his immediate followers produced few developed political doctrines. Unlike *Calvinism, Lutheranism involves no account of real or ideal *institutions, no clear theory of the *state, or of the relation between *church and state, and no very obvious economic analysis (although Luther accepted the doctrine of the *just price, together with a primitive version of the *labour theory of value). In *On Secular Authority,* 1523, Luther puts forward his own version of the *Two Swords doctrine, arguing that God has instituted two governments, the spiritual and the temporal, in order to combat the realm of Satan at the end of the world, which Luther believed to be imminent. The spiritual government is headed by Christ, who rules over all Christians in a spirit of love and mutual service. The realm thereby created is not of this world, but, like the City of God of *Augustine, is an internal possession and immortal ideal in the hearts of all believers.

The individual is held to commune directly with God, and not through the mediation of any merely human institution; hence no human institution can have an authority that enables it to override the call of conscience. The Christian can therefore refuse to comply with temporal laws that violate his faith, but always in a spirit of non-violent forgiveness, and never with a view to destroying the divinely ordained power of temporal government. The grace that is freely bestowed upon the soul may be expressed in social relations, but social relations are only ancillary to the life and duty of the spiritual being. Luther's famous polemic *Of the Bondage of the Will,* 1525, contains what many of his contemporaries saw as a denial of free will, asserting that God is always sovereign over the will and can direct it to his ends, faith being one result of God's power. This and related theories were uttered in the course of controversy with the more temperate *Erasmus, and most of Luther's voluminous writings are devoted to the expression and refinement of the themes rehearsed during that controversy. The religious movement which followed lent itself to the *universalist ideas of the *Enlightenment, and the Lutheran paradox (that the will is most free when most constrained by the grace of God) is reiterated, with resounding metaphysical and political effect, in *Kant's theory of *autonomy: that the will is only free when reason compels its obedience. The influence of Lutheranism over capitalism has been often discussed, e.g. by *Weber and by R.H. Tawney: *see* *Protestant ethic.

Luxemburg, Rosa (1870–1919)
Polish-born socialist and exponent of revolutionary *Marxism, who was one of the first to recognize the rise of despotism in the *bolshevik faction, and to warn against its influence. Luxemburg attempted to reconcile theoretical Marxism with respect for the 'will of the people'. She criticized Lenin for his dictatorial ways, his unscrupulousness and the innate tendency of his theory of the

*vanguard to lend itself to the advance of tyranny.

Luxemburg's most important theoretical work is *The Accumulation of Capital*, 1913, in which she argues that pure capitalism cannot create the conditions necessary to maintain its own development. Capital accumulates faster than demand within capitalist countries can increase: hence capitalism attempts to absorb underdeveloped areas and spheres of noncapitalist production, initiating a period of capitalist imperialism. This thesis was badly received by other communist theoreticians, and only with the Keynesian revolution was her theory that lack of purchasing power causes a breakdown in the capitalist system rehabilitated. However, she correctly predicted the subsequent course of Russian communism and, together with her fellow *Spartacist, Karl Liebknecht, had considerable momentary influence over the communist intelligentsia. She did not achieve political power, and was murdered by the Freikorps in Berlin in 1919.

Lycurgus
See *Sparta.

Lyotard, Jean-François (b. 1924)
French philosopher. *See* *postmodern, *postmodernism.

Lysenkoism
See *Lamarckism.

Maastricht Treaty

The Treaty made in 1992 between the member states of the *European Community which sought to redefine both their relation to one another and the entity under which they are subsumed. The Treaty renames the EC as the *European Union and contains articles, provisions and chapters which, if fully implemented, would have the effect of creating a federal state of Europe, with a single currency (*see* *monetary union), a common foreign policy and effective sovereignty over its members. The Treaty provides that all nationals of the member states will henceforth be *citizens of the EU – even, for example, the Queen of the UK. The rights and duties of citizenship are defined so as to include a duty to pay taxes to the EU, and a right to vote and stand for elections in any member state of the Union. The Treaty confirms the status of the European Commission as executive arm of the EU, and of the European Parliament as a legislative body. It confers on the President of the EU a right to formulate and apply a common European defence policy, and forbids the armies of member states from acting in any way 'contrary to the interests of the Union'. The Treaty also declares itself to be 'irrevocable' and 'irreversible', thus binding the parliaments of member states in perpetuity: though what this actually means is doubtful. In so far as the Maastricht Treaty is a treaty, those who signed it can also repudiate it, maybe citing as grounds its impertinence in declaring itself to be irrevocable. In these and other ways, however, the Treaty has involved a radical diminution of *sovereignty among those who are bound by it, a fact which it both acknowledges and mystifies by referring to the *subsidiarity of the national legislatures. The threat to national sovereignty has caused great controversy in the UK, and not only in the UK – the German government being charged before its own Supreme Court with having no constitutional right to give away so many of its powers. Furthermore, the Treaty contains a 'social chapter' (not ratified by the UK), which imposes conditions, for example, a minimum wage, and a maximum working time, that restrict the free market in labour. A minimum wage has since been adopted in the UK.

Machiavelli, Niccolò (1459–1517)

Italian political theorist and historian, who, in two controversial and superficially contradictory works – *The Prince*, and the *Discourses on the First Ten Books of Titus Livy*, both begun in 1513 – expounded a political vision which attempted to bring the observed facts of contemporary despotism into relation with general ideas about law, liberty and the state. Machiavelli has often been thought of as the first theorist of the modern state – the first, that is, to isolate for study this particular political arrangement, rather than the *polis*, the *church, or some body of universal, or potentially universal, law.

The Prince speaks entirely of *power, how it is obtained and how preserved. Its *Realpolitik* and close observation of people as they are, rather than as we might wish them to be, have caused the adjective 'Machiavellian' to be bestowed on anyone who, indifferent to questions of morality, devotes himself to the pursuit of power. It is now more normal to interpret *The Prince* in the light of the *Discourses*: it deals with the necessary conditions of government, rather than the sufficient conditions of good government, arguing that the *rule of law is natural to *rational beings, but that it must be established by power, and power may have to use unnatural means in order to impose itself.

In the *Discourses*, Machiavelli reflects on the character of Roman constitutional government as described by Livy, and tries to ascertain what the rule of law ideally should be.

(i) He rejects *Aristotle's division of governments into three good and three bad forms, and proposes as an ideal a form of mixed government, which is monarchical, aristocratic, and democratic at once. While he attributes this mixed government to *Sparta as formed by the laws of Lycurgus, it approximates in fact more nearly to the English constitutional monarchy that emerged from the Glorious Revolution of 1688. Machiavelli argues that, in mixed government, the separate classes will, through institutions of *representation, limit each other's power and so contribute to the *liberty of all. This defence of *limited government as a necessary condition of liberty began a tradition that continues to the present day.

(ii) Thus Machiavelli finds that dissent and *opposition are far from being the evils that they had been thought to be; on the contrary they might be necessary to the whole idea of a state in which liberty can be preserved. Such, at any rate, was the character of the opposition between Senate and Commons in Rome: without it, neither would have had the freedom which both enjoyed.

(iii) Machiavelli emphasizes the importance of the rule of law as superseding *faction and private vengeance; he therefore explores the constitution that might be necessary to uphold it. A constitution with established institutions, together with procedures whereby they may be renewed by 'being brought back to their beginnings', is defended, partly as a guarantee against *usurpation. Machiavelli also defends a distribution of power, sufficient to make possible the *impeachment of any officer of state, however highly placed. (His example is the impeachment of Coriolanus.)

This defence of *constitutionalism accompanies a detailed description of the political nature of man, as revealed in civil, military and religious usages. Machiavelli's view, voiced in both *The Prince* and the *Discourses*, that government is an artefact, made possible by force, and justifying all force that is used in its defence, has had many opponents and defenders. So too has his idea (influenced by Aristotle) that each constitution has its own peculiar *virtue, and that the value of a political arrangement cannot be discussed without reference to the human character that is engendered by it. The brilliant scepticism of Machiavelli's vision disguises from the sentimental mind the accuracy of many of his observations. His ultimate doctrine is less systematic than empirical, and its philosophical shortcomings are compensated for by its insight into human motivation.

Machtpolitik
German for *power politics.

macroeconomics
The economics of large aggregates, dealing with state finances, *fiscal

policy, unemployment, aggregate supply and demand, and so on. Macroeconomics tries to treat of the total influence of all relevant economic factors on each other, and to provide the means of understanding and predicting *national income (hence it is sometimes called income theory). Modern macroeconomics takes much inspiration from the work of *Keynes, and has been largely concerned with *equilibrium, and with the consequences of the possibility – elaborately described by Keynes – that equilibrium may occur at less than full employment.

Madison, James (1751–1836)

*Founding Father, friend of *Jefferson, and one of the principal architects of the US constitution. Madison gave voice to many of the underlying ideas of *federalism, arguing that a federal constitution is always a greater guarantee of stability and freedom than any attempted imposition of a unifying power. His writings in *The Federalist* are of exemplary clarity and power, and their translation of *Locke's and *Montesquieu's theories of natural right and limited government into real political terms was partly responsible for the philosophical consistency of the final constitution. In particular Madison was one of the main forces behind the adoption of the principle of a *separation of powers, and of a special process for amendment, which would 'guard equally against that extreme facility, which would render the constitution too mutable; and that extreme difficulty, which might perpetuate its discovered faults'.

magistrate

Traditionally any person, including the *sovereign, empowered to sit in judgement and to exercise judicial authority. Because of the important political role of magistrates in ancient Rome, the term was given wide application in the Renaissance, for example by *Machiavelli to denote any political *office whereby the affairs of state are regulated in accordance with law.

Maistre, Joseph Marie, Comte de (1754–1821)

French essayist and political thinker, a *reactionary *legitimist and *ultramontanist, who defended a modified, belated and high-toned version of the doctrine of the *divine right of kings. His scepticism towards received liberal and democratic ideas was trenchant and influential, although what he tried to put in place of them has seldom been found wholly satisfactory. He argued that constitutions are not created but found, and that the rage of constitution-making which characterized the governments of his day was in part founded on a misconception of the American constitution, which was no more than a document making explicit a spirit already present in the *common law from which it grew. All constitutions and all states are inseparable from the spirit of the society that is governed by them; the attempt to separate them means social and political death. This idea is associated with an attack on the liberal analysis of *political obligation. No obligation to the sovereign can have a basis in contract or consent, but only in *piety towards established things. The true object of that emotion is not the state, but God, and it is in religious duty that the obligation towards all human institutions must ultimately be founded. Moreover it is God, and not man, who is the maker of constitutions, and the ultimate *legislator, all French revolutionary thought on this subject being nothing but unseemly blasphemy designed to fortify human incompetence.

The Enlightenment, with its impious view of human perfectibility, was a collective manifestation of the sin of pride – an 'insurrection against God'. The violence of the Revolution was entirely what must be expected, when people attempt to deny the reality of original sin and take their destiny into their own hands. The events of the Terror were literally satanic, re-enacting the revolt of the fallen angels, and displaying what ensues, when human beings reject the idea of *authority, and imagine themselves capable of discovering a new form of government in the freedom from government.

De Maistre's thought is often criticized for its inexplicit character and its dismissiveness towards rival positions; however, he is still admired for his insights into human nature, particularly by those of conservative political sentiment. He was a diplomat in the service of the Sardinian crown, resident for many years in St Petersburg, and the works that he wrote there are among the masterpieces of French prose.

Maitland, F.W. (1850–1906)

English constitutional historian, who, in his posthumously published lectures, *The Constitutional History of England*, 1908, gave the classic statement of the theory that the constitution of the UK is a definite entity, even though tacit and procedural, to be deduced from *custom rather than from any written document. Maitland also attempted to establish that *limited government had been the rule rather than the exception in England, that the *rights claimed by seventeenth- and eighteenth-century theorists had always been implied in the *common law, and that the process of political *conciliation had been the principal organ of constitutional change. These ideas have played a large part in supporting both conservative theories of law and constitution, and the opposition to the thesis

of *historical materialism, which sees these things as developing in response to external (specifically economic) forces, rather than in response to innate principles of their own. Maitland also divided constitutional from *administrative law, in a manner that is now largely accepted, and developed a theory of *corporate personality, inspired partly by *Gierke and partly by the English law. He emphasized *equity and the law of *trusts, as being singular achievements of the English genius. Those institutions caused the emergence in England of a society in which free association and autonomous institutions limited the powers of a central state.

majesty

The ability to command respect through solemn and ceremonious (but not necessarily ceremonial) display. The majesty of the *state was emphasized by Roman writers, and is often defended as a condition of political *stability. This majesty may attach to the subordinate institutions of government (especially to the *judiciary, where it is often regarded as a necessary means to impose a sense of the objective authority of the law upon criminals and juries). What creates majesty or gives it cogency is hard to say: however, from the very definition, it is clear that it must, when it exists, have a role to play in generating political *allegiance. Robespierre, having as he thought discredited the old symbols which conveyed it, found cause to invent new ones (in particular the cult of Reason) in their stead; Napoleon, more perceptively, surrounded himself with all the old dignities, and all the new, consciously seeking to transfer monarchical ideas of majesty to himself. The modern *government through symbols is perhaps remarkable for its failure to create a similar effect of majesty, a fact which some say explains its frequent reliance on terror. The old crime of *lèse majesté* indicates the extent to which majesty was central to the political order, the sovereign being unable to tolerate more magnificence in a subject than he was able to display himself.

majoritarianism
The view that the will of the majority should determine the outcome of all political decisions. Advocated at the French Revolution by St Just and others, it is clearly a recipe for a new kind of tyranny, namely the *tyranny of the majority.

Malinowski, Bronislaw (1884–1942)
Polish-American anthropologist; *see* *anthropology, *myth.

Malthus, Thomas Robert (1766–1834)
English clergyman and *classical economist, who, in his *Essay on Population*, 1798–1803, argued that the natural rate of population growth is geometrical, while that of food production is arithmetical, thus posing a threat of ultimate starvation. Malthus also argued against *Ricardo's defence of *Say's law, and is now recognized as an original, perhaps eccentric, economist, and an important theorist of *economic growth. The adjective 'malthusian' is now used to describe theories that stress the possibility that human societies might exhaust their own resources: a novel version is implied by the *Gaia hypothesis. *See also* *famine.

management
Now an academic discipline in its own right, management has increasingly come to occupy a central place in business, in politics and in civil society. The *separation of ownership from control, the expansion of the corporation, the rise of the *multinationals and the state bureaucracies, and the complexities of modern organizations have all contributed to the process that has placed the manager at the centre of power. He may have no claims of ownership, and no long-term interest in the success of the organization that he manages, but his skills are regarded as indispensable in overcoming what might otherwise be insuperable problems of *coordination. Hence people can pursue a career in management, moving from firm to firm, and with no real interest in the product of any of them. By an insensible operation, managers redirect the firms that they control from the goal of production for profit, to the goal of managerial efficiency. Sometimes these goals coincide. But in certain areas – notably the field of education – the interests of managers and the goals of the institution may have little or no relation to each other.

managerial capitalism/managerial conservatism
Expressions sometimes used to denote the policies and ideas of the UK Conservative Party during the years prior to *Thatcherism and persisting as a strand in Conservative politics after Thatcher's removal. Managerial Conservatives need be neither conservative nor socialist, nor anything in particular. Their main concern is to manage the affairs of state and the economy so as to avoid upheavals and to 'move with the times'. They are sceptical towards beliefs and may very well have none, since beliefs are difficult to manage. They accept the *welfare state as a fact of history, and state *interventionism as the means to their own power. They are happy in the company of bureaucrats, and often behave like bureaucrats themselves. In many ways it would be right to describe them as *trimmers, though that term was invented before the formation of modern political parties. The Conservative Party has for a long

time been divided between the managerial and the *Tory factions, the first accusing the second of a nostalgic attachment to a vanished past, the second accusing the first of a dogmatic attachment to an uncomprehended future.

managerial revolution
Phrase gaining currency from the book of that title by *Burnham, 1941, which depicts the rise of 'managers' as a new social *class, common to *capitalist, *communist and *mixed economies, and argues that the 1939 war is the 'first great war of managerial society', just as *Lenin had argued that the war of 1914 was the last great war of *imperialism. Burnham's particular theories are largely discredited, but the phrase is still used to denote the shift of power from the legal owner of a business to the effective manager (see *management, *separation of ownership from control), and the changing patterns of ownership as family firms are progressively taken over by corporations run by professionally trained managers. The rise of the 'management consultant', brought about by the specialization of the managerial stratum of a firm, has exerted a strong influence over politics too, with managerial consultants being brought in to advise on issues that might previously have been referred to the civil service. Training in management and management consultancy is increasingly viewed as a way into politics, especially on the free-market Right.

Manchester school (also:
Manchesterism)
Term applied to the defenders of *free trade, and *laissez-faire, headed by Cobden and Bright and the Anti-Corn Law League, and relying for their intellectual credentials on the economic theories of *Ricardo.

mandate
Latin: something commanded. The doctrine of the mandate is highly influential in *democratic politics, although it is extremely difficult to see quite what it means, the problem here being inextricably bound up with the general problems of *collective choice. It is sometimes said that when a political *party stands for *election, it makes certain promises, and by virtue of this secures the vote of the electorate. In return for the voluntary act of the electorate, it therefore stands under a *contractual or quasi-contractual obligation to fulfil its promises, and has a 'mandate from the electorate' so to do. In other words, the relation between a party in office and the electorate is one of mandation. The mandate is held to be a sufficient (some say also necessary) condition for the legitimacy of acts performed in fulfilment of it. The whole structure of obligation stems therefore from the fundamental act of consent whereby democracies establish their claims to legitimacy. The problems for this view are several:

(i) The party programme may contain a variety of independent policies, and each voter might have been in a minority of party supporters on the issue that secured his vote; in which case, to whom has the ruling party promised what? (This case is in all probability the normal one.)

(ii) A large number of votes cast in favour of any party are cast independently of its programme, out of habit, allegiance or a liking for a certain 'style' of government. In which case, why is the obligation to keep promises the overriding one?

(iii) Political necessity, social policy, etc. may make it desirable or expedient to change a policy after election: does the party then no longer have a mandate? If parties were to promise only what they knew to be politically possible, then probably they would promise nothing. The electorate presumably knows this, and presumably this tacit understanding between the two changes the structure of the obligation created by the party programme.

At the same time, a party programme seems to express some kind of commitment. It may be that the correct response is to say that there is a mandate after election, but that its basis is not to be found in contract, or promise-keeping; alternatively, that there is no such thing as a mandate, in which case, with what authority does the ruling party act? Some answer the question by distinguishing mandation from *representation and from *delegation.

mandates system
A system which transferred the government of certain territories and colonies of Germany and Turkey to a special commission of the League of Nations after the First World War. A related system of *trusteeship under the United Nations Organization was introduced after the Second World War to deal with the provisional government of certain territories of Italy and Japan.

mandation
See *mandate.

Mandeville, Bernard de (1670–1733)
Dutch-born English doctor and satirist, who, in his *Fable of the Bees*, 1705, set out, to illustrate the political message contained in its subtitle: 'private vices, public benefits'. He tried to show, for example, how the accumulation of wealth through the egoistic pursuit of power and luxury leads to the public welfare, since vanity requires that wealth be redistributed after death in order to achieve posthumous fame for liberality. (Mandeville's

arguments about luxury and leisure, and about their contribution to aggregate demand, are to be found also in *Veblen's theory of conspicuous consumption.) Mandeville's caustic style disguised a serious economic theory, and he is often regarded as one of the founders of the *invisible hand justification of the market economy.

manichaeism (or: manichaeanism)
A form of *gnosticism founded by Mani, and originating in Persia in the early days of Christianity. Manichaeans founded their religion on a metaphysical doctrine: the division of the world between light and darkness, the first representing the forces of good, the second those of evil. The world itself, suspended between these two principles which are in eternal conflict, offers to the individual soul a path to salvation. The soul must throw off its attachment to matter (i.e. to the body, which issues from the principle of darkness), and ascend towards the light, which is the substance of the spirit and of God. The sect spread rapidly and caused numerous heresies within the Christian church, the most striking being that of the Albigensians in thirteenth-century Provence: see *crusade.

The term 'manichaeism' has been appropriated to name any all-embracing doctrine which sees the world in terms of a fundamental division and opposition between two irreconcilable forces, one good, the other evil; e.g. certain naive forms of *progressivism and *utopian socialism. The actual religion of Mani was, however, apolitical and ascetic in tendency.

manifesto
Italian: I manifest. The *Oxford English Directory* defines a manifesto as 'a public declaration, usually issued by or with the sanction of a sovereign prince or state, or by an individual or body of individuals whose proceedings are of

public importance, for the purpose of making known past actions, and explaining the reasons or motives for actions announced as forthcoming'. In fact many important manifestos – such as the *Communist Manifesto* – have been issued by bodies of little consequence at the time of their utterance, and have neither summarized past actions nor given any very concrete explanation of future ones. Indeed, 'manifestos of accusation' are now the rule rather than the exception (typical being Zola's famous *J'accuse*, issued apropos the *Dreyfus case). Such manifestos serve not so much to inform people as to give political *identity to the groups that issue them, by focusing their antipathies.

Mannheim, Karl (1893–1947)
German sociologist, and one of the founders of the *sociology of knowledge, which he argued must come to replace traditional philosophical theories of knowledge. In *Ideology and Utopia*, 1929, he argued that all knowledge is situation-bound, each age develops its own style of thought, and comparison between the styles is impossible. Within each age there is a conflict between the tendency to conserve a style of thought, and the tendency to renounce it in favour of some other; conservatism produces 'ideologies' (modes of *false consciousness which make the world seem more stable than it is), while the impetus towards change produces 'utopias' (over-valuations of the future and celebrations of the dynamic forces of history). Mannheim admits the possibility of a realistic vision between ideology and utopia, but prefers the theory that society is polarized into hostile camps, from whose conflict a 'dynamic synthesis' may be forged by the impartial intellectual observer. The Marxian influences are everywhere

apparent; in later life, however, Mannheim advocated 'planning for freedom', which he thought would overcome both the anarchy of liberal thought and the totalitarian implications of communism. He remains influential in sociology, and the discipline that he founded – the sociology of knowledge – has received a boost from the radical theories of *Foucault. However, the theory of 'relationism', whereby Mannheim attempted to escape the charge that his vision left no room for the idea of truth, has been rejected by most practitioners.

manumission
The freeing of a *slave. In Roman law this was effected in a variety of ways, often by using *legal fictions of gift or purchase. The church later introduced simpler procedures, and conferred a right of manumission *in ecclesia*, thus effectively abolishing slavery.

Mao Tse-Tung (Tse Toung, Zedong, or plain Mao) (1893–1975)
Chinese communist leader, who imported Marxist politics into China, where the peasantry, rather than the industrial proletariat, was the main focus of social discontent. Mao modelled himself, both theoretically and practically, on the example set by Stalin. During the 1960s his theories were extremely influential in leftist circles in Europe, though recent research into his policies and character have made it extremely difficult to view either him or his ideas with anything but revulsion. The main features of Maoism are these:

(i) 'Political epistemology'. Socialism requires us to 'revolutionize self and things'. People must realize that they are capable both of securing changes in things, and of changing themselves, before genuine revolution is possible. At the same time, material transformation is necessary in order to achieve the required transformation in consciousness. The circle here is not vicious, but 'dialectical'.

(ii) The priority of practice. Practice is the supreme test of truth, and all theory must be tested through its application, and rejected where required.

(iii) 'The necessity for error'. Mao argued that 'to say that mistakes can be avoided . . . is an anti-Marxist proposition . . . it amounts to denying the law of the unity of opposites'.

(iv) The law of the *dialectic. For Mao 'the correct line is formed in the struggle with the incorrect line': i.e. opposition and conflict are necessary to all historical change, and to deny them is to deny the law of contradiction. This law pervades all social formations, classes, individuals and the Communist Party itself, and is not abolished by the achievement of socialism or communism. Revolution is not a final 'resolution', but simply a move forward in the desired direction; contradictions continue unabated, and it is folly to attempt to extinguish them by dictating a solution from above. 'Marxist philosophy holds that the law of the unity of opposites is the fundamental law of the universe. This law operates universally, whether in the natural world, in human society, or in man's thinking. Between the opposites of a contradiction there is at once unity and struggle, and it is this that impels things to move and change.'

(v) The priority of politics. Ideological and political transformation is integral to the accomplishment of all economic objectives. There is no priority of the economic over the political; rather, they advance in concert, no revolution can succeed merely by devoting itself to increasing production, and when politics and economics conflict, politics must prevail. *Cultural revolution may often be more important than *industrial revolution, since

it creates the new modes of knowledge which enable the people to perceive the value of industrialization.

(vi) The emphasis on the community. The aim of revolution is the achievement of a particular kind of community, based in cooperative principles, without specialization, and without distinctions of right, class or privilege among the members. Manual labour is ideologically superior to intellectual labour, and the latter must gradually be eliminated. The existence of a fundamentally peasant society must be taken as a premise in political planning. (But *see* *Great Leap Forward.)

(vii) Criticisms of Soviet domestic policy, particularly agricultural policy, which 'drains the pond to catch the fish'. Mao retains a kind of *democratic centralism, but refers constantly to the wisdom of the masses, as though he had some interest in consulting them. Democracy and centralism are not only compatible but positively complementary: perhaps because they illustrate the 'unity of opposites'. Criticism and self-criticism provide the only methods of resolving contradictions among the people.

Maoism was an important force in international affairs, first because it effectively brought *international socialism to an end, by splitting the world communist parties into a Russian and a Chinese camp, secondly because it seemed for a brief while to provide a model for communism in the Third World, with its predominantly agricultural economies. Maoism has been repudiated by the Chinese Communist Party and its success in winning so many converts among the Western left is, in retrospect, little short of miraculous. At every point of difficulty the theory presents gobbledygook instead of argument: the unity of opposites, dialectical circles, the need for contradictions, unity in struggle, and so on. And Mao's ruthless destruction of the economy, culture, law, religion and happiness of the Chinese people, not to speak of his arguably unmatched achievements in the field of mass murder, ought to have been notorious long before his death.

Marcuse, Herbert (1898–1979)
German-American political philosopher, former member of the *Frankfurt school, and interesting partly for the intellectual *fashion which he inspired through his later libertarian and utopian writings on the subjects of sexual *repression and social *liberation. In *Reason and Revolution*, 1941, Marcuse presents a re-examination of *Hegel's political philosophy, and tries to show its centrality to the theories that had been expressed in the early 1844 manuscripts of *Marx. He explored the Hegelian distinction between *state and *civil society in order to analyse fascist *totalitarianism (in which civil society rules the state), modern communism (in which the state rules civil society), the withering away of the state, and civil liberty, which he regarded as the freeing of society from the bonds of the state. He emphasized the dialectical elements in both Hegel and Marx, and attempted to elaborate Marx's theory of *alienation in order to provide a thoroughgoing critique of modern industrial society. In subsequent writings (notably *Soviet Marxism*, 1958 and *One-Dimensional Man*, 1964) Marcuse mounted a sustained critique of 'technological rationality', which subordinates all human values to the single end of technological productivity. Society falls into the hands of a managerial ideology, and the motive to escape from this dwindles with the constant supply of material comforts.

In later life Marcuse joined the movement for *liberation, criticized American society as promoting *bourgeois freedoms at the expense of true *self-realization, and described the benign acquiescence which greeted his criticisms as a form of 'repressive tolerance'.

marginal analysis
The analysis of relations between marginal (i.e. small) increments or decrements of variable quantities. Principally used in economics, but with applications elsewhere in the social and political sciences, it involves the application of differential calculus to the analysis of *cost and benefit. The 'marginal principle' (held by some to denote an essential feature of *rational conduct) holds that it is rational to proceed with a course of action to the point where marginal benefits are balanced by marginal costs; use of this principle underlies much *welfare economics.

In political theory marginal analysis is always important in situations where behaviour is affected not by the actual quantity of, say, armaments, goods, productive forces, but by the effect of increments and decrements. It seems plausible to suggest that in many areas (e.g. wages and food consumption), once above the level of subsistence, people are more affected by changes in the level of their expectations than by the level itself, so that predictions and decisions will respond to marginal rather than to actual costs and benefits.

marginal productivity
The increase in output which results from increasing the quantity of an input (e.g. labour, capital) by one unit, the quantities of all other inputs remaining constant. *See* *marginal utility.

marginal utility
Marginal utility is the change in *utility resulting from an incremental unit

of a good. The 'marginal utility theory of price' holds that the price of a good in *equilibrium conditions is the price that the consumer is just prepared to pay for the last unit consumed. A good may have a very high utility and a very low marginal utility, for example water, and the marginal utility theory is held to explain why the price of such a good may yet remain so low, even when it is (as in this case) necessary to life. It thus explains what *classical economists called the 'paradox of value' – that the *use-value of a commodity might be very high, even when its *exchange-value is very low, and vice versa. It also replaces the classical idea that use-value and exchange-value are separate properties, by identifying the second in terms of the first.

The 'law of diminishing marginal utility' holds that, after some point, successive equal increments in the amount of a good yield successively smaller increases in utility, so that marginal utility always diminishes after a certain point. All such conceptions assume that utility may be measured in definite units, which is perhaps more plausible in the theory of price than in other areas. This much critized assumption has led to the replacement of marginal utility theory by analysis based on the *indifference curve, which makes no such assumption.

marginalism

Economic, political and strategic thinking which gives special importance to *marginal analysis. The term can also mean the emphasis on small increases and decreases, for example in political conciliation, or in arms control and strategic planning, whether or not marginal analysis is also invoked. *Cf.* *incrementalism.

maritime law

The law of the sea and of shipping, governing salvage and related matters.

It is part of the *municipal law of the individual state, and not a branch of *international law, although it has everywhere been formed in obedience to international *conventions agreed between sovereign states.

market

A system of exchange where the demands of buyers interact with the supply made available by sellers, thus, in *free markets, determining the resulting *price. More often, in practice, law, government intervention and the activities of *cartels and *monopolies exert some kind of control over its operation. Analysis of the market under various conditions is a major preoccupation of economists. It is also a preoccupation of political theorists, some of whom argue, on a variety of grounds, first that the market is unique to capitalism (but *see* *market socialism), secondly that it is to be preferred to every rival form of distribution, e.g., because it permits the emergence of *equilibrium despite the fact that buyers and sellers remain largely ignorant of each other's desires (whereas – a point often made by economists of the *Austrian school – equilibrium under a socialist *planned economy requires an immense amount of, probably unavailable, information about the consumer); or because it produces *collective choices which are also rational and perhaps even *optimal *social choices; or because it contains what *Hayek has called a 'harsh discipline' with which to regulate supply and demand, and to reduce profits and prices. Others have attributed to the market opposite effects, together with deleterious consequences of a more intangible order, such as *commodity fetishism, and the emergence of a 'market ideology', according to which even the human being and his faculties are thought of as 'alienable' – i.e. as bought and sold like commodities. (This play on the word *alienation is partly responsible for its modern use in political rhetoric.) Some have praised the market as an ideal form of social union, involving the peaceful and occasionally festive expression of social projects, in an atmosphere of conciliation, agreement and tacit understanding.

market forces

In a modern economy, market forces are identified as the forces of *supply and *demand which together are held to determine prices and quantities bought and sold. The idea that these are forces, in the sense of having a power in themselves to generate economic activity, is sometimes critized as a form of *fetishim by *Marxists (corresponding to Marx's 'capital fetishism'). The only *force* here, says the Marxist, is the productive force of labour; there is therefore a real ideological difference between those who explain price in terms of supply and demand, and those who explain it in terms of the *labour theory of value.

It is hard to know how to assess those claims, since if *x* really does *explain y*, it can be assumed that *x* is also a *cause of y*, and if a cause is not a force generating its effect, then what precisely *is* meant by 'force', and why should forces matter? Nevertheless, this controversy is often taken very seriously, since it connects directly with the Marxist critique of *bourgeois economics, as building assumptions about production relations into the explanation of production relations, and also with the more general criticism that ideology finds all its explanations in appearances, and not in the essence that they conceal. (*See* *essence/appearance.)

market socialism

Term sometimes used to denote a theory which attempts to reconcile the belief in the *market, as a system of exchange, with belief in *social ownership of the means of production. The argument is roughly this: a market is (at least to some extent) a self-regulating mechanism, and allocates resources without recourse to tyrannical measures designed to force an unwanted pattern of distribution on a reluctant society, and without all the manifold incompetences and inhumanities witnessed in the state-controlled systems of communism. At the same time, private ownership of the means of production leads to exploitation and injustice, together with unacceptable *accumulations of capital in the hands of the few. The ideal would therefore be to combine the benefits of the market mechanism with a social ownership that would remove its injustices. One suggestion has been that there should be cooperative ownership of every productive enterprise, but that each cooperative should be in free and open competition with others, thus stimulating production, and leading to the economical and useful exchange and distribution of the product. Supply and demand would determine prices, and the state would intervene where necessary only by adjusting supply or demand. Marx criticized all such theories on the grounds that *production, distribution and exchange are organically connected, and it is not possible for there to be private ownership only of one part of the chain. A certain measure of interest was aroused by market socialist schemes in the 1930s (notably by the theories of the Polish economist O.R. Lange) and more recently, following the introduction of a kind of market socialism into Yugoslavia in 1950, and the writings of the Czech theorist Ota Šik, who influenced the brief experiment in 'socialism with a human face' in Czechoslovakia, brought to an end by the Soviet invasion of 1968.

The Yugoslav experiment never proved itself to be viable, and the arguments of the *Austrian school, against which Lange fruitlessly pitted himself, have prevailed. It is now widely argued that private ownership is an integral part of the market mechanism, since it is the feature which ensures that costs and benefits are borne by individuals and which therefore compels each economic agent to work towards a rational budget of his own.

marriage

According to Christian theological doctrines which were, until recently, widely accepted, the marriage bond is unbreakable and eternal, and generates a peculiar 'affinity' between the partners (it is the impossibility of creating this affinity between blood relations and between people of the same sex that is supposed to explain the interdiction on incest and *gay marriage, respectively). This doctrine can be seen as in part a rationalization of the more widespread view, enshrined in law, that marriage is an autonomous institution, with peculiar internal aims and constraints, arising out of and generating *obligations which are not contractual, and not to be explained merely in terms of promises given or benefits received. These obligations cannot be specified in advance, and although marriage begins with a kind of contract, it is a contract to be united precisely by a non-contractual obligation: this is part of the difference in connotation between a promise, which is the index of a specific intention, and a vow, which dedicates one's being and not just one's acts.

The philosophical idea of the non-contractual obligation has been explored in this connection by *Hegel (who used it partly to counteract the *social contract theory of the *state), and reflects intuitions embodied in the law. Laws relating to marriage are nowhere reducible to laws of contract, and have incorporated striking elements not to be found in any other sphere of law (but *cf.* *industrial law). Such laws always attempt to prevent rather than to facilitate divorce, to guarantee the duration of marital obligations even beyond divorce, and to make the grounds of divorce correspond to a socially accepted idea of the permanence of marriage. Many liberals find this feature puzzling, and often seek to reformulate the law in contractual terms – not 'till death us do part' but 'till death or mutual consent us do part'. The older conception is given its most extreme legal expression in the English common law doctrine that husband and wife are one *person (namely, the husband), a conception that nowadays causes considerable offence to the other person. The rival 'contractual' view strives to make divorce as easy as marriage (provided there is agreement), and to make all legally enforceable obligations transmutable into monetary terms; it also sees no reason for the announcement of a marriage through the adoption of the husband's name by the wife, or for any other symbolic or ceremonial display. Some defenders of the contractual view in the US even advocate 'no fault divorce', effectively ending the jurisdiction of the courts over the obligations arising through marriage. The upshot of this contractarian view is, in effect, the abolition of marriage as a separate institution: it ceases to be intelligible that people should make *vows* of marriage, rather than contracts of cohabitation. Between the two extremes there is room for the conception of the 'limited vow': i.e. of non-contractual obligations that are regarded as extinguished by the fulfilment of certain conditions, and this is in effect what the modern law of marriage upholds.

Those inspired by certain *feminist and socialist arguments concerning the relation between the family and *patriarchy, or family and private property might similarly seek to abolish marriage. To the Christian, for whom marriage is a *sacrament, such arguments have no obvious force.

Bigamy (i.e simultaneous marriage to more than two or more people) is a crime in most Western systems of law, though not in *Islamic law. The immigration of polygamous Muslims into Europe has brought about the strange situation in which only the first marriage of an incoming patriarch is recognized by the law, the remaining wives being classified as unmarried mothers, entitled therefore to the welfare benefits which that condition, in many European states, now attracts. In other words, the Muslim immigrant is rewarded by the state for a condition that in the indigenous citizen would attract a substantial term of imprisonment. Not surprisingly this has produced explosive tensions, especially in France.

Marsilius of Padua (Marsilio dei Mainardini, 1275/80–1342)
Italian political theorist, rector of the University of Paris in 1313, subsequently excommunicated as a heretic and forced to flee to Bavaria. Marsilius's penetrating attack on the claims of the *papacy to authority in secular affairs (the *Defensor pacis* (Defender of the Peace), 1324) raised political theory to a new level and anticipated many of the concepts of political thought as we know them in the modern world. The papacy and priesthood, he argued, must be subject in all 'temporal' affairs to the people, constituted as a republic and making laws for itself which will be enforced by a secular authority. Even the Church should be constituted as a republic, since the hereditary and monarchical constitution of the papacy provides less guarantee than a system of popular councils that the ensuing doctrine will capture the divine intention. The state should be seen as a secular institution, issuing laws whose validity does not depend upon *natural justice but on the procedure whereby they are made and enforced. Law must be unitary and coercive, in order that human conflicts should be resolved; it should be made by the 'weightier part' of the citizens, either directly or through elective representatives, and the citizens must retain the right to elect and depose any government. The state itself is an association for the good of the citizens – where 'good' is given an Aristotelian meaning of happiness or fulfilment. The priesthood has a place in the state, but only because the citizens depend for their fulfilment upon a proper preparation for the 'future world'. So far as the present world is concerned, priests have no authority.

martial law
Law applied through the *courts martial or military tribunals established under the directorship of military institutions. Only exceptionally can martial law be imposed within the state *jurisdiction rather than in foreign territory temporarily occupied. In the UK it cannot be declared in time of peace. Its principal characteristics are procedural: justice is administered according to provisions laid down by military councils, standards of evidence are changed, and the right of appeal constrained or abolished.

It is commonly said that 'martial law' was declared in Poland in December 1981. This seems to imply (i) that after the declaration the law was administered by different tribunals, or by differently constituted tribunals, from those that had administered it before; (ii) that legal procedure became that of a military tribunal rather than a civil court; (iii) that the military institutions were separate from those of the *state; or else (iv) that there was genuine judicial independence under the former law that was removed by the imposition of martial law. In fact it is doubtful that any of (i) to (iv) is true, and it would therefore be better to refer to a sudden imposition of severe laws under a system that in any case never fully recognized judicial independence or the *rule of law.

The expression 'martial law' is also used (although legally this is not approved) to denote military law, i.e. the special bodies of law applicable to members of the armed forces during the course of their duties as such. In this sense it *could* be said that martial law in Poland was extended to the whole population.

Marx, Karl (1818–83)

A *Young Hegelian turned social scientist, who lived for much of his life in exile, having lent support to the revolutionary activity of 1848. Together with *Engels he wrote the *Communist Manifesto*, and developed a philosophy of man, history and politics that would give hitherto unprecedented authority to the communist cause. This philosophy has undergone many changes (*see* *dialectical materialism, *Marxism-Leninism, *neo-Marxism). The form in which it is found in Marx has three distinct, but interdependent, parts.

(i) Human nature. This theory shows the influence of *Hegel and finds fullest expression in Marx's early writings (e.g. *The 1844 Manuscripts*). The nature of man is not immutable but historical, changing in accordance with social and economic conditions. But the prime mover of history is man himself who, through labour, remakes the world in his own image and changes his image in accordance with his powers. The nature of man therefore depends upon the conditions in which he labours. *Private property creates the division between the classes, and also the condition of *alienation which is overcome only by overthrowing the institution which creates it. With the abolition of private property man ceases to be a mere object or means; he is restored to his dignity as subject, or end in himself. He then becomes free, and his social relations become classless.

(ii) History. The philosophical idea of the 'historical essence of man' is recast in the later writings (notably *Capital*, vol. I, 1867) as a scientific claim concerning the evolution of human societies. All social forms have a function, and this function explains their existence, their survival and their destruction. Marx's theory is a form of *materialism: history is propelled by material forces – the *productive forces – whereby nature is transformed into *use-values and *exchange-values. These productive forces compel the creation and destruction of successive systems of *production relations between people. These systems, or economic structures, form the material *base of society upon which the many-tiered superstructure of institutions is erected. Among the possible production relations are those of *feudalism, *capitalism, *socialism and *communism. The superstructure consists of the legal and other institutions which consolidate these arrangements, together with the *ideology that pertains to them. Productive forces have an intrinsic tendency to develop, as human knowledge of and mastery over nature increase. As they develop successive economic structures arise and give way, and the social superstructure changes along with them. At a particular point of development the productive forces and the production relations enter into conflict: the latter being unable to contain the former. Society then enters a period of *revolution. People become conscious of this by recognizing the existence of *class struggle, between those whose activity fits them for the new economic structure, and those who are guardians of the old. This consciousness is not the cause, but the effect, of the material conflict which generates revolution.

(iii) Economics. Marx put forward a version of the *labour theory of value. Since exchange-value enters the world only through labour, attribution to it of autonomous power is a form of fetishism (see *commodity fetishism). Exchange-value is in reality 'congealed human labour'. The accumulation of *surplus value is explained as the extortion of hours of unpaid labour; exchange-value therefore accumulates in the hands of the capitalist, and never in the hands of the worker. This is the only explanation of regular capital accumulation that is compatible with the truth of the labour theory (but cf. *primitive accumulation); it follows that capitalism is of necessity a form of exploitation.

The combination of these views leads to a prediction. At a certain point of development the economic structure of capitalism will no longer be able to contain and facilitate the ever-developing productive forces. Hence there will be a *crisis of capitalism to be resolved by revolution. This revolution will transfer power to the proletariat, and there will follow a development towards an economic arrangement that will be communist (since that is the only arrangement suited to the final mastery of nature), and also classless. Marx is famous for his attacks on 'utopian' socialism, describing his own form of socialism as 'scientific'. In retrospect, however, the motive of his thinking in all its forms appears decidedly utopian, and

its brilliance no longer disguises the fact that Marx's scientific pretensions are illusory.

Marxian/Marxist
Two terms which are not now generally synonymous. 'Marxian' means pertaining to one or other of the theories expounded by *Marx: for example, to the theory of exploitation and surplus value, or the theory of historical materialism. 'Marxist' means pertaining to the theory or (more usually) practice of *Marxism: i.e. forming some part of the complex revolutionary movement that derived its initial inspiration from the writings of Marx. Thus a Marxian economist might well not be a Marxist economist – he might even be opposed to all revolutionary activity. It seems that there are even Marxian conservatives, just as there are Marxists who believe very few of the theories of Marx.

Marxism
Marxism has two distinct parts: theoretical, and practical. Theoretically it involves adherence to the ideas of *Marx, together with a political commitment to proletarian *revolution of the kind described and foretold by Marx. Practically, it involves Marxist *praxis, within the context of a 'bourgeois' state, which in turn involves, not necessarily revolutionary activity, but a preparation of the ground for revolution in social and institutional life.

Marxism is, or was until recently, a vast movement and its theoretical and practical aspects do not necessarily correspond. Moreover, there have been currents, strains, heresies and rival interpretations in the theoretical sphere which make it additionally difficult to pin down any particular doctrine as giving the essence of Marxism. It is normal to distinguish the 'scientific' strain of Marxism, with its emphasis upon the supposedly rigorous analysis of the economic structure and 'law of development' of capitalist society, from the 'Marxist humanism' which, because it seems committed to less bold predictions and less monumental claims about the nature of society, has recommended itself to many who cannot quite believe either the economics of Marx or the many available versions of *historical materialism. Marxist humanism involves the application of the concepts found in Marxian theory to the description of human consciousness, to social and cultural phenomena, and to all aspects of life in which classes and their ideologies gain ascendancy. It is humanistic not only in its emphasis on consciousness, but also in its concern for values which may seem to have no place in the 'scientific' claims of historical materialism. Within these two broad movements one must distinguish, as versions of the 'scientific': *dialectical materialism, *technological determinism, and some of the theories concerned with *exploitation and the *labour theory of value; as versions of the 'humanistic': *critical theory, the *Frankfurt school, and the work of *Lukács and (possibly) *Gramsci. Within those intellectual currents many more influences are felt – some pay more or less attention to the work of *Engels, to the *Leninist theories of *imperialism and *revolution and to attempts made by *Luxemburg and others to prevent the theoretical justification of *tyranny. Some have tried to synthesize Marxism with other theories, for example with *structuralism (see *Althusser), with *cybernetics (see *crisis theory), with *liberalism (see *left-liberalism), with *feminism and so on.

Marxist practice has been more uniform than the theory. Revolutionary movements which call themselves Marxist tend to see the world in terms of a *class struggle, and attempt to align themselves with the oppressed party in that struggle. They may be very little influenced by either of the two main theoretical movements mentioned, but nourish themselves instead upon a variety of *left, *socialist and *egalitarian doctrines, associating themselves with the name of Marx on account of the successful revolutions carried out in his name.

In communist parlance many heresies within Marxism were singled out for condemnation (see, e.g., *deviationism). This practice was begun by the *bolsheviks, and continued by *Lenin, Stalin and their successors, with a fervour that is rarely encountered outside *religion – a fact that has been instrumental in persuading many to see the actual Marxist movement more as a quasi-religious than as a political phenomenon. Thus contemporary Marxism has been called by Raymond Aron 'the opium of the intellectuals', parodying Marx's own description of religion as 'the opium of the people'.

Marxism-Leninism

Term coined in the USSR after *Lenin's death, in order to denote the philosophy which Stalin held up as the true philosophy of the Russian Revolution. It purported to combine Marx's analysis of capitalism with Lenin's theories of revolutionary action – notably *democratic centralism and the theory of the *Communist Party as *vanguard. The question whether the two strands of thought are consistent with each other is not usually raised, although it is arguable that they are contradictory. Until 1989, communist parties would usually describe themselves as 'Marxist-Leninist'. Those few that survive today hide coyly behind a democratic facade and, while respectful towards Marx, make no mention of

Lenin, still less of any 'Marxist-Leninist' doctrine.

marxizing (sometimes French: *marxisant*)

Scattering references and allusions to *Marxian thoughts and technicalities through one's speech or writing, often in order to establish one's credentials as a serious member of the intellectual *left. Marxizing literary criticism had a vogue in France and Italy in the 1960s and 1970s (e.g. in the early work of Roland Barthes), and some dismiss the work of the *Frankfurt school as marxizing, meaning to imply that it presents no new theory, and does not involve a serious application but only an affectation of Marxist language – an accusation that can plausibly be made, for example, against the music criticism of *Adorno. The use of the term is, however, not necessarily pejorative. It may be thought that some degree of marxizing is necessary, e.g. in the composition of a dictionary of political thought, in order to give a modern perspective on the subject.

Masaryk, Tomáš (or Thomas) Garrigue, (1850–1937)

Czech philosopher and statesman, first President of Czechoslovakia and one of the architects of the post-imperial settlement in Central Europe. Masaryk was a highly cultivated man, with a literary gift that enabled him to argue simultaneously at the highest intellectual level and in terms designed to gather the support of ordinary people. He had no philosophical system, since he believed systems to be the enemy of reasonable conduct and the cause of social and political instability. Influenced in his philosophy by the moral law of *Kant and by contemporary *phenomenology, Masaryk sought to reconcile a *humanitarian *universalism with a belief that the small *nation has a special historical role in modern politics. The 'humanitarian ideal' must always be before us, even when we work to re-establish the historical claims of a nation over a particular territory. A nation must be conscious of its history as grounds for its own legitimacy, but it should not seek to establish itself by large-scale transformations or revolutionary actions. The true work of politics is always 'small-scale work' (*drobná práce*), which will slowly turn the face of society towards the future, while retaining a consciousness of the past. Masaryk saw in communism, and especially in the theories of Lenin, the greatest threat to the peace of Central Europe; the false universalism of the communists threatened to absorb all the nations of Europe in a collective act of submission to Russia. Communism was the heir to *pan-Slavism and to the diabolical *nihilism of the Russian romantics. While ostensibly hostile to all religion, communism involves a frenzied inversion of the religious instinct, and while promising to liberate man from slavery it in fact enslaves him more completely than any previous form of servitude.

Masaryk's popularity, his position as *philosopher king and his percipient analysis of the communist threat caused *Lenin to denounce him as communism's most dangerous living enemy. (*See also* *half education, *Havel, *suicide.)

mass culture

Term of American sociology, now widely used, but perhaps without theoretical basis, to denote that part of popular *culture which is produced consciously for the *masses, rather than the traditional 'high culture' that had been the property of a ruling élite. (*See*, e.g., D. Macdonald: *A Theory of Mass Culture*, 1957.) Mass culture is sometimes thought to be a product of the *industrial revolution, which destroyed the previous 'folk culture'. The mass culture is also said to be 'consumed' by those who enjoy it, to be 'manufactured', usually under conditions of intense stimulation of demand, and without any suggestion that the value of any cultural product is to be measured in terms other than its price. That a cultural commodity is wanted by someone is said to be the sole criterion of its worth; that the want is artificial, say, produced by the stimulus of advertising or by the peculiarly riveting form of the product, that the want is depraved, and can exist only in a nature that has been in some way morally or spiritually degraded – all such factors supposedly play no part in determining the calculations either of the producer or of the consumer.

In such accounts terms from the theory of *commodities are used, and it is indeed normal to associate this kind of culture with *consumerism – i.e. with the reduction of all values to those of the market. Debate over the value of mass culture is therefore at least as old as the *cultural conservatism that arose in response to the massive stimulation of production during the nineteenth century. The cultural conservative is apt to argue that a critical stance, with an eye to moral and aesthetic values, is an essential part of the understanding of cultural products. Without it 'culture' forms a great tide of stimulation in which true human attachments are dissolved. The opponent of that line of thought may sometimes rest his case in the trivial and disputable ground that *de gustibus non est disputandum* (there is no argument about taste); alternatively he may adopt the more serious argument that the complaints of the cultural conservative are concealed justifications of *élitism, and have the effect, whether or not intended, of confining all serious recreation to a *leisure class.

mass hysteria

The phenomenon of infectious reaction in *crowds, where each member, with no understanding of the cause or object of his emotion, may respond sympathetically to the joy, pride, anger, fear or anxiety of his neighbours. Without this 'cohesive' principle crowds would have no character of their own, *demagogues would be without power, and revolutions hardly conceivable. Since two favoured candidates for explanation of historical transformation are the *leadership theory, and the theory of *revolution, this may support the belief that all such transformations are really promoted by unconscious agency, of which mass hysteria is the immediate expression.

mass media

See *media.

mass production

Does the mass production of a commodity change its nature, or the nature of the appetite for it? *Cultural conservatives and romantic *socialists have both answered yes to that question, the first on the ground that replication devalues the object that is copied, the second on the ground that mass produced goods become symbols of, and ways of attaching people to, the industrial process, and so divorcing them further from their own autonomous powers. Thus there arose in the nineteenth century a reaction against mass production which joined conservatives like *Ruskin and Emerson with socialists like *Morris and *Thoreau against the tide of industrial change. Ripples of this movement can be felt in twentieth-century *agrarian movements, and in the attack on 'instrumental reasoning' initiated by Horkheimer and passed by him, through the Frankfurt School to *Adorno, *Benjamin, *Habermas and *Marcuse.

mass society
See *masses.

masses
'There are no masses, only ways of seeing people as masses', writes Raymond Williams (*Culture and Society, 1780–1950*, 1958), who further argues that the term 'masses' has arisen in modern English to replace the once familiar 'mob' as an expression of indiscriminate abuse. In representing a class in its undifferentiated totality the term represents it also as random, irrational and without human qualities. (*Cf.* the French *canaille*.) In *The Revolt of the Masses*, 1930, José Ortega y Gasset expresses some of the disdain of an old ruling class for the uncontrolled and destructive activities of people no longer obedient to traditional moral and social order, and argues, not that the 'masses' exist only because they are perceived as such, but that they exist because a new form of political organization has made them possible. He identifies this as the modern kind of democracy, in which individuals are regarded as having equal rights regardless of power, and all privilege is treated with hostility and, where possible, undermined, so as to restore the uniformity of the whole.

The idea of the masses as instruments of progressive and irresistible historical forces is the Marxist equivalent of the French Revolution's idea of the *people, as the sole source of *authority. Among the practitioners of Marxism many have allowed little leeway to the masses, although *Mao assigned to them an enormous role in every political transformation, involved them actively in his policies, and killed large numbers of them when they resisted.

massive retaliation
In January 1954, J.F. Dulles declared that 'the way to deter aggression is for the free communities to be willing and able to respond vigorously at places and with means of our own choosing'. This was interpreted as advocating a *strategy of massive retaliation, i.e. immediate complete response to all identifiable attacks using all available means. Subsequently in 1966 NATO affirmed a policy of 'flexible response', i.e. the maintenance of forces designed to conduct any conflict at the lowest possible level until negotiation can be begun and with the hope of avoiding 'escalation' towards nuclear war. The original NATO policy was in fact one of 'aggressive defence', Dulles intending to signal not a commitment to massive retaliation but rather a preparedness to overreach in counter-aggression the scope and consequences of any attack.

master and servant
The terms previously used in English law for the legal relation of employment, based in the *wage contract, but now overlaid and qualified by statutes that belie any simple contractual interpretation. (*See* *industrial law.*) The master was vicariously liable in tort or delict to any third party injured by fault of the servant when acting in the course of employment – an old *common law doctrine that survives in UK and US law. This doctrine had always acted, even in the absence of statutory provision, to constrain conditions of employment so as to prevent acts dangerous to the public.

The survival until recently of the old terms is one indication of the way in which the wage relation has been conceived in law, as a web of mutual duties, one party being dominant and the other subservient. The 'wage relation of the new type' prefers the terms 'employer' and 'employee', in order to deny the implication of dominance and subservience.

master and slave

A famous passage in *Hegel's *Phenomenology of Spirit*, 1807, describes a transition, represented as both historical and also essential to the individual self-consciousness, from the 'life and death struggle' in the *state of nature, to the acceptance of universal moral law. The transition is described as the 'moment' of lordship and bondage, or master and slave. One party to the original struggle overcomes and enslaves the other, so as to use the other as a means to his ends. The result is that the victor (the master) retires into a life of leisure and consumption which distances him from reality, while the loser, the slave, continues, even in his bondage, to imprint on the world the mark of his individual will. As producer, the slave is enabled to acquire a consciousness of himself as agent, and a sense of the world as containing not only means but also ends; as consumer, the master loses that consciousness, and with it the sense of the ends of his existence. The 'inner freedom' of the slave grows with the 'inner bondage' of the master, until the slave is in a position to rise up and bind his oppressor, so beginning the process again with a reversal of roles. The toing and froing between command and obedience is supposed to exemplify the structure of the *dialectic, and it is resolved only by the transition from this 'moment' of consciousness to that higher 'moment', in which each party sees the other as end and not as means, and thereby accepts the governance of a universal moral law (*see* *Kant).

The parable has many complex details and has had great influence on nineteenth- and twentieth-century political thought, inspiring philosophies of true (as opposed to 'artificial') *freedom, of *revolution and 'revolutionary consciousness', of *alienation, and so on. The influence was immediate on *Young Hegelians, and survived in *Marxist humanism. It has entered political thinking with renewed vigour as grounds for the theory of *recognition advanced by *Kojève and *Fukuyama.

materialism

1. Metaphysics. A somewhat outmoded label for the philosophy that denies that the mind and its contents have a peculiar nature separate from physical reality and subject to autonomous laws of constitution and development. The 'materialism' of the *Enlightenment held that nothing exists except matter, and that the processes which we interpret as mental are really material processes seen in a peculiar and erroneous light.

The *dialectical materialism of *Engels, and *historical materialism generally, have held, not that mental processes *are* material, but rather that their development is in essentials dependent upon transformations in material circumstances, so that what is perceived as a change in consciousness is only the effect, and never the cause, of a transformation in material states of affairs (for example a transformation in *production relations). Milder forms might say only that *some* mental processes (e.g. those constitutive of a social and political vision) are dependent upon material circumstances, and powerless to influence them.

Philosophically speaking, historical materialism should be seen as an answer to a certain kind of *idealism. The term 'materialism' is often now avoided by philosophers, since it seems to imply adherence to the view that 'matter' is the fundamental stuff of the universe, a view long ago disproved by physical science. The modern preferred term is 'physicalism', which holds merely that whatever exists is subject to the laws which govern physical reality, and is, in that sense, part of physical reality. But what is physical reality? The best answer is: whatever is governed by the laws of physics.

As that paragraph intimates, there is a philosophical problem in identifying precisely what is being affirmed, and what denied, by those who say that the mind is, or is not, a physical entity. It is fair to say that the current philosophical debate over this issue surpasses in minuteness and sophistication anything that was envisaged by eighteenth-century materialists, or anything that occurred to the defenders of historical materialism.

2. Morals. The attachment to material *values, i.e. to those pleasures and profits which are intrinsically connected with the body, and might equally be attributed to beings without reason or self-consciousness (such as the pleasures of food, drink, sex), together with an attachment to *money, as material means to pleasure. Usually contrasted with attachment to the 'true' realm of human values in which reason and self-consciousness are implicated, involving such intangibles as loyalty, love, courage, justice and *virtue generally.

materialist theory of history

See *dialectical materialism, *historical materialism, *historicism, *materialism.

matriarchy

The system of *kinship relations whereby authority tends to be vested in mothers rather than in fathers (*see* *patriarchy), and in which some or all of those rights and powers traditionally associated with the 'head' of the family belong to the mother (including the right to inherit and bequeath property). The study of matriarchy has done much to support *relativism concerning domestic values and institutions, and to illustrate part of the *feminist argument that many of the apparent distinctions between men and women (and in particular those associated with the granting of power and authority to men rather than to women) are not innate but 'culturally determined' (i.e. acquired).

Maurras, Charles (1868–1952)

French writer, right-wing activist, and polemicist, *see* *intégrisme, *royalism, *trahison des clercs.

maximin

1. A technical term of *decision theory and *game theory, denoting a strategy in which the player acts so as to achieve the best outcome that he can, given the worst possible pay-off that could result from the actions of the other players. Thus, the player maximizes the minimum pay-off.

2. A principle of social *justice according to which the best distribution of goods among a class of recipients is that in which the amount obtained by the worst off is the highest (in other words, which maximizes the minimum received). This criterion has recently been advanced by *Rawls as essential to the concept of distributive justice – it seems to capture the idea that justice must concern itself first and foremost with the situation of the worst off.

Rawls's appropriation of the term 'maximin' from game theory reflects his view that the theory of justice, like game theory, involves an application of principles of rational choice in a situation of conflict and coordination. It should not be thought to imply, however, that the reasoning underlying judgements of justice on this view is simply a special case of the reasoning behind the maximin strategies discussed by game theorists.

Mazzini, Giuseppe (1805–1872)

Italian nationalist and revolutionary, who participated in the 1848

Revolutions and was briefly head of the short-lived Roman Republic. Mazzini was a republican, though the cause of Italian unification that he espoused was achieved only when Garibaldi and others turned to the royal House of Savoy to provide the necessary unifying figurehead. Mazzini advocated national *self-determination as the collective correlate of individual liberty: the liberation of Italy from Austrian yoke was, for him, identical with the liberation of the individual Italian, who could be himself only as an autonomous member of a free nation. This synthesis of liberal individualism and nationalist collectivism had an intoxicating effect on a Europe already inflamed by romanticism and by the literary and artistic reinvention of Italy in the works of Goethe, Byron, Berlioz and others. Mazzini's 'Young Europe' society, founded on the model of his 'Young Italy', in order to spread nationalist ideas across the continent, was therefore influential in changing the climate of opinion and stimulating *irredentist movements across the continent.

McCarthyism

Attitudes and policies named after the Republican Senator Joseph McCarthy (1908–56), Chairman of the 'House Un-American Activities Committee', who in February 1950 alleged that he had the names of 57 'card carrying communists' in the State Department, and that 205 people employed by the department were well-known communist sympathizers. This, combined with the previous scandal caused by the trial of Alger Hiss for espionage, and Senator McCarthy's subsequent attacks on universities and intellectuals, led to a kind of hysteria which saw all liberal and socialist opinion as both communist and 'un-American'. Some recent writers have doubted that McCarthy deserved either the support that he initially achieved or the condemnation which his activities finally brought on him. *See also* *anticommunism.

McLuhan, Herbert Marshall (1911–80) Canadian communications theorist. *See* *communication, *media.

media

'The media of communication': i.e. all those means whereby the public receives *communications, whether or not they also lie within public control. Much recent thought has been devoted to the issue of the *control of the media, and the difference made to the content of communication by that control. Social theorists such as Vance Packard (*The Hidden Persuaders*, 1957) have done much to display the power of *advertising in stimulating demand and in creating artificial appetites, often by means that bypass completely the reasoning powers of the subject. To the extent that this is regarded as deleterious, it has been normal to advocate some legal control over advertising. So far no one has been able to describe what form that control should take without advocating the introduction of extensive powers of *censorship, or else forbidding or controlling the advertisement of potentially harmful products such as tobacco and alcohol.

Socialists and Marxists were given to argue that the media in any *class society automatically fall into the hands of the class that owns the economy, and so become directed to supporting the interests of that class. This aspect of the theory of class *hegemony was extremely influential, partly because it countered what were seen as *bourgeois celebrations of the 'freedom' of the media in Western societies. The view has been routinely propagated by departments of 'media studies' in UK universities, and conservatives often complain that it has so infected the graduates of that peculiar discipline, as to explain the drift of the mass media in general, and television in particular, towards the *left, as the new recruits set about the task of undoing the old hegemony. Indeed, it is now far more usual to hear complaints that the media are biased *against* capitalism, *against* wealth, *against* the old middle-class values and middle-class culture, than in favour of them.

Whatever the practical consequences of such Marxist theories, their intellectual credentials are unimpressive. It is a trivial consequence of certain theories of hegemony that the *ruling class controls all major sources of social and political power. Hence that class must also control the media. But the ruling class may be defined so vaguely as to mean nothing more than 'the class that controls the sources of political power', so making the accusation vacuous. In the absence of a better theory, the only serious distinction that could be drawn is that between control by forces within *civil society, which may be exerted against the state, and control by the *state. On all these issues *see* *communication.

The slogan of Marshall *McLuhan, that 'the medium is the message', captures the idea, familiar to literary critics, that form and content are never completely separable, so that *how* something is said partly determines *what* is said. On this view it becomes impossible for a medium that is modelled stylistically on the advertisement to convey the same thing as a medium modelled stylistically on *propaganda, so that the media in a market society and those in a totalitarian state will never be in full agreement about anything, and all appearance of agreement will be an illusion which lasts just as long as the stylistic contexts of the two are ignored. There must, naturally, be some exaggeration in a theory that has that consequence but, as literary critics have discovered, it is extremely difficult to see quite where the exaggeration lies.

There is no doubt, nevertheless, that the message is influenced by the medium, and the argument is prevalent that the mass media have entirely changed the character of politics, by forcing politicians to simplify or caricature their message, by obscuring the distinction between argument and propaganda and by generally emphasizing the sensational, fleeting and eye-catching aspects of life at the expense of the reflective, permanent and soul-touching matters which ought to be our real concern. It can hardly be doubted that television operates at a lower level intellectually than the traditional political pamphlet; some insist that it operates at a lower level emotionally and spiritually also, and that the need to adapt all political messages to its sensationalist parameters and minimalist attention-span has in effect destroyed the possibility of politics as a serious meditation on social problems and their solutions. This pessimistic view is not one that can be put across on television; hence it will remain the view of a minority.

mediation

The intervention of a third party in an attempt to resolve a conflict, especially an international conflict, where mediation is a recognized and sometimes mandatory procedure under the Charter of the United Nations. Mediation differs from *arbitration, since there is no agreement to accept the suggestions of the third party, and from *good offices, in that it involves active involvement in the negotiation. In US labour law mediation is recognized as a procedure for resolving industrial disputes.

mediocracy

Term coined by the French commentator and political theorist Régis Debray (b. 1940), to denote the rule by the mediocre, and also the rule by the media, with the implication that these amount to the same thing.

meme

Term introduced by the biologist Richard Dawkins (*The Selfish Gene*, 1989), as part of an explanation of human irrationality. A meme is a mental entity, such as an idea, a belief or a theory, that colonizes a human brain in the manner of a parasite, using the energy of that brain in order to promote its own reproduction, and so spreading through the human population by making use of the brain's achievements, such as language, media of communication, coercion, institutions and laws. Dawkins singles out religion as a particularly successful example which, once implanted, can infect an entire population with beliefs that sustain themselves in defiance of rational thought. The theory of the meme is supposedly an application of Darwin's theory that organisms survive if they can find an environmental niche that favours reproduction and if their competitors reproduce less successfully. It has been criticized as too metaphorical to be scientific, and as misdescribing the way in which ideas are 'reproduced'. Nevertheless it has a following in political thought, since it lends charm to *disenchantment.

memory

The importance of memory in political thinking has been frequently emphasized by conservatives. It is only by remembering our dead, conservatives are apt to argue, that we acquire a clear conception of who we are (the important point being that we unavoidably distinguish 'our' dead from the others). From Thucydides to Churchill the conservative calls for a politics of memory have fed into feelings of patriotism and given shape and credibility to policies that would otherwise seem to involve too great a sacrifice of present goods for the sake of people on whom we can no longer confer a benefit. The problem of building a concept of public memory into a political philosophy was one that exercised *Burke, whose principal complaint against the French Revolution was that, by destroying the past, it removed all foundation for the future. The experience of the First World War, captured in the line that Kipling took from the book of Ecclesiasticus – 'Their name liveth for ever more' – and which is inscribed on the mysteriously beautiful cenotaph built by Sir Edwin Lutyens in Whitehall, led in the UK to the establishment of a national Remembrance Sunday, observed by the *Anglican Church, and one of the last remaining state occasions in which almost everybody, including the mockers and the sneerers, feels called upon to join.

There is an interesting philosophical question raised by the political evocation of memory, which is this: do the dead have rights, and if so are they harmed by our abuse of those rights? The desecration of a grave, for example, arouses strong feelings of revulsion in all of us, even in those who have no vestige of religious faith. But do we believe that the act of desecration violates the rights of the dead man himself, and if so, do we believe that he is harmed thereby? Whatever the answer to those questions, acts of desecration are never lightly regarded, and the vandalizing of Jewish and other cemeteries in recent times has led to widespread political tension in Europe.

Mencius (Meng Tzu) (371–289 BC)
Chinese philosopher and politician;
see *Confucianism.

mensheviks

The *moderate faction within the
Russian Social Democrat Party. At the
party congress in London in 1903,
directed by Plekhanov (1856–1918)
and Martov (1873–1923), a division
arose between those favouring revolution and those favouring reform. The
first were the bolsheviks, the second
the mensheviks (from the Russian
menshinstvo, a minority, due to the
minority vote which they received as a
result of *Lenin's manipulation,
though in fact they were in the majority). The mensheviks formed a separate
political party in 1917, despite a nominal reunion with the bolsheviks in
1906, and were a majority in most
soviets after the February revolution.
They were ousted by the bolshevik
coup d'état in October, and then gradually liquidated or sent into exile.

The mensheviks were *Marxists,
who believed that Russia must pass
through a phase of capitalist development before proletarian revolution
would be possible; they also rejected
Lenin's theory of the role of the party in
establishing a socialist administration.

mental illness

See *psychotherapy.

mercantile law

Old term for business and commercial
law. Not a distinct branch of the legal
system in *common law countries, but
often so in those countries with a legal
system founded in *Roman law.

mercantilism

Economic doctrine much favoured
between the mid-sixteenth and late
seventeenth centuries, which explored
the relation between national prosperity and *international trade, and

which recommended intervention by
the state to encourage exports and
limit imports, and so increase both
wealth and power. A leading exponent
was Gerald Malynes (1586–1641), who
advocated such measures as *exchange
control, and made various important
additions to the concepts of political
economy. Later advocates of *free
trade criticized the mercantilists,
partly on the ground that their equation of prosperity simply with the
difference between export and import
showed an insufficient grasp of the
structure of the economy and of the
potential gains from trade.

mercenary

A professional soldier who fights for
pay, and regardless of political allegiance. Common from the thirteenth
century in Europe, the widespread use
of mercenaries was deplored by
*Machiavelli, on the ground that it
transferred power to untrustworthy
bands without interest in the political
stability or integrity of the state for
which they fought. Mercenary armies
declined, and virtually disappeared,
after the Revolutionary and Napoleonic
practices of *conscription had become
universal. Moral indignation against
mercenaries reflects acceptance by
many of the idea that *war can be legitimately carried out only by *states and
that individuals can legitimately
involve themselves in it only to the
extent that the state commands them.
Otherwise their responsibility for what
they do is personal, and they are no
better than murderers. The paradoxical
consequences of this doctrine are,
however, evident. It implies that the
command of a state can exonerate the
individual from moral blame (which
seems to imply that the state has some
near-divine dispensation). It may also
imply that the result – including *total
war, in which every citizen is bound by
terrifying oaths and penalties to wage

war absolutely and mercilessly and for whatever time his rulers should choose to commit him – is morally preferable to the activities of the self-seeking *condottiero*. The thought here is that there is something morally dubious about someone who fights and kills for money, and for whomsoever pays best, and something praiseworthy about someone who fights only when his country is in danger, and for the good of that country.

Standards of behaviour among mercenary soldiers have varied enormously, from the rapine and plunder of the *condottieri* to the disciplined fighting of the Gurkhas, circumscribed by a precise *ethic and with great emphasis on *honour. The small minority of British citizens who know some history look on the Gurkhas with gratitude and admiration.

meritocracy

Term coined in 1958 by Michael Young (*The Rise of the Meritocracy*), to denote government by those thought to possess merit (*cf.* *aristocracy). 'Merit' means, roughly, intelligence plus effort, both of which capacities are early identified and selectively nurtured through an education system designed to advance 'merit' as rapidly as possible, so that it will emerge in the form of an *élite prepared to take charge of government. In addition all jobs and positions will be obtained on the basis of merit alone, with the implication that, wherever you are, whether at the top or the bottom of the pile, it is where you deserve to be. In this way meritocracy has been thought to provide a remedy for *ressentiment*.

Meritocracy has been characterized as promoting rule by *status group rather than by *class; it indicates a large measure of *social mobility selectively obtained. Many regard meritocracy as a distinguishing feature of

modern government, and deplore, praise or ignore it accordingly. It was anticipated by Napoleon, with his advocacy of a society in which careers would be 'open to the talents'.

messianism

Belief in and adherence to the Messiah, i.e. to one who comes as a messenger from God. More broadly, messianic movements are those which are led by someone who claims to be, or to be licensed by, the Messiah. 'Messianism' is used to denote any social or political movement which importantly resembles the religious pattern, with emphasis on *leadership, inspiration, enthusiasm, or a vision of the promised land. Such movements frequently contain elements of *millenarianism, and even *mass hysteria, and tend to involve the deployment of *crowds rather than the building of *institutions. They are important in modern Asian and African politics, where they often build on existing religious sentiments, and upon an existing tendency to experience the world in terms of a 'mission'.

Methodism

Religious movement begun within the Anglican Church by John Wesley (1703–1791) and his brother Charles (1707–1788) in 1729. Fired by missionary zeal the brothers went to America in order to preach against strong drink and the slave trade, returned disappointed to England and, under the influence of the Moravian Church, began preaching in the open air, wishing to renew the faith of the English people, and to bring the principles of Christianity closer to their everyday lives. They emphasized hymn-singing (at the time only doubtfully legal in Anglican churches), doctrine, and communal study of the Bible, but tried, despite these evidences of religious conviction, to stay within the Anglican fold, breaking away only in 1784 when the Church refused to consecrate Methodist bishops.

Methodism thereafter became a *nonconformist church with a large and growing following. It spread to the US and throughout the nineteenth century formed the backbone of many communities (especially in large connurbations) both there and in Britain. It is responsible for much of the rooted protestant feeling in the American hinterland, and its ripples can still be felt in British politics. It is in essence serious, democratic, participatory and puritanical, but with a penchant for restrained joy. The Methodist emphasis on hymn-singing sparked brilliant literary endeavours on the part of Charles Wesley, and a long musical tradition involving serious composers (Wesleys included) throughout the nineteenth century. This tradition was incorporated into the Anglican liturgical legacy, to become one of its lasting treasures.

methodology

A word that should mean the study of methods, but is often used simply to mean 'method', as in 'the methodology of the social sciences'. If there is a subject then there is a method of investigation appropriate to it. There may be more than one method used to discover some matter, and in this case (which is probably more rare than commonly imagined) it is possible to speak of methodology, as the discipline which attempts to describe the method which best achieves the required result. Thus there is a 'methodology' of medical diagnosis, partly because diagnosis does not give the *theory* of what it discovers. In general the existence of a genuine methodology implies the absence of a conclusively established theory, since

a theory of something will automatically deliver an account of the correct way of making and validating discoveries about it. When people, following *Schumpeter, speak of 'methodological individualism' this implication is precisely what they wish to convey: that they do not know whether or not individualism is true, but they are going to act as though it were. (*Cf.* also methodological *holism.)

metropolitan power

The controlling power within an empire or colonial state: that part of the empire which is the privileged recipient of the benefits of expansion, from which the expansion originally occurred, and towards which all relations of accountability ultimately flow.

microeconomics

Branch of economics which treats of small 'decision units' – the *consumer, the *household, the *firm – in order to show how their decisions jointly determine relative *prices and quantities, and the allocation of resources to production. Microeconomics is distinct from macroeconomics, which is the study of the aggregate national income and those features of the economy that are associated with it. In a completely *planned economy, in which all economic activity occurs at the behest of and in response to central decision, it is not clear that the two studies could be truly separate.

middle classes

In the eighteenth century the term 'middle ranks' was used increasingly to denote the expanding section of society that was composed neither of 'nobility' nor of 'common people', and by the nineteenth century the term 'middle classes' was widely used to commend themselves by those to whom it applied. In current sociological usage the expression does not seem to denote a *class, but rather a large and fluid *status group, characterized most of all by its extent and flexibility, and by the ease with which someone can join, and the difficulty with which he can leave it. It is increasingly common to distinguish the 'upper' from the 'lower middle class', in order to accommodate the pronounced and growing distinction between those who wield real power in corporate and administrative organizations, and those whom they organize, and who, while not being strictly working class, since they do not dirty their hands, are nevertheless unable to enjoy the kind of control over their lives that comes with executive power. The flexibility and many-tiered character of the British middle class has been suggested as an explanation of the social stability of the kingdom, and its relative freedom from revolutionary upheaval: see David Cannadine, *Class in Britain*, 1999. *Cf.* *bourgeois.

middle England

Expression which attempts to summarize the supposedly moderate, unambitious, settled and unvocal majority of English people, whose attitudes are captured in *The Diary of a Nobody* by George and Weedon Grossmith, 1892, and whose support will always be needed by any politician who wishes to stay in office.

military-industrial complex

Phrase coined by President Eisenhower and popularized by *Mills. It denotes a pattern of relations sometimes thought to exist between high-ranking industrialists concerned in the manufacture of military technology, and military advisers, concerned in making themselves useful (perhaps even indispensable) to a government. The thought is that the two groups act in concert, perhaps even in collusion, so

as to maintain high levels of spending on defence, and a military approach in international politics.

Mill, James (1773–1836)

Scottish philosopher, historian and economist, influential in propagating the *utilitarianism of *Bentham, and forming on the basis of it a radical reforming political movement, dedicated to the extension of the franchise, and the representation of working-class interests in Parliament. His *Philosophical Radicals included *Ricardo. Mill himself was a keen student of the new political economy, and attempted to combine a respect for private property, dogmatic utilitarianism, sympathy for the under-privileged, and a libertarian attitude that extended to all aspects of production and trade. He devoted much attention to the problems of education, and was influential partly through his advocacy of the view that intelligence is as much acquired as inherited; the education that he gave to his son, *J.S. Mill, is vividly described in the latter's autobiography.

Mill, John Stuart (1806–73)

English philosopher and political economist who made contributions to almost all aspects of political thought.

(i) Political economy. Mill wrote an updated version of *Smith's *Wealth of Nations* (*Principles of Political Economy*, 1848), in which *classical political economy is summarized and given what is perhaps its most accessible expression. Mill offers a qualified defence of *laissez-faire*, but argues that it can lead to just and orderly economic development only if trade unions exist, in order to restore parity of bargaining power between the owners of industry and those employed by them. Price is regarded as determined by the equality of demand and supply – i.e. prices rise until demand has fallen to the level of supply. (Mill thus saw no cause to adopt *Ricardo's version of the *labour theory of value.) Mill makes various proposals for redistribution in the interests of social justice, mostly through taxation, especially on death, and presents a classic statement of the argument against the *hereditary principle.

(ii) Utilitarianism. One of the more famous of Mill's writings is the pamphlet of this name (1863), in which he amends and restates the Benthamite view of morality that had been bequeathed to him by his father *James Mill. While criticizing many of the assumptions of that view, Mill endorses the 'greatest happiness' principle as the criterion of what is right. He argues that the principle is defensible only if one distinguishes happiness from pleasure (or at any rate recognizes that there are qualitatively different pleasures). He sometimes sees, sometimes does not see, that this vitiates the quantitative approach that had been a principal motive behind Bentham's *hedonism. Mill also offers various thoughts about human nature in order to justify his amendments. *Utilitarianism* has fascinated many subsequent philosophers, partly for its passionate conviction, partly for its failure wholly to reveal why it is so convinced about what.

(iii) Liberalism. Mill's essays *On Liberty*, 1859, and *The Subjection of Women*, 1869, written 1861, contain classic statements of liberal thought about law, liberty and rights. The first defends the view that 'the sole end for which mankind are warranted, individually or collectively, in interfering with the liberty of action of any of their number, is self-protection', from which premise Mill argues at length in favour of basic freedoms, guaranteed by law, and of a radical distinction between the public sphere of law and the private sphere of morality. In the

course of this Mill adumbrates another view of law and liberty, the first as a system which maximizes, or ought to maximize, the second. In this sense liberty is seen not in terms of permission, but in terms of the opportunity for *self-realization, for example, through conducting 'experiments in living' in an environment that permits all faculties to be developed in harmony. *The Subjection of Women* is a classic argument in the *feminist cause, defending the proposition that there is no known difference between men and women that would justify attributing to them different *rights.

(iv) The theory of government. In *Considerations on Representative Government*, 1861, Mill outlines and defends an ideal system of government, based on *proportional representation, in which minorities will find spokesmen in the institutions of government, and in which the rights of all citizens will be effectively guaranteed, while allowing to them maximum occasion for self-development.

While Mill devoted most of his social and political writings to questions concerning law, constitution and economics, it seems clear that an *individualistic view of human nature underlies much of his sense of the value of the liberty that he defends. For this he has been criticized, by those opposed to individualism. He has also been accused of a certain naivety about human nature. He himself recognized the possibility of such an accusation and sometimes thought that he had cured himself through studying the *cultural conservatism of *Coleridge and *Carlyle, and absorbing, if not their political ideas, at least the German romantic view of the significance of culture which had inspired them. In any case, Mill's thinking about law, liberty and emancipation has been widely accepted in Anglo-Saxon jurisprudence, as giving the basic principles upon which legal reform should proceed. Much of the inner conflict in Mill's moral and political thought has been seen by later philosophers as the result of an intrinsic tension between the standards of liberty and utility, and this tension is expressed equally in the legal reforms (e.g. those concerning sexual conduct) which Mill's thinking has partly inspired.

millenarianism

Belief in the 'millennium' i.e. a future thousand-year period of blessedness. Based in the prophecy contained in Revelations 20, it has been spasmodically popular among Christians throughout the centuries. The term is now extended to denote any outlook based in the promise of an eventual release from earthly miseries by an enduring security, preferably without political institutions: e.g. *Marx's belief that communism will bring the prehistory of humanity to a close, as interpreted by certain of his early disciples. Such 'eschatological fantasy' (Norman Cohn: *The Pursuit of the Millennium*, 1957) is common to many political ideas, ancient, medieval and modern.

The religious idea is sometimes thought to be particularly predominant in countries which have formed their social and political identity in response to *colonialism (*see*, e.g., G. Balandier: *The Sociology of Black Africa*, 1970). An interesting example is the New Guinea 'cargo cult' in which the Western 'cargo' is thought to be about to arrive, bringing the spirits of the dead and ushering in the millennium. The nostalgia of *Islamism for a restoration of the supposedly pure and godly jurisdiction of the Prophet must surely also be traced to the same source in the human psyche as other enthusiasms more properly described as millenarian.

millet system

(Turkish: *millet*, from Arabic *millah*, a religious community.) The system of administration adopted under the Ottoman Empire which combined two kinds of *jurisdiction – territorial and ethnic-cum-spiritual. The criminal and commercial law of the Sultan (the Majalla, distantly adapted from the *sharî'ah*) prevailed over the entire territory; but in personal matters, to do with marriage, family and religion, the various communities had their own law, subject to appeals to the religious leaders – to Pope, Patriarch or Mufti. The system provides an important instance of dual jurisdiction, and represents one viable solution to the problem of ethnic *minorities: although it is significant that the Shi'ites, regarded as heretical by the Sunni authorities, were never granted a *millet* of their own – a fact that has had important (and destructive) repercussions in our time.

The millet system survives in the Constitution of Lebanon, in which the state law is qualified by a *statut personnel*, varying according to the confession of the citizen. The Lebanese experiment goes further, with an unwritten *Pacte nationale* that divides the offices of state between the confessions, so that, by convention, the President must be a Maronite Christian, the Prime Minister a Sunni Muslim, the Speaker of Parliament a Shi'ite, and so on. The system has been praised as providing the only stable instance of a quasi-democracy in the region (apart from Turkey itself and Israel, both of them very special cases). Although it is true that the presidents and ministers of Lebanon have gained and lost office without the aid of bullets, the constitution has rendered the country inherently fragile and without a true central authority. Lebanon has therefore been unable to defend itself from its neighbours and the constitution has for the past 20 years been a *legal fiction, used to disguise effective Syrian control.

Mills, C. Wright (1916–62)
American radical sociologist whose criticisms of the American political system, and especially of the decision-making mechanisms inherent in it, have provided the American *left with much rhetorical ammunition. *See* *military-industrial complex, *power élite.

Miłosz, Czeslaw, (b. 1911)
Polish poet and diplomat who, after succumbing for a while to the *totalitarian temptation, defected in Paris and then migrated to the US, to become one of the most penetrating critics of the communist system, and of the mentality from which it stems. In *The Captive Mind*, 1955, Miłosz describes the way in which the Marxist virus took over, one by one, the minds of his contemporaries, providing a false substitute for their lost religion, making theft, murder and torture into virtues in the eyes of the one who commits them, and in general colonizing the mind and the emotions of its victim. Miłosz's poetry (for which he was awarded the Nobel Prize in 1988), combining sincere Catholic sentiment with a kind of quizzical inwardness and a recognition of the depth to which the alien virus could penetrate, struck a chord in post-war Polish intellectuals, and inspired them in their resistance to communism. *See* *Asiatic despotism, *ketman*, *New Right.

minimal state
The *anarchist ideal of a state with the minimum concentration of power necessary to sustain a *civil society. *See* *Nozick.

minimax
Technical term of *game theory. A minimax strategy is one in which a player attempts to minimize his opponent's maximum gain. If there is such a strategy open to either party in a two-person *zero-sum game, then the game has a 'solution', i.e. a strategy with an acceptable guaranteed result. In the case of such games, the minimax strategy is also a *maximin strategy; the two terms are here synonymous. However, there are games in which maximizing one's minimum gain is not also minimizing another's maximum gain; in these cases it may be important to distinguish the two kinds of strategy by employing two distinct terms to refer to them.

minorities
Exactly what constitutes a minority is an extremely difficult question. Numerically speaking, the English upper class is a minority, so, probably, is the lower middle class. But neither would be referred to as a 'minority' in a political discussion, largely because a grouping in terms of *class suggests a socio-economic theory, whereas a grouping in terms of 'minority' suggests that the important facts are *ethnic or *cultural. A minority might, however, form a class – either a ruling class (the Alawites in modern Syria) or a subordinate class (the Tamils in Sri Lanka) – but this does not seem to be essential. There is a minority whenever there are (a) habits of association among members which involve an idea of separateness – perhaps imposed by the majority, perhaps accepted by the minority, perhaps both; (b) a sense of separate social *identity which expresses itself in differentiated behaviour. Clearly (a) and (b) reinforce each other: a majority may single out a particular group as *not* belonging to it and, by denying to it privileges and rights, reinforce the group's own sense that it constitutes a separate social identity, perhaps causing the group to seek a corresponding political identity.

The basis for this pattern of social division may be religion, language, race or any other factor that is socially perceivable, though in fact the division of a people into 'majority' and 'minority' often becomes prominent as a result of nationalistic sentiment.

The existence of minorities has generated the problem of *integration and minority rights. On one view the state is a set of legal institutions, not to be identified with the civil society that they govern. The state legislates, society obeys, but there is no other reason for the state to take an interest in the composition and habits of civil association. On this view, unless there is legal provision to the contrary, the rights guaranteed by law must be extended to all, and minority status cannot be legally acknowledged. That used to be the position in English law, which protected the rights of minorities by refusing to recognise them, directing its fire instead against the *tyranny of the majority. However, positive moves by the legislature in the US to rectify the position of minorities has led to the adoption there and elsewhere of *group rights as a legal category. This implies that membership of a minority group entitles the citizen to special protections not available to everyone. (See *reverse discrimination.)

The practice of making treaty stipulations guaranteeing minority rights has been known since the Reformation. As part of the peace settlement of 1919–20 most Central and Eastern European countries were required to make treaties or sign declarations protecting the rights of minorities. Such treaties proved unenforceable, in particular when faced with the persistent human tendency to seek vengeance for unexplained ills by attributing them to people regarded as *alien. *Islamic law, which expressly discriminates against all non-Muslim minorities, continues to engender enormous conflicts in the few countries where it has been adopted, notably in Indonesia.

Mises, Ludwig von (1881–1973)
Leading economist of the *Austrian school and social philosopher whose critical appraisal of socialism (*Socialism*, 1921) argued that a planned economy is inherently wasteful and even irrational, in that it must act so as to deprive itself of the information necessary to formulate a coherent plan. (*See* *calculation debate.*) Mises explored the possible forms of a socialist economy, and argued that none of them could deliver what they promised but that all of them would produce a stagnant society presided over by bureaucrats and a mass of legislation which would stifle the creative impulse. His description of the socialist future accurately prophesied the course of events in the USSR and elsewhere, and he was belatedly recognized, through the work of his pupil *Hayek, as one of the most important critics of the socialist idea. In his later writings – and especially in *Human Action*, 1947 – he attempted to set economic reasoning within a comprehensive philosophy of rational action, which would embrace the whole of politics and institution-building. This theory – which he called 'praxeology' – attempted to give an account of our rational and social nature which would show the folly of the 'planning mentality' which had colonized modern politics and which would at the same time vindicate the spontaneous practices of problem solving, among which the free market is only one.

mission civilisatrice
The 'civilizing mission' through which French colonial expansion in the nineteenth century justified itself, it being held that the introduction of legal,

political and cultural institutions was so much to the advantage of the developing countries as to justify their subordination to a *metropolitan power. Because of the deliberately *meritocratic nature of Napoleonic institutions, French law and especially French systems of education took root more effectively than those of many other colonial powers, and led, for example, to a uniform system of examinations throughout the French colonies and a comparatively flourishing colonial literature.

Mitbestimmung

German: co-determination. Legislation in Germany, compelling directors of private companies to ensure that workers are represented on their supervisory boards, began under the Weimar Republic with the *Betriebsrätegesetz* (Works Council Act) of 1920. The inspiration came from both social democracy and Roman Catholic social teaching. Further legislation in 1951, 1952 and 1976 now provides that there should be equal representation from the company (shareholders') side and the work force side on the supervisory board, though the provisions for electing a chairman ensure that the shareholders always have a casting vote. Defenders of the free market argue that the process of consultation involved in securing agreement for policy – and especially for changes in product, marketing, and timescale – have served to make German industry less and less competitive. Defenders of *industrial democracy dispute the evidence for that conclusion, and argue that, given the historical circumstances of postwar Germany, the practice of consultation has served greatly to ease social and political tensions.

mixed economy

An economy in which private enterprise and state-controlled (or *socially owned) enterprises exist side by side, interacting and perhaps even competing with each other. All economies are to some extent mixed even if illegally (say, through the existence of an extensive black market, as formerly in communist states). The UK economy has been one of the most important examples, in that it has contained extensive private and extensive public ownership which came, over a period of many years, to depend upon each other. The arrangement has been praised for its supposed flexibility, continuity and responsiveness to social change, together with its ability to permit government action in times of crisis, and private enterprise in times of stability. It has been criticized by thinkers of the *New Right, for supposedly allowing too much public ownership, and so undermining the conditions for economic prosperity, equilibrium and the free market. Moves towards *privatization have therefore been adopted, with results that suggest that state-controlled industries will soon be a thing of the past.

mixed government

Government which is neither monarchical, nor aristocratic, nor oligarchic, nor democratic, but some mixture of two or more of those categories. No government entirely corresponds to the traditional categories, which must be considered to be *ideal types; but some show a definite tendency towards stable synthesis of rival modes. Mixed government was recommended by *Machiavelli as the appropriate form of government for a class society, and it provides an example of *limited government in which the limitation comes as much from the balance of forces within the government as from any specific constitutional provisions.

model

1. In the social sciences a model of a situation is a simplified version which supposedly imitates the features that need explaining, without encumbering them with other features that are not connected. A military *chain of command provides a model, in this sense, of certain forms of totalitarian government. By understanding the simplified command structure that governs an army, we can understand the core institutions of the totalitarian state.

2. An example to be followed. Thus *Nicholas of Cusa proposed the Council as a model for the government of both church and empire, in opposition to the top-down command structure then prevailing.

3. In the philosophy of science, a model of a scientific theory is a situation that is governed by the laws of the theory, while possessing other features that are theoretically redundant, but which are chosen in order to make the theory intelligible. Thus Bohr's theory of the atom is made easier to grasp when we envisage the atom as a solar system, with protons and neutrons packed in the 'sun', and the electrons in orbit around it. The laws of atomic theory govern the operation of such a system, but the model also possesses features – for instance the precise location of each electron at any moment – which the theory does not predict. When it is discovered that these features are in fact misleading (as in this case) then the model is abandoned.

moderate

Used in two related senses, first to describe political opinions, secondly to describe a mode of government.

Opinions merit the label 'moderate' in popular usage when no one is particularly offended by them other than those who demonstrate, by their offence, that they are not moderate. The definition is not circular, so long as the form and content of inoffensive opinion can be described. The first three of the following conditions attempt to display its form, the last two its content:

(i) Primarily, a desire for *conciliation rather than *confrontation.

(ii) A preference for reform over revolution – which at one level is simply an expansion of the requirements implicit in (i).

(iii) A belief that political transformation should be gradual and involve no great violence to institutions.

(iv) Belief that there exists a *consensus among right-minded people, and that the process of politics consists in part in disovering this consensus and translating it into law. The consensus will shift with changing circumstances, which is why politics is necessary, but the coincidence between government and *public opinion is or should be the ultimate aim of politics, and the premise from which conciliation begins.

(v) Tolerance towards views which do not match the consensus, provided that they are expressed in accordance with the formal principles (i) to (iii), all other views being disliked as instances of *extremism.

Features (iv) and (v) lead to some confusion between moderate and *centrist positions, the latter being defined in polar terms (as a mean between extremes), the former being defined, as here, quite independently of any contrasting position.

A government is called 'moderate' not necessarily on account of the opinions that motivate it, but rather because it attempts to balance and conciliate, rather than to confront or eliminate, rival powers within civil society. A characteristic of moderate government is that it should permit the existence of an *opposition. Some argue that only a *limited government can do that, and that the combination of limited government and permitted opposition requires a *rule of law. Those plausible ideas depend, however, on intricate connections among institutions which can be laid bare only with the greatest intellectual labour.

modern/modernity

The adjective 'modern' has two senses: first, as the description of a period in Western civilization, and second, as the description of a style or attitude. In the second sense it is roughly equivalent to 'modernist', and will therefore be dealt with under modernism in this dictionary. This entry deals purely with the concept of the 'modern', as opposed to the premodern and the supposedly '*postmodern' world. The term 'modern' was introduced at the Renaissance, in order to draw a contrast between the ancient and the modern worlds. But in its modern sense, in which it does not merely describe but also expresses the spirit of modernity, the term is really an invention of the *Enlightenment, occurring for the first time clearly in the writings of *Rousseau.

In the realm of ideas the modern age began with *Bacon and Descartes. It is coterminous with the rise of science, the *secularization of European society, and the replacement of traditional by 'legal-rational' authority (concerning which, see *Weber). Its intellectual flowering in the Enlightenment coincided, however, with the first of many political disasters wrought in its name – the French Revolution of 1789, which sought to transcribe the modern ideas of *liberty, *equality and *fraternity into a new social order, and as a result destroyed freedom, law, peace and security, leaving, according to recent estimates, two million dead out of a population of 14 million. Revolutionary politics on the French model continued, however, into the twentieth century, as a distinctively modern phenomenon. Equally characteristic of the modern period is the assumption by *intellectuals of a right to rule, and the rise of the various political philosophies which would justify their doing so. Modern intellectuals have frequently entertained *progressivist theories, believing themselves also to have been granted a revelation of the movement of history and of the need to guide mankind into a new order of being. Such beliefs, characteristic of the *Young Hegelians, and also of the *utilitarians, have played an important part in the attempt to seize political power from the old and world-weary élites who seem destined for what *Trotsky called the 'dust-heap of history'.

*Nationalism too is a distinctly modern phenomenon, and has again been espoused by intellectuals, in their search for a *constituency in whose name they act against the moribund powers of an *ancien régime*. Modern creeds involve an attempt to recapture something thought to be threatened or lost, or, alternatively, a wholesale repudiation of the past in the name of the revealed future. It was perhaps Hegel who gave the first, and in many ways most penetrating, analysis of the state of mind that leans towards such beliefs. The modern person for Hegel is one who is not merely part of history, but conscious of history as part of himself.

In this sense modernity, as the self-conscious placing of oneself in history, can take optimistic and pessimistic forms. In either version it has demanded changes not only in the rhetoric, but also in the substance of political thinking. The modern person exists in *conscious* relation to history; if he acts out of custom and tradition it is in a certain measure from a sense of irony: if he commits himself to a future it is either recklessly, or with a battery of predictions designed to tell him how history *must* proceed. Some argue that conservatism too is a peculiar product of this modern consciousness; emerging perhaps for the first time clearly in the works of *Burke, *Maistre and Hegel, and consisting in celebration of custom and prejudice by people whose very self-consciousness distanced them from the object of their veneration. If revolution owes its currency to the modern spirit, it is perhaps because revolution destroys the history with which this spirit is constantly comparing itself. (The contrast between conservatism and revolution as just described, is captured in *Mannheim's polar division of thought between 'ideology' and 'utopia'.) Some have argued that the essence of modernity is *nihilism, combined with the recognition of the impossibility of nihilism (thus Turgenev, *Nietzsche, Dostoevesky). However, it may be more plausible to describe Nietzsche's philosophy as announcing the birth of a *postmodern outlook – one which has ceased to believe in the myths and arguments that legitimized modernity, and which either repudiates the idea of legitimacy altogether, or looks on it with a faint sarcastic smile.

modernism

Two things seem to be meant by 'modernism'. First, the active participation in the currents of intellectual and social change which created the *modern era. In this sense both *Marx and *J.S. Mill were, for all their differences, modernists. Second, a cultural and artistic *movement, armed with *manifestos, principles and paradigms, which attempted to rectify the *sentimentality and exhaustion of *romanticism. It is a curious fact that many of the most important artistic modernists have been *conservative in their social and political beliefs: witness *Eliot, Pound, Yeats, Matisse, Valéry and Stravinsky. Indeed, most of the artistic modernists rationalized their experimental gestures through the idea of *tradition; like Schoenberg and Eliot, they thought of themselves as keeping an artistic tradition alive, in defiance of the vulgarizing process of modern life. Many of them (Schoenberg, Stravinsky, Eliot, Britten, Messiaen and Matisse, for example) were in open rebellion against secularization, and all of them were suspicious of the *Enlightenment and its cheerful view of human nature as containing the potential to solve the problems that it also causes.

Only in the case of *architecture has modernism aligned itself with the modern world, and seen itself in *progressivist terms. To its conservative critics, architectural modernism's espousal of the modern is the cause of the popular reaction against it. Modern architecture is a visible symbol of the *alienation of modern man, precisely because it has tried to provide this homeless creature with a home – a home which is in constant flight from history. In architecture, therefore, the battle between modernism and *postmodernism encapsulates some of the deepest political conflicts of our time.

modernization

This term is generally used without reference to the ideas surveyed in the last two entries to denote the attempt to amend practices, institutions, laws and customs in order to align them with the modern world, the assumption being that it is they, and not the modern world, that must change. In the case of machinery, or anything else that is a means and not an end, this assumption is clearly reasonable. In the case of love, friendship, worship or anything else that is an end and not a means, it is absurd. This partly explains the conflict between those who favour, and those who oppose, the modernization of some institution or practice – the *liturgy, for example. The modernizers see the practice as a means; the traditionalists see it as an end.

This conflict has spilled over into politics, especially in the UK, where the conscious attempt to modernize has led to a complete overhaul of the Labour Party (*see* *New Labour), and a similar, though vaguer, attempt to bring the Conservative Party into line with social change.

monarchy

Literally, rule by one. As now understood, however, the form of government in which the *head of state holds office, usually with the title of King or Queen, either for life or until voluntary renunciation (by *abdication). Monarchies are of two fundamental kinds: absolute monarchy, and limited monarchy (of which the modern *constitutional monarchy is a variant). In the latter, the person who reigns does not necessarily rule, in the strict sense of *controlling the outcome of *executive decisions, but may perhaps exert no more than a merely ceremonial, or perhaps partly regulative, function. The absolute monarchy is obsolete, in one sense: that is, those who hold absolute *power* for life nowadays rarely do so as a matter of *law*, and tend to dignify themselves not with the title of King or Queen, but with that of Chairman (when government is through the machinery of a *party) or President. The distinction is a nice one. It is not that the title King is hereditary, while that of Chairman is not. There have been elected kings (as in Poland), and hereditary 'lord protectors' (Richard Cromwell): there might easily be hereditary party chairmen, and there are hereditary

Presidents in Syria and North Korea. It seems rather that a monarch is identified by a law of succession to office, and by a ceremonial and perhaps slightly mystical unity with the nation which he rules, whereby he takes its name, and becomes the personal embodiment of all its dignities and rights. (This has been called 'existential *representation' by *Voegelin.) A chairman derives his dignities more abstractly, and speaks for a doctrine and for the party that embodies it, as much as for a territory over which that party exercises its authority, while the office of President is expressly stripped of the *charisma of kingship. Clearly, there need be no great difference in the kinds of power that are exercised in the various kinds of case: the distinction is one of law, history and *ethos.

Hereditary monarchy is often praised, on the ground that it enables the head of state to achieve office without having to scramble for it, and on the ground that it implants an idea of continuity and legitimacy at the heart of popular sentiments towards the state. It is criticized, like all applications of the *hereditary principle, on the ground that it is arbitrary – i.e. there is no relation between the office filled and the qualifications of the person destined to fill it. Some accept this argument, and reply either that in this area arbitrariness is a virtue (it is part of the mystical quality of the 'head of state' and therefore of the allegiance towards the state that he symbolizes), or that every other mode of filling so high an office must be equally arbitrary, and usually more dangerous. Whatever the truth of these arguments, it seems that the popularity of monarchy remains great, perhaps because the monarch now has so little actual power. By contrast the party chairman attracts popularity not usually as holder of an office but rather because, like Hitler or Stalin, he embodies qualities of personal *leadership.

monetarism

Name given to an economic policy which sees the control of the *money supply as crucial to the control of *inflation and which, by implication, condemns government attempts to *reflate the economy through public spending (which must in normal circumstances increase the money supply). The policy is now normal in all free economies; the money supply is typically controlled through the base rate of interest on money loaned by a central bank (usually owned or controlled by the state). Raising interest rates increases the cost of borrowing, and therefore reduces the amount of money in circulation.

The theoretical basis of modern monetarism is the so-called 'quantity theory of money': a long-established but disputed theory based in acceptance of the 'Fisher equation' (after the economist Irving Fisher (1867–1947)): $MV = Py$, where M is the stock of money, V is the velocity at which money circulates through the economy, P is the average price level of goods and services, and y is a volume measure of the flow of those goods and services (i.e. the flow of *real income). Since the total money value of goods bought (= stock of money × velocity of circulation) is necessarily the same as the money value of goods sold (price level × goods and services sold), the equation is valid *a priori*. Thus V is sometimes defined as Py/M. The theory receives its empirical application by assuming that y is constant (or growing at a given rate), that the economy is at *full employment and will remain there, and that V is constant, determined by independent and unchanging facts concerning the institution of money, such as the time

intervals between wage payments. In which case M determines P, so that price level rises and falls with money supply. To keep down inflation (rising prices) it is therefore necessary, and sufficient, to keep down the money supply.

It is easy to find difficulties with the assumptions (a) of full employment (which here need only mean maximum possible employment), and (b) of constancy in the velocity of money circulation (which has certainly changed drastically with computerization and universal credit). *Friedman, one of the most recent defenders of monetarism, has argued that, nevertheless, although V varies, it is an 'endogenous variable' – one whose value is determined by institutional facts of the economy and not in a random way, so that, for the purposes of policy, V can be regarded as stable. Friedman has therefore argued that control of the money supply is still the one thing that governments can do which will exert a predictable effect on inflation, and cites in support of his theory the supposed empirical facts that only where such control exists has inflation been forced down, and only in the absence of it has it escalated to the point of *hyperflation. None of this shows, however, that it is or is not easy to control the money supply.

monetary union

The adoption by independent *sovereign states of a single currency as legal tender' – i.e. as the legally enforceable measure of any debt. If money supply is, as argued by the *monetarists, the major factor in causing and controlling *inflation, monetary union grants to each member state an ability to inflate the economy of its partners, and so to raise an indirect *taxation on the earnings of their citizens. This is one of many reasons offered by those who object to monetary union within the *European Union. In response, it is argued that exchange rates and other barriers to transactions across frontiers impede the creation of a single market. The existence of a single currency effectively removes from any member state the power to establish favourable terms of trade through devaluing its currency. Devaluation was the normal way for the Italian economy to regain equilibrium, and the removal of this possibility has caused a continuous political crisis.

money

Anything acceptable in payment of a debt can be called money, provided its acceptance is sufficiently widespread, but the principal application of the term is to any sufficiently universal medium of exchange, such as 'coin of the realm' (i.e. liabilities of the government) and bank credit notes. In less sophisticated economies the coin itself has a value – i.e. an intrinsic capacity to exchange against other goods, independently of the government's promise to sustain or enforce that exchange – as when the coin is made of gold. The reliance on 'valueless' tokens as embodiments of official promises indicates a confidence in the stability of the economy: where this confidence disappears, *barter may come to replace the monetary system. (See *hyperflation.)

Money has the following functions: it is a medium of exchange which replaces barter, and so facilitates transactions; it is a store of value, which facilitates saving; it is a unit for the measurement of value, which facilitates accounting. In all of these its value lies in no use apart from its potentiality to exchange against what is useful independently. The 'money illusion' is the propensity to respond to changes in money magnitudes as though they were changes in *real

terms and not simply a revision in terms of measurement. Thus when offered double income and double prices, someone may suffer from the illusion that he is being offered something real, rather than a change in his habits of accounting. (See *real terms.)

The 'money illusion' is to be distinguished from certain illusions associated with money by *Marx, but more metaphysically characterized. Marx argued that there is a mystery contained in the very fact of exchange-value, and in particular in money as its principal embodiment. The possession of value in exchange is an appearance only, and does not correspond to the essence of money. (See *essence/appearance.) This essence consists in the socio-economic relations (the *production relations) which generate exchange-value from the only thing (*labour) that *can* generate value. The institution of money creates the permanent illusion of value as embodied in the things, including money, which are exchanged, rather than in the labour that produces them. (See *commodity fetishism.) This particular application of the essence/appearance distinction is highly controversial, and while it seems to be saying something extremely important, it is hotly disputed what that something is. Part of its appeal lies in the echo of old religious ideas about the deceptiveness of money and of the worldly goods that it seems to crystallize.

money supply

Many definitions of this are offered by economists. However, the most generally accepted is: the amount of *money (i.e. items conventionally accepted in payment of debt) which circulates in an economy at any given time. This generally includes current accounts at banks as well as coin of the realm. Difficulties arise in trying to ascertain which, if any, is the most appropriate way of conceiving of the money supply for the purposes of government policy. Instruments used by governments in the control of the money supply include interest rate policy (changing the lending rate at a central bank), and operations of the 'money market', as when a central bank buys or sells government bonds. Governments may also try to control bank lending and the rate of interest more directly (*see* *credit control). All these instruments are used in the instigation of monetary policy.

monism

1. The belief that there is only one thing, or one kind of thing, that constitutes or explains events: or else that there is only one basic law or form of law which governs all transformations within a certain field. A monist is anyone who says 'one' to his opponents' 'many'.

2. Hence, the opposite of *pluralism, in particular the advocacy of a unitary state, in which one people obedient to one system of laws, and with one set of values and social relations, enjoys a single continuous territory. *See* *nationalism.

Monnet, Jean (1888–1979)

French statesman and bureaucrat, principal architect of the *European Union and first president of the European Coal and Steel Community which he had planned. Following the horrors of the First World War, Monnet conceived the life-long goal of creating a united states of Europe, as the condition of a lasting European peace. He left public office in 1955 to form the Action Committee for the United States of Europe, dedicated to lobbying on behalf of transnational institutions that would be capable of overriding national sovereignty. This idea was opposed by *de Gaulle, who favoured a Europe of sovereign nation

states, and with whom Monnet was at loggerheads during the 1960s. As a result Monnet developed the 'Monnet method' of 'integration by stealth', in which unification would be advanced step by step without the goal ever being clearly perceived or clearly perceivable. This method has been pursued ever since, and is largely responsible for the growing *democratic deficit of the EU and its institutions.

monopoly

A monopoly exists when a firm, organization or individual is the sole seller of a given commodity. Lesser degrees of monopoly can be recognized, and in UK law an enterprise can be referred to the Monopolies and Mergers Commission if it possesses one third or more of the market sales of a commodity. The commission makes reports upon which a minister may act in order to control or destroy the monopoly. Monopolies have been a common grievance throughout history, and were made illegal, with certain exceptions, by the English Statute of Monopolies 1624, a fact which did not, however, prevent the creation of state monopolies by postwar socialist governments. Exclusive control of a market naturally enables a firm to fix prices in its own favour and, it is argued, a *just price could never result from this. Some also argue that the existing strictures against monopoly still permit the same effects, through permitting or encouraging *oligopoly in its place.

The argument therefore gained currency during the 1960s that antimonopoly laws have not been truly effective, and that the monopolization of industry presents one of the most significant crises of modern capitalism. Thus Paul A. Baran and Paul M. Sweezy (*Monopoly Capital*, 1966) argued that competition in a market economy leads to the concentration and centralization of capital, and this, in turn, leads to the formation of monopolies. This transition from competitive to monopoly capital was held to have profound and far-reaching effects, on accumulation, on the structure of profits and prices and on economic growth, the principal sign of which is the increasing stagnation of the economy, as monopolies attempt to protect their markets. The argument is now widely rejected, and even among its defenders it is not always held to imply that capitalism is in a state of crisis. In fact, capitalist economies (which means, in effect, developed economies everywhere) seem to be currently entering a period of diversification in which the only sustainable monopolies are those (usually the legacy of socialist governments) enforced by the state.

Certain deviations from a competitive market towards monopoly may lead to a situation in which many firms are in competition with each other, say, because their products are close to each other and can be substituted one for the other, and yet each possesses a downward-sloping demand curve. This situation is described by economists as monopolistic or *imperfect competition.

Monroe doctrine
The doctrine enunciated by President Monroe in 1823, and still important in rationalizing US foreign policy, that the US can countenance no intervention in the American continent by a foreign power and would not itself intervene in disputes in Europe.

Montesquieu, Charles-Louis de Secondat, Baron de (1689–1755)
French philosopher and political theorist who attempted, in *The Spirit of the Laws*, 1734, to study human society 'scientifically', and to arrive at the

principles of government which would explain the nature and extent of law, and the constitution best suited to guarantee the liberties of the subject, while maintaining order over all. Montesquieu admired *Locke and the English constitution (or what he took to be the English constitution), praising it as 'the mirror of liberty'. He advocated a *separation of powers, and was the first to give the modern formulation of that idea, as part of a theory of *limited government. Montesquieu argued that only an aristocratic government on the English model could create an effective balance of powers within the state, avoiding the despotic tendencies inherent both in absolute monarchy and in government by the common people. He defended liberty, but his desire was to restore old liberties which the *absolutism of Louis XIV had eroded, rather than to advocate the new, and what he saw as dangerous, liberties of the *Enlightenment.

According to Montesquieu, law and constitution are ultimately founded in the 'spirit' of a people. While there is a universal *natural law, it is not to be supposed that the conditions for its enforcement exist everywhere and at every time: on the contrary, only within the ideal constitution can the natural law be used effectively to guarantee the rights of the citizen, and this constitution is in turn dependent for its power upon a spirit that is in part determined by geographical, climatic and historical conditions. (It is no accident, therefore, that the liberties of the English subject are guaranteed by jurisdiction over an *island*.)

Montesquieu gave interesting, and often penetrating, accounts of the spirit of a people under monarchy, and under the various forms of republican government, arguing that to each form of government there corresponds a fundamental moral sentiment that binds the citizen to the political order: in monarchy the sentiment is honour, in a republic it is 'political virtue' (see *virtue), manifest in a sense of public responsibility. These separate spirits are exhibited even in the smallest transactions. Montesquieu modified his constitutionalism by such sociological observations, tending to the conclusion that a constitution expresses a social condition that is not, in the end, detachable from it. (*Durkheim praised these observations as the first manifestation of modern sociology.) Thus, while Montesquieu influenced the liberal constitutionalists who attempted to divide state and civil society as far as possible, he himself did not countenance that division but, on the contrary, regarded the customs and *ethos of civil society as giving content to its laws. In this he influenced *Burke, who admired him, also, for what he took to be a thorough-going attempt to articulate the idea of liberty in terms of a conservative vision of *privilege.

moral majority

Term popular in the US during the late 1970s and 1980s and used to denote the ordinary, decent and supposedly clean-living citizens who, while forming a majority within the body politic, have little or no voice among the purveyors of *opinion. The supposition is that public debate is monopolized by assorted *liberals, *radicals, sceptics and *modernists, who ignore or disparage the old-fashioned and largely *conservative values of the majority so as to cultivate exquisite disagreements among themselves. The term was adopted as its name by a US pressure group in 1979 (although the name was changed to 'Liberty Federation' in 1986). (*See also* *silent majority.)

moral rearmament

The slogan of a political campaign, founded in Oxford (as the 'Oxford Group') by F. Buchman (1878–1961), an American Lutheran minister, with the aim of reinvigorating the Christian countries through a regeneration of moral values, an opposition to corruption, and a strengthening of international ties. The movement at times had an *anti-communist tendency, but its fervour was expended in the attempt (in the event, futile) to resist the liberalization of the law.

moralism

The disposition to moralize – i.e. to cast judgement of a moral kind upon actions which are not appropriately so judged. Moralism in art and literature is a familiar phenomenon, and some dismiss all moral judgement *of* art and literature as mere moralism, since it applies moral values in a sphere where they supposedly have no application. That view is no doubt already implausible; it is even less plausible to dismiss the relevance of moral judgement to actions done in the name of politics, although the Leninist theory of 'revolutionary morality' in effect dismisses as moralism most criticism of Leninist policies that anyone could ever be in a position to make. Here, as elsewhere, there is a dividing line between moral sense, which recognizes a moral issue when it sees one, and moralism, which curtails the possibilities of action by seeing everything in a moral light. But what that dividing line is depends upon a theory of *responsibility, which will settle the all-important questions of when the consequences of a politician's action are morally significant and when they are properly to be attributed to *him*.

morality and politics

What are the distinctions between moral and political judgement, and between morally and politically motivated action? Should moral values enter into political decision-making? If so, when and how? Those large questions have their parallel in all spheres where the actions of one person have consequences in the lives of others, but where the relation between the two is mediated by an *office or a *role. Thus a judge who condemns someone to punishment in accordance with the law is not normally thought to be acting *in propria persona*, but rather as the holder of an office; we do not normally criticize him in moral terms unless he exceeds that office – i.e. acts *ultra vires*, say by condemning someone of proven innocence in order to settle a private account. Intuitively, some such distinction might also apply in politics. How could war be conducted, unemployment created, or people left homeless or property-less, if there were not some way of exonerating the politician whose actions initiate these things? If we could never carry out this exoneration, then most normal politics would have to be condemned as immoral. The issue is complex, and requires clarity in the following areas:

(i) The nature of roles and offices, in particular those through which political power is channelled. Is it really possible for a role or an office to change the moral nature of the act performed by its occupant? Or, if not, to change his responsibilities?

(ii) The concept of responsibility. Can responsibility for the known consequences of an act depend upon roles and offices?

(iii) The concept of political *virtue. Can one think of political actions as justifiable in terms of the virtuous character that is expressed through them? *Aristotle, *Cicero, *Machiavelli and many others have argued that moral virtues express themselves in the political sphere, but in a manner

that responds to the needs of politics. The politician is like a soldier: although the activity in which he is engaged may require him to harm people, there are only some things which a virtuous character will tolerate. Moreover, there are forms of virtue which find their highest expression in the political (as others in the military) sphere. It may also be part of virtue to accept the problems of political expediency and to adapt one's conduct to them, for what the just, wise and courageous person will do depends partly upon the circumstances in which he is required to do it.

(iv) To what extent can the sphere of politics be seen (as e.g. Machiavelli saw it) as a sphere of necessity, in which the freedom of choice which permits moral thought and action is constrained or abolished?

(v) Most importantly, the nature of moral judgement. Moral judgement is an expression of *value, where the object is a human act or character. According to one popular view, given system by *Kant, moral judgement takes the form of commitment to universal and exceptionless laws, governing the behaviour of all rational beings as such, irrespective of circumstances, consequences and roles. This view would not countenance the distinction between spheres of personal responsibility and political expediency, but at best allow that expediency may sometimes place the agent in a dilemma. According to a rival view – that of Aristotle – moral judgement concerns itself not with universal rules of conduct but with the specification of the dispositions of character that we all have reason to admire (the virtues).

Whatever the answer to those problems, it is intuitively clear that political *ideals are not independent of moral values, and that even a moderate, who thought of all politics on the model of conciliation, must recognize that some courses of action are ruled out as morally impossible, and that some forces ought to be, not conciliated, but confronted. (This might be one underlying intuition governing the idea of a *crime – as an act expressing a state of mind that will not admit of conciliation within well-ordered government.) Thus the imposition of any form of government also implies the preparedness to use *force; it could even be, as *Machiavelli suggested, that a *rule of law can be achieved only through violence.

Even if that were to prompt us to take a lenient view of politicians, it would not permit us to abolish the distinction between moral and immoral *procedure* in politics. Lenin's 'revolutionary morality' – which concerns itself only with ends, never with means – abolishes that distinction. Hence it is not surprising if arguments from *natural justice and *human rights leave Leninists unmoved, since these concern essentially the way things are done. The more or less universal horror at *terrorism suggests that the sense of moral and immoral procedure is deeply seated in the ordinary conscience, and whether there can be a morality without it is open to doubt.

More, Sir Thomas (1478–1535)
English humanist and Lord Chancellor who was executed by Henry VIII and subsequently canonized as a Roman Catholic martyr; *see* *property, *utopia.

Morris, William (1834–96)
English painter, designer, poet and social critic, inspired by the writings of *Ruskin, who founded, in 1861, the organization which was later to be known as the Arts and Crafts movement, and, in 1884, the Socialist League. The Arts and Crafts movement opposed what it saw as the degradation of labour by the industrial process, and sought for ways to restore to labour the dignity and wholeness which it felt to have been characteristic of *craft. This would not be possible, Morris thought, without radical social transformation, and he advocated a policy of socialist reform, with *common ownership, and workers' cooperatives dedicated to manufacture that would be conducted as nearly as possible in the spirit of craft, with a concern for aesthetic values, and a leisurely involvement of the whole person of the labourer in his task. This ideal of labour was associated by Morris with medieval morality and society, on the assumption that the ideal form of labour, in which all participants had been on equal footing and equally fulfilled, was the construction of the medieval cathedral, through common industry, unmediated by property, and performed for the greater glory of God. On the other hand, Morris's utopian vision, expressed in *News from Nowhere*, 1891, makes no mention of religion, and concentrates merely on describing a world without industrial production. This caused some of his critics to condemn his views as romantic and even *reactionary, but his peculiar synthesis of socialism and *cultural conservatism has been highly influential in the English-speaking world, and finds echoes in contemporary thought.

movement
Movements should be distinguished from *parties, *institutions and *associations, in that they come into existence without any need for formal organization or for a clearly defined common strategy and have a history and causality distinct from the history and causality of any institutions that are associated with them. There is a

great difference between a political party that derives its credentials from a movement and one that derives it from its own peculiar history and policies. Thus the UK Labour Party arose from the *labour movement and expressly associated itself with the goals of that movement. The dwindling of the labour movement in recent times is partly responsible for the Party's recent attempts to reorganize itself as a modern democratic party which favours no particular movement or social class. There has never been a Conservative 'movement' in British politics – a fact which perhaps explains the comparative success until recently of the Conservative Party.

Fascism, communism and national socialism all began life as movements, and defined themselves as such. Parties founded in their name have usually ignored or eliminated opposition and believed themselves to enjoy an unlimited store of legitimacy. It has been argued (e.g. by *Oakeshott) that the goal-directed character of movements inevitably leads the parties which arise from them in this totalitarian direction. On this view (which was first adumbrated by *Burke) a political party provides a greater guarantee of individual liberty if it has no over-arching purpose, other than that of government, and adapts its goals to the needs and interests of the given historical society in which its *constituencies live.

multiculturalism

It is widely assumed that modern societies, shaped and reshaped by migration, contain many different *cultures, associated with ethnic and religious *minorities. The question arises, therefore, how the law, the state and the educational system should treat the *minority cultures. Multiculturalism signifies the approach which tries to give as much representation as possible, within legal, political and educational institutions, to minority cultures. It is often resisted, on the grounds that the majority culture is integral to the stability and continuity of society and is the true foundation for the authority of social and political institutions. The attempt to change its status from the 'given' of social experience to a mere option therefore poses a threat to the social order, since it offers to remove the foundations for civil obedience. (*See* *assimilation.)

The dispute here is difficult to assess, partly because the concept of a culture is so obscure. For instance, Western societies regard the law as an impartial and universal instrument which grants no privileges to people on grounds of race, class or social connections and which must be applied without reference to any group or community to which the subject belongs. Is this a peculiar feature of Western *culture*, and if so, ought a multiculturalist to set it to one side when dealing with people who, for cultural reasons, have no understanding or respect for the idea of impartial justice? In the face of this, it has been argued (for example, by Alain Finkielkraut, *La Défaite de la pensée* (*The Undoing of Thought*), 1987), that Western civilization is precisely *not* a culture, but a civilization, in which cultures can thrive side-by-side, but only so long as the *universalist ideas of the Enlightenment are respected. Moreover, the high culture of the West rises above all disputes between cultures (in the anthropologist's sense), and impartially surveys the human world for its material, without regard for cultural distinctions. On this view multiculturalism constitutes an attempt to reduce Western civilization to the status of a culture, and so abolish it. (*See further* *Kultur/Zivilisation*.)

The principal influence of multi-culturalism has been on the curriculum, especially in universities, where multiculturalists argue that study in the humanities has focused exclusively on the work of 'dead white European males' and ignored the achievements of other cultures. Whether this charge is just may be doubted: the *traditional* curriculum in the humanities involved the intensive study of other cultures – especially those of ancient Greece and Rome, and of ancient Palestine and Egypt. Moreover it extended, through the work of the historians and anthropologists, to the furthest reaches of the world. The art, literature and music of the West has always had a multicultural focus, from Boccaccio's versions of Arabic tales, to the re-creation of Japanese culture at the hands of Puccini and Britten. This does not alter the fact that Boccaccio, Puccini and Britten are dead white European males. Their curiosity towards other cultures might be dismissed as *orientalism, a part of the cultural *imperialism which, while ostensibly respecting other cultures, aims principally to absorb and so abolish them. As that last sentence indicates, it is impossible to mount an effective reply to the multiculturalists, since all arguments against them merely confirm their claims. Argument, after all, is one of the weapons of the European Enlightenment, a peculiar speciality of Western culture. Nevertheless, it is undeniable that multiculturalism has lost much of its appeal since the *Islamist atrocities of recent years, which have seemed to many to indicate that cultures cannot always occupy the same space on peaceful terms, and that some kind of shared way of life is the only solution to fragmentation and conflict.

multilateralism
See *bilateralism.

multinational corporations
The multinational corporations or enterprises are usually defined as those producing at least a quarter of their output outside their country of origin (which may or may not be the country where they are legally based). Because of the internal organization of such corporations they may form powerful international influences outside the direct control of particular governments, and so are now much discussed. The facts here are disputed: for example the extent of the involvement of such corporations in political *coups d'état* in order to secure governments favourable to their operations; the extent of the unseen network of influence or control which gives them power in governments generally; the extent to which they can evade one jurisdiction by transferring to another. What seems to be generally agreed is that all such power is potentially dangerous, and calls for new organizations (notably the Organization for Economic Cooperation and Development) with the responsibility to devise codes of conduct with which to regulate the behaviour of multinationals, so as to sever their economic power from all political influence. Moreover, since multinationals have neither armed forces, nor territory, nor *jurisdiction, and since their physical and financial assets are always potentially hostage to the countries in which they are situated, it is hard to see their power as a form of *control, rather than *influence. *See also* *World Trade Organization.

multiplier
A term introduced into economics by *Keynes, to denote a measure of the effect on the *national income or employment of a change in some autonomous component of aggregate demand. For example, suppose that firms increase their rate of investment

expenditure on plant, machinery etc.; this initial stimulus to the economy will generate new income and expenditure, which in turn generates further income and expenditure and so on. The result will be that the increase in national income will be several times larger than the increase in investment. The multiplier is the ratio between the overall increase in national income and the increase in investment expenditure that stimulates it. The overall effect of the initial investment increase is called the multiplier effect.

The multiplier plays an important role in Keynesian macroeconomics, being applied not only to investment, but also to export demand, and in particular to government spending, and taxation. Because of the multiplier, Keynes argued, government *fiscal policy may be a highly efficacious way of stimulating aggregate demand.

multipolar

A system is multipolar if it contains many poles (i.e. points of concentrated force) upon which the equilibrium of the system depends. In international politics 'multipolar equilibrium' is now widely thought to be the only available kind. It is contrasted with the 'bipolar' equilibrium which might exist between two powers who are either sufficiently dominant, or sufficiently isolated in their dealings with each other, to be able to determine the conditions of equilibrium between them, independently of any other power. With the concentration of economic and political potential in several different areas the problem of the conditions of multipolar equilibrium has become extremely important, but it is clear that nothing simple could be said concerning it.

municipal law

Since, in *Roman law, a *municipium* was any self-governing body within the Roman Empire, the term 'municipal law' has come to have two meanings:
1. The law of a state or nation, as opposed to *international law.
2. Laws made by a municipality, such as byelaws, through *delegated powers of legislation.

Murray, Charles (b. 1942)

US sociologist and political scientist. *See* *bell curve, *dependency culture, *family, *underclass.

music

*Plato laid down strict provisions concerning the kinds of music that would be allowed in his ideal republic, arguing that music both forms and imitates character, and that by moving, marching and dancing to the wrong things we become misshapen citizens. Plato's view has never been finally driven from the stage of political theory, and arguments over musical taste and styles of dancing continue to generate political fall-out. Many who are outraged by the violent, sexual and sexist imagery of much 'rap' music are tempted to repeat Plato's call for some kind of censorship, and revulsion against the more egoistic and barbaric trends in popular music has been common throughout the twentieth century. At the same time it should be noticed that Western pop music played a notable part in inspiring the youth in Soviet-occupied Europe to despise the regimes under which they lived, that jazz has for a century been a lingua franca that acknowledges no boundaries, and that, at the height of the Cold War it was a pop group, the 'Plastic People of the Universe' consciously inspired by the Beatles, who became the symbol of Czech resistance – a position that cost them a time in prison following the Soviet invasion of 1968. Hence *Havel's remark, on being questioned as to his political views, that he was 'more Lennonist than Leninist'.

Among those who have made music central to their political vision none has been more censorious in our time than *Adorno, whose dismissal of American popular music as a form of *fetishism (at a time when American popular music included Cole Porter, Glen Miller, Hoagey Carmichael and a thousand others whose innocent melodies have shaped the culture of the modern world) belonged to a comprehensive attack on tonality itself, as the exhausted remainder of bourgeois sentimentality. The true revolutionary consciousness, Adorno argued, required adherence to the 12-tone serialism of Arnold Schoenberg and the Second Viennese School, while tonality in general, and film music in particular, exhibits the false consciousness of capitalist society in its terminal decline.

Muslim Brotherhood
*Islamist movement founded in Egypt in 1929 by *al-Banna. It aimed to reimpose the law of Islam which is 'creed and worship, fatherland and nationality, law and culture, tolerance and strength . . . religion and state; and Koran and sword'. The movement has been from the outset anti-Western and founded in an ideal of Islamic self-sufficiency. Hasan al-Banna advocated dual allegiance, to the 'particular nationality', and to Islam as the overriding principle, and although he was concerned that there should be peaceful relations with the non-Islamic powers, the Brotherhood became increasingly militant, advocating the use of violence in the name of Islam even within the Islamic states, and recruiting activists from those states who were to pursue violent revolution in the name of the faith. The Brotherhood was for a long time regarded as a criminal organization in Egypt, and its most influential leader, *Qutb, was imprisoned and eventually executed by Gamal Abdul Nasser, following the latter's seizure of power. The Brotherhood today divides into a legal wing, with seats reserved for it in the Egyptian Assembly, and an underground movement which continues the Islamist activism of the founders. Variants and offshoots have made serious attempts in recent years to destabilize other Arab countries with Western-leaning governments – notably Lebanon and Algeria – and the movement now has links with *al-Qa'eda.

Muslim League
Movement founded in Dacca in 1906, which became the largest Islamic party in India, and which is largely responsible for the *separatist politics of Indian Muslims, and for the subsequent foundation of Pakistan, as a constitutional Islamic republic.

Mussolini, Benito (1883–1945)
Italian statesman; see *aesthetics and politics, *concordat, *coup d'état, *fascism, *Gramsci, *Pareto, *Sorel, *violence.

mutualism
A system of voluntary association for the exchange of services, in which credit is offered at cost (i.e. without profit), and services likewise; advocated by *Proudhon, and often suggested as an integral part of any developed system of *market socialism.

mutuality
The requirement in an agreement that each party do something to or for the other. Absence of mutuality makes an agreement unenforceable at law, so that a contract 'without consideration' is nugatory. Common moral thought, however, also upholds the obligation contained in a unilateral promise. Law and morality seem to agree in the thought that someone who claims

rights over another, who has not bound himself by a promise, and to whom he concedes no rights in return, is asserting a claim which, in normal cases, has no force. Hence those who claim unearned rights are regarded as making unjust demands. Conservatives often reject *reformist claims of right on account of this absence of mutuality, although whether or not this is correct is never simple: never more simple, in fact, than the problem of *political obligation.

myth

Any false belief that is (a) of symbolic importance in the emotional life of the believer, (b) based in a need to believe rather than in rational conviction, (c) associated with stories that are not usually accepted as history (or at any rate not on historical evidence), but as illustrations or parables, (d) endowed with a 'sacred' quality, which it can confer on the social relations, institutions or political arrangements associated with it, so granting them an air of legitimacy. It is a familiar thesis of anthropology that myths are natural to man, and that they do not exist in isolation, but interconnect, so that to accept one myth is to accept a system of which it forms a part. *Structuralists, for example, believe that the true meaning of any myth is revealed only in the context of such a system. A rival view (that of Malinowski) sees myth in terms of *functional explanation: myths exist *because* of their capacity to justify institutions, rights and laws. (Although it is fair to say that such explanations are not the prerogative of modern anthropologists: David Strauss, *Feuerbach and other *Young Hegelians also advanced them.)

Whether or not Malinowski is right, it is not uncommon to find philosophers who think that he ought to be. Plato, for example, famously argued both that the myths associated with the religion of his contemporaries ought to be rejected because of their harmful nature, and also that no one could hope to govern without the 'noble lie' whose untruth could be perceived only from the height of philosophy, but whose symbolic and sacred force was necessary in order to motivate the citizen to obedience.

Plato's view is the ancestor of certain Marxian ideas concerning *ideology, although it is used to justify myth as a means to political stability, rather than to condemn a particular form of stability because of its foundation in myth. It is to be compared with *Sorel's view of myth (specifically the myth of the 'general strike') as the means to construct a new reality. Like many modern conservatives, and like Sorel, Plato sought to defend myths, without giving any reasons for believing them – an enterprise as precarious as politics itself. But if he was right, so that myth not only does, as Malinowski argues, underpin ideas of legitimacy, but is necessary for that end, then the precariousness of this exercise cannot be conclusive ground for not engaging in it.

Hence the modern art of 'mythopoeia', which is the deliberate creation of myth for others' consumption. This is sometimes known as 'remythologizing' and it has occupied many of the political practitioners of our century, notably those, such as Stalin and Hitler, who tried to dignify the forms of *totalitarian government. Some argue that much of the rewriting of history that occurs in totalitarian states should be attributed to mythopoeia, rather than to the desire simply to hide the record of crimes. A quieter form of mythopoeia has been practised by certain intellectual conservatives – e.g. W.B. Yeats, T.S. Eliot, Ezra Pound – and through them has had a certain influence on modern conservative thought.

There is a tradition in artistic and psychoanalytic thought which regards myth as revealing truth – not religious truth, but truth about the human psyche. This view, associated with the composer Richard Wagner, for whom myth is the background to all serious drama, and the fund of allegory from which the picture of the human soul can be constructed, was passed to *Freud and to Freud's pupil C.G. Jung (1875–1961), who saw myth as representing certain 'archetypes' in the 'collective unconscious'. These archetypes show us what we really are, and how we really respond to one another and the world. They are primordial attempts to make sense of the human condition, and all religions are anchored in them.

Nanny state

Term of *journalese, used disparagingly of a certain kind of socialist attitude to the state, which sees the role of the state as that of caring for the citizen 'from cradle to grave', providing for all physical and medical needs, relieving poverty, and providing a shield against the effects of unemployment, family breakdown and natural disasters. Opponents of the nanny state tend to argue that it creates an *underclass of *welfare dependents, erodes personal responsibility and removes the incentives on which a healthy and free economy depends.

Napoleonic law

The 'Napoleonic code' (*code napoléon*) is the unofficial name given to the codes of law adopted in France at Napoleon's instance between 1804–11, and exported in whole or in part to territories in Europe that came under Napoleon's sway, and also to other places (including some states of South America). The Napoleonic code still forms the basis of French law, and while its composition is rooted in conceptions inherited from the pre-revolutionary period, in *Roman law, and in doctrines of *natural law, it remains one of the most complete and masterly systems of *statute law in existence. The primary source of the law is *legislation, and reliance on *common law, *custom and the doctrine of *precedent is kept to a minimum. Decisions are not binding precedents, but rather examples of judicial interpretation of the requisite statute. (However, there is intellectual pressure to attempt to achieve consistency between successive interpretations, and this leads to an enhanced role of *jurisprudence and academic commentary in determining the interpretation of the codes.) There are a few overriding principles, corresponding to ideas of *equity and public order, which may be consulted in case of gaps in the law, but their invocation is exceptional, and equity, for example, does not play the constitutive law-making role that it has played in Anglo-American law (*see* *trust).

The supreme court in France is the Cour de Cassation, to which appeal lies in law only, and it is composed of a first president, four presidents, 60 judges, a procurer-general and advocates-general: this type of supreme court is the model for Napoleonic systems of adjudication, and sits as a kind of permanent intellectual commentator on the statutes.

narodnik

Russian: *narod*, common people. A follower of Narodnism, a socialist movement which arose in the 1870s in Russia. According to the narodniks capitalism arises here and there by chance, is not a necessary stage of development, and might never develop in Russia. If revolution is possible, then it is equally possible in the form of a peasants' revolt, although this could succeed only if organized by leaders with charismatic force. However, revolution is not necessary, since constitutional reform, *decentralization and *redistribution might suffice to remove existing evils.

nation

A term often used rather vaguely to mean any *sovereign state with political *autonomy and settled *territory. That usage represents a confusion between *country and *nation state. The definition given here is not political but social:

A nation consists of a people, sharing a common language (or dialects of a common language), with common customs and traditions, which may have become sufficiently conscious to take on the aspect of *law, and who recognize common interests and a common need for a single *sovereign. (The idea is that there is an *explanatory* unity among all the things mentioned.)

In this sense Czechoslovakia, for example, consisted of two nations within the *jurisdiction of a single state, a fact recognized in Czechoslovak law, while the Germans were, between 1945 and 1989, a single nation formed into two states. (The UK is a single state, but probably at least two, possibly four, nations, although here the decline of Celtic languages makes the matter difficult to decide.) Some argue that a further ingredient in nationhood is national *identity, in the form of a sentiment of unity – for, which *see* *nationalism.

One of the most interesting questions concerning the nation is the role of *territory in fixing national identity. A nation can exist without territory of its own, as the Jews existed following the diaspora. And even before that catastrophe the Jews tended to regard their territory as a recent gift – a 'promised land' – and themselves as more often 'strangers and sojourners' in the place where they might be. History presents other examples of *nomads with aspirations towards sovereignty and no territorial jurisdiction over which it may be exercised: certain of the tribes of North America, for example, and the Mongol

hordes which swept the plains of Eastern Europe. Modern definitions of nation and nationality often incorporate a reference to territory, even making this central to the idea. This is appropriate only if we think of the nation in political terms, as a community organized according to the needs of a sovereign jurisdiction, and only if we think of jurisdiction as defined by territory, rather than, for example, religious affiliation. (*See* *millet system.*) In fact, the concept of the nation has been used by groups who wish to lay claim to a territory and to justify their occupation of it – the Jews being an evident example. It would be self-defeating for such a group to define itself in terms of the territory claimed, which would make true by definition a proposition which it wishes to make true by historical right.

Nation of Islam

A movement founded by W.D. Fard (a British citizen of mixed Jamaican and English descent) in Detroit in the 1930s, which promised a new and redemptive way of life to American blacks. The bizarre beliefs of the Nation of Islam have some elements of Sunni Islam, though the emphasis is on the dignity and rights of the black man in the American context, and the actual theology has little that an orthodox Muslim would endorse. The movement has exhorted blacks to develop their own institutions, their own rules and their own businesses, and above all to lift their heads high in the presence of whites. It supports a strict code of sexual ethics, has taken a strong stand against illegitimacy, prostitution, drug abuse and *welfare dependency, and exhorts its members to dress respectably and to be in everything aware of their dignity and the threats to it. The movement was badly shaken in the early 1960s by the split between its formal leader, Elijah

Muhammad, and the charismatic Malcolm X, prior to the latter's assassination by a Black Muslim in 1965. It is now led by Louis Farrakhan who, despite frequent explosions of apparent *anti-semitism, has won support for his civic initiatives.

nation-state

A state organized for the government of a *nation (or perhaps of two or more closely related nations), whose territory is determined by national boundaries, and whose law is determined, at least in part, by national customs and expectations. The nation-state is often compared and contrasted with the Greek *polis*, or city-state, and its emergence from the various international jurisdictions of Europe has been regarded as one of the major facts of modern political history. For the theory of the nation-state, *see* *nationalism.

national bolshevism

An attempt, begun in Germany by Karl Radek in 1919, to found a doctrine which would reconcile the seemingly incompatible outlooks of *bolshevism and *nationalism, in order to create a truly German revolution, and resist both the Western alliance and bolshevik Russia. The movement did not survive the rise of *national socialism, despite a certain similarity of rhetoric.

national debt

The total outstanding debts of the central government. How one calculates the national debt depends upon which public bodies are regarded as liabilities of central government. For example, should one include or not include nationalized industries? Local authorities? And so on. The largest item of all in the UK national debt is government securities, for loans received from private individuals. These provide a maximum security

investment, since no enterprise within a state is less likely to default than the state itself. Thus, by holding government securities individuals can obtain a safe return in money, if not in real terms, and banks can improve their own security, while, through buying and selling securities, the government can meet its financial requirements and exercise a convenient form of influence over the *money supply.

national health

The English Poor Relief Act 1601 was the first of a long series of statutory provisions governing the *health and social *welfare of the poorer subjects of the Crown, which led to the creation of a ministry of health in 1914. The process culminated in the founding, in 1948, of the National Health Service (NHS), by the then Labour government, thus providing the name by which this kind of welfare legislation is known in the UK, and also reinforcing, in the public consciousness, the connection between welfare provision and the *labour movement. (However the details of the NHS had been worked out by a Conservative politician, Sir William Beveridge, during the war, and were understood at the time as a cross-party commitment: *see* *social security.) The NHS aims to provide free medical treatment of an acceptable standard to every citizen, financed through taxation. Although the subsequent disputes over 'national health' focused tempestuous feelings, among those who regarded this as the most important achievement of modern socialism, and those who attacked it as a monstrous pile of inefficiencies, the debate has simmered down, and the health service is accepted as a legitimate, although increasingly expensive, part of government. Recent attempts to reform the NHS, by introducing competition between providers, private insurance and local hospital trusts, seem not to have cured its basic inefficiencies, and wholesale *privatization is still discussed as a viable option. (For the arguments, *see* *health.)

national income

The money measure of the total flow of goods and services produced in the economy of a state over a given period. (*See* *gross domestic product, *gross national product.) The national income can be calculated through the total of incomes received in the state, through the total expenditure of all individuals and institutions (including investment), or through the total price of all goods and services sold, net of tax, subsidies, etc. In principle the three measurements should give the same result, but technicalities of estimation and measurement mean that they do not do so exactly in practice.

National income is a measure of the flourishing of an economy, but not necessarily of the economic well-being of those contained within it, since that also depends upon how the income is distributed. A high *per capita* national income may in fact exist alongside a very low real income in the hands of the majority.

national interest

Something is in the national interest if it helps the *nation to survive, or to flourish in the way that nations flourish. Thus national *interests are really national *needs. But what is a nation, and how do nations flourish? The question is not a quibble, since the term 'nation' is used ambiguously, denoting *either* the *state, *or* *civil society, *or* both (on the assumption that they have the kind of unity canvassed by advocates of the *nation-state). A *despotic state is one that flourishes at the *expense* of civil society, so that if the national interest means the interest of such a state, there may be every

reason for the members of society to act against it. If, however, it means the interest of society, then in this case the state itself is not in the national interest. This ambiguity is clear enough in times of peace, where the state may be opposed by its subjects without any consciousness of *treason; it is far less clear in times of war, when the state provides the necessary means to the society's survival, and where the interests of the two, however briefly, coincide.

It is characteristic of traditional monarchy to attempt to personify the national interest in the monarch, by making him head of the armed forces, negotiator of all treaties, and symbolic substitute for the people in every act where their collective well-being is at stake. This idea of the king as 'father to his subjects' is one that was also borrowed by Stalin to considerable effect. (*See* *raison d'état.*)

national liberation

Literally, the freeing of a nation from a foreign power, but now also used to denote the *creation* of a nation by force from within, perhaps in defiance of some ruling élite which thrives on regional divisions. The liberation movements in Africa did not always aim to free nations from subjection, but often to break down institutions thought to be *neo-colonial, so as to remake the state as a nation, obedient to local customs and identity.

national socialism

Political movement founded in Germany in 1919, and subsequently led to power by Hitler. Theoretically national socialism was a mixture. As its name implies, it presented itself at first as a *nationalist answer to *international socialism, and appealed to those who could not envisage any resurgence of government after the débâcle of the First World War except along socialist and nationalist lines. However, it was from the beginning combined with *racist doctrines and military ambitions, which reflected both the outlook of the peculiar leaders of the party and also the underlying ideology. Part of the nationalist idea consisted in a belief in *Lebensraum* or 'living space' (*see* *geopolitics), and in a 'master race', or ruling people with a right to expand into that space, expelling those inferior peoples who stood in their way. There thus resurged the idea of the *Volksstaat*, a state in which there would be no distinction between political institutions and natural human relations, so that all political activity would bear immediately on society, and all social activity bear immediately on the state. In practice this meant the emergence of the one-party state (*see* *party), with the ruling party devoted to ensuring maximum social unity; this in turn led to *totalitarian government. The socialist element survived largely in the form of commitment to extensive *welfare programmes and a *mixed economy, together with hostility towards the historical *ruling class, whose rule was to be replaced by that of the *leader (*see* *Führerprinzip). The survival of some forms of private ownership, the adoption of virulent *anti-semitism, and hostility to the *labour movement and to the left generally, serve to distinguish Hitler's transformation of national socialism from Stalin's, in other ways comparable, transformation of its international counterpart.

Like Stalin, Hitler was fascinated by *eugenics, and influenced by the propaganda of *Sanger and others into believing that the genetic endowment of a nation is a prime concern of politics. Hence his anti-semitism led inexorably to the *holocaust. The same eugenic reasoning that prompted his hostility to the Jews prompted an equal aversion to

Gypsies and homosexuals, who were also victims of mass murder.

The name 'Nazi' is formed from the abbreviation for 'National Socialist German Workers Party'. *See also* *fascism.

nationalism

1. The sentiment and ideology of attachment to a *nation and to its interest.

2. The theory that a state (perhaps every state) should be founded in a nation, and that a nation should be constituted as a state. Hence, the attempt to uphold national *identity through political action. National identity is something more than nationhood: it involves, not only the territorial integrity, common language, custom and culture noted above as essential to the idea of a *nation, but also *consciousness* of these, as determining distinct rights and duties. This consciousness is held to render intelligible and to justify the habits of association among neighbours. (In its extreme form nationalism might involve the emergence of an *ethnocentric or even *racist ideology.)

Nationalism has often been thought to be a political reaction to the Napoleonic conquest of Europe, and to the break-up over the centuries of the Empire in Central Europe. However, that is misleading, if it is meant to imply, e.g., that the ideology of national self-determination neither preceded Napoleon in Europe, nor occurred independently elsewhere. It is more plausible to say that there emerged from the Napoleonic attempts at European government an association of nationalism and legal and political ideals of the *nation-state. These ideals attempt to find the ingredients of *political obligation and political *identity in *allegiances which are in some sense less than wholly political – matters of geographical, cultural and ethnic association. The motive is to find some binding force between people that is stronger than any revocable agreement to be governed, wider than any merely personal affection, and sufficiently public to lend itself to the foundation of political *institutions and laws. (*See* *pre-political order.*)

Some oppose nationalism to *patriotism. Any number of contrasts might be intended; for example, that between a sentiment of attachment (patriotism), and an ideology of national superiority (nationalism); or that between a respect for political institutions and laws (patriotism), and an attachment to race, language and custom (nationalism). Modern nationalism is often decried, on account, e.g., of its attempt to found political obligation in purely *social* allegiances, or its alleged irrationalism, or its opposition to *universalist doctrines, or its nascent belligerence or *xenophobia. Patriotism might then be proposed as a beneficent alternative, a sentiment which fills the gap between obligations incurred and obedience required, without having recourse to a bellicose fiction of national integrity. However, both 'nationalism' and 'patriotism' are used loosely, and, as defined in this dictionary, they are clearly compatible.

The defence of a politics of national identity is part of the legacy of Central European *romanticism, and found early expression in the writings of *Herder and *Fichte. In the UK nationalism is confined to the Celtic fringes, where, it has been associated with movements for *home rule in Ireland, Scotland and – to some extent – Wales. English nationalism is virtually unknown, at least under that description. The same could be said of American nationalism, although the US has defined itself successfully as a nation, has

attached itself firmly to a cherished territory, and generated the strongest form of contemporary patriotism.

Perhaps the greatest rise in nationalism in recent years has been in *postcommunist Europe – especially in the provinces of the former Yugoslavia and the republics of the former USSR. The emergence of nationalist *movements in these places is commonly attributed to one or other or both of two causes: first, the existence of ethnic, religious and social conflicts which the communist system had suppressed but not resolved, and which have suddenly come to the surface; second, the need to find grounds for the *legitimacy of a new social and political order without relying on the discredited search for a unifying *ideology. Perhaps the matter can be put in more simple terms: in the communist state, *they* are in charge. After the overthrow of communism, *we* are in charge. But who are *we*? This is the question to which nationalism provides the easiest and the most emotive answer.

nationalization

The acquisition by the state of property previously held by private persons or companies. This is one of the many uses in which 'nation' means 'state', and has no connotations of language, territory or custom. The acquisition by the state is sometimes thought of as a temporary phase in the transfer of property from private into *social ownership (i.e. ownership by society, and not by any political institution). Nationalization may involve *expropriation, or compulsory purchase. The purpose may be overtly political – in order to abolish or reduce private ownership, say – or simply one of economic or social expediency – for example, in order to uphold and keep in existence a network of railways vital to the economy as a whole, but which could not be run at a profit. (*See* *public goods.*) Alternatively, nationalization may be deemed advantageous in order that the state should occupy a dominant position within the economy; or in order to prevent individuals from exploiting those industries which lend themselves to the creation of monopolies (e.g. electricity).

Defenders of the *mixed economy see nationalization in this second light, *socialists often see it in the first. Those who argue for complete *privatization of the economy regard nationalization as the creation of enterprises which are inefficient, subsidized, protected from control by the market and inherently monopolistic.

natural justice

The substantive idea of natural justice has to be distinguished from the procedural idea often referred to in systems of *administrative law.

1. Substantive. 'Natural justice' denotes justice that does not depend on *convention but only on *nature, so as to contain within itself a criterion of validity that is independent of *positive law. This criterion is human nature itself, which supposedly leads us towards natural justice just as reasoning and observation lead us towards scientific truth. Thus it is given to all people to see the injustice of rape, murder and (perhaps) theft, without having to consult a body of law that expressly forbids them. In this sense 'natural justice' simply means 'justice', in its philosophical sense of a set of principles of right that exists independently of human prescriptions.

2. Formal. Those procedures that ensure the minimum standards of justice in *adjudication, whether or not the matter adjudicated involves natural justice in sense 1. The two standard principles accepted are that no person shall be judge in his own cause (*nemo judex in parte sua*), and

that each side shall be heard and no one condemned unheard (*audi alteram partem*) – two principles that come down from *Roman Law, and from *Augustine. The first requires a judge to be disinterested (e.g. not to have a financial interest in the result, or a motive for seeking a criminal conviction); the second requires that the person judged be given adequate opportunity to prepare and deliver his case. Neither *show trials nor revolutionary tribunals adhere, or can adhere, to those principles. The violation of natural justice is a fundamental ground of appeal, especially in UK administrative law.

natural law

Natural law and natural rights are those recognized by *natural justice, and the attempt to uphold them is the fundamental aim of any theory of *justice that is not merely sceptical of the whole idea.

Natural law, if it exists, is a system of law binding on people by virtue of their nature alone, and independently of all convention or *positive law. (*See* *nature and convention.*) The usual attribute of human nature that is chosen as the basis for this law is reason, or *rationality. It is because we are rational beings that we recognize natural law, and it is because we recognize it that it binds us. (Thus animals without reason are not bound by natural law, and the lion who eats his prey does no injustice.)

*Roman law sought for a body of principles – the *jus gentium* – that would apply to all peoples over which the Roman law was required to exert jurisdiction, and which would therefore be independent of all customary law, and of the specific rights reserved for citizens of Rome. As the *jus gentium* developed theorists sought for an intellectual basis, and therefore turned their attention to *jus naturale*, natural law, relying on theories of justice expounded by Greek (and especially *Stoic) philosophers. The *jus naturale* came to function as a standard against which all civil law could be judged, and was elevated by *Cicero into the repository of reflective criticism and justification of positive law. It is, in intention, a résumé of all those truths about justice that have universal application.

There are many theories of natural law mentioned throughout this dictionary, but it is important to distinguish two fundamental kinds. The medievals often attempted to derive natural law from a higher law (the divine law), which would express the will of God (*see* *Aquinas), while it is a characteristic of post-Renaissance thought (beginning with *Grotius and culminating in *Kant) to think that this reference to divine law is unsatisfactory, since it reduces natural law to positive law (i.e. natural law becomes the special case of a positive law laid down not by men but by God). Kant went further, and said that the reference to God's will is pernicious, since it absolves us from the responsibilities contained in the idea of an objective justice to which God himself must by his nature conform. The two kinds of theory are therefore quite different, not only in their theological claims, but also in the basis that they offer for natural law.

Theories of natural law have often been used to prescribe *natural rights, i.e. principles which tell us, without reference to custom or institutions, how human beings ought to be treated.

natural light

A name given by *Descartes to the faculty of reason, whereby we perceive the immediate and certain truth of ideas. The phrase 'it is manifest to the natural light' is another way of expressing the view that a truth or maxim is *a priori*, or shown valid by reasoning alone. Many seventeenth- and eighteenth-century theorists of *natural law appealed to this 'natural light' as the ultimate source of their theories.

natural rights

Rights which belong to all human beings by nature, and independent of *positive law. The theory of natural rights, recast in the rhetoric of *human rights, is an important tenet of modern liberalism, even though described by one liberal theorist, *Bentham, as 'nonsense on stilts'. It is necessary to distinguish four questions: Are there natural rights? *Which* rights are natural and how do you know? Under what conditions will people recognize or believe in them? Under what conditions will people uphold them?

In response to the third question, some legal *realists argue that natural rights are recognized only where there is legal procedure that conforms to *natural justice, and are, as it were, the psychological after-image of this procedure. The procedure seems to enshrine rights which transcend those merely legal rights that it adjudicates. Conversely, the attempt to secure recognition of natural rights in those states which have no *rule of law conforming to natural justice is a vain one.

Many philosophers have tried to give positive answers to the first question based on a theory of *natural law (notable examples being *Hobbes, *Locke and *Kant). Recently the emphasis on procedural ideas of justice has been significant. If there are to be *any* rights, it is sometimes said, there must be a legal procedure whereby to uphold them; so that there cannot be any positive rights at all, unless there is *adjudication. Hence, in this sense, there are either no rights at all, or else a universal right to adjudication in order to determine rights; hence a natural right to adjudication. This is one case of a popular modern form of argument, which has as its conclusion 'if there are any rights, then there is *this* one . . .', an argument which bears the mark of a procedural idea of justice. (*See* *justice.)

By contrast most traditional views have given detailed systems of natural rights, such as were offered by Locke in defence of life, limb, liberty, and property. Locke went on to suggest that at least some of these rights are *inalienable* – notably the right to life. Otherwise it would seem possible for someone to argue that, under the *social contract constitutive of some particular state, all citizens had forsworn that right, thus permitting their wholesale slaughter. If this possibility were allowed, then the doctrine of natural rights would no longer perform its desired function of providing a court of appeal in which the justice of every constitution and every law might be tried. Some have seen here a deficiency in the language of rights, and preferred to return to ideas of natural law. A right, they argue, is always alienable by agreement, but a law may still persist, imposing an independent obligation on the other party. Thus, whether or not I forswear my right to life, there will always be an obligation that binds you not to kill me.

Among sceptics it is necessary to distinguish those who dismiss the idea of natural rights in its entirety from those who, while thinking it to have no objective basis, yet find that it is part of human nature to believe in it, so that the idea that there are natural rights remains as an immovable illusion, which must therefore condition all political decision-making designed to govern people suffering from that

illusion. This sophisticated idea may go on to incorporate 'natural' rights into a system of law, even though motivated in doing so purely by *Realpolitik*. A sceptical observer of the postmodern world might also say that natural rights (in the form of human rights) have become a kind of *noble lie, and that all politicians must claim to respect this lie, just as anyone wishing to rule over a Muslim country must claim to acknowledge the divine origin of the Koran.

naturalism

Ambiguous term with at least the following meanings:

(i) The theory that human beings are part of the natural world and are to be understood and explained in terms of laws which govern nature as a whole.

(ii) The theory that laws derive their validity from a body of *natural law: legal naturalism.

(iii) The theory that moral judgements derive their validity from human nature: ethical naturalism, sense 1. (Typified by *Hume.)

(iv) The theory that moral predicates like 'good' and 'ought' denote 'natural' properties, i.e. properties that can be discerned by the ordinary methods of perception and inference: ethical naturalism, sense 2. (Defined by G.E. Moore, *Principle Ethica*, 1902, in the course of an attempt to refute it.)

(v) The presentation of human life as it is and unadorned, in literature, painting, poetry or drama – as in the novels of Zola.

naturalization

The acquisition of citizenship on the part of someone who had previously been an *alien.

nature and convention

The ancient contrast between nature and convention (Greek *phusis* and *nomos*) was elevated into a principle in the discussion of moral, political and social problems by the *sophists, and through them influenced Greek and Roman philosophy and law. As defined in this work, conventions include all regular practices which issue in intentional action, and which may vary from place to place and time to time. Conventions indicate laws that people happen to obey, rather than those laws which they *must* obey by nature. Unfortunately that 'must' is ambiguous: it may indicate the necessity to act according to the laws which explain our actions, or according to the laws which justify them. What we *must* do in the second sense, we need not do in the first. For the second 'must' indicates moral obligation, the first scientific necessity – and the distinction is enshrined in the double sense of '*natural law', as denoting either the laws which explain things, or the laws which tell us what is right. If the two sets of law coincided, then there would be no need for the second: people would be naturally good.

Nazism

See *national socialism.

Nechayev, Sergei Gennadevitch (1847–82)

Russian anarchist and terrorist; *see* *nihilism.

needs

Needs form a special class of *interests. I have an interest in anything that I would, on rational consideration, desire, but not every such thing is necessary to me. I need only that without which I would cease to exist or cease to flourish in accordance with the norms of my nature (*see* *normality). This definition needs to be extended slightly, in order to cope with artificial needs, i.e. needs that arise because human nature is artificially

changed, and with 'relative' needs, i.e. needs which a normal human being may have in a certain context (e.g. the need of a wounded man for treatment), as opposed to the absolute needs which stem directly from common human nature.

It is plausible to hold that I always have greater reason to pursue what I need rather than what I merely desire, even though the desire in the second case is far stronger than the desire in the first. (*See* *rational, for some of the difficulties caused by this fact for mathematical models of decision-making.) Thus someone may need to abstain from drinking and yet desire to drink far more than to abstain.

negotiation

A means for settling disputes, whereby each party declares what he desires, and attempts to obtain as much of it as possible by making concessions to the other side, or by displaying his purposes. Negotiation is characteristically the first step in international disputes, and made obligatory by the UN Charter, prior to any invocation of the jurisdiction of the Security Council. Likewise, in industrial disputes, negotiation is customarily regarded as the first step, and other measures are uncalled for until negotiation has broken down.

négritude

A term adopted by French-educated black intellectuals in Africa and the Caribbean, and current since the 1930s, used to denote a sense of common Negro *identity. The Negro is a distinct social and political being, with needs and emotions that are not necessarily catered for by the constitutional governments invented by the white man; he stands in need of a self-consciousness of his own devising, that will dignify his separateness, and generate institutions adapted to his needs. *Négritude* denotes a common inheritance, and perhaps a common destiny, among blacks, which would be sufficient, if respected, to unite them all against *colonialism and similar forms of exploitation. Its principal elements are nostalgia for traditional African society, and elevation of emotion, intuition and spontaneous social interaction over the rationalistic *hellenism of the white man's forms of government. Its principal exponents have been L.-S. Senghor and Aimé Cesaire.

neo-classical economics

Two schools of economic thought have been described as 'neo-classical', and there seems to be no agreement among economists as to which is correctly so-called:

1. The school which emerged after 1870 and which became dominant by the end of the nineteenth century, its main original theorists being *Jevons, Menger (*see* *Austrian school), Marshall, and particularly Léon Walras. Such economists were marked by their strong leaning towards *microeconomics, and the study of independent decisions made by many households and firms, in competitive market conditions. They analysed the *equilibrium conditions of markets, and attempted to explain *prices, quantities and income distribution; one of the major instruments used in this explanation was the theory of *marginal utility, the principle of diminishing utility being supposed to apply to the satisfaction of each particular desire. Members of this school tended to exaggerate their differences from their predecessors, although Alfred Marshall's influential version of neo-classical theory tended strongly to emphasize continuity. They stressed the scientific claims of economics, although some have suggested that this stress too is exaggerated, and that the neo-classical economists were

significantly less concerned with empirical evidence than were *Smith or *Ricardo. The theory was concerned with the elaborating of *ideal types, such as *perfect competition, and with giving mathematical models appropriate to the behaviour of ideally rational beings.

2. The school of economists which emerged after the Second World War in opposition to *Keynesianism and the *Cambridge school, which, while sharing many of the preoccupations of 1., has dispensed with the theory of marginal utility, and *marginalism generally, emphasizing consumer *preference as the fundamental factor in the explanation of economic activity, and the main determinant of value.

Both 1. and 2. have been variously criticized by *institutionalists, *Marxians, *Keynesians and others; in either case the term 'neo-classical' seems to indicate the similarity of their overall perspective to that of the classical economists, and an emphasis on competitive markets and equilibrium conditions, and on the general principles and operations of a liberal economy.

neo-conservatism

1. The kind of intellectual conservatism which arose in the US, partly in reaction to the social and political movements of the 1960s, and partly in support of US foreign policy during the *cold war. The leading neo-conservatives were urban intellectuals, academics and publicists, many of them converts from *social democracy, who had been disturbed by what they saw as the immanent breakdown of American society, as a result of sexual liberation, *multiculturalism, *political correctness and the *dependency culture. Prominent among them were writers associated with *Commentary* (under the editorship of Norman Podhoretz) and *The Public Interest*

neo-liberalism

(under the editorship of Irving Kristol).
Gertrude Himmelfarb, wife of Irving
Kristol, has, in her historical scholarship, mounted a sustained defence not
only of American culture, but also of
Western civilization in general. Their
son, Bill Kristol, was one of the major
architects of the Republican Party's
successful campaign during the 1994
congressional elections.

2. Growing from the original neo-
conservative position there has been a
movement in the world of politics, to
put into practice certain principles and
aspirations arising from the original
neo-conservative debates. Some
members of this movement have
obtained prominent positions in
government and administration in the
US, so that considerable attention has
been focused on their philosophy,
which does not always coincide with
neo-conservatism in sense 1. The
ruling idea is that American society
owes its success to its democratic tradition, and its respect for individual freedom. Threats to America come from
people who envy this success and do
not possess the institutions and
customs that enable them to emulate
it. The answer is not to contain them,
as in the past, within their borders. The
answer is to change the regimes that
foster them: to spread democratic institutions and free economies wherever
we can, so that the whole world can
enjoy the privileges that are presently
enjoyed in America. The Iraq war has
inevitably focused attention, much of
it hostile, on that position. Some of the
hostility comes from more traditional
conservatives (sometimes described as
'paleo-conservatives'), who defend an
*isolationist foreign policy, and a more
inward-looking and sceptical approach
to the democratic inheritance.

neo-liberalism
The return to the principles of classical
*liberalism. In particular, the defence

of the *free economy, *free trade, and
small government. Neo-liberals repudiate the quasi-socialist attitudes that
are typically described as liberal in the
American media, and advocate a
renewal of the *enterprise culture, and
a pursuit of market solutions to social
and political problems.

neo-Marxism
A term denoting various currents in
twentieth-century *Marxism – perhaps
starting with the work of *Lukács, and
continuing in the *Frankfurt school.
These currents diverge from traditional Marxism in emphasizing, not
*historical materialism, but the
description of consciousness, as the
central component in Marx's social
analysis. Some neo-Marxists find
inspiration in the elements in Marx
that derive directly from *Hegel,
emphasizing, for example, the analysis
of *alienation, the concept of the
*dialectic, the supposed movement of
history towards a *utopian ideal.
Others, in reaction, try to detach Marx
from Hegel, uniting his thought,
perhaps, with *existentialism (*see*
*Sartre), or with some kind of *struc-
turalism (*see* *Althusser).

neo-mercantilism
Term put about by the economist
Harry Johnson, which denotes modern
theories designed to justify the protection of home markets, by controlling
imports or subsidizing exports. The
term relates to the *mercantilism criticized in the name of *free trade by
*Smith, and is used to describe theories
which gained vogue in the 1930s,
during the Depression, and which were
revived in the 1970s and 1980s by
some *Keynesian economists of the
*Cambridge school. *See* *protectionism.

neutralism
Not the declaration of neutrality, but
rather the practice of showing an

intention to remain neutral in any eventual conflict, and to treat the parties to that conflict with total impartiality. It was practised before 1939 by the Belgian and Nordic states, and subsequently, especially by Third World countries who feared domination by either the Western or the Soviet bloc, and who were determined not to be drawn into the conflict between them. Now, although the concept of 'neutralism' is still used to describe this attitude, it was for a while replaced by that of *non-alignment, held to be a kind of 'positive neutrality', reminiscent of the 'armed neutrality' of eighteenth-century Russia.

neutrality
The position of a state that is not party to a war, which stands apart from it, and which treats each side impartially. It was fully recognized in international law only in the eighteenth century, but since then certain states have used the idea assertively in times of war, to show their determination not to be involved in it, as in the 'armed neutrality' of Russia, Sweden and Denmark in 1780. Under the UN Charter no member of the UN can remain neutral in a war in which the Security Council has called upon it to take action against a state guilty of aggression; otherwise a state is presumed to be neutral unless it declares by some act or word that it supports one side or another. A state may make a declaration of neutrality which binds it to help either side in ways specified in international law. The UN Charter illustrates a general point of significance, namely, that there is a tension between the idea of neutrality and that of *just war.

New Age
Term adopted during the 1980s to describe the social and spiritual condition of a world in which the old

religions have lost their credibility, in which authority of every kind is on the wane and in which nevertheless young people have not lost their need for *values or for spiritual sustenance. There are New Age movements, New Age religions, and New Age forms of art and literature. Their common features are these: easy-going attitudes to personal relations and sexual morality; a gentle toleration of weakness and aimlessness; a leaning towards *green politics and the defence of *animals; a genuine puzzlement over the nature and value of *civilization and a neo-pagan mysticism, sometimes rationalized in terms of the *Gaia hypothesis.

new class
Term coined by M. Djilas to denote the ruling élite formed through the Communist Party in those states in which it asserted supreme control in accordance with the principles of *democratic centralism. Djilas argued that, through the total permeation of all institutions by the Communist Party, the restrictions on membership and the advantages that accrue to membership a kind of self-perpetuating power structure asserts itself that has all the characteristics associated with a *ruling class (*The New Class*, 1957). Whether it is right to speak of a class in this context could be doubted: for the qualification for membership is radically different from anything historically encountered as definitive of class membership. (*See* *class, *élite, *status.) Djilas argued, however, that the new class had all the characteristics of earlier ruling classes, together with novel features of its own, in particular it comes to power not 'to complete a new economic order, but to establish its own and, in so doing, to establish its power over society'. The class is not identical with the Communist Party, but established through it; eventually, however, it

becomes stronger than the party, whose unity of belief and iron discipline it has exploited, and the party cannot control it. At the same time it is the upsurge of this new class that explained the unity and discipline of the party, and the party's rise to power. The Russian *nomenklatura seems also to correspond to the group that Djilas had in mind. The experience of *post-communist Europe suggests that the new class is able to retain its power even after the collapse of the communist system and the abolition or criminalization of the Communist Party.

New Deal

Expression introduced in President Roosevelt's nomination speech of 1932, and now used to describe the policies initiated during Roosevelt's first administration, 1933–37, when, in order to counteract the effects of the Depression, far-reaching measures of government intervention in the economy were introduced, including encouragement of private industry, together with state-financed industries and welfare legislation. The New Deal involved a radical departure from the previous US fiscal policy, of trying to secure a balanced budget, and had wide-ranging effects which have been both praised and criticized in subsequent discussions. It introduced the first substantial element of a *mixed economy into the US, together with expectations associated with welfare legislation. The New Deal is frequently criticized by *neo-conservatives as involving fundamental breaches of the spirit of the US Constitution, and setting America on the path towards the *dependency culture.

new diplomacy

The methods of 'open' as opposed to 'secret' diplomacy advocated and followed during the aftermath of the First World War, and presaged in President Wilson's 'Fourteen Points', in which he advocated 'open covenants, openly arrived at'.

New Labour

In the aftermath of *Thatcherism and three successive electoral defeats the UK Labour Party embarked during the early 1990s, on a series of internal reforms, led by a hitherto little-known faction within the Parliamentary party, whose most influential members were Gordon Brown and Tony Blair. Crucial aspects of the Old Labour outlook were abandoned or side-lined – including the notorious Clause 4 of the party constitution, demanding *social ownership of the means of production, together with the long-standing subservience to the Trades Union Congress. The party set out to present itself to the electorate as in harmony with the social and economic aspirations of ordinary voters; it endorsed the free economy and the trade-union reforms introduced by Margaret Thatcher; it distanced itself from the old agenda of class war and subversion; and it strove to appear pragmatic and compromising in all the areas where the old Labour Party had appeared dogmatic and out of touch. Through adroit use of public relations and *spin, it has succeeded in replacing the Conservative Party as 'the natural party of government', despite having embarked, in office, on radical constitutional reforms which have effectively balkanized the kingdom and left it without an effective second legislative chamber, and despite retaining much of the egalitarian outlook of Old Labour. New Labour has succeeded in focusing the class resentments of its old constituents on a single issue – that of *hunting – and in taking the country to war in Iraq as an affirmation of the Anglo-American alliance, something that would have been inconceivable under the Old Labour dispensation. It has sought to play an active role in the EU, and to present itself as a forward-looking, even 'cool' voice in British politics. Its domestic policies are informed by a systematic *political correctness, while its foreign policies seem to be based on *realism. Whether there is a consistent philosophical position behind New Labour may well be doubted. But it is undeniable that it has killed off socialism in the UK far more effectively than Thatcher did, and that little remains of its socialist legacy apart from the tendency to ban everything that its members dislike – a tendency that has led to the creation of over 900 new criminal offences since New Labour came to power.

New Left

Political tendency emerging during the 1950s, associated with an increasing disenchantment with Soviet communism and its offshoots. It led to the foundation, in the UK, of the *New Left Review*, which became one of the most important expressions of intellectual opinion on the *left. The New Left existed in a milder version in the US, and flourished in France, being grafted on to the native leftwing philosophies of *Sartre and other thinkers who had been shaped by the Second World War, to become a nationwide political movement of the 1960s, culminating in the events of May 1968. In so far as there is any single consistent position that can be ascribed to the New Left, it consists in a belief in the *democratization of all institutions, so as to eliminate every focus of established power. This belief naturally generated in support of itself many critical analyses of existing institutions and power structures, together with a proliferation of theories with which to describe and condemn them: it is partly due to the New Left that this dictionary is, if not necessary, at least possible. From this

critical analysis – which, while always left-wing in inspiration, did not necessarily involve the adoption of any specific Marxist theory (such as *historical materialism) – there arose an important school of English cultural critics and historians, among whom perhaps the most significant have been Raymond Williams, Perry Anderson and E.P. Thompson. This school has done much to develop a Marxist analysis of modern history, emphasizing the component of *class struggle, and attempting to interpret events in a way favourable to left-wing politics.

Critics of the New Left have sometimes objected to a supposed negativity, arguing that its diagnoses of existing power structures – because they accompany only schematic representations of alternatives – serve more as vehicles for *resentment than as serious proposals for a socialist future. Others even try to connect this resentment with the *sentimental anger of the German and Italian urban terrorists who arose from the movements of the 1960s. However, it is not at all clear that there is sufficient system in the opinions of the New Left to warrant those judgements. In the 1990s there emerged into the political arena in Germany several important figures from the New Left movements of 1968, one of whom, Joschka Fischer, became foreign minister. This 'domestication' of the New Left was perhaps more to be expected than its 'rustication' in the Baader-Meinhof gang; but the intellectual origins are probably indistinguishable.

New Right

Expression used to denote the resurgence of conservative and anti-socialist thought in the UK, the US and France which began in the 1970s and came to political prominence under Ronald Reagan and Margaret Thatcher.

There seem to be three distinct currents of thought in the New Right movement, at least as exemplified in the UK and the US, and it is not clear that they are compatible with one another:

(i) Revulsion against socialism as practised, together with an attempt to see the practice already implicit in the theories. A main stimulus for this attempt has come from Central European and Russian refugees from communism (*Milosz, Kolakowski, *Solzhenitsyn and others) who attempted to show that Marxist theories already contain the seeds of *Stalinism, because of their inability to envisage institutions that will be tolerant of *opposition, because of their *messianic fervour and *antinomian assurance that history must vindicate them, and because of their emphasis on historical necessity at the expense of individual choice.

(ii) Renewed attachment (especially in the US) to liberal values, and to libertarian justifications of the capitalist economy, sometimes tempered by an old-fashioned respect for institutions and customs (as in *Hayek), sometimes associated with a respect for the decencies of a *moral majority, sometimes based in a thoroughgoing individualism that comes close to anarchism (as in *Nozick).

(iii) Reaction to the excesses of *left-liberal *enlightenment opinion, in matters of law, morality and social consciousness, perhaps combined with the advocacy of more authoritarian forms of government or at least forms of government more sensitive to traditional values, customs and forms of association. The third current is likely to stand in partial opposition to the second, attempting to replace dogmatic policies with traditional conservative hesitations. It favours respect for institutions, pragmatism, conciliation and manoeuvre, all against a background of respect for the actual condition of civil society.

Examples of this third kind of thinking are to be found in Ian Gilmour, and other theorists of the UK Conservative Party, who acknowledge *Burke as their master. It should be pointed out, however, that the tension between the three positions is already manifest in Burke himself, who converted his reasoned hatred of the French Revolution (condemned on grounds resembling (i)), and his respect for the *free market and its ideology ((ii)), into a rhetoric which emphasized tradition and pragmatic politics as its fundamental ground (as in (iii)). The potential contradiction here provides one of the major objections raised against the New Right – that it seeks to be both conservative and liberal at once. Moreover, it is sometimes criticized for not tackling directly the problems of class and privilege as they are currently presented, and for a certain sentimental picture of tradition that seems to inspire it.

In the US, the New Right has centred on the *neo-conservative movement, with its serious social and political journals such as *Commentary*, *The Public Interest* and *New Criterion*. In the UK the New Right has relied more on newspapers than on weighty journals, although *The Salisbury Review* has made an attempt to reach the same kind of readership as the American neo-conservative publications.

In France and Italy the New Right has been less concerned with tradition and more interested in *libertarian theories of society and in the problems posed by life in a *secularized democracy. Some representatives of the movement (notably Alain de Benoist) have claimed *Nietzsche, *Spengler and *sociobiology as their sources of inspiration, emphasizing the biological need of human beings to assert, aggrandize and expend themselves.

Such thinkers argue against socialism as a form of mass domestication destined to bring about the degeneracy of the species, and against secularization as a *disenchantment of the world, which neutralizes hope and courage and stultifies the impulse to creative action. There has also been a trend within the French New Right – typified by the philosophers Alain Finkielkraut and André Glucksmann and the novelist Michel Houellebecq – to emphasize Enlightenment humanism and its universal values against the apologists for crime, whether socialist, communist, existentialist or Islamist.

New Urbanism

Movement associated with the Luxemburg-born architect Léon Krier (b. 1946) and circles of architects in Italy, the US and Spain, and to a lesser extent in the UK, which calls for a return to classical principles not only in the organization of buildings but in the lay-out of towns and cities, with the street as the principal public space. The New Urbanist movement extols the public spirit that maintained the city as the heart of Western political order, criticizes *suburbanization as unsustainable, and regards the US system of *zoning as responsible for a growing environmental and aesthetic disaster. It lays down 11 principles for humane development: walkability (returning the city to the pedestrian); connectivity; mixed use and diversity; mixed housing (in terms of size and aspect); quality design; restoring the traditional neighbourhood, with the public space at the centre; increasing density; smart transportation; sustainability; quality of life; overcoming zoning. The ideal is the Italian Renaissance city, which has survived and adapted itself in a way that no modern American city based on zoning laws has been able to emulate. There are already over a thousand new urbanist projects in the US, and the movement is part of a growing reaction against the modernist ideas of planning associated with Le Corbusier and the Bauhaus, which many blame for the socially and aesthetically disastrous developments of the 1960s.

Newman, John Henry, Cardinal (1801–90)
English divine and writer; see *cultural conservatism, *tractarianism, *universities.

newspeak

Term introduced by George Orwell, in his *dystopian novel, *1984*, to describe the imaginary language of a totalitarian state, in which words and syntax are remade so that only orthodox thoughts may be expressed by means of them. Orwell was consciously satirizing the language of the bolsheviks, some of whose terms appear in this dictionary (e.g. *agitprop, *Comintern). The word 'newspeak' is now more widely used, in order to describe the peculiar distorted syntax that emerges when people speak and write in conditions of totalitarian or rigidly bureaucratic control. Called 'wooden language' in both French and Russian, it has been analysed by Françoise Thom (*La Langue de bois*, 1987, translated as *Newspeak*, 1989), who emphasizes the following features:

(i) abstraction: it is not individuals which act, but 'forces', 'classes' or 'tendencies' (such as 'deviationism', 'rightism' etc.);

(ii) pan-dynamism: everything is in motion, and all reports of the world concern progress, reaction, revolution, crisis, liquidation etc;

(iii) *manichaeism: the subject matter is divided between good and evil, with 'no middle road';

(iv) the recourse to organic metaphors: the world is seen in terms of growth and decay, corruption and birth;

(v) hyperbole in praising the 'good' and euphemism in describing difficulties;

(vi) the use of emphatic tautologies, as a proof of the rightness of the underlying view of things – e.g. 'The theories of Marx are true because they are correct' (Stalin).

(vii) nominalization: verbs are replaced by nouns, as in the following instance, which illustrates most of the preceding features:

> In the nineteenth century, as a decision and an elucidation of the political conditions which had previously existed, the active mass of humanity divided itself into two groups: conservatives and revolutionaries. (Henri Barbusse, *Stalin*, 1935)

The syntax of newspeak derives from the fact that the criterion against which language is measured is not truth but power, and truth has itself become the servant of power. Newspeak is a system of spells cast over reality in order to silence it.

NGO

Non-Governmental Organization, a term that covers charities, US *non-profit organizations, and organizations devoted to social and political objectives. The NGO is now an important player in national and international politics, and can influence public policy both directly, through lobbying, and indirectly, through publicity campaigns and networking. This raises interesting questions of accountability: to whom is the NGO answerable for its actions, and how is it penalized for non-performance? Moreover, since each NGO has a specific purpose, through which it attracts funds and which defines its cause, it is under no obligation to reconcile its purpose with the many competing purposes that a government must take into account. To many observers, therefore, there is an air of unreality, even irresponsibility, about much NGO activity, especially in controversial fields such as *animal rights and the environment. An NGO devoted to ending the experimentation on animals is under no obligation to consider the impact on medical research; by defining itself through a single issue it can avoid all objections to its cause.

Nicholas of Cusa (1401–64)

Theologian, philosopher and mathematician of German extraction (Cusa = Kues on the Moselle), whose *De Concordantia Catholica* presented a comprehensive programme for the reform of the church and the empire. Nicholas's most important contribution to political thought was his theory of conciliar government, in which he elaborated the idea of the corporate personality of both church and state, and explored the nature of councils in generating a collective purpose and collective decisions. His main interests were in Neoplatonist cosmology and theology, however, and he left it to later thinkers to develop his political ideas.

Nietzsche, Friedrich Wilhelm (1844–1900)

German philosopher, critic and iconoclast, who gave an impassioned defence of *egoism, and who influenced some of the defenders of fascism, through his celebration of ancient values of strength, courage, pride and resolution. Nietzsche attacked first Christianity and all other forms of belief in a transcendent being, and secondly the modern 'secular religions' which had arisen in the place of it, and which had tried to perpetuate religious feeling through worship of a universal human nature.

He identified socialism, humanism, and above all egalitarianism, as principal manifestations of this bowdlerized religion, arguing that all of them display the deep corruption of the modern consciousness, which seeks to hide from the responsibility of existence by taking refuge in a *sentimental vision of universal brotherhood. In *Thus Spake Zarathustra*, 1884, Nietzsche presented his rival morality, arguing that man has only one duty, which is to realize in himself the *Übermensch* (superman, or 'transcended man') who has overcome in himself mere 'human' nature, rejected the 'herd instinct' of common morality, and asserted himself as master of his own experience, justified not in what he shares with others, but in what distinguishes him. Such a being will be disdainful of all attempts to ascribe to him some universal body of rights, and will act so as to rise above the herd which seeks only to bring everything down to its own level, living as it does in a state of permanent *resentment. His aim is not to obey a moral law, but to 'will his own desire as a law for himself'. He will elevate passion above reason, and regard the world with a scepticism that undermines all claims to right and truth that do not stem from himself and from his will to life, joy, and power. The principal disease of the will is not morality as such, but pity, which is the foundation of the 'slave morality' that Nietzsche attributed to Christ. Pity remorselessly seeks out objects over which to rejoice, taking pleasure only in weakness, and cutting off sympathy for the strong, the dominant and the successful – those, in short, who are good, not in the sense of common morality (which contrasts good with evil), but 'good specimens', who exhibit strength, power, and vitality (*Beyond Good and Evil*, 1886).

Nietzsche advocated in those terms a species of 'joyful wisdom' which he thought to be uniquely suitable to people without religious belief. From this standpoint he constructed many brilliant satires of the intellectual and political fashions of his age. His own political vision was almost entirely confined to the critique of *universalism; he left it to others to draw from his philosophical egoism what political conclusions they could. *See also* *postmodernism, *resentment.

nihilism

The belief in nothing, as opposed to the absence of belief. The word has been used in English since at least 1817, but gained currency later on account of the Russian nihilists, modelled upon the character Bazarov, in Turgenev's *Fathers and Sons* (1862). Bazarov, disliked by his creator, nevertheless inspired a generation of Russian radicals, who contrived to be politically active in the cause of nothing. Principal among them was *Nechayev, who collaborated with *Bakunin in writing *The Revolutionary Catechism*, 1869, in which the nihilist hero, a terrorist, without property, identity, morality or attachments, is described. The basic idea was that, since society is founded on lies, and all moral, religious and humanitarian beliefs are just instruments of concealment, all beliefs and values must be torn down and the disposition to hope and worship be eliminated, so that the world could be seen as it really is. For some reason it was thought that things would then be better for the people.

Nihilism, as a state of mind, rather than a doctrine, has often been thought to underlie many modern political philosophies, including *existentialism, some forms of *historical materialism, and even the various kinds of *conservatism which advocate the acceptance of what is, rather than the vain pursuit of what might have been.

nobility
1. A *class, identifiable in various ways, but usually thought to have arisen out of the social and economic position of *lord in *feudalism: i.e. the position of the owner of land, bound by duties towards the sovereign, and with feudal rights over the occupants of his land. In UK law the membership of this class was traditionally marked out by certain legal privileges, such as a title, and an associated *peerage which, until reforms brought in by *New Labour, conferred the political power consequent on membership of the upper chamber of Parliament. Since the office of peer has usually been hereditary (at least since the thirteenth century and until the nineteenth) this legal privilege reinforced the socio-economic position of the nobility as a hereditary class. Outside the UK nobility has been more widely defined, it having been common to recognize grades of nobility short of peerage – such as the *petite noblesse* of France, the little nobility of Russia, and the *szlachta* of Poland. The idea of a nobility does not extend to the description of classes in societies that have not known feudal modes of tenure, and while the nobility might still be referred to in modern Europe, it is always with the implication of feudal or semi-feudal arrangements, either still existing or recently extinguished.
2. A virtue, associated with 1., for a variety of good or bad reasons, one being that the feudal position of lord was traditionally granted by the sovereign in exchange or reward for military service, so that the nobility became responsible for the levying and maintaining of armies, so forming an 'officer class'. Hence its distinct social position tended to become

associated with the virtues proper to that class – e.g. courage and *honour. In addition, because of the *leisure consequent on its economic position, the nobility was able to cultivate refinements of culture, social interaction and display which have become mingled with the military virtues to form an elaborate and ritualized conception of what a nobleman might correctly do.

The connection of sense between 1. and 2. is obvious, as is the fact that they may not go together.

noble lie
See *myth, *Plato.

noble savage
An expression that became common in the eighteenth century, when it was associated with the philosophy of *Rousseau. The virtue of *nobility (sense 2.) being unobtainable in human society, it is necessary to imagine men and women in their pure, pre-social condition, in order to understand their moral capacities. In their savage condition they are higher than all the animals; in their civilized condition lower.

nomads
People who maintain social and even political organization among themselves, while remaining attached to no particular *territory, and owning only movable property, together with rights of pasture, often of a purely customary kind. Certain modern systems of law (notably *Islamic law and *Jewish law) are adapted for nomadic use, since they involve a flexible idea of *jurisdiction (based partly in racial and religious affiliation), and of *municipality.

Theories of the state do not always apply to nomads, since the absence of territorial jurisdiction leaves questions of legal *sovereignty undetermined. Nevertheless some nomadic peoples have developed political institutions, involving, for example, kingship, an aristocracy of tribal chieftains, a common law, and even parliaments and representative government. Modern legal conceptions of sovereignty attach, however, to territory, and such peoples will often find themselves subject to a jurisdiction which is not of their own law, and to *conflicts of law that can be resolved by no court.

Nomenklatura
Russian, a list of names. Under the communist system, privileged positions were reserved for those whose names were on the Communist Party list of approved candidates. To belong to the Nomenklatura it was not necessary to be a member of the Party, though only Party members could rise higher than the junior positions in society. The Nomenklatura in most communist states enjoyed higher salaries, better working and living conditions, and access to the special shops, selling imported or scarce commodities not available elsewhere. They were first in the queue for cars, houses, medical and educational services, and permissions to travel, and formed a particularly rigid upper class, whose privileges were guaranteed by the Party and withheld from the rest of society. The collapse of communism destroyed the class structure of communist society, but it did not prevent the Nomenklatura from using their effective monopoly of social power in order to secure equally high positions in the new arrangements. The term has therefore remained in use. (*See also* *new class.)

non-alignment
The active refusal of a state to align itself with either party to a dispute between superpowers, in particular the former dispute between the Western powers and the Soviet bloc. A conference of non-aligned powers took place (attended by 35 Mediterranean and Afro-Asian powers) in Belgrade in 1961, and the policies there advocated had considerable effect on world politics through the United Nations in the 1960s and 1970s. In all matters where the *cold war impinged upon their interests, however, the non-aligned states, usually under Yugoslav or Cuban influence, were decidedly anti-Western.

non-conformism
The non-conformist churches were formed from congregations within the *Anglican communion who found themselves, under the influence of evangelical and radical protestant ideas, unable to conform to the liturgical and doctrinal practice of the official church, and so gradually broke away from it – at first to form illegal churches of their own, subsequently to enjoy religious liberty as non-conformist churches within the Anglican tradition. The most important examples have been the *Methodist and Baptist churches, as well as the Calvinist church of Scotland and its offshoots.

Non-Government Organization
See *NGO.

non-intervention
Until the mid-nineteenth-century it was widely held that one state has the right to intervene in the affairs of another in order to protect its own citizens, property and rights that may be affected by the second state's inability or incompetence to protect them. Two Argentinians, Carlos Calvo in 1868 and Louis Drago in 1907, maintained that no sovereign state could have this right while still respecting the sovereignty of the other, and Drago's formulation of the idea of

non-intervention was incorporated as Article 1 of the second Hague Convention in 1907.

non-negotiable demands

Demands made during the course of negotiations which, it is implied, must be met if the negotiations are to be accepted, and their outcome *ratified, by the party who makes them. Non-negotiable demands have always been an important part of diplomacy, especially that of the communist states, it being assumed that the best way to advance your interests is to make sure that you negotiate only over those issues that do not really concern you.

The theory of the non-negotiable game has become an important part of *game theory, and points to important differences between the *strategies that are rational where negotiation is possible, and those which should be adopted where negotiation is ruled out.

non-profit organizations

Term of US law to denote institutions run by a board of unpaid trustees, which devote their funds and receipts to causes of general public concern, and which are forbidden by law to make a profit. Donations to non-profit organizations are tax-deductible, and the category is wider than that of charity in English law, permitting involvement in political research and certain kinds of campaigning. Hence there has been a proliferation of non-profit political organizations in the US, often in the form of policy think-tanks, such as the Hudson Institute and the American Enterprise Institute.

non-proliferation

In order to prevent the spread of nuclear weapons to states not subject to the familiar military and political constraints against their use, treaties of non-proliferation have been proposed,

and in 1968 a Nuclear Non-proliferation Treaty was signed by three of the major powers (the US, UK and USSR) who undertook not to transfer the appropriate technology, and by 100 or so minor powers, who undertook not to develop it. Several powers refused to sign (notably China, France, India, Israel and South Africa), on the ground that the treaty discriminates too heavily in favour of existing nuclear powers. The treaty remains open for signature, and although South Africa has since (1991) acceded to it, other powers – notably India, Pakistan, Israel, N. Korea and Iran – have either developed nuclear weapons of their own, or are in the course of doing so.

non-rival consumption

See *public goods.

non-violent resistance

Resistance, especially to the occupation of one's country without the use of *violence. (See also *passive resistance.) The policy was advocated by *Gandhi under the name of *civil disobedience, and can be successful when conducted from below against an unpopular government. However, its success in India is probably not independent of the fact that the British were no longer convinced that the occupation of India was to their advantage. Non-violent resistance has been more or less completely ineffective when conducted against an occupying power that is determined to remain – as in Norway during the Second World War, and in Czechoslovakia in 1968.

norm

An ambiguous term, which can mean either that which is normal, or that which is normative, i.e. required, say, by an ideal, a standard, or a moral code. Biologists would tend to use the term in its first sense, sociologists in its second, although in sociological usage the distinction is extremely difficult to draw, for reasons given below:

1. The idea of the normal. The normal is not the same as the statistical average. All surviving lions may be abnormal (say, because they all suffer from some hereditary disease). Thus the properties of the average lion may not be identical with those of the normal lion. The normal lion is the lion who possesses the properties necessary to the existence, continuance, reproduction and flourishing of his kind: i.e. he is the lion who obeys the laws of leonine nature. The idea of the normal is therefore no more clear than that of a law of nature – the subject of much debate in the philosophy of science, and beyond the scope of this dictionary. It is clear that this already raises special problems for the idea of human normality, since the concept of *human nature (and therefore that of the laws of human nature) remains *essentially contested. According to *Kant, for example, we have two natures, one empirical, governed by the 'laws of nature' as these are applied to all inanimate and organic things, the other 'transcendental', governed by 'laws of reason' which turn out to be norms only in the second sense, of ideals of conduct.

Much debate over the normal response of the normal person is uncertain partly because of deep uncertainties about the 'laws of human nature'. It could be that, while the average person enjoys pornography, the normal person is revolted by it. Until we know the nature and role of moral sentiment in the normal person we cannot determine whether this is true. It could be that the average person desires private property, while the normal person (the person 'restored to himself') does not. And so on. Likewise we speak of normal and abnormal societies, which presents parallel problems concerning the 'laws of social nature'.

2. The idea of the normative. Conduct is normative if imposed by *sanctions. While this covers moral codes and ideals, sociologists also tend to consider other sanctions besides the moral. Thus there are legal norms, customary norms, norms of good behaviour and manners, norms of dress, speech and deportment, all of which may be held to fall outside the domain of morality, at least as commonly understood. A new ambiguity enters the discussion, for the following reason: when a philosopher discusses normative judgements, he is concerned with those that are actually put forward as valid, and the reasoning used to support them. But the judgements that are so defended may not be the judgements that are obeyed. The sociologist is concerned not only with how people represent their codes of conduct, but with the *sanctions* that they apply. The two may not correspond, not because of hypocrisy or self-deception, but because of the intricate way in which social influences are spread. Thus it is quite possible for a sociologist to argue that there is a norm of male dominance in a given society, in which most people sincerely believe that sexual domination is morally wrong. This is because the sociologist recognizes the existence of sanctions beyond those laid down by morality: sanctions of custom, manners, and so on, which may be exerted through many channels, but may never issue in a moral condemnation. Such an observation would be possible only if there is some measure of conformity to the norm, otherwise the existence of *social* sanctions would be in doubt. Hence norms as observed by the sociologist are *also* records of what is normal (sense 1.) within society. Nevertheless, the sociologist's concern is not with what is normal, but with what is normative.

normal

See *norm.

normal profit

To be distinguished from *profit, normal profit is that profit which is just sufficient to induce an *entrepreneur to remain in his present enterprise. Thus it is the amount necessary to cover the cost of the services supplied, disregarding *opportunity costs.

normalization

Used after the Second World War to refer to the re-establishment of friendly relations between states, rulers and peoples. Also a euphemism for the forced resumption of unwanted ties, as in the normalization of Czechoslovakia after 1968, following the intervention of the Soviet army.

normative

See *norm.

North/South divide

It is notorious that many parts of the world seem unable to achieve any level of *development above the bare minimum needed for survival. In an attempt to understand this phenomenon, it used to be common to divide the world into three – the developed world of capitalism, the socialist (or communist) world and the *Third World, which enjoyed the material benefits of neither system. (See *three worlds theory.) The political collapse of the 'second world' and the ending of the *cold war have brought home the inadequacy of that division and led to the search for another language with which to express the vast distinction between rich and poor among the nations of the world. A report under the chairmanship of Willy Brandt, prepared for the use of the *United Nations, appeared in 1980 with the title: *North–South: a Programme for Survival.* This established the 'North/South divide' as the catch phrase in subsequent discussions of aid and development. The report recommended a massive 'transfer of resources from North to South', on the *Keynesian grounds that this would stimulate the Southern economies, permitting eventual 'take-off'.

The positions taken in response to the Brandt report are roughly the following:

(i) Agreement from those of a mild left-liberal persuasion, who either accept the Keynesian argument or believe that the transfer of resources is virtually the only course of action that is both humane and politically feasible.

(ii) Disagreement from the radical *left, which has condemned the Keynesian strategy as an attempt to buy off revolution in the South and so make the markets safe for further exploitation. (This response parallels that of classical Marxism to the legislative reforms that ushered in the era of 'welfare capitalism'.)

(iii) Disagreement from the *New Right, on the grounds that resources transferred to the poorer countries will always pass to the ruling élites and will therefore reward the policies that cause the poverty.

Key figures in the debate have been Immanuel Wallerstein and André Gunder Frank (who take the second position), and P.T. Bauer and Elie Kedourie (who take the third).

Definitions of the North/South divide are seldom forthcoming. Clearly the division is not geographical, since Australia belongs in the North and Mongolia in the South. If the division is simply that between rich and poor, however, the thesis that the North/South divide coincides with a distinction between rich and poor becomes tautological and nothing whatsoever is explained by it. The radical left argues that the poorer nations are poor because they are exploited by the richer – a version, at the international level, of the Marxist theory which holds that the working classes are poor *because* the upper classes exploit them. The credibility of the radical view has declined with the credibility of Marxist analysis, and it is safest to say that the explanation of the North/South divide is now a matter of puzzlement and concern on the radical left. It seems reasonable to suggest, nevertheless, that the rule of law, security of contract, democratic political institutions and a culture of trust between strangers have something to do with the success of private enterprise, and that private enterprise has something to do with the success of the economy as a whole. In which case, we should not be *too* surprised to find that the distinction between rich and poor coincides to a great extent with that between free economies under a rule of law, and economies that are either state-controlled or without a rule of law.

nostalgia

Greek: homesickness. Originally a yearning for home, but now used to mean any longing for an absent (and by implication past) state of affairs, accompanied by an idealization of that state, involving intemperate attention to its supposed virtues, together with a merely schematic representation of its faults. Nostalgia is a form of *sentimentality, and should be understood accordingly. It is normally thought to have the past as its object, and the accusation is often made against conservatives that their respect for what they take to be tradition is no more than nostalgia, i.e. sentimental attachment to something which can be loved with impunity partly because it has vanished, leaving only the memory of its virtues. When this objection comes from Marxists it

is sometimes countered by a *tu quoque* – on the assumption that there is an equivalent of nostalgia which has not the past but the future as its object, and which dwells on a similarly schematized state of being. (The communist future, like heaven, is usually only negatively described, and hence may readily be deprived of its vices.) If this extension of the idea is allowed, then it could be that nostalgia is an ingredient in all political thinking that is based on foregone conclusions.

Nozick, Robert (1938–2002)

US philosopher who, in *Anarchy, State and Utopia*, 1974, sets forth a complex restatement of what many have seen as a *Lockean theory of the state, justice, and private property. Beginning from the individualistic assumption that there is no true political entity other than individuals, and that only individuals have *rights, and relying on a *Kantian view of rights, he presents an influential defence of private property, of *accumulation, and of social and political inequalities, not as things good in themselves, but as things which can be removed only by denying the rights of individuals. He believes that conditions can be laid down for determining when property is justly acquired, and also justly transferred: crudely, the first when it is acquired without denying to anyone else any right or perpetuating any injustice, the second when property passes by voluntary and open transaction between fully knowing and responsible beings. He then attempts to formulate 'justice-preserving' rules of transfer: if property passes justly from *a* to *b* and justly from *b* to *c*, then *c* holds it justly if *a* held it justly. It can then be shown that there may be just holdings of large accumulations, just distributions which are vastly unequal, and so on. Any theory of 'distributive justice', which concentrates not on just transfer, but on the *end state of a distribution, is, Nozick thinks, bound to do violence to our far surer and more philosophically defensible ideas of the just transaction, and so should be rejected as a covert justification of injustice. In this way he argues against many (e.g. socialist) ideas of *redistribution, and in favour of certain kinds of private property.

Nozick's argument is essentially liberal: it proceeds by arguing that everyone should be free to do what he has a right to do, but not to interfere with another's rights. From the same idea Nozick derives a defence of private medicine (*see* *health), arguing that no doctor can be justly compelled to offer his services in accordance with an ideal distribution of medical benefits, and independent of his voluntary agreements. And likewise, for many other received ideas of *social justice. However, Nozick finds cause to uphold, not a traditional conservatism, but rather what he calls the *minimal state, i.e. the least powerful political arrangement compatible with the protection of rights. All political order is a *prima facie* interference with a natural right to pursue one's ends, and – having considered seriously the arguments for *anarchism – Nozick concludes that political order can therefore be justified only if it can also be shown to contribute to upholding individual rights.

In the course of his argument Nozick defends private property, private medicine, private schooling and private welfare services, and a variety of social and economic inequalities – not as good in themselves but as the unavoidable outcomes of the only concept of justice that we really understand: the concept of the 'justice preserving transaction'. It is not states of affairs, distributions or patterns of ownership that are just or unjust, but the human actions that produce them. Once we understand what justice means, in the real circumstances of human action, then we will see that we cannot respect the demands of justice, and also aim at a socialist or redistributive state. Indeed, distributions of power, property and privilege can never be guaranteed, even by the policies that set out expressly to produce them. Distributions arise by an '*invisible hand', and, Nozick argues, it is our failure to take seriously what Adam Smith meant by this phrase that has led us to over-estimate both the ability of politics to change the world, and its ability to respect the rights of individual citizens.

Nozick's arguments reformulate a debate that has long existed between those who think of justice in terms of patterns of distribution, and those who think of it in terms of transaction. His views have been criticized (a) because they do not take into account the difficulties posed by the idea of a 'just original acquisition'; (b) because they are based on an unargued individualism concerning human nature and human rights, which attempts to detach the individual from the history and social arrangement which has formed him; and (c) because Nozick seems not to attend to the many functions that a *state may fulfil besides that of policing the rights of its members. His views have been praised by those who see them as a fresh and challenging presentation of *Smith's defence of the free economy, and as a direct confrontation with the idea of *social justice.

nuclear family
See *family.

O **akeshott,** Michael (1901–90) English philosopher, who attempted to give a theory of human conduct and human experience that will be free from the *empiricist presuppositions of much modern political philosophy. He thereby tried in *Rationalism and Politics*, 1962, and *On Human Conduct*, 1975, to uphold a vision of 'civil association' that reconciles the conservative respect for custom, prejudice and tradition with certain liberal values. Oakeshott's thought has *idealist antecedents, but it eschews system and attempts to present a vision of political society and allegiance that will be respectful of the historical complexities contained in them, and of the actual nature of the beings that are subject to them. The main elements seem to be:

(i) An attack on *rationalism, by which is meant the attempt to subsume all political activity within an overriding aim or formula, to which social life must be made to approximate.

(ii) An attack on ideology, in the specific sense of principles and *doctrines detached from the historical circumstances of their utterance, political principles being acceptable only if they are, as it were, saturated with the conditions from which they spring. Oakeshott's use of the term 'ideology' does not coincide exactly with either of the senses given in this dictionary, although 'doctrine' is perhaps an equivalent. According to Oakeshott, the aims of political association are not made, but discovered, and doctrine can never be a substitute

for the 'intimations' which arise from active engagement in the political order.

(iii) An acceptance of certain forms of political life, and certain institutions, as 'given', i.e. as creating the framework within which political thought and activity are conducted, and therefore not to be construed as in any sense its product. Thus Anglo-American representative government is not to be thought of as a means to an end, or a solution to a given political problem, but as a form of political association, dictating both the end and the means, the solution and the problem.

(iv) A theory of political activity as the offshoot of, and dependent on, 'civil association'. This is the product neither of *contract, nor of any mutuality of purpose, but is to be construed rather on the model of a conversation, whose meaning and principle of development are to be seen at least partly in terms internal to itself. Hence the model for *political obligation is the diffuse obligation of *friendship rather than the precise and revocable obligation of contract – always remembering that civil assocation, unlike friendship, is compulsory. It is a conversation from which one cannot opt out.

Oakeshott develops a subtle, but somewhat elusive, view of human nature and human conduct with which to support those, and similar, views, and thereby to present a conservative defence of institutions, together with a critique of *dirigisme*, of *egalitarianism, and of the socialist ideal of a society without property or class.

obedience

The acquiescence to a *command, whether express or tacit; by extension, the acceptance in action of the *authority of a person or office. Emphasis on obedience as the master concept in political order is characteristic of *absolutism and *paternalism, and it is often thought that this emphasis gave way during the late seventeenth and eighteenth centuries to a similar emphasis on *consent, the distinguishing feature being that, in the second case, the subject, in obeying only what he has consented to, obeys himself, and so is not only subject but also sovereign of his political existence. Without consent, obedience is to some person or office other than oneself, and it is often thought that, until the grounds for such obedience can be discovered, political obligation and sovereignty will be without a foundation. Some thinkers do not believe that there is any foundation other than habit, or tradition, but that these are sufficient in themselves, and any attempt to replace them with an idea of *consent will be based in a fiction, and moreover a dangerous fiction. (See *legitimacy, *piety.) This is one aspect of the complex question of political obligation.

objectification

Term of *Hegel's metaphysics (German: Entäußerung), meaning the process of *self-realization through the 'positing' or creating of an objective world. For Hegel, *alienation (Entfremdung) is a specific 'moment' of objectification; this idea was taken over and amended by the young *Marx, who associated alienation with private property, and objectification with its overcoming, and 'the restoration of man to himself'.

objectivism

See *Rand.

obligation

1. Legal. A bond between two legal *persons, which confers enforceable *rights and *duties. For example, if x negligently injures y, then this confers on x the obligation in law to make due compensation to y, and y has a right to that compensation. (See also *jural relations.) In Roman law the law of obligations is extremely important, subsuming all of contract, quasi-contract and tort, and also any other civil relation in which one person imposes a legal liability on another.

2. Moral. The concept from which the legal notion derives is that of personal or moral obligation – the idea of being bound to do something. Some argue that this concept is primitive, in that it can be explained in no other terms; it is certainly one of the most difficult of all concepts to analyse, and creates major problems for moral philosophy. (See *duty.) The concept of moral obligation seems to be narrower than that of what is morally right: thus it is arguable that I have no obligation to save the life of a man who, unknown to me, is at this moment starving in Lesotho; nevertheless to do so would be morally right. The use of the language of obligation seems to imply an additional relation of *responsibility between the parties.

3. Political. See *political obligation.

Philosophical theories of obligation are of two kinds: those which take the concept as fundamental, and those which think it to be derivative from some other idea, such as that of *value. It is also important to distinguish subjectivist views, which see no ultimate justification for statements of obligation other than personal choice or *convention, from objectivist views, such as that of *Kant, who argues that there are obligations which are binding on all rational agents: to understand them is to be motivated to obey them.

obscenity

The attempt to define and suppress obscenity is an ancient one, and it has been recognized in English common law at least since 1727 that it is criminal to publish indecent matter. The Obscene Publications Act 1957 prohibited the publication of obscene matter but did not define 'obscene', although it provided a *test* of obscenity, namely, the tendency to corrupt and deprave those likely to come in contact with the material in question. It has been of considerable concern to attempt a definition, this being one of the areas where public law and private morality seem to enter into contact, and to generate conflicting intuitions. Without a definition of obscenity and a theory which accounts for its alleged evil, it becomes impossible to see how a law could forbid obscenity without also exercising an effective power of arbitrary *censorship. (Note that obscenity is not forbidden, but forbidden in *public*.)

Roughly speaking, obscenity is a property of representations and displays. The human body is not obscene, but it can be represented or displayed obscenely, in a photograph, picture, dance or gesture. The fault in the test given in the law is that it identifies obscenity through its effects, and these are largely unknowable. The common, and plausible, intuition is that the offence has already been committed in the very act of public display, whatever the consequences. (Hence obscenity is connected with indecency, which is a property of displays, gestures and descriptions, regardless of their effects.) Obscenity 'depersonalizes': it shows the human body, and the sexual act, as a mechanical performance, indicative of an animal pleasure detached from any expression of commitment between the partners; and moreover, obscenity *negates* that commitment or shows it

as irrelevant to the pleasures displayed. This need not be *true* of those engaging in the act, but the essence of obscenity is that that is how the act is *shown*. Thus the universal sexual attributes are divorced from the individual agents, and represented as interesting in themselves. In a similar way violence can be obscene, when it is used to display the human body as a mere object, a butcher's plaything and not the expression or incarnation of a human person. On the wider issue of legal control, *see* *pornography.

obsolescence

There are two kinds of thing which might suffer obsolescence, those with and those without a function. A machine with a function becomes obsolescent when it can no longer perform that function as efficiently as some available alternative. A village community – which exists for its own sake, and not as a means to an end – may become obsolescent, for example, because conditions essential to its survival have been changed. (Communications with the town may have improved, agricultural work may have become difficult or unattractive, local customs and ceremonies may have lost their appeal or authority.) In such a case it is normal to speak of obsolescence, even though the community is not being judged as inefficient. The lack of independent function is compatible with the existence of internal functions: for example, ceremonies within the village may have a function relative to the village's survival (such is the basic tenet of much *functionalist anthropology). However, the village itself is not made obsolescent by the appearance of an 'alternative'; there can be no alternative. Such thoughts underlie *organicist theories of society, and also certain conservative ideas concerning the nature of political institutions, e.g.

those voiced by *Oakeshott. The obsolescence of a political institution is often said not to be like the obsolescence of a machine, since an institution, while it may perform functions, also partly (perhaps sometimes wholly) creates the functions that it performs. It then becomes difficult or even impossible to compare institutions with alternatives so as to see which 'does the job best'. The dispute here is vital to the philosophy of *reform (i.e. does one 'reform in order to conserve', as *Burke put it, or in order to improve?), and also to understanding the implications of organicism.

'Planned obsolescence' is a much-criticized feature of large-scale manufacturing: objects are said to be made to perform a certain function, but with built-in faults, so that in the course of time they will perform it only imperfectly, by which time, however, the function will have become indispensable. Hence other objects will be needed to replace them, and demand need never fall to the point where the manufacturing process must come to an end. Some defend this practice, on the ground that it maintains employment and stimulates aggregate demand. Others criticize it for its inherent irrationality, and its wastefulness of natural resources, not the least of which is human labour.

occupation

A territory is occupied by a foreign power only if that power takes charge of government, and administers the territory with a view to maintaining its own position as the supreme authority in the land. A power can be given a right of administration under the UN *mandates system, in which it is assumed that the purpose will be to administer the territory with a view to its eventual independence. Or it might enter a territory in order to support some internal faction, and with a view

to withdrawing as soon as stability is achieved. In such cases the presence of the external power falls short of occupation. Likewise, a territory administered as a colony, or as part of an empire, is not, for that reason, occupied.

odium theologicum

'Theological hatred': a medieval expression denoting the extraordinary acerbity of abstruse discussions between theologians over matters which seem quite insignificant to the uninitiated. The venom of the intellectual in defence of a theory is thereby explained in terms of a real feeling that underlies it – in this case a religious feeling – while at the same time recognizing it to be slightly comic and perhaps misplaced. *Odium theologicum* recurs in the discussion of secular beliefs, particularly in the writings of the *New Left, and in Marxist intellectual propaganda, where it sometimes has a sinister side to it; an intellectual heresy might also show you to be an 'objective class enemy', and therefore for the chop.

office

Offices are specified by determining three things:

(i) rights and duties of the holder of the office;

(ii) conditions of entry;

(iii) conditions of exit.

(ii) and (iii) are collectively known as the rules of succession, and they cover almost every way in which political power may be transferred: for example, an office may be hereditary for life, or by election from a *college for a period of years, or by election from a *politbureau, but with no rules of exit; and so on. The rights and duties specified under (i) may be embodied in a law, a custom or a convention, or simply evident from the moral background against which the office is set. Offices must be distinguished into public and private, the former being characterized partly by the fact that the holder is entitled to influence the lives of others without their knowledge.

There is a tradition at least as old as *Aristotle which describes a *constitution as a set of public offices, united under law. There can be government without office, but such government automatically raises the question of how it might be limited. The only constraints on those who exercise power will be custom (ineffective in itself), and the criminal and civil law. But either the law will be too strong to allow political action (since every action will be grounds for at least civil redress, if not criminal prosecution), or else too weak to prevent *despotism, since it will be simply inapplicable to the rulers. Anything in between those extremes will be tantamount to a constitution of offices, since it will involve rules that circumscribe the responsibilities and define the obligations of someone when and in so far as he is acting in a certain capacity. Without such rules it is difficult to imagine such procedures as *impeachment, or redress for actions performed *ultra vires – procedures which, on one plausible view, are integral to the whole idea of *limited government. (See *Machiavelli.)

Offices may outlast their holders, and are often treated as symbols of political continuity, attracting to themselves the ceremonies and symbols of *majesty. Some welcome this process, thinking it part of wise government to assail the citizen with representations of a political order greater and more enduring than himself. Such thinkers may welcome too the association of offices with *honours, so symbolizing the unity of responsibility and power: power attached to an office is power limited by responsibility, and hence perceived in terms of a conception of legitimacy. Others dislike the ceremonial aspect of office, and wish for more 'informal' government, thinking that offices – when too much dignified with the majesties of state – place a veil between the rulers and the ruled, thus preventing the powerless from having access to or audience with power. In this connection *Weber argued for a *charisma of office: neither approving nor disapproving of its existence. See also *role.

official secrets

'Official' means pertaining to *office and in political contexts this means public office. However, this is not the meaning of an 'official' secret as defined, for example, in the UK Official Secrets Acts 1911 and 1920. Here an official secret is taken to be (roughly) any confidential matter relating to the state which may be disclosed so as to be 'prejudicial to the safety or interests of the state'. Whether purposes are prejudicial to the safety or interests of the state is a question for the court on hearing evidence from the Crown as to the interests of the state, and not a question for the jury on which the accused could give evidence concerning his ultimate intention.

The problem of reconciling a law of official secrets with freedom of information is so great as to remain unresolved. Recent parliamentary attempts to amend the Official Secrets Acts have proved fruitless, while the adoption by the US Congress of a Freedom of Information Act in 1966 has been much criticized for exposing the armed forces and the country to unnecessary dangers.

oligarchy

Greek: rule by a few. Quite what this means in practice is as difficult to determine as the meaning of *democracy. *Aristotle contrasted oligarchy (where the few rule in their own interest) with *aristocracy, or rule by the best, in which rule by the few is nevertheless in the interest of the many. However, 'aristocracy' now has a specialized meaning, implying a particular kind of *class organization, and it is not at all clear that this kind of government is in the interests of anyone. Oligarchy has been held to include the concentration of power under one-party government, that exhibited by the UK cabinet, and so on. Clearly, some of these arrangements might be in the interests of the people, some might not.

In general, since power is held in different degrees by different people, it is very likely that it will concentrate in the hands of a few, who, whatever the institutions and laws which limit their power, will nevertheless be able to recognize each other and to act instinctively in concert. It is therefore arguable that oligarchy is the natural condition of government, even in states which are legally *monarchies, or *democracies. (See *iron law of oligarchy.) Judgement of oligarchy must depend, therefore, on the principles whereby the élite is held together, and whereby its power is limited. In particular, can the people exert any *control over the oligarchy (e.g. by ejecting it from office at an election)? Or are they able to exert nothing more than *influence? Some argue that true oligarchy should be confined to the second case, whereas the first has a genuine democratic component.

oligopoly

Oligopoly relates to *monopoly as *oligarchy to *monarchy. It denotes the condition of a market in which a small number of firms control a large portion of the business. The various firms involved tend to recognize their mutual interdependence and potential power, and so try to come to whatever arrangements among themselves might be necessary to realize and retain that power. In practice such attempts may often be in vain, as mutual distrust and an underlying desire for individual power tend to prevail. However, agreements restricting price competition and similar attempts to control the market may emerge in a condition of oligopoly. Often governments attempt to prevent these and similar practices and this is one of the main purposes of *antitrust legislation.

In an oligopoly what is a rational act for each firm depends upon what the other firms will do. Hence *game theory has a very important role in the study of oligopoly. (See also *cartel, *imperfect competition.)

Olympic Games
See *sport.

ontology
Literally, the study of being; but usually used in political theory in a sense which ultimately stems from modern *phenomenology, to mean the underlying assumptions about reality, especially social reality, that are made in some given outlook. What is held to exist in itself, what only as a mode or determination of something else? Sometimes an institution is thought to exist independently of its members; sometimes a political outlook is nonsense without the assumption of the existence of God; sometimes the law is regarded as existing objectively and independently of men's conventional recognition of its imperatives. All these are 'ontologies', reflecting, in the last case, a belief in natural law.

The word 'ontology' is used in a similar sense by some analytical philosophers (e.g. Quine) to mean, not the study of being, but rather the class of things supposed to exist by a theory. Such a usage is also familiar among social scientists. It is often important to distinguish the ontology of a belief or practice from the ontology of the theory which explains it. Thus a *functional explanation of witchcraft, unlike the practice of witchcraft, will not normally imply the existence of disembodied spirits.

open door policy

Originally applied to a system for the economic development of China, proposed in 1899 by the US Secretary of State John Hay, according to which no nation was to have exclusive rights for the commercial exploitation of China. To put it cynically, China was to be made economically independent of each trading nation, by being made dependent upon all of them. The policy was rejected by the Chinese in the subsequent upsurge of *nationalist sentiment. The expression is now used to denote the policy of trading with all states on equal terms, without giving monopolies or preferences to any.

open society

Expression used by *Popper, to denote a society whose laws, customs and institutions are open to correction in the light of experience, as opposed to a closed society, founded on revelation or on a doctrine that is protected from refutation or dispute. An open society is one whose members may openly criticize the institutions and the structures of power without fear of reprisal; in which education is distinct from indoctrination; in which society is able to flourish freely in all the ways that are natural to it, without the impediment of supervision from the state; in which freedom of thought, action and belief is allowed to the greatest possible extent; and in which there is neither the overbearing discipline of *totalitarian government, nor the rigid political structure of *absolutism.

The positive description of the open society is less definite in the works of Popper than the trenchant attack on those taken to be its enemies – who include *Plato, *Hegel and *Marx (*The Open Society and its Enemies*, 1945). The rhetorical impact of the attack on Marx, in which Popper attempts to show that it is, to borrow a Marxist phrase, no accident that regimes based on Marxian doctrine end up as *totalitarian, has been great, although its intellectual content and value are inevitably disputed.

Open Source

A movement to achieve open access to the internet. In the information economy certain kinds of knowledge, encoded in simple algorithms, are vital for market entry, and the attempt to assert a monopoly over their use will present a vast and unprecedented barrier to economic transactions. Nevertheless firms like Microsoft, IBM and British Telecom attempt to copyright their software, so as to claim vital pieces of intellectual territory and demand a rent for their use. Their efforts illustrate the recent expansion in the concept of *intellectual property, and the way in which new forms of quasi-monopolistic power are being built from it.

Joining Open Source means rejecting all claims to copyright: programmers are compelled by a mechanism called 'copyleft' to distribute their code freely, allowing others to copy it, modify it and integrate it into their programmes. Within the programming community code is shared without any levy. Money comes in from outside the community, through the manufacture of hardware and through companies contracting for expertise, custom-design and support.

The theory behind Open Source is that programmes are improved more rapidly and efficiently the more people have access to them. Software progresses by continual 'tinkering'. Open Source has proved successful, and now dominates much of internet technology. Its success illustrates the peculiar nature of knowledge as an economic resource. Unlike land knowledge is not depleted by its use, so that there is no *tragedy of the commons involved in giving open access to it.

operations research

An interdisciplinary study which looks for the *optimal solution to problems in the management of a *firm, or any other complex organization dedicated to specifiable purposes. The normal method involves the construction of *models which are tested and then modified in order to approximate as nearly as possible to the actual situation which needs to be understood.

opinion

A 'matter of opinion' is a matter over which there may be reasonable disagreement, either because the subject forbids objective determination, or because the evidence and arguments available to either side are, in normal circumstances, insufficient to establish either view. In normal parlance, therefore, an opinion is either a judgement of *value, concerned with the ends of conduct, or a judgement of technique (concerned with the means) where matters are so complex as to remain unsettled by existing expertise, or a judgement of fact about the past, present or future, which cannot be established by available evidence. It is a respectable philosophical doctrine that in matters of value, the opinion of the majority converges on what is correct; the same cannot be

said about matters of technique, and the opinion of the majority in economics, law, and government, where these do not involve a reiteration of the *ends* of conduct, may be worthless, even when unanimous. *Opinion polls nevertheless range over both types of issue, so that it may often be rational (for this and other reasons) to ignore them.

Some have wanted to see a 'forum of opinion' in government: as was advocated once in *The Federalist* (vol. 49). This was part of the philosophy behind the upper chamber of Congress: it was supposed to generate an atmosphere of leisure and free discussion in order to represent, not *interests, but opinions, a process upon which 'all governments rest'. In so far as such an idea seems plausible it is because the institutional conditions are created under which opinions will be based on the maximum available understanding of their subject-matter. Other forms of consultation of opinion – say, through a poll of the majority – tend to be less credible as an instrument of government. Some see *representation as separating out the two kinds of opinion, allowing the majority to determine the ends of political life, without imposing their opinion about the means. (*See* *public opinion.) Others regard representation as a system whereby interests, rather than opinions, find expression in government.

Certain thinkers in the style of *Burke and *Tocqueville have fought against the 'tyranny of opinion' in all matters, believing that an opinion, as a conscious reflection, in words that the utterer may be unpractised to use, will probably reflect the attitude of the one who asks for it, rather than of the one who answers. This distrust of opinion was thought by Burke to be compatible with, and indeed one of the main reasons for, representative government. Others – notably *Lenin – have argued rather that since only the left intelligentsia is able to form opinions that approximate to the truth, only it should govern. That view, which smacks of *Plato's defence of the philosopher king, conveys a particular and much disputed conception of the relations between theory and practice, and between opinion and knowledge.

opinion polls

Attempts, through sampling, to test either the *opinions or the voting intentions of a population. As the definition suggests, opinion polls are of two kinds: one tries to ascertain what people think, the other what they will do. It is doubtful that any method exists which will reliably establish the first of those, since what people think is not necessarily what they say they think when asked. (Much depends upon who is asking and on the form of the question.) Tests of voters' intentions, however, seem to be more reliable, and various techniques have been developed, such as 'quota sampling', which will ensure that bias is filtered out. The most important problem posed by opinion polls is that, once published, they influence the facts they are supposed to measure, and so can be relied upon only if secret. Certain electoral systems – for example the French – therefore prevent the publication of polls during election campaigns.

opportunism

Term applied in 1876 to the French republican leader L. Gambetta, and since then adopted as an important item of political vituperation. In normal parlance, an opportunist is one who seizes every opportunity to advance himself and his cause, by compromise, pretended belief, and treachery. In Leninist parlance, it meant someone who renounced the 'revolutionary road to socialism', and showed a willingness to compromise with the *bourgeoisie.

opportunity cost

The opportunity cost of some chosen course of action is whatever benefit is offered by the best available alternative forgone. Opportunity cost is an important concept in modern economics, and in *cost–benefit analysis. It is generally assumed that it is rational to choose x if the benefit of x is greater than the opportunity cost of x. Further, on the assumption of *perfect competition in a market, the opportunity cost of every commodity is equal to its market price, which is a simple measure of the benefits forgone in purchasing it. As in other cases of cost and benefit the concept has wider application than to financial costs alone.

opposition

Some forms of rule cannot tolerate opposition, and root it out wherever it arises. Other forms not only tolerate it, but make room for it *within* the institutions of government. This feature of 'internalized opposition' has sometimes been taken as a mark of *limited, as opposed to absolute, government, and also as the mark of *politics, as opposed to *coercion. It is hard to imagine the feature without extremely complex institutions and constitutional devices: it is one of the principal problems of political thought, to discover what makes internal opposition possible.

The use of the term 'opposition', to denote forces within political institutions that resist the ruling officers or party, is comparatively recent. J. Cam Hobhouse, speaking in the House of Commons in 1826, remarked that 'it was said to be very hard on his majesty's ministers to raise objections to this proposition. For his own part, he thought it was more hard on his majesty's opposition to compel them to take this course.' Hansard records laughter at the phrase 'his majesty's opposition'. Although there are uses of 'opposition', to refer to a party or a caucus within an assembly, going back to the early eighteenth century, it seems that this suggestion of an *established opposition was relatively new. It is now, however, quite normal to refer to a 'loyal opposition', and to imply that the interests of the state are as well served by the opposition as by the government itself.

The 'opposition' in the modern UK Parliament consists not merely of opposition *parties or *factions, but principally of a 'shadow formation'. The offices of government are imitated within the opposition, which thereby forms itself into a body prepared to substitute for all the occupants of those offices at any time. The opposition has its leader, its base organization and committees, and usually responds to every move of the government with counter-proposals, representing, in theory, what it *would* do if it were in office.

The existence of such a structured opposition within the institutions of government contributes to the modern understanding of the idea of *party. It presupposes a form of government in which maximum unity within a party is combined with maximum separation between the offices of government and the party that occupies them. It is not surprising to find that this double feat of maximization is a rare achievement. (*See* *office, *representation.)

Governments which destroy opposition may do so in order to banish criticism from the process of government – such has been the case in most revolutionary regimes, beginning with that of the Jacobins in revolutionary France. It could be said that when the communists seized power in Russia in 1917 they made the greatest of all possible political mistakes – namely, that of destroying the mechanisms whereby mistakes are remedied. One of these mechanisms is opposition, and when, in the 1980s, *dissidents began to be semi-tolerated in the Soviet empire, it was because the communist party was beginning to recognize the need for criticism and to try its hand at listening to it. This toleration was possible, however, only because communism itself was on the verge of collapse, and the immediate effect was to remove the last shred of its credibility.

oppression

The use of *coercion, *force, or *violence by some holder of *power, in order to constrain another's freedom or deny his *rights. Defining oppression in that way explains the common thought that oppressed peoples have a right to rise up and throw off their yoke.

Oppression may be overt (as in the occupation of a country by an invader not acting in a just cause), or covert, as in the oppression exerted by organized criminals through a system of 'protection'. A disputed instance of covert oppression is that in which the oppression is also unintentional, while the force stems from social or economic power working upon economic need. This is the model of oppression adopted by virtually all left-wing movements, which set out to liberate the 'oppressed' from their unwitting captors, be they colonialists, capitalists, racists or simply people more comfortable than those on whose labour they depend. In the limiting case this kind of *persuasive definition tends to the view that oppression exists wherever there is inequality. The element of force is simply dropped from the concept.

Oppression must be distinguished from *repression, although some (e.g. *Marcuse, *Reich) have regarded the latter as an effect of the former.

optimal

A solution to a maximizing problem (e.g. a problem posed by the desire to achieve as much utility as possible from expenditure on goods, subject to remaining within one's income or budget) is optimal if it is as good as any other. There need not be a unique optimal solution: a problem may have several optimal solutions which are equally good. Optimal solutions must be distinguished from satisficing solutions, which merely meet certain requirements whether or not there is some superior alternative. The search for an optimal solution in social and political problems is now a large preoccupation of political science, and the concept has an important role in *operations research, *welfare economics, and even the theory of *justice. Problems of optimization arise when there are several objectives involved, and when the maximization of one objective is incompatible with the maximization of another. A typical example is that presented by inflation and employment. A government may seek to promote both employment and the reduction of inflation; it may be that these are so related that the maximization of one is incompatible with the maximization of the other. (*See* *Phillips curve.) Moreover there may also be a minimum below which one of the variables cannot be allowed to fall.

Criteria of optimality are contentious, especially in questions of distribution. The classical *utilitarian criterion, which seeks for the highest level of overall utility, is clearly compatible with vastly unequal distributions; the far weaker criterion of *Pareto optimality leaves many matters undetermined, while the *maximin criterion has often seemed to be applicable only in special cases.

Opus Dei ('the work of God')

A Roman Catholic organization, founded in Madrid in 1928, with the intention of fostering Christian principles of morality and religion. It maintains educational institutions, and has played an important, but covert, political role, both in Spain (originally in opposition to the Republican government, subsequently securing the restoration of Roman Catholic institutions under Franco), and elsewhere. Members of Opus Dei do not take holy orders; their duty is to bear witness to the Christian faith in everyday life: in the family, in the workplace and in the community. Opus Dei has awoken in certain circles the same suspicions that were once directed towards the *Jesuit order, but these suspicions are probably without foundation.

organic

Now used to mean: exhibiting the kind of organization that pertains to living organisms. The definition has an air of circularity, because of the etymologically identical term 'organization' that is used in formulating it. Attempts to clarify the idea have not proved very successful, and often run up against intractable philosophical problems. The usual contrast is between the organic and the mechanical, but that only helps if we have a clear idea of the mechanical: some things popularly described as 'machines' may obey principles of organization which also characterize organisms – such, at any rate, is one of the plausible assumptions of *cybernetics. An important idea seems to be that of function: it is plausible to suggest that all the parts of an organism bear a functional relation to one another. Each part is a means to the functioning of every other. Thus *Kant defined an 'organized natural product' as one 'in which every part is reciprocally both end and means' (*Critique of Judgement*). That is, of course, no clearer than the distinction between end and means. A related suggestion is that the *overall* function of an organism is internal – the maintenance of its own existence. That contrasts with the typical machine, which is constructed for an independent purpose, and which is not to be explained in terms of any principle of self-preservation. The two ideas are vague, but very important in political thinking. They underlie both the frequently made claim that societies are organic, and therefore not to be subjected light-heartedly to surgery, and also the opposing position that societies may occasionally be in need of a revolutionary 'purge'.

organicism

The view that certain composite entities – in particular social entities – are *organic, or sufficiently like organic things to be understood by the laws of organic life. The theory is usually put forward as a version of *holism, in order to argue that social entities, like organisms, cannot be understood merely as the aggregates of their parts, but only by invoking principles of organization that explain the functioning of the parts in terms of their relation to the whole. Organicist views are sometimes thought to be inherently conservative, since they suggest that social entities are delicate, not easily understood, and more likely to survive and flourish if not too much meddled with. However, some who accept that also advocate *revolution, out of a belief, for example, that the death of one society might involve the birth of another. (*See* *death.)

organization man

Expression introduced in a book of that title by William H. Whyte, in 1956, to describe the new human type supposedly generated by *bureaucracy and large-scale management. Whyte's analysis dwells on the conformity, mediocrity and mechanical responses of the organization man, together with the ideology which arises therefrom, and which replaces the impulse of morality and personal affection with the cold imperatives of impersonal order.

organization theory

The sociological theory of the function, mechanism and effect of organizations, especially of large-scale industrial organizations engaged in production. The foundations of the theory were laid by *Weber, but it is not clear that it is really a distinct branch rather than the whole of sociology.

oriental despotism

Term already used by travellers in the seventeenth century, and taken over by *Montesquieu. Traditional Chinese bureaucracy, the Mogul Empire, certain phases of the Russian Tsarist Empire, and even (although the intention here is no doubt ironical) the USSR, have been described as oriental despotisms. The principal characteristics are: concentration of power in the hands of a despot and his entourage; control of all social and political activity from above; absence of a rule of law, and immediate oppressive reaction to any challenge to the central power; emphasis on military power; rapid mobilization of the whole populace in order to override and eliminate *opposition, usually without regard to moral niceties. It is not clear whether 'oriental despotism' and '*asiatic despotism' are synonymous: it is possible that the second is described in relation to an economic system, the first in relation to habits of violence, and that the two do not necessarily coincide. Various theories have been advanced to explain oriental despotism, including the now largely discredited hypothesis (K. Wittfogel, *Oriental Despotism*, 1954) that it is a system made necessary by centralized schemes of irrigation.

orientalism

Term introduced by the American-Palestinian critic Edward Said (*Orientalism*, 1978) to describe the vision of Eastern and Middle Eastern peoples propagated by the literature of colonial expansion, and since adopted, according to Said, as the 'official version' in Western culture and politics. Orientalism sees the East as exotic, vaporous, idle, a realm of hints and fragrances rather than of action – and through this image seems to clear a space for the Western colonizer, for whom action is all and who is entitled to gratitude for his deeds. The Orientalist vision is held to be intrinsically demeaning, and based in a systematic refusal to take seriously the beliefs, achievements and way of life of oriental peoples. Said's thesis has been criticized as unscholarly and biased, and recent studies of the actual writings of orientalist scholars (e.g. Robert Irwin, *For Lust of Knowing: the Orientalists and their Enemies*, 2006), have suggested that the truth is the opposite of Said's claims. Even if the 'orientalists' had a tendency to caricature or stereotype the ways of life and habits of thought and feeling that they described, it would be pertinent to compare their writings with those of the orientals themselves. Did writers in Arabic or Hindi, for example, avoid all stereotyping when describing the occident? Comparative judgements are entirely absent from Said's work; in particular there is no attempt to compare the representation of the orient in Western art and literature with the representation of the West in the art and literature of Eastern peoples. Against that, it is argued that Said, errors of fact and emphasis notwithstanding, pointed to an important slant in Western perceptions, and one of which it is more than ever necessary to be aware.

original position

See *Rawls.

original sin

In *Christian theology, the sin which has belonged to all people since the fall of Adam. The doctrine is derived from St Paul's teaching that 'through one man sin entered the world' so that 'by the trespass of the one the many died'. According to *Aquinas, original sin consists in the loss of those supernatural privileges which had focused man's will upon his true eternal end; as a result of this loss man's reason is submitted to his senses. Original sin is transmitted, not because of Adam's personal failing, but because it is the condition of that human nature first exemplified in Adam, and growing organically from him. Original sin is redeemed in the sacrifice of Christ. The doctrine represents in mystical terms, and by way of a thesis concerning the structure of man's relation to God, a sentiment that also has many secular and political equivalents: the sentiment of man's 'fallen' condition, which has been rationalized in this and various other ways. The same sentiment emerges in the (typically conservative) theory of the inevitable imperfection of all human beings and their works, according to which too much hope and too much trust in human capacities constitute one of the most dangerous manifestations of that imperfection. Original sin is thus an important concept for such thinkers as *Maistre, who refers to it as 'explaining everything, and without which nothing can be explained'.

Ortega y Gasset, José (1883–1955)
Spanish writer and philosopher; *see* *hunting, *masses.

orthodoxy
Greek: the 'straight' opinion – i.e. the opinion that adheres as closely as possible to a given set of beliefs. Not every political doctrine or theory defines an orthodoxy. When writers refer, e.g., to 'liberal orthodoxy', it is extremely unclear what is meant, and even 'Marxist orthodoxy' is a dubious phrase, given the potential conflict between the scientific theory of *historical materialism and the *neo-Marxist critique of consciousness. Some conservatives argue that their view is characterized by the impossibility of orthodoxy, being founded in respect for the actual, and for all the variations, flexibilities and unpredictabilities that characterize the actual. But perhaps that rhetorical disclaimer has itself become a form of orthodoxy.

Orwell, George (pseudonym of E.A. Blair) (1903–50)
English writer and satirist, who deserves a place in this dictionary partly because his novel *1984*, 1949, well known for its description of an *ideal type of *totalitarianism, added certain words to political language which have proved irreplaceable. These words satirize the acronyms of bolshevism ('*Cominform', '*Comintern', 'Proletcult', etc.) and include *Newspeak (designed to meet the ideological needs of *Ingsoc*, or English socialism, and to make heretical thought – *thoughtcrime* – impossible), *prolefeed* (rubbishy entertainment and fictitious news for the masses, or *proles*), *unperson* (one who has been carefully removed from history) and *double-think*: 'the power of holding two contradictory propositions in one's mind simultaneously, and accepting both of them'. Orwell also invented the 'thought police', as the last word in despotic efficiency, and wrote, in *Animal Farm*, 1945, the most famous of all satires of *Stalinism, which he epitomized in the phrase 'all animals are equal, but some are more equal than others'.

Orwell was himself an important influence on English liberal socialism, although a severe and penetrating critic of the *left especially in respect of its anti-patriotism and its *fellow-travelling with the communists. His essays contain many effective and affecting attempts to define a humane and conciliatory form of patriotism, with which to oppose the sneering and iconoclasm of the intellectual left.

Ostpolitik
German: East policy. The West German policy, initiated by Chancellor Kurt Kiesinger in 1966, and emphasized afresh by Chancellor Willy Brandt in 1970, of attempting to end hostile relations with the Soviet bloc by agreements to renounce the use of force, to recognize *de facto* borders, and to encourage trade and cooperation. The policy was a forerunner of *détente.

ostracism
From Greek *ostrakon*, the potsherd used as a writing surface, on which citizens of Athens were invited each year (following a vote in the assembly) to write the name of any prominent citizen whom they wished to expel from the city. If 6000 or more potsherds were placed in the urns, then the citizen with the most votes was given 10 days (on pain of death) to leave the city, to which he could return only after 10 years. Ostracism involved no loss of status or property, and important citizens might be recalled from ostracism in times of emergency.

over-full employment

Empirical investigation and certain macroeconomic theories suggest that it is impossible to have completely full employment without inflation. If unemployment falls below a certain minimum, i.e. when there is excess demand for goods and labour, then demand becomes high relative to productive capacity, and prices and wages will tend to rise. When unemployment has sunk below this minimum, therefore, the economy might be said to be in a state of 'over-full employment'.

over-population

A state is sometimes called over-populated when no increase in population will generate an increase in production, so that all increases strain resources. Whether or not a state is overpopulated does not, on this definition, depend upon crowding, or density of population, but only on the actual ability to meet increased demand.

A state might also be called over-populated if increases in population fail to increase output per head, so that standards of living either remain stationary or fall with each addition to the population. Certain economists have attempted to provide theories of 'optimum population' along these lines, and have offered criteria in order to ascertain when population is at the optimum level. Such criteria are many and varied but oft-quoted versions include: that population at which average, or alternatively total, utility is maximized; that population at which income per head is maximized, and so on.

There is, however, more to life than economics, and it could be said that a state in which people in search of solitude cannot find it, in which wildlife is reduced to the vermin that feed on human waste, and in which woods and meadows exist only as parks or protected spaces, is over-populated.

ouvrièrisme

See *labour movement.

Owen, Robert (1771–1858)

British industrialist and philanthropist, early socialist, and pioneer of the cooperative movement. At his model cotton mills at New Lanark, Owen attempted to show that good wages and conditions for the workers are consistent with business success. Owen believed that social life is or should be continuous with work, and that the two are mutually dependent. He therefore built a model village for his workers, with communal facilities, education and welfare provisions. The great evil of competition is, he thought, the effect, and not the cause of social and economic institutions. Owen was hostile to established *religion, to the Victorian form of *marriage and to *private property, although he recognized the need for private property in the means of production (specifically a nation of 'small independent producers'). He hoped to combine this with socialized distribution (through common ownership of markets and redistribution in favour of the needy). Owen was close in his thinking and practice to *Fourier, and is sometimes claimed as a pioneer of *communitarian politics.

Owenism

The theory and practice of cooperative socialism on the model proposed by *Owen.

ownership

See *property.

Oxford Movement

See *Tractarianism.

Pacific blockade

Pacific blockade
Coercion short of *war from a more powerful state towards a less powerful one. It consists in the blockade of ports with minimum ancillary violence: its object is to avoid war, hence rights of warfare cannot be exercised against ships of other states involved in the blockade. It has been recognized as a distinct form of coercion at least since the Anglo-Swedish blockade of Norwegian ports in 1814. The Declaration of Paris 1856 required that blockades be effective; since then blockades have been used by the major powers in preserving peace. The practice has been to some extent superseded by the provisions of the Hague Convention 1907, no. 2, which forbids the use of armed force in the recovery of contract debts, unless arbitration is unsuccessful.

pacifism

The belief that all *war is unjustified, and that all international politics should proceed by arbitration and treaties under international law. Pacifism may arise out of religious or moral convictions so strong as to give grounds for *conscientious objection to military service, although the right to such objection is rarely recognized.

Attempts to build pacifism into a political doctrine have usually involved an element of *universalism – for example, a belief in universal *natural law, which is superior to, and ought eventually to replace, the municipal laws of states. This would abolish the nation state and subsume all human beings under a single universal jurisdiction. The thought here is that the main cause of belligerence is the sentiment of *territory associated with political division, and war will no longer be either necessary or possible when such division is removed. However, all that can really be inferred from the evidence is that war will then be called 'civil war'; experience also suggests that civil war is as bad as, if not worse than, war of other kinds.

Pacifism has been an important force in modern politics, partly because of its successful use as a strategy by *Gandhi (*see* *passive resistance), partly because of the unacceptable destructiveness of modern warfare.

Paine, Thomas (1737–1809)

English-born outlaw, one of the leaders of the American Revolution and elected member of the French National Assembly during the Revolution. Paine's pamphlet *Common Sense*, 1776, crystallized the sentiment that led to the Declaration of Independence, arguing that 'government even in its best state, is a necessary evil; in its worst state, an intolerable one'. Paine also wrote one of the major documents of radical reform, *The Rights of Man*, 1791, 1792. This, a response to *Burke's critical analysis of the French Revolution, contained a *universalist defence of the theory of *natural rights, and of revolution in the cause of such rights. His theory is in the spirit of *Locke (whom he claimed never to have read), and he used it to defend a kind of *minimal state, believing that society is so natural to man that government is barely necessary in order to maintain it (his acknowledged authority here being *Smith, whose concept of the *invisible hand he endorsed as containing the clue to the self-equilibriating nature of society when not imposed on by a *sovereign). Paine's arguments against the *hereditary principle were vehement, as was his hostility to monarchy in all its forms – although he opposed the Jacobin demands for the execution of the French king and almost lost his own head in doing so. Hereditary government, he argued, is a kind of fraud, and 'the idea of a hereditary legislators . . . is as absurd as an hereditary mathematician, or an hereditary wise man . . .'.

In fact, it was not the French but the American Revolution which provided Paine's chief inspiration. He took over the constitutional and democratic principles of the American revolutionaries and recommended them to the people of Britain and France. In his *Agrarian Justice*, 1796, however, he departed from the pure theory of natural rights and defended an *interventionist, rather than a minimal state. The treatise unfolds a scheme for a kind of *welfare state, based on redistributive taxation and involving a national system of poor relief, state-financed education, old age pensions, death and maternity grants, and other features which are now entirely familiar. All this was to be financed by systems of taxation calculated to redistribute the property of the rich and break down all hereditary accumulations of power and privilege.

palace revolution

A revolution against a *monarch or similar figure, or against the institution of monarchy, instigated by those close to the monarch, such as the higher nobility and officers of the court, and conducted within the precincts of the court, rather than in the towns or the country. Sometimes used to denote any relatively quiet change of government which occurs at the instigation of forces within a ruling faction or party, such as occurred within the *Politburo in the USSR in 1964 when Brezhnev ousted Khrushchev. The deposing of Ceauşescu by Iliescu in Romania in 1990 has also been described as a palace revolution, even though it was accompanied by the effective collapse of communism. See *post-communism.

pan-Africanism

A movement attempting to unite black Africans behind a consciousness of their distinct political *identity and common political destiny. Pan-Africanism began among US blacks in the 1850s, and achieved its first conference on African soil in 1958. Its doctrines have been various, and seldom systematic; for a while the ideals of *négritude were influential, particularly in French-speaking states.

pan-Germanism, pan-Slavism

Two movements which date from the late nineteenth century and which were strongly influenced by the intellectual currents of nineteenth-century *nationalism. They each aimed to unite under common political institutions people with a common language or related languages and, according to the theory, belonging to a common *race. Hitler's special brand of pan-Germanism tried to separate the ideas of language and race, in order to exclude those German speakers whom he found objectionable, while recent pan-Slavism in Eastern Europe has tended to emphasize common language, and to make no claims of a specifically racial character. Both movements have been largely discredited, the first because of its apotheosis in *national socialism, the second because of its role in legitimating the

Soviet conquest of Slavonic nations. *See* *Masaryk.

pan-Islam
Movement for uniting the Islamic nations, both socially and politically, which originated in the Ottoman Empire in the 1880s, and which has undergone a chequered history of anti-zionism, anti-communism and (most recently) anti-Americanism.

pan-Slavism
See *pan-Germanism.

pantisocracy
A form of social organization without government, all being of equal rank and social position, and none having any right of ascendancy over any other. (The term was introduced in the course of defending the idea by Southey, and promptly satirized by Byron.) Pantisocratists in the early nineteenth century were mostly comfortable English intellectuals, whose egalitarianism consisted in a desire to raise everyone to their own level (which they believed to be such that it rendered government unnecessary) rather than to reduce themselves to the level of anyone else.

papacy
The Pope, together with the papal curia, or administrative organs, of the Roman Catholic Church, whose headquarters are situated in the Vatican City in Rome. The Vatican is universally recognized as a *sovereign state, with the Pope as its constitutional *monarch. However, its *jurisdiction, even within its sovereign *territory (which is tiny, following the loss of the Papal states during the Italian Risorgimento) is confined to spiritual and civil matters, and cannot be enforced without the backing of another sovereign power.

The political influence of the papacy remains enormous, nevertheless. Through *encyclicals directed to the faithful the Popes have been able to influence social policy throughout the modern period, despite the decline in Roman Catholic observance. It is thanks to Pope John Paul II that the popular rising against communism in Poland was so effective and spread so rapidly through Eastern Europe, and the same Pope's lucid writings on philosophical and social issues have helped to provide political guidance in the post-communist confusion. (*See* *Centesimus annos*.)

An important recent controversy concerns the conduct of Pope Pius XII during the Second World War, with allegations (originating in the play *The Deputy*, 1963, by Rolf Hochhuth), that the Pope collaborated with the Nazis and endorsed their genocide against the Jews. These allegations have recently been traced to an orchestrated propaganda campaign pursuit by Soviet intelligence, and it has been argued that the Pope, whose possibilities of action were limited by the fact that both he and his clergy were hostage to ruthless powers, nevertheless played an important role in saving Jews from the holocaust.

paradigm shift
See *Kuhn.

paradox of democracy
A paradox, emphasized by *Rousseau, which has been stated in many versions; the essence of the paradox is this:

(i) If I believe in the legitimacy of democratic choice, then I believe that the policy chosen as a result of democratic procedure ought to be pursued.

(ii) There are two incompatible policies, A and B.

(iii) Believing that A ought to be pursued, I vote for A.

(iv) The majority vote for B.

By (i) and (iv), I believe that B ought to be pursued; by (iii) I believe that A ought to be pursued; I also know the truth of (ii), i.e. that A and B are incompatible. Hence I seem compelled by my belief in democracy to embrace conflicting – perhaps even contradictory – opinions. The paradox is not to be confused with the *voting paradoxes that arise in the theory of *social choice. The main attempts to resolve the paradox involve analysis of the particular belief contained in (i): what exactly *does* a democrat believe about the majority decision in this case? That it ought to be enacted? Or that it ought not to be opposed in any way other than that made available by democratic procedure? And so on.

paramilitary

An organization is paramilitary if it affects the style and method of military institutions – with military discipline, a hierarchy of command, directed towards violent ends, and self-licensed to kill – while existing within civilian institutions. Many revolutionary parties have passed through a paramilitary stage. The function seems to be at least partly that of making murder easier, not just physically, but also morally, by suggesting that killing is performed under orders, and so is no more murder than the killing of an enemy combatant in time of war. This further reinforces the command structure of the paramilitary organization, through the thought that something which may legitimately dispense so dreadful a licence must itself have the authority to govern.

parasitism

The charge of 'parasitism' was often levelled in the USSR and its satellites against citizens who did not work, and 'anti-parasite laws' were considerably strengthened in the late 1950s. The constitution guaranteed, in theory, a *right to work, and the citizen was in normal circumstances under an obligation to seek (and, when certain conditions were fulfilled, accept) work. The 'parasite' may in fact have been ejected for political reasons from his former employment, so that the charge was sometimes used to enforce a political judgement; however, it could normally be avoided, by working a certain minimum number of hours or earning a certain minimum wage. Thus arose a special kind of *unemployment, in which what is in effect unemployment benefit is paid out as a fictional wage, in exchange for a few hours of attendance at a place designated by the state.

Paretian liberal, impossibility of

A result in the theory of *social choice, due to Amartya Sen, which shows the inconsistency of three requirements: unrestricted domain (no individual preference orderings are ruled out *ab initio*); the 'weak Pareto principle' (if everyone prefers state x to state y, then x is socially preferred to y); and 'minimal liberty' (at least two persons have their own minimal 'personal sphere', such that, if one of them prefers x to y in his personal sphere, then x is socially preferred to y). The theorem is an example of an 'impossibility theorem', similar in spirit to *Arrow's theorem. Intuitively it seems to establish that there is a conflict between liberal values (which imply that at least some individuals are sovereign in at least some minimal private sphere), and a plausible criterion of social welfare (the weak Pareto principle).

Pareto, Vilfredo, Marchese (1848–1923)

Italian economist, sociologist and philosopher, one of the founders of modern sociology, and a vigorous political pamphleteer, who argued vehemently in the cause of *free trade on the one hand, and *authoritarian politics on the other, and against *socialism as enemy of the first, *liberalism as enemy of the second. Pareto was, however, no romantic conservative, but (at least in his own eyes) a hard-headed realist. His vision of politics and economics was founded in an ideal of rational conduct, which represented rationality as a perfect matching of end and means: his admiration for Machiavellian manoeuvres in politics came from this somewhat *scientistic vision of the rational man. Recognizing that most people do not behave according to his paradigms of rationality, he put forward ambitious (and often satirical) sociological theories of irrational conduct, the most influential being that many socially significant beliefs are *residues of socio-economic forces not themselves to be expressed in cognitive form.

Pareto is esteemed as a sociologist, partly because of his pioneering attempt to give an account of society as a 'system', with points of equilibrium, and mechanisms of adjustment, which may proceed independently of human attempts at voluntary control. (*Treatise of General Sociology*, 1921.) He emphasized the importance of problems of social integration, and the functional interdependence of seemingly disparate social phenomena. His theories of social integrity and interdependence profoundly influenced his economics, and Pareto is often considered to be one of the founders of modern *welfare economics. He argued that economics is a science, but must always be seen as part of a larger framework provided by the social sciences as a whole, social and economic phenomena being interdependent. He gave a theory of economic efficiency that took account, not only of the level of income, but also of its distribution within an economy, and this led him

to introduce certain important concepts, including the distinction between cardinal and ordinal utility (*see* *preference), many of the basic ideas of *marginalism, and the criterion of *optimality (or 'ophelimity') which has since become known as '*Pareto optimality'. Pareto optimality is the condition in which no one can be made better off without someone else becoming worse off – i.e. the position in which no change in *income will make *everyone* better off. This criterion contrasts, for example, with that proposed by classical *utilitarianism (the maximum welfare over all), and incorporates an intuition concerning *social justice, namely, that it is unacceptable to allow the welfare of anyone simply to be *sacrificed* to the interests of anyone else. Its utility in welfare theory has been doubted, partly because it does not determine a unique solution to welfare problems, and partly because it is compatible with every degree of social inequality between members of a society. However, various versions of the criterion have proved useful in giving the structure of *social choices. *See* *Paretian liberal.

Pareto's mind was far-ranging, and on almost every issue in economics and politics he had something (though not necessarily something lasting) to say. There is, for example, a 'Pareto's law', which holds, largely on the basis of empirical observation, that whatever the political conditions or mode of *taxation, income will tend to be distributed in the same way, with the lowest paid being the largest group. The law is, at best, only approximately confirmed.

Pareto was praised by the *fascist government of Mussolini, but since he lived to see only one year of its rule, it is impossible to know what he would have thought of it. Many of his political intuitions align him with some of

Mussolini's policies; on the other hand his keen sense of the ridiculous might have caused him to withhold commitment.

Pareto optimality

A criterion of social welfare (named from *Pareto's 'criterion of ophelimity'), according to which a situation is optimal if nobody in it could be made better off without someone being made worse off. Unlike the classic principle of *utilitarianism the criterion does not involve interpersonal comparisons of utility. Hence it can be applied to a social situation while making no assumptions concerning the relative force of individuals' preferences within that situation. For this reason the criterion has been extremely important in welfare economics, since it permits the theorist to drop one of the most contentious assumptions that have been made in that study. However, it suffers from the defect that there may be infinitely many Pareto optimal solutions to a single problem. For a weak 'Pareto' criterion of social welfare which similarly avoids interpersonal comparisons of utility, *see* *Paretian liberal.

parity

Comparability. When philosophers say that there is 'no parity' between say, the values of morality and the pleasures of the senses, they mean that the two cannot be set against each other in a rational equation, so that reasons of sensual pleasure cannot count for or against reasons of morality. The claim that there is no parity between two classes of benefit is often used to rebut the view that a single quantitative method can be applied to both of them – as in *J.S. Mill's attack on *Bentham's *hedonism.

Among specialized uses of the term, the following should be noted:

(i) to denote the exchange rate of a currency against some internationally accepted standard (such as gold), which the government declares to be the norm;

(ii) in 'parity index', which denotes an *index of the normal outgoings of US farmers, and is used to compute the 'parity prices' for agricultural products – i.e. the prices which must be set in order to support the farmer according to those expectations that cause him to continue farming;

(iii) in 'purchasing power parity theory', which states that exchange rates are determined by the price levels in the separate states compared (in other words, changes in exchange rate offset changes in price levels). This is a widely accepted theory which is sometimes held to undermine the assumptions behind *exchange control.

Parliament

A term often used for institutions of consultative government, but here discussed as the name of the institution of government by *bicameral *representation in the UK, which has evolved continuously since the eleventh century and which has been taken as a model by many other states (*see* *Westminster model). Many of Parliament's procedures, rights and duties are derived from convention and custom, and much of what is important concerning its role and power must be phrased as discovery rather than as legal rule – e.g. 'It seems that there is no legal limitation on Parliament's power', and not 'There shall be no limitation on Parliament's power.' The institutional structure with two houses (Lords and Commons) was established very early and its fundamental constitutional principles that all taxation without the consent of Parliament is illegal, that both houses must concur in legislation, and that the Commons have power to inquire into administration and accounts, and to impeach the King's ministers for maladministration – were asserted definitively in the reign of Edward III (b. 1312, r. 1327–77), thus establishing *limited monarchy in medieval England. Since then changes have occurred in the nature and quality of its membership, in procedures for election (the extension of the franchise beginning in 1832, and now reaching to almost every citizen over the age of 18), and by the emergence of *parties, a process which began in the late seventeenth century, but which took on its modern aspect after 1832.

Parliament is a system of representation, whose main present function is to legitimate and to limit in the name of the *Crown the power exercised by a political party, rather than that exercised by the monarch. Although legislation is still enacted by 'The Queen in Parliament', the thesis of the 'sovereignty of Parliament' – i.e. that Parliament is the true seat of sovereign power – has gained increasing acceptance since the seventeenth century; with the successive limitations of the powers of the House of Lords by the Parliament Acts 1911 and 1949, it would be more reasonable now to speak of the sovereignty of the Commons. That could not have been said before 1945, when the House of Lords played a major part in determining policy, providing ministers and amending legislation, and when the King himself was once (1931) required to intervene (under the 'royal *prerogative') in order to form a government.

Legislation must be passed first by the Commons, and then by the Lords, before gaining the 'royal assent'; the *Prime Minister is chosen, by convention, from the ranks of the majority party in the Commons, and is usually leader of that party. Most candidates for election to the Commons stand in the name of a party, and are subject to the discipline of a party, both before and after election. This has led to a radical change in the character of representation, which seems to be an inevitable result of the need to appeal to the electorate as a whole with a coherent legislative programme. (*See* *mandate.*)

Parliament has 'privilege' – that is, things spoken in the course of parliamentary proceedings are immune from proceedings in the courts; however, the Speaker of the House of Commons has power to discipline members for speaking out of order, or for using insulting or abusive language. Officially all legislation from the Commons is preceded by, and emerges from, debate. What debate there is, however, is at a fairly low level, and most legislation is passed unamended in the form that the dominant party has chosen. (But *see* *Committees.*) The House of Lords may introduce bills and these will tend to be debated, but the Commons is jealous of its power, and will tolerate bills in the House of Lords, or amendments to its own bills from the Lords, only if they relate to matters over which neither government nor opposition has strong feelings. If any dispute arises, the Commons may (by the Parliament Acts), override the decision of the Lords, after specified procedures have been complied with.

Originally the House of Lords consisted of *peers of the realm – hereditary nobility, bishops, the two archbishops and (after the Act of Union 1707) representatives from the peerage of Scotland. A quota of Irish peers was added, following the Act of Union with Ireland in 1800. Occasionally peerages were granted for life, the first in 1377, but this practice was challenged by the House of Lords in 1856, though passionately advocated then by *Bagehot and *J.S. Mill.

participation

It was resumed only in 1958, when a statute was passed to enable the practice. Since then virtually all peerages have been life peerages, created on the advice of the Prime Minister. The abolition by *New Labour of the right of hereditary peers to sit in the House of Lords has led to the anomalous situation that the second chamber of Parliament is now more or less exclusively composed of people nominated by influential members of the first, who are there for life regardless of merit or popularity. Calls for an elected upper house are resisted by both the Government and the Commons: an appointed second chamber is far easier to overrule, and in any case far more compliant, than one with its own title to legitimacy.

The sovereignty of Parliament is not officially diminished by the *European Union, since the treaties conferring legislative powers on the EU were passed by, and could be revoked by, Parliament. In practice, however, the legislative process has steadily passed from Westminster to Brussels, which is now responsible for nearly half of UK legislation. Moreover, any attempt to escape from the treaties, or to lessen their legislative impact, would encounter difficulties that could be overcome only by a unified cross-party strategy: something that is now unlikely.

parliamentarianism

The UK form of *constitutionalism, which upholds the sovereignty of *Parliament, and which argues that the constitution, procedure and structure of Parliament must not be overruled or damaged in the interests of a *party. It may argue for the wisdom of parliamentary institutions, or for the view that they are all we have got. Either way, it will assert that government without institutions is despotic, and that parliamentary institutions are

vital to *limited government, serving as the form which unites the content of successive acts of legislation, and which disciplines every change in the law in accordance with a recognized idea of sovereignty. Every act of government is performed, not by an individual, nor by a party, but by an officer, acting in the exercise of his office, who derives his authority in the last analysis from Parliament.

parochialism

Attachment to the parish; hence, any attitude which derives its sense and content from conditions too localized to permit generalization, and which evinces an unreasoning (and, by implication, unreasonable) attachment to those conditions. Just how circumscribed an attitude must be to be called parochial is not clear. Is Welsh Nationalism or Ulster Unionism parochial? Presumably not, since both seek political institutions that will correspond to real and enduring social forces. Likewise, many *nationalistic and *irredentist movements endeavour to produce a correspondence between forms of government and local *identity which could be seen to be reasonable even by those for whom that local identity provides no coherent motive.

participation

The ideal of participation is captured in the slogan: 'What touches all must be decided by all'; but who is included in the 'all'? How heavily must one be touched? The difficulty here explains a certain preference for the weaker slogan: 'Those affected by decisions must be involved in making them'. Again, however, it is not clear what 'involvement' amounts to. It could mean a right to vote, or a right to be heard, or a right to decide autonomous and circumscribed matters, or a right of veto, or a right of *representation, *delegation or *mandation. It is disputable whether any of these is tantamount to involvement in any independent sense – the issue here being that of the nature and validity of *collective choice. One aim is to ensure that decisions made are acceptable to those affected by them. But if that were *all* that involvement amounted to, then the real criterion would be consent, rather than some procedure of decision making. In which case, to consent to a situation in which all decisions are made by an independent body of managers is *itself* to be involved in their decisions. Clearly, therefore, something more active is meant by 'involvement'.

The call for participation has been extended from the institutions of state to all those subject institutions which have power, however limited and local, over the lives of people, particularly those which govern work. Hence the German call for *Mitbestimmung*, or coordination between workers and management in the place of work. Again, what is intended by this seems to vary from case to case, though the presence of workers or their trade union representatives on company boards is now a regular feature of German business. Similar calls have been made concerning the government of schools and universities, even armies and prisons. *See* *democracy, *democratization, *influence, *representation.

particularism
See *universalism.

partisan
1. Adjective: applies to someone who 'takes a party line' (which may or may not be the line of a *party) on any issue. To be partisan is to close one's mind to thoughts that present difficulties for an established outlook or opinion.

2. Noun: used to describe the Russians who attacked Napoleon's supply-line during the campaign of 1812, and now denoting any armed group offering resistance behind the lines of an enemy. Because of the Italian and especially Yugoslavian resistance to German forces during the war, it is particularly associated with guerrilla forces fighting within an occupied country.

partition
The political division of a territory into autonomous sections, with or without migration of the peoples resident there, in order to establish two governments. This may occur as a result of outside belligerency or influence (as in the partition of Germany), as part of a reorganization of government following the departure of a colonial regime (as in India), or as a result of internal unrest, perhaps also aided and fomented from outside (as in the partition of Cyprus). In the latter two cases it may involve *irredentism, or a desire for modes of government that recognize cultural, social or racial bonds which exist independently.

party
Exactly what constitutes a political party, and what distinguishes it from a *faction, is an extremely difficult question. In fact the term 'party' seems to denote – two distinct kinds of institution:

1. Under conditions of representative government, in which parties may succeed one another in office, according to the decision of an electorate, a party is a voluntary association of individuals, united for common political purposes, some of whom pledge their support, others of whom run for election, and some of whom will take office in government if the party is successful. It usually has a constitution, rules of membership, and procedure for determining officers. It tends to have agreed policies, divergence

from which may mean expulsion or discipline, but it does not necessarily align itself with any *doctrine, or with any *class. It seeks to increase its membership as much as possible, and holds office under a constitution that is superior to it, and which determines how it may conduct the affairs of state. It cannot make law, but only initiate legislation, law being made, not by the party, but by the sovereign institutions over which it exerts an influence, perhaps a dominant influence. Its constitution will be determined by the need to coincide with government offices as and when required or invited; it will therefore bear the stamp of the constitution under which it aims for power, with specific members picked out as spokesmen for the various ministerial portfolios.

2. In a so-called 'one-party state', there is an entity called a party, but which may have little in common with 1. It is not normally a voluntary association, but rather a corporate body of undetermined legal status, with powers to expel from and, by virtue of its monopoly over all office and advancement, to coerce to, membership. Its purposes are not only political (except under the assumption, which it accepts, that all purposes are political), but also social, and it seeks complete control over all institutions. It does not seek power through election, although it may rehearse a fiction of election every now and again, while forbidding any party other than itself to participate. It defines the offices of state, determines their membership, and permits no organized *opposition within them. It proceeds not by representation but by delegation from above, and generates permissions which extend from the hierarchy downwards, giving powers to local bodies and police to act with its authority. It controls the making of laws, supervises their application, and

is often bound by no precedent or constitutional constraint. It has a recognized doctrine and punishes all deviations from it, not only among its members but also among those who are excluded from membership. It does not necessarily seek to extend membership but often to curtail it, so as to exert the maximum discipline compatible with completely extended power. It usually makes other parties illegal, or else compels them to affiliate with itself. It infiltrates and gains possession of all autonomous institutions and often declares itself to be the enlightened *vanguard of a class. It recognizes no legal liability for its actions, and is usually unaccountable for its funds. Its lack of legal personality means that no action can be brought against it so long as it is in power – and even if an action could be brought, the party would control the outcome.

Enormous problems arise, therefore, when such an institution is accused of crimes. Although it lacks legal personality, it is clearly a *corporate person in the metaphysical sense: it holds assets, enjoys powers and privileges, decides and executes things, and is responsible for the result. (*See* *person.) The Nazi party, which lost power because of external defeat, was judged under *international law at Nuremberg and effectively treated as a legal person: it was dissolved, its assets confiscated and its leading executives charged with complicity in its crimes. The Communist Party, which lost power in its European dominions as a result of internal collapse, has suffered no such fate, its crimes have gone unpunished, its assets have disappeared without trace and its executive officers have reappeared as 'democratic' candidates in subsequent elections. This is only one of the many problems of *post-communism.

passive obedience

The doctrine of passive obedience, implied if not explicitly stated in the *Pastoral Rule* of Pope Gregory the Great (540–604), according to which the subject owes passive obedience to his sovereign, even if that sovereign is a tyrant. It is for God, not man, to punish the injustices of an evil ruler, and all attempts at rebellion will merely bring down a worse fate on the people. Even criticism of the ruler seems to have been condemned by Gregory: 'the acts of rulers are not to be smitten with the sword of the mouth, even though they are rightly judged to be blameworthy'. Gregory's position was periodically affirmed by the church, in somewhat milder forms, as an extension of the doctrine of the *Two Swords.

passive resistance

A policy of unarmed and *non-violent resistance to an occupying force, or a government imposed by such force. It involves deliberate neglect of official and administrative functions, refusal to attend interrogations, non-participation in government activities, and so on. The strategy was advocated and pursued by *Gandhi, in opposition to British occupation of India. It was followed also in Czechoslovakia, following the Russian invasion of 1968, but with little success. It is hard to organize passive resistance if opposition to it is determined, and the strategy is vulnerable to the self-interested defection of the majority.

passive revolution

The bringing about of revolution by withdrawing cooperation from all activities and institutions in which the existing *hegemony exerts itself, and so leaving it without a basis of power. The policy was advocated by *Gramsci as a form of non-violent social transformation from below, as opposed to the violent transformation from above practised by *bolshevism.

paternalism

'The principle and practice of paternal administration; government as by a father; the claim or attempt to supply the needs or to regulate the life of a nation or community in the same way as a father does those of his children': thus the *Oxford English Dictionary*, capturing what the first Duke of Buckingham meant when he said that 'a king is father to his subjects'.

The term can be used as one of praise or of abuse, depending upon whether the responsibilities or the advantages of a father are emphasized. The idea of 'paternal' government is, on the whole, one of a benign arrangement, such as its romantic admirers have sometimes imagined *feudalism to be. If a government is truly paternal, then it is bound by responsibilities which are the equivalent of the responsibilities of a parent. In this sense many sociologists describe relations which combine power and responsibility (e.g. that between employer and employee) as involving a paternal component (the inspiration here being *Weber).

The term is also used to denote the attitude which sees people as so helpless and childlike as to stand in the same need of authority and government as children. Kindness may be resented by its recipient if it stems from a paternalistic attitude, since it implies that he is weaker than self-respect admits.

Patočka, Jan (1907–77)

Czech philosopher, influenced by *phenomenology and by *Heidegger, who gave a novel account of the modern experience and of the peculiar political spirit that grew from it in Central Europe. According to Patočka, we belong to a 'natural world' – a world that is lived 'concretely' through our day-to-day perceptions and desires. But this world is shaped by the concepts of those who live in it and is therefore an historical world. Human beings have 'historicity' (*dejinnost*) and Europeans must 'confess to' the history that formed their civilization. Totalitarian philosophies like *Nazism and *communism invite us to ignore this history and to live in a state of exultation, ignoring or overriding the demands of the natural world, in pursuit of a militant nothingness. European politics, properly conceived, attempts to keep alive the vision of *Plato, who described the business of the *polis as the 'care of the soul'. This care of the soul occurs only when people's lives are informed by a 'morality of sense' rather than the 'morality of goals' that stirs the action of the modern revolutionary. The morality of goals blows the natural world apart and leaves us standing disinherited amid the ruins of history.

The loss of 'sense' (*smysl*), and of the morality which safeguards it, explains the character of twentieth-century wars, and of the twentieth century itself as a century of war. The morality of goals banishes death from everyday thought and action, in order to create a 'daytime' world full of illuminated promises. But this world is purchased at a price: it depends upon the night from which we flee but which is always with us. Others must be sacrificed in order that the night should be overcome. War becomes a permanent sacrifice of life for the sake of life, a propitiation offered to the night in order that death should play no part in our daily dealings. The new 'everyday' man, who has renounced the care of his soul and who therefore takes no responsibility for his own existence, secretly needs that other world of total destruction.

War, according to Patočka, has become the normal condition of modern man, who lives in a state of total mobilization, confronting now battle and now 'peace' in the same frame of mind. He takes responsibility for neither, and in neither is he confronted by a meaning that shows him how he might continue to care. Only at one point – the point of sacrifice – does he for a moment break out of the prison of everyday life, and there, in that 'life at the apex', he experiences the only form of *polis* to which he may attain: the 'solidarity of the shattered'.

The drastic quality of Patočka's thought reflects in some measure the drastic experiences of his country, first under Nazism and then under communism. But his attempt to synthesize phenomenology, cultural criticism and political analysis in a vision that would describe and explain the spiritual desolation of the totalitarian world accounts for his considerable influence. This influence increased in 1977 when Patočka became the first spokesman for Charter 77 (*see* *charter), a gesture which led to the police interrogation which cost him his life.

patriarchy
Literally, the rule by fathers. Used to denote:

1. Forms of *kinship relations in which the father is the bearer of authority, respect, property, and hereditary privilege (*cf.* *matriarchy).

2. In political writings, especially those of a *feminist persuasion, the dominance of social and political institutions by men, and the consolidation of male *hegemony throughout public and private life by means of law, especially family law. Since not all men are fathers, the term 'phallocracy' has been coined to replace this usage, generating the added implication that the dominion of men is also a form of irrational worship of the phallus.

3. The doctrine that political authority is inherited in the male line (perhaps from Adam), used as a justification for a particular kind of monarchy. *See* *divine right.

patrician

In early Rome, the privileged class of citizens who filled all magistracies and priesthoods until about 400 BC, when their power began to be limited by the *plebeians, so that, by the end of the Republic, their privileges were insignificant. Under the Empire only the Empress could create patricians, and, although the honour was hereditary, it was of no great political significance. The term is sometimes used of the European aristocracies, partly in order to denote the extent to which their class, like that of the patricians, is one determined by style and honour as much as by economic ascendancy.

patrimony

The inheritance from ancestors (the Latin root implies male ancestors, but the implication seems no longer to hold). The questions of patrimonial privilege and property are referred to under *hereditary principle.

patriotism

Love of country (literally, of fatherland). A vague term that is used differently for different purposes, and is in any case no clearer than the 'love' and 'country' employed in its definition. Patriotism is sometimes assimilated to, and sometimes sharply distinguished from, *nationalism. Thus the preamble to the USSR constitution declared that Soviet citizens are 'patriots and internationalists'. This makes it seem as though patriotism is more enlightened than nationalism, or at least, without the exclusiveness which is supposedly generated by too fervent an attachment to the *nation. If so, then 'country' may mean something like the laws

and institutions of the state, together with whatever customs and conditions may be supposed in their application. 'Love' means, not only the attachment to those things, but the determination to defend them, perhaps at cost to one's life, when necessary. According to many of the traditional defenders of patriotism, it is a higher feeling than that of obligation to the sovereign, and one that the sovereign himself may respond to. Thus Bolingbroke (*The Patriot King*, 1738–39) argued that the sovereign title is itself conditional upon patriotic acts, so that the country (both state and civil society) is the true object of all allegiance, for subject and sovereign alike.

Such ideas survive, and in normal parlance a patriot esteems not only the institutions of a state but also, more especially, the people governed by those institutions, and the language, history and culture that is theirs. Furthermore, patriotism involves sentiments of territory, and tends to feed itself on visions of landscape which, while they may have social order as their focus, are nevertheless saturated with *nostalgia towards a place and climate. In which case, the sentiments underlying patriotism could be distinguished only with considerable difficulty from those attaching to nationalism. If there is a serious distinction here, it is that between a natural feeling, and an artificial and perhaps belligerent *ideology. To put it another way: patriotism is an extension of the natural love of home; nationalism is a belief that my home is inherently superior to yours.

Some go further, however, and argue that patriotism has an essentially political dimension: the patriot is a citizen, whose respect is for the laws and procedures that define his rights and freedoms, and who therefore wishes to relate to his fellow countrymen as citizen to citizen rather than as members of the same ethnic, religious or national community. On this view – which is popular among *left-liberal writers – the patriot might also be a *cosmopolitan, and profoundly opposed to nationalist forms of politics.

pax

Latin: peace. The Roman 'peace' was imposed partly by conquest, partly by tribes petitioning to be included within it, for fear of more powerful neighbours, or from the recognition of political and economic necessity. Thus the 'pacification' of Europe and North Africa was simultaneously the creation of an empire and the imposition of a form of *international law, the *jus gentium* (*see* *Roman law). *Pagus* (French *pays*, Italian *paese*) meant a pacified, i.e. subdued, community, and hence a village or commune within the Empire. Thus the term *pax Romana* came to designate the peace that stems from common subjection to a higher power, in this case often taken to be a blessing, because of the *rule of law made possible by it.

Similar ideas are involved in the *pax Britannica*, brought about by Britain during the eighteenth and nineteenth centuries, and still persisting here and there within the Commonwealth, although with dwindling ability to assert itself as the separate legal and political systems diverge. In medieval Europe there was also a *pax Dei* (peace of God), which could be invoked or imposed from time to time. This was designed to bring quarrels to an end by the threat of spiritual punishments, and to protect certain categories of non-combatants in time of war. It was an antecedent of the modern law of *neutrality, and administered largely by the church. It must be distinguished from the analogous *truega Dei*, or 'truce of God', a more temporary measure, designed to permit diplomacy.

peace

In negative terms, the absence of *war. Peace is supposed in *international law to be the normal relation between states, and legislation for 'peacemaking' and 'peacekeeping' has proceeded on this assumption. Plans for peacekeeping have been frequently proposed, for example by the Abbé de Saint-Pierre in 1713 (a perpetual alliance of Christian states in Europe), by *Bentham in 1789 (international court of judicature and a common *legislature), and by *Kant, whose proposals are perhaps the most interesting. Kant envisaged 'perpetual peace' as requiring a reorganization of the constitutions of all potential belligerents. It is necessary, Kant thought, for all states to be republics, submitting to a public law based on a federation of free states. The basis of that law would be the universal imperative of reason – the 'categorical imperative' – acceptable to all rational beings, and the only true expression of freedom. The law would therefore provide an automatic guarantee of freedom to all who submit to it, and the cause of belligerency would cease to exist. (The inclusion of provisions designed to guarantee universal *human rights into modern agreements aimed at peace – such as the Helsinki agreement – can be seen as in part exemplifying Kant's underlying idea.) Until Trotsky's '*peaceful coexistence' it was also assumed by *international socialist movements that perpetual peace could be achieved only by complete social and political transformation of all potential belligerents and alignment behind a common principle.

A positive definition of peace is hard to produce. There are infinite shades of peace and conflict, from the absolute peace of reciprocated love in domestic security, to the internecine hatreds of civil war. In international law it is established that lack of belligerency is not sufficient for peace but only necessary, thus reflecting an intuition of daily existence. The ideal of pure personal tranquillity brings with it the notion of a complete rest from all consuming purposes. Poets have given us intimations of this condition, but it is unlikely that political thought can do any more than trouble it. War, with its concentrated purpose, is only one of many attitudes hostile to peace, in which the idea of a ruling purpose brings order into fragmented consciousness and exchanges small frustrations for absolute choices between life and death. Thus *Augustine argued that true peace requires not merely the absence of active hostilities but 'tranquillity in order'. Some have seen the *existentialist's philosophy of *commitment as construing personal fulfilment on the model of a transition from restlessness, not to rest, but to war, and have tried to explain its appeal accordingly. For nothing seems more tedious or futile than this state which, like heaven, can be only negatively described.

peaceful coexistence

Phrase coined by *Trotsky in 1917 (originally 'peaceful cohabitation'), and used first to designate the USSR policy of coming to terms with neighbouring capitalist states at the end of the First World War, and subsequently by Khrushchev to describe USSR policy towards capitalist states generally, despite the official commitment to supporting revolutionary working-class movements wherever they occur. China proposed its own form of 'peaceful coexistence' with India in 1954. The phrase has been interpreted very broadly in communist countries so as to permit the encouragement of wars of *national liberation, and the fomenting of unrest and civil disorder in neighbouring states.

peer

Latin: *pares*, equals. **1.** In sociological usage peers are those who compare themselves with one another, so that a peer group consists of those who, through whatever relation of interest, age, or social proximity, respond selectively to the advantages and disadvantages of other members of the group.

2. In the UK a 'peerage' is also a rank, often hereditary, conferring the title of 'lord' or (in some, mainly Scottish, cases) 'lady'. Originally the term 'peer' meant anyone 'on a par' with the sovereign, and entitled to be 'judged by his peers'. The peers in question were those barons and ecclesiastics recognized by the sovereign as having certain distinctive titles to land and jurisdiction, and parliamentary privileges appropriate to their military, economic and spiritual station. Until 2002 peers were entitled to sit in the House of Lords as of right: the only significant political privilege remaining to them (although it may be that a peer can still demand 'trial by his peers').

The House of Lords was abolished during the interregnum, but restored with the return of the monarchy, its legislative and administrative necessity being at the time indisputable. Its present composition – life peers, law lords and others appointed expressly for judicial, administrative or political reasons, together with a small body of hereditary peers elected from among their number – is hard to rationalize. It should be seen more as the residue of successive attempts to recruit the loyalty of powerful subjects by incorporating them into the process of government, than as an immovable part of the constitution. It is generally accepted that its function as a legislative body should be separated as far as possible from its function as a court of law, and that it must be so constituted as to reflect *opinions current within the nation as a whole.

Péguy, Charles (1873–1914)

French poet and essayist, and ardent polemicist in the cause of nationalism, Catholicism and his own variety of romantic socialism, which he presented as a kind of synthesis of Christian piety and the idea of France. In his influential journal *Cahiers de la quinzaine* (1900–14) he gave an outspoken defence of *Dreyfus, and in essays and poems he developed his highly charged iconography of Joan of Arc, whom he presented as the redeemer of his country, the embodiment equally of Christian sacrifice and patriotic duty. To meditate on Joan and her martyrdom was to see through the distractions of modern life to the spiritual core of France, which must always be re-awakened if the country is to live as it should. It was largely as a result of the campaign initiated by Péguy that Joan of Arc was canonized as a Saint of the Roman Catholic Church in 1920.

pensions

Ever since Bismarck's introduction of them into Germany, state pensions have been a subject of intense political dispute, some holding that they are the right of every citizen, others that they are a serious disincentive to save, and therefore a recipe for a spendthrift economy. The current crisis in state pension systems in Europe has two causes: first, the habit of governments (the French, German and Italian in particular) of regarding the state pension fund not as savings, but as a current account, which can be drawn upon to meet the immediate needs of government; secondly the rapidly increasing age of populations, which means that more people are drawing pensions, and living thereafter for longer. If the pension is merely a promise from the state to divert taxes from earners to support those who no longer earn, then the decline in the numbers of the first, and the rise in the numbers of the second, will sooner or later produce insolvency. It has been estimated that, after 2010, when the baby-boom generation retires, EU member states may not be able to afford their pension commitments. The exception is the UK, where state pensions are extensively supplemented by privately funded schemes – i.e where most pensions are supported by genuine saving.

people

1. Definite. The designation *le peuple* or 'the people', as the collective noun denoting those subject to government, came into prominence at the French Revolution: it first stood for *menu* or *petit peuple*, and denoted small businessmen, grocers, artisans, workers, employees, salesmen, servants, day labourers, the peasantry and the indeterminate poor. The term rapidly became of great rhetorical significance. *Arendt, for example, has held that 'the words *le peuple* are the key words for the understanding of the French Revolution, and their connotations were determined by those who were exposed to the spectacle of the people's sufferings which they themselves did not share' (*On Revolution*, 1963). On this view the term is saturated by the downward directed compassion of the privileged, towards *le peuple toujours malheureux*, as Robespierre described them. Since then, however, the term has become wider in its significance. 'The people' now designates all those subject to government within a jurisdiction, irrespective of status, class, or actual wealth and power: even happy people are people in the modern sense. Hence the modern usage recaptures the idea of the Roman *populus*, those subject to government, as opposed to the senate, those who govern. Such an idea is conveyed in the aim of 'government

of the people, by the people, for the people', and in the modern conception of the *sovereignty of the people, according to which those who are governed also exert ultimate *control (and not just *influence) over those who govern them. The 'will of the people' is, it is commonly supposed, what democratic election aims to discover, while the *interests of the people has provided a favoured criterion for the legitimacy of certain kinds of popular government – specifically in the now defunct *people's democracies. Here the term 'people' was used as part of the theory of *Marxism-Leninism, to denote 'the proletariat and its allies'.

2. Indefinite. When writers refer to 'a people', and discuss, for example, the rights, customs, and laws of that people, they intend to pick out a collective identity which is at least partly independent of political structure. A people has a history, and a continuity, which are not those of a state and, according to some *nationalist doctrines, it has a 'right' to that state which will express and conserve its existing identity. (*See* *Volksstaat.*) The idea presents difficulties similar to those presented by the idea of *race. However, it is clear that much modern controversy requires it, e.g. the dispute over the rights attributed to or claimed by the Palestinian 'people'.

people's democracy
Term first used by Soviet theorists after the Second World War, to denote the political and social organization of the socialist states of Eastern Europe and Asia, implying that ideologically such states were at a lower stage than the 'socialist democracy' of the USSR. In practice now used to denote the particular kind of supposed democracy, associated with rule by a tightly organized communist party, in which all consultation, representation and popular opinion achieve political expression through the machinery of the party, or not at all. This is democracy, it is agreed, since only the interests of the *people are consulted, and it is the people's, because it is their interest that counts. The expression is now usually dismissed as a piece of communist *newspeak, and only Vietnam and North Korea still describe themselves in this way.

perestroika
Russian: restructuring. Term introduced by Mikhail Gorbachev in 1987 to denote proposed changes to communist rule in the USSR. Perestroika would allow limited democratization at the local level and a measure of *industrial democracy, so as to achieve necessary social and economic reform without sacrificing the 'leading role' (i.e. ultimate control) exerted by the communist party. In the event little systematic change was initiated until the collapse of communism two years later. 'Perestroika', like '*glasnost', is probably best seen as a term of *newspeak, to be understood in terms of the power that speaks through it rather than the reality described.

perfect competition
A hypothetical condition important as an *ideal type in economic analysis. It is supposed that there are many buyers and sellers in the market, so that none individually can influence price, that there is no collusion between suppliers, and that both buyers and sellers are fully informed about prices throughout the market. Most actual competition deviates appreciably from this ideal, but it defines a model which, it is hoped, may be used to explain the actual behaviour of the actual markets that deviate from it. Some argue that it is absurd to explain actual competition in terms of perfect

competition, without further theory as to how the two are related. Others, notably *Friedman, argue that such objections are confused, since all scientific laws describe ideal situations, though this does not prevent them from generating explanations of a world to which the ideal only approximates.

Permanent Things

Phrase due to *Eliot, and taken over by the US conservative writer and activist Russell Kirk, who uses it to denote the features of the human condition that cannot be changed, and the accumulated wisdom which nevertheless enables us to deal with them. Love, death, procreation, suffering and religious need are all permanent; and modern life has to a great extent severed us from the emotional and intellectual tools that we need to deal with them. One task of *conservatism is to put us again in contact with the Permanent Things, in a way that overcomes our fear of them and which brings us both gentleness and peace.

permissiveness

The attitude of extreme *toleration towards all behaviour deemed to be *private – especially behaviour related to sexuality, human relations, forms of association, ceremony and leisure. The issue of how far permissiveness should be extended or prevented is identical with that of tolerance. The journalistic phrase 'permissive society' records the sense that a different form of social order may emerge from its widespread adoption. Hence arguments about the permission of individual actions may have to extend to the evaluation of a whole society. *See* *sexual conduct.

person

One of the problems posed by *human nature is that of relating the idea of person to that of human being. In Latin the use of the term *persona* to refer to human beings was late: previously it had denoted a dramatic role (as it still does in critical usage), and then a legal person (see below). Philosophies of the relation between the person and the human being are various: *Locke distinguished them on the grounds that the same human being might not be the same person and vice versa, and thought of consciousness and responsibility as the defining features of the person. *Kant distinguished them on the grounds of the wholly different laws that determine the behaviour of each, the human being belonging to the 'empirical' world of nature, the person to the 'transcendental' world where laws of reason alone prevail. Kant's view is, in effect, an attempt to recast the legal concept as the idea of a distinct category of being.

1. In law. A person is an entity with rights and duties recognized in law. There are natural persons (including most human beings, but perhaps not only them), and also artificial or 'juristic' persons, such as *corporations, which have a legal identity quite distinct from the natural persons who may at any moment constitute them, and which may survive as a set of unoccupied *offices, their rights and duties intact. (*See* *corporate personality.)

2. By extension, we can introduce the idea of the moral person, as the bearer of *moral* rights and duties. Such rights and duties are not the product of (although they may be confirmed in) a system of law, but have their basis in a system of moral values. They presumably include such natural rights as there may be. The metaphysical idea of the person introduced by Kant is meant to coincide with this idea, while also showing that persons are a distinct metaphysical kind of thing.

3. In politics it is clear that we are presented with many entities which, while not necessarily legal or moral persons, are analogous to them. They include the state (which is also an *international person in international law), many of its subject institutions, and even such socially defined entities as the *nation. These are thought to have rights and duties, although it is not always clear whether such rights and duties are legal or moral. The thought depends in part on the fact that states, nations and institutions contain natural persons as members. However, the membership may change completely, while the rights and duties remain (as when a state and its jurisdiction are repopulated by immigrants after a plague). The personal nature of the state is held by some (e.g. *Hegel) to go further, approximating indeed to the personal nature of human beings.

The construct of the legal person (sense 1.) has been of great interest, partly because of the suggestiveness of the idea that 'it is not the natural Ego which enters a court of law. It is a right-and-duty-bearing person, created by the law, which appears before the law' (Sir Ernest Barker). The idea of a *right as essential to that of the person creates many philosophical puzzles under sense 2. In particular, what is it about *human beings* that makes them moral persons? Kant attempted to identify a 'transcendental freedom' at the heart of human nature, and to show that all beings with that freedom must be treated as ends and not as means only. This can be seen as an attempt to show *why* humans are persons, and also to show just what is meant by a right. We have a sense that some human beings are not fully persons: a foetus, for example, or an unconscious relict made vegetable by a car-crash. Do we therefore think that they have *no* rights? That question is vital in considering issues of the *right to life. Again, *animals are protected

by the law: that is, we have legal duties towards them. Does that give them rights in law, and if so, are they too legal persons? More importantly, are they moral persons? Do they have moral rights, or are they merely the subject of moral duties? One reason for saying that they are not moral persons is that, while we have duties to them, they have, and can have, no duties to us. Hence it is misleading to speak of them as the bearers of rights. (*See* *animals.) Such views are much contested, and derive ultimately from a theory that the distinguishing mark of the person is *rationality, or perhaps, more accurately, rational *agency.

persuasive definition

Phrase coined by the American philosopher C.L. Stephenson (*Ethics and Language*, 1949), to denote the attempt to attach the value of one thing to the reality of another, by defining the second as the 'true' or 'real' example of the first. Thus: 'National socialism is true democracy' (Hitler). Here an important argument is 'won' by defining the desired conclusion as true. (Likewise the persuasive definition of 'democracy' in *democratic centralism.)

petit bourgeois

The class of small property owners, including those, such as small shop-keepers, with only indirect control over the economy. The *petit bourgeois* form an imprecise class since, if the qualification is by *amount* of property held, then it seems to include members of society with quite disparate functions, such as teachers, brass-band leaders, smallholders and fortune tellers, while if the qualification is functional (for example, control over exchange and distribution) then it includes every level of wealth, and possibly overlaps with the *haute bourgeoisie* and the proletariat. The term is used to denote a *spirit* in common to the small property owners in urban capitalism: the problem is to find a structural or functional explanation of that spirit, if there is one. *See* *Poujadism.

Petty, Sir William (1623–87)
English political economist and polymath. *See* *political arithmetic.

phallocracy
See *paternalism.

phenomenology
Philosophical method due largely to the German philosopher Edmund Husserl (1859–1938) (although the term had been introduced by Hegel in a somewhat different context). Phenomenology began as the theory of 'consciousness as such', studied in isolation from the material circumstances that surround it; the hope was to determine the nature and content of the various 'mental acts', such as belief, emotion, thought and desire. The term was later used to name a somewhat diffuse method in *sociology, which stays with the description of the perceived surface of social phenomena, believing that social consciousness represents the world in a unique way, and that until we understand the mode of 'representation' that is intrinsic to it, it is pointless to look beyond it to the material facts which provide its explanation, since we will not know what we are trying to explain. The principal exponent has been Alfred Schutz, but the language of phenomenology is frequently borrowed in the formulation of social and political theories. *See*, for example, *ontology, *Scheler.

philistinism
David's battle with the Philistine (literally Palestinian) Goliath became,

during the early nineteenth century, a symbol of the battle between the sensibility of the poet and the blunt calculation of the man of affairs. Following a German student usage popularized by Robert Schumann and *Carlyle, *Arnold developed an influential theory of the philistine consciousness, designed to provide an explanation and justification of *culture and *humane education, both of which the philistine is held to lack. The philistine is contrasted with the barbarian, the first being a type of the *middle class, the second a type of the *nobility. The philistine lives in a world entirely conditioned by material and commonplace values. His consciousness is so taken up with the pursuit of measurable profit and loss that he cannot perceive the world in other terms. For him, therefore, the world of culture and enlightened human understanding is not merely valueless – it is imperceivable. The philistine cannot be argued with, since he must always fail to see his opponent's point of view. Arnold originally criticized *utilitarianism as a form of philistinism, because of its desire to find a measurable quantity for every human value; others have criticized *vulgar Marxism in similar terms (because of its emphasis on the material explanations of human thoughts and feelings, and its lack of perception of their content).

Phillips curve
The relationship between *inflation and *unemployment estimated in 1958 by the New Zealand economist A.W.H. Phillips (1914–75). The curve is so shaped that as unemployment falls the rate of inflation rises, so, it is argued, it is never possible to reduce both together. The empirical evidence adduced by Phillips was fairly persuasive. However, the relationship measured by Phillips appeared to have 'broken down' in the 1970s, when

inflation and unemployment rose together (see *stagflation). Some, in particular the *monetarists, argue that there is no long-term relationship between inflation and unemployment, the latter being determined independently by market forces, the former depending upon the *money supply policy of the government. Opponents of this view point to the fact that attempts to reduce inflation by controlling the money supply have generally resulted in a rise in unemployment.

philosopher king
See *Plato.

philosophic radicals
Followers of *Bentham who attempted to translate *liberalism from philosophical premises into practical conclusions of law, economics and politics, and who formed, in the early nineteenth century in Britain, a kind of intellectual establishment, with some of the authority of the *left-liberal establishment formed (partly through the *Fabian society) in the twentieth century. They included *James Mill, *John Stuart Mill, *Ricardo, the jurist John Austin, and the historian George Grote.

philosophy
Greek: the love of wisdom. A term with three main current meanings:

1. Any very general (but not necessarily systematic) set of beliefs in which an outlook on the world is founded, and from which the motives of human action may be drawn.

2. Traditionally (as in 'natural philosophy'), any form of systematic science. This usage has largely disappeared, but marks an important intellectual tradition which saw science and philosophy, in sense 3. below, as continuous.

3. Specifically the *essentially contested subject-matter of philosophical writing, which treats all questions as abstractly as possible, and looks not for what is, but for what must be or might be. Philosophy examines the grounds of knowledge and the presuppositions of science (epistemology and method), together with the ultimate constitution of reality (metaphysics) and the essence of *value (ethics and aesthetics). Sometimes said to be the science of questions, philosophy asks for the ultimate meaning and justification of everything, including itself.

-phobia
Greek: fear. A suffix (comparable to the prefix *anti-) used to suggest an irrational and perhaps pernicious aversion to the substantive to which it is attached. By describing criticism of a practice as a phobia you suggest that the fault lies in the critic, not in the thing itself. Thus, in debates over *gay rights, the term 'homophobia' is used to denigrate the motives of those who criticize the gay agenda. In similar vein 'Islamophobia' is now a charge routinely laid against the critics of radical *Islam.

physiocrats
Group of French eighteenth-century economists, led by F. Quesnay (1694–1774), who argued against political interference in the 'natural' economic order, and thought that agriculture is the only source of wealth, and that it alone should be subject to taxation. (Physiocracy means 'the rule of nature'.) They argued that the state should play no part in directing economic activity, other than that of upholding the natural order and safeguarding property. Their defence of *free trade and *laissez-faire influenced *Adam Smith, while Quesnay himself made important beginnings in the science of *macroeconomics.

piecemeal engineering

An expression used by *Popper to denote his preferred manner of social reform: the replacement of worn-out parts of the mechanism, and the gradual sophistication of the whole, while keeping the machine in motion. The image, offensive to those who are opposed to mechanical models of political life (*see* *organicism), is not necessary to the thought that is expressed through it. *See* *reform.

piety

Latin: *pietas*. An important conception in Roman political thought, in Christian theology, and in certain (mainly conservative) theories of *political obligation. Piety contrasts with, and is also related to, justice, and in its basic meaning refers to the disposition to recognize and act upon obligations that are not based in contract nor in any other voluntary choice of the agent. Thus my duty to my parents (whom I neither chose nor chose to be related to, nor chose to be obliged towards) is one of piety, as is, on some views, my duty towards the state. (*See*, e.g., *Burke, *Hegel.) Piety is related to justice in that it involves a disposition to accord and to recognize obligations and rights; it is distinct from justice in that it is not concerned with the regulation of contract, exchange or distribution, or with the derivation of rights from free transactions. Hence it has often been thought to provide the model for theories of political obligation which deny the possibility of a *social contract, or of *tacit consent; and thus provides an important idea to anti-individualistic ideas of *legitimacy.

Since, if God exists, we owe him submission not by consent but by our natural position as created beings, the term 'piety' was early appropriated to describe the condition of sincere religious belief, although the Roman virtue, celebrated in the character of Virgil's *pius Aeneas*, already had a religious tone to it, and this tone survives, detached from any religious doctrine, in Wordsworth's evocation of 'natural piety'. Conservatives who are attached to that idea are often accused of 'pious cant' – i.e. fragrant venerating words which fail to give grounds for any true obligation. They are also accused – because a defence of piety towards existing institutions may involve a neglect of *social justice – of a lack of 'pity', to use a later Christian derivation from the same Latin root.

planned economy

1. A fully planned economy is one in which resources are allocated by a centralized administration, and not by the mechanism of *price. Decisions on outputs are taken by the administration, and the use of capital, land and labour is brought entirely within its supervision.

In the USSR the emphasis was on planned heavy industry, while in China it has been on planned agriculture; the first seems to present fewer administrative problems than the second, and it is significant that almost all planned economies have had to concede some element of *market economy in the agricultural sector.

For a long time during the twentieth century economists and politicians of the left argued for the necessity of planning, in order to deal with shortages, social upheaval, underdevelopment, *unemployment and collapse of confidence in the mode of production. To the extent that those problems can be identified independently of questions of ownership, it might seem to be an empirical matter whether a planned economy is better equipped to solve them than the market mechanism that it is supposed to replace. Comparison between fully planned and market economies in postwar Europe showed, however, that almost all of those problems had become worse in fully planned economies, and remained at least stable elsewhere. Some suggest that this is inevitable, the result of the insensitivity of the planned economy to *consumer preference, its susceptibility to large and devastating mistakes, and to large-scale corruption, and its lack of any natural tendency to *equilibrium.

It could be that the failures are in part due to dogmas of *common ownership which have led to the elimination of adequate incentives to produce – a fact (if it is a fact) which is independent of the existence of large-scale planning. However, it is also true that, while there is a theory of market equilibrium which has rough application, and which does suggest how equilibrium may come about without any deliberate striving towards it, there is no such theory for the planned economy, and this may be because it has no natural, but only a planned, equilibrium. Economists of the *Austrian school go further, and argue that it is not an empirical but an a priori matter, that the planned economy will exacerbate the problems that it sets out to solve. See *calculation debate, *Hayek, *Mises.

2. Partly planned economy. There has been increasing awareness during the twentieth century that, while markets have equilibrium conditions, it is not necessary that equilibrium will be reached or that the particular equilibrium reached will be compatible with other social and economic objectives, such as full employment and economic growth. Hence the emergence almost everywhere of partly planned economies, in which the government attempts to manage the flow of resources, while preserving as much of the price mechanism as is compatible with that aim. The partly

planned economy is now the rule rather than the exception; for particular examples, see *interventionism, *Keynesianism, *mixed economy, *prices and incomes policy. It is still an object of intense criticism from those who believe that the free economy is self-regulating, and delivers the only possible answers to the problems of *coordination in a modern society: see *anarcho-capitalism.

planning

1. The attempt to control the outcome of *collective choice, by adopting a comprehensive plan, as in *planned economy.

2. Specifically, the process whereby the built environment is subject to some kind of control by people other than the builders. Without planning towns could lack public amenities, contain impassable streets and dangerous structures; farmland and other necessary amenities beneficial to the whole community could be blighted and rendered unproductive. Hence some measure of planning control has been adopted from the beginning of human *settlement. Nevertheless the issue of *who* should control the process, *what* should be controlled and *how* has remained one of the liveliest questions of modern politics. Central planning by the state is likely to be insensitive to local perceptions, and biased in favour of the areas where politicians tend to live. Planning by the local community is likely to ignore or frustrate the larger needs of the country – such as the need for roads, for housing, for airports and so on.

As to the question *what* to control, a dispute exists between those who believe that planning should be sufficient to secure *public goods, with the market taking care of all problems of day-to-day coordination and amenity, and those who wish for control over social, aesthetic and historic aspects of the environment, on the grounds that these belong to future generations, and are at risk from the greed of their present tenants. Aesthetic and historic controls are a familiar feature of European planning laws, and notably those of the UK. In the US such matters are often referred to private initiatives, such as the 'scenic easements' whereby people agree – though encouraged by tax-breaks from the state – to enter legal limitations on use and construction into the title of their land.

As to the question *how*, there is again a great difference between the US model, which sees the fundamental feature of planning in terms of *zoning, whereby different areas of land are set aside for different uses, and the European model (especially that pursued by the *New Urbanism) which looks for mixed residential and industrial use, with the primary constraints residing in street plan and aesthetic order. The US system has been trenchantly criticized by Jane Jacobs (*The Death and Life of Great American Cities*, 1961), as bringing about a disaggregation of the functions of the city, isolating people from their work, producing a degraded environment in the centres of cities and a constantly expanding suburban rim, and in general destroying the city as a social, moral and aesthetic unity. To this it is sometimes replied that the American city is an example of the 'creative destruction' recommended by *Schumpeter, and that the process which has ruined the old order can always replace it with something better. Thus blighted cities renew themselves, and in time people move back from the suburbs to the rehabilitated centres. Nevertheless, it is not US-style zoning laws that created Paris, Venice or Bath, and some attempt at aesthetic *coordination would seem to be intrinsic to the goal of collective *settlement.

Plato (*c.* 428–348 BC)
Greek philosopher, whose two most famous political works – the *Republic* and *The Laws* – differ markedly in tone and emphasis, the first enunciating an ideal state organized according to a concept of *justice, the second describing varieties of constitutional government, illustrated from Greek city-states, and endorsing a constitution not wholly unlike that of *Sparta. The first is based in the highest metaphysical speculation, written with extraordinary literary imagination and philosophical skill, and moves towards conclusions that have always impressed for their cogency, if not for their practicality. The second is dry, discursive, and tempered by a cynical awareness of human imperfection.

The *Republic*: Plato's opening question is 'What is justice?' He dismisses, in a famous argument, the suggestion that justice is 'the interest of the strongest' (i.e. that *rights are really *powers). The interest of the strongest varies from time to time and from place to place, while justice is always one thing; moreover the exercise of any power, however great, can always be judged on its merits, and it is precisely the function of the idea of justice to provide the grounds for that judgement. Justice is a human attribute, and consists in a certain harmony in the human soul. In order to analyse this harmony, Plato compares the human soul with its highest earthly manifestation, an ideal city-state or *polis. This is a kind of super-person, constituted from the resolution of conflicting interests and aims. (The image here was to recur, notably in *Hobbes and *Hegel.) The just state contains a social *division of labour, and encourages the *virtues proper to each kind of labour. These virtues are all particularized forms of justice, and serve to fit those who possess them to the station that is theirs. Thus justice is the supreme virtue, which enables the citizen to accept his station, and the duties pertaining to it.

There are three social classes: the rulers or guardians, the soldiers, and those engaged in production. These classes correspond to fundamental faculties in the human soul – the rational, which commands, the spirited, which attacks, and the appetitive, which desires. Wisdom controls the first, courage the second, and temperance the third. Justice is the disposition of all to harmonize under the rule of wisdom. Hence the just state is the state in which wise guardians ensure mediation and reconciliation among the classes beneath them. Plato's conception leads to the ideal of the philosopher king, who holds power with complete entitlement, because he knows things as they are and has sought and found the truth in the realm of ideas. This conception is often satirized, or linked with suspicion to certain forms of *Leninism, according to which a *vanguard party, being in possession of the 'truth of history', has unlimited entitlement to the exercise of power. It is doubtful, however, that Plato meant to draw attention to anything except an ideal of just government, from which all actual government, and all tyranny, must diverge. Indeed much of Plato's incidental argument concerns not the philosophical ideal, but what he calls the 'second-best state', the state that could actually exist, given the imperfections of human nature.

In the course of elaborating his picture of the just state, Plato recommends abolition of the family (for the guardians), communal modes of ownership, censorship of art and letters, and propagation of the 'noble lie' which permits the multitude to acquiesce towards established power. (See *myth.) His discussion of the nature and place of education within the *polis* has been highly influential, along with his diagnosis of the various shortcomings of the actual forms of government in comparison with the ideal. He identifies these forms as *timocracy, whose principle is honour, *oligarchy, which is based on wealth, and *democracy, which is the rule of licence. In his description of democracy he satirizes the Athenian constitution, and provides one of the first and most trenchant critiques of *liberalism as a political doctrine.

The Laws: this contains detailed constitutional recommendations. Plato advocates a kind of *mixed government, or limited oligarchy, such as was later defended by *Machiavelli. Under Plato's system, power is concentrated in the old, whose main duties lie in the conservation of political institutions, and the holding of offices. Plato moves away from the communistic principles of the *Republic*, allowing to each citizen a wife, a family, and private property, at least in so far as this is necessary to form a *household. But each individual is subordinate to the state, of which he is an organic part, and law, which is the dispensation of reason, penetrates into every aspect of life, regulating and controlling even domestic functions. Once again Plato lays great emphasis on education, and its role in preparing the citizen for political life, but he adds to his discussion many additional provisions, defending the view that the state has an interest in the private life and development of the individual, and needs to make complex legal provisions for every aspect of social existence. Hence his philosophy, in both *The Laws* and *The Republic*, has been held to have *totalitarian leanings.

platoons

Term used by *Burke, who identified the 'small platoons' of a free society as the root of social and moral values, and the source of political allegiance. (Burke's phrase is frequently misquoted as 'little platoons'.) Burke's observation was repeated in other terms by *Tocqueville in his study of small-town and rural America, and has become a leading idea of conservative political thought. Society, it is argued, depends upon *trust, and trust develops at the local level, among people who know one another and who need to rely on one another in order to survive. It is at this level, therefore, that the true fund of *social capital is accumulated, and any political system which destroys or penalizes the small platoon – say through outlawing *charity, as the communists did – will destroy the social sentiments on which its own durability depends.

play

The disposition to enjoy doing something with reason, but for no independent purpose: the essential human activity from which on one view (that of Schiller, *Letters on Aesthetic Education*, 1801) all aesthetic experience derives, and which forms an important underlying structure in *leisure. Not all leisure involves play, since play is essentially active, a recovery from over-activity not through rest but through a rival activity that lacks the purposive character of *work. While there are games with purposes, such as winning, scoring a goal, etc., these are not detachable from the game itself. Thus play has no overall purpose besides itself, even if it has a function, e.g. the function, in a child, of preparing for adult life. Schiller had in mind the importance of such purposeless activities (among which art is the highest) in the formation of character and civic virtue: it is this which frees the human being from the instrumentality of work, and gives sense to his *labour.

plebeian

In Rome, the general body of citizens, other than *patricians. Originally the plebeians were excluded from office, but gradually were accorded democratic rights, until in 287 BC a *Lex Hortensia* made plebiscites (measures passed by the council of plebeians) binding on the whole people.

plebiscite

Nowadays, any means for securing an expression of popular *opinion (for example, by a *referendum) for the purpose of political decision-making. Originally, a measure passed by the council of the Roman *plebeians.

Plekhanov, Georgii Valentinovich (1856–1918)
Russian literary critic, philosopher and social reformer. Plekhanov was at first a *narodnik, became a convert to *Marxism and successfully advocated the adoption of Marxism by the Russian revolutionary movement. It is Plekhanov's version of Marxism (which he called *dialectical materialism) that was adopted by *Lenin and the *bolsheviks. *See also* *mensheviks.

plural society

A *civil society in which several *societies coexist in a single *territory, interacting in a peaceful way, perhaps so as to become socially, politically and economically interdependent. The normal assumption is that such a society is formed through a liberal constitution, which builds some principle of tolerance and *minority rights into its procedure, so as to break down isolationist and separatist tendencies among citizens belonging to various racial, religious and ethnic groups. It should be said that plural societies are rare, and usually dependent upon some kind of empire. *See* *millet system, *multiculturalism, *pluralism.

pluralism

1. The belief in the distribution of political power through several institutions which can limit one another's action, or through institutions none of which is *sovereign. Pluralism is the advocacy of a particular kind of *limited government.

2. The belief that the constitution of a state ought to make room for varieties of social customs, religious and moral beliefs, and habits of association, and that all political rights should be traced back to the constitution, and not to any social entity other than the state itself. In such circumstances the social and the political are as separate as can be, and uniform political institutions coexist with a *plural society. See *multiculturalism.

3. Any view which, in opposition to monism (and perhaps also to dualism), argues for a multiplicity of basic things, processes, concepts or explanations.

plutocracy

Rule by wealth – i.e. any form of government in which institutions are so formed (whether or not by express design) that only a person of considerable wealth can hold office, either because of the expenses necessary to achieve, or those necessary to maintain it. Plutocracy should be distinguished from government in which holding office is the occasion for acquiring wealth. US democracy has a tendency to be plutocratic, whereas the non-plutocratic system of *democratic centralism seems to lead to vast acquisitions of wealth by important officeholders.

pogrom

Yiddish, from Russian, 'like thunder'. An organized extermination or persecution of an ethnic group, named after the attacks on Jewish ghettoes in Russia and the Ukraine during the latter years of the nineteenth century. Pogroms caused the large-scale exodus of Jews from Russia and its dependencies, many of them making their way to America, others believing, with lamentable lack of foresight, that they would be safe in Poland, Lithuania or the Austro-Hungarian Empire.

police

A recent invention, the paid police force dates from 1829 in the UK, although it was familiar before then in France, Russia and elsewhere. It rapidly grew in power and complexity, and is now considered to be necessary almost everywhere and by almost everyone. Its powers vary from place to place, and in accordance with the political structure; being the instrument to enforce the law, its nature is partly determined by the character of the law that it enforces. The following variables should be noted:

(i) extent, i.e. the quantity of policemen per head of population;

(ii) powers, e.g. powers of search, with or without warrant, of arrest, detention, interrogation and restraint;

(iii) provisions for redress; to what extent may the citizen (*de jure), and to what extent can he (de facto) obtain redress (e.g. through a controlling body, or a court of law) against a police officer who has acted *ultra vires?;

(iv) openness; to what extent can the police operate secretly, and in such a way as to penetrate the private life of the citizen? (See *police state);

(v) armaments; what weapons may the police use in enforcing the law, and when?

It is necessary to distinguish those systems which provide for constant active invigilation of the police, and those which merely provide redress for violations. Given the power which, on one plausible view, the police must possess in order to fulfil their function, it may be that legal provisions for redress are insufficient, in that they do not override the powers of intimidation which the police can bring to bear on any potential complainant. For this reason there have evolved, in many Western countries, commissions of inquiry which attempt to invigilate independently, and also to prevent abuses before they have become widespread. In English *common law, unlawful arrest and imprisonment have from early on been crimes, and since 1967 a distinction is made between 'arrestable offences' and 'non-arrestable offences' (where arrest requires a warrant), in order to curb police powers while replacing the traditional distinction (still upheld in the US) between 'felonies' and 'misdemeanours'.

police state

A state in which political stability has come to be, or to seem to be, dependent upon police supervision of the ordinary citizen, and in which the police are given powers suitable to that. The police force is extended, and operates secretly, with powers to detain for interrogation without charge, to search, to interrupt correspondence and to tap telephone calls, and in general to keep detailed records on citizens accused of no crime, in order to enforce measures designed to extinguish all *opposition to the government and its institutions. The powers here may not be legally granted but that is not normally an obstacle, since there is a presumption that there is no *rule of law in these circumstances, and the acquisition of large *de facto* powers by the police will simply be one aspect of a widespread defiance of *natural justice.

policy

Greek *politeia*, government. The general principles which guide the making of laws, administration, and executive acts of government in domestic and international affairs. Policy has to be distinguished from *doctrine – the system of beliefs and values which generate policy, and which purport to describe the ends to which policy is the means – and from *philosophy, the underlying justification given for doctrine and policy together. (This tripartite distinction is emphasized by *Oakeshott.) Political outlooks differ radically over whether policy is or should be a reflection of some underlying philosophical position, but most agree that policy should be consistent, reasonable and acceptable to those with power to oppose it. Some argue that it cannot have those qualities unless it also has the support of a (perhaps unexpressed) doctrine, which identifies, even if it does not justify, the ends that are pursued.

polis

The Greek city-state, i.e. a system of independent *jurisdiction over a city. Usually the population was small enough for most citizens to be acquainted with those in power, and usually the economic life of the city involved trade with neighbours, supported by more or less extensive territories in the surrounding countryside and elsewhere. Western political thought began with the study of the *polis*, and its transference to the study of modern states and nations involves an extension of theory and concept that some have criticized as unwarranted. The *polis* was surrounded by other states whose citizens spoke the same language; it competed openly with its neighbours for territorial and economic privileges; its institutions were the object of observation, criticism and emulation from only twenty miles away; often it seemed to have a tribal character in which relations of kinship were as important as relations of law; and the Greek city-states were constantly at war with each other.

Such features distinguish the city state, in part, from the modern *nation state; nevertheless it is not at all clear that they render the observations of *Plato and *Aristotle inapplicable to modern constitutions.

politburo (sometimes: politbureau)
The 'political bureau', i.e. ruling committee of the USSR *Communist Party, and the effective bearer of executive power within the state. Established as a subcommittee of the Party Central Committee in 1919 (members, Lenin, Trotsky, Stalin, Kamenev, Krestinsky) it gradually grew, until abolished in 1952, when it was replaced by a 25-member presidium. This subsequently contracted to 10 members and was often called the Politburo from a sense that its nature and function were indistinguishable from those of the previous committee of that name. (Likewise for other ruling communist parties on the Soviet model.)

political
A term that is used in at least two important ways, first in the distinction between the political and the social, in which 'political' means, roughly, pertaining to the *state and its institutions; secondly in the distinction between political and other models of *government, for which *see* *politics.

political arithmetic
Term of seventeenth-century economics, made current by *Petty, who used it to denote the whole science of political economy. Petty put economics on a new footing through attempting to give a mathematical analysis of the balance of trade, and to expose fallacies in the currently accepted forms of *mercantilism.

political class
The class, increasingly important in modern democratic politics, of people who have made a career in political and administrative institutions, but who have not had any experience of the ordinary workplace. The political class has long been recognized as a reality in France: see *énarque*. It has also been remarked that the parliamentary members of the Labour Party under *New Labour are for the most part drawn from this class: people who have had posts in local government, in the civil service, in *quangos, in *NGOs close to Labour Party policy, in think-tanks and policy units, but who have not, on the whole, had to live from any direct contribution to the economy. The *European Union is likewise a fiefdom of the political class, there being few avenues for advancement within it that do not require a long apprenticeship in political or quasi-political institutions. Some think that this decisively influences the content of both EU and New Labour policies.

The distinctive feature of the political class is that it owes its social position to its political influence. In this it is the opposite of the old *ruling class, which owed its political influence to its social position. The political class therefore resembles the *new class described by Djilas, and the *Nomenklatura under Soviet communism.

political correctness (PC)
During the course of the twentieth century people became increasingly aware of the ways in which language and behaviour can serve to *stereotype and denigrate, and thereby to reinforce attitudes that promote *discrimination. A gradual but systematic reform of political language began, with words like 'nigger' and 'yid' disapproved and eventually expelled from the language. What began as a commendable pursuit of objectivity and courtesy soon took on a life of its own, however, so that each new way

of labelling people – however accurate – could be deemed 'politically incorrect' by someone, and so become a target of hostility. Thus 'negro', which replaced 'nigger', was soon disapproved, to be displaced by 'black', to be displaced in turn (in the US context) by 'African-American'. Harmless though these linguistic reforms might appear, they generated minefields for the unwary who, having inadvertently referred to some hitherto disfavoured minority with the wrong label, or even used that label in a way that could be misunderstood, might be accused of a *thoughtcrime – as illustrated by Philip Roth in *The Human Stain*, 2000. For this reason the concept of 'political correctness' has become a topic of intense controversy in the US and elsewhere, those on the *right attacking it as a threat to free speech and an excuse for witchhunts, those on the left endorsing it (though seldom under this description, which has now acquired a perjorative flavour) as a necessary preliminary to fair and respectful public dialogue.

The controversy has been fuelled by recent tendencies to judge not just language but also behaviour and even opinions in terms of their political correctness. It has been judged politically incorrect to open doors for women, to invite homosexuals to dinner without their current partners, to hunt animals, or to advocate a traditional curriculum in the humanities: though again, someone who thought in that way would not describe those practices as 'politically incorrect', but find some other and more neutral expression with which to condemn them. PC has advanced beyond good manners to become a social policy, directed towards a multicultural, inclusive, caring and non-judgemental society. Those who will not or cannot live in such a society are therefore the victims of PC, which seems to exclude them from institutions where its advocates are in the ascendant. The effect on university life in the US has been welcomed and deplored with equal vehemence, PC being used not only to police the language and attitudes of the professoriat, but also to advance and destroy careers within it, on grounds that many feel have little to do with academic excellence. Moreover, recent studies have shown that PC acts not merely to marginalize opinions, but also to marginalize facts, so that the UK Home Office, for example, has issued a report attributing the increase in HIV cases to increased sexual activity among the young, for fear that the truth – that the increase is due to immigration from Africa – would be unacceptable to *bien pensant* opinion.

political development

A topic in political science, arising from the assumption (common to *Comte, *Marx, *Durkheim and *Weber) that there is a definite sequence of changes undergone by political systems, which move always in the same direction. Hence societies can be described as more or less politically developed, and theories constructed as to which institutions lead to which in the avenue of political *progress. The assumption may be plausible in the case of Western democracies but seems to have little relevance elsewhere.

political economy

In contrast to domestic economy, political economy studies the economic behaviour and interest of the entire state. The term was introduced in 1613 by A. de Monchréstien, and became established in English usage with James Steuart's *Inquiry into the Principles of Political Economy*, 1767. It survives from subsequent eighteenth- and nineteenth-century usage, but retains, in the word 'political', an implication that factors other than the economic may be relevant to questions of political economy. *Welfare economics is an example of a theory of political economy, which attempts to build into its conception of 'welfare' some idea of the 'politically acceptable' which is not just reducible to the 'economically efficient'.

The term was for a while current among thinkers of the *New Left, in order to denote systems of economics which take seriously the political implications of the science, and which (in contrast to 'mainstream economics') attempt to describe arrangements which are radically different from the capitalist market. Such thinkers often complain that *neo-classical economics relies on being able to isolate the economic from the political, and that this cannot be done. Defenders of the *free market are themselves now returning to the use of the term.

political obligation

Roughly, the obligation of the *citizen towards the *state, or of the *subject towards the *sovereign. The expression is sometimes used to denote the reverse obligation from sovereign to subject, or the reciprocal obligation between the two.

The definition is rough since some theories of political obligation deny that there can be obligation towards a state, but admit the possibility of obligation towards *society; others deny even that, and argue that political obligation is held neither towards the state, nor towards society, nor towards any other abstraction or office, but towards each member of society individually. (The basis of this last view might be some sort of *individualism or, at any rate, a denial that abstract entities can be *persons.) The problem of political obligation – what it is and how it is justified – has come

to be one of the central problems of political philosophy. The major theories can be classified thus:

(i) Social contract theories, according to which the obligation arises from a contract, either with all members of society individually (Hobbes, *Locke), with society itself (*Rousseau), or with the sovereign (*Bodin).

(ii) Theories of consent which fall short of contract – e.g. *tacit consent, whereby the citizen shows his acceptance of an arrangement as so acting under its protection as to bind himself in an obligation towards it. This is often presented as a part of (i), as by *Locke.

(iii) Theories of non-consensual obligation, which describe political obligation as arising independently from any choice of the subject, say from *piety (as in *Burke and *Hegel), or from the sovereign's right to *obedience.

(iv) Theories (of which (iii) provides some examples) which are framed in terms of conditions for *legitimacy, arguing that there is an obligation from the subject towards every legitimate sovereign. The *divine right of kings is such a theory, as is the very different theory of the *mandate, and similar theories emerging from the idea of *election.

(v) Negative theories. For example, the theory that the citizen is always under an obligation towards the state unless and until the state acts unjustly, or so as to negate some necessary human good, such as freedom. Most such theories can be rephrased as special theories of legitimacy, which argue that the concept of legitimacy is 'defeasible' – i.e. every government is legitimate unless . . . – upon which might follow a possibly open-ended series of conditions. It is possible that Aristotle's theory of political obligation was of this type, and that his reference to justice as the binding principle of the state was meant to indicate one among several unspecified conditions, the absence of which would suffice to take legitimacy away.

All the above theories are discussed elsewhere in this work.

political offence

The right of *extradition usually suffers exception in the case of 'political offences', although what counts as a political offence has not been defined authoritatively in UK or US law. Two criteria have been suggested:

(i) Do the facts alleged amount to a known crime, discounting political motivation?

(ii) Was there political motivation?

If the second criterion is used, then you can get away with quite a lot, perhaps even murder and terrorism. If the first criterion is used, then a suspect can be extradited only for those things recognized as crimes in the court before which he is brought. This will suffice to grant *sanctuary to victims of many oppressive laws, which make it a crime, say, to publish criticisms of the state, but not to an assassin or a terrorist. The UK courts tend to view as political any offence committed 'in connection with' a 'political disturbance', but the two apostrophized phrases indicate that this criterion is as vague in practice as the notion which it is used to define.

Why should there be this exclusion under extradition agreements? One plausible answer is that, without it, rights of sanctuary are ineffective. Another is that a foreign power may be in the course of being overthrown, and may attempt to make itself secure by inventing 'political crimes'. To return people wanted for such crimes is in effect to take sides in a political struggle which may result in a new regime offended by the fate of its supporters, and therefore disposed to regard with hostility those who had surrendered

them. But many other considerations are relevant; it is, for example, important for extradition agreements to avoid what might amount to a declaration of war through judicial action.

political participation
See *participation.

political realism
See *realism.

political science
See *political thought.

political sociology
See *political thought.

political theology

The transfer of theological concepts to the political sphere, emphasizing man's fallen character, the defect of *original sin, and the need for an authoritative legal order that would do justice to the longing for redemption. Political Theology can be discerned in the writings of Rousseau and Hegel, both of whom are given to describing the political reality in terms borrowed from Christian theology, and in the writings of many Russian political thinkers, including *Kojève. It was attacked by *Schmitt (*Political Theology*, 1927), as involving a dangerous tendency to deify the state.

political thought

This may mean any one of four things:

1. Political thought, in the sense of the title of this dictionary: thoughts, theories and values which motivate *policy and political behaviour. Political thought includes the theories through which people attempt to explain each other's political behaviour, the values by which they judge it, and the mechanisms (such as law) whereby they attempt to control it.

2. Political theory. The theory of political institutions. This includes the

theories of the state, of law, of representation and election. It is a comparative and explanatory science, exemplified in works of constitutional history and analysis.

3. Political philosophy. This seeks the most general answers to the most general questions of method and justification raised by the concepts and theories employed in 1. and 2. Thus the concept of justice, which may form a part of ordinary political thought, may also be a subject of philosophical analysis, with a view to determining its grounds.

4. Political science. An academic discipline which includes 2. and 3. along with *political economy, and perhaps also *sociology (in which case it might go by the name of political sociology). It involves a developing synthesis of many contrasting disciplines, and incorporates all studies which have politically significant thought and action as their subject-matter. It is probably too wide and too ambitious to be an independent subject with a method of its own, and remains influential only as a projected unity rather than as an actual one.

political union

See *European Union, *federalism.

politicization

To 'politicize' is to transform an activity that seemed to have no political connotations into one that is consciously bent towards political ends. Thus *Benjamin recommended that, in the interests of revolution, it is necessary to 'politicize art', meaning that the facade of impassive contemplation presented by art must be broken down, and its real potential as an agent of political transformation revealed.

Often advocates of politicization argue that all institutions and practices are already tacitly politicized, in the interests of the *status quo*. There has thus arisen a movement among *leftist and *feminist scholars to politicize their teaching, not in order to inject politics where previously there was none, but in order to expose the covert political *agenda of the existing curriculum and to open up the possibility of political choice. For example, feminists argue that *humane education, as traditionally conceived, was really a complex process for the *legitimation of *patriarchy, and that the duty of the scholar is not only to show that this is so, but in the course of doing so to subvert the traditional curriculum by opening up the possibility of another, built around a rival political agenda.

Opponents argue that the traditional curriculum was built around an *intellectual* and not a political agenda, and that there is all the difference in the world between a curriculum that indirectly supports a certain political order and one which is constructed with the sole purpose of doing so. The second, they argue, is characteristic of *totalitarianism and is precisely not a curriculum in the true sense of the word since it substitutes *indoctrination for *education. Such, they imply, will be the result of the feminist programme, should it succeed. The debate here is fascinating, complex and not to be resolved within the space of a dictionary entry.

politics

Sometimes used as a plural noun, sometimes and now more usually as a singular, 'politics' began its career in English as a term of abuse for the activities of those engaged in *faction (and is rhymed with 'knavish tricks' in the National Anthem), but gradually became respectable as modern forms of *representation evolved. Definitions are many and varied, ranging from the conciliatory ('the art of the possible' –

Bismarck), through the cynical ('the art of governing mankind through deceiving them' – Isaac D'Israeli), to the wilfully assertive ('the art of carrying out the life struggle of a nation for its earthly existence' – Hitler). As now used 'politics' denotes a kind of activity associated with *government, but there are conflicting views as to what this activity amounts to. Some follow the English legal theorist Sir John Fortescue in his praise of the English constitution (*De Laudibus Legum Angliae, c.* 1470), and distinguish political from regal forms of government, both involving the imposition of law, but the former distinguished by the attempt to gain consent for that law through representation and *conciliation. Others, similarly motivated, frame their definition in terms offered by *Aristotle, and see politics as the art of controlling and reconciling the diverse *interests* within a state. This influence can be seen in the following definition: 'Politics . . . can be simply defined as the activity by which differing interests within a given unit of rule are conciliated by giving them a share in power in proportion to their importance to the welfare and survival of the whole community. And . . . a political system is that type of government where politics proves successful in ensuring reasonable stability and order' (Bernard Crick, *In Defence of Politics*, 1962).

Such definitions are appealing, since they emphasize the centrality of balance and conciliation to the art of politics; however, in the looser sense exemplified in this dictionary there are activities and doctrines called 'political' which have no ability to tolerate *opposition, and a rooted antagonism to all conciliatory gestures – e.g. *democratic centralism, *Leninism, *Gleichschaltung. Moreover the definition is far from clear, even if we can take for granted some understanding of the terms (such as 'interests', 'rule', 'welfare' and 'community') that are employed in it. What of a share in power that is *not* according to the welfare of the whole? What if conciliation is accomplished by some other means than power-sharing? What kind of power is in question? (If we say, 'political power' then we are beginning to run in a circle.) Nevertheless, the idea of politics as involving the recognition and conciliation of conflicting interests is now widely accepted. Some draw the conclusion that politics is therefore opposed to *sovereignty, although this is clearly wrong, since no conciliation can be effected between diverse interests without there being an entity more authoritative than both, even if that entity is nothing other than the contract or agreement that they will live in harmony. Out of that contract sovereignty is automatically born. More plausibly, sovereignty is its necessary pre-condition, and the condition of its enforcement.

Among writers who have given wide application to the idea of politics, one of the most influential in recent times has been *Arendt, who arranges human life in a threefold hierarchy – Labour, Work and Action – and identifies politics as the central feature of the last and highest sphere (*The Human Condition*, 1958). Politics has a special significance, since it is only in the realm of action that the uniqueness of the human individual, and his absolute right to exist, are brought into play. The goal of politics is to create the public realm in which individuals can exist freely side by side, while protecting the private space required for personal development.

polyarchy

Greek: rule of the many. Term used by the American political scientist Robert Dahl (b. 1915) to define modern democracies, in which government, while apparently vested in the *people, is in fact conducted by a plurality of competing *interest groups, formed by and in response to free elections, free opinion and freedom of association. (Robert Dahl, *Polyarchy: Participation and Opposition*, 1971.)

polycentrism

The splitting of a political organization into independent centres of power. Used to describe developments in world communism after the twentieth congress of the USSR Communist Party in 1956. The term was popularized by the Italian communist leader P. Togliatti, to refer to the general emergence of independent communist parties, a process which began with the dispute between the USSR and Yugoslavia, continued in the breach between Soviet and Chinese political practice and interests, and was subsequently exemplified in the various attempts by Western European communist parties to find an identity independent of the USSR (*see* *Eurocommunism), and by Eastern European communist parties to assert forms of national communism more appropriate to local conditions than those imposed on them by Stalin.

poor laws

The 'old poor law', created by the Poor Relief Act 1601, charged the relief of the poor to every parish, which had to provide work and to tax all residents in order to provide both the work and the relief that was earned by it. Parishes began to combine into poor law unions so as to administer this charge, and to appoint elected boards of guardians. The 'new poor law' of 1834 set up a central board of Poor Law Commissioners, and from then on social welfare was considered in the UK to be a national and not just a local

concern. This can be seen as in part a response towards the increased mobility of labour, and the rapidity with which towns were growing and declining. Legislation culminated in the creation of the *welfare state during the twentieth century, and the end of the requirement that poor relief would be given only to those who suffered what was increasingly regarded as the ignominy of the 'workhouse'. 'Unemployment benefit' is now regarded as a right.

Popper, Sir Karl Raimund (1902–96)

Viennese-born philosopher whose study of scientific method has been extremely influential, both in the philosophy of science, and (because of his own application of it to political theory) in political thought and practice. Popper argues in *The Logic of Scientific Discovery*, 1935, that all serious science is 'hypothetico-deductive', that is, it involves, not induction from accumulated instances, but rather the postulation of a hypothesis from which deductions are made. Since the hypothesis is universal, it can be confirmed by no finite number of instances; but it can be disconfirmed by one, and that is the clue to scientific method, which proceeds by 'conjecture and refutation' – i.e. the postulation of a hypothesis and the attempt to refute it through finding a counter-example. (*See also* *Kuhn.)

Pseudo-science is recognizable, therefore, by the fact that either it is unfalsifiable, or else it shuns falsification, by the constant adoption of qualifications so as to accommodate every conceivable fact. One example of such pseudo-science is the Ptolemaic system of 'epicycles', which have no other rationale than to avoid empirical disproof of the Ptolemaic cosmology. Another example is the Marxian theory of history, which makes only wrong predictions, and yet which constantly amends itself so as never to regard itself as refuted in its fundamental tenets. That is an example of *historicism – the attempt to subsume all of history under a single principle which 'explains' everything. In *The Poverty of Historicism*, 1957, Popper sets out to refute all forms of historicism on two grounds, the first being that the growth of knowledge itself exerts an influence on the course of history, hence neither the growth of knowledge nor its general effects can be predicted, since to predict knowledge is already to possess it. The second ground is that social science is of such a nature that it cannot generate laws of total social development, but only laws for fragmented and isolated social units. From this 'methodological individualism' Popper draws the conclusion that there is no rational approach to social problems which can give grounds for total change, since to attempt such change is necessarily to act on assumptions about the whole of things, i.e. to act blindly. The only kind of social reform that can be rationally contemplated is *piecemeal engineering. In the earlier *The Open Society and its Enemies*, 1945, Popper had attacked three historicist views – those of *Plato, *Hegel and *Marx – and tried to show that the search for total explanations of society was in each case combined with visions of government that were totalitarian in their aims and principles. He suggests that the only scientifically acceptable answer to the question, Who should rule? is to reject it, and to ask instead, How can institutions be devised that will minimize the risk of bad rulers?, a question to which Marxism, for example, has never addressed itself. (*See also* *holism, *open society, *individualism.)

populism

1. The populist (in Russian, *narodnik, where it is associated with a specific political movement) is one who wishes to solve all political problems by appealing to the 'will of the people', believing the people to have instincts and reactions which, if properly tapped, will be alone sufficient to provide guidance and authority to the statesman. The narodniks believed the people to have some special role in the process of social evolution; the US 'Populist Party (founded 1891) thought that the people required support from the government, in their attempt to maintain the American tradition of small private enterprise and self-sufficient farming. English conservatives often look for the 'roots' of their doctrine in the spirit of a people thought to be deeply and inarticulately loyal to its main provisions. (A view which was entertained and in part endorsed by *Coleridge and by *Carlyle.)

2. The term is now also used in a somewhat pejorative sense, to denote the behaviour of the politician who appeals at every juncture to popular sentiment, and enlists ignorant opinion to his side, even in matters of the utmost delicacy where the people lack the expertise to make a sound decision. In this sense the populist has much in common with the *demagogue, and his type is prominent in many *nationalist movements in the former communist countries.

pornography

The definition of this term is much contested. A first shot might be: pornography is the production of an *obscenity which provides a fantasy object for *sexual desire. That definition can be extended to any object which provides a gratification for fantasy and which shows the structural characteristic of obscenity (i.e. which represents the human body as voided of human personality). Thus there can be, in an extended sense, a pornography of eating, of violence, and so on.

The dispute over the value of pornography concerns two concepts which are instruments of confusion: that of obscenity, and that of fantasy. Given the definition offered of obscenity, it would seem that no one would think that a sexual impulse that sought to gratify itself through obscene representations could ever be a vehicle of personal feeling, and if it is true that sexual impulses ought to be vehicles of personal feeling, then pornography can reasonably be said to minister to debased desires. In addition it is sometimes said that fantasy is in itself a species of corruption, in that it permits the indulgence of impulses that would otherwise be inhibited, and so nurtures what we wish to suppress. One reply is that the fantasy gratification of a desire acts as a safety-valve for feelings which might otherwise be expressed in more damaging ways. Those two thoughts about fantasy are seldom attached to any theory of human nature which would enable us to determine which is true.

The problem of pornography and the law is in part independent. Those who see the law as a protective device, designed to safeguard the innocent from *harm, but to permit to the guilty whatever perversions constitute their delight, may think that the law should content itself merely to forbid the open sale of pornography. One of the problems, even for that view, lies in the peculiar nature of the 'offensiveness' of pornography: to discover such things by accident may have a devastating effect, and the mere knowledge that it is possible to obtain pornography proves to be an irritant to the morally susceptible. Moreover, with the increasing sophistication of the electronic *media, it is unlikely that legislation could be devised which would be able to arrest the flow of pornographic images.

To some extent the confused debates over this issue reflect the confusions in the criterion of harm. However, there is a real question, in the case of sexuality, as to where the boundary between the private and the public might lie. (See *law and morality, *sex) The debate has acquired an added twist in recent years, on account of the *feminist claim that pornography exploits and oppresses women and that its real but tacit function is to perpetuate their bondage. And the explosion of child pornography through the internet brings home the extent of the injustice and exploitation involved in the creation of pornographic material.

positive discrimination

Synonymous with *reverse discrimination.

positive economics

1. Economics of the actual, rather than the ideal: economics which takes its scientific pretensions seriously, and attempts to establish hypotheses that might be refuted by empirical evidence. (See *Popper.)

2. Alternatively, economics which attempts to detach itself from all statements of a *normative kind, on the grounds that the factual and the normative are distinct, and that science concerns itself only with facts, and never with *values.

positive law

Law 'posited', or laid down, by a particular body of *conventions; for example, through the will of a *sovereign, through the enactments of a *legislature (see *statute), or through the accumulation of customary rights. Positive law is distinguished from *natural law, being entirely the product of human design. Whether it can be justified by referring to some independent standard is one of the fundamental questions of political thought

– whether, for example, there is an independent standard of *justice (which is the doctrine of natural law), or whether the only standard is utility.

positivism
1. The philosophical and political doctrine propagated by *Saint-Simon and extended by *Comte, who gave it reputation. 'Positive' here means that which really exists and can be observed, as opposed to the dubious fancies of theology and metaphysics. Comte advocated a scientific sociology, and attempted to show that the *progress which attaches to scientific thought can be, and perhaps has been, transferred to the human condition generally. By extending scientific knowledge, the problem of providing for human needs in this life can be solved without referring to another, hence the worship of humanity was to replace the worship of God.

2. Certain schools of sociology, notably those influenced by *Durkheim, which concern themselves with questions of method, and regard their subject-matter as the realm of *social facts.

3. 'Positive science', i.e. the exhortation to study facts rather than values, and to eliminate all statements of a *normative character from scientific explanations. (*See* *positive economics.*)

4. Logical positivism. The philosophy associated with the 'Vienna circle' of the 1920s and 1930s, and influenced in England and America by Bertrand Russell and the early Wittgenstein. Logical positivism was based on the 'verification principle', according to which the meaning of every sentence is completely determined by its method of verification and by nothing else. Unverifiable propositions – such as those of theology and metaphysics – are meaningless. Logical positivism has had little

effect on political philosophy, except indirectly through the work of *Popper (who changed 'verification' to 'falsification' in his criterion for scientific method), and through the ethos of resolute scepticism and hard-headed anti-mysticism which it briefly inspired. Sometimes a particular interpretation of, e.g., *liberalism or *historical materialism, is denounced as 'positivist', the intention being to condemn a narrowness of outlook concerning what can, and what cannot, meaningfully be said.

5. Legal positivism. The view of law which advocates the study of actual legal systems, and eschews the search for independent justifications in terms of *natural law: i.e. the view which assumes that all law is *positive law. The leading positivists are Austin, who defined law as a command of the sovereign, expressing his wish, and backed by sanctions, and *Kelsen, who saw all law as a system of directives to apply coercion in accordance with a basic constitutional principle, or *Grundnorm*. Such theories see law as a system of rules backed by coercion, which do not owe their status as law to any independent criterion, such as that supposedly provided by natural law. Both Austin's and Kelsen's theories have difficulty, e.g. in accounting for the law of *contract or *trust (*see* *equity), but both have been highly influential, the first in particular on the *utilitarians (who were inspired also by an earlier positivist, *Bentham). Modern positivists attempt to preserve the spirit of such theories, while giving more sophisticated accounts of the process whereby a decision is 'validated as law'.

possession
What is it to possess something? I possess many things: my mind and talents; my *labour power, and certain things that I have produced or

acquired through exerting that power; a house, a garden, a set of books, a family. Do I possess all these in the same sense? *Locke argued that there is a *natural right of property which emerges from 'mixing my labour' with an object. This doctrine seems to give an affirmative answer, to say that the 'property' that I have in any object is like the property that I have in my labour power, which is in turn like the property that I have in my own limbs and talents. This transition from a 'natural' relation to a relation of *right has proved fascinating, but also unsatisfactory, to later thinkers. Despite Locke's argument, the concept of possession and its role in the notion of *private property remain obscure.

In *land law attempts have been made to define possession more precisely, with interesting political consequences. Possession seems to mean either *de facto* *control over some object or territory, or such control backed also by the sanction of the law (= legal possession). It is normal to consider legal possession to require two things: physical control, and an intention to exert it (an *animus possidendi*). The first element may be absent, as when a legal owner of property temporarily turns his back on it, and the law protects his right. But if the second element disappears, so too does the possession. This is what establishes the squatter's right to land. If John has resided at a place for some time without recognizing Alfred's right to it, and if Alfred has not asserted that right in any way, then, after a certain time (*see* *limitation) the law will step in to protect (or rather, to create) John's right to remain, thus conferring on him 'possessory title'.

post-communism

The condition of countries emerging from the collapse of communism.

Already in the last years of communism, *dissident writers (for example *Havel) had described the contemporary society as 'post-totalitarian'. There is now a widespread recognition that the social and political character of societies released from communism cannot be easily captured by the concepts of traditional political science. Among the special features are these:

(i) The dissolution of the Communist Party without any coherent legal process whereby to punish its crimes or to confiscate its unjustly acquired assets. (*See* *party.)

(ii) The retention by the old *Nomenklatura of high positions in the state bureaucracies and in the state-controlled enterprises.

(iii) Schemes for the wholesale *privatization of state enterprises, often to their former managers but sometimes by distributing coupons to the citizens at large.

(iv) Restitution of property to private owners and to the churches.

(v) Emergence of new political parties in which dissidents figure prominently, but which quickly lose popular support as they show themselves unable to deal with the inherited economic catastrophe.

(vi) Incipient democratic institutions, with a free press and a rule of law, though without the benefit of investigative journalism, and in the context of widespread apathy among the public, which has lost faith in politics of every kind.

(vii) The existence of a vast army of state dependants – employees in state enterprises, bureaucrats, collectivized farmers, and so on – who have no skills with which to survive in free market conditions, and who form a solid vote against all radical economic change.

Those conditions create a new cultural and political context. On the one hand there are the former dissidents and denizens of the *samizdat* culture, with European ideals and a sophisticated urban outlook but with little ability to govern; on the other hand there are the former *apparatchiks, worldly, materialistic and cynical, who nevertheless are the kind of people a Western investor or politician can 'do business with' and who are accepted by the people as the devil they know. The contest between the two factions is uneven, but in general agrarian societies like Poland, Romania and Hungary have leaned towards the apparatchiks, while urban and industrialized societies like the Czech Republic have leaned towards the ex-dissidents. In places where the *samizdat* culture did not exist, or existed only in minimal form, the ex-communist élites make great use of *nationalist ideologies, with which to *legitimate a power which previously depended on totalitarian control.

postmodern

The term 'postmodern' was made current by Ibn Hassan (*The Dismemberment of Orpheus: Towards a Post-Modern Literature*, 1976), though its wider use, to refer to the social and cultural condition of Western civilization following the end (as it is supposed) of the *modern period, is of more recent provenance. Theories of the postmodern condition are now commonplace, but credit must go to the French philosopher Jean-François Lyotard for grafting the concept on to the intellectual agenda of the *left. In *The Postmodern Condition*, 1979, he argues that modernity was distinguished by certain 'metanarratives' of *legitimation – by which he means theories and projects that justified human action in terms of a future state, usually a state of *emancipation from oppressive structures. Traditional societies derived their legitimacy from

some previous state, in which the gods themselves had authorized the tribe; the metanarratives of modernity, by contrast, confer legitimacy directly on the present moment, by showing how it might be seized for the benefit of all. Their legitimizing power stems from their universality – the good that is promised (freedom, enlightenment, socialism, prosperity, progress, etc.) is promised to all mankind, and the project of modernity is *cosmopolitan, involving the dissolution of traditional communities and their release into the collective future. The postmodern condition is one in which those metanarratives have lost their justifying force – the paths of emancipation have all been explored, the promises have been fulfilled, and we find ourselves released from tradition, free and equal members of a world community in which every lifestyle and every *value becomes openly available, only to lose its flavour. What exactly we should do about this, Lyotard does not say. However, other writers take up the point, arguing with *Fukuyama, for example, that capitalist democracy has finally overcome the contest of history and released us into a world of freedom and abundance from which we cannot turn back, in which all problems are inherently soluble and in which nothing is really worth dying for (*The End of History and the Last Man*, 1989). This is the world prophesied by *Nietzsche, the world of the 'last man', in which human aspiration will dwindle to such a point that all of life can be organized by a team of managers.

There is something that rings true in these attempts to write the 'history of the present moment', although whether what is being described is a postmodern condition, as opposed to the modern condition in its latest version, is debatable.

postmodernism

This seems to mean two things:

1. The sequel to *modernism. In music, painting and architecture, for example, the modernist schools have all but exhausted themselves and an eclectic mixture of styles has come in place of them. These could be called 'postmodernist', without implying any conscious adoption on the part of the artists themselves of a stance towards the *postmodern condition.

2. An attitude which affirms the postmodern world in the same way, and perhaps even with the same vehemence, as modernism affirmed the modern world, although quite what there is to affirm in a world that is based on the impossibility of affirmation it is hard to say. Usually a postmodernist in art is a skilled practitioner of irony who places elegant inverted commas around the naive beliefs of others.

In the English-speaking world the term was first propagated in both senses by Charles Jencks, in the course of describing postmodernist architecture. The postmodernist style, in Jencks's perception, is a style of quotation. Postmodernist architects do not build, but 'build' in inverted commas. And in doing so they mean to emphasize the peculiar nature of the world in which we live, a world in which all is permitted, in which the past has been divested of its authority, and in which all the cultures of mankind have been torn from their roots and spread before us on the smorgasbord.

It is not clear what a postmodernist politics would be. The *New Left Marxist critic Fredric Jameson has described postmodernism as the 'cultural logic of late capitalism', by which he seems to be condemning it (on the assumption that he is still sufficiently modern, or insufficiently postmodern, to believe that *late capitalism will one day be replaced by something better). Others have invoked *Nietzsche as providing the foundations for a postmodernist politics in which self-affirmation, free choice of lifestyle and defiance of convention go hand in hand with a recognition that there is no justification for this or for anything else. The problem for the *left is how to reconcile this posture with the instinctive commitment to democracy and equality – neither of which Nietzsche himself had any time for. The problem for the *right is how to redraw across the unbounded landscape of permission the old lines of authority, duty and responsibility, on which the future of mankind depends. Or is it true that we have reached the age of Nietzsche's last man?

post-structuralism

The movement of ideas, centred on the French *left and in particular on the journal *Tel Quel* (edited by Philippe Sollers), which followed the brief ascendancy of *structuralism in literary and political circles in Paris during the early 1960s. Not a school, but a loose assembly of thinkers who flirted with structuralism and then rejected it, looking elsewhere for cultural and political foundations. *Foucault is usually described as a post-structuralist, as is *Derrida; *deconstruction is also said to be a form of post-structuralism.

Poujadism

Attitudes associated with a political movement, the 'Union for the Defence of Small Shopkeepers and Artisans', founded in France in 1954, by Pierre Poujade (1920–97), and sometimes thought to be the quintessence of *petit bourgeois* politics: hostility to *taxation, to state ownership of industry, and to most forms of large-scale development and *modernization. There were also elements of anti-Semitism, Gaullism, and even fascism, among the Poujadists at the 1955 election.

poverty

An idea that is intuitively clear, but which is difficult to define except as the polar opposite of *wealth. A polar definition is unsatisfactory since, below a certain point, the difference between wealth and poverty is not just one of degree, but one of kind. Hence various analysts since the late nineteenth century have attempted to draw the 'poverty line' – the point below which *true* (non-relative) poverty exists. Charles Booth, in *The Poverty of the People*, 1899, took the average expenditure of families on food, rent and clothes and defined the poor as those with an income just equal to providing this average (but no more), and the very poor as those with less. Such ways of drawing the poverty line have since been attacked, in particular because they are insensitive to the different requirements and budgets that emerge in the state of poverty. Nevertheless poverty lines are still drawn for official purposes and used to define the 'poverty gap', which is the amount by which the aggregate income of the poor falls below what the line requires.

Two ideas seem important: first, that, in the polar sense, poverty consists in a relative absence of choice; i.e. the poor person is always circumscribed in his activity in ways which are overcome by wealth. Secondly, that the 'transition from quantity to quality' seems to occur when the inability to obtain what is desired becomes an inability to obtain what is needed. (*See* *need.*) Hence the poverty line corresponds to the point below which freedom of choice is so curtailed that a person cannot obtain what he needs. The difficulty in defining it is a result of the difficulty inherent in the concept of need: what a person needs for animal subsistence is not what he needs for effective survival as a social being; and what he needs as a social being may not suffice for his thriving as a rational animal. (E.g. does he *need* a family? Does he *need* education?) Needs are controversial, partly because of disagreements over *human nature, partly because of the social relativity of that nature.

Some distinguish poverty from pauperism, which is the state in which a person has less than he needs for survival, and so is unable to maintain himself at all without outside assistance. Pauperism (unlike poverty) has often been regarded not only as a misfortune, but as somehow intrinsically shameful – an idea variously rationalized in terms of *caste, *providence, idleness, but in all of its forms imposing on the pauper a sense of himself as falling not merely materially, but also morally, below a *norm. At the same time, traditional moralities have tended to argue that some (relative) poverty is not only compatible with virtue, but perhaps more naturally suited to it, and more naturally productive of happiness, than the extremes of wealth.

power

The ability to achieve whatever effect is desired, whether or not in the face of opposition. Power is a matter of degree; it can be conferred, delegated, shared and limited. It may be based on *consent or on *coercion. The power of a charismatic leader may be based on consent, while that of a tyrant usually is not; the power of the first may yet be very much greater than that of the second. Power may be exercised through *influence, or through *control (although it should be noted that, for no very good reason, political scientists often distinguish power from influence, thus restricting the term 'power' to relations that are exerted through control).

Because power (unlike *authority, *legitimacy and *right) is an indisputable fact, and easily understood as such, and because it seldom exists without also being exercised, there have arisen various *power theories of politics, which see power as the fundamental substance of which politics is the form. On these views, the important feature of every institution lies in its transformation, limitation and rationalization of power.

Power may be economic: ability to influence or control the economy; it may be political: ability to influence or control the institutions through which law is made or applied; it may be personal: ability to exert influence and control over people for whatever reason. Some theories argue that all political power is to be explained in terms of economic power (e.g. the common forms of *Marxism). Others regard all forms of power as different forms of a single thing, none of which is more basic to the explanation of human society than any other (e.g. *Foucault). In all its forms power involves both the ability to make or influence important decisions, and the ability to prevent others from doing the same.

One of the important questions in political thought concerns the relation of power to authority. We distinguish: power with authority; power with the common belief in its authority; and 'naked power', such as that exerted by a lawless gang. Politics can be seen as the attempt to transform the third into the second: to eliminate from public life all powers that do not have the sanction of a public acceptance of their authority. Thus, even when there is no 'political process' – no way in which new powers emerge into the public forum and seek the authority that is there bestowed – there may still be a process of *legitimation, whereby the naked power of the ruler attempts to represent itself as sanctioned by right. Naked power is weaker than the same power publicly accepted, and so this process can still be seen as a pursuit of power. Only if we believe that there really is an objective authority to be gained, can we see the pursuit of authority as something other than the pursuit of power.

The above sense of 'power' must be distinguished from the legal sense, where it denotes, not *de facto* ability, but *de jure* permission. The 'powers' conferred by law are permissions to do things without legal sanction. An agent who exercises such powers can be legally restrained only from exercising them *ultra vires* (i.e. beyond the powers granted), in which case he is not exercising them.

power élite

Phrase coined by *Mills, to denote those who wield *power within the ruling institutions of modern society, and who act, sometimes collusively, and in any case from common interests, to preserve and enhance that power.

power politics

German: *Machtpolitik*. The conducting of politics (including domestic politics) entirely as though there were no factor involved besides power, so that groups without power are not considered, and those with power considered only to the extent that they possess it.

power theories of politics

Theories of political practice and institutions which attempt to describe and to explain those things in terms of the existence, transfer, development and division of *power, as opposed to the *rights theories of politics, which see their subject matter in terms of *rights. (*See* *rights and powers.) Among power theories the theory of *sovereignty offered by *Machiavelli in *The Prince* is perhaps the most striking, in that it regards the central fact of politics as the concentration and maintenance of supreme *control over all people within a certain territory, and evaluates all institutions as means to this end. Justice and law are admitted into the theory only because the human disposition to believe in those things is itself one of the powers that have to be subsumed by the sovereign.

pragmatism

1. A philosophical theory associated with the names of the American philosophers C.S. Peirce (1839–1914), William James (1842–1910) and John *Dewey, which identifies the meaning and justification of beliefs through the practical results of holding them. Pragmatism can be seen as a form of *empiricism which tries to make due allowance for the fact that the subject of knowledge is not just a recipient of sensation, but also an active inquirer. Even 'truth' is subordinate to practice for James, since the only credentials of true belief are that, in holding it and acting from it, we find ourselves more successful than we otherwise might have been. Pragmatism has been enormously influential, both on American philosophy and on American political science. It seems to give a grounding to concepts not only of science, but also of law and social theory. By explaining political thought in terms of its survival value, it also justifies political thought as a beneficial feature of the human condition. Recent advocates of pragmatism, notably *Rorty, have seen in it the only coherent metaphysics for dealing with the *postmodern condition and an instrument for the *emancipation of all those groups who have been trapped by the 'realist' concept of truth. For Rorty the pursuit of truth must be replaced by the pursuit of

community, since there is no other constraint on our discourse. Hence pragmatism points towards a *communitarian politics.

2. More generally used as a name for any approach that emphasizes what can be done in the actual world rather than what ought to be done in an ideal world.

praxeology

See *Mises.

praxis

Derived from the Greek for action, the term *praxis* is used by Aristotle to denote practical reasoning, as opposed to *theoria*, or theoretical reasoning. Through *Hegel's use of the term, and the occasional reference in *Marx, 'praxis' came to denote the general capacity to act so that one's projects and beliefs are in harmony with the world represented through them, together with a presumption that belief and action are not so sharply separable as *empiricist theories of knowledge would require them to be. The term is much used in *neo-Marxism (which contains a 'praxis school'), and means something like this: praxis is activity that removes the necessity for *false consciousness. It sustains itself without *ideology, since it is directed to the essential nature of social reality. At a time of incipient revolution, the only true praxis is 'revolutionary praxis'. All other forms of activity falsify the world, and hide from the participant his true social nature. Through praxis we not only overcome false consciousness, but also manoeuvre ourselves into a position from which we can assess the claims of Marxism and perceive that they are true. (*Cf.* *faith.)

precautionary principle

A principle often invoked, but seldom defined, by those who argue for caution in all matters that might have long-term damaging effects, especially on the environment or on health. A footnote to the 1982 Stockholm environmental conference recommended the precautionary principle as the acceptable approach to scientific innovation – but did nothing to define it. Thereafter the principle was repeatedly mentioned in European edicts, as authority for a creeping regime of regulation which ostensibly had the protection of the public as its rationale, but which also (according to its critics) has had the stifling of innovation as its consequence. In 1998 a gathering of lawyers, scientists, philosophers and green activists in the US produced the Wingspread Statement, which defined the Principle thus: 'When an activity raises threats of harm to the environment or human health, precautionary measures should be taken even if some cause and effect relationships are not fully established scientifically' – which is a definition of nothing, since any activity can be deemed to comply with it. Finally, in 2000, the European Commission published a 29-page communication on the principle, purporting to clarify its use, but again answering the need for a definition with a fudge. The principle, it said, may be applicable 'where preliminary scientific evaluation indicates that there are reasonable grounds for concern that the potentially dangerous effects on the environment, human, animal or plant health may be inconsistent with the high level of protection chosen for the Community'. The words 'preliminary', 'potentially', 'may' betray the essential retreat from precision that this statement involves. And the reference to a 'high level of protection chosen for the Community' naturally leads to the question 'chosen by whom?'. The statement is in fact a licence to forbid

any activity that a bureaucrat judges, on whatever flimsy grounds, to have a possible cost attached to it.

Despite this vagueness – or maybe because of it – the precautionary principle is now routinely invoked to justify the regulation of businesses which have a potential impact on the environment, on health and safety, and on animals.

precedent

In law the 'doctrine of precedent' holds that in all judicial proceedings, previous decisions by superior courts are binding. More precisely, each such decision contains a principle (*ratio decidendi*, i.e. reason for deciding) which, if *applicable* to the present case, must be *applied* in the present case. The principle can be revoked, but not by any court inferior to the one that first applied it. In the US, where the doctrine of precedent is far less influential than it is in the UK, principles can be revoked by the courts that first applied them. In the UK they can be revoked only by a superior court, although the embarrassment that this causes in the highest court has led to the House of Lords on several occasions refusing to be bound by its own decisions.

The *ratio decidendi* of a precedent may not be easy to discover, and it is part of the judicial function in the lower court to interpret the judgement of the higher so as to bring the *ratio* to light. Alternatively, the judge of the lower court may leave the *ratio* unformulated, and decide either that the decision in the previous case does apply to the present case, or that it does not. In the latter judgement, known as 'distinguishing a case', the judge must point to material differences between the present case and the previous one and argue that the differences are relevant, so that the previous decision does not bind him.

The judge can do this without formulating the *ratio decidendi* of the preceding case; it suffices to show that the differences are so great that the *ratio*, whatever it was, does not apply.

The doctrine of precedent raises in a vivid form the question of judicial *legislation. The older theory in English law was that, in following precedents, judges were simply declaring the law that had always existed in custom and in previous decisions; but, this custom being the custom of judges, it must surely be the case that judges were the agents who created it. So such a theory is not a theory at all – it gives us no answer to the question of where law comes from when cases are distinguished and precedents made. The reasoning involved in following a precedent is in fact extremely complex, and it is very hard to present clear answers to philosophical questions as to its nature. What happens, for example, when a superior court *overrules* a precedent? Does it change the law, or does it rather record the conviction that the law had been wrongly understood? If the higher court changes the law, then it seems that it violates the *sovereignty of Parliament and the *separation of powers. If it declares that the law had been misinterpreted, then it says in effect that all previous cases under the precedent were wrongly decided, which seems hardly consistent with the fact that these cases can (as a rule) no longer be retried.

predestination

The divine decree under which certain persons are inexorably guided to eternal salvation, and perhaps others to damnation. The doctrine of predestination is a cornerstone of *Calvinist theology, according to which salvation is offered to the elect alone. Some have accepted predestination and sought to reconcile it with the view

that the others nevertheless have a chance. (Such seems to have been *Augustine's position.) Secular forms of the doctrine exist, as in the *Nazi idea that the Aryan race was predestined to world domination, and as in certain *vulgar Marxist views to the effect that history is *on the side of* the proletariat. In all its forms the doctrine may lead to *antinomianism and, according to *Weber, a disorderliness of such a deep-seated kind that a new kind of self-discipline and public regimentation may come in the place of normal moral sanctions. (*Cf.* *determinism, *fatalism.)

prediction/decision

A prediction is a statement about the future which expresses a belief, and which is founded (if at all) in evidence for its truth. A decision is also a statement about the future, but it expresses an intention, and is founded (if at all) not in evidence but in reasons for action. The distinction between the two is fundamental to the understanding of practical reason, and has exercised the ingenuity of several recent philosophers. On one account, *alienation is the state of mind which ensues from the renunciation of intention in favour of prediction, even in those spheres where the self and its *agency might be supposed to hold sway.

Decisions involve responsibility towards the future, whereas predictions do not. Hence some say that *historicist doctrines, which subsume all politics within a vision of the inevitable course of history, leave no room for responsible action. The view is dubious, but some milder version of it may nevertheless be correct.

preference

A concept of increasing importance in both economics and political theory, and now replacing, for many theoretical purposes, older ideas of *utility, both because preferences can be associated with direct empirical tests (*see* *revealed preference), and because preferences may be treated mathematically in ways which do not raise unanswerable problems of measurement. For the purposes of mathematical treatment, a preference is an ordering of alternatives: when *a* is not preferred to *b* and *b* not preferred to *a* the choice between them is said to be indifferent. The relation between preference and indifference has been important in the adoption of the *indifference curve, as a theoretical device in the explanation, e.g., of prices.

A 'preference ordering' may be of three or more alternatives (when *a* is preferred to *b*, and *b* to *c*, etc.). This has led to important questions concerning the consistency of preferences. If preference is a transitive relation (i.e. if it follows from the fact that John prefers *a* to *b* and *b* to c that he prefers *a* to *c*), then the following preference ordering is inconsistent *a* preferred to *b*, *b* to *c* and *c* to *a*. *Social choice theories explore problems posed by the search for a 'social preference ordering' based on individual preference orderings (*see* *social welfare function). They often attempt to show that, under certain conditions, no such ordering can be guaranteed to be consistent. (*See* *voting paradox, and *cf.* *Arrow's theorem, *Paretian liberal.)

Other problems of preference ordering can present themselves, for example, in the matter of preferences that concern different times. Given limited jam, preference for jam today over jam tomorrow is inconsistent with preference for jam tomorrow. The synthesis of preference theory and statistical analysis of *risk and uncertainty is the basis of *decision theory.

preference ordering

See *preference, *social choice.

prejudice

Belief without reasoned support, which serves as a premise for practical reasoning, and which is a constituent part of some *Weltanschauung resistant to refutation. Prejudice is held to be a vice in those who are capable of thinking, but some conservatives (e.g. *Burke) hold it to be a virtue in those who are not. Prejudice is a fixity of unreasoned belief, while *bigotry is a fixity of unreasoned *values; both contrast with *dogmatism, which is the tendency to translate both belief and value into articulate form, and to regard them as thereby conclusively established. Dogmatic beliefs are beyond argument because they have been put beyond argument; prejudices are beyond argument because they do not recognize that argument is possible. The fact that a prejudice is unreasoned does not imply that it is unreasonable. Indeed the desire for a reasoned basis for all one's beliefs is an unreasonable desire, a fact which partly explains the conservative rejection of *rationalism in politics.

pre-political order

Even if it is true that all social order has a political side, it may still depend upon a pre-political order – an order that pre-exists, and may perhaps outlast, the adoption of political institutions. Theories of the *social contract imagine people coming together for the purpose of government – but what brought them together? *Kinship? *Friendship? Shared *interests? Or is every human being to be party to the contract? Such questions suggest that all ideas of legitimacy depend upon a pre-political distinction between us and *them*, between those who have a claim to be protected by the political order and those who are outsiders or *aliens. *Nationalism should be seen as a theory of pre-political order – of the unity between people that makes politics possible – rather than a theory of political institutions. In theory at least, a nationalist can be a liberal, a socialist, a conservative or an anarchist. What matters is that these rival systems gain their authority for *us* in part because they are *ours*. To put it another way: political thinking requires a 'first-person plural', and nationalism is one of the easiest ways, in the modern world, of defining it.

prerogative

The pre-eminence which the sovereign retains in the UK constitution, and which other *heads of state retain elsewhere, consisting in certain rights of action allowed to no one else in law. In the UK the royal prerogative is created and governed by *common law, in certain instances modified by statute; it includes not only immunities from prosecution but also powers to initiate actions, exercised usually with the advice of ministers or of the courts. Among these actions the conduct of foreign affairs is particularly important. The powers exercised through the courts include the prerogative writs, such as *habeas corpus*; it has been this common law doctrine of royal prerogative that has enabled the courts to assert some of the basic *freedoms associated with the English constitution. The royal prerogative has been defined and limited several times, notably in Magna Carta 1215, the Petition of Right 1628, the Bill of Rights 1689, and the Act of Settlement 1700.

prescriptive right

A right created by lapse of time. In *Roman law, and in English and US law, such rights tend to be most prominent in the case of *land law, occupation of land continuously and peaceably from time immemorial being sufficient to warrant the presumption that such occupation is an indefeasible right. ('From time immemorial', in English law, means 'from time whereof the memory of man runneth not to the contrary' which, curiously, means from the beginning of the reign of Richard I; 20 years being sufficient to presume that such occupation has obtained.)

president

The name usually given to a *head of state in a *republic. The powers of the president vary from constitution to constitution: they may be minimal, as when the president is a figure of ceremonial significance only; or they may be absolute, as when he appoints himself president by virtue of his existing powers as leader of a party which has taken control of the state. The most interesting intellectual invention which bears this name is the US Presidency, constructed in part on principles laid down by *Montesquieu. The President is not only ceremonial and titular head of state, but also the chief *executive (i.e. fount of the executive power) and leader of the armed forces.

pressure group

An *interest group which has sufficient *influence on central government to be able to put pressure on behalf of its interests. Examples include the Confederation of British Industry, which tries to impress on the UK government the interests of managers, and the Trades Union Congress, which does the same for its members. On one view the activity of *politics is facilitated by pressure groups, since they can obtain the ear of government; on another view it is hindered by them, since they drown out the individual voice. A pressure group that is consulted regularly, and which has enduring institutions and a body of legislation to protect its aims, has ceased to be a pressure group, and has become instead part of the *establishment. Such was once the case with the Trades Union Congress. Not all interest groups are pressure groups: the difference is one both of intention and of power.

price
The rate at which an item exchanges against *money. (*See also* *exchange-value.) More generally, the rate of exchange between any two goods. Price theory attempts to explain the prices at which goods exchange, and it usually confines itself to the study of price in *equilibrium conditions. Theories are of various kinds. The older, 'classical' theory tended to explain price in terms of the *cost of production, the most sophisticated version of this being the *labour theory of value. This proposes a 'law of value': in those simple conditions of production, where there is no *profit, but simply the exchange of products by the producers, price at equilibrium will be directly proportional to the quantity of 'embodied labour'. This theory was severely criticized, partly because of difficulties over the idea of 'embodied labour', and alternatives were suggested, notably theories of the market, which find the determinants of price in the interaction between buyers and sellers, against certain background conditions. One such theory is the theory of *marginal utility, which gives an underpinning to the theory that price is determined by the equilibrium between *supply and *demand. Writing in the 1920s the economist Piero Sraffa revived the classical analysis in modified form, and gave new credence to some of the intuitions underlying the labour theory of value.

The 'price system', or price mechanism, is the system whereby price serves to coordinate activities within an economy, regulating supply and demand, and (so it is claimed) directing economic energy to areas where it is most profitably employed. The price system can be regarded as a mechanism which establishes economic equilibrium more readily and more surely than any government action, although governments sometimes try to control prices in order to control inflation (*see* *prices and incomes policy). The condition under which the price system can operate to produce an *optimal distribution of resources and incomes forms one of the major preoccupations of welfare economics.

price control
See *prices and incomes policy.

prices and incomes policy
A policy that aims to restrain prices and incomes, thus reducing the rate of *inflation (e.g. by fixing a legal limit to pay rises and price rises). A prices and incomes policy was introduced in autumn 1974 by the then Labour government in the UK, as a 'social compact' between government and the trade unions (the curious language being derived from *Locke). In its direct form the policy involves *interference in the *price system, and has been criticized on the grounds that this leads to serious misallocation of resources and unpredictable imbalances in a dynamic economy, and also on the grounds that the policy is based on mistaken assumptions about the causes of inflation, and can at best ameliorate the symptoms, but not cure the disease.

primary elections
Elections carried out usually by a *party, but in theory by any group, in order to determine who shall stand as candidate in some other, wider election. The person chosen in a primary

election is chosen as candidate for his group or party: the next, 'true', election, determines whether or not he will also be received as a 'representative' under the constitutional office for which he contends. Whom, then, does he 'represent': the party that chose him in the primary, the people who voted at the second election, or both? This is one of the difficult problems posed by the theory of *representation.

primary relations

Sociologists and anthropologists sometimes distinguish primary from secondary relations between people, the first having an inevitable and unchosen character, the second being formed through agreements and associations into which the agent enters, and from which he might also withdraw. (For a comparable distinction see *Gemeinschaft/Gesellschaft*.) Among primary relations the most important are those of *kinship, and in particular those kinship relations within the *family which are regarded as defining responsibility for the nurture of the child – e.g. relations with parents in the nuclear family. *Marriage involves the generation of new primary relations. This has sometimes been held to explain its peculiar status in most societies, as a bond that is not easily to be broken, and not to be construed in contractual terms. It is even said to be a *sacrament, i.e. a relation in which a third party, the divinity, intervenes.

prime minister

The officer charged with leading and speaking for the government in the principal assembly of the legislature: in UK the 'first minister of the *Crown'. The role of a prime minister as leader and instigator of *executive acts is greater or less, depending upon the executive power of the *head of state. In *constitutional monarchies, where the executive power of the head

of state has declined almost to the point of extinction, the executive power of the prime minister is such as to confer effective political leadership. In republics, the president may be elected precisely in order to exert executive power (it being one of the ruling conceptions of democracy that executive power must be transferred by election, which is the real reason why a constitutional monarch, with purely hereditary entitlement, could never bear it). In a republic, therefore, if the office of prime minister exists, the prime minister becomes accountable to the president; if the president exerts major executive powers then this accountability will restrict the executive powers of the prime minister. Whether or not a prime minister exerts full executive power depends therefore on the powers that are vested in the head of state. (Here 'powers' is used in a *de facto sense, and not in the legal sense mentioned in the definition of *power. In the legal sense the prime minister in the UK has no executive powers, and merely 'advises' the monarch, in whom all executive powers remain. Clearly many gradations can be envisaged here between legal fiction and political truth.)

primitive

Behaviour, institutions, customs and laws are primitive when they are 'first', that is 'early', examples of their type, the supposition being that there is some natural course of evolution which they have not yet undergone. That supposition is often in fact rejected in the case of those societies that were most frequently (until the development of modern *anthropology) called primitive. It is not at all clear that the societies of Africa which were contemporaneous with their nineteenth-century explorers were early examples of something else, nor is it at all clear how such an hypothesis could be proved. The archaeological division of human *prehistory into ages (stone age, bronze age, iron age, and so on) seemed at first to give some objective idea of development against which all societies could be measured. Modern archaeology has, however, cast doubt on the division, and on the theory which it is used to support, so that the main basis for the use of the label 'primitive' rests in ideas of human progress which probably seemed more believable in the nineteenth century than now. Naturally there is scientific progress, and therefore the technological progress that accompanies it. But it does not follow that other aspects of human existence – the building of institutions, laws, customs and values – can be assimilated to the model of scientific development, although some (e.g. Lucy Main: *African Societies*, 1974) recognize similar principles of development in the political sphere. In these crucial respects it may be seriously misleading, and at any rate highly theoretically loaded, to speak of primitive political systems. But *see* *political development, *primitive communism, *primitive law, *progressivism.

primitive accumulation

If there is to be wage labour, there must be someone who controls the means of production, and the labourer who, owning only labour power, must work for someone else. Hence the structure of a capitalist economy can rise only if control over the means of production first accumulates in some hands, but not in others. This process, called 'previous accumulation' by *Adam Smith, is called 'primitive accumulation' by *Marx. The acts of accumulation which bring the division between capital and labour into existence (e.g. enclosures) are called 'primitive' in that they are antecedent to the genuine *process* of capital *accumulation which

they make possible. Marx compared primitive accumulation to *original sin, and asserted that the history of primitive accumulation is 'written in the annals of mankind in letters of blood and fire'. Nevertheless *Trotsky and his followers advocated it, as the necessary means to establish communism in Russia, by abolishing rural and pre-capitalist modes of production and creating an 'accumulation' in the hands of the state. The necessary consequence – the simultaneous creation of the rootless, propertyless labourer – was regarded as a necessary means towards socialist modes of production and also (as in late medieval Europe) as a justified act of emancipation. In retrospect, the whole Marxian story of primitive accumulation seems to be as drastic and exaggerated as the biblical story of *original sin.

primitive communism

Expression coined by *Engels to refer to an *ideal type of economic relations, which he supposed to be exemplified, in part, by tribal communities, and which, according to the theory of *historical materialism (which justifies, if true, this use of the term 'primitive'), precedes the formation of *slavery. Primitive communism is like an economic *state of nature in the Marxian theory of history. It is a society without true political organization, without exchange and barter, and in which food is produced for common needs by the whole tribe working together without the sense of private property. It differs from 'true communism' in that it is a state of subjection to, rather than mastery over, nature; true communism can be achieved, according to the theory, only by passing through the intermediate stages of feudalism, capitalism and socialism, in order to permit the full development of human potential.

primitive law

The *conventions whereby *primitive communities are governed, and under which disputes within those communities are resolved. It has been much doubted that primitive law is really law, since it seems often to dispense with vital distinctions – e.g. between law and morality, law and etiquette – that are made in the legal systems of most modern societies. However, definite procedures of adjudication exist even in the most primitive communities, together with rights that can be defined independently of the particular person who claims them. Complex bodies of customary law have been identified, together with judicial offices whereby they are applied. The study of primitive law – 'legal anthropology' – has done much in recent years to clarify the nature of these systems. See Simon Roberts: *Order and Dispute*, 1979.

primitivism

An admiration for the primitive in man, which supposedly survives as a *residue even in the most civilized conduct, and which it may be necessary to recapture in order to be fully human. Primitivism played a large part in the political development of *national socialism, which allied its *racist doctrines to ideals of the tribal warrior. It has also been influential in modern literature, partly through the writings of D.H. Lawrence (although Lawrence's primitivism is sometimes described as callow), in modern art, partly through Picasso's admiration for African artefacts, and in modern music, through Stravinsky and the Ballets Russes. Primitivism is thus one of the major themes of modern culture, and *modernity is part of what makes primitivism possible.

prior restraint/subsequent punishment

A distinction sometimes made between two remedies for libellous or in other ways injurious publication, or for illegal or harmful meetings, demonstrations, or actions. Subsequent punishment is a threat which may be ignored by someone determined to act, whether for gain or from conviction. It does not protect the aggrieved party, if the one who seeks to embark on a course of injurious action has grounds for thinking that he can, by doing so, mobilize public opinion to protect him from sanction. Prior restraint is usually available in UK law in the form of an *injunction, which can be sought by the individual at any stage. The effect of this is to transform all injurious action from a civil to a criminal wrong, since the action will be tantamount to 'contempt of court'. This has had considerable significance in the development of US *labour law.

An injunction can also be sought by any citizen against any threatened crime. But the effects of disobedience are simply the effects of crime, and obedience to an injunction can itself be ensured only through the threat of punishment. The only kind of prior restraint that is independent of the threat of subsequent punishment is the actual imprisonment of someone *lest* he should commit a crime. This is illegal in the UK, in the US, and in most systems of law which guarantee elementary *freedoms. (*See *habeas corpus*.)

prison

See *punishment.

prisoner's dilemma

A situation in *game theory which has been thought to be particularly significant in revealing the complexities of political choice. Two partners-in-crime have been arrested and put in separate cells. They can be convicted of robbery, if prosecuted; and could be convicted of murder, if either were to confess. Each is promised by the police that both charges against him will be dropped if he alone confesses to murder, thus condemning the other. If both confess, both will get a somewhat reduced sentence for murder. If neither confesses, both will be convicted of robbery. Each reasons that he does better to confess, if the other confesses; and also better to confess, if the other does not. So each confesses regardless, and so helps to produce an outcome worse for both. The formal structure of this 'game' has been applied to the arms race, the failure of voluntary incomes policies, the over-fishing of the seas and many other aspects of social life, where norms which would benefit all fail to emerge. It captures a kind of insight about the contrary effects of individually rational decisions, found in *Hobbes, in *Hegel, in *Marx, and in many other earlier thinkers.

privacy

A condition imperfectly defined and imperfectly respected in many legal systems, despite the Universal Declaration of Human Rights (adopted but not enforceable by the United Nations Organization) which denounces interference with privacy, family, home and correspondence (implying, with intuitive plausibility, that these four are intimately connected). It was first argued in 1890 that there is a right of privacy, and that this right should be protected by law (Warren and Brandeis, in *Harvard Law Review*, 1890). Such ideas have continued to be important in US constitutional thinking, and definitions have been attempted. A report to the US President's Office of Science and Technology in 1967 asserted that 'the right to privacy is the right of the individual to decide for himself how much he will share with others his thoughts, feelings and the facts of his personal life.' That is vague, but it is difficult to replace it with anything

more precise. Such definitions are in part attempts to define the *sphere* of the private (as opposed to the public), in part attempts to describe matters in which the individual can tolerate no right of control in anyone but himself. (*See further* *private and public.*) In the controversial case of *Roe* v. *Wade* (1973) the Supreme Court affirmed that there is a right to privacy implied in the US Constitution, and that it could, in certain circumstances, be used to justify a right to *abortion. While many jurists question the validity of this judgement, it seems that the '*right to privacy' is now recognized in US law.

The 'right to privacy' is not recognized, at least under that description, in UK law, however, and those things which fall under 'privacy' must be protected through the laws of nuisance, libel, breach of confidence, breach of trust, etc. It is not clear, therefore, that a crime is committed by someone who spies on another, or that the tort involved is any more than a nuisance.

private and public

The distinction between private and public is drawn in one way in economics (*see* *private property, *private sector), in another way in law, and in another way for the purposes of political thought, where it denotes separate but overlapping spheres of activity: the private is the sphere of personal affection, personal antipathy and individual satisfaction, while the public is really two spheres (as *Hegel and others have pointed out): *civil society and *state. Civil society involves all those larger, more open relations between people that do not depend upon affection, but rather upon recognized purposes and upon an ability to cooperate through *contract and *consent. The state involves all those relations which are mediated by *law.

In law the distinction between private and public is equally unclear. The distinction is familiar in *Roman law, and the accepted boundary is that between affairs among individuals, and affairs among states, or between individuals and the state. The two spheres overlap inextricably so that, e.g., many *torts are also *crimes, and many individual contracts must have the state as a third and controlling party.

Some liberal views of the relation between law and morality argue that the 'private' (in the political sense) is a sphere which is, or ought to be, free from the supervision of the law. It is often argued that such a view is either tautological (the 'private' being defined as the realm in which individual choice is sovereign), or else crucially imprecise (e.g. is murder between consenting adults 'in private' to be permitted?). *See* *law and morality.

private enterprise

The undertaking of any economic activity using privately owned *capital and with a view to private gain. Ownership of capital may be single, joint, or through an association, such as a company. In private enterprise risk is undertaken, and the possibility of profit is essential to induce anyone to undertake that risk. *See* *enterprise.

private property

*Property is a *right of use. Not all property is private property, and it is in fact not easy to state the distinguishing conditions of the private. The following features seem to be important.

(i) The right to exclude. That is, what I own privately I can exclude you from using. This right may be conditional, as in a tenancy that is forfeited upon immoral use, or upon breach of some condition in the lease. Indeed all such rights may be conditional – in that the state may retain *eminent domain in all property. Moreover, exclusiveness is a matter of degree. I cannot exclude a police officer with a search warrant from my flat, nor the town surveyor, and so on. Nevertheless if I can exclude *anybody* from my flat, to that small extent it is mine.

(ii) The right to use as I will. This too is only limited. Nobody has the unqualified right in UK law to destroy his house, nor, if it is a Grade I listed building, to alter it in any material particular. And so on.

(iii) The right to transfer. Some forms of transfer may be forbidden, or penalized by taxation (e.g. by a gift tax, or capital transfer tax). But without some right of transfer the 'freedom to alienate', which classical liberal thought has often considered to be particularly important among property rights, would not exist.

It is vital to separate (i) and (iii), since it is (iii) that opens the possibility to *accumulation, and to the inequalities of wealth which, according to some (e.g. *Nozick), can be prevented only by injustice, and according to others (e.g. most socialists) are an injustice in themselves. Many arguments against private property are really arguments against (iii) and not against (i). Many defenders of private property and many attackers seem not to realize that all of (i) to (iii) are matters of degree, and therefore that their arguments may be directed for or against only some degree of private property and not for or against the institution as a whole. Furthermore it should be noted that private property is a legal right, and may or may not be a natural right, even if the existence of that legal right is justified. For a brief summary of the arguments on this issue, *see* *property.

private sector

In a *mixed economy, that part of the economy which is not under government *control. In other words, all *private enterprise, together with non-profit-making organizations, and exchanges between individuals.

privatization

The creation and upholding of a right of *private property in an object formerly owned socially or publicly, or perhaps not formerly owned at all. The term is intended to denote the converse of *socialization; the privatization of *nationalized industries has been increasingly implemented in the UK, by governments opposed to public ownership. It has been one of the platforms of the *Conservative Party, and is now accepted also by *New Labour.

Privatization is a major issue in *post-communist conditions. Almost all post-communist countries recognize the need to privatize the economy, and the question has arisen how this should be done in the absence of domestic investors with sufficient capital. One solution is to sell off state enterprises to any investor who can afford to purchase them at their value: this generally means a foreign investor, so that much of the economy is likely to end up in foreign hands – as in the Czech Republic today. An alternative method is to issue privatization coupons to the citizens, so that they can acquire shares in the former state enterprises – which is a way of privatizing the economy while ensuring that the profits are distributed among the people and not merely returned to the state. However, the customs and institutions that are required for this to be effective – stock exchange, company law, insurance, and the habit of taking responsibility for business decisions and accounting to shareholders – had all been destroyed by communism, so that coupon privatization led to widespread fraud and bankruptcy. One problem is that state enterprises were previously protected from failure by artificial modes of accounting, enabling them to pass on their losses to the state, which kept the enterprises afloat rather than face the need to make other provisions for those who worked in them. Needless to say, the fragile nature of post-communist legal systems, and the absence until recently of any serious law of commerce, bankruptcy or corporate liability, have opened the way to massive corruption, with firms being deliberately undervalued, sold off to their managers, who finance the purchase with loans brokered through the *Nomenklatura-ridden banking system, and finally sold to foreign investors at enormous profits.

privilege

1. In law, an entitlement or authorization to do or not do something which may involve, for example, immunity from prosecution or civil liability. A privilege is a kind of legally recognized *liberty which, by implication, is not generally available, but attaches, for whatever reason, to a certain role, office or organization. Thus trade unions have wide privileges in UK law, and there is a special privilege associated with actions for defamation, which is granted to parliamentary and official communications (where it is absolute), and to medical communications (where it is qualified). One of the important privileges in UK law is parliamentary privilege, granting freedom to each house to conduct its proceedings without interference from the Crown, the courts, bodies outside Parliament, or the public. Such privilege exists either by common law or by statute, but neither house may by its own resolution create new privileges. It was established in *Stockdale* v. *Hansard*, 1839, that the extent of this privilege is determined by law and could be examined by the courts, though the House of Commons has

not subsequently relinquished its claim to decide for itself whether any privilege exists. Abuse of privilege is now frequently complained of, but it seems that there is no serious redress available to the victim.

2. General. A privilege is a benefit which cannot be claimed as a *right. (NB. In some philosophical sense it might *be* a right; but the point is that it cannot be claimed as such.) Many of the disputes about the nature of welfare legislation concern whether or not some benefit is a privilege or a right, the difference being that in the second case, but not in the first, it would be an injustice to withhold it.

Privileges may attach to class, to membership of a party, to wealth, or to any other social position which enhances the power, status or well-being of the recipient. Hostility towards privilege may proceed from envy, and the consequent desire to destroy privilege come what may, or from the sense of justice, based on the thought that a privilege has been unfairly acquired by the other, or unfairly lost by oneself. In the extreme case it may be argued (perhaps on *universalist grounds) that, because there are no distinctions among human beings sufficient to justify the conferring of *any* privilege, all privilege is unjust. That view is tantamount to *egalitarianism, and may additionally involve the (probably mistaken) assumption that all privilege is *conferred*. (Depending upon whether or not judgements of justice require a presumption of *agency.)

The usual object of dispute is political privilege. Some argue that all political offices should be, in a real sense, open to all, so that all have a right to compete for office on an equal footing. One main problem for such a view is how to ensure that all people really *do* compete on an equal footing, since clearly an equal right does not imply

an equal ability. *See* *access, *egalitarianism, *equal opportunity.

procedural justice
Justice which attaches to a process rather than an *end state. If I steal the clock that stands in your dining room I acquire the clock unjustly. Unknown to you and me, however, the clock was stolen by your ancestor from mine, who acquired it by honest means. Your possession of the clock was therefore unjust, and I was the rightful owner. This fact does not invalidate the judgement that the transfer from you to me involved procedural injustice. Some philosophers have argued that the concept of justice is, deep down, reducible to this procedural idea, and that the rules of *natural justice distinguish just from unjust dealings but do not determine how resources should be allocated. Socialists tend to favour *distributive justice, or *social justice, as their paradigm: advocates of procedural justice regard these applications of the concept as either subordinate to the procedural paradigm, or else matters simply of *persuasive definition.

production, theory of
1. The branch of economics concerned with determining the choice of inputs, given the *price of those inputs, the *production function relating them to outputs, and the level of output desired. It is based on the assumption that firms will seek to minimize the cost of inputs.

2. More widely, sometimes used to describe the attempt to explore the *factors of production in their full social relationship, and to compare the various modes of production from the social and political point of view.

production, distribution, exchange, consumption
Four distinct but interdependent parts of the economic process, which are

sometimes separated for the sake of theory, and sometimes brought together, in order to argue that they are in some way organically interdependent. Goods are produced from nature either by cultivation or manufacture, they are distributed through mechanisms such as a *market, exchanged against other goods or money, and finally consumed. It is a fundamental tenet of *Marxist theory that the first three, at least, and probably all four, are interdependent, so that every system of *production relations also determines systems of exchange, distribution and consumption.

Some socialists have argued that the important thing that they wish to prevent is private property in the means of production, other kinds of private property being permissible or even necessary. Thus many concede that it is hard to imagine life without private property in the 'means of consumption', by which is usually meant the household and all that pertains to it. But those very same arguments that urge an organic interdependence between production, exchange and distribution, extend to consumption too. Consider the case of a nomadic tribe whose main product is carpets. Carpets are produced at home, primarily for domestic use but, when necessary, they are exchanged against other goods. Where does private ownership in the means of consumption end and private ownership in the means of production begin? Should we take away the needle that has dared to make a carpet for *sale*? Or should we allow only small-scale production in the home, and permit factories only when they are *socially owned?

production function

The relation between the quantity of output of some commodity and the quantity of inputs required to make it.

The production function varies from economy to economy and from firm to firm.

production relations (or: relations of production)

*Marxian and Marxian-influenced term for the relations between people in economic production and between people and *productive forces, which are enshrined in laws of *property, and which define the *base structure of society. Thus *capitalism is held to be a system of production relations, in which the capitalist controls the means of production and the worker controls his own labour power; by bringing the two into relation through the *wage-contract, production is made possible. Likewise *feudalism, *socialism and *communism are all, for Marx, systems of production relations, whose other features are explained in terms of this basic fact.

The rise of the *service economy, of information technology, of *managerialism, consultancies, *lobbying and all the other features of modern employment, have endowed the single-minded emphasis on production with a quaint Victorian air. The modern economy is to a great extent a virtual economy, in which little is produced, but in which people keep each other afloat by contracting out services that none of them need and which may, indeed, be entirely fictional.

productive forces (or: forces of production)

*Marx's theory of production attempts to separate the productive forces from the *production relations that channel them. The assumption is that all production involves both a dynamic and a fixed part, rather as a water turbine consists of a fixed piece of machinery which is set in motion by the force of water, but which, left to itself, does not move. The turbine channels the energy from the water to the electrical cable that runs from it.

The classical Marxian position is that, among the factors of production, labour, and labour alone, is a productive force. People often think that capital too is such a force. But, Marx argued, there is nothing in the status of an object as *capital* which causes it to produce (to think otherwise is to suffer from 'capital fetishism'). A piece of machinery may be owned as capital: but even if not owned at all it might still serve as an instrument of production. What makes it productive is that someone works with it and produces by means of it. That person, the producer, provides the productive force. The machine enhances his productivity, and is itself the product of force, including the force of intellectual labour. The mode of ownership or control does not contribute any power of production to the machine, but simply situates it in a system of production relations.

Some regard such arguments as attempting to prove the primacy of labour by *persuasive definition of the term 'force'. (For is not the electricity that powers the machine *also* a productive force? Why is it so important that someone had to do something to *make* it produce? Why isn't investing your savings in a piece of machinery *doing* something? Why is the Marxist worldview anything better than 'labour fetishism'?) Others hold that Marx's arguments formulate a profound truth about the nature of production, and provide the basis for a theory of history.

productivity

A measure of the rate of output from the use of given quantities of *factors of production. Thus there is labour productivity, capital productivity, and land productivity. (Economists also talk of 'total factor productivity'.) The productivity of a factor of production can be measured either in average, or in marginal terms, usually the former. Where labour is plentiful labour productivity will tend to be low, since it will be more economical to employ 'labour intensive' methods – i.e. methods in which large amounts of cheap labour are employed in preference to small amounts of expensive labour in conjunction with expensive machinery.

productivity bargaining

A kind of *collective bargaining in which employers agree to pay more for the more efficient use of labour time. In other words rewards are offered for more effort, or more effective effort, at the place of work. It has been common in the UK since the 1960s, and is perhaps the natural consequence of a conventional maximum to the length of the working day.

profession

The distinctions between employment, trade and profession are difficult to draw precisely, and might be drawn differently for different purposes. It is widely held that membership of a profession is an important determinant of social and political attitudes, even though it is not at all clear that the professions form, as such, either a *class or a distinct *status group.

The term 'profession' was originally applied to the three 'learned professions' of divinity, law and medicine, but now includes, for example, teaching and accounting. The surface features that seem relevant to the classification (and which may or may not identify a significant class) are:

(i) acquisition of learning as a requirement of entry;

(ii) a presumption of learning in practice;

(iii) self-direction, and control over the pace and scheduling of work;

(iv) the possibility of advancement, from level to level, *within* the profession;

(v) the relation to a client or clients, who pay a fee for professional services.

The first four features clearly go together, since what gives credence to the idea of advancement *within* a profession (rather than by means of the profession) is the fact that learning is cumulative; given talent for its acquisition, a professional will steadily master what he has to know.

A 'professional' is someone who has acquired the skills necessary to some practice, whether or not that practice is a profession in the above sense. In this sense there are professional criminals, and professional politicians.

professional ethic

The *ethic of a *profession. Sociologists tend to give a *functional explanation of the professional ethic (*cf.* *business ethic), arguing that what explains the existence of certain beliefs and *values among members of the professions is the fact that those beliefs and values facilitate the successful performance of professional tasks. Thus the professional believes that he is bound by a duty towards his client, and not by a wage contract: such a belief facilitates the adoption of irregular working hours, and the undertaking of highly demanding tasks. Similar beliefs concerning professional responsibility and decorum enable the members of a profession both to learn from one another and to avoid entering into the overt competition that would destroy the *career structure, and so remove one of the incentives to acquire more professional skill. Thus members of the legal profession in the UK were, until recently, forbidden to advertise their services; they also form into clubs and societies where they meet socially. There is nothing that *forbids* other professions from advertising, but it is regarded as very bad form in doctors, and for most teachers it suggests a position of relative failure. In the US the professional ethic is nearer to the business ethic, and indeed is continuous with it. Even the relation of a preacher to his congregation can take a business-like form in the US.

profit

Profit is the aim of private *enterprise, but there is little agreement over what produces it. Accountants distinguish gross profit (total receipts from sales, less immediate costs of production) from net profit (gross profit less interest on loan, and depreciation). But the real economic distinction is that between normal profit and *excess profit. The former is the income (i.e. the residue left after subtracting all *opportunity costs of inputs), which is just sufficient to keep the firm in business. In other words, it is the opportunity cost of remaining in business, rather than switching to some other activity. Excess profits are all profits above normal (sometimes called 'super-normal' profits), and sometimes regarded as the (risky) return to the entrepreneurial activity.

The theory of profit is an important part of classical economics. This tended to support the thesis of the *falling rate of profit, upheld by *Smith, *Ricardo and *Marx. It is not at all clear that the thesis is true, or what the consequences of its truth might be. The Marxian theory of profit relies on the notion of *surplus value. Marx argued that surplus value is not identical to profit, and therefore tried to give an account of how profit is determined by surplus value. The problem of deriving the one from the other is part of the 'transformation problem', and thus forms one part of the *value controversy in Marxian economics.

progress

Movement forwards. Condorcet is usually cited as the first major theorist of the modern version of the idea of progress. However, the rhetorical importance of the idea is sometimes dated from the seventeenth century, e.g. by J.B. Bury (*The Idea of Progress*, 1920), who argued that the entry of this concept into the realm of human values was part of the scientific revolution, and the consequent *secularization of thought, that occurred in the post-Reformation world. The belief in progress is a form of optimism, with two aspects – first, the belief that things *do* progress; secondly the belief that there is a recognizably 'progressive' *outlook* on the world, which involves distinctive values as well as distinctive beliefs. The second is sometimes called 'progressivism', and tends to take its credentials from the tradition of liberal *humanism. It regards all reform and social movement as tending towards the complete emancipation of the individual from oppressive *superstition. The first aspect – the belief that progress is the natural order of things – is a form of *historicism, and has itself been condemned (by Dean Inge) as a 'pernicious superstition'. It involved three thoughts:

(i) some states of affairs are better than others, and all reforms that advance towards the former and away from the latter are to be commended;

(ii) this advance occurs, in fact, through the passage of time;

(iii) scientific knowledge leads to the ever-increasing control over human destiny and understanding of the human condition.

(i) is a near tautology; (ii) involves, as it stands, a fallacy (the fallacy, pointed out by *Kant, of believing that time alone can have causal properties); (iii) is almost certainly false. However, the use of (iii) in support of (ii) is still given as a ground for the belief in progress. If the accumulation of scientific knowledge enables us to master our fate, then, since this accumulation is progressive, the human condition must steadily improve under its influence. (A very sophisticated version of that idea is contained in *technological determinism; a naive version is to be found in the *positivism of *Comte.)

It is often said that the belief in progress involves a confusion between ends and means. Science, which enables us to improve the second, always stands in need of the guidance of the first. But our knowledge of ends, unlike our knowledge of means, is, it is sometimes said, not progressive, but rather rests in those enduring values which define the invariable aspirations of human nature. In which case one might agree with *Adorno that 'no universal history leads from savagery to humanitarianism, but there is one leading from the slingshot to the megaton bomb'.

progressivism

See *progress.

proletariat

Latin: *proletarius*, one who breeds, from *proles*, offspring. Under the Servian constitution of the sixth century BC those who could not pay taxes were required to lend their offspring in military service to the Roman state. The term *proletarius* reappears in the fifteenth and sixteenth centuries, to name men similarly required to give services, only this time in the form of their own wage labour, being made landless by enclosures or eviction. Its modern use first occurs in the Swiss economist Sismondi, from whom it was borrowed by the French radicals, and passed to *Marx and his followers. The proletariat is the class of labourers under capitalist industrial production, who are, supposedly, propertyless, having nothing to sell but their *labour power, and being cast loose from all bonds of obligation and all attachment to place and land. They form a rootless, mobile, needy mass, united only by their similar station in the capitalist system, and by whatever class *identity might emerge from that. The proletariat as it features in Marxist literature is at best an *ideal type, at worst a *myth.

propaganda

The sacred congregation Propaganda Fidei ('for the propagation of the faith') was established in Rome by Pope Gregory XV in 1622. Since then the term 'propaganda' has come to denote any attempt – however disrespectful of truth, reason and the human intellect – to win acceptance for a cause, system, or state, either by praise of the thing itself, or by vilification of its known and unknown alternatives.

The emergence of the 'propaganda machine' in the twentieth century is largely due to the attention paid by the *bolsheviks and the *national socialists to the task of *legitimation. Their techniques have been the subject of much comment, and the attempt at mind-control (called 're-education' in China and Vietnam) has been contemplated with alarm by outside observers. The similarity of Nazi and bolshevik propaganda – despite the supposed contrast in their ideals – has seemed to suggest that there are patterns to which all propaganda must adhere. What matters is not so much the content of the resulting beliefs, as the feelings of loyalty to friends and hostility to enemies which they inspire. Thus the concept of the 'enemy' has become very important in modern propaganda, alerting people to the ever-present dangers by which they are surrounded. The Jew and the 'anti-socialist' class enemy are distinguished by the fact

that the first is what he is from birth, while the second may become what he is by corruption, and perhaps without realizing it himself. This means that you can never feel sure under bolshevik propaganda that you are *not* one of the enemy. The consequent failure (in comparison with Nazi propaganda) to generate a sense of security has been held responsible for some of the rejection of the propaganda message in the USSR. The subject is a mysterious one, and study is made additionally difficult by the fact that those who have had sufficient experience of the propaganda machine to know what it is like do not usually preserve the peace of mind necessary to examine it.

property

The fullest right that can exist over anything, which includes (in its maximum extent) the right to possess, use, lend, alienate, use up, consume and destroy. More simply, property can be described as a right of use, which can exist in various degrees, and subject to various conditions. There is no limit to the kinds of thing in which property rights may exist – copyright, for example, is a right of *intellectual property, and there can be rights in land, in debts or other obligations, in movable goods, in human beings (in which case at least one of the parties is a *slave). Principal questions raised by the concept of property are: is there any basis for property rights other than convention? And: ought there to be rights of *private* property? In considering both questions it is necessary to remember that property rights are both composite and also a matter of degree. Thus my property right in this computer is a right to use, to destroy and to transfer; to lend, to give and to hire. It is clear that a philosophical justification of one of those rights may not be a justification of the others. Moreover a justification of any of those rights might only show it to be conditional, or defeasible. Thus the right of use of land is normally regarded as conditional upon loyalty to the sovereign; the right of transfer of food conditional upon truthful declaration of its nature; the right to destroy food as conditional upon a minimum level of abundance, and so on. All the rights, therefore will be justified to a certain degree only, and it should not be thought that property is unjustified simply because no property right can ever be made absolute.

The arguments for and against private property invoke need, justice, freedom and utility. Arguments from all of those conceptions have been put forward to justify (a) universal *common ownership; (b) ownership by small *communes; (c) ownership by units small enough to be considered private, e.g. *companies, *families; (d) private ownership by individuals. It is generally hoped by socialists that an argument can be given for (a) or (b) which will not also permit (d). Thus if it can be shown that there is a right of common ownership in all land and in the means of production (say, because we have common needs and an equal right to satisfy them, or because we hold all land and its products in trust for ourselves and future generations), then the assertion of a private right of ownership is inherently unjust, since it is an attempt to exclude people from what is rightly theirs.

Arguments for private property should be distinguished into those which generate conclusions about particular property rights, and those which justify the existence of an institution of property rights without determining what should belong to whom. An argument of the first kind is *Locke's, to the effect that, given certain conditions, someone can create a *natural right to property in that with which he has mixed his

labour. All just transfers will preserve this natural right, so that it is, in theory, possible to trace the lineage of all present property to its original acquisition, and determine which item is rightly and which wrongly held. An argument of the second kind is *Hegel's, to the effect that the institution of private property is necessary for people to assert their full individual freedom. This argues that there must *be property rights, but says nothing about who should own what.

The major problem for defenders of a right of common ownership is to give an argument for it that will not also permit the right of detachment – i.e. the right of the individual to detach his share from the common fund, say, through exerting himself with the consent of the others. The major problem for the defender of private property is to show why its existence is not a massive interference in the freedom and rights of others, who are excluded from the enjoyment of every item that is privately owned. Some defenders of common ownership recognize the force of arguments such as Hegel's, and conclude that each individual needs a sphere of private right where he can exert himself exclusively. They therefore advocate private ownership of the 'means of consumption', while arguing against private ownership in the means of production, distribution and exchange. Whether it is possible so to separate production from consumption is, however, a matter of doubt: see *production, distribution, exchange and consumption.

The battle over private property is not new: it occurs in the dispute between Plato and Aristotle over common ownership, and is rehearsed in much medieval natural law theory (see *Aquinas). Sir Thomas *More criticizes private property in these terms: 'so long as private property remains, there is no hope at all that [social evils] may be healed and society restored to good health. While you try to cure a part, you aggravate the disease of other parts. In redressing one evil another is committed, since you cannot give something to one man without taking the same from another' (*Utopia*). Thus More argues against *redistribution and *sumptuary laws as remedies for the evils of private property, and advocates its abolition, just as the *Communist Manifesto* was to do later.

proportional representation

The form of *representation in which the strength of the representation of a *party in the assembly is directly proportional to the strength of its support among the electorate. It does not exist in the UK or the US but does exist in certain European assemblies. Thus in the UK candidates stand for election in a constituency, and they represent the people of that constituency once elected. On this system a party with minority support may procure *no* seats in Parliament; in the general election of 1974, for example, over a third of those elected to the House of Commons were elected on a minority vote, and the Liberal Party, with nearly 20% of the vote, secured only 2% of the seats. Some argue that such a result is inherently absurd, and that the House of Commons cannot really claim to represent the people if its institutional structure is so impervious to minority voting. It is replied either that *adversarial politics requires a two-party system if political stability is to be achieved, and hence requires a form of representation which filters out minority parties, or else that representation ought to be by constituency if the interests of the people (rather than the interests of the parties with which they may wrongly identify themselves) are to be consulted. Various suggestions for reform are made, sometimes accepting both sides of that argument. *See*, for example, *alternative vote, *single transferable vote.

prosecution

Legally sanctioned action by the state against a citizen in charging with, and preparing the proof of, a crime. Often a public officer is appointed to take charge of prosecutions (as in the US and France), but in England anyone may undertake prosecution in the name of the *Crown, and then ask for an authorized officer to take over. When a police officer prosecutes for a summary offence he is in theory acting as a private individual.

protectionism

The theory and practice of protecting home markets by curtailing or prohibiting competition from abroad, traditionally by the imposition of *tariffs or quotas to restrict the flow of imports (*see* *mercantilism, *neo-mercantilism). Some *Keynesian protectionists argue that import controls will raise national income, and in the long run lead to a higher total level of imports than existed before. Hence the control of imports may be to the benefit, not only of home markets, but also of international trade, so that other states, perceiving this, will not necessarily resort to retaliatory measures.

protectorate

In international relations and UK constitutional law, a protectorate is not a colony, but a form of guardianship, with the emphasis on the duty of the protecting state to foster the social, economic and political development of the protectorate to the point where political independence is feasible. Many of the British colonies enjoyed protectorate status (e.g. Rhodesia), although it is disputed how far they were treated as the term implies. Czechoslovakia was made a 'protectorate' of Germany in 1939, but here the term simply denoted *annexation. Likewise the 'protectorate' exercised over Britain by Oliver Cromwell and his son Richard had no precise legal status, either in *municipal or in *international law.

Protestant ethic
See *Protestantism.

Protestantism
The systems of Christian faith and liturgical practice based on the principles of the *Reformation. (In 1529, the reforming members of the Diet of Spyer had issued a *protestatio* against the decision of the Roman Catholic majority, hence the name.) The three original branches were *Lutheranism, *Calvinism and Zwinglianism, with *Anglicanism as a disputed case, sometimes regarded as a parochial synthesis of the principles of the Reformation and the practices of the Roman Catholic Church. The chief items of belief are acceptance of the Bible as the only source of revealed truth, the doctrine of justification by faith alone (*see* *Lutheranism), and that of the universal priesthood of all believers, which is tantamount to the rejection of the church as an independent source of authority, rather than a voluntary association of believers. With the rejection of the church is associated also a rejection of papal indulgencies (which relieve the individual of his necessary *conscience), and of the rituals, liturgies and ceremonies through which the church has dignified its worldly offices, together with an *iconoclasm towards all practices and beliefs that are merely local in significance (such as the veneration shown towards local saints).

The rise of Protestantism is associated with complex social and political developments. The growth of trading towns and manufactures, the movement of the population from the land, the decline of serfdom and the swelling of the journeyman class – these and many related changes are regarded as important factors, to be taken into account in any assessment of the political impact of Protestantism. Hence in 1905 *Weber put forward the proposition that, while some measure of *capitalism is inevitable under normal conditions, the peculiar thriving of capitalism in Western Europe and its dependencies, its indomitable progress, accumulation, and economic despotism, were the effect of what he called the Protestant ethic: the spirit of self-dependence and individual autonomy which flowered at the Reformation, and took powerful political form in the writings and activities of Calvin (*see* *Calvinism). The phrase has stuck, although the theory is much criticized, both by those who think that it mixes cause and effect (e.g. *Marxists, who believe that Protestantism is part of the ideology of modern capitalist production relations rather than their cause), and by those who believe that it is not founded in fact, pointing, for example, to the spread of capitalism in pre-Reformation Italy, and to the effect of the Counter-Reformation.

There are significant differences between Calvinism and Lutheranism, the first involving a sustained attempt to develop new political institutions, the second being content to refer large areas of social and political life to the jurisdiction of the individual conscience. The interaction of conscience and commerce lent a peculiar tone to the ideology of modern capitalism in Protestant countries, and whether or not Weber's thesis is accepted, it is normal to recognize that Protestant capitalism has had, as a result, a distinctive character – see e.g. R.H. Tawney: *Religion and the Rise of Capitalism*, 1926, in which the connections with *individualism and the *universalism of the *Enlightenment are emphasized.

Proudhon, Pierre-Joseph (1809–65)
The first writer deliberately to accept the title 'anarchist', and since sometimes regarded as the father of modern *anarchism. In *What is Property?*, 1840, Proudhon attacked many of the rights of property prevalent in nineteenth-century France, and in particular all those rights of property which conferred effective *control of another human being. At the same time he rejected communism, and upheld the individual's right to independence, and to the measure of private property necessary for that. Communism, he argued, was dependent upon authority and control for its enforcement, and was therefore not, in the end, preferable to the system of private property relations which it sought to replace. Thus property, and communism, while antithetically related, must both be transcended in their synthesis, which is anarchism.

Proudhon envisaged a world-wide working-class organization, founded not in political but in economic principles, specifically in the practice of *mutualism, whereby everything needed for production would be made available on mutually beneficial, but non-profit-making, terms. He founded a newspaper, was elected to the Constituent Assembly, and later imprisoned for his attacks on Louis Napoleon and his regime. His posthumous *On the Political Capability of the Working Class*, 1865, summarized his lifelong dedication to the labour movement, although he is perhaps best remembered for the maxim 'property is theft'.

providence
That which is provided specifically by God, through his foreknowledge and beneficent care of human things. Providence is a theological conception akin to that of *destiny, which rationalizes and makes acceptable the widely disputed and also widely confirmed hypothesis that human affairs are largely outside human control.

provocation
A term difficult to apply since, in its common usage, it refers to an idea of *normality. An act constitutes provocation if the normal person would be provoked by it, but precisely what features such a person might have is hard to determine. In law the test is that of the *reasonable man, which is designed to capture the idea of normality, and to give to it legal cogency. Thus an act or series of acts done by one person to another constitutes a provocation in law if it could cause in a reasonable man, and actually does cause in the victim, a sudden and temporary loss of self-control. (This is not a defence, but rather a fact which changes the nature of the crime – e.g. which changes murder to manslaughter.)

In international relations provocation seems to mean any warlike or declamatory gesture that promises a threat to the interests of one state by another. It has no precise meaning in international law.

prudence
1. One of the cardinal *virtues, prudence consists in the disposition to take account of the consequence of action, to fit the means to the end and the end to the means, and to behave in all things so that fulfilment is, in the circumstances, as likely as it is possible. That sentence contains a summary of *Aristotle's account of the

virtue of *sophrosune* (practical wisdom), which he regarded as the root of all other virtues. Without prudence, ancient philosophers argued, courage becomes rashness, wisdom becomes obstinacy, and justice becomes sentimental pity or rage. Prudence is thus integral to the other virtues which, without it, are merely the vicious simulacra of virtue in a spirit that does not possess it.

2. In moral philosophy, however, prudence is often used in a technical sense, in order to draw a contrast between the prudential and the moral. Prudence is the virtue of the rational egoist, or *economic man, who weighs every consideration in the balance of his own reasoned preferences, and does not show that 'irrational' attachment to absolute *values which is the distinguishing mark of the moral being.

psychotherapy

This has become an issue in political thinking on several accounts, among which the following are noteworthy.

(i) *Freud's theory that civilization rests upon the *repression of fundamental instincts, and contains, therefore, an internal conflict and discontent. The actual political consequences that Freud drew from this theory were marginal. He seemed to accept the process of repression, and the sublimation associated with it, as essential to family and social life, and to the transformation of the infantile libido, activated by its 'pleasure principle', into the mature *universalism of adult moral sentiment.

(ii) The general effect of Freudian and post-Freudian analysis on received ideas about the human condition. The most important has been the theory of unconscious motivation, and the associated idea that the reasons given for an action may be *rationalizations, unconnected with the motive, despite

the agent's own sincere conviction to the contrary. This view echoes in the sphere of individual psychology the fundamental tenet of *historical materialism. There has been, indeed, a movement to combine the two approaches, so as to argue that the repression which drives the libido underground, and so provides the reservoir of unconscious motives, is an instance of that *oppression which drives labour underground, to become the great motivating force of history, developing unseen from the illusory world of *bourgeois ideology. (See, for example, *Herbert Marcuse: *Eros and Civilization*, 1962.)

(iii) The emergence of schools which attempt to *politicize the theory and practice of psychotherapy, e.g. that of *Reich, the schools associated with the name of *Laing in the UK and Lacan in France, and recent schools of *feminist therapy. Some of these schools draw on *phenomenology, on theories propounded by *Sartre concerning the 'existential' significance of mental illness, and on theories given by *Foucault, concerning the nature of clinical treatment. From Sartre is derived the thesis that the patient diagnosed as psychotic suffers from an 'ontological insecurity' – i.e. a sense that either he does not exist as a *person, or else has no right to exist. From Foucault comes the thesis that it is the function of the therapist in bourgeois society to silence the voices of unreason, and to return the patient to the normality for which 'reason' is the arbitrary name. The Laingian school sees ontological insecurity not as the cause but as the effect of institutionalized treatment, and also of the strenuous conflicts of family life, which require conformity to social norms and a submission to authority. In the light of these alleged facts the Laingians propose a 'politics of experience', whereby the cure of the psychotic lies in upholding, rather than denying, the validity of his fundamental experiences. (*See also* *authenticity.)

(iv) Political questions are raised in addition by certain psychotherapeutic practices, such as the USSR practice of subjecting *dissidents to forced psychotherapy, often of a brutal and damaging kind (thus acting as though the Laingian thesis in (iii) were indeed true).

(v) The epidemic of psychoanalysis among the US middle classes, in which American *individualism has taken a new and surprising form, with a priesthood of psychoanalysts who, through the confessional, reassure the individual of his irreplaceable value as an end in himself, while exploiting, according to some, his evident value as a means.

(vi) The equally surprising epidemic of psychotherapeutic theories in France, in the wake of the seminars conducted by Jacques Lacan (1901–81), who claimed to be Freud's only heir, and who argued that the unconscious is structured like a language, and should be understood by applying the technicalities of Saussurian linguistics, mathematical logic and a variety of other disciplines. Whether Lacan had any understanding of the theories that he applied has been doubted, but his influence over the style and content of French philosophy and criticism has been enormous.

public choice

The theory associated with the US economists James Buchanan, Gordon Tullock and others associated with the Center for the Study of Public Choice in Fairfax, Virginia (the 'Virginia School'), which tries to apply the methods of economic analysis to the political process. Essentially, the political process in a democracy should be seen as a free or partly free market, in which parties offer public policies in exchange for votes and seek to maximize the votes that are cast in their favour. Members of political institutions should also be seen as maximizing the benefit and minimizing the cost of their positions. Bureaucracies expand partly because those within them acquire a *rent on the social product – a permanent and guaranteed income from the state, to which no real risk is attached. Bureaucratic tasks are proposed in order to raise this income and to expand the positions available, but have no necessary connection to any social or political need. Public choices should be seen as the private choices of the individuals who propose them and carry them out.

One of the most important developments in modern politics is therefore the growth of *rent seeking in the public sector. To obtain a rent on the social product, groups form in order to press for government funding or in order to find some safe niche within the existing system of benefits. Ideological fashions within state-funded industries can be explained in terms of this goal. Thus the state educational system will tend to be colonized by groups with socialist ideas, advocating egalitarian policies. For these ideas will (a) rationalize the constant expansion of the state system and make state funding of education permanent; (b) inhibit competition from the private sector; (c) ensure that minimum labour is required of those within the system, since the goal of education, according to the egalitarian premise, is not quality but uniformity. The *politicization of state bureaucracies can be explained in similar terms. By adopting an ideology which favours the needy, the minorities, and the powerless, the bureaucrat legitimizes the transfer of funds to his own profession, and makes available to himself and his colleagues the means to live comfortably at public expense while enjoying enhanced social status as the purveyor of official charity.

public goods

The term public good can be narrowly defined to include goods characterized by non-rival consumption (consumption by one person does not prevent consumption by another) and non-excludability (people who do not pay cannot be prevented from gaining access to the good). Examples include street-lighting, police protection and defence. Sometimes the expression 'public good' is used to include two other goods that have one, but not both of those characteristics. 'Near-public goods' have non-rival consumption, but excludability. 'Common-property goods' have rival consumption, but nonexcludability (*see* *common pool resources). All three types of goods – public goods (pure), near-public goods, and common-property goods – can be efficiently produced and allocated only through some kind of government involvement. The nature of these goods helps to explain, in the eyes of many economic theorists, the basic functions of government. No economy, however weighted towards the *private sector, can rely on private enterprise to supply public goods, since no entrepreneur would have the power to compel payment for them. The evolution of modern economies might be seen as involving a progressive recognition of the extent to which this is true of the goods that are ordinarily needed by the citizen.

public interest

Politicians and lawyers often refer to the 'public interest', arguing that such and such a policy is or is not in the public interest, or that publication of a document is or is not a public benefit. However, it is not clear what these and similar phrases mean. The public cannot be identified with the state, since a state can exist that is not in the public interest (e.g. a *tyranny). Nor can it be identified simply with the majority, since it might be in the majority interest to dissolve all social union and emigrate to the ends of the earth (say, when the state is threatened with extinction by powerful neighbours), but it is doubtful that such a course could ever be in the '*public* interest'. It may be suggested that the public interest is the interest of a *civil society, and has, as one necessary component, the cohesion of that society and its continuance as an entity with interests of its own. It is then possible to define *interest as recommended in this dictionary: but what would be a *measure* of the public interest will always be hard to determine. Some argue that there is no 'essence' captured by the term 'public interest', which functions, rather, as a term of contrast, used differently for different purposes. For related problems *see* *collective choice, *common good, *social choice.

public morals

It has been held in England to be a crime to conspire to corrupt public morals. However, the most important recent case (*Shaw* v. *DPP*, 1962), although a decision of the House of Lords, is now doubted, on account of the vagueness of the charge. It has also been held to exhibit unwarranted judicial *legislation, in that there is no law forbidding the corruption of public morals, so that the acts alleged (publishing a directory of prostitutes) were rendered criminal through a legislative application of the law of *conspiracy. However, it seems that the concept of conspiracy can, and arguably should, permit just such judicial legislation. The more problematic issue is that of 'public morals': what are they, and to what extent should the law attempt to protect them? It has been argued in the UK Parliament that fur farming and *hunting are both offences against 'public morality', and for this reason must be criminalized. The argument was in both cases successful. Meanwhile old attempts to enforce a code of 'public morality' in sexual behaviour have been removed from the statute book, as instances of oppressive puritanism. This suggests that, while opinions as to what is or is not immoral may change, the desire to align the law with a code of public morality remains unaltered. It also suggests a definition of public morality as the part of a moral code that the law might legitimately enforce, while private morality is presumably the part which is purely the concern of the individual. *See* *law and morality.

public opinion

Not the *opinion of the majority but the opinion that is active in the public realm. Public opinion can thus be liberal at a time when the majority opinion is illiberal (as perhaps now in the UK, at least over matters of crime and punishment), revolutionary at a time when the majority are reactionary (as happens from time to time in France), and even reactionary when the majority opinion is mildly liberal (as perhaps has happened in Japan). The consulting of public opinion is an important part of politics, and presumably a necessary prelude to the conciliation which, on some views, is the essence of the political process.

Public opinion must always be distinguished from the criteria whereby it is estimated – such as opinion polls, pronouncements through the *media and so on. Nevertheless, there must be some relation between these and public opinion, and in the absence of any of them it is doubtful

that public opinion exists as an independent force in politics. Thus it is doubtful that there is such a thing as public opinion in states where all means of expression are used for propaganda on behalf of the existing rulers; and, if there is it is neither possible nor necessary to consult it. Others have doubted the utility of consulting public opinion even in ostensibly democratic states. Thus Walter Lippmann, in *Public Opinion*, 1922, argued that modern *communications have the effect of condensing all information into brief slogans. These slogans, he thought, create a wall of stereotypes between the citizen and the issues to which he is expected to respond.

public ownership

Ambiguous term which may mean:

1. *social ownership and control;

2. ownership and control by the *state;

3. ownership and control in part by the state;

4. any of 1. to 3. without ownership, or any of 1. to 3. without control. (*See* *separation of ownership and control.)

Defenders of 1. sometimes denounce 2. as *state capitalism, and feel that it is particularly pernicious to identify the public with the state, rather than with society. Defenders of *private enterprise feel that 'public ownership' is often in practice a euphemism for state control, and argue against it on a variety of grounds, such as the inefficiency, corruption, and tyranny that stem from state control. *See* *social ownership, for some of the counter-arguments.

public sector

That part of economic activity which is not privately owned, either because vested in the state, or because subject to *common ownership. It includes central government and local authorities, in addition to *nationalized industries and public corporations. It currently accounts for over one-fifth of the *gross national product in the UK, as well as in most European countries, and often has a shortfall of receipts over expenditure which creates a semi-permanent 'public sector borrowing requirement'.

public spirit
See *consensus, *Montesquieu, *virtue.

Pufendorf, Samuel, Baron von (1632–94)
German jurist and philosopher who vigorously defended, in *De jure naturae et gentium*, 1672, a theory of *natural law with which to replace the medieval defence of it. Pufendorf's influence on eighteenth-century legal thinking was immense, and he provided a corrective to revolutionary enthusiasms with his defence of the view that rights always correlate with *duties, and that duty stems from the very essence of social life. *See also* *eminent domain, *international law.

punishment
Punishment may be defined as (i) the infliction of pain, privation or disadvantage, (ii) on the grounds of some wrong committed by the sufferer, (iii) by someone authorized to do so. Condition (iii) is sometimes disputed, partly because it involves the difficult concept of *authority. Perhaps it should be said only that the person who punishes must *think* himself authorized to inflict pain; however, he may derive this authorization merely from the belief that his victim deserves pain, i.e. from condition (ii).

The question of the justification of punishment, and of particular forms of punishment, is a major issue in legal and political philosophy, and one where conflicting intuitions abound. Theories of justification may be divided into the forward-looking and the backward-looking, the former finding the reason for punishment in its effects, the latter in its antecedents. It is also necessary to distinguish theories which attempt to give a justification for each punishment case by case, and theories which seek to justify only the practice of punishment, but which give no answer to questions concerning who should be punished when.

Forward-looking views may refer to the 'reforming' effect of punishment, to its effect as a 'deterrent', and to its effect as a 'restraint', it being clear that when maimed, dead or in prison a person is less likely to commit crime. In addition there is the 'expressive' theory, which justifies punishment in terms of its ability to express and relieve the feelings of public outrage at crime and to reaffirm the common moral sentiments of the community. The thought here is that, if not expressed through punishment, outrage will turn to private revenge, thereby endangering social order. All four forward-looking reasons might be offered together, and all may be used to justify the practice of punishment, and also the particular punishments that stem from it.

Among backward-looking views the most important is the 'retributive' theory, which says that the reason for punishing someone is simply that he deserves it because of what he has done. Punishment is, or tries to be, 'just retribution'. One defender of that view (*Hegel) even goes so far as to say that the criminal has a *right* to punishment, and that not to inflict it is to treat him, not as a person, but as a thing. Hegel's idea, or something resembling it, is often offered in opposition to those who advocate forms of 'therapy', designed to 'cure' the criminal of his 'disease', in the place of the vivid sanction that picks him out as responsible for a wrong, and so acknowledges his freedom and the dignity that stems from it.

Against the retributive view it is sometimes said that it does not *justify* punishment, but only describes it: for this backward-looking reason is simply the element of the idea of punishment contained in condition (ii) above. Something more needs to be said if the practice is actually to be *justified*, and for those of a *utilitarian cast this something more must always be sought in the future and not in the past.

On the question of what form punishment should take the main dispute has concerned *capital, and, to a lesser extent, corporal punishment. Some argue that these forms of punishment are never justified, since both violate a *human right of the victim, the first his right to life, the second (perhaps) his right to be treated so as to respect his dignity as a person. The US constitution forbids 'cruel and unusual' punishments, as do certain internationally applied treaties and charters of human rights, but the interpretation of this phrase seems to vary from place to place and from time to time. Some argue in favour of capital punishment on the grounds of its awe-inspiring effect, and perhaps of its power to 'concentrate the mind', as Dr Johnson put it. It is also sometimes said that, without this extreme punishment, there will be no way effectively to distinguish crimes like theft from crimes like cold-blooded murder which inspire a peculiar horror in the normal conscience. In this area it is clear that arguments of very different force and character are offered on both sides.

puppet regime

A *regime controlled by officials who act in the interests of, and under instructions from, the government of another state, usually sustained by threats of violence and economic coercion.

puritanism

1. The extreme forms of *Protestantism, in which the idea of the sovereignty of conscience is taken to require constant and scrupulous vigilance over one's every sentiment and action (and usually over everyone else's) in order to track down and extirpate all impure and irreligious thoughts and motives.

2. The secular survival of that doctrine, especially in Northern European and Anglo-Saxon countries, without its theological commitment, but with its same restless vigilance and self-examination, especially in matters of sexual morality, but also in any other area of personal life in which the self is of sufficient interest to provide the major subject of its own researches.

The influence of puritanism on English and American politics in the seventeenth, eighteenth and, to some extent, nineteenth century, has been so great that nothing brief can be said about it. It has often been observed, however, that the puritan self-obsession goes hand in hand with a vigilant concern that others be as miserable as oneself. Hence H.L. Mencken's definition of puritanism as 'the haunting fear that someone, somewhere, might be happy'.

Q

quango

'Quasi-autonomous non-government organization.' A body, often set up by a government and usually financed from the public purse, charged with investigating, recommending or arbitrating in some matter that is relevant to official policy, but which does not itself make policy and which is, in theory at least, attached neither to the government nor to any political party. An example is the UK 'Commission for Racial Equality', which is charged with receiving and acting upon complaints of racial discrimination, and which collects information and, where necessary, takes action through the courts in order to see that the law is upheld. Quangos are, as in this case, highly controversial. They have been denounced as self-perpetuating, expensive and meddlesome, busy most of all in justifying their own existence by finding problems where there are none, issuing reports where none are needed and engaging in expensive court cases which are all too frequently lost. Nevertheless, the number of quangos continues to grow, and *interest groups have recognized in them a novel way of getting the general public to pay for their activities and to provide a comfortable life-style to their leading representatives.

quantity theory of money
See *monetarism.

Quesnay, Francois (1694–1774)
French economist, defender of *laissez faire*, and intellectual leader of the *physiocrats.

quietism

Originally the name of a seventeenth-century mystical sect founded *c.* 1675 by a Spanish priest, M. de Molinor, which condemned all human effort, believing that perfection and salvation come only from God, and that man's task is to abandon himself passively to God's will, even to the extent of not caring about his own salvation. The term is now used to refer to any state of mind, or policy, that recommends prostrate acceptance of the principal fact – be it a conquering power, an economic order, an 'historical necessity', or whatever. Thus R.H. Hutton, in 1871: 'He was, in political and social conviction, a democratic quietist; one might almost say a fatalist'.

Quine, Willard van Orman (1908–2000)
American philosopher. *See* *ontology, *relativism.

Qutb, Sayyid (1906–66)
Egyptian writer, philosopher and *Islamist, who became the effective leader of the outlawed wing of the *Muslim Brotherhood while imprisoned under Nasser. Qutb began life as a secular reformist, writing novels and essays, while working in the Egyptian Ministry of Education. He subsequently spent two years in the US (1949–51), and was impressed by its godlessness (as he saw it) and hedonism. He was also influenced by *existentialism, and saw the problem of the Muslim in the modern world in terms made familiar by *Heidegger: the Muslim had been trapped by Westernization and colonialism into a stance of inauthenticity;

in response he must recapture his authentic self, by rejecting the otherness of the surrounding order. Western influence was not merely alien and alienating: it threatened a return to the state of *jâhiliyya*. Qutb saw Islam as providing the moral and spiritual leadership with which to avert that threat; he also found in Islam a recipe for *social justice, superior to any offered by the fashionable forms of socialism and communism. His thoughts were developed in two works written while in prison: a tract, *Milestones*, published in 1964, and a 30-volume commentary on the Koran – *In the Shade of the Koran*. The Western idea of secular government, he argued, is no solution to the problems of modern life, but merely a way of perpetuating man's alienation. It is also a form of idolatry. God alone is capable of laying down laws for mankind, and the human assumption of the right to do so involves placing the human on the level of the divine. All human political institutions are marked by the same taint of blasphemy, and the only hope for mankind resides, therefore, in the adoption of the *sharî'ah* and in studying and submitting to the Koran, which contains complete instructions for a life of peace and reconciliation with God.

Qutb was aware that ordinary people were not ready for this radical return to the pure source of Islam, and therefore argued for the necessity of a vanguard, not unlike the *vanguard party of Lenin, which would seize power in a single Islamic state and impose a strict Islamic orthodoxy there, in order to establish a secure base from which to influence or coerce its neighbours. His single-minded advocacy of this strategy, his persuasive style and his sincere and timely convictions marked him out in the eyes of the Egyptian authorities as a seriously dangerous man, and he was finally executed in 1966. He remains a major influence on Islamists, notably the leadership of *al-Qa'eda.

Race

A term of varying significance, originally used to
denote any class of people
related by common descent in a
manner significantly connected with
their location, language and customs.
Its use was extended to express what
might be called a 'moral idea' of affinity. According to this usage, a race is
defined by a significant common
history, which causes people to react
selectively towards one another, identifying with the triumphs and sufferings of the race to which they 'belong',
and regarding the history, customs
and outlook of that race as in some
way closer to their own personal existence than those of any other race.

The moral idea is not to be confused
with the later scientific and pseudo-
scientific attempts to divide humanity
into separate 'races' or subspecies,
supposedly exhibiting separate genetic
characteristics. This extension of the
idea of kinship beyond all connection
of place, language and custom was
common in the nineteenth century.
Thus *Gobineau thought it necessary to
distinguish between races in order to
explain the diverse physical characteristics and diverse states of development
of mankind. Later it was even thought
that human customs should be
explained in these same 'racial' terms,
and not, for example, in terms of
climate (as *Montesquieu had
attempted). Some see the *nationalist
theory of the *Volksgeist as inherently
racialist (i.e. as exhibiting a belief in the
disparity of races); and certainly its late
manifestation in *national socialism

involved a deep commitment to that
belief.

In the light of modern genetics the
issue of whether there are separate
human races in some scientifically
acceptable sense has come to seem
much harder to settle than was once
thought, although there is a body of
evidence to suggest that there are
slight variations in genetic make-up
between negroid, mongoloid and
Caucasian peoples. It seems that characteristics such as skin colour and
physiognomy, which are popularly
taken as indicators of race, are geneti-
cally very superficial. The question
whether there is something deeper
and more significant in behaviour, of
which these differences are a sign, is
extremely hard to answer. Recent work
in the US, by Charles Murray and
others, suggesting a distinction in
average IQ between US blacks and US
whites, has been taken very seriously.
(See *bell curve.) However, as the case
shows, the issue has become too
emotive to be treated with scientific
objectivity. Moreover the evidence
seems to suggest that the IQ of a population changes over time, and is radically affected by education. Thus East
European Jews coming to the US in the
late nineteenth and early twentieth
centuries performed badly in IQ tests,
whereas their direct descendants now
occupy the highest positions in political, intellectual and administrative
circles.

The term 'race' is still used in the
popular sense of common descent, of
which the supposed signs are skin
colour and physiognomy. It is in this

sense that the term is involved in the consideration of *racism.

racism

The terms 'racialism' and 'racism' are sometimes used interchangeably. It is probably best to use the first to mean the belief that there are significant distinctions (whether moral, intellectual or cultural) between *races, and the second to denote the belief not only that there are such distinctions, but that they provide adequate grounds for different treatment, in particular for granting rights and privileges to members of one race, and withholding them from members of another. Such a belief may or may not be accompanied by some *theory* of the differences between races. The emotional root of racism lies in a sense that some people are *alien, not necessarily on account of those physical characteristics that are used to identify them (although the appeal to such characteristics is a very important part of racism). Some have tried to explain this sense of the 'alien' in sexual terms – thus *Sartre, in his attempted diagnosis of *anti-semitism. Others have looked for economic causes, such as the need to recruit and also to confine a class of slave labourers, and the associated need for ready signs whereby to identify members of that class. Neither explanation can really account for the variety and extent of modern racism. 'Racial discrimination', i.e. *discrimination on grounds of race, is now the subject of legislation in many states, which often expressly reaffirm as illegal practices that were illegal already.

radical

From Latin *radix*, a root, the radical is one who wishes to take his political ideas to their roots, and to affirm in a thoroughgoing way the doctrines that are delivered by that exercise. It is a mistake to think that a radical must be on the *left, although the popular association between the radical and the *extremist is not so far-fetched as it might appear. The radical will tend to be hostile to the *status quo*, and anxious for sweeping changes, since the *status quo* generally expresses a balance between conflicting opinions and temperaments, and presents a loose imperfect order that lacks the ready intelligibility of systematic ideas. For this reason, while there may be 'radical right' views, 'radical conservatism' is apt to seem oxymoronic.

radical chic

Phrase coined by the American writer Tom Wolfe, to denote the affectation of radical left-wing views among middle-class intellectuals in order to achieve *status. *See also* *snobbery.

raison d'état

French: reason of state. A reason for state action which is of such importance as to involve the welfare and interests of the entire society, and to override all countervailing considerations, in particular those of an international character. The idea of the 'reason of state' entered political thinking during the sixteenth century, following the collapse of *ecclesiastical jurisdiction in international disputes. The principle that there are and must be such reasons was expounded by Giovanni Botero (1544–1617) (*Della Ragione di Stato*, 1590), and is implicit in *Grotius; it has been acknowledged in *international law since the Peace of Westphalia, 1648.

raison de guerre

A doctrine in international law, analogous to *raison d'état*, which permits violations of the rules of *just war if the overriding military purpose can be achieved by no other means. An act is justified by this doctrine only if the purpose itself is recognized as just. The bombing of civilian targets in order to bring about the surrender of combatants that are hiding among them is one possible action that might be justified by this doctrine.

Rand, Ayn (Alice Rosenbaum) (1905–82)

Russian-born writer and philosopher who emigrated with her parents after the Revolution and who was inspired by her vision of America to mount a sustained defence of *capitalism and critique of *socialism which have been highly influential in the US and to some extent elsewhere. Rand delivered her philosophy through essays, through novels (such as the famous *Atlas Shrugged*, 1957), and through newspapers and journals, some of which she inspired or founded. The principal influences on her thinking were *Nietzsche and social *Darwinism, and she saw in capitalism the mechanism whereby societies create the élites needed to govern them, by hardening both will and wit in the flame of competition. She described her philosophy as 'objectivism', believing that it shows people as they are, rather than as we should, in our sentimental moments, like them to be. She believed that her vision had the backing of science and was as dismissive of religion as the Marxists against whom she waged her lifelong intellectual battle. Rand argued that it is a mere illusion to believe that the poorer specimens of mankind will benefit from socialism, since socialist policies merely prevent the best and most useful people from exercising their skills and talents. But we all depend upon the success of these people, who create the material and moral space in which lesser beings can find their niche. (*The Virtue of Selfishness*, 1964.) In her novels Rand several times attempted to paint the portrait of the Nietzschean *Übermensch*, and, although the result does not appeal to everyone, it clearly appealed to her many followers, whose fervent support ensured that she became one of the most successful writers of her time, and one prepared ostentatiously to live the life of the *Übermensch* herself.

rank

Unlike *class and *status, rank seems to have no theoretical status in *sociology. Hierarchical societies – monarchies in particular – often have carefully composed rankings of subjects, with privileges, rights and duties allocated differently to the different ranks. In the UK this has the form of an order of 'precedence', in which the monarch takes precedence over the peerage, the peerage over the lesser aristocracy, and so on. Within the ranks of peers there are further divisions – between the various 'degrees of nobility' (baron, viscount, earl, etc.), the offices accorded to them (thus the Archbishop of Canterbury takes precedence over all other peers) and the ancestry of the title. In military organizations a system of ranking is still universal, but in this case it corresponds to a precise structure of *command, with lower ranks dutybound to obey orders from higher. Although formal ranks are more or less defunct in modern societies, informal equivalents are constantly emerging to replace them, so creating a 'ladder of success'. Rank plays a major part, therefore, in providing people with a motive to better themselves, especially within the *professions. The use of the term 'executive' to denote a social rank (as in 'executive homes') is one instance.

Rastafarianism

See *Ethiopianism.

rate of interest

The rate of interest is the difference between what is lent and what must be repaid after a specified time, expressed as a proportion of the amount lent; it is the price paid for borrowing a unit of money over that time. At any one time there tend to be different rates of interest prevailing for different types of loan. There are various explanations offered for the existence of a positive rate of interest:

(i) *time preference: money lent represents a sacrifice of present consumption for future income;

(ii) sacrifice of *liquidity: the lender may not be able quickly to convert the asset back to money, except perhaps by selling it, which may be risky;

(iii) risk and uncertainty: e.g. the borrower might not repay.

ratification

1. In *international law, the confirmation of a treaty or agreement. In UK ratification is by the *Crown, in US by the Senate. Since treaties are not binding unless ratified, this gives to the Senate large powers in international relations which might otherwise – had the English model been followed – have vested in the President.

2. The endowing of a *de facto power with *authority, whether legal, moral or political, either by express act, as when a parliament legalizes the activities of an autonomous organization (for example, the initial legalization of the free trade union movement in Poland), or implicitly, by the progressive *establishment of a power within the constitutional structures of a state. Ratification is a process whereby *power transforms itself into *authority, by gaining its title from offices and institutions which already possess it.

ratio decidendi

See *precedent.

rational

Human beings are rational beings, in that they are able to present and be guided by reasons for belief, reasons for action, and reasons for feeling and desiring. Moreover their choices and beliefs may or may not comply with the demands of reason. Hence 'rational' has two related senses in political discourse: it denotes the rational (as opposed to the non-rational) being, and the rational (as opposed to the irrational) act.

1. The rational being: a being who thinks and acts for reasons. Some philosophers argue that such a being must possess language, and that the possession of symbolism and reasoning powers is not an isolated capacity that can be thought of simply as an addition to the mental repertoire of a living being. On the contrary, reason permeates and transforms every element of the life of the being that possesses it. A rational being acquires intentions (in addition to desires), self-consciousness (in addition to consciousness), remorse and regret (in addition to disappointment), hope and determination (in addition to expectation), *values and ends (in addition to preferences and means). In short, it is argued that a rational being is a being of a different kind from a non-rational being, and this is often presented as a ground for the views that only rational beings are natural *persons, and that only rational beings have *rights.

None of the above thoughts is uncontroversial, but it is accepted on every hand that rationality is no simple matter, and makes the greatest possible difference to the life of the being who possesses it. *Aristotle argued that all and only rational animals are political animals: if this is so, then it would be right to be suspicious of political theories that apply equally to rational beings and to the biological affinities of herds and shoals. It seems implicit in the Aristotelian thesis that the rational being is essentially social. Some argue further and construe rationality as a social artefact, something that we possess, as we possess language, *by virtue of* our social relations. That is sometimes offered as a criticism of *individualism, which supposes that the individual can exist outside society, in a *state of nature, and still possess the rational capacities from which choices and values spring.

2. Rational choice. What makes a choice rational? This question has been subjected to extended quasi-mathematical treatment, e.g. in *decision theory, *game theory and the theories of *social choice. All such theories begin from premises concerning the ends of action (i.e. what is preferred), and try to examine the conditions under which ends may be rationally combined, and conditions for the rational choice of means. One obvious way of being irrational is to have inconsistent ends – and the exploration of inconsistency of choices plays a large part in all these theories. Another kind of irrationality is that involved in choosing means with a higher probability of failure than some equally feasible and equally desirable alternative. Furthermore, we have intuitions concerning time and rational choice: to choose a good now, rather than later, all other things being equal, may be more rational than to choose it later rather than now (*see* *time preference). All such intuitions can be built into the structure of a theory of rational choice, and the consequences delivered, and this is the main aim of decision theory.

Note that the intuitions mentioned concern either the choice of means to ends, or the reconciliation of ends. They do not settle the outstanding question of moral philosophy, whether there can be reasons given for an end of action which do not reduce it to a means. Aristotle thought that a

rational being is fulfilled only through *virtue, and that virtue circumscribes the ends of conduct. Hence the ends of the vicious person, however consistent, ordered and susceptible to *optimal solution, are against reason. *Kant argued, from a quite different standpoint, that a rational being is constrained by reason to accept only some ends of conduct, and to reject others as inconsistent with reason's demands. This whole subject, while of the greatest importance, remains shrouded in darkness.

rational economic man
See *economic man.

rationalism
1. The philosophical theory that the world is knowable to reason, and only to reason, and that the deliverances of the senses stand to be corrected in the light of reason. Rationalism has its origins in ancient metaphysics, especially in *Plato, but it is particularly associated with the modern 'rationalists', i.e. with the philosophers belonging to the movement which began with Descartes and which reached its culmination in the German academic philosophy of the *Enlightenment, to be rebutted by Kant in his *Critique of Pure Reason*. The principal exponents of rationalism were *Spinoza and (the main object of Kant's critique) Leibniz. Rationalism survived Kant's attacks, and indeed incorporated them, to re-emerge in the metaphysical idealism of *Hegel and his immediate followers. The debate between rationalism and *empiricism over the nature and object of knowledge still continues.

2. In *Weber, rationalism denotes the preference for 'legal-rational' over traditional and customary modes of *legitimation. Weber's thesis, that modern society has suffered a progressive *rationalization of all institutions,

is often accepted as casting light on the peculiar difficulties that the ideas of *allegiance and *obedience present to members of those societies, since there will always be some point at which the appeal to rules of legitimation gives out, and what then?

3. Sometimes used as a general designation of the search for rational solutions in the place of prejudices, and for scientific explanations in the place of what are regarded as mysteries. *J.S. Mill called himself a rationalist in this sense, although he was far from being a rationalist in sense 1.

4. More widely, 'rationalism' is used to denote the disposition to favour clear and explicit solutions, based on principles, whatever the problems, and to attempt to force reality into the mould of an ideal of reason-governed behaviour. According to some (e.g. *Oakeshott), rationalism is a political vice, involved in every attempt to force political realities into the convenient contours of pre-established theory. Rationalist doctrines are held to conceive human nature as better fitted to the solutions proposed for it than to those that it would discover through its own innate capacity to adapt itself to reality and reality to itself, e.g. through *custom and *tradition. As *Hayek expresses the point, rationalism exhibits a preference for instrumental over evolutionary rationality, and as a result destroys the information needed for its own success. (*See also* *tacit communication.)

5. Sometimes, in sociology, 'rationalism' is used to denote the thesis, due to *Dilthey, that the action of a rational being is *sui generis*, to be understood through *hermeneutics, and by reference to assumptions of rationality, rather than through scientific prediction and explanation of a kind that might equally be applied to the rest of nature.

rationalization

1. In *Weber, the appeal to *authority based on 'legal-rational' principles, i.e. principles that can be formulated as laws, and given the structure of a rational justification, however lacking in ultimate foundation. To rationalize the institution of monarchy, for example, is to give, a theory of the nature and function of the monarch that justifies his authority in terms of legal precepts and constitutional rules, rather than in terms of his inherent right to *obedience.

2. In normal parlance, and also in *Freudian theory, the justification of a course of action by proposing a reason that is not its motive. Rationalization is a way of justifying action in terms that do not explain it. The *Marxian theory of *ideology involves the thought that rationalization might be both *systematic*, and determined by class.

3. Reforming an organization (e.g. a firm) so as to eliminate all those parts and activities that do not serve the given purpose.

raw materials

Those *factors of production that are not artefacts, excluding *labour. Raw materials include land, and the contents of land, e.g. iron ore.

Rawls, John (1921–2002)

American philosopher who, in his *Theory of Justice*, 1971, attempted to reconcile a liberal ideal of political obligation with a redistributive conception of *social justice. The elements are:

(i) *Social contract. The contract is neither explicit nor tacit, but hypothetical: to determine the justice of an arrangement involves asking whether it *would* be the outcome of a social contract made under certain conditions.

(ii) The original position. The idea of the just arrangement is formed by abstraction from all actual social conditions so as to appeal to rationality alone. We suppose a 'veil of ignorance' to be drawn over social reality, and we choose from behind this veil the social arrangement that would then be acceptable to all. (The idea here has its roots in *Kant's categorical imperative.)

(iii) The original position is fair, and what is chosen in it is just, since it makes no ungrounded discrimination among members of society. Hence the resulting theory is one of 'justice as fairness'.

(iv) Two principles supposedly emerge from the thought experiment involved in the postulation of an original position. An arrangement is just if and only if (a) each person has an equal right to the most extensive basic liberty compatible with a similar liberty for all; (b) social and economic inequalities exist only if they are reasonably expected to better the position of the least advantaged, and are attached to offices and positions open to all. Condition (b) is not supposed to apply until (a) is satisfied, and is itself an application of the *difference principle, which will be chosen in the original position because, by virtue of the element of abstraction (ii), rational choice must concern itself with the position of the worst off, whoever he might be. (See *maximin.)

The two principles define the just original position; all other arrangements are just to the extent that they can be traced back, via just transactions, to such a position. The resulting theory is worked out in considerable detail, and is interesting partly for its attempt to incorporate results from theories of *rational choice, while being expressly anti-*utilitarian (although some commentators have argued that the theory is in fact very utilitarian, differing largely in the constraints that it imposes on rational

choice). It is often criticized (e.g. by *Nozick) for its supposed emphasis on the *end state of a transaction at the expense of the rights that are upheld and abused in the *course* of a transaction. (See *procedural justice.) Moreover, the status of the theory is unclear. It is not certain that it provides an account of justice that is binding on all rational beings, rather than a rationalization of moral intuitions which may themselves be rationally rejected. Nevertheless, the theory has been highly influential, partly, because of its attempt to reconcile intuitions taken respectively from liberal and from socialist standpoints.

reactionary

The idea of 'forces of reaction' which seek to arrest or reverse the achievements of revolution or reform was introduced into political thought by the philosophical radicals of the nineteenth century. At the time it was normal to identify these forces as the church, the aristocracy, and the institutions of the *ancien régime*. The term is still the property of the *left, although it has been used by *national socialists and *fascists. A reactionary is anyone who opposes changes that the left desires, or who seeks to re-establish a political order that has been overthrown in the name of left-wing ideals. The implication is usually that such a one merely 'reacts' to change and does not initiate change, so that he has no claim to be heard, being without serious recommendations.

real terms

The value of some variable, such as price or wages, when adjusted for changes in the purchasing power of money. Thus, if my income in money remains unchanged over a year during which inflation runs at 10%, my income in real terms decreases to 100/110 of its initial rate – i.e. by 9%. The 'real wage' is given by the money wage divided by an *index of the over-all price level. Aggregate values, such as total investment or national income, are often expressed in real terms.

realignment

Term of political science used to describe the emergence of new voting habits within recognized electoral groups – as when middle-class profes-sional women who have traditionally voted Republican begin to identify with the Democratic Party. The sugges-tion is that such changes involve deep changes in the *interests of the group in question, or in the policy and image of the parties that contend for its vote.

realism

1. Political. The disposition to see things as they are, rather than as they ought to be, and to recognize that the principal aim of all agents in the political sphere is power and self-aggrandisement. Certain critics of US postwar foreign policy have commented on its lack of realism, meaning, whether fairly or not, that it has taken a 'legal-moralis-tic' view of international conflict, rather than perceiving it in terms of the real struggles for power and influ-ence which the profession of legal and moral values tends to conceal. Such critics (including H.J. Morgenthau, *American Foreign Policy*, 1982) argue, not that ideals, values and law are irrelevant to international relations, but that they must be tempered by a vision of the real underlying tendency in terms of power, and that the *national interest must be rendered secure enough to make action in the name of values effective.

2. Legal. *See* *law.

3. Metaphysical. A realist is some-one who believes some object, class of objects, or property to be real and independent of our perceptions. Thus 'social realism' denotes a belief in the reality of social entities, such as society, the state and institutions, over and above the individuals who compose them (to be contrasted with *reduc-tionism); 'moral realism' denotes the view that moral values are part of the fabric of reality and not merely a projection of human attitudes: and so on.

Realpolitik

German: politics of the real. A term introduced by the German publicist Ludwig von Rochau in his *Grundsätze der Realpolitik*, 1853, in which he criti-cized the lack of *realism in the poli-cies followed by German liberals during the revolutionary years of 1848–49. The term was popularized later, since it seemed to capture the essence of Bismarck's policy during and after the years of German unifica-tion: a scrupulous attention to what is possible, a shrewd estimation of what one's opponent really wants, rather than what he says he wants, and a preparedness to assert *force when necessary. This particular brand of political realism should be distin-guished from *power politics, or from the politics of the *non-negotiable demand, neither of which need be realistic.

reasonable man

A creature known at *common law (which has yet to recognize the reasonable woman), as the standard against which human conduct is to be judged, and who remains undefined except through the social judgements of courts and juries. The 'reasonable man' test (for example, for negligence) suggests that the fundamental charac-teristics are prudence, stability and foresight, but not so much of any of these as would prove offensive or unnatural to others. The use of the attribute of 'reasonableness' to define what is in effect *normal human conduct has the interesting implication that human nature is to be defined at least partly through the study of ratio-nality. The invocation of the reasonable man in a proposed test for *obscenity (*The Williams Report*, 1979) suggests that reasonableness can also be under-stood as qualifying susceptibilities.

rebellion
Violent opposition by a substantial body of persons against the state, in the attempt to overthrow it. A rebel-lion can succeed in installing in power members of the same *class as those whom they replace; this is sometimes supposed not to be the case in a *revolution.

recession
A temporary period of under-use of labour and capital resources, produc-ing unemployment and decline in production. *Cf.* *depression. The term may also be used to denote the decline of an economy, i.e. the falling of the level of activity.

Rechtsgefühl
German: the feeling for law. A topic explored by nineteenth- and early twentieth-century German jurists, who argued that the application of a legal code requires a prior disposition to see the human world as already in some sense organised by ideas of right, law and justice. *Rechtsgefühl* might also be translated as 'the sense of justice'.

recognition
1. In *international law, any political and executive act which expresses or implies a legal significance in the acts of another state. An extremely complex idea, which has led to the need to distinguish *de facto* from *de jure* recognition, the first being extended, in the absence of any legal constitution, to powers with which it is necessary to deal while they last.

2. In the life of the individual recog-nition means the acknowledgement by others of one's worth, and the search for recognition has been identified as one of the primary motives of political life, and one of the social forces that have worked towards *democratiza-tion. *See* *Kojève, *Fukuyama.

redistribution
1. A reorganization of the boundaries between electoral districts in order to change the relation of *representation. This has often taken place in the UK, in response to the growth of towns and the depopulation of the country-side, although time-lags have led to notorious anomalies. Thus during the early nineteenth century, a country district of a few hundred might return two members to Parliament, and a swelling industrial town only one. (The problem of the 'rotten boroughs'.) On the larger issue of justice, *see* *representation.

2. The redistribution of *land, in accordance with conceptions of effi-ciency, justice or jurisdiction. *See* *land reform.

3. The redistribution of income and rewards in order to achieve some economic or social objective, usually that of *social justice in the distribu-tion of goods. Modern moves in this direction have tended to advocate either direct state control over salaries and wages, usually combined with public ownership of large-scale enter-prises, or else progressive *taxation, designed to ensure that the differential between the highest and the lowest paid is offset by a heavier burden of taxation on the former. Some argue that these measures do not work and that income distribution will always remain unaffected by them (*see* *Pareto). Others argue that questions of distribution cannot be separated from questions of ownership, so that effective state redistribution must

accompany state control of production. Others reject progressive taxation, as involving an injustice towards the rich, in asking them to surrender not just a higher amount, but a higher proportion of what they earn. It is sometimes added that a person has a high earning capacity because of his social function, and progressive taxation will therefore discourage the most useful from taking on the work that is required from them. On these issues, *see* *sumptuary laws, *taxation.

reductionism
The attempt, in philosophy, the social sciences, and elsewhere, to avoid reference to entities regarded as non-existent, usually by systematic replacement of the language which seems to refer to them. Thus a philosopher might attempt to replace all reference to social entities by references to individuals, and suggest some systematic replacement for sentences in which terms like 'state', 'society', and 'institution' occur. In political thought reductionism is often not carried through in that way, although in the debate concerning methodological *individualism, as opposed to *holism, the discussion is very much influenced by analytical philosophy, and therefore directs itself at least to the *possibility* of such systematic reduction.

Recent philosophy has suggested that there may be fundamental errors involved in the assumption that reduction could be carried through (e.g. it seems that any replacement for the offending sentences will either fail to capture the original meaning, or else be unintelligible because infinitely complex). In the face of difficulties, reductionists tend to take refuge in an appeal to common sense, characteristically making use of the locution 'nothing but' as in: 'authority is nothing but established power'; 'values are nothing but ideology'; or 'law is nothing but

the will of the ruling class'. This sophistical 'nothing-but' was decisively refuted by *Plato at the beginning of *The Republic* (arguing against 'justice is nothing but the interests of the stronger'). Needless to say, Plato's argument has done nothing to cure lesser mortals of the disease.

re-education
The process whereby political opinions and attitudes are deliberately changed or suppressed, through education and *propaganda, sometimes accompanied by threats and *coercion. The process is sometimes called 'rectification' (term introduced by *Mao in 1929), and may have a relatively benign significance. In the West, however, it is normally thought to be a euphemism for a process designed to change the outlook of the victim regardless of reason, involving forced attendance at institutions of a disciplinary nature.

Threats are irrelevant to the inculcation of belief, but they may certainly cause their victim to simulate belief. When the re-educated individual emerges, therefore, he may be an adept at *ketman* and, as such, regarded with yet greater suspicion by those in power. Hence the process of re-education tends to be never-ending.

referendum
The referring of a political question to the *electorate for a direct decision by popular vote. In some constitutions (e.g. that of Australia) the constitution can be amended only with the consent of the electorate at a referendum, and the device is frequently used (although not required) in France, in order to validate constitutional change. It has been used in the UK, but is unknown in the US, at least at the federal level.

A referendum involves a decision by the electorate without the intermediary of *representation, and therefore exhibits a form of *direct democracy. However, to say that is to assume that the question asked of the electorate is intelligible to the majority, and also that it is one that is sensibly submitted to its vote. Some have doubted that either of those conditions was fulfilled in the case of the UK referendum on the Common Market; but it seems that in any case a referendum has no legal or constitutional authority in the UK. (This is part of the doctrine of the *sovereignty of *Parliament.)

referendum democracy

Term introduced by Robert A. Dahl (*After the Revolution*, 1970) to denote the kind of democracy exemplified by Switzerland, in which the citizens can insist that any particular legislative decision be subject to a *referendum. To be distinguished from *direct democracy and *representative democracy, being a mixture of the two.

reflation

The deliberate policy of expanding aggregate demand in the economy, e.g. by expanding the *money supply. According to *monetarists reflation automatically causes *inflation, and indeed *Hayek has referred to 'reflation' as 'a fraudulent term meaning inflation'.

reform

A process of political change within the framework of a *constitution, and without questioning the *legitimacy of the *sovereign power. The net result of continuous reform may be a change of constitution (whether in fact or in law), but the essential feature is the absence of challenge to the received political process. 'Reform' in the UK has meant, from the nineteenth century at least, electoral reform, particularly the extension of the *franchise through the Reform Act 1832 and the Representation of the People Acts 1867, 1884 and 1918.

reform communism

The attempt by communist parties during the late 1980s, and notably in the USSR, under the leadership of Mikhail Gorbachev, to combine one-party rule with social and economic reform in order to avert the impending economic collapse. The attempt was made to encourage limited private enterprise, market mechanisms and public debate while retaining communist control over all major decisions affecting domestic and foreign policy. In the event, reform communism achieved little, since the Party's monopoly of social and political power was incompatible with the legal structures that were required (e.g. laws of contract, tort, corporate liability and bankruptcy) for economic reform to be anything more than a token.

Reformation

The religious movement that swept through Europe in the sixteenth century challenging the authority, doctrine and liturgy of the *Roman Catholic Church, and leading to the rise of *Lutheranism, *Calvinism and the *Protestant churches. The Reformation must not be confused with the changes introduced into the Church of England during the 'Reformation Parliament' of 1529–36, which were of a political rather than a religious nature, designed to unite the secular and religious sources of authority within a single sovereign power: the *Anglican Church did not until later make any substantial change in doctrine.

reformism

The advocacy of improvement by *reform, rather than by *revolution, either out of the conservative respect for constitution, as embodying unspoken wisdom condensed and applied in customary usage (*cf.* *Burke: 'one must reform in order to conserve'), or out of a sense that, without a frame of constitution and legitimacy, no political change is sufficiently predictable to be cogently intended. Many also regard the absence of any provision for reform as dangerous, arguing that a rigid constitution will not adapt to changing social circumstances, will therefore enter into ruinous conflict with social forces that it cannot control, and will so precipitate revolution, anarchy and, in the wake of anarchy, tyranny. Reformism is often identified as the principal enemy of revolutionaries who wish to exacerbate existing conflicts, and not to conciliate or soften them.

regime

French: a regimen, i.e. a form of rule. Now frequently used to denote the actual holders of office within a government, considered independently of the offices which they hold. On this definition there can be a change of regime without a change of *constitution or *office, and vice versa, as when a ruling party recasts the constitution in order to preserve its power. (An example of the former. the change of ruling party after a UK election; an example of the latter, the proposals of the Zanu Party in Zimbabwe to perpetuate its own power through the creation of a one-party state.) Since the nature of a regime is determined in part by the offices that it occupies, 'regime' and 'government' may be used synonymously, but on the definition given they are no more synonymous than are 'the Queen' and 'the Crown'.

regionalism

The advocacy of forms of government which permit and encourage the development of indigenous culture and institutions within separate regions of the *jurisdiction, and which involve the *delegation of substantial political and legal powers to regional authorities with less than full *sovereignty but more than merely administrative functions.

Regionalism has become an important issue in European politics. The principal threat to the sovereignty claimed by the *European Commission and its institutions comes from the *nation-states of Europe. To promote regionalism in the European nations is therefore to undermine the main source of opposition to the project of European Union. This was already perceived by *Monnet, and now seems to be a settled policy. The official map of Europe does not, for example, mention any place called England: but it does mark out four English 'regions', which have, under *New Labour, received their regional assemblies. This particular project for the *balkanization of England seems to have faltered, however, in that the voters clearly do not want these assemblies to be elected, preferring another layer of bureaucrats to another layer of politicians. Some people hope that the project will backfire, by provoking the English into demanding a Parliament of their own – something that they have lacked since the Act of Union 1707. At present there seems little likelihood of this.

regulation

Regulations are issued by bodies charged with the overseeing of some activity and may have the force of law if backed by a legal provision that they are mandatory. The growth of regulatory bodies, backed by legislation authorizing their decisions, has been the inevitable result of the expansion of government and also of the institutions of the *European Community. In the UK and the US the deregulation of industry and commerce has therefore become a respectable political aim, with rival bodies set up by the government to undo the regulations of previous regimes. It is widely recognized that in *post-communist societies a great work of deregulation is necessary if the economy is ever to move forward.

rehabilitation
Term of political science used, for example, of the posthumous restoration to favour and acquittal of a victim of a purge, under a *Stalinist regime. Often the victim will have been already executed, and the process of rehabilitation will involve careful planning in order to avoid bringing law and government into total disrepute. Thus only six of those convicted in the notorious Moscow Trials were rehabilitated prior to the collapse of communism although statements were made implying that all were innocent. Some observers have referred to 'de-rehabilitation', when some rehabilitated politician is again denounced as a traitor.

Reich, Wilhelm (1897–1957)
Psychoanalyst, and student of *Freud, who attempted to *politicize Freud's theory of sexual *repression. In modern society (both socialist and capitalist) the libido is repressed in ways that profoundly affect the individual character, and the nature of political institutions. Reich disagreed with Freud's view that repression performs a functionally necessary role in society, and argued (in *The Invasion of Compulsory Sex-Morality*, 1932) that the patriarchal family suppresses individual expression and fulfilment, and causes those subject to its influence to experience all social relations in terms of sanctions and fear. It is misguided to attempt to overcome this stultification of the individual by transforming the economic *base of social relations, as Marxists seek to do. Class distinctions

too are largely irrelevant, since the oppression which Marx rightly discerned at the heart of the social order occurs at a deeper level; it is there, on the plane of individual sexuality, that it must be overcome.

Reich criticized both fascism and communism ('red fascism') for their coercive nature, and saw them both as expressions of the same warped instincts, and as inherently exploitative of the masses' propensity to submit to external control (*The Mass Psychology of Fascism*, 1933–34). His naïve and sentimental view of human sexuality was shared by *Marcuse, and he had, at one point, considerable influence over *libertarian thinking.

reification
German: *Versachlichung* or *Verdinglichung*. Term introduced by Marx and popularized by *Lukács (see *History and Class Consciousness*, 1971), and by *Marcuse and others of the *Frankfurt school, in order to describe the process whereby, in a society organized according to the principles of capitalism, workers endow commodities, *exchange-values, the economic laws which seem to govern them, and the institutions which protect them, with a real existence independent of themselves. By virtue of this process, Lukács argues, the worker is unable to perceive that he alone is responsible for the existence and nature of these things, their reality being derived entirely from his own labour. Reification is a form of *false consciousness. It also causes the worker to see himself as diminished, unreal, inert, to the extent that he transfers through his actions the real powers that belong to him to the illusory world which commands his attention. The concept thus brings together the two Marxian ideas of *alienation and *commodity fetishism.

relativism

1. Moral. The view that *ideals and *values do not have universal validity, but are valid only in relation to particular social and historical conditions. ('What is truth on one side of the Pyrenees, is error on the other' – Pascal.) Moral relativism is to be distinguished from moral subjectivism, which says that no moral judgements have any validity whatsoever, beyond the fact of recording someone's subjective conviction. The relativist might think that moral judgements are objective while denying that they are universal.

2. Cultural. 'Cultural relativism' is the view that particular beliefs and practices make sense in one cultural context but not in another, and cannot be transplanted into another culture. Such views tend to be *organicist, and to argue that cultural transplants are a surgical impossibility.

3. Epistemological or cognitive. The view, associated with such philosophers as *Quine and *Kuhn, that observation and theory are inseparable, so that 'data' are intrinsically interpreted in terms of a theory, and cannot be regarded as 'given' independently. Epistemological relativism also implies (according to Quine) a relativism of *ontology. It has been extremely influential both directly, in philosophy, and also indirectly in the social sciences and the *sociology of knowledge.

4. 'Conceptual'. The view that the world itself is relative to the concepts with which we order it, and that there is no constraint on our concepts that is independent of our own decisions. This view, associated with *Nietzsche, who maintained that 'there are no truths, only interpretations', has enjoyed a renewed favour in recent years, as part of the *postmodernist conception of social and political reality. Taken to its limit, it seems to result in an 'absolute relativism' – the contradiction implied in this phrase being already implicit in the original idea.

In its more exuberant manifestations, postmodernism seems to embrace every kind of relativism, and to endorse the conclusion that there really are no truths, not even this one.

relevance

A movement within the theory and practice of education, growing from ideas associated with *Dewey, has aimed to make education 'relevant' to the children for whom it is designed. The assumption is that the traditional curriculum is too much preoccupied with matters (dead languages, abstract sciences, vanished cultures, moribund religions) which are of no relevance to the modern child since they make no contact with his experience. In place of the traditional curriculum we must introduce an education focused on the child and his interests – in other words, we must introduce a 'child-centred' curriculum. This means using the tools that are familiar to the child (videos rather than books, for instance), addressing the questions that already trouble him ('Where do bananas come from?' rather than 'Who won the battle of Marathon?') and referring to the cultural landscape that he knows (pop music and TV soap operas rather than Shakespeare). And so on. The 'relevance revolution' has been criticized on the grounds that by making education relevant to those who have yet to acquire it you deprive it of its sense. Indeed, the whole concept of 'child-centred' education has come under attack in recent debates as placing the emphasis on the wrong term in the educational relationship: instead of conceiving knowledge as a means to improve the child, it is argued, we should view the child as a means to pass on knowledge. In reply it is argued that if the law obliges all children to attend school then it ought also to find something useful for them to do there.

religion

Religion has two components: first, the habits of *piety and a sense of the holiness of human life. Second, the belief in, worship of, and attempt to obey, transcendent beings, usually on the assumption that they possess the power to regulate affairs in this world, and to distribute rewards and punishments in another. The two components are psychologically linked but logically independent, and there are religions which emphasize the first while remaining vague about the second (Shintoism, for example), and religions which emphasize the second while being vague about the first (some strands within *Protestantism, for example).

For some commentators religion is the single most powerful motive in human history, for others a mere device whereby the injustice of the existing social order is made tolerable to those destined to suffer it, and due to decline with the eventual mastery over nature and the tearing away of the veil of *ideology. Others still see religion, in the manner of *Durkheim, as the fundamental expression of our social nature and the true record of our dependence on a community that is greater than the sum of its members. In recent years there has also been a revival of the *humanist view that religion is a kind of poison of the human mind, which we can and ought to cure, since it is a major cause of conflict and aggression. A particular form of that last view is the theory, due to the biologist Richard Dawkins, of the religious *meme, which conceives religion as a parasitical organism that destroys the brains that it colonizes.

Religion and politics can never be separated in the minds either of believers or of those who seek to govern them, and religious conceptions have influenced almost all of the concepts and institutions of modern Western government: the law, through *canon law and *natural law; *sovereignty, through the doctrine of international *jurisdiction; property, through the doctrines of the *just price and *usury; social welfare and education, through the command of *charity and the concept of *social justice; political obligation, through the commands of *piety and *obedience: and political stability, through the belief that perfection belongs not to this world but to another.

Religion has re-entered politics in a massive way since the rise of *Islamism, which is motivated by the desire to establish forms of government authorised by God and, failing that, to destroy the alternatives along with those who live by them. This has led to important attempts to explore the Judaeo-Christian legacy, which has opted for *secular government as expressing the true will of God (see *Two Swords), and to understand the position of unbelievers under *Islamic law.

rent

1. In economics, a technical term, defined as the factor price received *minus* the lowest factor price which would have induced the factor unit in question to remain in its current employment. (Thus a philosophy lecturer earning £15 000 who would stay in his job even at £10 000 (though not less) has a 'rent' of £5000. This hypothetical surplus is often called 'economic rent'.)

2. The economic advantage attached to a position, regardless of what is done by the person who occupies it. Thus an officer in a factory whose job it is to inspect goods for

defects of a kind that no longer occur, has a rent on the productive process equivalent to his salary. The pursuit of rents, in this sense, is an important motive in modern societies and, according to the theory of *public choice, explains much political behaviour. (*See* *rent-seeking.*)

3. In normal parlance, the price paid per unit of time for the use of something durable, especially land and the buildings upon it. The problem of the nature of rent, and the factors which determine it, exercised the *classical economists – *Malthus, *Ricardo, and others – who produced, in effect, a *marginal productivity theory of the rent accruing to agricultural land.

The moral and legal problems of rent (particularly of residential accommodation) and of rent control have been important in European politics during the twentieth century. Some argue that rent control is intrinsically unacceptable, in that it involves massive interference in contractual relations in favour of one party, and sometimes after the bargain has been struck. This, it is sometimes said, infringes a requirement of *natural justice, so that rent control and, in particular, legislation providing security of tenure, are unjust, as well as interfering with the free economy in ways that are bound to have unwanted side-effects. Others argue that the payment of rent for land and buildings should not be considered under the ordinary philosophy of contract, but rather under the philosophy of *land law, in which *prescriptive right and security of tenure are of the essence. The arguments here are various, but one important consideration is obviously that security of tenure of property is at the root of every other security that a person may enjoy. In which case statutory controls over rent and tenure serve merely to ratify what

ought already to be judged as a tenure of land. The effect of rent control legislation introduced by successive Labour governments in the UK has been to destroy rented accomodation in town centres, except for businesses, which do not enjoy the same level of statutory protection. This in turn has led to a decline in town centres and a flight to the suburbs. A similar effect has been observed in France, notably in Paris, whose population is now in serious decline.

rent-seeking

The efforts of businesses, individuals or groups to obtain, through law or administrative regulation, either some kind of monopoly status or an increase in their incomes beyond what a competitive market might deliver. For example, the effort of a firm to introduce 'health and safety' regulations that, for historical reasons, it can easily comply with, but which impose serious costs on its competitors. The term was first employed by Anne O. Krueger in an article in the *American Economic Review*, 1976, and then taken up as part of a general theory by Gordon Tullock, *The Economics of Special Privilege and Rent Seeking*, 1989. Tariffs are, in this sense, a source of rents afforded by law to domestic producers; the salaries achieved by the directors of state monopolies are legally enforced rents on national income. The term may be used more widely to refer to any activity in which one person achieves, through law or the administrative process, a share in the profits of an activity undertaken by someone else. *See* *public choice.

reparations

A form of war indemnity, whereby the loser pays large sums to some party of the winner's choice, usually the winner itself. Reparations were demanded of Germany by the peace treaties of 1919–20; the demand was heavily criticized by economists, especially *Keynes, and is thought to have furthered the economic collapse of Germany, to have absorbed money in unpaid loans from the victors, and to have contributed to the turmoil from which Germany was to emerge with another burden of reparations, this time to Israel.

representation

1. The process whereby the interests of the governed are 'represented' to those who govern them, for example through parliamentary institutions. The practice of representation in the UK is as old as the English Parliament, although its form has changed radically over the centuries. It is still not wholly clear what representation consists in, or what conditions determine its just and efficient functioning. *Burke made a celebrated distinction between representation and *delegation thus: 'a delegate merely mirrors and records the views of his constituents, whereas a representative is elected to judge according to his own conscience'. However, it is clear that if the representative's conscience told him to disobey all petitions from those who elected him, it would be odd to describe him as continuing to represent them. A further complication is introduced by the idea of mandation, and the doctrine of the *mandate, which suggests obedience to promises as a criterion for the legitimacy of a representational office. It is probably most useful to distinguish representation, delegation and mandation as three separate relations between an officer and those to whom he is answerable. These relations may or may not occur together:

(i) mandation: the relation between an office-holder and an electorate, by virtue of the promises of the former to the latter, under which he is obliged to fulfil those promises, and also exonerated from the effects of doing so (since he has been 'given a mandate' to do just this);

(ii) delegation: the relation between an officer and an electorate, when the electorate has instructed him to convey certain requests and commands to another body;

(iii) representation: the relation between an officer and an electorate, who have no power over the officer other than that provided by an election, and in which the officer is bound (a) to obey the principles and constitution of the assembly in which he sits, and (b) within that framework, to urge consideration of the interests of his constituents.

The essential feature here is that a representative is bound by a double duty, that towards the institution in which he sits, and that towards the electorate. Neither duty is the result of a promise, but each must be upheld in obedience to the constitution under which the representative holds office. Thus representation is a conventional relation, mediated by conventions and rules, while delegation and mandation are both natural relations, founded in obligations undertaken by the appointee.

On this view, what makes someone a representative of a constituency or a group is not to be found in the existence or extent of the franchise. For example, representation may be by command from the sovereign; it seems that this was the case in the early days of the English Parliament, when representation of a borough was often undertaken with great reluctance by those commanded. However, many argue that it is impossible that someone should really represent the interests of a group if that group has no power either to elect or to eject him from the assembly, and hence that representation without franchise is not really the same thing as representation with it. The point here is that the representative must be not just *influenced but, in some crucial sense, *controlled, by those whose interest he represents – otherwise he will represent the state to its subjects, but not the subjects to the state. (*Cf.* *democratic centralism.)

This raises, however, the problem of the nature of the franchise. Some argue that a representative is more likely to respond to the interests of those who appoint him if they are identified with a specific place, where he himself is resident, and with the social and economic conditions with which he is familiar. In which case, the idea of the *constituency, as enshrined in UK electoral law, emerges as denoting the second term of the relation. Others argue, perhaps in favour of *proportional representation, that the UK system does not lead to an assembly which fairly represents the differences of opinion within the country, and that representation by interest ought therefore to be made explicit. For example each candidate ought to state, say, through his allegiance to a party, where his interest lies, the votes of the electorate for the various parties then determining how many seats in the chamber are allotted to each. Roughly speaking, the first conception reflects a view of representation as involving an obligation towards a group of people identified in terms of an existing social and territorial relation, the second involves a view of representation as involving obligations towards a group identified in terms of their *opinion. In fact, under the second view, parties and not people take the leading role as the principal channel through which public opinion influences government, and some argue that this makes representation of the *people* less likely, and not more.

2. Existential representation. Term coined by *Voegelin, in order to designate the traditional relation between a prince and his subjects, whereby the prince took the name of a territory, and was identified by the people of that territory as a personal embodiment of their political unity.

representative democracy
The kind of democracy in which voters elect representatives, as opposed to *direct democracy. *See* *representation.

representative government
See *representation.

repression
A term introduced into the theory of psychoanalysis by *Freud, to refer to two supposed processes whereby impulses are buried in the unconscious: primal repression, whereby the young child defends itself from mental tension by endowing objects with the power to overcome that tension, and repression proper, which is the defence mechanism against those unconscious wishes and impulses that might, were they to rise into consciousness, cause unbearable tensions in the 'ego'. Repression involves mechanisms and subterfuges whereby such wishes and impulses are kept blocked in the unconscious.

The Freudian language is dense with dubious metaphors of the mind; nevertheless it has had a wide influence on political thought, proving persuasive in its redefinition of the process of moral education, and also useful to certain *neo-Marxist theories of *structural violence, which construe the allegedly oppressive character of bourgeois society in terms of the repression of instincts vital to *self-realization. *See also* *Reich.

reprisals
When a state has failed to secure redress against another for a legal

wrong by diplomatic means it may, in certain circumstances, commit injurious acts short of war, of a kind which would otherwise be illegal. Frequently what one state calls reprisals the other state will call acts of *aggression, and in modern times reprisals have usually come from greater powers towards smaller ones, so ensuring that war will not be the outcome. Reprisals are not permitted in the case where the delinquent state discharges whatever vicarious responsibility it might have for the injurious acts of its officials or armies. Reprisals may be performed only by the state or its officials or forces, and against everything belonging to the delinquent state and its citizens. Negative reprisals consist in refusals to perform obligations, such as the repayment of a debt. Reprisals should be proportionate to the wrong done and limited to the compulsion necessary to obtain redress. In times of war reprisals may also exist, in this case to compel the other side to obey the laws of war.

republic

Latin: the public thing, in other words the state and its institutions. The term is now normally used to denote any state that is not a monarchy, or any non-monarchical federated part of a state which retains sufficient autonomy to exercise its own *jurisdiction.

Debates concerning the utility or otherwise of republics as opposed to monarchies now have a slightly antiquated air, and, although the Irish Republican Army was 'fighting' in a cause said to be republican, it is clear that the abolition of the UK monarchy would not have removed its grievance. In comparison with a modern *constitutional monarchy, a republic tends to be distinguished by the enormous concentration of power in the head of state. This fact, which accords with the eminently progressive character of republics, was not foreseen by Ambrose Bierce when in *The Devil's Dictionary*, he defined 'republic' thus: 'a nation in which, the thing governing and the thing governed being the same, there is only a permitted authority to enforce an optional obedience. In a republic the foundation of public order is the ever lessening habit of submission inherited from ancestors who, being truly governed, submitted because they had to. There are as many kinds of republics as there are gradations between the despotisms whence they came and the anarchy whither they lead.' Bierce's definition usefully suggests that the distinction between republic and monarchy has, historically, corresponded to two rival theories of political obligation, one based in an idea of *consent, the other in an idea of *obedience. In the classical literature of political theory, therefore, the term 'republic' has been used to denote a state in which citizens are directly or indirectly involved in public life, in which there is a rotation of officeholders, and in which there is an *ethos of public service and duty – such is the meaning of the term in *Harrington, *Machiavelli, *Montesquieu and *Rousseau. Hence republics have *citizens, while monarchs rule over *subjects.

Republican Party

The US Republican Party was founded in 1792 by *Jefferson, in order to defend agrarian interests and *states' rights, although the lineal heirs of Jefferson's Republicans are probably to be counted among today's Democrats. The Republican Party was re-formed as an anti-slavery coalition in 1854, and since then has gradually fitted itself into the common mould which the US constitution imposes on the main parties contending for office. It has gradually incorporated sections of public opinion that could be said to be *right of centre, but has shifted from the rural federalism of Jefferson to the free enterprise urban capitalism defended by the economists of the *New Right. The successes of the party since 1932 have been spasmodic, but it is now able to call upon considerable popular support through its image of tough-minded patriotism and international *Realpolitik.*

The name of the party originally signified Jefferson's theory that truly republican government required a federal constitution, and that only by the constant affirmation of states' rights could the office of President be kept from becoming monarchical. (For Jefferson the idea of monarchy was the idea of executive power of an overbearing, whether or not absolute, kind, vested in a single person.) The name persisted, as did the emphasis on states' rights, but it is now of no more than vestigial significance. In popular parlance and *journalese, the party is referred to as the GOP or Grand Old Party, in honour of its history. Parties calling themselves republican exist elsewhere, even in one-party states, but they are united by no common principles, not even that contained (under Jefferson's interpretation) in their name.

republicanism

Usually used to denote a particular tradition in political thought, which defends government of offices, representation of the people and the rule of law, as the pre-conditions of a free citizenry. Associated with *Machiavelli, *Montesquieu and *Kant, among others, republicanism is not necessarily opposed to monarchy, being concerned with the way in which the power of the state is deployed and limited, and in the fundamental accountability of the state towards the citizens that compose it. Kant's argument for a 'League of Nations' as the guarantee of 'perpetual peace' was premised on the assumption that the 'Nations' joining the League would be republics – in other words, states accountable to their citizens.

Rerum novarum

An *encyclical of Pope Leo XIII, issued in 1891, concerning the condition of labour, and defining the position of the Roman Catholic Church towards socialism and capitalism. The encyclical aims to 'define the relative rights and mutual duties of the wealthy and the poor, of capital and labour', and to find 'some remedy ... for the misery and wretchedness which press so heavily at this moment on the large majority of the very poor.' It argues that private property is a necessary institution and the object of a sacred right, since it is the means to express and realize individual choice and to make provision for one's family. The problems of the modern economy concern responsibilities as well as rights, and the social classes are not by nature hostile to each other, since labour and capital are mutually necessary. The encyclical holds that 'the main tenet of socialism, the community of goods, must be utterly rejected'. So must the socialist idea of equality: human difference is god-given and a necessary precondition of the mutuality on which human communities are built. This does not mean that all is well with the capitalist system: it is necessary to rectify its imbalances, to recognize that wealth is created by labour, and to further the creation of trade unions, welfare provisions and ways of establishing a *just wage. Capitalism has a tendency to treat working people as chattels; the remedy is not to embrace socialism, which makes them chattels of the state, but to cease treating them as chattels.

resale price maintenance

The practice whereby a producer requires distributors to resell a product at a certain minimum *price. There have been major inquiries by governments in the UK with the object of determining whether or not this practice is in the public interest. In 1964 it was decided (the Resale Prices Act) that all resale price agreements are to be deemed against the public interest, and therefore unenforceable at law, unless proved otherwise in court. One such agreement – the net price agreement in the book trade – endured until 1995.

resentment

Identified by *Nietzsche as a leading force in modern society, resentment (or *ressentiment*, to use Nietzsche's borrowing from the French) is the feeling entertained towards someone who is more fortunate than oneself when one knows that his good fortune has not been purchased at one's own expense but when one wishes, nevertheless, to deprive him of it. *Envy is the desire to possess what another has; resentment the desire to destroy it. The opposite of resentment is admiration, and resentment often arises as a defence against admiration – a grudging acknowledgement of another's virtues, which also cannot abide the thought of them. Resentment, according to Nietzsche, expresses the herd-instinct in man – the instinct which acts to enforce conformity and to prevent the individual from emerging as a law unto himself and so transcending human nature. (*See *Übermensch*.) It is the normal state of mind of the 'poor in spirit', those whom Aristotle would describe as 'naturally slaves'; and it attempts to enforce its vision by impeding all forms of human excellence and domination. It is satisfied only by *equality, but cannot welcome anything, not even equality, with joy. When people speak of socialism, social justice, rights or democracy, then it is the voice of resentment that is heard.

Nietzsche's exaggerations are now recognized as such; but the element of truth in what he wrote is less readily acknowledged. Nietzsche's suggestions were, however, taken up in a more temperate idiom by *Scheler, who used them to formulate a comprehensive critique of socialism, not as an economic doctrine but as a philosophy of man.

residue

A term used by *Pareto to denote fundamental impulses that motivate human conduct and which, while they appear to the agent as 'ideas', 'values' and 'convictions', exist independently, as enduring features of the human condition, unaffected by any rational argument or intellectual change. The theory of the relation between an idea and its residue bears some similarity to Marx's theory of the relation between an *ideology and its material conditions. The difference is that, for Pareto, a residue is not historically variable, but a more or less permanent datum of human nature.

resistance

*Opposition which is denied legal recognition, either because all opposition is denied legal recognition, or because it is of such a character as to fall outside those categories of opposition recognized in law. Resistance must therefore be either clandestine (as in the underground resistance in the Second World War) or *passive.

resources

Another name for the *factors of production, and conventionally classified into land, labour and capital, the first being given a wide sense to include *raw materials, the second covering every known employment, including book-keeping, accounting, etc., the last covering all produced means of production (goods made to produce other goods).

Resources are always scarce relative to the desired level of production, and hence there is major political dispute over their allocation, and over the role of government in determining their allocation. It has been a familiar anti-capitalist thesis that capitalism is wasteful of resources. It is a familiar anti-socialist thesis that socialism is even more wasteful. Both claims are clearly true.

responsibility

1. The feature of *agency without which there can be neither praise nor blame for what is done. If you and I are forcibly confined in a sealed container, then every breath of mine deprives you of air; but I am not responsible for your death by asphyxiation, as I would be were I to confine you and then deliberately to extract the air. The difference is intuitively obvious, but not easy to define. Old ideas of metaphysical *freedom, according to which the uncaused spontaneous act of will intercedes in the processes of nature, tend now to be rejected, not the least because they cannot account for responsibility. (Responsibility is often said to involve a *kind* of causation, not freedom from causation.) Lawyers are used to laying down negative conditions for responsibility, i.e. conditions in which someone is *not* responsible for the consequences of his acts, as when he is *coerced into doing them, and likewise conditions of 'diminished responsibility'. But the attempt to specify positive conditions meets with nearly insuperable obstacles, deriving in part from obscurities in the idea of agency. We hold people responsible for the consequences of negligence, even though negligence is not something 'done'. And among things done and done deliberately we still distinguish cases where responsibility is lifted. Self-defence is an obvious example; less clear is the case of the soldier acting under orders. (The concept of a *war crime is that of an action that cannot be excused, even by orders from a superior officer.) Some argue that responsibility is affected by *office, and that this must be borne in mind when assessing the responsibility of President Truman for the deaths that resulted from the bombing of Hiroshima. Others go further and argue that responsibility may even be affected by belief, so that, for example, Lenin's belief that the powers assumed in the name of the party would be temporary, exonerates him from the terrible consequences that ensued from that. All those cases are disputed (*see* *morality and politics), and it is fair to say that nothing is very clear about the concept of responsibility, not even its purpose. (Some say that the purpose is to channel praise and blame towards those actions which they might actually influence; others say that it is simply to describe the character of the person who is held responsible.)

2. Sometimes 'responsibility' is used to denote an action or sphere of action which is part of someone's duty, either as holder of an office, or as moral or political agent. In this sense responsibility is the converse of *accountability, and a person's responsibilities may indeed determine that sphere in which he is also responsible, in sense 1., for the outcome of whatever he does or neglects to do.

ressentiment

See *resentment.

restrictive practices

All practices which, while they may be valid in *common law, have the deliberate effect of restraining open *competition in a market. In the UK the Restrictive Practices Act 1956 created a new judicial tribunal to investigate such practices, for example, *resale price maintenance agreements. Some restrictive practices have always been considered invalid under common law rules of restraint of trade and conspiracy.

retaliation
Response to an act of *aggression; see especially *massive retaliation. It is sometimes regarded as proof that international relations remain in a *state of nature that the threat of retaliation is still the main factor to be considered in aggressive foreign policy, and the main force behind a policy of *deterrence. However, if it is possible to *recognize* aggression, and to distinguish it from retaliation, to that extent the state of nature has been superseded by something else, even if not by a *rule of law.

retribution
See *punishment.

retroactive legislation
Sometimes called 'retrospective legislation'. A law which expressly or by implication renders illegal, or otherwise affects, actions performed before it was passed. There is a presumption against such legislation in both UK and US law, but it is not unknown, especially where the consequences of not rectifying a legislative oversight might be politically or socially disastrous (see, for example, *Burmah Oil Co. Ltd.* v. *Lord Advocate*, 1965) or in the levying of taxes, where deliberation might have to come later than enforcement. Whereas retroactive legislation in civil law may sometimes be tolerated, it seems that it is almost never explicitly tolerated in criminal law, and may even be unconstitutional in the US. The grounds upon which it is criticized

are two: (a) it is an offence to *natural justice, since it implies that a person cannot know the legal consequences of an action for which he is subsequently judged; (b) it violates *judicial independence, since it enables the legislature to reverse judicial decisions. The two criticisms are independent: Frederick the Great reversed judicial decisions in the *interests* of natural justice in the famous case of Miller Arnold, 1779, in which judges were prosecuted for applying the law as it was. It is sometimes said that (b) is not in itself an objection, since *judicial independence is tantamount to judicial legislation, which is in turn tantamount to retroactive legislation (on which, *see*, e.g., *hard cases, *judiciary).

revanchisme
The policy and procedure of revenge (French: *revanche*) as a coordinated political activity. Revanchists are those with a grievance which they seek to rectify at all costs, the world being out of joint for them until retribution is exacted. Often the victim of a revanchist act is connected only remotely with the person or persons who perpetrated the original offence. Examples among modern political movements include certain movements within the Palestine Liberation Organization, and others within Armenian separatist groups in Turkey.

revealed preference
A preference that is revealed in an actual choice of one bundle of goods over another. Revealed preferences are said to provide an empirical test of economic theories. The resulting theory is associated with the name of P.A. Samuelson, who uses the concept of revealed preference rather than the classical and, it is supposed, less empirically based ideas of utility.

reverse discrimination

*Discrimination in favour of members of a certain group, in order to rectify an inherent inequality of opportunity experienced by that group. Reverse discrimination has been advocated in the cause of the rights both of women and of blacks, and in the US it is occasionally practised. It has been criticized on the ground that it exhibits precisely the kind of injustice (favouring someone on grounds irrelevant to the purpose) that it is supposed to overcome. The reply is sometimes made that the aim is to rectify a 'structural' injustice, and therefore that there are competing claims for justice – that of the present contenders for advantage, and that of social groups as a whole – which must be balanced against each other. It is only by practising reverse discrimination, for a period, that such 'structural' injustice will be overcome. The US Supreme Court, asked to decide on the constitutionality of reverse descrimination, as exemplified by certain programmes of *affirmative action, has sat on the fence, allowing the particular instance, but giving reasons that cannot be generalized. It therefore remains unclear whether reverse discrimination is permissible under US law.

revisionism

1. Defined by *Lenin as 'opposition to Marxism from within Marxism itself' (*Marxism and Revisionism*, 1908). The charge of 'revisionism' was first levelled by *Kautsky, in a polemical attack on the *social democrat Eduard Bernstein (1850–1932), and denoted a critical reinterpretation and partial rejection of Marxist theories, so as to make room for the social democrat vision of institutional change.

2. The label 'revisionism' is sometimes used to denote those American historians who reinterpret the history of the *cold war, so as to transfer blame on to the US. In recent years there has also emerged a 'holocaust revisionism' – i.e. historians who deny the existence, or play down the significance, of the *holocaust, something that is now a crime in Austria. There now seems to be a right-wing revisionism in historical studies, which lays the blame for twentieth-century destruction on communists, socialists and their fellow-travellers, and which reassesses, for example, the *New Deal as a social and political catastrophe.

revolution

Political scientists are deeply divided concerning both the meaning of the term 'revolution' and the true explanation of the phenomena denoted by it. To some extent the chosen explanation will determine the chosen meaning, so that theoretical discussions over whether the American Revolution, say, was a 'true revolution' will not be resolved merely by a dictionary definition. It is clear that the meaning of the term has changed, since it was first used of the 'Glorious Revolution' in England of 1688. What was then meant was the 'revolution' to some previous and lamented state of affairs, the term denoting the turning of the wheel of fortune. Now it seems to mean any major transformation that occurs simultaneously on the social and the political level, upsetting expectations and conformities that were sufficiently well established to define all important forms of association under the preceding order. The element of violence is sometimes considered necessary – although this is partly because those who advance this idea are influenced by a theory of 'revolutionary transformation' which requires it. An exception to such a thesis is the American Revolution, which was relatively pacific, and culminated in the calm and reasonable adoption of a constitution that has sometimes been thought to be the most imaginative piece of applied political science in human history. *Arendt (*On Revolution*, 1963) chooses to regard this example, not as exceptional, but as the prime example of a successful revolution. She argues that all political transformations called revolutions are united by the straining of subject peoples towards liberty, and the search for a constitution that will guarantee liberty. The Glorious Revolution, and the American Revolution, thus seem to be examples of revolutions which have achieved their ends, partly because they avoided the violence and social upheaval of later revolutions, and partly because transformation occurred at the political level, while retaining sufficient social continuity to guarantee stability.

Modern theorists are for the most part unpersuaded by Arendt's account, which, in the light of such phenomena as the 'Islamic Revolution' in Iran, can only seem stipulative. They tend to argue that violent transformations are of a different kind from nonviolent ones. The ancestor of such a view is the theory of *Marx, which regarded the French Revolution as the paradigm; and which was, if not obsessed, at least fascinated by the enormous and hitherto undiscovered *forces* which that revolution unleashed. Thus there emerged the Marxian theory of revolution, which exists in two possibly compatible versions. The first version holds that revolutions occur when *productive forces develop to the point where *production relations begin to fetter them and, those enormous forces having been contained only briefly, the fetters burst asunder, toppling all institutions along with them. The second version says that revolution is the product of *class struggle, which grows until all existing institutions are invaded by it, when open conflict

breaks out, leading to the replacement of the *ruling class by those that had been ruled by it. This second version of the theory originates in French revolutionary thinking, and gains some inspiration from *Hegel's diagnosis of the relation between *master and slave. The two theories are usually held together, partly because both are thought to explain revolution in terms of the existence of a *contradiction within the foundations of the social order. It is thus a fundamental thesis of Marxism that revolutions involve the defeat of one class by another; hence there are two revolutions involved in the transition from feudalism to socialism: that in which the bourgeoisie overthrows the aristocracy ('the bourgeois revolution'), and that in which the proletariat overthrows the bourgeoisie ('the proletarian revolution'). USSR propaganda described the *bolshevik *coup d'état* in October 1917 as the Great October Proletarian Revolution, on the assumption that it was the natural sequel to the 'bourgeois' revolution that had occurred in February.

*Leninist theories of revolution emphasize the role of the revolutionary *agent*, believing that revolutions occur at least in part because their 'subjective' conditions (and not only the 'objective', or what Marx had called 'material' conditions) are fulfilled. The important difference between Leninist and Marxian views is that the former regard the accumulation of political power as an essential element in revolution, whereas the latter think of revolution primarily in social terms. Modern theorists tend to recognize that the important modern events called revolutions have always involved the seizure of political power, usually by soldiers or intellectuals – hence the element of *coup d'état* has, since the Russian Revolution, come to seem indispensable (thus John Dunn, e.g.: *Modern Revolutions*, 1972). However, this does not settle the question of how the violent transformation of political power comes about, nor whether there is any single end towards which all revolutions are directed. The manifest lack of agreement among observers has a strong ideological cause: it seems to validate a *coup d'état* to say that it was part of an inevitable, and socially based, revolution; to confess candidly that it was motivated by the desire for power is to suggest that its credentials are no better (and probably worse) than those of the regime that it sought to replace.

The anti-communist revolutions that occurred across Eastern Europe in 1989 are notable for their lack of violence – that in Czechoslovakia going by the name of 'The Velvet Revolution'. Unlike the communist *coups d'état* which had imposed communism on Eastern Europe, these anti-communist upheavals involved the whole population, expressed a longing for a free economy, the rule of law and secure property rights, and were in every way the opposite of revolutions as described by Lenin and as theorised in standard works of political science. Indeed they were the first examples in history, in which the working class rose up in protest against the people who had enslaved it. Since these events, Marxist and neo-Marxist thinking about revolution – include much written about the French Revolution – has lost its credibility.

rhetoric

The presentation of thought in accessible language, esteemed as a fundamental component in political *virtue by *Cicero, and considered to be an important part of all *education in the medieval systems of schooling. The conflict between rhetoric – the art of persuasion – and philosophy – the pursuit of truth – is responsible for much of the brilliant synthesis of the two which *Plato called 'dialectic'. To understand this conflict remains crucial to social criticism and to political theory. A belief has political appeal only to the extent that it is persuasive and it may be persuasive without being true, and even because it is not true. For example, a belief which hides an unpleasant reality appeals on account of its falsehood, and the art of rhetoric may be to dress that belief up to the point of *doctrine, with associated theories, policies, and ideals, all expressed in a language accessible to the common political animal. Much of the success of *Nazi ideology and of *Maoism has been attributed to rhetoric, as has the appeal of the belief that *revolution will bring *emancipation, despite the weight of historical evidence to the contrary.

ribâ

Arabic: increase. *See* *usury.

Ricardo, David (1771–1823)

English economist and, after *Smith, perhaps the greatest of the *classical economists, and a founder of nineteenth-century *political economy. Ricardo's *Principles of Political Economy and Taxation*, first edition 1817, set out 'to determine the laws which regulate the distribution [between the different classes of landowners, capitalists and labour] of the produce of industry'. The emphasis was on land and the use of land: demand grows as a result of increasing population and therefore more and more land of a less and less fertile nature is brought into cultivation, until the *diminishing returns to land make the process unprofitable. However, if profits were higher at one place than another, this would encourage capital to be invested there until, by the law of diminishing returns, profit falls to the profit in the previous least profitable area. Since labour costs are the same everywhere a surplus will be earned on non-marginal land, and this surplus is *rent. Ricardo's *labour theory of value, adapted from *Smith, was also to prove profoundly influential in purporting to explain natural *price and distribution without reference to demand.

right, the

Defined by contrast to (or perhaps more accurately, conflict with) the *left, the term 'right' does not even have the respectability of a history. As now used it denotes several connected and also conflicting ideas. To be 'on the right' is to believe (or for the political realist, to affect to believe) some bundle of the following:

(i) *conservative and perhaps *authoritarian doctrines concerning the nature of *civil society, with emphasis on *custom, *tradition, nationality and *allegiance as social bonds;

(ii) theories of *political obligation framed in terms of *obedience, *legitimacy and *piety rather than *contract, *consent and *justice;

(iii) reluctance to countenance too great a divorce between *law and morality – i.e. between the enactments of the state, and the sentiments of society, hence a resistance to *liberalizing reforms in the law;

(iv) *cultural conservatism;

(v) respect for the *hereditary principle and *prescriptive rights;

(vi) belief in *private property, not as a *natural right, but as an indispensable part of the condition of society;

(vii) belief in elementary *freedoms, and in the irreplaceable value of the individual as against the collective;

(viii) belief in *free enterprise, *free markets and a capitalist economy, as the only mode of production compatible with human freedom, and suited to the temporary nature of human aspirations;

(ix) varying degrees of belief in human imperfectibility and *original sin.

Other items might be added to the list, and the above is suggested only as a cross-section of current significances. It should already be clear that not everything attributed to the 'right' is compatible with everything else, a fault that may lie either with the right itself or with those who so describe it. Thus the emphasis on freedom and the market may not be compatible with the belief in tradition and obedience, free-market relations being the great solvent of social allegiance based on custom and authority, rather than on the 'legal-rational' principles that *Weber attributes to the world structured by contract. Nor is the belief in *human rights underlying (vii), with its individualistic emphasis, obviously compatible with respect for prescriptive right and the hereditary principle. These ideological conflicts are to some extent internal to the conservative position, which, if founded in 'intimations' of social order (as *Oakeshott suggests), is bound to suffer conflicts in an age of social flux. To some extent they stem from the fact that the right is defined by opposition to the left, which, while it discerns contradictions in history, is adamant that it contains none within itself. Since the left sometimes opposes economic liberalism, sometimes individualism, and sometimes social conservatism, the term 'right' is applied indifferently to all of those outlooks, and also to *fascism, despite its leftist origins, on the grounds that the great conflict of the twentieth century, which erupted in the Second World War, involved an alliance of *progressive forces against fascism.

right to life

This is often given as a basic *right in systems of rights, and is sometimes said (e.g. by *Locke) to be inalienable, meaning that I can never confer on someone else the permission to take my life away. Problems arise, however, concerning the basis of this right, and its extent. It would seem that, if it exists at all, it exists universally, i.e. in every possessor of rights. For without it, no other right would seem to be possible, the holder having no right to endure long enough to exercise it. Nevertheless there are many who think that the right does not extend to the unborn human being, and others who believe that it may be relinquished by the aged and incurable. (*See* *abortion, *euthanasia.) In the first case it is sometimes argued that the foetus, while indisputably a living human being, is not a *person, and therefore cannot bear rights. It is often replied, first that the question of its personhood is undecided at best, secondly that rights may perhaps be possessed by things other than persons, thirdly that in any case we have duties of *piety (i.e. not founded merely in *justice, or the respect for rights) which extend to all human life. That is what explains, for some, the duty to respect human *life*, as a mysterious quality which inspires our awe and dread, in itself, and without reference to any idea of 'just transaction'.

right to privacy

See *privacy.

right to work

This expression has acquired two conflicting meanings:

1. The right to go about one's work unimpeded. This right has an important place in US labour law, where it is taken to conflict with the practice of picketing, for example, in which workers are (or may be) intimidated from entering the place of work. More importantly, it has been held to justify a trade union member who attends the place of work even when his union has declared a *strike, so that the union can take no punitive action against the member. Many US states have passed 'right to work' legislation which, by guaranteeing this right, effectively limits trade union power.

2. The right to *have work provided*. Unlike 1. this right, if it exists, establishes a claim rather than a liberty. (*See* *jural relations.) It is often objected that rights define obligations, and therefore if this right exists someone must be obliged to provide work for those who would otherwise be jobless. Who is this someone? The only realistic answer is the state. Hence affirmation of the right to work is tantamount to endorsing a *planned economy.

The reference to a 'right' to work is probably no more than a rhetorical emphasis on a supposed obligation of the state to endeavour to the best of its abilities to provide work. In which case, I do not have a right to work; the best that I have is a right that the state endeavour to provide work, whether or not for me. On the other hand, on some Hegelian views of the person, *self-realization requires labour, so that without labour, life is not truly human. Thus the right to life and the right to labour are on a par: both must be respected if there are to be rights at all. But this only supports the belief in a right to work if 'labour' and 'work' are synonymous. *See* *labour, *work.

rights

In law rights form one of the subclasses of legal advantage, the others being liberties and powers, the three advantages corresponding to the three legal burdens of duty, disability, and liability – *see* *jural relations. Some think that there are also *natural rights, in which case rights do not exist only in law, but also independently, through binding precepts of morality that do not depend upon a legal code for their validity. However, not every moral code is formulated in terms of rights: the Ten Commandments, for example, impose obligations, but do not specify rights, unless it is thought that every obligation creates a right in some other party. It is unclear whether that is the case. For example, it may be my moral duty not to be gluttonous, but whose rights are violated by my gluttony? Or, more contentiously, it may be my moral duty not to treat *animals cruelly, but does that fact alone confer rights on animals? (There may be independent arguments for saying that animals are not *persons, and therefore can have no rights.)

Nevertheless, it seems to be the case that every right defines an obligation. To deny someone his rights is to do what ought not to be done (the 'ought' being legal or moral depending upon whether the right is considered to be a positive or a natural right). Rights are also advantages which may legitimately be claimed: which would illuminate the concept of a right only if the idea of *legitimacy was clear, whereas in fact it is commoner to explain the idea of legitimacy through its relation to the concept of right than vice versa. The idea of a right seems, indeed, to be as basic as any other. We might even define *justice in terms of it, as the disposition to accord to every person his rights – or his 'due'. (It is thus that justice is defined, for example, in Ulpian's digest of the Roman Law.)

Many philosophers and jurists have tried to detach the concept of right from the bewildering complexities that surround such ideas as legitimacy and justice, and have affirmed, instead, that the only true rights are created by *positive law. In other words, a right is simply the creation of some convention or rule (whether or not a legal rule), and the only fact of the matter here is that people are given to make and to respect such rules, not that there are independent rights that correspond to them.

Whatever the plausibility of that view, it is certainly not what is commonly believed. Most rights that are asserted with immediate confidence are asserted independently of any law or convention – such as the right to life and the right to limb. It is the sense that these *are* rights which causes people to rebel against laws which violate them.

The language of rights has the function in moral and legal discourse of setting limits to what can be done: a right is 'to be respected', and can be disrespected only by doing wrong. That idea was taken up by *Kant in his ambitious philosophy of practical reason. (Kant argued that all persons must be treated as ends in themselves, that this is the fundamental right, and that reason alone compels us to comply with it.) It also plays an important part in the legal philosophy of *Dworkin, who argues that rights cannot be simply set aside in the interests of policy, precisely because 'rights are trumps' in the hands of the individual who possesses them.

Declarations of Rights have occasionally been made, as conditions to be complied with by every power that wishes to rule legitimately, e.g. by *Jefferson following the American Revolution, and also in the aftermath of the French Revolution under the influence of *Paine. The surprising degree of agreement as to which rights to declare has suggested to many that, even if we cannot presently find an objective basis to the idea of right, there certainly must be such a basis, else it would be impossible to understand how it is that people so readily and immediately reach agreement over so complex a matter. But there are contentious cases, and three articles above discuss three of them.

Lawyers distinguish positive and negative rights (e.g. my right that you fulfil your contract, and my right that you do not injure me); also rights *in personam*, availing against a definite person, and rights *in rem* (in a thing) availing against persons generally in respect of that thing (of which the most important is the right to exclude that lies at the heart of *private property). These distinctions are technicalities that do not bear on the central questions.

rights inflation

The habit of demanding as a *right what is at best a *privilege leads to a steady increase in the number of rights claimed by the citizens of modern states, and a corresponding increase in the burden of duties that must finally be shouldered by the state. Thus all the following privileges have been redefined in recent laws and charters as rights: health, education, esteem, creative work, family, love, happiness. Since no individual has a duty to provide those things, except under the terms of special relationships, the obligation to provide them falls upon the state, which finds in due course that it is no more capable of providing them than anyone else.

rights theories of politics

Political theories which use such concepts as right, obligation, law and justice in describing and explaining political arrangements; to be compared and contrasted with *power theories of politics. Rights theories include the major varieties of Western constitutionalism, in particular the systems of *Aristotle, *Locke and *Hegel. For Hegel, for example, the political world is identical with the sphere of right, and is constituted, and evolves, in accordance with the principles contained in that notion. Hegel's view contrasts radically with the power theory of *Marx, who saw all rights as institutional reflections of underlying relations of power. Thus for Hegel my power to exclude you from my home is to be explained in terms of a right of property; while for Marx all property rights are to be explained in terms of powers rooted in economic relations.

risk

To take a risk is either (a) to pursue a hoped-for good by means that might in fact incur a far greater evil, in the belief that the good is more probable than the evil or (b) to pursue an improbable good in the belief that it is so great a good that the more probable evils do not rule against the attempt. The ability and desire to take risks may be more prevalent in some cultures than in others, and it is often argued that a firm but reasonable disposition to expose oneself to risk is a *virtue – namely the virtue of courage. Some go further, arguing with *Rand, for example, that risk-taking is *the* human virtue, since it is the one that enables us to find solutions to our problems, to provide benefits for ourselves and others, and to live in freedom. Rand is not alone in adding that *socialism has a tendency to produce a 'risk-averse' society, since it rewards people who don't take chances and penalizes those who do. This argument is common in *post-communist societies, where it is often claimed that the 'new man' of socialism has, after all, been invented, and that he lacks the ability or the desire to fend for himself in conditions of risk.

That claim suggests an important connection between risk and freedom. A risk-averse society is one in which people are prepared to relinquish their freedom to others, and in particular to the state, in exchange for protection from normal hazards. The growing regime of health and safety regulations, which has begun to extinguish many traditional forms of risk-taking (in particular adventure holidays for children), provides a novel example of the way in which human freedom is gradually extinguished by the state – not intentionally, but by an *invisible hand.

risk and uncertainty

A technical expression in *decision theory, in which mathematical values are assigned to the degrees of *risk. In this context 'risk' denotes the situation where precise numerical probabilities can be assigned to the various possible outcomes of a choice: uncertainty the situation where they cannot. In the former case the odds can be calculated, and a decision made on the basis of them; in the latter case this is not so.

The economic theory of risk and uncertainty, based on the calculus of probability first formulated by D. Bernouilli (1700–82), provides a theoretical explanation of one of the most important aspects of the modern economy – the notion that an *entrepreneur's *profit is offset by his risk.

rites of passage

Expression coined by the French anthropologist Arnold van Gennep, in a book of that title (1909), to denote the *ceremonies that accompany the transition of an individual or group from one socially important condition to another – e.g. ceremonies of birth, puberty, maturity, marriage and death. The ceremonies tend to involve three components: *separation* of the individuals or groups from their previous condition; *transition* (French: *marge*) when the subjects remain suspended in limbo; and *incorporation* (*agrégation*) of the subjects as participants in their new condition. Such ceremonies survive in a variety of forms in modern communities, and are sometimes thought to have an important function in securing transformations of *identity that would otherwise be hard to bear, and in reinforcing a sense of the objective validity of social *norms. The relative absence of public, and publicly endorsed, rites of passage is sometimes offered as an explanation of the 'youth culture' of the modern city, in which young people must provide their own forms of initiation – perhaps through gangs and gang warfare.

ritual

An action which follows a repeatable pattern, which has the sanction of *custom, and whose meaning is symbolic, even though it cannot usually be captured by what the agent may say in explanation of it. Ritual tends to be inflexible, or resistant to change, and to be understood as compelled by a moral, or spiritual command that it would be sacrilegious, or at least outrageous, to disobey. Ritual is often thought to be an essential instrument of social cohesion, since it unites people behind a common form of action saturated by social significance. Hence the importance of ritual in military and civil institutions, in trade union gatherings, coronations, and trials.

Although psychologists sometimes misleadingly call the routine activities of animals 'rituals', it is arguable that only a rational being could feel the intimation of transcendent significance that provides the motive of ritual behaviour.

Robespierre, Maximilien de (1758–94) French revolutionary statesman. *See* *Jacobinism, *legislator, *majesty, *people, *social question, *terrorism.

role

A term with at least two meanings, and which has won an important place for itself in contemporary sociology.

1. Dramatic role, or 'persona': the character or state of mind which the actor simulates. From this idea have grown many modern usages of the term 'role', as a form of 'representation'.

2. In sociology. Sometimes defined as the 'dynamic aspect of a social position', i.e. the form of *agency connected with a social position. The social position is usually defined in terms of *norms of behaviour. Roles are like *offices, in that they are distinct from the person who occupies them, and bear their normative character independently. However, they are less well defined than offices, and arise more naturally out of social conditions, so that it is hard to see them as matters only of convention. Hence the 'norms' in question are not usually seen as matters only of responsibility and right.

There is a close connection between 1. and 2., and some sociologists (e.g. E. Goffman: *The Presentation of Self in Everyday Life*, 1956) regard the occupation of a role in sense 2. as very close to the kind of representational activity described in 1. The individual uses the roles that he occupies to control the impression that others may have of him: what is represented is not a dramatic character, but the self, in a particular, quasi-dramatic aspect.

Natural relations, such as 'father' or 'uncle', may be as much associated with roles, as artificial relations ('doctor', 'judge' etc.). Both may be matters of responsibility and competence, and both serve a like function of mediating between the individual and society, and providing circumscribed fields of intelligible action. Roles are sometimes important in *casuistry: since they define responsibilities, they may also limit them, so that, for example, the doctor who obeys the ethic intrinsic to his role may be released from blame for at least some unfortunate consequences. (*Cf.* *morality and politics.)

Roman Catholicism

The *church centred on the Bishop of Rome, which has represented itself as the mysterious body of Christ incarnate, has throughout the development of modern forms of government exerted a continuous influence upon law, upon ideas of sovereignty, and upon the institutional structure of societies developing under its tutelage. It is called 'catholic' because it claims universal validity, 'Roman' because this claim has, since the *Reformation, been disputed by other equally 'catholic' churches of *Protestant believers. It is through its claim to universality that the Roman Catholic Church has exerted a powerful political influence, and it is through the Roman Catholic Church that many of the distinctive institutions of *Christian countries took their form. The ideas of international jurisdiction and of a combined rule of *natural law and *sacrament were put forward from the earliest times, and built into a Christian political theory by *Augustine. It is sometimes held to be a significant achievement of Christianity (in contrast, say, to *Islam) that the institutions thereby founded and authorized were able to survive with their full political effectiveness even after the collapse of the Christian faith among those governed by them. Thus the doctrine of natural law, and the specific application of it through *canon law, have entered most of the legal systems of Europe. The idea of *limited government, and of the inviolable rights of the individual, repeatedly upheld in the name of the papacy by medieval jurists and theologians, achieved early acceptance, and endured to form the basic premise of most forms of liberal constitutionalism; the claims to international jurisdiction have persisted in modern international law, to a great extent founded on speculations already active in the ecclesiastical jurisdiction of the Middle Ages; the recurrent attempts to forbid or control usury and speculation, which have been a striking characteristic of Western governments, also have their origin in Roman Catholic teaching, as have the ideas of the just war, and the just practice of war, which have been important in shaping the forms of treaties and alliances among the European nations.

The Catholic Church retains its significance as a major force of international politics, and papal *encyclicals continue to project moral and spiritual doctrine from Rome to the comers of the earth. It is almost impossible to summarize the political tenor of this doctrine. On issues such as *abortion and contraception, for example, its doctrines have seemed to many to be illiberal, while its defence of an international code of *human rights reiterates a piece of liberal orthodoxy. Its internal structure is authoritarian, and it supports an important hierarchy of offices which has, through its penetration of secular institutions, tended to uphold hierarchical organization everywhere (notably in Spain, where the church entered into open conflict with forces of radical reform during the twentieth century). At the same time it seems bent on discarding hierarchical principles of government, and has recently begun to encourage the *laicization of its functions, and the revision of its *liturgies.

Roman-Dutch law

A legal system produced by the fusion of medieval Dutch law with the *Roman law as recorded in Justinian's *Digests* and *Institutes*. It was accepted at the Reformation, and applied in Holland during the sixteenth, seventeenth and eighteenth centuries, after which it was replaced by the *Napoleonic law. It was exported to the Dutch colonies, including South Africa, and has there remained as the main basis of the legal system. Since it upholds ideas of judicial independence and natural justice it proved an obstacle to the application of some of the oppressive legislation of *apartheid; this led to judicial qualifications of executive acts, notably over the right of residence in the black townships.

Roman law

A system of law developed over 2000 years, and largely identified through the *Digests* and *Institutes* commanded in AD 530 by order of the Emperor Justinian, in which the whole body of existing law was condensed and *codified, providing a unique system of rationalized legality, which purports to describe the nature of jurisdiction throughout the Empire.

Roman law as applied to citizens consisted in the *jus civile* – the civil law of contract, tort, property etc. – together with the criminal law, in so far as it dealt with the private affairs of individuals (all those branches constituting the *jus privatum*), and also the criminal law governing the relations between the individual and the state (the *jus publicum*). The civil law introduced many of the conceptual achievements upon which later codes have rested. Thus Roman law introduced the ideas of the juristic *person, of the corporate person, of *legal fiction, of the distinctions between kinds of *right, and kinds of association, of 'quasi-contract' (actions which must be adjudicated as though they formed part of a contract), of implied and explicit contracts – in short, the ideas required for a complete description of civil obligation in legal terms.

It was therefore inevitable that many later political theorists should phrase their conceptions of the state and political obligation in terms borrowed from Roman law (*Kant and *Hegel being noteworthy examples). The prominence of the civil law in the Roman system has led to this name being used to denote the system as a whole – a fact that causes frequent confusions. (*See* *civil law, *civilian.)

In addition to the *jus civile* Roman law acknowledged also a *jus gentium* and a *jus naturale*, the first being a system of international law designed to adjudicate disputes among those subjects of the Empire who were not citizens, whatever their local and customary legal practice, the second being largely a philosophical rationalization of the first by jurists influenced by the writings of Greek philosophers.

The *jus gentium* was free from the technicalities of the civil law, and involved principles of *natural justice and procedures of appeal from local tribunals to the jurisdiction of Rome. The *jus naturale*, or *natural law, seems to have been more or less identical with it, except in one particular, that *slavery was recognized as legitimate in the *jus gentium* but not in the *jus naturale* (although this may be due to a philosophical gloss). The two systems are interesting in showing the extent to which the search for a universal jurisdiction involves the invocation of rights thought to be natural rather than conventional. Thus the relation between the *jus gentium* and the *jus naturale* has come to symbolize the relation, both in power and in authority, between *positive and natural law.

romanticism

Primarily used to denote the artistic and cultural movement which began in eighteenth-century Europe, and of which the following are regarded as early manifestations: in France, the writings of *Rousseau; in Germany, the *Sturm und Drang* movement; in Britain, the poems of 'Ossian' and the literary movement that culminated in the publication of Wordsworth's and Coleridge's *Lyrical Ballads* in 1798. However, the various phenomena attributed to the romantic movement are so many and various – from Gothic novels to the French Revolution – that it is impossible to describe the phenomenon without invoking contentious critical and philosophical theories.

The romantic movement is usually thought to have marked the transformation of the intellectual's self-image from objective to subjective: the intellectual ceased to be an acknowledged part of the world and became a suffering observer of the world, passing from social being to outcast. (Hence the fascination of Goethe, who seemed to be social being and outcast together.) The romantics sought to show how the suffering and aspiration of the solitary individual were nevertheless a route to salvation; and so produced visions of peace and renewal which were dependent upon no society for their realization. An example of the latter is Wordsworth's idyll of a unity between the self and nature unmediated by social artifice; that idea has since become a familiar datum of the *modern consciousness.

Through Rousseau romanticism was to recast the eighteenth-century vision of the social contract as a eulogy of the *state of nature; through *Herder it translated itself into a philosophy of *nationalism; through *Hegel it attempted to reconcile its idea of the ultimate validity of the self and *self-realization with a philosophy of institutions; through *Coleridge it provided the foundations of later *cultural conservatism, and through Shelley it produced the greatest existing poetic invocation of *utopian socialism. It must therefore be considered to be a fundamental ingredient of modern thought, which cannot be summarized in a single political outlook.

By extension, the term 'romanticism' is often applied to any philosophy or state of mind that is more than normally redolent of the sentiments of the original romantics: for example, it has been applied to the writings of the *Frankfurt school, to the early *Marx, and to the irrationalist philosophy of *Sartre.

Roosevelt, Franklin Delano (1882–1945)
American statesman and US President. *See* *democratic parties, *four freedoms, *freedom, *good neighbour policy, *New Deal.

Röpke, Wilhelm (1899–1966)
Swiss economist and political theorist of German extraction, whose defence of the *social market economy was influential in the rebuilding of the German economy after the Second World War. Röpke was a disciple of *Mises and the *Austrian school, who defended the free market and spontaneous order in terms similar to those used by *Hayek. However, he recognized the potential damage done to local communities and traditional virtues by the globalizing tendency of markets, and sought to reconcile capitalism with communal values in a 'third way' that would avoid the errors both of unbridled economic freedom and of the socialism that was being advocated as its only alternative. (*A Humane Economy*, 1960.) He found confirmation for his 'localist' views in the village communities of Switzerland, where he lived as a refugee from Nazism, and attempted to develop theories of the local economy that would show how the services that socialists wished to provide

through the state could become spontaneously available at the local level. He was a fervent critic of the *welfare state as this emerged in the postwar period, believing that it would inevitably destroy the human capacity to take charge of destiny and to vanquish misfortune through mutual aid. The state should obey the principle of *subsidiarity, and allow local communities to find their own way to social welfare, calling on help only when needed, and only in ways that enabled them to retain local control. Röpke was a Roman Catholic, and much of his philosophy can be seen as an attempt to reconcile the teachings of the Church with those of the Austrian economists.

Rorty, Richard McKay (b. 1931)
American philosopher, and advocate of *pragmatism, who has used the pragmatist arguments to disestablish the concept of truth, and to jettison objectivity in favour of *relevance. Strongly influenced by both *Dewey and *Kuhn, Rorty sees all language and thought as instruments for coping rather than representations of reality. He defends a radical subjectivism and relativism in the theory of knowledge, and advocates a *liberal feminist politics as the way forward for the human community.

Rousseau, Jean-Jacques (1712–78)
Swiss-born writer and philosopher, whose *Social Contract*, 1762, and *Émile*, 1762, contain one of the first attempts to translate the spirit of *romanticism into political theory. *Émile* describes the education of the free being, and the process whereby the liberty and nobility which man possesses by nature can be preserved and enhanced through self-expression, and through an education that encourages at every point development rather than inhibition of the moral sentiments.

The *Social Contract* begins with the famous words 'Men are born free, yet everywhere they are in chains.' It can be read either as a celebration of liberty and the rights of man, which condemns all forms of absolute or arbitrary government, or as a recipe for the abolition of human liberties and the absorption of the individual into a sovereign collective. The work is unsystematic, rhetorical and fraught with paradoxes. Nevertheless its fundamental conceptions have been highly influential, and its very contradictory nature has often been esteemed, as the mark of a vision that recognizes the contradictions implicit in all social order.

Man is good by nature, just as he is free by nature. He is made bad, as he is made unfree, only by institutions which negate his powers. (The doctrine of the 'noble savage' to some extent summarizes these intuitions, although the phrase is not Rousseau's, and he himself argued that the savage requires society if he is to be *truly* free – in other words if he is to make something real and rewarding of his natural freedom.) *Direct democracy is the only form of decision-making that can preserve man's natural liberty, since it is the only form in which his consent is the sole ground of legitimacy. But this extreme form of (non-representative) democracy has its paradoxes. In particular, in surrendering to it, the citizen chooses to be overridden by the rest of the community whenever his choice conflicts with theirs (*see* *paradox of democracy); in this way he surrenders part of his freedom to the community. This act of surrender has the form of a *social contract, between each member of society and every other, for the *common good. This contract creates an association which has corporate identity and personality. The association is called, when passive, 'the state', when active,

'the sovereign'. Like any legal person it has will. Rousseau calls this will the *general will, which is to be distinguished from the 'will of all' (the aggregate will of individual members of society). The resulting theory of sovereignty, which influenced *Hegel among others, shows in turn the influence of *Roman law conceptions of corporate personality.

It seemed to Rousseau to follow that he whose will conflicts with the general will is in conflict with himself. Such a man attempts to live a *contradiction; if he is not made to bend to the general will his own freedom will therefore be negated, so he must be 'forced to be free'. This paradox of freedom was very influential, as was the idea of the 'lived contradiction'. Rousseau himself saw that it admitted of *tyrannical interpretation, but did not avoid that consequence, since he believed that the problem of political freedom is genuine and serious, and certainly more mysterious than the empiricists had represented it to be. Such paradoxes were to be expected in any serious attempt to cast light on law and freedom. Thus Rousseau compared the problem of the *rule of law with that of squaring the circle, and argued that every freedom which the law provides, it must also curtail. Rousseau rejected Locke's version of the social contract theory, and also the idea of a *natural right. The condition of society is one in which all rights are alienated to the sovereign power.

routinization

Term used by *Weber, to denote the transformation of *charismatic *leadership into institutionalized leadership, where an office takes the place of a personality as the focus of authority.

royalism

The belief in the *legitimacy of monarchical government, and of a particular person's or *dynasty's title under that government. Royalism has been influential in modern French politics, particularly through the anti-parliamentarian movement, Action Française, founded in 1899 by Léon Daudet and Henri Vaugeois, and given direction by Jacques Bainville and by Charles Maurras, who was its major theorist. According to Maurras the true France (*pays réel*) must be distinguished from the republican system (*pays légal*) that had been imposed on it. All political practice requires certainty, which comes only through knowledge of the immediate environment; no abstract idea of legitimacy can be a motive to action until made part of a 'subjective synthesis' which relates to the actual historical conditions in which it must be applied. The embodiment of this synthesis in the person of a monarch gives to the legal idea of legitimacy its true 'particularized objectivity' – the sovereign has objective authority through law, and also subjective power, through his immediately intelligible identity with the traditions and social condition of the nation.

rule of law

The form of government in which no power can be exercised except according to procedures, principles and constraints contained in the law, and in which any citizen can find redress against any other, however powerfully placed, and against the officers of the state itself, for any act which involves a breach of the law.

The rule of law is an artefact, and the fundamental search involved in modern theories of *constitution is for the conditions which make it possible. It is obviously not enough for a constitution to *declare* that the law is supreme; it must also be possible for any citizen, however placed, to enforce that law. This suggests

*judicial independence as a minimum requirement, at least if the law is to be enforced against the state. But that notion involves paradoxes, as does the idea of a *separation of powers upon which it is founded. In the end it is the state that controls the appointment and dismissal of judges, as it is the state that makes and revises the law.

In conditions of social collapse, or widespread terror and intimidation, a rule of law will no longer be possible; hence a rule of law also requires laws of *sedition and public order through which it may be upheld against the busy subversion of the lawless. This leads to a further paradox, noted by *Machiavelli, namely that a law of sedition must be as determined and as violent as the forces which it may need to overcome, and, since these include the extremes of military violence, it must itself be prepared to resort to extremes (although not to the same extremes, since that would be tantamount to permanent civil war). This means, in effect, that the rule of law must be prepared to disregard *natural justice and judicial procedure while combating some types of offender. At the same time, it must in other cases give untrammelled freedom to judicial procedure, and to the natural justice which, on one plausible view, is repeatedly invoked in it. So that the rule of law is itself indebted to the violence that it seeks to condemn.

ruling class

A *class which, by whatever mechanism, is able to fill all important offices within the state, or every important position through which power over the people is exercised. Whether or not such a class will exercise power in its own interest is a question which *Aristotle, for one, regarded as open, thinking that it all depends upon the nature and education of the ruling class. That it *will* exercise power in its own interest (whatever it in fact *intends*) is a familiar doctrine of *historical materialism.

For the notion to be a useful one, there must be some way of determining membership of the ruling class other than through the occupancy of positions of power, else the 'ruling class' simply means 'those in power'. Many criteria proposed have proved unsatisfactory, and many discussions of the nature and value of a ruling class seem to peter out in the helpless tautology that 'power belongs with the powerful', often with some kind of protest against that elementary and indeed necessary truth.

The idea of a ruling class ceases to be empty if, for example, class membership is determined by economic control, and 'rule' by political control. Then the idea that there is a ruling class is in effect the idea that those who control the economy will, for that reason, control the government. That is, in effect, the *Marxian position with regard to the *bourgeois state (whether or not true). The inverse of that is the view that control of political power leads to the control of economic power: in which case it would be better to speak of a class of rulers, rather than a ruling class. Such, in effect, has been the position in modern communist societies, at least as described by Djilas (*see* *new class).

In Western democracies *social mobility has made it difficult to give a clear identification of a ruling class, and indeed the concept now has a certain air of quaintness, being a survival from debates that are all but dead. But *see* *political class.

rural politics

The domination of modern politics by the towns and the people who live in them has been frequently deplored, and has led in recent times to *agrarian movements, which seek to protect both the rural way of life and the environment on which it depends. These movements have been important in European politics, and have also had a certain following in the US. In Britain the advocacy of the rural way of life was made central to the socialist project by H.J. Massingham (a *guild socialist, writing between the wars), central to the conservative cause by Lady Eve Balfour (*see* *Soil Association), and central to liberal values and the pursuit of freedom by A.G. Street, whose broadcasts on farming were a major source of comfort to the British during the dark years of the Second World War. The British rural movement was joined by many of the leading intellectuals between the wars who, in an important publication entitled *Britain and the Beast* (1938), pressed for legislation to protect the countryside from ribbon development and suburban sprawl. This publication influenced the *planning acts that were passed after the end of the war, which imposed a 'green belt' around the towns, and attempted to concentrate development in already urbanized areas.

Rural movements are still important, attracting the support of the new refugees from the cities, many of whom are anxious to find ways of supporting the farmers who maintain the view from their window. In Britain the rooted hostility of the Labour Party to *hunting and other such rural pursuits has to some extent galvanized a rural reaction; but it remains true that rural movements are dismissed by the new *political class as minority affairs, motivated more by *nostalgia and *romanticism than by any real understanding of the modern world.

Ruskin, John (1819–1900)

English writer, painter and social critic. Ruskin began his literary career with striking books on painting and architecture, including *Modern Painters* (1843–60) and *The Stones of Venice* (1851–53). Already these works announced his true vocation as a social critic and moralist. Art was of importance for Ruskin because he saw in the art of the past a spiritual wholeness and social cohesion which were, he believed, vanishing from the world of industrial capitalism. All that is most valuable in life depends upon transcending the motive of profit and the spirit of calculation. The machine age had degraded not only work into a means; it had done the same for leisure – and therefore for art. For the medieval craftsman work was an act of *piety and was sanctified in his own eyes as in the eyes of his God. For such a labourer, end and means are one and the spiritual wholeness of faith is translated into the visual wholeness and purity of his craft. Hence his craft was also art, a permanent testimony to the reality on earth of man's spiritual redemption.

From such ideas Ruskin mounted a sustained and passionate defence of the Gothic revival in architecture, denouncing almost all the buildings of his day as unfeeling products of the profit machine. He was fervently anti-capitalist, and yet he distanced himself from socialism, writing dismissively of the *egalitarian and *materialistic values which socialists espouse. It is perhaps more accurate to describe Ruskin (as he described himself) as a Tory – though of a highly peculiar and romantic kind. His ideas came from art, and from brilliant insights into the moral and spiritual significance of the aesthetic enterprise. But he applied these ideas in the social sphere with an uncompromising élitism. His prolific social writings are really lay sermons exhorting his countrymen to Christian morality and pious works and to the acceptance of a faith in which he himself only half believed. He wrote intensely (and to a feminist, shockingly) on the differences between the sexes, and regarded the working classes as more in need of a statement of their duties, than a list of their rights. His carefully wrought style borders at times on *sentimentality, and expresses in its every rhythm a deep sense of disappointment with the human species, together with a memory of the angelic visions from which his life began. *See also* *aesthetics and politics, *architecture, *craft, *cultural conservatism, *Morris.

Russell, Bertrand Arthur William, third Earl Russell (1872–1970)
English mathematician and philosopher. *See* *empiricism, *gentleman, *positivism.

Sacrament

According to the Book of Common Prayer: 'an outward and visible sign of an inward and spiritual grace given unto us, ordained by Christ himself, as a means whereby we receive the same, and a pledge to assure us thereof.' A sacrament is an act whose significance, while it may sometimes be understood in earthly terms, is so great that it must eventually direct us towards the transcendental. It is through the idea of a sacrament (as exemplified in the communion) that Christian thinkers have tried to make sense of the non-contractual and peculiarly binding nature of *marriage, and of like human relations in which *piety seems to be the ruling principle. Similar views can be found in other religions, which tend to call God to witness to those transactions which are of enduring and formative importance, including sometimes the appointment of a ruler (*see* *caliphate).

Saint-Simon, Claude-Henri de Rouvroy, Comte de (1760–1825)

Founder of French socialism, and initiator of the critical analysis of social conditions that was to prevail in nineteenth-century political thought. Saint-Simon was associated with *Comte in the founding of *positivism; however, he was less systematic, more analytical and, although without Comte's rhetorical gifts, indisputably less naive and more circumspect. He developed a theory of *class conflict, identifying the principal classes as the producers (*indus-triels*) and the parasites (bureaucrats), and further argued that revolutionary and reforming activity is always useless if not accompanied by a proper theory of the conditions that determine and mould political change. He dismissed *utopian socialism for its indifference to the real facts of history, and advocated what he took to be a realistic theory of historical transformation, together with an ideal constitution of the socialist society which he wished to bring about. He thought that the time had come when the *industriels* could take control of society and organize it according to the actual needs of its members. The resulting constitution would consist of three chambers, that of invention, that of examination and that of deputies. The first would consist of artists and inventors, the second of critical scientists, the third of the 'captains of industry' who would initiate change and control education. It was so clear to Saint-Simon that this arrangement would be perceived to be in the public interest that he neglected to propose any laws that would enforce it. However, he thought that this kind of constitutional organization, combined with common ownership of the means of production and redistribution in the cause of *social justice, would, taken together, ensure that the future society would embody as much of socialism as is compatible with the historical conditions from which it must arise. (*De l'organisation sociale*, 1825.)

samizdat

Russian: self-publishing. The name for the literature in the USSR and Eastern Europe which, while being denied official publication, circulated in legally permitted (but nevertheless illegally persecuted) ways, as duplicated typescript. It included all significant literature expressing political views opposed to the thought and practice of the ruling Communist Party. The *samizdat* culture became a major force during the 1970s and 1980s, when publication in the West helped to broadcast its message, and its leading figures, such as *Havel and *Solzhenitsyn, laid the foundations for a *postcommunist politics. This dictionary appeared in a *samizdat* edition in Czech in 1985, translated by Petr Pithart.

Samuelson, Paul Anthony (b. 1915)

American economist. *See* *compensation criterion, *revealed preference.

sanction

1. In law. Any provision for the enforcement of a law, by rewarding its obedience or punishing its transgression. Legal *positivism tends to regard sanctions as essential to law, thinking that this *power is the material reality which exists in appearance as the law's *authority. (*See* *command)

2. In *international law, punitive action by one state against another, usually of an economic kind, designed to force a change of policy without resorting to overt aggression. Opinions differ as to the relation between sanction and *pacific blockade, and as to the precise extent to which either is inevitably the prelude to belligerence. Sanctions can be ordered by the Security Council of the UN, as a way of enforcing compliance with international law, or with resolutions passed by the General Assembly. They are supposed to avert belligerence, though

recent events in the Middle East suggest that they merely delay it.

sanctuary

The practice of fleeing to a sacred place for refuge, especially from criminal proceedings. Sanctuary has more or less ceased, although it was long protected in English law, and by 'sanctuary and abjuration' (i.e. forswearing all civil rights and leaving the jurisdiction) a criminal could often escape prosecution. Now the term is used in a wide and vague sense for the protection offered – e.g. by a criminal organization – to persons who enter into a certain place in order to escape the law that may prevail there *de jure*, but not in fact.

Sanger, Margaret (1879–1966)

US feminist and socialist, who devoted her life to the cause of birth control. Sanger's tireless advocacy led to the introduction of sex education into American schools, and the gradual acceptance of contraception as a normal and even necessary practice. She was heavily influenced in her thinking by the early twentieth-century studies of human sexuality – notably that by Havelock Ellis – and she was a devotee of *eugenics, which she helped to make briefly respectable, influencing people as widely different as *Shaw and Hitler. She was the originator of organizations that led in time to the Planned Parenthood Federation of America.

sansculottism

The *sansculottes* ('without breeches') formed the undisciplined and destructive mass which emerged at the French Revolution, endowing republican principles with a promptness and barbarity of execution that until then they had not possessed. Hence sansculottism came to be used to name any violent republican fervour thought to be based more on unthinking resentments than on a reasoned comparison between the virtues of monarchical and republican government. (The *sansculottes* wore trousers instead of breeches, as a symbol of their energy and social position.)

Sapir–Whorf hypothesis

The hypothesis, defended (though not under this description) by the US anthropologists Edward Sapir and Benjamin Lee Whorf, that the language we speak shapes the world that we know – in other words that reality is to some extent invented by our concepts and categories. Sapir and Whorf had made a thorough study of native American languages, and were surprised by the very unEuropean ways in which these languages conceptualize the world. The hypothesis is sometimes cited in defence of radical relativism or subjectivism in the theory of knowledge, but the ability of Sapir and Whorf to present evidence for the hypothesis as a general truth refutes any such conclusion. Exactly what the hypothesis implies, however, remains a matter of controversy.

Sartre, Jean-Paul (1905–80)

French philosopher, novelist and playwright, a leading advocate of *existentialism and, since 1945, one of the most important and influential of French left-wing intellectuals. Sartre's political philosophy evolved from an attempt to synthesize existentialism and *Marxism, towards a complex philosophy of 'revolutionary *praxis', and a rejection of what Sartre took to be the central theses of *dialectical materialism (*Critique of Dialectical Reason*, 1960).

Through his initial involvement with the French Communist Party, and subsequently with the student *movement of 1968, and through his

active opposition both to the French during the Algerian war and to the Americans during the war in Vietnam, Sartre stood always at the helm of leftist disaffection. His ability to turn a blind eye to the crimes of communism (from which he nevertheless distanced himself during the 1950s) was matched by the penetration with which he saw crime in almost every aspect of the Western way of life. His rhetorical gifts enabled him to exert an influence which, in the eyes of his opponents, was by no means justified by the quality of his thinking. Whatever the verdict of history, however, Sartre remains one of the most important of all influences in the formation of the modern French intellectual, and of the modern world in general. It is difficult to synthesize the many and varied strands in Sartre's political thought, which was constantly in a state of flux, but the following picture is perhaps not wholly inaccurate. (Sartre's interesting views on *sex are dealt with under that entry.)

The essence of man's stance towards the world is freedom, which condemns him either to exercise true 'existential' choice, or to lose himself in the 'bad faith' of otherness. In bad faith a person is for himself what he takes himself to be for others; in particular he loses his freedom by adopting *roles, and moral codes, that bind him to public expectations in a public world. This attempt at a spurious 'objectivity' constitutes the loss of the true 'subjectivity' of freedom. The only remedy for bad faith is *commitment, construed as the total identification with one's freedom and the casting in of one's lot with life. (Sartre gives a trenchant and poignant account of this subjective freedom in his great work of *phenomenology, *Being and Nothingness*, 1945.)

But towards what should I commit myself? By Sartre's own theory that question should have no answer, since the self and its freedom are strictly transcendental – i.e. knowable only in action and not as objects in the empirical world. However, Sartre also accepts the idea of the intellectual as the agent of social transformation, and believes that there can be no *authenticity that does not involve, through its transcendence of all publicly available roles, moralities and classes, identification with the *proletariat of Marxist theory. On the other hand, the Marxist theory of history gives a partial and mechanistic account of man's situation in the world, and does not speak directly to the free agent. No historical materialism will ever provide a substitute for political action, and no theory of the *dialectic will ever make room for the agent's own perspective on the social world in which he is condemned to act. The role of praxis is to transcend all such partial theories, and to 'totalize' the experience available to the modern consciousness. This totalization occurs *in* action, and also shows the world as *open* to action, and transformed through action.

Such totalization can be achieved only by the person who rejects all bourgeois morality and custom, and for the modern intellectual the true saint or hero is not the man of 'good heart' but rather the demonic anti-hero, the traitor, the person who turns morality inside out to reveal its empty inside. Such a saint (the writer and criminal Jean Genet is Sartre's example, *Saint Genet*, 1952) speaks directly to the modern spirit, by *showing* all values to be subjective, and by inciting the free being to disobey all laws that are not affirmed subjectively, from the totalizing viewpoint of revolutionary praxis.

By a deft stroke of rhetoric, Sartre tries to recommend his philosophy to others (although no such recommendation can be obeyed without bad faith). Many have found in it the ultimate expression of the ethic of *autonomy that Kant brought into the world, while others have condemned it as a tissue of rhetorical confusions. It can be seen equally as an imaginative dramatization of the post-romantic soul, which rejects both the world and its own isolation from the world; and as a fine flight of intellectual snobbishness, in which bourgeois values are mocked in the name of a criminal chic.

satellite state

A state that is bound by economic, political and ideological gravity to another and more powerful state, which dictates its policies while permitting a fiction of self-government. States within the USSR *sphere of influence were in fact more usually described as satellite states, since 'influence' is in this case a euphemism for *control.

satisficing

See *optimal.

Savigny, Friedrich Carl von (1779–1861)
German jurist, see *historical jurisprudence, *Volksgeist.

saving

The practice of accumulating resources, in the form of money, land, goods and other forms of *capital, with a view to earning either *interest for the time being or a profit on their eventual deployment. Saving cannot occur in an economy that does not allow accumulation, unless it is saving by the state, whose current officers have no motive to save. This is one explanation often given for the collapse of socialist economies. On the other hand, taxes that discourage saving – such as *wealth taxes, and taxes on *gift – are now a widespread feature of modern economies. And the UK tax provisions that describe all forms of interest as 'unearned income' reflect a deep hostility to saving – or at least to the people who are able to do it. That the free economy depends upon saving is, however, no longer doubted.

Say's law

The 'law of markets' (*loi des débouches*) proposed by J.B. Say (1767–1832). The basis of the law is that resources are never under-used, or, in common language, 'supply creates its own demand'. *Keynes criticized the law as underlying many of the errors of what he called classical macroeconomics.

scarcity

In economics, any condition where there is less of something than would be demanded at zero price (i.e. if it cost nothing). Thus cars are scarce, air is not – or at any rate, not yet. It is usually assumed that, in a market economy, scarcity is a necessary condition of positive price, so that absolute *abundance of something means that it will cost nothing.

Scheler, Max Fedinand (1874–1928)

German philosopher, who presented a synthesis of Roman Catholic wisdom and Husserlian *phenomenology, which he called 'personalism', based on the distinctive place of the human person in the cosmos. Unlike the animals we are self-conscious, both objects and subjects in our own eyes and the eyes of others, and this shapes all the emotions and attitudes that we have towards each other. We are not just social beings, but beings who judge and are judged, whose self-conception is shaped by the incessant dialogue between self and other. Hence the vital importance of emotions like guilt and shame, which illustrate the complex way in which we hold ourselves accountable to others, in all our dealings with them. Human sexuality should be understood in the same light, as shaped by our intrinsic accountability, so that shame, for example, remains an immovable part of it, even in the feelings of the shameless.

Scheler's thought was wide-ranging and disorganized, but he made a substantial contribution to political theory in his study of *resentment, in which he takes up Nietzsche's idea, that *ressentiment* (as they both call it) is a fundamental part of the human condition, a state of mind into which we fall when deprived of ideals and higher purposes. (*Ressentiment*, 1925.) Scheler argues against Nietzsche's view of Christian morality, as the morality of the resentful slave, and argues that, on the contrary, the Christian doctrine of forgiveness and the Christian morality of love are a prophylactic against resentment. Take them away and resentment flows unhindered into our social relations, and is responsible for the *egalitarian orthodoxy and *socialist politics that threaten to undermine the culture of Europe. Scheler develops this argument in a subtle and interesting way, connecting his anti-socialist critique with the ideas of *Augustine and others, concerning the nature of love.

Scheler's influence in Germany was short-lived; but his disciples founded a school of personalist phenomenology in Poland, centred in the Catholic University of Lublin, which endured as the only free university in the Soviet bloc through the years of communist oppression. It was here that Karól Woityła, later Pope John Paul II, acquired his philosophical training, so that Scheler's ideas now play a significant part in Roman Catholic social philosophy.

Schelling, Thomas Crombie (b. 1921) American strategic theorist. *See* *brinkmanship, *strategy.

Schiller, Friedrich von (1759–1805) German poet and essayist. *See* *play.

Schleiermacher, Friedrich Daniel Ernst (1768–1834)
German protestant theologian, whose impact on political thought came through his theory of *hermeneutics. In interpreting Biblical texts it is not sufficient to give a literal translation; nor can we put ourselves in the position of those who first wrote them down. But we, like they, are rational beings, who have reasons for what we say and do. We discover these reasons in dialogue, and the interpretation of a text must therefore be seen as a kind of dialogue, in which we offer a partial interpretation and elicit from the text a kind of reply to it. Building up in this way, we establish an enduring conception of what is being said to us across the centuries.

Schleiermacher's ideas were later taken up by *Dilthey, who generalized the notion of hermeneutics so as to apply it to all kinds of human action, institution and forms of knowledge.

Schmitt, Carl (1888–1986)
German political theorist, sometimes identified with *Nazism, but more reasonably thought of as a *realist in the tradition of *Hobbes, whom he much admired. Schmitt was a Roman Catholic, who was shaken by the experience of Germany's collapse during the First World War, and by the instability that he observed in the Weimar Republic. He believed that no social order was viable without effective *sovereignty, and that a lack of realism concerning human motivation and a failure to perceive the fragility of human institutions had led to a naive confidence that democracy and law would generate a sovereign state of their own accord. In *Political Theology* (1927) he argues that law decides only how decisions should be made, not who should make them. To understand who or what is sovereign one should attend not to the normal case, in which codes, laws and conventions determine the running of the state, but to the exceptional case, in which laws and procedures are suspended and there is 'unlimited authority'. 'Sovereign is he who decides on the exception', for he is the one to whom power returns in every emergency and from whom power flows when things have quietened down.

No state could survive, Schmitt believed, without a concentration of power, and this power will always be vested in the one who is able to take command in a crisis. The real sovereign, therefore, is not necessarily identical with the parliament, the monarch or any other entity appointed to this role by law. The real sovereign is revealed by the crisis, and it is the task of politics to know who this is. It was the crisis of *hyperflation which revealed the institutions of the Weimar Republic to be a sham, and the effective sovereign who emerged from behind them briefly elicited Schmitt's approval, although Hitler's subsequent conduct alienated Schmitt from the Nazi party, which regarded him with such suspicion that he henceforth kept his thoughts to himself.

Schmitt held that all significant concepts of the modern theory of the state are really secularized theological concepts: 'the idea of the modern constitutional state triumphed together with deism, a theology and metaphysics that banished the miracle from the world.' The 'politicization of theological concepts' is found at its most developed in *Rousseau, for whom the sovereign may do what he will but can do no evil, since his will is the general will, sanctified by the people's consent to it. Schmitt saw himself as reacting against the dangerous consequences of this deification of the state and building instead on realistic foundations.

Schumpeter, Joseph Alois
(1883–1946)

US economist and sociologist of Austrian extraction, whose *Capitalism, Socialism and Democracy*, 1942, did much to revise prevailing sentiments concerning each of the phenomena referred to in its title. Schumpeter argued that capitalism, as it had been known in the West, was gradually giving way to a new economic order which, if it was not called socialism, would differ from socialism only in name. He identified certain main processes which were contributing to this transformation: constant increases in scale which, if extrapolated to their natural limit, would eventually entail *socialization of the means of production; an increasing tendency to rationalization and bureaucratic management, and an erosion of the role of the innovative *entrepreneur; the decay of vital features of the social and institutional framework of capitalism, with the loosening of family ties and inheritance, which undermines the motive to *accumulation; the corrosive role of intellectuals, who will always tend to take an anti-capitalist stance in any dispute; and the sheer success of capitalism in raising the *absolute* standard of living, and improving the *relative* power of the lower classes. Schumpeter was a staunch critic of democracy detached from the traditional institutions that would serve to direct the democratic choice, and sometimes advocated, sometimes merely predicted, 'socialism', by which he meant massive central planning of all economic activity within the political

framework that would make that possible. He believed that capitalism has been successful as a form of 'creative destruction' – always destroying what is dysfunctional, by putting something functional in competition with it. However, he thought that the days of capitalism are numbered, and that the new forms of human society, with their emphasis on equality and individual rights, would destroy the habit of *saving on which capitalism depends.

scientific method

The method of the 'natural sciences', based in observation and experiment, and usually displaying the following four features: (i) the search for laws of cause and effect; (ii) the introduction of theory which may involve reference to entities not normally observed (e.g. the atomic theory); (iii) the derivation of predictions from theory; (iv) the division of reality into 'natural kinds' – i.e. fundamental classifications (such as those involved in (ii)) which reflect, not actual human interests, but rather independent laws of nature (e.g. the classifications introduced by the periodic table of the elements). In addition, some (notably *Popper) emphasize the importance of refutation in the logic of scientific inference. Exactly what that logic involves is one of the major points of controversy in modern analytical philosophy. In particular philosophers disagree concerning the nature of scientific laws (for example, are they universal and necessary truths, or can there be irreducible probabilities in the laws of nature?), the nature of theoretical entities such as electrons and electromagnetic waves, the relation between a theory and its *models, the existence and nature of natural kinds, and so on.

It is disputed whether the scientific method can be applied in all areas of human enquiry. In particular the *humanities seem to contain knowledge, concepts and forms of enquiry that are concerned not with explanation but with meaning, and therefore demand another method if they are really to be methodical. (*See* *Verstehen.*) Whether there can be a social or political science in the understanding of that term sketched in the above paragraph remains one of the most important questions in political thought. *Sociobiology says that there can be; *hermeneutics that there cannot.

scientism

The belief that scientific method is applicable to all human problems, and that it will generate the only possible solution to them. 'Scientistic' is usually contrasted with 'scientific'. The first involves an unlicensed extension of scientific concepts into areas where the writ of science may not run; the second is simply scientific method in its legitimate application.

Many oppose scientism on the grounds that scientific method cannot be applied universally, say, because of human metaphysical *freedom. Others oppose it on the slightly more sophisticated ground that, while it may apply universally, it is not the only way of understanding (or even of explaining) that to which it is applied, and in certain cases is the more misleading of the available ways (*see* *Verstehen*). Others oppose it on the grounds that it gives a false sense of knowledge in a state of actual ignorance – as, for example, in certain nineteenth-century theories of history and society which, by generating confidence in their 'scientific' basis, have also justified appalling mistakes which human intuition would have instinctively avoided.

Others, of course, accept scientism, or some modified form of it, although not under that label, which is always applied with denigratory intent; *see*,

for example, *Comte, *positivism, *progress.

Scots law

The system of law prevailing in Scotland. Although part of the UK, Scotland has always retained its own legal system and its own judiciary, and has never been fully integrated into English legislative practice, despite the Act of Union (1707). The law is more fully codified than English law, being based on *Roman law rather than Anglo-Saxon *common law, and it was one of the strongest arguments given for *devolution that laws conceived and made in the English Parliament should not be automatically imposed on a legal system that is often structurally recalcitrant to their judicial application. Final appeal is now to the UK House of Lords, and this has tended to impose uniformity and to force some of the structure of the common law on to the previously codified arrangement. Nevertheless the complexity of Scots law and its acknowledged adaptation to the customs of Scotland are such that it constantly reasserts itself, and causes uncertainty as to how UK statutes can be applied within its *jurisdiction. The creation of a Scottish Parliament has meant that laws made for Scotland may once again have no application in the rest of the UK, and these laws are of necessity part of Scots law.

secession

The voluntary removal of a state from some *federation of which it forms a part, most famously exemplified in the secession of the 11 southern states of the US in 1860–62, to form the 'Confederate States of America', thus precipitating the American Civil War.

secondary action

See *industrial action.

secrecy

Secret societies (e.g. the Fijians, the Coronary, the Ku Klux Klan) are not easily tolerated within any political arrangement which permits freedom of assembly, since, unless purposes and membership are declared, it is unclear whether or not an assembly is also a *conspiracy. However, at least one secret society – the *freemasons – has established an international identity, with some political consequences. *Official secrets are, however, everywhere reserved as a right of government which no citizen can challenge in open court. At the same time, there must be some limits on secrecy if the *rule of law is to be maintained, and those limits must be public, so that, if we cannot know what the secrets are, we can, so to speak, know where they are. The existence of secret laws (as at times in the former USSR) is a fundamental violation of the rule of law, since it makes it impossible for any citizen to know that he is obeying the law. There is a common-sense presumption that too much secrecy undermines trust, and that a state which relies on secret laws, and a secret police to survey its citizens, is at least partly dependent upon terror. See *police state.

sectarianism

The advocacy of *separatist policies by, or on behalf of, a group which has broken away from an established religion due to differences over doctrine or religious practices, while being neither sufficiently organized, nor sufficiently distinct in terms of belief, to found a new religion. The word is sometimes used more loosely, to denote any kind of separatist movement, where the group possesses a national, linguistic, even political, rather than religious, identity. The term comes from Latin *sequi*, to follow, and denotes the followers of a religious practice.

'Sectarian violence' may occur in the absence of sectarianism; i.e. groups may express their antagonism towards each other violently while desiring to continue in the close proximity which renders their mutual hatred so inspiring.

secularization

The transfer of *authority from religious institutions to secular bodies. Secularization has both a subjective and an objective aspect. The first involves the gradual disappearance of religious thought, feeling and imagery from the understanding of worldly things, so that religion either ceases to exist as an independent force, or else is confined to an abstract worship of the transcendental. As a result people experience the obligations, transactions and institutions of everyday life in terms that make no reference to the divine. This may be evident, e.g., in relations between the sexes, which some religions view as *sacramental; it is also evident in the gradual decline in the felt significance of nonconsensual grounds of *political obligation, such as *piety and *obedience. Some have even argued that the associated secularization of political theory has been the most momentous of the intellectual changes which brought about the modern consciousness (e.g. J.N. Figgis: *From Gerson to Grotius*, 1916).

The objective aspect of secularization consists in the process whereby religious offices, institutions and ceremonies are extruded from public life – in education, law-making, administration and government. Conservatives sometimes oppose this objective secularization, on the assumption that the subjective secularization that would warrant it has not occurred, or is undesirable, or is precipitated by objective secularization. In *Islamic states this sentiment is very strong, and desecularizing movements abound; some argue that this is because the complete secularization of Islamic institutions of government would leave no remainder. *See* *secular government.

secular government

Government in which all political institutions – including the law and the legislature – are independent of religion, and make no discrimination among citizens on religious grounds. Secular government has been promoted in Europe and its diaspora since the *Enlightenment, and some argue that it was endorsed by Christ, in the parable of the tribute money (Matthew 22, v. 21), and also by the early church, in the doctrine of the *Two Swords. The clause in the US constitution that tells us that 'Congress shall make no foundation of religion' (the 'no foundation' clause) is often held to express a commitment to secular government, as is the principle of *laïcité* in the constitution of France. How far these provisions should be taken, however, has become controversial – in the US because of a movement to ban religion entirely from all public institutions, in France because of the desire of the growing Muslim population to display its religious affiliation in schools. In response to the first of those it is sometimes argued that the constitution is opposed merely to the *establishment* of a religion, as an official religion of the state. It is not opposed to the free exercise of religion by citizens, nor does it wish to banish the shared Judaeo-Christian heritage to the periphery of political life. Thus a court that displays the Ten Commandments is not, on this interpretation, violating the 'no foundation' clause, but merely drawing attention to shared values which the majority of citizens wish to see respected. Likewise for prayers in schools, and all the other disputed practices. Against that it is argued that the state can free itself from religious commitments, and deal impartially with all citizens, only if it meticulously purges state institutions, schools included, of any religious symbols or commitments. There is room here for many intervening positions. The question is: which measures bring peace and reconciliation between the various religions within the state, and which set them at loggerheads? This question has become extremely serious in Europe, on account of the *Islamist rejection of the secular state as a form of idolatry.

security

The guarantee of safety: i.e. the political arrangements which make *war less likely, which provide for negotiations rather than belligerence, and which aim to preserve peace as the normal condition among states. 'National security' also denotes all purposes of defence: i.e. the preparation for belligerence in order to deter or deflect it; in certain conditions therefore policies of national security may precipitate insecurity (the problem of the arms race and *arms control). Sometimes the term 'national security' is used so widely as to refer to any 'vital' interest. The United Nations Security Council is a body designed to mediate in all conflicts that threaten war, in order to avert it. Its core consists of those powers strong enough to coerce the others.

sedition

A crime less serious than *treason, but provided for under various names and descriptions in all systems of law, and consisting in the *subversion of the state through words and preparatory acts rather than through deeds. In the UK it is a *common law offence, described thus in *R.* v. *Burns*, 1886: 'acts, words or writings published with the intention to bring into hatred or contempt, or to excite disaffection against, the person of Her Majesty, her heirs, or successors, or the government and constitution of the United Kingdom . . . or either House of Parliament, or the administration of justice, or to excite the Queen's subjects to attempt, otherwise than by lawful means, the alteration of any matter in Church or State by law established, or to incite . . . crime . . . or to raise discontent or disaffection amongst Her Majesty's subjects, or to promote feelings of ill-will and hostility between different classes of subject'. The definition is clumsy, but the intent is clear: to make criminal all those acts which seek to undermine the conditions that make the *rule of law under a given constitution possible. It is plausible to suggest that every rule of law requires a law of sedition, but it is clear that the crime here described is committed every day by those who try to stir up racial or class hatred.

segregation

The establishment by law or by custom of separate institutions of education, separate facilities of leisure and recreation, and perhaps even separate kinds and places of work, for people belonging to different groups, usually defined in terms of *race or *caste. *Apartheid is an extreme case, and the 'Jim Crow' legislation of certain southern states of the US another. *Integration aims at reversing segregation.

self-defence

An act performed in self-defence may not be criminal in law, even if of a kind that normally would be considered such. Thus violence offered in self-defence is permitted, provided, roughly speaking, that it is such that a *reasonable man would have thought it to be necessary in order to avert or reduce the risk of serious harm to himself.

Under *international law every state has a right of self-defence against armed attack, but the right is vague, subject to abuse, and also subject, under the UN Charter, to review by the Security Council. 'Collective self-defence' denotes agreements between states for mutual assistance in the event of armed attack.

self-determination

1. The aspiration of some group – grounded in some existing sentiment of national or racial *identity associated with common territory, language or religion – to form its own sovereign state and to govern itself. This aspiration was recognized and encouraged in President Wilson's 'Fourteen Points', upon the breaking up of the Austro-Hungarian Empire, and has provided a powerful political motive in modern Africa, where tribal affinities provide the *pre-political background to its emergence, and also in *post-communist Europe, where the pre-political background is provided by a sense of national identity. This background is always presupposed, otherwise there is, so to speak, no 'self' to 'determine'. Only if a single social entity can be identified before and after the change – first as a society, and then as a state – can there be any recognizable process of self-determination.

2. Literal translation of German *Selbstbestimmung*, term introduced by *Fichte and subsequently exploited by *Hegel and the Hegelians. The process whereby the self achieves freedom, self-knowledge and self-mastery, by situating itself in an objective and public world. The process is one of 'determination', i.e. rendering determinate, concrete, individual, as opposed to indeterminate, abstract, universal. *See* *self-realization.

self-help

1. The ethic popularized during the nineteenth century through the writings of Samuel Smiles, advocating as a virtue the frame of mind that will promote *social mobility. Natural disabilities and low inherited social status are to be overcome by dedicated effort, by self-reliance and saving. This policy will invariably prove to be the best one, since it is the least dependent upon unpredictable social transformations for its success.

2. 'Self-help' groups: i.e. groups with common interests that they seek to promote through association amongst themselves, rather than through influence over government, or appeal to other bodies.

3. In international relations, activities, such as reprisals, aimed at compelling a state to obey a law or agreement, without recourse to adjudication.

self-realization

Literally, the making real of the self i.e. the actualization of those potentialities for thought and action which are distinctive of self-knowledge and self-identity, and which provide the individual with a sense of who he is, that he is someone, and that he has an intrinsic value which justifies his existence. The concept of the 'self' is so puzzling that few philosophers would be happy with the implications of that, or of any other, definition. However, most people have an intuitive understanding of what is meant by 'I', and of the value to us of the unique perspective on the world of thought and action which that word encapsulates. And the idea that the self exists first as potential, and then as reality, seems to be fairly common. Few thinkers are agreed over the nature of this process, and the term 'self-realization' is perhaps best considered to be a technicality of idealist philosophy, occasionally put to polemical use by psychotherapists and popular moralists, but without fixed significance outside the context that gave it sense.

Thus *Fichte used the term *Selbstbestimmung*, which means literally the 'determination' or 'making determinate' of the self, but which has the popular sense of 'resolution', in order to describe the process whereby the self becomes an object of its own self-knowledge. This self-knowledge is not theoretical only, but also practical, and involves an *alienation of the self – a sundering of the subject into subject and object – and a final restoration of the self, when the 'self as object' (the 'Not-I') is incorporated into the subjective point of view.

That basic scheme survives in *Hegel, as does the term *Selbstbestimmung*, used in Fichte's sense. But the theory has become part of a sustained critique of *individualism. Freedom is the property of the self – i.e. of the self-identifying, self-conscious centre of thought and action. But the self is not 'given' in a state of nature, nor is its existence an all-or-nothing affair. The self exists to a certain degree, and its realization is brought about through a process of *dialectical interaction with its kind. The process has various stages, including that of *master and slave, and involves the eventual 'positing' of the world of ethical life (or *Sittlichkeit) in which the individual achieves free agency, and the perspective of the 'I', by understanding the world in moral terms. Hegel's fundamental point is that the process whereby we advance to true individuality, freedom and self-knowledge is also one in which we build institutions, laws and a public political world. We achieve subjective freedom only by building objective constraints.

Outside idealist philosophy the

term may be used more loosely, in order to emphasize the role of expression in the making of the individual. Thus, broadly, political philosophies may be divided into the 'expressive' and the 'instrumental', according to whether they see the fulfilment of an individual in terms of internal self-development (*Rousseau), or in terms of external utility and success (*Hobbes). For the first kind of philosopher, categories such as *alienation will replace ideas of disutility, and labour will be seen as an externalization of the self rather than as a 'cost' or investment. The idealist theory of self-realization is part of the metaphysical attempt to uphold the expressive view, by showing that the individual described in the instrumental view is the achievement, and not the initiator, of social order.

senate

1. Under Roman government, the assembly of senior men, which succeeded the council of kings. Membership depended upon wealth and hereditary privilege, and the senate evolved into a body not unlike the UK House of Lords as it was until recently, with nominal sovereignty and vestigial legislative powers.

2. The upper house of the US *Congress, composed of two senators from each state elected for six-year terms by popular vote, and presided over by the US Vice-President. It operates largely through standing committees, and enjoys wide executive powers.

3. In general, any upper house in *bicameral government constructed on the US model, which is not a house of *peers, and which reflects political divisions exemplified equally in the lower house.

The problem of the nature and powers of a senate exercised the makers of the US constitution.

Originally the US Senate was designed to be a forum of *opinion, in which issues of public concern could be discussed with the leisure necessary for their proper consideration. It was intended that the chamber should serve, not merely as a revising and endorsing chamber, but as an additional organ of government, able to take a wider perspective than that forced on the House of Representatives by its representational function. This contrasts with the UK House of Lords, at least as it now is, which has virtually no powers other than powers of revision and endorsement. The problem of the ideal composition of a senate continues to exercise political theorists. It is widely felt that a senate must consist of experienced statesmen and people of public repute, who are not necessarily politicians, but who have wide knowledge and understanding of political matters. Otherwise it adds nothing that is not available in the lower house.

sentimentality

The enjoyment of emotion for its own sake, without regard to the true character of its object. The fundamental feature of sentimental emotion is that it is founded, not in a belief about and desire to understand its object, but rather in a belief about and admiration for the subject, as the vehicle of heroic, dignified or tender responses. It is essentially self-directed. Hence it generates a lack of real interest in its object, a preference for fantasy over reality, and a disposition not to observe but to falsify the world. It has even been described (by Oscar Wilde) as the other side of cynicism and, contrary to its own self-image, is apt to seem cold-hearted to those directly affected by it. The thought of the true lover is 'This deserves my love', that of the sentimental lover, 'I am admirable, loving this'; it is evident that the first has, while the second has not, an interest in, and a motive to understand, the object of his emotion.

In politics sentimentality is an important motive, since it is a public and recognition-seeking state of mind. Thus there is sentimental grief, such as the frequent conservative regret over the nation and its lost traditions, and also sentimental anger, which searches the world for supposed injustices in order to say 'I am admirable, being angry at this.'

separation of ownership from control

The development of the *joint-stock company, and corporations of limited liability, in which the managers and directors have no more than a limited financial interest, is part of the process whereby, in modern economies, ownership has become separated from *control. Thus a large industry may be owned by shareholders who have next to no control over what occurs in any particular part of it. The separation has been taken further by the *managerial revolution, so that ownership is now of no consequence in establishing the character of work.

Most large corporations now have boards of directors, under a Chief Executive Officer, who take the important decisions on behalf of the firm. The directors are often rewarded with enormous salaries and bonuses, which must be approved by the shareholders, but which are decided by themselves. They stand to the true owners – the shareholders – in a fiduciary relationship, being under an obligation to try to increase the value of the shares, or in other ways to carry out the wishes of the shareholders. However, they are few, active and with their own agenda, while the shareholders are many, passive, unknown to each other and often unable to mount any effective action that will change the conduct of the

firm. This means that the new forms of ownership create large areas where accountability is vague and unenforceable, and where corruption and self-interest can take root. *See* *stakeholder.

separation of powers (sometimes: division of powers)

The theory of the separation of powers, implicit in *Aristotle, but first given independent expression by *Harrington and *Locke, is known in its modern form largely through the writings of *Montesquieu, who thought that this separation was already exhibited by the English constitution, providing one of the principal safeguards of the *liberty of the English subject. Following Montesquieu, the three powers normally considered to be separable in the exercise of government are the *legislature, the *executive, and the *judiciary, the first of which formulates policy and enacts it as law, the second of which carries policy into action and the third of which applies the law according to rules of procedural justice, and resolves disputes. (There is some confusion over what, in fact, the executive power comprises; foreign policy and the waging of war had been assigned to a separate power by Locke, but are incorporated within the executive by Montesquieu.) The sign of the despot, Montesquieu argued, is to subsume these powers under one, and to hold that one to himself. In particular, the despot will never permit an independent judiciary, who might impede him from having his way in every dispute. In this condition of despotism nothing in the structure of power acts as a brake upon power, and hence no freedom can be *guaranteed*. In order to limit power, Montesquieu thought, the three powers that he had identified must be separated as much as possible, and balanced against each other. Thus the executive power should not be exercised by members of the legislature but (Montesquieu thought) by a monarch, subject to *impeachment for actions performed *ultra vires*. (This notion was carried into reality with the creation of the office of *President under the US constitution.)

In the UK it is now clear that the executive power lies with the *cabinet, which is formed from members of *Parliament (i.e. of the legislature), and which effectively controls the operation of Parliament. Moreover, in the UK the highest court of the land – the House of Lords – is also part of the legislature, and judges in that court can, and do, influence legislation. A convention prevents peers without judicial office from sitting in judgement, so that in effect the complete collapse of the powers does not occur. Nevertheless, it is clear that the UK constitution is very far from being as Montesquieu imagined it; and whatever guarantees of liberty are contained in it cannot be attributed simply to a separation of powers. Even the US constitution does not separate the powers completely, nor indeed could it do so without destroying the necessary unity of government. If the three powers ceased to function in harmony, then clearly government would be impossible. Thus, laws enacted by the legislature must be applied by the executive, and upheld by the judiciary, and if a judge acts *ultra vires*, it must be possible for the legislature to hold him to account, and for the executive to remove him from office. In contemplating the relation between the three powers we therefore encounter a problem not unlike that of the Holy Trinity: these things said to be three must also be one. In practice it seems that the greatest guarantee of liberty under the UK constitution is the existence of an independent judiciary, but, as Montesquieu himself observed, the judiciary is less a power than a brake upon power. The other two powers are instigators of policy, and must therefore always act in concert.

*Democratic centralism is strictly incompatible with any separation of powers, and this is manifest most of all in judicial procedure when the executive (the party) has an interest in the outcome. The expression 'telephone justice' was common in the Soviet empire, as a description of court procedure in all politically inspired cases: meaning that the party officials would telephone the judge to inform him of the verdict the night before the trial.

separatism

1. The aim of some group within a state to renounce allegiance to that state, and to form a sovereign state of its own. (*See also* *irredentism, *nationalism, *self-determination.)

The ambitions of a separatist movement must inevitably raise two vital questions: is there sufficient *pre-political cohesion to achieve a true political *identity? And: is it in the interests of either party that this identity should be brought into being? Clearly not every group which has a social identity can also have a political identity; economic, institutional and other dependencies may forbid it. (In that sense my street can have no political identity, although, thanks to the residents' association, it is a definite social entity.) Equally a group with the capacity for political identity may well not wish to achieve it: the Protestant community of Northern Ireland being perhaps one example, the Sardinians another.

2. The aim of some radical *feminists, who maintain that, in the company of men, women are bound to be oppressed and so must seek only each other's company for social and political purposes.

serf
See *feudalism.

service/manufacture
A service industry produces services rather than goods – for example, haircuts, banking, railways, communications, and so on. A manufacturer produces physical commodities. The shift from manufacture to service industries is one of the most remarkable features of modern economies, and one that was not, in general, foreseen before it occurred. *See* the next entry.

service economy
An economy in which the principal activity, involving the greatest transfer of funds, is the provision of services. Even where there is a product manufactured for sale, a corporation may contract with all kinds of service providers (bankers, consultants, public relations experts, lobbyists, health and safety advisers, lawyers) and offer services of its own (advice, invitations to visit, entertainment, and so on), so that its net contribution to the economy is weighted more towards services than towards commodities. It seems that all modern economies are moving in this direction, as people think of ever more ingenious ways of selling themselves. In the nineteenth century there was no such thing as a management consultant or a public relations expert: now every corporation needs both.

People providing services are more likely to be self-employed or members of partnerships than those engaged in manufacture. The growth of the service economy has therefore involved a retreat from the old wage contract. This tendency has been amplified by systems of taxation and employment law which provide a counter-incentive to anyone who wishes to employ another. The service economy therefore only distantly resembles the picture of capitalism painted by the nineteenth-century writers who railed against it. Instead of large-scale manufactures in the hands of a minority, employing large work forces engaged in producing objects for sale, we are seeing on the one hand a multiplication of small businesses, in which there are few or no wage contracts, and in which nothing is manufactured for sale, and on the other hand large, possibly *multinational, conglomerates, which change their economic focus with every change in demand, and whose employees live in the business like citizens of a new species of state, moving from specialism to specialism and enjoying social and educational advantages that attach them to the firm.

servitude
1. The state where one person is controlled by another, without being owned by him (*cf.* *slavery). Servitude is not necessarily an evil, and mutual servitude by consent is often a good. Love is a familiar form of involuntary servitude, and one that has been generalized into highly abstract visions of the government of the universe by Aristotelians and neo-Platonists. However, in the absence of consent, love, or friendship, servitude is sometimes regarded as an outward form of *alienation; since the *wage contract seems to give control to one party and not to the other, it is sometimes thought to be a form of servitude. (*See* *master and servant.)
2. Technical term in Roman and Scots land law roughly equivalent to easements and profits in English law (i.e. a qualification in a property title that 'runs with the land').
3. In *international law a servitude is an international agreement imposing a certain permanent status – e.g.

that of a demilitarized zone – on a certain territory (a development from 2.). A servitude may exist, e.g., in order to provide to a *landlocked state a means of access to the sea: it is analogous to a burden, such as a covenant, in land law.

settlement

The process whereby a human community becomes attached to a particular territory, lays claim to it as 'ours', and begins to cultivate the land, to build permanent homes and to invest its social and economic energies in the common home. Settlement marks the transition from *hunter-gatherer to *agricultural communities, and occupies a deep and important place in the collective psyche, underpinning locality, nationality and *territorial jurisdiction. Settled communities have resident gods, for whom they build temples, so that settlement usually involves a radical break with the old totemic forms of religion.

sex

The biological difference between men and women, which is identified in terms of reproductive function, provides the material basis of a distinction that is perceived and experienced in many ways. (*See* *gender.) Human sexuality presents philosophical and psychological enigmas which have their repercussions in political thought and practice, and not only when it comes to deciding questions of the role of law in mediating relations of erotic love, but also in questions concerning *sexism, *marriage and its political significance, the relation of civilization to *repression, and *sexual conduct generally.

Roughly speaking, philosophers and psychologists may be distinguished into those who think that human sexuality is simply a special case of animal sexuality, overlaid perhaps with distinctive but artificial rituals, and those who think that it is an altogether distinct phenomenon, sharing with the sexuality of animals nothing significant besides the reproductive function. Thinkers of the first kind include *Freud, and those of the second kind *Hegel, *Sartre and *Scheler. The problem arises because, while human beings are animals, they are also persons, and their personality seems to be deeply compromised in all their sexual acts: hence they may feel embarrassment, shame, and many other vulnerabilities that it would be nonsense to attribute to a creature without the idea of self. Moreover, human sexual desire does not seem to have the same object as animal desire. The animal desires stimulation of its sexual organs; the human desires another person, the particular him or her who captures his attention. And this personalized object is also *individuated* by sexual desire: it is James who is wanted, not someone else, and no other will 'do just as well'. This is one of the group of peculiarities in human sexuality which have led some philosophers (including Hegel and Sartre) to think that sexual desire contains a contradiction. As Sartre puts it, I want to possess the individuality of the other, which is his freedom: I want to possess him in his freedom, and therefore I desire that he be both wholly free and also wholly enslaved. From this account Sartre attempts to describe the peculiar relation of the human to his sexual organs, and to the pleasures of these organs, which seem to compromise him in a way that no other pleasures do.

By contrast Freudian and related schools of psychoanalysis have tried to understand human sexuality, and its admitted peculiarities, in terms of the simultaneous repression and preservation of animal instincts. These may be 'sublimated' into the strange activities of erotic love, but retain their inherently 'general' character, and can be studied as impersonal drives in all human beings.

On either view, it cannot be denied that sexuality is affected by and affects many of the customs, manners and attitudes of social life, so that the distinction between the sexes has gathered to itself a kind of universal social significance, leading to the recognition of a masculine and a feminine in everything, from the tone of a voice to the movement of a finger. This penetration of the human world by a radical division of kind (the transformation of sex into gender) is regarded by some as beneficial, by others as unjust or even disastrous, and by all as a fact. What to do with this fact is a question the answer to which has inevitable political overtones. A society that builds upon the biological distinction between the sexes further distinctions of *role, obligation, activity, dress, custom, and style, in effect creates two societies, interlocking and influencing each other in ways that perhaps reinforce the distinctions further. A society which abolishes those distinctions is a different kind of entity. Whether it can retain the same institutions – such as marriage and the family – may be doubted.

sex education

Two views of sex education now compete for dominance in modern societies. One holds that sex education is an education in restraint, designed to safeguard children against exploitation and to promote chastity, decency and the possibility of lasting sexual relations; the other holds that sex education is an education in practical knowledge, which makes no judgement as to right and wrong, but helps pupils to avoid unwanted pregnancy

and sexually-transmitted diseases, so that they can enjoy the fruits of temptation without the traditional cost. Needless to say, conservatives tend to the first of those views and are dismayed by curriculum reforms (initiated by a long series of activists beginning with *Sanger) which promote the second. The issue is of growing concern in Europe, as Muslim parents react against lessons that they believe to be deeply offensive to their way of life. In the US the *home schooling remedy is more readily available; but the controversy is nevertheless every bit as vehement.

sexism

1. Mild: the view that distinctions of gender are morally or politically significant, in such a way as to justify assigning different rights and different standards of behaviour to the two sexes.

2. Strong: the view that one of the sexes is in some respect inferior to the other, in such a way as to justify assigning inferior rights (or perhaps no rights at all) and devaluing those tasks and characteristics which traditionally pertain to the 'inferior' sex.

Either sex may be the object of sexist attitudes (in sense 2.); however, it is commonly held that, in developed societies, women have been the usual victims. Sexism in its mild form need not mark out either sex as the 'victim', and must therefore be sharply distinguished from the stronger version with which it tends to be confused. As currently discussed, the strong form of sexism is considered to be, not merely a view about the rights of the two sexes, but a systematic way of perceiving and evaluating their activities and relations. It is sometimes claimed by *feminists that many men, perhaps most men, tend to perceive women as sex objects, or as instruments for the gratification, consolation and reproduction of men, rather than as persons, and that this attitude may be expressed in as many ways as male dominance can secure. It is claimed, for example, that men dominate and control the employment of women, their domestic lives, their relations to each other and to their children, even the language which they speak. Some go so far as to argue that the persistence of gender distinctions in language and the use of the pronoun 'he' to refer indifferently to people (as in this dictionary) are vestiges of a sexism so intransigent as to have enshrined itself in grammar. It is sometimes replied that the fact that men are dominant in the public sphere is a fact of nature, to be offset by the dominance of women in the private sphere. (Metaphysical embellishments of this theory may – e.g. in the thought of *Hegel – add 'active' and 'objective' to 'public', 'passive' and 'subjective' to 'private'.) The accusation of sexism, it is said, fails to take account of the need, experienced by every social being, for a public and a private sphere, and for the cultivation of different talents, achievements and susceptibilities within the two spheres. This need, which explains the appearance of male dominance, could never be satisfied by the fact of it. It requires, rather, a social framework which effectively divides roles, employments, and attitudes, and which then facilitates the separate but complementary development of the two sexes within that division.

Needless to say, the dispute between the two views just outlined is bitter and confused. In both forms, sexism must raise the question of when a difference is relevant to a determination of rights. If it is true that some men do not think that women are persons, then this may explain the claim that some men seek to deny *all* rights to women, on the assumption that all and only persons

have rights. For the most part, however, argument over 1. and 2., in so far as it concerns rights, tends to focus on the practice of assigning *different* rights to the two sexes – as in the argument over *equal pay. If we think that all persons have or should have equal rights, since the only ground for the possession of any rights is the mere fact of being a person, then presumably we shall oppose both forms of sexism. However, it is possible to believe that personality can be of two kinds, and that the division of kinds is relevant to the assigning of rights. Thus it could be that female sexuality is so different from male sexuality as to determine in a significant way the nature of the female person (a view that we are likely to hold if we think that the personality of the agent is involved in and moulded by the sexual act – *see* *sex). Thus it seems that there are many crimes, notably sex crimes, which tend to be differently regarded according to whether the victim is male or female, and many rights in civil law, such as property rights, which are or have been differently specified for men and for women, usually greatly to the detriment of the woman who seeks to free herself from unwelcome bonds of marriage or guardianship. Matrimonial law is replete with such unequal rights, and the inequalities follow an obvious pattern. Thus UK and US law recognize a superior right for a mother to be with her children than for a father to be with his, and a superior right to support upon the breakdown of a marriage. It is clear that such inequalities reflect the fact that the law upholds existing divisions of roles, the superior rights granted to women in the private sphere being offset by the inferior rights granted to them in the public sphere of contract and employment. The greatest inequalities of all, however, lie in the domain of obligations rather than in that of rights (e.g. the obligation of women to care for their children, that of men to fight in wars), and can be attributed to a similar cause.

sexual conduct

Political questions concerning sexual conduct include:

(i) The general question of *law and morality. To what extent is sexual conduct really a *private matter, of no *public concern? And should the law seek to free itself of the marks of a moral code that does not have universal assent?

(ii) The politics of the sexual act. To what extent does the sexual act express and reinforce a political vision? Some (e.g. *Reich) have argued that the nature of sexual conduct is the crucial factor in social well-being. Others have devised forms of sexual 'protest' which, whether because they shock others, or because they liberate the agent, serve as a main vehicle for political sentiment.

(iii) The issue of rape. *Feminists claim that rape should be seen not just as a sex crime, but as a way in which men assert and maintain their dominion over women. The peculiarity of rape is that only men commit it, and, in normal circumstances, only against women. It is therefore seen as a 'political' act; the threat of it, and the fear of it, are active forces within a community, which cow women into submissive *roles.

(iv) The problem of the sexually normal. Is this a coherent idea, and if so, should the law take cognizance of it? For example, is there a concept of 'normal sexual relations' which requires that the parties be of different sex? (*See* *homosexuality.)

(v) The problem of *sexual harassment.

sexual harassment

*Harassment of someone either with a view to sexual relations, or in order to dominate sexually, or in some other way to awaken a consciousness of one's own or the other's sex. There is no definition of sexual harassment in English law, and, although the US judiciary is increasingly recognizing sexual harassment as a *tort, there seems to be no settled meaning in US law either. The narrow definition, which holds that A sexually harasses B when (and only when) A uses threats in order to induce B's consent to sexual relations, can be used as grounds for legal action in both systems of law – e.g. for unfair dismissal, breach of contract, etc. in civil law, and, in the extreme case, for indecency or even rape in criminal law. But many people, especially American feminists, are increasingly dissatisfied with this narrow definition, which simply makes sexual harassment a special case of threatening behaviour, and wish to introduce a wider definition that will capture the peculiar nature of sexual power and its misuse. Wider definitions may extend to constant sexual jibes, the use of suggestive language, even to wolf-whistles and suggestive 'body language'. Many object to these wider definitions, on the grounds that they tend to attach severe penalties (such as loss of employment) to behaviour which expresses no malign intention but only an attitude to the other sex which falls short of some standard of politeness, or even some standard of *political correctness. On the other hand, the narrow definition offers little protection to victims of a known form of wrongdoing. Part of the problem seems to stem from the collapse of traditional codes of sexual behaviour, which ruled out the possibility of obscene language, sexual gestures or unwanted intimacies with any member of the other sex who was not already a willing partner, usually a spouse.

sexual orientation

The orientation towards a particular sex as the object of desire. The concept of sexual orientation arose during the 1970s as part of a movement to normalize *homosexuality, the idea being that orientation is innate, a feature of the human being as closely tied to his nature and destiny as the colour of his eyes or the size of his brain. Whether this is so is a matter of dispute, partly because the concept of 'orientation', unless given some secure physiological or psychological basis, is vacuous as an explanation of conduct. (*Cf.* an 'orientation towards chocolate', cited as an explanation for chocolate eating.) Homosexuality, it seems, is of many kinds, and its prevalence or otherwise is strongly influenced by cultural factors. Nevertheless, sexual orientation has now been accepted as a fact, and laws forbidding discrimination on grounds of orientation have been adopted by many states and by the *European Union.

shame culture and guilt culture

A distinction introduced into *anthropology by Ruth Benedict (*The Chrysanthemum and the Sword*, 1946), and for a while highly influential. The distinction is between those cultures which rely on 'external sanctions for good behaviour', and those which rely rather on 'an internalized conviction of sin'. In the first the offender is shamed publicly before his fellows; in the second he confines his guilt within his troubled heart. The superficial appeal of the distinction (which to some has seemed to capture some of the difference between Mediterranean Catholicism and Northern Protestantism) should not lead us to exaggerate its explanatory potential. Rather it refers to two distinct but intimately related ways in which remorse may express itself. The sufferer may regard himself as horrible in the eyes of others, and redeemed when others re-accept him; or he may regard himself as horrible in his own eyes, and therefore as alone responsible for the expiation of his sin. It has sometimes been thought that guilt must therefore engender a heightened consciousness of oneself as an individual, with unshiftable burdens of responsibility – hence its association with the *Protestant ethic and other codes which might be thought to be based on a philosophy approximating to individualism. Shame, on the other hand, has an intrinsically social quality, and represents the sufferer as an organic part of the community which condemns him. The role of shame in ancient societies – the Greek in particular – has been singled out as the basis of the perceived distinction between the ancient and the modern world. Bernard Williams (*Shame and Necessity*, 1992) has described Greek shame in terms of a rival conception of human *responsibility to that exhibited in the modern world and a rival conception of the nature of the cosmic forces which govern us.

shadow economy

That part of an economy that escapes official notice, because it involves illegal procedures, tax evasion, or the provision of services outside the regimes of health and safety, employment law and social security that are imposed by the state. Now responsible for 15% of GDP in many European states, the shadow economy continues to grow as the burdens of the official economy increase. Advocates of *anarcho-capitalism welcome this tendency, believing that the shadow economy is the only genuinely free part of the economy: the only part in which goods and services exchange exactly at the *opportunity cost of providing them. Others regret the growth of the shadow economy, not least because it implicates a growing proportion of the population in illegal activity, and so brings the law into disrepute.

sharî'ah
See *Islamic law.

Shaw, George Bernard (1856–1950)
Irish dramatist, critic and social reformer, who, in the prefaces to his plays and *The Intelligent Woman's Guide to Socialism and Capitalism* (1928), defended, with consummate wit, an iconoclastic socialism, as the way not only to solve all problems of scarcity, competition and human conflict, but also to release the human potential that is otherwise exhausted in the business of making money. Idealist and cynic by turns, Shaw delighted in shocking his contemporaries, and was an outspoken defender of the bolsheviks, travelling to Russia in the Stalin years, to become a willing dupe of Soviet propaganda. His own socialism, however, was not revolutionary but gradualist, and he was a founding member of the *Fabian society, for which he became the most famous spokesman.

Shi'ism
From Arabic, *shî'ah*, party (i.e. the 'party of 'Ali'). Shi'ites believe that the Prophet founded an imamate, or succession of religious leaders. Each imam has some residue of the authority of the Prophet (who, however, is the only one to have been granted a divine revelation). The imamate resides in the *ahl al-bayt*, the 'people of the (Prophet's) house', in other words the Prophet's direct family. Succession therefore belonged first to 'Ali, the Prophet's cousin and son-in-law, and thereafter to those stemming from him. Who these are is a matter of dispute; hence there are three forms of Shi'ism: Zaydis, Isma'ilis, and – the most significant – the *ithna 'ashâris*, or 'twelvers', who recognize 12 genuine imams as successors to the Prophet. All were murdered, saving the last, Muhammad al-Mahdi (the Messaiah), who was, however, occulted in 940 AD, to return at the last day – meanwhile living secretly among us as the guarantor of God's law. Shi'ites do not differ from the Sunnis in the matter of the obligations or the laws that are binding on Muslims, although they recognize only one school of jurisprudence. Fiercely persecuted under Sunni domination, they cultivated the art of religious concealment or *taqîyya* (Persian: *ketman*). Shi'ite devotions involve an annual lament for the second imam, Husayn ibn 'Ali, who was massacred with his followers in 680 AD at the battle of Karbala, in what is now Iraq.

show trials
1. Trials on the model of the Moscow trials of the 1930s. The essential features are: large publicity, and a carefully selected victim, who is chosen as an example of some characteristic which the state wishes to eradicate. The verdict is predetermined by the prosecution and the judge instructed accordingly, so that there is no separation between judge and prosecution, no application of *natural justice, and no genuine *adjudication. The purpose of such trials is to stage a large-scale threat, directed at the population as a whole; they are 'trials' only in the sense that someone appears in court.

2. More loosely, any trial which is made into a public spectacle, in order to emphasize a political point, like the trial of the Nazi Eichmann in Jerusalem. Such a trial need not violate canons of procedural justice.

Sidgwick, Henry (1838–1900)
English philosopher; see *immigration, *utilitarianism.

Sieyès, Emmanuel-Joseph, Comte (1748–1836), normally known by his original religious title as the Abbé Sieyès French revolutionary pamphleteer and statesman, whose writings injected an element of nationalism and fanaticism into the rhetoric of the Revolution – especially his seminal 'What is the Third Estate?' (1789), written to justify the rise of the people to the highest position of political power. In this he gives prominence to the 'Nation' as the expression of the *general will of the people, and argues that it does not matter how the Nation exercises its will, or with what degree of violence, just so long as it does so. Sieyès was elected deputy for Paris, and gave the Third Estate the title by which it is now known – the National Assembly. From 1793 he withdrew from public life, survived the Terror which his writings and speeches had done not a little to inspire, and took part in the *coup d'état* of 1799 which brought Napoleon to power.

silent majority

Term used by US President Reagan to refer to those who have no voice in the *media, who dissent from the alleged *liberal (in sense 1.) consensus of the media and who supposedly form the majority of decent US citizens. The same idea as *moral majority.

single-issue fanatics

Expression probably due to the English Journalist Bernard Levin and used to denote *interest groups which focus on a single question and work to make it the sole or dominant public concern while showing complete intolerance towards any view on the matter save their own and a refusal to work for a compromise solution. Single-issue fanatics have emerged on both sides in the debates over *abortion, *animal rights, *homosexuality and many other fashionable causes. A conciliatory view of them would argue that they serve an important function in awakening the public to real problems, but that they should be prevented from dictating the answers. However, because they form an important input into the new *political class, they very often do dictate the answers, by being entrusted to provide them.

single-party system

Any system of government in which only one *party holds power, whether *de facto or *de jure. The party in question either arranges token *opposition or removes opposition entirely. Such is the 'party of the new type' introduced by *Lenin. It would be quite wrong to describe a system in which a party of the old type is invariably returned to power at elections as a single-party system, for reasons made clear in the entry devoted to *party.

single transferable vote

A method of *proportional representation designed to be maximally sensitive to the preference ranking of the electors. Votes cast for unsuccessful candidates are redistributed as in the *alternative vote system, and the 'excess' votes cast in favour of successful candidates are also allocated proportionally to the alternative choices of those who voted for them. The system is used in the Republic of Ireland, and is often held to give the best available match between the candidates elected and the wishes of the electorate.

Sismondi, Jean Charles Leonard Simon de, (1773–1842)
Swiss author, *see* *proletariat.

Sittlichkeit

German: morality or ethical life. Often used in the specific sense given to it by *Hegel, where it includes customary behaviour, respect for *persons, and a comprehensive stance towards the social world, rather than obedience to any specific moral code (*Moralität*), the assumption being that *Sittlichkeit* is a phase of development of the soul or *Geist*, through which it must pass if true individuality and freedom are to be achieved. See also *self-realization.

Skinner, Burrhus Frederic (1904–1990) US psychologist; see *behaviourism, *social engineering.

slavery

A slave is someone who is controlled and also owned by another, and who has either no *rights against the other, or only diminished rights. (*Cf.* *servitude.) The crucial factor here is that of ownership. It is fairly normal for people to possess legal or moral rights in others: such as the right to redress possessed against the person who has injured you. But rights of *private property are not normal. These rights have been interpreted as involving the right to exclusive use of the labour of the slave (restricted, however, by law), and the right to transfer ownership in the slave to another. It is clear that the owner of a slave does not have to be an individual human being. The state may assert rights of exclusive use in the labour power of its citizens, commanding and controlling them in all activities in which labour is expended, and it may even exert a limited right of transfer. But the slave himself is normally considered to be an individual human person, and the injustice of slavery is held to follow from this.

It is generally thought that an individual person cannot be owned without also denying to him at least one of his (presumably *natural) rights: his right to dispose of his labour power as he wills. When classical writers – e.g. *Aristotle – defended slavery it is not clear that they were defending any

absolute form of it. Slaves had extensive rights in Roman law, the practice of *manumission was not only widespread but also normal, and the actual conditions of slave labour were often to be favourably compared with the conditions of much factory labour in the nineteenth century (although the state slaves of Athens were forced to work the silver mines). This makes it additionally clear that abolitionist arguments need to be carefully phrased if they are to show that this arrangement is unjust, but comparable arrangements not so. Some, for example, think that the abolitionist arguments can be made cogent only by also denouncing the rights that a husband may exert over his wife's body under some laws of marriage.

The English *common law has never recognized rights of ownership in persons, although slavery was a feature of Anglo-Saxon society. The Church opposed slavery and it died out in the early Middle Ages, since when it has been virtually unknown in Britain. Its history elsewhere is, however, far more chequered, and British merchant seamen were active in exporting slaves from Africa (where the slave trade was indigenous) to other parts of the world – especially to America. The abolitionist movement began in eighteenth-century England, largely under Quaker influence, and took heart from Somersett's Case (1771), in which Lord Mansfield upheld an escaped slave's right to freedom, arguing that ownership of one person by another is not recognized in the English law. The first Slave Trade Abolition Act came into effect in 1806. Subsequently Parliament, under pressure from an articulate and influential anti-slavery faction led by William Wilberforce, declared slavery to be an evil of such proportions that HM Government was entitled to take action on the high seas to eradicate it.

Naval patrols were maintained from 1819 until 1861, with the purpose of intercepting slave traders and freeing their cargoes.

The abolitionist movement spread rapidly to America, where an antislavery society was founded in Philadelphia in 1775. Jefferson condemned the slave trade in the first draft of the Declaration of Independence, though this draft was not carried and Jefferson himself remained a slave-owner to the end of his life. Nevertheless, by 1787 all the Northern States had excluded slavery by Ordinance. Its persistence in the South was one cause of the secession of the Southern States, and therefore of the civil war of 1861. In 1865, following the victory of the Northern States, the Thirteenth Amendment to the Constitution was passed, declaring the emancipation of all slaves.

In recent times slavery has been introduced on a massive scale in the USSR, China and elsewhere, either in the form of compulsory 're-education' or in the form of labour camps. This has not aroused the same measure of disapproval as the slavery which blots the record of the US, largely because the slaves in question have been owned by the state and therefore not treated as private property but merely as property. Like everything owned by the state, however, they have been more carelessly treated than they would have been had someone had a personal interest in their efficiency. The miserable story, told by *Solzhenitsyn and others, has been the most important cause of the total collapse in recent years of the communist idea.

Current evidence suggests that the indigenous African slave trade has not entirely died out, and that slavery is still practised in certain Islamic countries – notably in Sudan, in which Christian women and children are routinely enslaved by Islamic militants. The Koran seems to take the existence of slavery for granted, as a normal feature of the human condition.

Smith, Adam (1723–90)
Scottish philosopher and political economist, whose *Theory of the Moral Sentiments*, 1759, presented an influential account of the emotional life of the moral being, and whose *Inquiry into the Nature and Causes of the Wealth of Nations*, 1776, completely transformed the subject of *political economy, and introduced many of the thoughts, problems and conceptions which have since lain at its heart. In the *Theory of the Moral Sentiments* Smith gave an account of justice as a negative virtue, which consists in refraining from injuring another and from taking what is rightfully his. This virtue is the essential foundation of a well-ordered society, but it is a sentiment too feeble to exist without the firm support of law. Smith later developed this view and made concessions towards some kinds of egoism, which he came to think to be a social value. In *The Wealth of Nations* he opposed the *mercantilist beliefs that a state's power depends upon its wealth, and that the best policy for a state is to retain as much of it within its borders as possible; on the contrary, Smith argued, there are great potential gains from trade and exchange, and he praised the virtues of competition. Thus Smith also rejected the idea of the primacy of agriculture (*see* *physiocrats), and gave a systematic account of the importance of manufacture in production.

Smith also pointed to the benefits, in terms of increasing production, which stem from specialization and the *division of labour, the products of which could be exchanged in the marketplace. Productivity depends on the skills of the labour force and the proportion of productive to unproductive labour. The detail division of labour enhances the first, while the accumulation of capital enhances the second. Smith thus initiated the inquiries into the nature and function of *capital that were to dominate nineteenth-century political economy.

Smith emphasized the distinction between *use-value and *exchange-value, suggesting labour as a measure of the second. However, he did not subscribe to the *labour theory of value in its subsequent form, since he thought prices to be determined by supply and demand. He defended *laissez faire*, and believed that a market economy left to itself, while not without its evils, nevertheless has a natural tendency to *equilibrium possessed by no rival economic system. In it: 'Every individual is continually exerting himself to find out the most advantageous employment for whatever capital he can command.' This will be in producing and selling the goods which satisfy as many needs as possible. So that, through intending his own gain, a capitalist contributes to the general welfare, 'led by an invisible hand to promote an end which was no part of his intention'. This justification of capitalism, which echoes various thoughts of *Mandeville's, was to prove extremely influential, and still has its adherents. In fact what it justifies is not capitalism as such, but rather the profit motive, attached to the equilibrating mechanism of the market, which produces benefits for all. Critics tend to point out that without attention to problems of distribution, the market system may produce vast inequalities, and that this may in itself destroy the possibility of equilibrium in the political sphere.

Smith produced important recommendations concerning public finance and *taxation. In particular, he argued

that a tax ought to be proportionate to the ability to pay, an argument that was influential in forming taxation policy after Pitt. Smith's long-term influence on political thought, however, lies in his subtle development of the *invisible hand conception of human society, and in the idea that collective solutions may be most effective when not directly intended. This argument, embellished with the conceptions underlying the *calculation debate, has, in the hands of *Hayek and others, produced a comprehensive answer to the socialist philosophy of planning.

snobbery

The affectation of a *class or *status, by cultivating the manners and society of those thought to possess it. It is usually accompanied by contempt for the class or status to which the subject least wishes to belong. If the class or status aspired to is lower than the one denied, then snobbery is called inverted: a special case of that is *radical chic, in which political posturing is regarded as an index of class membership.

Snobbery is possible only given the belief that there is something to class or status *other* than the affectation of it; hence its widespread persistence suggests that, whether or not class and status are mere appearances, there is a common belief that they are something more than that.

sobornost

Russian: commonality, from *sobor*, a gathering. A term of Russian Orthodox theology used to denote generally the ineffable unity of the faithful, and specifically the unity between clergy and laity that prevails in the Orthodox Church, as opposed to the hierarchical arrangement promoted by Roman Catholicism and the *individualism of the Protestant sects. The concept became central to

Russian conservative thinking in the nineteenth century, partly as a result of the *pan-Slavist writings of Aleksei Khomyakov (1804–60). According to Khomyakov, the truth of religion is contained in the entire community of believers, and stems not from reason but from the corporate identity that emerges as people join together in charity, hope and prayer. *Sobornost* is still proposed as a social ideal by modern Russian conservatives, notably by *Solzhenitsyn.

social capital

A concept of increasing importance in sociology, which draws on the language of economics in order to describe the accumulated social resources inherited by each new generation from its predecessor. These resources are used in managing the day-to-day affairs of social existence, and include customs, language, manners and morals – in short, all the practices that are taught to us by our parents in order to make us fit members of society. These things cannot be invented anew by each generation, since they are the distillation of a long process of accommodation and are presupposed in the process of learning.

According to Robert Putnam, the US political scientist who has made social capital his particular area of study, the term 'refers to features of social organizations such as networks, norms, and social trust that facilitate coordination and cooperation for mutual benefit.' In *Making Democracy Work* (1993) Putnam argues for the political, institutional, and economic value of social capital, and in *Bowling Alone* (2000) he presents a scholarly and provocative account of America's declining social capital. Numerous findings of comparative economic studies by the World Bank and the United Nations corroborate Putnam's

thinking: i.e., some regions of the globe lag behind while others thrive due to their social capital.

social choice

A technical term meaning a choice for a society derived from the choices of its individual members. The aim of social choice theory is not, typically, that of the theory of *collective choice (although as noted, the term 'collective choice' is also used to refer to what is here described as 'social choice'). The theory is concerned not so much to describe and explain the actual inputs to social choices or to determine how the various kinds of influence and control regulate the making of political decisions, but rather to investigate the relation between social choices and individual preferences, when the second are taken as the ground and justification of the first. The theory of social choice is a complex area of applied mathematics, and many definitions are in fact current in the literature, both of 'social choice' itself, and of the *social welfare function which is the theory's principal device (the device which generates a statement of social choice from the statement of individual preferences). Much current work studies the derivation of social choices from the choices and *preference orderings of *all* individuals, and pays great attention to 'impossibility theorems'. These are results such as *Arrow's theorem and the *Paretian liberal which imply that, given certain requirements (e.g. that no member of society should dictate the outcome, that a social choice satisfies some given principle of *optimality, etc.), it is impossible to derive a social welfare function for a society. In other words, those requirements turn out to be inconsistent with the desire that social choices be determined by individual choices. The impossibility theorems have sometimes been thought to capture intuitive difficulties in the concept of *voting, and of collective choice generally.

social contract

Expression introduced into political theory by *Plato, and taken over by *Locke (who also spoke in his connection of a 'social compact'), and now used as a general label for views which try to found all ideas of *legitimacy and *political obligation in a contract, whether express, implied, or hypothetical: e.g. the views of *Hobbes, *Locke, *Rousseau and *Rawls. The essence of the view is this: since to contract is to put oneself under an obligation, the grounds of political obligation would be objectively determined if all such obligation could be traced to a contractual promise. For Hobbes the contract is between *subjects, to set up and obey a *sovereign; in accepting the sovereign's protection, the subject implicitly contracts to obey him. Hobbes wavers between the view that this obedience is absolute and the view that it is circumscribed by *natural law (i.e. by a system of rights that cannot be alienated under the terms of the contract). Locke similarly argued that sovereign power is not a party to the contract but at best the result of it; the contract is between the members of society, who mutually forswear certain freedoms that they enjoy in a *state of nature for the benefit of the security provided by society. But the terms of the contract do not permit the alienation of certain inalienable *natural rights. (Locke wished to oppose *absolutism in the name of *limited government, and foresaw the objection that absolute government might be precisely what had been contracted for.) Rousseau developed more fully the idea that sovereignty is the *outcome* of the contract, and countenanced a partial return to the more absolutist stand of Hobbes. The *general will that

emerges from the contract has indisputed sovereignty over the particular wills that might conflict with it.

There are four possible kinds of social contract theory, according to whether the contract is construed as explicit, as implied, as hypothetical or as quasi-contractual:

(i) Explicit. Political obligations actually stem from explicit contracts. For example, a contract may be held to have preceded the formation of society. Or a constitution may be thought to be a contractual document, which is held before the citizen as he reaches the age of consent, and to which he then may signify his assent. (Hence the importance of a *bill of rights, as in the US constitution, or Magna Carta, and the importance of an 'oath of allegiance'.)

(ii) Implied. The contract is to be inferred from social behaviour, but is not explicit, for example because the faculty to make explicit contracts emerges in the individual only long after his behaviour has shown his *tacit consent to the arrangement that surrounds him.

(iii) Hypothetical. A state is legitimate to the extent that a contract *could* be constructed that its subjects *would* accept, and which does confer on them an obligation towards the state. This is the basis of views offered by *Kant and *Rawls, and it is sometimes criticized on the ground that nobody could be *really* bound by a hypothetical contract, so that the problem of political obligation remains.

(iv) Quasi-contractual. On the analogy of *Roman and *common law doctrines of quasi-contract, it could be held that contract provides the best *model* for the understanding of obligations which arise through the mutual encouragement of interacting parties, and that a quasi-contractual obligation is to be inferred wherever this interaction is voluntary and accompanied by manifest and intended advantages to the participants. This is perhaps the most plausible view, but it stands in need of theoretical elaboration. Moreover it does little to solve the general problem of political obligation, and can therefore be thought not to have succeeded in its principal purpose, which is one of justification rather than explanation.

social credit parties

Based on the theory, advanced by C.H. Douglas (1879–1952), that the weakness of modern capitalism lies in a deficiency of purchasing power. Social credit parties arose during the Depression with the aim of instigating monetary reform designed to make 'social credit' available to consumers – e.g. by discounts paid to retailers. The success of such parties was greatest in Canada, but is now dwindling, along with the belief in the underlying idea.

social Darwinism

See *Darwinism.

social democracy

1. 'Social democracy' is sometimes used to mean the theory and practice of *democratization, applied to all social institutions and all social rewards, and not merely to the institutions of government.

2. The theoretical and practical attempt to reconcile democracy with *social justice, through the use of state power.

3. In a more specialized sense, 'social democrats' are defined by political affiliation. Originally all parties affiliated to *international socialist movement assumed the title 'social democrats', but the modern use of the term emerged in 1905 following the split between the *bolshevik and the *menshevik wings of the Russian Communist Party, the second adhering

to the label 'social democrat' in order to emphasize its adherence to a policy of peaceful social change by popular consent.

Now 'social democrat' denotes, roughly, any view, with some elements of socialist belief, which seeks reform rather than revolution, that respects constitutional procedures (even when the reform of the constitution is part of its aim), and which adheres to the principles of democratic election. The underlying belief is that a party must rule, not merely in the name and the interests of the people, but also by consent from the people. This means that social democrats must seek to retain the means whereby consent is offered, and must accept the existence of *opposition parties, and of elections which might lead to their own removal from office. Social democrat parties were originally dominated by Marxists, whether orthodox or *revisionist, but in Germany, where the movement has dominated politics, the Social Democrat Party (SPD) definitively broke with Marxism in 1959. As the leftist sentiments have dwindled, so have the social democratic parties in Europe moved towards the bland definition of their aims given in 2. above.

social engineering

The planned reconstruction of society. The phrase was used, for example, by the American jurist Roscoe Pound to denote the rule of law in a democratic society, but has often been thought to have rather sinister overtones. Hence it is contrasted with *piecemeal (social) engineering (by *Popper), and with social architecture, the first expressing hostility to the *totalitarian, the second hostility to the *utilitarian, implications of the phrase. A variant is the 'behavioural engineering' advocated by B.F. Skinner; *see* *behaviourism.

social fact (also: societal fact)

An expression used, especially by *Durkheim, to indicate acceptance of the fundamental tenet of *holism in sociology. There are statements about society which cannot be rephrased as statements about individual members of it, and therefore there are facts about society over and above facts about its membership (*see* *reductionism). An example of such a social fact is the existence of a state of war between two societies; or the existence of a rule of law, or of any other constitutional artefact. Not all social facts are intentional artefacts of that kind: e.g. unnoticed *norms are also social facts. Durkheim argued that sociology is the study of social facts; and that their existence provides the refutation of *individualism. In other words, sociology is inherently *katascopic.

social justice

An application of the concept of *justice to the wealth, assets, privileges and advantages that accumulate within a society or state. The idea has its origins in Christian writings from the nineteenth century – both those of the British *Christian socialists, and those of the Roman Catholic conservatives, such as the *Jesuit Luigi Taparelli (*Reflections on Natural Law*, 1855), who argued that social justice arose from fair dealings between individuals, and not from some distributive scheme. However, with the rise of socialism, the concept became attached to that of *distributive justice, so as to denote an obligation not of the individual but of the *state.

As currently applied the idea seems to be this. Consider a state or system of laws; this identifies a society and ultimately determines, through those laws, the distribution of distributable benefits within it. We can then ask, which system of laws would achieve an equitable distribution of benefits?

And that seems like a reasonable application of the concept of distributive justice.

Some people object, however, that until something is produced, there are no benefits to distribute, and the very fact of production might create *rights* in the thing produced which would be violated by any distribution that does not have the consent of the producer. (*See* *Locke and, for the inverse application, *exploitation.) If that is so, then the whole picture of social justice as a form of distribution might involve a covert affirmation of a kind of *agency in an area where there is no agency, and a right of *control where there is no such right. (Such is the view, for example, of thinkers like *Nozick.) It is certainly true that appeal to this idea involves, if it is to be consistent, a radical rethinking of all existing rights of acquisition and exchange which, while they may be allowed to survive that process, are also put in question by it. Some find it paradoxical or impossible, arguing that it involves an extrapolation of our common ideas of justice to a point outside the situations which make them applicable. Others (notably *Rawls) argue that, on the contrary, it is just such a rethinking that occurs in every application of the concept of *justice.

One source of confusion concerning this topic is that European discussions have tended to introduce, under the idea of 'social justice', questions of *need, *welfare, and *poverty, giving arguments designed to be as responsive as possible to relations of social interdependence. American discussions, on the other hand, have emphasized the concept of *justice*, and so seen the discussion largely in terms of individual rights. Tensions arise partly because 'social' and 'justice' pull in different directions, the first towards the whole condition of society, the other towards the rights of the individual. Some thinkers – notably *Hayek – argue that the concept of justice is a procedural notion, concerned with rectifying abuses, and that its application to society as a whole, without settling the question 'who did what to whom?' is meaningless.

social market

Term introduced by *Röpke, to denote a market economy that would take due account of the needs that cannot be satisfied by markets, either because they depend on *public goods, or because they are met by other forms of social order than those generated by free exchange. At the local level, Röpke thought, social needs are spontaneously met by charity, religious foundations, and the associations that form the community. It is through civil society that the seeming harshness of capitalism must be remedied, and not through the socialist state. Through the influence of Röpke and Germany's postwar finance minister Ludwig Erhardt the 'social market economy' was adopted as the distinctive German solution to the problem of combining a free market with a welfare state.

social mobility

The movement of individuals, families and groups from one *class or *status group to another. For example, the ascent of a nineteenth-century shopkeeper to the upper middle class through the profits of trade, or to the aristocracy through the acquisition of a peerage. Or the ascent of a party member within the Communist Party system. Social mobility is in both directions, although inertia and the manner in which upper echelons legitimate and dignify their position tend to make the downward descent less frequent – at least in so far as status is concerned, since the loss of a fortune or public disgrace are not sufficient for

loss of status. On the other hand, European royalty have been spectacularly downwardly mobile, since the French Revolution – there being in any case no way of moving in the opposite direction.

The description of the process is as difficult as the description of the classes and status groups between which people are alleged to move. Thus 'upward mobility' is often thought to be a feature of modern 'post-industrial' society, on account of the increasing importance of skilled, and the decline of unskilled, labour. But whether this is mobility from one class or status group to another, rather than the reformation and reconstitution of the lower class, is extremely difficult to determine. For it is not possible for *everyone* to move upwards, without *someone* moving downwards. (The entire Congolese army was once promoted by one rank, though it is doubtful that any member of it was gratified.)

Social mobility is one of the phenomena that have led sociologists to doubt the utility of nineteenth-century theories of class membership, which suggest easily recognized gradations of 'higher' and 'lower', but which rely on theories of economic control that no longer clearly apply.

social ownership

A form of *common ownership which is put forward by some *socialists as their defining purpose, and in reference to which 'socialism' originally acquired its modern significance. Social ownership is to be contrasted with private ownership on the one hand and 'state ownership' on the other. The latter is still a form of exclusive ownership, but by a public rather than a private individual, whereas social ownership is supposed to be genuine ownership in common. It is exemplified in some forms of *cooperative, but the aim of many socialists is that it should extend more widely than that (since cooperatives still may thrive under systems of private property). How wide it can be while still being a form of ownership (i.e. a right of use) is debatable.

social question

Term used since the eighteenth century to denote that area of political concern which calls not merely for conciliation, adjudication and legislation in the interests of stable government, but for positive action in order to ameliorate social conditions. It was the 'social question' that was partly responsible for the changed role of European government since the French Revolution and its transformation into an active instigator and purveyor of social change. Thus the programme of the French revolutionists was drawn up in response to what Robespierre called 'the most sacred of all laws, the welfare of the people, the most irrefrangible of all titles, necessity'. Throughout the nineteenth century in UK politics the 'social question' was used to denote the condition of people who until then had not had a vote; it was therefore an important phrase in the rhetoric surrounding the introduction of the second Reform Bill. Now that the legitimacy of government action to alleviate want is acknowledged, except perhaps by a small hard core of thinkers from the *New Right (though *see* *underclass), the phrase has tended not to be used; the question is no longer debated, only the answer.

social security

Social security legislation, introduced into Germany by Bismarck in the form of state pensions, and into the UK in 1908 by Asquith's government, is now a common feature of Western democracies, and usually invoves compulsory contributions from all tax-payers,

in return for guarantees from the state. The Beveridge Report to the UK Parliament in 1942 proposed a social insurance scheme intended to cover every citizen against 'interruption or destruction of earning power, and for special expenditure arising at birth, marriage and death.' This led to the creation of the *National Health Service and subsequently to the expansion of *social services to include measures of support that Beveridge himself would almost certainly have rejected, as undermining the responsibility of the citizen.

social services

Those services which are provided by the state for the benefit of society. What they include varies from case to case, but it is common to count *education, *health, some *communications, and the maintenance of law and order as social services which a government can be expected to provide and maintain, under the conditions in which a modern government must inevitably find itself. To what extent social services benefit from, or are damaged by the co-existence of private services, catering for the same benefits – i.e. private schools, private medical facilities, private means of communication – is one of the major issues of European politics discussed in this dictionary under the various separate headings. Equally important is the question of limits: are there areas in which the state should not attempt to provide support? The *nanny state is often accused of intruding into and taking over the *family, by offering itself as a better provider of income, better source of security and well-being, even a better guardian of children, than can be obtained through the market in human relations. But if we exclude the state from the family, then the question arises: who is to clear up the mess? *See* *underclass.

social stratification

The development of systematic inequalities of wealth, power, influence, education and privilege within a society. Such inequalities are normally seen as discontinuous that is, difficult of access from outside, so that each stratum is separated by a barrier from its neighbours. It might be part of a theory of the *systematic* nature of stratification to explain this phenomenon of the barrier.

Social stratification may not exhibit the neat divisions of ownership or control invoked in theories such as the classical theories of *class. As in the case of class, however, the problem of describing the true character of social stratification is not separate from that of explaining it. Those who favour *functional explanations in social matters may identify the strata of society in terms of certain functions performed in upholding and facilitating the social order. Those who adhere to *power theories of politics might identify strata in terms of levels or types of power. Without those explanatory aims 'social stratification' has the vague sense of 'discontinuous inequality'. *See* *status.

social welfare function

1. A relationship which associates a number with each possible allocation of resources within an economy; the higher the number, the higher in the social *preference ordering is the associated allocation of resources, while two resource allocations with the same number are 'indifferent' from the social point of view.

2. In the theory of *social choice, the term 'social welfare function' is usually used in the sense given to it by K.J. Arrow, i.e. a set of procedures for devising an entire social preference ordering over alternative states of society, given the set of preference orderings over those states possessed by the individuals in society. Such a function is compared by Arrow to a 'constitution': it is a way of translating individual desires and choices between alternative states of affairs into a social choice between them. For an application of this device that has been thought to be of considerable importance in political thought, *see* *Arrow's theorem.

socialism

A wide term, with two principal related meanings:

1. In Marxian theory and official communist language, socialism denotes a social and economic system that is supposed to be the transitional stage between *capitalism and (full) *communism. The means of production are taken into *social ownership, and the state persists as an administrative machine, upholding a new order of legality, and a new system of rights, in such a way as to permit the emergence of true *common ownership, and the eventual abolition of the state. This fantasy has little or nothing to do with:

2. 'socialism', construed as a broad and comprehensive outlook on the human condition. As a political theory, socialism is a relative newcomer, and probably lacks both the system of traditional *liberalism, and the pragmatic character of *conservatism. But its influence over modern politics is none the less great for its lack of clear foundations. The principal ideas seem to be these:

(i) The belief in *equality. This may be variously stated in terms of *equal opportunity, *egalitarianism, etc. The main consideration is that human beings are equally entitled to the things of this world, since they are equal in every respect relevant to their entitlement. All inequalities must therefore be justified, and the onus is on the one who defends them to produce the proof.

(ii) The state as administrator. The state is seen, not as the legal and ceremonial manifestation of civil society, but rather as a complex administrative device, designed to guarantee individual entitlements, and to distribute benefits among the citizens accordingly. The state is, therefore, primarily concerned with *distribution, and must provide and maintain the institutions which ensure that human goods – food, medicine, education, recreation – are made available to everybody on terms that are as equal as possible. Law is necessary as a means to good order, and to effective administration. But neither it, nor any other aspect of the state machinery, is an end in itself. Moreover, the state should be *confined* to administrative functions, and not, for example, set up as the propagator of religious doctrine, or nationalist ideology.

(iii) The elimination of systems of *control. People exert control over each other in various ways – e.g. through the *class system, through political institutions, and through hereditary privileges. All such systems violate the fundamental axiom of equality. While most socialists in sense 2. deny the Marxian thesis that *all* private property in the means of production is a form of control over other men's lives, they accept that *some* is. Hence private property, while in itself right and permissible, and perhaps even a proper expectation of a citizen in a well-ordered society, should not be allowed to accumulate inordinately or to escape accountability for its use, lest vast systems of private control should emerge and prove damaging to the interests of society. Socialists used to draw the conclusion that the state must therefore be prepared to *nationalize major assets, and should curtail or forbid the transactions that lead to large-scale private accumulation – such as gifts

and inheritance. A softer kind of socialism has emerged in recent years, in which the role of the state is confined to regulating, taxation and preventing oligarchies and cartels, without itself directly owning or controlling economic assets. (*See* *New Labour.)

Those three main principles explain most of the details of socialist policy: in particular the attempt to eliminate privilege in all its forms, the opposition to the *hereditary principle, and the defence of the *welfare state. Historically socialism has had strong affiliations with the *labour movement, for the obvious reason that, while it promises very little and threatens much to the class of property owners, it promises much and threatens little, or seems to threaten little, to the workers. It has been an important force in European politics, and has acquired some of the pragmatism and ability to compromise which is integral to parliamentary government, so that, under the actual conditions of Western government, none of the three principles is expressed or applied in its pure, theoretical form.

Critics of socialism have argued, for example, that there is a potential conflict between principles (ii) and (iii). The massive control that needs to be exerted by the state if it is to be seen as an administrator with full responsibility for everyone's welfare is incompatible with the attempt to free people from the control of others. All that will be achieved is the transfer of control from an old *ruling class of aristocrats to a new *élite of bureaucrats. Moreover, some add, a ruling class with a monopoly of government is a better guarantee of freedom and justice than a bureaucracy of self-made men. Others object to the idea of the state as a means, and argue instead that the true character of the state is as an end in itself – only as such can it command the obedience and allegiance of the citizen. As means the state comes to seem arbitrary and dispensable, and therefore holds increasing power with increasing instability. Others reject the premise of equality, on a variety of grounds mentioned elsewhere in this dictionary, while others still argue that the ideal of *social justice implied in (i) to (iii) is incompatible with the assertion of *natural rights and *freedoms. Finally, it has been argued with great force (e.g. by economists of the *Austrian school) that economic failure is generic to the socialist idea of a state-supervised economy. These arguments, together with the experience of socialist governments in Europe, have recently led to a decline in support for the socialist idea.

Socialist International

Founded as the Labour and Socialist International in 1923 in order to bring together those parties which, while descending from the original *Internationals, had renounced revolution in favour of *gradualism. The Socialist International was reconstituted in 1951, following its suspension during the Second World War. It now brings together most parties of a moderate *socialist or *social democratic persuasion and has 56 affiliated parties from 52 states. Its vice-presidents in recent years have included Golda Meir of the Israeli Labour Party and Walid Jumblatt (Janbalat) of the Lebanese 'Progressive Socialist Party', which is, however, neither socialist nor progressive nor a party, being a sectarian organization of the Druze loyal to the Jumblatt family.

socialist law

General term for the system of law developed in the USSR from the 1930s, but especially from 1967, and adopted by East European regimes subject to

Soviet control. Socialist law was the result of an attempt to fill the legal vacuum left by the Russian Revolution, by using traditional Romano-Germanic law as a vehicle through which communist conceptions of property relations and contract, and of the role of the party, could be expressed. The basis of civil and criminal law was retained, in so far as was necessary for the regulation of common social relations and the prevention of crime. The technical terms of Roman and German law were also retained, although the outlawing of many property transactions and private associations made it uncertain how some of them applied. Moreover, although there were written codes of law in all the countries affected, the absence of *judicial independence made the passage from the written statute to its meaning and application uncertain, and laws ostensibly guaranteeing rights, liberties or privileges to the citizen were not applied against the state or its agents.

Not only was socialist law erratically applied, it also contained enormous gaps – especially in the areas of tort, contract, the law of corporations, bankruptcy, etc. – which rendered it entirely useless in any context other than that created by the absolute rule of the communist party. As a result, it has been abandoned by all *post-communist states, which now have the immense task of drafting codes that will be suited to their new conditions – a task made additionally complex for those which have joined the *European Union, by the requirement that they incorporate into their legal code the totality of the *acquis communautaire, a body of law running to 100 000 pages, rooted in concepts that have no equivalent in socialist systems.

socialist parties

Any party with socialist aims, which seeks power within, and also seeks to preserve, a constitution permitting organized opposition to those aims. (*See* *labour parties, *social democrats.) Most such parties are affiliated to the *Socialist International.

socialist realism

First proclaimed by the writer Maxim Gorky and such politicians as *Bukharin, socialist realism summarizes the artist's duty to the party under communism. He must eschew all *formalism, and represent the world of the proletariat in a dignifying, optimistic and generally intelligible manner so as to achieve 'the reflection of reality in its revolutionary development'. He must also endeavour not just to interpret the world, but to change it, in the direction prescribed by 'party mindedness'. Socialist realism is often condemned as a form of *philistinism, and is now more or less universally despised for its cliché-ridden sentimentality. However, there were occasional revivals of the idea in the USSR during its final spasms, and a version of it has been influential in China, where it is still affirmed under Article 12 of the 1975 constitution. Almost without exception socialist realism in art, literature and music has been *kitsch of a singularly depressing kind, its only virtue being the blatant display that its optimism is self-deceived.

socialization

1. In sociology, the process whereby the individual acquires the characteristics that fit him for membership of society, including, most importantly, the perception of himself as an immovably social being, guided by *norms, *roles, and relations with others.

2. In politics, the transfer of an object from private into *social ownership. *See* *nationalization.

socially responsible investment,
or SRI

Investment in funds and businesses that have an acceptable ethical profile. Many banks and financial agencies offer portfolios that adhere to some code of SRI, in the hope of attracting funds from investors anxious that their money be invested in enterprises of which they approve. Industries that threaten the environment (mining, oil and gas), health (alcohol, tobacco), life (weapons) and public morals (gambling) are dropped from the SRI portfolio – all those mentioned being, however, star performers on the stock exchange. SRI has been compared to CSR (*corporate social responsibility): a way in which the capitalist economy buys off the more fanatical of its critics by adopting a stance of *political correctness.

societal fact

See *social fact.

society

Any aggregate of individual human beings who interact in a systematic way, so as to determine criteria of membership. There are as many ways of counting societies as there are forms of systematic social interaction, and the distinction – essential to political thought, although often ignored by it – between *state and society is by no means easy to draw. In one sense the UK includes countless societies; in another sense only one. Here the *Hegelian concept of *civil society, as a 'moment' of the very same entity which is also a state, is useful. We might then describe the UK society as a collection of societies united into a single civil society. A civil society is a social system which bears the marks of political organization, and is ordered according to the constitution and legislation of a state. Such a society might precede and survive the state, just as a mass of bronze might precede and survive the statue into which it is cast. At the same time, it is no more *separable* from the state than the bronze is separable from the statue (while it lasts). To construe the relation between state and society thus – on the model of form and matter – is not wholly satisfactory, partly because the relation between form and matter itself presents conceptual difficulties. But it enables us to know more or less what we are talking about. Consequently the expression 'civil society' is used in this dictionary to denote a society identified through its political order.

Society in the wider sense is the subject-matter of *sociology; it includes every group of people who selectively respond to other members of that group: all groups of people who form 'systems' in the sense of *cybernetics. The narrower term *association refers to those systems which are also socially recognized as such, and perhaps accorded, on that account, separate status in law. Thus the upper class may form a society, given to systematic interaction, but it does not form an association.

sociobiology

Alternatively: evolutionary psychology or evolutionary sociology. Any theory or would-be theory which studies *society and social behaviour as a feature of the biology of the participants, and which thus hopes to cast light on the social nature of man by studying the 'social' behaviour of other animals and its biological causes. Some doubt that such a science is possible, arguing that social behaviour is essentially connected with *rationality, i.e. the attribute of men that animals are often supposed not to possess. For such thinkers sociobiology involves an illegitimate *reductionism. Others defend the utility of such a

science, thinking that it helps to resolve the perennial question of *human nature, and also to remove some of the mystery that human social arrangements display.

The theory of evolution implies that the human mind has evolved through long periods of adversity, and is what it is because of its capacity to adapt. At the same time it must contain important and immovable residues from earlier periods of evolution, in particular residues from the social feelings necessary to survival in the conditions of the *hunter-gatherer. Institutions that promote the survival of a community in the face of life-and-death competition from its rivals can also be explained by applying the method of Darwinian biology. Religion, on one plausible position, is such an institution. Likewise the division of roles between the sexes, believed to be a cultural artefact by *feminism, might more plausibly be explained as a deeply implanted sociobiological fact, an inevitable by-product of sexual selection in the conditions that our ancestors encountered.

It seems, therefore, that sociobiological theories do not necessarily inherit the progressivist optimism of nineteenth-century *Darwinism. Indeed, they have increasingly been used to defend a fundamentally conservative position regarding institutions, customs and laws.

sociology

The study of *society, in its widest sense. Rival schools of sociologists emerged during the nineteenth century, perhaps the most important being the *individualists, who thought that all true explanations of facts about society must show them to be the consequences of separately identifiable facts about individuals, and the *holists, who believed that individuals are unintelligible outside their social context. Some now remain neutral with regard to that debate, or take an intermediate position; and for the most part prevailing schools no longer present themselves as rivals so much as complementary *models of inquiry into facts so unsystematic that it is not to be expected that any premature system will cast light on them. The most important theoretical device that has found its home in sociology is that of *functional explanation; apart from that, the main attempt has been to find either illuminating classifications of social phenomena, or else underlying mechanisms of social change (as in *Marx and *Weber).

Sociology has had enormous influence on political thought, partly through Marx and Weber, who revolutionized the understanding of class relations and their role in social coordination as a whole, partly through theories, such as *Durkheim's trenchant critique of individualism, which have seemed to undermine the foundations of many political beliefs. Dispute still remains, however, concerning the pretensions of sociology. Some regard it not as a science, but as a *scientistic substitute for what should be, if it were to exist at all, a *humanity. Such critics tend to point to the mass of unexplained jargon (sometimes called 'sociologese') which the discipline has generated, together with its more or less complete failure to present a body of established results, or falsifiable predictions. (See *Popper.) Others defend the subject on the grounds that one should not criticize it simply on the basis of the products of its second-rate adherents, nor denigrate the real achievements of the great sociologists (such as Marx, Weber, and Durkheim) who have transformed not only our vision of society, but also our vision of all political institutions within it. Some of the disputes in this area concern the

extent to which sociology can be, or ought to be, *value-free. Some concern the nature of scientific method and its relation to the 'human' world (see *Verstehen). Some concern the extent to which societies are really intelligible to those who do not belong to them (see *relativism).

sociology of knowledge
The branch of *sociology, first proposed by *Mannheim, which concerns itself with discovering the social causes (if there be such) of beliefs and ideals. 'Knowledge' is a misleading term, since it implies the truth of what is known. 'Belief' would be better, since the sociology of knowledge often concerns itself with explaining beliefs in ways that show that they are neither caused by, nor in any other way related to, the truth of what they describe: a good example being the *Marxian theory of *false consciousness, which presents in a striking form the epistemological problem to which all such explanations give rise.

The sociology of science is a burgeoning area of sociology, partly because of the growing influence of epistemological *relativism, of the kind typified by *Foucault. See also *postmodernism.

socio-technics
Term due to Polish sociologists (e.g. A. Podgorecki: *Principles of Socio-Technics*, 1966) which became the preferred term in the Soviet bloc for *social engineering. 'Socio-technics' has a practical and progressive air which helped to overcome the party's ideological suspicion of *sociology.

Socrates (469–399 BC)
Greek philosopher, who left no writings of his own but who appears in dramatized form in the pages of Xenophon and *Plato. In Plato's

version, Socrates is portrayed as a defender of a kind of intellectual aristocracy and a critic of *Athenian democracy. Right decisions are based on knowledge and wisdom, and it is therefore absurd to entrust the government of a *polis to the mass of ignorant people. Political knowledge, like all knowledge worthy of the name, must be grounded in philosophy – which means that it must arise from a constant questioning of received ideas. Socrates scoffs at Athenian freedoms and offers a mischievous defence of the rigid oligarchies of *Sparta and Crete. Since Athens was in the process of losing its recurrent war with Sparta, it is not surprising that the Athenian jury condemned Socrates to death when he was arraigned before them – the charges, however, being 'impiety' and 'corrupting the youth'. At the same time, Socrates is portrayed by Plato as a model citizen, obedient in every particular to the Athenian state, even to the point of refusing to escape from prison when condemned. He compared the state to his father, and argued that his duty was first and foremost to obey the law, even when the law was in error.

Soil Association

Founded by Lady Eve Balfour in 1946, in order to put into practice the philosophy expounded in her *The Living Soil*, 1944, and in the hope of regenerating the local food economy, based in organic methods, renewable resources and a commitment to home production. These, she argued, had once existed, and the need for them had been proved by the Second World War, in which the British people came close to starvation. The Soil Association took over the philosophy of the pre-war *agrarian movements, and set itself up as an unofficial monitor of farming practices, devoted to defending *agriculture against *agribusiness, to advising

farmers on organic production and local markets, and lobbying on behalf of the small family farm. In due course the Association became an established NGO with an officially recognized role in authenticating farmers as 'organic producers', and is now recognized as such by the *European Union.

soixante-huithard (French: a sixty-eighter)

Someone who acquired his cultural and political outlook through inspiring, participating in, or sympathizing with the student 'revolution' of May 1968 in Paris and elsewhere (*'les évènements de Mai'*). In particular those, like *Foucault, *Althusser and *Derrida, who are either upstream or downstream from the intellectual ferment of those days, and whose thought is indelibly marked by the *antinomian enthusiasms of which May 1968 is the enduring symbol. The appearance of the *soixante-huithards* in suits and ties, sporting titles like Foreign Minister (Joschka Fischer), Member of the European Parliament (Rudi Dutschke), Speaker of the House of Commons (Peter Hain), European Commissioner (Neil, now Lord, Kinnock) is one of the ironies of recent European history.

solidarism

A posture espoused by leading parties in the French Third Republic between the two World Wars. Solidarism is opposed both to *laissez-faire capitalism and Marxist *collectivism, and advocated a *mixed economy, *welfare legislation, and support for voluntary associations as partners in the state's overriding task of social reconciliation.

solidarity

Common attachment which is so strong as to create a 'solid' resistance to attack. Originally a term of sociology, e.g. in *Durkheim, who used it to denote the internal forces of social cohesion, it later became a left propaganda word, used to describe the political consciousness of an emerging class struggling against *oppression. The term was taken over by the Polish free trade union which emerged in 1980 in opposition to the dictatorship exerted in Poland by the Communist Party.

Solzhenitsyn, Aleksandr (b. 1918)

Russian novelist, essayist and leading *dissident whose brilliantly written account of the Soviet labour camps (*The Gulag Archipelago*, 1973), made it virtually impossible for Western intellectuals to make excuses for the USSR in particular, or *communism in general. Himself for many years an inmate in the gulag, Solzhenitsyn briefly found favour during the temporary 'thaw' following Khrushchev's denunciation of Stalin. However, he was subsequently silenced and persecuted, and at last forced into exile in the US, a society which welcomed him but failed wholly to please him. While denouncing communism as the devil's work, he has also criticized the spiritual condition fostered by modern *capitalism – and in particular the rootlessness and self-centredness which supposedly stem from *secularization. His political vision is *Christian, *nationalist, and *conservative, based in a belief in man's fallen condition (*see* *original sin) and in the *sacramental character of our relation to the history and territory in which we have been placed by the hand of God. His social philosophy involves a revival of the theory of *sobornost, in the form given by the theologian and *pan-Slavist Khomyakov, and elements of romantic Russian conservatism pervade his didactic writings. He remains one of the most outspoken and powerful critics of contemporary decadence, and also of the *dependency culture made necessary by human selfishness, which prompts us to hand over the duty of *charity to an impersonal state.

Sombart, Werner (1863–1941)

German economist and social theorist, who, in *Der Moderne Kapitalismus*, 1902, 1916–27, tried to overthrow the analysis of *capitalism given by *Marx, by refuting the fundamental premise of *historical materialism. Sombart argued that the modern Western consciousness is not a consequence of the development of the capitalist economy, but that this economy is the consequence of a particular spirit, the 'Faustian' spirit of expanding knowledge and opportunity (also described by *Spengler in his less rigorous account of the condition of modern man). Sombart attempted to show how social, cultural and economic values interpenetrate in such a way as to generate the *dialectical movement of history. He repudiated Marxism completely after the Russian Revolution, denouncing it as 'uninhibited Mammonism', i.e. as a congeries of utilitarian values and pure hatred. His work remains important because of its attempt to formulate an intuitive objection to historical materialism, based on the fact that capitalist development seems to have been a local phenomenon, the product of a particular culture, rather than the inevitable result of the growth of knowledge and economic power.

sophists

From Greek *sophia*, wisdom. The sophists were itinerant and professional teachers of the art of *rhetoric (hence the word 'sophism' for a spurious but deceptive argument), who thrived in Greece around 400 BC. The most influential doctrine associated with this heterogeneous body was that of the distinction between *nature and convention. The sophists also gave some of the earliest formulations of the idea of *natural law.

The sophists were noteworthy for their belief in *progress, and for their attempt to persuade people that *virtue, and therefore the art of government, could be taught to all rational beings. This had a revolutionary impact on Athenian society, and also was partly responsible for Plato's attacks on them, by virtue of which so many of their ideas have survived, albeit perceived only darkly through Plato's bias. The sophists have sometimes been taken as the archetypal 'liberators', those who induce in their hearer the confidence in human capacities, and the confidence to make the world anew. As Plato portrays them, they also had a pronounced leaning towards scepticism and relativism, and in many ways foreshadowed, in their sophistry as well as in their assaults on objective knowledge, the *postmodernist fashions of the twenty-first century.

Sorel, Georges (1847–1922)

French philosopher and social theorist, a Marxist turned *revisionist, turned eccentric, who lent his weight to the *anarcho-syndicalist movement, and influenced the development of modern political thought through his *Reflections on Violence*, 1908. In this he argues that *violence is not the single phenomenon normally described by that name, but extends through all social order, so that there is a 'violence of principles' exerted in the name of morality and religion, and various forms of *structural violence contained within the law and institutions of every enduring society. All serious political opposition must develop its own form of violence if it is to be successful; *confrontation, rather than *conciliation, is the true political process. Sorel proceeded to advocate the general strike as the preferred way of precipitating radical social change. He gave a curious theory of *myth in support of this idea. Having opposed Marxism on account of its *deterministic attitude towards the future, he argued that people control the future not through scientific understanding but through myth. The role of a myth is to rehearse the imminence of some event, and to concentrate human will towards it, so as eventually to bring it about. There are only two attitudes to the future – that of myth, which eventually masters the future, and that of *utopia, which swoons away from it. Some have found this analysis useful in the sociology of modern *fascism and Marxism, the first of which Sorel influenced through Mussolini.

Southern agrarians

A group of writers from the Southern States of the US, centred around the poet Allen Tate and including novelists like Eudora Welty and historians like M.E. Bradford, who, partly in reaction to the *New Deal, and partly out of *nostalgia for the rural life of the South, wrote extensively in praise of the unique social order that had been destroyed by the Civil War, renewing the call for *states' rights against the Union in order to recapture the indigenous virtues of the American *agrarian way of life.

sovereign

1. General: the person, body, or system of offices in which *sovereignty is vested.

2. Specific: the person who, under a *monarchy, exercises the functions associated with the *head of state. Who this person shall be is determined in the UK by the Act of Settlement 1700, which can probably be altered only with the consent of those states within the Commonwealth which are also monarchies presided over by the sovereign of the UK.

The divergence between 1. and 2. is illustrated by the theory that sovereignty in the UK vests not in the sovereign but in Parliament.

sovereignty

'There is and must be in every state a supreme, irresistible, absolute, and uncontrolled authority, in which the . . . right of sovereignty resides.' Thus wrote Blackstone in the *Commentaries on the Laws of England*, 1765–70, arguing that this absolute authority lies not with the sovereign, but with 'the Queen in Parliament'. It is now unclear what is meant by sovereignty, and the concept seems to focus disputes in political science and philosophy which no dictionary article could possibly resolve. Moreover, it has been argued that the concept (at least, as Blackstone understood it) is a distinctly modern one, and that medieval conceptions of monarchy saw the monarch as standing side by side with his parliament in the business of government, beneath a law which both were bound to respect, and that in such a state there is no 'absolute' or 'uncontrolled' authority. (*See* *absolutism.) On the other hand, a power can be internally divided and still be sovereign (*see* *separation of powers).

The concept derives its contemporary significance from *Bodin, *Hobbes *Rousseau, *Hegel, and many more, and seems to have at least two distinct parts:

1. External sovereignty. This is an attribute which political bodies possess in relation to other such bodies. Thus 'sovereignty' in *international law implies the recognition of a *state as having rights of jurisdiction over a particular people and territory, and being solely answerable for that jurisdiction in international law. This legal idea is meant to correspond to an actual power to assert itself over the territory in question. However, legal sovereignty can diverge from actual power, as in the case of the communist states of Eastern Europe, which were sovereign states in international law, but which had no real power to act independently of the Soviet Union in any matter which concerned the Soviet interest. Here, it might be said, employing a distinction elaborated below, that legal and coercive sovereignty diverge.

There are many theories of external sovereignty, perhaps the most important distinction among them is between those which regard sovereignty in instrumental terms (e.g. as an institution existing in order to protect a society from internal and external violence), and those which see it in expressive terms, as the 'realization' or embodiment of social and political order. Hobbes's theory is an example of the first, Rousseau's an example of the second.

2. Internal sovereignty. This is an attribute possessed by a political body in relation to a society that falls under its government. Sovereignty in this sense lies in supreme *command over a *civil society, and it has a *de jure* (legal) aspect, as well as a *de facto* (coercive) aspect. Legal sovereignty vests in that person, office or body whose decisions cannot legally be challenged in the court. Coercive sovereignty vests in that person, office or body which in fact *controls the powers exerted and enforced in the name of government. *Schmitt famously argued that sovereignty in this second sense is vested in the one who is able to take control in a crisis – i.e. when custom and habit give way to obedience and command. And ultimately, he implied, this is the only kind of sovereignty that matters, since all else depends on it.

In the UK legal sovereignty is vested in the Queen in Parliament, whereas all *executive decisions are made by the *cabinet, which some say controls the political process as best it can (although it may be that the cabinet's *influence falls short of control). It is arguable that, because of constitutional pressure, coercive sovereignty can only be exercised in accordance with the law, and that all exercises of political power are thus eventually subject to scrutiny by Parliament. This 'coming together' of the legal and the coercive seems to be the ideal of internal sovereignty. It can be described as a uniting of power and (legal) authority. Quite what it involves has remained disputed since Bodin.

The US constitution purports to vest internal sovereignty in itself, but that seems incompatible (a) with the fact that the constitution can be amended, (b) with the fact that, unless some body can *enforce* the constitution, it is without coercive power. In this case legal and coercive sovereignty seem to fall apart.

Once a body – e.g. a *legislature – has legal sovereignty there is clearly no limit to its legislative competence; it can be challenged by no one and is not bound by its own decisions. The UK Parliament used to conform to that rule (although the great extent of *judicial independence might lead one to doubt that Parliament really could enact legislation that is in flagrant breach of *natural justice). Appeal can now be made against Parliamentary legislation, however, either to the *European Court of Justice, which oversees conformity to the treaties that form the EU, or to the *European Court of Human Rights. The second has only persuasive authority; but the first can effectively disqualify legislation, and has frequently done so. Hence it is doubtful that Parliament is now sovereign.

Nor is the US Congress sovereign according to the above rule, since its legislative powers are limited by the constitution, the interpretation of which constantly changes as Congress presses up against its previously defined limits, and as *judicial

activism in the Supreme Court reinvents the *Founding Fathers. Some legal *positivists try to argue that, in such a case, true legal sovereignty must lie with whomsoever has power to change the constitution, but this seems absurd, since the body empowered to do this has hardly ever met and does not exist continuously. It is interesting to note, therefore, that the application of the concept of sovereignty to modern states such as the US and the UK seems to be inherently problematic.

sovietology

An academic discipline which arose during the 1950s and 1960s, with the intention of studying the nature of the *USSR and its institutions. The credentials of a sovietologist depended upon his ability to travel to the USSR and report back on his findings; but he could obtain the visa to travel only if his findings were approved by the ruling *Communist Party. Hence sovietology tended to paint a rosy picture of soviet society, so continuing a tradition initiated by *Shaw and the *Webbs. For this reason the discipline was widely regarded with suspicion, especially by those who lived under the Soviet system. Almost all predictions made by official sovietologists turned out to be wrong, and virtually no sovietologist foresaw the collapse of the USSR and the consequent collapse of the academic salaries that depended on it.

Sparta

Greek *polis*, whose remarkable constitution, attributed to the legendary *legislator Lycurgus, provided one of the two most important *ideal types for ancient discussions of government (the other being *Athens). The following features (which seem to have existed from the sixth century BC onwards) are noteworthy: the division between citizens and helots (the latter being a conquered race destined from birth to a condition of slavery); the forbidding of the alienation of land within the city; the hereditary transfer of land to the head of the household; the forbidding of all with full citizenship from carrying on commerce or trade; the lack of a monetary system (the last four features amounting to a more or less complete absence of the phenomena of exchange and *price); collective education of a military rather than academic kind until the age of 30, and collective meals for all men until the age of 60. The political system consisted of two hereditary kings, a senate of elders which also functioned as a supreme court, an assembly of all male citizens over 30 and 15 elective *ephors*. The last gradually came to acquire legislative, judicial and executive power, and could even sentence the king to fine or imprisonment. The whole organization of the state was directed towards war, and towards the continuing suppression of the ever-rebellious helots. Nevertheless, the communal organization of Spartan social life, together with its strict curtailment of all property dealings, were often admired, e.g. by *Plato, whose admiration was later shared by *Rousseau.

Spartacists

Members of the movement founded as the Spartacus League in 1916 in Germany, by *Luxemburg and Karl Liebknecht, and named after the Roman slave Spartacus, who led an unsuccessful rebellion of slaves, and who died in 71 BC. The Spartacus League was a revolutionary Marxist organization, strongly opposed to the war, and later became the nucleus of the German Communist Party.

species-being (or: species life)

Normal English translation of the term *Gattungswesen*, introduced by *Hegel

and used by Feuerbach to signify the social essence of man (i.e. the fact that human beings are not truly such in isolation but only when joined in social relations with their kind), and taken over by *Marx in his early writings, in the hope that it indicated a theory of society that would be materialist in its assumptions and anti-individualist in its results.

speciesism

Term invented by Richard Ryder, and favoured by the Australian philosopher Peter Singer, and by other advocates of *animal liberation, and used to denote the unjustified discrimination in favour of our own species and against the other animals when deciding questions which affect the interests of both. The assumption is that in a great many areas of social and political life the considerations that determine our treatment of people are exhibited also by animals: they too feel pain and hunger; they too need safety, shelter and a healthy environment; they too have affections and desires. To this the reply is often made that, although those claims are true, animals are not moral beings and therefore have neither *rights nor *duties. Racism and sexism are condemned because they deprive moral beings of their rights; there is no equivalent to this in our treatment of animals, and the term 'speciesism', therefore, is an invitation to confusion. Besides, how are we to weigh animal against human interests? Locusts too feel pain and hunger, they too need safety and a healthy environment. Should we politely make way for them as they storm across the land?

speculation

Buying and selling with a view to profit as a result of changes in price. From the earliest times this practice has been condemned, the idea being that the speculator makes no contribution to the economy, either as producer or distributor, and furthermore that he profits from instabilities and that his activities may even encourage them.

The most common defence of speculation lies in the argument that it is an integral part of the self-regulating price mechanism, and facilitates the return of the market to *equilibrium. *See* *arbitrage. Moreover the speculator takes a risk, and his profit (should it occur) is the compensation for that risk.

Spencer, Herbert (1820–1903)
British philosopher and social theorist; *see* *Darwinism, *evolutionism, *taxation.

Spengler, Oswald (1880–1936)
German philosopher of history whose *Decline of the West*, 1919–22, presents in Wagnerian imagery a compendious vision of world history, as the 'comparative morphology' of cultures. Each culture has a life cycle of about 1000 years, and Western culture is now at its end, entering the period of 'civilization' where administration and technology take over from the flowering of the spirit in its summer forms. (*See* *Kultur/Zivilisation.*) The Western spirit is 'Faustian', consisting in a constant urge to reach out into infinite space and fill it with significances – it is this spirit that explains the soaring gothic cathedrals, the perspectival paintings, the ever expanding contrapuntal forms of music. The ancient Graeco-Roman spirit, by contrast, was 'Apollonian', confined in a local finite space, practising the severe circumscribed life of the *polis. Spengler's vision was unscholarly and impetuous, but his very modern version of the cyclical theory of history proved influential,

and his poetry was captivating to a generation that had seen the crimes committed in the name of progress. His later adulation of the 'beast of prey' and the nobility of the 'irrational' man lent some support, or at least hot air, to the Nazi ideology, although he himself disapproved of Nazism, arguing, in reference to Hitler, that Germany stood in need of a hero, not a heroic tenor. The conception of the 'Faustian' spirit was shared with *Sombart, who put it to comparable use.

sphere of influence
Territory over which some powerful state claims preferential rights of a political and economic kind, but which may be united with that state neither by direct alliance, not by any imperial or quasi-imperial tie. Spheres of influence may be proclaimed unilaterally (as under the *Monroe doctrine), or by agreement, as between the UK and Russia in 1907 in the case of Persia.

It is normal to distinguish *influence from *control. The Soviet 'sphere of influence' in Eastern Europe, for example, was also a sphere of control, even of *force, and is probably better understood in such terms. The US 'sphere of influence' in Latin America may be similar, although many doubt this. The boundary between influence and control is difficult to draw, and is always drawn differently by the two sides in an international dispute.

spin
Term of *journalese, probably derived from the techniques of bowling in cricket, which signifies the artful presentation of policy or the disguising of lack of policy through the media and through publicity, in order to distract attention from the substance and focus it instead on the form. Spin has been an important feature in the

rise of *New Labour, whose leaders have worked hard at image and presentation, believing that the true goal of government is to be re-elected, regardless of policy.

Spinoza, Baruch (Benedict de) (1632–77)

Dutch Jewish philosopher of Portuguese extraction, a thoroughgoing *rationalist, and a *determinist, who nevertheless believed that intellectual freedom was the goal of civil order. Spinoza's *Tractatus Theologico-Politicus*, 1670, written under the influence of *Hobbes, presented a systematic treatment of the nature of the republic, expressing many modern liberal ideas. Like Hobbes, Spinoza believed that the essence of government is power, and he made no distinction between *rights and powers (partly because of a metaphysical theory which implied that rights *are* powers). Nevertheless he defended a doctrine of *natural rights, supported by *natural law, which in turn is revealed to the *natural light of reason. Like *Grotius, Spinoza argued that the natural law is not law because it is laid down by God, but because it is the expression of necessities perceivable to all reasonable beings. All *positive law should be seen as an attempt to maintain the discipline of government, while conceding and protecting natural rights. Political obligation arises from an implicit *social contract, and consent rather than fear must establish the true authority and power of government. Hence the aim of government is liberty, since without liberty there can be no consent.

Spinoza attempts to reconcile a near-absolutist view of *sovereignty (arguing that the natural rights of the subject are, with a few exceptions, transferred to the sovereign), with a defence of *limited government, for which he sees *judicial independence as a necessary condition. The conflict here is redolent of similar conflicts in Hobbes; and like Hobbes, Spinoza is not anxious to place people in a state of nature, believing that, even though there are natural rights, they can be perceived only in the state of society. Hence, without political power, the value of limiting that power could never be understood. The right of the sovereign must be as absolute as his power; however, although it may seem supreme to the senses, it must always be limited by reason, whose power in the end is higher than that of anything that would oppose it. Here Spinoza relies on *Socrates' defence of the life of the intellect as the exercise of true freedom. (The defence is developed further in Spinoza's posthumously published *Ethics*.) Hence the absurdity of all laws designed to control human thought, or the expression of human thought. Spinoza's metaphysical determinism implies that the only freedom available to us is that of understanding the necessities which govern us, and it is to this intellectual freedom that political freedom is the means.

Spinoza's impassioned defences of free speech and religious toleration were highly developed. He argued that the real disturbers of the peace within any commonwealth are not those who express their sincere opinions, but rather those who seek to curtail the liberty of judgement over which they cannot tyrannize. Such people force a contradiction into the structure of law, and so bring it into disrepute, remove its limiting function, and destroy the sovereignty which the law proclaims.

Although he upheld Hobbes's idea of sovereignty, Spinoza concluded that the ideal sovereign is not a monarch, but a democratic assembly filled by those who represent the owners of property: i.e. those who exercise the powers that must be ruled.

spontaneous order
See *Hayek.

sport
A leisure activity recognized as the common property of every class, and the focus of much political interest in both domestic and international affairs on account of its inherently associative character, and also because it is the most available form of *play, and therefore the most common active relief from *work. Institutions of sport are institutions of society, and it is significant that ideologies, such as fascism, which attempt to close the gap between society and state, requiring a point-by-point correspondence between law and social life, have invaded the institutions of sport and attempted to policize them. This is partly because sport provides, through the player, the team and the captain, ready objects of human allegiance symbolic of local, territorial and national virtues. The identification between a team and its home town and the idea of organized competition between towns are both of great interest in the study of nationalism, since they embody in embryo the feelings of locality, associated with prowess and a right to rule, which are tapped by that political movement. Nationalism has, in fact, more or less completely dominated the major attempt to use the institutions of sport to further peaceful international relations – the Olympic movement, founded in 1894 by the Comtean optimist Baron Pierre de Coubertin (1863–1937). The ceremonial and ritualistic character of the Olympic contest was exhibited in the Olympic Games of Antwerp in 1920, and later put to dramatic use by Hitler at the Eleventh Olympiad, in Berlin, 1936. (However, to Hitler's disgust, an American black, Jesse Owens, failed to demonstrate the inferiority of his race.)

Sport is pursued for its own sake, and exhibits the characteristics that go with that: intense social togetherness, reckless disregard for cost, and a sense of being at home in the world. At the same time, like children's play, of which it is a derivative, sport serves a function: in pre-modern societies it prepares people for war and hardship, and furthers the goal of sexual selection. Like art and literature, sport is a preparation for life which is also a form of life and, noticing this, *Veblen made the following characteristically cynical comment: 'Athletics has an obvious advantage over the classics for the purpose of leisure class learning, since success as an athlete presumes, not only a waste of time, but also a waste of money, as well as the possession of certain highly unindustrial archaic traits of character and temperament'. (*Theory of the Leisure Class.*)

The ceremonial aspect of sport has often been commented upon. Pindar's odes, dedicated to athletes at the Pan-Hellenic games, are intensely religious works, which see victory in the hippodrome as a tribute to the gods, and which describe the contest as something sacred, consecrated to higher powers and to the renewal of Greek society. Certain sports, especially those involving animals – horse racing, bull-fighting, *hunting – recall the quasi-religious and festive character that is invoked by Pindar, and this has suggested to some observers that our feelings for sport are residues of deep-seated needs in the world of the *hunter-gatherer. This might explain the profound involvement of the fan, and the enormous investment of emotion in the fate of national and local football teams.

stabilization
1. Political. The securing of a *regime from the threat of internal overthrow

by revolution or rebellion. Stabilization has been a major preoccupation of US foreign policy in Latin America, where precarious regimes are stabilized through economic and military support. However, political stability does not depend only upon money and arms, but also (so it seems) upon ideology and felt social unity, both of which may be provided by a religion. Neglect of the vital role of religion has sometimes been held responsible for the failure of the policy of stabilization in Iran, although that is clearly only one element in a complex episode.

2. Economic. The attempt by governments to reduce the extent of fluctuations in both income and level of employment.

stagflation

The situation in which rapid *inflation accompanies stagnation of production and high and rising unemployment. It is one of the most difficult of all problems faced by a government since there seems to be no remedy for the one evil that will not also exacerbate the other.

stakeholder

A neologism, denoting any person or group that has a vital interest (a 'stake') in the success or conduct of an enterprise. In discussing business enterprises the stakeholder is usually contrasted with the shareholder. The latter has risked his money in the firm, which is therefore bound to him by a fiiduciary obligation not to waste or squander it. The former simply has an interest in the firm, whose obligation towards him is only that laid down by the general principles of morality and law. Stakeholders include all those whose interests are affected by a business – local communities, the general public, passers-by, in addition to consumers, employees and suppliers, who are also bound to it by contract.

Sometimes a distinction is made between a narrow and a wide definition of the term. In the narrow sense stakeholders are all those groups who are vital to the survival and success of the firm (employees, customers, suppliers and so on), while in the wider sense stakeholders include any group that can affect or be affected by the firm. Clearly a firm has an interest in satisfying the interests of its stakeholders in the narrow sense, that it does not have in satisfying the interests of its stakeholders in the wider sense.

Emphasis on the stakeholder is part of the growing attempt by businesses (especially large multinational corporations) to present an appealing public image, and to avert negative campaigns by lobbyists and pressure groups. It has even been seen as an attempt to align the capitalist enterprise with the principles of *Kant's moral philosophy. (E. Freeman and W. Evan, *The Stakeholder Theory of the Modern Corporation: Kantian Capitalism*, fourth edn, 1994.) *See* *corporate social responsibility.

Stakhanovism

In 1935, Alexei Stakhanov, a miner in the Ukraine, increased output by organizing a group of subordinate workers, and thus became the hero of Soviet labour, a kind of ideologically purified version of the entrepreneur, motivated not by material but by 'moral' incentives, and paid accordingly. As a result, a system of 'norms' was introduced which determined the minimum amount which must be produced by every labourer at a certain wage. Stakhanov, hated ever since by Soviet workers, gave his name to the system of organized labour and pay differentials in the USSR.

Stalinism

The form of *despotism exemplified by Stalin's exercise of power in the USSR, the main characteristics of which are: complete control of all media for propaganda purposes; systematic elimination of opposition, without respect for morality or law (although suitably glossed by ideas of 'revolutionary morality' – *see* *Lenin – and *socialist legality); mobilization of popular support around the leader; 'five-year plans' designed to secure production by force; elaborate propaganda designed to reconcile every aspect of policy with Marxist-Leninist principles; unswerving dogmatism in all matters, regardless of competence; fear of and pitiless retribution against all those thought to be traitors to the ruling party and its purposes.

Some argue that Stalinism is implicit in Leninism, and the necessary consequence of the attempt to use Marxist doctrine as a programme of action rather than a theory of history (*cf.* *myth, *Sorel). The infrequency of Marxist-Leninist governments without dictatorship might be held to confirm this. Others prefer to see Stalinism simply as the offshoot of the criminal characteristics of Stalin himself, although this thought continues to present difficulties to a certain kind of historical materialist, since it seems to imply that history is made by individuals, rather than by the 'material forces' that project them into eminence.

stare decisis

More precisely: *stare decisis et non quieta movere*: to stand by decisions and not to move what has been settled. *Stare decisis* is the fundamental axiom of the doctrine of *precedent, and the root of all *common law, according to which previous judicial decisions must be followed if applicable. A decision can in fact be questioned, but only by a higher court, and when deemed binding by the highest court is immune from appeal in law. However, a decision is binding only in

respect of its **ratio decidendi* – i.e. the principle of the original judgment – and not in respect of *obiter dicta*. The *ratio decidendi* may be implied rather than express, and hence there is still room for the judicial manoeuvre of 'distinguishing a case', whereby it is decided that a precedent, while binding, does not apply. Making sense of the doctrine of *stare decisis* is vital to understanding both law and judicial independence.

state

A term which derives its modern usage from *Machiavelli, but concerning which there is no commonly accepted definition. A fundamental divide separates those who adhere to the *rights theory of politics, from those who adhere to the *power theory, and this is often reflected in definitions of 'the state'. As an example of the first, consider *Hegel: 'the state is the actuality of the ethical idea'; as an example of the second, *Weber: the state is the organization which 'monopolizes legitimate violence over a given territory' (where a 'legitimate' power is simply one that has bestowed upon itself the artificial sanction, itself no more than a special kind of power, of law).

Both views begin from the same fundamental distinction, that between state and *society, and both recognize that law is essential to the first, but may not be essential to the second. This same intuition underlies the idea of the state in *international law: an *association of persons, living in a determinate part of the earth's surface, legally organized and personified, and associated for their own government. Two special cases recognized in the literature are the city state, (**polis*), and the *nation state, both of which accord well with that definition. While somewhat perfunctory, the legal idea serves to identify the class of objects that have been discussed by such thinkers as Machiavelli, *Hobbes, *Bodin and Hegel. The many obscurities are revealed, however, once we break down the definition into its components:

(i) association among persons for the end of government;

(ii) legal organization: i.e. the power of the government is exercised partly through law, and hence may be determined and limited in certain cases by a *constitution;

(iii) attachment to a particular *territory over which *jurisdiction is exercised;

(iv) personification: i.e. the state is both a juristic *person in international law, and a kind of quasi-person in popular thinking, with rights, obligations and also a personal identity over time distinct from the identity of its members. Furthermore the state has *agency and *responsibility, whether or not in law.

Each of the four components presents difficulties, some of which are explored elsewhere in this dictionary. It is worth noting that (ii) is not the same as a *rule of law, which exists only as a special case of it; there can also be states which are without *constitutions. (Despite those legal positivists, such as *Kelsen, who try to identify a state with a system of *positive law.) Moreover the idea of *sovereignty is not explicitly mentioned in any of (i) to (iv), although, on some views, it could be thought to be implied by (i) and perhaps also by (iv).

Since (i) to (iv) are probably all independent, or at least separately discussable, it is open to theorists to deny any of them while attempting to keep the remainder. Thus some would deny (i), arguing that political association is not 'for an end' and, even if it were, it would not be for the end of *government*. (*See*, e.g., *Oakeshott.)

Others might deny (ii), on the grounds that it is parochial, over-influenced by the procedures of Western politics, and does not take account, for example, of *oriental despotism, whether historical or 'actually existing'. Condition (iv) too meets with opposition, largely on ideological grounds, from those *individualists who think that only human beings can have rights and obligations, and that to personify the state in any other than a legal sense is to begin to worship it (*see* *minimal state). Finally (iii) can be seen to be of a different character from the other conditions, on account of the extralegal reference to territory. Again this might be thought to be a parochial condition, expressive of the localized sentiments of attachment to the *polis* and the nation state. Could there not be a state without territory (e.g. the Jewish state, at certain periods during its history: *see* *Jewish law)? On the other hand it is very difficult to detach the idea of *jurisdiction from that of territory, just as it is difficult to imagine the fully political being who has *no* local attachments.

That last idea, however, introduces a fairly common use of the concept of the state, in which the state and the citizen are collectively contrasted to the sovereign and the subject; it being supposed that the first two define a distinctively modern kind of relationship, and a corresponding virtue of citizenship, which abstracts from blind obedience and unthinking attachments towards a reasoned respect towards the law. Thus the state might be held to be a name for a special sub-class of associations conforming to (i) to (iv): that in which the 'legal-rational' system of authority has come to replace the traditional system of obedience. (Such a view takes inspiration from Weber.)

state of nature

The state of man outside society which is invoked by political philosophers either as a deliberate fiction, in order to separate *nature from convention in human affairs, or as a hypothesis about the condition of man before the existence of society, or as a hypothesis about his condition should society be taken away. If there is a *natural law, then it is valid in a state of nature. However, it may not be *upheld* there, and *Hobbes, who believed in natural law, thought that, without a coercive *sovereign, such a law would not and could not be enforced, so that the life of man in the state of nature is 'solitary, poor, nasty, brutish and short'. Others (e.g. *Locke) have taken a more sympathetic view of it, while yet others (especially *Hegel and *Marx) have rejected the whole conception as incoherent, for example because it supposes the existence of rational, autonomous *persons outside the condition of society which alone makes the existence of such beings possible (Hegel), or because it imagines men in a state of nature disposed to form just those relations which capitalism and the market economy fit them for (Marx, glossed by C.B. Macpherson).

states' rights

The US constitutional doctrine that the states of the Union should enjoy exclusive exercise of any powers not expressly granted to the federal US constitution. Advocates of states' rights have been active in US politics since the beginning of the Union, their initial inspiration coming partly from *Jefferson's insistence upon the principle of *federalism as essential to a certain kind of limited government. Movements for the advancement of states' rights continue to oppose the accumulation of legislative and political authority in the federal government, especially in matters of local concern. In this they may often enter into conflict with bodies such as the *civil rights movement, which attempt to force local communities to conform to strictures contained in the federal constitution.

statism

See *étatisme.

status

A term sometimes used by sociologists (notably *Weber) to denote a kind of *social stratification that is not a matter either of *class or of political position. The term is used vaguely and inconsistently, but the main idea is that of a stratification based in social recognition rather than in any kind of material power, although, because social recognition is itself a kind of power, it is hard to draw the line with precision. Thus a group that sets itself apart through social relations, style and manners, may be composed of members from a variety of economic divisions within society, and yet be regarded, both by itself and by others, as somehow 'at the top' of a social scale. Some think that this might still be true of certain traditional European aristocracies, despite their more or less total loss of control over economic and political life.

It is sometimes argued that 'status groups' have replaced classes as the recognizable social divisions in modern societies. Such groups are characterized by rapid *social mobility within the *hierarchy, and the absence of any hereditary qualification for membership: hereditary power and influence may be a sufficient condition for membership of a high status group, but it is never a necessary condition.

Some sociologists estimate status in terms of the 'reward system' in a society, where reward includes every kind of advantage offered by social life. This leads to more status groups than traditional class theories cater for, but it is not clear whether the status group theory is supposed to replace those theories or merely to add to them. Others, influenced by Weber's original claims that the system of privilege and honour is independent of the system of economic control (the class system), try to analyse status groups in terms of the opinion of distinction that is attached to each of them. Some even argue that the *media are one of the most important influences in the creation of modern status groups, so that TV personalities lie at the highest point in the social scale, with subordinate positions identified in terms of their greater or lesser proximity to that position of eminence. Defenders of traditional class analysis are apt to say that opinions of distinction are to be *explained* in terms of class, and do not define it. The area is one of confusion, exacerbated by the fact that social groupings have all been subjected to the solvents of *democratization and the media.

status quo

'The existing state of affairs', or 'previous state of affairs' (*status quo ante*). The expression has been in use since the 1830s to refer to the maintenance of or return to an existing social or political order. There is always a *status quo* at the back of conservative thinking on society, which furnishes the idea of an imperfect but nevertheless achieved social order which it would be better to conserve than to destroy.

statutes

Those laws which are laid down in statutes and statutory instruments, as distinct from *common law, which is the sum of principles contained in and developed through the decisions of judges, but not otherwise sanctioned

by a legislative body. Statutes may be written, or they may be preserved (as were certain parts of Anglo-Saxon law) in the form of an oral tradition of maxims. The verse form of some of the ancient systems of law (e.g. the fragments of Solon that remain to us) may be explained by the need to memorize the law for recital at the critical moment.

Under UK law statute is in theory of higher authority than common law, and always prevails when the two conflict. However, statutes can usually be applied only after judicial interpretation, so that, despite being supreme as the expression of the will of the Queen in Parliament, they may be made to conform to the common law. While it may sometimes be inexpressible, the common law is always by its nature intelligible; the same is not true of statutes.

stereotype

A summary characterization of a human group, usually arising from and fortifying prejudices for or against that group, and used as a template into which individual members of the group are made to fit. Stereotyping is probably a necessary element in any attempt to cope with groups of which one is not a member, but the possibilities of injustice to which it gives rise are now all too familiar. It has all the virtues, and all the vices, of *prejudice, of which it is a special case.

Stirner, Max (pseudonym of Johann Caspar Schmidt) (1806–56)

German philosopher and polemicist who defended, in his book *The Ego and its Own* (1844), a radical *individualism which anticipated *Nietzsche, and which also influenced nineteenth-century political thinkers such as *Marx and the anarchists. Stirner's philosophy is based on the idea that nothing is justified for me except the expression and extension of my own will, there being no external authority or morality which has any objective force. God is dead, and all religion is a ploy by other people to make me surrender some part of my 'own'. In the face of the absurd demands of modern society, I must act so as to enhance my power – over things, over people, and over my own instincts and appetites. Stirner's influence, in later periods was largely confined to *fascists and *national socialists. *See* *egoism, *Young Hegelians.

stoicism

A system of teachings named after the *stoa poikile* (painted porch) in Athens, where Zeno of Cilium began to lecture around 300 BC. Stoicism flourished for over 500 years, and it is normal to distinguish the early, middle and late stoas, the last being exemplified by Epictetus and Marcus Aurelius (slave and emperor) in Rome. Stoicism was a systematic attempt to describe nature, beginning from principles of reason or *logos*. The resulting view of the world was a form of *materialism. Human reason is of the same stuff as the cosmic reason, which we understand as fate, necessity or providence, and to which we must submit in consciousness of its governance over our lives. That consciousness is our highest freedom and aim, and the thing which secures our happiness. This stoic paradox of freedom – that freedom is the consciousness of necessity – recurs throughout the history of social and political thought, for example in ideas that might be attributed to *Spinoza, to *Kant and to *Hegel. Actual stoic morality was varied, and although all stoics preached the need for virtue, and identified the happiness of man with a kind of spiritual calm (*apatheia*), not all of them accepted (what their name now implies) a strenuous resignation in the face of suffering and misfortune. The stoic political doctrines tended to be *universalist, founded in a conception of man as *rational agent, with universal rights as a citizen of the 'cosmopolis' (*see* *Cicero, *cosmopolitanism).

strategic capability

The military capacity of a state with 'strategic' weapons (*see* *strategy). First-strike capability is possessed by a force which can itself be destroyed by an enemy strike, and so which must be deployed first, in a 'pre-emptive strike'. Second-strike capability is possessed by a force that can survive a strike sufficiently intact to inflict unacceptable damage. Counter-value capability is that of a force sufficient only to destroy the enemy's cities and installations; counterforce capability is that of a force that may cripple the adversary's strategic military powers and still leave room for the destruction of his cities and industries. These technical terms are of some use in formulating the various levels at which strategic thinking must be conducted in modern conditions.

strategy

Greek: *strategos*, the office of a general, from *stratos*, an army. The art of the commander-in-chief, i.e. the art of projecting and achieving the larger objectives of a campaign; as opposed to 'tactics': the art of local deployment and small-scale manoeuvre through which a strategic purpose is achieved. The division is not exact, but corresponds to a division among weapons between the strategic (those which intimate the final aim of battle), and the tactical (those that are employed during battle as a matter of course). Roughly speaking this distinction has come to mean, weapons which will bring the show to an end, and those that will ensure its continuance. (*See* *strategic capability.)

The term 'strategy' has been given a more precise meaning in *decision theory, where it means a set of plans to cover all contingencies, and the study of those conflicts which require such overall planning is now an important part of *game theory, recent thinkers having attempted to use that theory to cast light on the nature of strategic problems. (Although it should be noted that, in game theory, 'strategy' may sometimes mean simply 'option'.) It is sometimes argued that certain modern strategies are based on illegitimate or ill-considered attempts to extend the solutions for two-person games to what are essentially *n*-person games, and that a proper attention to the theory of the latter will show such strategies as *deterrence; for example, to be far from *optimal. Game theory has thus influenced both the vocabulary in terms of which strategy is discussed, and the situations with which it is compared. One theorist writes: 'Strategy . . . is not concerned with the efficient *application* of force but with the *exploitation of potential force*. It is concerned not just with enemies who dislike each other but with partners who distrust or disagree with each other. It is concerned not just with the division of gains and losses between two claimants but with the possibility that particular outcomes are worse (better) for *both* claimants than certain other outcomes. In the terminology of game theory, most interesting international conflicts are not "constant-sum games" but "variable-sum games": the sum of the gains of the participants involved is not fixed so that more for one inexorably means less for the other. There is a common interest in reaching outcomes that are mutually advantageous' (Thomas C. Schelling, *The Strategy of Conflict*, 1960).

stratification
In sociology, the formation of social strata – such as those of *class, or *status. Not a process, but a condition, which is generally understood either in *functional terms, or in terms of *power relations.

Strauss, David (1808–74)
German writer on religious and philosophical themes. *See* *Young Hegelians.

Strauss, Leo (1899–1973)
Political theorist of German-Jewish origins and student of *Heidegger. On the advent of the Third Reich, Strauss emigrated first to the UK and then to the US, there to found a school of political science which has been enormously influential in establishing the subject in American universities, as a humane rather than a scientific discipline. Strauss was influenced by his study of ancient philosophy (especially *Plato), by *Schmitt, and also by his reading of the US Constitution and the thinking that created it. His own views were unsystematic, but involved a defence of the *rule of law and the balance of interests achieved by the US Constitution. Strauss was opposed to *historicism, by which he meant the habit of referring all ideas to the historical context from which they arose. Political science, he believed, must aim for the trans-historical perspective, from which ideas could be judged for their validity. Strauss believed that he had found that perspective in the idea of *natural right, which he understood in the sense of the American Declaration of Independence, rather than in the sense adopted by *Aquinas.

Even if historicism is the enemy of political science, however, Strauss believed that in studying the classics of political theory it is always necessary to 'read between the lines' in order to discover the rhetorical goal of the writer. Political theory is itself part of politics, and politics is the sphere in which people can achieve, by painstaking and arduous means, the accommodation required for their common fulfilment. Strauss deplored the fascist, communist and socialist movements that were tearing Europe apart, and deplored equally the failure of American intellectuals to appreciate the profound thinking behind their legal, political and social institutions, and the fact that these things are far more easily lost than won. Much US political science has been stamped with Strauss's *conservatism, so that the adjective 'Straussian' has acquired a distinct sense in the world of political theory – meaning roughly conservative, *constitutionalist, and rooted in deep readings of the classics (readings, however, which expose the complexity and ambiguity of the author's real intentions). Strauss's more distinguished pupils include Allan Bloom and Harvey Mansfield.

Strauss's achievement, in founding a school of political science within the American academy, has had repercussions outside the academy also, with 'Straussians' obtaining influential positions in government and administration under the conservative presidency of George W. Bush. This in turn has led to an industry of scholarship devoted to exposing Strauss as a malign and perverse influence, responsible for *neo-conservatism, *tort reform and the war in Iraq. It could be, however, that the critics are thinking of Johann Strauss the younger.

strict liability

In the law of *tort, the kind of liability that may often be created by statute, but which, until *Rylands* v. *Fletcher*, 1868, was not known in *common law; strict liability occurs when a person may be held liable for the consequences of some act or omission, whatever the state of mind from which it flows, and whether or not he has acted as a *reasonable man. It is an important feature of English and American common law that they do not tolerate strict liability in the criminal law, and judges will interpret statutes which create crimes in such a way as to suppose that an element of 'guilty mind' is required, unless the statute is very carefully worded.

Some criminal codes allow a distinction between 'felonies and misdemeanours' (abolished in UK law, though not in US law), and allow only the latter to include offences of strict liability. It is also normal to provide that offences of strict liability cannot later be cited so as to damage the interests of the person who committed them.

strike

1. A form of *industrial action.

2. A term used in the theory of *strategic capability, as in 'first-strike', and 'second-strike' strategies.

structural unemployment

Unemployment created by some basic change in the structure and conditions, especially technological conditions, in an economy. It may persist for a long time, because such change tends to make the skills of a whole class of workers redundant. To overcome structural unemployment governments have paid much attention to the problem of the location of industries and the retraining of the work force. (*Contrast* *frictional unemployment.)

structural violence (also: structural oppression)

An expression used by *neo-Marxist critiques of liberal and democratic society, probably under the influence of *Sorel. The supposition is that *violence can take many forms besides that of *confrontation, and is often concealed within the 'structures' of a society, so as to oppress particular classes or particular groups of opinion within it. Thus some argue that the economic structure of capitalism does repeated and systematic violence to people who are employed in it. This structural violence may be contained even within those institutions – such as parliamentary representation – that are most often put forward as proof of the peaceable and conciliatory character of the 'bourgeois' state. This is because the 'freedoms' and 'rights' thereby protected are selectively defined, so as to coincide with the existing privileges of the bourgeoisie. Hence (supposedly) the institution is used (rather like a court of law in a *show trial) to legitimate the continuing violence which one class directs against another.

The idea has been very influential; a notable use of it was by the French *New Left philosopher Maurice Merleau-Ponty (1908–61), who in his *Humanism and Terror*, 1947, excused some of the crimes of *Stalinism by comparing them advantageously with the more concealed, insidious and ineradicable crimes contained within the capitalist economic order.

structuralism

A much misused term for any science, pseudo-science or critical method which finds the significance of human things (especially social and cultural products) in their structure. Structuralist theories have been proposed for the interpretation of all of the following: actions, rituals, religions; texts, clothes, buildings; poetry, music, architecture; and, most important perhaps, since it is often thought to be the root product of any culture, language.

To have structure, an object must have parts united under ordered relations. To say that structure is *the* determinant (rather than *a* determinant) of meaning is to say that it is not the parts themselves but the relations among them that are significant. This does not mean that the meaning remains unchanged when parts are changed, but that it remains invariant with respect to any *systematic* change of parts. Thus a short tone followed by a long tone has a Morse Code meaning. If the short tone becomes long, the signal may retain its meaning, provided the long tone becomes proportionately longer.

Confusion has been caused by the fact that there are two kinds of theory which might be called 'structuralist':

(i) the structuralist *anthropology of Claude Lévi-Strauss and his followers, which finds significances by discovering repeated patterns. It is supposed that relations (exemplified, e.g., by rituals) remain unchanged from culture to culture, while the parts related may be systematically different. It is then argued that meaning attaches to the recurring pattern of relations (the 'structure') and not to the local variants that are fitted into it;

(ii) the linguist's theory of grammatical structure, according to which the meaning of a sentence is determined in part by its structure – i.e. not merely by the words employed, but by the rules governing their conjunction.

In case (i) what is interpreted is the pattern divorced from its component parts; in case (ii) what is interpreted is the *whole*, as structured from its parts. The two kinds of interpretation are entirely different, since only in the first is the structure thought to have an independent significance. (Hence the word 'meaning' does not mean the same in (i) and (ii).) The confounding of the two has led to the impression that everything that has significant structure (architecture, music and literature, for example) also has the structure of language, and is to be interpreted in terms that might be equally used in the interpretation of linguistic signs. (One of the thoughts behind 'structuralist' criticism.) The confusion has even been extended to political theory, e.g. by *Althusser.

Structuralism in literary theory has its roots in the work of the Swiss linguist, Ferdinand de Saussure, whose *Course in General Linguistics* (1906) contains the famous (perhaps also notorious) thesis that 'in language there are only differences *without positive terms*', meaning not merely that words have no meaning in isolation, but that their meaning is exhausted by the distinctions and contrasts between them – so that the meaning of 'hot' is given by the contrast with 'cold'. Saussure's theories seemed to support the view that meaning in language is *entirely* a matter of structure. French literary theorists worked this thesis together with two others: the *formalist claim that form is the true conduit of artistic meaning, and the *Marxist claim that the meaning of cultural arte-facts lies in their *ideological function. The result, in the writings of Roland Barthes and other writers of the 1960s, was a kind of trenchant and pseudo-technical approach to literary texts which was stiff with anti-bourgeois sarcasm. The obscurity of the literary analysis was compensated for by the charm of the political commitment, with the result that 'structuralism' became part of the repertoire of Parisian leftism during the 1960s and 1970s. Those who rebelled against it on the left often did so because they were hostile to structure as such – either because it is the embodiment of social *power (*Foucault), or because meaning is revealed only in the act of *decon-struction (Derrida). Hence arose the broad church of *post-structuralism, which combined the leftist commit-ment of the Parisian intellectual, a

magpie-like accumulation of glittering technicalities and a kind of nihilistic rejection of all organized meanings, whether artistic, social or political.

subject

1. Subject of consciousness. The subject features in Kantian, post-Kantian and idealist philosophy as the central protagonist in a complex drama. In *Fichte, *Hegel and their successors, the subject is distinguished by its character as a 'for itself': it is that which is revealed to itself and whose character is connected with its self-revelation. The fissure between subject and object is the place at which all metaphysical, moral and religious questions congregate. The self-conscious being is both subject and object, and it is one of the striking claims of Hegelian idealism that I can come to know myself fully as subject only if I am also realized as object, in a world of objective rights, duties and moral relations. (*See* *self-realization.) The metaphysics of the subject played a crucial role in the development of nineteenth-century German political thought and is fundamental to the philosophies of *Marx, *Nietzsche, *Heidegger and *Sartre, to name but four.

2. A being subject to the power of another, and compelled therefore to obey the other's commands. *Spinoza wrote that 'it is the fact of obedience, not the motive for obedience, which makes a man a subject', meaning to imply that the relation of subject to sovereign is not dependent upon consent but simply upon the ability of the second to command the first.

It is often pointed out that the rela-tion sovereign/subject has been super-seded in political thinking by that of state/citizen. The change is not merely a change in words, since it has been accompanied by changed ideas of *sovereignty and *political obligation.

The relation between sovereign and subject is one of *command and *obedience, whereas (it is supposed) that between state and citizen is one of mutual *obligation. However, the distinction is not as clear cut as that implies, since the two relations are not incompatible, and on some views occur together in all political arrangements.

subsidiarity

Term of Roman Catholic theology, given its current sense in an *encyclical by Pope Pius XI in 1931, in which it is used to describe the decentralization of power and authority in the Roman Catholic Church, through the institution of the episcopate. This institution allows decisions to be taken always at the lowest level compatible with the overarching authority of the church. From this source it was appropriated by *Röpke, in his effort to develop a social and political theory in which the market economy would be reconciled with local community and the 'little platoon'. Subsidiarity, in Röpke's understanding of the term, refers to the absolute right of local communities to take decisions for themselves, including the decision to surrender the matter to a larger forum. Subsidiarity places an absolute brake upon centralizing powers, by permitting their involvement only when requested.

The term was adopted by the *European Community during the early 1990s, in order to describe the residual powers that would be withheld by the member states following the achievement of full political union. In this use it has the opposite sense from that intended by Röpke, providing a comprehensive authorization to the EU institutions to expropriate whatever powers they might deem to be theirs. By purporting to grant powers in the very word that removes them, the term 'subsidiarity' wraps the whole idea of decentralized government in mystery. Many commentators therefore assume that it simply denotes the project of a *federal Europe, with national governments autonomous only at the 'subsidiary' level, and the European institutions uniquely empowered to determine which questions belong to the 'subsidiary' and which to the 'European' level. If this is so, then subsidiarity simply means the replacement of sovereignty by delegated powers.

subsidy

See *subsidization.

subsidization

The payment of sums by a government in order to make the price of a good lower, and the reward to the producer higher, than free *market forces would otherwise cause them to be. Subsidies have played an important part in *interventionist policies, especially in the field of *agriculture. Since farmers are vulnerable to conditions, such as bad weather, animal diseases and general environmental degradation that they cannot control, their survival from year to year is always in doubt. Although in a bad year food can be imported from more hospitable climates, dependence on imports renders a country dangerously vulnerable in times of war or international turmoil. Hence many governments have assumed an obligation to subsidize famers in harsh years, so that they will still be around when things get better. The debate over the wisdom of this began in the UK in the nineteenth century, when Parliamentary liberals led by Bright and Cobden attacked the protectionist 'corn laws'.

During the twentieth century the regime of subsidies expanded under its own momentum, so that land use, crops, 'set aside' and even unproductive residence on a piece of farm land now attract subsidies from the state. In France, where the Napoleonic inheritance law has led to the minute subdivision of land among members of farming families, the burden of subsidies has become enormous, and the effort to externalize the cost of this through the *Common Agriculural Policy of the *European Union has created both internal dissension within the EU itself, and adverse effects on developing nations, which can no longer export food to Europe because of protectionist measures.

substitution

1. Economics. In many areas one consumer good may provide a substitute for another should conditions prevail which prevent attainment of the good desired initially. Thus two goods are substitutes if a rise in the price of one causes an increase in demand for the other. Such substitute relationships depend on the goods in question having similar functions or administering to a similar taste. Burgundy and claret, for example, may be mutual substitutes.

Third World countries often adopt 'import substitution policies', i.e. policies encouraging the substitution of home-produced goods for imported ones, and it seems that the 'politics of substitution' is increasingly important, as governments attempt to persuade citizens to buy the goods made at home.

2. Politics. A *strategy advocated by *Trotsky, whereby a militant organization (in the particular case, the Red Army) takes over the functions of the professional classes – especially schools, hospitals, local councils – and substitutes for the holders of every office some individual allied to the central cause. At a certain moment the whole of the *bourgeoisie finds itself suddenly and unexpectedly without effective power.

subversion

Undermining of an institution or of the state, often by *infiltrating offices and turning them against themselves, but also by any clandestine activity designed to influence the victim or to leave him without the support of the institutions upon which he relies. (*Cf.* *substitution.) The possibility of subversion is often not recognized in Western law, except in relation to military institutions. However, the US Subversive Activities Control Act 1950, designed to root out communists from offices of state, recognized subversion as a danger to which the US was exposed, while leaving the question of what constitutes subversion more or less unanswered, apart from the stipulation that it requires an intention to damage the interests of the Union.

A 'war of subversion' is one carried on by giving military means and moral and economic support to subversive groups within another state.

succession

The passing on of a title, whether to property, to kingship, or to rights of government. Expectations about *legitimacy are active in determining legal rights of succession. The principle of the 'entail' in feudal and quasi-feudal law, whereby an estate is held under a right of use for life, and then passed to a legally determined successor or heir, is not accepted in modern systems as a normal property right. In English law, all entails become *trusts of property, and are construed so as to permit transfer of the property during the lifetime of any tenant. Some feudal laws operate as though all property reverts on death to the sovereign, to be redistributed by him in accordance with the law (which is also his will). The idea that someone might *appoint* his successors, by will, seems to imply the right to transfer property even after death, and so has the effect of making a person sovereign over his own property. The feudal principle of 'succession according to law' still applies to titles of nobility and kingship (the latter subject to the Act of Settlement 1700 in the UK). Moreover, the idea of the sovereign as party to all succession has re-entered political practice, in the form of taxes designed to return property to the state on the death of the tenant. *See* *death taxes.

succession problem

Political systems ought to last longer than those who control them. There therefore arises the 'succession problem': how are the successors to the highest offices of state discovered or appointed? One way of seeing democracy is as a general answer to that problem. In tyrannies the problem is acute, since all procedures for appointing a successor depend on the will of the existing tenant, who will usually refuse to relinquish power when alive and who will be powerless when dead. Hereditary monarchy can be seen as another, and more mystical, solution to the succession problem – one that lifts the appointment of the successor out of the realm of human choice entirely, even the choice of the monarch himself, so that political continuity acquires a 'God-given' character.

succession states

Those states which, on the break-up of the Austro-Hungarian and Ottoman empires in 1918, succeeded to the full sovereign rights previously possessed over their territories by the Emperor or the Sultan.

Sufism

The religion and practice of the Sufi sect of *Islam. The etymology of the term (*tawassuf*) is disputed: it is probably from *suf* – wool – on account of the woolly garments of the Sufi fraternities; but it could be from Greek *sophia* – wisdom – recording the pronounced influence of Greek philosophy, notably that of *Plato and Neoplatonism, on the early practitioners of Sufism. Schools of Sufism arose during the eighth to eleventh centuries under the Abbasid caliphs, in Basra and Baghdad, and also in what is now Northern Iran. Their doctrine is a-political and directed to the salvation of the individual soul. Salvation comes from the effort to achieve, first, the 'stations' (*maqâmât*) which come through suppressing the ego by means of spiritual exercises so as to arrive at a selfless trust in God, and secondly the 'states', which are gifts of God's grace, leading to the final bliss, in which the individual soul is absorbed into the divine essence, enjoying mystical knowledge and all-embracing love. Sufism was at first regarded as a heresy, but the philosopher al-Ghazali (d. 1111) persuaded the theologians that it is compatible with the teachings of the Koran. It became institutionalized in fraternities and orders, and received its most comprehensive statement in the monumental work on 'the unity of being' by Ibn 'Arabi (d. 1240). The close parallels with Christian mysticism, and the philosophy of forgiveness and love, have made Sufism a source of reconciliation in the otherwise dangerous conflicts of faiths in the Middle East.

suffrage

Originally an intercessionary prayer, then a vote or opinion for or against something, finally the power to vote at an election. 'Universal suffrage' thus denotes the right of all to vote, and 'extension of the suffrage' an extension of that right to persons formerly deprived of it. Hence, since 1906, a 'suffragette' has meant any woman active (or perhaps militant) in the cause of the right of women to vote in an election.

suffragette
See *suffrage.

suicide
The causes of suicide are as many as the ways in which the will to live may fail. *Durkheim argued, however, that suicide in modern society owes its extent to the upsurge of a single set of closely related causes which show this most private and individual of acts to be, he thought, a gesture whose meaning is inherently social. Suicide does not occur outside the social context, and has to be seen as a response to social conditions, rather than to individual misfortune. The normal condition responsible is that of *anomie* in the social order, which causes the individual to become obsessed with the arbitrariness of his own existence to the point of finding no answer to the question, Why not die? In effect, *anomie* causes the rejection of the individual from the social organism in which he has his being, so that his suicide can be seen as analogous to the death of an amputated limb.

Durkheim also identifies other kinds of suicide, e.g. that inspired by a spirit of *fatalism, and draws a broad division between 'altruistic' and 'egoistic' motives for suicide, all having a social explanation similar to the one given. His statistical methods have, however, been criticized, since they may serve to explain variations, but not the actual level of suicide at any particular moment. Moreover, there seem to be patterns of suicide which are preserved through all changes in social and political conditions. Since records have been kept, for example, the Hungarians have been far more disposed to kill themselves than the people of any other nation. The imposition and overthrow of communism made little difference to this vital statistic.

Durkheim's theory was one of many offered during the early decades of the twentieth century, at a time when people were alarmed at the seeming rise in the number of suicides. Another theory, propagated in an influential book by *Masaryk, attributed the rise in the suicide rate to *half-education. Studies of the phenomenon continue to emerge, one of the most interesting from the contemporary point of view being that of the US psychotherapist Leslie H. Farber, which discusses the 'life of suicide' (*The Ways of the Will*, 1990). The suicide, according to Farber, is both toying with the arbitrariness of his life, and endeavouring to overcome it. By acting as though, at every moment, dying is within his grasp, he makes the arbitrariness of existence into his own doing, and so exerts a kind of terminal control over it. The final gesture acquires a kind of meaning, by advertising its lack of meaning.

None of the prevalent theories seems adequate, however, to the new phenomenon of the 'suicide bomber' – which began with the *kamikaze* pilots of Japan in the Second World War and has reached monstrous proportions with the new breed of *Islamist 'martyr'. Here the desire to die is only part of the motive: the desire to kill is integrally connected with it.

sultanate
The dominion of a sultan (Arabic: sovereign or sovereign power). 'Sultan' was the title normally borne by an Islamic prince or ruler under monarchical government. A sultanate is to be distinguished from the *caliphate, which, while technically a form of rule, has its ultimate significance in religious conceptions of legitimacy. The difference between the title Caliph and the title Sultan roughly corresponds to the distinction between *authority and *power. The former title has often been held by

men who were the subjects, even the near prisoners, of the 'sultans' whose rule they authorized.

summit diplomacy

(from 'parley at the summit', a phrase from Winston Churchill's election speech of 1950). Personal negotiations between heads of state or ministers of government, usually of *superpowers.

sumptuary law

A law restricting extravagance and display in food, drink, furnishings, dress, and so on. In other words, a law controlling *conspicuous consumption. Originally such laws had the function of confining ostentation to the sovereign and his immediate court, but they were also imposed for moral and religious reasons. Their effect was to separate economic power from the display of power, so that people could not, by the mere fact of *accumulation, create about themselves the magnificence and dignity which attracted sentiments of obedience.

Sunni

From Arabic *sunnah*, custom. Sunni Muslims are the orthodox believers, who hold that infallible guidance ended with the death of the Prophet, so that the Koran and the *sunnah* (the deeds and sayings of the Prophet) represent the final authority in matters of faith and good conduct. The Prophet's successors owe their entitlement to their election by the community of the faithful, and have no additional authority that enables them to add to those sources of the law. (*Cf.* *Shi'ites.*) Sunni Muslims have accepted the existence of four equally authoritative schools of jurisprudence, whose duty is to derive the law from the guidance given in the Koran and the *sunnah. See *fiqh.*

superpower

A term which seems to mean any state able to threaten and negotiate on behalf of uncountably many, and which in practice has denoted the US and the former USSR.

superstition

From Latin, *superstare*, 'to stand over or against something' (i.e. in awe). Superstition means any unreasonable awe and reverence towards non-existent things, or towards actual things on the supposition that they are signs of something which is in fact non-existent. Superstition is to be distinguished from *myth, in that it is based on a sense of human fragility before the unknown, while myth may indicate human confidence, leading to a description of the world as already shaped by and adapted to human will and agency. Superstition is also to be distinguished from other kinds of unreasoning belief – such as *prejudice.

Traditionally superstitions were associated with *religion. However, some profess to find 'secular superstitions' in the beliefs of modern people, such as that in inevitable human *progress. This is regarded as a superstition on the ground of a structural similarity with traditional examples: it is an unreasoning belief caused by awe and by fear of the unknown.

superstructure

See *base.

supply

The quantity of a good or service which suppliers make available for purchase at a given price; it generally varies (often increasing) with the price; hence the 'supply function', or 'supply curve', which plots that variation.

supply and demand, law of

Supply and demand are often identified as the principal market forces, which make themselves felt through the *price system. The 'law of supply and demand' states that these forces have a *natural* tendency to equilibrium, since if supply exceeds demand, price will fall, causing supply to fall and demand to rise; and vice versa when demand exceeds supply.

supply of money
See *money supply.

supranational
Institutions and laws are supranational when not confined in their power and application to any one *state, and when not of such a kind as to have power and application internationally (i.e. to all sovereign states). For example, the *European Union is a legally organized supranational body.

supreme court
1. In common parlance, a court from whose decision there is no appeal. The function of a supreme court is usually to settle, either by interpretation of statute, or by exercise of judicial reasoning under the principles of common law, questions of law that have been disputed in some lower court. It does not normally concern itself with questions of fact, but has a decisive political influence in settling the interpretation of law. The powers of the supreme court may indicate the nature and the extent of the rule of law in a jurisdiction. For example, the US Supreme Court is a third body, separate from either house of Congress, which has supreme powers of *judicial review, and which can question the legality of all executive decisions under the constitution. Its judges can be removed only by *impeachment, and its special relation to the constitution, of which it is guardian and interpreter, endows it with enormous political power, exercised for example during the controversies over the *New Deal. (*See* *judicial activism.)

In the UK, by contrast, there is no supreme court separate from the legislature. The House of Lords (which might otherwise deserve the name) sits sometimes as a court, sometimes as a legislative body. Judges may influence legislation, and usually have a great impact when criticizing the technicalities of the drafting of a statute. But apart from that their political influence is secured only by the normal provisions of judicial independence.

2. The phrase 'supreme court' is in fact a technical term in UK constitutional law and applies, under the Judicature Act 1873, not to the House of Lords but to the Court of Appeal and the High Court, which rank successively as inferior courts. Hence the term 'supreme court' is used highly ambiguously in discussing the UK judicial, system: appeal to the highest court is *from* the supreme court. This quirk of usage in fact serves further to reveal the great difference between appeals to the House of Lords and invocation of the US Supreme Court. The second is an essential recourse in securing constitutional rights, whereas the first is simply a final measure in the judicial process, and provides no special guarantee of the rights of the appellant. Hence, political controversies concerning judicial powers have a completely different character under the two constitutions.

surplus value
A term from the *labour theory of value, specifically in its Marxian variants. The capitalist pays the labourer the *exchange-value of his day's labour, which is, it is supposed, the value required to reproduce his *labour-power. This value is in fact produced by hours of work less than the amount contracted for under the wage contract. During the remaining hours of work the labourer produces surplus value – i.e. value over and

above that which the capitalist pays him. This surplus value, it is supposed, accumulates not in his hands but in the hands of the capitalist.

surrender

In *international law, cessation of resistance by one belligerent. Traditionally, 'surrender' has been taken to mean 'surrender on terms', the terms including at least survival and often survival as a political unit, even a unit of a certain sort. The terms may or may not include *capitulations. The idea of surrender has, therefore, been that of an 'arrangement for ending war', a social practice in which reciprocal concessions are made. The demand for 'unconditional surrender' is a new departure, a refusal to abide by that practice. (Unconditional surrender is not a legal concept, but simply a reference to the absence of any informal agreement established through diplomacy, or any express or implied assurance on the part of the victor.) Roosevelt's insistence on unconditional surrender after the Second World War has been denounced, not only for its breach of traditional conventions, but also as a 'theoretical' mistake, and an 'incomprehension of the relations between strategy and policy' (Raymond Aron: *Peace and War*, 1962).

sustainability

The much-trumpeted goal of the environmentalists, which is not always clearly defined. An activity that depends on non-renewable resources which it also depletes is not sustainable, since there will come a point when resources are exhausted. An example is the use of fossil fuels to power motor vehicles. It does not follow that the use of motor vehicles is not sustainable, since they could be powered in another way. A sustainable economy embodies the knowledge of how to renew or replace all the resources on which it depends. The growing recognition that economies depend upon *social capital provides an ecological argument for *conservatism, one goal of which is to renew trust, responsibility, humility, and the little *platoons and family structures which produce those things. The most important of our renewable resources is human beings: social conditions which discourage reproduction, or which impede the transfer of social capital from one generation to the next, are radically unsustainable, since their situation cannot be rectified by new technology.

syndicalism

French: *syndicat*, a trade union. Syndicalism was a militant trade union movement begun in France in the 1890s, and which for a time had the support of *Sorel, who gradually attempted to synthesize the syndicalist ideas with anarchism (*see* *anarcho-syndicalism), and to import his ethic of violence into the practice of *industrial action. The syndicalists wished to transfer all control over the economy not to the state but to the trade unions, conceived as free associations of workers. The syndicalists were influenced by *Proudhon's attacks on the state and property, and rejected politics in favour of industrial action, seeing the strike as the true place of the *class struggle, and the only means of guaranteeing that when control of the means of production was lost by one class it would be gained by the other, rather than transferred to some new centre of privilege and power.

Syndicalism was influential at the turn of the century, leading to the Charter of Amiens, 1906, in which its fundamental claims were enunciated, and to the formation of the American Industrial Workers of the World (the

'Wobblies'). Its influence declined, partly through suspicion among workers of its anarchist tendencies, but a kind of syndicalist spirit has remained alive in French trade union activity, manifesting itself with some force in 1968.

systems theory
See *cybernetics.

Taboo

A Polynesian word, used to mean any activity which is prohibited, or object which is untouchable or unmentionable, as a result of some deep and inarticulate fear of a superstitious or religious kind. On account of *Freud's attempt to explain taboo, and to relate it to states of mind that he thought to be civilized survivals of taboos, it is normal for the word to be used of all kinds of activities that are morally forbidden, but which fall outside the range of our moral rationalizations, incest being the most important example. Freud thought that in this case what is forbidden is also unconsciously desired; because of the strength of the passion, the interdiction must be absolute and unquestionable, and therefore surrounded by superstitious fears. *Sociobiology takes the opposite view: namely that the revulsion against incest gives an evolutionary advantage to those groups who possess it; hence this revulsion is selected over time and requires no other explanation.

tacit communication

*Communication which takes place without exchange of words, or explicit agreement – for example the communication between two car drivers at an unmarked intersection, resulting in one giving way to the other. Such communication may take the form of 'tacit bargaining', in which each participant acts from a sense of what the other may concede in return for a favour; or it may take the form of a 'team spirit', whereby collective *strategy emerges spontaneously among people with an immediate common purpose. Such phenomena are of great importance in social action, underlying foreign policy and military strategy, as well as the *free market and most other forms of *association. The fundamental element consists in the usually rapid and often mysterious exchange of information about reflexive states of mind – i.e. states of mind of the following kind: 'He intends that I intend that he intends that . . .' or 'She expects that I expect that she intends that I intend that . . .'. Some thinkers estimate the importance of *tradition, *culture and *custom as lying, at least partly, in their ability to bring order and intelligibility to the tacit communication upon which social cohesion rests. Some conservative hostility towards *rationalism could be seen as an attempt to define the large area of tacit bargaining in which our greatest efforts towards the rational solution of conflict are expended, and to defend it from the oversimplification which purely explicit bargaining inevitably requires.

tacit consent

Consent that is not expressed but is to be inferred from the intentional activities of the agent. In *Locke's version of the *social contract theory tacit consent to a political arrangement can be inferred when an individual knowingly stays subject to its laws, even when free to leave to some 'vacant place' where he will be subject to no laws at all. *Hume pointed out that even if this is a criterion of consent, it is one that can never be applied, since most places fall under *some* jurisdiction and those that do not are without the necessary comforts and conveniences of the present arrangement, whatever the grounds of its legitimacy. Some reply that, even if alternatives are unattractive, this does not mean that people are *compelled* to remain where they are, so that the existence of consent can be inferred from their remaining. A sovereign who expressly forbids emigration, however, cannot argue that his subjects consented, even tacitly, to his rule.

By analogy other theories of *political obligation can be given a 'tacit' form. Thus some speak of the relation between sovereign and subject as one of tacit *command, meaning that the two parties intentionally behave as though one were commanding the other, even though no commands are actually issued.

tactical voting
Casting one's vote with a view to the final outcome, but not for the candidate or party that one would prefer, say because the preferred candidate has no chance of election and the vote would therefore be a 'wasted vote'. Tactical voting is extremely important in the UK system of elections, where the existence of 'safe seats' and 'marginal constituencies' ensures that only a minority of the seats in the House of Commons regularly change hands. It is less important in systems of *proportional representation, which are designed precisely to avoid the problem of the 'wasted vote'.

tactics
See *strategy.

taliban
Collective noun from Arabic *tâlib*, a student. The title *tâlib* has been common among the *Wahhabi Muslims who have aimed to defend Islam against the infidel: it indicates a status lower than that of the *'ulema*, or religious scholars, while suggesting a life dedicated to the study and practice of Islam. In taking charge of the state, the self-declared Taliban of Afghanistan showed how ineffective their studies had been in equipping them for government.

tariffs
Import tariffs are taxes imposed on imports which may have the purpose either of raising revenue or, more usually, of effecting some long-term economic policy, such as the diminution of a *balance of payments deficit. (*See also* *protectionism.) Tariffs may also be used to counter 'dumping', to protect an industry, or to retaliate against some other state's tariffs. Export tariffs are less frequent, although they may be used to protect or prevent the exportation of essential *raw materials or works of art.

taste
The ability to discriminate among the objects of rational choice when these are chosen for their own sakes – as ends rather than means. In eighteenth-century *aesthetics the concept of taste played an important part in characterizing the nature of aesthetic judgement and the significance of art. Thus *Kant identified the 'judgement of taste' as an essential feature of reason, argued that it proposes a 'common sense' or agreement among rational beings, that it is 'disinterested' in the sense of abstracting from both cognitive and practical concerns, that it sees its object not as a means but as an end in itself, and that it aims to understand the world as purposeful (though without attributing a purpose). Taste reveals to us the meaning of the world as an object of sensory

contemplation – though exactly how this faculty should be cultivated Kant did not reveal.

The term plays a less prominent role in modern aesthetics. Nevertheless, the idea of discrimination between the objects of attention remains as a significant input into all social and political thinking. Our conduct is governed not merely by *morality and *law, but by rational preference: we seek out objects, works of art and people for our own entertainment, and we are in the habit of discriminating between them. Manners are a matter of taste, as is the company one keeps and the language one uses. On the whole people must share their tastes if they are to live together in harmony, and things judged to be in bad taste may cause offence and indignation. Thus *pornography and *obscenity are judged to be in such bad taste that many people believe them to be immoral – proof that taste and morality are, as Kant argued, continuous.

Some leftist thinkers (e.g. Terry Eagleton, *The Ideology of the Aesthetic*, 1990) have argued against Kant that taste is not the property of all rational beings everywhere, but that both the phenomenon and the concept used to describe it are *ideological products of the *bourgeois forms of society. Against this it has been argued (a) that the concept of the bourgeois is here used so widely that almost any mature society could correspond to it, and (b) that, on any narrower definition, it is clearly false to say that non-bourgeois societies (that described by Homer, for instance) lacked either the habit of discrimination or some equivalent of the distinction between good and bad taste.

*Postmodernists tend to argue that all discrimination is arbitrary, and that in *postmodern conditions we do not discriminate, but only 'discriminate' in inverted commas, affecting the habit of judgement because this seems momentarily agreeable, and by way of playing with a culture that we no longer truly possess – or rather, which no longer truly possesses us.

Tawney, Richard Henry (1880–1962)
British historian and social critic; *see* *gentry, *Lutheranism, *Protestantism.

taxation
A lawful levy by the state on the property of its citizens. Taxation can be of income or of capital. The first has been preferred in capitalist countries, in order not to damage accumulations of capital thought essential to continuing *private enterprise. Capital taxation is often the declared aim of those who seek to make large-scale private enterprise impossible. Capital transfers and capital gains may also be taxed: the first is a tax on capital (which occurs, however, only at the moment of transfer); the second is a tax on income from capital. However, as the example illustrates, the boundary between capital and income taxation is a fine one, and, viewed from one point of view, capital gains tax can also be seen as a tax on capital, especially if it applies to all profit, whether or not there is a profit in *real terms (i.e. whether or not there is a real income). Capital transfer tax is a penalty on the exchange of property, whether by sale, gift or will. It therefore restricts the right of transfer which many have thought to be fundamental to the right of property.

The questions of the justice of taxation and of its ideal form have exercised political theorists and philosophers repeatedly. Clearly taxation has a different significance in socialist and in capitalist economies: in the latter the disposition of private capital is essential to production under existing economic relations, so that taxation – if it is not to be an instrument of radical social change – has to respect capital. Within that broad requirement, however, there are many possibilities. Roughly speaking, theorists divide according to whether they see taxation as a necessary burden which should be distributed as justly as possible upon those destined to bear it, or whether they see it rather as an *instrument* of justice (specifically *social justice) which should be used in part to secure a more equitable distribution of material goods than currently obtains. It is true that there are some eccentrics who reject taxation more or less entirely. Thus *Nozick (following *Spencer) seems to regard taxation as an intrinsic violation of justice, since it involves forcing the citizen to work for the state for a certain number of hours without reward. (This is like the Marxist view that the worker is compelled to work a certain number of hours in each day for the capitalist and is therefore exploited.) The obvious reply – namely that the state returns the benefit received in the form of *public goods and services – is argued not to be sufficient, since the exchange, even if mutually profitable, is forced. Others take for granted that, since the *rule of law is itself based in force, and since there can be no rule of law without the government necessary to sustain it, taxation is a precondition of the arrangement in which voluntary transactions, of the kind esteemed by Nozick, may occur. Moreover, it is argued, it is the state which makes private accumulations possible, by guaranteeing the law under which they are held, whether or not they are also held justly. It is therefore entitled to address itself to the question whether they *are* held justly and to redistribute them accordingly.

Whether our view of taxation is of a relation conditioned by justice, or of an instrument of justice, two questions seem particularly important in determining its preferred nature: (i) should there be total taxation on death? (for which *see* *death teaxes, *hereditary principle, *succession); (ii) should there be progressive taxation? The latter is assumed now to be normal, although it should be noted that there is a sense in which it requires different classes of citizens to be treated 'unequally', the rich being compelled to part with a greater portion of their wealth than the poor. This is not because the government seeks to protect the very poor from the burden of taxation: that is an independent provision, usually secured by allowing all income below a certain amount to go tax free. It would seem then that the advocacy of progressive taxation goes more naturally with the second view of taxation, as an instrument of justice, rather than as a necessity conditioned by justice. For progressive taxation certainly has an effect of redistribution, but it is uncertain that it makes any serious difference to government revenues, since it may depress economic activity. (The arguments here are topical, complex and seemingly inconclusive; however, it should be noted that in the UK in the 1980s, following the reduction of the higher rate of taxation to 40 per cent, the total income of the state from taxes *rose*.) Another view of progressive taxation is as a kind of highly sophisticated *sumptuary law; but that is perhaps too anachronistic an idea to be of any great contemporary relevance.

Some have suggested the need for a *negative* income tax, as a means of supporting those whose income is too small to supply their needs, although clearly the problems of administration here would be enormous.

technocracy

1. The 'rule by technicians', proposed in 1919 by the Californian engineer

W.H. Smyth, and celebrated in *Veblen's *Engineers and the Price System*, 1921. In fact the ideal of technocracy had already had its supporters in the nineteenth century, such as *Saint-Simon and *Comte. Under the universal *separation of ownership from control real power vests increasingly in those who are able to control the means of production, and chief among these are the technicians with the knowledge necessary to operate the complex machinery of modern production. Hence the actual economic power of technocrats is always increasing. That they should also rule, i.e. translate that power into political terms, is a suggestion that is sometimes greeted with horror, perhaps on the assumption that the technician's view of his fellow human beings is likely to be somewhat *utilitarian, perhaps even *philistine. In the modern *service economy, however, the technician is quite unlike the engineer celebrated by Veblen: he is a software expert, a person who makes links in cyberspace rather than in machinery; and he himself is a link rather than a controlling manager.

2. By extension, those who believe that technocracy in sense 1. would be a good thing are now called technocrats.

technological determinism

The interpretation of *historical materialism which sees the steady growth of *technology as the principal factor in the development of *productive forces, and which therefore regards all major historical transformations as effects of technological change.

technology

1. Any practical application of scientific method and scientific conclusions whether in peace or war. Technology is the science of means, and as science advances so does technology. It seems that the increasing sophistication of

means must also affect the ends of human conduct: some ends which were not previously possible may now be seriously intended. Hence technology, which solves many problems, also poses a problem for the moralist as much as for the politician. During the nineteenth century *cultural conservatism set itself against the harsh purgative effect of technological transformation, believing that the multiplication of possibilities was in danger of destroying the seriousness of human attachment to all of them. The believers in *progress seemed, on the other hand, to take inspiration from technology, whether in the form of an economic theory of constantly developing productive capacity, or in a more *scientistic vision of moral improvement. Most modern thinkers take some intermediate position; it is impossible not to recognize the profound change in human aspirations that has been precipitated by the technology of *communications; or the irreversible changes that have occurred in the nature of social relations, partly as a result of that. But it is also difficult to contemplate the result with complete satisfaction. The major divide is between those who think of technology itself as the only cure to the ills that it generates, and those who seek to control and inhibit it directly, and by other means.

2. Now commonly used as a shorthand for information technology, or IT: an expression that covers the technological aspect of computer software and hardware, telecommunications and all other applications of digital algorithms in the transfer of information.

teleological explanation

Any explanation of some event or process in terms of its end rather than its origins. For example, an explanation in terms of purpose ('he did it in order to annoy her'), which must be contrasted (at least initially) with an explanation in terms of antecedent conditions ('he did it because of indigestion'). In both cases, a crucial factor is singled out as providing an explanation, but in the first case this factor lies (or seems to lie) in the future, in the second in the past. The distinction here was known in Aristotelian science as that between 'final' and 'efficient' causation; now it is more normal to distinguish two kinds of explanation, the first teleological, the second causal. Among teleological explanations it is important to distinguish those which refer to a definite mental process, e.g. intention or desire, those which refer to a teleological motivation while remaining open as to whether that motivation should be described in mental terms ('the cat is stalking in order to catch the bird'), and those which apply in circumstances where mental processes are not in issue ('the plant turns in order to catch the sunlight'). Philosophers of science sometimes argue that the last are really *functional explanations – i.e. a special kind of causal explanation. *Functional explanation has sometimes been thought to be a kind of teleological explanation, but this seems wrong, since a function is not a condition which postdates the occurrence of what it explains.

Many philosophers of science have wondered *how* there can be teleological explanations, and whether all such explanations involve the invocation of purpose. Such explanations are certainly frequent in all the human sciences, but whether they can be introduced elsewhere is doubtful: a fact which might suggest that the reference to purpose is indeed necessary. Nevertheless social scientists still wonder whether the purpose invoked in teleological explanation has to be a human purpose, or whether there might be a 'social teleology' which

proceeds independently. This may or may not reduce, in the end, to the question of the possibility of functional explanation in the social sciences.

teleology
The study of the end (Greek: *telos*), goal or purpose of something. The term is now often used to refer to the theory that all evaluation should be by reference to consequences: i.e. to *consequentialism.

television
See *addiction, *communications.

terms of trade
The ratio of the *index of export prices to that of import prices. An improvement in the terms of trade is therefore a consequence of export prices rising more rapidly than import prices.

territory
Portion of the earth and its atmosphere which is such that it may fall under the *jurisdiction of a sovereign state. Modern international law recognizes territorial claims over part of the sea, and over air space, but how far these claims extend or should extend is a constant source of dispute. Modern territorial sovereignty has developed from the personal sovereignty exercised by feudal and absolute rulers, which was conceived in terms of an actual property right, albeit under a law more hypothetical than enforceable. The frequent redress of sovereigns to the Pope or to some individual said to be *Caliph in order to establish this property right led to important attempts to develop an international law of territory. The rise of *nationalism can be seen as involving, at least in part, an attempt to replace a conferred property right by a *prescriptive right, by identifying a particular tract of land with the

immemorial customs of people associated partly because of it, and also through their language, customs, race or kinship. Modern international jurisdiction begins from the premise that the world is divided up haphazardly into territories by irreversible facts of history, and that *prima facie* rights to jurisdiction must be accorded to those governments which currently claim them. It then seeks to confine each state to that territory currently claimed by it, by the 'principle of territoriality', which holds that a sovereign state ought not to engage in jurisdictional acts outside the limits of its territory.

Certain *sociobiologists have identified the search for territory as a fundamental human instinct, the equivalent of which is to be found in many of the lower animals, who are presumably not motivated by any sense of the right of ownership or jurisdiction. Whether there is anything in common between animal and human territorial behaviour is open to doubt; nevertheless there is something about the manner in which people fight for territory which demands explanation in other than legal terms.

terrorism

Defined in the UK Prevention of Terrorism Act 1976, s. 14 (1) as: 'the use of violence for political ends [including] any use of violence for the purpose of putting the public or any section of the public in fear'. This definition seems to confuse two ideas: the use of *violence for political ends, and the use of violence in order to put the public in fear. Clearly it is the second idea that is important: the intentional creation of widespread fear and dismay by violence, in particular by violence of a random and arbitrary kind. It has frequently been defended, most famously by Robespierre: 'They say that terrorism is the resort of despotic government. Is our government then like despotism? Yes, as the sword that flashes in the hand of the hero of liberty is like that with which the satellites of tyranny are armed . . . The government of the Revolution is the despotism of liberty against tyranny.' Robespierre's defence is the one that is often offered, and is usually generalized by making use of the idea of *structural violence. Terrorism merely opposes violence with violence in the name of freedom from violence. Whether this is so depends in part on the meaning of the term 'violence'. Alternatively, terrorism is a response to deep injustices of which the terrorist is the victim, and to which he can call attention in no other way.

In the modern context state terrorism of the kind advocated by Robespierre is of less interest than terrorism conducted by private initiatives, either by insurgent groups wishing to disrupt or overthrow a government, or by groups like *al-Qa'eda which have no clear political intentions. The extreme violence of Islamist terrorism, its frequent recourse to suicide attacks and its deliberate targeting of non-combatants, hostages and bystanders, have made it clear that terrorism is not just a tactic used in the pursuit of some goal, but in many cases an end in itself, an act of vengeance against a world condemned. The old excuses frequently offered on the left, that terrorists are people reduced by poverty, oppression and injustice to a last recourse, whose goals need to be understood and who would choose peaceful means to achieve them if these means were available, have now worn too thin to be repeated. The new kind of terrorism, conducted by rich, privileged and hate-filled people bent on destruction, needs another kind of explanation. And that explanation should surely be read back into all those other acts of terrorism which thinkers of the left have been in the habit of excusing, in particular those that climaxed in the Russian Revolution and which have been documented by Anna Geifman (*Thou Shalt Kill*, 1989). Some argue that Nietzsche's concept of *ressentiment* (*see* *resentment) provides an explanation; others follow Dostoevsky and Conrad in seeing terrorism as the presence among us of evil. Either way, it seems that the desire to inflict suffering, fear and destruction is far more important than any goal that could be achieved thereby.

Hence we should distinguish two kinds of terrorism: instrumental terrorism, in which terror is used as a means to an end, and 'teleological' terrorism, in which terror is an end in itself, pursued as the intrinsically interesting and possibly redemptive thing that it is. Instrumental terrorism is habit-forming, and may become teleological in time. But the true teleological terrorist is in search of an exultation that is largely indifferent to any finite or definable purpose, and which can be gained only by some stupendous act of destruction. (*See* *war on terror.)

Thatcherism

The outlook and philosophy associated with the policies of Margaret Thatcher, leader of the UK Conservative Party from 1975 until 1990, and Prime Minister from 1979 until 1990. The principal features of Thatcherism seem to be these:

(i) Advocacy of a 'politics of conviction', rather than the *managerial conservatism of Thatcher's predecessor, Sir Edward Heath.

(ii) Economic *monetarism, rather than the previously orthodox *Keynesianism.

(iii) Extensive *privatization of state-controlled enterprises.

(iv) Curtailing of the powers of large organizations, and especially of *trade unions.

(v) Hostility to *restrictive practices and *monopolies in every field – especially those exercised by professional organizations and bureaucrats.

(vi) The attempt to break the hold of local government bureaucracies over education and to introduce a quasi-market into the health service and into the provision of schools.

(vii) Adherence to national sovereignty in all dealings with foreign powers – including the *European Community, as it then was, and the former USSR.

(viii) Emphasis on *law and order at home and strong defences abroad.

(ix) In general an attempt to reduce the extent and the power of the state in domestic matters and to maintain its power as the representative of the British people abroad.

(x) Hence, an attempt to lower taxation and to apply taxation to the genuine needs of the state, such as defence and education.

Those policies were not all successfully carried out. Nevertheless, they follow logically from philosophical principles defended by *Hayek and others, and Thatcherism can be seen as the first attempt to *modernize British *conservatism, by discarding the *Butskellite consensus and acting from a consistent philosophical foundation. The popularity of Lady Thatcher (as she later became) was due in part to the clarity of her public statements and her ability to persuade the electorate that her convictions corresponded to their wishes – particularly in matters of taxation and opportunity. Her unpopularity among the intellectual and media élite was due both to her right-wing philosophy and to her confrontational approach to those who disagreed with her. It is significant, however, that the main items of her political legacy have been accepted by the leaders of *New Labour, with an air of quiet relief that it was she, not they, who had the trouble of achieving them.

theft

Dishonestly appropriating property with the intention permanently to deprive another. A statutory offence since 1968 in the UK, and defined more or less as above in a badly drafted act. Theft has always been recognized under a variety of names (larceny, embezzlement, fraudulent conversion) at *common law. It is still a common law offence in US and Scots law.

When *Proudhon declared that 'property is theft' he meant that all *private property involves the exclusion of others from what is, in effect, a *natural right of common possession. If that is so, then it may seem that no theft is greater than that involved in the maintenance of private property relations through a law of theft. Others argue that everything possessed lawfully either is, or has been made from, something which has been wrongfully appropriated, so that theft is merely a 'conventional' crime, a creation of arbitrary stipulations of positive law, designed to protect existing relations of *control.

However, the important point is not who has the right to own some object (whether or not this be a natural right or a right of some other kind), but rather who is being dishonest in taking and retaining something. The arguments about the thief's act focus not on the question whether his victim had a right to what he held, but rather on the question whether the thief acted dishonestly. Dishonesty is not an easy notion to define. It involves such things as deceit, covert dealing, breach of agreement – in short a whole range of human activities in which one person is abused by

another. What is wrong with theft is what is wrong with that abuse. *Kant held that all such abuse involves the use of a rational being as a means only, and that that is the essence of inter-personal wrongdoing. In which case theft is morally the same kind of thing as (although no doubt less serious than) rape or murder. The problem here is immensely complex, but it is what is really at issue between Robin Hood and those whom he seeks to rob.

theocracy

Literally, 'government by God', but often, in common usage, 'government by priests'. The term was coined by the Greek-speaking Jewish historian Josephus, to denote the Jewish conception of government as embodied in the Torah, where divine laws are treated as creating both religious and civil obligations (*see* *Jewish law). Theocracy as practised in the ancient world involved not direct government by priests, but the tenure of judicial and legislative offices by priests, and this idea has survived under *Islam into the modern world.

The ruling conception of a theocracy according to *Spinoza (*Tractatus Theologico-Politicos*, XVII), is that all civil obligations are thought to stem from a covenant with God, and no other source of authority (such as a contract with the sovereign, or with other members of society) is recognized as binding. Even the 'general-in-chief or dictator' rules only because chosen by God to do so. Spinoza points out that in ancient Jewish custom the office of interpreter of the law was vested, not in the sovereign, but in the Levites who had no part in government. The sovereign, however, was not normally a priest. Hence there was an effective *separation of powers within the state, leading to the *limitation of the powers of the sovereign. Here, therefore, the idea of divine governance produced an effective *rule of law.

The case should be contrasted with Iran under Khomeini, where both executive and judicial offices were held by divines. (But *see* next entry.) In so far as *Islamism has a goal, it is to establish a theocracy, in which the *sharī'ah* is the sole or primary system of law, with non-Muslims either forcibly converted or reduced to *dhimmī* status.

theocratic guardianship

A political stance advocated by Ayatollah Khomeini, according to which there should be secular government and the institutions necessary to that end, superintended by religious institutions, which provide the means to resolve difficult moral, legal and social problems, and to redirect the 'political will' so as to align it with the will of God.

theodicy

Term coined by Leibniz, to denote any theory which shows the order of the world to be compatible with God's absolute goodness, and so justifies the ways of God to man. (Greek: *dikē*, justice.) An example is Leibniz's own famously satirized view that the actual world is the best of all possible worlds: a view the subtlety of which is badly misrepresented when thus quoted out of context.

third way

Advocacy of a 'third way' between conflicting viewpoints is a recurring feature of modern politics – in particular the proposal of a third way between socialism and capitalism, made by *Röpke in his defence of the 'social market', by the Czech economist Ota Šik in his defence of *market socialism, by Daniel Bell in *The End of Ideology* (*see* *end of ideology), and most recently by Tony Giddens, ideologist

of *New Labour. After initial excitement the slogan quickly loses it appeal, as it is discovered that it has little or nothing to announce in the way of concrete policies.

Third World

See *three worlds theory.

thirdworldism

Term of recent coinage to denote the shift of *left opinion away from the defence of *socialism against *capitalism, towards the advocacy of the Third World against the developed countries and their interests (alternatively, the advocacy of the South against the North). (*See* *North/South divide, *three worlds theory.) Thirdworldists are of many kinds, as are people of the left generally, and it is necessary to distinguish the radical position, according to which the poverty of the South is caused by the wealth of the North and is the result of injustice and exploitation, from the more moderate position that Northern states have a duty to provide aid to Southern states in order to achieve a measure of world-wide *social justice. Followers of *Nietzsche, *Rand and certain strands within the *New Right accuse thirdworldists of organized *sentimentality and view them as part of the *victim culture. But this stock reaction overlooks the great variety of motives behind this new form of advocacy, and the distinction between those who are merely exulting in the problem and those who are trying hard to find a reasonable and acceptable solution to it.

Thompson, Edward P. (1924–93)

British historian and social theorist; *see* *Althusser, *class consciousness, *New Left.

Thoreau, Henry David (1817–62)

US writer and philosopher, whose meditations on the life of solitude,

Walden, 1854, defend a distinctively American individualism. Alone by Walden pond, absorbing works of literature and philosophy, intently observing nature and reflecting on real human needs, Thoreau arrived at a purified vision of humanity, strongly influenced by Emerson and by *Plato's *Republic*. The task of the philosopher, he argued, is to achieve an 'equable life', which is one of 'simplicity, magnanimity and trust'. Existing institutions are by no means necessary to satisfy our needs, and in everything we should strive for a heroic independence. *Walden* has exerted a lasting influence over American political ideas, through its vision of civilized independence, in which man rediscovers his true self through communion with nature.

In an earlier essay ('Resistance to Civil Government', 1849), Thoreau introduced, in the course of defending it, the idea of *civil disobedience, justifying his refusal to pay a poll tax as part of a philosophical protest against slavery and imperialism.

thoughtcrime

Term of *newspeak, as described by *Orwell, to denote the crime of thinking what is forbidden by the party or its ideology. Thoughts have generally been regarded as lying beyond the reach of the criminal law, and Orwell's intention was to satirize the communist desire nevertheless to control them. However it is sometimes argued that accusations of thoughtcrime are increasingly rife in the modern world, and that this is illustrated by the more extreme forms of *political correctness. Inadvertently using a 'forbidden' word ('darling' of the girl working next to you), you 'reveal' your forbidden (sexually demeaning) thoughts, and this in turn leads to punishment (accusation of *sexual harassment, followed by the loss of your job).

threat assessment

The analysis of the ability and will of a potential enemy to engage in aggression and warfare. In *strategy, the threat assessment is a matter for diplomatic and political analysts, who provide the military with a 'worst case' scenario. The strategist must then plan to deal with that scenario in order to achieve the best possible output from the worst possible inputs.

three worlds theory

The Third World (French: *tiers monde*) comprises those states and territories which exhibit neither developed capitalist nor developed socialist economies, many of which have recently 'emerged' from colonial or primitive rule, to adopt untried political institutions, sometimes bequeathed by or borrowed from states in another 'world'. 'Three worlds' theory has consisted in the comparative analysis of the economic (and to some extent political) conditions of the three 'worlds', and an attempt to understand the Third World, perhaps as an *ideal type (in comparison with the ideal types of capitalism and socialism). The description of Third World economy is extremely difficult; it is not possible to think of it either as 'pre-capitalist' or as 'pre-socialist', because all developments take on a character that is *sui generis*, there being little competence in economic management, only a very rudimentary *middle class, and little 'national consciousness' (as opposed to local or tribal consciousness) to which a government may appeal in its attempts to mobilize the economy. There is a dominance of subsistence production, very little unemployment (since much employment is of low productivity), a low accumulation rate, a small public sector, a low *per capita* income, and a markedly unequal income distribution. The Third World countries rarely have an interdependent market network, with prices tending towards uniformity and moving flexibly. The absence of this mechanism, which provides immediate signals for economic decisions, is often held to be a key feature in under-development.

The assumption of 'three worlds' is no longer credible. When China declared herself a Third World country at the Bandung Conference in 1955 she was merely confessing to a general truth about the so-called 'second' world. The subsequent collapse of communist economies has led to the discrediting of standard theories of development. In so far as any attempt is made to discuss the issue it is now in terms of the *North/South divide.

thrift

Originally the fact of thriving or being prosperous, and hence, by transfer, the virtue traditionally thought necessary for that end. Thrift is a species of narrow *prudence – so narrow, some think, as not really to be prudence, and not a *virtue. Thrift involves the disposition to save rather than spend, to invest wisely, and accumulate diligently; above all to avoid debt. Thrift is sometimes described as a peculiarly capitalist virtue, part of the ideology which consolidates and legitimates the activity of capital accumulation. However, capitalism depends upon borrowing, and the thrift of one person is often what makes the risk taken by another possible. It should also be pointed out that the parable of the prodigal son, from which much of the morality of thrift traditionally took its authority, was uttered in pre-capitalist Judaea, by someone who regarded prodigality as an eminently forgivable failing.

tiger economies

Expression of *journalese to denote the economies of certain South-East Asian countries on the Pacific rim, which during the 1990s suddenly began to expand into far-reaching export markets, while generating hitherto unheard of prosperity at home. One cause of this was the ending of local wars, and the subsequent importation of Western technology and expertise into a labour force in which *family values and tightly-knit communities gave an added impetus to productive labour.

time preference

Preference for present as opposed to future consumption. Consider the question: Suppose there is no inflation, then how much money would I have to give you in one year's time to induce you to forgo £1 now? The existence of this (positive or negative) 'subjective rate of interest' is of crucial importance in all economic decisions concerning time, and must be taken into account, for example, when constructing a model of the *rational agent in terms of *decision theory.

The concept of time preference is important in certain theories of *interest and *profit. It is also a factor that seems to be overlooked in many traditional arguments concerning the justice or injustice of *usury. Pure time preference is to be distinguished from preferences arising from risk. Thus there are further grounds for preferring satisfaction now rather than at any later time, since I exist now, and it is always to some degree possible that I will not exist later.

timocracy

Term used by *Plato to denote the government of honour, which arises out of *aristocracy (government by the best), when the military character of the state comes to be the focus of all ambition. Culture, philosophy and the arts of peace decline, and are respected only in so far as they confer honour on those who achieve military prowess and public power. Such a description might perhaps be applied to Sparta, to certain orders of medieval knighthood (e.g. that of Malta), to the local rule by the samurai in Japan, and perhaps to the (first) Napoleonic state.

Tocqueville, Alexis, Comte de (1805–59)

French politician and historian, whose shrewd observations of France and America have become classics of social and political analysis. In his first major work, *Democracy in America*, 1835, he argues that the 'principle of equality', whereby all distinctions of social status are gradually eroded, is the ruling principle of modern history. The tendency towards equality had, he thought, been dominant since the Middle Ages and, with the American and French Revolutions, had entered its final stage. The major problem facing modern society is that of reconciling equality with liberty, in the increasing absence of the diversity of power that had characterized traditional aristocratic regimes. The lower classes undermine the upper by increasing centralization, which erodes all social hierarchy, regionalism and local feeling, and results in an unprecedented concentration of power. Nevertheless, in a prescient and in many ways laudatory account of the US constitution, Tocqueville praised the American system for its ability to encourage decentralized government, even in a condition of complete democracy, and the constitution as an instrument able to shape society in accordance with democratic expectations, while still retaining the mechanisms by which the blunderings of democratic politics could be rendered revocable errors. He described the *jury as a political system, enacting the sovereignty of the people in the courtroom; at the same time he saw judicial independence in the US as endowing the judiciary with some of the stabilizing influence and inherent political privilege of the European aristocracy. Tocqueville's criticisms of American democracy and of the ethos of equality were many and various. He argued that liberty is threatened by public opinion ('the *tyranny of the majority') which, with the egalitarian loss of individuality, self-assurance and social ease, must increasingly tend towards uniformity. Not only liberty, but also culture and intellectual distinction are threatened by equality; all class distinctions are destined to be replaced by increasingly arbitrary-seeming distinctions of status, without the dignifying attributes of culture and leisure that might render them permanent and authoritative. The 'imperfect phantom of equality' haunts the mind of all, destroying alike obedience, honour and the capacity to command, so that people, increasingly unable to find solace in the social order, will be confined within the solitude of their hearts. To some extent, however, this tendency to fragmentation is countered by the American genius for association, which leads to a proliferation of clubs, churches and societies in which long-standing and genial hierarchies are recreated.

In *The Old Regime and the French Revolution*, 1856, Tocqueville gave a highly influential account of the causes and effects of the French Revolution, arguing that revolutions occur when things begin to improve, or when things go wrong after a period of improvement – a view that many have seen confirmed in subsequent history. Although revolution speeds up the real change, that change – towards centralization, bureaucracy, and the increasing levelling of social hierarchy – is not caused by revolution but precedes it, being itself one of the major causes of revolution, since it undermines the old privileges which made preventive measures possible. Tocqueville blamed the old aristocracy for much of its loss of power; it had become a *caste* and, unlike the English gentry, had been willing to exchange political power for social exclusiveness and fiscal privilege, thus becoming both obnoxious to the majority, and unable to defend itself.

tokenism

The attempt by a firm, institution or association to show that it is open to some category of potential members by including a 'token' instance or two. For example, the attempt by a school to show that it is open to children of all ethnic groups by including a few token pupils from ethnic minorities, or the attempt by a university to show that it is open to all opinions by including a few token conservatives among its academic staff.

tolerance

The habit of permitting disagreement and not disapproving of opinions that you do not share or lifestyles that are other than yours. To be distinguished from *toleration.

toleration

The policy of patient forbearance towards that which is not approved. There is toleration only where there are also things that are disapproved; if people were perfect, toleration would be neither necessary nor possible.

The extent to which toleration can and should be extended has occupied many political theorists in modern times, most famously *Locke, whose *Letter on Toleration*, 1688, put forward arguments which are now widely accepted. Locke's concern was with religious toleration; he argued that no sovereign could found his right to rule on the truth of his religion, for it is not within the competence of a state to discern the truth of religious doctrines,

nor is it the function of a state to save men's souls; rather the state exists to protect men's rights, and may use force to that end alone. Hence there ought to be tolerance in all matters of religion. Locke did not think that toleration should be extended to Roman Catholics, however, since he doubted that somebody could be a Catholic and still owe first allegiance in political matters to the English sovereign. The principles behind Locke's view were soon widely accepted, and later extended from the religious to the moral sphere by *Mill, although Mill's arguments are widely disputed. (*See* *law and morality.)

Modern discussions tend to concern the further extension of toleration not just to that which is spiritually alien or morally disapproved, but also to that which is politically opposed. Toleration of *opposition to communism has been rare in communist states but it is sometimes argued that toleration ought to be extended so far as is consistent with political stability (perhaps even further) in those political arrangements which recognize the legitimacy of opposition, and seek to permit freedom of *opinion. The position of the US in relation to communism illustrates to some extent the difficulties of the position. Some argue that in so far as communists can be supposed to be bent on destroying the existing form of government they can be compared to the Catholics whom Locke wished to exclude from toleration. (An argument influential at the time of *McCarthyism.) Others think that it is a right, that either is or ought to be protected under the US constitution, to work by peaceful means for whatever form of government is sincerely judged to be best for the American people. It is, however, reasonable to suppose that if the form of government projected is one that explicitly rejects the legitimacy of opposition then there is no real right to political toleration, since anybody who claims that right must himself be prepared to grant it. Moreover anybody who seeks to overthrow the US constitution and replace it with one that does not guarantee civil rights cannot claim to be protected by any right under the US constitution.

The question of the limits of toleration has now come to the fore on account of the confrontation with *Islamism. The Koran is not a tolerant document, and those who wish to take it as the foundation for political order are committed thereby to a series of intolerant attitudes, towards other faiths and forbidden practices. Western states tolerate the practice of Islam, and expect loyalty to the secular law that upholds this toleration. But should they tolerate the *Wahhabi mullahs who incite their congregations to overthrow the secular law and to impose *Islamic law in the place of it?

Tolstoy, Lev Nikolayevich, Count (1828–1910)
Russian novelist and social theorist; *see* *anarchism, *country, *leadership.

Tönnies, Ferdinand (1855–1936)
German sociologist; *see* *Gemeinschaft and *Gesellschaft*.

tort
The term in *common law for all wrongs that are actionable in civil law, in contrast to crime on the one hand, and breach of contract on the other. The law of tort is a branch of the law of obligations, where the legal obligation arises, not under an agreement, but under a general obligation to refrain from harming another, or to make good any harm done. The principle is to endeavour to shift the loss sustained to the person responsible for

it. An important consequence is that a person who is injured through another's fault receives damages in law, while a person injured through no one's fault does not. Some argue that there is an injustice in this, since an injured person ought to be compensated simply because of his injury, and not because of any wrong done. However, it is clear that for the law to function as a law of obligation it must continue to enforce sanctions on grounds of responsibility; it is an instrument not of *distributive but of *commutative justice.

tort reform
In US law damages in *tort are awarded by the jury. Moreover procedures exist whereby trial lawyers can seek to disqualify particular members of the jury, on a variety of grounds that might prove prejudicial to the case. These facts, together with the possibility of 'class actions', brought in soft jurisdictions by clever lawyers against large companies, has led to a series of judgements in which juries grant astronomical damages for small faults, or for no faults at all, simply because the plaintiff is dramatized as a victim, and the defendant as tough, large, successful and able to pay. Tort cases now absorb 2% of US GDP, lawyers have grown rich on the proceeds, and small businesses have been driven to bankruptcy – notably in a rash of cases concerning asbestos, which have been brought against all those who manufactured, sold, delivered or used that product, by people whose injuries as a result of contact with it are often purely hypothetical. To date there have been 700 000 plaintiffs filing suits against 8400 different defendants, 85 of which have been forced into *bankruptcy. This continuing saga threatens to undermine a whole section of the national economy, from the small-town ironmonger to the

large-scale developer, and there is no end in sight. Hence 'tort reform' has become a major domestic cause in the US, businesses calling for it, the *Association of Trial Lawyers of America denouncing it. The answer is perhaps that of the English law, which is to forbid juries to award damages, except in matters, like reputation, where they alone are competent to decide.

torture

Any form of violence that causes, and is intended to cause, acute and sustained mental or physical pain to the victim. Torture may be used as a form of *punishment, or as an act of vengeance upon defeated enemies. In its more institutionalized forms, however, torture is to be distinguished from punishment, being a means of coercion of the victim, intended to elicit evidence or confession. Thus torture has been part of the legal system of most of the European powers, and 'judicial torture' generated its own jurisprudence, rules, treatises and doctors of law.

In England torture as punishment and as coercion was, officially at least, virtually abolished in 1640, and most modern states explicitly rule out the use of torture either by statute or by constitutional provisions. Its persistence, however, is widespread, despite a declaration issued in 1975 by the United Nations Organization forbidding the use of torture by any member state. The question of its justification has once again come to the fore in the *war on terror. Is it legitimate to torture, when this is the only means to obtain information that will foil a terrorist plot? Can you torture to avoid torture? Most people would like to draw an absolute line at torture, and say that you must not cross it – in other words, that *consequentialist reasoning here must stop. But the horrendous possibilities presented by *weapons of mass destruction in the hands of terrorists may cause a shift in popular opinion.

Even if torture is allowed on those grounds, the *enjoyment* of torture would presumably still be regarded as a sin. Only rational beings are able to take pleasure in torturing each other, since only rational beings have the capacity to relish what another is feeling. Sadistic torture is sometimes said to proceed from a state of mind that not only overrides respect for persons, but which also desires to show persons as unfit for respect, by showing the ease with which the person can be overcome by the animal. According to *Sartre, sadism of this kind is present in much sexual desire, as a 'reef upon which desire may founder'.

Toryism

Philosophy and policies associated with the English *Conservative Party, and its predecessor, the 'Tory' faction in English government since the Restoration. (The term comes from the Irish *tóraighe*, a pursuer, used in the seventeenth century to denote the dispossessed Irish who subsisted by plundering and killing English settlers, and extended later to those with Popish sympathies, and then to the loyalists who opposed the exclusion of James, Duke of York from the succession to the Crown.) Toryism has never been one thing, and is often divided into 'high' Toryism, which has a traditionalist and aristocratic flavour, and 'low' Toryism, more redolent of the *business ethic and the spirit of *free enterprise. The modern Conservative Party, with commitment to *monetarism, *free trade, the *market economy, widespread *democracy and *human rights, is partly a product of the recent import of ideas that first took root in America, and which were for a long time regarded as alien to the

British way of doing things. Tory suspicion of the idea of human rights was not traditionally directed at the American experiment, however, but at the French imitation of it. The leading document here is that of *Burke, denouncing what had been done in the name of liberty and rights by the French Revolution. Burke's argument is situated at the 'high' end of the thermometer where the following features seem important:

(i) Belief in a *legitimacy founded in *custom, history and the *status quo, rather than in *doctrine.

(ii) Belief that the devices of *legitimation should not be political – e.g. should not consist in published opinion or propaganda – but social, lying in popular morality, religion and ordinary patriotic sentiment.

(iii) Belief in the role and value of a *ruling class, and adherence to the view that politics is a natural activity of that class, but a dangerous device in the hands of any other.

(iv) Belief in the validity of private property, combined with a certain contempt for *mere* property, or for property that has been acquired too quickly or too recently.

(v) Belief in political restraint of economic activity in the interests of larger social questions, leading to a suspicion of unbridled capitalism, free trade, and perhaps even of *industrialization.

(vi) Belief in 'one nation', and the 'feudal principle' (both phrases bequeathed to Tory rhetoric by Disraeli), according to which class divisions may be legitimate and beneficial, but only so long as they are tempered by *conciliation and reciprocal obligations. (A view which sometimes leads to 'welfare Toryism' – the active fostering of a *welfare state in the interests of social continuity.)

(i) to (vi), overlaid and eroded by varying degrees of commitment to *democracy, to *liberalism, and to the *market economy, form the infinite grades of opinion that are now thought of as 'Tory'. All of (i) to (vi) could be thought of as survivals of a feudal aristocratic mentality, although they all have received the backing of serious political thought, both before and after Burke. 'Tory democracy' – initiated by Disraeli – to some extent marked the break with the old high Tory mentality. People question whether *Thatcherism is really a form of Toryism, rather than *liberalism in its classical sense.

total war

War involving the participation of all citizens, military and civilian, and in which all social and economic forces are directed towards the military effort. Since the *levée en masse* of the French Revolution, conscription of all capable citizens has been the norm in warfare, and is even thought by some to be a democratic duty. Hence total war is a repeated occurrence, unlike the *limited war of previous times.

totalitarian temptation

Expression introduced by the French political scientist Jean-François Revel to denote the tendency of intellectuals to embrace totalitarian political systems – specifically Marxism – on account of their apparently reasoned responses to the problems of human society, and on account of the distinguished role that they promise to the intellectuals themselves.

totalitarianism

A state is totalitarian if it permits no *autonomous institutions, i.e. if the aims, activities and membership of all *associations are subject to the *control of the state. For this to be the case freedom of association cannot be permitted – and it is significant that the value of this freedom is doubted both by *Hobbes and by *Rousseau, two thinkers who offer arguments useful to totalitarian government, despite the fact that totalitarianism, as distinct from *absolutism and *autocracy, is a distinctly twentieth-century invention. Complete state control of the means of communication is also essential, together with an *ideology (sense 1.); for the sole origin of all legitimation is the state itself, there being no autonomous institutions, such as church, universities, clubs and societies, through which respect for the civil order can be independently inculcated. If such institutions exist it is only by permission of the state, and in accordance with strict instructions from the state.

Totalitarianism is not necessarily violent, but it is frequently argued to be unjust, since it involves encroachment by the state on many *natural rights, and an abolition of all forms of society that are not coerced from above. This 'withering away of society' often takes place under a rule that promises the *withering away of the state. It is, however, disputed that *collectivization, or *social ownership, or any other aim of communist and related systems, in itself requires totalitarian government.

Totalitarianism is a matter of degree, and much academic study has been devoted to distinguishing its subvarieties. In all versions, however, the fundamental feature is that of central control, usually through a *party.

town and country

The division between town and country is geographical, economic and ideological, and the question of their relation has moved steadily up the political agenda, as the border between them has become indistinct. Suburbanization has sucked the heart out of many towns, and also destroyed much of the countryside. Thanks to the *internet jobs that were confined to urban areas can now be performed from remote country cottages. And the steady replacement of *agriculture by *agribusiness has meant that the business of farming is more and more the concern of absentee corporations than of people resident on the land. Inevitably this has led to tensions, as incomers drive up the price of rural accommodation, and the old forms of rural employment disappear. For a long time in the UK there have been NGOs and pressure groups striving to protect the countryside from unnecessary or unsightly development; but the decline of farming has made it impossible to guarantee the future even of the most established rural economy. The formation of the Countryside Alliance in 1997 was in part a response to this problem, in part the beginnings of a campaign to protect *hunting, the dispute over which is for many people iconic of the town and country divide.

Thinkers of the left have taken exception to the 'rural idyll', as they describe it, with the critic Raymond Williams (1921–1988) leading the attack on 'English pastoral', denouncing it as part of the ideological mask that hides the exploitation of the peasantry by those who own the land. (*The Country and the City*, 1973.) Williams's study initiated a series of attacks on the vision of England that had been so important in war-time propaganda, and which owed its continuing prominence – as Williams argues – to an extended literary and artistic tradition lasting from the eighteenth to the twentieth centuries. In reply it has been pointed out that the rural theme in English literature has been as much concerned with farming and the farm-labourer as with the country house, and that the idioms of English folk-song and folk-poetry testify to a universal engagement with the countryside as an icon of England.

Tractarianism

Name given to the early stages of the 'Oxford Movement', derived from *Tracts for the Times*, 1833–41, many written by J.H. (later Cardinal) Newman, defending the Apostolic and Catholic claims of *Anglicanism, and presaging the subsequent defection of many tractarians to the Roman Catholic Church. Tractarianism involved criticism of *liberalism in social and moral matters, and hostility to the Reformation, and to many of the effects of *industrialization. It had roots in a conservative and even reactionary view of English religion and society, and sought to articulate many tenets of *cultural conservatism in the form of doctrine, while at the same time claiming religious sanction for its views.

trade cycle (also 'business cycle')

Regular oscillations in the level of economic activity, in which *depressions and *recessions follow upon periods of high employment and accelerating production. Theories of the trade cycle include most of the more important modern macroeconomic analyses, such as Keynes's theory (according to which depressions result from *aggregate demand's falling below the productive potential of the economy), and the theory of *monetarism, which sees the money supply as the key factor in the regulation of economic activity.

trade dispute

A concept introduced into UK law in order to designate the disputes in which trade unions claim a right of intercession, and in respect of which they may be granted legal privileges. It was defined in the Trades Disputes Act 1906, and again in the Trade Union and Labour Relations Act 1974, as a dispute between employers and workers or between workers and workers, relating to: terms and conditions of employment; allocation of work or duties; discipline; membership or non-membership of a union; facilities for union officials; negotiating machinery.

The sub-classes of dispute recognized, and the provision that dispute may be between workers and workers, illustrate the extent to which *industrial law can no longer be considered as part of the law of contract, the relation of employment having achieved a separate legal structure.

trade-related intellectual property (TRIP)

Term that covers trade-marks, trade secrets, copyright and the fruits of 'research and development' when these have been protected by some patent or similar legal device. TRIPs have become a major object of political dispute as a result of the treaties negotiated and enforced by the *World Trade Organization, which aim to offer world-wide protection to patents and copyrights. A patent filed in the US can in this way be enforced throughout the world, including places where a similar product has been developed but no patent filed. Thus a US pharmaceutical company synthesized and then patented the medicinal ingredients in turmeric, which had been grown and sold for medicinal purposes in India for centuries. Indian farmers were suddenly deprived of the right to sell their produce, since it had been patented by a multinational trading within their borders. In the event the Indian government was able to secure a cancellation of the patent; but similar cases constantly arise, and prompt reflection on a wider problem of *globalization, which is the extent to which *intellectual property really can be or ought to be protected. *See* *Open Source.

trade union (or: trades union)

Originally an association for the self-protection of employees, particularly in response to the conditions of industrial production, and existing since the eighteenth century. Deemed a *conspiracy in restraint of trade at *common law, trade unions were finally fully legalized in the UK in 1871, by a Conservative government under Disraeli, after several decades of agitation. In 1875 the modern concept of a *trade dispute was adumbrated in a statute which, by implication, permitted peaceful picketing. Finally, after a case in which a union was held liable in damages for the loss caused by a strike, the Trades Disputes Act 1906 made most forms of trade union association and *industrial action legal. Since then the legislation concerning trade unions conferred on them privileges beyond those of any other associations (with the exception of the churches) which are not themselves branches of government. The objections to these privileges take two basic forms: first, that they seem to countenance the violation of essential freedoms and rights (*see*, e.g., *closed shop); secondly that they make certain actions initiated by trade unions injudiciable, despite their enormous social consequences, and therefore destroy the correspondence between grievance and legal remedy defended by some advocates of the conciliatory role of government (*see* *industrial action). *Thatcherism saw a radical break with the tradition of granting legal privileges and tried to bring unions more into line with other organizations enjoying power over their members.

The UK and US examples are of the 'free trade union' – i.e. unions formed under a law permitting freedom of association, and not disciplined from above by the state (although perhaps disciplined from within by a *party, it being important, in the UK, that the trade unions and the Labour Party, having emerged together from the *labour movement, remained, until

recent moves by *New Labour, closely affiliated). In modern communist countries trade unions were not free in that sense, nor was there a 'right to strike' such as has been recognized for l00 years in English law. Trade unions were conceived, rather, as representative devices within the framework of *democratic centralism, whereby the opinions of workers may be heard, and local disputes adjudicated, without disturbing the discipline of production. A similar concept of the trade union was adopted by Italian *fascism, with its defence of *corporatism.

The *de facto* power of unions in the UK, together with the legal recognition of that power, and the role given to trade union officials in negotiations over policy and economic planning, changed the trade union movement during the twentieth century from a movement of protest within the lower class to a slightly disputatious but more or less *accommodated part of the *establishment. The growth of self-employment and the *service economy, have now initiated a serious decline in the importance of the unions, which in many trades and professions have already all but disappeared.

tradition

A highly charged and often commendatory term, which is used by certain forms of *conservatism in order to assert the validity of its respect for the past, together with a belief that the present must be understood as a continuation, and never as an initiation, of social and political *identity. The term substitutes for a considerable lack of theory, and indeed is apt to embody the important conservative theory that theories (and especially theories of history) are dangerous – perhaps even, in the area of political practice, nonsensical. The following elements seem to be contained in the idea, as standardly invoked:

(i) A tradition denotes a class of intentional actions, together with the thoughts, beliefs, perceptions and associations that motivate them. Like *custom, tradition must be distinguished from *habit, and from mechanized response.

(ii) In virtue of (i), traditions contain a principle of development. Intentional actions are founded on reasons, thoughts and perceptions, and develop as understanding develops.

(iii) Nevertheless the reasons for traditional behaviour are 'immanent'; that is, they exist not as explicit doctrines, but as perceptions of the validity of an act while performing it, together with an intimation of further reasons which it may be impossible, and perhaps undesirable, to state.

(iv) Traditions are essentially shared, and understood as such. There are solitary habits, but no solitary traditions. And part of the motive of traditional behaviour is *that* it is shared; it involves the sense of a practice as possessing social and not just individual validity, so that, in conforming to it, the agent enjoys the sanction of a social norm.

(v) Traditions create a background of shared expectations, against which deviance and originality can be achieved. It is also partly by seeing people against this social background that their individual moral character is perceived. Hence, on one view, traditions are an essential ingredient in the production of the individual. The individual is an artefact, who becomes individual only because he has first absorbed into himself the common background of social behaviour against which to define himself.

(vi) Genuine traditions are not invented, but arise by an *invisible hand from the process of social interaction over generations.

The ruling thoughts of those who seek to uphold tradition are two: first, that tradition indicates a form of wholly peaceful attachment to a place, a time, a past, and the many social and institutional arrangements which make that past present; secondly, that a tradition is a form of knowledge, that cannot be contained in a single human head but condenses into itself, so to speak, information that is otherwise irretrievably dispersed. (That last thought unites *Burke and *Hayek in the defence of custom.)

It is characteristic of British conservatism to emphasize (iii) (*see*, e.g., Burke, *Oakeshott), and to underplay (v), which in turn is a preoccupation of German idealists and their progeny (*see* *Hegel). Moreover, it is more characteristic of the English than of the French or German defence to oppose tradition to *doctrine as a mode of *legitimation, although all seem to agree that tradition is required if other political values are to be realized, since all such things as justice, liberty and community can be achieved only in a condition of social continuity. (*See also* *tacit communication.)

Traditions can be both social and political. The emphasis is usually placed on the former, on the grounds that the state and its institutions are themselves offshoots of *civil society. Left-wing critics of tradition tend to focus on feature (vi) above, arguing that all traditions are invented (in the manner of Scottish country dancing or Trooping the Colour), and therefore that all traditions can be changed without structural damage. In response conservatives sometimes distinguish true traditions (the *common law, the Western orchestra, the male suit) from their invented competitors.

traditionalism

Any doctrine or policy founded in the defence of tradition, but specifically the philosophy of history and political programme developed by the *counter-revolutionary movement in eighteenth- and nineteenth-century France. Its main exponents were *Maistre, the Vicomte de Bonald (1754–1840) and F.R de Lammenais (1782–1854). All were *ultramontanists, and defenders of a religious view of civil obligation, together with some sophisticated variant of the doctrine of *divine right. As a doctrine traditionalism was condemned by a papal decretal in 1855. Its spirit was revived in the twentieth century in *intégrisme and the associated *royalism.

tragedy of the commons

Term introduced by Garrett Hardin ('The Tragedy of the Commons', *Science* 1968), to denote the form of *counterfinality to which *common pool resources are subject. All commons, whether land or sea, food or raw materials, are relentlessly depleted by those entitled to take from them, since each argues that if he holds back then others will deprive him. Hence every form of common ownership ends in tragedy, as the resource is exhausted. This happened to common land in medieval Europe; it is happening now to the oceans.

trahison des clercs

French: the treason of the clerks; in other words, betrayal by intellectuals. The title of a book by Julien Benda (1927), directed in the first instance against the political agitation of certain right-wing French intellectuals (notably *Maurras) but including a more general criticism of the role of the intellectual in modern politics, and of the increasing addiction of intellectuals to *Plato's myth of the 'philosopher king' – i.e. the myth that knowledge bestows the right to rule. The phrase has therefore been applied to the *fellow-travellers on the French

intellectual left, and in particular to Maurice Merleau-Ponty and *Sartre.

transcendentalism

Romantic anti-rationalistic movement in nineteenth-century New England centred on the poet and essayist R.W. Emerson (1803–82), who shared with *Coleridge and *Carlyle a view of human nature derived from German idealism, and who attempted to synthesize that view with native American individualism. Transcendentalists were inspired by *Kant's 'transcendental idealism', which invites us not to focus on our experience but to study its preconditions – to see the world as already marked out with the forms of human knowledge. Emerson criticized the civilization generated by industrial production, and all modes of mass existence, advocating self-knowledge, self-reverence and self-determination as universal ideals. In this he influenced his pupil *Thoreau, who also followed him in his admiration for Kant. Transcendentalist communities flourished for a while in New England, and Henry James senior (father of the novelist Henry and the psychologist William) was an important member of one; but they had little lasting influence.

transnational institutions

Bodies which operate over more than one nation state, without being fully international in the manner of the *United Nations and its associated institutions. The *European Union is an example, as are various *NGOs, such as Greenpeace or the Red Cross. The transfer of political disputes and law-making capacities to transnational bodies has been one of the most important and far-reaching of recent political changes.

transport

A bone of contention in British politics, ever since *Ruskin set his heart against the railways, as intrusions into the majesty of God's world. The construction and maintenance of roads has been regarded as a prerogative of central government since ancient times, and even in the US local and federal authorities have the right to acquire land for road-building by *eminent domain, and to fund the work out of taxes – with results that are both irreversible and frequently disastrous. The railways, by contrast, began life in Europe and America as private projects. Their early profits quickly turned to deficits, by which time they had become so fundamental a part of the communications system that governments everywhere saw fit to *nationalize them, in order to keep them running. Even in the US the vestigial rail network now receives large subsidies from public funds. Schemes to exclude cars from city centres, to favour bicycles and to maintain effective and efficient networks of public transport are now a routine part of the *green agenda and of local government politics in Europe, and the destruction of the environment by roads and motor transport has led, both in the US and in Europe, to a renewed attachment to railways, and arguments in favour of their status as *public goods. Critics argue that public transport, and the railways in particular, are an inefficient allocation of resources, and that the market will solve problems of transport more effectively than any central plan. Transport has therefore become a new area in which the battle between statism and the free economy is being fought out.

treason

Breach of *allegiance to the *sovereign. Treason is defined in UK law by the Statute of Treasons 1351. It comprises, e.g., levying war against the sovereign in his realm, being an adherent to his enemies in his realm, or giving them aid and comfort elsewhere. The US constitution defines treason as levying war against the US or adhering to their enemies. There have been very few treason trials in the US and relatively few in the UK. Their relative abundance in the USSR is sometimes attributed to the fact that sovereignty rested, at least *de facto, with the ruling party, which had to impose its rule by force.

treaty

An agreement, normally written, concluded between two or more states or other subjects of *international law, intended to create rights and obligations between them that will be governed by that law. The word 'treaty' is normally reserved for the more formal kinds of agreement; *conventions and pacts are generally either less important or less formal. But to some extent the three terms, along with 'charter', 'act', 'declaration', 'protocol', can be used interchangeably, besides having various technical uses of their own.

In many respects the principles of private contract apply to treaties, but with one important exception: treaties are not made invalid by *duress, a party who enters a treaty by duress still being taken to have consented to it. Reasons for this rule are not hard to find: treaties must be dictated to the vanquished at the end of every war; moreover, there is no coercive sovereign in international law who can restrain the parties, so that both will threaten force (however covertly). Dictated treaties cannot, however, be contractual, and other treaties, to the extent that they share the nature of dictated accords, must be seen as exhibiting the peculiar synthesis of force and law which constitutes much of international adjudication. Moreover, it is sometimes argued that if the terms of a treaty are manifestly unjust, then they are not binding.

Treaties are not normally valid unless *ratified (the exceptions concern for the most part minor matters). Each constitution contains its own provision as to the agent in whom this power of ratification is vested. In the UK it is the monarch; in the US in theory it is the President, but he can ratify a treaty only with the consent of two thirds of the Senate, so that in fact the power of ratification vests in the Senate, with the President as solely empowered to *make* treaties.

Many problems of interpretation arise. Treaties are framed in order to deal with present exigencies, and later inherited by *regimes either unable or reluctant to fulfil, or even to understand, the original terms. Some international lawyers argue that in every treaty there is implied a clause which provides that the treaty is to be binding only so long as things stand as they are (*rebus sic stantibus*), so that a treaty is never more than conditional. But conditional on what? If the only answer is 'conditional on the present disposition of power' the function of a treaty as limiting the exercise of power is effectively denied, since as soon as a state emerges from the necessity that induced it to accept a treaty, it could repudiate it.

tribe

A form of social organization which is founded on *kinship (or a fiction of kinship) rather than on *territory, but which nevertheless retains a distinct *chain of command. Legal anthropology has tended to the conclusion that no tribe is wholly without law, if only in the form of customary procedures for settling disputes. Law implies *jurisdiction, and jurisdiction *sovereignty. However, it seems that tribal jurisdiction is not like modern forms of territorial jurisdiction: those who come under the law are defined only by their kinship relation. This has meant that no tribe is in fact recognized as sovereign in international law, or as an *international person. The clash between modern territorial notions of sovereignty and older ideas of allegiance based on kinship is responsible for much political disorder in Africa and elsewhere.

tribunals

In French law a tribunal is a lower court. In the UK it is not a court, but a quasi-judicial institution from whose rulings appeal may be made to 'appeals tribunals', and eventually to a court, on grounds such as breach of *natural justice. (*See* *administrative law.) The growth in the number and variety of tribunals since the 1950s follows the creation of new and complex relations between people that do not clearly fall under the traditional laws of contract, family or tort. *See* *industrial law.

trimmer

A term borrowed from nautical usage to mean someone who adjusts his position ('trims'), between opposing parties or factions, inclining now to the one, now to the other, as interest requires.

The term was originally applied to Lord Halifax and his associates in 1680–90; the description was accepted by Halifax as a compliment, since it suggested to him that he always acted so as 'to keep even the ship of state'. It is now largely a term of abuse, on account of the prevalent idea that allegiance is owed, and perhaps primarily owed, to a doctrine or party. That idea is coherent in a one-party state, but Halifax's response would perhaps be more reasonable in a state that aims to have authority and sovereignty over and above the authority and influence of a party.

Trotsky, Leon (Lev Bronstein)
(1879–1940)
Russian revolutionary, writer and
orator; *see* *Trotskyism.

Trotskyism
A collection of *Marxist doctrines and
policies associated with Trotsky, who
organized the first soviet in 1905, at
first opposed and then supported
Lenin, and was later Stalin's unsuccessful rival for leadership of the USSR
Communist Party on the death of
Lenin. Trotsky was expelled from the
USSR in 1929, organized opposition to
Stalin among exiles, and founded a
fourth *International in 1938. He was
murdered at Stalin's instigation in
1940.

Trotsky's opposition to Stalin
ostensibly had a theoretical base, in
that Trotsky remained wedded to the
ideal of an international socialism,
and opposed Stalin's policy of 'socialism in one country'. He continued to
advocate 'world revolution' after his
exile, making repeated use of a rhetorical phrase derived from Marx's
Address to the Communist League, 1850,
which became the identifying slogan
of Trotskyism: permanent revolution.
Trotsky was also one of the first
Marxists to proclaim that the initiative for anti-capitalist revolution in
the twentieth century would come
from underdeveloped countries, and
advocated a theory of multiple
systematic development which he
thought would account for this, while
remaining compatible with some
form of *historical materialism. (*See*
law of uneven development.) He
wrote widely and eclectically on many
themes, and was an acute analyst of
culture and institutions.

Apart from his doctrines Trotsky
remains influential, first, because of
the tactics with which he helped to
lead the *bolsheviks to power: *entryism, *substitution, the use of *front

organizations, and the organization of
the 'Red Army', which was a crucial
factor in the ultimate triumph of the
bolshevik **coup d'état*; secondly because
of his trenchant criticisms of the
'Bonapartist bureaucracy' that he saw
emerging under Stalin's dictatorship.

Trotskyists usually claim to have
more respect for democratic procedure
and human rights than *Stalinists,
which is plausible enough, since they
could hardly have less. They also argue
against centralization and bureaucracy, emphasize the role of politics in
social transformation, and argue that
revolution requires the transformation
of *all* institutions, however small.

truce
Originally truth or fidelity to a
promise, often given by one belligerent to another. The term now means
the cessation of hostilities between
belligerents, usually by declaration
and common consent, and usually for
a specified period. For 'truce of God',
see *pax.

Truman doctrine
The doctrine contained in a message
from President Truman to the US
Congress in March 1947, which
pledged US support for 'free peoples
who are resisting attempted subjugation by armed minorities or outside
pressures'. This marked the break with
the *isolationism implied in the
*Monroe doctrine, and laid the ideo-
logical foundation for subsequent US
policy towards communist regimes.

trust
1. The disposition to rely on another
to behave openly, honestly and trans-
parently towards his fellows. Trust has
been identified as a vital part of *social
capital, a precondition of the capitalist
economy, and one explanation of the
difference between places where that
economy has taken successful root,

and places where it has not. (This has been argued for example by Robert Putnam and *Fukuyama.)

The importance of trust in a free society was pointed out by *Hume, who argued that the institution of promising depends upon trust, and that without promises there can be no long-term relations and therefore no effective society. Studies of 'low trust societies' (for example Edward C. Banfield's study of the village of Montegrano in Calabria: *The Moral Basis of a Backward Society*, 1958), have suggested that societies develop economically by forging trust between their members, and that in the absence of trust nothing is done for others and nothing achieved for oneself. (*See* *platoons.)

2. The legal arrangement whereby a trustee holds the legal title to property subject to the interest of a beneficiary, and bound by trust to safeguard that interest. In UK and US law, because of the doctrine of the primacy of *equity, the beneficiary's interest will be protected, and the beneficiary is, in equity, the true owner of the property. Thus the separation of legal from equitable ownership has become an important legal conception, by which judicial decision has created a network of property rights either unrecognized, or even denied, by the law. From medieval times the device has been used to avoid the effect of property statutes, and in particular to avoid taxation on property, by transferring the legal title to an untaxable trustee.

Trusts may be created expressly, by statute, declaration or will. Or they may arise through the operation of the law of equity, as in the 'constructive trust', where a judge, in the interests of justice, infers the existence of a trust that might have been known to neither party. (An important example is the constructive trust sometimes

discerned when property is acquired with the help of another – e.g. a mistress – who is then dismissed without reward.) The law of trusts therefore has two important political applications: to override legal provisions in the interests of what might be argued to be *natural justice; and to uphold classes of extra-legal property rights through technicalities and fictions of ownership. The first use is often applauded, the second often denounced, in particular because it constantly acts so as to remove property dealings from the supervision of the legislature, and so permits the creation of *monopolies, *cartels, and other objectionable agreements, even when these are forbidden by statute. The purpose of *anti-trust legislation is in part to break down the influence of equity in this area (although here the term 'trust' has a slightly different sense, and such legislation may be directed against things which are not trusts in the precise legal sense).

Some charitable trusts show private property at an extreme point of attenuation, where the legal holders of the property (the trustees) may have no rights, but only obligations, and where the beneficiaries may be impossible to list, so that the funds of the trust cannot be divided among them. This case is sometimes cited as an example of the immense complexity of *private property rights, so that, if private property is objectionable, it is unlikely that it is in every case for exactly the same reason.

3. In a less formal sense, the idea of trust has been highly influential in political thinking. *Locke, for example, argued that the earth was given to men in common and that civil society holds it in trust. In *Burke we find the view that the present generation are always trustees of a patrimony that has been inherited from the dead and is to be

passed to those unborn. That ecological idea of *conservatism connects with modern *environmentalism, and both would agree in denouncing many forms of modern political decision-making for implicitly breaking the obligation of trusteeship.

trusteeship
1. The position of the legal owner of property under a *trust.

2. In *international law, the relation of the United Nations Organization, through its 'trusteeship council', to certain 'trust territories', about which the council concerns itself, formulating questionnaires, reporting on their political, social and economic conditions, and doing what it can to foster progress in those respects. The 'trust territory' stands to a *sovereign state roughly as equitable ownership stands to legal ownership in the doctrine of the *trust in law. The ownership of these territories vests in the people there resident, but they have yet to achieve the recognized sovereignty whereby their rights over the territory may be recognized in international law. A state which is appointed trustee of such a territory is held accountable to the UN for its government, and also to the people in the territory concerned.

The trusteeship system replaced the *mandates system, and now applies only to very few territories. It is, nevertheless, of considerable intellectual interest, in that it attempts to transfer a highly developed section of *municipal law into the international sphere.

Two Swords doctrine
Doctrine of the Church, derived from the New Testament and from *Augustine, and given authoritative statement at the close of the fifth century by Pope Gelasius I, who announced that God had granted 'two swords' for earthly government: that of the Church for the government of men's souls, and that of the imperial power for the regulation of temporal affairs. Although in doctrinal matters the emperor must submit to the clergy, in temporal affairs he is sovereign. The doctrine thus secured a sphere of autonomy for the church, while conceding the supremacy of secular law in the government of human communities. Already, therefore, the seeds of the Enlightenment vision of politics, as a sphere outside the provenance of religion, were sown, and the doctrine exerted an influence down the centuries which served entirely to distance Christian communities from those founded on *Islamic law.

tyranny
From Greek: *turannos*, an absolute ruler. For *Aristotle (and following him *Cicero and *Aquinas) a tyrant is one who rules exclusively in his own interest. The word tyranny is now used more or less synonymously with '*despotism', to denote any form of government which is oppressive, cruel, and without a rule of law, and in which there is considerable concentration of power, in the hands of a single individual or a single organization. The fascination of tyrants, for whom all spheres are seemingly spheres of will, so that the objective is absorbed into the subjective, has led to their frequent deification by poets. *Nietzsche's injunction to each man to will his own desire as a law for himself was accompanied by a respect for tyranny, as the highest example of that principle. The poet's refusal to recognize a world beyond the subjective is redeemed by a gift of imagination, whereby he may, in Hamlet's words, be bounded in a nutshell, and yet count himself king of infinite

space. The tyrant, who lacks that gift, may yet have the grandeur of vision which substitutes for it, and this may be one reason why he is so frequently extolled.

The question of the justification of tyrannicide exercised ancient moralists and philosophers. One answer seems to be that it is justifiable in the circumstances where, were the tyrant an alien, war would be justified: so that the problem becomes identical with that of *just war.

tyranny of the majority

Phrase used by both *J.S. Mill and *Tocqueville to signal the danger that democracy might degenerate into tyranny if minorities and eccentrics are not protected from oppression by the majority. It is possible for a policy of *genocide, for example, to achieve the consent of the majority; without constitutional guarantees – and specifically a law which upholds elementary *rights and *freedoms – democracy may therefore become the enemy of liberty.

Übermensch

The 'overman' or 'super-man', a concept introduced in *Nietzsche's philosophy of self-mastery and later vulgarized in the Nazi doctrine of the 'master race' (*Herrenvolk*). According to Nietzsche human nature defines the essence, not of an individual, but of a class, and the individual owes it to himself to transcend every class, and every principle, creed or custom that might confine him to one (including, incidentally, the class of the *Herrenvolk*). The individual is essentially *contrasted* with the universal. Hence human nature must be overcome, and true excellence belongs to the creature who emerges from this overcoming: the *Übermensch*. The doctrine relies on a rather dubious metaphysics, but has its parallel in certain *existentialist ideas concerning the priority of 'existence' over 'essence'. Nietzsche used it to revive ideas from *Aristotle's ethics. Aristotle argued that all people ought to cultivate *virtue, that virtue belongs to the entire character, and that its highest form is that of the *megalopsuchos*, or great-souled person, who surveys the human scene with a kind of lordly disdain that is unavailable to the mass of common mortals.

ultra vires

'Beyond the powers': i.e. beyond those *powers conferred by law. Action *ultra vires* is an important ground for legal proceedings in all areas where powers are conferred on individuals who are tempted to exceed them: e.g. administration, delegated government, police action, company direction. The ability to bring such proceedings, and to enforce judgement against all officers of government should they exceed their *office, is often held forth as the principal mark of genuinely *limited government, since it is the sign that a citizen can effectively confine the powers of those who govern him, to those sanctioned in law. This is one part of that 'negative power' which *Calhoun celebrated in his *Discourse on the Constitution of the United States*, 1852, when he argued that 'it is . . . the negative power which makes the constitution, and the positive which makes the government'. However, Calhoun argued, the proceeding for actions *ultra vires* is not enough. He proposed the far stronger 'rule of concurrent majority', according to which 'every major interest in the country . . . is to possess a veto power on political decisions directly affecting it'. This power to prevent the very formation of policy is of a quite different order from the power to prevent the exceeding of office in its execution: it is arguable that, being a *veto, it must limit government to the point of non-existence.

ultramontanism

('Beyond the mountains'; meaning, beyond the Alps.) The tendency in the *Roman Catholic Church to favour the centralization of authority in the papacy and its court (the *curia*) and to oppose national and diocesan independence in religious matters. After two centuries of vacillation ultramontanism triumphed in 1814, with the revival of its principal advocate, the *Jesuit order. It became a political force among French *traditionalists, who invoked the support of the papacy for their *legitimism, and who regarded the universal spiritual authority of the church as necessary to all civil order born out of Christian conceptions of sovereignty. During the course of the nineteenth century, however, the Jesuit influence declined, and the principle of *subsidiarity was gradually accepted, and stated as an official doctrine of the Church in 1931.

ummah

Arabic: nation or people, by implication the world-wide Muslim community (the *ummah muhammad*), which identifies itself as a people without definite frontiers or territory, united by their submission to God's law.

underclass

Term of American sociology, given currency by Charles Murray, used to describe the new class of state dependants produced by the *welfare system and by the supposed habit in modern states of subsidizing idle, feckless and irresponsible behaviour. The unmarried mother with six children by different men can, it is argued, be more comfortable on welfare than the married mother of two who works to provide for them. Children of the first mother grow up in the underclass, and tend to remain there, in a lifelong dependency on the state. The underclass is a genuine *class, in that it is brought into being entirely by economic factors – namely, the subsidies available to those who join it. But to join it you also have to behave irresponsibly, since the subsidies are not available on any other terms.

underground

A name applied to movements and associations opposed to some established order, which are compelled to conceal their opposition for fear of official reprisals. The name is sometimes appropriated by movements and associations that openly defy censure from an *establishment, and also by certain non-political associations which continue peacefully within a *police state, even when not forming a genuine *opposition, as in the underground universities, schools and religious associations that struggled for survival in the USSR and its dominions. Here opposition was not the *purpose* of association, although it was the normal result; hence there arose a real need for concealment.

unemployment

Used to denote involuntary, rather than voluntary, lack of paid employment, and divided into various kinds: e.g. cyclical, *frictional, seasonal, and structural. It is a feature of much *neoclassical economics, and of the economic assumptions that are sometimes encapsulated in *Say's law, that structural unemployment, and any other enduring unemployment, become inexplicable; it is a virtue of *Keynesian economic theory that it attempts to explain such kinds of unemployment, in terms of lack of effective demand. The Keynesian theory and its offshoots are not generally accepted as explaining every kind of unemployment, and the emphasis on technological factors has become increasingly important. If the means of production become so sophisticated that enormous productivity can be achieved while employing only a fraction of the work force, then, at some point of development, demand can be met in a condition of less than full employment.

In actual conditions it is socially necessary to work in order to enjoy any measure of material comfort. Most postwar governments have therefore taken it as a major policy objective to keep the level of unemployment to a minimum. Various more or less arbitrary figures have been suggested as the 'acceptable' maximum of unemployed members of the workforce: it was once 2%, then, throughout the 1950s and 1960s, 1.5% was considered normal. The 'acceptable' maximum has perforce risen as unemployment has risen; some even argue that unemployment below a certain level (Lord Beveridge argued 3%) marks a condition of *overfull employment, which cannot be sustained without damage to the economy. Moreover, in the *service economy, in which individuals frequently change their jobs, unemployment may be constantly at a fairly high figure, since it is constantly boosted by the interim unemployment of people who are changing from one job to another. Nevertheless it is now assumed that 5% unemployment (the UK) indicates a healthy economy, 10% an unhealthy economy (Germany), 25% a continuing national crisis (Algeria).

Many economists believe that reduction of unemployment is incompatible with certain other basic economic objectives, such as control over the rate of *inflation (*see* *Phillips curve), or a stable *balance of payments. Alternatively it may be that the seeming difficulty of reconciling control of inflation with full employment is the result of deep structural factors within the economy, and that the two objectives could be reconciled only by overthrowing the economic order that makes each of them desirable.

unification of laws

The elimination of national peculiarities from law, so that states which frequently deal with each other commercially and politically should be able to do so without unnecessary legal impediment, and so that *international law should be able to connect as easily as possible with *municipal law. A movement for the unification of laws began in the nineteenth century, and has continued, despite serious obstacles and interruptions, up to the present. Important agencies of the movement have been the Universal Postal Union (established 1874), the *International Labour Organization (established 1919), and the Hague Conference (begun 1893).

unilateral act

An act which affects the relations of two or more parties, but in which only one party is involved as an *agent. The contrast is with bilateral, trilateral, etc. acts, in which there is always some element of agreement, collusion or common responsibility.

unilateral nuclear disarmament

Voluntary renunciation by one side to a potential conflict of at least some (including the most destructive) of the weapons of war. The usual argument given for unilateral nuclear disarmament has been this: if nuclear armaments are kept by both sides then there is a probability of war by accident and war will in this case mean total destruction; if nuclear armaments are kept only by one side then there is a probability of deliberate war, which will involve conquest but not total destruction. However small the first probability and however large the second, the negative value of total destruction is incommensurably greater than that of conquest, so that it would always be irrational to choose the first alternative over the second.

The strength of such arguments depends upon the method for assigning probabilities, and also upon assumptions about accidental war, and about the destructive effects of nuclear weapons. It is always to be supposed, however, that, if people have not yet invented a weapon that will destroy the world, this is only through lack of time.

unincorporated association

See *incorporation.

united front

A term once popular on the left to denote coalitions formed for the purpose of achieving a specific objective – as with the Anti-Fascist United Front in the UK during the 1930s, which effectively prevented the British League of Fascists from making any headway in the political arena. United fronts were subsequently viewed with suspicion, following their use by the communists to seize power with an appearance of legitimacy in postwar Eastern and Central Europe. Having joined with other parties of the left in order to eliminate their main opponents, the communists then seized control of government and proceeded to eliminate their friends. 'United fronts' persisted as masks for communist totalitarianism, and the term is now rejected in *post-communist countries as a particularly cynical piece of communist *newspeak.

UK, constitution and laws

The United Kingdom comprises the kingdoms of Scotland and England, the principality of Wales, and Northern Ireland (which is that part of the former kingdom of Ireland which elected in 1920 to be bound by the Act of Union 1800, and which has in that sense remained loyal to the *Crown). The UK is not a federal state, since although there are sovereign legislative bodies outside Westminster (the Scottish Parliament, e.g.), they cannot legislate on matters that affect the country as a whole, and possess all their legislative powers by grant from the Westminster Parliament. Nor is it a true unitary state, in that there has

been and still is *delegation of power and regional autonomy on a scale more familiar in federations. Scotland, Wales and Northern Ireland have their own legislative, or quasi-legislative, chambers (the last somewhat fitfully). And the legal systems of Scotland and, to some extent, Northern Ireland are substantially different from that of England and Wales, necessitating separate systems of courts and judicial offices (*see* *English law, *Scots law). It is usual, therefore, to acknowledge that, constitutionally, the UK is *sui generis*, and to be understood neither on the federal nor on the unitary model.

Furthermore the constitution remains unwritten and probably unwriteable, contains large elements that are the effect and residue of long-established custom and convention, rather than legal or executive recognition, and is completely open to amendment in every particular, containing (and probably able to contain) no equivalent of the *entrenched clause. *Sovereignty resides, according to many observers, in 'the Queen in Parliament', an expression which indicates the peculiar combination of hereditary monarchy and parliamentary representation that has led to present institutions. The actual locus of this sovereignty is in fact hard to determine: *executive power has been thought to reside not with the monarch but with the *Prime Minister or, to be more exact, the *cabinet, while legislative power resides in the two Houses of Parliament, as well as being exercised by judges through the operation of *common law and *equity. The *separation of powers is incomplete and dependent largely on convention, although *judicial independence seems to be as well guaranteed as anything else, by the nature of the law, and by rights and privileges enshrined in custom. Custom is in fact the most important part of the arrangement, and provides the background from which Parliament emerges as a definite shape, but without which parliamentary institutions are far from easy to understand.

United Nations Organization

The UN, successor to the League of Nations established in the wake of the First World War, came into existence after the Second World War. Its constitution is embodied in a Charter, ratified in 1945, following negotiations between the UK, US, USSR and China begun in 1942. The membership consists of the original 50 states which adopted the Charter, and states later admitted, which are peace-loving, accept the obligations of the Charter and are deemed able and willing to carry them out. States are recommended by the Security Council and admitted by a two-thirds vote of the General Assembly. The General Assembly comprises representatives of all members, and it initiates studies and makes recommendations concerning all matters, but without legislative power. The Security Council is composed of five permanent members (the UK, US, France, China and Russia as successor to the former USSR) and six others elected for two years by the General Assembly. The functions of the Security Council are primarily executive and members agree to accept and carry out its decisions: the power of *veto possessed by each of its members ensures that these are few. In addition to those two principal bodies there are the Economic and Social Council, concerned with the promotion of better living conditions and the support of human rights throughout the member states; the Trusteeship Council, concerned with the administration of *trusteeship territories, and the *International Court of Justice.

The partial effectiveness of the United Nations in adjudicating at least some disputes which might otherwise be settled violently has given some credibility to these institutions; however, the number of petty tyrannies and totalitarian states represented in the General Assembly, and allegations of corruption against the administration of the organization, and especially against its subordinate bodies, have led to a loss of confidence in recent years. Indeed many states, including the US, now seem to be deliberately withholding contributions due under the Charter, so that the UN is constantly facing bankruptcy. At the same time, because the US is the most powerful member of the Security Council, and able to use it effectively, since the collapse of communism, to legitimize peace-keeping operations outside the US, the UN has also been condemned as an instrument of US foreign policy.

US, constitution and laws

Although the United States of America has the most famous of all written *constitutions, its actual constitution at any moment can be determined only by examining two centuries of judicial decision, and observing the extent to which the written words have been qualified, clarified and 'interpreted' in their application. The constitution of 1788 establishes a federal system of government, with considerable limits to its power, but with absolute sovereignty in all matters that concern the existence of the US as a single state. The federal government consists of legislative, executive and judicial branches, interrelated but distinct, and constructed expressly so as to accord with the theory of the *separation of powers, as this had been understood by the *Founding Fathers. The federal legislature is the *Congress, in which two main parties contend for power, while the federal executive is the *President, affiliated to one of the parties in Congress (although not necessarily to the majority party). The President has power to appoint a *cabinet, who are not members of Congress, in order to facilitate the exercise of executive power. The judicial power resides in, and depends on, the *Supreme Court which, because it can interpret and enforce the constitution, has considerable political influence.

The legal system is dualistic, with federal and state courts acting side by side to determine the rights and obligations of the citizen, the federal courts having jurisdiction in all matters arising under the constitution or in connection with the existence of the US as a sovereign state, the state courts adjudicating in most matters of civil and criminal law. The federal courts also exercise the supremely important function of *judicial review of administrative decisions.

Case law is as important as legislation, and the doctrine of *precedent is effective in practice, even if not fully recognized in law. Hence, although there is not a true *common law system in the US, the law of the separate states exists against a background of accepted decisions which are tantamount to common law, and which usually evolved out of an inheritance of European (e.g. English) common law. (Originally the settlers had tended to prefer written codes of law, and the Carolinas had a complete written code, compiled by *Locke, from 1668; this code gave way in 1712 to the English common law, as the only workable system, and this return to common law was universal by the time of the federal constitution.) The division between common law and *equity was originally recognized in the US, but has since been gradually diminished, and the enshrining of ideas of *natural justice in the *Bill of Rights has led to an automatic expectation of equitable remedies, which therefore have needed no procedural guarantee.

universalism

1. In Christian theology, another term for 'apocatastis', the doctrine that all moral agents – angels, human beings and devils – will ultimately be saved.

2. In political thought, the belief in universally valid principles of government and individual rights, usually founded in a theory of universal human nature. Typical universalist doctrines are those of *international socialism, *human rights, and the moral law of *Kant. Opposition to universalism is exemplified by *nationalism (sometimes called, in this context, 'national particularism', to emphasize that the universal is being contrasted with the particular), and by those varieties of conservatism which stress the view that man as a political animal is always the product of, and always incorporates into himself as part of his political nature, local conditions and attachments.

The opposite of universalism should be called particularism, and not individualism, which is a theory about human nature, and may well be compatible with universalism. Thus the universalist doctrines of *liberalism are also often individualistic. Only some individualists, notably *Nietzsche, have also advocated forms of individualism which have particularism as a consequence.

universities

Associations incorporated by charter or statute, for the purpose of the development and transmission of knowledge. The idea of a university is ecclesiastical in origin, and derives from the *Roman law concept of the *universitas*, a corporation created for a specified purpose. The distinctive structure, powers and educative role of the universities for a long time reflected their medieval origin, although the newer universities in the US and the UK are institutions of a kind that have very little outward resemblance to their medieval forebears.

The question of the ideal nature of university education, and of the role of the university in public life, are in fact older than the universities themselves. The medievals recognized their predecessors in the academy of *Plato, and in the school of Constantinople, founded AD 425, while the question of the nature and function of university education has its antecedents in the ancient dispute between *rhetoric and philosophy. Philosophy – the pursuit of wisdom – seems sublime but useless, while rhetoric – the art of persuasion – seems useful but degrading. Plato set out to show that philosophy is not only useful but indispensable both to the happiness of the individual and to the good government of the *polis. The debate now centres on the relative merits of arts and sciences, but it has the same structure. On the one hand there are the graceful but useless accomplishments of the humanities; opposed to them stand the useful-seeming sciences. Defenders of *humane education have tried to describe further, and more serious uses, which the arts satisfy through their very uselessness; while defenders of the sciences have emphasized the need for new recruits to management. The conflict between *utilitarians and *cultural conservatives in the nineteenth century led to several important attempts to examine the nature of universities as institutions and their role in the modern state, notably that of Cardinal Newman, in *The Idea of a University*, 1852.

In more recent years, discussions have centred upon the question, How widely distributed should university education be, and who should finance it? (*See* *education.) The extent to which universities have been funded and expanded under public initiative in the UK is some indication of the acceptance of their utility (and perhaps of the fact that those who gain high office tend to be university graduates).

urban planning
See *planning.

use-value
Classical economists' term for *utility, normally contrasted (following a usage introduced by *Smith) with *exchange-value which is explored by theories of *price. It is often held that 'use-value as such lies outside the sphere of investigation of political economy' (Marx), meaning that, from the economic point of view, the fact that someone has a desire which some object satisfies is the ultimate fact. The structure of the desire itself, and its merit, depth and moral or spiritual significance lie outside the economist's purview. Thus an apple has use-value, so does a work of art. But the desire for an apple is based on physical need, that for a work of art on a conception of aesthetic value. Many are unhappy with theories that treat these two things as on a par and have sought to take account in their economics of the multifarious nature of human desire. Is, for example, a desire for medical treatment to be considered as similar to a desire for cosmetics? And if not, what does this entail for the use-value of each? Reflections on this type of question motivated J.K. Galbraith's *The Affluent Society*, 1958, and for a while made their way into the centre of economics, only to retreat again under the influence of the theory of *revealed preference.

usurpation

The illegitimate seizure of political power. Usurpation is to be distinguished from *revolution, in that the power seized in the first case precedes the seizure, and endures through it. Revolution consists not in the seizure of power but in its abolition and replacement by another power (sometimes represented as temporary). 'Illegitimate' means either illegal or (more widely) contrary to *natural justice.

usury

Originally, lending at a profit, and hence lending money for *interest. This is the narrow interpretation sometimes given to *usuria* (literally: putting to use) in *canon law, and to *ribâ* (literally: increase) in *Islamic law. However, what has been intended by both terms has been a matter of considerable dispute, so that, while both *usuria* and *ribâ* are forbidden, this has not always meant that people have been unable to lend at interest. It is now more normal to reserve the term 'usury' for interest judged to be unjust or excessive, which denotes the original idea only if *all* interest is such. Over this issue both Christian theologians and Islamic jurists have given contradictory opinions and there seems to be no settled view in either religion. The transition from the original to the modern meaning has sometimes been thought to be explained by the rise of capitalism, but this is now doubted.

Clearly, lending money at a rate of interest equal to the rate of inflation is not lending money for profit in real terms. The blanket condemnation of usury also seems to neglect both the concept of *time preference, and the fact that individuals independently prefer goods now to the same goods later (there being, for example, a probability that I may not be here to enjoy them at a later time). Suppose I could be induced to forgo £1 now only if I could receive £1.10 in a year's time; does it not follow that someone who wishes to borrow £1 from me must offer 10% interest if he is to have my consent? One can imagine all kinds of sophisticated variants of that case and of the accompanying question. Moreover, according to the *Austrian school of economic thought, resources that are saved can be put to productive use in order to produce *more* goods in the future (*see also* *capital). Such considerations clearly influenced the Islamic jurists, who developed elaborate *legal fictions on this principle in order to avoid the charge of *ribâ*: for example, I sell you my piano for £110, payable in a year's time; I then promptly buy it back from you for £100. The net result of the transaction is a loan of £100 at 10%; technically, however, it is a double contract, neatly capturing the idea of time preference in its terms.

Philosophical condemnations of usury have been of two kinds: the general and the particular. The first purports to find something wrong in any human relation in which someone enjoys a (legal) right to part of the product of another's labour, while not himself producing. Such arguments include criticisms of the feudal practice of *corvée*, and Marxist arguments concerning the *exploitation of the worker by the capitalist, who extorts hours of 'unpaid labour'. Such arguments are of a great generality, and clearly do not invoke any quality specific to usury. The more specific arguments tend to criticize, not usury in its original sense, but rather the modern idea of an unjust, oppressive, or exploitative loan. It may be, indeed, that this is what has always been intended by critics of usury. Typically critics concentrate on the case where one person grants a loan to another who is genuinely needy, in order to secure his dependence, making sure that the rate of interest is so high that the loan can never be repaid, so that the borrower in effect binds himself for life to provide an income to the lender. Some find elements of this kind of usury in modern credit systems – particularly the system of the bank card, which tempts people to spend to the limit of their capacity, and then binds them by interest rates that force them to try to raise their earnings. It is not clear that the cases are exactly parallel, although it is certain that no medieval moralist could have tolerated such modern forms of credit. A celebrated defence of usury on utilitarian grounds was offered by *Bentham (*Defence of Usury*, 1787), but here 'usury' means 'lending at interest, according to the market rate'.

'Usurocracy', the rule by usurers, is a coinage of Ezra Pound's, in which he mixes Latin and Greek etymology for expletive effect.

utilitarianism

The philosophy of morals, politics and legislation, associated with the names of *Bentham, *James Mill, *J.S. Mill, and Henry Sidgwick (1838–1900), which founds all practical reasoning in the concept of *utility, and argues that the right action, the good character, and the right law are those that maximize utility. Utilitarianism exists in many forms, but its most representative definition is that given by J.S. Mill, partly in order to endorse, and partly in order to criticize, the moral philosophy of Bentham: 'The creed which accepts as the foundation of morals Utility, or the Greatest Happiness Principle, holds that actions are right in proportion as they tend to promote happiness, wrong as they tend to produce the reverse of happiness. By happiness is intended pleasure and the absence of pain; by

unhappiness, pain and the privation of pleasure'. Mill's definition has the merit of showing the strong point of utilitarianism, which is that it can deliver comparative judgements of moral worth: in other words it connects the idea of good with those of better and best, in a way that facilitates rational choice. Critics of utilitarianism often commit themselves, whether or not intentionally, to an absolutist position which renders all comparisons of moral value impossible. The theory can be divided into three parts:

(i) the merits of an action lie in its consequences, and not in the motive or character from which it springs. Hence utilitarianism is often criticized as a form of *consequentialism and held, as such, to countenance injustice for the sake of however slight an increase in the overall good.

(ii) Consequences are to be assessed in terms of something first called happiness, and then later identified in terms of pleasure and pain. The theory therefore provokes (as Mill realized) two powerful objections: that there is not one single end of human conduct, and that, even if happiness is an end, it is not to be described merely in terms of pleasure or pain. Happiness is the fulfilment of the *person or *rational agent, and is not reducible to the pleasures which an animal might equally feel. ('Better Socrates dissatisfied than a pig satisfied'.) The emphasis on pleasure and pain stemmed from Bentham's *hedonism, itself an attempt to reduce ethics to measurable quantities, and so to solve the problems of morals and legislation through *cost–benefit analysis.

(iii) The *optimum to be achieved is overall maximization, untempered by any idea of distribution or desert. The theory has therefore prompted objections from those who, while perhaps accepting (i) and even (ii), wish to adopt a more just, intelligible, or politically feasible criterion of optimality: *see* *Pareto optimality, *maximin. (When *welfare economists refer to the 'utilitarian criterion of optimality' they have this idea of overall maximization in mind, whether or not conjoined to (i) and (ii).)

There are further difficulties – especially the practical difficulties of applying such a principle – and philosophers, attracted by what seems to be the eminent common sense of the doctrine, have sought to overcome some of them by distinguishing act utilitarianism (just discussed) from rule utilitarianism. According to the latter an action is judged right by its conformity to some rule, and the rule itself judged right by its conformity to the greatest happiness principle. It is sometimes argued that no such sophistications will escape a general difficulty for consequentialist doctrines, which is that they describe, not the moral reasoning of the agent, but the moral rationalizations of the observer, and hence provide no guide to action. It has also been argued, by *Hegelians and their progeny, that utilitarianism is founded in a mistaken and unduly *individualistic view of human nature.

utility

A term sometimes used by economists to denote what was classically called *use-value, and by philosophers to denote a variety of things, for example happiness (*see* *utilitarianism), pleasure (sometimes identified with happiness), and function. Modern economics, however, tends to dispense with the concept of utility, employing only the notion of *preference orderings. All these things are brought together in the thought that an object with utility is a means to an end, and is desired for that reason. If the ends of human conduct are given, then the utilities of all objects can be estimated in relation

to them. *Bentham thought that, if I desire something, then I desire it as a means to pleasure. By adroit manipulation of that idea he came to believe that the utility of every object is a measurable quantity, to be estimated in terms of the intensity, duration, propinquity, fecundity and probability of the pleasure to which it is a means. Philosophers have objected that many less measurable dimensions have been left out of this account – e.g. those of depth, seriousness, and *value. Moreover we distinguish in our practical reasoning between desires, needs, whims, and values: yet all these distinctions seem to have no place in the Benthamite calculus. It may be replied that the objection is not to the actual terms of measurement that Bentham used, but to his claims as to what he was measuring. If 'utility' is thought of simply as another name for preference, and, if preferences are construed in the terms of *decision theory, then comparative utilities can be seen as parts of a preference ordering. To say that one state of affairs has greater utility than another for John, is simply to say that John prefers the first to the second. This replacement of any real notion of utility with the notion of preference ordering is often thought to signal a great advance. It does not overcome the philosopher's worries about the incommensurability of the many things that might be weighed in the balance of preference, but it satisfies the economist's worries that the theory of utility might be associated with nothing empirically discernible whatsoever. (*See* *revealed preference.)

utility function

A mathematical device for representing a consumer's preference orderings.

utopia

Term coined by *More (*Utopia*, 1516), to mean (although the Greek derivation is incorrect) 'No place'. More portrays a social arrangement without violence, oppression, or property, and presents a comprehensive view of ideal institutions. The term has since been appropriated to name any such picture, usually with the implied criticism that a 'utopia' must idealize human nature, and gain its plausibility from neglecting recalcitrant facts. However, in the vast literature devoted to the construction of idealized societies one may distinguish the following quite different endeavours:

(i) to make political recommendations, in the form of an ideal, without examining the actual policies that might realize it. More's *Utopia* is an example of this.

(ii) To show what it would be like for an 'ideal' to be realized, thereby criticizing it; Huxley's *Brave New World* is an example of this. (On one theory of the literary imagination (ii) is always a greater imaginative task than (i) since it involves the labour of concrete description.) Huxley's utopia might also be described as a *dystopia.

(iii) The construction of an *ideal type of political arrangement, in order to explain actual forms of government. It is possible that Plato's *Republic* is at least partly of this kind, as are certain parts of Aristotle's *Politics*. Such a theory may attempt to give a full account of human nature, and to illustrate the ways in which actual arrangements fall short of the ideal.

(iv) The construction of an ideal in terms of which to *justify* actual approximations to it. Plato's theory is also of this type.

Early socialists such as *Fourier and *Owen were sometimes criticized for

their 'utopian' character by the Marxists (in particular by Marx and Engels): their theories were of type (i), and involved the postulation of an ideal without the investigation of the actual conditions which must make it unrealizable. By contrast the socialism of Marx was held to be 'scientific', not just in the sense of being based on a scientific theory of social development, but also in the sense of taking account of actual social conditions, and of the transformations that will be necessary if a socialist community is to be brought into being. Some socialists try to justify utopias as *myths, which have the function of spurring people to action, so *hastening* the conditions which will make them actual. (*See* *Sorel.)

Objections to utopianism have been made not only in the name of so-called 'scientific' socialism (which ought perhaps to be called 'scientist socialism'), but also in the name of political *realism, and of the conservative attachment to existing social conditions. Some argue that much type (i) utopianism, in its reluctance to accept the proven realities of human nature, shows a diseased and egocentric consciousness. On this view, it is not surprising to find that those who are galvanized by utopian ideals are so often able to perpetrate cruelties, with consciences that are automatically washed clean by the never-ending absolution from that source. Much *terrorism has a utopian component, and reveals the contempt for others and for the human condition that, on one plausible view, underlies the utopian mentality. *See* *antinomianism, *millenarianism.

Value

Worth, desirability, goodness: an idea that generates more questions than it answers. It is important to distinguish two uses:

1. In economics it is normal to follow *Smith in distinguishing *utility – or *use-value – from *price – or *exchange-value. Thus Smith wrote: 'The word value, it is to be observed, has two different meanings, and sometimes expresses the utility of some particular object, and sometimes the power of purchasing other goods which the possession of that object conveys. The one may be called "value in use", the other "value in exchange".' Smith adds that 'the things which have the greatest value in use have frequently little or no value in exchange; and, on the contrary, those which have the greatest value in exchange have frequently little or no value in use'; he gives water as an example of the first, a diamond as an example of the second. This observation is sometimes referred to as the 'paradox of value', and it is one of the things that theories of value have attempted to explain (success in explaining it being one argument sometimes offered for the *marginal utility theory).

2. Generally, the term 'value' is applied to all those objects thought to be worthy of human pursuit, say on moral, aesthetic, or religious grounds. Thus value attaches to goods in economics; but to ideals, motives, sentiments, actions and so on in the wider context. The principal question in the theory of value is that of the objectivity of moral value judgements: judgements of what is good, right or worthy. In normal philosophical usage, such judgements are of two kinds: (i) judgements of the worth, goodness or intrinsic desirability of a state of affairs, or of the *virtue of a character, or of the admirable quality of a motive; (ii) judgements of obligation, of the rightness or wrongness of an act, of duty, of what ought to be done, and so on. Sometimes the expression 'value judgement' is reserved for type (i), in order to separate what are thought to be the distinct logical structures of 'good' and 'ought'. Sometimes type (ii) is taken as primary, since it captures explicitly the normative element that is already implicit in (i).

The philosophical question may be expressed thus: are such value judgements mere expressions of preferences, dressed up in a language that claims the concurrence of others, or can they be objective, binding on all who understand them? Theories of the objectivity of value judgements can be divided into two: (a) 'realism', which holds that value judgements, like any other judgement in the indicative mood, describe reality and are therefore true or false according to whether or not they correspond to reality, (b) theories of practical reason which deny (a), e.g. because value judgements are not really indicatives but imperatives, but which go on to assert that, despite the fact that there is no 'moral reality', value judgements are still binding on all rational beings as the essential expression of the principles of practical reason. *Kant's view is an example of type (b), certain types of *utilitarianism may be of type (a), while *Aristotle's theory of *virtue contains a subtle mixture of both.

Theories of *justice are more or less useless if they accompany a sceptical or subjectivist theory about the value of justice. In general, any political ideal which seeks not only to exist but also to recommend itself must, in the end, uphold the objectivity of judgements of value. It is sometimes said that Marxism can never so recommend itself, since it dismisses value judgements as *ideology.

value-free
German: *wertfrei*. A judgement is sometimes held to be more 'scientific', and therefore more suited for incorporation into a scientific theory of society, if it is freed from all expressions of *value (in sense 2.). So at least thought *Weber, who introduced this usage, and who recommended a 'value-free' social science while also doubting its possibility. Some have argued that there can be no value-free social science, because there is no value-neutral language for the description, and therefore analysis and understanding, of social life. Others have argued that a value-free social science is necessary since value judgements are subjective, or unscientific, or possess some other defect that forbids them from serving as vehicles for an objective science of man.

vanguard
Those who are foremost in a battle. The term was appropriated by *Lenin, to denote the role of the Communist Party in the Russian Revolution and subsequently. Since the proletariat is disorganized, easily subverted, and without an understanding of its revolutionary mission, it stands in need of a disciplined organization that will organize and lead it, and which will articulate its needs and ideals: this is the vanguard, which represents the synthesis of the 'objective conditions' of revolution (i.e. the development of *productive forces and the beginnings of 'class warfare'), with the 'subjective conditions' – the understanding of past, present and future that will enable the cogent formulation of policy and tactics. The Leninist theory of the vanguard has also been influential in *Islamism, through the writings of *Qutb.

The French translation of the term – *l'avant-garde* – has entered common usage as the name for innovative movements in the arts and culture, and it is probably no accident that the Leninist idea of the vanguard and the aesthetic addiction to avant-garde art for a while coincided.

Vatican Councils
The two 'Vatican Councils,' 21st and 22nd 'Oecumenical Councils' respectively, were called, first, by Pope Pius IX in 1868, when *ultramontanism resurged and was victorious, with the affirmation of the doctrine of papal infallibility, second, by Pope John XXIII in 1962 (lasting until 1965), in which far-reaching liturgical reforms were instigated, together with measures of *secularization from within.

A Vatican Council is a convocation of bishops and others holding high office within the *Roman Catholic Church, in order to settle disputed questions of vital importance to the role of the church in society. The effect of the first was to redefine the role of the church as an international (but 'apolitical') organization; the effect (though not the intention) of the second was to emphasize social transformation and secular morality, rather than faith, mystery, and eternal truth. Pope John Paul II, whose outlook was partly shaped by the Second Vatican Council, which he believed to have laid the foundations for a new work of evangelism, later did his best to moderate its radical image and apparent compromises with the secular world, and to interpret its message as one of continuity with the long-standing traditions and teachings of the Church.

Veblen, Thorstein Bunde (1857–1929)
American economist and sociologist, whose imaginative description of the transformation of social relations under the impact of technology and mass production has had a lasting influence on modern social and political science. Veblen was influenced by *Marx, and accepted the latter's dichotomous view of social development, replacing the dualism of *productive forces and *production relations with his own close equivalents, technology (which is the dynamic and constantly developing force) and institutions (the static and constraining structures which are functionally related to that force). However, Veblen was sceptical about the idea that there might be general 'laws of motion' of capitalist society, as of virtually everything else in Marxian social analysis. (See especially *The Theory of Business Enterprise*, 1904.) He argued that capitalist institutions would differ from place to place according to cultural factors, and that the class structure could not have a single universal form or function. His *Theory of the Leisure Class*, 1899, identified the function of the *leisure class at a certain stage of technological development in terms of a propensity towards conspicuous consumption. This tendency causes the class of parasites to act as a stimulus to production, and also an impediment to production beyond a certain level, while impressing on the labourer an image of the social distinction which consumption confers, thus prompting the labourer to emulate the wastefulness of the leisure class. Such a theory is characteristic of Veblen's irony: it is both a serious piece of social analysis, and also a satirical portrait of human futility. He was pessimistic, and although he sometimes allowed a socialist vision to break through his thin-lipped smile at modern capitalism, he was convinced of nothing so much as the inevitable 'triumph of imbecile institutions over life and culture'.

Verstehen
German: understanding. A term appropriated by philosophical anthropologists during the nineteenth century (notably by *Dilthey and others influenced by *Kant's philosophy of human nature), in order to denote the peculiar mode of understanding necessary for the perception of human affairs. It is supposed that scientific explanation sees the human being as an organism motivated by physical causes; *Verstehen* sees him as a *person, acting from reasons, and in accordance with fundamental *values. The two visions represent the world in contrasting, perhaps even conflicting, ways. Some argue that without *Verstehen* no social reality is perceivable, since its lived essence lies outside the observer's grasp.

The idea of a duality of vision, the scientific (explanatory) and the human (justificatory), is often mooted, but not always in these terms. Fundamentally it involves an attempt to recast the old metaphysical idea of *freedom – that there are events outside the laws of nature – in a less paradoxical form, by saying that events can be seen under two aspects that of nature, and that of 'freedom'.

The term was later imported into *sociology by *Weber, who accepted the broad outline of Dilthey's theory. *See also* *hermeneutics, *humane education.

veto

Latin: I forbid. A right to prevent an act or policy by a single negative vote. The veto is an important device, since, by granting it to every member of a body, you also ensure that no action can be undertaken unless they all consent to it. Hence the existence of a veto is an essential part of the *social contract. In international affairs the veto has also seemed essential, if there is not to be recourse to force. Thus the veto granted to permanent members of the United Nations Security Council ensures that no issue will be decided by the United Nations Organization against the perceived interests of its more powerful members. This is sometimes thought to be necessary if those powerful members are to accept the rulings of its international jurisdiction.

Elsewhere the veto is often criticized, as tending to paralyse policy in emergencies i.e. at the very moment when policy is needed. Debates over the future of the *European Union now focus on the extent of the veto retained by member states: if the veto disappears entirely, then national *sovereignty becomes a pretence.

Vico, Giambattista (1668–1744)

Italian philosopher of history, who, in his *Scienza Nuova*, 1725, final version 1744, presented what was perhaps the first theory of history in the modern sense. He also anticipated the theory of *Verstehen, and made a pioneering study of *myth and its social significance.

Vico rejected the idea of a fixed, static human nature, and believed that the essence of man changes with historical development. All *social contract theories ultimately assume that man can be abstracted from his social conditions and yet be seen as a freely choosing being, obeying laws of natural justice and able to engage in contracts and exchanges with his kind. On the contrary, such theories simply project into a hypothetical state of nature the image of man at one particular historical moment, and then suppose that the historical conditions which created him are also part of 'nature'. Such theories are examples of 'pseudo-myths', which misrepresent the early stages of man's development in accordance with a theoretical requirement. True myths, like poetry, art and language itself, should be seen as the embodiment in imaginative form of genuine perceptions of surrounding social conditions and preoccupations.

Vico thought that history exhibits a pattern, and that all events at a given moment bear some intrinsic relation to each other – although he presented no developed theory as to what this relation might be. The law of historical development is that of the recurring cycle, and the understanding of history ('the world of nations') is a special case of that human understanding which has people rather than physical processes as its object. Human nature must first be understood in terms of its expressions in language, culture and myth; then it will be seen that there is an underlying cyclical movement in all things. From bestial conditions men emerge, through an 'age of heroes', to an oligarchical society which gradually transforms itself into the law-governed communities of the 'age of men', established through class conflict. Upon the achievement of democracy and equal rights, society gradually disintegrates, lacking internal authority and cohesion, so giving way to a renewed bestiality.

That doctrine contains in embryo some of the most important of the thoughts that are characteristic of the *modern mind (including the thesis of the *end of history); hence the interest in Vico, who seemed to anticipate by 100 years the ideas that have lent tone to the confusions of the post-romantic consciousness.

victim culture

Pejorative expression popular on the US *right to denote the supposed habit on the *left of scouring the world for victims in order to construct a political agenda around the goal of rescuing them. The victim culture is alleged to shift its attention just as soon as the victim proves to be less downtrodden or more canny than at first appeared. The working class is less attractive, therefore, than ethnic minorities or abused women; and these two may be less attractive than *animals, who are not only victims of human abuse but also unable to protest on their own behalf, and – what is perhaps even more important – unable to protest against those who claim to speak for them.

The victim culture is also expressed by those who claim the special status and privileges of 'victimhood', and who, by parading their wounds, seek an easy avenue to sympathy and to the advantages that spring from it.

vigilante

Italian: a look-out. Vigilantes are members of a volunteer police force, exercising rough justice in the absence of adequate enforcement of the law, on the model of those that were formed in the West of America during the 'gold rush', when groups of adventurers spread lawlessly into the wilderness.

It is usually thought that no state can recognize the legitimacy of a vigilante force, since this would be to grant to legislative and executive powers to a body independent of the state, in which case the state ceases to be *sovereign, and so ceases to have authority to grant those powers. It is sometimes replied that, if the state does not enforce the law, then it does not really make law, so that it has in any case renounced its jurisdiction and therefore its sovereignty, once a vigilante force becomes necessary. (At times these arguments have been relevant in describing the situation in Northern Ireland, and even on the subways of New York.)

violence

Violence is a property of *force. A force is violent if it 'violates', i.e. if it breaks and destroys that to which it is applied. It is an act of violence to strike my neighbour, an act only of force to steer him uninjured but against his will from the room. (*See* *coercion.)

Questions concerning violence repeatedly recur in political dispute, and while some of them are semantic, there is usually a serious issue of justification involved. Thus it is generally assumed that an act of violence needs to be justified; if no justification can be offered then violence is always a violation of right, unless it is of such a kind as to impute *responsibility to no *agent (e.g. the violence of the wind, or of some uncontrollable human passion). It is for this reason that certain radical thinkers have tried to find violence concealed within existing social structures, for if there really is such *structural violence contained in seemingly peaceful institutions, then violent opposition to them would be more easily justified.

One advocate of that position – *Sorel – did not much care whether violence was justified or not, so long as the proletariat could be brought to perceive its necessity. In his *Reflections on Violence*, 1908, he argued that all existing class conflicts must be exacerbated to the point of open violence, since attempts to render them peaceful served the interests of neither protagonist. Curiously, he argued that the bourgeoisie too would be vitalized by genuine conflict; through violent conflict energy would again enter social relations, changing them from uncreative apathy to dynamic instruments of change. Moreover, open violence, construed in a spirit of war, is free from hatred – in this it differs from the persecutions carried on through the law courts in the name of the state. Sorel's romanticized view of the essential decency of war enabled him to attack all the 'prejudices against violence' that he discerned in the parliamentary socialists of his day, and to advocate a politics of 'violence enlightened by the idea of the general strike'.

Sorel's encomium of violence (which contains no attempt to define what he praises) has been the object, from time to time, of veneration, by such romantics as Mussolini and the French *New Left of 1968. The question that he raises, and which has interested subsequent philosophers, is that of whether a particular class may be in such a position that, without violence, it could never achieve rights which it ought to enjoy.

Virginia school

See *public choice.

virtue

Excellence of character, or 'dispositions that we praise' (*Aristotle); the subject-matter of much ancient morality, and of theories that have been profoundly influential, through Aristotle, *Plato and *Cicero, on Western political thought.

It was a commonly accepted view among ancient political thinkers that each kind of state generates and is generated by a character in its citizens, and that each particular virtue will correspond to its own political order.

(This idea recurs in *Machiavelli and in *Montesquieu.) It is also an important thesis, advanced both by Plato and by Aristotle, that *true* virtue is one; to be truly courageous a person must also be wise, to be wise he must be just, to be just he must be prudent, and so on. Only the virtuous person can be happy, and hence there is, in the end, only one ideal state, that in which the true virtues flourish in the harmonious relation which defines their unity. In Plato the idea is taken further; the ideal state is itself conceived on the model of a human character, and Plato tries to find in it the harmonious disposition of human virtue. But in all versions, the implication of a deep correspondence between the character of the citizen and the order of the *polis* is defended. Some modern thinkers have regretted the fact that this idea has entered a decline, and that questions of constitution are discussed in terms of such abstractions as freedom, right, and distribution, rather than in terms of the quality of individual experience with which they are conjoined. Others have rejected the ancient enterprise as over-ambitious, perhaps even dangerous in its imputation of a political significance to every aspect of personal life.

The best account of virtue is Aristotle's. A virtue is a disposition; it is expressed in intentional action; it involves characteristic thoughts and motives; it consists in a readiness to obey reason, whatever the opposing temptations; it 'mediates' between emotions, by permitting the subject to make up his mind in defiance of them (the doctrine of the 'mean'); it is intrinsically connected to success in action; it defines the ends of action and not only the means (the distinction between virtue and technique); its application is more likely in the long run to lead to fulfilment than any of the emotions that it counters, and it defines the type of the fulfilled rational being. An example is courage, the disposition to face present danger in defiance of the two warring passions (fear and aggression) which tempt us, the one to cowardice, the other to rashness. Courage always makes a general contribution to success in action, by providing the motive to overcome obstacles and to do what is right despite the temptations of passion. Its motive is honour, and this provides the end of action, in circumstances however terrible.

Courage, when not conjoined to prudence, is merely the disposition to give way to that passion (aggression) which wars naturally with fear. Hence 'true' courage requires prudence. And so, it is hoped, through all the virtues, showing that the courageous man must also be just, temperate and wise. Justice presents a special problem, since it is an 'other-regarding' and not only a 'self-regarding' disposition. However, Aristotle thought that without justice no man could experience friendship, and that without friendship a rational being, who is also by nature a social being, could not be fulfilled. Without justice, moreover, courage is mere bullying, prudence small-mindedness, and wisdom no more than the cunning of the fox. To complete the picture Aristotle argued that virtue is a constituent part of happiness (which is the ultimate end of rational conduct). So all men have reason to acquire virtue. That was Aristotle's answer to the question of *value: there are objectively desirable states of character, and every rational being must see that he has reason to acquire them. (Unlike the editor of this dictionary, however, Aristotle did not mean 'men' to refer to all human beings: he thought that there were distinctive virtues in the two sexes, and that those of women fitted them

for the successful conduct of another kind of life from that led by men.)

In an influential book (*After Virtue*, 1981) the philosopher Alasdair MacIntyre has identified the Aristotelian philosophy of virtue as lying at the heart of the tradition of moral philosophy which has animated Western civilization. Recent attempts to shore up that tradition from the premises of *liberal *individualism are, he argues, destined to fail, as is *Nietzsche's final assault on the whole concept of morality in the name of the 'higher man'. MacIntyre seems to recommend a return to the Aristotelian tradition, as the most promising foundation for a morality that is both communal and secular and which takes seriously the social essence of humanity.

The concept of virtue was important in Machiavelli, in Montesquieu, and in *Rousseau, all of whom associated it with the idea of *republican government. Recent defenders of *communitarianism have revived the idea, arguing that there are 'virtues of citizenship' which are presupposed by any durable *civil society, and that the cultivation of these virtues is one of the primary tasks of the community.

Voegelin, Eric (1901–85)
German political scientist; *see* *gnosticism, *monarchy, *representation.

Volksgeist
German: the spirit of a people; a term employed by writers of the late eighteenth century, especially by *Herder, and used to give theoretical foundation to the *nationalist position, by arguing that each people has its own 'spirit', from which language, customs and institutions emerge organically, and which constitutes the real bond of unity among them. (This is the nationalist basis for *political obligation.) Thus the jurist F.C. von Savigny

(1779–1861) argued against *codification, in favour of customary law, on the grounds that the latter was the immediate expression of the *Volksgeist*, and that law inconsistent with the *Volksgeist* is law inconsistent with the people that it seeks to rule. This opposition to codified law was highly influential, and overcome only in 1900. The idea requires that it be possible to identify a 'people' independently of a state, and then in turn to identify the spirit which unites them, and with which the state must be brought into harmony.

Volksstaat

The people's state. The unified social and political arrangement which is supposed to emerge from aligning state institutions with the *Volksgeist of the people who will be ruled by them. Based on *nationalist doctrines of the nature of a *people, it was an attempt to recast in terms intelligible to the people themselves the famous and flattering doctrine of their *sovereignty. In theory every institution is to be animated by the single spirit of the *Volksgeist*. The idea was popular with some Nazis.

Voltaire, François-Marie Arouet (1694–1778)

French writer and philosopher, leading figure of the French *Enlightenment, who wrote in every milieu and defended a kind of *deism (i.e. belief in a transcendental and inaccessible God) against the orthodox Christianity of his day. His famous satire of Leibniz's optimism – *Candide*, 1759 – was read as a call to return to reality from the entrancing illusions of religion, and his frequent attacks on the evils committed in religion's name made Voltaire into a hero of subsequent *humanist thinkers. To his critics he remains shallow as a philosopher and rhetorical as a poet; but his reputation for a century

after his death was that of the greatest sage of the French Enlightenment.

voluntarism

In the context of the theory of historical development, 'voluntarism' denotes any view that emphasizes (or perhaps over-emphasizes) the role of human design and intention, as against the role of the 'material' factors emphasized by *historical materialism. The thesis that the human will is a determining factor in history seems uncontentious to the innocent, nor is it refuted by the manifestly true assertion that the will itself is determined by other (perhaps 'material') things. (*See* *determinism.*) Nevertheless it might still be true that the overall *pattern* of history (the 'course of events') can best be explained by a theory that does not mention the will, not even the will of Napoleon or of Lenin. If that were the case then one fairly plausible form of voluntarism would have been refuted.

voluntary associations

See *associations.

voting

The expression of a preference as a contribution to a *collective choice. Voting by a show of hands is to be distinguished from voting by secret ballot. The second is no more than a contribution to a collective choice, while the first is a way both of making a choice and at the same time of declaring one's choice to others. It is determined, therefore, not only by one's preference, but also by one's attitude to others' opinions of one's preference. This is why the introduction of the secret ballot is often regarded as a necessary condition of 'free elections'. (*See* *elections.) *Tactical voting occurs when people vote for a candidate who is not their preferred candidate, but who may, e.g., be more likely to win than the better alternative, or likely to precipitate another election sooner, and so on. It is important in that it shows that voting cannot be taken as a direct index of *ultimate* preferences.

voting paradox

One of the paradoxes in the theory of *social choice, which suggests that there may be no *social welfare function that will deliver a consistent social preference ordering from individual preference orderings. Suppose a vote shows a majority preference for policy x over policy y, and also for y over z; it does not follow that there is a majority preference for x over z. (Suppose there are three citizens, A, B, and C; A prefers x to y and y to z; B prefers y to z and z to x; C prefers z to x and x to y.) The discovery of this paradox is sometimes attributed to Condorcet.

vox populi, vox dei

The voice of the people is the voice of God. The expression occurs in a letter to Charlemagne from the poet Alcuin in 800 and was also used by Archbishop Reynolds when crowning Edward III in 1327. This extreme version of the doctrine of the *sovereignty of the people, which suggests that the people are right whenever they believe anything at all, is compatible with any kind of government, on the assumption that for the most part the people have no beliefs. Their 'voice' is heard only at those moments of crisis in which God too enters the fray.

vulgar Marxism

Expression sometimes used to denote crude forms of *historical materialism, which attempt to explain all beliefs and values as the offshoots of economic factors and class position, and which then imagine that, in providing the explanation of a belief, one is relieved of the need to refute it.

W

age
Remuneration under a contract of employment, usually extended on a weekly basis, and outside the special terms and expectations associated with a *profession. The distinction between wages and salaries (which are usually paid monthly) is at first sight a superficial one; however, it may be of considerable sociological interest, since it is often thought to correspond roughly to a distinction between kinds of employment (manual and administrative), and even (according to some) between classes, that of *wage labour, and that of the 'salariat'. (*See* *class, *social stratification, *status.) The contractual nature of the wage relation is nominally upheld in law, but the institution of *collective bargaining and the recent developments in *industrial law make the idea of a contract into a *legal fiction.

Explanations of the level of wages include the *classical 'wage fund theory' (the theory that in the short run there is a given amount of savings to pay the wages of the labour force); *Marx's theory that wages are the *exchangevalue of *labour power (*see* *surplus value); and the *marginal productivity theory of wages. One thing that needs to be explained by such theories is why the wages of manual labourers are so often lower than salaries.

wage labour

The condition of someone who, in order to exist, sells his labour, and does so under the terms of a *wage contract. Practical reasoning for such a person is determined by a weekly cycle of labour and reward. It is clear that wage labour creates an important structural component in most modern societies. Wage labourers must associate with each other, since they are employed as a 'work force'; they share values, expectations, and institutions of *leisure, which may have a functional relation to the economic role that they play. Hence wage labour will always be a plausible candidate for a social *class, whatever the actual standard of living associated with it.

Wahhabism

A form of radical *Islamism known after its founder, Muhammad ibn 'Abd al-Wahhab (1703–1792), from the Najd area of Arabia, ruled by local sheikhs of the house of Saud. In 1744 Ibn al-Wahhab launched a campaign of purification and renewal, whose aim was to restore true Islam in the holy places where the Prophet had lived and governed, and to destroy all the later accretions and abominations which had grown in its place. He gathered around him a following of *muwahhidoun* – believers in unity: i.e. in the unity of God and the unity of the faithful. Contained in the name is the attitude for which al-Wahhab soon became notorious, namely total intolerance towards anyone who disagreed with him. Supported by the local Saudi rulers, the Wahhabis spread their campaign, after their founder's death, by force of arms, and even sacked the holy Shi'ite city of Karbala in Iraq. The campaign was crushed by the Ottoman sultan, and the Saudi emir was decapitated. But Wahhabism lived on, spreading to other areas, and notably to Afghanistan and British India. Its message was puritanical, and its enemy was modernization in all its forms, especially that associated with Western colonial rule. Its aim was to create a pure heart of Islam, and to spread from that heart to every limb of the Islamic *ummah.* A century after Ibn al-Wahhab's death another Saudi chieftain (Ibn Saud) took up the cause, conquered Arabia in the early twentieth century, during the years of Ottoman decline, and established the dynasty that now protects the Wahhabite clergy and funds their missionary outposts around the world. Hence Wahhabism remains one of the principal inputs into *Islamism.

war

A forcible contention between states with the purpose of overpowering each other by armed force, in order to secure certain demands or claims. All wars involve a measure, however small, of *violence. War is to be distinguished from domestic upheavals and rebellions, however violent, in that it occurs between *states or powers seeking to constitute themselves as states; as such it is recognized and regulated by *international law, which incorporates legal rules originating in traditional discussions of the *just war.

The problem of enforcing laws of war is a perpetual one: if a party is already fighting, then it is not usually disposed to take legal advice. The threat of reprisals offers some coercion, but the *fact* of reprisals tends to lead only to escalation and ever more horrifying breaches of the law. The recent concept of the *war crime has arisen partly from the need for international judicial procedures (preferably conducted at a time of *peace) whereby to emphasize the binding quality of the law of war.

The study of war distinguishes various kinds of war, some of which are discussed elsewhere in this dictionary: *cold war, *insurgency, *limited war, and so on; also 'catalytic war' (conflict between two states deliberately catalysed by a third which has an interest in respect of one or the other or both). To some extent these classifications stem from the desire to relate the kinds of war to the causes of war. There seems to be, for example, a broad distinction between wars which result from the aggressive and expansionist policies of one of the belligerents, and wars which arise out of a mutual and perhaps longstanding hostility which may not, in itself, reflect any territorial claims. (Wars of religion are perhaps examples of this, as are some modern 'wars of ideology'.) The attempt to explain war *as such* involves going behind all such distinctions, in order to find that thing in human nature which requires violent resolution of *conflict. Some assert that there is an innate principle of belligerence which may be diverted into peaceful uses, but which is always ready to break out in violence when prompted. It was fashionable among post-romantic philosophers to sing the praises of this alleged instinct (thus *Nietzsche, *Sorel), although it has less following now that everyone has reason to fear it. Whether or not we accept the theory of innate belligerence, there is still a problem in explaining the outbreak of *war.* Those who attach belligerence to ideas of territory, purporting, say, to bring evidence from *sociobiology in order to demonstrate the primitive nature of the territorial instinct, may not in fact succeed in explaining war. For this is to explain how whole masses of people, who do not wish to fight, and who have no ambitions over the territory of their opponents, may yet find themselves acting under orders in ways from which their nature normally recoils. Further, modern anthropological studies of warfare between tribes, e.g. in Africa and North America, have emphasized the relative insignificance of territorial factors, in comparison with such motives as revenge (the blood-feud, which may become so institutionalized as to confer on war the character of a customary obligation), religious duty, e.g. towards a 'god of war', and personal prestige. The last motive is particularly important in tribes where the exhibition of personal prowess in war is the means by which a young man can increase his influence in the community and induce his fellows to bestow on him the political authority that normally vests in the elders. All the above motives are perceptively characterized by Homer, and underlie many of the systems of *honour that still prevail in modern societies.

war communism
Term used to describe the aims of the Red Army during the civil war which followed the Russian Revolution: i.e. the establishment of communism by the *substitution of communist military personnel for all civilian officers, and the total military organization of all production and distribution. The term gained currency as part of the need to persuade people that the harsh conditions initially prevailing were temporary, and in order to shift blame for them on to the 'imperialist war' that was taking place elsewhere. The fact that conditions remained harsh for the next 70 years has lent a somewhat ironical tone to the expression.

war crime
Conduct during war which harms either combatants or civilians, and which goes beyond legitimate hostilities under the laws of war. The allied powers set up a United Nations War Crimes Commission in 1943, which introduced the new category of the 'crime against humanity', partly in order to cover those atrocities that were being committed against people who were citizens of the very state whose agents were oppressing them. The problem with the jurisdiction over both kinds of crime is that, in the nature of the case, it is the victor who tries the vanquished, and similar crimes committed by the first may remain unmentioned or deliberately concealed behind the persecutory venom directed against the second (although there have been exceptions to this rule). Very rarely therefore has a state either tried, or been in a position to try, one of its own citizens for a 'war crime'. The US is an exception to this (the case of My Lai during the Vietnam War, and of Abu Ghraib prison in Iraq.) However, there have been trials in other jurisdictions of military personnel who have 'overstepped the mark of duty', although usually without reference to the concept of a war crime.

The Nuremberg and Tokyo trials conducted in the wake of the Second World War, in which the victors tried leading members of the defeated belligerents, set a precedent that was subsequently approved by the UN General Assembly and by the International Law Commission. A permanent 'war crimes tribunal' now exists in The Hague, before which individuals can be brought for trial at the instigation of the UN General Assembly. Leading figures in the Balkan conflict following the break-up of Yugoslavia have been arraigned before this court, the most famous being President Milosevic of Serbia.

war on terror
Following the terrorist attacks of 11 September 2001, the US declared a 'war on terror', which would involve searching out terrorists around the

world and destroying their networks, and also belligerently confronting the states that harbour them. The policy has been criticized on the grounds that terror is a means employed by the enemy, not itself an enemy, and that to declare war on terror is to introduce a crucial vagueness into military planning and foreign policy. Moreover, the US has, in the past, supported movements that others have described as terrorist, and many of its own citizens give active support to terrorist organizations such as the IRA. In reply it might be argued that the threat is so serious, and the enemy so elusive, that a new kind of war must in any case be envisaged, if the security of the US is to be guaranteed, given the existence of *weapons of mass destruction.

warfare state

A state whose main economic, social and political structure is created by or directed towards conditions of war, and which exists by virtue of perpetuating those conditions, or by engaging in ceaseless preparations for war, whether or not under the guise of self-defence (expression introduced by Archbishop Temple (1941)).

Washington consensus

A series of proposals, first presented in 1989 by John Williamson, to introduce market solutions to the problems of South America, and to free South American economies from the burden of regulation that has prevented them from achieving equilibrium. So-called because it summarizes the received wisdom of Washington-based institutions with an interest in Latin America: the *International Monetary Fund, the *World Bank and the US treasury department, in particular.

wealth

The total stock of possessions, tangible or intangible, which have *value.

Wealth may be regarded as a stock of provisions, to be slowly expended in catering for present requirements, or as *capital, to be invested in the expectation of an *income. Moralists tend to favour the first use, economists the second (in so far as they regard *accumulation and *investment as necessary). It is sometimes said to be a peculiar feature of capitalism that wealth can generate an income for the holder of wealth; it could be that wealth might exist without that power.

Objections to wealth tend to be objections to capitalist investment, either as a form of *usury, or as a form of *exploitation. Taxes on wealth are sometimes proposed, partly in order to give voice to those objections, partly because it is thought economically or socially justified to bring all large accumulations under the control of the state. Sometimes the intention is to formulate a kind of *sumptuary law, designed to diminish the prestige and potency of property and to make sure that no private citizen can dispose of an actual power greater than that of the state. Sometimes the intention is the redistribution of wealth; in accordance with an ideal of *social justice. Wealth taxes are increasingly disapproved of, however, as destroying the motivation to save and invest and as promoting the habits characteristic of a *consumer society. Nevertheless they have been introduced in France, and have had the effect of lowering the price of land and property, relative to their price in neighbouring states.

wealth taxes

See *wealth.

weapons of mass destruction (WMD)

Idiom emerging in the course of the *war on terror, to denote weapons that will seriously disable a country by killing large numbers of its citizens or destroying vital infrastructure. WMD refers both to nuclear weapons, and to other forms of destructive ordinance, such as chemical agents and biological weapons, which can destroy whole populations, even without damaging a single building. Until the end of the *cold war strategy was founded on the assumption that such weapons, if used at all, would be used by a sovereign state, which could be deterred by threats of retaliation. The assumption now is that, if used, they will be used by terrorists who are undeterrred by the threat of retaliation. The strategic problem that this poses is possibly insuperable, although it might seem to justify the *war on terror.

Webb, Beatrice (1857–1943), and Sidney (1858–1947)
British socialists and social theorists; see *Fabianism, *gradualism, *sovietology.

Weber, Max (1864–1920)
German sociologist and economic historian (not to be confused with his brother Alfred), who is often regarded, together with *Comte, *Durkheim and *Marx, as laying the foundations of modern sociology. Weber defended the idea of a *value-free social science. Social phenomena are identified in terms of a 'sense', which is attached by social beings to all their actions, and which is the true object of social knowledge. 'Sense' can be understood only by *Verstehen, which therefore becomes the distinguishing mark of the social sciences. However, Verstehen needs to be supplemented by causal explanation, and both require a theoretical model or *ideal type. (This last expression has probably acquired a significance other than the one that Weber gave to it. For Weber an ideal type describes what an agent *would* do, if he were acting entirely rationally in accordance with the 'sense' of his own

behaviour.) The ideal type facilitates *Verstehen* by providing the language with which the far from ideal social reality can be described; it also suggests (but does not provide) causal explanations of reality. The concept of the ideal type was applied by Weber to the analysis of capitalism, and, in *The Protestant Ethic and the Spirit of Capitalism*, 1920–21, Weber tried to show that the Marxian theory of economic determination could not explain the actual history of capitalist development, which must be understood at least partly in terms of the ascetic and secular morality of *Calvinism.

Weber attempted to update the nineteenth-century theories of *class, distinguishing class from *status, and trying to show the importance of socially nurtured opinions in determining status. In general, he felt that the neglect of the peculiar categories through which we observe and create our social behaviour had been responsible for many of the failings that he claimed to discover in the older theories of class.

Among the theories associated with the name of Weber is his treatment of the idea of *authority. He tried to define authority in terms of statistical laws, which express 'the probability that a command with a given specific content will be obeyed by a given group of persons'. He thought that command and obedience can be observed only by *Verstehen*. He then made his famous distinction between traditional authority (which rests on *custom and *prescription), *charismatic authority (which is a major source of social change), and 'legal-rational' authority of the kind exercised by the modern bureaucrat, where legitimacy rests on a belief in the legality of a pattern of normative rules, and the right of those elevated to power under those rules to issue commands.

Weber's theory is not really an analysis of the concept of authority, but rather a sociological explanation of why it is that people come to believe in it (command and obedience already involving the ideas of authority). Nevertheless it is often taken as a starting point for discussions of the idea.

Weil, Simone (1909–43)
French essayist and philosopher of Jewish extraction, and a modern proponent of *stoicism. Weil's mystical Christianity, and identification with the victims of modern European politics, compelled highly influential, if eccentric, reflections on the state of contemporary society, together with proposals for its political revitalization (*The Need for Roots*, 1949). She identified the chief evil of modern civilization as *déracinement*, and attempted to analyse the nature of the *enracinement* (putting down of roots) that had protected humanity in the past, and might again protect it in the future, from social corrosion. A human being has roots by virtue of his active participation in a collectivity, which conserves in living form an inheritance of social existence, and which continues to offer presentiments of a future continuity. Weil attempted to reconcile that emphasis on particularized attachments with *universalist views of obligation, derived from *Kant, and also with a respect for *hierarchy, diversity, *private property and *territory. This led her to support true *patriotism (a local intimation of world citizenship) against *nationalism (a form of *déracinement* comparable in its effects to the corrosiveness of industrial production). At the same time she claimed both Christian and Marxian inspiration for her rejection of the effects of industrialization, and proposed *utopian schemes for the amelioration of the condition of labour, by preventing the emergence

of large-scale industry. She wished labour to be an exercise in willing obedience, founded in allegiance to others and to the social order. Her profoundly moral view of economic life influenced also her idea of law, which she thought (with Kant) could enforce morality without infringing freedom. She admired the UK constitution as a seeming expression of that ideal of law, came to England as a refugee from Nazism, and died there before realizing her ambition of returning to France and sacrificing herself for her country.

welfare
A disputed concept, meant to describe the flourishing or happiness of human beings, but defined by *welfare economics in terms of *preferences. Some philosophers have argued that the individual may not be better off simply for having what he prefers, and that, although *values, for example, are preferences, not all preferences are values. Some of our preferences (e.g. those concerning food) we regard as reflections of our own constitution – as *mere* preferences that we are under no obligation to justify when challenged. Values (sense 2.) on the other hand have an authority greater than that, and indeed we learn to perceive and understand the world in terms of them. Thus a value seems to have not only strength, like a preference, but also 'depth', a quality whereby it brings order to experience by determining the interpretation of experience. It is said to be absurd to incorporate such a thing into a system of measurement, and some have for this reason looked with scepticism upon the aims of welfare economics. However, it is better to see that theory as concerned with a limited set of questions concerning economic values (values in sense 1.) and the distribution of goods, rather than with the

larger philosophical issue of the 'good for man'. At the same time, that larger issue cannot be neglected in any consideration of the social significance of 'welfare legislation'.

welfare economics

Branch of economics concerned with economic efficiency and resource allocation, as a means to the welfare of society. For the most part welfare economics tries to avoid assumptions regarding ethics, justice, and political desirability, and proposes instead measures of efficiency which are *value-free. Efficiency is usually taken to mean *optimality (often *Pareto optimality) in the satisfaction of *preferences. The theory inquires into the relative economic efficiency of the various economic systems, such as the price system. Welfare economics has generated the theory of *social choice, and the problem of the *social welfare function, and has thereby come to have far-reaching significance for political theory.

welfare state

Colloquial term (originally introduced by Archbishop William Temple (1881–1944), in *Citizen and Churchmen*, 1941) for a state which makes substantial provision through law and administration for those in need: e.g. the sick, poor, elderly, disabled and indigent. Even the US is now a welfare state in this sense, though clearly less so than many. Moves in the direction of the welfare state, through *poor laws and welfare legislation, accelerated appreciably during the nineteenth century, in particular with Bismarck's social welfare legislation of 1883–89, which was later taken as a model by other European states. In post-Second World War Europe, both capitalist and communist, *health services, *education, unemployment benefit and pensions have been in almost every

case provided out of government funds. This has met with opposition on the ground that it involves illegitimate government expenditure, and therefore illegitimate taxation, perhaps because it is held to encourage indigence and discourage *self-help. The favoured alternative, of private insurance schemes as practised in the US, is often attacked for the abuses and injustices to which it seems to give rise, while the welfare state is defended as involving not only social justice, but also a task for government which (unlike many of the tasks that it seems to arrogate to itself) is both necessary and could be effectively performed by no other *agent. The controversy was for a long time more or less dead, but has recently been revived by the perceived need to reduce expenditure on welfare, and by the rise of the *dependency culture. (*See also* *health.) The declining birth-rate and increasing longevity of European populations make it inevitable that the current welfare provisions will soon cease to be affordable. Recent radical proposals from the US sociologist Charles *Murray advocate replacing the welfare state with a yearly income offered by the state to all adults, a portion being dedicated by law to health and pension insurance. Murray argues that within a few years the policy will be far cheaper than welfare provisions, while avoiding the worst effects of the dependency culture and contributing to a healthier and more charitable social order.

Weltanschauung

German: world outlook. A general conception of the world, in which beliefs, values and metaphysical presuppositions are all woven together so as to instil the world with significance, and facilitate the transition from thought to action.

West

The West, if it were defined geographically, would be defined by contrast with the East – and the term first entered currency during the nineteenth century, in order to distinguish Western from oriental civilizations. In the course of the twentieth century, however, 'the West' came to denote, first, the civilization which arose out of Christianity and took on an expansive and increasingly *secularized form at the *Enlightenment and, second, the loose association of nation states which, as heirs to that civilization and under pressure of common threats such as *fascism and *communism, began to cohere as a *bloc. *Spengler's highly influential *Decline of the West* was one of many books written in the earlier decades of the twentieth century purporting to identify the peculiar spirit and destiny of Western civilization. (For Spengler the key component has been the 'Faustian' spirit – the spirit of adventure and experiment. Others have emphasized the ability to construct and to obey comprehensive systems of law, and to regulate all transactions between people by a conception of rights and duties.)

As now understood, the West is the association of peoples, nations and states which share a sufficient number of the following features – all of them, directly or indirectly, legacies of the ancient Mediterranean civilizations, whether Greek, Roman or Jewish, and all shaped by the *world-historical force of Christianity:

(i) The *rule of law.

(ii) *Representative government (tending, as a rule, to some kind of *democracy).

(iii) *Capitalist economy.

(iv) Universal *education.

(v) Permanent or semi-permanent *alliances and *treaties with other states possessing features (i) to (iv).

(vi) A large Christian population.

(vii) Secular institutions of government.

(viii) Religious freedom and an ethos of *toleration towards *minorities.

(ix) Other *freedoms of a *liberal kind, and especially the freedom of the press. Much of the West is now situated in the East, and in any case the world is round. *See also* *North/South divide.

westernization

The importation of customs and institutions characteristic, or thought to be characteristic, of the *West. In fact the term denotes two processes:

1. The deliberate adoption of institutions formed on the Western model. In this sense westernization was advocated by the Tsar Peter the Great of Russia, who sought to lift his empire out of the backwardness in which he believed it to be mired, and to modernize its institutions. It was also proposed as a serious policy by influential figures in the Ottoman government in the nineteenth and twentieth centuries, and much more wholeheartedly by Atatürk, on the supposition that the Western way of doing things was necessary if Turkey was to adapt its social structure and political institutions to the conditions of modern life. (*See* *Kemalism.) Atatürk's policy has been imitated elsewhere – notably in Iran, where it precipitated an Islamic reaction, and in the Pacific basin.

2. The unintended but seemingly inexorable process whereby the capitalist economy and the *consumer society take root wherever they are not deliberately exterminated, bringing customs and habits which many find objectionable but which nobody seems able to resist. This process is facilitated by the local search for *status and the confused idea that somehow the Western way of doing things is more *modern and more

glamorous than the local traditions. But it is much more the effect of mass communications, and of the vast stimulation of appetite for consumer goods and the consumer culture which has occurred through *advertising and the world-wide search for markets.

Westernization in sense 2. is the core of *globalization, and is a major factor in modern politics. It is often advocated in the hope that an attachment to the commercial aspect of Western civilization will, in time, bring about an attachment to the democratic institutions that have been associated with it. It is attacked by those who believe that westernization merely destroys local traditions and moral absolutes while putting nothing effective in the place of them – democracy having a limited ability to survive outside the Western climate.

Westminster model

*Bicameral government on the model of the UK *Parliament, i.e. with a lower house of representatives answerable to the electorate, with extensive legislative powers, and a *cabinet exercising major executive powers; together with an upper house structured in some other way, so as to embody the dignity and durability of the state and of the interests within it, but with limited legislative power, consonant with its non-representational character. Normally the upper house would be thought of as a revising chamber, while the lower house contains the principal powers and the principal initiators of policy.

Whig

The 'whigs' were rebels who held out in the Scottish lowlands in 1679, resisting the Act of Uniformity 1662, in the interests of their own religious eccentricities. The label is borrowed, from 1680 onwards, as a name for the English political faction that sought the transfer of power from the monarch to Parliament. Primarily the Whigs were a faction of Protestant noblemen, united in opposition to *Toryism, as it then was. However, because of their *parliamentarian leanings, they gradually became identified with the more liberal movements in English politics and, during the course of the eighteenth century, brought about the realignment of parliamentary forces which permitted the emergence of the UK Liberal Party. By 1868 the term 'Whig' was no longer widely used, except as the name of the peculiar mixture of ardent eccentricity and rooted belief in the right of aristocrats to govern irrespective of their views, which some saw as a persisting principle in English politics. Later thinkers (e.g. *Eliot) have continued to identify 'whiggism' with the liberal faction and have thought of it as a progressive, perhaps individualistic and even capitalistic, movement within the aristocracy, rather than as a form of *liberalism in the modern sense. *See* *Whig interpretation of history.

Whig interpretation of history

Expression coined by Sir Herbert Butterfield in a book of that title (1931), to denote the vision of history as generated by a conflict between *progress and *reaction, in which the first is always, in the end, victorious, bringing about the ever increasing prosperity, enlightenment and emancipation of mankind. The identification of this view as 'Whig' reflects the theory that the aristocratic faction which went by that name was given to an exaggerated estimate of its historical mission. However, it is clear that, in so far as anything so schematic can be believed as doctrine, there have been plenty of American, French and German whigs in history.

withering away of the state
Phrase coined by Engels to denote the process whereby, according to Marx, and also to Lenin who made much of the idea, the state under socialism gradually becomes redundant, its existence as an instrument of *coercion being necessary only in order to sustain the oppressive economic relations of capitalism, and only so long as people have the character and expectations induced by those relations. Gradually, under the practice of *collective choice, as the friendliness of the social order without private property in the means of production is recognized, law is no longer required, and people enter a condition ('full communism') in which society exists and flourishes without a controlling state. Then the 'government of people' gives way to the 'administration of things' (Marx). It is sometimes said that communism fulfilled this prediction, by administering people as things.

Wollstonecraft, Mary (1759–97)
English philosopher and novelist, wife of *Godwin, and champion of the libertarian and egalitarian ideals which she associated with the French Revolution. Wollstonecraft's *Vindication of the Rights of Men*, 1790, a reply to *Burke's *Reflections on the Recent Revolution in France*, defended the liberal position that 'The birthright of man . . . is such a degree of liberty, civil and religious, as is compatible with the liberty of every other individual with whom he is united in a social compact . . .'; the work argued rhetorically for reason against prejudice, for impartiality and equality against privilege and hierarchy, for a political system dedicated to the satisfaction of human needs against one dedicated to the accumulation of power. Wollstonecraft's attack on the *hereditary principle and on the vested power of the family presaged her subsequent rejection of all self-perpetuating systems of control and, in *A Vindication of the Rights of Women*, 1792, she argued vigorously for the view that women, as rational creatures, should reject the vision of their nature, role and education that had been imposed on them by men, and cease to regard themselves as creatures subject to the control of another and stronger sex. The weakness and dependency of the female are, she argued, largely a consequence of the education chosen for her, while the sexual role and *mores* to which women conform are likewise the creation of men, designed for the advantage of the male, who confines the female within a sphere of submissive chastity while permitting himself the conduct which extends his influence and power.

Wollstonecraft's thoughts were disjointed and unsystematic: nevertheless they provoked widespread reaction, and have since been regarded as important early statements of the modern *feminist position.

women's movement
The movement to promote the *emancipation, *liberation, *rights and interests of women, as these are defined *by* women, which has existed as a political force in modern times since the early nineteenth century. While individual eighteenth-century writers (both men and women) made statements in support of *feminism (the most important being, perhaps, *Wollstonecraft's *A Vindication of the Rights of Women*, 1792), there was no organized movement to which women, and particularly working-class women, substantially contributed, over which they had control, and through which their particular interests could be fostered. During the nineteenth century the demands for female suffrage came through the *labour movement and other agents of

reform, but were not as a rule associated with any attempt to articulate the thoughts which are characteristic of modern feminism. An exception was the Nottingham Female Political Union (1838); it had few successors until 1889, when the Women's Franchise League began to campaign, not only for female suffrage, but also for complete equality of women in divorce, inheritance and the custody of children. Subsequently, many similar organizations emerged, the most influential being the US National Organization for Women (NOW), founded by the feminist Betty Friedan (1921–2006) and 27 others in 1966. NOW has a decidedly left-wing identity, and many who endorse the women's movement would not endorse NOW. Since the granting of female suffrage the main concerns of the movement have included *equal pay, *equal opportunity, equal *access, and the eradication of *sexism. Equal pay has been widely achieved in the *professions, but not in wage labour; statutes forbidding sexual discrimination have been adopted in the UK and the US, and women have begun to ascend to high offices of government, though not necessarily the kind of women of whom feminists would approve.

work

An activity which is of such a nature that it will not be voluntarily undertaken without reward. It is sometimes thought that the activity should be part of the economic process of *production, distribution, exchange and consumption, but that requirement is perhaps too stringent, except in the trivial sense that all paid employment is a part of the process of distribution, even that of the entertainer.

Some theorists (e.g. Arendt: *The Human Condition*, 1958) distinguish work from *labour, taking inspiration, e.g., from the earlier writings of Marx. Labour is seen as an essentially expressive activity, the activity in which *self-realization and the creation of human life have their cause. Labour becomes the social essence of man, and it is labour, rather than reason, which distinguishes man from the other animals. On this view 'work' might be usefully reserved as a name for that excrescence of the labouring process in which things are produced not for consumption but for exchange. Work is the instrumental, as opposed to the constitutive, aspect of human production. Too great an emphasis on work leads to the 'instrumentalization' of the world, the devaluation of everything to a means. Thus work becomes *alienated labour.

The 'work ethic' is the outlook which sees a major value of human existence in work, and which deprecates idleness as a deviation from a human norm. It involves a belief that people are, as it were, created through their employments, and a disposition to judge everyone in terms of his employment, so that the question 'What do you do?' stands in place of the question 'Who are you?'. For this attitude someone without work is existentially disturbing, since he continues to appear like a ghost at social gatherings, despite the fact that he does not exist. The work ethic is sometimes held by sociologists to be associated with the emergence of *status distinctions in the place of distinctions of *class, but it is part of a large phenomenon of social transformation which probably cannot be explained so simply.

In popular parlance the name 'worker' is reserved for the person whose work is a form of *wage labour, thus reflecting some measure of conscious or unconscious acceptance of the view that only wage labourers really *produce* anything. The growth of the *service economy has led to an increasing reluctance to use the term 'worker' in this somewhat antiquated sense.

workers' control/workers' ownership

Expressions that denote the partial or complete ownership or control over an enterprise by those whose work is necessary if it is to function. Ownership involves the legal right to transfer, and to realize the *value of the enterprise as a capital asset. This may be vested in an individual, a company or the state, even though workers have effective control over the enterprise in every other respect. Workers' ownership in effect amounts to the creation of a *cooperative.

Workers' *control was an ambition of many radical and even anarchist elements within the nineteenth-century socialist movement, and was the express aim of *anarcho-syndicalism. It is often advocated on grounds of justice, since the workers are a major factor of production (and, on some views, the only force of production), and therefore ought to exert rights of control over the means of production: on grounds of utility, in that the increased interest that they might then take in the enterprise can only increase their disposition to work; on more philosophical grounds, such as that workers' control is the solution to *alienation and the abolition of the treatment of the worker as a means. It is criticized as utopian, and as failing to take account of the fact that business involves both work on the part of those employed in it, and risk-taking and investment on the part of those who set it up, and that the state of mind required in the worker will inevitably undermine the ability to take that kind of risk.

working class

1. In common parlance, the class (if it be such) of *wage labour, whether or not that class has substantial holdings of *private property, and whether or not it has ownership in or control over the means of production.

2. In Marxist theory, another name for the industrial *proletariat.

1. includes some peasants, 2. does not. 1. is based in intuitions and *class consciousness; 2. is based in a theory, which seeks to explain those intuitions and not merely to reiterate them. The expression is now going out of fashion, partly because it is associated with dead theories and policies, such as those of the nineteenth-century socialists, partly because of the growth of the *service economy and the disappearance of old social and economic roles.

World Bank

The International Bank for Reconstruction and Development set up in 1944 under the *Bretton Woods Agreement (for which, *see* *bilateralism), in order to assist in the reconstruction of those developed economies that had been shattered by the Second World War, and to offer support for those developing countries which were without indigenous powers of investment. Membership of the Bank is restricted to those states that are also members of the *International Monetary Fund. The bank offers loans, and can raise money by borrowing in private capital markets, which are now its principal source of funds. It applies commercial and free-market principles, charging a commercial interest on its loans.

world government

The *universalist ideal of a single unitary system of government, in which all disputes between people would be settled not by *force but by *adjudication, under a single *jurisdiction, and a *rule of law upheld through truly representative institutions of government. Under such a government there cannot be war, but only crime, and all disputes take on the air of justiciable grievances.

World government has been the dream of many exponents and theorists of international law. It was advocated by *Kant, as the logical corollary of the universal validity of the moral law, and has inspired many of those active in founding the League of Nations (a term taken from Kant), and the subsequent *United Nations Organization. Sceptics argue that world government will mean simply that wars are no longer called wars, but insurrections, that nations are equal only because they are equally oppressed by the central power, that law is universal only because all local disputes are governed not by law but by force. Clearly vast issues of theory and practice are invoked by these contentions. To what extent, for example, could the differences between customs and languages be recognized under world government, and *how* would they be recognized? To what extent could the citizen from Cambodia make his grievance heard by a judge appointed from the Peruvian judiciary and expect equal treatment with a Peruvian? And so on.

world-historical

Adjective introduced by *Hegel to denote those individuals, forces and events which cannot be understood in terms of their immediate circumstances, but which must be referred to the transformation of world history which they cause. Thus Christ and Muhammad were world-historical figures, whose thoughts, words and deeds changed the course of human history. Christianity is a world-historical force, but so too are *socialism and *westernization (sense 2.).

world organizations

See *international organizations, *United Nations organization.

World Trade Organization (WTO)

Set up in Geneva in 1995 as the successor to the *GATT, the WTO provides a forum in which its members can debate and resolve disputes over trade, with a view to promoting free trade between them. The WTO exists in order to prevent tariff wars, *protectionism, counterfeiting and trade-mark piracy, and in order to promote multilateralism and the general liberalization of the global economy. It is based on six principles: non-discrimination, progressive reduction of trade barriers, transparency, fair competition, special arrangements for developing countries, and 'predictability' – the last meaning that states should not increase tariffs or bypass the rules through quotas or other restrictions. In international law, WTO agreements have the status of treaties, though it has set up its own procedure for mediating and resolving disputes, with internal sanctions by way of enforcement. Although the WTO now has 134 members, with 31 further applicants (compared with the 22 original signatories of GATT), it has less than 20 disputes requiring resolution each year, representing an infinitesimal proportion of world trade. Despite this success it has become the focus of important political controversies: first because of conflicts with the *protectionist policies of the *European Union, secondly because of organized protests by green activists and advocates of the interests of *developing countries at its recent conferences. One focus of these protests has been the ability of the WTO to impose legal or quasi-legal constraints that abolish customary rights and expectations of producers in poorer countries, in the interests (so it is alleged) of the predatory ambitions of *multinationals. *See* *trade-related intellectual property.

world wars

Wars which involve a substantial proportion of existing states. Such wars are precipitated by alliances and treaties which bind nations in a chain of belligerence. But their cause is often held to be deeper than that, for why were such alliances and treaties originally made, if not to contend with a 'common enemy'? Hence many seek to trace such wars to underlying economic interests, which need to be exerted over a larger area than that contained in any single jurisdiction. The classical exposition of such a theory is *Lenin's theory of the *imperialist war that was fought in Europe in 1914–18. However the theory is not widely accepted, and the Second World War is very implausibly described in terms of it. More plausible is the suggestion that war is contagious, and spreads through alliances and unstable frontiers until whole regions are embroiled.

Xenophobia

Pathological fear of strangers, usually accompanied by a conviction that they belong to a group that is *alien. Some forms of *racism are also forms of xenophobia, just as some anti-racism is motivated by 'xenophilia', the pathological love of strangers caused by contempt for one's traditional community. Xenophobia arises most readily where there is a conflict of interest between the two groups, for example, when an immigrant group appears to an existing working class to be competing with it for scarce jobs and resources. Hence it is sometimes thought to be rarer among those classes for whom strangers are not competitors, such as the traditional European aristocracy in times of peace.

Y eats, William Butler (1865–1939) Irish poet and dramatist; *see* *ceremony, *myth.

Young Hegelians

Philosophers, theologians, and political theorists in the 1830s and 1840s, with whom both Marx and Engels came into contact, and who attempted to adapt and transform Hegel's philosophy so as to give it a coherent critical and practical application. They included the theologians David Strauss (1808–74) and Bruno Bauer (1809–82), who were strongly influenced by Hegel's theory of universal history, the reactionary individualist *Stirner, a brilliant polemicist who foreshadowed Nietzsche's philosophy of self-enhancement, and the critic and philosopher Ludwig Feuerbach (1804–72), whose sophisticated iconoclasm had a profound effect on the younger generation of intellectuals. Feuerbach was interested in giving a *materialist version of the Hegelian philosophy of the self. He argued that man's essence is social, and resides in the *species-being that he shares with his kind. Only man has species-being, since only man has to *find* his own nature, by interacting with his kind. The alienated character of religion, as Hegel had described it, comes about because men carry that search beyond their social existence, into a transcendental realm which they do not understand. They then project out of themselves, and make into properties of the divinity, the perfections that might have been theirs. These perfections can have no reality outside man's social life, but there they have real existence. In removing his perfection from himself and bestowing it on a transcendent being, man makes his own perfection unobtainable, since it now lies outside the sphere of social action. This is the *fetishism which constitutes the essence of religious belief, and also the true divorce between man and his species-being (*The Essence of Christianity*, 1841).

All the Young Hegelians shared this interest in, and to some extent reaction against, religion, and all of them endeavoured to detach the Hegelian philosophy from its uncompromising metaphysical idealism. Feuerbach's theories recur in the early theories of Marx, particularly that concerning *alienation and were profoundly influential on Richard Wagner, and on the idea of myth and its significance that inspired *The Ring of the Nibelung*.

yuppie

'Young upwardly mobile professional'. The 'new class' emerging from the service economy of the modern capitalist state, which has brought about radical and to some extent unforeseen changes in lifestyle and voting habits, especially among urban electorates.

Zeitgeist

The 'spirit of the times'. A term belonging to *Hegel's philosophy of history, denoting the successive stages of development of the universal *Geist* or spirit, as it generates history from itself in accordance with the logic of the *dialectic. The term is used more simply and vulgarly to imply that, when two events in the human world are contemporaneous, they must each be expressions of a single *Zeitgeist* which compels them. This is one of the simplest fallacies of *historicism, and consists in interpreting the retrospective order that we impose on history through our cultural and critical classifications, as a kind of *causal* order. The fallacy is often identified in historians and critics of art, where it is sometimes said to have done much harm.

zero-sum

Term from *game theory, denoting the situation in which one player's gain is another's loss, as in a duel, so that the several pay-offs of the players add up to zero for every possible choice of strategies. The idea of the zero-sum game has proved intriguing to political theorists, since it seems to provide a model for war, diplomacy, and some domestic politics. Some have even argued that political *freedom is a zero-sum game, on the ground that every freedom that is granted to one person involves restricting the freedom of others so as to make room for it.

zero tolerance

A term used to describe harsh forms of policing, or radical legislative measures, designed to enforce standards in some matter where excuses, legal delays, and evasive tactics have given the advantage to the miscreant. Introduced by Mayor Giuliani into the policing of New York, the policy involved instant arrest of those discovered damaging or defacing buildings, criminal charges against all those reported as intimidating neighbourhoods, and a strong police presence on the streets in all areas where crime had taken a root. The spectacular drop in the crime rate led to the policy being copied in other places. Often a politician will try to gain credibility for a policy by describing it as showing 'zero tolerance' towards wrongdoers; but this is unlikely to be true.

Zionism

Jewish movement to establish, or re-establish, a Jewish *nation, so as to resurrect the Zion of the Jewish kings and prophets. The movement has been characterized by nationalist aspirations, based on a religion, law, custom and language which have survived without jurisdiction and without the territory over which it could be exercised. Zionism was founded in modern times by Theodor Herzel at the World Zionist Conference in Basle in 1897. Many different suggestions were made as to where the new Zion might be established – including parts of Africa and South America, where local resistance would, it was hoped, be minimal. In the end, however, the decision was taken to establish a Jewish state in Palestine. In 1917, as a result of enquiries from leading British Jews, and following a meeting of the war cabinet, the British Foreign Secretary, A.J. Balfour, wrote to the then Lord Rothschild, conveying the government's permission for Jews to settle in Palestine as their homeland, provided that the rights of the existing population were respected. At the time Palestine was part of the Ottoman Empire, though the Sykes-Picot accords between Britain and France had assigned it as a protectorate to Britain, in the inevitable event of an Ottoman collapse. The letter entered history as the Balfour Declaration of 1917.

Zionism stands for the aspiration of Jews everywhere to gain the territory with which to complete the legal and political identity of the Jewish state. The claims to the particular territory now known as Israel are founded in an idea of the unbroken connection of the Jews with the Biblical lands celebrated in their religion and literature, and forming the object of God's original promise to his chosen people. These claims are not strictly part of Zionism, but form an ancillary and powerful motive in the actual history of the movement. The Zionist claim to a territory is founded rather on the absolute need for the Jews to combine as a state, and no longer to seek to survive merely as a loosely joined international society. It is this absence of a state, Zionists often claim, that led to the *holocaust.

The tensions caused by the birth and growth of Israel, in an area where its existence has never had the endorsement of the indigenous peoples, have led to radical anti-Zionist movements, among Arabs and Muslims in particular, which have seldom stopped short of *anti-semitism. Hence anti-Zionism has now taken on an unpleasant flavour which has little or nothing to do with the question of the justice or injustice of the Zionist project.

Zivilisation
See *Kultur/Zivilisation.

zoning
The process, under US *planning law, of assigning separate social needs to distinct geographical zones, and forbidding what are thought to be unacceptable or antisocial mixtures of use. Industry is allocated to one area, residential estates to another, shopping facilities to a third, and so on. The practice has been much criticized as causing a fragmentation and suburbanization of the towns, and as contributing to the over-use of cars and the under-use of legs as instruments of human mobility. *See *New Urbanism.*